Enron: Corporate Fiascos and Their Implications

ABOUT THE EDITORS

NANCY B. RAPOPORT is Dean and Professor of Law at the University of Houston Law Center. After receiving her B.A., *summa cum laude,* from Rice University and her J.D. from Stanford Law School, she clerked for the Honorable Joseph T. Sneed on the United States Court of Appeals for the Ninth Circuit and then practiced law (primarily bankruptcy law) with Morrison & Foerster in San Francisco. She started her academic career at The Ohio State University College of Law in 1991, and she moved from Assistant Professor to Associate Professor to Associate Dean for Student Affairs and Professor in 1998 (just as she left Ohio State to become Dean and Professor of Law at the University of Nebraska College of Law). She served as Dean of the University of Nebraska College of Law from 1998–2000. She has been the Dean at the University of Houston Law Center since 2000. She has developed a lifelong interest in the intersection of the fields of bankruptcy law and professional responsibility. When Enron imploded—more or less in her own backyard—she began her obsession about the causes and lessons of Enron.

BALA G. DHARAN is the J. Howard Creekmore Professor of Management at the Jones Graduate School of Management, Rice University, Houston. He has extensive research and consulting experience in financial reporting and accounting issues, as well as investment analysis and business valuation, and he is frequently cited by media on accounting issues. He has been invited twice to testify before Congress on Enron's financial reporting and on accounting standard-setting process. He has been a visiting professor at business schools at Harvard, Berkeley, and Northwestern. He is a graduate of Indian Institute of Technology-Madras, Indian Institute of Management-Ahmedabad, and Carnegie Mellon University.

CONTRIBUTING AUTHORS (IN ALPHABETICAL ORDER)

DOUGLAS G. BAIRD is the Harry A. Bigelow Distinguished Service Professor of Law at the University of Chicago Law School.

MATTHEW J. BARRETT is a Professor of Law at Notre Dame Law School.

WILLIAM R. BUFKINS is Managing Director of Organization Analytics, a management consulting firm specializing in executive compensation.

W. AMON BURTON, JR. is a corporate attorney in Austin, Texas, with a practice that encompasses both ethics consulting and business representation. Mr. Burton also teaches professional responsibility at the University of Texas School of Law.

ROGER C. CRAMTON is the Robert S. Stevens Professor of Law, Emeritus, at Cornell Law School.

JOHN C. COFFEE, JR. is the Adolf A. Berle Professor of Law at Columbia University Law School.

LYNNE DALLAS is a Professor of Law at the University of San Diego School of Law.

BALA G. DHARAN is the J. Howard Creekmore Professor of Accounting at Rice University.

JOHN S. DZIENKOWSKI is the John S. Redditt Professor in State and Local Government Law at the University of Texas School of Law.

LAWRENCE J. FOX is a partner at Drinker Biddle & Reath LLP.

VICTOR B. FLATT is the A.L. O'Quinn Chair in Environmental Law at the University of Houston Law Center.

MICHELLE MICHOT FOSS is the Executive Director of the Institute for Energy, Law and Enterprise at the University of Houston Law Center. Dr. Foss is also an Assistant Research Professor at the Law Center.

ROBERT W. GORDON is the Chancellor Kent Professor of Law and Legal History at Yale Law School.

LESLIE GRIFFIN is the Larry and Joanne Doherty Chair in Legal Ethics at the University of Houston Law Center.

MICHELE M. HEDGES is Senior Vice President and General Counsel of NextiraOne, LLC.

EDWARD J. JANGER is a Professor of Law at Brooklyn Law School.

SUSAN P. KONIAK is a Professor of Law at Boston University School of Law.

GEORGE W. KUNEY is an Associate Professor of Law and the Director of the Clayton Center for Entrepreneurial Law at the University of Tennessee College of Law.

JOHN H. LANGBEIN is the Sterling Professor of Law and Legal History at Yale Law School.

COLLEEN E. MEDILL is a Professor of Law at the University of Tennessee College of Law.

GERALDINE SZOTT MOOHR is an Associate Professor of Law at the University of Houston Law Center.

FRANK PARTNOY is a Professor of Law at the University of San Diego School of Law.

PAUL D. PATON is a Fellow of the Keck Center on Legal Ethics and the Legal Profession and a J.S.D. Candidate at Stanford Law School. He is also a lawyer with PricewaterhouseCoopers LLP in Toronto, Canada.

TROY A. PAREDES is an Associate Professor of Law at Washington University School of Law.

NANCY B. RAPOPORT is Dean and Professor of Law at the University of Houston Law Center.

ROBERT K. RASMUSSEN is Associate Dean for Academic Affairs and Professor of Law at Vanderbilt Law School.

DEBORAH L. RHODE is the Ernest W. McFarland Professor of Law at Stanford Law School.

CHARLES J. TABB is the Alice C. Campbell Professor of Law at the University of Illinois College of Law.

JEFFREY D. VAN NIEL is a former Master Commissioner for the Ohio Supreme Court in the area of public utilities law and is currently an environmental law consultant.

JACQUELINE LANG WEAVER is the A.A. White Professor of Law at the University of Houston Law Center.

STEVEN H. WILSON is an historian who received his B.S., M.S., and Ph.D. in History from Rice University.

DUANE WINDSOR is the Lynette S. Autrey Professor of Management at Rice University.

Enron: Corporate Fiascos and Their Implications

Nancy B. Rapoport and Bala G. Dharan, editors

Cover art by *Jeffrey D. Van Niel*

Front cover art: Jeffrey D. Van Niel, "Enron, Titanic, and the Perfect Storm."
Back cover art: Jeffrey D. Van Niel, "Employees and Shareholders May Now Board the Lifeboats."

© 2004 By FOUNDATION PRESS

    395 Hudson Street
    New York, NY 10014
    Phone Toll Free 1–877–888–1330
    Fax (212) 367–6799
    fdpress.com

Printed in the United States of America

ISBN 1–58778–578–1

 TEXT IS PRINTED ON 10% POST CONSUMER RECYCLED PAPER

CONTENTS

ACKNOWLEDGMENTS

So many people contributed to this book that we scarcely know where to begin. We, of course, owe a great deal of gratitude to our contributors, who gave us the opportunity to publish their scholarly essays in our book and worked with us to deliver them on a timely basis. In addition, we are very grateful to Steve Errick, our publisher at Foundation Press, who developed the idea for this textbook and suggested that we take on this project. Thanks to the guidance and patience of Steve and his colleagues at Foundation Press and at West, working on this book project was a very enjoyable experience for both of us. We are also grateful to several people at Foundation Press who worked hard to make this book look so professional, especially Sharon Ray, the book designer, Jim Coates, the production manager, and Iris Griedlinger, our editor.

Several of our colleagues and friends put a lot of effort into this book, discussing the issues with us, commenting on our ideas, reading drafts, and suggesting the names of possible contributors. We are grateful to Paige Barr, Seth Chandler, Michael Cinelli, Kelli Cline, Luddie Collins, Eric Gerber, Susan Hartman, James Highsmith, Harold and Ferne Hyman, Christian Liipfert, Harriet Richman, Shelby Shanks, Catherine Vance, Teresa Watts, Duane Windsor, Michelle Wu, and Stephen Zeff. Much of the support work in getting the papers in the book ready for publication, including citation checks, was done by some talented students at the University of Houston Law Center: Laura Armiston, Gloria Bluestone, Magdalene Conner, Patrick Flanagan, James Halvatsis, Julia Hernandez, Mikel (Colby) Lewis, Brandy Monge, Julia Stoebner, Charles Williamson, and Gary Wright, as well as other students who worked for Harriet Richman in the O'Quinn Law Library. We also had help from an outstanding undergraduate from George Washington University, Sara McPherson. Finally, we are grateful to several people involved with Enron and Andersen who shared their insights with us off the record.

NBR and BGD

Nancy Rapoport's Additional Acknowledgments

I'm grateful to my co-editor, Bala. His experience, perspective, and encouragement (not to mention his sense of humor) turned this project into reality.

I also want to thank my parents, Morris and Shirley Rapoport, who have always encouraged me to test my boundaries and try new things (and who will always read my drafts, even when they're about the more esoteric aspects of bankruptcy ethics).

My most heartfelt thanks go to my husband and partner in all things, Jeff Van Niel. Jeff is the unofficial third editor on this project: it's because he's a "real person" with real-world business and law experience that his edits were so valuable. He worked tirelessly on every aspect of this book, including the art work, the "big picture" view of this book, the line-by-line editing of the essays, and the organization of the actual manuscript process. Even more important was Jeff's willingness to work with me, far into the night, while giving up months of "couple time" to get the book done. Jeff, I cannot imagine my life without you, and any success I have is due in large part to your guidance and support.

NBR

Bala Dharan's Additional Acknowledgments

I am grateful to my co-editor, Nancy, and thankful for the opportunity this project gave me to get to know her personally and experience first-hand the boundless energy and enthusiasm she brings to everything she does.

I also want to express my heartfelt thanks to my wife of twenty-five years, Vidya, and our beloved son, Anand, for their love, encouragement and support, and for letting me spend many countless hours of our family evenings and weekends on this project.

BGD

INTRODUCTION

Enron. Like the national scandals that preceded it—Teapot Dome; Watergate; the "Keating Five"—the very name connotes more than just the story of one company in Houston, Texas. "Enron" connotes extreme greed and extreme cunning. It connotes a corporate culture run amok, relying on corporate cronyism to support heretofore unsupportable business deals. The key players were larger than life, and their collective fall from grace was cushioned by millions of dollars in salaries, bonuses, and stock options. The story of Enron is still being written.

And yet, we're not waiting to write this book until the full story is known. Why? For one thing, waiting until "the whole truth" comes out would mean waiting for years (and possibly forever) while the legal system grinds on. There is too much to study and learn *now* to justify waiting until all of the testimony is in, all of the cases have been resolved, and all of the punishment has been meted out.[1] For another thing, both of us[2] are enjoying the opportunity to explore and react to news while it's fresh. And the news keeps coming. First, Enron was a scandal unto itself. Then along came WorldCom, Tyco, Adelphia, and ImClone, and the stories of greed and cunning continue unabated. In case anyone thought these stories were unique to America, Elan and Royal Ahold showed that Europe could provide equally sordid sagas.

The amazing thing about these corporate scandals is the sheer excess involved. Who could have imagined that Tyco CEO Dennis Kozlowski and ImClone founder Sam Waksal would both be charged with tax fraud for the same reason: trying to avoid paying sales tax on expensive works of art? Who could have imagined that Enron's Ken Lay would have gone from making the "A" list at all of the top national social events to being relegated to social obscurity? Who (outside Hollywood) could have imagined paying $6,000 for a shower curtain *a la* Kozlowski?

More important, who could have imagined the ripple effect that Enron and its progeny would have on the market—tens of billions of dollars of market capitalization destroyed, workers' retirement plans devastated, shareholders' dreams ruined, arts organizations' budgets hit by dried-up philanthropic dollars, and individual investors' trust in the market shattered?

---

[1] Just as in other great tragedies, we suspect that many people deserving of punishment may never be subjected to it, while some undeserving people will have their reputations dragged through the mud.

[2] A third one of us (Nancy's husband, Jeff Van Niel) has also become integral to this book. Like the other two of us, he is here in Houston, in the thick of it all; unlike the two of us, he knows energy deals exceptionally well, and he has also been editing all of the essays.

Certainly, Enron is not to blame for all of the market's woes. The lingering effect of the burst dot.com market bubble, along with September 11, 2001 and of the recent war in the Middle East, are also contributing to the market's current stagnation. But Enron marks a permanent change in how the public views corporate governance and the amount of trust accorded to corporate leaders. Unlike the savings and loan crisis of the 1980s, Enron dealt a huge blow to the public's confidence in the whole system of corporate governance—including boards of directors and auditors. When the officers of Enron engaged in repetitive self-dealing, parlaying thousands of dollars into millions, seemingly overnight, Enron's board of directors *waived its own ethics rules* to permit such self-dealing. When the officers of Enron crafted Rube-Goldberg-like financial transactions, in what appears to have been a deliberate effort to create financial statements that *could not be understood* even by experts, they did so by working hand-in-glove with Enron's outside auditors[3]—Arthur Andersen, one of the oldest, largest, and most venerated accounting firms.[4] And that's not the worst of it: investment banks, consultants, outside lawyers, and financial analysts apparently bent over backwards to curry favor with Enron.[5] Did they believe that exaggerated claims of Enron's success would mean millions of dollars in future business, or were they bullied by some of Enron's chief cheerleaders?

Enron, in some sense, is a larger-than-life disaster, much like the *Titanic*. Both tragedies had more in common than one might think. *Titanic's* tragedy stemmed from human error and arrogance (as did Enron's). *Titanic's* failure was tied to the unrealistic faith in technology to keep the passengers safe from harm. Enron's failure was tied to the unrealistic faith that formal and informal checks and balances could always keep the market honest. In both tragedies, on average, the rich (top management, in Enron's case; the upper class, in *Titanic's*) survived while the working class (Enron's employees and small investors; *Titanic's* employees and steerage passengers) bore the brunt of the loss.

What do we hope that you'll get from this book? First, we want you to explore Enron from a variety of different aspects. Business schools have perfected the case study,[6] and Enron is the quintessential case study. Through essays written by scholars and experts in their fields, we hope to examine the causes and consequences of Enron's

---

[3] In Neal Batson's Third Interim Report, Batson makes a convincing case that some of Enron's most senior officers deliberately concealed relevant facts from Andersen in order to effectuate certain improper transactions. Neal Batson, Third Interim Report of Neal Batson, Court Appointed Examiner, *In re* Enron Corp., No. 01-16034 (Bankr. S.D.N.Y. June 30, 2003), Appendix C, at 38–44. Such concealment would cut against an allegation that Andersen worked hand-in-glove with Enron to effectuate the transactions. Of course, the jury's still out on an *actual* finding of concealment

[4] Wrongly venerated, it seems in retrospect. Arthur Andersen's list of clients includes a who's who of corporate scandals such as WorldCom, Waste Management, Sunbeam, and the Baptist Foundation of Arizona.

[5] The jury is also out on whether the lawyers (inside and outside counsel) crossed the line in terms of encouraging Enron to defraud investors, but even the Enron Board's own report—the Powers Report—faults the lawyers for not looking more critically at some of the business deals.

[6] Law schools have perfected the study of *cases*. That's not the same thing at all.

failure from business, financial, legal, and ethical perspectives. Some essays analyze the business-government interactions and decisions that laid the foundations for Enron's growth and subsequent demise. Others describe and detail the complex web of partnerships and accounting tricks used by Enron to hide bad news and project inaccurate good news. Still others focus on the ethical and legal dimensions of the Enron crisis and their lessons for business and law students as well as society. Don't worry if you're unfamiliar with some of the topics. Each essay is designed to walk you through the basics, so that you can get a sense of how different Enron really was. The notes and questions after the essays will give you an opportunity to put yourself in the place of some of the cast of characters and to think through some of the thorniest problems for yourselves.

Second, we hope that you will learn how destructive corporate greed can be to the very system of wealth creation on which we all depend. The 1990s and early 2000s were marked by a bitter contempt for "real" assets and for modest returns on investment. The dot.com failure—and the corporate scandals that followed—jolted us back to reality, so much so that Richard Kinder (who used to work with Ken Lay at Enron) has taken to describing the successful Kinder Morgan business plan as "real assets, real earnings, real cash."[7] The same greed that encouraged the cutthroat culture of Enron led to its downfall.

Finally, we hope that you will see Enron as a cautionary tale. For far too long, business schools have graduated MBAs who don't know enough about law, and law schools have graduated JDs who don't know enough about business. This is the main lesson from Enron, where some very intelligent people made some horrific mistakes, in part because everyone assumed that someone else was "taking care of it." The financial engineers assumed that the lawyers were taking care of the "legal stuff," and the lawyers assumed that the accountants were taking care of the "financial stuff." Instead, legal and financial niceties were ignored, forgotten, or distorted. Enron showed us that the workings of a modern corporation involve complex interactions between diverse fields of expertise, such as finance, accounting, ethics, law, and management. If we learn nothing else from Enron, we must learn that deliberate ignorance about related fields will cause professionals to offer incomplete advice, at the very least, and may cause them to lose their licenses if the incomplete advice leads to malpractice. Perhaps the traditional separation of business schools and law schools can morph into a world in which business and law schools work together, joining forces to create better-educated professionals. If we are to restore public trust in corporate governance and the market, then we must learn to take responsibility for more than our particular assignments—to take responsibility for solving problems, rather than merely answering questions.

NBR & BGD 2003

---

[7] http://www.kindermorgan.com/investor/presentations/presentations.cfm?Archive=Y.

Chapter 1

Enron in Perspective

We designed this chapter to give you a bird's-eye view of Enron: not just a general overview of what happened, but also a sense of the legal and social history leading up to Enron's actions, as well as a sense of the other corporate scandals that emerged after Enron's own scandal broke. One of us (NBR) has a father who often repeats the adage, "he who does not learn from history is doomed to repeat it."[1] As you read through the essays, think about lessons that you can take from this background material when you face your own potential Enrons in "real life."

---

[1] *See* GEORGE SANTAYANA, THE LIFE OF REASON 284 (1905) ("Those who cannot remember the past are condemned to repeat it.")

Enron—The Primer *

Jeffrey D. Van Niel

The stage was set for the collapse of the collection of companies known as Enron long before Enron existed.[1] Corporate governance issues, including mismanagement and outright fraud, have plagued our free-market system since it was created. It seems we feel compelled to revisit these same issues once every generation.[2] From my perspective, a company operating in a free market attempts to maximize its profits by taking every advantage of the gaps that exist within and between the various rules and regulations that form the boundaries of that market. Unfortunately, corporate focus has shifted towards the "what can I get away with?" perspective and away from a business model bounded by common sense and ethical norms. The problem with this view is that it ignores the distinction between legal and illegal (and moral and immoral) conduct.

---

* © Jeffrey D. Van Niel 2003, all rights reserved. During the last year, I have helped my wife edit many of the papers gathered together to form this book. Given the breadth of topics in this compilation work, we believed that you, the student, would prefer not to read virtually the same historical recitation of Enron's meteoric rise and crash into bankruptcy in every paper of every chapter in this book. So I have undertaken in this Primer to set forth a coherent, factual statement of the events leading up to the collapse of Enron. In order to make this primer as accurate as possible, I have relied upon and made liberal use of virtually all of the authors' papers in this book. For their research efforts and help in making this primer understandable and accurate, I am particularly grateful for the research of Victor Flatt and Jacqueline Weaver, whose works formed the backbone of this primer, to Bala Dharan for his editing, and to Nancy Rapoport, for her help with the accounting section.

[1] The company known as Enron was actually several separate companies (Enron Energy Services, Enron Broadband Services, Enron Capital and Trade, later called Enron Wholesale Services, and Enron Transportation Services) that were owned wholly or in part by Enron Inc., *see* Enron Annual Report 2000, *available at* http://www.enron.com/corp/investors/annuals/2000/ar2000.pdf.

[2] "National Student Marketing in the 1970s, OPM in the early 1980s, Lincoln Savings & Loan during the S&L crisis of the 1980s, and the huge BBCI bank failure and fraud of the 1990s." Roger Cramton, *Enron and the Corporate Lawyer: A Primer on Legal and Ethical Issues*, 58 BUS. LAW. 143, 143 (2002) (footnotes omitted).

But I digress. Although this text and its updates do not focus exclusively upon Enron and its meteoric rise and fall into bankruptcy, the events surrounding Enron's collapse (and the subsequent corporate scandals—and current corporate governance upheaval—that occurred relatively soon thereafter) makes for an excellent learning opportunity. To that end, this primer attempts to set forth, briefly, the political, legal, and energy policy environment within which Enron grew to be what it became—the most influential energy-trading and market-creating company ever seen. The purpose of this primer is to provide you with sufficient background so that you can engage in a basic discussion of the events and circumstances surrounding the collapse of Enron and the most recent crisis of corporate governance. Consequently, I have not provided an exhaustive dissertation on the history and evolution of Enron or of its actions in the California energy crisis (not that we will ever really know *all* of the facts and circumstances surrounding the collapse of what was once the seventh largest company in the Fortune 500). The individual essays in this book and your professors will help you study Enron (and "Enron-esque") issues in more detail.

SETTING THE STAGE FOR THE CREATION OF ENRON

Long before electricity or natural gas, people used coal, wood, and various animal fats and oils to heat and light their homes. None of these resources was efficient or clean, and the smell permeated everything. As population centers grew more dense, something needed to change in the manner in which individuals were supplied with heat and light. Soon enough, companies were competing with each other to supply natural gas or other flammable liquids and gases to urban dwellers. Since no company at this time had exclusive rights to serve any of these customers, the streets and rights-of-way were constantly torn up as each company installed its own pipelines to serve its customers. Eventually, municipalities brought this chaotic practice to a halt, and the first monopolistic utilities were born.[3] Delivering electricity to the masses followed a similar competitive infrastructure growth pattern, with wires and power poles filling all of the available space in the rights-of-way. Additionally, the electric industry fought a more fundamental internal war to determine whether to distribute direct current (DC)[4] or alternating current (AC) to the prospective customers. (Light bulbs and small engines run equally well on either power supply.)[5] Eventually, alternating cur-

---

[3] AMY FRIEDLANDER, POWER AND LIGHT: ELECTRICITY IN THE U.S. ENERGY INFRASTRUCTURE 1870–1940 at 81–92 (1996).

[4] Thomas Edison, credited with inventing the incandescent electric light bulb, was a strong advocate of the distribution of direct current electricity, and owned at least one direct current electric company that distributed power to urban dwellers in New York City. *Id.* at 40.

[5] *See, e.g.,* Dennis Bernaal, *Electricity: Transformers and Delivery of Electric Power, in* MACMILLAN ENCYCLOPEDIA OF ENERGY, 392 (John Zumerchik ed., 2001); *see also Direct Current, available at* http://www.sunblock99.org.uk/sb99/people/DMackay/dc.html; WhatIs?Com, *DC, available at* http://whatis.techtarget.com/definition/0,,sid9_gci213659,00.html.

rent won out over direct current, because alternating current was capable of being transported longer distances, and electric utilities sprouted across the county.

Although local electricity and natural gas distribution systems are functionally similar, providing heat and light to customers, the industries evolved in dramatically different ways. At its most basic level, natural gas is extracted from the ground as a naturally occurring molecule that must be refined to meet certain purity standards before it is considered capable of entry into and transmission in the national interstate pipeline system. You can, if you want, physically track an individual molecule of natural gas through the various pipelines from the well to your house. But, since every molecule of natural gas is fungible, no one makes the effort to physically track individual molecules of gas. Customers simply take what they need from the gas system and pay the bill when it arrives. Natural gas can also be pressurized and stored for long periods of time for later use. An electron of electricity, on the other hand, is created using a process that turns an alternating current generator. Unlike natural gas, technology does not yet permit us to track individual electrons as they pass down an electric wire. Nor can electricity be stored for later use, except through the use of batteries. Fortunately, an electron is an electron, so there is no need to be able to track electrons over the wires. Again, customers simply use what they need and then pay the bill when it arrives.

Functionally speaking, local gas and electricity utilities put their products into the hands of the end-use customer in very similar ways. The product is first produced (either generated or pumped from a well). It is then transported to the local distribution area using a bulk transport system (interstate and intrastate pipelines for gas and interstate and intrastate transmission lines for electricity). Once the product reaches the local distribution area, the local utility converts the product into volumes that can be used by local consumers (reducing the pressure for the gas and reducing the voltages for electricity to voltages usable by individual customers). The local utility then transmits the product to the end-use customer. Functionally speaking, the production chain looks like what you see in Chart A.

1. Natural Gas

During the regulated or monopolistic time in gas history, each aspect of the natural gas delivery chain (well-head, pipeline, local distribution company ("LDC"), end-user/customer) was regulated, with some level of governmental review and price approval and control. The type and number of potential sellers and buyers for the gas were also limited. At that time, only pipeline companies were permitted to sell gas to municipalities for resale to end-users.[6] In that context, the pipelines were filling the merchant and delivery functions in the delivery chain. Similarly, only LDCs, which were frequently municipalities, were permitted to sell gas to the residents and industries within their

---

[6] PAUL W. MACAVOY, THE NATURAL GAS MARKET: SIXTY YEARS OF REGULATION AND DEREGULATION 16 (2000).

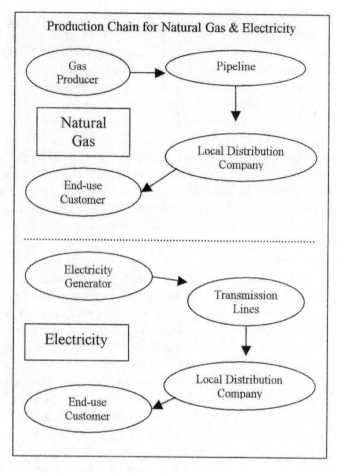

Chart A

distribution areas. Within this system, the entity filling the merchant function had an obligation to serve *all* of the customers who requested its service within its area of operations, whether it wanted to or not. In other words, if you ran a pipeline, all of the municipalities that tied into your pipeline were your customers and you had to provide them with gas. The same was true for an LDC or a city; it had to serve all of the customers within its area of operations that requested service. The obligation to serve flowed directly from the benefit received by the distributing entity for being the only service provider—i.e., having a monopoly. If you were the only service provider, you had to serve those who sought service.[7] The only part of this production chain that did

---

[7] *Id.*

not have an obligation to serve were the gas producers. They could sell to whom they wanted and withhold supply from those whom they did not want to serve.

The current restructuring of the electric and natural gas energy markets, or deregulation, as it is now known, began as a direct consequence of the oil crisis in the 1970s. Politically, the government had to do something to prevent a total collapse of the U.S. economy.[8] Restructuring initially began in 1978,

> when Congress passed the Natural Gas Policy Act ("NGPA"), and began the march towards a competitive retail natural gas marketplace.[9] Pursuant to the NGPA, the Federal Energy Regulatory Commission ("FERC") issued several orders both to forcibly open the natural gas industry to competition and to control the competitive behavior of the various industry participants, including the pipelines, marketing and aggregating companies and local gas utilities.[10] Ultimately, FERC issued Order 636, to "promot[e] competition among gas suppliers . . . [and to] benefit all gas consumers and the nation by 'ensur(ing) an adequate and reliable supply of (clean and abundant) natural gas at the lowest reasonable price.'"[11]

Restructuring efforts for the natural gas delivery chain have now eliminated virtually all of this governmental regulation, and replaced it with market-based economic theory (freedom to choose your supplier of each service, be it product, transportation, or ancillary service). In other words, customers are now generally free to shop for a

---

[8] Susanna McBee, *U.S. Governors Eschew the Old Freebies and Get Serious*, WASH. POST, Aug. 31, 1978, at A5 (". . . natural gas pricing bill, which [President Carter] considers a key part of his energy package, and which [State Governors] consider crucial to the nation's economy and thus their own states' well-being.")

[9] 15 U.S.C. §§ 3301–3432 (2001).

[10] *Regulation of Natural Gas Pipelines After Partial Wellhead Decontrol*, Order No. 436 ("FERC Order 436"), 50 FR 42408 (Oct. 18, 1985), FERC Stats. & Regs. (Regulations Preamble 1982–1985) 30,665 (1985), *vacated and remanded*, Associated Gas Distrib. v. FERC, 824 F.2d 981 (D.C. Cir. 1987), *cert. denied*, 485 U.S. 1006 (1988), *readopted on an interim basis*, Order No. 500, 52 F.R. 30334 (Aug. 14, 1987), FERC Stats. & Regs. (Regulations Preambles, 1986–1990) 30,761 (1987), *remanded*, American Gas Ass'n v. FERC, 888 F.2d 136 (D.C. Cir. 1989), readopted, Order No. 500-H, 54 F.R. 52344 (Dec. 21, 1989), FERC Stats. & Regs. (Regulations Preambles 1986–1990) 30,867 (1989), *reh'g granted in part and denied in part*, Order No. 500-I, 55 FR 6605 (Feb. 26, 1990), FERC Stats. & Regs. (Regulations Preambles 1986–1990) 30,880 (1990), *aff'd in part and remanded in part*, American Gas Ass'n v. FERC, 912 F.2d 1496 (D.C. Cir. 1990), *cert. denied*, 111 S.Ct. 957 (1991).

[11] Jeffrey D. Van Niel & Nancy B. Rapoport, *"Retail Choice" Is Coming: Have You Hugged Your Utilities Lawyer Today? (PART I),* 2002 No. 2 NORTON BANKR. L. ADVISER 2 (citing FERC Order 636, 57 F.R. 13267, 13269 (April 16, 1992), Order on Reh'g, Order 636(A), 57 F.R. 36128 (Aug. 12, 1992), *Order on Reh'g*, Order 636(B), 61 F.R. 61272 (Nov. 27, 1992), *Order on Reh'g*, Order 636(C), 78 FERC 61186 (1997)) [hereinafter *Retail Choice*].

better price or terms from any supplier they can find.[12] The final and most recent step in this restructuring effort permits residential consumers to purchase their own gas supplies from any number of willing sellers in the marketplace. This step must be accomplished on an individual state-by-state basis, as retail sales are beyond the purview of federal regulation.

As a result of these various FERC Orders, any customer seeking to acquire and/or transport natural gas over an interstate pipeline may do so, so long as that customer acquires the necessary transport rights from that pipeline, as Chart B indicates.

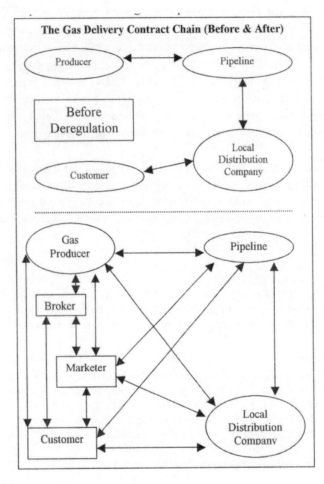

Chart B

---

[12] *Id.* at 3.

Moreover, some industrial and large commercial customers currently may, depending upon their state, individually acquire and transport their own natural gas to their facilities, paying the pipelines and LDC only a transport fee to deliver the gas. As individual customers have acquired more and more rights to buy and transport gas on the interstate pipeline system, there has been a corresponding increase in companies willing to perform these services for the customer. These middlemen are known by many names: agents, marketers, brokers, etc. Their function is to ease the burden on individual customers by buying and arranging for the transportation of the gas to the customer or the customer's facility. As a result of these middlemen, the nice, clean contract days of the past are long gone. As reflected in Chart B, contract relationships are now as potentially complex as the number of individuals that may get involved in the transaction. A customer or his broker or marketer can contract directly with any or all aspects of the supply or delivery chain in order to obtain and deliver gas.

2. Electricity[13]

Historically, each electric utility generated virtually all of the power necessary to service the customer needs in its service territory and then transmitted that power to its service territory over transmission lines that it also owned. Since virtually all of these utilities competed with each other for retail customers and service territory, the concepts of free flowing electrons between service territories to enhance competition never entered the, production, construction or transmission development equation. Accordingly, the national electric grid more closely resembles a patchwork quilt than the free-flowing system design of the natural interstate gas pipelines and distribution system.

Although neighboring service territories do interconnect at various points, these interconnections were historically designed only to assist neighboring utilities in case of an emergency, not to facilitate efficient electron flow between, among and across several service territories. Contrary to the gas industry, no national high voltage transmission system exists to enhance the transmission of electricity from region to region across the country. These utility-owned generation, transmission, and distribution assets were constructed and are being maintained at huge expense to the local utility and its customers. Accordingly, requiring these same utilities to give up their monopoly rights and potentially guaranteed profits, not to mention the control and sometimes ownership of their facilities, has been and will be an uphill battle.

---

[13] I took this part of my essay directly from an earlier piece that I co-authored. *See Retail Choice, supra* note 11, at 2. We said it just fine the first time, and I saw no need to reinvent the wheel.

The Energy Power Act of 1992 started the competitive march in the electric industry by instructing FERC to order electric utilities to permit third parties to use the utilities transmission assets to transmit ("wheel") blocks of wholesale power through the utilities' service area. Essentially, FERC was requiring the transmission line owners to convert their transmission patchwork quilt into a national freeway system for transmitting electricity across and through states. FERC implemented the Energy Policy Act's mandates by issuing FERC Orders 888 and 889, as well as the Independent System Operator ("ISO") and Regional Transmission Organizations ("RTO") orders, each of which seeks to eliminate constraints on the movement of power across regions and permit non-utility power purchasers to buy and transmit blocks of power over large distances to different regions and states.

The ISO and RTO orders seek to have independent third-party entities operate the high voltage transmission lines in order to facilitate the movement of electricity across regions and state boundaries, thereby enhancing competition by reducing (1) the cost to move power long distances, and (2) the transmission owners' opportunities to manipulate the power markets.

Sadly, notwithstanding considerable recent and public discussion, the federal government has no comprehensive electric industry restructuring policy or statute in place. Although the California . . . [energy crisis] has focused attention upon retail electric competition, it remains highly unlikely that any comprehensive restructuring legislation will pass in the near future. Thus, at least in the near term, the transition to a fully competitive retail electric marketplace will be controlled by the states on a state-by-state basis. Therefore, we can look forward to more differences than similarities between states when considering retail utility competition legislation or programs.... As a result of the federal efforts, state legislators and regulators have been compelled to take steps to promote a more competitive local natural gas, and electric marketplace. Given the ever-changing competitive environment and limited space available in . . . [this primer], we have not attempted to generate an exhaustive list of the individual state efforts to open the various retail utility industries to competition. Nor will we discuss these individual state efforts in detail. Additional information regarding the status of an individual state's utility restructuring efforts may be found on each state's utility commission website.[14]

[14] *Retail Choice, supra* note 11, at 2–3 (citing Promoting Wholesale Competition through Open Access Non-Discriminatory Transmission Services by Public Utilities, Docket No. RM95-8-000, 888 at 280 (April 24, 1996) 61 Fed. Reg. 21,540 (May 10, 1996), FERC Stats. & Regs. P31,036 (1997), *Order on Reh'g,* Order No. 888(A), 62 Fed. Reg. 12,274 (1997), FERC Stats. & Regs. P31,048 (1997), *Order on Reh'g,* Order No. 888(B), 81 FERC P61,248 (1997), *Order on Reh'g,* Order No. 888(C), 82 FERC P61,046 (1998); *Inquiry Concerning the Commission's Policy on Independent System Operator,* Docket No.

B. THE BIRTH OF ENRON[15]

In 1985, Enron was born of the merger of Houston Natural Gas with Internorth, creating the first nationwide natural gas pipeline network.[16] In early 1986, Ken Lay was named chairman and chief executive officer of Enron.[17] A few years later, Enron began opening overseas offices in England in order to take advantage of the privatization of the United Kingdom's power industry.[18] An extremely ambitious company, Enron pushed the envelope and shifted from the regulated transportation of natural gas to the unregulated energy trading markets, under the impression that there was more money in buying and selling financial contracts linked to the value of energy assets than in actual ownership of physical assets.[19] Jeffrey Skilling entered the scene in 1989, launching a program under which buyers of natural gas locked in long-term supplies at fixed prices.[20] In the following years, Enron continued to expand worldwide, with pipelines in South America and power plants in England and India.[21] Over this period, Enron spent billions of dollars in acquiring and building new sites and companies, even as it tried to shift away from "old market" ideas (like real assets) toward "new market" ideas (Skilling's "asset-lite" philosophy).[22]

At its zenith, Enron was named the "most innovative" company in the United States by *Fortune* magazine *every year* between 1996 and 2001.[23] In mid-August 2000, *Fortune* magazine named Enron as one of the top ten stocks that would last the decade because Enron had so successfully transformed itself from a stodgy gas utility into the

---

PL98-5-000, and *Regional Transmission Organizations*, Docket No. RM99-2-000 (December 20, 1999) 65 Fed. Reg. 12,088 (March 8, 2000), 90 FERC Stats. & Regs. P31,092, *Order on Reh'g*, Order No. 2000(A) 90 FERC Stats. & Regs. P61, 201.

[15] This section has been taken nearly verbatim from an earlier draft by Victor Flatt. Victor B. Flatt, *The Enron Story and Environmental Policy*, 33 ENVTL. L. REV. 10485 (2003).

[16] HOUS. CHRON. ONLINE, *Enron Timeline* (2002), *available at* http://www.chron.com/cs/CDA/ printstory.hts/special/enron/1127125 (last visited June 18, 2003) [hereinafter *Enron Timeline*].

[17] *Id.*

[18] *Id.*

[19] Mark Jickling, *The Enron Collapse: An Overview of Financial Issues*, Cong. Research Serv., (March 19, 2002), *available at* http://fpc.state.gov/documents/organization/9110.pdf (March 28, 2002).

[20] *Enron Timeline, supra* note 16.

[21] *Id.*

[22] Lanny J. Davis, *Enron? We're Missing the Point*, WASH. POST, Jan. 6, 2002, at B01 ("Jeffrey K. Skilling actually once boasted about the company's absence of hard assets. He proudly described its approach as 'asset lite,' adding: 'In the old days, people worked for assets. We turned it around—what we've said is, the assets work for people.'").

[23] David Ivanovich, *Everybody Knows Enron's Name But Pop Icon Status Probably Won't Last,* HOUS. CHRON., Oct. 21, 2002, at 1A; *accord,* PETER C. FUSARO & ROSS M. MILLER, WHAT WENT WRONG AT ENRON: EVERYONE'S GUIDE TO THE LARGEST BANKRUPTCY IN U.S. HISTORY (2002) at 75; *see also* Daniel Altman, *Finding Gems of Genius Among Enron's Crumbs*, N.Y. TIMES, Feb. 3, 2002 at 6A.

largest online broker of energy.[24] Obviously, there is a lot more to the birth and growth of Enron than is represented in this section. The other essays in this book, especially those of Jacqueline Weaver and Michelle Foss, will delve more deeply into the structure (and exploits) of Enron.

C. THE COLLAPSE OF ENRON[25]

Enron was well known for its aggressive stance on nearly virtually every energy-related issue. Some call that perspective "arrogance." Over time, Enron developed a veritable buffet of financial strategies to skirt and sometimes defy the boundaries of the law, all of which created the façade of profitability.[26] These strategies, which will be discussed in more detail later, helped to camouflage and hide Enron's precarious financial position. In fact, Enron's strategies to conceal information regarding its true financial status were so successful that several billion-dollar Wall Street firms registered—or at least feigned—surprise when Enron's house of cards collapsed.[27] What caused the ultimate downfall of Enron? Several issues contributed to Enron's downfall, although two in particular sealed its fate: 1) Enron lived and died by the "deal"—and many of its deals went horribly wrong, losing millions of dollars;[28] and 2) when Enron's sham accounting schemes came to light, the company collapsed, virtually overnight, as people sought to distance themselves from the company and its stock.

Following Enron's collapse, California's deregulation nightmare, energy traders' manipulation of the natural gas and electric indices and swap trades, and the economic and financial effect of the stock market plunge, consumers have become significantly more conservative in their perspectives towards taking on additional risks.[29] The net effect of these events has been a significant slowdown in states' movement towards a fully competitive retail marketplace. In that regard, California has taken steps to rees-

---

[24] David Rynecki, *Ten Stocks to Last the Decade*, FORTUNE, Aug. 14, 2000 at 114, 117.

[25] This section is primarily the result of an earlier draft by Victor Flatt, but some portions are derived from the work of Jacqueline Weaver. Jacqueline L. Weaver, *Can Energy Markets Be Trusted? The Effect of the Rise and Fall of Enron on Energy Markets*, 3 HOUS. BUS. & TAX L. J. (forthcoming Fall 2003); *see also* Flatt, *supra* note 15.

[26] PUBLIC CITIZEN'S CRITICAL MASS ENERGY & ENVIRONMENTAL PROGRAM, BLIND FAITH: HOW DEREGULATION AND ENRON'S INFLUENCE OVER GOVERNMENT LOOTED BILLIONS FROM AMERICANS (2001), *available at* http://www.law.wayne.edu/mcintyre/text/Blind_Faith_mjm.pdf; *see also* nn. 34–58 and accompanying text.

[27] *Id.*

[28] Deals "gone bad" include the Dabhol gas-fired power plant in India, the Azurix foray into privatizing water markets in England and Argentina, and Project Braveheart's rush into selling broadband capacity in a glutted market. *See* Weaver, *supra* note 25, at 15, n. 41.

[29] Jeffrey D. Van Niel & Nancy B. Rapoport, *"Retail Choice" Is Coming: Have You Hugged Your Utilities Lawyer Today? (PART II)*, 2002 No. 8 NORTON BANKR. L. ADVISER 2 (August 2002) at 1 (citations omitted).

tablish a fully regulated retail environment, effectively killing the first efforts at retail competition for electricity in the U.S.[30]

D. THE GATEKEEPERS' ROLE IN THE COLLAPSE OF ENRON

Regardless of your personal opinion regarding Enron's outside accounting firm, Arthur Andersen ("Andersen"), or Enron's lawyers, Enron was likely not capable of creating and implementing the various schemes used to artificially inflate its earnings without the help of its in-house and outside accountants and its in-house and outside lawyers. It is possible that no single outside law firm knew all that Enron was trying to do. We don't yet know what the lawyers said in advising Enron,[31] although the Third Examiner's Report may reveal more facts.[32] Other contributors to this book will delve more deeply into the roles and potential liability of the accountants and lawyers. I mention them here, simply to set the stage for their inclusion later in the text. As to Andersen, the laundry list of corporate misdeeds and accounting scandals, fraud, and other issues with which the company was intimately involved belies the argument that the Enron situation resulted from the acts of a single rogue employee (even, say, a Skilling or a Fastow),[33] notwithstanding the Andersen criminal jury's willingness to pin the blame on in-house counsel Nancy Temple.

Accounting Games and Enron[34]

One of the first questions that the public asked, after the Enron scandal came to light, was "why didn't we/the Board of Directors/the market know that Enron's business plan was doomed to fail?" Part of the problem was that Enron used and abused the accounting rules to obscure its true financial condition. Two of the most well

---

[30] *Id.*, citing Howard Horn, *Unplug Deregulation in Texas,* HOUS. CHRON. at C1 (August 4, 2002).

[31] *See* Neal Batson, Second Interim Report of Neal Batson, Court-Appointed Examiner, *In re* Enron Corp., No. 01-16034 (Bankr. S.D.N.Y. Jan. 21, 2003), *available at* 2003 Extra Lexis 4, 2003 WL 1917445 (stating that the Third Examiner's Report would explore the actions of the professionals in more detail).

[32] *Editors' Note:* In fact, in Batson's Third Interim Report, Batson alleges that some of Enron's senior officers kept pertinent information from Andersen in order to get Andersen's approval on the fraudulent deals. *See* Neal Batson, Third Interim Report of Neal Batson, Court-Appointed Examiner, *In re* Enron Corp., No. 01-16034 (Bankr. S.D.N.Y. June 30, 2003), Appendix C, at 38–44 [hereinafter Third Examiner's Report]. We are eagerly awaiting Batson's Fourth Interim Report, which we expect we'll discuss in the supplement to this text.

[33] Among Andersen's most notorious accounting clients are Adelphia Communications, Baptist Foundation of Arizona, Boston Chicken, Global Crossing, McKesson-HBOC, Qwest Communications, Sunbeam, Waste Management, WorldCom, and, of course, Enron. BARBARA LAY TOFFLER & JENNIFER REINGOLD, FINAL ACCOUNTING: AMBITION, GREED, AND THE FALL OF ARTHUR ANDERSEN 1 (2003).

[34] This section is derived in substantial part from an earlier draft by Victor Flatt, but Nancy Rapoport has made significant contributions as well. *See* Flatt, *supra* note 15.

known examples of the use and abuse of accounting rules were Enron's use of "special purpose entities" ("SPEs") and its use of "mark-to-market" accounting.

SPEs and mark-to-market accounting are both important parts of many businesses' operations, as are such other traditional accounting tools as pro forma reporting.[35] These tools are not, in themselves, good or evil. It's how they're used that makes them good or evil.

Drug companies and movie studios use SPEs to move the risk of a new product or movie off the balance sheet of the main company. An SPE will let a new or potentially risky project obtain financing, without increasing the risk exposure of the main company.[36] Without SPEs, there would be few new miracle drugs in development, few breakaway hits like *My Big Fat Greek Wedding*[37] (as well as fewer disasters such as phen-fen). SPEs let companies take on more risk than they (or their lenders) might otherwise choose to do. The SPEs let companies move risk off their main (consolidated) balance sheets by creating a separate, independently controlled entity, with a portion of the ownership separate from the main company's ownership.[38] The risk exposure of the SPE must also be severed from the exposure of the main company, or the SPE's structure becomes nothing more than smoke and mirrors.[39]

Enron violated both of the basic SPE principles. First, the ownership wasn't truly independent.[40] The partnerships that represented the 3% independent ownership of many of Enron's SPEs were partnerships controlled by Enron's Chief Financial Officer, Andrew Fastow. In essence, Fastow-the-CFO-of-Enron was negotiating with Fastow-the-general-partner-of-the-SPE. Not surprisingly, Fastow, not Enron, profited most from the deals that Enron made with the SPEs. Second, Enron guaranteed the SPEs that Enron would make good any losses that the SPEs suffered as a result of the deals with Enron. Therefore, Enron still retained substantial risk exposure and should have disclosed the debt on its consolidated balance sheet.[41]

Enron was able to manipulate reporting, hide debts, and hide poor-performing assets through these related-party transactions.[42] These internal business transactions also allowed Enron to meet its earnings expectations and sustain its stock price. Although GAAP requires detailed disclosure of related-party transactions in financial

---

[35] In pro-forma reporting, financial information is reported "as if" certain assumptions applied.

[36] WILLIAM C. POWERS, JR. ET AL., REPORT OF INVESTIGATION BY THE SPECIAL INVESTIGATIVE COMMITTEE OF THE BOARD OF DIRECTORS OF ENRON CORP., 38 (Feb. 1, 2002), *available at* http://news.findlaw.com/hdocs/docs/enron/sicreport/sicreport020102.pdf [hereinafter POWERS REPORT].

[37] MY BIG FAT GREEK WEDDING (IFC Films 2002).

[38] POWERS REPORT, *supra* note 36, at 5.

[39] *Id.*

[40] Walter M. Campbell, *Enron's Aggressive Accounting*, 22 No. 5 FUTURES & DERIVATIVES L. REP. 12 (2002).

[41] POWERS REPORT, *supra* note 36, at 14.

[42] *Id.* at 4.

statements,[43] Enron never disclosed sufficient details to determine exactly how it had structured the SPEs.[44] Enron also failed to report its indebtedness to creditors in guaranteeing the debt of its SPEs.[45] GAAP requires that material indebtedness be disclosed; yet Enron failed to disclose this indebtedness. It remains to be seen whether the court-appointed bankruptcy examiner for the Enron cases finds that Enron failed to make those disclosures on its own or based on advice from its professionals.[46] The Third Examiner's Report, due to be released after this essay has been proofread for publication, may shed some light on that question.

Like its SPEs, Enron misused mark-to-market accounting as well. Under GAAP, an enterprise cannot recognize revenue until the business has substantially completed performance in a bona fide exchange transaction.[47] In essence, mark-to-market accounting lets a company book all expected profits in the first year of a long-term deal. (If, later, the deal does not produce the expected profits, the company is required to restate the original profit figures.) Enron misused mark-to-market in two ways. First, because the deals that Enron was creating were usually "never before seen" types of deals (like Weather futures and markets in broadband), Enron was free to make up the projected profit figures. Since there were no other competing figures to challenge the profit projections that Enron was using, no one could challenge Enron's figures. Second, even when a deal was going poorly, Enron did not restate the original profit estimates. The first type of misuse is, possibly, understandable. After all, innovative companies *don't* have accurate profit projections for "never before done" deals. The second type of misuse, though, likely constitutes an intentional misrepresentation.

Let's now consider the pro forma reports. Enron used pro formas (and made up the underlying assumptions) to misrepresent its net income from its operations by labeling billion dollar expenditures as "one-time" or "non-recurring" charges.[48] (The memo from Andersen's in-house lawyer, Nancy Temple, to the Andersen partner in charge of the Enron account, David Duncan, dealt with precisely this issue.) Moreover, Enron engaged in active "earnings management," timed to ensure that it made "profits" every quarter. In effect, Enron overstated its restructuring charges to clean up its balance sheet, took a large one-time earnings hit, then reversed some of those charges at a later date and added them back into income in a period where true earnings fell short.[49]

---

[43] *Id.* at 179.

[44] *Id.* at 178.

[45] *Id.* at 197.

[46] *Editors' note: See* Third Examiner's Report, *supra* note 32, at Appendix C (role of Enron's officers). We expect the Fourth Examiner's Report to discuss the role of some of Enron's other professionals.

[47] Manuel A. Rodriguez, *The Numbers Game: Manipulation of Financial Reporting by Corporations and Their Executives*, 10 U. MIAMI BUS. L. REV. 451, 462 (2002) (citing Arthur Levitt, *The Numbers Game: Manipulation of Earnings in Financial Reports*, THE CPA J., Dec. 1998, at 14.).

[48] *Id.* at 3.

[49] *Id.* at 125.

Although this type of earnings management is not unheard of in the normal course of businesses, it does not follow GAAP.[50] Excluding the non-recurring items allowed Enron to meet and exceed its estimated earnings when, in actuality, Enron was unable to match investor expectations.

Enron also provided incomplete financial statements as far back as 1996. To be considered "complete," financial statements require several components, including a balance sheet, an income statement, and a statement of cash flow.[51] Enron repeatedly failed to provide these components on a timely basis.[52] The failure to provide such information deprived investors of critically needed information. Decisions based on the income statement alone could not provide the full financial picture necessary to make informed investor decisions. Enron's misleading financial statements distorted the information needed by investors, creditors, and lenders and, ultimately, undermined the credibility of the capital markets.[53]

If we're generating a laundry list of Enron's accounting abuses, we have to include one that is controversial—stock option grants. The use of stock option grants to compensate employees actually started as a reaction to a $1,000,000 cap on salaries for top-level employees. In order to "pay" those employees more than $1,000,000, Enron (as well as numerous other companies, both established and start-up) granted the employees stock options. Like most of these other companies, Enron did not treat stock option grants to employees as a form of compensation and did not list the grants as expenses. Though not illegal, this practice allows the posting of financial data that is not complete, especially in Enron's case, where stock options represented a very large and important form of employee compensation. Had Enron reported the granting of stock options in the manner proposed by the Financial Accounting Standards Board (FASB), Enron's profits from 1998 through 2000 would have been reduced by approximately $188 million.[54]

Additionally, Enron's auditors were compromised. An auditor examining these transactions should have been able to correctly interpret and understand what had occurred, required the proper reporting of such transactions, and ordered Enron to change its practices for future transactions. That did not happen. The Securities Exchange Commission ("SEC") uses auditing as its primary method of regulation of informa-

---

[50] *See* Rodriguez, *supra* note 47, at 460–61.

[51] *Id.* at 451.

[52] CBS.MarketWatch.com, *Enron, OPEC, Chevron Texaco and More*, CBS MarketWatch (2001) ("Enron, accused repeatedly of withholding critical financial information, provided investors Wednesday with a financial update of the company and its plans for the future as it heads toward a merger with Dynegy.").

[53] Peter Behr, *Lay Leaves Enron Board; Founder Severs Last Ties to Firm*, WASH. POST, Feb. 5, 2002, at A4 ("Powers told members of the House Financial Services Committee yesterday that the failure of Lay and other directors to police accounting and ethics violations at Enron was "appalling." Disclosures of executives' self-dealing and false financial statements by Enron shattered its credibility with investors and customers, forcing it into bankruptcy.").

[54] Julie Kosterlitz & Neil Munro, *Full Disclosure*, NAT'L J. (Feb. 23, 2002).

tion and financial documents for large publicly traded companies. The failure of the audits to reveal the problems, therefore, hampered any possible SEC enforcement actions. Enron's auditors also sold Enron some very creative financial structuring advice—advice that allowed Enron to book losses sufficient to prevent Enron from having to pay much income tax for many years, despite the vast profits that Enron was simultaneously reporting to shareholders and the SEC.[55]

The use of large accounting firms simultaneously to perform auditing and non-auditing services created a huge conflict of interest between auditor dependence and company pressures. During 2000, Enron paid a total of $52 million to Andersen: $25 million for auditing services and $27 million for non-auditing (consulting) services. The consulting services provided Enron with advice for structuring its business deals. Andersen estimated that keeping Enron as a client would generate $100 million a year in revenues.[56] In order to satisfy auditing standards, auditors must remain independent. Andersen's extensive consulting work for Enron may well have compromised its independence and its judgment in determining the nature, timing, and extent of audit procedures. Further, the $27 million in consulting fees may also have been lucrative enough to deter Andersen from asking Enron to make revisions to its financial statements.[57] Certainly, Andersen failed to live up to its founder's policy that the firm would always "[t]hink straight, [t]alk straight."[58]

E. ENRON AND THE CALIFORNIA ENERGY CRISIS[59]

It will take years to determine the exact roles played in the California energy markets by the various market participants (independent power generators, energy traders, pipeline capacity owners, the California Independent Service Operator ("ISO"), the California Power Exchange ("PX"), FERC, and state and federal politicians) and other factors, including the retail price caps, drought, and environmental laws. Armed with hindsight and internal Enron legal memoranda detailing the manipulation schemes[60]

---

[55] David Cay Johnston, *Wall St. Firms Are Faulted In Report on Enron's Taxes*, N.Y. TIMES, Feb. 14, 2003, at C1.

[56] Reed Abelson & Jonathan D. Glater, *Who's Keeping the Accountants Accountable?*, N.Y. TIMES, Feb. 15, 2002, at C1.

[57] *Id.*

[58] TOFFLER & REINGOLD, *supra* note 33, at 9.

[59] Large portions of this section come from the work by Jacqueline Weaver, whose detailed discussion of this topic covers nearly 50 pages. Additional contributions to this section were taken from an earlier draft by Victor Flatt. *See* Flatt, *supra* note 15; *see also* Weaver, *supra* note 25.

[60] The schemes Enron developed and used in California may not have been clearly illegal. But if using these schemes did not directly cross the line of illegality, Enron certainly cast its shadow across the line. Indeed, Enron's counsel advised the company of this fact prior to their implementation. *See* Harvey Rice, *Enron Was Told Strategy in California Could be Illegal*, HOUS. CHRON., December 12, 2002, at A1.

developed by Enron for use in the California market,[61] we now know that Enron and several other companies successfully "gamed" the California energy markets between 2000 and 2001. During that time, these companies reaped *huge* profits. One-hundred-fifty different companies have been called to task by the FERC over their involvement in these market manipulation schemes.[62]

California sought to restructure its retail energy markets to reduce its energy costs.[63] Eager to be the first state with this new market structure, both of California's state legislative houses unanimously passed the restructuring of the energy market. Sadly, the assumption that a deregulated retail market could not drive prices up and make matters worse was wholly erroneous. The hastily developed legislation restructuring California's energy market was subject to rampant abuse and has since been proven a horrible failure.[64]

A brief history of California's power generation and delivery system is relevant in understanding the complex nature of restructuring California's electric power generation and delivery system. California's energy problems began in earnest in 1973 with rolling brownouts. Utility companies could not build power plants fast enough to keep up with rapid population growth in the west.[65] Finally, environmental pressures to pursue energy conservation and to refrain from building nuclear power plants hampered the growth of new power plants. Under this pressure, in the 1960s, many power plants began burning oil, which was cleaner and cheaper than coal.[66] Unfortunately, the oil embargo and oil shortages of the 1970s resulted in huge cost increases for consumers. California's energy conservation movement continued to promote the use of energy conservation instead of continued power plant construction. Utility companies lacked the broad-based public support needed to justify their continued monopoly status.

The Energy Policy Act of 1992 allowed restructuring of the regulatory landscape and set the stage for deregulation.[67] The 1992 Act required power generators to

---

[61] On May 6, 2002, memos written by Enron's Oregon lawyers were given to FERC by Enron's bankruptcy attorneys and posted on FERC's website. The memoranda are on the FERC website, http://www.ferc.gov/ferris.htm, in Docket No. PA02-2-000 (last visited June 27, 2003).

[62] Order to Show Cause Why Market-based Rate Authority Should Not Be Revoked, Fed. Energy Reg. Comm'n Rep. (CCH) Docket No. PA02-2-00, 99 FERC P 61,272 (2002), *available at* http://www.ferc.gov/Electric/bulkpower/PA02-2/showcause-06-04-02.pdf.

[63] Mike Stenglein, *The Causes of California's Energy Crisis*, 16 NAT. RESOURCES & ENV'T 237 (2002).

[64] David Penn, *California's Electric Deregulation Debacle and Enron's Bankruptcy in Perspective: an Analysis*, (June 26, 2002), *available at* http://www.appanet.org/pdfreq.cfm?PATH_INFO=/legislativeregulatory/legislation/Pennenron.pdf&VARACTION=GO (last visited June 27, 2003).

[65] Jamaca Potts, Book Note, *Power Loss: The Origins of Deregulation and Restructuring in the American Electric Utility System, by Richard F. Hirsh*, 26 HARV. ENVTL. L. REV. 269, 273 (2002).

[66] *Id.*

[67] Timothy P. Duane, Essay, *Regulation's Rationale: Learning from the California Energy Crisis*, 19 YALE J. ON REG. 471, 496 (2002).

compete on the wholesale level and allowed states to begin retail competition as well.[68]

After marathon closed-door negotiations, the California legislature unanimously passed deregulation legislation commonly known as AB 1890.[69] The legislation became effective January 1, 1998, and it split California's electricity market into three areas: (1) generation of electricity, (2) transmission of bulk electricity flows, and (3) distribution of the electricity to the retail customer.[70] AB 1890 and CPUC created new rules for selling electricity into California. These new rules included the creation of two non-profit companies, the California PX and the California ISO.[71] The PX provided the marketplace for buying and selling electricity, known as the "wholesale power pool." The ISO managed the day-to-day operations and ensured the reliability of the transmission grid under the supervision of the FERC.[72] Since the PX and the ISO were non-profit companies, with no corresponding profit motive, they were supposed to prevent one segment of the industry from exercising its market power and manipulating the marketplace. Both the PX and the ISO failed in this effort.

The legislation froze retail rates at levels 10 percent below those in effect in June 1996.[73] Freezing retail rates proved to be one of the two major flaws in California's retail competition experiment. By eliminating the market-based pricing incentives from the retail market, consumers had no incentive to reduce their usage under this new regime. Beginning in May 2000, the demand for electricity began to exceed the supply, causing wholesale costs to skyrocket. The wholesale rates from December 1999 had increased by 938% in December 2000.[74] The retail price freezes affected Pacific Gas & Electric ("PG&E") and other retail power suppliers because they were required to absorb all the high wholesale costs.[75] On April 6, 2001, PG&E, California's largest IOU, filed for Chapter 11 bankruptcy protection.[76]

---

[68] A.B. 1890 § 854, 1996 Cal. Stat. 854, codified, in relevant part, at Cal. Pub. Util. Code §§ 330-398.5 (Deering 2001) [hereinafter AB 1890]. Federal jurisdiction over electricity is limited to wholesale transactions and power sales made in interstate commerce, while state jurisdiction over the retail marketplace is exclusive. *See* Transm. Access Policy Study Group v. Fed. Energy Regulatory Comm., 225 F.3d 667, 690–92 (2000).

[69] Duane, *supra* note 67, at 497.

[70] Harvey Wasserman, *California's Deregulation Disaster* (2001), *available at* http://www.nirs.org/mononline/califdereghw.htm (last visited June 27, 2003).

[71] Sam Weinstein & David Hall, *The California Electricity Market—Overview and International Lessons*, Public Services International Research Unit (February 2001), *available at* http://www.psiru.org/reports/2001-02-E-Calif.doc (last visited June 27, 2003).

[72] Stenglein, *supra* note 63, at 237.

[73] *Id.*

[74] *Id.*

[75] *Id.*

[76] *Id.*

1. Structural Flaws in the System[77]

Because of its poor design, the California energy market was ripe for the picking, and numerous companies swarmed over that market like buzzards to a kill. From what we know today, several design features of the California system combined to create the crisis: (1) the PX's market design and structure flaws; (2) the ISO's market design and structure flaws, (3) CPUC's prohibition on long-term contracts and other risk-reducing tools; (4) CPUC's forced divestiture of the IOU's generation and the corresponding obligation to serve load in California; (5) FERC's failure to timely respond to the crisis;[78] and (6) the market participants' ability to find and exploit multiple schemes to manipulate the market and extract huge profits from the market.[79] I leave the details of the market design flaws to the individual authors later in this text.

2. Game-Playing in California

California's market design had flaws, but the crisis was caused more precisely by a failure to understand the inherent rationale of regulation or to regulate despite those flaws.[80] Some of Enron's schemes appear to violate ISO rules, which expressly prohibit gaming the system. The ISO tariff prohibits (1) "gaming" (defined as "taking unfair advantage of the rules and procedures") of either the PX or ISO; (2) "taking undue advantage" of congestion or other conditions that may affect the grid's reliability or render the system "vulnerable to price manipulation to the detriment of [the ISO Markets'] efficiency"; or (3) engaging in anomalous market behavior, such as "pricing and bidding patterns that are inconsistent with prevailing supply and demand conditions."[81] Contrary to these express prohibitions, Enron and other companies created

---

[77] This section is derived from an earlier draft by Victor Flatt. *See* Flatt, *supra* note 15. Jacqueline Weaver also presents a comprehensive discussion of this topic in her essay on energy markets, *this book, infra* at 237–299.

[78] Stenglein, *supra* note 63, at 239.

[79] FED. ENERGY REG. COMM'N, FINAL REPORT ON PRICE MANIPULATION IN WESTERN MARKETS I-17 (Mar. 26, 2003).

[80] *Id* at I-12.

[81] Stoel Rives memo, dated Dec. 6, 2000, at 8, *available at* http://news.findlaw.com/hdocs/docs/enron/stoelrives120800mem.pdf (last visited July 7, 2003) [hereinafter Rives]. A different law firm wrote the second memo to Richard Sanders, assistant general counsel at Enron, after it reviewed the December 8 memo and then met with Enron traders, including the head trader in the Pacific Northwest, Tim Belden. This later memo explained that some of the analysis of the effect of the trading schemes on electricity prices or supplies in the earlier memo was erroneous. Severin Borenstein, an academic expert, concluded that some strategies were pretty clear violations of ISO rules. HOUS. CHRON., May 12, 2002 at 1A, 18A. In August 2002, FERC released a report that attempted to analyze the impact of Enron's trading strategies on Enron's profits and on California's electricity market. Staff Report of Federal Energy Regulatory Commission, *Initial Report on Company-Specific Proceedings and Generic Reevaluations; Published Natural Gas Price Data; and Enron Trading Strategies*, Docket No. PA02-2-2000, Aug. 2002 at 83–100.

and tested techniques that did all of the above. These techniques had names like Death Star (a phantom power transfer), Fat Boy (an artificial increase in demand), Ricochet (see Ricochet Chart and description below), Load Shift (megawatt laundering—see Load Shift Chart below) and others to extract huge profits from the California market.[82] Let's look at some of these games in a bit more detail.

Under several of the schemes, companies would intentionally over-schedule power into a transmission and power transfer interface in order to take advantage of the most obvious loophole in the system, in which the ISO would pay congestion relief charges to companies that failed to deliver power to the interface. In other words, the companies would schedule loads for delivery that they had *no intention* of providing, so that they could be paid by the ISO not to deliver that power. Enron called this particular scheme "Load Shift."[83] Chart C illustrates this scheme.

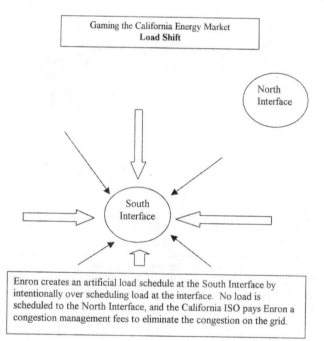

Chart C. Load Shift Chart

---

[82] We will examine some of these schemes in detail below.

[83] Rives, *supra* note 81, at 5.

Enron had another game called "Ricochet." Remember: 1) the PX was selling power on an hour-ahead and day-ahead basis, 2) the generators had no obligation to sell their power to the PX or keep it in state, and 3) the ISO had an obligation to import power from out-of-state if there was inadequate power available to meet the expected demands. Using this weakness in the system, Enron and others simply bought power from the PX, shipped it out of state to a confederate, then when prices were high enough in California, wheeled that same power back into California at prices that were sometimes 200 times higher than the price that was paid for the same power earlier that day.[84] See Chart D below. Simply put, Enron and other power suppliers exploited the system.

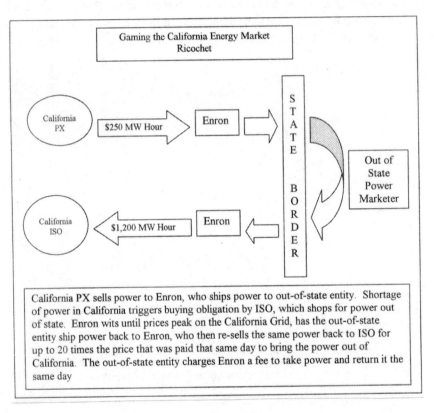

Chart D. Ricochet Chart

3. Other Abuses and Games[85]

One of the most popular abuses employed was "wash trades," "swap trades," or "roundtrip trades." Under this mechanism, there appears to be two purchases and two

---

[84] *Id.* at 6–7; LOREN FOX, ENRON: THE RISE AND FALL 197–98 (2003).

[85] This section is derived from an earlier draft of Jacqueline Weaver's essay on energy markets. *See* Weaver, *supra* note 25.

sales between two market participants. In reality, these trades exist only on paper: no power or money ever changes hands, as the two transactions take place simultaneously and cancel each other out completely. See Chart E below. Electricity was not the only commodity manipulated using the roundtrip trade method; roundtrip trading was also used for natural gas and broadband capacity. Dynegy, AEP, CMS, El Paso, and Williams admitted that some of their traders had engaged in roundtrip trades.[86]

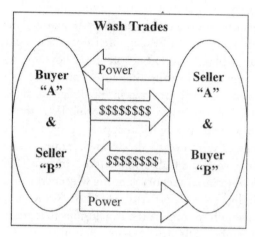

Chart E. Wash Trades Chart

Another abuse arose from withholding generation from the California market.[87] Many felt that, just as traders could profit from market manipulation, power generators could make billions if they could successfully game the system. As reflected in Jacqueline Weaver's essay in Chapter 2, power generators did game the system and reaped obscene profits as a result. Additionally, the market participants saw fit to manipulate the gas and electric trading indices. In other words, companies were reporting erroneous prices for natural gas sold onto the spot markets in California. Given the close tie between the industries—a lot of electricity is generated using natural gas—manipulating the published prices for the spot market would cause significant swings in electric prices.[88]

---

[86] Dynegy was the first company to settle with the CFTC over the practice of submitting false data to publications, paying a $5 million fine. Michael Davis, *$5 Million Settlement for Dynegy*, HOUS. CHRON., Dec. 20, 2002. at C1.

[87] The gaming tactics revealed in the Enron memos were those of a trader, not a power generator. Experts believed that electricity suppliers made billions of dollars through two mechanisms: (1) physical withholding, *i.e.,* not running power plants; and (2) economic withholding, *i.e.,* bidding supplies into the market only at very high prices or refusing to bid supply into the market David Ivanovich, *Enron Opens a Pandora's Box*, HOUS. CHRON., May 12, 2002 at 1A, 18A (quoting Severin Borenstein).

[88] FERC STAFF REPORT, COMPANY SPECIFIC SEPARATE PROCEEDINGS AND GENERIC REEVALUATIONS; PUBLISHED NATURAL GAS PRICE DATA; AND ENRON TRADING STRATEGIES, Docket No. PA02-2-000, Aug. 2002.

4. Where Was the FERC?[89]

FERC's role in the California crisis has been correctly criticized in light of this deregulation disaster. Since the major suppliers came from out of state, they were under FERC's *exclusive* regulatory jurisdiction. Most important, FERC failed in its duty to deter and discipline the anti-competitive behavior that was driving the pricing increases.[90] FERC was, from the inception of California's deregulation efforts, advised about the potential problems that might arise in that market.[91] It obtained reports as early as 1996 commenting on the potential for price manipulation and weakness in California's deregulation scheme.[92] FERC ignored all of these reports and signed off on California's deregulation plan. A recent report notes how few resources FERC then spent (and currently spends) on controlling anti-competitive behavior in the energy market.[93] FERC blamed on all of the flaws in the design of the California system on the California CPUC, California PX, and California ISO, thus deflecting attention from its own deficiencies and culpability in approving such a system.[94]

Other federal agencies were not so shy when it came to assessing FERC's poor performance in dealing with the California market. In June 2001, the General Accounting Office (GAO) released a report assessing why energy prices in California had increased so dramatically.[95] The report criticized FERC's study of outages, stating that it was not thorough enough to support the conclusions that generators had not withheld supply.[96] In November 2002, the Senate Committee on Governmental Affairs released a report regarding FERC's oversight of Enron. The Report found that FERC "was no match for a determined Enron."[97]

Had FERC acted in a timely manner, "it could have saved Californians billions of dollars."[98] At the most critical moment of the California crisis, FERC abandoned its role as a regulator, leaving the market vulnerable to massive profiteering.[99] FERC chose to investigate the various schemes being used to game the California energy market

---

[89] This section is derived from an earlier draft by Victor Flatt. *See* Flatt, *supra* note 15. Jacqueline Weaver also presents a comprehensive discussion of this topic in her essay on energy markets. *See* Weaver, *supra* note 25; *see also this book, infra* at 237–299.

[90] Duane, *supra* note 67, at 516.

[91] Stenglein, *supra* note 62, at 241.

[92] *Id.*

[93] David Ivanovich, *Report Raps FERC Over Enron Schemes*, HOUS. CHRON., November 12, 2002, at 1B.

[94] *Id.*

[95] GENERAL ACCOUNTING OFFICE, ENERGY MARKETS: RESULTS OF STUDIES ASSESSING HIGH ELECTRICITY PRICES IN CALIFORNIA (GAO-01-857) (June 2001).

[96] *Id.*

[97] U.S. SENATE STAFF REPORT OF COMMITTEE ON GOVERNMENTAL AFFAIRS, COMMITTEE STAFF INVESTIGATION OF FERC'S OVERSIGHT OF ENRON CORP. at 2 (Nov. 12, 2002), *available at* http://www.senate.gov/~gov_affairs/111202fercmemo.pdf.

[98] Stenglein, *supra* note 62, at 242 (quoting Senator Feinstein).

[99] Duane, *supra* note 67, at 517.

only after the disclosure of an internal legal memo at Enron. Sadly, prior to the release of that memo, FERC was convinced that California's problems were merely the result of poor design and a supply and demand imbalance.

5. Enron's Political Clout[100]

As the California market was crumbling, Enron and the in-state power generators launched a public relations campaign to convince the world that California's problems were not the result of market abuse, but instead were a self-inflicted supply and demand imbalance combined with a drought. Simultaneously, these companies flexed their lobbying clout with Vice President Dick Cheney and the FERC commissioners, arguing against imposing wholesale price caps in the California market.[101] As Enron put it, the crisis was created entirely by California's own hand, and California could solve that crisis itself.

Throughout Enron's lifespan, Enron aggressively lobbied Congress, the Commodity Futures Trading Commission ("CFTC"), the SEC, and the FERC for less regulation and oversight. Enron's lobbying success is impressive. Through a series of decisions, FERC authorized "power marketers" like Enron to operate with little oversight in its energy market.[102] Following FERC's decisions freeing Enron from regulatory oversight, Enron petitioned the chairwoman of CFTC, Wendy Gramm, to exempt energy derivatives from regulation. Ms. Gramm initiated rulemaking in favor of Enron's petition to be exempt from CFTC oversight.[103] Five weeks after stepping down from her governmental position, Ms. Gramm was named to Enron's board of directors, and she was compensated "between $915,000 and $1.8 million in salary, attendance fees, stock options and dividends over . . . eight years."[104] Coincidence? Perhaps.

---

[100] This section is derived in part from an earlier draft of Jacqueline Weaver's essay on energy markets and in part from an earlier draft by Victor Flatt. *See* Flatt, *supra* note 15; *see also* Weaver, *supra* note 25.

[101] On April 17, 2001, Ken Lay met with Vice President Dick Cheney to discuss the California crisis and reportedly gave Cheney an eight-point memo that advised the administration to reject price caps, even temporary price caps. The day after the meeting, Cheney said price caps would not solve California's problems. Patty Reinert, *FERC to Focus on Enron's Role in Calif. Energy Crisis*, HOUS. CHRON., Feb. 1, 2002 at A1. *See also* U.S. SENATE STAFF REPORT OF COMMITTEE ON GOVERNMENTAL AFFAIRS, COMMITTEE STAFF INVESTIGATION OF FERC'S OVERSIGHT OF ENRON CORP., at 41–46 (Nov. 12, 2002), *available at* http://www.senate.gov/~gov_affairs/111202fercmemo.pdf (regarding Enron's lobbying).

[102] MINORITY STAFF COMM. OF GOV'T REFORM, FACT SHEET: HOW LAX REGULATION AND INADEQUATE OVERSIGHT CONTRIBUTED TO THE ENRON COLLAPSE (2002).

[103] *Corrections*, S.F. CHRON., Feb. 1, 2002, at A2 ("A story Jan. 13 reported that Wendy Gramm, when chairwoman of the Commodity Futures Trading Commission in January 1992, led a majority vote in favor of a rule that exempted Enron Corp.'s electricity contracts from CFTC oversight. The vote, in fact, was to initiate the rulemaking in favor of Enron. Final approval of the rule occurred after Gramm had left the board.").

[104] Robert Manor, *Gramms Regulated Enron, Benefited From Ties*, CHI. TRIB., Jan. 18, 2002, at 17N. Senator Phil Gramm, Wendy Gramm's husband, was the senior Republican on the Senate Banking Committee, which participated heavily in the drafting of the 2000 legislation.

Enron's lobbying efforts were so aggressive and successful that "staff members of one Congressional committee asked a lobbyist for an Enron-led industry group to negotiate major aspects of the bill directly with regulators."[105] In 2000, the CFTC was further removed from regulating energy traders when Congress passed the Commodity Futures Modernization Act, which codified the CFTC's decision exempting energy contracts from regulatory oversight.[106]

6. Where Are the Manipulators Now?[107]

The glare of publicity about their gaming, manipulation, and accounting fraud has nearly bankrupted many of the companies involved in the California market and energy trading scandals. Most have now disposed of their energy trading businesses and are trying to preserve the remaining aspects of their companies. By December 2002, one year after the Enron bankruptcy, the stock prices of the companies that once rode the wave of deregulation have, with 3 exceptions, dropped by at least 80% (Dynegy, 97%; El Paso, 87%; Williams, 92%; AES Corp., 82%; Calpine, 87%; Mirant Energy, 93%; Reliant Resources, 88%; Duke Energy, 50%; Enron, 100%; and CMS Energy 60%):[108]

FERC has issued motions to show cause to 150 companies regarding their behavior in the California markets.[109] As of early 2003, it appears that in excess of $3.3 billion in refunds will be given back to California by these companies.[110]

CONCLUSION

Obviously, Enron's various business dealings, its ability to affect national policy, and its ultimate effect on markets is more complex than this primer reflects. The rest of the text will elaborate on each of these issues, as well as on many other issues (legal issues, business issues, and social and psychological issues). The beauty of Enron as a case study is that it presents so many complex issues—and so many learning opportunities.

---

[105] Michael Schroeder and Greg Ip, *Out of Reach: The Enron Debacle Spotlights Huge Void in Financial Regulation*, WALL ST. J. Dec. 13, 2001, at A1.

[106] Commodity Futures Modernization Act of 2000, Pub. L. No. 106-554, 114 Stat. 2763 (codified as amended in scattered sections of 7 U.S.C.).

[107] This section is derived from a previous draft by Jacqueline Weaver. *See* Weaver, *supra* note 25.

[108] The data is the decreased stock price from Oct. 15, 2001 to December 2002. John E Olson, *Energy Markets at a Crossroads: Has Deregulation Failed?*, Int'l Ass'n of Energy Economics Conference, Houston, Tex., Dec. 12, 2002.

[109] Order to Show Cause Why Market-based Rate Authority Should Not Be Revoked, Fed. Energy Reg. Comm'n Rep. (CCH) Docket No. PA02-2-00, 99 FERC P 61,272 (2002), *available at* http://www.ferc.gov/Electric/bulkpower/PA02-2/showcause-06-04-02.pdf.

[110] The Administrative Law Judge at FERC reviewing the complaints regarding market manipulation and violations issued an order assessing refunds in the amount of $1.8 billion. That order was reviewed by the FERC, and FERC determined that the proper refund amount was more like $3.3 billion. Richard A. Oppel, Jr., *Panel Finds Manipulation By Energy Companies*, N.Y. TIMES, March 27, 2003, at A14.

Enron and the Energy Market Revolution

Dr. Michelle Michot Foss*

What was Enron: cheater or innovator? Schemer or revolutionizing force? Was the company's impact overrated, or did it make a fundamental contribution? And is the energy market revolution, of which Enron was a part, alive or dead? For some time to come, the role of Enron and its executives in U.S. and global energy markets will be hotly debated and analyzed. More obviously, Enron will remain in the news, since Enron's chapter 11 filing is one of the largest and most complex bankruptcy proceedings in U.S. history.

Given the assumptions about the role and function of energy merchants in more competitive natural gas and electric power industries, and conditions in the aftermath of the spectacular collapse in this segment, a key question in the post-Enron era is whether energy policy experimentation will or can continue. Speculation is that the "Enron effect," coupled with electric power market dysfunctions in California and broader repercussions from the bursting stock market-dotcom-technology bubbles, has so tarnished important actors (energy companies, regulators, accountants, attorneys, financial analysts and houses and, yes, even university-based researchers) and so destroyed credibility that a new paradigm may be needed.

The passage of time and ultimate resolution of investigations, inquiries, and litigation as the Enron bankruptcy continues to unfold will begin to inform the post-Enron legacy, for better or worse. The Enron story can be distilled into four bold ideas that took root and were implemented in practice.

* Executive Director and Assistant Research Professor, Institute for Energy, Law & Enterprise (IELE), University of Houston Law Center. I have worked on natural gas industry issues for about 20 years. Enron was a corporate sponsor of IELE (formerly the Energy Institute at the C.T. Bauer College of Business, University of Houston) as well as the preceding Natural Gas Project, which Dr. Kenneth L. Lay, Enron chairman and CEO, helped to create during his tenure as member and chairman of the UH Board of Regents.

- A belief that "stranded value" inherent in the natural gas and electric power value chains could be captured and redistributed to shareholders and customers by breaking down regulated barriers to entry and by introducing competition and innovation.
- A gamble to create competitive advantage via sophisticated price risk management practices and businesses such as gas and utility portfolios and the "Gas Bank" concept. These activities, linked to a new "social compact," could both produce new revenues and profits (as Enron arbitraged across market differentials) *and* alleviate the impact of volatility on customers, as heavily regulated industries transitioned to more light-handed regulatory regimes.
- The new "social compact" that would replace the regulatory covenant and allow the public interest to be served through more efficient, competitive enterprises providing the same levels of reliability and security as regulated entities.
- A desire to export these strategies to international markets where, Enron managers and staff believed, the introduction of privatization and reduction in state control of energy sectors would yield premium returns to investors and shareholders and numerous benefits to customers in these countries and regions.

All of these ideas flowed out of the historical context for energy in the U.S. and elsewhere. They reflected an emerging mindset, well beyond Enron's own charter, that favored market-based over government-directed approaches to energy development and delivery. This emerging mindset partly mirrored long-term political, social, and economic shifts, but the more important drivers were dissatisfaction with the government-centered policies that grew out of the 1970s energy disruptions; the search for new, more profitable business models for the U.S. natural gas pipeline industry; economic need and cost and service quality associated with state-controlled energy enterprises in other countries; and changing technologies that fundamentally altered the cost structure of the natural gas and electric power industries and how business is conducted.

ENRON'S BOLD IDEAS

Enron was partly an artifact of the history of energy policy and politics in the U.S., including fundamental shifts in the market-government balance, as well as a change agent forged out of the battles to create a modern, market driven, natural gas industry. But Enron mostly needed to make money, and it was the drive toward revenues and profitability within the framework of the reconstituted natural gas industry that set Enron's ultimate course toward bankruptcy.

Capturing "Stranded Value" in Natural Gas and Electricity

As Enron managers began to formulate critical strategies, a number of competitive arenas had been defined through the restructuring process (see diagram below).[1] Pipeline companies had participated in the upstream businesses in the past. Enron initially expanded its upstream presence, but later spun off the domestic businesses (renamed EOG Resources). Gathering and storage continued to play important roles in the midstream mix. Most aggressively in its midstream businesses, Enron acquired additional pipeline systems (Transwestern and Northern Border, to name two of the more critical acquisitions). The company never acquired gas utility assets. While the acquisition of Portland General, an electric utility in Oregon, was one of the higher profile moves, Enron became adept as a non-utility developer of electric power generation, and began to dip into other businesses that had fallen in or out of vogue, liquefied natural gas ("LNG") as one specific example.

More significant to the emerging corporate strategy, however, were two key concepts. The first was the idea of *natural gas as a premium product*. Enhancing the value of natural gas was, of course, a driver for and outcome of restructuring, and a target for the industry as a whole—witness the Natural Gas Council activities.[2] Perhaps more than its peers, Enron understood how to position around this fresh take on the value of gas relative to other fossil fuels. The second key idea, both compatible with and in

---

[1] It is important to emphasize that during the process of natural gas restructuring, and as it morphed into electric power, the affected organizations included roughly 10,000 natural gas producers (among them the largest, publicly traded companies); about 100 interstate and intrastate pipelines; about 100 investor owned gas utilities (and probably 1,000 small and municipal systems); about 100 investor-owned electric power utilities; seven federal power authorities; approximately 10,000 public electric utilities and member cooperatives; 48 state legislatures (the U.S. natural gas system is, thus far, confined to the contiguous 48 states); 48 public utility commissions (slightly more for those states, like Texas, which split responsibilities between two agencies); the FERC; and the U.S. Congress.

[2] During this time frame, image was everything. The curtailments in the 1970s, wretched financial performance following the pipeline "take or pay" ("TOP") settlements, and sharp political conflict both between the industry and government and within the industry raised serious questions for the industry about reliability, market power, and price manipulation (was open access just a means to this end?). Within the industry, blame was shifted around as businesses in each segment struggled to contain the financial fall out from the restructuring process. The Natural Gas Council was formed in 1992 to unite the industry and provide quick response to customer concerns, establish industry-wide coordination to address reliability (a Natural Gas Reliability Council, like the North American Electric Reliability Council, was envisioned), position natural gas as the environmental fuel of choice, and encourage growth in demand (a stated target at the time the Natural Gas Council was formed was a 2.5 tcf increase nationwide by 1996). The focus on reliability quickly centered on information, use of electronic bulletin boards ("EBBs") and related issues, and fostered creation of the Gas Industry Standards Board ("GISB") to help build consensus on standards and protocols. The GISB has since become the North American Energy Standards Board, or NAESB, to reflect the growing consensus on standards across the continent, and the increased focus on electric power and gas/power convergence.

U.S. (Canada) Natural Gas Value Chains

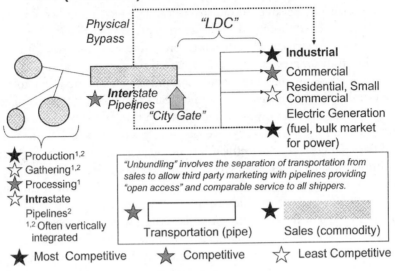

Note: provided by the author.

contrast to the first, was the notion of *creating private markets to extract business from regulated services,* part of which hinged on Enron's ability to manage risk. If natural gas was a premium fuel, in high demand by a large, lucrative industrial and commercial customer base, then Enron could compete with utilities to provide this service. But natural gas had also been commoditized, and everyone was a price taker. Risk management, of great concern to these customers, was a key component of Enron's new gas services approach. And while utilities often viewed Enron as a predator, stealing their large customers, they also used Enron as a gas supplier and risk manager either through bilateral contracts or through their own trading and marketing activities with Enron as their counterparty. Upstream of the large customers and utilities were producers who needed financing and risk management as well. Enron could integrate across the segments, re-bundling diverse services that were outside of regulatory jurisdiction and capturing value from price risk that had otherwise been stranded, in a sense, in the pre-restructuring, regulated environment.

As these businesses developed, Enron needed to press into action a workable formula for its risk management functions. The Gas Bank was the first step.[3] Until this

---

[3] While still at McKinsey, Jeff Skilling launched the "Gas Bank" concept during 1989–1990, which grew into Enron Capital and Trade (which Skilling later led), and then into a host of energy service businesses that optimized assets through financial market positions, took speculative positions (Enron traded for its own accounts), and bundled energy supplies and services into packages with risk management strategies that provided benefits to major customers (from hospitals and schools to major industrial customers) and lucrative incentives back to Enron.

innovation, producers typically financed production out of cash flow, if large enough, or from secured financing from a variety of sources, such as commercial banks. Imbedded in producer finance were returns that Enron could capture both from production cash flows and, more important, from the risk management function that producers had not faced during wellhead price control. Following the Gas Bank innovation, Enron needed an "angle" to successfully pitch risk management to utilities, at a time when state regulators were quite leery of approving risk management schemes for their client industry. Rethinking the social compact for public utilities became the mantra. As the company acquired skills in its new business activities, the logical extension was to include electric power. By the mid 1990s, Enron Gas Services became Enron Energy Services, which combined natural gas, power, and other fuels with incentive pricing, trading, and risk management, and related infrastructure services (like transportation arrangements) into total, value-added packages.[4]

Dealing in Risk

Enron became so competent at dealing in risk that, by 2001, most estimates were that the company controlled roughly 40 percent of the wholesale market for both natural gas and electric power.[5] Within Enron, the instinct on long-term portfolios for gas, and the Gas Bank, represented the earliest glimmer of the "asset-light" strategy for which Enron was credited, and blamed, later on. The prevailing sense was that broad and liquid financial markets and risk portfolios could be created for gas and, eventually, power and other commodities. These instincts arrived early on, at least by 1991, although the "asset-light" phrasing and explicit strategy did not come into play until 1999.[6] Enron was transforming itself and the marketplace in a very distinctive way. The company was rapidly becoming a financial business and pushing its peer group in that direction.

The initial concept for the Gas Bank was directed to the specific problem of producer finance in the more volatile natural gas marketplace. Underlying the bank and the products that extended from it was the right to market existing "proved and developed production" ("PDP"). PDP assets are less risky than "proved and undeveloped" production ("PUD") or "proved, developed, but non-producing" ("PDNP") assets. PDNP assets still, however, represent a critical phase for producers, who must assemble financing to move from the initial exploration well to development of a field.

---

[4] The author's interpretation of Enron's strategies is based on information accumulated in the years since 1991 from Enron staff and managers (including Rob Bradley, Margaret Carson, Cathy Abbott, Bruce Stram, Mike Muckelroy, Steve Kean, Jeff Skilling, and Ken Lay) in both written and verbal communications (on file with author).

[5] *Power Marketer Sales Statistics*, POWER MKT. WK., Mar. 19, 2001, at 15.

[6] Current and former Enron managers have speculated that the asset-light strategy did not pre-date 1999 (various communications, late 2002) (on file with author). However, it is clear that the fundamentals were in place well before then.

The essence of Enron's suite of offerings for producers is shown in the table below, with E&P risk increasing to the right. In 1991, the first year of operation, Enron completed roughly $100 million in producer finance transactions through the production payment/prepay mechanism. By 1993, Enron had almost $500 million in producer finance, with more than one-third provided through other mechanisms, and by 1994 transactions exceeded $1.5 billion, including equity, joint ventures, limited partnerships, loans, and production payment/prepay. Volumetric Production Payments ("VPPs") were designed to compete with senior debt provided by commercial banks but with more favorable terms (more flexibility with regard to risk-weighted reserves, slightly cheaper interest rates). (See table on the next page for terminology.)

Mezzanine financing for producers offered through an entity like was another innovation. The cost to producers was higher, but Enron was willing to accept a higher level of risk as well. Equity financing through development partnerships helped to launch the riskiest ventures targeting probable production based on geologic information—no preliminary well data, or only data inferred from production near the prospective area. Enron did establish some constraints, declining to finance activities like ultra-deep onshore plays (below 16,000 feet) or offshore prospects in water deeper than 275 feet.

Enron's success with its producer finance programs quickly attracted additional entrants. Other energy merchants moved in. Industry majors like Shell set up producer finance groups. Outside of Enron, most competitors focused on mezzanine products, creating something of a boom. Like energy derivatives, producer finance transactions were reportedly using mark-to-market models as current revenue.[7]

With the collapse of the fleet of producer finance programs associated with energy merchants, these contracts had to be unwound, fortunately with little impact for the producers but with substantial implications for the merchants. The consequences of shuttering the energy merchant producer finance businesses are more serious going forward. Both VPP and mezzanine products have largely exited the capital markets. In addition to producers, developers of midstream and power assets are also likely to be heavily affected, adding to the potential for market disruptions and price pressure as the U.S. economy recovers.

Changing the Regulatory Covenant

As natural gas restructuring progressed, natural gas supply procurement altered dramatically. Before 1983, both producers and local distribution companies ("LDCs") were locked into rigid arrangements that, while they provided guaranteed markets for producers and supply security for LDCs, also posed a host of problems. What if market conditions changed? Producers had no other options for marketing their production. What if LDCs needed less capacity than contracted for? Take or pay clauses

---

[7] Based on market trends documented by Oil & Gas Investor (various issues) and industry sources (on file with author).

Enron Gas Services Producer Finance

Increasing Reserve Risk →

	Gas Purchase Contracts	Gas Bank	Volumetric Production Payments (VPPs)	Net Profits Interests (NPIs), Junior VPPs	Development Partnerships
Purpose:	Right to market existing PDP	Purchase gas at fixed price under prepaid contract	Acquire reserves at fixed price	Provide capital to facilitate acquisitions	Provide capital to exploit reserves
Reserve Categories:		Evaluation primarily based on PDP (some acreage dedicated, PUD)	Evaluation based primarily on PDP (some PDNP and PUD)	Based on PDP residual cash flow, PDNP & PUD	Based on PUD and probable
Market View of Financing:		Viewed as fixed price contract with partial prepayment	Viewed as non-recourse senior financing	Viewed as non-recourse mezzanine financing	Viewed as equity financing

Source: Information provided by Doug Hurley, Enron Gas Services, 1994.

and minimum bills would apply. No flexibility existed for short term or seasonal variations. It was as if demand elasticity was a forgotten principle, the tradeoff being certainty.

By the mid 1980s, with special marketing programs ("SMPs") and the first stage of open access through FERC's[8] Order 436 on deregulation underway, innovations were dropping into place. The short-term spot market developed; producers could market their available supplies elsewhere, and opportunities existed for value capture at points other than the wellhead. In the lead-up to FERC's proposed "Mega-NOPR" (notice of proposed rulemaking), which was implemented as Order 636, seasonal pricing had emerged and variations in contract length were under experimentation. Post-636, the variety of offerings continued to increase, to reflect peak and off-peak demand requirements, firm and interruptible service with various conditions, and, of course, the abundance of available, unregulated products that marketers and brokers could package, such as balancing, peak-shaving storage, emergency assistance, and so on.

For LDCs, there were two considerations. The first, another form of cultural adaptation in the industry, was the acceptance of marketers as reliable providers of supply. LDCs were suspicious that, among other things, marketers were unreliable and would unfairly price contracts, that their access to supply was not firm, that they were not creditworthy and did not have the financial strength to back their commitments, and that they would drop the ball on critical balancing and administration requirements. The second problem was exposure to risk.[9] With greater flexibility also came greater volatility. The spot and short-term markets could be quite variable, especially around seasonal peaks, and market conditions could change drastically over the term of a contract. LDCs needed to be able to manage these issues, but had little encouragement from Public Utility Companies ("PUCs") to do so or, if the encouragement was there, then the skill sets and internal leadership to create them were missing.

Enter Enron's utility portfolio concept. Enron managers deduced that risk essentially was being shifted from the federal jurisdiction to states. PUCs were bottlenecks, mandating least-cost purchases and preferring that LDCs procure supplies on the spot market, based on a presumption that spot markets were where the most competitive bargains could be found. Consumer advocates liked these approaches and lobbied hard to encourage PUCs to maintain them, but at Enron the opinions were that consumer advocates were not fully recognizing the element of risk. Buying spot gas introduced a greater chance of price volatility and reduced supply security. The gas market had essentially flipped—from the rigid tradition of long-term contracts pre-1983, to the post-636 world where upwards of 70 percent of gas was trading in the 30-day spot market. In addition, Enron managers felt that too much risk was shifting to consumers, who were already saddled with Order 636 transition costs. The idea was that LDCs could have better demand-side management with fixed-term pricing, more flexible condi-

---

[8] "FERC" is the Federal Energy Review Commission.

[9] *See* JOHN HERBERT, NATURAL GAS CLEARINGHOUSE REPORT (1993).

tions, and price risk management supplanting the long-term contracts in the pre-636 world. Accordingly, Enron launched a campaign to convince PUCs and LDCs that the portfolio management approach (a mix of supply contracts that reflected variations in pricing, term, and risk) would be more effective. In 1991, 45 percent of the customer product mix at Enron Gas Services was long-term sales, with LDCs accounting for 56 percent of those sales. Spot sales accounted for 55 percent, with LDCs constituting 46 percent. Enron's goal was to shift some portion of LDC spot sales into the more lucrative long-term arrangements. Long-term sales did not include only gas, but all of the other services Enron wanted to provide, including risk management, to LDCs.[10]

The choices for LDCs were many, with firm contracts that enabled fixed, truncated, dampened, or floating prices as well as short-term fixed (indexed/negotiated) and floating/negotiated options. Beyond LDCs, Enron pushed the portfolio concept for gas-fired electric power generation and expanded its offerings of products. These products included 15-year fixed price commitments, 25-year market-based commitments, and flexible delivery. For both LDCs and power generation, the suite of risk management programs unbundled physical delivery from price and included swaps (forward hedges), participating swaps (participating hedges), maximum price hedges (caps), and maximum/minimum hedges (collars).[11] Of course, as time passed, the products became even more sophisticated, but the basic point remained—gas and electric power utilities could, with judicious use of portfolios and risk management, vastly improve their gas supply options and provide benefits to consumers in return.

Enron's arguments were compelling, but gas utilities were bound by the "regulatory covenant" that granted franchise protection in return for assurances of "just and reasonable" rate regulation. Instead, Enron managers argued that LDCs needed to be free to set flexible contract provisions that not only would better serve their consumers (the utility portfolio concept) but also would reflect conditions in the vital upstream businesses, thus linking Enron's innovations for utilities with their innovations in producer finance. LDC supply contracts would be arms-length from regulators, but they would reflect negotiated understandings about the role of private contracts in LDC obligations to serve. The utility portfolio scheme also would include light-handed, more cost-effective regulation that allowed LDCs to experiment and, importantly, to extend open access principles into the gas utility segment.[12]

As with most of Enron's initiatives, other motives were present for the company's strategic moves. A high-profile case had dominated the natural gas supply scene, one that pitted Canadian producers against the California regulators. At stake were long-

---

[10] All details in this section are based on information provided by Enron. This information includes meetings and follow-up conversations with Ken Lay and Jeff Skilling in September 1991 and with Bruce Stram in October 1991 (on file with author).

[11] For a good glossary of energy trading terminology, go to http://www.nymex.com/media/glossary.pdf.

[12] *See* Bruce Stram & Terry Thorn, *Beyond Regulation: A 'Social Compact' for Gas and Electricity*, PUB. UTIL. FORT., Mar. 1, 1993, at 19.

term export supply contracts that had been negotiated by the producers and approved by Canada's National Energy Board or NEB, Canada's equivalent to FERC, with Pacific Gas Transmission Company ("PGT"). Hard into its philosophy that spot market purchases were best for utilities, the CPUC was sympathetic to consumer advocate arguments that the contracts presented excess rents to the producers, and that regulators should disallow some $200–500 million in alleged overcharges. The heated Alberta-California "gas war" spilled over into sharp jurisdictional disputes between the state and the FERC over pipeline capacity releases by Pacific Gas & Electric ("PG&E") on the PGT system.[13] The disputes were eventually settled, with considerable effort by the Canadians, but they left a decidedly sour note on the issues of spot or long-term gas purchases, state or federal authority, and interests of marketers and producers as opposed to regulators and consumer advocates. Ironically, these disputes reflected the host of issues that surfaced in California energy markets by 2000.

From the time the notion of a social compact was articulated until Enron's collapse, Enron pushed hard for state regulators to adopt, and adapt to, this way of thinking. And, again, Enron was not the only company making these arguments. What differed was the intellectual ground from which Enron argued and the vast research and supporting opinions that it marshaled in its effort. Also, Enron had a vast army of willing supporters, given the philosophical shift toward markets and the willingness to rethink regulation.

"Going International"

After Enron's dominance in the U.S. became evident, and before its adventures in broadband and other businesses, Enron looked to the international arena. Restructuring in the U.S. had rapidly depleted profit margins as firms "competed away" gains, and new sources of growth were needed. Emerging markets and many developing countries offered fertile ground for new infrastructure investments. Consequently, Enron stepped out of America with a first gas-fired generation IPP at Teeside in the U.K. From there, the company quickly took strategic positions in locales such as Argentina (with gas pipelines and power), and it pursued and won the high visibility Bolivia-Brazil gas pipeline and engaged in its high-profile Dabhol power project in India. Apart from infrastructure, Enron also led the way to help establish nascent wholesale markets and constantly searched for risk management opportunities and vehicles around its international asset base.

Enron's investments were supported, as usual, by creative analysis and persuasive arguments. There was no objection to the case for international development. Institu-

---

[13] Based on Arlon Tussing, *An Overview of FERC's Mega-NOPR,* Address at the Conference of the Independent Petroleum Association of Mountain States and the International Association for Energy Economics (Feb. 13, 1992); *see also* UH IELE, PROPRIETARY REPORT ON U.S. NATURAL GAS MARKETS (2001) (prepared for SRIC Corp.) (on file with author and available by request *at* http://www.energy.uh.edu/publications.asp).

tions like the World Bank and U.S. Agency for International Development were pushing international energy companies to move into new terrain, especially where capital constraints were greatest. Support for international risk taking was ample, through export import banks, credit agencies, risk insurance providers and guarantors, and so on. But international markets were quite uneven. Regulatory frameworks were nascent and immature. Demand was artificially boosted by rampant tendencies for governments to subsidize energy prices, presenting the danger that returns could be thin. Economies were fragile. Politics were stubborn and privatization programs uneven. Enron, a quick first-mover for international natural gas and electric power investments, also became the "go to" firm for risk assessment that financial analysts could use to evaluate projects undertaken by Enron and its competitors. Unlike oil, which has long been an international business, natural gas and electric power were typically domestic industries, dominated by public utility or public service constraints and, outside of the U.S. and Canada, always sovereign-owned. Assessing the risks undertaken by publicly traded firms that had, up to that point, often been protected by utility regulation in the U.S. was not easy. Enron staff and managers made the job easier with ample access (on the company's own terms) to information, data, and opinion.[14]

There were many underlying problems in Enron's international strategies, but one in particular was the tendency to value international transactions using the same accounting techniques as in its U.S. contracts.[15] Given the level of risk Enron was assuming, that exposure easily could deplete reserves. The investment requirements on large projects could rapidly exceed what the company could sustain. (Enron often used a strategy of taking large equity positions to launch new projects and then selling down to reduce exposure, so that delays in these transactions contributed to risk.) Enron's aggressive accounting on extremely high-risk, opaque international transactions created undue pressure on the company's balance sheet and income statement. More than other factors, Enron's international projects most likely caused the company's eventual downfall.[16]

---

[14] For example, *see* Margaret Carson, *Global Power Privatization and Deregulation Trends, in* THE 1997 NATURAL GAS YEARBOOK (Robert E. Willet ed., 1997). For information and analysis on international energy investment trends, including trends, role of institutions, and issues, see Michelle Michot Foss, *Latin American Gas: Progress, Potholes and Pitfalls* in NATURAL GAS YEARBOOK (Financial Communications Company, Houston, 2001); Michelle Michot Foss, *Perspectives on the International Exploration Business,* in INTERNATIONAL OIL AND GAS EXPLORATION: A BUSINESS PERSPECTIVE (American Association of Petroleum Geologists, Tulsa, Oklahoma, 2000); Michelle Michot Foss, *Worldwide Transitions: Energy Sector Reform and Market Development,* in NATURAL RESOURCES AND ENVIRONMENT (ABA Section, Natural Resources, Energy and Environmental Law, Spring 1998).

[15] Information on accounting for international transactions was provided by a colleague then at Enron in 1997 who prefers to remain anonymous.

[16] An opinion on the contribution of Enron's international investments to its collapse was provided anonymously by a former international project developer at Enron, December 2002. His comments supported the author's own analysis and conclusions.

CONCLUSIONS: FORESTS AND TREES

The personal losses and traumas associated with Enron's downfall have made it difficult, at best, to draw objective conclusions about this company and its role in, and contribution to, the energy market revolution that was launched in the 1970s. It has been easy to dismiss Enron as yet another example of capitalist excess and simple to attribute both Enron's collapse and the collateral damage caused by that collapse on deregulation, the incursion of markets, and the inability to manage and govern risks and behaviors. However, private companies can achieve astounding levels of creativity and innovation when presented with market incentives and given a willingness to take chances. Out of the chaos of energy disruptions in the 1970s, and the high political conflict of natural gas restructuring and gas/power convergence, Enron employees mobilized and deployed strategies for new products and businesses that were stunning. Enron's collapse was stupid—there is no other way to put it. The loss to society and the energy marketplace of Enron's creativity and innovation must be added to the total burden in diminished wealth, jobs, trust and credibility, and momentum to continue the energy market revolution.

We can draw a number of lessons.

- With respect to the excesses of capitalism, Enron's collapse triggered many inferences to Samuel Insull and Joseph P. Kennedy, two of the more colorful figures in American business history who provide strong analogies to the Enron story. With Thomas Edison, Insull helped to launch the modern electric power industry by seeking public utility regulation by the states as a means of ordering a chaotic new marketplace and providing reasonable returns for the early investors. His intention was that the need for regulation would be short-lived, only until the propensity toward "destructive competition" declined and the industry was established. (He was not fond of government intervention.) The historic record indicates that Insull also was guilty of financial engineering practices that stretched the truth about his enterprise, Middle West, which had grown into a vast holding company that exerted market power and abused privilege. Middle West also collapsed, of course, and Insull died a poor man. Kennedy, on the other hand, managed to recover from his indiscretions (wash-trading techniques that artificially pumped up the value of stocks and seem suspiciously similar to what energy traders are thought to have practiced). Kennedy's misadventures led to the creation of the SEC and regulatory oversight of trading and financial markets.[17] Apart from corporate abuse, what the combined stories of Insull,

---

[17] For recent treatments of Insull and Kennedy, *see* Rebecca Smith, *Enron's Rise and Fall Gives Some Scholars A Sense of Déjà vu*, WALL ST. J., Feb. 4, 2002, at A1; Eric Rau, *Making the Street Safe*, FIN. TIMES, June 27, 2001, at 13.

Kennedy, and Enron really demonstrate is the tension between creating new markets (and the desire for all of the economic benefits that this entails) and the need for government oversight. Building new markets is hard, and the dance between business and government is not easily consummated. We prefer not to think that history will repeat itself, because this implies that we never learn any lessons. Yet, history still repeats itself.

- To that point, the rise of Enron and the energy market revolution are best captured in the concept of the "evolving bargain" between business and government, as put forth by Willis Emmons.[18] Market structures are moving targets. Firms that pursue first-mover strategies risk getting burned as new and emerging markets and the regulatory frameworks that underpin them evolve. Firms both respond to, and push for, market structures. The dynamics of the process are complex and troublesome to anticipate. Was Enron too much of a first-mover, faced with having to cover mistakes from the drive to be a market leader?

- Another useful line of query comes from Peter Senge, who pioneered the idea that companies are learning organizations. His case study on People's Express[19] also is a commentary on first-movers and new markets that are moving targets as a matter of evolving bargains, but he shows how easy it is to miss the obvious. In the case of People's Express, the lesson was that airline travelers want more than just discount prices and will choose providers who also offer other benefits like on-time service.[20] In the case of Enron, creativity and innovation were not enough. Trust and credibility have turned out to be desirable options as well.

- With the downfall of the company, the Enron "asset-light" strategy of emphasizing revenues and profits from financial operations rather than from a hard asset base has been sufficiently disparaged. Monday-morning quarterbacking has dictated a return to hard-asset businesses for the energy sector. These observations miss the point. What Enron demonstrated, if anything, is that there truly is value associated with information and knowledge. It may seem that Enron was a perverse practitioner of its own corporate philosophy, attaching the greatest value to information and knowledge that could obfuscate the company's true financial health. But, in fact, information and knowledge provide comparative advantages to a company's core business, just as good information and knowledge about what companies

---

[18] WILLIS EMMONS, THE EVOLVING BARGAIN: STRATEGIC IMPLICATIONS OF DEREGULATION AND PRIVATIZATION (2000).

[19] PETER M. SENGE ET AL., THE FIFTH DISCIPLINE: THE ART AND PRACTICE OF THE LEARNING ORGANIZATION 127–35 (1990).

[20] *Id.* at 132.

do and how they do it is invaluable for the marketplace to function well. These would seem to be lessons that everyone could take to heart.

- Time and again during the saga of Enron's collapse, and as other energy merchants were imploding, the question was raised of what was proper and what was not in the fast-moving energy markets that were being created. What were the rules of the game that Enron and other companies were playing? One thought is that the advent of online exchanges removed the possibility of formal rules imposed on the NYMEX by the SEC and CFTC, providing some market ordering and governance.[21] This lesson is under active debate, as industry and government engage in their evolving bargain dance to determine the proper extent of oversight for online exchanges.

- Finally, as always, what is the role of government when it comes to new markets? How is government accountability assessed? The "bums" can be thrown out, but can a case be made for regulatory malfeasance and, if so, what would that imply? The search for the proper role of government has been long underway in U.S. business history. Those of us who are in the business of thinking this out can be assured of employment for some time to come.

---

[21] This idea was voiced by Deniese Palmer-Huggins, former NYMEX director in Houston, in a private conversation with the author on Mar. 11, 2003. Aberrant trading behavior is monitored and penalized at NYMEX, which is subject to the formal rules of the U.S. Securities and Exchange Commission (SEC) and Commodities Futures and Trading Commission (CFTC). For an overview of NYMEX's regulations, see NYMEX, Safeguards and Standards, *available at* http://www.nymex.com/jsp/about/ss_main.jsp (last visited Aug. 18, 2003).

Malefactors of Great Wealth: A Short History of "Aggressive" Accounting

*Steven Harmon Wilson, Ph.D.**

In December 2001, soon after being celebrated as the seventh largest corporation in the country, the Enron Corporation of Houston, Texas, filed the then-largest bankruptcy action in the nation's history.[1] Enron's stock price crashed, depriving shareholders of billions of dollars of stock value. The collapse threw thousands of Enron employees out of their jobs and, simultaneously, wiped out their retirement plans (which largely consisted of Enron's own stock). Enron's failure has been since been attributed to corporate mismanagement and over-reaching to the point of hubris.[2] It has also become apparent, moreover, that the energy trader's rise to the short list of top corporations, and its high profits, had been mostly elaborate illusions. According to a report of the Senate Committee on Governmental Affairs reviewing the Enron debacle, Enron's stock value was largely sustained by "aggressive" accounting practices that were at best misleading, at worst fraudulent.[3]

These aggressive accounting practices also were, it now appears, widespread. The Enron shock was followed by similar troubles at other Wall Street stars, including Adelphia, Tyco, and WorldCom. A quick succession of major corporate bankruptcies

---

* Steven Harmon Wilson received his doctorate from Rice University. He is an Assistant Professor of History at Prairie View A&M University. He also works as a litigation and management consultant.

[1] In re Enron Corp. et al., Chapter 11, Case No. 01-16034 (Bankr. S.D.N.Y. 2001). Documents pertaining to all of the Enron bankruptcy proceedings are available at http://www.elaw4enron.com/.

[2] Enron's main business was the trading of "energy" commodities—especially electricity and natural gas—as might be expected for a corporation with its headquarters in Houston, Texas, but it also traded commodities ranging from broadband telecommunications services to weather insurance. Tom Fowler, *The Fall of Enron*, HOUS. CHRON. Oct. 20, 2002, at A1.

[3] U.S. STAFF OF SENATE COMM. ON GOVERNMENTAL AFFAIRS, 107TH CONG., FINANCIAL OVERSIGHT OF ENRON: THE SEC AND PRIVATE-SECTOR WATCHDOGS 75 (Comm. Print 2002), *available at* http://www.senate.gov/~gov_affairs/100702watchdogsreport.pdf; *see also The Fall of Enron: How Could It Have Happened: Hearing Before the Senate Governmental Affairs Comm.*, 107th Cong. 376 (Jan. 24, 2002), *available at* http://www.access.gpo.gov/congress/senate/senate12sh107.html.

(incredibly, WorldCom's bankruptcy superseded Enron's bankruptcy as the nation's largest)[4] contributed to a national economic downturn. Wall Street analysts had been providing "buy" recommendations on questionable stock for all sorts of reasons other than their own personal beliefs in the strength of particular companies;[5] moreover, those analysts had accepted, apparently without question, the financial reports from many companies that based profit projections on such aggressive accounting. The analysts' transgressions, and the widespread nature of the recent corporate scandals, resulted in a crisis in investor confidence, which is delaying the economic recovery.[6] This news revealed that the apparently robust stock market of the 1990s—which had already weathered the rapid collapse of high-technology "dot.com" stocks—had been surviving under a speculative bubble. Federal prosecutors and congressional investigators are now attempting to unravel the tangled web of facts and fictions that fed the rise and subsequent fall of the market. The official search for the truth will last many months, perhaps years, but lawmakers believe that enough is already known about the Enron affair and the other corporate shenanigans to allow them to enact reforms that the lawmakers hope will prevent repetition.[7]

What follows will approach the subject of discreditable and possibly illegal behavior by high-flying executives from another perspective. This essay will begin with the past and move forward, seeking to make a preliminary assessment of how closely the present-day events echo earlier historical cycles of scandalous revelation and scandalized reform. The nineteenth century saw the westward expansion of the United States as well as the industrialization of the American economy. Many Americans grew rich simply by providing traditional goods and services to a rapidly expanding population. Some achieved great wealth by investing in novel goods and services made possible or newly profitable by emerging production, transportation, and communications technologies. Others reaped enormous rewards by despoiling vast natural resources, ex-

---

[4] Simon Romero & Riva D. Atlas, *WorldCom's Collapse: the Overview; WorldCom Files for Bankruptcy; Largest U.S. Case*, N.Y. TIMES, July 22, 2002, at A1.

[5] U.S. STAFF OF SENATE COMM. ON GOVERNMENTAL AFFAIRS, 107TH CONG., FINANCIAL OVERSIGHT OF ENRON: THE SEC AND PRIVATE-SECTOR WATCHDOGS 75, 69–70 (Comm. Print 2002), *available at* http://www.senate.gov/~gov_affairs/100702watchdogsreport.pdf; *see also* Barton Aronson, *The Enron Collapse and Auditor Independence: Why the SEC Should Go Further in Regulating Accounting Firms*, Jan. 24, 2002, *available at* http://writ.corporate.findlaw.com/aronson/20020124.html.

[6] U.S. STAFF OF SENATE COMM. ON GOVERNMENTAL AFFAIRS, 107TH CONG., FINANCIAL OVERSIGHT OF ENRON: THE SEC AND PRIVATE-SECTOR WATCHDOGS 75, 6 (Comm. Print 2002), *available at* http://www.senate.gov/~gov_affairs/100702watchdogsreport.pdf.

[7] The Sarbanes-Oxley Act of 2002, Pub. L. No. 107-204, 116 Stat. 745 (codified in scattered sections of 11, 15, 18, 28, and 29 U.S.C.), for example, strengthens the oversight of accountants, takes steps to reduce the conflicts of interests faced by auditors and stock analysts, and enhances the SEC's enforcement tools. President George W. Bush has also signed an executive order creating a national task force to pursue corporate fraud. *See* David Ivanovich, *The Fall of Enron; Enron's Legacy: Massive Change—Reformers' Ideas Lauded, Loathed*, HOUS. CHRON., Dec. 1, 2002, at A1.

ploiting a large, uneducated, and unorganized labor force, and taking advantage of weaknesses in the financial, political, and legal systems. A handful of the shrewdest industrialists amassed truly staggering fortunes, which allowed them to wield unprecedented power in the marketplace and, contemporary critics charged, to exercise undue and corrupting influences on politics. The times were ripe for financial and political scandal, but, in the absence of legal rules, the line separating legitimate profit from sorry plunder was very thin. During the decades following the Civil War, the so-called Gilded Age, epic battles for domination of the new economy often disrupted it, bringing windfall profits to a select few but leading to panic and poverty for many others. The indifference of members of the millionaires' club to the negative economic, political, and social effects of their profit-seeking practices earned them enduring fame, and lasting infamy, as "Robber Barons."[8]

This essay will review the careers of the most celebrated Barons—industrial and financial giants such as Cornelius Vanderbilt, J.P. Morgan, Andrew Carnegie, and John D. Rockefeller—and also several of their lesser-known contemporaries (sharp operators like Jay Gould and Jim Fisk), who were nearly as influential but are perhaps more accurately to be called plain Robbers. This is a useful distinction because it describes their different business models. Robbers sought profitable advantage mostly by clever machination and manipulation. Barons were guilty of their share of market manipulations (not to mention despoiling, exploiting, and advantage-taking), but they also developed complex financial, organizational, and management tools that enabled them to help bring about, and not just to dominate, the nation's industrial transformation. Perhaps another way of stating the distinction is that the Barons attempted to control whole industries, while the Robbers sought to corner the markets. Yet both Robbers and Barons were tempted to increase the potential for their private profit by exploiting the public's ignorance, the politicians' corruptibility, or both. Moreover, despite the distinction between Robbers and Barons, the shared penchant for what

---

[8] CHARLES R. GEISST, WALL STREET: A HISTORY 64-98 (1997); *see also*, MORTON KELLER, AFFAIRS OF STATE: PUBLIC LIFE IN LATE NINETEENTH CENTURY AMERICA 244-245 (1977); RON CHERNOW, TITAN: THE LIFE OF JOHN D. ROCKEFELLER SR. 98-99 (1998). In his portrait of the great nineteenth-century entrepreneurs, Matthew Josephson describes them as akin to "the ancient barons-of-the-crags—who, by force of arms, instead of corporate combinations, monopolized strategic valley roads or mountain passed through which commerce flowed." MATTHEW JOSEPHSON, THE ROBBER BARONS: THE GREAT AMERICAN CAPITALISTS, 1861–1901, at vi (1962). The term Gilded Age, coined by Mark Twain in his satirical novel of that name published in 1873 (and written in collaboration with his neighbor, Charles Dudley Warner), expressed Twain's disillusionment with his fellow citizens' rampant greed. This theme is announced in the preface: "In a State where there is no fever of speculation, no inflamed desire for sudden wealth, where the poor are all simple-minded and contented, and the rich are all honest and generous, where society is in a condition of primitive purity, and politics is the occupation of only the capable and the patriotic, there are necessarily no materials for such a history as we have constructed." MARK TWAIN & CHARLES DUDLEY WARNER, THE GILDED AGE: A TALE OF TODAY v (Oxford Univ. Press 1996) (1873).

contemporary observers would label misbehavior means that the compound characterization—Robber Baron—may continue to make perfect sense.[9]

It is not the intent of this brief history to draw direct comparisons between the scandals of the past and those of the present. That is a perilous endeavor. Nevertheless, one of the great pleasures—and uses—of history is the occasional shock of recognition. The spectacular collapse of Enron, featuring charges of malfeasance and close relations between the fallen firm's leaders and the nation's officials (including President George W. Bush and prominent members of his administration), may recall to the public imagination the scandalous waste, fraud, and abuse of the nineteenth century.[10]

THE RELEASE OF ENERGY

Because government restraint on business—such as corporate taxation and securities regulation, not to mention environmental protection and labor laws—was weak or did not exist at all, the nineteenth century was a time of extraordinary opportunities for fortune hunters. This is not to imply that governments took a laissez-faire stance towards the economy. To the contrary, politicians actively encouraged westward expansion and industrialization with generous subsidies, land grants, or other favorable legislation. The era's judges also encouraged business enterprises by allowing corporations to pass much of the risks—financial, but especially physical risks—onto the general public.[11] The point of government was not to be hands-off, but to facilitate "the release of energy" that would spread the prosperity of a free people across the expanding nation.[12] The public sector ceded responsibility for developing the nation's economic potential to private interests. The result, as Howard Zinn has noted, was that "most of the fortune building was done legally, with the collaboration of the government and the courts."[13]

The dream of westward expansion came to the new republic earlier than the urge to industrialize, and speculation in western lands was a popular pastime among members of the founding generation. Unfortunately, even they were not immune to temptation.

---

[9] For management challenges and innovations as "big business" emerged in the Gilded Age, see THOMAS C. COCHRAN, 200 YEARS OF AMERICAN BUSINESS 53–69 (1977).

[10] Peter Carlson, *High and Mighty Crooked: Enron Is Merely the Latest Chapter In the History of American Scams*, WASH. POST, Feb. 10, 2002, at F01.

[11] *See* MORTON J. HORWITZ, THE TRANSFORMATION OF AMERICAN LAW 1780–1860, at xv, 1–36 (1979); *see also id.* at 63–108 (1979); *see also* Michael Les Benedict, *Laissez-Faire and Liberty: A Reevaluation of the Meaning of and Origins of Laissez-Faire Constitutionalism*, 3 LAW. & HIST. REV. 293 (1985); Lawrence M. Friedman & Jack Ladinsky, *Social Change and the Law of Industrial Accidents*, 67 COLUM. L. REV. 50 (1967).

[12] *See* JAMES WILLARD HURST, LAW AND THE CONDITIONS OF FREEDOM IN THE NINETEENTH CENTURY UNITED STATES 3–32, 50–51 (1956; *see also id.* at 50–51.).

[13] HOWARD ZINN, A PEOPLE'S HISTORY OF THE UNITED STATES, 1492–PRESENT 254 (rev. ed. 1995).

In January 1795, Georgia's governor signed a bill committing the state to sell 35 million acres of the state's Yazoo territory, so named for the river winding through it, to the Georgia Co., the Georgia-Mississippi Co., the Upper Mississippi Co., and the Tennessee Co. These four companies agreed to pay $500,000 for a vast tract that encompassed much of present-day Alabama and Mississippi.[14] The rival Georgia Union Co. had offered $800,000, including a $40,000 deposit in hard money. But the state rejected the higher bid, perhaps because U.S. Senator James Gunn was a stockholder in the successful companies, as were a number of the Georgia legislators. The Yazoo sale was perhaps the most audaciously corrupt real estate deal in early American history. The facts soon were revealed, Georgia voters tossed out the rascals at the first opportunity, and new legislators rescinded the sale. In February 1796, the reformers collected the records of the offensive bill on the lawn of the state capitol (then in Louisville), there to be consumed by a "Holy Fire" they summoned with the aid of a magnifying glass.[15]

Although no doubt cathartic, the state's quick legislative (and pyromanic) remedy proved problematic once it was tested in the courts. Georgia sought to refund the original purchase price, but some of the land had already been sold to third parties. On the same day that the law authorizing the sale was repealed, for example, an 11 million acre tract was sold to the New England Mississippi Land Co. for $1,138,000.[16] Because Georgia did not recognize the speculators' rights to sell the land, the title was considerably clouded. In 1802, along with the cession of other western claims, Georgia sold the disputed land to the federal government for $1.25 million. The Yazoo controversy seemed to be a case for the courts. As a consequence of the 11th Amendment, however, the New Englanders could not sue Georgia in federal court. Moreover, as a result of a state act that revoked jurisdiction, the speculators were also barred from suing in the Georgia courts.[17]

---

[14] This was not the first effort to conclude a mass sale of Yazoo land. In December 1789, Georgia authorized the sale of 20 million acres of the Yazoo territory for $207,000. The deal fell through when the three purchasers, the Virginia Yazoo Co. (which boasted Patrick Henry as a partner), the South Carolina Yazoo Co., and the Tennessee Co. sought to pay for the land with essentially worthless Revolutionary-era paper currency.

[15] It has been reported that every member of the state legislature, save one, had accepted a bribe (even so, the bill only passed the house 19 to 9, and prevailed in the senate 10 to 8). On the Yazoo land fraud and the lawsuits that followed it, see C. PETER MAGRATH, YAZOO: THE CASE OF FLETCHER V. PECK (1966).

[16] That is, in 13 months, the original buyers had reaped a 650% profit on that land.

[17] Other early attempts to settle the territory had failed, due in part to the presence of native people of the Cherokee, Creek, Choctaw, and Chickasaw tribes. The failure led to *Chisholm v. Georgia*, 2 U.S. (2 Dall.) 419 (1793), in which the U.S. Supreme Court held that a citizen could sue a state in federal court, in this case on the grounds of diversity (Chisholm was from South Carolina). The ruling led the debt-ridden states, and early proponents of states' rights, to ratify the 11th Amendment to bar such action in February 1795. President John Adams did not formally declare the 11th Amendment part of the Constitution until January 8, 1798. Later, it was agreed that Presidents have no authority concerning constitutional amendments.

One option for the speculators was to collude to build what we would now call a "test case." John Peck of Massachusetts bought Yazoo land from someone who could trace title to the state of Georgia. He then sold 15,000 acres to Robert Fletcher of New Hampshire, based on a warranty deed (that is, one warranting clear title). In June 1803, Fletcher, now alleging that the title was bad, sued Peck in federal court on the basis of its diversity jurisdiction, since the two parties were citizens of different states. After some delays, the federal circuit court concluded that the warranty deed was good, and held in favor of Peck. Fletcher appealed to the U.S. Supreme Court. In *Fletcher v. Peck*,[18] Chief Justice John Marshall, for the Court, struck down the 1796 Georgia Reform Act as unconstitutional, ruling the state had infringed on a valid contract. In 1814, Congress awarded the claimants over $4 million.[19]

ROBBERS VS. BARONS

Cornelius Vanderbilt (1794–1877) was perhaps the first person in American history to truly merit the label of Robber Baron. He established his first business around the time the Yazoo cases were concluded, well before the Gilded Age, and thus, he carried a lifetime of fortune-making lessons into that opportunistic era. Vanderbilt was born on Staten Island in 1794. In 1810, the sixteen-year-old farm boy purchased a small sailboat with $100 he borrowed from his mother and started a ferry service between Staten Island and New York City. Vanderbilt's timing was good: the government authorized him to transport provisions to regiments stationed in the New York area during the War of 1812. He was able to establish a small coastal fleet and formed a steamboat company in 1829. Vanderbilt was able to charge lower fares than his competitors and soon dominated the shipping business. By 1846, the "Commodore" (a name he claimed for himself as a fleet owner) was a millionaire.[20]

Vanderbilt accumulated a fortune of $20 million by 1860. Already in his mid-60s, he might have retired in luxury. Instead, he saw new moneymaking opportunities then emerging in railroad development. Vanderbilt entered that business by purchasing stock in the New York and Harlem Railroad in 1862. By 1863, he controlled that line and used it to start streetcar service in New York City. Between 1862 and 1869, he

---

[18] Fletcher v. Peck, 10 U.S. (6 Cranch) 87 (1810).

[19] In the circuit court, Peck was represented by John Quincy Adams, a Massachusetts Senator and future President. At the Supreme Court, Peck was represented by future Justice Joseph Story and Robert Goodloe Harper, a South Carolina Congressman who had been an investor in the South Carolina Mississippi Company, one of the land speculation companies involved in the scandal. Fletcher was represented by Luther Martin, an Anti-Federalist at the time of the Constitutional Convention, but now a long-time Federalist. The political congruence of counsel suggests strongly that the dispute was feigned. This collusion was necessary to obtain a ruling, because the Supreme Court's jurisdiction extends to "cases and controversies," not to advisory opinions. *Id.* This was a point made in a separate opinion by Justice Johnson, who announced his disinclination for the Court to hear a "feigned case." *Id.* at 143 (Johnson, J., concurring).

[20] *See generally* GEISST, *supra* note 8, at 76–77.

gathered up seventeen local lines and forged them into the New York Central Railroad. His acquisition of the Lake Shore and Michigan Southern Railroad completed the first New York-to-Chicago rail line. In this fashion, Vanderbilt amassed $100 million, the first fortune in America of such magnitude.[21]

Vanderbilt usually increased the value of his acquisitions through capital investment, unified management, reduced costs, and improved efficiency. When he found it expedient, however, he was not above increasing the apparent value of his companies simply by printing and selling more shares, a dilution known as "watering the stock." On at least one occasion, in one of the most colorful episodes of stock manipulation in American history, he famously fell prey to that very manipulation.[22] That event provides an excellent introduction to the unscrupulous business activities that transformed the nation during the Gilded Age.

The Erie Railroad War began when Vanderbilt attempted to drive out of business the last real competitor to his New York Central. The target was the Erie Railroad, controlled by three of the sharpest operators on Wall Street. Vanderbilt's nearest contemporary of the three was Daniel Drew (1797–1879), who was born in Carmel, New York. Drew served briefly in the War of 1812 before beginning a livestock business, driving cattle and horses to New York City from upstate, and later from as far away as Illinois.[23] In 1857, Drew became director and treasurer of the Erie Railroad line. Vanderbilt had battled Drew for control of the Hudson River Railroad, clashed with Drew again over the New York Central, and now fought Drew and his partners in the Erie Railroad War. The second of the three operators, Jay Gould (1836–1892), although much younger, nonetheless had a lot in common with Vanderbilt. Born on a farm in Delaware County, New York, Gould grew up in relative poverty and received little formal education.[24] Gould began speculating in railroads around 1860 and became a director of the Erie in 1867. Like his two partners in the Erie business, Jim Fisk (1834–1872) received little formal schooling and in his youth held a variety of jobs—from waiter to ticket agent for a circus—before finding the railroads and becoming a director of Erie Railroad.[25]

---

[21] *Id.* at 78. Seeing the connections between transportation and communication, Vanderbilt also bought control of America's dominant telegraph company, Western Union. Rockefeller claimed to have been inspired by the Western Union's consolidation of smaller telegraph lines. CHERNOW, *supra* note 8, at 149.

[22] JAMES W. ELY, JR., RAILROADS AND AMERICAN LAW 83-84 (2001).

[23] Drew is among those credited, probably apocryphally, with feeding salt to his cattle and letting them drink themselves full in order to increase their weight. This alleged fraud may (or may not) have inspired the name given to his later Wall Street practice known as "stock watering." GEISST, *supra* note 8, at 69.

[24] Nonetheless, earnings from his three years as a surveyor and the profits from the book he was able to write from his experience, *A History of Delaware County*, enabled him to open a Pennsylvania tannery. *Id.* at 58.

[25] With the proceeds gained from his Wall Street endeavors, Fisk lived the conspicuously decadent life of a Robber Baron until January 6, 1872, when he was shot by a rival following a quarrel over business and the affections of a mistress, an actress named Josie Mansfield. *Id.* at 72.

In 1868, Vanderbilt instructed his brokers to buy every Erie share they could find, and the Erie's sharp operators saw an opportunity to swindle Vanderbilt out of millions. Drew, as the Erie's treasurer, ordered 100,000 new stock certificates to be printed, which Vanderbilt's agents promptly bought. Eventually realizing that the stocks had no value, Vanderbilt prevailed upon a judge he had on his payroll to issue an injunction forbidding Erie to issue any more stock. Drew responded by getting a judge who was on *his* payroll to order Erie to keep on printing the stock. Vanderbilt once more appealed to his pocket judge, who issued a warrant for the arrest of Drew, Fisk, and Gould. The trio fled across the Hudson River with $7 million of Vanderbilt's money. They took up residence in a Jersey City hotel and hired armed guards to protect them from arrest. Their battle then shifted to the legislatures of New York and New Jersey, as agents for each side generously spread around cash. Gould himself traveled to Albany, carrying a trunk that was, the *New York Herald* reported, "stuffed with thousand-dollar bills." Gould reportedly spent upwards of $1 million to encourage the cooperation of the New York legislature, which obliged by confirming the legality of the Erie sales.[26]

The Erie's directors—surely the Robbers in the story—took Vanderbilt's money and went on to devise other schemes. In 1869, for example, Gould and Fisk sought to corner the market in gold. They encouraged someone close to President Ulysses S. Grant, apparently a brother-in-law of the President, to convince the President to end regular sales of federal gold reserves. Gould and Fisk had gained control over enough of the private supply of gold to bid up prices. Grant eventually saw the scheme for what it was and released $4 million in bullion. That action drove gold prices back down, but the shock caused stock prices to fall generally. A panic began on September 24, 1869, a day known as "Black Friday."[27]

The spectacle of the "Erie War" briefly entertained the public, and "Black Friday" outraged it. Both affairs indicate one of the emergent features of the Gilded Age business environment, namely, an unprecedented concentration of power to affect the marketplace in a few not always steady hands. The real losers in the Erie affair were the rank-and-file stockholders, who had no control of the market, and could only watch as their share value was being diluted. What began as a private competition for the domination of New York's rail system soon involved rampant public corruption and ultimately disrupted the market for many more than just the millionaires personally involved in the struggle. Vanderbilt, out-maneuvered but unbent, managed to unload his 100,000 Erie shares onto unsuspecting London investors.[28]

[26] ZINN, *supra* note 13, at 254; *see also* GEISST, *supra* note 8, at 69–71; LAWRENCE M. FRIEDMAN, A HISTORY OF AMERICAN LAW 513 (2d ed. 1985).

[27] GEISST, *supra* note 8, at 60–61.

[28] Although he was bested in the Erie affair, Vanderbilt emerged victorious in his other struggles with Drew, and so merged the New York Central with the Hudson River Railroad in 1869. *Id.* at 78.

TRANSCONTINENTAL CORRUPTION

The legal system placed few if any restraints on those with access to such large pools of investment capital, and the political system frequently worked to increase the size of the pool. Business and government entities both became larger during the Civil War, but the public sector's expansion proved temporary. By contrast, private enterprises continued to grow during and after the Reconstruction Era. Peace brought the return of cheap—and with new immigration, ever cheaper—labor, and opened access to land and other natural resources. Moreover, the federal government used its power—and the public's money—to encourage industrialization, especially the building of railroads. The dream of building a transcontinental railroad had excited Americans since victory in the Mexican War brought the acquisition of the Southwest and California. The U.S. Congress spent $150,000 during the 1850s to survey three possible routes from the Mississippi River to the Pacific Ocean. Democrats and Whigs deadlocked over the route—Northern or Southern?—as well as the level of public support to be lent to the effort. Only after the Southern Democrats left the Union with their seceding states did Republicans take control of Congress and pass a stream of long-stalled legislation they felt was crucial for economic development.[29] These statutes included the Homestead Act (1862),[30] the National Banking Act (1864),[31] and the Pacific Railroad Act (1864).[32]

The Pacific Railroad Act led to the creation of the Union Pacific Railroad, which would lay its rails west from Omaha, Nebraska, and the Central Pacific, which would build east from Sacramento, California. The federal government supported the project by granting the companies right of way or outright title to millions of acres of public land, and by paying each company a fixed sum for each mile of track they completed. The subsidy was $16,000 for each mile of flat land, $32,000 per mile of hilly terrain, and $48,000 per mile through mountains. The linking of East and West coasts by rail was completed on May 10, 1869, with a golden spike hammered home at Promontory Point, Utah.[33]

It was not long at all before the lucrative provisions of the massive transcontinental project led, almost inevitably, to corruption on an equally grand scale. The Credit Mobilier affair is the classic example of how the government's encouragement of railroad construction for the public good instead made for shady business practices. In the late 1860s,

---

[29] ELY, *supra* note 22, at 52–53; *see also* STEPHEN E. AMBROSE, NOTHING LIKE IT IN THE WORLD: THE MEN WHO BUILT THE TRANSCONTINENTAL RAILROAD, 1863–1869, at 59–60 (2000); *see also id.* at 94–96, 172.

[30] Homestead Act of 1862, 43 U.S.C. § 161 (repealed 1976).

[31] National Bank Act of 1864, ch. 106, 13 Stat. 99 (1864) (codified as amended in various sections of 12 U.S.C.).

[32] Pacific Railroad Act of 1862, ch. 120, 12 Stat. 489, *amended by* Act of July 2, 1864, ch. 216, 13 Stat. 356 (1864); *see also* AMBROSE, *supra* note 29, at 59–60; *see also id.* at 94–96, 172.

[33] AMBROSE, *supra* note 29, at 363–66.

the Union Pacific's management formed a construction company called Credit Mobilier and hired U.S. Representative Oakes Ames of Massachusetts to be its president. Ames sold stock in Credit Mobilier at discounted prices to fellow Congressmen and other influential officials. Schuyler Colfax and Henry Wilson, President Ulysses S. Grant's first and second-term Vice-Presidents, were among those so favored by Ames. To build a major portion of the railroad, Credit Mobilier charged the Union Pacific almost $100 million, nearly twice the actual cost of the work. Once this overcharging was exposed in 1872, angry editorials, Congressional hearings, and a federal lawsuit ensued, but the masterminds behind the scheme went essentially unpunished. They were disgraced, of course, but left public life considerably richer than when they entered.[34]

Even without the taint of scandal, the transcontinental railroad project seemed to be cursed with financial difficulties. In 1864, to encourage the building of a railroad to the Northwest, Congress chartered the Northern Pacific on terms similar to the earlier lines. Jay Cooke, the Philadelphia investment banker who had gained a virtual monopoly on the sale of the government bonds that financed the Union's Civil War effort, now began to market Northern Pacific bonds across the United States and Europe. It was a daunting task, since, by the end of the decade, construction was costing $1 million a month. In part because President Grant supported a proposal to refinance the Northern Pacific with a $300 million government loan, Cooke spent a great deal to help Grant win re-election in 1872.[35]

Unfortunately for Cooke, the Grant administration was tarred with charges of rampant corruption—with some justification, given the Vice President's role in the Credit Mobilier affair.[36] The adverse publicity hurt bond sales, both at home and abroad.

---

[34] GEISST, *supra* note 8, at 66–67. The Credit Mobilier scandal was not an isolated example of corruption. The Contract and Finance Co., which was the Central Pacific's counterpart of the Credit Mobilier, charged back $121,000,000 for $58,000,000 worth of work. The Central Pacific was led by Leland Stanford, Collis Huntington, Charles Crocker, and Mark Hopkins, known as the "Big Four." These industrialists prevented other railroads from competing in California, reaped enormous profits from their monopoly, and dominated California politics (Stanford was later elected Governor and U.S. Senator). AMBROSE, *supra* note 29, at 374–375. Unlike the leaders in the Credit Mobilier scandal, however, the Big Four escaped even the minor repercussion of disgrace, in part because the records of the Contract and Finance Co. were destroyed before an investigation got underway. It was left to novelist Frank Norris to fictionalize the story of their monopoly in *The Octopus: A Story of California* (1901).

[35] For Cooke's activities marketing the Union's debt to finance the war, see David M. Gische, *The New York City Banks and the Development of the National Banking System, 1860–1870*, 23 AM. J. LEGAL HIST. 21 (1979).

[36] Grant's two terms were boom times for corruption. In addition to Gould's and Fisk's gold-cornering scheme, for example, there was the Whiskey Ring. In 1875 a group of liquor distillers, with the assistance of Treasury officials, conspired to defraud the federal government of millions dollars in taxes. The ring included Grant's personal secretary, Orville Babcock, who was indicted along with hundreds of others. Babcock was acquitted after deposition testimony given by Grant in his defense was read to the jury. Timothy Rives, *Grant, Babcock, and the Whiskey Ring*, 32 PROLOGUE 143 (2000).

Cooke found that he could only sell enough bonds to cover $200,000 of the $1 million needed monthly by the Northern Pacific. Cooke was forced to purchase the remaining $800,000 in bonds himself. About the time the Congressional debate over the loan commenced, the *Philadelphia Ledger,* which already had attacked the proposed refinancing, printed a rumor that Jay Cooke & Co. itself needed the $300 million to bolster its own credit, which had been impaired by its close connection with the "failing" railroad. The refinancing proposal was defeated in Congress in February 1873. Northern Pacific bonds became harder to sell. In September, Cooke received a telegram and learned that his partner had closed the doors of his New York branch. The doors to Jay Cooke & Co. in Philadelphia closed that same day. Perhaps Cooke's embarrassment was compounded by the fact that, when the fateful telegram arrived, President Grant was breakfasting at Cooke's home. Jay Cooke's failure shook Wall Street. The ensuing Panic of 1873 was the worst economic collapse of the nineteenth century. Ten thousand businesses were forced to close and the ensuing depression lasted for five years.[37]

THE TRUSTWORTHY

Most suffered after the Panic, but others profited. J. Pierpont Morgan (1837–1913), the heir of an established investment banking family with connections in London, was an up-and-coming financier who prospered during the unsettled marketplace ushered in by the Panic of 1873. In 1871, Morgan's family had entered into partnership with Anthony Drexel, who had been Cooke's wartime partner. It turned out that Drexel had lent newspaper editor G.W. Childs the money he needed to establish the *Philadelphia Ledger,* which emerged as Cooke's great bane over the Northern Pacific refinancing deal. It might have been merely a coincidence, but Cooke's troubles made money tight everywhere—for example, the price of gold soared in London—and, as major dealers in the money markets, Drexel, Morgan & Co. profited by the uncertainty.[38]

Morgan began his career at a time when investment bankers were beginning to play a key role in the industrialization of the expanding economy. Throughout the 1870s, he sparred often with Gould and other shrewd players in the securities markets. Morgan pioneered many of the techniques for securing the financing of ever-larger undertakings. He profited most handsomely by his ability to make the deal for others, either by taking a large commission off the top, accepting stock or securities certificates, reserving a seat for himself or a trusted lieutenant on a board of directors, or a combination of these methods. By the turn of the century, he controlled much more capital than he personally owned, and was known as "Jupiter" on Wall Street, the mythic god

---

[37] GEISST, *supra* note 8, at 61–63.

[38] RON CHERNOW, THE HOUSE OF MORGAN: AN AMERICAN BANKING DYNASTY AND THE RISE OF MODERN FINANCE 33–37 (1990).

to whom all others deferred. Morgan embodied for many Americans the financier variant of the Robber Baron.[39]

Despite his reputation, and his own record of profit-taking during the various Panics, Morgan actually was a champion of order and stability rather than laissez-faire, which he knew led to "ruinous competition." By the 1890s, for example, competition had bankrupted many of the nation's railroads. The Union Pacific itself finally collapsed into bankruptcy during the Panic of 1893. Morgan formed a group of investors and established control over the faltering lines. The wasteful competition in the steel industry also drew his attention. At a social gathering in 1900, Morgan approached financier Charles Schwab, a friend of Andrew Carnegie, the infamous Baron who dominated the steel industry, and Morgan indicated his desire to bring order out of the chaos. Carnegie, on hearing of the plan, scribbled his selling price on a slip of paper. Morgan agreed to the $480 million figure and, with Carnegie Steel as the nucleus, he created United States Steel, the first corporation capitalized in excess of a billion dollars.[40]

That Andrew Carnegie (1835–1919) was in the position to sell a business for half a billion dollars is a testament to his own business acumen. He was born in Scotland, but immigrated to the United States with his family in 1848. Carnegie found work in a textile mill, taught himself to be a telegraph clerk, and, astonishingly, rose to become the head of the Pennsylvania Railroad. Carnegie briefly entered the oil business when oil was discovered on a property he owned, but he made his mark on industrial history when he bought into the steel business. By employing the Bessemer method, an efficient process already being used in England, Carnegie revolutionized steel production in the United States. Among other contracts, his firm was in the position to profit handsomely by providing steel rails to replace the aging iron rails used for early railroad construction. Moreover, he had been financially involved with J.P. Morgan since the 1870s, when the House of Morgan (then still Drexel, Morgan) marketed the bonds to bankroll one of his early steel mills.[41]

Carnegie ultimately led world steel production. But it was his ruthless control of his organization as well as his domination of the market that earned him his reputation as a Robber Baron. Carnegie gained control over all of the materials that went into making his product. Where he could, he purchased his sources and suppliers outright. Where he could not, he brought the owner into his business network as an

---

[39] Morgan paid a $300 bounty to avoid being drafted during the Civil War. He had then profited from that conflict by purchasing 5,000 obsolete (and in many cases dangerously defective) rifles from an arsenal in New York for $3.50 apiece, then selling them to the Union Army in Virginia for $22 each. *Id.* at 21–22.

[40] *Id.* at 83–84.

[41] *Id.* at 39.

associate or partner, as he did with Henry Clay Frick, who became Carnegie's vice-president.[42]

The true master of consolidation and control was neither Morgan the banker nor Carnegie the steel magnate, but John D. Rockefeller, Sr. (1839–1937) the oilman. No less than Jay Gould noted that Rockefeller possessed "the highest genius for constructive organization" in American business history.[43] Like Vanderbilt, Rockefeller was born on a farm in New York. He migrated with his family to Cleveland, Ohio, at age 14. Rockefeller found work selling for commission at a commodities firm and prospered enough to open his own business by the age of 20. In 1859, oil was discovered in Northwestern Pennsylvania, which was soon overrun with speculators. One of them was Rockefeller, who soon realized that refining oil, rather than getting it out of the ground, was the key to success. He bought his first refinery in 1862, and he quickly purchased others. He formed companies with associates in other states as he bought competing firms and brought their most talented managers into his service. To consolidate his growing empire, he created the Standard Oil Co. of Ohio in 1870.[44]

Like Carnegie, he gained an early advantage by investing in the newest technology. Rockefeller's scientists learned to refine the cleanest-burning kerosene. Standard Oil found new markets, especially as industrial lubricants, for the previously wasted residues of the refining process. His researchers developed new processes that enabled Standard Oil to make money on oil that other refiners could not use at all. For example, one variety of Indiana oil was known as "polecat" oil because of its high sulfur content. Only Standard Oil was able to refine and sell it. Yet Rockefeller showed his true gift, like Carnegie, by organizing. He perfected management practices that allowed his Standard Oil to grow into a complex national operation, the prototypical example of corporate consolidation and efficiency. Instead of buying oil from middlemen (called jobbers), Rockefeller saved the jobbers' profit for himself by sending his own employees into the oil patches to buy crude at wholesale prices. His marketing and distribution agents used their own barrels and wagons and, at their employers' direction, kept detailed records of every dollar spent in the course of doing business.[45]

---

[42] Frick was a man after Carnegie's own heart. He had coal mines and coke ovens in western Pennsylvania, and he also owned the duplex houses where his workers lived and ran the only store where they could buy their supplies. He has been largely remembered for his decision to break the 1892 Homestead Strike at Carnegie's plant by hiring armed detectives. Seven strikers died, and many criticized Frick. WILLIAM M. WIECEK, THE LOST WORLD OF CLASSICAL LEGAL THOUGHT: LAW AND IDEOLOGY IN AMERICA, 1886–1937, at 76 (1998). Rockefeller, however, sent a congratulatory telegram. CHERNOW, *supra* note 8, at 334.

[43] CHERNOW, *supra* note 8, at 112.

[44] *Id.* at 129–132.

[45] *Id.* at 284–288.

Rockefeller often gained market share simply by trading ownership of smaller refineries for stock in Standard Oil, but, if a refiner refused to sell, he would sell Standard Oil products below cost and force the smaller refiner into bankruptcy. Meanwhile, he made up the difference by jacking up the prices in the markets where Standard Oil had no more competition. Rockefeller also used the railroads to his advantage. He shipped vast amounts of oil—often in his own cars—and insisted that the railroads give him a rebate. Rockefeller later insisted on "drawbacks," in which the railroad raised its rates for other shippers and gave him a portion of the profit (naturally, Standard Oil was still getting its rebate). Thus, Rockefeller's competitors were subsidizing Standard Oil's transportation costs. When the drawback Standard Oil had arranged with the Pennsylvania Railroad was made public, Rockefeller ended it, but he continued to demand the drawbacks from other lines. These practices led inexorably to Standard Oil's domination of the nation's refining capacity at precisely the time that oil—already the source of illumination and lubrication, and later to become the major source of energy—became indispensable to America's rapidly industrializing society.[46]

Standard Oil's evolution from being merely the largest to being virtually the only oil refiner of consequence in the United States was completed through the creation of the Standard Oil Trust in 1882. The original Standard Oil Co. was an Ohio corporation, which was prohibited by law in many states from owning plants in those states, or, in some cases, even holding stock in out-of-state corporations. One of Rockefeller's attorneys, Samuel C. T. Dodd, conceived the "trust" in order to find a way around such state laws governing corporations. Dodd's clever solution was to place corporate control in a board of trustees, naturally chaired by Rockefeller. That is, Standard Oil became a "trust" that issued "trust certificates," rather than remaining a corporation that issued stock. Through this new device, Rockefeller snapped up the rest of his remaining competitors without worrying about breaking corporate anti-monopoly laws. Thirty years after he entered the refining business, Rockefeller's company enjoyed a greater than 90 percent market share.[47]

REGULATORS AND REFORMERS

Rockefeller's organizational innovation was soon adopted by other industrialists. By the 1890s, thousands of once separate and competing companies had been organized into a few hundred industrial trusts. The public's worry that such economic power was being concentrated in just a few hands finally gave rise to reform movements, including Populism and Progressivism, all calling for some kind of government regulation of business. Proposed regulatory remedies varied—some critics concluded

---

[46] *Id.* at 112–117.

[47] *Id.* at 226–227; *see also* KELLER, *supra* note 8, at 435.

that a radical restructuring of society, such as some form of socialism, was the answer to rapacious business and industry—but most reformers simply demanded that the "special interests" be regulated for the greater good of the common people.[48]

The U.S. Congress answered these calls for regulation, beginning in 1887, with the creation of the Interstate Commerce Act, the first "major affirmative exercise of federal regulatory authority under the commerce clause."[49] Congress created the Interstate Commerce Commission ("ICC"), which, among other responsibilities, was empowered to review railroad rates. Congress focused on the specific fear of monopoly in 1890, when it passed the Sherman Antitrust Act, which banned "[e]very contract, combination in the form of trust or otherwise, or conspiracy, in restraint of trade or commerce among the several States or with foreign nations."[50]

The Sherman Act was mostly unsuccessful in restraining business, because the era's judges feared government encroachments on property rights of corporations more than they feared the increase of industrial power over the economy. The major test of the Sherman Act came when the American Sugar Refining Company bought the E. C. Knight Company, gaining control of 98 percent of American sugar refining. In *United States v. E.C. Knight*,[51] the U.S. Supreme Court upheld the lawfulness of the acquisition because refining was not interstate commerce subject to congressional regulation. The Court's permissive attitude toward business consolidation disappointed many reformers.[52]

The *E.C. Knight* decision gave the green light to mergers. The irony was that the Standard Oil Trust itself lasted only until the 1890s, when the firm was transformed into yet another novel entity—a "holding company," organized under a New Jersey statute that allowed a corporation to "hold" the stocks of other firms. Standard Oil of New Jersey, holding diversified interests including the Chase Manhattan Bank, became the flagship of Rockefeller's empire. Like the earlier trust, Rockefeller's holding company presaged the future. General Electric, American Telephone and Telegraph ("AT&T"), and International Harvester all emerged from this frenzy for mergers. More than one thousand companies disappeared in mergers in 1899. Morgan's 1901 creation of the billion-dollar U.S. Steel—encompassing more than 200 companies, 1,000

---

[48] WIECEK, *supra* note 42, at 176–179; *see also* KELLER, *supra* note 8, at 565–587; CHARLES W. MCCURDY, JUSTICE FIELD AND THE JURISPRUDENCE OF GOVERNMENT-BUSINESS RELATIONS: THE PARAMETERS OF LAISSEZ-FAIRE CONSTITUTIONALISM, 1863–1897, 61 J. AM. HIST. 970 (1975); Arnold M. Paul, *Legal Progressivism, the Courts, and the Crisis of the 1890s*, 33 BUS. HIST. REV. 495 (1959).

[49] JAMES W. ELY, JR., THE GUARDIAN OF EVERY OTHER RIGHT: A CONSTITUTIONAL HISTORY OF PROPERTY RIGHTS 97 (2d ed. 1998); *see also* KELLER, *supra* note 8, at 423–28.

[50] Sherman Antitrust Act, 15 U.S.C. §§ 1–7 (2002); *see also* KELLER, *supra* note 8, at 435–438.

[51] U.S. v. E.C. Knight, 156 U.S. 1 (1895).

[52] *See generally* HOWARD GILLMAN, THE CONSTITUTION BESIEGED: THE RISE AND DEMISE OF LOCHNER ERA POLICE POWERS JURISPRUDENCE 1–2 (1993).

miles of railroads, and 170,000 workers—was the ultimate symbol of consolidation and combination.[53]

The House of Morgan had ample reason to doubt the wisdom of the advocates of regulation, since the government had such trouble keeping its own house in order. During the 1890s depression, for example, the U.S. Treasury's gold reserves shrunk to dangerous levels. Outstanding drafts, if presented, would have thrown the federal government into default. Since the majority of foreign investment in the U.S. (much of it represented by Morgan) depended on the stability of gold and the government's credit, Morgan had to take action. In 1895, he put together a syndicate to buy gold. The syndicate then immediately exchanged the gold for U.S. bonds. Morgan, having thus restored the federal government's solvency and credit rating, promptly resold his bonds at a profit. Far from earning him the acclaim of a grateful nation, however, Morgan's rescue of the national honor underscored for many Populist critics the danger of leaving such concentrated power unchecked.[54]

The regulators eventually prevailed in the courts, and the first major victory was won against no other than J. P. Morgan. Around the time of the U.S. Steel deal, Morgan had also ended the "ruinous" competition between owners of the nation's largest rail lines by combined their control in a holding company, Northern Securities. To the surprise of many, and the irritation of Morgan, President Theodore Roosevelt authorized the Justice Department to file a suit attacking the combination under the Sherman Act. In 1904, in a 5–4 decision, the Supreme Court decided against Morgan's Northern Securities Company.[55] Justice John M. Harlan, who had dissented from the *E.C. Knight* majority decision, now wrote for the majority that "[t]he mere existence of such a combination . . . constitute[s] a menace to, and a restraint upon, that freedom of commerce which Congress intended to recognize and protect, and which the public is entitled to have protected."[56] The *Northern Securities* decision reversed *E.C. Knight,* but the Court did not fully embrace a stronger reading of the Sherman Act. Instead, the Justices later favored a fact-based "rule of reasonableness."[57] Nevertheless, for re-

---

[53] Ida Tarbell, the daughter of an oil producer whom Rockefeller had put out of business, published scathing articles on the rise of Standard Oil in 1904, in *McClure's* magazine, and she did as much as any "muckraking" journalist to give the Robber Barons their reputation. Her articles were later compiled into a book. *See* IDA M. TARBELL, THE HISTORY OF THE STANDARD OIL COMPANY (Peter Smith, 1950) (1904). For slightly less muckraking, see RALPH W. HIDY & MURIEL E. HIDY, HISTORY OF STANDARD OIL COMPANY (NEW JERSEY), 1882–1911: PIONEERING IN BIG BUSINESS (1955). For a modern biography, warts and all, but recognizing the epic proportions of Rockefeller's achievement, see CHERNOW, *supra* note 8.

[54] CHERNOW, *supra* note 38, at 73–76.

[55] Northern Sec. Co. v. U.S., 193 U.S. 197 (1904).

[56] *Id.* at 327.

[57] ELY, *supra* note 22, at 235. For more on Harlan, whose career on the bench—1877 to 1911—spanned the Gilded Age, see G. Edward White, *John Marshall Harlan I: The Precursor*, 19 AM. J. LEGAL HIST. 1 (1975). Justice Oliver Wendell Holmes, in dissent, credited this verdict to an unsophisticated, but widespread, belief among the public, Congress, and the courts that big must necessarily be bad. Northern Sec. Co., 193 U.S. at 364.

formers, the decision implied that the mere existence of a powerful combination now could be presumed to be a threat to trade and therefore unlawful. Bolstered by the success, reformers called for more regulation and better enforcement of the antitrust laws. Lending his support to the cause, President Theodore Roosevelt referred pointedly during a speech at a Gridiron Club dinner to "malefactors of great wealth," while Morgan was in the audience.[58]

Finally, in 1911, in another landmark case, the Supreme Court ordered that Rockefeller's Standard Oil organization be dismantled and shared out into a handful of individual refining companies.[59] In 1914, another federal statute, the Clayton Act,[60] was passed to supplement to the Sherman Act. The Clayton Act imposed restrictions on proposed mergers and acquisitions and empowered the federal courts to enjoin anti-competitive conduct before it caused harm. Congress also established the Federal Trade Commission ("FTC"), with authority to monitor enforcement of the Sherman, Clayton, and other acts.[61]

Although Morgan was embittered at the adverse judgment, he once more served the nation, after his fashion, during the Panic of 1907. He gathered the leading business figures in New York in his library on Madison Avenue and led them in a concerted effort to halt a Wall Street sell-off by providing much-needed funds to stave off bankruptcies. The Wall Street Panic subsided, but public suspicions were rekindled against Morgan and his associates. Although long-delayed by lobbyists, national banking reform legislation finally emerged from Congress in 1913.[62]

In 1912, a Congressional panel known as the Pujo Committee called an outraged Morgan to testify about his activities. Morgan survived the ordeal, but died the next year.[63] The Pujo investigators found no proof of Morgan's alleged "Money Trust," but nevertheless concluded, as Louis Brandeis, a reform-minded lawyer and future Supreme Court Justice who assisted the committee, stated it, that Morgan too often profited by risking "other people's money." In the book of that name, which he subsequently wrote about bankers, Brandeis concluded: "They control people through the people's own money. The power and growth of power of our financial oligarchs comes from wielding the savings and quick capital of others."[64]

[58] RON CHERNOW, THE DEATH OF THE BANKER: THE DECLINE AND FALL OF THE GREAT FINANCIAL DYNASTIES AND THE TRIUMPH OF THE SMALL INVESTOR 102 (1997).

[59] Standard Oil v. U.S., 221 U.S. 1 (1911).

[60] The Clayton Antitrust Act, 15 U.S.C. §§ 12–27 (2000).

[61] GABRIEL KOLKO, THE TRIUMPH OF CONSERVATISM: A REINTERPRETATION OF AMERICAN HISTORY, 1900–1916, at 261–267 (Quadrangle Books, 1967) (1963).

[62] CHERNOW, supra note 38, at 121–130.

[63] The Armstrong investigation in New York, directed by lawyer and future Supreme Court Chief Justice Charles Evans Hughes, came in 1905. KOLKO, supra note 61, at 84, 94.

[64] LOUIS D. BRANDEIS, OTHER PEOPLE'S MONEY, AND HOW THE BANKERS USE IT 12–13 (1914).

CONCLUSION

With J.P. Morgan's passing, the power of the "financial oligarchs"—Robber Barons, if you will—described by Brandeis shortly came to an end. This was probably inevitable. The concentrated power that he and his generation wielded was an artifact of the tension created when the momentum of industrialization overwhelmed the rather primitive, even clubby, financial system of the nineteenth century. Morgan and his contemporaries held power because they were among the few men with the connections and the knowledge to bring off the deals. That power was diminished somewhat by the "democratization" of the market in the twentieth century, which brought a flood of new investment capital from the growing number of middle class individuals. This influx of cash allowed corporate directors, investment bankers, and stock manipulators to play the market, and often profit enormously, by placing other people's money at risk. But the era when a handful of wealthy industrialists or financiers could make or break the market at will was ended by the general distribution of more modest wealth. The calls for reform regulation lasted for a few more years, but the movement waned as the government faced the challenges of fighting World War I.[65]

Fresh revelations of public corruption in the 1920s, however, brought to mind the Robbers of old. In 1921, Albert B. Fall, Secretary of the Interior under President Warren Harding, received $400,000 worth of "loans" in cash and stock from oilmen Edward L. Doheny and Harry Sinclair, as well as a separate gift of $100,000 from Doheny. The Interior Department soon leased California's Elk Hills and Wyoming's Teapot Dome—sites of the nation's naval oil reserves—to Doheny and Sinclair. In 1924, when the "Teapot Dome" scheme was uncovered, Fall was indicted and convicted of bribery. He was fined $100,000 and sentenced to one year in prison, becoming the first cabinet member to go to prison. The two oilmen escaped conviction.[66]

Worse than such influence peddling was the return of stock speculation on a large scale. After a credit-fed run-up in the 1920s, financial markets began collapsing in October 1929, touching off a financial panic. The stock market hit bottom in 1932. The crash revealed fundamental weaknesses in the economy and contributed to the Great Depression. Soon after his inauguration in 1933, President Franklin D. Roosevelt, seeking to save capitalism from its own excesses, began by criticizing corporate arrogance and greed. Roosevelt denounced bankers as "money changers," and declared a national bank holiday even before he introduced the earliest of his New Deal legislation.[67]

The New Deal reforms included significant measures intended to restore stability and confidence to the financial markets. In 1933, Congress adopted regulations requiring companies to disclose specific financial information before issuing stock or

---

[65] KOLKO, *supra* note 61, at 286–287. On the changes in the investment market, *see* CHERNOW, THE DEATH OF THE BANKER, AT 40–41, *supra* note 58.

[66] WILLIAM E. LEUCHTENBURG, THE PERILS OF PROSPERITY, 1914–1932, at 93, 145 (1958).

[67] *See* SUSAN ESTABROOK KENNEDY, THE BANKING CRISIS OF 1933, at 152 (1973); ELMUS WICKER, THE BANKING PANICS OF THE GREAT DEPRESSION, at 128–129 (1996).

securities.[68] Next, the 1933 Banking Act (the "Glass-Steagall Act")[69] separated investment banks from commercial banks—finally forcing the break-up of firms like the old Morgan bank.[70] The Securities Exchange Act of 1934 compelled publicly traded firms to provide listings of their assets and liabilities and outlawed various practices that had been used to manipulate stock prices for speculative purposes. This act also created the Securities and Exchange Commission ("SEC"), which was empowered to monitor the behavior of publicly traded companies.[71]

The label Robber Baron continues to be popular shorthand for a business leader who exhibits a will to dominate his or her chosen marketplace, especially through ruthless tactics, up to and including public and private corruption. In the same way, commentators often invoke the term "Gilded Age" to describe a period that shows such economic features as a widening gap between an underclass of the poor and an upper class of the super-rich (who exhibit unbridled avarice and conspicuous consumption). The 1980s, which brought corporate raiding and massive leveraged buyouts, invited such comparisons. That decade began with junk bond-insider trading scandals and ended with the federal government's rescue of failed savings and loans—and other so-called "thrift institutions"—that had been ruined by foolish or unscrupulous managers. It seems that the modern details of manipulation and malfeasance change, but the traditional theme that great riches (or the promise of them) bring too much political influence always recurs.[72]

---

[68] The Securities Act of 1933, 15 U.S.C. §§ 77a–aa (2002); *see* LOUIS LOSS & JOEL SELIGMAN, FUNDAMENTALS OF SECURITIES REGULATION 29–31 (4th ed. 2001); JOEL SELIGMAN, THE TRANSFORMATION OF WALL STREET: A HISTORY OF THE SECURITIES AND EXCHANGE COMMISSION AND MODERN CORPORATE FINANCE 39–40, 561–62 (rev. ed. 1995).

[69] The Banking Act of 1933, ch. 89, 48 Stat. 162 (1933) (codified as amended in scattered sections of 12 U.S.C. (2000)).

[70] CHERNOW, *supra* note 38, at 374–77.

[71] The Securities Exchange Act of 1934, 15 U.S.C. §§ 78a–jj (2002).

[72] KEVIN PHILLIPS, ARROGANT CAPITAL: WASHINGTON, WALL STREET, AND THE FRUSTRATION OF AMERICAN POLITICS 97-99 (1994). Indeed, one account of the S&L scandal invokes Brandeis's usage. *See* PAUL ZANE PILZER WITH ROBERT DEITZ, OTHER PEOPLE'S MONEY: THE INSIDE STORY OF THE S&L MESS (1989). For an official history of these events, see DIVISION OF RESEARCH AND STATISTICS, FEDERAL DEPOSIT INSURANCE CORPORATION, HISTORY OF THE EIGHTIES—LESSONS FOR THE FUTURE: AN EXAMINATION OF THE BANKING CRISES OF THE 1980S AND EARLY 1990S (1997), *available at* http://www.fdic.gov/bank/historical/history/vol1.html. For a memoir of an official, see L. WILLIAM SEIDMAN, FULL FAITH AND CREDIT: THE GREAT S&L DEBACLE AND OTHER WASHINGTON SAGAS (1993). For a scholarly examination, see KITTY CALAVITA ET AL., BIG MONEY CRIME: FRAUD AND POLITICS IN THE SAVINGS AND LOAN CRISIS (1997). For popular outrage, see JAMES RING ADAMS, THE BIG FIX—INSIDE THE S&L SCANDAL: HOW AN UNHOLY ALLIANCE OF POLITICS AND MONEY DESTROYED AMERICA'S BANKING SYSTEM (1990); JAMES R. BARTH, THE GREAT SAVINGS AND LOAN DEBACLE (1991), KATHLEEN DAY, S&L HELL: THE PEOPLE AND THE POLITICS BEHIND THE $1 TRILLION SAVINGS AND LOAN SCANDAL (1993), NED EICHLER, THE THRIFT DEBACLE (1989), JAMES O'SHEA, THE DAISY CHAIN: HOW BORROWED BILLIONS SANK A TEXAS S&L (1991); and MARTIN MAYER, THE GREATEST-EVER BANK ROBBERY: THE COLLAPSE OF THE SAVINGS AND LOAN INDUSTRY (1990).

Whether any of the fallen executives of Enron and other discredited companies can best be regarded as modern-day analogues of the Gilded Age's Robbers, Barons, or Robber Barons remains to be seen—prosecutions are underway and lawsuits have been filed, and Americans await the judgements of juries. Yet the nature of the allegations gives some early idea of the correspondence between past and present.

According to the staff of the Senate Committee on Governmental Affairs reviewing the debacle, Enron created a maze of hidden debts, false assets, and self-dealing partnerships. The partnerships were kept off the company's balance sheets completely or were obscured by complex misleading descriptions.[73] These off-balance sheet entities appear to have been created either to generate false profits to be counted in Enron's favor, or to cloak real liabilities that would have been counted against the bottom line. That is, by spending millions of dollars on an army of lawyers, accountants, and all manner of consultants—bright individuals from the top schools and the best firms, all apparently willing either to be dazzled or corrupted outright by the blizzard of bonus cash (again, we cannot be certain, but many cases are pending)—Enron was able to fool a range of public and private entities that ought to have played some role in monitoring its activities.[74]

Enron sustained the illusion of meeting its earnings projections every quarter, and, as a result, the stock price remained strong, much stronger than it deserved to be. In

---

[73] See *The Role of the Board of Directors in Enron's Collapse, Hearing Before the Permanent Subcomm. On Investigations, S. Governmental Affairs Comm.* 107th Cong. 511 (2002), *available at* http://www.gpo.gov/congress/senate/senate12sh107.html; *The Role of Financial Institutions in Enron's Collapse, Hearing Before the Permanent Subcomm. on Investigations, S. Governmental Affairs Comm.*, 107th Cong. 618 (2002), *available at* http://www.gpo.gov/congress/senate/senate12sh107.html. PSI also has issued a report on the role of the Board of Directors in its collapse. *See* PERMANENT SUBCOMM. ON INVESTIGATIONS, S. GOVERNMENTAL AFFAIRS COMM., 107TH CONG., THE ROLE OF THE BOARD OF DIRECTORS IN ENRON'S COLLAPSE 70 (Comm. Print 2002), *available at* http://www.access.gpo.gov/congress/senate/senate12lp107.html.

[74] So much is apparently clear, and Congress has passed the Sarbanes-Oxley Act to tighten oversight of accounting practices, to strengthen criminal penalties for corporate fraud, and to mandate changes in corporate governance, stock research, financial reporting, and other pertinent areas. Pub. L. No. 107-204, § 307, 116 Stat. 745 § 307 (2002). President Bush's executive order created a rapid-reaction squad of experts—FBI investigators and U.S. Attorneys—and charged them to focus on complex corporate crime. These changes will not be effective if they are not enforced, of course. The same Senate Committee found that the SEC has failed to review any of Enron's financial filings since 1997, even though the company was undergoing significant growth and substantially changing the nature of its business. The Senate investigators suggest that, had SEC investigators reviewed these filings, they might have uncovered some of the problems with the company's "aggressive" accounting. The Senate Committee staff concluded that, at least with respect to Enron, credit rating agencies also failed to exercise the proper diligence. The agencies did not consider factors affecting the long-term health of the company, particularly accounting irregularities and overly complex financing structures. U.S. STAFF OF SENATE COMM. ON GOVERNMENTAL AFFAIRS, 107TH CONG., REPORT ON FINANCIAL OVERSIGHT OF ENRON: THE SEC AND PRIVATE-SECTOR WATCHDOGS 75, 4–6 (Comm. Print 2002), *available at* http://www.senate.gov/~gov_affairs/100702watchdogsreport.pdf.

the absence of a convenient printing press, Enron's "aggressive" accounting seemed to be the next best way to water stock. For the historian, it is ironic that current executives of J.P. Morgan Chase & Co.—successor to financial institutions founded by two great Barons, Morgan and Rockefeller—claim that Enron duped them into engineering several of the complex financial transactions that enabled the company to hide debt and inflate revenues.[75] Surely, that is an old Robbers vs. Barons trick worthy of the likes of Messrs. Gould, Drew, and Fisk.

QUESTIONS

1. If you were in the state legislature, how would you devise a way to use the law to promote economic expansion without also encouraging mismanagement or malfeasance? Would your answer change if you were a member of Congress?

2. Which branch of government—Congress, the judiciary, or the executive branch— is best suited to monitor corporate behavior in the marketplace?

3. How can clients and their lawyers construct new forms of business without running afoul of claims that, in hindsight, the new forms of business have "gone too far"?

---

[75] *J.P. Morgan Official Says Deals "Innovative,"* HOUS. CHRON., Dec. 27, 2002, at B2; Karen Masterson, *Enron Deals Bring Rebuke; Bank Executives Say They Were Duped by Energy Giant,* HOUS. CHRON., Dec. 12, 2002, at A4. Chase merged into J.P. Morgan on December 31, 2000. For the Rockefeller's connection to Chase Bank, see CHERNOW, *supra* note 8, at 377.

Brandeis, Business Ethics, and Enron

Edward J. Janger*

Business ethics, or the lack thereof, is big news these days. Enron, Adelphia, and WorldCom are three of the biggest bankruptcies in the history of our country. All three appear to arise, in roughly equal parts, out of individual venality and a failure of corporate governance structures to identify a fraud before huge damage could be done to employees, investors, retirees, and people who hoped someday to retire. To generations X and Y, this all seems very new, very unfamiliar—a fundamental breach of trust. What happened to the invisible hand and the new economy? As it turns out, the invisible hand (when we found it) was reaching into the till, and the new economy wasn't all that much different from the old economy. When someone tells you to invest on the basis of undemonstrated revenues, or an oil well that hasn't been dug, there is a lot of risk, and don't believe anybody who tells you otherwise.

Enron is nothing new, but getting to Enron has taken a fair amount of collective forgetting. Bubbles and busts were familiar attributes of the laissez-faire ethos that prevailed at the turn of the century. The Progressives, and Louis D. Brandeis, their most eloquent advocate, identified the evils that led to the Enrons of that era (particularly the consolidation and collapse of the railroad industry), and proposed a regulatory regime as well as corporate governance rules to deal with them. Indeed, our current three-part architecture of internal and external regulation of securities markets by the regulators, professionals (lawyers and accountants), and shareholders was largely the brainchild of Brandeis and the Progressives.[1]

---

* Professor, Brooklyn Law School. This essay is based on the Andrew R. Cecil Lecture on Values in a Free Society, delivered October 14, 2002 at the University of Texas at Dallas.

[1] PHILIPPA STRUM, LOUIS D. BRANDEIS: JUSTICE FOR THE PEOPLE 383–84 (1984). Indeed, Bruce Murphy has suggested that Brandeis, through Frankfurter, may have played a role in the drafting of these laws, even while he was on the bench. BRUCE ALLEN MURPHY, THE BRANDEIS/FRANKFURTER CONNECTION 131–38 (1982).

Conceived during the first two decades of the new century, the Progressives' ideas formed the basis for the disclosure-based program that was enacted into law as part of the New Deal, in the wake of the stock market crash of 1929.[2] Since that time, and particularly since 1980, that architecture has steadily eroded, as the spirit of deregulation has prevailed.[3] What was that architecture? What is it that Brandeis saw that former SEC Chairman Harvey Pitt and Congress did not?

Brandeis was particularly concerned about what he called the "Money Trust," consolidation in the financial and railroad industries, and the plight of labor.[4] While these were the specific financial issues of his time, his writings on these topics during the ten years before he was appointed to the Supreme Court transcend their historical context. Brandeis constantly returned to four basic themes: transparency (or disclosure and accountability); undivided loyalties (or prevention of conflicts of interest); manageable enterprise size (or the curse of bigness); and (for my purposes, most intriguingly) business as a profession. Each of these four themes is implicated in the Enron story, and particularly in the story of Enron and its interaction with its accountants, its lawyers, and government regulators.

THE ENRON STORY

Before mapping Brandeis onto Enron, let's take a moment to outline the Enron story itself. What did the folks at Enron do, and how did they get away with it for so long? The Enron story is by now familiar. Enron overstated the value of its assets, understated its liabilities, and in the process pumped its stock price to extreme highs, while the underlying business was sliding toward bankruptcy. How did Enron hide its lies from the marketplace, and would we have caught up with Enron sooner if we'd listened to Brandeis?

The principal tool that Andrew Fastow, Enron's Chief Financial Officer, appears to have used in the creation of the celebrated LJM, Chewco, and Raptor partnerships is called "structured finance."[5] The magic was accomplished through manipulation of

---

[2] MURPHY, *supra* note 1, at 131–38.

[3] *See, e.g.,* Garn-St. Germain Depository Institutions Act of 1982, Pub. L. No. 97-320, 96 Stat. 1469 (1982) (Bank Deregulation); Gramm-Leach-Bliley Act of 1999, Pub. L. No. 106-102, 113 Stat. 1338 (1999) (codified in scattered sections of 12 and 15 U.S.C.) (repealing the Glass/Steagall wall between banks and investment banks).

[4] *See* LOUIS D. BRANDEIS, OTHER PEOPLE'S MONEY AND HOW THE BANKERS USE IT (Frederick M. Stokes, 1914).

[5] The transactions described here are based on the Remarks of Joseph F. Berardino, Managing Partner-Chief Executive officer, Andersen, to the United States House of Representatives Committee on Financial Services, December 12, 2001, *available at* http://financialservices.house.gov/media/pdf/121201jb.pdf (last visited April 16, 2003) and the Criminal Complaint filed against Andrew Fastow by the United States Department of Justice, *available at* http://news.findlaw.com/hdocs/docs/enron/usfastow103102ind.pdf [hereinafter, Fastow Complaint].

legitimate structures[6] and the malleable accounting rules for "off balance sheet" treatment of entities.[7]

Let's start with a legitimate use of structured finance, and then explore how Fastow manipulated that device. Let's assume that Enron entered into a deal to sell a piece of heavy equipment for $500,000, and the buyer promised to pay for it over the next ten years, at a steady rate of $50,000 plus interest. Let's further assume that Enron wanted the cash now, instead of the income stream. Enron would have two options: it could borrow $500,000 against the income stream (an "account"[8] or an "instrument"[9] or "chattel paper,"[10] depending on how the deal was structured), or it could sell the income stream (or "financial asset") for $500,000. Under either transaction, it would have cash of $500,000 in hand now, but the accounting consequences of the two transactions would be slightly different. The loan transaction would alter both the left side and the right side of the balance sheet. Cash would increase by $500,000 on the left side, while $500,000 would be booked as debt on the right side of the balance sheet. The sale transaction, by contrast, operates only on the left side of the balance sheet. One asset (a piece of heavy equipment) would first become an account (or other type of financial asset), and then would become cash. All of these changes would occur on the asset side of the balance sheet. One important thing to note, however, is that neither the sale nor the loan transaction alters the book value of Enron. Shareholder equity remains constant.

Neither of these transactions is controversial. Neither of them is deceptive. The advantage of the sale transaction, for Enron's purposes, is that after the sale, Enron would book the full $500,000 value of the receivable as income in the quarter on which the asset was sold. This is permissible under accounting rules if the sale is a "true sale" to a "separate entity."[11] In other words, Enron must have truly transferred the benefits and risks of ownership to the purchaser. It must have sold an asset worth $500,000 and received $500,000 in return.

---

[6] Securitization and other "structured finance" arrangements, when properly used, can have a number of efficiency creating advantages over more traditional forms of secured credit. Steven L. Schwarcz, *Rethinking Freedom of Contract: A Bankruptcy Paradigm*, 77 TEX. L. REV. 515 (1999); Steven L. Schwarcz, *The Inherent Irrationality of Judgment Proofing*, 52 STAN. L. REV. 1 (1999); Steven L. Schwarcz, *Judgment Proofing: A Rejoinder*, 5 STAN. L. REV. 77 (1999). *But see* Lynn M. LoPucki, *The Death of Liability*, 106 YALE L.J. 1, 25–26 (1996); Lynn M. LoPucki, *The Irrefutable Logic of Judgment Proofing: A Reply to Professor Schwarcz*, 52 STAN. L. REV. 55 (1999).

[7] Statement No. 140 of the Financial Accounting Standards Board, *Accounting for Transfers and Servicing of Financial Assets and Extinguishments of Liabilities B a replacement FASB Statement No. 125. available at* www.fasb.org [hereinafter FASB] (providing standards for distinguishing transfers of financial assets that are sales from transfers that are secured borrowings).

[8] U.C.C. § 9-102(2) (2003).

[9] *Id.* at § 9-102(47).

[10] *Id.* at § 9-102(11).

[11] *See* FASB, *supra* note 7.

Here's where the smoke and mirrors come in. What if the value of the income stream is $500,000, but Enron chose to book it as a $1,000,000 deal? Well, that is a fraud, and that is basically what Enron did. How could Enron have done this without being detected? This sleight of hand was accomplished by manipulating and pressing the limits of the accounting rules for off-book transactions. Since nobody would pay $1,000,000 for a $500,000 asset, Enron sold it to a partnership that it controlled, and Enron guaranteed to the purchasing partnership that the $500,000 asset would in fact yield $1,000,000. In the case of the LJM and Chewco partnerships set up by Fastow, the enhancements took different forms for each partnership, but in both cases, Enron essentially guaranteed (in various ways too complicated to detail here) that, if the buyer defaulted on its obligation to pay for the assets, Enron would make up the difference.[12] In the case of the LJM partnerships, the alleged promise from Enron to the partnership was called the "Global Galactic" agreement.[13] The problem is that Enron never disclosed this recourse.[14] In this simplified example, Enron essentially borrowed $500,000 from the buyer and didn't list that debt on the balance sheet.

Having explained what Enron did, recognize one other important fact: these numbers were made up. In the real Enron deals, the undisclosed recourse totaled $1.2 billion. When the magnitude of the undisclosed recourse was finally disclosed, the value of Enron's stock collapsed.[15] What is striking to me, and has been striking to many commentators, is not that Enron pushed the limits of a financial form. At some level, we expect businessmen to do that. What is striking is that three sets of professionals—Enron's officers, with their fiduciary duty to shareholders; Enron's lawyers, with their duty to the corporation; and the accountants, with their duty to the public investors—either failed to detect, or failed to speak out about, the fraud.

---

[12] Fastow Complaint, *supra* note 5, at ¶ 11, 21–26 (Chewco); *id.* at ¶ 30–39 (LJM).

[13] *Id.* at ¶ 34.

[14] Fastow apparently never disclosed the Global Galactic Agreement to the Enron Board. *Id.* at ¶ 35. According to one participant, the

> Transactions between Enron and LJM were mere "warehousing" deals in which there was an understanding that LJM would hold Enron assets only for a short time, with Enron agreeing that LJM would make a profit on those assets. Fastow and others caused LJM to "purchase" underperforming assets from Enron for prices that often bore no relation to the assets' true value. These assets were referred to as Enron's "nuclear waste." In undocumented side deals, Enron agreed that LJM would not lose money even if the market value of an asset declined, because Enron would attempt to arrange a sale of the asset to a third party at a profit to LJM or, if no such third party could be found, Enron itself would repurchase the asset.

Id. at ¶ 38.

[15] When Enron restated its earnings on October 16, Enron stock was trading in the mid-$30s. A month later it fell below $10. *See* Lee Cearnal, *Graphic, An Enron Timeline: The Rise and Fall,* HOUS. CHRON., Oct. 21, 2002, *available at* http://www.chron.com/cs/CDA/story.hts/special/enron/1625635 (last visited April 23, 2003).

What would Brandeis have had to say about Enron? Brandeis was a Progressive, and Progressives are remembered for their belief in "good" government. The focus is usually on the public sector, but Brandeis's Progressivism included reform of the private sector as well. In his view, for markets to function, they needed information—accurate information. Investors in public companies needed accurate disclosure of material information.

DISCLOSURE AND ACCOUNTABILITY

The key to Brandeis's Progressive vision was what we now call "transparency"—accountability in both the public and private spheres. "Sunlight," Brandeis said, "is . . . the best of disinfectants; electric light the most efficient policeman."[16] Brandeis was probably a Progressive before such a term existed. For example, "When [B]randeis was ten years old[, he] leveled against the treasurer of a debating society to which he belonged the charge of inaccurate accounting: the amount involved was forty cents. Only after an explanatory interview given by the treasurer did Brandeis agree to drop the investigation."[17]

Throughout his career as the "People's Lawyer," a common theme was his demand that public officials and business people account accurately and publicly for their use of funds. As he saw it, accurate disclosure of financial information by public and private actors was essential for citizens to exercise their franchise in an informed fashion and for shareholders to provide effective supervision to corporate managers. A formative chapter in Brandeis's career was the campaign to force the New Haven Railroad to divest itself of the Boston and Maine Railroad, and thereby to prevent a railroad monopoly in New England. A key piece of his strategy was to force the Morgan interests to provide accurate disclosure of the state of the Railroad's finances. Brandeis wrote his brother Alfred: "I think, before we get through, the estimable gentlemen who scrambled for the chance of exchanging their B&M stock for New Haven will find that they have been served a gold brick."[18]

Alpheus T. Mason, Brandeis's early biographer, wrote:

> When [the New Haven Railroad's Annual Report] appeared in the fall of 1907, he was very surprised. He knew the company's fixed charges had increased tremendously, yet the report failed to reveal this. The balance sheet listing contingent liabilities did not include certain items which he knew existed. What startled him was the absence of a full statement of resources—a conspicuous departure from accounting practices.[19]

---

[16] LOUIS DEMBITZ BRANDEIS, *supra* note 4.

[17] ALLON GAL, BRANDEIS OF BOSTON 22 (1980).

[18] ALPHEUS T. MASON, BRANDEIS: A FREE MAN'S LIFE 182 (1946).

[19] *Id.* at 182–183.

Indeed, Brandeis wrote the chairman of the Massachusetts Board of Railroad Commissioners: "One might study the report filed with your board from end to end and never know that the New Haven held any interest in the Boston & Maine railroad stock, or in the Rhode Island Railway System, or in any of the Massachusetts Street Railways controlled by the New England Investment Security Company."[20]

Note what is being complained of. Brandeis is, in effect suggesting that "off balance sheet accounting" for related entities led to an understatement of the contingent liabilities faced by the New Haven Railroad. Does this sound familiar?

The resonances become even sharper. The shortcomings in the New Haven's Annual Report led Brandeis to write a pamphlet.

> Brandeis's chief point . . . was that the New Haven's "change from financial strength to weakness has been accomplished in an extraordinarily short period of time; the published reports of the company have been so framed as not to disclose its real condition." For example, Brandeis could find no provision for maintenance. On the other hand, he found the ordinary expenditure of about ten million dollars for rolling stock, repairs, etc., charged not to operating expenses in the regular way but to profit and loss. If the amount had been charged in the conventional way, he pointed out, the New Haven would have fallen $1,171,550.82 short of paying its 8 per cent dividend.[21]

It is difficult to discern precisely what Brandeis is complaining about here, but it looks as if the New Haven was capitalizing expenses. In other words, it was counting operating expenses as assets. While Enron did not try this trick, this is precisely what WorldCom did, to the tune of four billion dollars.

This piece of financial detective work was not an isolated incident in Brandeis's career. The theme of accurate disclosure also showed up in Brandeis's early police power opinions on the Court, and might be described simply as a belief in truth-in-advertising. For example, in a 1916 decision concerning, of all things, ice cream,[22] Brandeis wrote an opinion for the Supreme Court upholding Iowa and Pennsylvania statutes that said a frozen dessert could not be called "ice cream" unless it contained at least 12% butterfat.[23] He declared:

> The ice cream of commerce is not iced or frozen cream. It is a frozen confection—a compound. The ingredients of this compound may vary widely

---

[20] *Id.* at 183.

[21] *Id.* at 185.

[22] Edward J. Janger & Michael Berkowitz, *Brandeis, Zionism and Other People's Money* 36 (1998) (unpublished manuscript, on file with author); *see also* MASON, *supra* note 18, at 441–464.

[23] MASON, *supra* note 18, at 441–464.

in character, in the number used and in the proportions in which they are used. . . . The facts show that in the absence of legislative regulation the ordinary purchaser at retail does not and cannot know exactly what he is getting when he purchases ice cream. . . . He presumably believes that cream or at least rich milk is among the important ingredients, and he may make his purchase with a knowledge that butter-fat is the principal food value in cream or milk. Laws designed to prevent persons from being mis-led in respect to the weight, measurement, quality or ingredients of an article of general consumption are a common exercise of the police power.[24]

Just as with the New Haven Railroad, and with the Pennsylvania and Iowa laws regarding the butterfat content of ice cream, to Brandeis, if investors, consumers, and/or voters were likely to be deceived, it was the appropriate role of the law to require complete and accurate disclosure.

At bottom, the Enron and WorldCom cases are about false advertising. Undisclosed "contingent liabilities" brought Enron down. Operating expenses booked improperly as capital investment brought WorldCom down. In both cases, inattention to basic accounting principles left shareholders unable to distinguish ice cream from sorbet.

PREVENTING CONFLICTS OF INTEREST

The second component of Brandeis's vision was individual loyalty. In a 1915 series of articles initially published in *Harper's Magazine,* and later reprinted as a book entitled *Other People's Money,*[25] Brandeis catalogued the evils of what he called the money trust. He described a network of "interlocking directorates,"[26] where a small number of commercial and investment banks controlled the boards of directors of, and access to capital for, virtually every major industry. As he put it:

Investment bankers, like J.P. Morgan & Co., *dealers in bonds*, stocks and notes, *encroached upon the functions of the three other classes of corporations* with which their business brought them into contact. They became the directing power in railroads, public service and industrial companies through which our great business operations are conducted—the *makers of bonds and stocks*. They became the directing power in the life insurance companies, and other corporate reservoirs of the people's savings—the *buyers of bonds and stocks*. They became the directing power also in banks and trust

[24] Hutchinson Ice Cream Co. v. Iowa, 242 U.S. 153, 157–58 (1916).

[25] BRANDEIS, *supra* note 4.

[26] "There is obvious consolidation of banks and trust companies; the less obvious affiliations—through stockholdings, voting trusts, and interlocking directorates—of banking institutions which are not legally connected; and the joint transactions, gentlemen's agreements, and "banking ethics" which eliminate competition among investment bankers." BRANDEIS, *supra* note 4, at 4.

companies—the *depositaries of the quick capital* of the country—the life blood of business, with which they and others carried on their operations. Thus four distinct functions, each essential to business, and each exercised, originally, by a distinct set of men, became united in the investment banker.[27]

This consolidation of power in a small number of hands presented a number of dangers. As Brandeis saw it:

> The practice of interlocking directorates is the root of many evils. It offends laws human and divine. Applied to rival corporations, it tends to suppression of competition and to violation of the Sherman law. Applied to corporations which deal with each other, it tends to disloyalty and to violation of the fundamental law that no man can serve two masters. In either event it tends to inefficiency; for it removes incentive and destroys soundness of judgment. . . .[28]

Further, "protection to minority stockholders demands that corporations be prohibited absolutely from making contracts in which a director has a private interest. . . . For when a company's important contracts are made through directors who are interested on both sides, the common presumption that money spent has been properly spent does not prevail."[29]

Again, Brandeis's concern about conflicts of interest resonates throughout the Enron story. At the single-firm level, stock options held by key officers created strong incentives to pump up the stock price, and maintain it at a certain level, until the options could be exercised and the stock unloaded.[30] The Fastow partnerships further became

---

[27] *Id.* at 5 (emphasis added).

[28] *Id.* at 51.

[29] *Id.* at 61–62.

[30] Tom Fowler, *The Pride and The Fall of Enron,* HOUS. CHRON., Oct. 20, 2002, at 1, *available at* http://www.chron.com/cs/CDA/story.hts/special/enron/1624822 (last visited April 16, 2003).

> In theory, Enron had mechanisms in place to raise such questions, to assess risk and accurately report financial numbers . . . . But the system was easily overridden. Deal originators could determine the total value of their proposals by manipulating such factors as the long-term price for whatever was being bought or sold. Their bonuses were based on the total value of the deal, not the cash it brought in.
>
> All this was designed to pump up the quarterly reports, made possible by "mark-to-market" accounting, a system Skilling pushed Enron to adopt in 1991 that allows a company to report as current revenue the total value of a deal over its projected lifetime.
>
> Mark-to-market as it was used at Enron made earnings look good, pumping up the stock price and increasing the value of the thousands of stock options executives received as compensation.
>
> "It was a moral hazard being able to record your profits immediately," one former executive said. "It created many temptations."

Id.

a mechanism through which Enron could manipulate earnings (using the sale device described earlier), could conceal losses by manipulating the rules for off balance sheet accounting, and could transfer assets to insiders through a device known as "tranching."[31] Through tranching, Fastow managed to take advantage of the fact that even bad assets produce some income. The Fastow partnerships sometimes issued multiple "layers" of securities against a particular asset. The senior levels would get paid off first, and so on down the chain. Through this device, Enron was both able to move bad assets off its balance sheet, and transfer the limited value of those assets to insiders.

At the multi-firm level, a number of additional conflicts of interest appear. First, there is the conflict of interest faced by Arthur Andersen, who served both as auditor and consultant to Enron. Zealous attention to accounting principles might have jeopardized the consulting business. Indeed, it might also have jeopardized the auditing business itself. The investment banks, who sold both analysis and underwriting services, had a tremendous incentive to report favorably on their underwriting client.[32] Finally, the lawyers, who may have issued "true sale" opinions in the structured finance transactions, also risked losing business if they complained.[33]

One of the most troubling conflicts faced by all of the "professionals" in a case like Enron is the fact that the accountants are hired by officers of the company to represent the company. As noted above, those officers themselves face certain conflicts. When the professionals are called upon to counsel the "company" with regard to interested transactions, there is an inherent tension between honoring the duty to the client (the corporation), and making the person who hired you (the officer) happy. These are not easy lines to walk.

But Brandeis recognized a further "conflict" created by this web of relationships. For Brandeis, these conflicts of interest infected not just the company itself, but the political process.[34] They were a threat to "industrial and political liberty." To understand this point, we need to examine Brandeis's third evil—the curse of bigness.

---

[31] SPECIAL INVESTIGATIVE COMMITTEE OF THE BOARD OF DIRECTORS OF ENRON, REPORT OF INVESTIGATION 144 (Feb. 1, 2002) [hereinafter POWERS REPORT].

[32] The New York Attorney General, Eliot Spitzer, the SEC and others recently settled claims against investment banks for such conflicts of interest for over $1.2 billion. Press Release, NY Attorney General, *NASD, NASAA, NYSE and State Regulators Announce Historic Agreement to Reform Investment Practices* (Dec. 20, 2002), *available at* http://www.oag.state.ny.us/press/2002/dec/dec20b_02.html (last visited April 16, 2003).

[33] In one of her memos imploring Enron to launch an investigation of accounting practices, Sherron Watkins wrote, "Can't use V&E due to conflict—they provided some true sale opinions on some of the deals." *See* David Koenig, *Vinson and Elkins has Forged Close Ties with Enron*, HOUS. CHRON., January 27, 2003, *available at* http://www.chron.com/cs/CDA/story.hts/special/enron/1228517 (last visited April 16, 2003).

[34] BRANDEIS, *supra* note 5, at 62 ("For even more important than efficiency are industrial and political liberty; and these are imperiled by the Money Trust.").

THE CURSE OF BIGNESS

Brandeis's suspicion of "bigness" was rooted in his admiration for Jeffersonian democracy, and more deeply in Plato. As he saw it, self-governance was only possible on a small scale. Humans have limited capacity to understand complex enterprises, and large-scale enterprises fall prey to agency (i.e., conflicts). First, once a corporation gets too large, it is too complicated for one mind to comprehend, and the result is likely to be "agency" and inefficiency. In describing Harriman's control of various railroad interests, Brandeis quips:

> [L]ess than twelve years after Mr. Harriman first became a director in the Union Pacific, he died from overwork at the age of 61. But it was not death only that had set a limit to his achievements. The multiplicity of his interests prevented him from performing for his other railroads the great services that had won him a world-wide reputation as manager and rehabilitator of the Union Pacific and the Southern Pacific.[35]

Second, once a corporation gets too big, it becomes too powerful and seeks to restrain the market[36] and to use the political process to gain advantage. Brandeis's concern about interlocking directorates and the money trust was not just that the interlocking relationships created inefficiency. They also infected the political process.

Again, both dangers of bigness infect the Enron story. Not only is it clear that Enron grew so big that no one person could understand all of the transactions that it was doing, but something even more pernicious appears to have been going on. Enron appeared to have been constructing its deals with the express purpose of making it difficult for outsiders to understand the underlying economics. Lack of transparency reinforced the problem of bigness. Second, while we don't know the extent, it does appear that Enron worked hard to garner and maintain influence in the political process.[37] It appears that Brandeis may have been right to worry that large enterprises like Enron can pose a danger to democracy.

---

[35] *Id.* at 169.

[36] *Id.* at 152 ("The fact that industrial monopolies arrest development is more serious even than the direct burden imposed through extortionate prices.").

[37] Ken Lay is believed to have lobbied Vice President Cheney with regard to energy policy. David Lazarus, *The Enron Collapse: Memo details Cheney-Enron links*, SAN FRAN. CHRON., January 30, 2002, at A1, *available at* http://www.sfgate.com/cgi-bin/article.cgi?f=/c/a/2002/01/30/MN46204.DTL (last visited April 23, 2003). Between 1990 and 2002, Enron and Enron executives contributed $5.8 million to various political candidates. Nearly three quarters of this went to Republicans. *Graphic, Enron's Political Contributions*, HOUS. CHRON. *available at* http://www.chron.com/content/chronicle/special/01/enron/index.html (last visited April 16, 2003).

BUSINESS AS A PROFESSION

The fourth theme, "business as a profession," was not so much a problem as it was a proposed solution. In most respects, this was Brandeis's most controversial suggestion, and the one that has had the least influence. In a number of his writings, Brandeis advocated a view of business people, not as profit seekers, but as professionals. In his view, business people, like lawyers and accountants, had professional duties to shareholders, to employees, and to the public, and should be trained and should think of themselves in terms of those duties.

In a 1912 commencement speech at Brown University, Brandeis said the "peculiar characteristics of a profession," are:

> First. A profession is an occupation for which the necessary preliminary training is intellectual in character, involving knowledge, and to some extent learning, as distinguished from mere skill.

> Second. It is an occupation which is pursued largely for others and not merely for one's self.

> Third. It is an occupation in which the amount of financial return is not the accepted measure of success.

In his view, a corporate charter carried with it a public trust. Particularly where railroads, utilities, and large industrial concerns were involved, corporate officers had a duty to society, not just to shareholders. Brandeis stated that "[b]usiness should be, and to some extent already is, one of the professions. It is an occupation in which the amount of financial return is not the accepted measure of success."[38]

What then was the measure of success?

> True, in business the earning of profit is something more than an incident of success. It is an essential condition of success. . . . But while loss spells failure, large profits do not connote success. Success must be sought in business also in excellence of performance; and *in business, excellence in performance manifests itself, among other things, in the advancing of methods and processes; in the improvement of products; in more perfect organization, eliminating friction as well as waste; in bettering the condition of the workingmen, developing their faculties and promoting their happiness; and in the establishment of right relations with customers and the community.*[39]

---

[38] LOUIS DEMBITZ BRANDEIS, BUSINESS—A PROFESSION (1912), *reprinted in* BRANDEIS ON DEMOCRACY 119 (Philippa Strum ed., 1995).

[39] *Id.* at 121 (emphasis added).

Brandeis's ideal businessman was based on a pair of clients that he had early in his career, a shoe manufacturer named William H. McElwain, and the Filene family of Boston retailers. Both were financially successful, but both also placed an emphasis on building a quality workplace, along with selling quality goods at a fair price.[40]

It is a measure of how far we have come that Brandeis's vision seems quaint and perhaps hopelessly naive. Ben and Jerry may have given 1% for peace, but now they've been purchased by Unilever.[41] On one level Brandeis's ideal is inconsistent with the demands and duties placed on managers of public companies. Both Filene's and McElwain's shoe factory were privately held enterprises. Both Filene and McElwain were free to share profits with employees. Not so, perhaps for the officers of a publicly held company.

Moreover, there are risks associated with Brandeis's "do the right thing," vision of professional ethics. In a public company, it is tough enough to expect managers to look out for the shareholders' interests, let alone the interests of the employees and society at large. Was Brandeis asking for trouble? He may have been. Indeed, even he had trouble implementing his own idea of professionalism. He applied a similar view of professionalism to lawyers, and often described himself, not as the lawyer for his client, but as the "lawyer for the situation." This periodically exposed him to criticism. Indeed, one particular case became a *cause celebre* when he sought confirmation as a Justice of the Supreme Court.

Brandeis was approached by Mr. Lennox, the owner of a tannery that was insolvent. Brandeis disclosed to Lennox that he (Brandeis) had represented another creditor of the tannery. Mr. Lennox, after consultation with his father, told Brandeis that he wanted to pay 100% to the creditors and he wanted to hire Brandeis. Brandeis then advised him to do an assignment for the benefit of creditors and, along with his family, to make up any shortfall, paying the creditors 100%. Since the tannery was a corporation, Lennox was not obligated to pay the creditors 100%. When Lennox asked Brandeis if he was acting as his counsel, Brandeis said: "Not altogether as your counsel, but as trustee of your property." In short, Brandeis informed Lennox that Brandeis represented the company, not Lennox. This was the right thing to do, but Lennox does not appear to have understood what Brandeis meant. Upon realizing that he did not have to contribute personal assets, he refused to turn them over and sued Brandeis for deceiving him.[42]

This story illustrates how Brandeis's idea of "do the right thing" professionalism may muddy rather than clarify lines of duty. It makes it difficult to determine exactly for whom you, the "professional," are acting. Indeed, it creates some of the same conflicts that Brandeis inveighed against. Should a corporate officer work for the shareholders? The workers? The customers? Or the community? When should one of these subsidiary duties override the duty to the shareholders? On the other hand, there is a

---

[40] *Id.* at 119.

[41] *Ben and Jerry's Financial History, available at* http//lib.benjerry.com/our_company/research_library/fin/index.html (last visited May 27, 2003).

[42] MASON, *supra* note 18, at 232–37.

degree to which "professionalizing" business ethics along Brandeisian lines might be appropriate. The principal component of professional ethics, for doctors, lawyers and accountants, is the idea that there is a duty owed to someone else. For the doctor, it is the patient. For the lawyer, it is the client. For the accountant, it is the public, which relies on the financial statements.

On this level, Brandeisian business ethics can be distinguished from Enronian ethics. Even when there may be a conflict of interest, the conflict is created by a Brandeisian desire to do good for someone else, not by a desire to make money for oneself. One thing is clear about the officers of Enron: they had no sense of duty to anybody but themselves. And it was not just the business people. The lawyers appear to have lost sight of the fact that their client was the corporation, not the CFO who hired them. The accountants appear to have lost sight of their duty to the public when it conflicted with their own profit motive, and the investment banks appear to have shaded their analysis in order to protect their underwriting business.

In sum, Brandeis may have demanded too much of businesspeople, but his ideas remain useful. Operating against a background of *laissez-faire,* he advocated professional behavior and saw a role for businessmen in protecting consumers and rank and file employees. The folks at Enron demanded too little. When one compares the cost of Brandeis's train wreck (Lennox) to the cost of Enron, Brandeis's approach appears to have much to recommend it. Brandeis had one unhappy client and suffered professional embarrassment. The costs of Enron are still being totaled up.

Brandeis would have been horrified by Enron, but not surprised. He had seen it all before. He would have been appalled by the lack of professionalism of businesspeople, and by the lack of professionalism exhibited by the professionals themselves. Mostly, however, Brandeis would have been disappointed. He would have bemoaned our failure, over almost 100 years, to learn the lessons of his own time. We should have seen it coming. The bigness of Enron, the culture of non-transparency, and the conflicts of interest faced by its officers, directors, attorneys, and accountants undercut their ability to act professionally, and more important, prevented them from identifying fraud when committed by their colleagues.

Brandeis demanded more, and so should we.

QUESTIONS

1. Do the Sarbanes-Oxley reporting and certification requirements encourage officers and directors to act more like Brandeisian professionals?
2. Do the SEC's "up the ladder" rule and the proposed "noisy withdrawal" rule encourage lawyers to behave more in the manner that Brandeis advocated?
3. What conflicts of interest are created by the "up the ladder rule?" By "noisy withdrawal?" Are they more or less troublesome than the conflicts that exist without those rules?
4. Are lawyers effective regulators of client conduct? What about accountants? Are they better or worse than government regulators? Than judges?

Dr. Jekyll & Mr. Skilling: How Enron's Public Image Morphed from the Most Innovative Company in the Fortune 500 to the Most Notorious Company Ever*

Jeffrey D. Van Niel** & Nancy B. Rapoport***

Prior to its collapse into bankruptcy, only a few people knew Enron Corp, or any of its various subsidiaries ("Enron"), from direct dealings with the company. Most people, however, were familiar with Enron from what they had read or heard.[1] Following disclosure of the company's accounting problems and of the California electric market manipulation in 2001, the company's public image—as well as its stock price—plummeted. It is the ebb and flow of Enron's public perception that we scrutinize in this essay.

After reading about the various corporate and accounting scandals and watching former managers do their "perp walks" on television, we have had an opportunity to consider how a company that was once placed on a pedestal and touted as the most innovative company in the United States for six years in a row[2] could deteriorate into

* © Jeffrey D. Van Niel and Nancy B. Rapoport 2003. All rights reserved.

** Jeffrey D. Van Niel is currently licensed to practice law in Nebraska and Ohio and is actively pursuing licensure in Texas. He practiced utilities regulation and utilities law in Ohio for 10 years as an Assistant Ohio Attorney General representing the Public Utilities Commission of Ohio, as a Master Commissioner on behalf of the Supreme Court of Ohio, and in private practice with Kegler, Brown, Hill & Ritter and McNees, Wallace & Nurick. Mr. Van Niel also practiced utilities law for two years in Nebraska with Woods & Aitken.

*** Nancy Rapoport is Dean and Professor of Law at the University of Houston Law Center.

[1] For example, during his 12 years practicing in the utility law arena, Mr. Van Niel had many opportunities to interact with Enron personnel (including its lawyers) on numerous issues, including retail competition and the deregulation of the natural gas and electric industries.

[2] *See, e.g.,* Harry Hurt III et al., *Power Players Enron Has Shaken Up the Sleepy Gas Pipeline and Power Businesses by Aggressively Embracing Risk and Continually Remaking Itself. So What's Not to Like?*, FORTUNE, Aug. 5, 1996, at 94 [hereinafter *What's Not to Like*] ("Competitors voted Enron the most innovative company in the U.S. in FORTUNE's poll of "America's Most Admired Corporations" this year, ahead of high-tech highfliers like Intel and Microsoft."); *America's Most Admired Companies*, FORTUNE, Mar. 3, 1997, at F1; *America's Most Admired Companies*, FORTUNE, Mar. 2, 1998, at F1; *America's Most Admired Companies*, FORTUNE, Mar. 1, 1999, at 68; *America's Most Admired Companies*, FORTUNE, Feb. 21, 2000, at F1; *America's Most Admired Companies*, FORTUNE, Feb. 19, 2001, at F1.

a seething mass of accounting scandals, civil litigation, and criminal indictments. What struck us most was the apparent dramatic shift in the public perception of Enron—at least that was the premise when we started writing this essay. As with most academic pieces, we thought we knew what we wanted to say. Unfortunately, our research provided a different conclusion from the one that we had expected.

What do we mean? Simply put, everything that happened to Enron in 2001 was predicted—and used as a reason to avoid the company—as early as 1996.[3] A careful reader of Enron-related articles in the press might have seen this coming and avoided Enron like the plague.[4]

So what happened between 1985 and 2001 that launched Enron on the road to becoming the fifth largest company in the *Fortune 500*?[5] Why, that meta-mantra of the late 1990s and early 2000s: "thinking outside the box." Enron was considered the

---

[3] So aside from envy, what's not to like about Enron? According to some critics, the very things that have made the company a success: management's penchant for risk taking and innovation; the parent corporation's aggressive accounting practices and allegedly Byzantine methods of "managing earnings" via no fewer than six separately traded subsidiaries; an alleged overemphasis on short-term performance, symbolized by the daily posting of stock prices in the headquarters building; and the unusually complex intracompany transactions needed to drive profit growth. "Enron's just got too much hype in it for us," says a member of a multibillion-dollar Houston-based investment firm that specializes in blue-chip stocks. "A few years ago, they were promoting natural gas-powered automobiles. Then they dropped that idea like a hot potato, and started building power plants and spinning them off. It's hard to figure out what the fresh feed for this month is going to be."

What's Not to Like, supra note 2, at 94.

[4] In fact, some very high-profile investors stayed away from Enron stock because Enron's financial statements were simply not making sense. *See, e.g.,* MIMI SWARTZ WITH SHERRON WATKINS, POWER FAILURE: THE INSIDE STORY OF THE COLLAPSE OF ENRON xi–xiii (2003) [hereinafter POWER FAILURE]; LYN M. FRASER & AILEEN ORMISTON, UNDERSTANDING THE CORPORATE ANNUAL REPORT: NUTS, BOLTS, AND A FEW LOOSE SCREWS 17–21 (2003).

[5] *Fortune 500 Largest U.S. Corporations*, FORTUNE, Apr. 15, 2002, at F1 (listing Enron fifth, even though by then it was in Chapter 11). For an explanation of why it still made the list, *see* Carol J. Loomis, *And the Revenue Games People (like Enron) Play; Got energy trading contracts?*, FORTUNE, Apr. 15, 2002, at 190 ("We will explain these wacky revenue leaps. But first, an explanation as to why the Greatest Leaper of them all, Enron, is fifth on our 2001 list.... [W]e decided to rank Enron based on its nine-months['] revenues [because Enron had yet to release fourth quarter results]."). However, the irony of Enron's high ranking was not lost on the editors of FORTUNE who, in the same issue, published a poem with the concluding stanza:

Oh, somewhere the sun is shining, somewhere the stars are bright;
Somewhere there are investors who sleep like logs at night;
Consider these 500—how they grow! They burn! They strive!
And could someone please explain here—Exercise your brain here!
Can someone please explain here—Why is Enron still No. 5?

Stanley Bing, *The Auditor*, FORTUNE, Apr. 15, 2002, at 402.

best company at identifying talented employees who were willing to be innovative.[6] By 1996, Enron was creating a new business every other year.[7] Ken Lay, Enron's CEO both before and after Jeffrey Skilling, explained the company's changed focus (from a stodgy natural gas pipeline company to a cutting-edge entrepreneur and moving force in electric deregulation) in an August 5, 1996 *Fortune* magazine interview by pointing out that 40% of the company's earnings in 1995 came from businesses that did not exist in 1985.[8] Lay was confident that the trend would continue: "We expect that 5 years from now, over 40% of our earnings will come from businesses that did not exist 5 years ago. It's a matter of re-creating the company and the businesses we're in."[9] Enron re-created its businesses right into the ground.

1. ENRON BEFORE THE FALL—THE PUBLIC PERCEPTION

Enron started out as a somewhat sleepy natural gas utility in 1985, when Houston Natural Gas Corp. and InterNorth Inc. merged. It is safe to assume that, other than the people being directly served by that utility in 1985, most people still had never heard of Enron. Seven years later, virtually everyone had heard of Enron.[10] By 1992, Enron owned the largest natural gas pipeline network in the country and had already begun its efforts to revolutionize the natural gas industry. Finally, Enron stepped out of the shadows and into the spotlight with its revolutionary concept for the "Gas Bank."[11] With the Gas Bank, Enron forever altered not only the gas industry, but also the company itself.

---

[6] Some of Enron's mechanisms to obtain innovative thinking were draconian in nature. Every employee was ranked within his or her group each year, and the bottom 20% were let go. The pressure to produce was intense, and the internal competitions were brutal and cutthroat. *See infra* note 47 and accompanying text. Notwithstanding these factors, potential employees beat down the doors to get placed with Enron, including the "best and brightest," 20% of which would be ground into next year's compost.

[7] *What's Not to Like, supra* note 2.

[8] *Id.*

[9] *Id.*

[10] Early in 2003, NBR taught a group of 10th graders at the Schlenker School in Houston. Almost all of the students had heard of Enron and could describe in some detail what had happened to the company.

[11] [I]n 1989, Skilling, who was still working at McKinsey as an Enron consultant, realized that there was plenty of gas available—from producers who were being freed from federal price controls—and there was plenty of demand, from new utilities that wanted to burn gas to make electricity. But there was no intermediary that could aggregate—and more important, *balance*— the gas supplies coming from the producers with the demand coming from consumers. Why not create a mechanism that would allow them to hook up? Skilling called his idea the Gas Bank.

ROBERT BRYCE & MOLLY IVINS, PIPE DREAMS: GREED, EGO, AND THE DEATH OF ENRON 54 (2002) [hereinafter PIPE DREAMS].

A. The Puff Pieces

To the casual reader of business weeklies, Enron was riding high at the turn of the 21st century. In 1996, the *Washington Post* referred to Enron as a "titan in the natural gas industry."[12] In 1998, *Fortune* called Enron "the world's leading integrated natural-gas and electricity giant."[13] In 2000, *Fortune* again fawned over Enron, ranking it 25th among "the world's most admired companies."[14] In early 2001, the *Economist* still referred to Enron as "a highly successful energy brokerage."[15] Enron symbolized everything that was glitzy and go-go-go—the perfect morphing of a staid energy company into an *uber*-dot.com business.

The early 1990s were times of explosive change in many areas, including the development and use of personal technology and computerization, communications and mobile phones, and most important, the perceptions of workers and their intellectual capacity (and capabilities as company assets). These changes accelerated in the mid- and late 1990s, with the advent of the dot.com bubble. Simultaneously, Enron was evolving as well—creating new businesses, pushing the envelope and morphing itself from an energy utility to a growth company.[16] Here's the question—how do you make your energy utility look as good as a dot.com growth stock? Hindsight helps us respond with the obvious answer: you cook the books. Some people knew that Enron's

---

[12] Daniel Southerland, *You've Heard of Big Oil. This is the Story of Big Gas . . . and It Begins with Enron Corp., Which Wants to Be No. 1 in World*, WASH. POST, Feb. 4, 1996, at H1.

[13] Erin Davies, *Enron: The Power's Back On*, FORTUNE, Apr. 13, 1998, at 24.

[14] Nicholas Stein, *The World's Most Admired Companies*, FORTUNE, Oct. 2, 2000, at 182.

[15] *The Slumbering Giants Awake*, ECONOMIST, Feb. 10, 2001, at 6.

[16] Enron originally wanted to become "The World's Leading Energy Company," *see* POWER FAILURE, *supra* note 4, at 112, but eventually, even that sobriquet was too limiting. According to Cokie Roberts at ABC, "You start back in January of 2001. There was a big party, lavish party in San Antonio where Kenneth Lay declared Enron the 'world's greatest company.'" *ABC News: This Wk.* (ABC television broadcast, Feb. 10, 2002). It's not far to go from calling yourself "The World's Greatest Company" to being the butt of jokes like this one:

> Making the rounds of Wall Streeters while markets were in the dumps this week was a recording from the following number: 510-809-4466: "Thank you for calling Enron, please listen closely to the following options as our menu has changed.
>
> If you wish to serve a subpoena on a current or former Enron executive, press 1; If you are an Enron shareholder, and would like to learn how to turn your Enron stock certificates into decorative origami, press 2; If your Enron 401(k) plan is worthless and you'd like some tips on how to survive your retirement eating nothing but mac and cheese, press 3; If you are an Enron executive and would like to find out which prison inmate will be making you his b***h, press 4; If you would like to invoke your constitutional right against self[-]incrimination, press 5. If you are Dick Cheney, press 6 and thanks for nothing[,] Dick.
>
> Thank you for calling Enron, the World's greatest company."

Beth Piskora et al., *Bull's Eye*, N.Y. POST, Feb. 24, 2002, at 31.

accounting was questionable, long before Skilling abruptly retired as CEO and Enron's world came tumbling town.

B. The Early Critiques

Remember the old adage, "if it looks too good to be true, it usually is"? Enron illustrated that adage perfectly, and some very smart people figured out that Enron's financials were a sham. Others might not have known that Enron was cooking the books, but they looked askance at those books anyway. Even the normally effusive *Fortune* ran a story describing the impenetrability of Enron's financial information.[17] And the publication *Inside F.E.R.C.'s Gas Market Report* noted that, on December 21, 1995, Robert Christensen Jr. had downgraded Enron from a "buy" to a "hold," warning that "[t]he thin trading liquidity of these [gas derivatives] products can cause financial windfalls as well as huge potential losses. From the outside looking in, we cannot tell which way it will go for [Enron]."[18] A few outsiders looked at Enron and did not like what they saw.

There were clues as early as 1995, when *Fortune* reported Enron's losses on the power plant in Dabhol, India.[19] Also in 1995, there were rumors that Enron was "facing margin calls of hundreds of millions of dollars because it had a 'short' position on contracts to deliver natural gas in January."[20] Mind you, these problems only involved Enron's hard assets, rather than its later, "asset-lite" businesses.[21] And don't get

---

[17] To skeptics, the lack of clarity [in Enron's financials] raises a red flag about Enron's pricey stock. Even owners of the stock aren't universally sanguine. "I'm somewhat afraid of it," admits one portfolio manager. And the inability to get behind the numbers combined with ever higher expectations for the company may increase the chance of a nasty surprise. "Enron is an earnings-at-risk story," says Chris Wolfe, the equity market strategist at J.P. Morgan's private bank, who despite his remark is an Enron fan. "If it doesn't meet earnings, [the stock] could implode."

Bethany McLean, *Is Enron Overpriced?*, FORTUNE, Mar. 5, 2001, at 122.

[18] *Huge Spread in Basis Differentials Complicates Hedging, Say Analysts*, INSIDE F.E.R.C.'S GAS MARKET REP., Dec. 29, 1995, at 9.

[19] Rajiv M. Rao, *Enron's power outage in India*, FORTUNE, Oct. 2, 1995, at 34.

[20] Bill Mintz, *Enron shares recover as buyback announced*, HOUS. CHRON., Dec. 23, 1995, at B1.

[21] Skilling often touted his "asset-lite" philosophy. A mere two months before his sudden resignation, Skilling argued, "'Today the key to success is we don't need to own assets, as long as we can use [them] to acquire information such as knowledge about gas pipelines and natural gas. Once we have the information and knowledge, we no longer need to own the assets.'" Dr. Nikolai Dobberstein, *Creating Global Winners*, MALAYSIAN BUS., June 1, 2001 (quoting Jeffrey Skilling and encouraging Malaysian companies to follow similar business models). Skilling was a master at convincing people of this doubtful logic. For example, this interview on CNBC:

HAINES [Newscaster]: . . . Joining us now is Enron's CEO, Jeffrey Skilling. And in spirit of full disclosure, I have some shares of Enron in my IRA. Mr. Skilling, how does revenue go up so much and the bottom line doesn't benefit more?

us started on Enron's political maneuverings, both in the U.S. and abroad,[22] or its manipulation of the California energy markets.[23]

Why didn't more people question Enron's financial statements and business plans? Enron was well-known for bullying analysts who disagreed with Enron's own rosy pictures of its financial health.[24] Still, a smattering of analysts and reporters stood firm in their criticism of Enron's murky financial statements—enough to convince us that

---

MR. JEFFREY SKILLING (Enron CEO): Well, we had a net income increase, Mark, of over 40 percent and earnings per share up 32 percent, so I—I think it was a—a real good quarter.

HAINES: Yeah, but that doesn't answer the question: Well, how can revenue go up, like 150 and—and—and the bottom line only benefit 40—40 percent?

MR. SKILLING: What—what drives our net income, Mark, is the increase in physical volumes delivered. Revenues are impacted by price levels and price revel—levels really don't impact us because we don't own the generation facilities, we don't own gas production assets. So prices move up and down. That impacts our revenue. But ra—what really matters to us is, how much volume are we delivering to customers? And our volumes this quarter are up 58 percent, which drove that increase in our wholesale income.

CNBC: Squawk Box (CNBC television broadcast, July 12, 2001).

[22] For a discussion of Enron's political influence in the U.S., *see* Kevin Phillips, *The Company Presidency; Enron and the Bush family have boosted each other up the ladder of success. But have their ties created a Teapot Dome?*, L.A. TIMES, Feb. 10, 2002 at M1 (detailing the exchange of money and favors between various political figures and Enron); Eliane S. Povich, *Gramms and Enron: A Mutual Aid Society; Rules backed by senator, wife helped company*, NEWSDAY, Feb. 10, 2002, at A6 (explaining that as chief of the Commodities Futures Trading Commission, Wendy Gramm drafted rules exempting energy trades from government regulation, then shortly afterwards accepted a lucrative position on Enron's board of directors; and noting Enron "donated almost $100,000 to Sen. [Phil] Gramm [(R-Texas), and Wendy's husband] over the past decade."). Apparently, Enron attempted similar tactics abroad. However, Enron wasn't always popular overseas, and not just because of its failed businesses worldwide. A particularly colorful example of nasty press overseas occurred in 1998:

In the hurt tone of a nun rejecting accusations of Satanism, executives and Government propagandists denounced our revelation last week that Enron, a US energy company which has bought American politicians wholesale, was sponsoring the Labour Party conference. Their protestations of injured innocence grew louder on Thursday when, as we predicted, Peter Mandelson allowed the multi-national accused of complicity with the beating and false imprisonment of Indian peasants to take over the Wessex Water monopoly in southern England.

Nick Cohen, *Hold on a minute . . .* , OBSERVER, Sept. 13, 1998, at 32.

[23] *See, e.g.,* Rebecca Smith & John R. Wilke, *Leading the News: Enron Ex-Trader Admits to Fraud In California Crisis*, WALL ST. J., Oct. 18, 2002, at A3 ("The former head of Enron Corp.'s Western energy-trading desk admitted he conspired to manipulate California's electricity market and extract illegal profits for his employer, giving federal prosecutors a valuable witness who will help them develop cases against executives at Enron and other big energy-trading companies."); Robert Gavin, *Did Utilities Aid 'Ricochet' Trades?*, WALL ST. J., May 24, 2002, at B4 (explaining "the so-called Death Star strategy in which Enron scheduled fictitious electricity deliveries on overburdened transmission lines, in order to receive congestion relief payments . . .").

[24] PIPE DREAMS, *supra* note 11, at 249–56.

our original theory (that no one knew about Enron's risky business model until after Skilling resigned as CEO) was wrong.[25] After Skilling resigned, of course, everyone began to understand what these few analysts had been saying all along.

2. ENRON AFTER THE FALL—THE PUBLIC PERCEPTION

Enron seemed to go from "most admired" status to "most despised" status in record time, once the revelations about the company's behavior became public. Nightly news broadcasts depicted the very real tragedy of retirees (and those close to retirement age) whose lives were forever changed by Enron's plummeting stock price.

Even in the midst of tragedy and anger, some were able to find humor in the situation:

Enron Business Haikus

Business model
Too complex to understand
It's a house of cards.

Buy low and sell high.
Our intermediations
Raise energy costs.

Our profits are made
At the consumer's expense
Pass the caviar.

Stock price fell today.
Management says, "Don't fear."
I am still afraid.

Chaos reigns within.
Reflect, repent and sell short.
Even down can be up.[26]

---

[25] *See, e.g.,* Todd Mason, *Houston Oil Analyst Wouldn't Buy Enron's Story,* FORT WORTH STAR-TELE-GRAM, Apr. 11, 2002, at A1 (describing John Olson's negative views of Enron and Enron's use of pressure to get him to retract his views); Jeff Donn, *Rise and Fall of Enron; Energy Giant Fed on Chaos and Change; Did Arrogance Boomerang?,* COM. APPEAL, Jan. 22, 2002, at B7 (same); Tom Fowler, *The Fall of Enron; A Year Ago, Enron's Crumbling Foundation was Revealed to All When the Company Reported Its Disastrous Third-Quarter Numbers. It's Growth-At-Any-Cost Culture Led It to Bankruptcy—and Ignominy,* HOUS. CHRON., Oct. 20, 2002, at A1 (John Olson fired by Merrill Lynch for refusing to change his views on Enron); *Courageous Warnings on Enron,* ST. PETERSBURG TIMES, Jan. 27, 2002, at 2D (Bethany McLean, a reporter for *Fortune,* wrote an article critical of Enron despite Enron's attempts to get the magazine to quash the story).

[26] TIM BARRY, THE TOTALLY UNAUTHORIZED ENRON JOKE BOOK 18 (2002) [hereinafter JOKE BOOK]. Another part of the book describes:

These jokes, and others like them, indicate how much Enron's demise—as well as the demise of other companies after Enron—has entered the public consciousness.[27] We can trace Enron's entry into the world of late-night TV jokes[28] starting roughly after Jeffrey Skilling, Enron's CEO, resigned on August 14, 2001.

What may have triggered the media's focus, in part, was the unlikely proposition that Skilling would have resigned "for personal reasons" and to spend more time with

---

Shareholder Haikus From Enron's Last Days

CNN today
Says Enron distress increased.
This is not good news.

Dynegy retreat
Leaves few options available.
My foreboding grows.

The merger now dead.
Hope fades to a mere glimmer.
Chapter 11 looms.

The official news
Now has tolled. Enron is gone.
So is my money.

Id. at 29.

[27] We can't resist this one, describing "Enronism" as different from capitalism and communism:

You have two cows. You write-down and set aside the debt incurred by one of the cows to an off-sheet entity. You sell all three of them to another publicly listed joint trading venture company, using equity derivative transactions created by your brother-in-law at the bank. The trading company sells to a vehicle that is capitalized with a promise of Enron stock based on the increased valuation of the third cow, with the understanding that the first 33% of the future profit is returned to the partners of the venture in the form of more cows. Then execute a debt/equity swap with an associated general offer so you get all four cows back, with a tax exemption for five cows (debt depreciation of the first [cow]). The recognized future milk funds flow of the six cows are brought forward and transferred via an intermediary to a Cayman Island company secretly owned by the majority shareholder, who "enhanced" the capital structure by selling the rights to all seven cows back to your listed company. You hire Arthur Andersen to audit your books. The annual report says the company owns eight cows, with an option on one more.

Iconoclast website, http://www.iconoclast.ca/issue/9001,3,0402,17,1.html (last visited Jan. 12, 2003).

[28] For a sampling of these jokes, *see* http://politicalhumor.about.com/library/blenronscandal.htm (last visited July 22, 2003). *See also* JOKE BOOK, *supra* note 26, at 87 (listing Enron jokes by late-night comedians). Other corporate scandals have also gotten late-night notice. *See, e.g.,* http://members.aol.com/mrdejim/oct02.html (quoting Jay Leno: "Martha Stewart's stockbroker's assistant is going to testify against her. She may have sent a coded message to him on her show today when she demonstrated how a canary with a broken neck can't sing.") (aired on *The Tonight Show with Jay Leno* (NBC television broadcast, Oct. 2, 2002)) (last visited July 22, 2003).

his family.[29] Did anyone really believe that such a hard-driving, aggressive CEO was leaving in order to stop and smell the roses?[30]

The news stories kept coming fast and furious (both literally and figuratively furious), and our morning ritual of reading the newspapers while eating breakfast expanded from 15 minutes to 30 minutes to sometimes over an hour, just to keep up. Politicians started incorporating Enron references into their speeches.[31] Late-night

---

[29] Skilling's resignation was the triggering event that caused Sherron Watkins to write her now-famous one-page anonymous memo to returning CEO Ken Lay. *See* POWER FAILURE, *supra* note 4, at 275–89.

[30] There were problems with Skilling's story. To begin with, Skilling was never considered much of a family man. He was divorced. He and his ex-wife had three children. Skilling loved his kids, but few saw him as a fanatical family man. Second, by quitting, Skilling left lots of money on the table. In 2000, Skilling's pay package had totaled some $10.1 million, more than double the amount he'd been paid in 1999. By leaving early, he was forgoing millions of dollars—perhaps tens of millions. Finally, it just didn't fit. Skilling had always been in it for the power, for the glory, for the thrill of having people think he was important. And *now,* now that he was finally in charge of the whole enchilada, he was throwing in the towel? No way.

PIPE DREAMS, *supra* note 11, at 293. *Compare* Dan Balz & Mike Allen, *Hughes to Leave White House; Key Bush Aide Wants to Return to Texas with Family*, WASH. POST, Apr. 24, 2002, at A1 (reporting that Presidential Counselor Karen Hughes is resigning to focus on her family and rediscover her Texas roots); Bill Sammon, *Hughes to Leave Bush White House; Key Advisor Will Give Up Position in Summer, Focus on Her Family,* WASH. TIMES, Apr. 24, 2002, at A4 (describing Hughes's devotion to her family and her resolve to put their happiness ahead of her service to the government); Jim Vandetlei & Jeanne Cummings, *Bush Counselor Karen Hughes Will Step Down*, WALL ST. J., Apr. 24, 2002, at A5 (noting that while Hughes will officially resign, Bush asserts that she will remain in his "inner circle").

[31] As all of you know, life is about more than the 30 second soundbites on television or slogans in campaigns. Life is about choices, and so is politics when practiced properly.

And one of the first things worth fighting for is fairness, fundamental fairness.

And Enron, Enron makes it crystal clear: No worker in America should be robbed of years of labor by unconscionable personal greed. No employee, no employee should see retirement savings wiped away by arrogant executives who live by special privilege.

One of my colleagues compared the executives of Enron to the Corleone family. I think that's an insult . . . to the Corleones.

Senator John F. Kerry, Remarks at the California Democratic Party State Democratic Convention (Feb. 16, 2002), *available at* http://www.gwu.edu/~action/2004/kerry/kerry021602sp.html (last visited July 23, 2003). Even a local Democratic Committee inserted Enron jokes into its meeting minutes:

Attorney General Bill Lockyer and his top 10 elements of the new periodic table:

. . . .

7. Fundraisium: combines with Graydium to make governium.

6. Enronium: unstable, only attracts subpoenas.

. . . .

1. DickCheneyum: Must be stored in a remote location; used to extract fundraisium from petroleum.

Minutes of the Santa Clara County Democratic Central Committee Meeting (Mar. 7, 2002), *available at* http://www.scc-democrats.org/minutes/020307.html (last visited July 23, 2003).

comedians continued their assault on Enron's executives, many of whom (Skilling, Fastow, Lay) were now household words.[32] And, appropriately enough, editorials[33] and political cartoons made short shrift of Enron's willingness to sacrifice employees at the altar of executive greed. We've kept several of these cartoons, and one of them nicely expresses the public's denunciation of Enron.[34]

---

[32] JOKE BOOK, *supra* note 26, at 87.

[33] One of our favorite articles begins this way:

There's a great and honorable tradition about disaster at sea: Women and children first, and the captain goes down with the ship. For Enron, it's been just the opposite. Kenneth Lay and the rest of the top executives paid themselves an average of $5 million apiece as the huge corporation staggered toward bankruptcy. And ordinary employees lost their jobs and most of their savings. The best they have been able to negotiate so far is severance pay capped at $13,500 apiece.

Enron's Disaster, BANGOR DAILY NEWS, June 22, 2002, at 8.

[34] Cartoon reprinted with permission of the HOUSTON CHRONICLE. HOUS. CHRON., June 21, 2002, at 32A.

Even before Enron filed for bankruptcy, books on Enron began to crop up every-where.[35] Since the bankruptcy filing, of course, Enron books (yes, we're counting this one, too) have become their own cottage industry.[36] Of all of the books listed in foot-

[35] HUMAN RIGHTS WATCH STAFF, THE ENRON CORPORATION: CORPORATE COMPLICITY IN HUMAN RIGHTS VIOLATIONS (1999); ICON GROUP LTD., ENRON CORP.: LABOR PRODUCTIVITY BENCHMARKS AND INTERNATIONAL GAP ANALYSIS (2000); ICON GROUP, ENRON OIL & GAS COMPANY: INTERNATIONAL COMPETITIVE BENCHMARKS AND FINANCIAL GAP ANALYSIS FINANCIAL PERFORMANCE SERIES (2000); ICON GROUP, ENRON OIL & GAS COMPANY: LABOR PRODUCTIVITY BENCHMARKS AND INTERNATIONAL GAP ANALYSIS LABOR PRODUCTIVITY SERIES (2000); JOEL KURTZMAN & GLENN RIFKIN, RADICAL E: FROM GE TO ENRON—LESSONS ON HOW TO RULE THE WEB (2001); ABHAY MEHTA, POWER PLAY: A STUDY OF THE ENRON PROJECT (2000); VAULT REPORTS, ENRON: THE VAULTREPORTS.COM EMPLOYER PROFILE FOR JOB SEEKERS (1998).

[36] The books vary in terms of audience (popular culture genre versus business analysis genre), quality (some are self-published—need we say more?), and viewpoint. As of May 27, 2003, we found these books listed at Amazon.com via an "Enron" search: See, e.g., ALVIN A. ARENS ET AL., AUDITING AND ASSURANCE SERVICES AND ENRON CASE PACKAGE (9th ed. 2002); RICHARD E. BAKER ET AL., ADVANCED FINANCIAL ACCOUNTING (5th ed. 2002); DIRK J. BARREVELD, THE ENRON COLLAPSE: CREATIVE ACCOUNTING, WRONG ECONOMICS OR CRIMINAL ACTS? A LOOK INTO THE ROOT CAUSES OF THE LARGEST BANKRUPTCY IN U.S. HISTORY (2002); JOKE BOOK, supra note 26; GEORGE J. BENSTON ET AL., FOLLOWING THE MONEY: CORPORATE DISCLOSURE IN AN AGE OF GLOBALIZATION (2003); DANIEL L. BERGER, ACCOUNTANTS' LIABILITY AFTER ENRON (2002); ARTHUR L. BERKOWITZ, ENRON: A PROFESSIONAL'S GUIDE TO THE EVENTS, ETHICAL ISSUES, AND PROPOSED REFORMS (2002); CRISTA BOYLES, ENRON PROOF YOUR 401(K): STEPS TO KEEP YOUR MONEY SAFE (2002); JULIA K. BRAZELTON & JANICE L. AMMONS, ENRON AND BEYOND: TECHNICAL ANALYSIS OF ACCOUNTING, CORPORATE GOVERNANCE, AND SECURITIES ISSUES (2002); LYNN BREWER & MATTHEW SCOTT HANSEN, HOUSE OF CARDS: CONFESSIONS OF AN ENRON EXECUTIVE (2002); PIPE DREAMS, supra note 11; HENRY R. CHEESEMAN & MICHAEL BIXBY, BUSINESS LAW—ENRON CASE STUDY (2003); CHARLES J. CICCHETTI ET AL., RESTRUCTURING ELECTRICITY MARKETS: A WORLD PERSPECTIVE POST-CALIFORNIA AND ENRON (2003); CORPORATE AFTERSHOCK: THE PUBLIC POLICY LESSONS FROM THE COLLAPSE OF ENRON AND OTHER MAJOR CORPORATIONS (Christopher L. Culp & William A. Niskanen eds., 2003); BRIAN CRUVER, ANATOMY OF GREED: THE UNSHREDDED TRUTH FROM AN ENRON INSIDER (2002) [hereinafter ANATOMY OF GREED]; LOREN FOX, ENRON: THE RISE AND FALL (2002) [hereinafter RISE AND FALL]; PETER C. FUSARO & ROSS M. MILLER, WHAT WENT WRONG AT ENRON: EVERYONE'S GUIDE TO THE LARGEST BANKRUPTCY IN U.S. HISTORY (2002) [hereinafter WHAT WENT WRONG]; CHERYL DE MESA GRAZIANO, ENRON AND THE POWERS REPORT: AN EXAMINATION OF BUSINESS AND ACCOUNTING FAILURES (2002); JOE BEN HOYLE, ADVANCED ACCOUNTING, UPDATE EDITION WITH ENRON POWERWEB (2002); ARIANNA HUFFINGTON, PIGS AT THE TROUGH: HOW CORPORATE GREED AND POLITICAL CORRUPTION ARE UNDERMINING AMERICA (2003); IDC, ENRON: A REMINDER ON FREE MARKET FUNDAMENTALS (2001), available to download at http://www.amazon.com; GREG JENKINS, ENRON COLLAPSE (2002); PAUL JORION, INVESTING IN A POST-ENRON WORLD (2003); STANLEY KELLER, DISCLOSURE AND OTHER LESSONS LEARNED AFTER ENRON: WHAT YOU NEED TO KNOW NOW TO FILE 10-K AND OTHER FORMS (2002); E. JOHN LARSEN, MODERN ADVANCED ACCOUNTING WITH POWERWEB: ENRON (9th ed. 2002); BETHANY MCLEAN & PETER ELKIND, SMARTEST GUYS IN THE ROOM: THE RISE AND FALL OF ENRON (2003); WILLIAM F. MESSIER JR., AUDITING & ASSURANCE SERVICES: A SYSTEMATIC APPROACH WITH ENRON POWERWEB (2002); DANIEL QUINN MILLS, BUY, LIE, AND SELL HIGH: HOW INVESTORS LOST OUT ON ENRON AND THE INTERNET BUBBLE (2002); CATHY PETERSON, FLASHLIGHT WALKING: THE INSPIRING STORY OF ONE FAMILY'S STRUGGLE THROUGH CANCER AND THE ENRON LAYOFF (2003); JAMES POST ET AL., BUSINESS AND SOCIETY:

note 36, a few have emerged as useful, mass-market studies of Enron's culture as well as its downfall.[37]

One such book, PIPE DREAMS, helps to put the Enron scandal in perspective, albeit in an admittedly liberal perspective:

CORPORATE STRATEGY, PUBLIC POLICY, AND ETHICS (10th ed. 2003); VIJAY PRASHAD, FAT CATS AND RUNNING DOGS: THE ENRON STAGE OF CAPITALISM (2002); PRABIR PURKAYASTHA & VIJAY PRASHAD, ENRON BLOWOUT: CORPORATE CAPITALISM AND THEFT OF THE GLOBAL COMMONS (SIGNPOST 6) (2002); JACK C. ROBERTSON ET AL., MP AUDITING AND ASSURANCE SERVICES W/ APOLLO SHOES CASEBOOK AND POWERWEB: ENRON (10th ed. 2002); PETER S. ROSE, MONEY AND CAPITAL MARKETS (8th ed. 2002); ANTHONY SAUNDERS & MARCIA MILLON CORNETT, FINANCIAL INSTITUTIONS MANAGEMENT : A RISK MANAGEMENT APPROACH (4th ed. 2002); ANTHONY SAUNDERS ET AL., FINANCIAL MARKETS AND INSTITUTIONS: A MODERN PERSPECTIVE (2nd ed. 2003); RICHARD J. SCHROTH & A. LARRY ELLIOTT, HOW COMPANIES LIE: WHY ENRON IS JUST THE TIP OF THE ICEBERG (2002); CHRIS SEAY & CHRISTOPHER BRYAN, THE TAO OF ENRON: SPIRITUAL LESSONS FROM A FORTUNE 500 FALLOUT (2002); REBECCA SMITH & JOHN R. EMSHWILLER, UNCOVERING ENRON (2003); THEODORE F. STERLING, THE ENRON SCANDAL (2002); J. DAVID SPICELAND ET AL., INTERMEDIATE ACCOUNTING (UPDATE EDITION) WITH COACH, ESSENTIALS OF ACCOUNTING, ALTERNATE PROBLEMS AND S&P PACKAGE W/ POWERWEB (2nd ed. 2002); J. DAVID SPICELAND ET AL., INTERMEDIATE ACCOUNTING VOLUME 1 WITH COACH CD-ROM AND POWERWEB: FOCUS ON ENRON, ALTERNATE EXERCISES, PROBLEMS AND NET TUTOR (3rd ed. 2002); J. DAVID SPICELAND ET AL., INTERMEDIATE ACCOUNTING VOLUME 2 WITH COACH CD-ROM AND POWERWEB: FOCUS ON ENRON AND NET TUTOR (3rd ed. 2002); IRIS STUART & BRUCE STUART, ETHICS IN THE POST-ENRON AGE (2003); POWER FAILURE, *supra* note 4; U.S. GOVERNMENT, 2002 COMPENDIUM OF MAJOR FINANCIAL REPORTS TO THE SEC BY TWELVE COMPANIES UNDER SCRUTINY OR IN THE NEWS: ADELPHIA COMMUNICATIONS, AOL TIME WARNER, ENRON, GLOBAL CROSSING, HALLIBURTON, IMCLONE SYSTEMS, MARTHA STEWART LIVING OMNIMEDIA, MERRILL LYNCH, POLAROID, QWEST, WORLDCOM, AND XEROX (Progressive Management CD-ROM, 2002); U.S. GOVERNMENT, 21ST CENTURY COMPLETE GUIDE TO ENRON: SECURITIES AND EXCHANGE COMMISSION [SEC] FORMS AND FILINGS FROM 1994 PLUS HOUSE AND SENATE HEARING ON THE COLLAPSE OF ENRON AND ITS IMPACT ON PENSIONS AND AUDITING, WITH REPRODUCTIONS OF INTERNAL DOCUMENTS (Progressive Management CD-ROM, 2002); U.S. GOVERNMENT, 21ST CENTURY GUIDE TO ENERGY AND COMMERCE POLICY AND OVERSIGHT: LAWS, LEGISLATION, HEARINGS, HOUSE ENERGY AND COMMERCE COMMITTEE—ENRON, HEALTH CARE, HDTV, TELECOMMUNICATIONS, ENVIRONMENT, HAZARDOUS MATERIALS, TOBACCO INDUSTRY (Core Federal Information Series Progressive Management CD-ROM, 2003); U.S. GOVERNMENT, ENRON'S CREDIT RATING: ENRON'S BANKERS' CONTACTS WITH MOODY'S AND GOVERNMENT OFFICIALS: REPORT (2003); U.S. GOVERNMENT, THE ENRON COLLAPSE AND ITS IMPLICATIONS FOR WORKER RETIREMENT SECURITY: HEARINGS BEFORE THE COMMITTEE ON EDUCATION AND THE WORKFORCE, HOUSE OF REPRESENTATIVES (2002); U.S. GOVERNMENT, THE FINANCIAL COLLAPSE OF ENRON: HEARING BEFORE THE SUBCOMMITTEE ON OVERSIGHT AND INVESTIGATIONS OF THE COMMITTEE ON ENERGY AND COMMERCE, HOUSE OF REPRESENTATIVES (2002); GORDON YALE, ENRON: AN ACCOUNTING ANALYSIS OF HOW SPEs WERE USED TO CONCEAL DEBT AND AVOID LOSSES (2002); YANKEE GROUP, BANDWIDTH TRADING AFTER ENRON (2002), *available to download at* http://www.amazon.com; *see also* FRANK PARTNOY, F.I.A.S.C.O.: BLOOD IN THE WATER ON WALL STREET (1997); FRANK PARTNOY, F.I.A.S.C.O.: THE INSIDER STORY OF A WALL STREET TRADER (1999); FRANK PARTNOY, F.I.A.S.C.O.: GUNS, BOOZE AND BLOODLUST: THE TRUTH ABOUT HIGH FINANCE (1998); FRANK PARTNOY, INFECTIOUS GREED: HOW DECEIT AND RISK CORRUPTED THE FINANCIAL MARKETS (2003).

[37] These books include PIPE DREAMS, *supra* note 11; POWER FAILURE, *supra* note 4; WHAT WENT WRONG, *supra* note 36; RISE AND FALL, *supra* note 36; ANATOMY OF GREED, *supra* note 36; *see also* BARBARA LEY TOFFLER, FINAL ACCOUNTING: AMBITION, GREED, AND THE FALL OF ARTHUR ANDERSEN (2003).

The Enron failure is the biggest political scandal in American history. Tea-pot Dome—a scandal about payoffs to Secretary of the Interior Albert Fall by a couple of greedy oilmen—was memorable, but involved very few people. The Watergate scandal was bigger and more pernicious than Tea-pot Dome, but it, too, involved relatively few people: Tricky Dick Nixon, a dozen or two of his henchmen, and a few inept plumbers. Enron was different. By the time of its bankruptcy, Enron owned—or perhaps was just renting—politicians in the White House, Congress, state courts, state legislatures, and bureaucrats at every level.

It's the biggest scandal ever to hit Wall Street. The problems at junk-bond trading house Drexel Burnham Lambert in the 1980s were tiny in comparison to Enron. That scandal involved Michael Milken (who went to jail for securities fraud) and a handful of others. The Enron debacle has ensnared every major investment bank in New York, including Merrill Lynch, Citigroup, J.P. Morgan Chase, UBS, and dozens of others. . . .

Enron is the biggest derivatives-trading firm to go bust since the failure of the hedge fund Long-Term Capital Management in 1998. . . . [Long-Term's] positions involved so many banks that the New York Federal Reserve organized a multi-bank, $3.6 billion bailout, lest Long-Term's failure cause a global financial meltdown. And though Long-Term was big, Frank Partnoy, a law professor at the University of San Diego, told Congress in January 2002, that Enron's derivatives business made Long-Term "look like a lemonade stand."[38]

Bryce goes on to note that Enron's collapse also was "the biggest scandal ever to hit accounting,"[39] as well as "the most egregious example of executive piracy in American corporate history."[40]

Ultimately, corporations don't make mistakes—their leaders do. And Enron is more a tale of greed and ego run amuck than it is a tale of why certain business models fail. When the people at the top lose their moral grounding (or, worse yet, if they never had any moral grounding), that's when Enron-sized scandals are likely to occur. Someone at the top has to provide a moral compass for the organization.

Character shapes an organization's culture. It always has, and it always will. For every executive willing to take responsibility for bad decisions[41] or willing to go above

---

[38] Pipe Dreams, *supra* note 11, at 5–6 (footnotes omitted).

[39] *Id.* at 6.

[40] *Id.* at 7.

[41] *See, e.g.,* James P. Miller, *Buffett Offers A Mea Culpa For Bad Year,* Wall St. J., Mar. 13, 2000, at C1 ("'Even Inspector Clouseau could find last year's guilty party: your Chairman,' Mr. Buffett told investors in the letter.").

"Overall," he tells holders, "you would have been better off last year if I had regularly snuck off to the movies during market hours." . . . Mr. Buffett says, "Here, I need to make a confession (ugh): The portfolio actions I took in 1998 actually decreased our gain for the year." In particular, he says

and beyond for his employees,[42] there's one who is willing to sacrifice his employees or customers. Take a look at one glimpse into Skilling's character in WHAT WENT WRONG:

> A story from Jeffrey Skilling's HBS [Harvard Business School] student days may provide a telling glimpse into his character. HBS classes are typically conducted using the case method. Most cases are based on real business incidents, and students are presented with the problems that a business faced and must come up with solutions for themselves. Discussion of the cases, which helps determine a student's grade, is led by the professor in a pitlike classroom. A forceful student unsure of the facts is quick to be ripped to shreds by other students looking to make their mark. In one such class, Jeffrey Skilling was asked what he would do if his company were producing a product that might cause harm—or even death—to the customers that used it. According to his professor at the time, former Congressman John LeBoutillier, Jeffrey Skilling replied: "I'd keep making and selling the product. My job as a businessman is to be a profit center and to maximize return to the shareholders. It's the government's job to step in if a product is dangerous." In an Enron culture seemingly obsessed with *Star Wars,* Skilling's bloodless demeanor led his colleagues to refer to him as "Darth Vader" behind his back.[43]

Keep in mind that, after Skilling joined Enron, Enron focused on hiring relatively young[44] people who were considered to be the "best and brightest," both in Enron's

---

his decision to sell McDonald's Corp. shares, a process Berkshire began in 1997, has proven to be "a very big mistake." McDonald's shares have risen 82.7% since January 1998.

James P. Miller & Joseph B. Cahill, *Buffett Says Berkshire Would Have Benefited If He Hadn't Made Any Stock Actions in 1998,* WALL ST. J., Mar. 15, 1999, at C2; James P. Miller, *Buffett Offers A Mea Culpa For Bad Year,* WALL ST. J., Mar. 13, 2000, at C1 ("'Even Inspector Clouseau could find last year's guilty party: your Chairman,' Mr. Buffett told investors in the letter.")

[42] *See, e.g.,* Mitchell Pacelle, *Through the Mill: Can Mr Feuerstein Save His Business One Last Time?—Textile Owner Overcame Fire and Changes in Fashion; Creditors May Be Tougher—Needed: $92 Million by July 31st,* WALL ST. J., May 9, 2003, at A1; Carey Goldberg, *A Promise Is Kept: Mill Reopens,* N.Y. TIMES, Sept. 16, 1997, at A14 (congratulating Aaron Feuerstein for keeping his employees on payroll while he rebuilt his burnt-down factory).

[43] WHAT WENT WRONG, *supra* note 36, at 28. Skilling was tone-deaf when it came to insensitive comments. One of his legendary comments during the California energy crisis was "'You know what the difference is between the state of California and the *Titanic?* At least when the *Titanic* went down, the lights were on.'" *Id.* at 112.

[44] *See id.* at 50.

estimation and in their own.[45] Young people have the relative advantage of cutting-edge training, but they have the relative disadvantage of less experience in a variety of situations. Imagine the pressure on brand-new, inexperienced Enron employees to behave like their leaders:[46] to act like them, to dress like them, to drive the same cars that they do, and to disregard the same social mores that they did.[47] (The pressure to conform to expected "Enron" codes of behavior was reinforced by Enron's "rank and yank" system of evaluating employees.[48]) The profligate spending at Enron,[49] the

---

[45] *See id.* at 43. Contrast Skilling's focus with that of Enron's old guard, represented by Richard Kinder. Kinder's group represented the "old Enron": pipelines that were real assets that made real cash profits. *See* PIPE DREAMS, *supra* note 11, at 123.

[46] "'It *is* just a small group of people . . . but those people were created by the Enron System—a system that also creates hundreds of other sheep who are easily led by others.'" *See* ANATOMY OF GREED, *supra* note 11, at 180.

[47] One of Enron's most well-known secrets was its tolerance of sexual escapades, whether adultery, sexual harassment, or just plain poor taste. *See* PIPE DREAMS, *supra* note 11, at 144–48. As Robert Bryce puts it so succinctly, "[f]ish rot at the head. . . . Enron failed because its leadership was morally, ethically, and financially corrupt." *Id.* at 12.

[48] "Enron employees were ranked every six months on the same 1-to-5 scale as new recruits; however, 15 percent of all employees were required to be in the lowest category (1), and they were yanked from Enron." WHAT WENT WRONG, *supra* note 36, at 51. For those of you more statistically inclined, imagine that you are selecting your employees from the right-most hand of a bell-shaped curve (the best and the brightest); now take that small group of employees and spread them out over a 1-to-5 scale. What you've done is take people who are roughly the same and use meaningless distinctions to separate them, yanking those on the left-hand side of this second curve out of the organization. Moreover, you're taking the glue of the organization—not the flashy superstars but the reliable team-players—and throwing them out. *See* PIPE DREAMS, *supra* note 11, at 129. Robert Bryce explains it well:

> Although the process was designed to advance the careers of top performers and punish the low performers, it quickly mutated into a numbers game. . . . The people who were rated 1's and 2's were golden. "It was all based on how much money you were able to make," said one source. With millions of dollars at stake in each annual rating, the fights over individual rankings became intense. "It was a pit of vipers. You can't believe how brutal that process could be. You had people attacking other people's integrity, morality, and values. It wasn't about supporting up, it was about tearing down."
>
> . . . . [Most of the benefits of the ranking system went to the deal-makers, not to the administrative staff. And most of the deals were ranked on profits.]
>
> Perhaps most insidious, the [rank and yank] committee gave Enron's Masters of the Universe a baseball bat they could use to intimidate the people who might stop one of their bad deals—and therefore limit their bonuses.

Id. at 129–30.

[49] Bill Murphy, *THE FALL OF ENRON; Enron's art hopes just a pipe dream; Buying spree now drawing fire*, HOUS. CHRON., July 29, 2002, at A1 (art committee at Enron Corp. given $20 million budget); Carol Vogel, *Enron's Art to Be Auctioned Off*, N.Y. TIMES, Apr. 16, 2003, at C6; Paula Span, *The Gavel Falls on Enron Artworks; Auction Puts Tiny Dent in Company Debt*, WASH. POST, May 16, 2003, at C1.

self-dealing and selfishness,[50] the rudeness[51]—all signaled to Enron's employees what sorts of behavior were rewarded. Is it really so hard to figure out why Enron, as an organization, was willing to lie and cheat?

---

[50] [T]he independence and objectivity of the Enron Board had been weakened by financial ties between Enron and certain directors. These financial ties, which affected a majority of the outside Board members, included the following.

—Since 1996, Enron paid a monthly retainer of $6,000 to Lord John Wakeham for consulting services, in addition to his Board compensation. In 2000, Enron paid him $72,000 for his consulting work alone.

—Since 1991, Enron paid Board member John A. Urquhart for consulting services, in addition to his Board compensation. In 2000, Enron paid Mr. Urquhart $493,914 for his consulting work alone.

—Enron Board member Herbert Winokur also served on the Board of the National Tank Company. In 1997, 1998, 1999, and 2000, the National Tank Company recorded revenues of $1,035,000, $643,793, $535,682 and $370,294 from sales to Enron subsidiaries of oilfield equipment and services.

—In the past 5 years Enron and Kenneth Lay donated nearly $600,000 to the M.D. Anderson Cancer Center in Texas. In 1993, the Enron Foundation pledged $1.5 million to the Cancer Center. Two Enron Board members, Dr. LeMaistre and Dr. Mendelsohn, have served as president of the Cancer Center.

—Since 1996, Enron and the Lay Foundation have donated more than $50,000 to the George Mason University and its Mercatus Center in Virginia. Enron Board member Dr. Wendy Gramm is employed by the Mercatus Center.

—Since 1996, Enron and Belco Oil and Gas have engaged in hedging arrangements worth tens of millions of dollars. In 1997, Belco bought Enron affiliate Coda Energy. Enron Board member Robert Belfer is former Chairman of the Board and CEO of Belco.

—Charles Walker, a noted tax lobbyist, was an Enron Board member from 1985 until 1999. In 1993–1994, Enron paid more than $70,000 to two firms, Walker/Free and Walker/Potter, that were partly owned by Mr. Walker, for governmental relations and tax consulting services. This sum was in addition to Mr. Walker's Board compensation. Enron was also, for more than 10 years ending in 2001, a major contributor of up to $50,000 annually to the American Council for Capital Formation, a non-profit corporation that lobbies on tax issues and is chaired by Mr. Walker.

Permanent Subcommittee on Investigations of the Committee of Governmental Affairs, The Role of the Board of Directors in Enron's Collapse, S. Rep. No. 107-70, at 51–52 (2002); *see also* Pipe Dreams, *supra* note 11, at 256–66 (use of corporate jets for private business).

[51] On April 17, 2001, analyst Richard Grubman (of Highfields Capital Management) participated on a conference call run by Jeffrey Skilling to discuss Enron's first-quarter results. Grubman pointed out that Enron hadn't

provide[d] the analysts with more information prior to the conference call . . . [including cash flow statements and balance sheets]. Skilling responded that Enron had never provided those reports before analyst calls. Grubman wasn't satisfied. "You're the only financial institution that can't produce a balance sheet or a cash flow statement with their earnings" prior to conference calls, he said.

"Well, thank you very much," replied Skilling. "We appreciate that. Asshole."

Pipe Dreams, *supra* note 11, at 268–69.

When Enron was flying high, there were some who remained skeptical about all of its claims of greatness and brilliance.[52] During Enron's prominence as one of *Fortune* magazine's "most innovative" companies,[53] it bought, cajoled, and bullied to get what it wanted, from favorable deals to exemptions from rules. Once Enron began its downward slide, all of those over whom Enron had run roughshod enjoyed Enron's comeuppance. The gloves came off: aggrieved employees, customers, and competitors were happy to talk to any and all who asked about how Enron had behaved. Even those who had never spent a millisecond of their time thinking about Enron before the scandal broke came away from all of the stories with a horrible impression of a company that had also, in fact, had some very good business ideas, hired some wonderful people, and given widely to the Houston community.

The lesson? Remember that phrase that you learned when you were a kid: the bigger they are, the harder they fall.

QUESTIONS

1. When you take all of the essays in Chapter 1 together, you can see how hard it is for companies to innovate while still "coloring inside the lines" of regulation. Is it always the case that true innovation *has* to be linked with a disregard for the letter of the law (or at least the spirit of the law)? What kind of regulatory scheme could you envision that would encourage true innovation while discouraging the type of regulatory game-playing that has, historically, accompanied that innovation?

2. Assume that you are the chair of a board of directors and you are looking for a new CEO. What characteristics would you like that CEO to have? Would you want different characteristics for your CEO depending on the nature of the company's business, or its place in the market? During your interview with aspiring CEO candidates, how would you go about ascertaining that your CEO has the characteristics that you want? Would you ask for a personality test? A psychological profile? Testimonials from business partners or from other companies in the same market?

---

[52] *See supra* notes 17–45 and accompanying text; *see also* ANATOMY OF GREED, *supra* note 36, at 19 (quoting a research analyst explaining to a friend, and recent Enron hire, that the company had serious financial problems based on a close examination of the company's 2001 Annual Report).

[53] "At its zenith, Enron was named the 'most innovative' company in the United States by FORTUNE magazine *every year* between 1996 and 2001." Jeffrey D. Van Niel, *Enron—The Primer,* in NANCY B. RAPOPORT & BALA G. DHARAN, ENRON: CORPORATE FIASCOS & THEIR IMPLICATIONS 11 (2004) (citing WHAT WENT WRONG, *supra* note 36, at 172; Daniel Altman, *Finding Gems of Genius Among Enron's Crumbs,* N.Y. TIMES, Feb. 3, 2002, at D6).

Chapter 2

Enron and the Business World

One of the reasons that we wanted to create this textbook is our belief that part of what brought Enron down was the over-compartmentalization of the professionals advising Enron. Enron's officers conceived of various business deals, some of which were clearly illegal, and some of which were borderline at best.[1] The lawyers gave legal advice, and the accountants gave financial advice (and, apparently, never the twain did meet). If the officers, the lawyers, and the accountants had all talked over the intricacies of the deals together, perhaps Enron would not have made so many bad decisions.

Don't assume that it's only corporate debacles that involve such compartmentalization. *Most* organizations use compartmentalization and, frankly, such specialization helps organizations survive and thrive. It's no accident that many companies have an organization chart with an alphabet soup of specialized executives (CEO,[2] CFO,[3] COO,[4] CIO,[5] etc.), each of whom has a particular function to fill within the organization. Companies also need lawyers and accountants, and they need them precisely because of their expertise.

But we see an alarming trend developing, not just among professionals but among the executives as well. There's a tendency to draw lines in the sand, to say that a particular issue or problem "isn't my job," and thus to avoid dealing with troubling or complex situations. There's a lack of joint ownership of issues. A wise CEO will rely on the talents of the CFO and COO (and others) to help set priorities and solve problems. An even wiser CEO will want the CFO, COO, and others to get input from each other and from the professionals who advise the company. The foolish CEO lets

---

[1] *See* Neal Batson, Third Interim Report of Neal Batson, Court-Appointed Examiner, *In re* Enron Corp., No. 01-16034 (Bankr. S.D.N.Y. June 30, 2003), Appendix C, at 38–44.

[2] Chief Executive Officer.

[3] Chief Financial Officer.

[4] Chief Operations Officer.

[5] Chief Information Officer.

turf problems fester, permitting each executive and professional to preside over individual fiefdoms.

Executives, lawyers, and accountants can contribute to this over-compartmentalization or contribute to a solution. Part of the solution must include a working knowledge of each other's fields. This chapter is designed to give those of you who are less familiar with the workings of the business world some familiarity with the business issues surrounding Enron, and therefore some familiarity with business principles generally. If you are already familiar with business principles, then use this chapter to test your assumptions about how various theories worked in Enron's case.

Red Flags in Enron's Reporting of Revenues and Key Financial Measures

Bala G. Dharan* & William R. Bufkins**

1. INTRODUCTION

In this article, we analyze the forensic warning signals, or red flags, that started showing up in the financial statements of Enron Corp. a year or two before its eventual fall from grace and bankruptcy in 2001. Since many of the warning signals are primarily related to how Enron measured and reported its total revenues, we will focus on revenues first. We will then review the other red flags, including profitability and cash flows.

Enron used revenues—not profits—as its primary financial objective, performance driver, and measure of success. Enron's use of distorted, "hyper-inflated" revenues was more important to it in creating the impression of innovation, high growth, and spectacular business performance than the masking of debt in special purpose entities. Indeed, Enron's president and CEO Jeff Skilling promoted revenues as the primary measure of performance to achieve his objective of propelling Enron to the status of the "world's leading company." And, by the time of its demise, Enron had used its hyper-revenue growth to claw its way up to Number 7 on the widely followed *Fortune 500* list of the world's largest companies.[1]

That Enron used a variety of deceptive, bewildering, and fraudulent accounting practices and tactics—legal and illegal—to obfuscate its financial statements is a given. But Enron's phenomenal four-year revenue growth from $13.3 billion in 1996 to $100.8 billion in 2000[2] awed politicians and heads of state, and attracted the attention of Wall

* Bala G. Dharan, Ph.D., CPA, is J. Howard Creekmore Professor of Accounting at the Jesse H. Jones Graduate School of Management, Rice University, and Houston.

** William R. Bufkins, CCP, is managing director of Organization Analytics, Houston, an executive compensation consulting firm.

[1] *Fortune 500 Largest U.S. Corporations*, FORTUNE, Apr. 16, 2001, at F1 [hereinafter FORTUNE 500].

[2] ENRON: 2000 ANNUAL REPORT (2001), *available at* http://www.enron.com/corp/investors/annuals/2000/ar2000.pdf (last visited June 11, 2003) [hereinafter ENRON: 2000 ANNUAL REPORT].

Street. The revenue growth amounted to an average annual growth of over 65%, unprecedented in the slow-moving energy and utility industries, and with that growth, Enron succeeded in fooling the best and the brightest among Wall Street analysts, the news media, their own employees, and countless investors. When Enron collapsed, it was labeled as the "largest bankruptcy in history,"[3] on the basis of its illusory revenue size.

Past discussions of the Enron accounting scandal have focused mainly on Enron's efforts to shift assets and liabilities off balance sheet with Byzantine structures and special purpose entities.[4] What has been largely overlooked is an analysis of how Enron effectively used the "mark-to-market" ("MTM") accounting rule and other revenue-boosting accounting methods as a business strategy to create the illusion of being a "larger" company than a General Electric, Citigroup, or IBM. This certainly contrasts with all of the publicity Enron received by using off balance sheet financing in special purpose entities. Dynegy, Reliant Energy, and El Paso also moved up to the top 50 ranks of the *Fortune 500* by using these accounting methods.[5]

It was not profitability that was driving Enron's stock price and high price-to-earnings multiples, since, as we show, Enron's return on equity and profit margins were in the bottom ranks of the largest energy companies. Ironically, Enron's most profitable segment was the asset-intensive Transportation & Distribution group. By contrast, the divisions that were the focus of Enron's famed "asset-light" business strategy reported small accounting profits and certainly did not generate operating cash flows.

As opaque and impenetrable as Enron's financial statements have been characterized, they do provide several forensic accounting red flags with regard to profits and cash flows, suggesting major weaknesses in the company's financial foundations. The evidence we present in our analysis suggests that the business media and sell-side financial analysts must have been in denial over Enron's financial fundamentals, which just didn't add up according to common profitability and valuation measures, regardless of how much debt was hidden in special purpose entities and masked from the public.

2. THE *TITANIC* ANALOGY

Even before Enron collapsed, 2001 was shaping up to be a year of major shocks for the U.S. economy, which was reeling from the collapse of the stock market bubble in 2000 and the September 11, 2001 terrorist attacks on New York and the Pentagon. The tech stock and dot.com market collapse had already ushered in a new period of

---

[3] *E.g.,* Chris Kraul et al., *Enron Files Chapter 11, Sues Ex-Suitor Dynegy Energy: Bankruptcy Filing is Largest Ever*, L.A. TIMES, Dec. 3, 2001, at A1.

[4] *See e.g.,* Wendy Zellner & Stephanie Anderson Forest, *The Fall of Enron*, BUS. WK., Dec. 17, 2001, at 30.

[5] FORTUNE 500, *supra* note 1.

economic uncertainty as investors saw their life savings decline by as much as 75% in two years. Then Enron, propped up by the media and management experts alike as one of the world's most innovative and admired companies, struck an iceberg, in the form of the unexpected and inexplicable resignation of Skilling on August 14, 2001. Within months, Enron sank like the *Titanic*.

In fact, the *Titanic* analogy is quite apt for Enron. Like the *Titanic* that was described by its admirers as "unsinkable," Enron had been characterized by *Fortune* magazine in August 2000 as one of the "10 stocks to last the decade . . . that should put your retirement account in good stead and protect you from those recurring nightmares about stocks that got away."[6] Like the *Titanic's* reckless decision to race through iceberg-infested waters to beat a Trans-Atlantic crossing record, Enron's management made increasingly larger investments into ill-conceived projects and businesses, even as the U.S. and world economy was starting to slide into a recession as a result of the popping of the largest stock market bubble in history. Finally, like the *Titanic's* inadequate number of lifeboats, the management of Enron seemed to operate without adequate corporate controls and checks as the company's compensation system kept rewarding managers for coming up with new investment ventures of every stripe—and deals that turned out to be egregiously unprofitable.

Like the *Titanic*, the human tragedy from Enron is all too well known—a devastating loss for Enron employees and shareholders as Enron's stock plunged to less than a dollar, with collateral damage extending to virtually every other energy merchant company, including Dynegy, Reliant Energy, El Paso, and Williams, all of whom modeled themselves in various degrees after Enron. Enron's fall also directly led to the indictment, subsequent conviction, and collapse of Arthur Andersen, one of the world's preeminent accounting firms.

As Bala Dharan stated in his testimony to Congress, "How could this tragedy have happened while the company's management, board of directors, and outside auditors were supposedly watching over for employees and investors?"[7]

3. STRATEGIC IMPORTANCE OF REVENUE SIZE AND GROWTH

By the time *Fortune* issued its list of 500 biggest companies in April 2001, Enron had made it to Number 7, surpassing the ranks of corporate giants such as Citibank and IBM.[8] In four short years from 1996 to 2000, its revenues had increased by more than 750 percent, rising from $13.3 billion in 1996 to $100.8 billion in 2000.[9] From

---

[6] David Ryneck, *10 Stocks to Last the Decade*, FORTUNE, Aug. 14, 2000, at 114.

[7] *Developments Relating to Enron: Prepared Witness Testimony Before the House Comm. on Energy and Commerce*, 107th Cong. (2002) (testimony of Dr. Bala G Dharan Ph.D., CPA) [hereinafter Dharan Testimony].

[8] FORTUNE 500, *supra* note 1.

[9] ENRON: 2000 ANNUAL REPORT, *supra* note 2.

1999 to 2000, Enron's revenues increased 151% from $40.1 to 100.8 billion.[10] This growth of over 65% per year is unprecedented in any industry, let alone the staid energy industry that normally views even a two or three percent a year growth as a decent achievement. Another two or three years of 60% growth would have pushed Enron well past ExxonMobil and Wal-Mart as the world's largest company. Indeed, Enron reported pre-bankruptcy revenues of $138.7 billion for the first nine months of 2001, pushing it up to Number 6 on the *Fortune Global 500*, passing DaimlerChrysler, Royal Dutch/Shell, General Electric, Toyota and ChevronTexaco.[11]

By the end of 2000, the hyper-growth in Enron's revenue placed the company squarely in the company of the energy "supermajors." With over $100 billion in revenue, Enron was twice as large as Chevron ($50.6 billion revenue in 2000 before merger with Texaco), and foreseeably would catch up rapidly to BP ($161.8 billion in 2000) and ExxonMobil ($231.8 billion in 2000). Enron's chairman, Ken Lay, could soon claim to be heading the "world's leading company," and not just the world's leading energy company. The rapid revenue growth and the rapidly climbing *Fortune* rankings undoubtedly attracted media attention, and Enron was soon also propelled into *Fortune's* ranks of the world's most innovative, "admired companies."[12]

As can be seen by the use of revenues as the basis for *Fortune's* annual ranking of companies, annual revenues can be an important psychological measure that carries a lot of weight among investors and the public as an indicator of success and economic size, in the same way GNP determines the economic stature of a nation-state. It has long been understood by managers that firm size carries important implications for the prestige of the company, its influence in the marketplace, its ability to command the attention and respect of the media and Wall Street, and its ability to attract talented students from Ivy League business schools as employees. Firm size also can help a company's image in terms of branding.

Management models developed in the 1970s postulated large firm size as a negative indicator of higher political costs (due to potential anti-trust regulations, pricing regulations, etc.). However, changes in the business-government environment in the 1980s and in more recent years, and in particular, structural changes in the way companies are able to contribute to and influence political campaigns, have fundamentally altered this relation between firm size and political cost. Indeed, we claim that larger firm size provides increased relief from regulatory costs because larger firms are able to leverage their ability to support political campaigns through donations to political action committees and are able to acquire greater political influence and goodwill. This is particularly true in regulated industries with high entry costs, such as the energy and utility industries. The benefits of getting regulatory relief, such as electricity deregulation, are disproportionately greater for larger firms in these regulated and high-entry cost indus-

---

[10] *Id.*

[11] *Fortune Global 500: The World's Largest Corporations,* FORTUNE, July 22, 2002, at F1.

[12] Nicholas Stein, *The World's Most Admired Companies,* FORTUNE, Oct. 2, 2000, at 182.

tries. Finally, investors may also perceive a reduced risk of bankruptcy for large firms, mainly due to U.S. and global regulators' often-demonstrated unwillingness to let large corporations fail. Not surprisingly, corporations in the energy industry in recent years have initiated mergers and other actions to increase their overall size and influence.

The linkage of revenues with executive compensation was also a factor that probably led to Enron's focus on boosting its total revenue figures. There is some evidence from Enron's description of its compensation plans provided in its annual proxy statements that Enron linked the level of compensation of its key executives to its reported revenues. For example, the following excerpts from a proxy statement filed by Enron in 1997 highlight Enron's pay targeting policy: "Base salaries are targeted at the median of a comparator group that includes peer group companies... and general industry companies similar in size to Enron."[13] Similarly, a proxy statement from 2001 says: "The [Compensation] Committee determined the amount of the annual incentive award taking into consideration the competitive pay level for a CEO of a company with comparable revenue size, and competitive bonus levels for CEO's in specific high performing companies."[14] The implications of revenue size as factor in setting competitive pay levels is illustrated by a widely used Hewitt Associates executive compensation survey. For example, Hewitt reported that average annual total compensation was $10 million for a CEO of a $25 billion company and $25 million for a $100 billion company.[15] By comparison, Ken Lay's year 2000 total compensation was $40.8 million,[16] 62% higher than the $25 million for a $100 billion company and 24% higher than the $33 million pay average for a $140 billion company.

4. ENRON'S REVENUE ACCOUNTING TECHNIQUES

While most energy companies were trying to grow large through mergers, Enron adopted a different strategy for growth. Mega-mergers in the energy industry led to ExxonMobil, BP Amoco (now BP), ChevronTexaco, ConocoPhillips, RWE, and Total Fina Elf. But Enron was not growing on this scale by acquisitions. Instead, it simply grew by exploiting two revenue recognition accounting rules. First, it used mark-to-market accounting for its energy contracts, which it treated as financial contracts for this purpose. This allowed Enron to report expected benefits from future transactions into current period income. Second, Enron adopted an aggressive accounting inter-

---

[13] ENRON CORP., 1997 PROXY STATEMENT 15 (1997), *available at* http://www.namebase.org/enron/ enron98a.txt (last visited June 12, 2003).

[14] ENRON CORP., 2001 PROXY STATEMENT 14 (2001), *available at* http://www.namebase.org/enron/ enron01a.txt (last visited June 12, 2003).

[15] HEWITT ASSOCIATES, *Total Compensation Measurement, Executive Long-Term Incentives and Regression Analysis Report, 2002,* Apr. 1, 2002 (note: total compensation includes base salary, cash bonuses and the value of long-term incentives such as stock options and restricted stock grants).

[16] ENRON: 2000 ANNUAL REPORT, *supra* note 2.

pretation of what constitutes revenues in the trades that took place over its "Enron Online" trading platform. Specifically, by adopting a so-called "merchant model" of revenues, Enron reported the entire value of each trade on which it was a counterparty as its revenue, rather than reporting as revenues only its trading or brokerage fees. Traditional trading firms such as Goldman Sachs and Merrill Lynch use a more conservative "agent model" of revenue reporting, in which only the trading or brokerage fee would be reported as revenue. Each of these revenue-distorting accounting techniques is discussed in more detail below.

The revenue effects that arise from the methodology of MTM accounting, which is required by generally accepted accounting standards for financial assets, are counter to what most accounting students are taught in Accounting 101 as to how revenues should be recognized. The two basic criteria for revenue recognition are that revenue is reported after (1) service has been provided or mostly provided, and (2) cash collection has taken place or is reasonably certain. Contrast this conservative revenue recognition technique of accountants with the financial economist's theory of valuation of financial assets and projects, which says that an asset's value is the present value of *future cash flows,* i.e., net cash flows that will only be generated in the future as a result of service activities that will need to take place in those future periods, after subtracting costs that will need to be incurred. Under MTM, changes in the fair values of financial assets classified as trading securities are reported as income. In other words, in the MTM valuation method, revenue recognition depends on the initial estimates of, and subsequent changes in, the estimated future actions of companies and future costs of performance of service, rather than on actual past transactions.

In effect, the MTM method for financial assets allows revenue to be recognized as earned even before service is provided. As an example, let's say a company such as Enron enters into an agreement with a customer to deliver gas or electricity at set amounts and prices for the next ten years. As applied to financial contracts such as these, the MTM technique permits a company to report as revenues in the current period the net present value of all future period revenues of the multi-year transaction, even before any service is provided or products are delivered. By contrast, if the financial contract is treated as a normal business deal, the firm would have reported only the fees or revenues received in one year after the gas or electricity is delivered.

The MTM technique requires companies to estimate what would happen over very long periods, such as the ten-year period in the above example. Since there are often no quoted prices for these complex and often-unique energy contracts, it is difficult to calculate a valuation of these contracts using real market prices, so companies are free to develop and use discretionary methods based on their own assumptions and methods.[17] Regulators and analysts have long worried that the MTM technique can be used

---

[17] C. William Thomas, *The Rise and Fall of Enron; When a Company Looks Too Good to Be True, It Usually Is,* J. OF ACCT., Apr. 2002, at 41.

by aggressive companies to overestimate future unrealized profits, or to hide or understate future unrealized losses from soured contracts. In the case of Enron, it is no wonder revenues grew the way they did, especially since incentive plans were based on the hypothetical total net present value of the deal, not the actual cash flow that would result from the deal. Starting from as early as 1992, Enron started applying the MTM technique to its financial contracts, capitalizing on the fact that this approach to revenue reporting, as applied to energy trading and energy contracts, results in a gross distortion in reporting revenues.

In addition to using the MTM methodology for its energy contracts, Enron also adopted the "merchant" model of reporting revenues for its trading activities, especially the booming volume of trading that took place over its proprietary Enron Online trading platform. To understand the merchant model, consider a retailer, such as Wal-Mart, who buys products from manufacturers, takes possession of the goods, and takes the risks of selling the goods as well as the risks of collecting from the end-user. Because of the risks taken, the merchant is allowed to report the entire selling price of the products as revenues and the cost of purchases as "cost of goods sold." By contrast, an "agent" is someone who provides a service to the customer (such as facilitating the purchase of an airline ticket), but does not really take up the risks of possession and risks of collection. Under the agent model, the service provider is allowed to report the trading fee, brokerage fee, etc. as revenue, but not the entire value of the transaction.

All of the major financial companies with trading operations, such as Goldman Sachs and Citigroup, used the agent model to report their "spreads" and fees from trading transactions. However, Enron's apparent logic for using the merchant model for its energy trades was that it was not merely an agent but was the legal "counterparty" in almost every transaction that took place on Enron Online.

The combined effect of using the MTM methodology and the merchant model for revenue reporting was that Enron's revenues and cost of goods sold, reported in the income statement, were increased as much as fifty times compared to what they would have been under more traditional accounting. However, this artificial boosting of revenues and cost of goods sold did not increase the net of these two income statement numbers, known as "gross profit."

It is interesting to examine how much smaller Enron would have been in revenue terms if it had not used MTM for energy contracts and if it had used the agent model for energy trades. We estimate that an adjustment for both MTM accounting and merchant accounting would have pushed down Enron's reported revenues to $6.3 billion in 2000 instead of the reported $100.8 billion.[18]

This can be seen from examining the gross profit reported by Enron in each of the last five years, since the gross profit is a reasonable proxy for the amount of revenue that would have been reported by Enron under the agent model and without the help

---

[18] ENRON: 2000 ANNUAL REPORT, *supra* note 2.

from the accounting assumptions of MTM. Table 1 shows the revenues, cost of goods sold, and gross profit data from 1998 to 2000.

Table 1. Projected "Real" Revenues—1998–2000[19] (Dollars in millions)

Item	1998	1999	2000
Operating Revenues, as reported	$31,260	$40,112	$100,789
Less Cost of Goods Sold, as reported	$26,381	$34,761	$94,517
"Real" Revenues (gross profit)	$4,879	$5,351	$6,272
% Revenue growth, as reported by Enron		28.3%	151.3%
% "Real" revenue growth		9.7%	17.2%
Projected Fortune 500 Rank			287
Actual Fortune 500 Rank			7

The adjustment for revenue would have pushed Enron down in the Fortune 500 list from number 7 to number 287. A similar analysis of revenues and Fortune rank prompted *New York Times* reporter Morgenson to conclude that Enron was the "master of obfuscation in its financial statements."[20]

The story of how Enron got to use the MTM accounting for its energy contracts illustrates the importance that Enron gave to its dealings with regulators. One of Jeff Skilling's first major acts after being hired to work for Enron in 1991 was to seek the approval of the Securities and Exchange Commission to adopt the mark-to-market accounting method for the energy contracts entered into by his Enron Gas Services group. With the approval of the SEC in place in January 1992, nine months after Skilling was hired, Enron became the first company outside the financial services industry to use mark-to-market accounting.

This event marked a major turning point for the company, since it was the beginning of a change in focus (for performance evaluation purposes) to revenue growth, rather than cash flow and profitability, thus sewing the seeds of Enron's decline and fall. It was also the genesis of the transformation of Enron to a trading and financial deal-making company.

The extent of inflation of Enron's revenues due to the use of MTM and merchant model accounting varied by business units. The two methods were primarily used by Enron's "Wholesale" business unit, and to a lesser extent, by the "Broadband" and "Retail" business units. Table 2 depicts revenues and operating income by business unit, as reported for 2000.

[19] Numbers as reported, although obscured and not calculated, in ENRON: 2000 ANNUAL REPORT, *supra* note 2; ENRON: 1999 ANNUAL REPORT (2000), *available at* http://www.enron.com/corp/investors/annuals/annual99/pdfs/1999_Annual_Report.pdf (last visited June 13, 2002); ENRON: 1998 ANNUAL REPORT (1999), *available at* http://www.enron.com/corp/investors/annuals/annual98/pdfs/1998_Annual_Report.pdf (last visited June 13, 2002).

[20] Gretchen Morgenson, *How 287 Turned Into 7: Lessons in Fuzzy Math*, N.Y. TIMES, Jan. 20, 2002, at C1.

Table 2. Revenues and Operating Income by Business Units, 2000[21] (Dollars in millions)

	Trans. & Dist.	Whole- sale	Retail	Broad- band	Other*	Total
Revenues	$2,955	$94,906	$4,615	$408	$–2,095*	$100,789
% of Corporate Total	2.9%	94.2%	4.6%	0.4%	NA	
Operating Income (loss)	$565	$1,668	$58	$–64	$–274*	$1,953
% of Corporate Total	28.9%	85.4%	3.0%	NA	NA	
Operating Margin (Op. Income/Revenue)	19.1%	1.8%	1.3%	–15.7%	NA	1.9%

*Corporate costs, intercorporate eliminations, and others.

As Table 2 indicates, the Transportation and Distribution unit was profitable from an operating income perspective, with an operating profit margin of 19.1%. By contrast, Wholesale, with 94.2% of Enron's revenues, generated only 1.8% of operating income. This illustrates the extent of revenue inflation in Wholesale (i.e., Enron's trading operation) due to MTM and merchant model accounting. Without these accounting methods, the Wholesale unit would have been 50 times smaller in size.

This practice of reporting inflated trading revenue was not limited to just Enron in the energy industry. Many other companies in the energy trading industry felt the need to meet the competitive pressure from Enron's rapid ascendancy, and most of the main competitors of Enron adopted financial reporting methods that were identical to Enron's. Soon, several energy companies with substantive trading operations moved into the elite top 50 of the *Fortune 500* category, including Duke Energy, El Paso Corporation, Reliant Energy, and Dynegy Corp.[22]

5. FORENSIC ACCOUNTING: OTHER RED FLAGS

The media and the analyst community were late to the game of deciphering Enron's accounting numbers. As Enron's stock was on its way to reaching its high of $90 in late 2000, the investment banking and analyst community was still "snowed" by the level of media hype and market euphoria surrounding Enron's ascendancy in size, stature, and political influence. However, by the end of 2000, some analyst reports and articles in the media began to dig deeper into Enron's opaque and impenetrable financial statements and ask questions. Enron was also attracting negative attention from a growing number of independent financial analysts, who just didn't see the profitability numbers adding up in Enron's financial statements. In early 2001, Enron's CEO Skilling berated an analyst during a conference call for asking for a balance sheet (and allegedly used an obscene word to refer to him, while the microphone was still on).[23]

---

[21] Numbers as reported in ENRON: 2000 ANNUAL REPORT, *supra* note 2.

[22] *Fortune 500 Largest U.S. Corporations,* FORTUNE, Apr. 15, 2002, at F1.

[23] Julia Boorstin, *The Insider,* FORTUNE, May 14, 2001, at 242.

An article in the Texas edition of the *Wall Street Journal* on September 20, 2000, was one of the first to raise concerns about the inflated revenues and profits of energy traders.[24] The article referred to the soaring stock prices of Enron, El Paso Corp., and Dynegy Inc., and continued: "But what many investors may not realize is that much of these companies' recent profits constitute unrealized, noncash gains. Frequently, these profits depend on assumptions and estimates about future market factors, the details of which the companies do not provide, and which time may prove wrong."[25]

An analyst report in February 2001 from John S. Herold, Inc., written by Lou Gagliardi and John Parry, also expressed concerns about Enron's reported profitability. At a celebrated analyst meeting on January 25, 2001, Jeff Skilling made a "New Valuation Metrics" presentation proclaiming that Enron should be valued at $126 a share. The Herold report observed that Enron's profits for its Wholesale Energy Division had been steadily declining from 6.5% in 1995 to 2.7% by 2000 and that a realistic Enron valuation would be $53.20 per share.[26] The report questioned the sustainability of Enron's market leadership, citing that low barriers to entry and low cost revenue growth made it attractive for competitors Dynegy, El Paso, Reliant, Duke, and Williams to chip away at Enron's market share and propel their revenues into *Fortune 50* territory as well. Herold also contrasted the average profit margins of Goldman Sachs, Merrill Lynch, and Lehman Brothers of 66% with Enron's low 3.6% profit margin,[27] pointedly asking whether Enron's market premium was warranted, based solely on future super-revenue growth.[28]

A month later, this theme was expanded by *Fortune* reporter Bethany McLean, who published a cover story in March 2001 questioning Enron's valuation.[29] These early reports were the first to raise red flags about Enron's low profit margin and questionable accounting disclosures. The reports asked why Enron traded at 50 to 100 times earnings while comparable firms like Duke Energy and Goldman Sachs traded in the range of 15 to 22 times earnings.

Financial analysis of ratios can try to discover anomalies in valuation, such as overpriced or under-priced stocks, and can also call attention to poor performance of managers and corporate divisions. However, it is well known that financial ratio analy-

---

[24] Jonathan Weil, *Energy Traders Cite Gains, but Some Math is Missing*, WALL ST. J., Sept. 20, 2000, at T1.

[25] *Id.*

[26] The percentages given are for earnings before interest, taxes, depreciation and amortization (EBITDA) of this division, divided by the division's revenues.

[27] These percentages represent the earnings before interest, taxes, depreciation and amortization (EBITDA) of Enron and the other firms, divided by their respective revenues.

[28] John S. Herold, Inc., *The New, New Valuation Metrics: Is Enron really worth $126 per share?* Herold Industry Studies analyst report by Louis Gagliardi, John Parry, and Arthur Smith, Feb. 21, 2001.

[29] Bethany McLean, *Is Enron Overpriced?*, FORTUNE, Mar. 5, 2001, at 122.

sis alone cannot generally discover management fraud, especially if the fraud is pervasive in the company and senior management takes an active part in perpetuating it. With this caveat, in this section we examine several common financial ratios commonly used in financial analysis and valuation of companies and highlight the warning signals, or red flags, from the financial statements that would have alerted investors that Enron's real financial performance was a lot less than what its managers and Wall Street analysts proclaimed.

Profitability Measures

Enron's reported net income grew from $584 million in 1996 to $979 million in 2000, an average of 16.9% per year, totaling 67.6% profit growth for the five-year period.[30] Enron appeared to be exceeding even the magic "Jack Welch" (of General Electric) standard of 15% annual earnings growth. Maintaining a high earnings growth contributed to the perception that Enron was among the elite of "high performing" companies. However, as Table 3 indicates, Enron's reported profits were microscopic relative to revenues. Net income did not grow at anything near the same rate as revenues, which grew a phenomenal 164.6% per year for the same five-year period. As a result, there was a steady decline in net profit margin, from 4.4% in 1996 to a paltry 1% in 2001. Similarly, Enron's gross profit margin (gross profits as a percent of revenues) declined from 21.2% in 1996 to 13.3% in 1999, and took a dramatic drop to 6.2% in the following year as earnings more than doubled. Enron's rapidly declining profitability was not questioned by Wall Street analysts, as long as the reported net profits continued to grow at 15% plus per year—regardless of how small these profits actually were as a percentage of revenues.

Table 3. Declining Gross Profit Margin and Net Profit Margin, 1996–2000[31]

	1996	1997	1998	1999	2000
Revenues	$13,289	$20,273	$31,260	$40,112	$100,789
Gross profit	$2,811	$2,962	$4,879	$5,351	$6,272
Gross profit % of Revenues	21.2%	14.6%	15.6%	13.3%	6.2%
Net Income	$584	$105	$703	$893	$979
Net Income as % of Revenues	4.4%	0.5%	2.2%	2.2%	1.0%

Table 4 shows data comparing the profitability of major global energy companies. In terms of net profit margin, return on assets and return on equity, Enron's financial performance was at the lowest end for this group. Only El Paso Corp. had worse profitability and return ratios.

---

[30] *See supra* note 19.

[31] *See supra* note 19.

Table 4. Profitability and Return Ratios for Global Energy Companies[32] (Dollars in millions)

	2001 Revenues	Profit Margin	Return on Assets	Return on Equity
ExxonMobil	$191,581	8.0%	10.7%	20.9%
BP	174,218	4.6%	5.7%	10.8%
Royal Dutch/Shell	135,211	8.0%	10.0%	19.3%
ChevronTexaco	99,699	3.3%	4.2%	9.7%
Total Fina Elf	94,312	7.3%	9.0%	22.7%
American Elec. Power	61,257	1.6%	2.1%	11.8%
Duke Energy	59,503	3.2%	3.9%	15.0%
El Paso	57,475	0.2%	0.2%	1.0%
ConocoPhillips	56,984	5.7%	5.1%	15.5%
Petròleos de Venezuela	46,250	7.9%	6.0%	9.9%
Reliant Energy	46,226	2.1%	3.1%	14.3%
ENI	44,637	15.5%	6.0%	28.4%
Dynegy	42,242	1.5%	2.6%	13.7%
Enron (2000 data)	100,789	1.0%	0.4%	2.3%

The rapid decline in Enron's gross profit margin revealed a major red flag—the increasing use of the merchant model of revenue accounting by Enron to report both revenues and costs from energy trading, and the application of MTM accounting to increasing volumes of gas and electricity sold. As discussed earlier, the combination of merchant model and MTM accounting allowed Enron to book the whole value of the commodity traded as revenues, rather than just the trading fees or commissions.

Even the small profits reported by Enron in 2000 were eventually determined to be only a mirage by court-appointed bankruptcy examiner Neal Batson.[33] Batson's report reveals that over 95% of the reported profits in these two years were attributed to Enron's misuse of MTM and other accounting techniques.[34] But while financial analysts could not be expected to know that the company illegally manipulated the earnings, the reported profit margins in 2000 were so low and were declining so steadily that they should have merited ample skepticism from analysts about the company's profits.

Segment Profit and Mark-to-Market Accounting

Enron's segment disclosures, providing detailed revenue and profit data for its various operating segments, provided further red flags regarding the true profitability of

---

[32] Revenues as reported in *Fortune Global 500 The World's Largest Corporations*, FORTUNE, July 22, 2002, at F1.

[33] Second Interim Report of Neal Batson, Court-Appointed Examiner, *In re* Enron Corp., No. 01-16034 (Bankr. S.D.N.Y. Jan. 21, 2003) *available at* 2003 WL 1917445 (CORPSCAN).

[34] *Id.* at 36, 47–48.

the company. In particular, the segment data indicated that operating divisions that used mark-to-market accounting, such as the Wholesale Energy and Retail Energy divisions, showed increasing profits, while divisions that did not have the ability to use this method showed no profits. In other words, Enron's reported profits came mainly from mark-to-market accounting gains in derivatives. The non-derivatives business—including trading—was growing rapidly but generated no profits. Table 5, taken from Partnoy's congressional presentation on Enron's derivatives problem,[35] illustrates this issue.

Table 5. Enron's Income from Derivatives and Non-Derivative Businesses[36] (Dollars in millions)

	2000	1999	1998
Non-derivatives revenues	93,557	34,774	27,215
Non-derivatives expenses	94,517	34,761	26,381
Non-derivatives gross margin	(960)	13	834
Gain (loss) from derivatives	7,232	5,338	4,045
Other expenses	(4,319)	(4,549)	(3,501)
Operating income	1,953	802	1,378

As Table 5 shows, the non-derivatives business of Enron had a gross margin of negative $960 million in 2000, compared to a gain from derivatives business of $7,232 million.

Cash Flow

Perhaps the biggest red flags in Enron's financial statements were signs of poor earnings quality as indicated by several key cash flow measures.

One of the most common measures of earnings quality used by financial analysts, debt-rating agencies, and accounting academics is the so-called accruals, which is the difference between net income and cash flow from operations ("CFO"). Accruals are positive when net income is greater than CFO. When this happens, it usually indicates poor earnings quality issues. Interestingly, Enron was apparently very aware of the importance of CFO for analysts and bond rating agencies. In fact, Enron ensured by whatever means necessary that the annual reported CFO always exceeded the net income, as shown by panel A of Table 6.

---

[35] *Collapse of Enron Corp., Hearing Before the Senate Comm. on Governmental Affairs*, 107th Cong. (2002) (testimony of Frank Partnoy, Professor of Law, University of San Diego School of Law) (testimony included in this book under the title, ENRON AND THE DERIVATIVES WORLD, starting at page 173).

[36] *Id.*

Table 6. Enron's Net Income and Cash Flow from Operations[37] (Dollars in millions)

Panel A: Annual Data, 1998–2000

	1998	1999	2000
Net income	703	893	979
Cash flow from operations	1,640	1,228	4,779

Panel B: Quarterly Data for year 2000

	Q1	Q2	Q3	Q4
Net income	338	289	292	60
Cumulative net income	338	627	919	979
Cash flow from operations	(457)	(90)	647	4,679
Cumulative cash flow	(457)	(547)	100	4,779

However, as panel B of Table 6 shows, this was not the case when one examines Enron's quarterly financial data. As the data illustrate for the year 2000, Enron reserved almost all of its financial management of cash flow data to the fourth quarter. Similar troubling contrasts in the behavior of Enron's cash flow from operations for Quarters 1–3 and Quarter 4 existed for previous years as well, including 1998 and 1999.

Another cash flow measure called free cash flow also signaled both earnings quality and valuation concerns. Free cash flow is defined as the difference between cash flow from operations and cash flow from investments.[38] When free cash flow from operating activities is negative, the firm will have to make up the difference through debt or equity financing. In the long run, the valuation of an enterprise is determined by the free cash flows. No firm can remain viable for long if its free cash flow from operations is consistently negative. Yet, as Table 7 shows, Enron reported large negative free cash flows for much of 1997 to 2000. In fact, the large positive cash flow from operations reported by Enron for 2000 helped understate the real bleeding of free cash flows during that year. The 2000 cash flow from operations included $5.5 billion in deposits received by Enron from its California electric utility customers, $2.35 billion of which Enron had to repay.[39] Subtracting this payable from the calculated positive free cash flow for 2000 results in negative free cash flow of $1.835 billion for 2000.

---

[37] *See supra* note 19.

[38] This is a simplified definition, used here to illustrate the concept. *See generally* STEPHEN PENMAN, FINANCIAL STATEMENT ANALYSIS & SECURITY VALUATION 308-24 (2001) (discussing free cash flows and their calculation).

[39] Morgenson, *supra* note 20.

Table 7. Free Cash Flow, 1997–2000[40] (Dollars in millions)

	1997	1998	1999	2000
Cash Flow from Operations	$211	$1,640	$1,228	$4,779
Less: Cash flow from investments				
(Cash investments in operations)	($2,146)	($3,965)	($3,507)	($4,264)
= Free Cash Flow from Operating Activities	($1,935)	($2,325)	($2,279)	$515

In summary, the red ink as indicated by free cash flows from 1997 to 2000 was massive. This had to be made up by constant trips to capital markets for equity and debt issuance, speeding its collapse when the capital market windows finally shut down in late 2001 in response to its accounting revelations.

Given that Enron's net income margins had also declined from over 4% of revenue to less than 1%,[41] the negative free cash flows should have been a major red flag for any analyst trying to value Enron's equity. It certainly caught the attention of hedge fund manager Jim Chanos of Kynikos. He was quoted as saying, "No one could explain how Enron actually made money. . . . Not only was Enron surprisingly unprofitable, but its cash flow from operations seemed to bear little resemblance to reported earnings."[42]

6. CONCLUSION

One could go on with more red flags. There are the pro-forma earnings headlined by the company with increasing audacity in every quarterly earnings report, starting from late 1999. Or those inscrutable footnote disclosures about related party transactions, including ventures controlled by a "senior officer" of the company. Or the deal-based compensation system, which rewarded managers for bringing in projects with estimated profits rather than for executing ventures to generate real profits.

While there were red flags aplenty, the fact that there were all these accounting red flags that could be identified through financial analysis does not in any way shift the blame of Enron's failure to its investors. As Dharan stated in his address to Congress, the Enron meltdown was the result of a massive failure of corporate control and governance.[43] Enron did make numerous bad business decisions, including expensive energy projects such as Dabhol, overpaid investments in water projects such as Azurix, and ill-timed ventures into broadband trading. But in the end, the revelations in late 2001 of the company's Byzantine efforts to hide assets in special purpose entities,

---

[40] *See supra* note 19.

[41] *See supra* Table 3, p. 15.

[42] Bethany McLean, *Why Enron Went Bust*, FORTUNE, Dec. 24, 2001, at 58.

[43] Dharan Testimony, *supra* note 7.

whose viability and existence depended on maintaining the high value of inherently fragile Enron stock, caused the company to implode—revealing to investors how the company's board and management had failed at even the most basic aspects of corporate governance and control.

Enron's problems were also exacerbated by a compensation and performance management system[44] that contributed to a dysfunctional culture that in turn fostered an excessive short-term earnings focus. The obsessively compensation-driven culture encouraged high volume deal-making, often without regard to the quality of cash flow or profits, and getting accounting numbers booked as fast as possible to maintain the fragile underpinning of Enron's stock price, thus assuring that the deal-makers and executives would receive large cash bonuses and stock option exercise gains.

Although the Enron debacle has passed into history, the wide ranging dysfunction, conflicts of interest, and breakdown of governance standards and management practices have gone a long way to damage investor confidence and weaken the credibility and effective functioning of our governance institutions. Until more reforms and strengthened corporate governance practices are implemented, it will be a difficult road ahead to restore investor confidence and the healthy functioning of market intermediaries in the accounting, consulting, legal services, banking, investment advisory, and credit rating sectors. We hope that Enron will be a catalyst for stimulating innovative solutions to address these wide-ranging business challenges.

---

[44] Paul Healy & Krishna Palepu, *Governance and Intermediation Problems in Capital Markets: Evidence from the Fall of Enron*, J. OF ECON. (forthcoming 2004) (Harv. Bus. School working paper 03-027).

Enron's Accounting Issues: What Can We Learn to Prevent Future Enrons?

Dr. Bala G. Dharan*

Mr. Chairman and members of the Committee, I want to thank you for inviting me to present my analysis of the accounting issues that led to Enron's downfall. I am honored to be given this opportunity.

I am Bala Dharan, Professor of Accounting at the Jesse H. Jones Graduate School of Management, Rice University, Houston. I received my Ph.D. in accounting from Carnegie Mellon University, Pittsburgh. I have been an accounting professor at Rice University since 1982. In addition, I have taught accounting as a professor at Northwestern University's Kellogg School of Management, and as a visiting professor at the Haas School of Business at University of California, Berkeley, and the Harvard Business School. I am also a Certified Public Accountant and a Registered Investment Advisor in the state of Texas. I have published several articles in research journals on the use of financial accounting disclosures by investors.

The Enron debacle will rank as one of the largest securities fraud cases in history. Evidence to date points to signs of accounting fraud involving false valuation of assets, misleading disclosures, and bogus transactions to generate income. I have had several invitations to speak on Enron's accounting issues over the last few months. In my talks and lectures, I am asked two questions most frequently: One, how could this tragedy have happened while the company's management, board of directors, and outside auditors were supposedly watching over for employees and investors? Two, what can we learn from this debacle so that we can avoid future Enrons? Undoubtedly the first question will be the focus of the many investigations currently underway, including your Committee's efforts. In my testimony, I will focus on what we can learn from the accounting issues related to Enron's use of mark-to-market ("MTM") accounting and

---

* BALA G. DHARAN, Testimony, in LESSONS LEARNED FROM ENRON'S COLLAPSE: AUDITING THE ACCOUNTING INDUSTRY, S. Doc. No. 107-83, at 87–96 (Feb. 6, 2002), *available at* http://energycommerce.house.gov/107/action/107-83.pdf.

special purpose entities ("SPEs"). These two issues are very closely related, especially as they were practiced by Enron. In addition, I will address the related accounting issue of pro-forma disclosures, and also how Enron's failed business strategy contributed to the accounting errors. I hope other invited panelists addressing this Committee will talk about the critical roles played by Enron's management, board, auditors, lawyers, consultants, financial analysts, and investment bankers in Enron's fall. I conclude with recommendations for regulatory changes and improvements in the accounting and auditing rules governing special purpose entities, mark-to-market accounting, and financial disclosures in general.

1. LOSS OF INVESTOR TRUST

My analysis of the Enron debacle shows that Enron's fall was initiated by a flawed and failed corporate strategy, which led to an astounding number of bad business decisions. But unlike other normal corporate failures, Enron's fall was ultimately precipitated by the company's pervasive and sustained use of aggressive accounting tactics to generate misleading disclosures intended to hide the bad business decisions from shareholders. The failure of Enron points to an unparalleled breakdown at every level of the usual system of checks that investors, lenders, and employees rely on—broken or missing belief systems and boundary systems to govern the behavior of senior management, weak corporate governance by the board of directors and its audit committee, and compromised independence in the attestation of financial statements by the external auditor.

Enron started its transformation from a pipeline company to a "risk intermediation" company in the 1980s. It adopted a corporate strategy of an "asset-less" company, or a "frictionless company with no assets." The company's Chief Financial Officer said in a 1999 interview to a management magazine (which awarded him a "CFO Excellence Award for Capital Structure Management") that the top management transformed Enron into "one engaged in the intermediation of both commodity and capital risk positions. Essentially, we would buy and sell risk positions." What this description of the company implies is that, unlike any other major company in the U.S., Enron's corporate strategy was virtually devoid of any boundary system that defined the perimeter of what is an acceptable and unacceptable investment idea for managers to pursue. Since any business investment basically involves some risk position, this strategy is not really a strategy at all but an invitation to do anything one pleases. Enron's top management essentially gave its managers a blank order to "just do it," to do any "deal origination" that generated a desired return. "Deals" in such unrelated areas as weather derivatives, water services, metals trading, broadband supply, and power plants could all be justified and approved by managers under this concept of an asset-less risk intermediation company. The company even briefly changed its tagline in a company banner from "the world's leading energy company" (which implies some boundary system for investments) to "the world's leading company." It is no wonder that this flawed business strategy led to colossal investment mistakes in virtually every new area that the company tried to enter.

While bad business strategy and bad investment decisions can and do contribute to a company's fall, it is a company's desperate attempt to use accounting tricks to hide bad decisions that often seals its fate. My analysis of cases of major stock price declines shows that when news of an unanticipated business problem, such as a new product competition or obsolescence of technology, is released to the market, the company's stock price does take a hit, but it often recovers over time if the company takes appropriate and timely management actions. However, when a company loses the trust and confidence of the investing public because of discoveries of accounting wrongdoings, the net result on the company's stock price and competitive position is mostly devastating and long-lasting. This is because accounting reports are the principal means by which investors evaluate the company's past performance and future prospects, and a loss of trust effectively turns away investor interest in the company.

My analysis also suggests that it is not possible to recover from a loss of investor confidence by some quick management actions. Before re-admitting the company to their investment portfolios, investors would demand and seek evidence that the accounting numbers are again reliable, and this process of rebuilding of trust often takes place through several quarters of reliable financial disclosures. If the company's finances are not fundamentally sound to begin with, then it is quite likely that the company would not survive this long trust-recovery phase intact. This is exactly what happened in the case of Enron. Burdened with dozens of failing investments and assets hidden in special purpose entities whose very existence and financing often depended on the high stock price of Enron's shares, the company quickly entered a death-spiral when investors questioned its accounting practices and pushed its share price down to pennies.

2. USE OF PRO-FORMA EARNINGS

Enron's loss of investor faith started with the company's 2001 third quarter earnings release on October 16, 2001. As earnings releases go, this one must rank as one of the most misleading. The news release said, in an underlined and capitalized headline, "Enron Reports Recurring Third Quarter Earnings of $0.43 per diluted shares." The headline went on to reaffirm "recurring earnings" for the following year, 2002, of $2.15 per share, a projected increase of 19% from 2001. But an investor had to dig deep into the news release to know that Enron actually lost $618 million that quarter, for a loss of ($0.84) per share. A net loss of $618 million loss was converted to a "recurring net income" of $393 million by conveniently labeling and excluding $1.01 billion of expenses and losses as "non-recurring."

The practice of labeling certain earnings items as non-recurring or "one-time" has unfortunately become widespread in the U.S. and has corrupted the corporate disclosure environment to the detriment of investors and the public. Companies ranging from General Motors to Cisco mention some form of pro-forma earnings in their earnings disclosures. Of course, there is nothing "one-time" or "non-recurring" about the $1.01 billion of expenses and losses that Enron chose to label as such in its 2001 third quarter earnings release. In other words, neither accountants nor managers could assure that what they call non-recurring would not recur.

My ongoing research also shows that the adoption of pro-forma earnings reporting is often a company's desperate response to hide underlying business problems from its investors. As an example, Enron did not always use pro-forma earnings in its news releases. Its earnings release as late July 24, 2000, for 2000 second quarter did not contain any reference to recurring earnings. In its 2000 third quarter earnings release on October 17, 2000, Enron started using the recurring earnings in the body of the news release. We know from the Enron board's internal report, dated February 1, 2002, that this was also the time when the senior management started worrying about the declining value of many of their merchant investments. By the following quarter, recurring earnings had been elevated by Enron to news headline.

Not all companies, of course, use pro-forma earnings or use them in blatantly misleading ways. Companies like Microsoft do report their earnings without having to resort to misleading pro-forma disclosures. However, we need to ensure that misleading pro-forma disclosures are halted altogether. In a recent speech, the Chairman of the Securities and Exchange Commission has warned companies that pro-forma earnings would be monitored by the SEC for misleading disclosures. However, this does not go far enough. The SEC should recognize all pro-forma disclosures for what they really are—a charade. They may differ from one another in the degree of deception, but the intent of all pro-forma earnings is the same—to direct investor attention away from net income measured using generally accepted accounting principles, i.e., GAAP earnings.

Enron's 2001 third quarter earnings press release, on October 16, 2001, contained another major shortcoming—lack of information about its balance sheet and cash flows. While the company's press release provided information on net income, the company failed to provide a balance sheet. This is inexplicable—we teach in Accounting 101 that the income statement and the balance sheet are interrelated ("articulated") statements. This essentially means that we cannot really prepare one without preparing the other. Not surprisingly, almost every major company's earnings release contains the balance sheet along with its income statement. Financially responsible companies would also provide a cash flow statement. Analysts and investors puzzled with Enron's lack of balance sheet disclosure had to wait until after the markets closed on October 16, 2001, when the senior management disclosed—in response to a question during the earnings conference call—that it had taken a $1.2 billion charge against its shareholders' equity (a balance sheet item), including what was described as a $1 billion correction of an accounting error. The experience suggests, that along with reforms on pro-forma earnings usage, we should mandate a fuller, more complete presentation of financial statements in the earnings news releases so that investors can truly be in a position to interpret the quality and usefulness of the reported earnings numbers.

3. SPECIAL PURPOSE ENTITY ACCOUNTING

3.1. Business Purpose of SPEs

Enron's internal report, released on February 1, 2002, makes clear that Enron used dozens of transactions with special purpose entities ("SPEs") effectively controlled by the company to hide bad investments. These transactions were also used to report over $1 billion of false income. Many of these transactions were timed (or worse, illegally back-dated) just near ends of quarter, so that the income can be booked just in time and in amounts needed to meet investor expectations. However, SPEs were not originally created as mere tools of accounting manipulation. Surprisingly, the SPE industry did start with some good business purpose. Before discussing the accounting issues related to SPE accounting, it would be useful to have a brief description of what these entities are and how they arose.

The origin of SPEs can be traced to the way large international projects were (and are) financed. Let's say a company wants to build a gas pipeline in Central Asia and needs to raise $1 billion. It may find that potential investors of the pipeline would want their risk and reward exposure limited to the pipeline, and not be subjected to the overall risks and rewards associated with the sponsoring company. In addition, the investors would want the pipeline to be a self-supported, independent entity with no fear that the sponsoring company would take it over or sell it. The investors are able to achieve these objectives by putting the pipeline into a special purpose entity that is limited by its charter to those permitted activities only. Thus a common historical use of SPE was to design it as a joint venture between a sponsoring company and a group of outside investors. The SPE would be limited by charter to certain permitted activities only—hence the name. Such an SPE is often described as brain-dead or at least on auto-pilot. Cash flows from the SPE's operations of the project are to be used to pay its investors.

In the U.S., the use of SPEs spread during the 1970s and 1980s to the financial services industry. In the early 1980s, SPEs were used by the financial services firms to "securitize" (market as securities) assets that are otherwise generally illiquid and non-marketable, such as groups of mortgages or credit card receivables. Because they provide liquidity to certain assets and facilitate a more complete market for risk sharing, many SPEs can and do indeed serve a useful social purpose.

3.2 Accounting Purposes of SPEs

These examples illustrate that SPEs can be motivated by a genuine business purpose, such as risk sharing among investors and isolation of project risk from company risk. But as we have seen from the Enron debacle, SPEs can also be motivated by a specific accounting goal, such as off-balance sheet financing. The desired accounting effects are made possible because of the fact that SPEs are not consolidated with the parent if they satisfy certain conditions. The accounting effects sought by the use of SPEs can be summarized into the following types:

1. Hiding of Debt (Off-Balance Sheet Financing). The company tries to shift liabilities and associated assets to an SPE. The main purpose of forming the SPE in this case is to let the SPE borrow funds and not show the debt in the books of the sponsoring entity. The so-called "synthetic leases" are examples of this type of SPE. In the 1980s, SPEs became a popular way to execute synthetic lease transactions, in which a company desiring the use of a building or airplanes tries to structure the purchase or use in such a way that it does not result in a financial liability on the balance sheet. Though Enron's earlier use of SPEs may have been motivated by this objective, the key SPEs formed by Enron since 1997, such as Chewco, LJM1 and LJM2, were intended more for the other accounting objectives described below.

2. Hiding of Poor-Performing Assets. This objective has a major factor in several SPE transactions of Enron. For example, Enron transferred poor-performing investments (such as Rhythms NetConnections) to SPEs, so that any subsequent declines in the value of these assets would not have to be recognized by Enron. In 2000 and 2001 alone, Enron was able to hide as much as $1 billion of losses from poor-performing merchant investments by these types of SPE transactions.

3. Earnings Management—Reporting Gains and Losses When Desired. This accounting objective has also been a fundamental motivation for several of the complicated transactions arranged by Enron with SPEs with names such as Braveheart, LJM1, and Chewco. For example, Enron was able to transfer a long-term business contract—an agreement with Blockbuster Video to deliver movies on demand to an SPE and report a "gain" of $111 million.

4. Quick Execution of Related Party Transactions at Desired Prices. Enron's use of SPEs such as LJM1 and LJM2, controlled by its own senior managers, was specifically intended to do related party transactions quickly and when desired, at prices not negotiated at arms-length but arrived at between parties who had clear conflicts of interest. For example, the Blockbuster deal above was arranged at the very end of December 2000, just in time so that about $53 million of the "gain" could be included in the 2000 financial report. (The rest of the gain, $58 million, was reported in 2001 first quarter.) The purpose of this and several similar transactions by Enron seems to have been to use these transactions with SPEs controlled by its own senior executives to essentially create at short notice any amount of desired income, to meet investor expectations.

There are three sets of accounting rules that permit the above financial statement effects of SPEs. One deals with balance sheet consolidation—whether or not SPEs such as synthetic leases should be consolidated or reported separately from the sponsoring entity. The second deals with sales recognition—when the transfer of assets to an SPE should be reported as a sale. The third deals with related party transactions—whether transfers of assets to related parties can be reported as revenue. Of these, the accounting problem that needs immediate fixing is the one dealing with consolidation of SPEs. This is addressed next. With respect to sales recognition rules and related party transaction rules, the problem may lie more with Enron's questionable accounting and corresponding auditor errors, rather than the rules themselves. However, Enron's revenue recognition from SPE transactions often depended on the so-called mark-to-market accounting rules, which gave Enron the ability to assign arbitrary values to its energy and other business contracts. These rules do have certain problems that need fixing, and this issue is addressed in section 4.

3.3. Consolidation of SPEs

Despite their potential for economic and business benefits, the use of SPEs has always raised the question of whether the sponsoring company has some other accounting motivations, such as hiding of debt, hiding of poor-performing assets, or earnings management. Additionally, the explosive growth in the use of SPEs led to debates among managers, auditors, and accounting standards-setters as to whether and when SPEs should be consolidated. This is because the intended accounting effects of SPEs can only be achieved if the SPEs are reported as unconsolidated entities separate from the sponsoring entity. In other words, the sponsoring company needs to somehow keep its ownership in the SPE low enough so that it does not have to consolidate the SPE.

Thus consolidation rules for SPEs have been controversial and have been hotly contested between companies and accounting standards-setters from the very beginning. In the U.S., the involvement of the Financial Accounting Standards Board ("FASB"), the accounting standards-setting agency, in SPE accounting effectively started from 1977, when the FASB issued lease capitalization rules to control the use of off-balance sheet financing with leases. Corporate management intent on skirting around the new lease capitalization rules appeared to have led to the rapid development of SPEs to do the so-called "synthetic leases." In the first of several accounting rules directed at SPEs, in 1984, the Emerging Issues Task Force ("EITF") of the FASB issued EITF No. 84-15, "Grantor Trusts Consolidation." However, given the rapid growth of SPEs and their ever-widening range of applications, standards-setters were always a step or two behind (and were being reactive rather than proactive) in developing accounting rules to govern their proper use.

The question of whether a sponsoring company should consolidate an SPE took a definitive turn in 1990 when the EITF, with the implicit concurrence of the SEC, issued a guidance called EITF 90-15. This guidance allowed the acceptance of the infamous "three percent rule," i.e., an SPE need not be consolidated if at least three percent of its equity is owned by outside equity holders who bear ownership risk. Subsequently, the FASB formalized the above SPE accounting rule with Statement No. 125, and more recently Statement No. 140, issued in September 2000.

An analysis of the development of the three percent rule suggests that the rule was an ad-hoc reaction to a specific issue faced by the FASB's Emerging Issues Task Force and was intended as a short-term band-aid, but has somehow been elevated to a permanent fix. More importantly, the rule, in many ways, was a major departure from the normal consolidation rules used for other subsidiaries and entities. In the U.S., we generally require full consolidation if a company owns (directly or indirectly) 50 percent or more of an entity. Thus the three percent rule is a major loosening of the normal consolidation rule. The motivation for this seems to have been that the SPEs were restricted in their activities by charter and thus the parent company could claim lack of control. The parent company only had to show that some other investors did indeed join the SPE venture with a significant exposure (signified by the three percent rule) in order to make the SPE economically real and thus take it off the books.

Clearly the accounting for SPE consolidation needs to be fixed, starting with the abandonment of the three percent rule and its replacement with a more strictly defined "economic control" criterion. The need to fix consolidation rules has also been amply recognized by the FASB, which has been working for several years on a comprehensive "consolidation" project. However, the Enron debacle should give our standards-setters the needed push to rapidly complete this critical project and issue new rules for the proper consolidation of SPEs whose assets or management are effectively controlled by the sponsoring company. The rules should emphasize economic control, rather than rely on some legal definition of ownership or on an arbitrary percentage ownership. Economic control should be assumed unless management can prove lack of control.

4. MARK-TO-MARKET ACCOUNTING AND EARNINGS MANAGEMENT

In the U.S., financial assets, such as marketable securities, derivatives, and financial contracts, are required to be reported on the balance sheet at their current market values, rather than their original acquisition cost. This is known as mark-to-market ("MTM") accounting. MTM also requires changes in the market values for certain financial assets to be reported in the income statement, and in other cases in the shareholders' equity as a component of "Accumulated Other Comprehensive Income" ("OCI"), a new line item that was required for all public companies by FASB Statement No. 130 from 1997.

MTM was implemented in FASB Statement No. 115, issued in 1993, for financial assets that have readily determinable market values, such as stocks and traded futures and options. In 1996, FASB Statement No. 133 extended MTM to all financial derivatives, even those that do not have traded market values. For some derivatives, a company may have to use complex mathematical formulas to estimate a market value. Depending on the complexity of the financial contract, the proprietary formulas used by companies for market value estimation may depend on several dozen assumptions about interest rate, customers, costs, and prices, and may require several hours of computing time. This means that it is hard, if not impossible, to verify or audit the resulting estimated market value. Of course, a consequence of this lack of verifiability is that MTM accounting can potentially provide ample opportunities for management to create and manage earnings. Thus MTM accounting represents the classic accounting struggle of weighing the trade-off between relevance and reliability—in this case the relevance of the market value data against the reliability of the data. In the end, the accounting standards-setters took the position that the increased benefit from reporting the market value information on the balance sheet justified the cost of decreased reliability of income statements and the earnings number.

It will be useful to consider an example of how Enron recognized value with MTM accounting, in order to understand how MTM can be easily manipulated by a company to manage earnings, especially with respect to financial contracts that do not have a ready market. Assume that Enron signed a contract with the city of Chicago to deliver electricity to several office buildings of the city government over the next twenty years, at fixed or pre-determined prices. The advantage to the city of Chicago from this "price risk management" activity is that it fixes its purchase price of electricity and allows the city government to budget and forecast future outlays for electricity without having to worry about price fluctuations in gas or electricity markets.

Enron sought and obtained exemptions from regulators to allow it to report these types of long-term supply contracts as "merchant investments" rather than regulated contracts, and obtained permission from accounting standards-setters to value them using MTM accounting. Without MTM, Enron would be required to recognize no revenue at the time the contract is signed and report revenues and related costs only in future years for actual amounts of electricity supplied in each year. However, MTM accounting permits Enron to estimate the net present value of all future estimated revenues and costs from the contract and report this net amount as income in the year in which the supply contract is signed. The idea for such an accounting treatment seems to be based on the notion that the financial contract could have been sold to someone else immediately at the estimated market value, and hence investors would benefit from knowing this amount in the balance sheet and correspondingly in the income statement. Enron used similar MTM procedures not only to value merchant investments on its books but also to determine the selling price, and hence gain on sale, for investments it transferred to the various SPEs it controlled.

A major problem with using MTM accounting for private contracts such as the one described above is that the valuation requires Enron to forecast or assume values for several dozen variables and for several years into the future. For example, the revenue forecasts may depend on assumptions about the exact timing of energy deregulation in various local markets, as well as twenty years of forecasts for demand for electricity, actions of other competitors, price elasticity, cost of gas, interest rates, and so on.

While there are strong conceptual reasons to support MTM accounting, the Enron crisis points to at least some need to revisit and revise the current accounting rules for reporting transactions and assets that rely on MTM values. In particular, MTM rules should be modified to require that all gains calculated using MTM method for assets and contracts that do not have a ready market value should be reported only in "Other Comprehensive Income" in the balance sheet, rather than the income statement, until the company can meet some high "confidence level" about the realization of revenue for cash flows that are projected into future years. Normal revenue recognition rules do require that revenue should be recognized after service is performed, and moreover that revenue should be "realized or realizable," meaning that cash flow collection should be likely. In the absence of satisfying this condition, revenue rules (such as those explained in SEC Staff Accounting Bulletin 101) normally compel a company to wait until service is performed and cash collection probabilities are higher. Extending this logic to MTM accounting would protect the investing public from unverifiable and unauditable claims of gains being reported in the income statement.

5. RECOMMENDATIONS

The Enron meltdown is a result of massive failure of corporate control and governance, and failures at several levels of outside checks and balances that investors and the public rely on, including an independent external audit. In my testimony, I have focused on the accounting issues, and in particular on the possible changes we need to make in these areas in order to prevent future Enrons. My recommendations are summarized below.

1. The SEC, the New York Stock Exchange ("NYSE"), and the Nasdaq should adopt new rules severely restricting the format and use of pro-forma earnings reporting. All earnings communications by companies should emphasize earnings as computed by Generally Acceptable Accounting Standards. Any additional information provided by the company to highlight special or unusual items in the earnings number should be given in such a way that the GAAP income is still clearly the focus of the earnings disclosure.

2. Companies should be reminded by regulators and auditors that the use of terms such as "one-time" or "non-recurring" about past events in earnings communications implies certain promises to investors about future performance, and therefore should not be used except in rare cases.

3. Companies should present a complete set of financial statements, including a balance sheet and a cash flow statement, in all their earnings communications to the general public, in order to permit investors to evaluate the quality of the reported earnings numbers.

4. The FASB needs to accelerate its current project on consolidation accounting, and in particular, fix the consolidation rules in the accounting for Special Purpose Entities to prevent its continued abuse by corporations for earnings management. The current consolidation rules, including the "3 percent" rule for SPEs need to be abandoned and replaced with an "economic control" rule. The new rules need to emphasize economic control rather than rely on some legal definition of ownership or on an arbitrary percentage ownership. Economic control should be assumed unless management can prove lack of control. Similar rules should be extended to lease accounting.

5. The FASB and the SEC need to consider requiring new disclosures on transactions between a company and its unconsolidated entities, including SPEs. In particular, more detailed footnote disclosures on the sale or transfer of

assets to unconsolidated entities, recognition of income from such transfers, and the valuation of transferred assets should be required.

6. The mark-to-market accounting methodology, while theoretically sound, needs to be modified in the light of what we have learned from the Enron meltdown. Traditional revenue recognition rules, such as the realization principle, should be extended to the recognition of gains and losses from MTM accounting. Forecasted cash flows beyond two or three years should be presumed to have a low level of confidence of collectibility. Gains resulting from present values of such cash flows should be recorded in the Accumulated Other Comprehensive Income in the balance sheet, rather than the income statement, until the confidence level increases to satisfy the usual realization criterion of collectibility.

Understanding Enron: "It's About the Gatekeepers, Stupid"*

*John C. Coffee, Jr.***

What do we know after Enron's implosion that we did not know before it? The conventional wisdom is that the Enron debacle reveals basic weaknesses in our contemporary system of corporate governance.[1] Perhaps, this is so, but where is the weakness located? Under what circumstances will critical systems fail? Major debacles of historical dimensions (and Enron is surely that) tend to produce an excess of explanations. In Enron's case, the firm's strange failure is becoming a virtual Rorschach test in which each commentator can see evidence confirming what he or she already believed.[2]

Nonetheless, the problem with viewing Enron as an indication of any systematic governance failure is that its core facts are maddeningly unique. Most obviously, Enron's governance structure was *sui generis*. Other public corporations simply have not authorized their chief financial officer to run an independent entity that enters into billions of dollars of risky and volatile trading transactions with them; nor have they

---

* Originally published at 57 BUS. LAW. 1403 (2002). Reprinted with permission.

** Adolf A. Berle Professor of Law, Columbia University Law School.

[1] As a result, proposals to reform corporate governance through legislation, codes of best practice, and heightened listing standards are proliferating. *See, e.g.,* Tom Hamburger, *Corporate-Governance Bill Weighed,* WALL ST. J., May 3, 2002, at C-10 (discussing proposed "Shareholder Bill of Rights"); Kate Kelly, *Stock Exchanges Fortify Watchdog Roles,* WALL ST. J., April 30, 2002, at C-1. The SEC has proposed changes in financial reporting, which proposals have encountered mixed reviews. *See* Gretchen Morgenson, *Information Sooner, Yes, But Make It Better Too,* N.Y. TIMES, May 5, 2002, at § 3-1. Other recurring legislature proposals address auditors and the Financial Accounting Standards Board. *See* Michael Schroeder, *Tauzin Bill Aims to Bolster FASB With Firms' Fees,* WALL ST. J., April 30, 2002, at A-4.

[2] This observation applies with special force to academics. Those who doubted stock market efficiency before Enron doubt it even more afterwards, pointing to the slow fall of Enron stock over the last half of 2001. Those who are skeptical of outside directors are even more convinced that their wisdom has been confirmed. For example, my Columbia colleague, Jeffrey Gordon, has proposed a new model of "trustee/directors" to populate the audit committee and perform certain other guardian roles. *See* Jeffrey N. Gordon, *What Enron Means for the Management and Control of the Modern Business Corporation: Some Initial Reactions,* 69 U. CHI. L. REV. 1233 (2002).

allowed their senior officers to profit from such self-dealing transactions without broad supervision or even comprehension of the profits involved.[3] Nor have other corporations incorporated thousands of subsidiaries and employed them in a complex web of off-balance sheet partnerships.[4]

In short, Enron was organizationally unique—a virtual hedge fund in the view of some,[5] yet a firm that morphed almost overnight into its bizarre structure from its origins as a stodgy gas pipeline company. The pace of this transition seemingly outdistanced the development of risk management systems and an institutional culture paralleling those of traditional financial firms. Precisely for this reason, the passive performance of Enron's board of directors cannot fairly be extrapolated and applied as an assessment of all boards generally.[6] Boards of directors may or may not perform their duties adequately, but, standing alone, Enron proves little. In this sense, Enron is an anecdote, an isolated data point that cannot yet fairly be deemed to amount to a trend.

Viewed from another perspective, however, Enron does furnish ample evidence of a systematic governance failure. Although other spectacular securities frauds have been discovered from time to time over recent decades,[7] they have not generally disturbed

---

[3] Although no substantive findings have yet been made by any court or agency, these are essentially the findings of a special committee of Enron's own board. *See* William C. Powers, Jr. et al., REPORT OF INVESTIGATION BY THE SPECIAL INVESTIGATIVE COMMITTEE OF THE BOARD OF DIRECTORS OF ENRON CORP. (the "Powers Report"), Feb. 1, 2002), 2002 WL 198018.

[4] Although complete information is still lacking, Enron appears to have established nearly 3,000 subsidiaries and partnerships in Delaware, the Cayman Islands, the Netherlands, and elsewhere. *See* Glenn Kessler, *Enron Agrees to Let Congress See Tax Returns,* WASH. POST, Feb. 16, 2002, at A13.

[5] Indeed, some commentators view Enron as virtually a hedge fund. *See Enron and Derivatives: Hearings Before the Senate Comm. On Gov'tal Affairs* (2002), *at* Frank Partnoy, "Enron and Derivatives" (available on Social Sciences Research Network at www.ssrn.com at *id.* 302332) (testimony of Professor Frank Partnoy, Professor of Law, University of San Diego School of Law before Senate Committee on Governmental Affairs).

[6] No doubt, there are other corporations in which an entrepreneurial founder has dominated the board and caused it to approve dubious self-dealing transactions. WorldCom Inc. and Global Crossing quickly come to mind, and the resignation of the former's chief executive and the bankruptcy of the latter suggest that firms with weak corporate governance do not perform well during market downturns. *See* Rebecca Blumenstein & Jared Sandburg, *WorldCom CEO Quits Amid Probe of Firm's Finances,* WALL ST. J., April 30, 2002, at A-1. The starting point of this article is not the premise that contemporary corporate governance is fundamentally sound, but rather that there is high variance among boards—some very good, and others quite bad. Its conclusion is, however, that reliable corporate governance is not possible without reliable gatekeepers—because boards necessarily depend on professional assistance from gatekeepers.

[7] Many of these frauds have involved far more sinister and predatory conduct than has yet come to light in Enron. For example, officers of Equity Funding of America counterfeited bogus insurance policies in order to convince their auditors that their product was selling. *See* Dirks v. United States, 463 U.S. 646, 648-50 (1983) (discussing the basic fraud in the course of analyzing the liability of a tippee who advised clients to sell this stock). More recently, officers of Bre-X Minerals Ltd. apparently salted mining samples taken from the firm's properties in Indonesia to convince the market that it had discovered one of the largest gold mines in history. During the period that these false statements were issued, Bre-X's stock price

the overall market. In contrast, Enron has clearly roiled the market and created a new investor demand for transparency. Behind this disruption lies the market's discovery that it cannot rely upon the professional gatekeepers—auditors, analysts, and others—whom the market has long trusted to filter, verify, and assess complicated financial information. Properly understood, Enron is a demonstration of gatekeeper failure, and the question it most sharply poses is how this failure should be rectified.

Although the term "gatekeeper" is commonly used,[8] here it requires special definition. Inherently, gatekeepers are reputational intermediaries who provide verification and certification services to investors.[9] These services can consist of verifying a company's financial statements (as the independent auditor does), evaluating the creditworthiness of the company (as the debt rating agency does), assessing the company's business and financial prospects vis-à-vis its rivals (as the securities analyst does), or appraising the fairness of a specific transaction (as the investment banker does in delivering a fairness opinion). Attorneys can also be gatekeepers when they lend their professional reputations to a transaction, but, as later discussed, the more typical role of attorneys serving public corporations is that of the transaction engineer, rather than the reputational intermediary.

Characteristically, the professional gatekeeper essentially assesses or vouches for the corporate client's own statements about itself or a specific transaction. This duplication is necessary because the market recognizes that the gatekeeper has a lesser incentive to lie than does its client and thus regards the gatekeeper's assurance or evaluation as more credible. To be sure, the gatekeeper as watchdog is typically paid by the party that it is to watch, but its relative credibility stems from the fact that it is in effect pledging a reputational capital that it has built up over many years of performing similar services for numerous clients. In theory, such reputational capital would not be

---

rose from $2.85 per share to $224.95; on discovery of the fraud, the stock collapsed and the company went into bankruptcy. *See* McNamara v. Bre-X Minerals Ltd., 2001 U.S. Dist. LEXIS 4571, 197 F. Supp. 2d 622 (E.D. Tex. March 30, 2001). Similar observations could be made about other recent scandals, including OPM in the early 1970s, Lincoln Savings & Loan in the 1980s, or the massive BCCI bank failure in the 1990s. Each dwarfs Enron in terms of the culpability of senior management. Nor are the market losses greater in Enron. The stock declines in 2000 in Lucent Technologies and in 2001 in Cisco Systems were considerably greater in terms of decline in total market capitalization, even though neither of these cases has elicited any public enforcement proceeding. *Companies Face a Record Number of Shareholder Lawsuits*, INVESTOR RELATIONS BUSINESS, April 22, 2002 (citing Cornerstone Research, Securities Class Action Filings: 2001: A Year in Review, *available at* http://securities.stanford.edu/clearinghouse_research/2001_YIR/yir_Filings.pdf (last visited March 12, 2003)).

[8] The term "gatekeeper" is not simply an academic concept. In Securities Act Release No. 7870 (June 30, 2000), the SEC recently noted that "the federal laws . . . make independent auditors 'gatekeepers' to the public securities markets." 2000 SEC LEXIS 1389 *Revision of the Commission's Auditor Independence Requirements, Exchange Act Release No. 33-7870, 65 Fed. Reg. 43148-01 at 43150 (July 12, 2000).

[9] For a fuller, more theoretical consideration of the concept of the gatekeeper, see Reinier Kraakman, *Corporate Liability Strategies and the Costs of Legal Controls*, 93 YALE L.J. 857 (1984); Reinier Kraakman, *Gatekeepers: The Anatomy of a Third-Party Enforcement Strategy*, 2. J.L., ECON. & ORG. 53 (1986); Stephen Choi, *Market Lessons for Gatekeepers*, 92 NW. U. L. REV. 9116 (1998).

sacrificed for a single client and a modest fee. Here, as elsewhere, however, logic and experience can conflict. Despite the clear logic of the gatekeeper rationale, experience over the 1990s suggests that professional gatekeepers do acquiesce in managerial fraud, even though the apparent reputational losses seem to dwarf the gains to be made from the individual client.[10]

Why has there been an apparent failure in the market for gatekeeping services? This brief comment offers some explanations, but also acknowledges that rival explanations lead to very different prescriptions. Thus, the starting point for responding to the Enron debacle begins with asking the right question. That question is not: why did management engage in fraud? But rather it is: why did the gatekeepers let them?

I. THE CHANGING STATUS OF THE GATEKEEPER

In theory, a gatekeeper has many clients, each of whom pays it a fee that is modest in proportion to the firm's overall revenues. Arthur Andersen had, for example, 2,300 audit clients.[11] On this basis, the firm seemingly had little incentive to risk its considerable reputational capital for any one client. During the 1990s, many courts bought this logic hook, line, and sinker. For example, in *DiLeo v. Ernst & Young*,[12] Judge Easterbrook, writing for the Seventh Circuit, outlined precisely the foregoing theory:

> The complaint does not allege that [the auditor] had anything to gain from any fraud by [its client]. An accountant's greatest asset is its reputation for honesty, closely followed by its reputation for careful work. Fees for two years' audits could not approach the losses [that the auditor] would suffer from a perception that it would muffle a client's fraud. . . . [The auditor's] partners shared none of the gain from any fraud and were exposed to a large fraction of the loss. It would have been irrational for any of them to have joined cause with [the client].[13]

Of course, the modest fees in some of these cases (the audit fee was only $90,000 in *Robin v. Arthur Young & Co.*)[14] were well less than the $100 million in prospective annual fees from Enron that Arthur Andersen & Co. explicitly foresaw. But does this

---

[10] This observation is hardly original with this author. *See, e.g.,* Robert A. Prentice, *The Case of the Irrational Auditor: A Behavioral Insight Into Securities Fraud Litigation,* 95 Nw. U. L. Rev. 1333 (2000).

[11] *See* Michelle Mittelstadt, *Andersen is charged in Enron case; Shredding allegations imperil firm's survival; it calls case flimsy,* Dallas Morning News, Mar. 15, 2002, at 1A.

[12] DiLeo v. Ernst & Young, 901 F.2d 624 (7th Cir. 1990); *see also* Melder v. Morris, 27 F.3d 1097, 1103 (5th Cir. 1994); Robin v. Arthur Young & Co., 915 F.2d 1120, 1127 (7th Cir. 1990) (mere $90,000 annual audit fee would have been an "irrational" motive for fraud).

[13] DiLeo, 901 F.2d at 629.

[14] *See* Robin, *supra* note 12, at 1127.

difference really explain Arthur Andersen's downward spiral? After all, Arthur Andersen earned over $9 billion in revenues in 2001.[15]

Once among the most respected of all professional service firms (including law, accounting, and consulting firms), Andersen became involved in a series of now well-known securities frauds—e.g., Waste Management, Sunbeam, HBO, McKesson, The Baptist Foundation, and now Global Crossing—that culminated in its disastrous association with Enron. Little, however, suggests that Arthur Andersen was more reckless or less responsible than its peers.[16] Instead, the evidence suggests that something led to a general erosion in the quality of financial reporting during the late 1990s. During this period, earnings restatements, long a proxy for fraud, suddenly soared. To cite only the simplest quantitative measure, the number of earnings restatements by publicly held corporations averaged 49 per year from 1990 to 1997, then increased to 91 in 1998, and finally skyrocketed to 150 and 156, respectively, in 1999 and 2000.[17]

What caused this sudden spike in earning restatements? Because public corporations must fear stock price drops, securities class actions, and SEC investigations in the wake of earnings restatements, it is not plausible to read this sudden increase as the product of a new tolerance for, or indifference to, restatements. Even if some portion of the change might be attributed to a new SEC activism about "earnings management,"[18] which became an SEC priority in 1998,[19] corporate issuers will not voluntarily expose

---

[15] Arthur Andersen's website reports that revenues for 2001 were $9.34 billion. *See* www.andersen.com; Matt Krantz, *Andersen Faces Fight for Survival,* USA TODAY, Jan. 14, 2002, at 1B.

[16] Compared to its peers within the Big Five accounting firms, Arthur Andersen appears to have been responsible for less than its proportionate share of earnings restatements. While it audited 21% of Big Five audit clients, it was responsible for only 15% of the restatements experienced by the Big Five firms between 1997 and 2001. On this basis, it was arguably slightly more conservative than its peers. *See* Devin Gordon et al., *Periscope: How Arthur Andersen Begs for Business,* NEWSWEEK, Mar. 18, 2002, at 6. In discussions with industry insiders, the only respect in which I have ever heard Andersen characterized as different from its peers in the Big Five was that it marketed itself as a firm in which the audit partner could make the final call on difficult accounting questions without having to secure approval from senior officials within the firm. Although this could translate into a weaker system of internal controls, this hypothesis seems inconsistent with Arthur Andersen's apparently below-average rate of earnings restatements.

[17] *See* George B. Moriarty & Philip B. Livingston, *Quantitative Measures of the Quality of Financial Reporting,* 17 FIN. EXECUTIVE 53, at 54 (July/Aug. 2001).

[18] Accounting firms have sometimes attempted to explain this increase on the basis that the SEC tightened the definition of "materiality" in the late 1990s. This explanation is not very convincing, in part because the principal SEC statement that tightened the definition of materiality—Staff Accounting Bulletin No. 99—was issued in mid-1999, after the number of restatements had already begun to soar in 1998. Also, SAB No. 99 did not truly mandate restatements, but only suggested that a rule of thumb that assumed that amounts under 5% were inherently immaterial could not be applied reflexively. *See* Staff Accounting Bulletin No. 99, 64 Fed R. 45150 (August 19, 1999).

[19] The SEC's prioritization of earnings management as a principal enforcement target can be approximately dated to SEC Chairman Arthur Levitt's now famous speech on the subject in 1998. *See* Arthur Levitt, *The Numbers Game,* Remarks at N.Y.U. Center for Law and Business (Sept. 28, 1998), *available at* http://www.stern.nyu.edu/clb/.

themselves to enormous liability just to please the SEC. Moreover, not only did the number of earnings restatements increase over this period, but so also did the amounts involved.[20] Earnings restatements thus seem an indication that earlier earnings management has gotten out of hand. Accordingly, the spike in earnings restatements in the late 1990s implies that the Big Five accounting firms had earlier acquiesced in aggressive earnings management—and, in particular, premature revenue recognition—that no longer could be sustained.

This apparent pattern of increased deference by the gatekeeper to its client during the 1990s was not limited to the auditing profession. Securities analysts have probably encountered even greater recent public and Congressional skepticism about their objectivity. Again, much of the evidence is anecdotal, but striking. As late as October 2001, sixteen out of the seventeen securities analysts covering Enron maintained "buy" or "strong buy" recommendations on its stock right up until virtually the moment of its bankruptcy filing.[21] The first brokerage firm to downgrade Enron to a "sell" rating in 2001 was Prudential Securities, which no longer engages in investment banking activities.[22] Revealingly, Prudential is also believed to have the highest proportion of sell ratings among the stocks it evaluates.[23]

Much like auditors, analysts are also "reputational intermediaries," whose desire to be perceived as credible and objective may often be subordinated to their desire to retain and please investment banking clients. One statistic inevitably comes up in any assessment of analyst objectivity: namely, the curious fact that the ratio of "buy" recommendations to "sell" recommendations has recently been as high as 100 to 1.[24] In

---

[20] According to Moriarty and Livingston, supra note 17, companies that restated earnings suffered market losses of $17.7 billion in 1998, $24.2 billion in 1999, and $31.2 billion in 2000. Moriarty & Livingston, *supra* note 17, at 55. Expressed as a percentage of the overall capitalization of the market (which was ascending hyperbolically over this period), these losses for 1998 through 2000 came to 0.13%, 0.14%, and 0.19%, respectively, of market capitalization. *Id.* In short, however expressed, the losses increased over this period.

[21] *The Collapse of Enron: The Role Analysts Played and the Conflicts They Face: Statement Before the Senate Comm. on Gov'tal Affairs*, 2002 WL 2011028 (2002) (statement of Frank Torres, Legislative Counsel, Consumers Union); *see also Collapse of Enron Corp.: Hearings Before the Senate Comm. on Gov'tal Affairs*, 2002 WL 2010033 (2002) (statement of Frank Partnoy, Professor of Law, University of San Diego School of Law) (discussing similar sixteen out of seventeen tabulation).

[22] *See* Lauren Young, *Independence Day*, SMARTMONEY, May 1, 2001, at 28.

[23] *Id.*

[24] A study by Thomas Financial/First Call has found that less than one percent of the 28,000 stock recommendations issued by brokerage firm analysts during late 1999 and most of 2000 were "sell" recommendations. *Analyzing the Analysts: Are Investors Getting Unbiased Research from Wall Street?: Hearing Before the Subcomm. on Capital Mkts., Ins., & Gov't. Sponsored Enters.* (2001) (opening statement of ranking democratic member Paul E. Kanjorski) (citing and discussing First Call study) [hereinafter Opening Statement]. A study by Thomas Financial/First Call has found that less than one percent of the 28,000 stock recommendations issued by brokerage firm analysts during late 1999 and most of 2000 were "sell" recommendations. *Id.*

truth, this particular statistic may not be as compelling as it initially sounds because there are obvious reasons why "buy" recommendations will normally outnumber "sell" recommendations, even in the absence of conflicts of interest.[25] Yet, a related statistic may be more revealing because it underscores the apparent transition that took place in the 1990s. According to a study by Thomson Financial, the ratio of "buy" to "sell" recommendations increased from 6 to 1 in 1991 to 100 to 1 by 2000.[26] Again, it appears that something happened in the 1990s that compromised the independence and objectivity of the gatekeepers on whom our private system of corporate governance depends.[27] Not surprisingly, it also appears that this loss of relative objectivity can harm investors.[28]

II. EXPLAINING GATEKEEPER FAILURE

None of the watchdogs that should have detected Enron's collapse—auditors, analysts or debt rating agencies—did so before the penultimate moment. This is the true common denominator in the Enron debacle: the collective failure of the gatekeepers. Why did the watchdogs not bark in the night when it now appears in hindsight that a massive fraud took place? Here, two quite different, although complementary, stories can be told. The first will be called the "general deterrence" story; and the second, the "bubble" story. The first is essentially economic in its premises; and the second, psychological.

A. The Deterrence Explanation: The Underdeterred Gatekeeper

The general deterrence story focuses on the decline in the expected liability costs arising out of acquiescence by auditors in aggressive accounting policies favored by

---

[25] "Sell-side" analysts are employed by brokerage firms that understandably wish to maximize brokerage transactions. In this light, a "buy" recommendation addresses the entire market and certainly all the firm's customers, while a "sell" recommendation addresses only those customers who own the stock (probably well less than 1%) and those with margin accounts who are willing to sell the stock "short." In addition, "sell" recommendations annoy not only the issuer company, but also institutional investors who are afraid that sell recommendations will "spook" retail investors, causing them to panic and sell, while the institution is "locked into" a large position that cannot easily be liquidated.

[26] *See* Opening Statement of Congressman Paul E. Kanjorski, *supra* note 24, at 1 (citing study by First Call).

[27] Participants in the industry also report that its professional culture changed dramatically in the late 1990s, particularly as investment banking firms began to hire "star" analysts for their marketing clout. *See* Gretchen Morgenson, *Requiem for an Honorable Profession*, N.Y. TIMES, May 5, 2002, at 3-1 (suggesting major change dates from around 1996).

[28] Although the empirical evidence is limited, it suggests that "independent" analysts (i.e., analysts not associated with the underwriter for a particular issuer) behave differently from, and tend to outperform, analysts who are associated with the issuer's underwriter. *See* Roni Michaely & Kent L. Womack, *Conflict of Interest and the Credibility of Underwriter Analyst Recommendations*, 12 REV. OF FIN. STUD. 653, 675–76 (1999).

management. It postulates that, during the 1990s, the risk of auditor liability declined, while the benefits of acquiescence increased. Economics 101 teaches us that when the costs go down, while the benefits associated with any activity go up, the output of the activity will increase. Here, the activity that increased was auditor acquiescence.

Why did the legal risks go down during the 1990s? The obvious list of reasons would include:

(1) the Supreme Court's *Lampf, Pleva* decision in 1991, which significantly shortened the statute of limitations applicable to securities fraud;[29]

(2) the Supreme Court's *Central Bank of Denver* decision,[30] which, in 1994, eliminated private "aiding and abetting" liability in securities fraud cases;

(3) the Private Securities Litigation Reform Act of 1995 ("PSLRA"), which (a) raised the pleading standards for securities class actions to a level well above that applicable to fraud actions generally; (b) substituted proportionate liability for "joint and several" liability; (c) restricted the sweep of the RICO statute so that it could no longer convert securities fraud class actions for compensatory damages into actions for treble damages; and (d) adopted a very protective safe harbor for forward-looking information; and

(4) the Securities Litigation Uniform Standards Act of 1998 ("SLUSA"), which abolished state court class actions alleging securities fraud.[31]

Not only did the threat of private enforcement decline, but the prospect of public enforcement similarly subsided. In particular, there is reason to believe that, from some point in the 1980s until the late 1990s, the SEC shifted its enforcement focus away from actions against the Big Five accounting firms towards other priorities.[32] In

---

[29] Lampf, Pleva, Lipkind, Prupis & Petigrow v. Gilbertston, 501 U.S. 350, 359–61 (1991) (creating a federal rule requiring plaintiffs to file within one year of when they should have known of the violation underlying their action, but in no event more than three years after the violation). This one- to three-year period was typically shorter than the previously applicable limitations periods, which were determined by analogy to state statutes and often permitted a five or six year delay—if that was the period within which a common law fraud action could be maintained in the particular state).

[30] Central Bank of Denver, N.A., v. First Interstate of Denver, N.A., 511 U.S. 164 (1994).

[31] *See* Securities Litigation Uniform Standards Act of 1998 (SLUSA), Pub. L. No. 105-353, 112 Stat. 3227 (1998), codified in scattered sections of 15 U.S.C. For an analysis and critique of this statute, see Richard Painter, *Responding to A False Alarm: Federal Preemption of State Securities Fraud Causes of Action*, 84 CORNELL L. REV. 1 (1998).

[32] This point has been orally made to me by several former SEC officials, including Stanley Sporkin, the long-time former head of the Commission's Division of Enforcement. They believe that the SEC's enforcement action against Arthur Andersen, which was resolved in June 2001, was one of the very few (and perhaps the only) enforcement actions brought against a Big Five accounting firm on fraud grounds during the 1990s. *See* Securities and Exchange Commission v. Arthur Andersen LLP, SEC Litigation Release No. 17039, 2001 SEC LEXIS 1159 (June 19, 2001). Although the Commission did bring charges

any event, the point here is not that any of these changes were necessarily unjustified or excessive,[33] but rather that their collective impact was to appreciably reduce the risk of liability. Auditors were the special beneficiaries of many of these provisions. For example, the pleading rules and the new standard of proportionate liability protected them far more than it did most corporate defendants.[34] Although auditors are still sued today, the settlement value of cases against auditors has gone way down.

Correspondingly, the benefits of acquiescence to auditors rose over this same period, as the Big Five learned during the 1990s how to cross-sell consulting services and to treat the auditing function principally as a portal of entry to a lucrative client. Prior to the mid-1990s, the provision of consulting services to audit clients was infrequent and insubstantial in the aggregate.[35] Yet, according to one recent survey, the typical large public corporation now pays its auditor for consulting services three times what it pays the same auditor for auditing services.[36] Not only did auditing firms see more

---

during the 1990s against individual partners in these firms, the Commission appears to have been deterred from bringing suits against the Big Five themselves because such actions were extremely costly in manpower and expense and the defendants could be expected to resist zealously. In contrast, during the 1980s, especially during Mr. Sporkin's tenure as head of the Enforcement Division, the SEC regularly brought enforcement actions against the Big Five.

[33] Indeed, this author would continue to support proportionate liability for auditors on fairness grounds and sees no problem with the PSLRA's heightened pleading standards, as they have been interpreted by some courts. *See, e.g., Novak v. Kasaks,* 216 F.3d 300 (2d Cir. 2000), *cert. denied,* 531 U.S. 1012 (2000).

[34] At a minimum, plaintiffs today must plead with particularity facts giving rise to a "strong inference of fraud." *See, e.g., Novak v. Kasaks,* supra note 33. At the outset of a case, it may be possible to plead such facts with respect to the management of the corporate defendant (for example, based on insider sales by such persons prior to the public disclosure of the adverse information that caused the stock drop), but it is rarely possible to plead such information with respect to the auditors (who by law cannot own stock in their client). In short, the plaintiff faces a "Catch 22" dilemma in suing the auditor: it cannot plead fraud with particularity until it obtains discovery, and it cannot obtain discovery under the PSLRA until it pleads fraud with particularity.

[35] Consulting fees paid by audit clients exploded during the 1990s. According to the Panel on Audit Effectiveness, who was appointed in 1999 by the Public Oversight Board at the request of the SEC to study audit practices, "audit firms' fees from consulting services for their SEC clients increased from 17% . . . of audit fees in 1990 to 67% . . . in 1999." *See* Panel on Audit Effectiveness, REPORT AND RECOMMENDATIONS, Exposure Draft 102 (May 31, 2000) (alteration in original) at 102. In 1990, the Panel found that 80% of the Big Five firms' SEC clients received no consulting services from their auditors, and only 1% of those SEC clients paid consulting fees exceeding their auditing fees to the Big Five. *Id.* at 102. While the Panel found only marginal changes during the 1990s, later studies have found that consulting fees have become a multiple of the audit fee for large public corporations. *See infra* at note 36 and accompanying text.

[36] A survey by the *Chicago Tribune* this year finds that the one hundred largest corporations in the Chicago area (determined on the basis of market capitalization) paid on average consulting fees to their auditors that were over three times the audit fee paid to the same auditor. *See* Janet Kidd Stewart and Andrew Countryman, *Local Audit Conflicts Add Up: Consulting Deals, Hiring Practices In Question,* CHI. TRIB., Feb. 24, 2002, at C-1. The extreme example in this study was Motorola, which had over a 16:1 ratio between consulting fees and audit fees.

profit potential in consulting than in auditing, but they began during the 1990s to compete based on a strategy of "low balling," under which auditing services were offered at rates that were marginal to arguably below cost. The rationale for such a strategy was that the auditing function was essentially a loss leader by which more lucrative services could be marketed.

Appealing as this argument may seem—that the provision of consulting services eroded auditor independence—it is subject to at least one important rebuttal. Those who defend the propriety of consulting services by auditors respond that the growth of consulting services made little real difference, because the audit firm is already conflicted by the fact that the client pays its fees.[37] More importantly, the audit partner of a major client (such as Enron) is particularly conflicted by the fact that such partner has virtually a "one-client" practice. Should the partner lose that client for any reason, the partner will likely need to find employment elsewhere. In short, both critics and defenders of the status quo tend to agree that the audit partner is already inevitably compromised by the desire to hold the client. From this premise, a prophylactic rule prohibiting the firm's involvement in consulting would seemingly achieve little.

While true in part, this analysis misses a key point: namely, how difficult it is for the client to fire the auditor in the real world. Because of this difficulty, the unintended consequence of combining consulting services with auditing services in one firm is that the union of the two enables the client to more effectively threaten the auditing firm in a "low visibility" way. To illustrate this point, let us suppose, for example, that a client becomes dissatisfied with an auditor who refuses to endorse the aggressive accounting policy favored by its management. The client cannot easily fire the auditor. Firing the auditor is a costly step, inviting potential public embarrassment, public disclosure of the reasons for the auditor's dismissal or resignation, and potential SEC intervention.[38] However, if the auditor also becomes a consultant to the client, the client can then easily terminate the auditor as a consultant (or reduce its use of the firm's consulting services) in retaliation for the auditor's intransigence. This low visibility response requires no disclosure, invites no SEC oversight, and yet disciplines the audit firm so that it would possibly be motivated to replace the intransigent audit partner. In effect, the client can either bribe (or coerce) the auditor in its core professional role by raising (or reducing) its use of consulting services.

---

[37] For the academic view that "auditor independence" is an impossible quest, in large part because the client pays the auditor's fees, see SEAN O'CONNER, THE INEVITABILITY OF ENRON AND THE IMPOSSIBILITY OF AUDITOR INDEPENDENCE UNDER THE CURRENT AUDIT SYSTEM (forthcoming in 2003, *available at* http://papers.ssrn.com/sol3/delivery.cfm/SSRN_10303181_code020311510pdf? abstractidW303181.

[38] Item 4 ("Changes in Registrants Certifying Accountant") of Form 8-K requires a "reporting" company to file a Form 8-K within five days after the resignation or dismissal of the issuer's independent accountant or that of the independent accountant for a significant subsidiary of the issuer. The Form 8-K must then provide the elaborate disclosures mandated by Item 304 of Regulation S-K relating to any dispute or disagreement between the auditor and the accountant. *See* Changes in Disagreements With Accountants on Accounting and Financial Disclosure, 17 C.F.R. 228.304 (2001).

Of course, this argument that the client can discipline and threaten the auditor/consultant in ways that it could not discipline the simple auditor is based more on logic than actual case histories. But it does fit the available data. A recent study by academic accounting experts, based on proxy statements filed during the first half of 2001, finds that those firms that purchased more non-audit services from their auditor (as a percentage of the total fee paid to the audit firm) were more likely to fit the profile of a firm engaging in earnings management.[39]

B. The Irrational Market Story

Alternatively, Enron's and Arthur Andersen's downfalls can be seen as consequences of a classic bubble that overtook the equity markets in the late 1990s and produced a market euphoria in which gatekeepers became temporarily irrelevant. Indeed, in an atmosphere of euphoria in which stock prices ascend endlessly and exponentially, gatekeepers are largely a nuisance to management, which does not need them to attract investors. Gatekeepers are necessary only when investors are cautious and skeptical, and in a market bubble, caution and skepticism are largely abandoned. Arguably, auditors were used in such an environment only because SEC rules mandated their use or because no individual firm wished to call attention to itself by becoming the first to dispense with them. In any event, if we assume that the auditor will be largely ignored by euphoric investors, the rational auditor's best competitive strategy (at least for the short term) was to become as acquiescent and low cost as possible.

For the securities analyst, a market bubble presented an even more serious problem: it is simply dangerous to be sane in an insane world. The securities analyst who prudently predicted reasonable growth and stock appreciation was quickly left in the dust by the investment guru who prophesized a new investment paradigm in which revenues and costs were less important than the number of "hits" on a website. Moreover, as the IPO market soared in the 1990s, securities analysts became celebrities and valuable assets to their firms;[40] indeed, they became the principal means by which investment banks competed for IPO clients, as the underwriter with the "star" analyst could produce the biggest first day stock price spike. But as their salaries thus soared, analysts' compensation came increasingly from the investment banking side of their firms. Hence, just as in the case of the auditor, the analyst's economic position became increasingly dependent on favoring the interests of persons outside their profession (i.e.,

---

[39] See Richard Frankel et al., Marilyn Johnson, and Karen Nelson, *The Relation Between Auditors' Fees for Non-Audit Services and Earnings Quality* (MIT Sloan School of Management Working Paper No. 4330-02 (2002) (available from Social Sciences Research Network at www.ssrn.com at id. 296557). Firms purchasing more non-audit services were found more likely to just meet or beat analysts' forecasts, which is the standard profile of the firm playing "the numbers game."

[40] For the view that investment banking firms changed their competitive strategies on or around 1996 and thereafter sought the "popular, high-profile analyst" as a means of acquiring IPO clients, see Morgenson, supra note 27, at Section 3-1 (quoting chief investment officer at Trust Company of the West).

consultants in the case of the auditor, and investment bankers in the case of the analyst) who had little reason to respect or observe the standards or professional culture within the gatekeeper's profession.

The common denominator linking these examples is that, as auditors increasingly sought consulting income and as analysts increasingly competed to maximize investment banking revenues, the gatekeepers' need to preserve their reputational capital for the long run slackened. Arguably, it could become more profitable for firms to realize the value of their reputational capital by trading on it in the short-run than by preserving it forever. Indeed, if it were true that auditing became a loss leader in the 1990s, one cannot expect firms to expend resources or decline business opportunities in order to protect reputations that were only marginally profitable.

C. Towards Synthesis

These explanations still do not fully explain why reputational capital built up over decades might be sacrificed (or, more accurately, liquidated) once legal risks decline and/or a bubble develops. Here, additional factors need to be considered.

1. The Increased Incentive for Short-Term Stock Price Maximization

The pressure on gatekeepers to acquiesce in earnings management was not constant over time, but rather grew during the 1990s. In particular, during the 1990s, executive compensation shifted from being primarily cash-based to being primarily equity-based. The clearest measure of this change is the growth in stock options. Over the last decade, stock options rose from five percent of shares outstanding at major U.S. companies to fifteen percent—a three hundred percent increase.[41] The value of these options rose by an even greater percentage and over a dramatically shorter period: from $50 billion in 1997 in the case of the 2,000 largest corporations to $162 billion in 2000— an over three hundred percent rise in three years.[42] Stock options create an obvious and potentially perverse incentive to engage in short-run, rather than long-term, stock price maximization because executives can exercise their stock options and sell the underlying shares on the same day.[43] In truth, this ability was, itself, the product of

---

[41] *See* Gretchen Morgenson, *Corporate Conduct: News Analysis; Bush Failed to Stress Need to Rein in Stock Options*, N.Y. TIMES, July 11, 2002, at C-1; *see also* Gretchen Morgenson, *Market Watch: Time For Accountability At the Corporate Candy Store*, N.Y. TIMES, Mar. 31, 2002, § 3, at 1.

[42] *See* Morgenson, *Corporate Conduct, supra* note 41, at C-1 (citing study by Sanford C. Bernstein & Co.). Thus, if $162 billion is the value of all options in these 2,000 companies, aggressive accounting policies that temporarily raise stock prices by as little as ten percent create a potential gain for executives of over $16 billion—a substantial incentive.

[43] This point has now been made by a variety of commentators who have called for minimum holding periods or other curbs on stock options. These include Henry M. Paulson, Jr., chief executive of Goldman, Sachs, and Senator John McCain of Arizona. *See* David Leonhardt, *Corporate Conduct: Compensation: Anger At Executives' Profits Fuels Support for Stock Curb*, N.Y. TIMES, July 9, 2002, at A-1.

deregulatory reform in the early 1990s, which relaxed the rules under Section 16(b) of the Securities Exchange Act of 1934 to permit officers and directors to exercise stock options and sell the underlying shares without holding the shares for the previously required six-month period.[44] Thus, if executives inflate the stock price of their company through premature revenue recognition or other classic earnings management techniques, they could quickly bail out in the short term by exercising their options and selling, leaving shareholders to bear the cost of the stock decline when the inflated stock price could not be maintained over subsequent periods. Given these incentives, it becomes rational for corporate executives to use lucrative consulting contracts, or other positive and negative incentives, to induce gatekeepers to engage in conduct that made the executives very rich. The bottom line is then that the growth of stock options placed gatekeepers under greater pressure to acquiesce in short-term oriented financial and accounting strategies.

2. The Absence of Competition

The Big Five obviously dominated a very concentrated market. Smaller competitors could not expect to develop the international scale or brand names that the Big Five possessed simply by quoting a cheaper price. More importantly, in a market this concentrated, implicit collusion develops easily. Each firm could develop and follow a common competitive strategy in parallel without fear of being undercut by a major competitor. Thus, if each of the Big Five were to prefer a strategy under which it acquiesced to clients at the cost of an occasional litigation loss and some public humiliation, it could more easily observe this policy if it knew that it would not be attacked by a holier-than-thou rival stressing its greater reputation for integrity as a competitive strategy. This approach does not require formal collusion but only the expectation that one's competitors would also be willing to accept litigation losses and occasional public humiliation as a cost of doing business.

Put differently, either in a less concentrated market where several dozen firms competed or in a market with low barriers to entry, it would be predictable that some dissident firm would seek to market itself as distinctive for its integrity. But in a market of five firms (and only four for the future), this is less likely.

---

[44] Rule 16b-3(d) expressly permits an officer or director otherwise subject to the "short-swing" profit provisions of Section 16(b) of the Securities Exchange Act of 1934 to exercise a qualified stock option and sell the underlying shares immediately "if at least six months elapse from the date of the acquisition of the derivative security to the date of disposition of the . . . underlying equity security." *See* 17 C.F.R. 240.16b-3(d)(3) (2003). The SEC comprehensively revised its rules under Section 16(b) in 1991, in part to facilitate the use of stock options as executive compensation and to "reduce the regulatory burden" under Section 16(b). *See* Ownership Reports and Trading by Officers, Directors and Principal Security Holders, Securities Exchange Act Release No. 34-28869, 1991 SEC LEXIS 171 (Feb. 8, 1991). A premise of this reform was that "holding derivative securities is functionally equivalent to holding the underlying equity security for purpose of Section 16." *Id.* at *35–*36. Hence, the SEC permitted the tacking of the option holding period with the stock's holding period, thereby enabling officers and directors to exercise options and sell on the same day (if the option had already been held six months).

3. Observability

That a fraud occurs is not necessarily the fault of auditors. If auditors can respond to any fraud by asserting that they were victimized by a dishonest management, they may be able to avoid the permanent loss of reputational capital—particularly so long as their few competitors have no desire to exploit their failures because they are more or less equally vulnerable. Put differently, a system of reputational intermediaries works only if fault can be reliably assigned.

4. Principal/Agent Problems

Auditing firms have always known that an individual partner could be dominated by a large client and might defer excessively to such a client in a manner that could inflict liability on the firm. Thus, early on, they developed systems of internal monitoring that were far more elaborate than anything that law firms have yet attempted. But within the auditing firm, this internal monitoring function is not all powerful. After all, it is not itself a profit center. With the addition of consulting services as a major profit center, a natural coalition developed between the individual audit partner and the consulting divisions; each had a common interest in checking and overruling the firm's internal audit division when the latter's prudential decisions would prove costly to them. Cementing this marriage was the use of incentive fees. If those providing software consulting services for an audit firm were willing to offer the principal audit partner for a client a fee of 1% (or so) of any contract sold to the partner's audit client, few others within the firm might see any reason to object. If software consulting contracts (hypothetically, for $50 million) were then sold to the client, the audit partner might now receive more compensation from incentive fees for cross-selling than from auditing and thus had greater reason to value the client's satisfaction above his interest in the firm's reputational capital. More importantly, the audit partner now also had an ally in the consultants, who similarly would want to keep their mutual client satisfied. Together, they would form a coalition potentially able to override the protests of their firm's internal audit unit (if the firm felt that an overly aggressive policy was being followed). While case histories exactly matching this pattern cannot yet be identified, abundant evidence does exist for the thesis that incentive fees can bias audit decision-making.[45] Interestingly, Enron itself presents a fact pattern in which the audit firm's on-the-scene quality control officer was overruled and replaced.[46]

---

[45] One of the most famous recent accounting scandals involved the Phar-Mor chain of retail stores. There, after the audit partner for Coopers & Lybrand was denied participation in profit sharing because he had insufficiently cross-sold the firm's services, he sold $900,000 worth of business in the next year (most of it to Phar-Mar and its affiliates), but then failed to detect $985 million in inflated earnings by Phar-Mor over the following three years. *See* Prentice, *supra* note 10, at 184; Max H. Bazerman et al., *The Impossibility of Auditor Independence*, SLOAN MANAGEMENT REV. (Summer 1997) at 89.

[46] Carl E. Bass, an internal audit partner, warned other Andersen partners in 1999 that Enron's accounting practices were dangerous. David Duncan and Enron executives are alleged to have had Mr. Bass removed from the Enron account within a few weeks after his protest. *See* Robert Manor & Jon Yates,

III. IMPLICATIONS

A. Models for Reform

Does it matter much which of the foregoing two stories—the deterrence story or the bubble story—is deemed more persuasive? Although they are complementary rather than contradictory, their relative plausibility matters greatly in terms of deciding what reform are necessary or desirable. To the extent one accepts the deterrence story, we may need legal changes. In principle, these changes could either raise the costs or lower the benefits of acquiescence to auditors. To the extent one accepts the bubble story, the problem may be self-correcting. That is, once the bubble bursts, gatekeepers come back into fashion, as investors become skeptics who once again demand assurances that only credible reputational intermediaries can provide. To the extent one takes the reverse position, regulatory action is needed.

This comment is not intended to resolve this debate, except in one small respect. Alan Greenspan has recently espoused the bubble story and expressed the view that the market will largely self-correct on its own.[47] His arguments have some merit. Although reasonable people can certainly debate the degree to which markets can reform themselves and the reciprocal degree to which legal interventions are necessary, one special area stands out where regulatory interventions seem essential, because ultimately the market cannot easily self-correct within this area without external interventions. Enron has shown that we have a "rule-based" system of accounting that arguably only asks the gatekeeper to certify the issuer's compliance with an inventory of highly technical rules—without the auditor necessarily taking responsibility for the overall accuracy of the issuer's statement of its financial position. Understandably, the SEC has called for a shift to a "principles-based" system of accounting,[48] and this shift cannot come simply through private action.

Even as a matter of theory, the gatekeeper's services have value only if the gatekeeper is certifying compliance with a meaningful substantive standard. Yet, it is seldom not within the power of the individual gatekeeper to determine that standard of measurement. In

---

Faceless Andersen Partner in Spotlight's Glare; David Duncan Vital to Federal Probe After Plea, CHI. TRIB., April 14, 2002, at C-1. If nothing else, this evidence suggests that the internal audit function within one Big Five firm could be overcome when the prospective consulting fees were high enough.

[47] *See* Remarks by Chairman Alan Greenspan, *Corporate Governance*, Remarks at the Stern School of Business, New York University, New York, New York (Mar. 26, 2002) (available at the Federal Reserves website at www.federalreserve.gov/boarddocs/speeches). In his view, earnings management came to dominate management's agenda, and as a result: "[I]t is not surprising that since 1998 earnings restatements have proliferated. This situation is a far cry from earlier decades when, if my recollection serves me correctly, firms competed on the basis of which one had the most conservative set of books. Short-term stock price values then seemed less of a focus than maintaining unquestioned credit worthiness." *Id.* at 4. Specifically, he finds that "[P]erceptions of the reliability of firms' financial statements are increasingly reflected in yield spreads of corporate bonds" and that other signs of self-correction are discernible. *Id.* at 5.

[48] *See* Judy Mathenson and Neil Roland, *SEC's Pitt Calls for 'Principles-Based' Accounting*, BLOOMBERG NEWS, Feb. 19, 2002 (available on LEXIS/NEXIS; news; curnws file).

the case of auditors, organizational reform of the accounting firm thus will mean little without substantive reform of substantive accounting principles.

Again, reasonable persons can disagree as to the best means of improving the quality of the financial standards with which the auditor measures compliance. One means would be to require the auditor to certify not simply compliance with GAAP, but to read the auditor's certification that the issuer's financial statements "fairly present" its financial position to mean that these financial statements provide the necessary disclosures for understanding the issuer's overall financial position. This probably was the law (and may still be). Interestingly, the SEC's staff has recently sought to resurrect the classic decision of Henry Friendly in *U.S. v. Simon*[49] by arguing that compliance with GAAP was not itself the standard by which the auditor's performance was to be measured.[50] The alternative route, which does not involve greater reliance on litigation, is to depend upon substantive regulation: here, this would require greater activism by the Financial Accounting Standards Board ("FASB"), which in the past has been constrained by industry and congressional interference. Insulating the FASB and assuring its financial independence would thus be appropriate initial steps toward reform.[51]

B. Lessons for Lawyers

What are the lessons for lawyers that emerge from this tour of the problems and failings of our allied professions? Arguably, just as analysts and auditors do, securities lawyers serve investors as the ultimate consumers of their services. Conceptually, however, differences exist because lawyers specialize in designing transactions to avoid regulatory, legal, and other costly hurdles, but seldom provide meaningful certifications to investors. Still, the same "commodification" of professional services that reshaped the accounting profession has also impacted the legal profession. Thus, there may be handwriting on the wall that, as auditing firms evolved from offering a single professional service into a shopping center of professional services, they lost internal control. Bluntly, the same fate could face lawyers. Indeed, the audit firm always knew that the indi-

---

[49] 425 F.2d 796 (2d Cir. 1969).

[50] *See* Floyd Norris, *An Old Case Is Returning to Haunt Auditors,* N.Y. TIMES, Mar. 1, 2002, at C-1 (noting that SEC Chairman Harvey Pitt has taken to citing *Simon*).

[51] In this author's judgment, Congress has no more business legislating laws of accounting than it does legislating a law of gravity. But it can create a neutral and independent body to promulgate substantive accounting rules. At present, FASB receives much of its revenues from charitable contributions from persons interested in accounting. Unfortunately, those most interested in accounting (i.e., Enron) have the worst incentives. In addition, insulated bodies may need to be subjected to greater sunlight and transparency. These issues were recently the focus of hearings on June 26, 2002 before the Subcommittee on Commerce, Trade and Consumer Protection of the Committee on Energy and Commerce of the House of Representatives, at which this author testified. *See Strengthening Accounting Oversight: Hearing Before the Subcomm. On Commerce, Trade and Consumer Prot.,* 2002 WL 1381128 (June 26, 2002) (statement of John C. Coffee, Jr.), Federal Document Clearinghouse Congressional Testimony, June 26, 2002.

vidual audit partner serving the large client could become conflicted (because the audit partner's job depended on satisfying its single client), but the audit firm also knew
that it could monitor its individual audit partners to manage this conflict. For a long
time, monitoring seemingly worked—at least passably well. More recently, incentive-
based compensation has exacerbated the monitoring problem, and similarly, the evolution of the auditing firm into a financial conglomerate has seriously compromised
old systems of internal control.[52]

Whatever the control problems within accounting firms, law firms have nothing
even remotely approaching the substantial system of internal controls employed by
audit firms (which still did not work for them). The contrast is striking. Both audit
firms and broker-dealers have far more advanced systems of internal quality control
than do law firms. For example, audit firms typically have an in-house "internal standards" or "quality assurance" division, and they rely on periodic "peer review" of their
audits by similarly situated firms. Although peer review, at least as a formal system,
may not work for law firms (because law is an adversarial profession, and also one
obsessed with protecting the attorney-client privilege), this conclusion only raises the
larger question: what will work?[53]

In overview, law firms are today positioned on a learning curve that seems at least a
decade behind auditing firms, as the law firms are moving, much later than auditing
firms, from "ma and pa" single office firms to multi-branch organizations. Across the
legal landscape, the combination of lateral recruitment of partners, based on revenues
generated, plus the movement toward multi-branch law firms means that law firms as
an organization are at least as (and probably more) vulnerable to quality control problems as auditing firms. Yet, they lack the minimal institutional safeguards that the
latter have long used (with only limited success) to protect quality control. Logically,
law firms should perceive the need to institutionalize a greater quality control function. Realistically, however, law firms have not experienced the same pattern of devastating financial losses that, during the 1980s, threatened the very viability of auditing
firms.[54] Thus, as a practical matter, law firms will probably not respond before the first

---

[52] Enron itself shows this pattern, as the Andersen audit quality partner who challenged some of the
aggressive accounting policies that Enron wanted to pursue was outflanked and eventually transferred. *See*
Manor & Yates, *supra* note 46.

[53] This short comment is not the best vehicle in which to outline specific reforms. Nonetheless, one
could imagine law firms creating a "quality control" office and staffing it with the sixty-year-old partners
who today tend to be pushed into retirement because they no longer can work the around-the-clock pace
of young partners. Precisely because such partners have experience, they would have credibility with their
peers in the firm in seeking to maintain firm quality.

[54] Various reasons can be given for the expansion of auditors' liability during the 1970s and 1980s.
Some stress the revision of the Restatement (Second) of Torts, whose Section 552, adopted in 1975, vastly
expanded the auditor's liability for negligence by substituting a foreseeability standard for the former
privity test. *See* Thomas L. Grossman, *The Fallacy of Expanding Accountants' Liability,* 1988 COLUM. BUS.
L. REV. 213, 221–225 (1998). Others emphasize the development of the class action in the 1980s, and in
particular, the "fraud on the market" doctrine, developed by the lower federal courts in the early 1980s

large financial disaster befalls a major law firm and motivates greater attention to internal control. Predictably but sadly, only then will "bottom line"-oriented law partners recognize that the "bottom line" includes liabilities as well as revenues.

CONCLUSION

This essay has sought to explain that Enron is more about gatekeeper failure than board failure. It has also sought to explain when gatekeepers (or "reputational intermediaries") are likely to fail. Put simply, reputational capital is not an asset that professional services firms will inevitably hoard and protect. Logically, as legal exposure to liability declines and as benefits of acquiescence in the client's demands increase, gatekeeper failure should correspondingly increase—as it did in the 1990s. Market bubbles can also explain gatekeeper failure (and this perspective probably works better in the case of the securities analysts, who faced little liability in the past), because in an environment of euphoria investors do not rely on gatekeepers (and hence gatekeepers have less leverage with respect to their clients).

Popular commentary has instead used softer-edged concepts—such as "infectious greed"[55] and a decline in morality—to explain the same phenomena. Yet, there is little evidence that "greed" has ever declined; nor is it clear that there are relevant policy options for addressing it. In contrast, focusing on gatekeepers tells us that there are special actors in a system of private corporate governance whose incentives must be regulated.

Reasonable persons can always disagree on what reforms are desirable. But the starting point for an intelligent debate is the recognition that the two major, contemporary

---

and accepted by the Supreme Court in Basic, Inc. v. Levinson, 485 U.S. 224 (1988), which dispensed with the need to prove individual reliance and thereby increased the likelihood of class certification. Whatever the cause of the litigation explosion, the impact of litigation costs on accounting firms is clearer. By 1992, securities fraud litigation costs for simply the six largest accounting firms accounted for $783 million or more than 14% of their audit revenues. In addition, they faced billions of dollars in potential exposure. See Private Litigation Under the Federal Securities Laws: Hearings Before the Subcommittee on Securities of the Senate Committee on Banking, Housing and Urban Affairs, 103rd Cong., 1st Sess. No. 103-431 (1993) (statement of Jake L. Netterville), reprinted in Fed. Sec. L. Rep. (CCH) No. 1696, (January 10, 1996). One major auditing firm, Laventhol & Horwath, did fail and enter bankruptcy as a result of litigation and associated scandals growing out of the savings and loan scandals of the 1980s. See What Role Should CPA's be Playing in Audit Reform?, PARTNER'S REPORT—THE MONTHLY UPDATE FOR CPA FIRM OWNERS (April 2002) (discussing experience of Laventhol & Horwath). The accounting profession's bitter experience with class litigation in the 1980s and 1990s probably explains why it became the strongest and most organized champion of the Private Securities Litigation Reform Act of 1995.

[55] Federal Reserve Chairman Alan Greenspan has coined this rhetorical phrase, saying that "An infectious greed seemed to grip much of our business community." See Floyd Norris, The Markets: Market Place; Yes, He Can Top That, N.Y. TIMES, July 17, 2002, at A-1. This article's more cold-blooded approach would say that the rational incentives created by stock options and equity compensation overcame the limited self-regulatory safeguards that the accounting profession had internalized.

crises now facing the securities markets—i.e., the collapse of Enron and the growing controversy over securities analysts, which began with the New York Attorney General's investigation into Merrill Lynch—involve at bottom the same problem: both are crises motivated by the discovery by investors that reputational intermediaries upon whom they relied were conflicted and seemingly sold their interests short. Neither the law nor the market has yet solved either of these closely related problems.

Auditors and Analysts: An Analysis of the Evidence and Reform Proposals in Light of the Enron Experience

John C. Coffee, Jr. *

I. INTRODUCTION

I want to thank the Committee for inviting me to appear today. Because I realize that you are covering a broad range of issues and have only limited time to listen to any individual witness, I believe that my contribution will be the most useful if I focus on just two issues: (1) What powers, duties, and standards should Congress include in any legislation that establishes a self-regulatory body to oversee the auditing profession? and (2) How should Congress respond to the evidence that conflicts of interest do bias the recommendations and research of securities analysts?

If we focus only on Enron, it cannot prove by itself that there is a crisis or that either auditors or securities analysts have been compromised by conflicts of interest. By itself, Enron is only an anecdote—bizarre, vivid, and tragic as it may be. But Enron does not stand alone. As I elaborated in detail in testimony before the Senate Commerce Committee on December 17, 2001 (and thus will not repeat at any length here), Enron is part of a pattern. As the liabilities faced by auditors declined in the 1990s and as the incentives auditors perceived to acquiesce in management's desire to manage earnings increased over the same period (because of the opportunities to earn highly lucrative consulting revenues), there has been an apparent erosion in the quality of financial reporting. Assertive as this conclusion may sound, a burgeoning literature exists on earnings management, which indicates that earnings management is conscious, widespread and tolerated by auditors within, at least, very wide limits.[1] Objective data also show a decline in the reliability of published financial results. To give only the simplest quantitative measure, from 1997 to 2000, there were 1,080 earnings restatements by

---

* JOHN C. COFFEE, JR. & ADOLF A. BERLE, AUDITORS & ANALYSTS: AN ANALYSIS OF THE EVIDENCE AND REFORM PROPOSALS IN LIGHT OF THE ENRON EXPERIENCE (Mar. 5, 2002), *available at* http://banking.senate.gov/02_03hrg/030502/coffee.htm.

[1] John C. Coffee Jr., *The Acquiescent Gatekeeper: Reputational Intermediaries, Auditor Independence and the Governance of Accounting* (May 2001) (unpublished Columbia Law and Economics working paper No. 0191), *available at* http://papers.ssrn.com/sol3/papers.cfm?abstract_id=270944.

publicly held companies.[2] Most importantly, there has been a significant recent increase in the number of earnings restatements. Earnings restatements averaged 49 per year from 1990 to 1997, then increased to 91 in 1998, and soared to 150 in 1999 and 156 in 2000.[3] Put simply, this sudden spike in earnings restatements is neither coincidental nor temporary.

Worse yet, the accounting profession is conspicuous by its lack of any meaningful mechanism for internal self-discipline. This void contrasts starkly with the governance structure of the broker-dealer industry, where the National Association of Securities Dealers ("NASD") administers a vigorous and effective system of internal discipline. Because both brokers and auditors ultimately serve the same constituency—i.e., investors—this disparity is unjustifiable.

Put simply, American corporate governance depends at bottom on the credibility of the numbers. Only if financial data is accurate can our essentially private system of corporate governance operate effectively. Today, there is doubt about the reliability of reported financial data—and also about the independence and objectivity of the two watchdogs who monitor and verity that data: namely, auditors and securities analysts.

What should Congress do about the crisis? While there is a case for raising the liabilities that auditors and analysts face, I am fully aware that many are skeptical of private enforcement of law through class and derivative actions. Essentially, this asks a third watchdog—the plaintiff's attorney—to monitor the failings of the first two (auditors and analysts), and plaintiffs' attorneys may have their own disincentives. Also, it may still be too early to ask Congress to revisit the Private Securities Litigation Reform Act of 1995 (the "PSLRA"). Thus, both in my December appearance before the Senate Commerce Committee and again today, I am urging the Congress to give fuller consideration to public enforcement through the creation or strengthening of self-regulatory organizations ("SROs"). An SRO already exists with jurisdiction over securities analysts (i.e., the NASD), but one needs to be created from whole cloth in the case of auditors. Thus, my comments will focus first on the creation of a new SRO for auditors and then how to strengthen the oversight of analysts.

II. AN SRO FOR AUDITORS: SOME SUGGESTED STANDARDS

The governance of accounting is today fragmented and indeed Balkanized among (1) state boards of accountancy, (2) private bodies, of which there are essentially seven, and (3) the SEC, which has broad anti-fraud jurisdiction, but less certain authority

---

[2] George Moriarty & Philip Livingston, *Quantitative Measures of the Quality of Financial Reporting*, FIN. EXECUTIVE, July–Aug. 2001, at 53.

[3] *Id.* 715 of these restatements involved Nasdaq listed companies; 228 involved New York Stock Exchange companies; the rest were listed either on the American Stock Exchange or traded in the over-the-counter market. Premature revenue recognition was found to be the leading cause of restatements.

under Rule 102(e) of its Rules of Practice.[4] Disciplinary authority is particularly divided within the profession. The Quality Control Inquiry Committee ("QCIC") of the SEC Practice Section of the American Institute of Certified Public Accountants ("AICPA") is delegated responsibility to investigate alleged audit failures involving SEC clients arising from litigation or regulatory investigations, but it is charged only with determining if there are deficiencies in the auditing firm's system of quality control. The Professional Ethics Executive Committee ("PEEC") of the AICPA is supposed to take individual cases on referral from the QCIC, but as a matter of "fairness" PEEC will automatically defer, at the subject firm's request, any investigation until all litigation or regulatory proceedings have been completed. In short, the investor's interest in purging corrupt or fraudulent auditors from the profession is subordinated to the firm's interest in settling litigation cheap, uninfluenced by any possible findings of ethical lapses.

Little in this system merits retention. Legislation is necessary to create a body that would have at least the same powers, duties, and obligations as the NASD. In truth, however, the legislation that created the NASD in 1938 (the Maloney Act) is not an ideal model, given its general lack of specific guidance. Rather, model legislation should have the following elements:

1. *Rule-Making Power.* The SRO should be specifically authorized to (1) address and prohibit conflicts of interest and other deficiencies that might jeopardize either auditor independence or the public's confidence in the accuracy and reliability of published financial statements, and (2) establish mandatory procedures, including procedures for the retention of accountants by publicly-held companies and for the interaction and relationship between the accountants and audit committees. This is a broad standard—and deliberately so. It could authorize the SRO to require that auditors be retained and/or fired by the audit committee and not by the company's management. In addition, the SRO should be authorized to affirmatively mandate the adoption and use of new or improved quality control systems, as they from time to time become accepted.

2. *Mandatory Membership.* All outside auditors preparing or certifying the financial statements of publicly-held companies or of companies conducting registered public offerings would be required to be members in good standing, and suspension or ouster from the SRO would render an auditor unable to certify the financial statements of such companies.

3. *SEC Supervision.* SEC approval of the initial registration of such an SRO and of all amendments to its rules would be mandated, just as in the case of the NASD. The

---

[4] 17 C.F.R § 201.102 (1998). The SEC's authority under Rule 102(e) was clouded by the D.C. Circuit's decision in Checkosky v. SEC, 139 F.3d 221 (D.C. Cir. 1998) (dismissing Rule 102(e) proceeding against two accountants of a "Big Five" firm). The SEC revised Rule 102 in late 1998 in response to this decision (see Securities Act. Rel. No. 7593 (Oct. 18, 1998) *available at* 1998 SEC LEXIS 2256 (last visited Jun 18, 2003)), but its authority in this area is still subject to some doubt that Congress may wish to remove or clarify.

SEC would also have authority to amend the SRO's rules in compliance with a statutory "public interest" standard. Finally, the SEC should have authority to sanction, fine, or suspend the SRO and to remove or suspend its officers or directors for cause.

4. *Enforcement Powers.* The SRO should have the same authority to impose financial penalties or to suspend or disbar an auditor from membership, or to suspend, disbar, fine, or censure any associated professional. Such fines and penalties should not require proof of fraud, but only a demonstration of negligent or unethical conduct. Subpoena authority should also be conferred, and a failure to cooperate or provide evidence should be grounds for discipline or dismissal.

5. *Duties of Supervisory Personnel.* A common response of organizations caught in a scandal or a criminal transaction is to blame everything on a "rogue" employee. Yet, such "rogues" are often responding to winks and nods from above (real or perceived) or to an organizational culture that encourages risk-taking (Enron is again symptomatic). The federal securities laws impose duties on supervisory personnel in brokerage firms to monitor their employees, and a parallel standard should apply to supervisory personnel in auditing firms.

6. *Governance.* The SRO should have at least a supermajority (say, 66 2/3%) of "public" members, who are not present or recently past employees or associated persons of the auditing industry.

7. *Prompt Enforcement.* The practice now followed by PEEC of deferring all disciplinary investigations until civil litigation and regulatory investigations have been resolved is self-defeating and unacceptable. It might, however, be possible to render the findings and disciplinary measures taken by the SRO inadmissible in private civil litigation.

III. SECURITIES ANALYSTS

A. What Do We Know About Analyst Objectivity?

A number of studies have sought to assess the impact of conflicts of interest upon the objectivity of securities analyst recommendations. Additional evidence was also recently collected at hearings held in June 2001 by the Subcommittee on Capital Markets, Insurance and Government-Sponsored Enterprises of the House Financial Services Committee. This data is probably more germane, and merits greater reliance, than the well-known statistic that an alleged 100:1 ratio exists between the "buy" recommendations and "sell" recommendations made by securities analysts. Although the actual ratio may be somewhat less extreme than 100:1,[5] the real problem with this

---

[5] A December 2000 Thomson Financial Survey reported that 71% of all analyst recommendations were "buys" and only 2.1% were "sells." Apparently, only 1% of 28,000 recommendations issued by analysts during late 1999 and most of 2000 were "sells." This study also finds that the overall "buy" to "sell" ratio shifted from 6:1 in the early 1990s to 100:1 by sometime in 2000. Of course, this shift also coincided with the Nasdaq bull market of the 1990s.

statistic is that it is not necessarily the product of conflicts of interest. That is, analysts employed by brokerage firms (as all "sell-side" analysts are) have a natural incentive to encourage purchase or sale transactions. For this purpose, "buy" recommendations are more useful than "sell" recommendations, because all clients can buy a stock, but only existing holders can sell, as a practical matter.

Other data better illustrates the impact of conflicts of interest on analysts. Among the most salient findings from recent research are the following:

1. *Conflict of Interests.* Several studies find that "independent" analysts (i.e., analysts not associated with the underwriter for a particular issuer) behave differently from analysts who are so associated with the issuer's underwriter. For example, Roni Michaely and Kent Womack found that the long-run performance of firms recommended by analysts who are associated with an underwriter was significantly worse than the performance of firms recommended by independent securities analysts.[6] They further found that stock prices of firms recommended by analysts associated with lead underwriters fall on average in the thirty days before a recommendation is issued, while the stock prices of firms recommended by analysts not so associated with underwriters rose on average over the same period. Finally, the mean long-run performance of buy recommendations made by analysts on non-clients is more positive than the performance of recommendations made on clients—at least for twelve out of fourteen brokerage firms.

Still another study by *CFO Magazine* reports that analysts who work for full-service investment banking firms have 6% higher earnings forecasts and close to 25% more "buy" recommendations than do analysts at firms without such ties.[7] Similarly, using a sample of 2,400 seasoned equity offerings between 1989 and 1994, Lin and McNichols find that lead and co-underwriter analysts' growth forecasts and, particularly, their recommendations are significantly more favorable than those made by unaffiliated analysts.[8]

2. *Pressure and Retaliation.* In self-reporting studies, securities analysts report that they are frequently pressured to make positive buy recommendations or at least to temper negative opinions.[9] Sixty-one percent of analysts responding to one survey reported personal experience with threats of retaliation from issuer management.[10] Similarly, former Acting SEC Chairman Laura Unger noted in a recent speech that a survey of 300 chief financial officers found that 20% of surveyed CFOs acknowledged withholding business

---

[6] R. Michaely & K.L. Womack, *Conflict of Interest and the Credibility of Underwriter Analyst Recommendations*, 12 REV. FIN. STUD. 653 (1999).

[7] Stephen Barr, *What Chinese Wall*, CFO (Mar. 2000).

[8] Hsiou-wei Lin & Maureen F. McNichols, *Underwriting Relationships and Analysts' Earnings Forecasts and Investment Recommendations*, 25 J. ACCT. & ECON. 101 (1997).

[9] Jane Cote, *Analyst Credibility: The Investor's Perspective*, 351 J. MANAGERIAL ISSUES (2000).

[10] Debbie Galant, *The Hazards of Negative Research Reports*, INSTITUTIONAL INVESTOR (July 1990).

from brokerage firms whose analysts issued unfavorable research.[11] This is a phenomenon that is almost certain to be underreported.

This data should not be over-read. It does not prove that securities research or analyst recommendations are valueless or hopelessly biased, but it does tend to confirm what one would intuitively expect: namely, conflicts of interest count, and conflicted analysts behave differently than unaffiliated or "independent" analysts.

B. The Regulatory Response

In light of public criticism regarding securities analysts and their conflicts of interest, the National Association of Securities Dealers ("NASD") proposed Rule 2711 ("Research Analysts and Research Reports") in early February 2002.[12] Proposed Rule 2711 is lengthy, complex and has not yet been adopted. Nonetheless, because its adoption in some form seems likely, a brief analysis of its contents seems useful as an introduction to what further steps Congress should consider.

Basically, Rule 2711 does seven important things:

(1) It places restrictions on the investment banking department's relationship with the "research" or securities analyst division of an integrated broker-dealer firms;

(2) It restricts the pre-publication review of analyst research reports by the subject company and investment banking personnel;

(3) It prohibits bonus or salary compensation to a research analyst based upon a specific investment banking services transaction;

(4) It prohibits broker-dealers from promising favorable research or ratings as consideration or an inducement for the receipt of business or compensation;

(5) It extends the "quiet period" during which the broker-dealer may not publish research reports regarding a company in an IPO for which the firm is acting as a manager or co-manager for 40 calendar days from the date of the offering;

(6) It restricts analysts' ability to acquire securities from a company prior to an IPO or to purchase or sell for a defined period before or after the publication of research report or a change in a rating or price target; and

(7) It requires extensive disclosure by an analyst of certain stock holdings or compensation or other conflict of interest relationships.

All of these prohibitions are subject to substantial exceptions and/or qualifications, and it is debatable whether some can be effectively monitored. Only time and experience with proposed Rule 2711 can tell us whether its exceptions will overwhelm the

---

[11] Laura Unger, *How Can Analysts Maintain Their Independence,* Remarks at Northwestern Law School (Apr. 19, 2001), *available at* http://www.sec.gov/news/speech/spch477.htm.

[12] S. REP. NO. 2002-21 (2002).

rule. Nonetheless, Rule 2711 represents a serious and commendable effort to police the conflicts of interest that exist within broker-dealer firms that both underwrite securities and provide securities research and recommendations. In this light, the most important question is: what else can or should Congress do? Are there topics or areas that Rule 2711 has not addressed that Congress should address? These are considered below.

C. Congressional Options

The overriding policy question is whether conflicts of interest relating to securities research should be prohibited or only policed. As I will suggest below, this question is not easily answered, because there are costs and imperfections with both options:

1. *Radical Reform: Divorce Investment Banking From Securities Research.* Congress could do what it essentially did a half-century ago in the Glass-Steagall Act:[13] namely, prohibit investment banking firms that underwrite securities from engaging in a specified activity (here, providing securities research to all, or at least certain, customers). Arguably, this is what Congress and the SEC have already proposed to do with respect to the accounting profession: i.e., separate the auditing and consulting roles performed by accountants. Here, the conflict might be thought to be even more serious because the empirical evidence does suggest that the advice given by conflicted analysts is different from the advice given by independent analysts.

But this divestiture remedy is here even more problematic than in the case of the original Glass-Steagall Act. Put simply, securities research is not a self-sufficient line of business that exists on a free-standing basis. To be sure, there are a limited number of "independent" securities research boutiques (Sanford C. Bernstein & Co is probably the best known and most often cited example) that do not do underwriting, but still survive very well. Yet, this is a niche market, catering to institutional investors. Since May 1, 1975 ("Mayday"), when the old system of fixed commissions was ended and brokerage commissions became competitively determined, commissions have shrunk to a razor-thin margin that will not support the costs of securities research. Instead, securities research (i.e., the salaries and expenses of securities research) is essentially subsidized by the investment banking division of the integrated broker-dealer firm. The problematic result is at the same time to subsidize and arguably distort securities research.

This point distinguishes the securities analysts from the accountant. That is, if the auditor is prohibited from consulting for the client, both the auditing and the consulting function will survive. But, in particular because the costs of securities research cannot be easily passed on to the retail customer, a Glass-Steagall divorce might imply that the number of securities analysts would shrink by a substantial fraction.[14] A cynic

---

[13] *See* Glass-Steagall Act of 1933, 12 U.S.C. § 36 et. seq. (separating commercial and investment banking).

[14] I recognize that the number of "buy side" analysts employed by institutional investors might correspondingly increase, but not, I think, to a fully compensating degree. Moreover, "buy side" analysts do not publish their research, thus implying increased informational asymmetries in the market.

might respond: why seek to maximize biased research? Yet, if the number of analysts were to fall by, hypothetically, one half, market efficiency might well suffer, and many smaller firms simply would not be regularly covered by any analyst. Hence, the divestiture approach may entail costs and risks that cannot be reliably estimated.

2. Piecemeal Reform: Policing Conflicts. Proposed Rule 2711 represents an approach of trying to police conflicts and prevent egregious abuse. The practical ability of regulators to do this effectively is always open to question. For example, although proposed Rule 2711 generally prohibits investment banking officials from reviewing research reports prior to publication, it does permit a limited review "to verify the factual accuracy of information in the research report" (see Rule 2711(b)(3)). It is easy to imagine veiled or stylized communications that signal that the investment banking division is displeased and will reduce the analyst's compensation at the next regular salary review. Such signals, even if they consist only of arched eyebrows, are effectively impossible to prohibit. Still, at the margin, intelligent regulation may curtail the more obvious forms of abuse.

Although proposed Rule 2711 addresses many topics, it does not address every topic. Some other topics that may merit attention are discussed below, but they are discussed in the context of suggesting that Congress might give the NASD general policy instructions and ask it to fine-tune more specific rules that address these goals:

1. An Anti-Retaliation Rule. According to one survey,[15] 61% of all analysts have experienced retaliation—threats of dismissal, salary reduction, etc.—as the result of negative research reports. Clearly, negative research reports (and ratings reductions) are hazardous to an analyst's career. Congress could either adopt, or instruct the NASD to adopt, an anti-retaliation rule: no analyst should be fired, demoted, or economically penalized for issuing a negative report, downgrading a rating, or reducing an earnings, price, or similar target. Of course, this rule would not bar staff reductions or reduced bonuses based on economic downturns or individualized performance assessments. Thus, given the obvious possibility that the firm could reduce an analyst's compensation in retaliation for a negative report, but describe its action as based on an adverse performance review of the individual, how can this rule be made enforceable? The best answer may be NASD arbitration. That is, an employee who felt that he or she had been wrongfully terminated or that his or her salary had been reduced in retaliation for a negative research report could use the already existing system of NASD employee arbitration to attempt to reverse the decision. Congress could also establish the burden of proof in such litigation and place it on the firm, rather than on the employee/analyst. Further, Congress could entitle the employee to some form of treble damages or other punitive award to make this form of litigation viable. Finally, Congress could mandate an NASD penalty if retaliation were found, either by an NASD arbitration panel or in an NASD disciplinary proceeding.

---

[15] Galant, *supra* note 10; Cote, *supra* note 9.

2. *A No-Selling Rule.* If we wish the analyst to be a more neutral and objective umpire, one logical step might be to preclude the analyst from direct involvement in selling activities. For example, it is today standard for the "star" analyst to participate in "road shows" managed by the lead underwriters, presenting a highly favorable evaluation of the issuer and even meeting on a one-to-one basis with important institutional investors. Such sales activity seems inconsistent with the much-cited "Chinese Wall" between investment banking and investment research.

Yet, from the investment banking side's perspective, such participation in sales activity in what makes the analyst most valuable to the investment banker and what justifies multimillion dollar salaries to analysts. Restrict such activities, they would argue, and compensation to analysts may decline. Of course, a decline in salaries for super-stars does not imply a reduction in overall coverage or greater market inefficiency.

Although a "no-selling" rule would do much to restore the objectivity of the analyst's role, one counter-consideration is that the audience at the road show is today limited to institutions and high-net-worth individuals. Hence, there is less danger that the analyst will overreach unsophisticated retail investors. For all these reasons, this is an area where a more nuanced rule could be drafted by the NASD at the direction of Congress that would be preferable to a legislative command.

3. *Prohibiting the "Booster Shot."* Firms contemplating an IPO increasingly seek to hire as lead underwriter the firm that employs the star analyst in their field. The issuer's motivation is fueled in large part by the fact that the issuer's management almost invariably is restricted from selling its own stock (by contractual agreement with the underwriters) until the expiration of a lock-up period that typically extends six months from the date of the offering. The purpose of the lock-up agreement is to assure investors that management and the controlling shareholders are not "bailing out" of the firm by means of the IPO. But as a result, the critical date (and market price) for the firm's insiders is not the date of the IPO (or the market value at the conclusion of the IPO), but rather the expiration date of the lock-up agreement six months later (and the market value of the stock on that date). From the perspective of the issuer's management, the role of the analyst is to "maintain a buzz" about the stock and create a price momentum that peaks just before the lock-up's expiration.[16] To do this, the analyst may issue a favorable research report just before the lock-up's expiration (a so-called "booster shot," in the vernacular). To the extent that favorable ratings issued at this point seem particularly conflicted and suspect, an NASD rule might forbid analysts associated with underwriters from issuing research reports for a reasonable period (say, thirty days) both before and after the lock-up expiration date. Proposed Rule 2711 stops well short of this and only extends the "quiet period" so that it now would

[16] This description of the analyst's role (and of the underwriter's interest in attracting "star" analysts) essentially summarizes the description given by three professors of financial economics: Rajesh Aggarwal, Laurie Krigman and Kent Womack. Rajesh Aggarwal et al., *Strategic IPO Underpricing, Information Momentum, and Lockup Expiration Selling*, J. FIN. ECON. (forthcoming).

preclude research reports for this first 40 days after an IPO. Such a limited rule in no way interferes with the dubious tactic of "booster shots."

IV. SUMMARY

The most logical and less overbroad route for Congress to take with regard to securities analysts and their conflicts is to pass legislation giving the NASD more specific guidance and instructions about the goals that they should pursue and then instruct the NASD to conduct the necessary rule-making in order to fine tune this approach. NASD penalties might also properly be raised. This approach spares Congress from having to adopt a detailed code of procedure, avoids inflexibility and rigid legislative rules, and relies on the expertise of the SEC and the NASD, as paradigms of sophisticated administrative agencies.

Enron and Andersen—What Went Wrong and Why Similar Audit Failures Could Happen Again

Matthew J. Barrett*

Years may pass before the public finds out exactly why Andersen's audits of Enron failed to uncover the pervasive accounting fraud at the company, but several factors likely contributed to the audit failure. Unconscious bias, compounded by organizational flaws and a culture at Andersen that emphasized marketing non-audit services to audit clients in an effort to boost profits; significant conflicts of interest and self-interest; and greed all help explain why Andersen did not (1) catch the problems at Enron, and (2) tell the world that such problems existed. Although Congress attempted to address some of the perceived problems in the Sarbanes-Oxley Act of 2002 ("SOx"), several significant gaps remain because the reforms do not adequately address unconscious bias.

Aren't audits supposed to be sign-offs on the appropriateness of a company's financial statements? Not exactly. Before we examine what went wrong in Andersen's audits, we should clarify what an audit hopes to accomplish. In an audit, the auditor evaluates the various representations that an enterprise's management asserts in the financial statements and related notes about the firm's assets and liabilities at a specific date and transactions during a particular accounting period so that the auditor can render a report on (and almost always express an opinion about) those financial statements and accompanying disclosures. Ultimately, the auditor seeks to express an opinion as to whether the financial statements present fairly, in all material respects, the enterprise's financial condition, results of operations, and cash flows in conformity with generally accepted accounting principles. If the examination of the entity's procedures and accounting records allows the auditor to reach an affirmative conclusion, then the auditor will issue an unqualified or "clean" opinion. Even an unqualified opinion, however,

*Professor of Law, Notre Dame Law School. The author gratefully acknowledges valuable research assistance from John J. Barber, a member of the class of 2005 and an Arthur Andersen alum, and helpful comments and suggestions from David R. Herwitz. Copyright © 2003 Matthew J. Barrett.

does not guarantee the accuracy of financial statements; such an opinion provides only "reasonable assurance" that the financial statements fairly present, in all material respects, the enterprise's financial condition, results of operations, and cash flows in conformity with generally accepted accounting principles.[1]

Differing perceptions exist between the assurance that investors and other users of financial statements expect and that which auditors provide.[2] An important study during the early 1990s revealed that almost half of the investors surveyed believed that audited financial statements provide absolute assurance against errors or unintentional misstatements. In that same survey, more than seventy percent expressed a belief that audited financial statements provide absolute assurance against fraud or intentional misstatements. Unfortunately, even in a properly planned and executed audit, fraud can more easily avoid detection than unintentional errors. As a result, investors set a higher standard for auditors to uncover fraud than to discover errors and their expectations exceed the assurance actually provided. The accounting profession has labeled these misconceptions as the "expectation gap."[3]

To reiterate, an audit provides only *reasonable assurance* against material misstatements, whether intentional or unintentional, in the financial statements. In reality, an audit does not guarantee that error or fraud has not affected the financial statements. Similarly, even an unqualified report does not offer any assurance that the enterprise presents a safe investment opportunity or will not fail. At the same time, however, then-existing generally accepted auditing standards required an auditor to assess the risk that errors and fraud may cause the financial statements to contain a material misstatement. In addition, the auditor faced a professional obligation to design the audit to provide reasonable assurance that the examination would detect material errors and misstatements, to exercise professional skepticism, and to perform and evaluate audit procedures to attain the required assurance.[4]

Didn't a jury convict Andersen for fraud in its audits of Enron? No. Although David Duncan, Andersen's former lead audit partner on the Enron account, pleaded guilty to

---

[1] *See generally* DAVID R. HERWITZ & MATTHEW J. BARRETT, MATERIALS ON ACCOUNTING FOR LAWYERS 180–82, 200–04, 215–17, 233–40 (3d ed. 2001).

[2] *Id.* at 227–33.

[3] Marc J. Epstein & Marshall A. Geiger, *Investor Views of Audit Assurance: Recent Evidence of the Expectation Gap*, J. ACCT., Jan. 1994, at 60.

[4] *See* CONSIDERATION OF FRAUD IN A FINANCIAL STATEMENT AUDIT, Statement on Auditing Standards No. 82 (American Inst. of Certified Pub. Accountants 1997) ("SAS No. 82"); *see also* HERWITZ & BARRETT, *supra* note 1, at 231–33. Effective for audits of financial statements for periods beginning on or after Dec. 15, 2002, SAS No. 99, *Consideration of Fraud in a Financial Statement Audit*, supersedes SAS No. 82. CONSIDERATION OF FRAUD IN A FINANCIAL STATEMENT AUDIT, Statement on Auditing Standards No. 99 (American Inst. of Certified Pub. Accountants 2002). In addition to previous expectations, SAS No. 99 now requires an auditor to extend the exercise of professional skepticism to the possibility that fraud may cause a material misstatement. In particular, auditors must evaluate specific fraud risks and document the plan and procedures used to evaluate those risks. *Id.*

obstruction of justice during the SEC's inquiry into Enron's collapse and a federal jury convicted Andersen on one felony count of obstructing justice, those crimes did not relate to the audits themselves.[5]

As to those audits, however, Andersen has acknowledged that its audits failed to require Enron to include two special purpose entities ("SPEs") in the company's consolidated financial statements as generally accepted accounting principles required.[6] Shortly before its bankruptcy filing, Enron restated its financial statements back to 1997 to include those two SPEs.[7] During his Congressional testimony in December 2001, then-Andersen Chief Executive Officer Joseph F. Berardino blamed Enron for withholding "critical information" about the larger SPE, an entity called Chewco. He candidly admitted that Andersen attributed the incorrect accounting on the smaller SPE, a subsidiary of the entity known as LJM1, to "an error in judgment."[8] At that time, financial accounting rules required that, among other things, unrelated parties own an investment equal to at least three percent of the fair value of an SPE's assets to avoid consolidation.[9] (Accounting rule-makers subsequently adjusted that threshold upwards to ten percent,[10] and they continue to study the consolidation requirements.[11] Those rule-makers also now refer to SPEs as "variable interest entities," or VIEs.)[12] In 1999, after reaching some conclusions on valuation issues involving various assets and liabilities, Andersen's audit team originally determined that unrelated parties held more than three percent of the subsidiary's residual equity, thereby meeting the required

---

[5] Flynn McRoberts et al., *A Final Accounting: Repeat offender gets stiff justice*, CHI. TRIB., Sept. 4, 2002, at 1, *available at* 2002 WL 26771271. For a discussion of the Andersen criminal case, see Amon Burton & John S. Dzienkowski, *this book at* 689–762.

[6] *Before the House Committee on Financial Services*, 107th Cong. (Dec. 12, 2001) (statement of Joseph F. Berardino, Managing Partner–Chief Executive Officer, Andersen), *available at* http://news.findlaw.com/hdocs/docs/enron/andersen121201tst.pdf [hereinafter Berardino testimony].

[7] *See* ENRON CORP., FORM 8-K, CURRENT REPORT PURSUANT TO SECTION 13 OR 15(d) OF THE SECURITIES EXCHANGE ACT OF 1934 (filed Nov. 8, 2001) (disclosing required restatement of previously issued financial statements), *available at* http://www.sec.gov/Archives/edgar/data/1024401/000095012901503835/h91831e8-k.txt; *see also* Jonathan Weil, *Enron's Auditors Debated Partnership Losses, Andersen Memos Show That the Accountants Knew of Raptor Status*, WALL. ST. J., Apr. 3, 2002, at C1, *available at* 2002 WL-WSJ 3390542.

[8] Berardino testimony, *supra* note 6.

[9] William W. Bratton, *Enron and the Dark Side of Shareholder Value*, 76 TUL. L. REV. 1275, 1306, n. 118 (2002) (explaining the origin and history of the three percent test); *see also* Gordon Housworth, *Enron & Arthur Anders[e]n: to comply is not enough*, CRITICALEYE, Aug. 2002, at 21–25, *available at* http://www.emeaconsulting.com/Critical_Eye/Critical_EYE_aug_2002.pdf.

[10] CONSOLIDATION OF VARIABLE INTEREST ENTITIES, FASB Interpretation No. 46, ¶¶ 9, C21–25 (Financial Accounting Standards Bd. 2003), *available at* http://www.fasb.org/interp46.pdf.

[11] FINANCIAL ACCOUNTING STANDARDS BOARD, *Project Updates: Consolidations Policy and Procedures* (Apr. 8, 2003), *available at* http://www.fasb.org/project/consol.shtml (last visited June 13, 2003).

[12] CONSOLIDATION OF VARIABLE INTEREST ENTITIES, *supra* note 10, at ¶ 6.

threshold for non-consolidation. In reviewing the transaction in October 2001, Andersen determined that the audit team reached its initial judgment in error and advised Enron to correct the error.[13]

Based upon testimony at Andersen's criminal trial, internal documents that Congressional investigators obtained, and a report by a special committee on Enron's board, an article in *The Wall Street Journal* immediately after Andersen's conviction highlighted inadequate disclosures, questionable transactions with other SPEs, the premature recognition of revenue, and the failure to insist that Enron record adjustments recommended in previous audits as other potential deficiencies in Andersen's audits.[14] Governmental investigations of Andersen's audits presumably continue, and civil litigation remains pending.[15]

So why did Andersen fail to catch the problems at Enron? Although numerous conflicts of interests permeated the relationship between Andersen and Enron, unconscious bias—the propensity to interpret data in accordance with our desires—best explains why Andersen's audits failed. Other explanations include the culture and organizational flaws at Andersen.

Unconscious bias. A recent *Harvard Business Review* article entitled "Why Good Accountants Do Bad Audits" argues that unconsciously biased judgments, rather than criminal collusion between auditors and management, often cause audit failures.[16] Two recent experiments, one with business students and the other with professional auditors, demonstrated that even the suggestion of a hypothetical relationship with a client distorts an auditor's judgments. Long-standing relationships involving millions of dollars in ongoing revenues can only magnify the results. The article posits that three structural aspects of the accounting industry—ambiguity, attachment, and approval—create significant opportunities for bias to influence auditing judgments. In addition, the article highlights three aspects of human nature—familiarity, discounting, and escalation—that amplify auditors' unconscious biases.[17]

Ambiguity. Accounting remains an art, not a science, which requires enterprises, and their auditors, to exercise professional judgment in preparing and auditing financial statements. Although we often hear accountants referred to as "bean counters" and may believe that accounting provides clear-cut answers to all questions, financial accounting requires various estimates that affect the amounts shown in the financial state-

---

[13] Berardino testimony, *supra* note 6.

[14] Ken Brown, *Andersen Staff Works to Tie Up Loose Ends, Andersen Might Face More Legal Problems Beyond Guilty Verdict*, WALL ST. J., June 17, 2002, at C1, *available at* 2002 WL–WSJ 3397879.

[15] *Id.*

[16] Max H. Bazerman, George Loewenstein & Don A. Moore, *Why Good Accountants Do Bad Audits*, HARV. BUS. REV., Nov. 2002, at 96.

[17] *Id.*

ments, including the reported amounts of assets, liabilities, revenues, and expenses. In addition, generally accepted accounting principles often allow alternative treatments for the same transaction or events and may not address a particular situation because business transactions evolve more rapidly than accounting principles. Witness the Internet's recent emergence and Enron's transformation from a regional natural gas company to a global energy and commodities trader.[18] Given the various accounting estimates and permissible choices in accounting methods, a typical business enterprise could potentially select from more than a million possible "bottom lines."[19] To illustrate, the fast-food chain Wendy's once advertised that its customers could order a hamburger 256 different ways. Wendy's offered eight different toppings and condiments, such as lettuce, tomato, cheese, ketchup, and mustard, which customers could request. Either selecting or omitting those individual extras translated to 256 options, a number that grew exponentially with each extra. For public companies today, generally accepted accounting principles allow even more choices. In this regard, entities must decide when to recognize revenue; estimate sales returns and allowances, warranty costs, useful lives, and salvage values; select inventory and depreciation methods; and decide whether or not to expense stock options. Bias thrives in such an environment.[20]

Attachment. The auditor's business interests in fostering a long-term relationship with a client's management encourage auditors to render "clean" audit opinions in an effort to retain any existing engagements and to secure future business. Auditors that issue anything but an unqualified opinion frequently get replaced.[21] During the late 1990s, the largest public accounting firms—first the Big Six and then the Big Five (now the Final Four)—increasingly provided non-audit services, such as consulting, internal auditing, and tax advising, often to the very enterprises they audited.[22] During 2000, Enron paid $52 million to Andersen—$25 million for auditing services, and an additional $27 million for non-auditing services, including $3.5 million for tax work—and ranked as Andersen's second-largest client.[23] Perhaps more significantly, an internal Andersen memo in February 2001 regarding the retention of Enron as an audit client refers to $100 million a year in potential revenues from Enron.[24] Even if

---

[18] *See generally* Matthew J. Barrett, *Enron, Accounting, and Lawyers*, NOTRE DAME LAWYER, Summer 2002, at 14, 15, *available at* http://www.nd.edu/~ndlaw/alumni/ndlawyer/barrett.pdf.

[19] HERWITZ & BARRETT, *supra* note 1, at 173 (citing R.J. Chambers, *Financial Information and the Securities Market*, 1 ABACUS 3, 13–16 (1965), *reprinted in* R.J. CHAMBERS, ACCOUNTING FINANCE AND MANAGEMENT, 185–88 (1965)).

[20] Bazerman, Lowenstein & Moore, *supra* note 16, at 98–99.

[21] *Id.* at 99.

[22] ENRON CORP., SCHEDULE 14A, PROXY STATEMENT PURSUANT TO SECTION 14(a) OF THE SECURITIES EXCHANGE ACT OF 1934 (filed Mar. 27, 2001), *available at* http://www.sec.gov/Archives/edgar/data/1024401/000095012901001669/0000950129-01-001669.txt; *see also* Barrett, *supra* note 18, at 16.

[23] Berardino testimony, *supra* note 6 (detailing non-audit fees that Enron paid to Andersen in 2001).

[24] Tom Hamburger & Ken Brown, *Andersen Knew of Enron Woes a Year Ago*, WALL ST. J., Jan. 17, 2002, at A3, *available at* 2002 WL–WSJ 3383224.

Andersen could absorb the loss of Enron as a client, individual careers and the Houston office depended upon retaining the Enron engagement. As the audit partner for the firm's second-largest client, David B. Duncan enjoyed clout not only in the Houston office, but throughout Andersen.[25]

Like the remaining Final Four accounting firms, Andersen encouraged its employees, especially those not likely to become partners, to take jobs with clients or potential clients when they left the firm. The resulting "revolving door" between Andersen and Enron only enhanced the financial attachment. From 1989–2001, eighty-six people left Andersen to work for Enron.[26] Andersen alumni at Enron included Richard A. Causey, its chief accounting officer and a former Andersen audit manager; Jeff McMahon, Enron's treasurer; and Sherron Smith Watkins, the vice president who unsuccessfully tried to blow the whistle on Enron's aggressive accounting.[27] Employees at Enron often referred to Andersen as "Enron Prep."[28] In the "up or out" environment at Andersen, everyone who worked on the Enron account had subtle incentives to keep both their bosses and the people at Enron happy.

The so-called "integrated audit" that Andersen employed at Enron and then sought to market more widely to other clients also documents attachment. Under this model, Andersen sought to combine its role as external auditor with internal auditing, the process whereby an enterprise checks its own books.[29] Paralleling and sometimes overlapping outside or independent audits, internal audits seek to ensure that an enterprise follows its procedures, safeguards its assets, and operates efficiently.[30] Under a five-year, $18 million contract that sought to create an "integrated audit," Andersen took over Enron's internal auditing in 1994, transforming dozens of Enron staffers into Andersen employees.[31] *The Wall Street Journal* reported that before Enron's collapse,

---

[25] Flynn McRoberts et al., *A Final Accounting: Ties to Enron blinded Andersen*, CHI. TRIB., Sept. 3, 2002, at 1, *available at* 2002 WL 26770980.

[26] Peter Behr & April Witt, *Concerns Grow Amid Conflicts*, WASH. POST, July 30, 2002, at A1, *available at* 2002 WL 24824440.

[27] ENRON AND BEYOND: TECHNICAL ANALYSIS OF ACCOUNTING, CORPORATE GOVERNANCE, AND SECURITIES ISSUES 156 (Julia K. Brazelton & Janice L. Ammons, eds., 2002) [hereinafter ENRON AND BEYOND]; *see also* John R. Wilke, Anita Raghavan & Alexei Barrionuevo, *U.S. Will Argue Andersen Knew of Missteps, Prosecutors Marshal Evidence About Role in Flawed Enron Work*, WALL. ST. J., May 7, 2002, at C1, *available at* 2002 WL–WSJ 3393942; *see also* Alexei Barrionuevo & Jonathan Weil, *Duncan Knew Enron Papers Would be Lost*, WALL. ST. J., May 14, 2002, at C1, *available at* 2002 WL-WSJ 3394733.

[28] Behr & Witt, *supra* note 26.

[29] Alexei Barrionuevo & Jonathan Weil, *Partner Warned Arthur Andersen On Enron Audit*, WALL ST. J., May 9, 2002, at C1, *available at* 2002 WL–WSJ 3394352; *see also* Barrionuevo &Weil, *supra* note 26 ("Andersen held out Enron as the prime example of its 'integrated' audit approach. . . .").

[30] HERWITZ & BARRETT, *supra* note 1, at 202–04.

[31] McRoberts et al., *supra* note 25; Alexei Barrionuevo, *Questioning the Books: Court Documents Show Andersen's Ties With Enron Were Growing in Early '90s*, WALL ST. J., Feb. 26, 2002, at A6, *available at* 2002 WL-WSJ 3386987.

more than 100 Andersen employees worked in leased space inside Enron's headquarters in Houston.[32] In videotapes that Andersen filmed to market the "integrated audit," people at both Andersen and Enron described how intertwined their operations had become. In one segment, Jeffrey Skilling, then Enron's president, commented: "I think over time we and Arthur Andersen will probably mesh our systems and processes even more so that they are more seamless between the two organizations."[33] Coupled with the inherent ambiguity in financial statements, such attachment can influence auditors to accept the "client's" interpretation and application of generally accepted accounting principles.[34]

Approval. Management has historically selected the accounting principles and estimates that an enterprise uses to prepare its financial statements.[35] An audit essentially endorses or rejects the accounting choices that the client's management has made.[36] Research has shown that self-serving biases become even stronger when people are endorsing someone else's judgments, provided those judgments align with their own biases, than when they are asked to make original judgments themselves. This research suggests that unconscious bias can cause auditors to accept more aggressive accounting treatments than the auditor might propose independently.[37]

Familiarity. People are less willing to harm individuals that they know relative to strangers. People are even less willing to harm paying clients, or individuals they consider paying clients, with whom they enjoy ongoing relationships.[38] Like lawyers for corporations, who represent the entity and not the officer who hired them, auditors' real responsibilities flow to the investing public, not the manager or individual who retained them.[39] An auditor who suspects errors or misstatements, whether intentional or not, must choose, perhaps unconsciously, between harming a known individual, and likely the auditor's own self-interest, by questioning the accounting, or injuring faceless others by failing to object to the possibly incorrect numbers. Such biases only grow stronger as personal relationships with the client's management, sometimes former auditing colleagues, deepen.[40] David Duncan and Rick Causey often vacationed together, annually leading a group of Andersen and Enron "co-workers" on golfing trips to elite courses around the county.[41] The "revolving door" between Andersen and Enron

---

[32] Ianthe Jeanne Dugan, Dennis Berman & Alexei Barrionuevo, *On Camera, People at Andersen, Enron Tell How Close They Were*, WALL ST. J., Apr. 15, 2002, at C1, *available at* 2002 WL–WSJ 3391766.

[33] *Id.*

[34] Bazerman, Lowenstein & Moore, *supra* note 16, at 99–100.

[35] HERWITZ & BARRETT, *supra* note 1, at 173.

[36] Bazerman, Lowenstein & Moore, *supra* note 16, at 99–100.

[37] *Id.* at 100–01.

[38] *Id.* at 100.

[39] HERWITZ & BARRETT, *supra* note 1, at 182–83.

[40] Bazerman, Lowenstein & Moore, *supra* note 16, at 100.

[41] McRoberts et al., *supra* note 25.

and the "integrated audit" model also strengthened the familiarity.[42] As a result of familiarity, auditors likely will believe assertions of managers with whom they have worked in the past because a relationship of familiarity and trust erodes the auditor's objectivity and neutrality.[43]

Discounting. Immediate consequences influence behavior more than delayed ones, especially when uncertainty accompanies the future costs. This tendency appeals to the propensity to place more emphasis on the short-term effect of decisions than their long-term ramifications. Immediate adverse consequences, including damage to the relationships with the client and its management, possible loss of the engagement, and potential unemployment, may dissuade auditors from issuing anything other than an unqualified opinion. By comparison, the costs arising from an audit failure, namely civil lawsuits, disciplinary proceedings, and reputational losses, appear distant and uncertain, or even unlikely.[44] After an earlier audit failure at Waste Management, for which Andersen agreed to the largest fine ever against an auditor, the firm did not fire the audit partners whom the SEC sanctioned.[45] Ironically, one of those auditors wrote the document retention policy featured in Andersen's criminal trial for obstructing justice in the Enron investigation.[46] The internal Andersen memo regarding the decision to retain Enron as a client documents Enron's aggressive accounting practices and potential conflicts of interest by then-Enron chief financial officer Andrew Fastow. Nevertheless, Andersen executives decided to retain Enron as a client because "we [have] the appropriate people and processes in place to serve Enron and manage our engagement risks."[47] As total audit and other fees from Enron grew to $52 million in 2000, Andersen willingly assumed increasing engagement risks for a client that the firm believed could potentially generate $100 million in revenues annually.[48]

Escalation. People often hide or explain away minor mistakes, often without realizing what they are doing. Unconscious biases may cause an auditor to accept small imperfections in a client's financial statements.[49] Over time, such misstatements can become material. At that point, correcting the situation may require admitting previous errors or biases, restating the financial statements, or even resigning. Rather than take those actions, the auditor may try to conceal the problem, thereby escalating unconscious bias into fraud.[50] For example, after Andersen approved the non-consoli-

---

[42] *See supra* notes 26–34 and accompanying text.

[43] Bazerman, Lowenstein & Moore, *supra* note 16, at 100.

[44] *Id.*

[45] Flynn McRoberts et al., *A Final Accounting: Civil war splits Andersen,* CHI. TRIB., Sept. 2, 2002, at 1, *available at* 2002 WL 26770609.

[46] *Id.*

[47] Hamburger & Brown, *supra* note 24.

[48] *See id.*

[49] Bazerman, Lowenstein & Moore, *supra* note 16, at 100.

[50] *Id.*

dated accounting for various SPEs, the auditors later adopted an interpretation that enabled Enron to avoid recognizing losses for declines in the value of underlying investments in certain entities known as the Raptors.[51] At Andersen's criminal trial, prosecutors also introduced evidence to show that the firm's prior audit failures at Waste Management and Sunbeam gave Andersen a motive to hide the problems at Enron.[52]

The culture and an ineffectual Professional Standards Group at Andersen. Shortly after its conviction, a four-part series in *The Chicago Tribune* traced Andersen's collapse from the position it held for decades—as the "gold standard" for auditing firms in the United States—to convicted felon.[53] After the 1989 decision to create separate business units and profit pools for Arthur Andersen and Andersen Consulting, Arthur Andersen aggressively marketed more lucrative consulting services to its audit clients, which enabled Andersen's top partners to triple their earnings during the 1990s. In retrospect, this pursuit of profits ultimately led to the firm's destruction.[54]

Although only symbolic of this change in culture, the firm abandoned its traditional trademarked icon, two mahogany doors, for an orange ball dubbed "the logosphere" and branded itself simply as "Andersen."[55] More importantly, the firm evaluated and compensated audit partners for their ability to cross-sell other services and adopted a program labeled "2X" that sought to generate two dollars in consulting revenues for every dollar in audit revenues.[56] In essence, auditing became a "loss leader" to very profitable consulting services.[57]

Perhaps even more significantly, unlike the other Big Five firms, Andersen marketed itself as a firm in which the audit partner could make the final call on difficult accounting and auditing questions without having to secure approval from the firm's team of experts that reviewed and reached conclusions on such questions that local offices encountered. Andersen called this team of experts the Professional Standards Group.[58] Relying upon accounting professionals at the SEC and elsewhere, *Business Week* reported that "unlike other firms, Andersen allow[ed] regional partners—the

---

[51] Weil, *supra* note 7.

[52] Barrionuevo & Weil, *supra* note 29.

[53] Flynn McRoberts et al., *A Final Accounting: The fall of Andersen*, CHI. TRIB., Sept. 1, 2002, at 1, *available at* 2002 WL 26770388 [hereinafter McRoberts et al., *The fall of Andersen*]; McRoberts et al., *supra* note 45; McRoberts et al., *supra* note 25; McRoberts et al., *supra* note 5.

[54] McRoberts et al., *The fall of Andersen*, *supra* note 53; *see also* McRoberts et al., *supra* note 45.

[55] Ken Brown & Ianthe Jeanne Dugan, *Sad Account: Andersen's Fall From Grace Is a Tale of Greed and Miscues*, WALL ST. J., June 7, 2002, at A1, *available at* 2002 WL–WSJ 3397111.

[56] ARTHUR ANDERSEN, U.S. 1999 ANNUAL REPORT, 17–19 (2000), *available at* http://www.nrri.ohio-state.edu/oss/admin/vendorprop/andersen/ander1999.pdf (last visited June 12, 2003).

[57] *See generally* John C. Coffee, Jr., *Understanding Enron: It's About the Gatekeepers, Stupid*, 14–16 (July 30, 2002), *available at* http://ssrn.com/abstract_id=325240; *this book at* 125–143.

[58] *Id.* at 16, 22.

front-line executives closest to the companies they audit—to overrule the experts," and Andersen's Enron audit team did so on at least four occasions, allowing Enron to hide debt and inflate reported earnings.[59] Equally troubling, Andersen honored Enron's request to remove Carl E. Bass, then a member of the Professional Standards Group from that team, because his accounting stances were too conservative.[60]

Significant conflicts of interest and self-interest. As previously mentioned, among the services that Andersen sold to Enron and other audit clients were internal auditing services.[61] In essence, Andersen's outside auditors were evaluating the firm's consulting services.[62]

Recall also that Enron paid Andersen $27 million for non-auditing services during 2000. When non-audit fees comprise a significant part of an auditor's income from the audit client, those fees might easily tempt an auditor to overlook an enterprise's "aggressive" accounting simply to retain the client's non-audit business. At a minimum, those fees paid to Andersen call the appearance of Andersen's independence into question.[63] To repeat, even if Andersen could absorb the loss of a client like Enron, individual careers and offices that depended upon keeping Enron as a client would certainly suffer.[64]

Finally, the "revolving door" between Andersen and Enron created additional incentives for auditors interested in employment at Enron to try to keep Enron's management happy.[65]

How does Sarbanes-Oxley address these problems? SOx Section 301 required the SEC to prescribe rules that direct the national securities exchanges and national securities associations, such as the New York Stock Exchange and The Nasdaq Stock Market, Inc., to prohibit the listing of any company that does not place in an audit committee—a committee of independent directors presumably better able to protect the company's interests—the responsibility for hiring, compensating, and firing the auditor.[66] In April 2003, the SEC issued rules that require each national securities exchange and national securities association to submit proposed amendments to their listing rules that comply with the SEC rules by July 15, 2003.[67] The rules set Decem-

---

[59] Mike McNamee, *Out of Control at Andersen*, BUS. WEEK, Apr. 8, 2002, at 32.

[60] *Id.*

[61] *See supra* notes 29–34 and accompanying text.

[62] McRoberts et al., *supra* note 45.

[63] Barrett, *supra* note 18, at 16.

[64] *See supra* notes 23–25 and accompanying text.

[65] *See supra* notes 26–28.

[66] Sarbanes-Oxley Act of 2002, Pub. L. No. 107-204, § 301, 116 Stat. 745, 775–77 (codified at 15 U.S.C.A. § 78j-1 (West. Supp. 2003)).

[67] Standards Relating to Listed Company Audit Committees, 68 Fed. Reg. 18,788, 18,817 (Apr. 16, 2003).

ber 1, 2003 as the deadline to obtain final approval. Under the SEC's rules, most domestic companies must comply with the new listing rules by the earlier of (1) their first annual shareholders meeting after January 15, 2004, or (2) October 31, 2004.[68] In the meantime, most publicly traded companies have given their audit committee the exclusive power to hire, compensate, and fire the firm's auditor.

SOx and new final SEC rules also strengthen statutory and administrative requirements regarding auditor independence. SOx Section 201 lists various services outside the scope of the practice of auditors, including bookkeeping services, financial information systems design and implementation, appraisal or valuation services, fairness opinions, internal audit outsourcing services, management or human resources functions, and legal services, as "prohibited activities."[69] Although auditors can no longer perform internal auditing and many other consulting services for their audit clients, the SEC's new final rules issued in January 2003 reiterate its long-standing position that an accounting firm can render certain tax services to audit clients without impairing the firm's independence.[70] SOx Section 202, however, requires the audit committee to preapprove all audit and most non-audit services.[71]

SOx Section 203 provides that most accounting firms may not provide audit services to a publicly traded company, usually referred to as an issuer, if the lead audit partner or the reviewing audit partner has performed audit services for the issuer in each of the issuer's previous five fiscal years.[72] Section 206 prevents an auditing firm from auditing an issuer that employs in certain high-level positions an individual who served on the audit team during the past year.[73] The SEC's new regulations, which (subject to various transitional rules) became effective May 6, 2003, specify that the receipt of compensation by an "audit partner" based upon procuring engagements with the audit client for services other than audit, review, and attest services destroys independence.[74] The SEC rules also require a one-year "cooling off" period prior to the commencement of audit procedures if certain members of an audit client's senior management have served as members of the firm's audit team.[75] Finally, the rules generally require the rotation of the lead and concurring partners on an audit team every five years.[76]

---

[68] *Id.* at 18,817.

[69] Sarbanes-Oxley Act of 2002, Pub. L. No. 107–204, § 201, 116 Stat. 745, 771–72 (codified at 15 U.S.C.A. §§ 78j-1 & 15 U.S.C.A. § 7231 (West. Supp. 2003)).

[70] Strengthening the Commission's Requirements Regarding Auditor Independence, 68 Fed. Reg. 6006, 6017 (Feb. 5, 2003) [hereinafter Auditor Independence].

[71] Sarbanes-Oxley Act of 2002, Pub. L. No. 107-204, § 201, 116 Stat. 745, 771–72 (codified at 15 U.S.C.A. §§ 78j-1 & 15 U.S.C.A. § 7231 (West. Supp. 2003)).

[72] *Id.* § 203, 116 Stat. at 773 (codified at 15 U.S.C.A. § 78j-1 (West. Supp. 2003)).

[73] *Id.* § 206, 116 Stat. at 774–75 (codified at 15 U.S.C.A. § 78j-1 (West. Supp. 2003)).

[74] Strengthening the Commission's Requirements Regarding Auditor Independence, 68 Fed. Reg. 6006, 6024–26, 6047 (Feb. 5, 2003) (codified at 17 C.F.R. § 210.2-01(c)(8) (2003)).

[75] *Id.* at 6007–10, 6044–45 (Feb. 5, 2003) (codified at 17 C.F.R. § 210.2-01(c)(2)(iii) (2003)).

[76] *Id.* at 6017–22, 6047 (codified at 17 C.F.R. § 210.2-01(c)(6) (2003)).

SOx also creates the Public Company Accounting Oversight Board ("PCAOB") to register, regulate, and inspect public accounting firms that audit publicly traded companies; to establish or adopt auditing, quality control, ethics, independence, and other standards; and to conduct investigations and disciplinary proceedings when appropriate to enforce compliance with the law and professional standards.[77] Section 102 requires auditing firms to register with the PCAOB and each application for registration must contain a statement of the firm's quality control policies for its accounting and auditing practices.[78] This requirement should lead to more effective internal review and consultation committees inside auditing firms.

Do any gaps remain? To the extent that conflicts of interest cause audit failures, SOx addresses the problems for publicly traded enterprises subject to the SEC's jurisdiction, with one significant exception. Even though management can no longer hire and fire the auditor and the audit committee must approve any non-audit services, under the guise of increasing auditor independence, management can still potentially recommend that the audit committee hire another accounting firm to provide tax or other non-prohibited consulting services. Thus, if the auditor does not approve, or at least acquiesce in, certain accounting treatments or disclosures preferred by the client's management, the audit firm may risk losing significant non-audit revenues.[79] Recall that Enron paid Andersen $3.5 million for tax services in 2000.[80]

SOx largely misses the mark, however, if unconscious bias explains most audit failures. As long as financial or other incentives tempt auditing firms and their executives and employees to try to retain an audit engagement, unconscious bias will remain present. Thus, unconscious bias suggests the need to require mandatory rotation of audit firms after fixed terms for preset fees to eliminate the threat that the client can fire or otherwise punish the auditor for failing to approve questionable accounting practices.[81] SOx Section 207 directs the Comptroller General to study and review the potential effects arising from a limit on the period of years in which an audit firm may serve as the auditor for a particular issuer and to submit a written report to certain Congressional committees within one year after SOx's enactment.[82] While mandatory rotation of audit firms will certainly increase auditing fees, given unconscious bias and the enormous losses and damage from Enron scandal and other recent audit failures,

---

[77] Sarbanes-Oxley Act of 2002, Pub. L. No. 107-204, § 101, 116 Stat. 745, 750–53 (codified at 15 U.S.C.A. § 7211 (West. Supp. 2003)).

[78] *Id.* at § 102, 116 Stat. 745, 753–755 (codified at 15 U.S.C.A. § 7212 (West. Supp. 2003)).

[79] *See generally* HERWITZ & BARRETT, *supra* note 1, at 173–74, 192–93.

[80] Berardino testimony, *supra* note 6.

[81] Bazerman, Lowenstein & Moore, *supra* note 16, at 102.

[82] Sarbanes-Oxley Act of 2002, Pub. L. No. 107-204, § 207, 116 Stat. 745, 775 (codified at 15 U.S.C.A. § 7232 (West. Supp. 2003)).

can companies any longer afford not to pay increased fees for the benefit of their investors, employees, and communities?

One final caveat: SOx (and the federal securities laws generally) does not apply to closely held firms and not-for-profit organizations that may require audited financial statements to obtain bank loans or for other reasons.[83] Those enterprises and their auditors remain outside the SEC's reach.

NOTES AND QUESTIONS

1. Even if the then-existing consolidation requirements under generally accepted accounting principles did not require Enron to consolidate the two SPEs, some commentators have argued that unconsolidated financial statements could not "present fairly" Enron's financial condition, results of operations, or cash flows. In other words, some critics of Andersen's audit reports believe that financial statements must both (i) comply with generally accepted accounting principles and (ii) "present fairly" the financial condition and results of operations. *See, e.g.,* Steve Liesman, *SEC Accounting Cop's Warning: Playing By Rules May Not Ward Off Fraud Issues,* WALL ST. J., Feb. 12, 2002, at C1, *available at* 2002 WL-WSJ 3385675; *see generally* DAVID R. HERWITZ & MATTHEW J. BARRETT, MATERIALS ON ACCOUNTING FOR LAWYERS 230 (3d ed. 2001). In *United States v. Simon,* 425 F.2d 796 (2d Cir. 1969), the Second Circuit upheld criminal convictions against three auditors of Continental Vending Machine Corporation after they challenged a jury instruction that described the "critical test" as whether the financial statements as a whole "fairly presented" the corporation's financial position and accurately reported its operations. *Id.* at 805–06. Various accounting experts testified that the financial statements did not violate generally accepted accounting principles. The Second Circuit declined to overturn the trial court's refusal to give a requested instruction that essentially would have given the defendants a complete defense to the criminal charges if the financial statements conformed to generally accepted accounting principles. In other words, the Second Circuit ruled that compliance with generally accepted accounting principles does not automatically shield an auditor from criminal liability. Presumably, the same conclusion would also apply in civil cases.

2. Did Andersen knowingly participate in the fraud at Enron? Alternatively, was Andersen reckless in overlooking the problems at Enron?

3. Do you accept the concept of unconscious bias as an explanation for the audit failure at Enron?

4. Might the identified factors that amplify unconscious bias—ambiguity, attachment, approval, familiarity, discounting, and escalation—also affect either cor-

---

[83] *See* HERWITZ & BARRETT, *supra* note 1, at 171.

porate executives and employees generally or lawyers in their relationships with their clients? If so, what can be done to reduce the consequences of such bias?

5. Tax work can fall into three broad categories—return preparation, tax planning and consulting, and tax shelters. In this last category, an advisor, such as an accounting firm, law firm, or investment bank, essentially attempts to use technical quirks in the Internal Revenue Code against the Internal Revenue Service and seeks to sell so-called "products" to companies and corporate executives to reduce taxes. In such an arrangement, the promoter assumes an advocacy role for the buyer. When officers at audit clients purchase such tax shelters, the accounting firm arguably must perform incompatible roles—the audit requires the accounting firm to act as a watchdog of management at the same time that the firm must act as an advocate for the officer in the tax matter. When an audit client purchases a tax shelter, the accounting firm must audit its own advice, which impairs its independence. Because accounting firms tend to sell similar tax-shelters, critics complain that even the attempt to sell a product to a non-audit client impairs independence.

The Wall Street Journal reported that, during 2002, General Electric Co. paid its auditor, KPMG LLP, more than $21 million in tax fees. Offering another example, the same article points out that Caterpillar Inc. paid its auditor, PricewaterhouseCoopers, $17.4 million for tax work in 2002, more than twice the $8.2 million that the company paid in audit fees. The amount for tax work included $13.9 million "'for services performed as a subcontractor for outside legal counsel.'" For 2003, a spokeswoman at Caterpillar estimated that the amount for tax work would fall to $13.5 million. Cassell Bryan-Low, *Questioning the Books: Keeping the Accountants From Flying High,* WALL ST. J., May 6, 2003, at C1, *available at* 2003 WL-WSJ 3966838; Cassell Bryan-Low, *Accounting Firms Still Earn More From Consulting Fees,* WALL ST. J., Apr. 16, 2003, at C9, *available at* 2003 WL-WSJ 3964987. Should audit committees refuse to preapprove such fees? Should audit committees insist that another accounting firm prepare the company's tax returns and provide tax planning services? Could unconscious bias affect audit committees?

Enron and the Derivatives World

Frank Partnoy[*][1]

I am submitting testimony in response to this Committee's request that I address potential problems associated with the unregulated status of derivatives used by Enron Corporation.

I am a law professor at the University of San Diego School of Law. I teach and do research in the areas of financial market regulation, derivatives, and structured finance. During the mid-1990s, I worked on Wall Street structuring and selling financial instruments and investment vehicles similar to those used by Enron. As a lawyer, I have represented clients with problems similar to Enron's, but on a much smaller scale. I have never received any payment from Enron or from any Enron officer or employee.

I. INTRODUCTION AND OVERVIEW

Enron has been compared to Long-Term Capital Management, the Greenwich, Connecticut, hedge fund that lost $4.6 billion on more than $1 trillion of derivatives and was rescued in September 1998 in a private bailout engineered by the New York Federal Reserve. For the past several weeks, I have conducted my own investigation into Enron, and I believe the comparison is inapt. Yes, there are similarities in both firms' use and abuse of financial derivatives. But the scope of Enron's problems and their effects on its investors and employees are far more sweeping.

According to Enron's most recent annual report, the firm made more money trading derivatives in the year 2000 alone than Long-Term Capital Management made in its entire history. Long-Term Capital Management generated losses of a few billion dollars; by contrast, Enron not only wiped out over $70 billion of shareholder value, but also defaulted on tens of billions of dollars of debts. Long-Term Capital Manage-

---

[*] Professor of Law, University of San Diego School of Law. FRANK PARTNOY, ENRON & THE DERIVATIVES WORLD (Jan. 24, 2002), *available at* http://www.senate.gov/~gov_affairs/012402partnoy.htm (last visited Sept. 4, 2003).

[1] The original testimony has been slightly edited for inclusion in this book.

ment employed only 200 people worldwide, many of whom simply went on to start new hedge funds after the bailout, while Enron employed 20,000 people, many of whom have been fired, and many more of whom lost their life savings as Enron's stock plummeted last fall. In short, Enron makes Long-Term Capital Management look like a lemonade stand.

It will surprise many investors to learn that Enron was, at its core, a derivatives trading firm. Nothing made this more clear than the layout of Enron's extravagant new building in which the top executives' offices on the seventh floor were designed to overlook the crown jewel of Enron's empire: a cavernous derivatives trading pit on the sixth floor.

I believe there are two answers to the question of why Enron collapsed, and both involve derivatives. One relates to the use of derivatives "outside" Enron, in transactions with some now-infamous special purpose entities. The other—which has not been publicized at all—relates to the use of derivatives "inside" Enron.

What are derivatives? They are complex financial instruments whose value is based on one or more underlying variables, such as the price of a stock or the cost of natural gas. Derivatives can be traded in two ways: on regulated exchanges or in unregulated over-the-counter ("OTC") markets. My testimony involves the OTC derivatives markets, the focus of Enron's activities.

Sometimes OTC derivatives can seem too esoteric to be relevant to average investors. Even the well-publicized OTC derivatives fiascos of a few years ago—Procter & Gamble or Orange County, for example—seem ages away. But the OTC derivatives markets are too important to ignore, and are critical to understanding Enron. The size of derivatives markets typically is measured in terms of the notional values of contracts. Recent estimates of the size of the exchange-traded derivatives market, which includes all contracts traded on the major options and futures exchanges, are in the range of $13 to $14 trillion in notional amount. By contrast, the estimated notional amount of outstanding OTC derivatives as of year-end 2000 was $95.2 trillion. And that estimate is most likely an understatement. In other words, OTC derivatives markets, which for the most part did not exist twenty (or, in some cases, even ten) years ago, now comprise about 90 percent of the aggregate derivatives market, with trillions of dollars at risk every day. By those measures, OTC derivatives markets are bigger than the markets for U.S. stocks.

Enron may have been just an energy company when it was created in 1985, but by the end it had become a full-blown OTC derivatives trading firm. Its OTC derivatives-related assets and liabilities increased more than five-fold during 2000 alone.

And, let me repeat, the OTC derivatives markets are largely unregulated. Enron's trading operations were not regulated, or even recently audited, by U.S. securities regulators, and the OTC derivatives it traded are not deemed securities. OTC derivatives trading is beyond the purview of organized, regulated exchanges. Thus, Enron—like many firms that trade OTC derivatives—fell into a regulatory black hole.

After 360 customers lost $11.4 billion on derivatives during the decade ending in March 1997, the Commodity Futures Trading Commission began considering whether to regulate OTC derivatives. But its proposals were rejected, and in December 2000 Congress made the deregulated status of derivatives clear when it passed the Commodity Futures Modernization Act. As a result, the OTC derivatives markets have become a ticking time bomb, which Congress thus far has chosen not to defuse.

Many parties are to blame for Enron's collapse. But as this Committee and others take a hard look at Enron and its officers, directors, accountants, lawyers, bankers, and analysts, Congress also should take a hard look at the current state of OTC derivatives regulation. (In the remainder of this testimony, when I refer generally to "derivatives," I am referring to these OTC derivatives markets.)

II. DERIVATIVES "OUTSIDE" ENRON

The first answer to the question of why Enron collapsed relates to derivatives deals between Enron and several of its 3,000-plus off-balance sheet subsidiaries and partnerships. The names of these byzantine financial entities—such as JEDI, Raptor, and LJM—have been widely reported.

Special purpose entities might seem odd to most investors, but they actually are very common in modern financial markets. Structured finance is a significant part of the U.S. economy, and special purpose entities are involved in most investors' lives, even if they do not realize it. For example, most credit card and mortgage payments flow through special purpose entities, and financial services firms typically use such entities as well. Some special purpose entities generate great economic benefits; others—as I will describe below—are used to manipulate a company's financial reports to inflate assets, to understate liabilities, to create false profits, and to hide losses. In this way, special purpose entities are a lot like fire: they can be used for good or ill. Special purpose entities, like derivatives, are unregulated.

The key problem at Enron involved the confluence of derivatives and special purpose entities. Enron entered into derivatives transactions with these entities to shield volatile assets from quarterly financial reporting and to inflate artificially the value of certain Enron assets. These derivatives included price swap derivatives (described below), as well as call and put options.

Specifically, Enron used derivatives and special purpose vehicles to manipulate its financial statements in three ways. First, it hid speculator losses it suffered on technology stocks. Second, it hid huge debts incurred to finance unprofitable new businesses, including retail energy services for new customers. Third, it inflated the value of other troubled businesses, including its new ventures in fiber-optic bandwidth. Although Enron was founded as an energy company, many of these derivatives transactions did not involve energy at all.

A. Using Derivatives to Hide Losses on Technology Stocks

First, Enron hid hundreds of millions of dollars of losses on its speculative investments in various technology-oriented firms, such as Rhythms NetConnections, Inc., a start-up telecommunications company. A subsidiary of Enron (along with other investors such as Microsoft and Stanford University) invested a relatively small amount of venture capital, on the order of $10 million, in Rhythms NetConnections. Enron also invested in other technology companies.

Rhythms NetConnections issued stock to the public in an initial public offering on April 6, 1999, during the heyday of the Internet boom, at a price of about $70 per share. Enron's stake was suddenly worth hundreds of millions of dollars. Enron's other venture capital investments in technology companies also rocketed at first, alongside the widespread run-up in the value of dot.com stocks. As is typical in IPOs, Enron was prohibited from selling its stock for six months.

Next, Enron entered into a series of transactions with a special purpose entity—apparently a limited partnership called Raptor, one of a several of similarly-named entities created by Enron, which was owned by another Enron special purpose entity called LJM1—in which Enron essentially exchanged its shares in these technology companies for a loan, ultimately, from Raptor. Raptor then issued its own securities to investors and held the cash proceeds from those investors.

The critical piece of this puzzle, the element that made it all work, was a derivatives transaction—called a "price swap derivative"—between Enron and Raptor. In this price swap, Enron committed to give stock to Raptor if Raptor's assets declined in value. The more Raptor's assets declined, the more of its own stock Enron was required to post. Because Enron had committed to maintain Raptor's value at $1.2 billion, if Enron's stock declined in value, Enron would need to give Raptor even more stock. This derivatives transaction carried the risk of diluting the ownership of Enron's shareholders if either Enron's stock or the technology stocks Raptor held declined in price. Enron also apparently entered into options transactions with Raptor and/or LJM1.

Because the securities Raptor issued were backed by Enron's promise to deliver more shares, investors in Raptor essentially were buying Enron's debt, not the stock of a start-up telecommunications company. In fact, the performance of Rhythms NetConnections was irrelevant to these investors in Raptor. Enron got the best of both worlds in accounting terms: it recognized its gain on the technology stocks by recognizing the value of the Raptor loan right away, and it avoided recognizing on an interim basis any future losses on the technology stocks, were such losses to occur.

It is painfully obvious how this story ends: the dot.com bubble burst and by 2001 shares of Rhythms NetConnections were worthless. Enron had to deliver more shares to "make whole" the investors in Raptor and other similar deals. In all, Enron had derivative instruments on 54.8 million shares of Enron common stock at an average price of $67.92 per share, or $3.7 billion in all. In other words, at the start of these deals, Enron's obligation amounted to seven percent of all of its outstanding shares. As Enron's share price declined, that obligation increased and Enron's shareholders were substantially diluted. And here is the key point: even as Raptor's assets and Enron's shares declined in value, Enron did not reflect those declines in its quarterly financial statements.

B. Using Derivatives to Hide Debts Incurred by Unprofitable Businesses

A second example involved Enron using derivatives with two special purpose entities to hide huge debts incurred to finance unprofitable new businesses. Essentially, some very complicated and confusing accounting rules allowed Enron to avoid disclosing certain assets and liabilities.

These two special purpose entities were Joint Energy Development Investments Limited Partnership ("JEDI") and Chewco Investments, L.P. ("Chewco"). Enron owned only 50 percent of JEDI, and therefore—under then-applicable accounting rules—could (and did) report JEDI as an unconsolidated equity affiliate. If Enron had owned 51 percent of JEDI, accounting rules would have required Enron to include all of JEDI's financial results in its financial statements. But at 50 percent, Enron did not have to.

JEDI, in turn, was subject to the same rules. JEDI could issue equity and debt securities, and as long as there was an outside investor with at least 50 percent of the equity—in other words, with real economic exposure to the risks of Chewco—JEDI would not need to consolidate Chewco.

One way to minimize the applicability of this "50 percent rule" would be for a company to create a special purpose entity with mostly debt and only a tiny sliver of equity for which the company easily could find an outside investor. Such a transaction would be an obvious sham, and one might expect to find a pronouncement by the accounting regulators that it would not conform to Generally Acceptable Accounting Principles. Unfortunately, there are no such accounting regulators, and there was no such pronouncement. The Financial Accounting Standards Board, a private entity that sets most accounting rules and advises the Securities and Exchange Commission, had not given a satisfactory answer to the key accounting question: what constitutes sufficient capital from an independent source, so that a special purpose entity need not be consolidated?

Since 1982, Financial Accounting Standard No. 57, Related Party Disclosures, has contained a general requirement that companies disclose the nature of relationships they have with related parties, and describe transactions with them. Accountants might debate whether Enron's impenetrable footnote disclosure satisfies FAS No. 57, but clearly the disclosures currently made are not optimal. In 1998, FASB adopted FAS No. 133, which includes new accounting rules for derivatives. Now at 800-plus pages, FAS No. 133's instructions are an incredibly detailed—but ultimately unhelpful—attempt to rationalize other accounting rules for derivatives.

As a result, even after two decades, there is no clear answer to the question about disclosures on related parties. Instead, some early guidance (developed in the context of leases) has been grafted onto modern special purpose entities. This guidance is a 1991 letter from the Acting Chief Accountant of the SEC in 1991, stating:

> The initial substantive residual equity investment should be comparable to that expected for a substantive business involved in similar [leasing] transactions with similar risks and rewards. The SEC staff understands from

discussions with Working Group members that those members believe that 3 percent is the minimum acceptable investment. The SEC staff believes a greater investment may be necessary depending on the facts and circumstances, including the credit risk associated with the lessee and the market risk factors associated with the leased property.

Based on this letter, and on opinions from auditors and lawyers, companies started pushing debt off their balance sheets into unconsolidated special purpose entities so long as (1) the company did not have more than 50 percent of the equity of the special purpose entity, and (2) the equity of the special purpose entity was at least 3 percent of its total capital. As more companies have done such deals, more debt has moved off balance-sheet, to the point that, today, it is difficult for investors to know if they have an accurate picture of a company's debts. Even if Enron had not tripped up and violated the letter of these rules, it still would have been able to borrow 97 percent of the capital of its special purpose entities without recognizing those debts on its balance sheet.

Transactions designed to exploit these accounting rules have polluted the financial statements of many U.S. companies. Enron is not alone. For example, Kmart Corporation—which was on the verge of bankruptcy as of January 21, 2002, and clearly was affected by Enron's collapse—held 49 percent interests in several unconsolidated equity affiliates. I believe this Committee should take a hard look at these widespread practices.

In short, derivatives enabled Enron to avoid consolidating these special purpose entities. Enron entered into a derivatives transaction with Chewco similar to the one it entered into with Raptor, effectively guaranteeing repayment to Chewco's outside investor. (The investor's sliver of equity ownership in Chewco was not really equity from an economic perspective, because the investor had nothing—other than Enron's credit—at risk.) In its financial statements, Enron took the position that, although it provided guarantees to unconsolidated subsidiaries, those guarantees did not have a readily determinable fair value, and management did not consider it likely that Enron would be required to perform or otherwise incur losses associated with guarantees. That position enabled Enron to avoid recording its guarantees. Even the guarantees listed in the footnotes were recorded at only 10 percent of their nominal value. (At least this amount is closer to the truth than the amount listed as debt for unconsolidated subsidiaries: zero.)

Apparently, Arthur Andersen either did not discover this derivatives transaction or decided that the transaction did not require a finding that Enron controlled Chewco. In any event, the Enron derivatives transaction meant that Enron—not the 50 percent "investor" in Chewco—had the real exposure to Chewco's assets. The ownership daisy chain unraveled once Enron was deemed to own Chewco. JEDI was forced to consolidate Chewco, and Enron was forced to consolidate both limited partnerships—and all of their losses—in its financial statements.

All of this complicated analysis will seem absurd to the average investor. If the assets and liabilities are Enron's in economic terms, shouldn't they be reported that way in accounting terms? The answer, of course, is yes. Unfortunately, current rules allow companies to employ derivatives and special purpose entities to make accounting standards diverge from economic reality. Enron used financial engineering as a kind of plastic surgery, to make itself look better than it really was. Many other companies do the same.

Of course, it is possible to detect the flaws in plastic surgery, or financial engineering, if you look hard enough and in the right places. In 2000, Enron disclosed about $2.1 billion of such derivatives transactions with related entities, and recognized gains of about $500 million related to those transactions. The disclosure related to these staggering numbers is less than conspicuous, buried at page 48, footnote 16 of Enron's annual report, deep in the related party disclosures for which Enron was notorious. Still, the disclosure is there. A few sophisticated analysts understood Enron's finances based on that disclosure; they bet against Enron's stock. Other securities analysts likely understood the disclosures, but apparently chose not to speak for fear of losing Enron's banking business. An argument even can be made—although not a good one, in my view—that Enron satisfied its disclosure obligations with its opaque language. In any event, the result of Enron's method of disclosure was that investors did not get a full picture of the firm's finances.

Enron is not the only example of such abuse; accounting subterfuge using derivatives is widespread. I believe Congress should seriously consider legislation explicitly requiring that financial statements describe the economic reality of a company's transactions. Such a broad standard—backed by rigorous enforcement—would go a long way towards eradicating the schemes companies currently use to dress up their financial statements.

Enron's risk management manual stated the following: "Reported earnings follow the rules and principles of accounting. The results do not always create measures consistent with underlying economics. However, corporate management's performance is generally measured by accounting income, not underlying economics. Risk management strategies are therefore directed at accounting rather than economic performance." This alarming statement is representative of the accounting-driven focus of U.S. managers generally, who all too frequently have little interest in maintaining controls to monitor their firm's economic realities.

C. Using Derivatives to Inflate the Value of Troubled Businesses

A third example is even more troubling. It appears that Enron inflated the value of certain assets it held by selling a small portion of those assets to a special purpose entity at an inflated price, and then revaluing the lion's share of those assets it still held at that higher price.

Consider the following sentence disclosed from the infamous footnote 16 of Enron's 2000 annual report, on page 49: "In 2000, Enron sold a portion of its dark fiber inventory to the Related Party in exchange for $30 million cash and a $70 million note receivable that was subsequently repaid. Enron recognized gross margin of $67 million on the sale." What does this sentence mean?

It is possible to understand the sentence today, but only after reading a January 7, 2002, article about the sale by Daniel Fisher of *Forbes* magazine, together with an August 2001 memorandum describing the transaction (and others) from one Enron employee, Sherron Watkins, to Enron Chairman Kenneth Lay.

Here is my best understanding of what this sentence means.

First, the "Related Party" is LJM2, an Enron partnership run by Enron's Chief Financial Officer, Andrew Fastow. (Fastow reportedly received $30 million from the LJM1 and LJM2 partnerships pursuant to compensation arrangements Enron's board of directors approved.)

Second, dark fiber refers to a type of bandwidth Enron traded as part of its broadband business. In this business, Enron traded the right to transmit data through various fiber-optic cables, more than 40 million miles of which various Internet-related companies had installed in the United States. Only a small percentage of these cables were "lit"—meaning they could transmit the light waves required to carry Internet data; the vast majority of cables were still awaiting upgrades and were "dark." As one might expect, the rights to transmit over dark fiber are very difficult to value.

Third, Enron sold dark fiber it apparently valued at only $33 million for triple that value: $100 million in all—$30 million in cash plus $70 million in a note receivable. It appears that this sale was at an inflated price, thereby enabling Enron to record a $67 million profit on that trade. LJM2 apparently obtained cash from investors by issuing securities and used some of these proceeds to repay the note receivable issued to Enron.

What the sentence in footnote 16 does not make plain is that the investor in LJM2 was persuaded to pay what appears to be an inflated price, because Enron entered into a "make whole" derivatives contract with LJM2 (of the same type it used with Raptor). Essentially, the investor was buying Enron's debt. The investor was willing to buy securities in LJM2, because if the dark fiber declined in price—as it almost certainly would, from its inflated value—Enron would make the investor whole.

In these transactions, Enron retained the economic risk associated with the dark fiber. Yet as the value of dark fiber plunged during 2000, Enron nevertheless was able to record a gain on its sale, and avoid recognizing any losses on assets held by LJM2, which was an unconsolidated affiliate of Enron, just like JEDI.

As if all of this were not complicated enough, Enron's sale of dark fiber to LJM2 also magically generated an inflated price, which Enron then could use in valuing any remaining dark fiber it held. The third-party investor in LJM2 had, in a sense, "validated" the value of the dark fiber at the higher price, and Enron then arguably could use that inflated price in valuing other dark fiber assets it held. I do not have any direct knowledge of this, although public reports and Sherron Watkins's letter indicate that this is probably what happened.

For example, suppose Enron started with ten units of dark fiber, worth $100, and sold one to a special purpose entity for $20—double its actual value—using the above scheme. Now, Enron had an argument that each of its remaining nine units of dark fiber also were worth $20 each, for a total of $180. Enron then could revalue its remaining nine units of dark fiber at a total of $180. If the assets used in the transaction were difficult to value—as dark fiber clearly was—Enron's inflated valuation might not generate much suspicion, at least initially. But ultimately the valuations would be indefensible, and Enron would need to recognize the associated losses.

It is an open question for this Committee and others whether this transaction was unique, or whether Enron engaged in other, similar deals. It seems likely that the dark fiber deal was not the only one of its kind. There are many sentences in footnote 16 regarding other related party transactions.

D. The "Gatekeepers"

These are but three examples of how Enron's derivatives dealings with outside parties resulted in material information not being reflected in market prices. There are others, many within JEDI alone. I have attempted to summarize this information for the Committee. Clearly it is important that investigators question the Enron employees who were directly involved in these transactions to get a sense of whether my summaries are complete.

Moreover, a thorough inquiry into these dealings also should include the major financial market "gatekeepers" involved with Enron: accounting firms, banks, law firms, and credit rating agencies. Employees of these firms are likely to have knowledge of these transactions. Moreover, these firms have a responsibility to come forward with information relevant to these transactions. They benefit directly and indirectly from the existence of U.S. securities regulation, which in many instances both forces companies to use the services of gatekeepers and protects gatekeepers from liability.

Recent cases against accounting firms—including Arthur Andersen—are eroding that protection, but the other gatekeepers remain well insulated. Gatekeepers are kept honest—at least in theory—by the threat of legal liability, but this threat is virtually non-existent for some gatekeepers. The capital markets would be more efficient if companies were not required by law to use particular gatekeepers (which only gives those firms market power), and if gatekeepers were subject to a credible threat of liability for their involvement in fraudulent transactions. Congress should consider expanding the scope of securities fraud liability by making it clear that these gatekeepers will be liable for assisting companies in transactions designed to distort the economic reality of financial statements.

With respect to Enron, all of these gatekeepers have questions to answer about the money they received, the quality of their work, and the extent of their conflicts of interest. It has been reported that Enron paid $52 million in 2000 to its audit firm, Arthur Andersen, the majority of which was for non-audit related consulting services, yet Arthur Andersen failed to spot many of Enron's losses. It also seems that at least one of the other "Big 5" accounting firms was involved in at least one of Enron's special purpose entities.

Enron also paid several hundred million dollars in fees to investment and commercial banks for work on various financial aspects of its business, including fees for derivatives transactions, and yet none of those firms pointed out to investors any of the derivatives problems at Enron. Instead, as late as October 2001, sixteen of seventeen securities analysts covering Enron rated it a "strong buy" or "buy."

Enron paid substantial fees to its outside law firm, which previously had employed Enron's general counsel, yet that firm failed to correct or disclose the problems related to derivatives and special purpose entities. Other law firms also may have been involved in these transactions; if so, they should be questioned, too.

Finally, and perhaps most importantly, the three major credit rating agencies—Moody's, Standard & Poor's, and Fitch/IBCA—received substantial, but as yet undisclosed, fees from Enron. Yet just weeks prior to Enron's bankruptcy filing—after most of the negative news was out and Enron's stock was trading at just $3 per share—all three agencies still gave investment grade ratings to Enron's debt. The credit rating agencies in particular have benefited greatly from a web of legal rules that essentially requires securities issuers to obtain ratings from them (and them only), and at the same time protects those agencies from outside competition and liability under the securities laws. They are at least partially to blame for the Enron mess.

An investment-grade credit rating was necessary to make Enron's special purpose entities work, and Enron lived on the cusp of investment grade. During 2001, it was rated just above the lowest investment-grade rating by all three agencies: BBB+ by Standard & Poor's and Fitch IBCA, and Baa1 by Moody's. Just before Enron's bankruptcy, all three rating agencies lowered Enron's rating two notches, to the lowest investment grade rating. Enron noted in its most recent annual report that its "continued investment grade status is critical to the success of its wholesale business as well as its ability to maintain adequate liquidity." Many of Enron's debt obligations were triggered by a credit ratings downgrade; some of those obligations had been scheduled to mature in December 2001. The importance of credit ratings at Enron and the timing of Enron's bankruptcy filing are not coincidences; the credit rating agencies have some explaining to do.

Derivatives based on credit ratings—called credit derivatives—are a booming business and they raise serious systemic concerns. The rating agencies seem to know this. Even Moody's appears worried, and recently asked several securities firms for more detail about their dealings in these instruments. It is particularly chilling that not even Moody's—the most sophisticated of the three credit rating agencies—knows much about these derivatives deals.

III. DERIVATIVES "INSIDE" ENRON

The derivatives problems at Enron went much deeper than the use of special purpose entities with outside investors. If Enron had been making money in what it represented as its core businesses, and had used derivatives simply to "dress up" its financial statements, this Committee probably would not be meeting here today. Even after Enron restated its financial statements on November 8, 2001, it could have clarified its accounting treatment, consolidated its debts, and assured the various analysts that it was a viable entity. But it could not. Why not?

This question leads me to the second explanation of Enron's collapse: most of what Enron represented as its core businesses were not making money. Recall that Enron began as an energy firm. Over time, Enron shifted its focus from the bricks-and-mortar energy business to the trading of derivatives. As this shift occurred, it appears that some of its employees began lying systematically about the profits and losses of Enron's derivatives trading operations. Simply put, Enron's reported earnings from derivatives seem to be more imagined than real. Enron's derivatives trading was profitable, but not in the way an investor might expect based on the firm's financial statements. Instead, some Enron employees seem to have misstated systematically their profits and losses in order to make their trading businesses appear less volatile than they were.

First, a caveat. During the past few weeks, I have been gathering information about Enron's derivatives operations, and I have learned many disturbing things. Obviously, I cannot testify first-hand to any of these matters. I have never been on Enron's trading floor, and I have never been involved in Enron's business. I cannot offer fact testimony as to any of these matters.

Nonetheless, I strongly believe the information I have gathered is credible. It is from many sources, including written information, e-mail correspondence, and telephone interviews. Congressional investigators should be able to confirm all of these facts. In any event, even if only a fraction of the information in this section of my testimony proves to be correct, it will be very troubling indeed.

In a nutshell, it appears that some Enron employees used dummy accounts and rigged valuation methodologies to create false profit and loss entries for the derivatives Enron traded. These false entries were systematic and occurred over several years, beginning as early as 1997. They included not only the more esoteric financial instruments Enron began trading recently—such as fiber-optic bandwidth and weather derivatives—but also Enron's very profitable trading operations in natural gas derivatives.

Enron derivatives traders faced intense pressure to meet quarterly earnings targets imposed directly by management and indirectly by securities analysts who covered Enron. To ensure that Enron met these estimates, some traders apparently hid losses and understated profits. Traders apparently manipulated the reporting of their real economic profits and losses in an attempt to fit the imagined accounting profits and losses that drove Enron management.

A. Using "Prudency" Reserves

Enron's derivatives trading operations kept records of the traders' profits and losses. For each trade, a trader would report either a profit or a loss, typically in spreadsheet format. These profit and loss reports were designed to reflect economic reality. Frequently, they did not.

Instead of recording the entire profit for a trade in one column, some traders reportedly split the profit from a trade into two columns. The first column reflected the portion of the actual profits the trader intended to add to Enron's current financial statements. The second column, ironically labeled the "prudency" reserve, included the remainder.

To understand this concept of a prudency reserve, suppose a derivatives trader earned a profit of $10 million. Of that $10 million, the trader might record $9 million as profit today, and enter $1 million into "prudency." An average deal would have prudency reserve of up to $1 million, and all of the "prudency" entries might add up to $10 to $15 million.

Enron's prudency reserves did not depict economic reality, nor could they have been intended to do so. Instead, "prudency" was merely a slush fund that could be used to smooth out profits and losses over time. The portion of profits recorded as "prudency" could be used to offset any future losses.

In essence, the traders were saving for a rainy day. Prudency reserves would have been especially effective for long-maturity derivatives contracts, because it was more difficult to determine a precise valuation as of a particular date for those contracts, and any "prudency" cushion would have protected the traders from future losses for several years going forward.

As luck would have it, some of the prudency reserves turned out to be quite prudent. In one quarter, some derivatives traders needed so much accounting profit to meet their targets that they wiped out all of their "prudency" accounts.

Saving for a rainy day is not necessarily a bad idea, and it seems possible that derivatives traders at Enron did not believe they were doing anything wrong. But prudency accounts are far from an accepted business practice. A trader who used a prudency account at a major Wall Street firm would be seriously disciplined, or perhaps fired. To the extent Enron was smoothing its income using prudency entries, it was misstating the volatility and current valuation of its trading businesses, and misleading its investors. Indeed, such fraudulent practices would have thwarted the very purpose of Enron's financial statements: to give investors an accurate picture of a firm's risks.

B. Mismarking Forward Curves

Not all of the misreporting of derivatives positions at Enron was as brazen as "prudency." Another way derivatives frequently are used to misstate profits and losses is by mismarking forward curves. It appears that Enron traders did this, too.

A forward curve is a list of forward rates for a range of maturities. In simple terms, a forward rate is the rate at which a person can buy something in the future.

For example, natural gas forward contracts trade on the New York Mercantile Exchange ("NYMEX"). A trader can commit to buy a particular type of natural gas to be delivered in a few weeks, months, or even years. The rate at which a trader can buy natural gas in one year is the one-year forward rate. The rate at which a trader can buy natural gas in ten years is the ten-year forward rate. The forward curve for a particular natural gas contract is simply the list of forward rates for all maturities.

Forward curves are crucial to any derivatives trading operation because they determine the value of a derivatives contract today. Like any firm involved in trading derivatives, Enron had risk management and valuation systems that used forward curves to generate profit and loss statements.

It appears that Enron traders selectively mismarked their forward curves, typically in order to hide losses. Traders are compensated based on their profits, so if a trader can hide losses by mismarking forward curves, he or she is likely to receive a larger bonus.

These losses apparently ranged in the tens of millions of dollars for certain markets. At times, a trader would manually input a forward curve that was different from the market. For more complex deals, a trader would use a spreadsheet model of the trade for valuation purposes, and tweak the assumptions in the model to make a transaction appear more or less valuable. Spreadsheet models are especially susceptible to mismarking.

Certain derivatives contracts were more susceptible to mismarking than others. A trader would be unlikely to mismark contracts that were publicly traded—such as the natural gas contracts traded on NYMEX—because quotations of the values of those contracts are publicly available. However, the NYMEX forward curve has a maturity of only six years; accordingly, a trader would be more likely to mismark a ten-year natural gas forward rate.

At Enron, forward curves apparently remained mismarked for as long as three years. In more esoteric areas, where markets were not as liquid, traders apparently were even more aggressive. One trader who already had recorded a substantial profit for the year, and believed any additional profit would not increase his bonus much, reportedly reduced his recorded profits for one year, so he could push them forward into the next year, which he wasn't yet certain would be as profitable. This strategy would have resembled the "prudency" accounts described earlier.

C. Warning Signs

Why didn't any of the "gatekeepers" tell investors that Enron was so risky? There were numerous warning signs related to Enron's derivatives trading. Yet the gatekeepers either failed utterly to spot those signs, or spotted those signs and decided not to warn investors about them. Either way, the gatekeepers failed to do their job. This was so even though there have been several recent and high-profile cases involving internal misreporting of derivatives.

Enron disclosed that it used "value at risk" ("VAR") methodologies that captured a 95 percent confidence interval for a one-day holding period, and therefore did not disclose worst-case scenarios for Enron's trading operations. Enron said it relied on "the professional judgment of experienced business and risk managers" to assess these worst-case scenarios (which, apparently, Enron ultimately encountered). Enron reported only high and low month-end values for its trading, and therefore had incentives to smooth its profits and losses at month-end. Because Enron did not report its maximum VAR during the year, investors had no way of knowing just how much risk Enron was taking.

Even the reported VAR figures are remarkable. Enron reported VAR for what it called its "commodity price" risk—including natural gas derivatives trading—of $66 million, more than triple the 1999 value. Enron reported VAR for its equity trading of

$59 million, more than double the 1999 value. A VAR of $66 million meant that Enron could expect, based on historical averages, that on five percent of all trading days (on average, twelve business days during the year) its "commodity" derivatives trading operations alone would gain or lose $66 million, a not trivial sum.

Moreover, because Enron's derivatives frequently had long maturities—maximum terms ranged from six to twenty-nine years—there often were not prices from liquid markets to use as benchmarks. For those long-dated derivatives, professional judgment was especially important. For a simple instrument, Enron might calculate the discounted present value of cash flows using Enron's borrowing rates. But more complex instruments required more complex methodologies. For example, Enron completed over 5,000 weather derivatives deals, with a notional value of more than $4.5 billion, and many of those deals could not be valued without a healthy dose of professional judgment. The same was true of Enron's trading of fiber-optic bandwidth.

And finally there was the following flashing red light in Enron's most recent annual report: "In 2000, the value at risk model utilized for equity trading market risk was refined to more closely correlate with the valuation methodologies used for merchant activities." Enron's financial statements do not describe these refinements, and their effects, but given the failure of the risk and valuation models even at a sophisticated hedge fund such as Long-Term Capital Management—which employed "rocket scientists" and Nobel laureates to design various sophisticated computer models—there should have been reason for concern when Enron spoke of "refining" its own models.

It was Arthur Andersen's responsibility not only to audit Enron's financial statements, but also to assess the adequacy of Enron management's internal controls on derivatives trading. When Arthur Andersen signed Enron's 2000 annual report, it expressed approval in general terms of Enron's system of internal controls during 1998 through 2000.

Yet it does not appear that Andersen systematically and independently verified Enron's valuations of certain complex trades, or even of its forward curves. Andersen apparently examined day-to-day changes in these values, as reported by traders, and checked to see if each daily change was recorded accurately. But this Committee—and others investigating Enron—should inquire about whether Andersen did anything more than sporadically check Enron's forward curves.

Even when the relevant risk information is contained in Enron's financial statements, it is unclear whether Andersen adequately considered this information in opining that Enron management's internal controls were adequate. To the extent Andersen alleges—as I understand many accounting firms do—that their control opinion does not cover all types of control failures and necessarily is based on management's "assertions," it is worth noting that the very information Andersen audited raised substantial questions about potential control problems at Enron. In other words, Andersen has been hoisted by its own petard.

But Andersen was not alone in failing to heed these warning signs. Securities analysts and credit rating agencies arguably should have spotted them, too. Why were so many of these firms giving Enron favorable ratings, when publicly available information indicated that there were reasons for worry? Did these firms look the other way because they were subject to conflicts of interest? Individual investors rely on these institutions to interpret the detailed footnote disclosures in Enron's reports, and those institutions have failed utterly. The investigation into Andersen so far has generated a great deal of detail about that firm's approach to auditing Enron, but the same questions should be asked of the other gatekeepers, too. Specifically, this Committee should ask for and closely examine all of the analyst reports on Enron from the relevant financial services firms and credit rating agencies.

Finally, to clarify this point, consider how much Enron's businesses had changed during its last years. Andersen's most recent audit took place during 2000, when Enron's derivatives-related assets increased from $2.2 billion to $12 billion, and Enron's derivatives-related liabilities increased from $1.8 billion to $10.5 billion. These numbers are staggering. Most of this growth was due to increased trading through EnronOnline. But EnronOnline's assets and revenues were qualitatively different from Enron's other derivatives trading. Whereas Enron's derivatives operations included speculative positions in various contracts, EnronOnline's operations simply matched buyers and sellers. The "revenues" associated with EnronOnline arguably do not belong in Enron's financial statements. In any event, the exponential increase in the volume of trading through EnronOnline did not generate substantial profits for Enron.

Enron's aggressive additions to revenues meant that it was the "seventh-largest U.S. company" in title only. In reality, Enron was a much smaller operation, whose primary money-making business—a substantial and speculative derivatives trading operation—covered up poor performance in Enron's other, smaller businesses, including EnronOnline. Enron's public disclosures show that, during the past three years, the firm was not making money on its non-derivatives businesses. Gross margins from these businesses were essentially zero from 1998 through 2000.

To see this, consider the table below, which sets forth Enron's income statement separated into its non-derivatives and derivatives businesses. I put together this table based on the numbers in Enron's 2000 income statement, after learning from the footnote 1, page 36, that the meaning of the "Other revenues" entry on Enron's income statement is—as far as I can tell—essentially "Gain (loss) from derivatives":

Enron's Income from Derivatives and Non-Derivative Businesses (in millions of dollars)

	2000	1999	1998
Non-derivatives revenues	93,557	34,774	27,215
Non-derivatives expenses	94,517	34,761	26,381
Non-derivatives gross margin	(960)	13	834
Gain (loss) from derivatives	7,232	5,338	4,045
Other expenses	(4,319)	(4,549)	(3,501)
Operating income	1,953	802	1,378

This table demonstrates four key facts. First, the recent and dramatic increase in Enron's overall non-derivatives revenues—the statistic that supposedly made Enron the seventh-largest U.S. company—was offset by an increase in non-derivatives expenses. The increase in revenues reflected in the first line of the chart was substantially from EnronOnline, and did not help Enron's bottom line, because it included an increase in expenses reflected in the second line of the chart. Although Enron itself apparently was the counterparty to all of the trades, EnronOnline simply matched buyers ("revenue") with sellers ("expenses"). Indeed, as non-derivatives revenues more than tripled, non-derivatives expenses increased even more.

Second, Enron's non-derivatives businesses were not performing well in 1998 and were deteriorating through 2000. The third row, "Non-derivatives gross margin," is the difference between non-derivatives revenues and non-derivatives expenses. The downward trajectory of Enron's non-derivatives gross margin shows, in a general sense, that Enron's non-derivatives businesses made some money in 1998, broke even in 1999, and actually lost money in 2000.

Third, Enron's positive reported operating income (the last row) was due primarily to gains from derivatives (the fourth row). (Enron—like many firms—shied from using the word "derivatives" and substituted the euphemism "Price Risk Management.") Excluding the gains from derivatives, Enron would have reported substantially negative operating income for all three years.

Fourth, Enron's gains from derivatives were very substantial. Enron gained more than $16 billion from these activities in three years. To place the numbers in perspective, these gains were roughly comparable to the annual net revenue for all trading activities (including stocks, bonds, and derivatives) at the premier investment firm, Goldman Sachs & Co., during the same periods, a time in which Goldman Sachs first issued shares to the public.

The key difference between Enron and Goldman Sachs is that Goldman Sachs seems to have been up front with investors about the volatility of its trading operations. In contrast, Enron officials represented that it was not a trading firm, and that derivatives were used for hedging purposes. As a result, Enron's stock traded at much higher multiples of earnings than more candid trading-oriented firms.

The size and scope of Enron's derivatives trading operations remain unclear. Enron reported gains from derivatives of $7.2 billion in 2000, and reported notional amounts of derivatives contracts as of December 31, 2000, of only $21.6 billion. Either Enron was generating 33 percent annual returns from derivatives (indicating that the underlying contracts were very risky), or Enron actually had large positions and reduced the notional values of its outstanding derivatives contracts at year-end for cosmetic purposes. Neither conclusion appears in Enron's financial statements or its management's discussion and analysis ("MD&A") section.

IV. CONCLUSION

How did Enron lose so much money? That question has dumbfounded investors and experts in recent months. But the basic answer is now apparent: Enron was a derivatives trading firm; it made billions trading derivatives, created through use of reporting tricks such as mismarking forward curves and managing prudency reserves, while it lost billions on virtually everything else it did, including projects in fiber-optic bandwidth, retail gas and power, water systems, and even technology stocks. Enron used its expertise in derivatives to hide these losses. For most people, the fact that Enron had transformed itself from an energy company into a derivatives trading firm is a surprise.

Enron is to blame for much of this, of course. The temptations associated with derivatives have proved too great for many companies, and Enron is no exception. The conflicts of interest among Enron's officers have been widely reported. Nevertheless, it remains unclear how much top officials knew about the various misdeeds at Enron. They should and will be asked. At least some officers must have been aware of how deeply derivatives penetrated Enron's businesses; Enron even distributed thick multi-volume Derivatives Training Manuals to new employees. (The Committee should ask to see these manuals.)

Enron's directors likely have some regrets. Enron's Audit Committee in particular failed to uncover a range of external and internal financial gimmickry. However, it remains to be seen how much of the inner workings at Enron were hidden from the outside directors; some directors may very well have learned a great deal from recent media accounts, or even perhaps from this testimony. Enron's general counsel, on the other hand, will have some questions to answer.

But too much focus on Enron misses the mark. As long as ownership of companies is separated from their control—and in the U.S. securities market it almost always will be—managers of companies will have incentives to be aggressive in reporting financial data. The securities laws recognize this fact of life, and create and subsidize "gatekeeper" institutions to monitor this conflict between managers and shareholders.

The collapse of Enron makes it plain that the key gatekeeper institutions that support our system of market capitalism have failed. The institutions sharing the blame include auditors, law firms, banks, securities analysts, independent directors, and credit rating agencies.

All of the facts I have described in my testimony were available to the gatekeepers. I obtained this information in a matter of weeks by sitting at a computer in my office in San Diego, and by picking up a telephone. The gatekeepers' failure to discover this information, and to communicate it effectively to investors, is simply inexcusable.

The difficult question is what to do about the gatekeepers. They occupy a special place in securities regulation, and receive great benefits as a result. Employees at gatekeeper firms are among the most highly-paid people in the world. They have access to superior information and supposedly have greater expertise than average investors at deciphering that information. Yet, with respect to Enron, the gatekeepers clearly did not do their job.

One potential answer is to eliminate the legal requirements that companies use particular gatekeepers (especially credit rating agencies), while expanding the scope of securities fraud liability and enforcement to make it clear that all gatekeepers will be liable for assisting companies in transactions designed to distort the economic reality of financial statements. A good starting point before considering such legislation would be to call the key gatekeeper employees to testify.

Congress also must decide whether, after ten years of deregulation, the post-Enron derivatives markets should remain exempt from the regulation that covers all other investment contracts. In my view, the answer is no.

A headline in Enron's 2000 annual report states, "In Volatile Markets, Everything Changes But Us." Sadly, Enron got it wrong. In volatile markets, everything changes, and the laws should change, too. It is time for Congress to act to ensure that this motto does not apply to U.S. financial market regulation.

Enron and Ethical Corporate Climates

Lynne L. Dallas[*][1]

With substantial inquiry concerning what individual Enron directors and officers knew or what they should have known, little attention has been directed to examining the institutional structure at Enron that may have spawned the unethical behavior—and to assessing responsibility for that structure. By institutional structure, I refer to Enron's ethical climate, which is a manifestation of its culture. Corporate culture is defined as a "complex set of common beliefs and expectations held by members of the organization," which are based on shared value, assumptions, attitudes, and norms.[2] The corporation's ethical climate refers to the ethical meaning attached by employees to organizational policies, practices and procedures. These policies, practices, and procedures influence moral awareness, the criteria used in moral decision-making, whether morals will have priority over other values, and moral behavior.

I. SOCIAL CONTEXT IS IMPORTANT TO INDIVIDUAL ETHICAL/UNETHICAL DECISION-MAKING

There is considerable reluctance to make directors liable for a legal violation committed by others. The assumption is that fault for such illegal decision-making lies solely in the individual characteristics of the persons committing the violations. Research makes clear, however, that "individual characteristics alone are insufficient to explain moral and ethical behavior."[3] One commentator summarizes this research as follows:

---

[*] Professor of Law, University of San Diego School of Law, San Diego.

[1] This essay is based on one of my articles: *A Preliminary Inquiry into the Responsibility of Corporations and Their Officers and Directors for an Ethical Corporate Climate: The Psychology of Enron's Demise*, 35 RUTGERS L. J. (forthcoming 2004).

[2] Vicky Arnold & James C. Lampe, *Understanding the Factors Underlying Ethical Organizations: Enabling Continuous Ethical Improvement*, 15 J. APPLIED BUS. RES. 1, 2 (1999).

[3] Bart Victor & John B. Cullen, *The Organizational Bases of Ethical Work Climates*, 33 ADMIN. SCI. Q. 101, 103 (1988).

> Theory and research related to the situational effects on ethical/unethical behavior offer strong support for situational variables having a profound effect on ethical/unethical behavior in most people. The clear implication is that it is inappropriate for organizations to rely totally on individual integrity to guide behavior. . . . Therefore, organizations must provide a context that supports ethical behavior and discourages unethical behavior.[4]

Although this research does not relieve the individual violator of responsibility, it does widen the net of responsibility to those responsible for the environment in which decision-making occurs. Having the persons responsible for a corporation's unethical climate bear some of the blame, thus giving them an incentive to improve their corporation's climate, is particularly important in a world where the actions of a few employees can have severe, adverse consequences.

While the social context of decision-making is extremely important, more attention has been given to the components of individual ethical decision-making and moral reasoning processes. An examination of these components and processes reveal, however, an important role for social context.

II. COMPONENTS OF INDIVIDUAL ETHICAL/UNETHICAL DECISION-MAKING AND THE IMPORTANCE OF SOCIAL ENVIRONMENT

James Rest, in his important publication *Moral Development: Advances in Research Theory,* identified four inner cognitive-affective processes that he called components in ethical decision-making. They are: (1) "moral awareness," which is awareness that an ethical issue exists, thus a situation is interpreted as raising moral issues; (2) "moral decision-making," which is deciding what course of action is morally sound; (3) "moral intent," which refers to deciding that moral values should take priority over non-moral values in the decision; and (4) "moral behavior," which constitutes executing and implementing the moral decision.[5]

The first component, moral awareness, is affected by the moral intensity of the issue involved. Two factors that are relevant to moral intensity are social consensus and social proximity. These factors suggest that corporations affect the moral awareness of their employees. Social consensus is defined by Thomas M. Jones as "the degree of social agreement that a proposed act is evil (or good)."[6] Kenneth D. Butterfield states that it is "the individual's perception of social consensus within the individual's rel-

---

[4] Linda Klebe Trevino, *Ethical Decision-Making in Organizations: A Person-Situation Interactionist Model,* 11 ACAD. MGMT. REV. 601, 614 (1986).

[5] James R. Rest, *The Major Components of Morality,* in MORALITY, MORAL BEHAVIOR, AND MORAL DEVELOPMENT 24, 24-36 (William M. Kurtines & Jacob Gewirtz eds., 1984).

[6] Thomas M. Jones, *Ethical Decision-Making by Individuals in Organizations: An Issue-Contingent Model,* 16 ACAD. MGMT. REV. 366, 375 (1991).

evant social sphere that is most important to determining whether an individual will recognize a moral issue."[7] His empirical study confirms that:

> [M]oral awareness is more likely to be triggered when an individual perceives a social consensus within the organization/profession that the activity in question is ethically problematic. Thus, although previous normative and descriptive writings have tended to suggest that ethical decision-making is an individual or personal process . . . research suggests that, in organizational contexts, it is very much a social process. If a decision-maker perceives that others in the social environment will see an issue as ethically problematic, she or he will be more likely to consider the ethical issues involved.[8]

Thus, the corporation plays an important role in determining the degree to which its employees are aware of ethical issues.

The corporation also affects moral awareness by influencing the moral intensity of an issue resulting from social proximity. Social proximity refers to the "feeling of nearness (social, cultural, psychological, or physical) that the moral agent has for victims (beneficiaries) of the evil (beneficial) act in question."[9] Moral awareness or sensitivity includes the "awareness that the resolution of a particular dilemma may affect the welfare of others."[10] Business practices and procedures determine the degree to which consequences of business decisions are made salient to the employee as decision-maker. Does the corporation, for example, require managers to "explicitly report on potential consequences" (both beneficial and non-beneficial) to corporate stakeholders of his or her decisions?[11] Is the employee evaluated on the basis of these consequences? Because an employee's perceptions and interpretations of particular situations affect his or her emotions, an understanding of the consequences of business decisions may create empathy, and thus moral awareness, in employees.

Management's framing of issues in ethical or moral terms may also affect the moral awareness of employees. For example, corporate norms at Ford dictated that employees deciding on the recall of the Ford Pinto not refer to the "problem" of the Pinto "bursting into flames" and killing people, but rather refer to the "condition" of the Pinto as "lightening up." Butterfield found a significant relationship between ethical

---

[7] Kenneth D. Butterfield et al., *Moral Awareness in Business Organizations: Influences of Issue-Related and Social Context Factors*, 53 HUM. REL. 981, 990, 999 (2000).

[8] *Id.* at 1001.

[9] Jones, *supra* note 6, at 376.

[10] Alice Gaudine & Linda Thorne, *Emotions and Ethical Decision-Making in Organizations,* 31 J. BUS. ETHICS 175, 179 (2001).

[11] Butterfield et al., *supra* note 7, at 989.

issue framing and moral awareness for those actions that are viewed by participants as ethically ambiguous. These findings indicate that the corporation, through issue framing, may have an impact on employees in situations that employees view as ethically ambiguous.

With respect to component two, moral decision-making (deciding what is the moral course of action), Rest offers two approaches that suggest the importance of social context to individual ethical/unethical decision-making. The social norms approach suggests that individuals determine the appropriate course of action by reference to social norms. According to this approach, "moral development is a matter of acquiring a number of social norms and being set to have those norms activated by specific situations."[12] Corporations have an important impact on the social norms adopted by employees. Perceived practices and procedures of corporations reflect workplace norms that involve ethics and that include "the perceived prescriptions, proscriptions and permissions regarding moral obligations" in the corporation.[13] For example, as discussed later in this article, various social norms operating in Enron's workplace influenced the employees' unethical decision-making.

The second approach to moral decision-making focuses on cognitive development. Lawrence Kohlberg developed a theory of moral development in which persons progress in moral reasoning through three stages. The stages reflect how persons interact with their environment, think about ethical dilemmas, and determine what is fair and just. For persons reasoning at the first two stages, social environment has a profound effect on individual decision making. According to Kohlberg, persons progress to higher stages of moral reasoning by experiencing ethical dilemmas and being exposed to higher-stage reasoning. Thus, corporations may increase the moral reasoning levels of their employees through work tasks, training programs, and education. Rest reports that such moral development programs do produce "modest but significant gains."[14] Training programs of particular use to employees are those that center on ethical dilemmas that are likely to arise in their jobs and workplaces. Rest also notes that programs "emphasizing peer discussion of controversial moral dilemmas" are particularly effective."[15]

Lastly, the third and fourth components of ethical decision making involve following through with what a person reasons to be morally sound. There is "moral intent," which is the decision to give priority to morals over competing values and "moral behavior," which is to actually engage in the execution and implementation of a moral decision.

A number of contextual factors encourage or discourage an employee from giving priority to morals and actually following through with a moral decision. First, general

---

[12] *See supra* note 5, at 31.

[13] Victor & Cullen, *supra* note 3, at 101.

[14] JAMES R. REST, MORAL DEVELOPMENT: ADVANCES IN RESEARCH AND THEORY 177 (1986).

[15] *Id.*

role expectations within the business environment can influence the ethics of decision-making. Bommer claims that employees are "ethical segregationists" in that they often apply different sets of values to work and home.[16] Bommer claims that "managerial decisions will correspond more closely to the humanistic, religious, cultural, and societal values of the society-at-large only when these values are made part of the job environment."[17]

A second factor is the employee's assessment of personal responsibility for corporate decision-making. Unethical behavior is more likely when responsibility is diffuse or attributed to others higher in the corporation. Through its expectation of employees and its policies and practices, the corporation determines whether and to what extent employees are held personally responsible for corporate decisions.

Third, the corporate environment influences whether empathy-based moral motives are encouraged or discouraged. Martin Hoffman notes that "[m]ature empathy . . . reflects a sensitivity to subtle differences in the severity and quality of consequences that different actions might have for different people, and it may therefore contribute to informed moral judgments about behavior."[18] Empathy may also increase the receptiveness of an individual to justice principles such as equality and fairness. Business practices and policies enhance employee empathy when they encourage employees to consider the consequences of their decisions on other stakeholders and facilitate extensive communication between employee decision-makers and those who will bear the consequences of their decisions.

Fourth, an important social factor in an employee's moral behavior is his or her choice of referent—or persons after whom his or her behavior is modeled. Referents in the work environment may be higher-level officials who are viewed as organizational heroes, direct supervisors, or peers. The differential association theory explains that unethical behavior is learned by employees while observing and interacting with members of primary groups such as peers and managers. Employees either internalize the primary group's definition of unethical behavior through a socialization process, or adopt it through peer pressure, and act on that basis. The beliefs and values of referents often are better predictors of behavior than the employee's own individual beliefs. In addition, the opportunity for unethical behavior is a necessary condition for unethical behavior. In this regard "corporate policies are moderating variables in controlling opportunity."[19]

---

[16] Michael Bommer et al., *A Behavioral Model of Ethical and Unethical Decision-Making*, 6 J. BUS. ETHICS 265, 268 (1987).

[17] *Id.*

[18] Martin L. Hoffman, *Empathy, Its Limitations, and Its Role in a Comprehensive Moral Theory*, in MORALITY, MORAL BEHAVIOR, AND MORAL DEVELOPMENT 283, 297 (William M. Kurtines & Jacob L. Gerwirtz eds., 1984).

[19] O.C. Ferrell & Larry G. Gresham, *A Contingency Framework for Understanding Ethical Decision-Making in Marketing*, 49 J. MARKETING 87, 92 (1985).

In conclusion, while the wider social environment, individual personality traits, and the nature of specific ethical issues are important to the ethics of employee decision-making, the corporation itself creates a social environment that can increase or decrease the likelihood of ethical decision-making.

III. ASCERTAINING CORPORATE CLIMATES AND THEIR EFFECT ON EMPLOYEE ETHICAL/UNETHICAL DECISION-MAKING

A. Methods of Ascertaining Ethical Climates

Ethical climates can be ascertained and studied. A number of methodologies exist for determining a corporation's ethical climate. Employee questionnaires are the most common. These questionnaires may focus on the main goals and values of the corporations, elicit information on the beliefs of top executives, supervisors, and peers, inquire about ethical and unethical behavior engaged in by employees or observed by them in the workplace (either generally or by specific categories), find out the employees' perceptions of whether their colleagues are ethical or unethical, and ascertain the corporation's commitment to, and support of, ethical behavior through questions about its policies, practices, and procedures.

B. Victor and Cullen's Ethical Climate Questionnaire

Bart Victor and John Cullen have developed a classification of ethical climates that has been widely used by academic researchers. They characterize corporate climates according to whether or not participants use egoism (instrumentalism), benevolence, or principle as the main ethical criterion. These decision criteria are defined in terms of whether the goals are "maximizing self-interest, maximizing joint interests [benevolence], or adherence to principle."[20] Most corporate climates have at least minimal degrees of caring and instrumentalism.

C. The Effect of Climates on Ethical/Unethical Decision-Making

A corporation's climate is important to decision-making by employees. One study, based on responses to projective vignettes, found that ethical climates measured by questions such as "what are the opinions of your colleagues concerning the ethicality of X," were positively related to ethical decision-making. Another study of twenty-two large mall department stores found that stores with well-defined codes of ethics and organizational values experienced less employee theft. In addition, a survey of employees from different companies found that an ethical compliance program that was values-driven resulted in lower observed instances of unethical conduct.

---

[20] Victor & Cullen, *supra* note 3, at 104.

In terms of Victor and Cullen's climate classification system, Wimbush proposes that the instrumental (egoism) climate will foster unethical behavior. He explains:

> This is expected to occur because only in an ethical climate based on an egoistic decision-making criterion would people most likely act in ways to promote their own exclusive self-interest regardless of laws, rules, or the impact their decisions have on others. . . . The deleterious effect of the decision-maker's decisions on others could mean, for example, taking from others what is rightfully theirs or intentionally not providing adequate or truthful information.[21]

These expectations are confirmed by Victor and Cullen's survey of employees in a number of corporations. They found that "[e]mployees were more satisfied with the ethics of their company when they observed greater levels of caring [benevolence] . . . and lower levels of instrumentalism [self-interest]."[22] Wimbush notes that without organizational policies encouraging ethical behavior the perception of workers may be that "anything goes as long as the organization's desired level of productivity is achieved."[23]

A recent study also used Victor and Cullen's classification system. It found that ethical climates have an important impact on an employee's perception of the nature of his or her relationship with the corporation that may, in turn, affect employee conduct. The study focused on "covenantal" relationships between employees and corporations, which are "based on mutual commitment to the welfare of the other party, as well as allegiance to a set of shared values, which may be expressed in the mission and objectives of the organization."[24] Covenantal relationships were contrasted with "transactional" employment relationships where the contract is based on an economic exchange in which the relationship "is limited to the offering of . . . skills and abilities that are instrumental to the outcomes sought by both parties."[25] The study found that employees' perception of the corporation's climate affects whether they believe they have a covenantal relationship with their corporation. Employees' perceptions of climates in which the ethical criterion was egoism were negatively associated with their beliefs in a covenantal relationship with the corporation. Benevolent and principle work climates were positively associated with the employee belief that a covenantal relationship existed. The covenantal relationship is deemed to encourage employees

---

[21] James C. Wimbush & Jon M. Shepard, *Toward an Understanding of Ethical Climate: Its Relationship to Ethical Behavior and Supervisory Influence*, 13 J. BUS. ETHICS 637, 641 (1994).

[22] Victor & Cullen, *supra* note 3, at 117.

[23] Wimbush & Shepard, *supra* note 21, at 641.

[24] Tim Barnett & Elizabeth Schubert, *Perceptions of the Ethical Work Climates and Covenantal Relationships*, 36 J. BUS. ETHICS 279, 287 (2002).

[25] *Id.* at 280.

"to engage in proactive behaviors, such as organizational citizenship behaviors, that promote the long-run interest of the organization."[26]

IV. FACTORS RELEVANT TO ETHICAL CORPORATE CLIMATES

Factors relevant to an ethical climate include the corporation's mission statement and code of ethics, the criteria for business decisions, the words and actions of leaders, the handling of conflicts of interest, the reward system, the guidance provided to employees concerning dealing with ethical issues, and the monitoring system. The relevance of the reward system to an ethical climate is briefly discussed below.

The type of reward system that is used appears to affect the likelihood of ethical decision-making. Two systems are identified: outcome-based systems and behavior-based systems. In an outcome-based system, employees are evaluated only on the basis of the outcome of their efforts, such as sales volume or profits booked. In a behavior-based system, consideration is also given by supervisors to the methods or techniques used by employees to achieve the desired outcomes. In a study comparing these systems, behavior-based systems were found to be associated with more ethical decision-making and a more ethical corporate climate.

Whether the compensation system is perceived by employees to be fair also appears to contribute to an ethical climate within the corporation. Doeringer notes the importance of fair compensation to the employees' perceptions of the legitimacy and the morality of corporate authority. He writes that "[t]he importance placed on fairness is related less to the possibility that pay inequities will result in lower effort among disgruntled employees than to a larger concern with creating a set of corporate values that will be perceived as legitimate and moral by the work force."[27]

By placing unrealistic expectations on employees and threatening them with dire personal consequence for not meeting certain ends, management places its relationship with employees on a transactional basis grounded in egoism. They fail to provide a climate for the maintenance of a covenantal relationship in which there is a mutual commitment to the welfare of the other party and allegiance to a shared set of values consistent with social responsibility.

Reward systems can also become unfair and, therefore, increase the likelihood of unethical conduct by tending to politicize the compensation and promotion system. An example is ranking employees at various levels, with those at the bottom rank being first in line for firing. These systems tend to magnify employee insecurity and increase the amount of employee time devoted to currying favor with superiors. Other adverse consequences include decreasing the likelihood of employees communicating problems to supervisors, less accountability for superiors who are not challenged by their employees, and over-confidence on the part of the more powerful managers. More-

---

[26] *Id.* at 287.

[27] Peter B. Doeringer, *The Socio-Economics of Labor Productivity*, in MORALITY, RATIONALITY, AND EFFICIENCY 108, 108–09 (Richard M. Coughlin ed., 1991).

over, for those department heads who are successful in attracting and motivating good employees, an intra-departmental rating system risks losing lower-ranked employees to less successful departments where they will be ranked higher. The system is unfair for several reasons: it discourages teamwork, which is a necessary component of many corporate jobs; it punishes the more successful manager who is able to attract good employees and motivate them; it requires the ranking of employees who often make incommensurable contributions to the success of a company; and it politicizes the compensation process. When Enron, for example, adopted its "rank and yank" system, it was observed that the "most visible consequence was the large amount of time people spent at the local Starbucks, buttering up superiors and bad mouthing peers."[28]

V. ENRON'S CLIMATE

Without extensive surveys and interviews of Enron's employees, it is not possible to give a definitive account of Enron's climate. A review of journalist accounts of Enron, however, indicates that many factors were present that did not support and encourage an ethical climate.

The officers and employees of the company viewed laws and company rules as something to get around or change if the rules did not serve the company's purpose of making money. As one employee explained, "Our job was to take advantage of the law to make as much money as we can."[29]

The employees were expected to work around the laws and company rules to make money. The law and rules were viewed as hindering innovation, creativity, and the entrepreneurial spirit rather than being a necessary foundation for them. Former CEO Jeffrey Skilling encouraged disrespect of rules and company authority. Skilling "set employees loose, encouraging them to push the edge of every rule, even without their supervisors' knowledge."[30] A particularly egregious example is an Enron employee who used $30 million worth of company hardware and enlisted the help of 380 Enron employees to develop a trading system that Skilling, then CEO, was on record as opposing. The employee was not reprimanded because the trading system made money. Current and former employees state that by 2001, "Enron had become less a company than a collection of mercenaries . . . ."[31] An Enron trader claimed that "[t]here wasn't anything they wouldn't try to make money at."[32] The lack of adult restraint apparently spilled over into relations among employees at Enron's offices.

Enron supported and encouraged unethical/illegal behavior by maintaining a reward system that was highly political. The following is a description of how the system

---

[28] James Lardner, *Why Should Anyone Believe You?*, BUSINESS 2.0, at 47 (Mar. 2002).

[29] David Streitfeld & Lee Romney, *Enron's Run Tripped by Arrogance, Greed; Profile: A Lack of Discipline and A Drive to Bend the Rules Were Key Factors in the Meltdown*, L.A. TIMES, Jan. 27, 2002, at A1.

[30] *Id.*

[31] *Id.*

[32] *Id.*

apparently worked. The company formed a twenty-person Personnel Review Committee ("PRC") to rank over 400 Enron vice presidents and a number of its other managers. There were substantial differences in bonuses among rankings and the possibility of firings for those with the lowest rankings. Every six months the PRC process would begin, requiring managers to obtain evaluations from supervisors, peers, and subordinates. The PRC could only rank by unanimous consent, which gave members of the PRC the incentive to lobby for favorable rankings for their employees. Andrew Fastow, Enron's chief financial officer ("CFO"), was willing to hold up the PRC for days to get what he wanted. The members who were not successful in negotiating for their employees would lose employees to other divisions and would often receive lower future evaluations themselves. One journalist noted that members developed "entourages" or "fiefdoms" of loyal employees who gravitated to them because of their ability to protect them in the PRC process.[33] As a result, the managers who emerged to run Enron's new businesses were not necessarily the most competent in those businesses, but they were the most competent in playing the game for power and recognition at Enron.

The system ensured that the powerful players would not be held accountable. Facing precarious futures but the possibility of huge bonuses, employees were fearful of criticizing powerful players. For example, members of the risk assessment group who reviewed the terms and conditions of deals were fearful of retaliation in the PRC from persons whose deals they were reviewing. Internal auditors at Enron may also have felt these pressures because some of them were placed under the authority of the separate business units they audited rather than under the jurisdiction of Enron's central internal auditing officer. In addition, those officers who dealt with the special purpose entities were required to negotiate, on behalf of Enron, with their bosses who had conflicts of interest with respect to these entities. Certain Enron officers, including CFO Fastow, were particularly feared by employees for their vicious retaliations. Enron's culture was described as "ruthless and reckless . . . that lavished rewards on those who played the game, while persecuting those who raised objections."[34] Employees reported that what resulted was a "yes-man" culture in which it became very important to be in the "in-group." As one former employee stated, "One day, you are viewed with favor, and the next day you are not. You know who is in the in-crowd and who is not. . . . You want to continue to be liked in that organization. You do everything you can do to keep that."[35] This system placed considerable power in top management. Some employees feared, for example, that "not giving enough to the chairman's favorite political candidate could send their careers into a dive."[36] An Enron former executive officer reported the effect of such an environment on CEO Skilling:

---

[33] Joshua Chaffin & Stephen Fidler, *Enron Revealed To Be Rotten to the Core*, FIN. TIMES (London), Apr. 9, 2002, at 30.

[34] *Id.*

[35] Joe Stephens & Peter Behr, *Enron's Culture Fed Its Demise*, WASH. POST, Jan. 27, 2002, at A01.

[36] *Id.*

Over the years, Jeff changed. He became more of a creature of his own creation. His hubris came to outweigh some of the more attractive parts of his personality. He became more intolerant, more opinionated, and more bombastic. Jeff was always right, and that got worse. He had a little bit of a God syndrome.[37]

Skilling's arrogance translated into an "institutional arrogance." Unthinking loyalty, homogeneity, and the rejection of outsiders characterized the system. Some employees noted how "loyalty required a sort of groupthink" and that you had to "keep drinking the Enron water."[38] One aspect of the loyalty was that problems were "papered over."[39] A myth was perpetuated that "there were never any mistakes."[40] The culture was self-perpetuating. As one young employee in the risk assessment group, which was mainly staffed by inexperienced MBAs, noted:

> If your boss was fudging, and you have never worked anywhere else, you just assume that everybody fudges earnings. . . . Once you get there and you realized how it was, do you stand up and lose your job? It was scary. It was easy to get into "Well, everybody else is doing it, so maybe it isn't so bad."[41]

Enron's socialization process was referred to as "Enronizing," and people who did not fit in were referred to as "damaged goods" or "shipwrecks."[42]

The lack of accountability is also reflected in the failure of the reward system to consider the manner in which profits were booked. According to former employees, "[e]mployee commissions were tied to the projected profits on long-term deals, with little concern for how the transactions actually worked."[43] Former employees from all divisions reported that "their units routinely engaged in aggressive accounting and financial manipulation, designed to conceal losses and make their operations appear highly profitable."[44] Over-estimations of profits and under-estimations of costs were endemic to the organization. Top management exerted substantial pressure. In discussing Enron's derivative traders, Frank Partnoy, in his Congressional testimony, noted "Enron derivative traders faced intense pressure to meet quarterly earnings targets imposed directly by management and indirectly by securities analysts who covered Enron"

---

[37] Evan Thomas et al., *Every Man for Himself,* NEWSWEEK, Feb. 18, 2002, at 26–27.

[38] Stephens & Behr, *supra* note 35.

[39] Bethany McLean et al., *Why Enron Went Bust,* FORTUNE, Dec. 24, 2001, at 62.

[40] *Id.*

[41] John Byrne et al., *The Environment Was Ripe For Abuse,* BUS. WK., Feb. 25, 2002, at 118.

[42] Johnnie L. Roberts et al., *Enron's Dirty Laundry,* NEWSWEEK, Mar. 11, 2002, at 26.

[43] Chaffin & Fidler, *supra* note 32.

[44] *Id.*

and that these traders "apparently manipulated the reporting of their 'real' economic profits and losses in an attempt to fit the 'imagined' accounting profits and losses that drove Enron management."[45] Insiders called the company "The Crooked E," which was "a word-play on [the company's] slanted logo and business practices."[46]

The reward system, which ranked employees against each other and which offered substantial bonuses, also did not encourage team work or caring among employees. The system discouraged sharing of power, authority, or information. As one employee stated, "People became proprietary about their deals. . . . Why should I help Johnny if I'm rated against Johnny?"[47] The system was "heavily built around star players."[48] A former employee reported that "I locked my desk every night so my colleagues wouldn't steal my work."[49] Enron traders were "afraid to go to the bathroom because the guy sitting next to them might use information off their screen to trade against them."[50]

Enron attracted individuals who wanted to make a lot of money fast. The competitive atmosphere was reflected in Skilling's personality which reportedly thrived "on one-upmanship and didn't mind trying to embarrass the less-quick-witted or anyone who challenged him."[51] Civility was apparently also not valued at Enron.

Enron had a code of ethics and company-stated values that were referred to as RICE, standing for Respect, Integrity, Communication, and Excellence. These values were not adopted after widespread company discussions; rather, they were personally selected by Kenneth Lay. The values were displayed on banners in the lobby of Enron's Houston headquarters and appeared on various items that were given as inspirational gifts to employees. Enron employees said, however, that Lay's interests were "limited to actions that boosted the company's bottom line—and ultimately its stock price."[52] Moreover, in terms of honesty and communication, Lay's statements to employees and the public prior to Enron's filing for bankruptcy on October 24, 2001, are problematic. On August 24, 2001, he stated, "The company is probably in the strongest and best shape it has ever been."[53] On September 26, 2001 he stated that Enron is "fundamentally sound," its third quarter is "looking great," and "we're well-positioned for a

---

[45] *Testimony of Frank Partnoy at the Senate Enron Hearings,* 21 FUTURES & DERIVATIVES L. REP. No. 11, Feb. 2002, at 10.

[46] Chaffin & Fidler, *supra* note 33.

[47] Streitfeld & Romney, *supra* note 29.

[48] Byrne et al., *supra* note 41.

[49] Streitfeld & Romney, *supra* note 29.

[50] McLean, *supra* note 39, at 61–62.

[51] Roberts et al., *supra* note 42, at 25.

[52] Chaffin & Fidler, *supra* note 33.

[53] Lardner, *supra* note 28, at 46.

very strong fourth quarter."[54] And on October 16, 2001, Lay stated "Our 26% increase in [profits] shows the strong results of our core wholesale and retail energy businesses and our natural gas pipelines."[55]

In addition, although Enron had a code of ethics, an anonymous hotline, and required new employees to sign the code, the Enron board waived the conflicts of interest provision in its code of ethics regarding related party transactions with special purpose entities. Moreover, the board members themselves had conflicts of interest.

The climate of Enron came from the top and was probably a long time in the making. It is significant that on the day when internal Enron whistleblower, Sherron Watkins, met with Lay to discuss her allegations of accounting irregularities, Enron's outside law firm delivered a memo to Enron on the "possible risks associated with discharging (or constructively discharging) employees who report allegations of improper accounting practices."[56]

After Enron's problems had become public and just before it filed for bankruptcy, Lay knew what to do. In September 2001, Lay sent out an employee survey, which, in comparing the corporation to the way it had been a year before, found that forty-two percent of Enron employees viewed the company as more self-serving, thirty-seven percent as less trustworthy, and thirty-nine percent as more arrogant. He wrote to employees: "Enron's values will have more importance in each employee's evaluation and feedback. . . . We are all responsible for how we treat our coworkers and customers."[57] It was, however, too little, too late.

The Enron climate did not encourage and support ethical behavior. At most, Enron adopted a compliance-based approach. It clearly did not adopt a values-based approach that would have encouraged employees to follow not only the letter, but also the intent, of laws. Enron also did not encourage compliance with its own rules, which supported an attitude that made it much more likely that employees would not only break company rules, but the law as well.

Although concern with quarterly earnings is an aspect of the current business environment that seeks to enhance shareholder value, Enron's culture was focused not so much on shareholder well-being, or on the well-being of other stakeholders, but on individual self-interest. Every six months, the entire organization geared up for performance reviews and consideration of bonuses. The PRC process affected decision-making throughout the organization at other times. The emphasis on individual bonuses detracted from concern for the impact of business decision-making on Enron's stakeholders. This individual self-interested climate created a situation where monitoring

---

[54] Rushworth M. Kidder, *Ethics at Enron*, Institute for Global Ethics, ETHICS ONLINE, Jan. 21, 2002, *available at* http://www/rider.edu/planc/coursed/us.pol/Enron?ethics.htm (last visited Sept. 13, 2002).

[55] Lardner, *supra* note 28, at 46.

[56] Peter Behr & Susan Schmidt, *Enron CEO Knew of Deals' Risk*, WASH. POST, Feb 20, 2002, at A1.

[57] Streitfeld & Romney, *supra* note 29.

was extremely important. But because of the cavalier attitude towards rules modeled by top management, and, at most, a compliance-based approach to laws and rules, the likelihood of effective monitoring at Enron was substantially reduced.

Enron's top management conveyed the impression that all that mattered was for employees to book profits. Although nothing is wrong with a profit objective, Enron placed this objective above all others. Moreover, the focus was on "paper," and not real profits. Aggressive accounting was encouraged and condoned. Unfortunately, this was also encouraged by the broader business environment in which Enron operated. In addition, Enron placed unreasonable pressures on its employees to book profits, possibly to increase the value of top management's stock options. This exclusive focus on profits and these pressures increased the likelihood of illegal/unethical conduct at Enron.

Enron further eroded the likelihood of ethical behavior by failing to make employees responsible for their decisions. Their responsibility was to "do the deal." Once the deal was closed, employees were rewarded without consideration of how the deal would work out in practice. The emphasis was on appearances and not on real performance. Moreover, the reward structure encouraged the pervasive "fudging" of accounting numbers throughout the organization. The ranking system increased the emphasis on individual self-interest and diminished teamwork (or a caring environment) among coworkers and the expression of empathy. The size of the bonuses also contributed to accounting transgressions and added to the viciousness of retaliations, which diminished open discussions of problems and accountability within the organization.

The ranking system and the PRC unanimity rule also increased the political nature of the system that created an unfair compensation system. Considerable power was placed in top management. Moreover, the system placed power in the hands of individuals who were willing to devote the necessary energies to office politics and political maneuvering. The net effect of such a system was to decrease the likelihood that employees would raise objections to the unethical/illegal conduct of powerful players because power, not real performance, was the driving force of the organization.

Enron socialized new employees to go along with the unethical/illegal behavior of their supervisors. The conduct was pervasive. With so many inexperienced employees, these employees understandably came to believe that ethics has nothing to do with business.

Although Enron had a code of ethics, which is a factor in an ethical climate, Enron's board of directors waived compliance with it on a number of occasions to permit conflicts of interest transactions by Enron's CFO. The lack of concern for conflicts of interest was also evident in the reward system for members of the risk management group and the association of Enron's internal auditors with business units. Additionally, a number of Enron's directors who waived the conflicts of interest rules also had conflicts of interests.

Enron has been described as having an arrogant climate. Such a climate is prone to greater homogeneity because differing views are not valued. This homogeneity can exaggerate the impact of various decision-making biases. Groups that are homogeneous experience group polarization that can result in more risk-adverse behavior or riskier decisions. At Enron, risky decisions were the norm and high risk was encouraged and supported by the lack of contrary views being expressed. To the extent that unethical/illegal activity is considered risky, such a climate can enhance the probability of unethical/illegal behavior. Moreover, this type of climate is likely to exaggerate the egocentric bias that "refers to the tendency for individuals to assume that others are more like them than is actually the case."[58] As a result, Enron's top management and its traders did not take account of the risk preferences of its shareholders, employees, and consumers. In addition, once Enron managers perceived Enron to be at risk, according to prospect theory, they were likely to adopt more risky strategies as they perceived themselves to be choosing between options that represented losses. Also, corporations with arrogant climates are likely to have less accountable employees due to the confirmation bias, which is the "tendency of group members to seek information that confirms their initial opinions."[59] Moreover, homogeneous groups are more likely than heterogeneous groups to rely on shared information, that is, information that they have in common. These tendencies adversely affect information-seeking processes and are likely to result in inadvisable decision-making.

VI. FINAL ANALYSIS AND RECOMMENDATIONS

Ethics and ethical compliance systems require consideration of (a) organizational values, (b) the nature of organizational decision-making, (c) the values and behavior of the organization's leaders, (d) the organization's reward system, (e) the handling of conflicts of interest, (f) the availability of ethical guidance for employees, and (g) the organization's monitoring system. These factors are relevant to the promotion of an ethical climate.

Concerning organizational values, the organization must highly value ethics and ethical behavior. Ethics must be as important as, if not more important than, profits. The organization must value business decisions that take into consideration their consequences to organizational stakeholders. Finally, the organization must take a values-based rather than a compliance-based approach to ethical compliance, which means that the organization places importance not only on compliance with the law and company rules, but also compliance with their intent.

The nature of decision-making within the organization is also relevant to the promotion of an ethical climate. In an ethical climate ethical standards influence decision-making. Business standards are taken into account in day-to-day decision-making by all employees, and business issues are framed in ethical terms. Employees are encouraged to consider the consequences of their decisions on stakeholders and to assume responsibility for those consequences. Employees understand that their role is to con-

---

[58] Lynne L. Dallas, *The New Managerialsim and Diversity on Corporate Boards of Directors*, 76 TULANE L. REV. 1363, 1402 (2002).

[59] *Id.*

sider ethical standards and the consequences of their business decisions on corporate stakeholders. Employees recognize that business decisions are based on compliance with the intent as well as the letter of the law and organizational policies.

The values and behavior of leaders are also relevant to the promotion of an ethical climate. In an ethical climate, leaders view their ethical responsibilities as being as important as, if not more important than, their other organizational responsibilities. Leaders model ethical behavior. For example, ethical leaders are truthful with the organization's stakeholders. They promote communications among employees throughout the organization of information and concerns, both good and bad. They are consistent in words and in actions in encouraging and supporting ethical behavior and discouraging unethical behavior within the organization. In this regard, they do not place on employees unreasonable expectations that may increase the likelihood of unethical/illegal conduct within the organization.

With respect to conflicts of interest, the organization enhances its ethical climate by determining organizational structure, appointments, and benefits with attention to actual or potential conflicts of interest. The organization must have policies that prohibit directors, officers, and employees from taking actions or having interests that make it difficult for them to act in the best interest of the organization.

The organization's reward structure promotes an ethical climate when employee compensation and promotion decisions take into account compliance with ethical standards. Ethical behavior is rewarded and unethical behavior punished. The reward structure also promotes an ethical climate when it provides a behavior-based system that not only considers employee outcomes (production) but also the manner in which those outcomes are achieved. The reward structure must also be perceived as fair by employees. It must not provide the prime motivation for employees and must not detract from the employee's attention to the real business of the organization. In addition, the compensation of leaders must include an assessment of the ethical/unethical behavior of the units that they oversee. Finally, employee compensation must not reflect retaliation for the good faith reporting of violations of ethical standards to appropriate persons within the organization.

In terms of the availability of ethical guidance to employees, the organization increases the likelihood of having an ethical climate when it adopts a code of ethics that provides guidance to employees in their decision-making. The code is most effective when it contains guidance for common ethical dilemmas faced by employees and when it is distributed to all employees, including managers and lower-level employees. The corporation increases the likelihood of having an ethical climate when it encourages and supports open discussions of ethics and ethical compliance among employees. Moreover, employees must know from whom to seek guidance within the organization concerning ethically ambiguous situations and must be encouraged to do so. The organization must emphasize training for employees, for both top managers and low-level employees, which programs are most effective when they provide opportunities for employee discussions and role playing, deal with business ethical dilemmas relevant to the employees involved, and make employees self-aware of factors leading to unethical/illegal decision-making.

As for the organization's monitoring system, an organization supports an ethical climate by having a person with high status and authority within the organization who has primary responsibility for gathering information, monitoring, and reporting on ethics and ethical compliance within the organization. This individual would also be responsible for recommending any changes in the corporation's policies and practices as they relate to ethics and ethical compliance.

An ethical climate is also supported by having the organization's board of directors, or a board committee, periodically review reports on ethics and ethical compliance within the organization, and having the board or its committee discuss and make decisions, when necessary, concerning organizational personnel, policies and practices relating to ethics and ethical compliance.

In addition, the organization enhances the likelihood of an ethical climate when it periodically makes self-assessment of its values, ethical climate, and ethical compliance record. This would involve conducting employee surveys that apply to the organization as a whole and separate surveys of employees in subunits, different job classifications, and hierarchical levels. These employee surveys would cover perceptions of organizational values, the nature of organizational decision-making, the values and behavior of leaders, conflicts of interest, reward structure, employee guidance, and monitoring and assessing the nature and extent of violations of ethical standards. In addition to employee surveys, the organization might conduct exit interviews and employee focus groups to assess ethics and ethical compliance and would periodically interview and survey organizational stakeholders.

The organization would also provide a method for employees to report anonymously violations of the code. It would require employees to periodically acknowledge their understanding and compliance with the organization's code of ethics. In addition, the organization's leaders would periodically certify that:

a. Ethical behavior is highly valued in the organization and is as important as, if not more important than, profit-seeking behavior;
b. The organization's climate encourages and supports ethical decision-making by employees;
c. Employees know that their decisions should comply with the intent as well as the letter of the law and company policies;
d. Ethical decision-making is rewarded, and unethical decision-making punished; and
e. A reasonably system is in place to review, monitor and if necessary, modify the corporation's climate.

Finally, the organization, when deemed advisable, would seek outside audits and advice on the organization's ethics and ethical compliance.

Based on these recommendations, the law does not go far enough in ensuring that corporations have ethical climates. It focuses almost exclusively on the adoption of a code of ethics by corporations and the disclosure of any waiver of the code. In the wake of Enron, Congress passed the Sarbanes-Oxley Act of 2002.[60] The Sarbanes-Oxley Act directed the Securities and Exchange Commission ("SEC") to promulgate rules and regulations that require public corporations to disclose whether or not they have a code of ethics for senior financial officers and, if they do not, to disclose the reasons why they do not have such a code. The Act also requires the SEC to promulgate rules that provide for prompt disclosure of any waivers of code standards. The Act defines codes of ethics to include "standards [that] are reasonably necessary to promote . . . honest and ethical conduct."[61]

In addition, the SEC in 2003 adopted rules required by the Sarbanes-Oxley Act that provide that reporting companies adopt a code of ethics and disclose any waivers (explicit or implicit) of the code. Consistent with the Sarbanes-Oxley Act, the SEC requires the code of ethics to provide for "(1) Honest and ethical conduct, including the ethical handling of actual or apparent conflicts of interest between personal and professional relationships; (2) Full, fair, accurate, timely, and understandable disclosure in reports and documents that a registrant files with . . . the Commission and in other public communications . . . ; [and] (3) Compliance with applicable governmental laws, rules and regulations."[62]

Similarly, the New York Stock Exchange ("NYSE") has proposed to the SEC rules that require companies listed on the NYSE to adopt a code of ethics and disclose any waiver of the code.[63] The NYSE proposed rules require the code of ethics to cover a number of topics, namely, conflicts of interest, corporate opportunities, confidentiality, fair dealing, protection and proper use of company assets, and compliance with laws, rules, and regulations.

A limitation of the Sarbanes-Oxley Act is that it requires the code of ethics to cover only senior financial officers. The Act does not require the code of ethics to apply to directors, other senior executive officers, or lower-level employees of the corporation. The SEC, in its rules applicable to reporting companies, has expanded this coverage to include the corporation's chief executive officer. The NYSE, in its proposed rules, has gone further, however, in requiring listed companies to have a code of ethics that applies to directors, officers, and lower-level employees.

---

[60] Pub. L. No. 107-204, § 406, 116 stat. 745, 789–790 (to be codified at 15 U.S.C. § 7265).

[61] *Id.*

[62] Disclosure Required By Sections 406 and 407 of the Sarbanes-Oxley Act of 2002, SEC Release No. 33-8177 (Jan. 23, 2003).

[63] NYSE Corporate Accountability and Listing Standards Committee, Recommendations Submitted for SEC Approval (2002); Self Regulatory Organizations; Notice of Filing of Proposed Rule Change and Amendment Nol. 1 Thereto by the New York Stock Exchange, Inc. Relating to Corporate Governance, SEC Release 34-47672 (April 11, 2003).

While having a code of conduct is likely to contribute to ethical behavior within an organization, it is the least effective means of decreasing the likelihood of unethical conduct when it is compared to the following: organizational consistency between ethical policies and actions, rewarding ethical behavior and punishing unethical behavior, ethical executive leadership, and open discussions of ethics within the organization. To some extent provisions included within a code of ethics that relate to compliance with the code goes some of the way in assuring that there is consistency between the organization's ethical policies and actions, some connection between rewards and unethical/ethical behavior, ethical behavior by executives, and an open discussion of ethics in the organization. The SEC rules, for example, require the code to provide for "prompt internal reporting of violations of the code to an appropriate person or persons identified in the code" and "accountability for adherence to the code."[64] The NYSE rules provide that corporations must proactively encourage ethical behavior by encouraging employees to report illegal or unethical behavior and consult with appropriate personnel about the best course of action when in doubt. The company must also ensure that "employees know that the company will not allow retaliation for reports made in good faith."[65] These compliance provisions, however, do not explicitly address organizational consistency, reward systems, ethical leadership by executives, and an open discussion of ethics throughout the organization. Moreover, no mention is made of the use of employee questionnaires or surveys to ascertain corporate climate, and there is no provision for leader certification of important ethical climate measures. There are also no guidelines that state that employees should consider the consequences of their decision on stakeholders, that the employee reward system should be fair, or that feedback on organizational conduct should be obtained from organizational stakeholders.[66]

Finally, the Sarbanes-Oxley Act also directed the U.S. Sentencing Commission to reevaluate its sentencing guidelines as applied to organizations. It has solicited comments regarding whether the U.S. Sentencing Guidelines should encourage organizations to foster ethical cultures to ensure more than technical compliance which "can potentially circumvent the purpose of the law or regulation."[67] Ethicists would answer this in the affirmative. They stress the importance to organizational ethics of a values-

---

[64] Disclosure Required By Sections 406 and 407 of the Sarbanes-Oxley Act of 2002, SEC Release No. 33-8177 (Jan. 23, 2003).

[65] NYSE Corporate Accountability and Listing Standards Committee, *Recommendations Submitted for SEC Approval* (2002).

[66] The only reference to fairness is that which is legally problematic. The NYSE rules state that "[e]ach employee would endeavor to deal fairly with the company's customers, suppliers, competitors and employees." Unfairness consists of taking advantage through "manipulation, concealment, abuse of privileged information, misrepresentation of material facts, or any other unfair dealing practice."

[67] Advisory Group on Organizational Guidelines to the United States Sentencing Commission, REQUEST FOR ADDITIONAL PUBLIC COMMENT REGARDING THE U.S. SENTENCING GUIDELINES FOR ORGANIZATIONS (2002).

based approach to compliance where the intent as well as the letter of the law is important. A climate that supports and encourages technical compliance alone will likely increase the probability of illegal conduct within the organization. The Commission has also sought public comments regarding what an "effective program to prevent and detect violations of law" should consist of. The Guidelines should provide that:

> The organization must periodically assess its employees' perceptions of organizational values, the nature of organizational decision-making, the values and behavior of leaders, the reward system, and employee guidance and monitoring systems in encouraging and supporting compliance with the letter and intent of laws and company policies.

Moreover, the Commission should add the following bracketed language to its Guidelines on appropriate organizational conduct:

> The organization must have taken reasonable steps to achieve compliance with its standards:
>
> [a] By utilizing monitoring and auditing systems reasonably designed to detect [and decrease the likelihood of violations of law and company policies] by its employees and other agents;
> [b] [By making a periodic self-assessment of its ethical climate];
> [c] By having in place and publicizing a reporting system whereby employees and other agents could report [to an independent ombudsman] [violations of law and company policies] by others within the organization without fear of retribution;
> [d] [By requiring employees to periodically acknowledge their understanding and compliance with the organization's code of ethics; and]
> [e] [By having the corporate CEO and CFO certify, to their knowledge and after reasonable inquiry, that:
> (1) Ethical behavior is as highly valued in the organization and is as important as, if not more important than, profit-seeking behavior; (2) the organization's climate encourages and supports ethical decision-making by employees; (3) employees know that their decisions should comply with the intent as well as the letter of the law and company policies; (4) ethical decision-making is rewarded, and unethical decision-making punished, within the organization; and (5) a reasonable system is in place to review, monitor, and if necessary, modify the corporation's ethical climate.]

VII. CONCLUSION

This paper has shown that corporate climates influence ethical/unethical decision-making by employees. In addition, ethical climates are ascertainable and there is considerable agreement about many of the factors that create and support ethical climates.

It is clear that, given Enron's climate, it was only a matter of time before Enron would have imploded. Thus, Congress and other regulatory organizations are justifiably directing their attention to codes of ethics and ethical climates. This paper has argued, however, that to assure legal and ethical decision-making, a corporation has to do more than merely adopt a code of ethics and disclose any waiver of it.

Giving attention to ethical climates will contribute to organizational compliance programs by eliciting employees' perceptions of ethics and ethical compliance within the organization. This inquiry adds an additional dimension to legal compliance programs. By focusing on ethical climates, the organization can take steps to decrease the likelihood of unethical/illegal decision-making that, as the demise of Enron and other corporations amply demonstrates, has devastating consequences for employees, shareholders, creditors, and the economy as a whole.

NOTES AND QUESTIONS

1. What are the components of ethical decision-making? How are the components of ethical decision-making affected by social context?
2. How are ethical climates ascertained? What are the different kinds of ethical climates identified by Victor and Cullen? What effect may these different climates have on ethical/unethical decision-making within the corporation?
3. Do you believe that the climate at Enron increased the likelihood of illegal/unethical behavior? If so, what were the factors that contributed to the unethical climate? Do you believe that Enron's directors and officers should be held responsible for Enron's climate?
4. What is an arrogant climate? What are the likely consequences of an arrogant climate?
5. In your view, has the law gone far enough in promoting ethical corporate climates? What do the SEC rules and NYSE proposed rules provide? What rules would you propose?
6. What are the concerns of the U.S. Sentencing Commission in the wake of Enron? What changes, if any, do you propose in the Commission's Guidelines?

Whistleblowing in the Business World

Leslie Griffin *

I. INTRODUCTION

In 1982, Certified Public Accountant Sherron Watkins began work at Arthur Andersen ("Andersen") as an auditor. After eight years at Andersen, she moved to New York, where she worked for MG Trade Finance. In October 1993, Andrew Fastow hired her to return to Houston to work at Enron. Over the years, she held a variety of positions there. Watkins moved to the Broadband Services Division of Enron in 2000, but lost that job in spring 2001.[1] She was then assigned to Chief Financial Officer Andrew Fastow's section in June. There she "was charged with reviewing all assets that Enron considered for sale."[2] This position gave the "eight-year veteran"[3] the opportunity to discover some problems with Enron's books. Her review of the so-called "LJM," "Condor" and "Raptor" transactions "led her to Enron's hollow center."[4] She was "highly alarmed" because, as an accountant, she knew that "a company could never use its own stock to generate a gain or avoid a loss on its income statement."[5]

---

* Larry & Joanne Doherty Chair in Legal Ethics, University of Houston Law Center.

[1] ROBERT BRYCE, PIPE DREAMS: GREED, EGO, AND THE DEATH OF ENRON 294 (2002); *see generally* MIMI SWARTZ WITH SHERRON WATKINS, POWER FAILURE: THE INSIDE STORY OF THE COLLAPSE OF ENRON (2003) [hereinafter SWARTZ/WATKINS].

[2] Sherron Watkins, *Prepared Witness Testimony on the Financial Collapse of Enron Corp.*, The Committee on Energy and Commerce, Subcommittee on Oversight and Investigations, February 14, 2002, *available at* http://energycommerce.house.gov/107/hearings/02142002Hearing489/Watkins801.htm (last visited February 27, 2003), at 2 [hereinafter Watkins, *Prepared Witness Testimony*].

[3] BRYCE, *supra* note 1, at 294.

[4] April Witt & Peter Behr, *Dream Job Turns Into a Nightmare*, WASH. POST, July 29, 2002, at A01. Watkins provided a summary of her career in Watkins, Prepared Witness Testimony, *supra* note 2.

[5] Watkins, *Prepared Witness Testimony, supra* note 2, at 2.

The discovery of questionable accounting entries worried Watkins, who made plans to leave the company and went on interviews with other businesses.[6] "Her plan was to sign a new job contract and confront Enron Chief Operating Officer Jeffrey Skilling on her last day at Enron."[7] Then Skilling surprised her by resigning suddenly on August 14, 2001.[8] Combined with what she had learned about the books in the Broadband Services Division, Skilling's resignation persuaded Watkins that the problems at Enron were serious.

After Enron's Chairman and Chief Executive Officer Kenneth Lay opened a suggestion box for Enron employees, Watkins wrote a one-page anonymous memorandum on August 15, the day after Skilling quit.[9] The message warned that the company might "implode in a wave of accounting scandals,"[10] and provided Watkins's suggestions for fixing the accounting problems.[11] She worried that some of the numbers could not be fixed; "it's a bit like robbing the bank in one year and trying to pay it back 2 years later."[12] She also warned that there could be some "disgruntled 'redeployed'" Enron workers "who know enough about the 'funny' accounting to get us in trouble."[13]

Lay held an all-employee meeting on August 16. "Reacting to a potential whistle-blower in their midst, Lay's top advisers drafted talking points for Lay to use at the meeting, in case the letter writer surfaced."[14] After Lay asked people at the meeting to notify him of problems at Enron, Watkins decided to confront him directly.[15]

Watkins admitted to Chief of Human Resources Cindy Olson that she had written the anonymous memo.[16] Olson encouraged Watkins to meet with Lay; an appointment was set for August 22. Watkins chose Lay as her audience because she feared that Fastow and Skilling might fire her.[17] She never confronted Skilling directly because she

---

[6] Jodie Morse & Amanda Bower, *The Party Crasher,* TIME MAG., December 30, 2002, at 55; *see also* SWARTZ/WATKINS, *supra* note 1, at 271.

[7] *Id.* at 55.

[8] BRYCE, *supra* note 1, at 294.

[9] Memorandum from Sherron Watkins to Kenneth Lay, August 15, 2001, *available at* http://energycommerce.house.gov/107/hearings/02142002Hearing489/tab10.pdf [hereinafter 8/15/01 Memorandum]; *see also* MORSE & BOWER, *supra* note 6, at 55. For Watkins's account of the memoranda, *see* SWARTZ/WATKINS, *supra* note 1, at 275–89.

[10] 8/15/01 Memorandum, *supra* note 9; *see also* MORSE & BOWER, *supra* note 6, at 55.

[11] WITT & BEHR, *supra* note 4, at A01.

[12] 8/15/01 Memorandum, *supra* note 9.

[13] *Id.*

[14] WITT & BEHR, *supra* note 4, at A01.

[15] MORSE & BOWER, *supra* note 6, at 55.

[16] BRYCE, *supra* note 1, at 295.

[17] Watkins, *Prepared Witness Testimony, supra* note 2, at 2; *see also* Tamara Lytle, *Lay Was 'Duped'; Whistle-Blower Blames Deputies,* ORLANDO SENTINEL, February 15, 2002, at A1.

"did not want to do that without the safety net of a job in hand. [She] felt like it would be an immediate job-terminating move. Frankly, [she] thought it would be fruitless, that nothing would happen."[18]

Because she feared that Lay might hire Fastow or Chief Accounting Officer Rick Causey to replace Skilling before their August 22 meeting, Watkins met with Enron Associate General Counsel Rex Rogers on August 17. She gave Rogers a copy of the anonymous memo, as well as two other short memos about the accounting problems.[19]

On August 20, Watkins called Andersen partner James A. Hecker, a former colleague from her days at the accounting firm, to use him as a "sounding board."[20] Hecker memorialized the conversation for his files and called a meeting of Andersen partners to discuss its implications. Watkins told Hecker that she had discussed Enron's financial situation with Enron's general counsel, who had assured her that Andersen and Enron's law firm, Vinson and Elkins ("V&E"), had appropriately authorized the financial statements.[21] Watkins also spoke with fellow Enron employee Jeffrey McMahon about the problems.[22] She sent him a copy of the one-page anonymous memo.[23] Fastow and other Enron employees speculated that Watkins and McMahon became allies so that one of them could succeed to Fastow's job.[24]

Watkins and Lay met for a half-hour on August 22. In preparation for that session, Watkins wrote a longer, seven-page memorandum (composed of five separate short memoranda) that elaborated on the concerns in her initial anonymous page.[25] It provided a detailed analysis of the accounting problems at Enron and the options available to Lay to manage them. The memo confirmed that Skilling's resignation prompted Watkins's action.[26] She warned Lay: "Skilling's abrupt departure will raise suspicions of accounting improprieties and valuation issues."[27] She reported that Enron's account-

[18] *The Financial Collapse of Enron: Hearing Before the House Subcomm. on Oversight and Investigations of the Comm. on Energy and Commerce,* 107th Cong. 107-89 (2002) at 18.

[19] These two short memos are part of the longer, seven-page memorandum that Watkins gave to Lay on August 22. *See* Memorandum from Sherron Watkins to Rex Rogers, August 17, 2001, *available at* http://energycommerce.house.gov/107/hearings/02142002Hearing489/tab14.pdf (last visited February 27, 2003).

[20] Memorandum from James A. Hecker to The Files, August 21, 2001, *available at* http://energycommerce.house.gov/107/hearings/02142002Hearing489/tab16.pdf (last visited February 27, 2003).

[21] *Id.*

[22] *The Financial Collapse of Enron, supra* note 18, at 37.

[23] *Id.* at 49.

[24] BRYCE, *supra* note 1, at 297; *see also* SWARTZ/WATKINS, *supra* note 1, at 303.

[25] *See* Memorandum from Sherron Watkins to Kenneth Lay, August 22, 2001, *available at* http://energycommerce.house.gov/107/hearings/02142002Hearing489/tab11.pdf (last visited February 27, 2003) [hereinafter 8/22/01 Memorandum].

[26] *Id.*

[27] *Id.*

ing (especially of "Raptor" and "Condor") had been "very aggressive."[28] She reiterated the earlier anonymous warning: "I am incredibly nervous that we will implode in a wave of accounting scandals."[29]

Although Watkins knew that Andersen had "blessed the accounting treatment" of those transactions, the memo noted that the Andersen accountants (who had paid millions of dollars to settle litigation over problems with their audit of Waste Management) could not "protect Enron" from the effects of its books.[30] She recommended that "objective experts in the fields of securities law and accounting" review Enron's books.[31] After such analysis was completed, Lay would have a choice. If the "probability of discovery [was] low enough," he could "quietly and quickly reverse, unwind" the positions. If not, he would have to "develop damage containment plans and disclose."[32]

Watkins's seven-page memo recommended specifically that Lay ask General Counsel James Derrick and Assistant General Counsel Rex Rogers to hire an outside law firm to examine "Raptor" and "Condor."[33] Watkins was savvy enough to recognize that a law firm could "give Enron attorney client privilege on the work product" and to oppose hiring V&E because "they provided some true sale opinions on some of the [questionable] deals."[34] Because of Andersen's and PricewaterhouseCoopers's conflicts ("AA&Co. (Enron); PWC (LJM)."), she suggested that the new outside law firm hire one of the remaining Big 6 accounting firms to review the transactions independently.[35]

Watkins's memorandum also referred to the President and CEO of Enron Industrial Markets, Jeffrey McMahon, with whom she had already discussed these problems. Watkins had worked with McMahon at both Andersen and MG. Now he worked for Enron. In March 2000, McMahon (then the company treasurer) had questioned Skilling about the accounting treatment of LJM and Fastow's compensation.[36] In response, Skilling had recommended McMahon's transfer to the president's job in the industrial subsidiary.[37] Watkins's memorandum complained that Skilling had ignored McMahon's warnings and warned Lay about Skilling's bad judgment.[38]

---

[28] Id.

[29] Id.

[30] Id. at 2.

[31] Id. at 3.

[32] Id. at 4.

[33] Id. at 7.

[34] Id.

[35] Id.

[36] Skilling disagrees with this. See William C. Powers et al., Report of Investigation by the Special Investigative Committee of the Board of Directors of Enron Corp., February 1, 2002, at 21, 166 [hereinafter POWERS REPORT].

[37] Chris Mondics, Enron's Auditor is Just as Guilty, PHILADELPHIA INQUIRER, February 14, 2002, at A01; 8/22/01 Memorandum, supra note 25, at 4.

[38] 8/22/01 Memorandum, supra note 25, at 5.

At that August 22 meeting, Watkins focused on the "Raptor" transactions.[39] Lay told Watkins that he would have the matter investigated,[40] and, according to some reports, promised to fire V&E and Andersen.[41] Watkins then requested a transfer within Enron. She wound up in Olson's Human Resources group.[42] About that position, Watkins wrote that "I haven't really had a real job since my first meeting with Ken re: these matters in late August."[43]

CFO Fastow was furious when he learned about the Watkins/Lay meeting. He entered Watkins's office and disconnected her laptop computer.[44] In order to protect Watkins's work, Human Resources Director Olson transferred Watkins's files to a new computer and gave Fastow the old hardware, without software or files.[45] On one account, Fastow tried to fire Watkins, stating "I want that bitch out of here tonight."[46]

Before his August 22 meeting with Watkins, Lay had given a copy of the one-page memorandum to Enron General Counsel James Derrick. Lay and Derrick agreed to hire V&E to investigate the matter. The two men thought that V&E was a good choice because those lawyers were already "familiar" with Enron and hence could perform a review "quickly."[47] V&E began a "preliminary investigation" into the allegations on August 23 or 24, to figure out if independent lawyers and accountants were needed for further review.[48] "A few weeks later, on September 21,[49] the law firm "assured Lay that the off-the-balance sheet matters were not a problem."[50]

Legal questions about Watkins's status at Enron were also addressed.[51] V&E attorney Carl Jordan sent an e-mail to Enron attorney Sharon Butcher about this "confidential employee matter" on August 24.[52] The e-mail addressed whether Enron's conduct

---

[39] Watkins, *Prepared Witness Testimony, supra* note 2, at 3; *see* 8/22/01 Memorandum, *supra* note 25, at 4–5.

[40] POWERS REPORT, *supra* note 36, at 174.

[41] Dan Ackman, *Sherron Watkins Had Whistle, but Blew It,* Forbes.com, February 14, 2002, *available at* http://www.forbes.com/2002/02/14/0214watkins.html (last visited February 27, 2003).

[42] *The Financial Collapse of Enron, supra* note 18, at 19.

[43] Memorandum from Sherron Watkins to Elizabeth Tilney & Cindy Olson, October 30, 2001, *available at* http://energycommerce.house.gov/107/hearings/02142002Hearing489/tab21.pdf (last visited February 27, 2003) [hereinafter Watkins to Tilney].

[44] BRYCE, *supra* note 1, at 298.

[45] *The Financial Collapse of Enron, supra* note 18, at 19.

[46] BRYCE, *supra* note 1, at 298.

[47] POWERS REPORT, *supra* note 36, at 173.

[48] *Id.*

[49] Kurt Eichenwald, *Company Man to the End, After All*, N.Y. TIMES, February 9, 2003, at § 3 at 1.

[50] BRYCE, *supra* note 1, at 298.

[51] MORSE & BOWER, *supra* note 6, at 53.

[52] E-mail from Carl Jordan to Sharon Butcher, August 24, 2001, *available at* http://energycommerce.house.gov/107/hearings/02142002Hearing489/tab18.pdf (last visited February 27, 2003) [hereinafter Jordan E-Mail]; *see also* SWARTZ/WATKINS, *supra* note 1, at 291.

toward Watkins could be perceived as retaliation against a whistleblower. Enron had one advantage; Texas does not recognize a cause of action for corporate whistleblowers.[53] Nonetheless, to avoid any possibility of a claim of constructive discharge, Jordan advised the company to emphasize that the transfer to Human Resources had occurred at Watkins's request. Enron should also give her someone to contact "in the unlikely future event that she believes she is being retaliated against."[54] Finally, her new position "should have responsibilities and compensation comparable to her current one."[55]

The Jordan memo also addressed the possibility of a "Sabine Pilot" claim by Watkins.[56] *Sabine Pilot* allows Texas employees to bring lawsuits alleging "discharge of an employee for the sole reason that the employee refused to perform an illegal act."[57] Jordan drew an analogy to cases in which

> an employee's duties involve recording accounting data that she knows to be misleading onto records that are eventually relied on by others in preparing reports to be submitted to a federal agency (e.g., SEC, IRS, etc.). . . . If the employee alleges that she was discharged for refusing to record (or continuing the practice of recording) the allegedly misleading data, then she has stated a claim under the Sabine Pilot doctrine.[58]

Jordan warned that *Sabine Pilot* lawsuits, even meritless ones, could subject a company's books to review during discovery and its finances to awards from confused juries. Hence "they are very expensive and time consuming to litigate."[59]

Finally, Jordan cautioned that Watkins might "seek to convince some government oversight agency (e.g., IRS, SEC, etc.) that the corporation has engaged in materially misleading reporting or is otherwise non-compliant. As with wrongful discharge claims, this can create problems even though the allegations have no merit whatsoever."[60]

Months later, Watkins told *Time Magazine* that she "was really shocked when [she] saw a detailed memo about the pluses and minuses of discharging [her]."[61]

In late August 2001, Watkins sold $47,000 of Enron stock.[62] Meanwhile, V&E proceeded with its investigation of Watkins's allegations.

---

[53] Austin v. HealthTrust, Inc.-The Hosp. Co., 967 S.W.2d 400 (Tex. 1998).

[54] Jordan E-Mail, *supra* note 52, at 1.

[55] *Id.*

[56] Sabine Pilot Service, Inc. v. Hauck, 687 S.W.2d 733 (Tex. 1985).

[57] *Id.* at 735.

[58] Jordan E-Mail, *supra* note 52, at 1.

[59] *Id.* at 2.

[60] *Id.*

[61] MORSE & BOWER, *supra* note 6, at 59.

[62] BRYCE, *supra* note 1, at 299; *but see* SWARTZ/WATKINS, *supra* note 1, at 344 (Watkins sold $31,000 of stock).

V&E interviewed Watkins on September 10 for roughly three hours.[63] During that interview, Watkins told Enron lawyers that Andersen was "'as guilty as Enron'" and "knew many of the details of suspect transactions."[64] V&E gave an oral report to Lay and General Counsel Derrick on September 21 and, on October 15, sent a letter summarizing the findings to Derrick.[65]

V&E's evaluation of Enron was very narrow. V&E did not review any of the underlying accounting transactions. The firm's inquiry was "confined to a determination whether the anonymous letter and supplemental materials raised new factual information that would warrant a broader investigation."[66] V&E focused on the fact that the Board of Directors and its Audit Committee had followed the proper "approval procedures"[67] for the numerous accounting decisions. "At Lay's and Derrick's request, the V&E lawyers also briefed Robert Jaedicke, the Chairman of the Audit and Compliance Committee, on the findings. The lawyers made a similar presentation to the full Audit and Compliance Committee in early October 2001."[68] V&E also recommended that Enron "assure [Watkins] that her concerns were thoroughly reviewed, analyzed, and . . . given serious consideration."[69]

The Enron Board of Directors finally learned of the anonymous letter at its October 8 Board meeting. The board did not learn the author's identity or request it, nor did the board see the letter itself or the text of the V&E report.[70]

On October 16, Enron announced major changes in its accounting, including a reduction in shareholders' equity by $1.2 billion.[71] On October 28, the Board of Directors appointed a special committee, under the leadership of University of Texas Law School Dean William Powers, to investigate the financial problems. The Powers Report was issued on February 2, 2002. The Powers Committee concluded that Watkins was "right about the problem," but not about all the facts. Her predictions were "strikingly accurate" on how the public would react to the transactions.[72] The Committee thought her letter was a good "road map" for understanding the "Raptors."

---

[63] POWERS REPORT, *supra* note 36, at 174.

[64] Chris Mondics, *Enron's Auditor is Just as Guilty,* PHILADELPHIA INQUIRER, February 14, 2002, at A01.

[65] Letter from Max Hendrick, III, Vinson & Elkins, to James. V. Derrick, Jr., Executive Vice President & General Counsel, Enron Corp., *Preliminary Investigation of Allegations of an Anonymous Employee,* 2001 WL 1764266, 10/15/2001.

[66] *Id.* at 2.

[67] *Id.* at 5.

[68] POWERS REPORT, *supra* note 36, at 175.

[69] SWARTZ/WATKINS, *supra* note 1, at 304; Watkins conversation with author, Feb. 24, 2003.

[70] STAFF OF PERMANENT SUBCOMM. ON INVESTIGATIONS OF THE COMM. ON GOVERNMENTAL AFFAIRS, 107TH CONG. 2D SESS., THE ROLE OF THE BOARD OF DIRECTORS IN ENRON'S COLLAPSE, 70 at 45 (Comm. Print 2002), LEXIS 2002 CIS S. Print 4025, *available at* http://frwebgate.access.gpo.gov/cgi-bin/getdoc.cgi?dbname=107_senate_committee_prints&docid=f:80393.pdf (last visited Feb. 27, 2002).

[71] POWERS REPORT, *supra* note 36, at 30.

[72] *Id.* at 176.

The Powers Committee also concluded that "[t]he result of the V&E review was largely predetermined by the scope and nature of the investigation and the process employed."[73] It determined that the Board of Directors "failed in its oversight duties."[74] Furthermore, although the Audit and Compliance Committee had "an opportunity to probe the transactions thoroughly," their review was "too brief, too limited in scope, and too superficial."[75] Although the Board and its sub-committees had numerous opportunities to review the LJM and Raptors transactions, they were not thorough and careful in doing so. The Board's oversight was not "rigorous"[76]; it avoided its responsibilities to request more information, and to raise substantive questions about the unusual accounting transactions.[77] The failures of oversight were pervasive across the company:

> There was an absence of forceful and effective oversight by Senior Enron management and in-house counsel, and objective and critical professional advice by outside counsel at Vinson & Elkins, or auditors at Andersen.[78]

Nonetheless, although the Committee concluded that Andersen and V&E deserved some blame, the accountants' and attorneys' conduct did not relieve the Board of its responsibilities.

In October 2001, Watkins netted $17,000 from the sale of her Enron stock options.[79]

On October 30, she met again with Lay,[80] offering him a new memorandum that included numerous public relations suggestions. Lay could defend himself by pointing out what Skilling, Fastow, and Causey had done wrong. He could "admit he had trusted the wrong people,"[81] especially that "Mistake #2" was to rely on V&E and Andersen.[82] After all, the law and accounting firms had been "motivated by self preservation"[83] rather than company interests. Watkins warned Lay that other Enron executives had "misled" and "duped" him.[84] She urged him to "publicly take responsibility

---

[73] *Id.*

[74] *Id.* at 22, 148.

[75] *Id.* at 23–24.

[76] *Id.* at 10.

[77] *Id.* at 22.

[78] *Id.* at 17.

[79] BRYCE, *supra* note 1, at 299; *see also* SWARTZ/WATKINS, *supra* note 1, at 345.

[80] Watkins to Tilney, *supra* note 43.

[81] *Id.*

[82] *Id.* at 1; *see also* Mondics, *supra* note 37.

[83] Watkins to Tilney, *supra* note 43.

[84] *Id.* at 2.

for the company's problems."[85] Although early reports indicated that Lay sold thousands of his shares of Enron stock in response to Watkins's memoranda and repeated warnings,[86] it now appears that through October 2001, Lay "held on to 1.2 million shares—and some five million vested options—as the price dove toward zero."[87]

In an October meeting with V&E lawyers, Watkins stated that "she believed 'Fastow was in effect blackmailing banks to become investors in LJM.'"[88] She learned "about this pressure from friends at Chase, Bank of America and Credit Suisse First Boston during 'cocktail conversations.'"[89] McMahon confirmed that he had warned Skilling in March 2000 that "Fastow was pressuring investment banks that did business with Enron to invest in LJM2."[90]

Enron filed for chapter 11 bankruptcy protection in December 2001. By January 2002, the House Energy and Commerce Committee was probing Enron's failure. Investigators discovered Watkins's seven-page memorandum among the 40 boxes of Enron documents. On January 15, Republican Representative Billy Tauzin of Louisiana released it to the press.[91] Only then did Watkins's actions become known outside Enron; she "became a reluctant public figure."[92]

Watkins testified before the House Subcommittee on Oversight and Investigations on February 14 and 15, 2002. She explained the details of the "funny accounting." Watkins told Congress that she believed that Skilling, Fastow, V&E, and Andersen "did dupe Ken Lay and the Board."[93] Before Congress, she reasserted what she had told V&E in October: that Fastow had pressured banks to invest in LJM.[94]

"In mid-May [2002], a bankruptcy court judge ordered Enron to pay her legal bills, in the amount of $220,000."[95]

Although Watkins retained her job at Enron until November 2002, it provided little interesting work. She now lectures around the country (earning up to $25,000

---

[85] MONDICS, *supra* note 37.

[86] BRYCE, *supra* note 1, at 299 ("Perhaps it's just coincidence, but that same day, August 21, Lay sold 68,620 shares of Enron stock, netting himself just over $1 million. The day before that, Lay had sold 25,000 shares, taking home nearly $387,000.").

[87] Kurt Eichenwald, *Company Man to the End, After All*, N.Y. TIMES, February 9, 2003, at § 3 at 1.

[88] Julie Mason, *Committee Widens Its Probe: Did Enron Pressure Banks?*, HOUS. CHRON., March 7, 2002, at 4.

[89] *Id.*

[90] POWERS REPORT, *supra* note 36, at 167; *see also* SWARTZ/WATKINS, *supra* note 1, at 218–19.

[91] Todd J. Gillman, *Seven-page memo warned of Enron's collapse*, DALLAS MORNING NEWS, January 17, 2002.

[92] Richard Lacayo & Amanda Ripley, *Persons of the Year: The Whistleblowers*, TIME MAG., December 30, 2002, at 32.

[93] *The Financial Collapse of Enron*, *supra* note 18, at 21.

[94] *Id.* at 54.

[95] BRYCE, *supra* note 1, at 360.

per appearance) and she co-authored a book about Enron with Mimi Swartz, with whom she shared a $500,000 advance.[96] *Power Failure: The Inside Story of the Collapse of Enron* was published in March 2003. Watkins resigned from Enron on November 15, 2002.

At the end of 2002, *Time Magazine* named "The Whistleblowers" as Persons of the Year 2002. The cover story honored Watkins, WorldCom accountant Cynthia Cooper, and FBI Special Agent Coleen Rowley for blowing the whistle on their respective organizations.[97] In the interview with *Time,* Watkins expressed regret that she had not "gone to the board"[98] with her discovery of the accounting problems.

> TIME: What would you have done if you had known?
>
> WATKINS: I would have gone to the board.
>
> TIME: Would it have made a difference?
>
> WATKINS: There's a slim chance Enron might not have imploded. It's hard to say. People are much more forgiving than we think. The scary thing is the amount of resistance we met.[99]

On this point, a contrast with fellow accountant and Person of the Year Cynthia Cooper is instructive. Cooper was Vice President of WorldCom's internal audit division, the unit she had founded in 1994.[100] Early in March 2002, John Stupka, the head of WorldCom's Wireless Division, complained to her that the company had taken $400 million from his division in order to "boost income."[101] Andersen was WorldCom's accountant, too. Cooper mentioned Stupka's concerns to Arthur Andersen partner Kenny Avery and WorldCom Chief Financial Officer Scott Sullivan, who ignored her argument. Indeed, Sullivan was "furious" and "angrily" ordered her to "back off."[102] Cooper mentioned the problem to the Audit Committee of the Board of Directors on March 6. On March 7, the Securities and Exchange Commission requested information from WorldCom as part of an investigation.[103]

Meanwhile, Andersen was looking unreliable because the Enron scandal had erupted in Congress in January 2002. Cooper led her internal audit team in an investigation of

---

[96] MORSE & BOWER, *supra* note 6, at 54.

[97] LACAYO & RIPLEY, *supra* note 92, at 32.

[98] MORSE & BOWER, *supra* note 6, at 54.

[99] *Id.* at 59.

[100] Amanda Ripley, *The Night Detective*, TIME MAG., December 30, 2002, at 45.

[101] *Id.*

[102] *Id.* at 47.

[103] Susan Pulliam & Deborah Solomon, *Uncooking the Books: How Three Unlikely Sleuths Discovered Fraud at WorldCom*, WALL ST. J., October 30, 2002, at A1.

WorldCom's books. The trio worked at night so that their colleagues would not become suspicious. During those quiet hours, by May 2002 they discovered a "gaping hole in the books,"[104] namely "$3.8 billion in misallocated expenses and phony accounting entries, part of the "largest [accounting fraud] in corporate history."[105]

On June 11, Sullivan asked Cooper to delay her audit.[106] Cooper re-contacted Max Bobbitt, the chairman of the Audit Committee, on June 12. He told her to report her discoveries to WorldCom's new accountants, KPMG, who agreed that WorldCom's practices did not comply with Generally Accepted Accounting Principles. Cooper's team and KPMG briefed the Audit Committee at a June 20 meeting; Sullivan tried to persuade the directors to continue supporting him. The Board gave Sullivan and company Controller David Myers the weekend to resign or be fired. Myers resigned; Sullivan was fired. Then WorldCom informed the world about the problem with its books.[107]

In contrast, Watkins criticized herself for not going to the Board, and "[s]ome laid-off Enron employees began blaming Watkins for not taking her concerns to the Securities and Exchange Commission."[108] Watkins's attorney, Philip Hilder, has defended her decision. "Watkins held off on notifying authorities outside of the company, believing Lay was conducting a thorough investigation. 'It's a false impression that she sat back and did nothing,' Hilder said. 'Her boss asked her for time to investigate, and it was only after the investigation was complete that she realized it was a whitewash.'"[109]

II. WHO IS A WHISTLEBLOWER?

Time Magazine identified Watkins as one of three Whistleblower Persons of the Year. *Time* reported that, in contrast to Rowley and Cooper, Watkins "does not shy away from describing herself as a whistle-blower or suggesting that her gender may have played a role in her decision to act."[110]

There have been numerous challenges, however, to this identification of Watkins as an authentic whistleblower. For example, the Watkins chapter title in Robert Bryce's respected book about Enron is "Sherron Watkins Saves Her Own Ass."[111] Bryce notes that her fellow employees found Watkins "calculating" and "vindictive,"[112] a "conniv-

---

[104] RIPLEY, *Detective, supra* note 100, at 49.

[105] PULLIAM & SOLOMON, *supra* note 103, at A1.

[106] RIPLEY, *Detective, supra* note 100, at 49.

[107] *Id.*

[108] MORSE & BOWER, *supra* note 6, at 56.

[109] *See* Julie Mason, *Watkins' Own Ethics Questioned; CPA Professional Standards Required Action, Experts Say,* HOUS. CHRON., February 15, 2002, at A21.

[110] MORSE & BOWER, *supra* note 6, at 54.

[111] BRYCE, *supra* note 1, at 293–99.

[112] *Id.* at 295.

ing, manipulative self-promoter to a dangerous extreme," and "poison in the well."[113] He wonders why, "given Watkins's knowledge of all the fraud and mismanagement at Enron Broadband Services [where she worked before her transfer to Fastow's division], she didn't mention any of those things in her letters to Lay."[114] Bryce demonstrates that, at the time she wrote the anonymous memo, she "was facing almost certain firing by Fastow."[115] Thus, he concludes, "though Watkins deserves kudos for her courage, there is another fact that cannot be denied: In writing the letter, [she] had little to lose and much to gain."[116] She "was able to mark herself as a whistle-blower without really going public. By writing the letter, she protected herself from getting fired."[117] In other words, "Watkins was not Enron's Mother Teresa."[118]

Such disparagement of Watkins is not surprising. Pejorative words—like "snitch" or "tattletale," "leper" or "rat"[119]—are frequently used about whistleblowers. Indeed, a leading book on whistleblowers profiles them as psychological narcissists;[120] they can be "quirky, anxious and irritable."[121] "Whistleblowers who engage in altruistic acts at greater personal costs are often considered cultural heroes, whereas those motivated by greed and revenge are typically viewed as dirty, rotten scoundrels."[122]

The more substantive criticism of Watkins's whistleblower status, as she admitted, is that she never reported her concerns about accounting improprieties to the Board or anyone outside of Enron. As a *Wall Street Journal* reporter observed: "A whistle-blower, literally speaking, is someone who spots a criminal robbing a bank and blows a whistle, alerting the police. That's not Sherron Watkins. . . . What she did was write a memo to the bank robber (Mr. Lay) suggesting he was about to be caught and warning him to watch out."[123] A UP story was even blunter:

---

[113] *Id.* at 297.

[114] *Id.*; *see also* SWARTZ/WATKINS, *supra* note 1, at 96 (identifying problems with Enron's accounting in 1996).

[115] *Id.* at 295.

[116] *Id.*

[117] *Id.* at 298.

[118] WITT & BEHR, *supra* note 4, at A01.

[119] David O. Weber, *"Still in Good Standing": The Crisis in Attorney Discipline*, ABA J., November 1, 1987 at 58.

[120] C. FRED ALFORD, WHISTLEBLOWERS: BROKEN LIVES AND ORGANIZATIONAL POWER 63 (2001).

[121] John Schwartz, *Playing Know And Tell*, N.Y. TIMES, June 9, 2002, at 4-2.

[122] TERANCE D. MIETHE, WHISTLEBLOWING AT WORK: TOUGH CHOICES IN EXPOSING FRAUD, WASTE, AND ABUSE ON THE JOB 15 (1999).

[123] Dan Ackman, *Whistleblower?*, WALL ST. J., December 24, 2002; *see also id.* ("But Ms. Watkins was no whistleblower and she had no impact. In fact, she looks like Time's worst choice ever. . . . But whistleblowers? They were most conspicuous by their absence. Take Enron. As it burned, analysts and auditors fiddled. To be sure there were accountants inside Arthur Andersen who questioned Enron's books. But they stayed inside—as did Ms. Watkins.").

Whistleblower Sherron Watkins certainly wasn't a heroine. For one thing, she didn't blow any whistles: She didn't go to the SEC; she didn't even go to *The New York Times*, which would have welcomed with open arms in August 2001 a female whistleblower with dirt on a Texas company with connections to President Bush and Vice President Dick Cheney. She went only to Ken Lay, and there the matter rested while she continued to earn—or at least receive—her munificent Enron salary.[124]

Even Members of the House of Representatives, who praised her brave testimony before the Committee on Energy and Commerce, noted that Watkins was not a whistleblower in the "conventional" or "traditional" sense.

> CHAIRMAN JAMES C. GREENWOOD: "Let me point out that Ms. Watkins is *not a whistleblower in the conventional sense.* She was, and is, a loyal company employee, who sought valiantly, and sadly in vain, to get the people in charge to face the facts and make the hard choices needed to save the company."[125]

> MR. STEARNS OF FLORIDA: "Your status is perhaps not, as the press might outline, that you are a whistleblower. *You are not the traditional whistleblower* in the sense that you are still working for the company. And the way you did it was commendable, in the sense that you went to different people and talked to them, and you asked for a transfer to another part of the company. But in a sort of *semantic way,* you are not a whistleblower in the traditional sense, and I am not sure if we have a word for—which describes when you stay within the company and work as you did, but it is—I think it was very effective and helpful for us."[126]

Because there is confusion about the "semantics" of whistleblowing in the corporate context, I distinguish two types of whistleblowers below: *retaliatory* whistleblowers and *reporting* whistleblowers.

First, employment and labor law offer some legal protections against firing or demotion for whistleblowers who report company misconduct or refuse to participate in illegal activities; this is the law of retaliatory discharge. Hence in the retaliatory whistleblowers section I identify which whistleblowers are protected from retaliation in common and statutory law. As the Jordan memorandum suggested, in early 2002, Sherron Watkins did not qualify for such protection. Hence, she was not a retaliatory whistleblower.

---

[124] Martin Hutchinson, *Is Skilling Enron's Ollie North?,* UPI, February 27, 2002.

[125] *The Financial Collapse of Enron, supra* note 18, at 3 (emphasis added).

[126] *Id.* at 10 (emphasis added).

A second aspect of whistleblowing identifies when and how employees must *report* their suspicions of illegality to others. As we have seen, the primary controversy over Watkins's whistleblowing was her decision to report the accounting irregularities to Lay, but not to the Board or the SEC. Hence Watkins was an "internal" but not an "external" reporter whistleblower.[127] As Professor Miethe explains:

> Whistleblowers are often distinguished according to the nature of their disclosures. There are two general types. "Internal" whistleblowers report misconduct to another person within the company who can take corrective action. This contact person may be an immediate supervisor, ombudsman, union representative, or company executive. "External" whistleblowers, in contrast, expose fraud, waste, and abuse in organizations to outside agents. Common sources for external reporting are law enforcement officials, lawyers, news media, and an assortment of local, state, and federal agencies. Both internal and external whistleblowers must resort to their action because they lack the power themselves to directly change organizational practices.[128]

After describing the academic "debate" whether internal reporting qualifies as whistleblowing, Miethe adopts a broad definition, namely *"employees or former employees who report misconduct to persons who have the power to take action."*[129] Under this phrasing, internal reporter Watkins qualifies as a whistleblower. Nonetheless, the debate explains why her status as whistleblower is controversial. Her critics believe that she should have made an external report of wrongdoing.

On both subjects, retaliatory discharge and reporting obligations, and largely in response to the Enron and WorldCom implosions, federal law has changed since Sherron Watkins wrote her anonymous memo to Ken Lay on August 15, 2001.[130]

III. RETALIATORY WHISTLEBLOWERS

Most whistleblowers (especially the non-famous ones) "face some kind of retaliation."[131]

A. Texas Law

Recall that V&E attorney Carl Jordan wrote an e-mail memorandum concerning Watkins's status as a whistleblower; he correctly concluded that she was not protected

---

[127] MIETHE, *supra* note 122, at 15.

[128] *Id.* at 15–16.

[129] *Id.* at 11.

[130] Sarbanes-Oxley Act, Pub. L. No. 107-204 (2002) (codified in scattered sections of 15 U.S.C. and 18 U.S.C.).

[131] *Whistle-Blowers Being Punished, A Survey Shows*, N.Y. TIMES, September 3, 2002, at A14.

under Texas law.[132] The Texas Whistleblower Act protects *public* employees against retaliation for good faith reporting of violations of the law to law enforcement authorities.[133] Retaliation includes firing, suspension, or other "adverse personnel action."[134] Because the statute covers "public employees" who work for a "state or local governmental agency,"[135] however, it did not protect Watkins. Moreover, Watkins did not report her concerns to a law enforcement authority.[136]

As Jordan noted, the Supreme Court of Texas has held that there is no common law cause of action for private whistleblowers in Texas; whistleblower protection is purely statutory.[137] Despite the arguments of plaintiffs' attorneys, the Court has refused to "create a judicial exception to the employment-at-will doctrine" because "the Legislature has been so proactive in promulgating statutes that prohibit retaliation against whistleblowers in many areas of the private sector."[138] These statutes prohibit retaliation against, e.g., physicians and nurses, nursing home and hospital employees, workers with hazardous chemicals, agricultural laborers, employees who report discrimination or file certain Workers Comp and employment grievances, and others.[139] Watkins's actions fit under none of these statutes.

Moreover, the Supreme Court observed that in 1995 the Texas Legislature rejected an amendment to the Labor Code that would have created a Whistleblower Act for

---

[132] *See supra* notes 52–60 and accompanying text.

[133] TEX. GOVERNMENT CODE ANN. § 554.002 (Vernon 1995).

[134] TEX. GOVERNMENT CODE ANN. § 554.002(a) (Vernon 1995).

[135] *Id.*

[136] *See* Duvall v. Texas Dep't of Human Servs., 82 S.W.3d 474 (Tex. App.—Austin 2002); Garay v. County of Bexar, 810 S.W.2d 760 (Tex. App.—San Antonio 1991, writ denied) ("statute applied to violation reports made to appropriate law enforcement authority.").

[137] *See* Austin v. HealthTrust, Inc.-The Hosp. Co., 967 S.W.2d 400 (Tex. 1998); Winters v. Houston Chronicle Publishing Co., 795 S.W.2d 723, 723 (Tex. 1990).

[138] *Austin*, 967 S.W.2d at 400.

[139] *Id.* The Court notes that:

[A] physician cannot be retaliated against for reporting to the State Board of Medical Examiners the acts of another physician that pose a continuing threat to the public welfare. Tex.Rev.Civ. Stat. Ann. art. 4495b, § 5.06(d), (q) (Vernon Supp. 1998). The Legislature has also enacted a statute that prohibits retaliation against nursing home employees who report abuse or neglect of a nursing home resident. Tex. Health & Safety Code § 242.133. Additionally, employers who use hazardous chemicals may not retaliate against employees for reporting a violation of the Hazard Communication Act. Id. § 502.017; see also Tex. Agric. Code § 125.013(b) (prohibiting retaliation against agricultural laborer for reporting a violation of the Agricultural Hazard Communication Act). Nor can employers retaliate against employees for opposing or reporting discriminatory practices in the workplace. Tex. Lab.Code § 21.055; see also Tex. Lab.Code § 411.082 (prohibiting employer from retaliating against employee for using the Workers' Compensation Commission's toll-free telephone service to report, in good faith, an alleged violation of an occupational health or safety law); Tex. Loc. Gov't Code § 160.006 (preventing county employee from being subject to

private employees.[140] That bill would have prohibited an employer from discharging an employee "who in good faith reports activities within the workplace that constitute a violation of law or would otherwise have a *probable adverse effect on the public*."[141] The Legislature later rejected another bill that deleted the italicized part and applied only when the reported activity "constitute[d] a violation of law."[142] Because the Legislature did not protect private whistleblowers, the Supreme Court refused to do so.

Attorney Jordan also considered the possibility that Watkins would file a *Sabine Pilot* lawsuit.[143] In that case, a deckhand alleged that "he was fired for refusing to pump bilges into water," which was illegal. The Texas Supreme Court identified a "very narrow exception" to the employment-at-will doctrine in these circumstances, and allowed a cause of action for the "discharge of an employee for the sole reason that the employee refused to perform an illegal act."[144] "In such cases, plaintiffs have the burden to prove that the discharge was *for no reason other* than his refusal to perform an illegal act."[145] Although Watkins might not have prevailed on the merits, Jordan's memo warned Enron that *Sabine Pilot* could cause the company problems from opening its books in discovery and being subject to awards from a confused jury (who might not understand the grey areas of accounting).

Outside of Texas, whistleblower protection "measures' content varies greatly" across the states.[146] In general, across the nation, the employment-at-will doctrine has been eroded "through the adoption of the tort theory of firing in violation of public policy."[147] Some states offer statutory and common law protection to more whistleblowers than Texas does.[148] Moreover, *Sabine Pilot* offers a more limited public policy exception to employment-at-will than that identified in other states' law.[149] Despite the changes in

---

retaliation for exercising a right or participating in a grievance procedure established under Chapter 160 of the Local Government Code). . . . Registered nurses [who] are required by law to report another registered nurse who "has exposed or is likely to expose a patient or other person unnecessarily to a risk of harm" or who "is likely to be impaired by chemical dependency." Tex.Rev.Civ. Stat. Ann. art. 4525a, § 1 (Vernon Supp. 1998). Beyond the protections provided by article 4525a, the Legislature has recently enacted another specific whistleblower statute for any hospital employee who reports illegal activity. *See* Tex. Health & Safety Code § 161.134.

Id. at 401–2.

[140] *Id.* at 400 (quoting Tex. H.B. 622, 74th Leg. R.S. (1995)).

[141] *Id.*

[142] *Id.* (citing Tex.C.S.H.B. 622, 74th Leg., R.S. (1995)).

[143] Sabine Pilot Serv., Inc. v. Hauck, 687 S.W.2d 733 (Tex. 1985).

[144] *Id.*

[145] *Id.*

[146] Elletta Sangrey Callahan & Terry Morehead Dworkin, *The State of State Whistleblower Protection*, 38 AM. BUS. L. J. 99, 100 (2000).

[147] *Id.* at 105.

[148] *See generally id.*

[149] *Id.* at n. 40.

employment-at-will doctrine, however, "the courts are relatively conservative in what they recognize as protected whistleblowing, and if the whistleblower cannot point to a well-established law, rule or regulation that is being violated, she or he is unlikely to be protected."[150] Watkins was unprotected.

B. Sarbanes-Oxley

In reaction to Enron and other corporate scandals, Congress passed new corporate responsibility legislation, the Sarbanes-Oxley Act, which was signed by President Bush and became effective on July 30, 2002.[151] The Act "protects employee whistleblowers in ways not seen before."[152] It expands both criminal sanctions and civil liability against retaliating employers, including any companies who file reports under the Securities and Exchange Act. The statute's reach is broad. "Unlike most other federal statutes that protect employees . . . the Sarbanes-Oxley Act holds individual executives, agents, and supervisors *personally liable* for unlawful retaliation, and it makes retaliation a *felony_offense* under federal criminal law."[153]

According to this new legislation, employers are subject to civil liability if they retaliate against employees who report suspected securities fraud, bank or wire fraud, or violations of securities law and regulations, or "[f]ederal law relating to fraud against shareholders."[154] The Act also protects employees who testify in or file proceedings

---

[150] *Id.* at 106.

[151] Sarbanes-Oxley Act, Pub. L. No. 107-204 (2002) (codified in scattered sections of 15 U.S.C. and 18 U.S.C.).

[152] Le Hammer, Nick Linn, Laurence E. Stuart, & Susanne K. Sullivan, *Navigating the Civil and Criminal Whistleblower Provisions of the Sarbanes-Oxley Act*, ACCA DOCKET, March 2003 at 21, 24.

[153] *Id.* at 30 (emphasis added).

[154] 18 U.S.C. § 1514A(a)(2) (2002). 18 U.S.C. § 1514A provides:

(a) . . . [No] officer, employee, contractor, subcontractor, or agent . . . [of a publicly traded company] . . . may discharge, demote, suspend, threaten, harass, or in any other manner discriminate against an employee in the terms and conditions of employment because of any lawful act done by the employee—

(1) to provide information, cause information to be provided, or otherwise assist in an investigation regarding any conduct which the employee reasonably believes constitutes a violation of [title 18] section 1341, 1343, 1344, or 1348, any rule or regulation of the Securities and Exchange Commission, or any provision of Federal law relating to fraud against shareholders, when the information or assistance is provided to or the investigation is conducted by—

(A) a Federal regulatory or law enforcement agency:

(B) any Member of Congress or any committee of Congress; or

(C) a *person with supervisory authority over the employee (or such other person working for the employer who has the authority to investigate, discover, or terminate misconduct); or*

(D) *any company employee with authority to investigate, discover, or terminate prohibited corporate misconduct.*

(emphasis added).

about such violations.[155] On the criminal side, it is a felony to retaliate against whistleblowers who "provide to a law enforcement officer any truthful information relating to the commission or possible commission of *any* Federal offense." Note the broad range of the criminal provisions: they apply to employees who report violations of any federal law, not just securities laws.[156]

Under Sarbanes-Oxley, retaliatory whistleblowers must file a complaint with the Department of Labor ("DOL") within 90 days of the retaliation.[157] If there is no decision from DOL within 180 days of the filing, the grievant may file a lawsuit in federal district court.[158] Reinstatement, back pay, compensatory damages, special damages, attorneys' fees, and costs are available as damages *against individual employers* as well as the corporation. The criminal penalty is a fine (up to $250,000 for individuals and $500,000 for organizations) and/or imprisonment of up to 10 years.[159]

Whistleblower statutes did not shield Sherron Watkins when she wrote her memoranda and met with Kenneth Lay. Enron "highlighted the absence of consistent state or federal protections for corporate whistleblowers, such as Sherron Watkins."[160] Sarbanes-Oxley offered her new support. As Houston labor and employment lawyer Laurence Stuart observed: "We call this the 'Sherron Watkins provision.' She would not have been protected before July 31 [2002] . . . no on July 30, yes on July 31."[161]

IV. REPORTING WHISTLEBLOWERS

Sarbanes-Oxley "also mandates up-the-ladder reporting of illegal or fraudulent conduct by corporate counsel."[162] Watkins is not an attorney. Like whistleblowers of all professions, however, she confronted the difficult issue of internal or external reporting of misconduct. When questioned before the House of Representatives in February 2002 about her decision not to report the accounting irregularities outside Enron, Watkins explained her hopes that the problems could be "fix[ed] calmly" and internally and her reluctance to "hasten the demise" of Enron:

> MR. GANSKE FROM IOWA: Did you ever think about, you know, *going to Treasury, Justice, the SEC, blowing the whistle* on this? This is—you know, you have outlined potentially criminal behavior.

---

[155] 18 U.S.C. § 1514A(a)(2) (2002); *see also* HAMMER, *supra* note 152, at 30.

[156] HAMMER, *supra* note 152, at 34 ("This provision of the law is particularly noteworthy because it protects a broader class of whistleblowers than do the civil protections of the Sarbanes-Oxley Act.").

[157] 18 U.S.C. § 1514A(b)(2)(D) (2002).

[158] 18 U.S.C. § 1514A(b)(2)(A) (2002).

[159] 18 U.S.C. § 1513(e) (2002).

[160] HAMMER, *supra* note 152, at 24.

[161] Laurence E. Stuart, Address at the Baker & McKenzie Breakfast Briefing on Sarbanes-Oxley (Feb. 13, 2003), Houston, Texas.

[162] HAMMER, *supra* note 152, at 24.

MS. WATKINS: . . . I don't want to *hasten our demise*. There are 20,000 employees here whose livelihood is at risk. If it appears that I *hastened the demise* of the company, I might be targeted by them. They might confuse the problem as something I caused. I did not want to *hasten the demise*.[163]

MR. GANSKE: Tell me what you were feeling about that time, specifically on whether you had an ethical obligation to let this be known.

MS. WATKINS: I wasn't thinking legally. I really felt like I could not go outside of the company. Enron was full of bright people. There were maybe *calm ways* of addressing this. Having it hit the press in an inflammatory way would definitely *hasten the demise*.

And I wanted to make sure that we have researched everything thoroughly, because what I wanted to do was restate, come clean, but with some contingency plans how to make sure our trade counter parties had confidence in our survival, maybe shore up some equity and finance deals, knowing that we were going to face hard times.

But to go to the press, or to go to the SEC, would not have given Enron a chance to try to *fix it calmly*. And most definitely this news would have been inflammatory, and we would be in the same position we are in right now.[164]

By December, however, in the interview with *Time*, Watkins expressed regret that she had not "gone to the board":

TIME: What would you have done if you had known?

WATKINS: I would have gone to the board.

TIME: Would it have made a difference?

WATKINS: There's a slim chance Enron might not have imploded. It's hard to say. People are much more forgiving than we think. The scary thing is the amount of resistance we met.[165]

A. Going to the Board

There are three tiers of review over public companies: "the board of directors, who are supposed to keep tabs on management inside the company; the independent auditors, who are supposed to make sure the company is keeping—and disclosing—its books honestly; and the SEC, which is supposed to watch over and keep tabs on the

---

[163] *The Financial Collapse of Enron, supra* note 18, at 50 (emphasis added).

[164] *Id.* at 51 (emphasis added).

[165] MORSE & BOWER, *supra* note 6, at 59.

whole system and make sure the other watchdogs are doing their jobs."[166] Auditors are expected to detect fraud "and report what they find to the Board, and if not appropriately dealt with at that level, to the SEC."[167] Accountants have debated whether CPA Watkins (who was not employed at Enron as an auditor) was obligated to make these notifications.[168]

About her judgment as a whistleblower, however, every indication is that Watkins's direct notification of the Board would not have influenced events at Enron. Both the Powers Committee and the Senate Subcommittee on Governmental Affairs concluded that the Enron Board of Directors failed spectacularly in its oversight duties.[160] For example, the Board was informed of "high-risk" accounting at Enron as early as February 1999.[170] It possessed enough information to understand the complexity of the "Raptors" and other transactions; nonetheless it approved both "LJM" and the "Raptors."[171] The Audit Committee exercised little control over Arthur Andersen and did not probe the details of its accounting decisions.[172] "The Board witnessed numerous indications of questionable practices by Enron management over several years, but chose to ignore them to the detriment of Enron shareholders, employees and business associates."[173]

Not only did the complex financial transactions escape the Board's attention. Although Watkins thought that Skilling's resignation would put investors and journalists on notice of the problems at Enron, the departure did not trouble the Board. Moreover, the Board knew about Watkins's anonymous letter. "Even in early October 2001, when told of an anonymous employee letter warning of company problems and an $800 million earnings charge from the Raptors termination, the interviewed Board members told the [Senate] Subcommittee staff they had left the October Board meeting feeling the company was still on track."[174] The Board was not ignorant of the facts; it had repeatedly believed the auditors, V&E, and top management. "High risk accounting practices, extensive undisclosed off-the-books transactions, inappropriate

---

[166] Staff of the Senate Committee on Governmental Affairs, 107th Cong. 2d sess., Financial Oversight of Enron: The SEC and Private-Sector Watchdogs 75 (COMM. PRINT 2002), 2002 WL 31267528, *14, *available at* http://frwebgate.access.gpo.gov/cgi-bin/getdoc.cgi?dbname=107_cong_senate _committee_prints&docid=f:82147.pdf (last visited Feb. 27, 2002).

[167] *Id.*

[168] *See infra* notes 188–94 and accompanying text.

[169] POWERS REPORT, *supra* note 36, at 148; *Role of the Board of Directors in Enron's Collapse, supra* note 70.

[170] *Role of the Board of Directors in Enron's Collapse, supra* note 70, at 15.

[171] *Id.*

[172] *Id.* at 57.

[173] *Id.* at 5.

[174] *Id.* at 15–16.

conflict of interest transactions, and excessive compensation plans were known to and authorized by the Board."[175] It is difficult to conclude that Watkins's "going to the Board" would have made a difference.

B. The Accountants

Auditors have the highest rate of reporting whistleblowing of any profession.[176] The experts argue that the accounting culture supports and encourages whistleblowers, and that whistleblowing is "largely role-prescribed behavior for these employees."[177] Long before the implosion of Enron and the passage of the Sarbanes-Oxley Act, "Congress expanded the 'whistle-blower' role of independent public accountants"[178] in the Private Securities Litigation Reform Act of 1995.[179] The 1995 legislation sought to ensure that Audit Committees, Boards of Directors, and the Securities and Exchange Commission would receive notification of illegal activity within corporations by establishing reporting requirements for audits of the "financial statements of an issuer by a registered public accounting firm."[180]

Whenever an "independent public accountant" discovers "information indicating that an illegal act . . . has or may have occurred," she must inform the Audit Committee or the Board of Directors of the illegality.[181] If the legal violation is material, and management fails to "take timely and appropriate remedial actions," the accountant shall notify the board of her conclusion that remedial action was not undertaken.[182] Any issuer who receives such a notification from an accountant must inform the SEC and copy its SEC report to the accountant.[183] If the accountant does not receive that copy, she must either resign or report her original complaint to the Commission.[184] Her resignation also triggers an obligation to send a report to the SEC.[185] The bottom line is that both the Board and the SEC are informed of the problem whether by the accountant or the issuer. Or, as Harvey Pitt explained, "by imposing a statutory 'whistle-

[175] *Id.* at 14.

[176] MIETHE, *supra* note 122, at 62–63.

[177] *Id.*

[178] William F. Dietrich, *Legal and Ethical Issues for Attorneys Dealing with Financial Data: Heightened Scrutiny After the Enron and Andersen Debacle*, 1325 PLI/Corp 925, 944 (2002).

[179] Pub. L. No. 104-67 (codified at 15 U.S.C. § 78-a (1995)).

[180] Private Securities Litigation Reform Act of 1995, Pub. L. No. 104-67, § 301(a) (1995) (codified at 15 U.S.C. § 78j-1(a) (1995)).

[181] 15 U.S.C. § 78j-1(b)(1)(B) (1995).

[182] 15 U.S.C. § 78j-1(b)(2)(B) (1995).

[183] 15 U.S.C. § 78j-1(3) (1995).

[184] 15 U.S.C. § 78j-1(3)(A), (3)(B) (1995).

[185] 15 U.S.C. § 78j-1(4) (1995).

blowing' obligation on public company auditors, the Reform Act has altered the relationship between companies and their accountants."[186]

In a 1996 lecture about the "practical implications" of the 1995 Act, Pitt anticipated some of Watkins's and Lay's conduct at Enron. He recommended that companies make an anonymous reporting mechanism available to their employees.

> Experience teaches that when employees have no internal mechanism to report their concerns, these concerns will be reported outside the corporation when they cause discomfort. It is difficult to imagine any benign recipient of this type of information who may reside outside a corporation. Likely candidates include reporters, the government, corporate competitors, short sellers, and lawyers who specialize in defending so-called "whistle blowers." Try as we might, we cannot come up with any positive benefits associated with restricting the ability of employees to divulge questionable corporate conduct solely to these categories of recipients![187]

Although Watkins was not employed by Andersen, the public accounting firm, or working for Enron as an accountant, some accountants have criticized her failure to report Enron's problems as a violation of accountants' professional standards.[188] For example, Mark Cheffers, CEO of AccountingMalpractice.com, stated that "there are at least three [places] where she would have been responsible for going outside of internal management to tell what she knew."[189] State regulators and professional organizations "require accountants to report irregularities, and the Securities and Exchange Commission requires insiders to disclose suspected financial frauds."[190] "'States typically have their own rules with regard to reporting of irregularities,' Cheffers said. Otherwise she risks losing her license."[191]

In contrast, Bob McAdams, past chairman of the Texas Society of Certified Professional Accountants, noted that "'[i]f you continue to be connected with a misleading financial statement, you are in the position of having your license revoked.' At the same time, McAdams said, 'It sounds like she acted judiciously to me. She wasn't a perpetrator, and she did what she thought was right.'"[192] Saint Louis University's James Fisher concluded that "'[s]he did exactly the right thing ethically, she reported it to

---

[186] Harvey L. Pitt et al., *Promises Made, Promises Kept: The Practical Implications of the Private Securities Litigation Reform Act of 1995*, 33 SAN DIEGO L. REV. 845, 846 (1996).

[187] *Id.* at 865–66.

[188] *See* Julie Mason, *Watkins' Own Ethics Questioned; CPA Professional Standards Required Action, Experts Say*, HOUS. CHRON., February 15, 2002, at A21.

[189] *Id.*

[190] *Id.*

[191] *Id.*

[192] *Id.*

Ken Lay, the top guy.'"[193] Finally, because "'Watkins was apparently not involved in falsifying any reports,'" Professor Ron Clay agreed with Fisher. "'I would assume if she brought it to the CEO she would at least be doing what she thought was the correct thing to do.'"[194]

Because of the accounting failures at Enron, Sarbanes-Oxley imposes stricter requirements on public accountants and mandates more communication between accountants and the Audit Committee. Nonetheless, everyone is aware that, at Enron, all three tiers of review (the Auditors, the Board, and the SEC) failed. Hence Congress and the public have demanded why a fourth tier did not step in to prevent the scandal. "Where were the lawyers?"[195]

C. The Attorneys

The ABA's Model Rule of Professional Conduct 1.13 establishes that the corporation (not the CEO, CFO, or any individual) is the corporate attorney's client. Hence the corporate lawyer must serve "the best interests of the organization,"[196] not individuals. The rule also permits attorneys who suspect illegality within the company to request a "separate legal opinion" on the matter.[197] Enron's in-house legal counsel Jordan Mintz did so in May 2001, long before Watkins wrote her memorandum.[198] Mintz was worried that COO Skilling repeatedly failed to sign required legal documents.[199] He questioned some of the partnerships' accounting arrangements as well as possible conflicts of interest over the compensation of Enron executives.[200] Accordingly, without telling any of his Enron colleagues, Mintz hired the New York law firm Fried, Frank, Harris, Shriver & Jacobson to investigate the partnerships. Fried, Frank recommended that Enron "'halt this practice' of special partnerships."[201] Mintz then wrote

---

[193] *Id.*

[194] *Id.*

[195] *See* Lincoln Savings & Loan Ass'n v. Wall, 743 F. Supp. 901, 920 (D.D.C. 1990) ("Where were these professionals, a number of whom are now asserting their rights under the Fifth Amendment, when these clearly improper transactions were being consummated?

Why didn't any of them speak up or disassociate themselves from the transactions?

Where also were the outside accountants and attorneys when these transactions were effectuated? What is difficult to understand is that with all the professional talent involved (both accounting and legal), why at least one professional would not have blown the whistle to stop the overreaching that took place in this case.")

[196] MODEL R. PROF'L CONDUCT R. 1.13 (b) (2001).

[197] MODEL R. PROF'L CONDUCT R. 1.13 (b)(2) (2001).

[198] Rone Tempest, *Enron Counsel Warned About Partnerships Probe*, LOS ANGELES TIMES, January 31, 2002, 2002 WL 2450218.

[199] *The Financial Collapse of Enron, supra* note 18, at 42.

[200] *Id.* at 45–47, 57.

[201] TEMPEST, *supra* note 198.

internal memoranda opposing some of the off-the-books partnerships.[202] Mintz never notified the Board of Directors about these flaws in the partnerships.

> MS. DEGETTE. And did you ever go to any of the board members, Mr. Winokur or others, and tell them of your concerns, that Mr. Skilling had not signed these sheets?
>
> MR. MINTZ. I didn't, Congresswoman.
>
> MS. DEGETTE. Why not?
>
> MR. MINTZ. In an organization like Enron, I try to work within the system and report to people who are senior to me who I felt had the direct responsibilities with the board.[203]

MR 1.13 permitted Mintz to notify the Board. The attorney who suspects misconduct within the corporation *may* "refer[] the matter to . . . the highest authority" within the organization, usually the Board.[204]

Lawyers are neither retaliatory nor reporting whistleblowers. In many states, including Texas, lawyers are not protected from retaliatory discharge in common or statutory law.[205] Moreover, because they zealously protect the attorney-client privilege and the confidentiality of their clients' communications, lawyers usually resist any reporting obligations to external authorities. For example, the ABA's Ethics 2000 Commission recently recommended an amendment to Model Rule 1.6, which protects the confidentiality of client communications. The new rule would have permitted (but not required) an attorney to reveal confidences to:

> prevent the client from committing a crime or fraud that is reasonably certain to result in substantial injury to the financial interests or property of another or to prevent, mitigate or rectify substantial injury to the financial interests or property of another that is reasonably certain to result or has resulted from the client's commission of a crime or fraud in furtherance of which the client has used the lawyer's services.[206]

The ABA also considered suggestions to modify MR 1.13. Some law professors urged the ABA to switch the *may* to *must*, requiring mandatory reporting to the Board of suspected violations of law.

---

[202] *Id.*

[203] *The Financial Collapse of Enron, supra* note 18, at 48 (he went to "Mr. Buy and Mr. Causey").

[204] MODEL R. PROF'L CONDUCT R. 1.13 (b)(3) (2001).

[205] *See* Bohatch v. Butler & Binion, 977 S.W.2d 543 (Tex. 1998); Willy v. Coastal Corp., 855 F.2d 1160 (5th Cir. 1988), *affirmed by* 503 U.S. 131 (1992).

[206] MODEL RULES OF PROF'L CONDUCT R. 1.6 (proposed amendment 2002); *see also* Geoffrey C. Hazard Jr., *Ethics, Etc.*, NAT'L L.J., October 16, 2000, at A25.

WHISTLEBLOWING IN THE BUSINESS WORLD

In August 2001, the ABA rejected both proposals: first, to allow permissive disclosure of financial fraud and, second, to mandate up-the-ladder reporting within the corporation. Those decisions did not go unnoticed by legislators struggling with massive accounting scandals:

> [T]he State bars as a whole have failed. They have provided no specific ethical rule of conduct to remedy this kind of situation. Even if they do have a general rule that applies, it often goes unenforced. . . . Similarly, the American Bar Association's Model Rules of Professional Responsibility do not have mandatory rules for professional conduct for corporate practitioners which require them to take specific action. The ABA merely has a general rule that an attorney must represent the best interests of an organization and suggests a number of ways an attorney could respond, including reporting illegal conduct to a responsible constituent of the organization, such as the board of directors. But this does not *mandate action*.[207]

Accordingly, Sarbanes-Oxley directed the SEC to set professional rules *mandating up-the-ladder reporting* for lawyers who appear before the Commission.[208] These rules are reminiscent of the earlier requirements for public accounting firms.[209] First, attorneys *must* "report evidence of a material violation of securities law or breach of fiduciary duty" to the company's CLO (Chief Legal Officer), CEO, or both. If those officials do not respond appropriately to the complaint, the lawyer *must* report the evidence to the Audit Committee or the Board. If she is still not satisfied, the lawyer must resign. The Securities and Exchange Commission has not yet decided how "noisy" the lawyer's withdrawal must be. It is currently considering alternative proposals, one that requires the lawyer to inform the SEC of the resignation and one that orders the issuer to do so. Under Congress's direction, corporate lawyers are becoming reporting whistleblowers. If the attorney is discharged for her reporting, she may inform the Board that this was the basis of her firing and (presumably) sue for retaliatory discharge.[210]

The controversies over Enron, and Congress's passage of Sarbanes-Oxley, also persuaded the ABA to reconsider its rules on corporate responsibility. The ABA Task Force on Corporate Responsibility issued its final recommendations on March 31, 2003. This "Cheek Report" recommended that corporations improve "reporting rela-

---

[207] 148 Cong. Rec. S6555 (daily ed. July 10, 2002) (statement of Sen. Enzi) (emphasis added).

[208] Sarbanes-Oxley Act of 2002, Pub. L. No. 107-204, § 307, 116 Stat. 745 (2002) (codified at 15 U.S.C. § 7245). *See also* SEC, *SEC Proposes Rules to Implement Sarbanes-Oxley Act Provisions Concerning Standards of Professional Conduct for Attorneys*, SEC PRESS RELEASE 2002-158, November 6, 2002, *available at* http://www.sec.gov/news/press/2002-158.htm (last visited February 27, 2003).

[209] *See supra* notes 178–86 and accompanying text.

[210] In-house attorney whistleblowers would presumably be protected as "employees" under Section 806 of the Act, but it is unlikely that this provision would provide protection to outside counsel.

tionships" among corporate counsel so that potential violations of law and breaches of fiduciary duty are reported directly to the general counsel.[211]

The Task Force also recommended two substantive amendments to Model Rule 1.13(b),[212] both to clarify the rule and to impose some *mandatory* reporting requirements on lawyers. The first amendment identifies the *trigger* that obligates the lawyer to report possible violations of law. The second amendment *requires* a lawyer to report up-the-ladder within the organization once the trigger is met. As noted above, the current Model Rule 1.13 does not *require* lawyers to "report up." The proposed Model Rule 1.13 states:

> (b) If a lawyer for an organization <u>knows facts from which a reasonable lawyer, under the circumstances, would conclude that an officer, employee or other person associated with the organization is engaged in action, intends to act or refused to act in a matter related to the representation that is a violation of a legal obligation to the organization, or a violation of law which reasonably might be imputed to the organization, and that is likely to result in substantial injury to the organization,</u> then the lawyer shall proceed as is reasonably necessary in the best interest of the organization. Unless the lawyer reasonably believes that it is not necessary in the best interest of the organization to do so, the lawyer <u>shall</u> refer the matter to higher authority in the organization, including, if warranted by the circumstances, the highest authority that can act on behalf of the organization as determined by applicable law.[213]

The Cheek Commission also recommended changes in the confidentiality rules so that lawyers may reveal fraud to third parties.[214] The confidentiality change is applied explicitly to corporate lawyers in the new Model Rule 1.13, which permits corporate

---

[211] James H. Cheek, III chaired the committee; its report is known as the Cheek Report. The report is available at http://www.abanet.org/buslaw/corporateresponsibility/home.html, last visited June 5, 2003, P. 32.

[212] *Id., supra* note 211, at 35.

[213] *Id., supra* note 211, at 44 (emphasis added).

[214] *Id., supra* note 211, at 52. The proposed Model Rule 1.6 states:

> (b) A lawyer may reveal information relating to the representation of a client to the extent the lawyer reasonably believes necessary: . . .
>
> (2) to prevent the client from committing a crime or fraud that is reasonably certain to result in substantial injury to the financial interests or property of another and in furtherance of which the client has used or is using the lawyer's services; [and]
>
> (3) to prevent, mitigate or rectify substantial injury to the financial interests or property of another that is reasonably certain to result or has resulted from the client's commission of a crime or fraud in furtherance of which the client has used the lawyer's services.

lawyers to reveal information to third parties "to "prevent substantial injury to the corporation."[215]

The ABA Task Force acknowledged that lawyers, unlike accountants, are not "gatekeepers."[216] Nonetheless, the Cheek Report does clarify and expand corporate lawyers' obligation to be internal and external whistleblowers, in the "relatively unusual situation" when a client violates the law.

V. CONCLUSION

"Whether whistleblowers are viewed as snitches or saviors depends, of course, on one's perspective."[217] After Enron and other corporate scandals, in 2002 the whistleblowers were viewed as saviors. The Whistleblower was *Time's* Person of the Year. Sarbanes-Oxley offered the strongest legal protection ever to retaliatory whistleblowers, and increased the ranks of reporting whistleblowers. The accountants, who were already whistleblowers under the 1995 securities laws, faced even stricter reporting requirements. The securities lawyers now join their ranks . . . reluctantly. Many lawyers do not want to "snitch" on their clients; they believe that lawyers save clients by keeping confidences.

Amidst the celebration of whistleblowing, it is timely to remember that, before 2002, the dominant metaphor for whistleblowers was the bee sting. No one anticipated what would result when Sherron Watkins wrote her anonymous memorandum on August 15, 2001. "One has only one sting to use, and using it may well lead to one's own mortality."[218]

Or to the cover of *Time Magazine*.

QUESTIONS

1. Assume that you are an associate in a law firm and you have noticed something in a client's file that doesn't "look right" to you. Would you investigate further?

---

[215] *Id., supra* at 56. The proposed amendment to Model Rule 1.13 states:

(c) Except as provided in Paragraph (d), if

(1) despite the lawyer's efforts in accordance with Paragraph (b) the highest authority that can act on behalf of the organization insists upon or fails to address in a timely and appropriate fashion action, or a refusal to act, that is clearly a violation of law, and

(2) the lawyer reasonably believes that the violation is reasonably certain to result in substantial injury to the organization,

then the lawyer <u>may</u> reveal information relating to the representation whether or not Rule 1.6 permits such disclosure, but only if and to the extent the lawyer reasonably believes necessary to prevent substantial injury to the organization.

[216] *Id., supra* at 21.

[217] Miethe, *supra* note 122, at 13.

[218] Gerald Vinten, *The Whistleblowers' Charter*, Executive Development, vol. 8, no. 2, 1995, at 27.

Would you ask someone at the client's business about your qualms? Would you report your qualms to the senior associate or partner in charge of the matter? Exactly how would you go about broaching the issue? What would you do if everyone with whom you spoke ignored your concerns?

2. Would your answers in Question 1 change if you were in-house counsel at the client? Why or why not?

3. Would your answers in Question 1 change if you were the partner at the law firm in charge of the client's matter? What if you were another partner in the law firm but you didn't have any contact with that particular client?

4. What should Model 1.13 require lawyers to do when they suspect a client is planning to act illegally?

5. Should lawyers be required to reveal confidences to "prevent the client from committing a crime or fraud that is reasonably certain to result in substantial injury to the financial interests or property of another"?

6. Should Sherron Watkins have reported the accounting improprieties to someone outside Enron?

7. Should the law permit Sherron Watkins to file a lawsuit against Enron for retaliatory discharge?

Can Energy Markets Be Trusted? The Effect of the Rise and Fall of Enron on Energy Markets

Jacqueline Lang Weaver*

I. INTRODUCTION

Greenspan Says Enron Cure Is In Market, Not Regulation. (Headline)

Mr. Greenspan defended the current approach to corporate governance, with its reliance on trust in the chief executive, as the best available.

—*New York Times,* March 27, 2002 (four months after the Enron bankruptcy).[1]

---

* A.A. White Professor of Law, University of Houston Law Center. This essay is excerpted, in revised form, from a longer article of the same title, with the copyright permission of the *Houston Business & Tax Law Journal,* an electronic journal at the University of Houston Law Center. The full article will appear on this journal's website at www.hbtlj.org in early fall 2003 and printed in hard copy in 4 HOUS. BUS. & TAX L. J. __ (2004). The version of the article excerpted here was largely completed by March 15, 2003, before FERC released its staff's *Final Report on Price Manipulation in Western Markets* on March 26, 2003. This essay briefly summarizes the findings of this report at relevant points in the text. The interested reader should consult the longer article on the journal website for a full account of post-March 15, 2003 findings and events at FERC, in industry, and in the academic and trade literature. A second excerpt from the essay appears in this book in Chapter 5-2, titled *Lessons for Teaching Energy Law.*

The author thanks Peter Egler, Research Librarian at the O'Quinn Law Library, and Ryan LaRue, Class of 2004, for their outstanding research assistance for this article. She also thanks the following reviewers for their substantial time commitment and perceptive comments on earlier drafts: Professor Fred Bosselman, Chicago-Kent School of Law; Professor Roger Sherman, Economics Department, University of Houston; Professor David B. Spence, McCombs School of Business, University of Texas; Darren Bush, Visiting Professor at the University of Utah School of Law (who will be joining the University of Houston Law Center in fall 2003); and Alan Raymond, former president and CEO of Shell Energy Services Company. Dr. Gurgen Gulen of the Institute for Energy, Law & Enterprise at the University of Houston Law Center provided comments on sections of the article. Kirk K. Weaver and Dr. Usha Shah also provided invaluable assistance. The University of Houston Law Foundation provided research grants to support this work.

[1] Richard W. Stevenson, *Greenspan Says Enron Cure Is in Market, Not Regulation,* N.Y. TIMES, Mar. 27, 2002, at C5.

The problem with socialism is socialism. The problem with capitalism is capitalists.

—Willi Schlamm, reformed German Communist,
as quoted in a *Wall St. Journal* editorial in
January 2002 that continues:

[The Enron scandal] is a problem for anyone who believes in free markets.[2]

The end of the Cold War signaled the "end of history," according to Francis Fukuyama.[3] Human progress had culminated in the triumph of a universal capitalistic and democratic order. With the demise of Marxist social engineering, Fukuyama next sought to explain what made some capitalistic societies more productive and secure than others. The answer: trust. Trust is the "expectation that arises within a community of regular, honest, and cooperative behavior, based on commonly shared norms."[4] Trust is the cultural capital that enables a society to create large, private business organizations rather than remain dependent on smaller economic entities formed along kinship ties. As Nobel laureate Kenneth Arrow has written:

> Trust is an important lubricant of a social system. It is extremely efficient; it saves a lot of trouble to have a fair degree of reliance on other people's word. Unfortunately, [trust] is not a commodity which can be bought very easily. If you have to buy it, you already have some doubts about what you've bought. Trust and similar values, [like] truth-telling, are . . . goods, they are commodities; they have real, practical economic value; they increase the efficiency of the system. . . . But they are not commodities for which trade on the open market is technically possible or even meaningful.[5]

Trust is also the most fragile of all forms of human and physical capital. Once dissipated, it may take decades to replenish, if indeed it can be renourished at all.[6]

When Enron, the seventh largest company in the Fortune 500 in 2001, collapsed virtually overnight, destroying billions of dollars of shareholder value, trust in capital markets fell, too. The steady, toxic drip-feed of revelations of corrupt accounting, executive greed, devious financing, and inept or absent regulatory policing exposed a web of conflict of interests permeating the corporate boardroom, Wall Street, and legislative halls. Trust in business executives and in the financial and accounting com-

[2] *Enron's Sins*, WALL ST. J., Jan. 12, 2002, at A10.

[3] FRANCIS FUKUYAMA, THE END OF HISTORY AND THE LAST MAN (1992).

[4] FRANCIS FUKUYAMA, TRUST 26 (1995).

[5] *Id.* at 151–52.

[6] *Id.* at 321.

munities plummeted. A 2002 poll showed only 16 percent of Americans trusted what any big company told them.[7] The toxic revelations then spilled into the energy markets, when state and federal investigations of the California energy crisis found Death Star and Fat Boy and other games played by Enron, and the new breed of energy traders and merchant generators that energy deregulation had birthed.

Most of the essays in this book address the corporate governance aspects of Enron's fall—the causes, consequences, and reforms in the duties of corporate boards and the accounting profession in general. Yet, Enron was synonymous with energy trading in the new gas and electric markets that developed with the liberalization of these markets in the United States and abroad. Enron was ranked the most innovative company in the United States for six years in a row by *Fortune* magazine, due to the novel businesses it launched in energy trading and services during the 1980s and 1990s. In the year since Enron declared bankruptcy on December 2, 2001, other companies that had entered the energy trading business, such as Dynegy, El Paso, Williams, Calpine, Mirant, and Duke, are struggling to survive. Many have seen their credit ratings reduced to junk bond status. They have quit the trading business and are rapidly selling their hard assets—their pipelines and power generating plants—to raise capital to bolster their balance sheets by reducing debt. Wholesale electricity trading volumes have plummeted on national exchanges. UBS Warburg, the large financial institution that bought Enron's most prized asset—its energy trading floor—has shuttered its Houston office. Retail electricity deregulation—a key driver of energy markets—has virtually halted at the state level.

Can energy markets be trusted ever again? This essay looks at Enron's role in the creation of these markets; the role of energy trading in the California crisis; the fall-out from the Enron scandal and the California-related investigations; the role of regulators in creating and restoring trust; and it concludes with some thoughts about the future of energy markets today. The account is necessarily incomplete. The files of press accounts, government reports, agency dockets, economic analyses, and industry and trade association documents surrounding the Enron scandal are massive. Many investigations have not yet concluded; discovery of documents is still ongoing in many lawsuits; new revelations appear almost daily, sometimes as part of settlements between companies and regulators and sometimes as part of guilty pleas by traders.

The reader must also be sternly warned: Many of the authors, both individual and institutional, of the reports and documents cited here have biases. Some biases might be easy to detect: California politicians certainly have a different view of many issues from that of federal regulators, and regulators certainly have different views from that

---

[7] The Lord Browne of Madingley, Group Chief Executive of BP, "Meeting America's Energy Needs," Speech delivered to the Houston Forum 9 (Aug. 1, 2002) (on file with author). A 1998 survey found that two-thirds of 160 chief financial officers of public companies had been asked by executives to misrepresent their companies' results. Twelve percent admitted to doing so. Alex Berenson, *The Biggest Casualty of Enron's Collapse: Confidence*, N.Y. TIMES, Feb. 10, 2002, Sec. 4, at 1.

of industry. Economists, who have played an enormous role in the deregulation debate, often have an ideological bent that suffuses their writings with an embrace of markets as an abstract goal that seems difficult to match with the reality of market performance in the electricity sector. Even empirical evidence is difficult to assess because authors frequently present only those data that support their viewpoint and neglect to either explain the data's limitations or present other conflicting data that gives a more balanced measure of market performance. All of these biases make it tremendously difficult to determine what the "real story" is, particularly at this early date. But enough is known that the reader who tackles this essay should be able to appreciate the contours of the battle among regulation, market power, and competition in the newly created electricity markets, and the ability of regulators to protect the public interest in these markets.

II. WHAT ENRON DID: THE BEST OF COMPANIES— THE WORST OF COMPANIES

> Enronitis: The tally of firms tarred by Enronitis, a lack of trust, is growing by the day.
>
> —*U.S. News & World Report*, Feb. 2002[8]

> The dripfeed effect [of revelations of corporate sleaze] has been devastating for investors' confidence, helping to prolong the longest and deepest bear market since the second world war. . . . Enronitis has been a big contributor to the past year's economic ills in America and the rest of the world.
>
> —*The Economist*, Nov. 30, 2002[9]

A. In the Beginning: The Landscape Before Deregulation.

In 1971, Dr. Kenneth Lay, a Ph.D. economist went to work for the Federal Power Commission, now called the Federal Energy Regulatory Commission, or FERC.[10] At that time, the natural gas pipeline industry looked like Figure 1.[11]

---

[8] Noam Neusner et al., *Confidence Lost—Lenders and Investors Come Down with 'Enronitis'*, U.S. NEWS & WORLD REP., Feb. 18, 2002, at 32. Even the doughnut company, Krispy Kreme, felt the Enron virus. The company decided not to use an accepted financing technique called a synthetic lease for fear of Enronitis. Its stock plunged 10 percent when its synthetic lease on a $30 million plant was called an "off balance-sheet trick." *Id.* Synthetic leases allow firms to keep real estate costs off the balance sheet while enjoying tax deductions as if they were the owner of the asset. Even participants in synthetic leases are confused by them, however, and have had to restate financial results. *Id.* at 33.

[9] *Investor Self-Protection*, THE ECONOMIST, Nov. 30, 2002, at 12.

[10] ROBERT BRYCE, PIPE DREAMS 28 (2002).

[11] FRED BOSSELMAN, JIM ROSSI & JACQUELINE LANG WEAVER, ENERGY, ECONOMICS AND THE ENVIRONMENT 435 (2000) [hereinafter EEE].

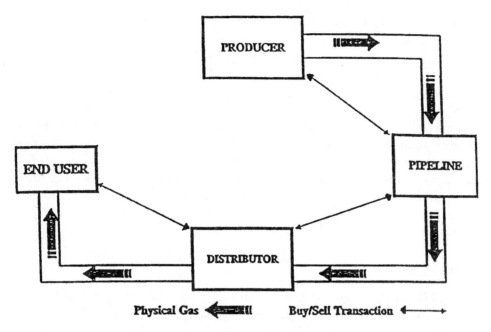

Figure 1.

Molecules of natural gas traveled from producer to end user in a completely regulated system. Both the price of natural gas sold by producers into the interstate market (from 1954 onward) and the transportation tariff for moving the gas in interstate pipelines were regulated by FERC on the basis of cost-of-service ratemaking. After lengthy hearings, FERC established prices and rates that would allow producers and pipeline owners to achieve a reasonable rate of return, say 13 percent, on their investment in gas wells and gas pipelines. Most gas was sold to local distributing companies at a city gate and the distributor then transported the gas in smaller pipelines to heat homes and stores and to fuel furnaces and factories. The distributing company operated under the grant of a local monopoly franchise on this business, so its tariff was also regulated by the state's public utility commission to protect consumers.

It was a steady, if not boring, industry of regulators, cost accountants, and lawyers who drafted fairly standardized, bilateral contracts between each participant in the market. Producers sold all of the gas from their wells to the pipeline closest to their field under long-term contracts of twenty years or as long as gas was produced from the field. The gas in the pipeline was owned by the pipeline company, which then sold it to the distributor, again under long-term contracts. Thus, pipelines provided a "bundled" service to end-users. The pipeline was both a gas merchant, buying and selling gas under long-term contracts, and a transportation service provider. In the decades of the 1930s through the 1950s, the pipeline was often both a monopsonist (the sole buyer in a field) and a monopolist (the sole seller to a distributing company or end user). Because the early pipelines, like railroads, had monopoly power, regulatory agencies were created to limit the rates they could charge so that consumers were protected from this market power.

In contrast to the pipeline industry, the gas production sector—the drillers and producers who undertake the search for oil and gas in reservoirs thousands of feet under the earth's surface—was composed of hundreds of participants, both large and small. Nonetheless, in 1954, in a poorly reasoned opinion, the U.S. Supreme Court held that the Natural Gas Act required the Federal Power Commission (now FERC) to regulate the maximum price of natural gas that producers could charge for sales of gas in interstate commerce.[12] Price regulation applied to a competitive industry predictably created shortages in natural gas by the late 1960s. When Middle East oil exporters embargoed sales of their crude oil to the United States in 1973 for geopolitical reasons, acute shortages of both oil and gas plunged the U.S. economy into the twin evils of stagnation and inflation, aptly named "stagflation."

B. Shortages and Inefficiency.

In 1978, Congress enacted a massive five-part National Energy Act to help the nation cope with serious energy shortages. One key part of the act was to gradually deregulate natural gas prices so that higher prices would encourage producers to drill more wells and encourage consumers to conserve its use. At the same time, FERC moved to restructure the gas pipeline industry so that sales of natural gas were unbundled from the transportation service provided by the pipelines. The pipelines would no longer own all of the gas carried inside them. Instead, end users of gas could deal directly with producers of the gas, bargain for the best price, and then ship their gas via open access pipelines to where the gas was in most demand. Pipeline rates would continue to be regulated by FERC, reflecting the natural monopoly power of this distribution system. The vision that FERC had, and that Ken Lay shared, now as CEO and President of Houston Natural Gas Company was of an industry structure that looked like Figure 2.[13]

The physical flow of natural gas remains the same as in the pre-1985 era, but the buy/sell financial transactions involve new players, such as gas marketers, brokers, and purchasing agents, and new risk management tools. Natural gas was increasingly sold into a spot market on thirty-day contracts rather than committed to twenty-year contracts at a fixed price. If gas producers or end users did not want to develop their own in-house expertise to buy and sell gas in the new fast-moving market, they could use gas marketers that specialized in matching supply to demand.

To realize this vision of a competitive gas market between producers and end users, FERC faced a daunting task. Under the Natural Gas Act, FERC had no power to require an interstate pipeline to transport gas for a third party. Starting in the early

---

[12] Phillips Petroleum Co. v. Wisconsin, 347 U.S. 672 (1954).

[13] EEE, *supra* note 11, at 436.

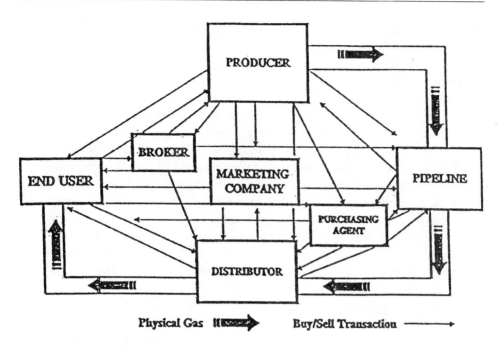

Figure 2.

1980s, FERC issued a series of orders aimed at transforming pipelines to "open access" carriers that were obligated to carry gas owned by third parties on equal terms with gas owned by the pipeline itself. FERC required pipelines to "functionally unbundle" their merchant gas sales function from their pipeline transportation function. FERC did not require that the pipelines actually physically divest themselves of one of these two functions. Rather, the companies had to set up separate affiliates and maintain an internal "firewall" between the two so that the pipeline affiliate would not give special information or treatment to its own gas producing affiliate or gas storage affiliate that was not shared equally with competitors for the pipeline space. Pipelines had to file published tariffs on electronic bulletin boards, so that all shippers could buy service at the same rate as the pipeline charged customers who bought gas owned by the pipeline.

FERC also created a new secondary market in pipeline space. A shipper who had committed to buy, say, 30 percent of the pipeline's space, could release unwanted space to other companies who could use it. Thus, contracts for released pipeline space could be bought and sold on the electronic boards.

In 1985, Ken Lay was CEO of Enron, a company formed by the merger of Houston Natural Gas with Internorth Natural Gas to create a company with 37,000 miles of pipelines in 1985, transporting about 17 percent of all the gas in the U.S. by the early 1990s.[14] In 1988, in a meeting called the "come to Jesus" gathering, Ken Lay announced

---

[14] BRYCE, *supra* note 10, at 31–33.

Enron's major strategy shift: to seek opportunities and growth in unregulated energy markets, leveraged off its stable base as a regulated pipeline company.[15]

By 1995, a preeminent scholar of gas markets gave FERC high marks for its performance in creating competitive markets for gas:

> The participants in the gas market have responded to the spur of competition by implementing numerous efficiency-enhancing commercial and technological innovations. Gas is being found, produced, stored and transported at much lower cost than was the case a decade ago. Gas is traded constantly at dozens of market hubs at constantly changing spot prices. Hundreds of new pipeline interconnections have transformed the previously fragmented transportation system into a closely integrated network that links all North American supplies with all markets in the United States and Canada. Electronic bulletin boards allow . . . continuous trade [in] transportation capacity so that all gas can move from supply areas to market areas over the least expensive route.
>
> The deregulated gas market performed extremely well during the unusually cold 1993–1994 winter. That performance was in sharp contrast . . . to the disappointing performance of the still-regulated electricity industry . . . [in which] all industrial, commercial, and governmental activities in the Middle Atlantic states had to be halted for a day in January 1994 to avoid a complete electricity blackout of that region.[16]

According to Professor Pierce, the "closely analogous" electricity industry was an obvious candidate for similar restructuring, which could "improve that industry's performance dramatically and reduce the nation's electricity bill by approximately $24 billion a year."[17] The choice was simple: Should markets or central planning dominate the performance of the electricity industry?[18]

C. Electricity Deregulation Begins

Beginning in the early 1990s, electricity restructuring began abroad in countries such as the United Kingdom, Argentina, and Australia. In many of these countries, the government actually owned the electricity systems. Restructuring was usually accompanied by an auction or sale of these government assets, placing the industry into the

---

[15] LOREN FOX, ENRON: THE RISE AND FALL *vii* (2003) (detailing a timeline of Enron events).

[16] Richard J. Pierce, Jr., *The Evolution of Natural Gas Regulatory Policy*, 10 NATURAL RESOURCES AND ENV'T, Summer 1995, at 53, 84.

[17] *Id.* at 84.

[18] Bernard S. Black & Richard J. Pierce, Jr., *The Choice Between Markets and Central Planning in Regulating the U.S. Electricity Industry*, 93 COLUM. L. REV. 1339 (1993).

hands of private investors (many of whom were U.S. companies). In the United States, most electric utilities are already privately owned and are commonly called "IOUs" or investor-owned utilities. Thus, privatization were not necessary, but eliminating the monopoly power of these franchised IOUs and opening up the electric grid to nondiscriminatory access for transmitting electricity was essential to competitive markets. Figure 3 illustrates in broad form the move from the old structure to the new.[19]

Under the traditional structure depicted on the left, one vertically integrated utility was granted a monopoly franchise to serve a particular area of a state. The utility operated its own generation plants (fueled by coal, nuclear, or natural gas), transmitted the electricity on high voltage transmission lines, and then distributed it to individual homes and businesses on lower voltage distribution lines. Customers had no choice of provider.

The grant of these monopoly franchises amounted to a "regulatory compact" between the state and the privately owned utility. The utility was granted a monopoly and in exchange had a duty to serve all customers in its territory. With a captive market guaranteed to it, a state public utility commission ("PUC") regulated the rates of the utility so that prices to end users would be just and reasonable. Rates were regulated under the traditional cost-of-service formula as follows:

Revenues = Capital Base × a Reasonable Rate of Return + Operating Costs.

Under this formula, the regulatory body limited the amount of revenues a utility could receive. The private utility could earn a reasonable rate of return on the capital it invested in generation and transmission facilities, but only if the capital was prudently invested in useful facilities. Utilities could also recover their operating costs—largely the cost of fuel—as long as these costs were prudently incurred.

Under cost-of-service ratemaking, a regulated utility has an incentive to over-invest in capital facilities because every dollar spent on capital improvements earns a rate of return. Economists call this incentive to over-invest the "Averch-Johnson" inefficiency of cost-of-service ratemaking, and it was this inefficiency that restructuring the power industry was to cure. Cost-of-service ratemaking involved lengthy hearings conducted by the state utility commissions to assess and project long-term future electricity demand in the area served by each utility and the most efficient fuel source or type of plant to serve that demand. These hearings became especially contentious during the 1970s when utility investments in nuclear power plants cost billions of dollars more than projected, greatly raising consumer rates and the ire of environmentalists.[20]

On the national level, FERC regulates the interstate sale of electricity at wholesale, by regulating both the wholesale price of electricity and the rates charged for use of the

---

[19] EEE, *supra* note 11, at 709.

[20] EEE, *supra* note 11, at Ch. 8 (presenting examples of traditional ratemaking; see especially pp. 541–43 on nuclear plants); Harvey Averch & Leland L. Johnson, *Behavior of the Firm under Regulatory Constraint*, 52 AMER. ECON. REV. 1052 (1962).

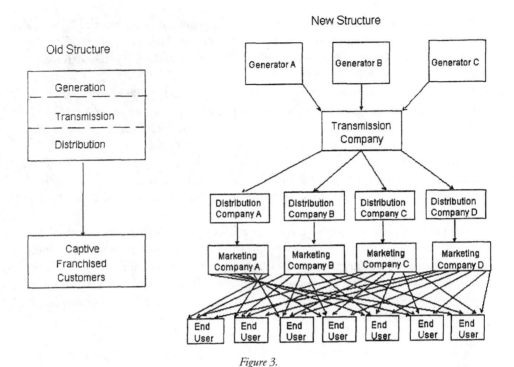

Figure 3.

transmission wires. These wires are the equivalent of a gas pipeline—an essential network industry that is often a natural monopoly. Unless it is rate-regulated, a bottleneck industry can extract monopoly rents from generators and end users who must use the transmission service to move electricity to market. FERC used cost-of-service ratemaking for interstate transmission of electricity. Similarly, state PUCs regulated the rates charged for distribution of electricity to retail users. State PUCs also regulated the siting of new generation facilities and transmission lines. Thus, complete deregulation of electricity markets from power plant to a homeowner's light switch would ultimately require restructuring the industry at two levels—the federally regulated, wholesale market for electricity and the state-regulated retail market.

The brave new world of restructured electricity would free the formerly captive end users to make deals directly with generators, using open access transmission and distribution wires to transmit electricity along the cheapest path. As part of the same National Energy Act of 1978 that eventually deregulated natural gas prices, Congress passed an act called PURPA (the Public Utilities Regulatory Policy Act) to promote competitive markets at the generation end of the vertically integrated industry. PURPA encouraged the growth of new wholesale providers of electricity called "Qualifying Facilities" or QFs. Only a certain type of generating facility could qualify for QF status, namely small, nonconventional producers of wind, solar, geothermal, hydroelectric or cogeneration plants. But these QFs became the first independent power producers, i.e., producers of electricity that were independent of the existing franchised utility.[21] To encourage their growth, Congress authorized FERC to require that the existing utilities purchase all the power produced by the QF at a price reflecting the utilities' "avoided cost" of generating power on their own. Under guidelines set by FERC, some state public utility commissions set a rather high rate for these required purchases. Thus, with both a guaranteed high price for their electricity and a guaranteed market, private capital flowed into the QF sector, especially in California with its geothermal potential.

In the Energy Policy Act of 1992, Congress added a different type of independent power producer to the landscape—an "e-wog," or EWG, which stands for an exempt wholesale generator. Such a generator is exempt from the regulatory constraints of a 1935 New Deal statute called PUHCA (the Public Utilities Holding Company Act) that regulated the activities of large, utility holding companies whose collapse in the Great Depression had caused great problems.[22] E-wogs, unlike QFs, can generate electricity using large gas- or coal-fired plants, but they cannot be vertically integrated and cannot own transmission assets. The E-wog, now more often called an independent power producer, or IPP, is the merchant power plant in the business of producing electricity to sell into the wholesale market. As long as the merchant plant does not sell electricity at retail, the plant's rates are regulated by FERC, not by the state PUC.

Both the growth of independent power producers and public dissatisfaction with high utility rates from cost overruns in the 1980s led state PUCs and FERC to experiment with different types of electricity rates. Both agencies adopted performance-based rates or incentive rates that allowed both utility shareholders and consumers to benefit if a utility's financial performance resulted in a rate of return higher than a cost-based return. Under these new ratemaking formulas, a utility had the incentive to reduce costs to gain a higher, but still controlled, rate of return. Performance indicators based on worker safety, system reliability (blackouts), and customer satisfaction would monitor the utility's non-price behavior, and financial rewards or penalties would be granted if the utility under- or over-performed against national standards.

For IPPs, FERC adopted the penultimate incentive rate—unregulated, market-based rates. IPPs would live or die based on the ability of their management to build more cheaply and operate more efficiently than existing power plants owned by utilities. If IPPs could undersell traditional utilities when electricity markets opened up to competition (which depended crucially on the IPPs being accorded equal access to the transmission lines owned by the utilities), their shareholders and managers would reap profitable rewards. If they could not produce competitively, the IPPs would suffer the

---

[21] EEE, *supra* note 11, at 717–20, 749–52.

[22] *Id.* at 747–49.

same fate as any unregulated business, including bankruptcy. Since IPPs, by definition, did not own transmission facilities (which were still regulated as a natural monopoly) and because they were often new entrants to a previously closed system, IPPs were given market-based rates on the grounds that they did not possess market power.[23]

In the middle of electricity restructuring sits the power marketer.[24] Traditionally, the vertically integrated utility was the only entity that bought and sold electricity in bulk in wholesale markets. Now, power marketers emerged as key players. They owned none of the hard assets of generation, transmission or distribution. A power marketer like Enron bought electricity from all types of generators—those still owned by IOUs, E-wogs or QFs—and then resold the power to another utility. FERC has jurisdiction over the power marketer because it makes sales of electricity in interstate commerce at wholesale. However, many of the regulations that governed traditional public utilities were waived for power marketers. Because most marketers do not own generation or transmission that could give them market power in certain geographical areas, they are permitted to charge market-based rates—that is, whatever price is agreed upon by buyer and seller. The power marketer did not need to file accounting records with FERC because no cost-of-service ratemaking is done. Nor did the marketer have to file individual contracts with FERC for its approval. The marketer simply had to file quarterly summaries of their transactions.

A FERC report in March 1999 described the "breakneck speed" of change in the electric utility industry, with power marketers as key players. Sales of electricity by power marketers had jumped from 2.6 million megawatt-hours of electricity in the first quarter of 1995 to 95 million megawatt hours in the fourth quarter of 1996.[25] The market at that time was still somewhat concentrated: 73 percent of all sales were made by only ten power marketers. One, Enron, had about 26 percent of the market.

By 1997, electricity futures contracts were being sold on the New York Mercantile Exchange, NYMEX, to serve the growing wholesale trade. Power marketers are the biggest users of futures, although investor-owned utilities that secure FERC approval of market-based rates will also use futures to hedge their risks in the more volatile world of energy markets. The power marketer that enters into a contract to sell power at a set price runs the risk that the price it must pay for electricity as a buyer will increase before the power is delivered to its customer. NYMEX allows the marketer to hedge risks on the futures market. Under traditional cost-of-service ratemaking, utilities did not need a futures market: they were guaranteed a rate of return that allowed them to recover their costs.

---

[23] *Id.* at 720–31.

[24] *Id.* at 780–88.

[25] *Id.* at 785–90.

D. Enron: The Next Big Idea

WMM

—Jeff Skilling's license plate: "We Make Markets"[26]

Better Reliability Through Markets.

—Motto of the California Independent
System Operator (CAISO)[27]

Enron's "genius" was to build a business model that tracked the opening of deregulated energy markets. This business model was accompanied by a powerful and well-
financed political lobbying arm that worked to push government regulation out of the
markets. Voted the most innovative company in America from 1996–2001, Enron
"synthesized existing ideas from the Texas oil business, Wall Street and Silicon Valley."[28] From the high-tech oil industry came the use of massive supercomputer processing capacity, built to analyze seismic data culled from soundwaves miles beneath
the earth's surface, and then transferred to use in complex financial modeling. From
Wall Street came the use of sophisticated risk management tools, such as hedging and
derivatives. From Silicon Valley came the use of the Internet to transact energy trades
in real time, like buying and selling on eBay. Enron started with a sound business
model that operated with deserved success in the early 1990s. This section describes in
more detail the innovations Enron introduced into energy markets.

As FERC deregulated gas markets, gas began to be traded as a commodity on spot
markets. Jeffrey Skilling, a Wall Street management consultant from McKinsey &
Company, quickly grasped the effect of this radical change on gas producers and gas
users. With gas no longer tied to fixed-price, long-term contracts, both sellers and
buyers in the market would need hedging tools to manage volatile prices.

The Gas Bank. Enron's first innovation, engineered by Skilling, was the Gas Bank.[29]
With the higher gas prices allowed under the Natural Gas Policy Act, new supplies of
gas came onstream at the same time that the Clean Air Act was creating a new demand
for gas as a far cleaner fuel than coal for electricity generation. The Gas Bank matched
the new supplies with the new demand. Producers deposited gas in the Bank under
long-term purchase contracts with Enron that guaranteed the producers a steady cash
flow, essential to their being able to secure financing for their drilling ventures. Gas

---

[26] PETER C. FUSARO & ROSS M. MILLER, WHAT WENT WRONG AT ENRON 70 (2002).

[27] Robert McCullough, *Revisiting California,* PUB. UTIL. FORTNIGHTLY, Apr. 1, 2002, at 28.

[28] FUSARO & MILLER, *supra* note 26, at 75; *see also* Daniel Altman, *Finding Gems of Genius Among
Enron's Crumbs,* N.Y. TIMES, Feb. 3, 2002, at 6.

[29] *See* BRYCE, *supra* note 10, at 52–59; FOX, *supra* note 15, at 22–40 (providing more detail about
Enron's start in gas trading in both physical and financial markets).

users entered into multi-year contracts with the Bank, paying a premium for a guaranteed gas supply of large volumes. Enron, as the middleman, pocketed the spread. Enron Gas Services was a smash hit with an old-fashioned product marketed in a new way. The Gas Bank created more demand for gas-fired power plants because these plants could get financing based on their assured gas supply.

Enron provided price stability through the use of financial derivatives such as swaps and options. Swaps allow a gas user to swap a floating price for a fixed price.[30] Options give gas buyers the right, but not the obligation, to buy gas in the future at a fixed price. As the middleman between buyers and sellers, Enron was the counterparty to both sides of the trade and made money on the spread. Of course, Enron was then exposed to the risk of holding gas contracts with an obligation to deliver at a fixed price when prices might zoom upwards in a shortage. Enron developed Enron Risk Management Services to hedge its own risks, and Enron Gas Services became Enron Capital and Trade Resources, headed by Skilling.

In 1992, the success of this business model was exemplified when Enron signed a twenty-year gas contract to supply gas for a large plant being built by an independent power generator, Sithe Energies.[31] Enron's "gas bank" concept allowed it to combine gas supplies from the Gulf of Mexico to Canada. FERC's open-access pipeline policies and Enron's own pipeline ownership let it transport gas over a wide grid to assure the power plant of reliable deliveries. Enron used derivatives to hedge its own price risk.

Financial derivatives. Enron's Gas Bank furthered the development of trading in gas futures. In 1990, NYMEX introduced a standardized gas futures contract on its exchange. A future is a simple form of derivative—a contract to buy or sell a commodity at a specified price on a certain day in the future. Most futures contracts are settled in cash, not by physical delivery of the commodity. A gas futures market serves two distinct types of users: the party who wants to offset risk and secure a fixed price in the forward market; and the party who thrives on and seeks out risk—the speculator hoping to profit on market volatility by accurately forecasting the direction of future prices and betting on these forecasts. The NYMEX market operates like a stock exchange—a liquid market where buyers and sellers can easily trade at transparent prices.[32] With NYMEX, a trader who agrees to supply a large volume of gas at a fixed price but has no offsetting deal to buy gas at a guaranteed lower price, can buy gas futures to hedge against the risk.

---

[30] Fox, *supra* note 15, at 27 (providing a nice example of hedging through use of a swap: Suppose an aluminum producer in Louisiana wants to buy gas at a fixed price. Enron would write a financial contract under which the aluminum company paid Enron a fixed price for the gas. Enron paid the fluctuating price of the gas bought in nearby fields. Enron's business was to make money on the difference between the fixed and fluctuating price). *See also id.* at 36.

[31] *Id.* at 32–33.

[32] In contrast, over-the-counter trading is still customized, face-to-face (or phone-to-phone) bargaining between traders, but these trades can be hedged in the NYMEX futures market.

In 1997, with electricity markets deregulating, Enron acquired Portland Gas and Electric, a large electric utility in Oregon. Enron started to engage in trades based on the spark spread, that is, the spread between gas prices (the input side of electricity production) and the price of electricity (the output). Power plant owners could use a spark spread to hedge the difference in price between the gas used to generate electricity and the electricity it sold. Other gas traders like NGC, Duke, and Aquila followed suit.

Still, as the biggest nationwide marketer of both gas and electricity, Enron had the reputation of being able to do the best deals. A buyer or seller looking for a particular deal would first go to Enron, just as traders today go to eBay. Suppose an electric utility in California wanted to buy electricity at $30 per megawatt-hour. Enron might find someone in the region to sell power to Enron at $29.50, with Enron netting the margin. But Enron had other options as well. If excess gas existed in the Northeast because of abnormally warm weather, Enron could buy cheap gas there and send it to a powerplant in New York, freeing up space in a Canadian pipeline that could then send Canadian gas to the Midwest, releasing midwest gas which could then be routed to California and traded for electricity costing $24 per megawatt-hour. Enron could earn a fatter margin on the more complicated trade.[33]

At the heart of Enron was the trader, intimately familiar with the markets that he or she worked. She would know the weather forecast for all parts of the United States, the timing of the Columbia River fish flush for spawning salmon,[34] the prices of natural gas at key hubs nationwide, pipeline capacities, gas storage inventories, and what power plants were scheduled to go offline for maintenance. By the end of the 1990s, nearly one-quarter of all gas and electric trades went through Enron, a dominance unheard of in the stock market. In 1997, Enron began to sell weather derivatives that allowed heating oil distributors, ski resorts, movie studios, and other businesses whose profitability was tied to the vagaries of Mother Nature to stabilize their revenues. Enron's research department, staffed by brilliant mathematicians, chess grandmasters, and modelers, would analyze gigabytes of weather data to forecast temperature trends that would make these "bets on the weather" profitable to Enron.[35]

Enron Energy Services (EES). This Enron unit, set up in 1997, marketed the sale of customized energy contracts to large industrial users. One of EES's most famous deals was signed with Owens Corning, the huge glass manufacturer, to supply Owens with its complete energy needs for twenty plants across the United States for ten years. Enron guaranteed Owens that it would save the company $60 million in energy costs over the ten-year period. Enron would also get a share of the savings in energy costs.

---

[33] See FOX, *supra* note 15, at 98–108 for more detail on Enron's electricity trading business.

[34] During spawning season, the operators of the large hydroelectric dams in the Northwest reverse the usual pattern of river flows, boosting prices for peak power. Daytime flows are cut to encourage salmon to spawn lower on the river bank; flows are raised at night (offpeak) to keep the eggs submerged.

[35] FOX, *supra* note 15, at 133–34.

Traders who successfully concluded huge deals like this, involving billion-dollar sales of energy, were rewarded large bonuses upfront.[36]

EnronOnline. By mid-2000, all the top executives at Enron came from the trading side rather than the hard asset side that operated the pipelines and power plants owned by Enron. In late 1999, Enron launched itself into cyberspace with EnronOnline. This proprietary Internet website quickly became the largest e-commerce site in the world, trading electricity, gas, coal, oil, refined products, paper, plastics, petrochemicals, clean air credits, and bandwidth on fiber optic cables. It offered over 800 products for sale.[37] Enron, the once-staid pipeline owner and operator, had taken the New Economy by storm, based not on hard assets, but on intellectual capital—the trader's intimate and superior knowledge of markets. Enron promoted the Kyoto Protocol to reduce greenhouse gas emissions that contributed to global warming. The protocol would allow trading of greenhouse gas credits, and Enron would be at the very center of another global market.

EnronOnline did not charge to join or use its exchange. Unlike eBay, which matches buyers and sellers for a fee, Enron was the principal in every trade. If a company sold Enron options to buy gas for $100,000 in the morning, Enron would make money by selling the options in the afternoon for $105,000. Profits came from making deals. Because Enron was the counterparty for every single transaction, buyers and sellers did not have to wait for another counterparty willing to take their deal. Enron was there, instantly, if its traders thought the price was right. It was as if one company ran the New York Stock Exchange and was also a party in every single trade on the exchange. EnronOnline displayed the prices for all the exchange transactions openly, providing valuable price information to all the players in the market.

This trading model required large amounts of cash. Enron might have to hold some commodities for days or weeks to get the price it wanted on its trades. Enron needed billions of dollars in ready cash to handle this "float." It also needed to remain creditworthy, or counterparties would refuse to do business with it.

In mid-August 2000, *Fortune* magazine named Enron as one of the top ten stocks that would last the decade because it had so successfully transformed itself from a stodgy gas utility to the largest online broker of energy—with broadband width to be its next big thing.[38] Skilling's license plate said it all: WMM—"We make markets."

E. Enron's Fall: What Went Wrong

> Relationships don't matter. Trust doesn't matter.
> They'll do it if the price is right.[39]
>
> —Jeff Skilling

---

[36] *Id.* at 114–21.

[37] *Id.* at 165–69; BRYCE, *supra* note 10, at 216–19.

[38] David Rynecki, *Ten Stocks to Last the Decade*, FORTUNE, Aug. 14, 2000, at 114, 117.

[39] BRYCE, *supra* note 10, at 124.

Other essays in this book discuss what went wrong with Enron's general business model. In short, nothing mattered except the deal, and Enron made some disastrous deals on the hard asset and non-energy sides of its business, such as the Dabhol gas-fired power plant in India, the Azurix division's failed foray into privatizing water markets in England and Argentina, and Project Braveheart's foolhardy rush into selling broadband capacity in a glutted market.[40] None of these projects generated any cash flow to repay the debt borrowed to finance them. EnronOnline also was a cash-hungry business. Addicted to quarterly earnings growth to maintain its share price, Enron hid its ill-performing assets, called "nuclear waste" by Enron insiders, in Special Purpose Entities created to keep debt off the books. When these accounting shams came to light, Enron collapsed, virtually overnight. But—were Enron's innovations, its energy trading and services businesses, profitable on their own?

The trading innovations might have been profitable in early years, but most of the ventures certainly were not as profitable as Enron's executives portrayed them to Wall Street. An accurate picture of profitability was virtually impossible to obtain because of Enron's use of mark-to-market accounting, more accurately described as "mark to model" accounting—or in Enron's case, it seems, "mark to maybe" or "mark to myth." Whichever "M to M" label is used, this type of accounting allowed Enron to book future revenues immediately. For example, Enron could estimate the value of the twenty-year contract it sold to Sithe Energies, based on projections of future prices ("maybe" prices) of natural gas run through financial models, and offer an optimistic, if not glowing, view of the contract's value. Jeff Skilling and the Enron Audit Committee adopted mark-to-market accounting in 1991 and then lobbied the Securities and Exchange Commission for its approval. In 1992, Enron became the first non-financial company to get this approval. Many of the contracts projected falling energy prices based on Enron's forecast of the pace of energy deregulation in various states.

Enron Energy Services ("EES") was built on long-term deals to supply energy to large users. It appears to have lost money in 1999, but was able to show a profit the next year.[41] In hindsight, it appears these profits often resulted from the magic of "M to M" accounting. For example, in February 2001, EES signed a deal to supply Quaker Oats with gas, electricity, and trained personnel for fifteen of its plants. It guaranteed Quaker that it would save $4.4 million a year in energy costs and then projected that Enron would make $36.8 million in profits over the ten-year contract, booking $23.4 million of that amount immediately. In many instances, users were enticed to sign the long-term contracts by being offered large amounts of money from Enron. EES paid Eli Lilly $50 million upfront to sign a 15-year contract.[42] The dealmakers at Enron who closed on such contracts were paid huge bonuses before Enron ever made a dime of profit.

---

[40] See generally BRYCE, supra note 10; FOX, supra note 15.

[41] Jeff Skilling created a fake trading room to impress analysts that EES was profitable. He spent $500,000 to outfit the room with slick computers and phones and then trained secretaries to act as busy traders. Jason Leopold, Enron Executives Helped to Create Fake Trading Room, WALL ST. J., Feb. 20, 2002, at A4.

[42] BRYCE, supra note 10, at 209.

In spring 2001, Enron moved EES into its wholesale trading department to hide its losses.[43] Enron had 28,500 customers worldwide who had signed onto deals with EES to manage all their energy needs and absorb the risks of volatile prices.[44] The proof that many of these contracts showed only illusory profits inflated by M-to-M accounting came in bankruptcy court, when Enron walked away from many of those contracts. Many of EES's former clients—the city of Chicago, Harrah's casinos in Las Vegas, and San Diego State University—now forced to find other energy providers, remarked on how happy they had been with the EES deals, which had indeed saved them money.[45] EES, far from being a surging profit center, was losing money on many of the contracts that had been pushed through Enron's management by traders incentivized to close the deal and get their upfront bonuses. Their assumptions of the future pace of energy deregulation and of prices were, not surprisingly, overly optimistic.

EnronOnline probably reduced the profits Enron made in trading.[46] By displaying prices openly, margins narrowed, making Enron more dependent on volume. At the start, EnronOnline could offset reduced margins with greater volumes. By one estimate, the average profit margin on a trade of a unit of natural gas went from five cents in the early days to one cent by 2000.[47] Other exchanges sprang up and competed with Enron.[48] Moreover, without fees or commissions to produce a steady source of cash, and with Enron as a counterparty to every trade, EnronOnline's business model put enormous pressure on staying creditworthy and liquid. By mid-2000, Enron was doing billions of dollars of trades in 800 products daily. Each hour or day that Enron held a commodity before reselling it required that Enron pay interest on money borrowed to support its position in the market.[49]

Enron Capital and Trade ("ECT"), later called Enron Wholesale Services, handled Enron's risk management services. Its energy derivatives business was clearly profitable from the start,[50] and Frank Partnoy concludes that this one aspect of Enron's business

---

[43] Tom Fowler, *Division's Motives For Hiding Losses May Be Unlawful*, HOUS. CHRON., Jan. 26, 2002, at A1.

[44] Alex Berenson, *Ex-Workers Say Enron Unit Had Only 'Illusory' Profit*, N.Y. TIMES, Jan. 25, 2002, at A1.

[45] Tom Fowler, *Enron Star Unit Loses Large Clients*, HOUS. CHRON., Dec. 6, 2001, at 1C; Melissa Clary, *San Diego State U. Drops Enron For New Provider*, THE DAILY AZTEC, Oct. 22, 2002 (Energy Central Professional Online).

[46] FUSARO & MILLER, *supra* note 26, at 75.

[47] FOX, *supra* note 15, at 131.

[48] BP, Royal Dutch Shell, Goldman Sachs, and others formed ICE, the Intercontinental Exchange, later joined by Duke, AEP, Aquila, Reliant, and Mirant. Others created TradeSpark, an online exchange. *Id.* at 234–35.

[49] BRYCE, *supra* note 10, at 220–21. In the first six months of 2000, Enron borrowed over $3.4 billion to finance its overall operations at a time when the company's cash flow was a negative $547 million. By June 2000, interest charges on debt amounted to over two million dollars per day.

[50] FOX, *supra* note 15, at 100.

model continued to bring in large amounts of cash even after Enron declared bankruptcy.[51] Although competitors entered the business, Enron had a clear advantage over them by having the most trading activity, so that a buyer or seller looking for a certain deal would most likely find it at Enron. But, as Enron's debt soared and its cash flow winnowed, Enron became a less creditworthy counterparty. Enron engaged in more than risk management services and trades. Its wholesale services division also placed unhedged bets that gas or electricity prices would head in a certain direction. Such bets are very risky.[52] Speculative trading on big bets was made by Enron's entire trading staff rather than by individual traders. The company had risk controls in place to limit the amount any trader could put at risk. When Wall Street and Enron's board became increasingly nervous about Enron's huge trading businesses causing massive losses, Enron tightened its internal risk controls in the late 1990s.[53] Nonetheless, the trading culture remained pervasive at Enron.

From its early days as king of the Gas Bank, Enron had inserted a clause in its derivatives contracts with gas producers assuring that if its counterparty suffered a "material adverse change," then Enron could demand that its counterparty put up collateral to protect Enron against a default by the contracting party.[54] The clause worked both ways, although no one expected it to ever work against Enron, the stronger party. But, once Enron's accounting shams began to surface and its real debt burden was exposed, its counterparties pulled the trigger under these clauses and demanded that Enron post more cash as collateral to support its contracts. Enron had no cash, and could not borrow it.[55] The $77-billion dollar company collapsed quickly in December 2001.[56]

At the time of Enron's collapse, a *Wall Street Journal* editorial writer marveled at the success of competitive energy markets in absorbing the giant's fall. No price spikes or supply interruptions had resulted because these markets were sufficiently deep and liquid. The fall of Enron was in itself a success story and a tribute to competition.[57]

---

[51] FRANK PARTNOY, INFECTIOUS GREED: HOW DECEIT AND RISK CORRUPTED THE FINANCIAL MARKETS 328–30 (2003).

[52] In 1994, a large German conglomerate, Metallgesellschaft (MG) lost nearly $1 billion on the oil futures market because it bet that oil prices would decline in the future. FOX, *supra* note 15, at 96.

[53] *Id.* at 94–97.

[54] BRYCE, *supra* note 10, at 219.

[55] *Id.* at 332–33. In its November 2001 filing, shortly before declaring bankruptcy, Enron had $18.7 billion in liabilities from derivatives and commodities futures contracts on its books, most of which needed to be collateralized.

[56] The bankrupt Enron sold its North American trading business to UBS Warburg in exchange for the promise of a share of future profits from the business, but Enron kept the billions of dollars of derivatives its traders had already bought. While some commentators took this transaction to mean that Enron's trading position had become unprofitable, Partnoy concludes that Enron made more than $1 billion in 2001 trading natural-gas derivatives alone and that the derivative trades provided billions of dollars of cash to the company while it was in bankruptcy. PARTNOY, *supra* note 51, at 329–30.

[57] Susan Lee, *Enron's Success Story*, WALL ST. J., Dec. 26, 2001, at A11.

III. ENRON AND THE CALIFORNIA ENERGY CRISIS

An imperfect market is better than a perfect regulator.

—Ken Lay[58]

A dysfunctional market can impose infinitely more harm on consumers than regulators on their worst day.

—Consumer Federation of America[59]

To most of the general public, Enron, energy markets, and the California energy crisis are inextricably linked. The days of rolling blackouts, spectacular price spikes for gas and electricity, Enron's gaming techniques of Death Star and Fat Boy, and the company's ultimate demise are all somehow lumped together in the public consciousness that there is grave danger in deregulated energy markets. Yet the causes of California's crisis are far more complex, and the failures in energy markets uncovered by subsequent investigations are far more serious, than any acts of Enron alone can possibly explain. California and Enron exposed fundamental problems of mitigating monopoly power, in devising restructuring plans that cannot be gamed, as well as inadequate monitoring by regulatory commissions at either the state or federal level, which can leave consumers in a far worse position than traditional cost-of-service regulation.

It will take many more months, if not years, to sift through gigabytes of evidence to establish more definitively the roles that independent power generators, energy traders, pipeline capacity owners, ISOs, FERC, state politicians, price caps, drought, and environmental laws played in the California energy markets. It is a daunting task— reading through reports of academics, the California Public Utility Commission, the California Independent System Operator ("CAISO"), California state auditors, FERC, the General Accounting Office, consultants, practicing lawyers, think tanks, the trade press, and testimony in House and Senate Committee hearings—to try to ascertain if the facts, opinions, and analyses from all these varied sources are solidly based or so slanted by the bias of the authoring parties as to be of little use. The economic and political issues are so permeated with ideology that is often difficult to separate the message from the messenger and fact from fiction.

Two simple examples suffice. First, the public was often told that the California crisis was caused by a huge demand for electricity from the tremendous growth in Internet use. In May 1999, at the height of the dot-com boom, a "policy wonk" declared that computers and the Internet now consumed 13 percent of total U.S. electricity demand, from virtually nothing ten years before—and this percentage was growing fast. The estimate was quickly used by the Greening Earth Society, a mis-

---

[58] FOX, *supra* note 15, at 200.

[59] MARK COOPER, CONSUMER FEDERATION OF AMERICA, ELECTRICITY DEREGULATION AND CONSUMERS 9 (2001).

named offshoot of a coal suppliers' trade association to spread the mantra: "Dig more coal—the PCs are coming." J.P. Morgan investment analysts then used the projections without attribution or qualification, and the assertion became an accepted fact. California's blackouts were not caused by Enron and merchant plants, but by the Internet's appetite for juice.[60]

Second, the public was also told that California's "greenies," environmentalists and local community activists, had caused the crisis because the state had created "monumental obstacles" to siting and granting permits to new power plants."[61] However, since 1974, California has had a one-stop omnibus permitting procedure that is superior to most states' procedures in minimizing the time for siting review while also protecting the public's right to participate in site evaluation. A thorough review of permitting since 1990 showed that plant developers did not seek siting permits until California had adopted its electricity restructuring program in 1997 and the "rules of the game" were known to investors. After that date, all of the 23 applications for new plants were approved by the California Energy Commission ("CEC") with an average approval time of 14 months.[62] CEC approval meant that all environmental standards of the state's Environmental Quality Act and all state and local agency approvals were met in one fell swoop. Moreover, when the energy crisis hit, California issued 21-day and six-month emergency approval processes for peaking power plants as an extraordinary response to the extraordinary situation it faced. Myth has often prevailed in the debate over energy markets.

Having read through a mountain of material in the past few months, I have emerged with some conclusions that might stand the test of time, regardless of what additional investigations may find. At the very least, the conclusions will provide a framework for the reader to proceed through this rather lengthy essay and make his or her own assessment. I would be delighted to look back on this essay during the coming years and find that these conclusions were unduly pessimistic.

1. In electricity, markets have met their match. Because electricity cannot be stored, because incumbents still hold substantial monopoly power, and because power markets operating in real time are so complex, regulators cannot assure that markets will operate competitively. Electricity is an essential good for most residential users and for many commercial and industrial users also. This means the demand for electricity is relatively inelastic, that is, consumers will continue to buy it even when its price rises. Under these conditions, it is extraordinarily difficult to discern when price rises and

---

[60] David Wessel, *Bold Estimate of Web's Thirst For Electricity Seems All Wet*, WALL ST. J., Dec. 5, 2002 (online).

[61] Susan Tierney & Paul J. Hibbard, *Siting Power Plants in the New Electric Industry Structure: Lessons from California and Best Practices for Other States*, 15 THE ELECTRICITY J. 35, 49 n.4 (June 2002).

[62] *Id.* at 37.

price spikes signal true scarcity and when they signal the abuse of market power or a design flaw in the restructured system. The power markets may be "made to work" but only by imposing on them a degree of market intervention that defies the label of "deregulation" and which may well be greater than the regulatory burden of cost-of-service ratemaking.

2. Businesses will seek to exploit loopholes and some people in business will always cheat. Even a few "legal loopholes" or outright acts of cheating can ruin a market, especially an emergent market created in a newly deregulated sector. These anti-competitive loopholes are difficult for regulators to detect. As Federal Reserve Chairman Alan Greenspan recently remarked with some chagrin: "It is not that humans have become any more greedy than in generations past. It is that the avenues to express greed [have] grown so enormously."[63]

3. Politicians, economists, and many industry lobbyists have promised that residential consumers will benefit from electricity deregulation, largely through lower prices. This promise is not easy to keep.

4. No matter what the cause, consumers will not consider large price increases in gas or electricity to be fair, especially when they have been promised price decreases. The business risk of operating in this political climate is significantly higher than that in regulated markets. In a capital-intensive industry like power generation and transmission, higher business risk increases borrowing costs and makes the promise of lower prices even more difficult to achieve.

5. The business lobby can run powerful political campaigns that successfully leave large loopholes in regulatory regimes which businesses then exploit legally. The business lobby can also run powerful public opinion campaigns championing free markets and consumer choice. When the two campaigns produce contradictory results in delivering actual consumer benefits, trust in business dissipates. The only institutions capable of restoring trust in "deregulated" markets in the United States at this time are governmental agencies that are themselves trustworthy because they have the staffing, expertise, and budgetary resources to restructure and police the markets effectively. The ultimate irony of "energy deregulation" is that it requires strong regulation and oversight to succeed.

With this preview in mind, the next section of this essay will address the four major areas where investigations have uncovered the most serious problems that have led to a crisis of confidence in deregulated energy markets:

---

[63] *When Greed Was a Virtue and Regulation the Enemy*, N.Y. TIMES, July 21, 2002 (online). The quotation is from Greenspan's testimony before the House Banking Committee on July 16, 2002. Greenspan acknowledged that he had been wrong in his long-held belief that the government should not regulate the accounting industry.

1. Gaming a flawed regulatory system.
2. Withholding generating capacity.
3. Affiliate abuse of pipeline capacity.
4. Manipulation of gas and power price indices.

But first, California's framework for competitive retail power markets must be described. In doing so, the uniqueness of electricity as a commoditized product will make apparent why electricity markets are so difficult to restructure through markets.

A. California's Electricity Deregulation Plan

> Enron bled California dry and used us as a cash cow to keep the price of its stock high so that insiders could sell out.
>
> —Senator Barbara Boxer of California, April 2002[64]

> Deregulation always benefits people. If it doesn't, you have to rework it until it does.
>
> —Pat Wood III, FERC Chairman, June 2001[65]

If any one state embraced competitive markets in electricity, it was California—the state that symbolized the New Economy and represented one-eighth of U.S. domestic production. In 1999 (before the chaos began), Professor Suedeen Kelly, a former state utility commissioner, thanked California for its "bold experiments that so richly benefit the rest of us."[66] In an article whose theme is that the new electric powerhouses will be an awesome change for society, but hopefully not a cataclysmic one, she noted that only California, of all the states, had leaped into restructuring rather than adopting a cautious, go-slow approach so often criticized by many economists. She attributed this leap, in her usual charming manner, to Californians' daily familiarity with living on earthquake faults, which probably numbed them to the fear of cataclysmic change.[67]

California's energy crisis began in May 2000 and ended in June 2001, although in a very real sense it will not end for many years. At the height of the crisis, California signed long-term power contracts with many independent power producers ("IPPs") and energy suppliers that will leave its citizens paying energy prices far above any other

---

[64] *U.S. Senate Probes Enron Calif. Price Manipulation,* REUTERS, Apr. 11, 2002 (online).

[65] Timothy P. Duane, *Regulation's Rationale: Learning from the California Energy Crisis,* 19 YALE J. ON REG. 471, 493 (2002).

[66] Suedeen G. Kelly, *The New Electric Powerhouses: Will They Transform Your Life?,* 29 ENVTL. L. 285, 295 (1999). In Connecticut Light & Power Co. v. FPC, 324 U.S. 515, 530, Justice Jackson wrote of state utility commissions that it is "wise to keep the hand of state regulatory bodies in this business, . . . [as] laboratories where many lessons in regulation may be learned by trial and error on a small scale without involving a whole national industry in every experiment."

[67] Kelly, *supra* note 66, at 291.

state and far above the level it began with before it embraced deregulation with such verve and fervor.

But, to start at the beginning. By the mid-1990s, wholesale electricity trading nationally had advanced rapidly. More than 400 power marketers had licenses from FERC to buy and sell electricity in wholesale markets.[68] Wholesale sales of electricity between large buyers and sellers, often using power marketers as middlemen, were well-established. A number of states were slowly opening their retail electricity markets, regulated by their state PUCs, to competition also. (Recall that the state PUCs, not FERC, have power over retail energy sales to the ultimate end user, such as residential, industrial, or commercial electricity users). California took the Big Bang approach to deregulation.

The basics of California's deregulation plan were as follows: California's three major investor-owned utilities with large monopoly franchises[69] were required to sell off their generating plants and buy electricity from a central pool called the Power Exchange. The utilities were discouraged from signing long-term bilateral contracts to replace their divested generation capacity.[70] After all, such bilateral contracts could simply reimpose the old vertically integrated, franchised structure and allow the three utilities to buy from their previously owned plants, squeezing out new entry by competitive merchant power plants, the IPPs (independent power producers).[71] The three utilities continued to own their transmission and distribution networks, still regulated under cost-of-service ratemaking by either FERC (for interstate transmission) or the Califor-

---

[68] FOX, *supra* note 15, at 196.

[69] Pacific Gas & Electric operated in northern California; San Diego Gas & Electric and Southern California Edison operated in the south.

[70] Contrary to many accounts, the California PUC did not prohibit, but merely discouraged, long-term contracts by not guaranteeing full cost recovery of these forward contracts should they be priced above spot market prices. The three large regulated utilities were thus buying electricity at wholesale in the spot market while the rates at which they could sell electricity to the bulk of their retail customers were frozen under the California plan, a rather risky business model even considering that everyone thought wholesale rates would fall with deregulation. It is not clear why the three utilities failed to hedge this spot market risk. Frank Wolak posits that the utilities believed that FERC would intervene and declare wholesale prices to be unjust and unreasonable if these prices rose to such a level that the utilities faced negative returns. Wholesale prices would have to double to put the utilities in this untenable situation, and a doubling from $35 to $70 per megawatt-hour was unfathomable. It could only occur by the exercise of substantial unilateral market power—which FERC would surely act to correct. No one foresaw the rise in natural gas prices that ultimately played a key role in the crisis. *See* FRANK WOLAK, LESSONS FROM THE CALIFORNIA ELECTRICITY CRISIS 7–8 (Apr. 2003), Univ. of California Energy Institute, Center for the Study of Energy Markets, CSEM WP-110, *available at* www.ucei.org.

[71] The lack of long-term bilateral contracting in California's market design has been heavily criticized, after the fact. But regulatory theorists (mainly economists) and potential market entrants persuaded regulators and legislators that competition would be jump-started by forcing most power sales through a central market. JOHN W. ROWE ET AL., COMPETITION WITHOUT CHAOS 3 (AEI-Brookings Joint Center for Regulatory Studies, Working Paper 01-07, June 2001). Great Britain, the leader in electricity deregulation, had such a system (which it subsequently revised because the system allowed too much monopoly power to be exercised by large generators).

nia PUC (for local distribution). Thus, the utilities would now have to buy electricity from the Power Exchange at market prices that fluctuated by the day, hour, and even by ten-minute segments, depending on demand. The California Independent System Operator, or ISO, played the role of air traffic controller, monitoring the physical flow of electricity along the transmission network from generators to users and assuring reliability.

The ISO has a crucially important role to play in electricity markets because of the physics of electrons and wires. Unlike oil and gas, electricity cannot be stored. Disaster in the form of blackouts can occur unless electricity suppliers generate exactly the amount of power that users demand at every single minute. Matching supply to demand—to the flip of any consumer's light switch—is the tricky business called "load balancing." The ISO is the entity that monitors the physical flows of electricity and balances the loads throughout the entire network grid. If any imbalance occurs anywhere on the grid, then the entire grid is in peril. It is as if, when one plane in the air develops trouble with a wing flap and starts nosediving, all other planes in the air simultaneously drop out of the sky. When a transmission line overheats or an ice storm brings down wires, when a power plant unexpectedly fails or demand surges in a heat wave, the ISO must have two capabilities: First, it must be able to reroute electricity flows instantaneously to keep the grid in balance. Second, the ISO must be able to provide what are called "ancillary services."

Ancillary services sound like a minor item, and in this regard they are quite misnamed. Ancillary services are really "essential services" that assure reliability of power flow-through techniques such as keeping a margin of spinning reserves. Spinning reserves are excess capacity in the form of spinning turbines whose electricity can be connected to the grid in minutes, if need be. ISOs also provide ancillary services such as voltage control and measurement. In short, the ISO is the traffic controller that coordinates the complex flow of electrons through the wires, preventing the wires from overheating due to congestion, and rerouting supplies and balancing load demand every minute of the day in real time. When utilities were vertically integrated monopolies, they could coordinate much of the supply/demand balancing within their own geographic territory, with some cooperation from neighboring utilities. When electricity markets are opened to competition, this coordination among generators and transmission companies must still be maintained for grid reliability, but the entities involved are now often rivals, and regulators must develop new protocols and rules to assure the smooth operation of a system now composed of many separate and competing parts.

The California plan was adopted after a lengthy stakeholder process that built a consensus for change among all participants; the legislation was passed unanimously by both houses.[72] In any restructuring plan, cost reallocation looms large as an enormously divisive issue between consumers and utilities (and their shareholders) because

---

[72] Kelly, *supra* note 66, at 296.

of stranded costs and cross-subsidized rates. Stranded costs are the costs of the existing power plants which the incumbent utilities will not be able to recover in rates after deregulation begins. If plants were built on the expectation that electricity would be sold for six cents per kilowatt-hour through cost-of-service rates, then when new lower-cost competitors invade what was once the utility's franchise territory and start selling electricity for four cents, the utility's high-cost plants will become uneconomic, "stranding" this investment.

At the same time, retail competition will usually disadvantage the small residential and commercial consumer because these customers will lose the rate subsidy built into traditional rate-making. State commissioners often designed retail rates so that large industrial users paid a little more and small consumers a little less than blind market forces would dictate. This cross-subsidy between large and small users cannot continue to exist under competition, meaning that rates for small consumers will rise relative to rates paid by large users. Championing a residential rate increase is political suicide for state commissioners and legislators. Both the rhetoric and reality of lower rates are a political necessity for passage of deregulation laws.[73] Given these two political imperatives—stranded cost compensation to utilities and lower rates to consumers—it is a virtual miracle that any states have managed to satisfy all constituents sufficiently to ensure passage of retail restructuring laws. The essential premise of restructuring is that competition will lower costs sufficiently to both fund stranded cost reimbursement and benefit consumers.

The restructuring states have adopted imperfect, but "common sense" methods of resolving these billion-dollar issues. Virtually all states have gerry-rigged systems that freeze or lower or place a maximum "cap" on rates to residential consumers for a period of years, while also devising methods that allow utilities to recover their stranded costs from consumers. Professor Kelly praised California for its political and economic balancing of these two issues. Utilities were assured a mechanism to recover their stranded costs, and rates for residential and small consumers were lowered by ten percent.[74]

A few cautionary voices from the academic world of economists raised concerns that markets in electricity were not easy to design properly and were too easy to manipulate. In February 2000, Severin Borenstein and James Bushnell at the University of California Energy Institute at Berkeley warned that too few lessons were being

[73] *Id.* at 299–300. Professor Kelly chides economists who tout the virtues of efficient markets without recognizing the political constraints imposed by the real world. Economists suffer the "fallacy of misplaced concreteness" that relies on abstract models which simply cannot be applied in the real world and which threaten the process of devising creative solutions to the uncommon problems posed by electricity restructuring. *Id.*

[74] While rates were decreased 10 percent, consumers were charged fees that paid for the bonds used to securitize the utilities' stranded costs and assure their recovery. Thus, the 10 percent rate decrease was offset by an 8 percent fee surcharge. Duane, *supra* note 65, at 501. Students at state universities are quite familiar with the phenomenon of fixed tuition rates and escalating fees.

learned from the experiences of countries or states that had already embarked on this path. They wrote:

> Probably the two most salient lessons are that the short-run benefits are likely to be small or non-existent, and the long-run benefits, while compellingly supported in theory, may be very difficult to document in practice.
>
> More concretely, market power among generators is likely to be a more serious and ongoing concern than has been anticipated by most observers. . . . In general, the non-storability of electricity, combined with very little demand elasticity and the need for real-time supply/demand balancing to keep the grid stable, has made restructuring of electricity markets a much greater challenge than was inferred from experience with natural gas, airlines, trucking, telecommunications, and a host of other industries.[75]

The authors then noted that almost every electricity market currently operating in the world uses some form of price or revenue cap to counteract these problems.[76] They also observed that, independent of restructuring, electricity prices were expected to fall in the 1990s as sunk investments in high-cost (largely nuclear) generating facilities were paid off or as long-term, high-priced contracts expired. The real question was whether restructuring would result in prices lower than what traditional regulation would have achieved.[77] While the authors acknowledged that introducing more competition into energy markets had enormous potential benefits, it also had serious risks due to the physics of electricity and the continued existence of monopoly power in the industry.

Just three months after the California ISO and Power Exchange began, a dramatic price spike for replacement reserve electrical capacity occurred in July 1998.[78] FERC had just issued an order deregulating the market price for replacement reserves, a form of stand-by power. Prices surged from the regulated range of $10 per megawatt to

---

[75] SEVERIN BORENSTEIN & JAMES BUSHNELL, ELECTRICITY RESTRUCTURING: DEREGULATION OR REREGULATION? 2 (Program on Workable Energy Regulation (POWER) at the University of California Energy Institute, Working Paper No. PWP-074, Feb. 2000), *available at* www.ucei.berkeley.edu.

[76] *Id.* at 11–12.

[77] *Id.* at 15–16. Econometric studies showed that prices exceeded competitive levels by 20 to 25 percent in Great Britain's deregulated power pool, and electricity prices in California were about 14 percent above competitive levels in 1998 and 1999. It appeared that restructuring was not achieving as low prices as had been hoped for. In 2001, Great Britain changed its regulatory system to decrease the market power of large generators during peak demand periods. *See generally* TIMOTHY J. BRENNAN, KAREN L. PALMER & SALVADOR A. MARTINEZ, ALTERNATING CURRENTS: ELECTRICITY MARKETS AND PUBLIC POLICY 36–37 (2002).

[78] Nicholas W. Fels & Frank R. Lindh, 22 ENERGY L.J. 1, 10–11 (2002). Just a month before, in June 1998, a huge price spike in electricity hit the Midwest. Wholesale power prices rose as high as $6,000 per megawatt-hour, 200 times the normal price. For the fallout from this event, *see* FOX, *supra* note 15, at 197–98.

$9,999 per megawatt. (The generators apparently assumed that the ISO's software program would not accept bids exceeding four digits.)[79] The California regulators filed an emergency motion with FERC for a stay of the generators' market-based rates. At this point, FERC had jurisdiction over the Power Exchange ("PX"), which traded electricity at wholesale. California's radical embrace of real-time markets operating through the power exchange system had divested the state of any control over these markets. FERC rejected the request for a stay of the market-based rates, although it allowed the California ISO to reject bids in excess of price levels it considered improper for ancillary services.[80]

No major problems emerged until the May 22, 2002 price tsunami hit. But the scene was certainly set. In the California ISO system, over half of the 288 generating units were designated as "must run" units for reliability purposes. "Must run" plants are so important to grid reliability that regulators will not allow market forces to determine whether the plant should run or not. As Borenstein and Bushnell put it: "What electrical engineers call reliability concerns, economists call local market power."[81] In a market system, high prices will send a signal to investors that it is profitable to build new power plants in certain areas. However, new plants take years to build. Importing electricity to shortage areas can occur quickly unless transmission lines are congested. When "load pockets" of demand arise, and imports cannot reach them, then the local generators in that pocket have very real market power. Building new transmission lines to assure competition from imported electricity is a long-term proposition and creates huge winners and losers among generators. A company that owns all the generation capacity in one area, say San Francisco, will not want additional transmission lines built to serve the area. The distributional effects of building transmission lines can easily exceed the efficiency effects, confronting policy makers in the real world with yet another political dynamic that makes restructuring painfully difficult, as FERC has painfully discovered in the past decade.

In short, electricity is not a simple commodity like wheat, pork bellies, or gas. Electricity markets are tricky to design because of physics, economics, and politics.

B. Gaming a Flawed Deregulatory Plan

> Like a casino, Enron has a house advantage in the energy markets.
>
> —Enron trading officials to Enron executives and directors[82]

---

[79] BORENSTEIN & BUSHNELL, *supra* note 75, at 11–12. The assumption was wrong. A bid in the millions of dollars would have been accepted.

[80] The ISO then capped prices at $250 per megawatt for all ancillary services, such as standby power. *Id.* at 12.

[81] *Id.* at 13.

[82] David Barboza, *Despite Denial, Enron Papers Show Big Profit on Price Bets*, N.Y. TIMES, Dec. 12, 2002, at A1. The trading officials gave the casino analogy to Enron's directors and executives when they sought to justify engaging in risky, speculative energy trades.

Do you want to do an ex-post type of game or you want to do a congestion
type of game plus ex post?
I don't want to crush the market too bad.

—Exchange between Xcel and Mirant traders, July 18, 2000.[83]

It never occurred to us in our innocence that something so vital to society
would be treated like a casino. We thought the hand of Adam Smith would
be benign.

—David Freeman, chair of Los Angeles Department of
Water and Power, after release of
Enron memos, May 2002.[84]

From May 22, 2000 until June 2001, the California electricity market was characterized by emergency alerts, rolling blackouts, and huge price spikes. Profits soared for
the generators that had bought power plants from the divesting California utilities
under the restructuring plan. Six companies, which now owned 40 percent of the
power generated in California, reported the following increases in net income for July,
August and September of 2000:

Dynegy—up 83%
Reliant—up 37% overall; its wholesale energy division up 642%
Duke—up 74%
AES—up 131%
NRG—up 221%
Southern Energy—up 59%

In addition, Calpine, a merchant power plant company that had built its own plants
in California, saw its net income rise 243 percent.[85] Enron reported fourth quarter profits up 34 percent in 2000, but Jeffrey Skilling, then Enron's president, told investment
analysts that California had little impact on these results because Enron owned no generating units in California.[86] Yet about one-quarter of all electricity trading in California's
wholesale market is estimated to have gone through Enron's traders, with their "house

[83] Scott Thurm & Robert Gavin, *Xcel, Mirant Traders Discussed 'Games' to Use in Energy Market*, WALL ST. J., June 10, 2002, at A4.

[84] Chris Taylor, *California Scheming*, TIME, May 20, 2002, at 42.

[85] *Profits Soaring for Power Suppliers*, HOUS. CHRON., Dec 17, 2000, at 17A.

[86] David Barboza, *Former Enron Officials Say Enron Hid Gains During Crisis in California*, N.Y. TIMES, June 23, 2002, at A1. If these profits had not been hidden in reserves, Enron would have doubled its reported profits. The practice of using "cookie jar" or "prudency" reserves as a sort of slush fund to doctor quarterly earnings, especially to assure smoothly rising earnings reports, may violate securities laws, but accounting experts say that the subjectivity of prudency reserves under accounting standards makes them easy to manipulate "legally."

advantage." Clearly, Enron had the opportunity to profit by buying and selling electricity during the crisis. According to several former Enron executives, Enron hid as much as $1.5 billion in trading profits off its books during the crisis to quell the political firestorm that was developing.[87] One Enron manager familiar with the California trading records disclosed: "There were days when we were making $100 million. When you're making that kind of money you have to ask yourself, 'Are we the market?'"[88]

Some of Enron's trades involved huge amounts of money. When a natural gas pipeline owned by El Paso exploded near Carlsbad, New Mexico, killing a family of twelve, Enron traders made almost $500 million in that one day on the ensuing price spike.[89] Large, speculative trades involve large risks. In another instance, one trader made a $485 million gain on December 4, 2000—followed by a $550 million loss on December 12 when gas prices unexpectedly plummeted.[90] All the while, Enron's top executives publicly asserted that they did not engage in speculative trading, but made money simply by being the middleman between buyers and sellers.[91]

While the California market was roiling, the in-state generators and Enron launched one of the most successful public relations campaigns ever promoted by industry, a campaign to convince the American public and legislators that California's agony was due to a largely self-inflicted supply and demand imbalance coupled with a bit of bad luck from Mother Nature. California had not built new generating plants, electricity demand had soared, and a drought in the northwest hydropower region hit at a particularly bad time. Also, if California would just free retail prices from the rate freeze, consumers could respond to the higher price signals and conserve, thus bringing prices back down. California politicians were foolish not to see the virtues of a free market in energy at the retail level.

At the same time, Enron and others used their lobbying clout with Vice President Dick Cheney and members of FERC to argue against imposing wholesale price caps in the California market.[92] Prices should be allowed to signal scarcity in a free market.

---

[87] *Id.* at A21.

[88] *Id.*

[89] *Id.* This is the same pipeline explosion that El Paso Corporation claimed as a defense to the allegations that it withheld supplies of natural gas from California during the crisis, thus causing gas and power prices to soar. *See* text *infra* accompanying notes 138–52.

[90] David Barboza, *Despite Denial, Enron Papers Show Big Profit on Price Bets,* N.Y. TIMES, Dec. 12, 2002, at A1.

[91] *Id.*

[92] On April 17, 2001, Ken Lay met with Vice President Dick Cheney to discuss the California crisis and reportedly gave Cheney an eight-point memo that advised the administration to reject price caps, even temporary price caps. The day after the meeting, Cheney said price caps would not solve California's problems. Patty Reinert, *FERC to Focus on Enron's Role in Calif. Energy Crisis,* HOUS. CHRON., Feb. 1, 2002, at 1A. See STAFF OF SENATE COMM. ON GOVERNMENTAL AFFAIRS, 108TH CONG., COMMITTEE STAFF INVESTIGATION OF FERC'S OVERSIGHT OF ENRON CORP. 41-46 (Nov. 12, 2002) for an account of Enron's lobbying.

Only then would new entrants respond by building new plants or transmission lines to ease the supply shortage. The crisis was created by California and could be solved by it.

Meanwhile, Governor Gray Davis and other California officials waged a vociferous and often strident public campaign branding merchant plants and energy traders as avaricious evil-doers and manipulators who were threatening the public health, safety, and jobs of all Californians. Because the energy market in California is not self-enclosed, price spikes spread to other western states on the interconnected grid. Eleven western governors urged President Bush to take action to end the market chaos.

For many months, FERC, the only entity with jurisdiction over wholesale rates for power traded on the Power Exchange, refused to act.[93] Academics and private consultants found mounting evidence of the exercise of market power that could not be explained by normal supply/demand factors.[94] Finally, in June 2001, a new chairman of FERC, Pat Wood III, took decisive action to impose wholesale price caps on the entire eleven-state western region that operated under an interconnected grid, and the crisis ended.

Even those who sympathized with California's position that FERC must intercede to stabilize the market acknowledged that California's market design was itself fatally flawed. The design encouraged generators to withhold bidding of supplies into the day-ahead market. (The day-ahead market allows the ISO to project expected demand and supply so that the ISO can bring sufficient generating capacity and reserves online from plants that might take several hours to start up). Because of underbid supplies, when the next day arrived, the ISO would find itself short of supply and would then ask for bids to supply power into the hour-ahead or minutes-ahead, real-time markets. Knowing that the ISO was now fairly desperate, generators could bid high prices into these real-time markets with little fear that they would lose the sale to a competitor, particularly in areas where local market power existed in load pockets. As the California State Auditor explained in the apt title of its March 2001 report on California's restructuring plan: "The Benefits of Competition Were Undermined by Structural Flaws in the Market, Unsuccessful Oversight, and Uncontrollable Competitive Forces."[95] Like other reports completed in 2001, the auditors did not see evidence of illegal market manipulation or collusion by generators. Energy marketers like Enron were not even discussed in the report. California had, unfortunately, created a system that allowed generators to bid strategically in ways that enriched the companies at the state's expense at a time when the state suffered from tight supply and high demand.

---

[93] FERC's role in the California energy crisis and the Enron-related fallout are discussed in Jacqueline Lang Weaver, *Can Energy Markets Be Trusted?*, 4 HOUS. BUS. & TAX L. J. (forthcoming 2004) (Part IV).

[94] See text *infra* accompanying notes 124–37.

[95] BUREAU OF STATE AUDITS, CALIFORNIA STATE AUDITOR, ENERGY DEREGULATION: THE BENEFITS OF COMPETITION WERE UNDERMINED BY STRUCTURAL FLAWS IN THE MARKET, UNSUCCESSFUL OVERSIGHT, AND UNCONTROLLABLE COMPETITIVE FORCES 88 (2001) *available at* www.bsa.ca.gov/bsa/ (summarizing the causes of the California crisis identified as of March 2001).

Not until after Enron's bankruptcy in December 2001 and subsequent investigations of its activities did evidence come to light showing all the schemes that Enron traders had invented to game the California system. Indeed, as late as April 2002, Enron's spokesman continued to assert that Enron had not manipulated prices and that California's problems were a result of its flawed deregulation system.[96] Then, on May 6, 2002, almost two years after the California market started running amok, memos written by Enron's Oregon lawyers during the California crisis were given to FERC by Enron's bankruptcy attorneys and put on FERC's website.[97] The impact was nothing short of stunning: California's rant against traders had real substance.

The outside lawyers' memos, written to help Enron prepare for the investigations and litigation that it expected to face soon,[98] were the first "smoking guns" to provide an inside look at the trading strategies used by Enron. The December 2000 memo, addressed to Richard Sanders, an assistant general counsel at Enron, outlined ten colorfully named strategies used by Enron traders, such as Death Star (a phantom power transfer), Get Shorty (sell high, buy low), Fat Boy (an artificial increase in demand), Ricochet (megawatt laundering), and Load Shift (trading loads). Many strategies involved structuring trades so that Enron could be paid congestion charges as high as $750 per megawatt, a price at which it was often profitable to sell power at a loss simply to collect the congestion fees.

The lawyers then summarized their understanding of whether the strategies helped to stabilize the grid or destabilize it and whether they were legal or not. For example, under one scheme, Enron would buy power at the maximum capped price of $250 per megawatt-hour in California,[99] and then ship it outside California and sell it back to the state for $1,200 per megawatt-hour. The lawyers concluded that "[t]his strategy appears not to present any problems, other than a public relations risk arising from the fact that such exports may have contributed to California's declaration of a Stage 2

---

[96] Richard Stevenson, *Enron Trading Gave Prices Artificial Lift, Panel Is Told*, N.Y. TIMES, Apr. 12, 2002, at C1. Enron's denials came in response to a U.S. Senate Commerce Subcommittee hearing at which Loretta Lynch, chair of the California Public Utility Commission, testified that Enron had engaged in sham trades of large volumes of electricity contracts with its own subsidiaries in order to drive up electricity prices. California State Senator Dunn also testified that a review of Enron's trading documents showed that Enron traders bet on higher prices for summer 2000, giving them a motive to drive up the price. Some Republicans remained skeptical, suggesting that Enron was being used as a whipping boy by California for its own botched market design.

[97] Enron's bankruptcy lawyers gave the memos to FERC, and Enron waived any attorney-client privilege regarding the memos. The December 8, 2000 memo describes how Enron's traders adjusted their models to deal with the generators' strategy of underscheduling into the day-ahead market to raise prices on the real-time hourly and ten-minute markets.

[98] The law firm memos were written in December 2000 after the California PUC obtained subpoenas for Enron documents and the state Attorney General threatened to prosecute Enron officials.

[99] FERC did eventually institute wholesale price caps on electricity in California, but not in the surrounding states, thus creating an obvious incentive to export power and then re-import it.

Emergency yesterday."[100] The Ricochet scheme, under which Enron bought power from the Power Exchange, exported it out-of-state to another party who then charged a small fee and sold it back to Enron to sell back to the ISO in the higher-priced real-time market "may increase the Market Clearing Price by increasing the demand for energy."[101] Another scheme was "obviously a loophole," which the ISO could close if it simply stopped paying congestion charges to entities that failed to deliver energy.[102] The Load Shift scheme was found to increase congestion costs and increase costs to all market participants in the real-time market. The Get Shorty scheme required submitting false information to the ISO.

Some of these schemes seemed to violate ISO rules, although the lawyers' memo did not directly analyze this issue. The memo simply quoted the ISO rules. The ISO tariff prohibited "gaming," defined as "taking unfair advantage of the rules and procedures" of the Power Exchange or ISO; "taking undue advantage" of congestion or other conditions that may affect the grid's reliability or render the system "vulnerable to price manipulation to the detriment of the [the ISO Markets'] efficiency"; or engaging in anomalous market behavior such as "pricing and bidding patterns that are inconsistent with prevailing supply and demand conditions."[103] The types of conduct prohibited by the anti-gaming rules certainly appeared to prohibit many of Enron's schemes, despite the lawyers' silence on this issue in the memos.

With the release of these memos, the world of energy trading would never be the same. The memos disclosed that the Enron traders told their lawyers that "everybody does this" when discussing some of the schemes.[104] The Washington trade group rep-

---

[100] Memorandum from Christopher Yoder & Stephen Hall of the Stoel Rives law firm to Richard Sanders, re: "Traders' Strategies in California Wholesale Power Markets/ISO Sanctions," dated Dec. 8, 2000, at 3, *available at* www.ferc.gov/ferris (Docket No. PA02-2-000).

[101] *Id.* at 6–7.

[102] *Id.* at 7.

[103] *Id.* at 8. The second memo to Richard Sanders, assistant general counsel at Enron, was written by Gary Fergus and Jean Frizzell of the Brobeck law firm on the subject of "Status Report on Further Investigation and Analysis of EPRT Trading Strategies," after Brobeck reviewed the December 8 memo from the Stoel Rives law firm and then met with Enron traders, including the head trader in the Pacific Northwest, Tim Belden. This later memo explained that some of the analysis of the impact of the trading schemes on electricity prices or supplies in the earlier memo was erroneous. After the memos were disclosed, consultants in the power business stated that the descriptions of the trading activity by Enron's lawyers were confused and distorted. Severin Borenstein, an academic expert, concluded that some strategies were "pretty clear" violations of ISO rules. David Ivancovich, *Enron Opens Pandora's Box*, HOUS. CHRON., May 12, 2002, at 1A, 18A.

[104] Within days of the California trading revelations, the media reported what "everybody" appeared to already know, according to a J.P. Morgan Securities analyst: that the big energy trading companies like Aquila, El Paso Energy, Enron, and Reliant Resources swapped broadband capacity in round-trip trades, also called wash trades, to give the impression that their operations had growing volumes and revenues. The companies repeatedly sold the same routes to each other at the same price on the same day. David Barboza, *Traders Also Swapped Broadband, Data Show*, N.Y. TIMES, May 17, 2002, at C1.

resenting the nation's independent power traders, the Electric Power Supply Association, quickly sought to distance itself from Enron's schemes, saying that they "cannot be condoned."[105] Four large energy trading companies, Dynegy, Mirant, Williams and Reliant, denied that they engaged in any illegal market manipulation.[106] On May 8, 2002, two days after the release of the memos, FERC gave 150 power marketers, independent generators and traders until May 22 to admit or deny under oath that they used trading strategies like those in Enron's lawyers' memos.

As a result of this order, transcripts (such as the one between Xcel and Mirant traders quoted at the beginning of this section of this essay) began to appear on the FERC website. The traders in the Xcel transcripts said Williams and Duke regularly overscheduled load to create "tons of congestion."[107] Duke and Williams continued to deny that they had engaged in Enron-type trading, although Duke admitted that its financial statements included $1 billion in revenue from wash trades that were done to "validate real-time prices," not to inflate revenue.[108] The Securities and Exchange Commission began an investigation of El Paso, Williams, and Duke centered on wash trades, also called round-trip trades, that inflated revenues. A federal grand jury investigation began in the Northern District of California and issued subpoenas to Dynegy, Southern Company, AES, Duke Energy, Mirant, Reliant, and Williams.[109] The world of energy trading was now locked in litigation and investigation.

Once the trading documents were made public, speculation began about the link between California's energy crisis and Enron's bankruptcy.[110] When FERC finally stepped in decisively in June 2001 and imposed interstate power price caps throughout the eleven interconnected western states, California's crisis ended. Prices plunged. Five months later, Enron was bankrupt. If Enron had bet on power prices in California staying high for a long time and had lined up long-term contracts to buy power at high prices, the price drop would have been devastating to its pocketbook.

By August 2002, ten other companies had admitted to engaging in some of the trading games disclosed in the Enron memos.[111] Spurred into action by the May release of the Enron memos, which validated much of what California officials, legisla-

---

[105] Richard A. Oppel, Jr., *How Enron Got California to Buy Power It Didn't Need*, N.Y. TIMES, May 8, 2002, at C1.

[106] Will McNamara, *How Will the Smoking Gun Enron Memos Impact the Energy Industry?*, ISSUEALERT SCIENTECH, May 8, 2002, at 4.

[107] Neela Banerjee, *New Questions on Handling of Power Prices in California*, N.Y. TIMES, June 8, 2002, at B1, B3.

[108] *Id.*

[109] *Id.*

[110] Alex Berenson, *California May Have Had a Big Role in Enron's Downfall*, N.Y. TIMES, May 9, 2002, at C1.

[111] David Ivanovich & Janet Elliot, *The Fall of Enron: Regulators Find Evidence Prices Distorted by Enron, West Coast Deals Probed*, HOUS. CHRON., Aug 14, 2002, at 1A.

tors, and the press had been finding in their own investigations, FERC finally began a serious review of the California power markets. FERC staff issued an initial report on price manipulation in the Western markets in August 2002, followed by a final report in March 2003.[112] These reports, described in more detail later in this essay, list many more companies that FERC found cause to believe illegally gamed the California markets in violation of the FERC-approved ISO rules.[113]

In mid-October, 2002, Enron's lead trader in the California markets, Timothy Belden, pleaded guilty to several counts of wire fraud for deliberately submitting false data to the California ISO.[114] With Belden's plea came the discovery of just how brazen Enron's traders could be and how overmatched the regulators were in monitoring the market. In May 1999, Belden decided to test the limits of the state's grid to find loopholes that could be exploited.[115] A small geothermal plant in Beowawe, Nevada generated 15 megawatts of electricity, enough for a small town. This power was sent to Silverpeak, Nevada where a Southern California Edison line carried it into California. On May 24, 1999, Belden made four bids to sell 2,900 megawatts of power to the California Power Exchange ("PX") for next-day delivery. The PX approved the bid and Belden told the ISO that Enron would use the Silverpeak line to move the electricity. This line can only handle 15 megawatts, so a load of 2,900 megawatts would explode the transformers or possibly melt the power lines. The automated software system running the grid would read this bid as causing congestion. Belden would then relieve the congestion and get paid for doing so. This one trade drove up the price of electricity by more than 70 percent that afternoon across the state. An ISO operator reported the anomalous trade to the compliance unit of the state's PX. Enron was fined $25,000 while California electricity customers were overcharged by $4.6 million to $7 million that day. A single fraudulent trade could destabilize the whole market. The traders had learned a lot. Between 1999 and 2001, revenues at Belden's trading unit rose from $50 million to $800 million.[116]

---

[112] STAFF OF FEDERAL ENERGY REGULATORY COMMISSION, INITIAL REPORT ON COMPANY-SPECIFIC PROCEEDINGS AND GENERIC REEVALUATIONS; PUBLISHED NATURAL GAS PRICE DATA; AND ENRON TRADING STRATEGIES 83-100 (Aug. 2002) [hereinafter FERC INITIAL REPORT 2002] (Docket No. PA02-2-2000); and STAFF OF FEDERAL ENERGY REGULATORY COMMISSION, FINAL REPORT ON PRICE MANIPULATION IN WESTERN MARKETS: FACT-FINDING INVESTIGATION OF POTENTIAL MANIPULATION OF ELECTRIC AND NATURAL GAS PRICES (Mar. 2003) (Docket No. PA02-2-200 [hereinafter FERC FINAL REPORT 2003].

[113] See text *infra* accompanying notes 176–99.

[114] Kurt Eichenwald & Matt Richtel, *Enron Trader Pleads Guilty to Conspiracy,* N.Y. TIMES, Oct. 18, 2002, at C1. Belden told the judge, "I did it because I wanted to maximize profits for Enron." With his plea, he returned $2.1 million, part of the bonuses that he had received from Enron.

[115] John R. Wilke & Robert Gavin, *Brazen Trade Marks New Path of Enron Probe,* WALL ST. J., Oct. 21, 2002, at C1.

[116] *Id.* at C12.

Enron's lawyers appear to have told Enron executives in December 2000 that these schemes were potentially criminal. On December 10, Enron's assistant general counsel, Richard Sanders, ordered them stopped, but the order was never put in writing.[117] At the December meetings in Portland, Oregon, Enron executives noted in handwriting that "[n]o one can prove [this], given the complexity of our portfolio," and then ordered that the notes be removed.[118] It appears that the traders continued to use these strategies until FERC imposed a price cap on all energy sales in the Western region in June 2001, six months after the traders were warned that some of their acts might be criminal.[119]

C. Withholding Generating Power

"We decided the prices were too low . . . so we shut down."
"Excellent. Excellent."
"We pulled about 2,000 megs off the market."
"That's sweet."

"Everybody thought it was really exciting that we were gonna play some market power."
"That was fun!"

—Exchange between Reliant traders in June 2000[120]

The capitalists are so hungry for profits that they will sell us the rope to hang them with.

—V. I. Lenin, 1920[121]

The gaming tactics revealed by the release of the Enron memos in May 2002 were those of a trader, not an electricity generator. The tactics aimed largely at affecting the

---

[117] Harvey Rice, *Enron Was Told Strategy in Calif. Could Be Illegal*, HOUS. CHRON., Dec. 12, 2002, at 1A, 20A.

[118] Richard A. Oppel, Jr., *Despite Doubters, Enron Waited To Stop Its Trades, Senate Is Told*, N.Y. TIMES, May 16, 02, at A1.

[119] Rice, *supra* note 117, at 20A.

[120] Ken Silverstein, *Reliant Settlement Accelerates Justice*, UTILIPOINT ISSUEALERT, Feb. 12, 2003, at 2. The transcripts of these exchanges were made public as part of FERC's $13.8 million settlement with Reliant for Reliant traders' withholding supply for two days in June 2000. Transcripts between a Williams trader and AES, a generator, also revealed discussions about withholding power with a feigned maintenance shutdown that would allow Williams to make more money by supplying replacement power. *Shares in Tulsa, Okla.-Based Energy Firm Sink After Release of Documents*, KNIGHT RIDDER NEWS, Nov. 16, 2002 (online).

[121] John E. Olson, *Energy Markets at a Crossroads: Has Deregulation Failed?*, Address at the Int'l Ass'n of Energy Economists Conference, Houston, Texas (Dec. 12, 2002) (quoting Lenin) (handout in author's files).

price of electricity in California rather than the actual physical supply of energy produced in the state. After all, Enron was largely a trader, not a generator, although it owned one utility in Portland, Oregon that could be used in some of its gaming tactics. The California ISO, in a November 2002 report, concluded that Enron's trading schemes had not caused blackouts.[122] Experts believed that the big money—billions of dollars rather than mere millions—was made, not by traders, but by the electricity suppliers, the owners of power plants, through two mechanisms: (1) physical withholding, i.e., simply not running power plants that could be run to meet market demand; and (2) economic withholding, i.e., bidding supplies into the market only at very high prices or refusing to bid supply into the day-ahead market, thus forcing the ISO to buy power in the real-time market where it would pay any price in an effort to avoid blackouts.[123] Because of the structure of the California market, generators could strongly affect prices by engaging in these two forms of withholding, even without colluding in any manner that might violate the antitrust laws.

Reliable evidence that substantial market power could be exercised in California's electricity sector was found only a few months after the California crisis began in May 2000. In September 2000, economists from the California Energy Center issued a report finding evidence that market power had raised electricity prices about 16 percent above competitive levels between June 1998 and September 1999.[124] Their analysis used assumptions that would tend to underestimate the degree of market power exercised. The study raised a red-flag warning of dire danger ahead. By the time the study was released in September 2000, California was already deep in the danger zone. Electricity prices during the summer of 2000 had soared to unimaginable heights of $200, $400, $500, and even $800 per megawatt-hour (compared to a normal price of about $35 per megawatt).

In January 2001, two reports appeared analyzing the post-May 2000 power crisis in California: one in a widely read trade publication and the other on the website of the AEI-Brookings Joint Center for Regulatory Studies. The first report was by an inde-

---

[122] The ISO's report attributed the blackouts to supply and demand imbalances and lack of transmission capacity between southern and northern California. The report concluded that the trading schemes affected power prices, but not system reliability. DR. ERIC HILDEBRANDT, CALIFORNIA INDEPENDENT SYSTEM OPERATOR, DID ANY OF ENRON'S TRADING AND SCHEDULING PRACTICES CONTRIBUTE TO OUTAGES IN CALIFORNIA? (Nov. 15, 2002) *available at* www.caiso.com. The ISO report became embroiled in controversy with state Senator Dunn of California, who was investigating the California energy crisis with great determination, and Robert McCullough, a private consultant, who had his own version of events. *See* text *infra* accompanying notes 125–29.

[123] David Ivanovich, *Enron Opens a Pandora's Box*, HOUS. CHRON., May 12, 2002, at 1A, 18A (quoting Severin Borenstein); FERC INITIAL REPORT 2002, *supra* note 112, at 83.

[124] SEVERIN BORENSTEIN ET AL., DIAGNOSING MARKET POWER IN CALIFORNIA'S RESTRUCTURED WHOLESALE ELECTRICITY MARKET (Sept. 2000) (National Bureau of Econ. Research, Working Paper No. 7868, Preliminary Report). Two of the authors were the same economists who had issued so many caution flags about deregulating energy markets without adequate attention to local market power. *See* text *supra* accompanying note 82.

pendent consultant, Robert McCullough, titled "Price Spike Tsunami: How Market Power Soaked California."[125] Going against the prevailing public opinion campaign then being waged by the industry, FERC commissioners, and the executive branch, McCullough asserted that all explanations about the price spikes that relied solely on drought, increased electricity demand, and increased natural gas prices were wrong.[126] Indeed, the Western System Coordination Council ("WSCC")'s "2000 Summer Adequacy Report," published on May 25, 2000, three days after the first price spike, indicated that sufficient resources existed in both California and the entire western region, with a satisfactory margin of 15 percent.[127]

McCullough attributed the price spikes to the California ISO's letting itself be gamed by the merchant power plant generators that did not have an obligation to serve a franchised area (as did the previous utility-owned generators). The ISO issued emergency alerts for power whenever offers of supply bid into the day-ahead market were insufficient to meet its reliability criteria in that market. The next day, sellers averted the declared emergency by finding electricity supplies but only at "murderous" market-clearing prices in the real-time markets. The mystery, to McCullough, was why the ISO allowed itself to be so repeatedly deceived. The ISO board did consist of a substantial number of representatives from generating companies, calling into question its status as an "independent" system operator.[128]

McCullough also noted that the pattern of capacity utilization of generating units was very odd. Cleverly using data from the EPA's Acid Rain database of power plant emissions from generation and a WSCC database that no regulators appeared to have looked at, McCullough concluded that the California market had deviated from any normal pattern of utility practice. Generators did not generate, peakers did not peak, and emergencies lacked justification.[129] The ISO and Power Exchange did not exchange data between them, and they operated on automatic pilot, rather like Hal the computer in the movie *2001: A Space Odyssey.* Divestiture had put generating capacity in the hands of only a few companies. Generators could simply reverse-engineer the computer software and game the system with strategic bidding. Indeed, the ISO col-

---

[125] Robert McCullough, *Price Spike Tsunami: How Market Power Soaked Calif,* PUB. UTIL. FORTNIGHTLY, Jan. 1, 2001, at 22–32.

[126] *Id.* at 25. McCullough's report presented the following data: From May to August 2000, Columbia River inflows were at 98 percent of their historical average, hardly a drought condition. Regional load demand in May 2000 was lower than loads during several previous months, and roughly equivalent to the load in May 1999. In May 2000, hydroelectric generation from the Columbia River was 120 percent of the May averages from 1986 through 1999.

[127] *Id.* at 26.

[128] *Id.* A few months later, FERC issued a series of proposed remedies for the California wholesale electric market, including the removal of generator representatives from the ISO board. *See* San Diego Gas & Elec. Co., 93 FERC ¶ 61,121 (Nov. 1, 2000).

[129] *Id.* at 30. Peakers are power plants that are brought online only during periods of peak demand. They are almost always gas-fired power plants that can be started up very quickly.

lected and distributed the hourly operating data for its generating suppliers, so each company knew the production levels of its competitors.

The second January 2001 study used an entirely different methodology of analyzing the California market. Paul Joskow, a professor of economics and management at M.I.T., and Edward Kahn, an expert consultant, simulated competitive benchmark wholesale prices for electricity in California during summer 2000, taking into account changes in the four market fundamentals—natural gas prices, demand, imports of electricity from other states, and changes in the prices of nitrogen oxide (NOx) emission permits—which had been identified as the root causes of the soaring prices.[130] While these factors were found to explain a significant percentage of the changes in wholesale electricity prices, a large unexplained difference remained.[131] The two economists then examined whether the abnormally high prices were due to physical withholding of supplies by generators during peak hours. Using some of the same databases as McCullough, their preliminary conclusion was that unexplained "output gaps" strongly suggested physical withholding.[132] Something other than "market fundamentals" was at work in California. In a later study, the California economists from the energy center at Berkeley estimated that 51 percent of total electricity expenditures in the summer of 2000 could be attributed to market power, usually exercised during peak demand periods.[133]

On April 1, 2002, Robert McCullough revisited his earlier study of market power in California.[134] By this time, no one denied that physical or economic withholding of supply to inflate prices had occurred. The only issue was whether the withholding was done legally or illegally under the market rules set up by the ISO, FERC and antitrust laws. His report again lambastes the California ISO for its passive market surveillance,

---

[130] PAUL L. JOSKOW & EDWARD KAHN, A QUANTITATIVE ANALYSIS OF PRICING BEHAVIOUR IN CALIFORNIA'S WHOLESALE ELECTRICITY MARKET DURING SUMMER 2000 (AEI-Brookings Joint Center for Regulatory Studies, Working Paper 01-01, 2001). Paul Joskow is a professor in M.I.T.'s Center for Energy and Environmental Policy Research. This Working Paper was based on research commissioned by Southern California Edison Co.

[131] Id. at 16–17. Actual electricity prices ranged from 20 percent to 50 percent higher than competitive prices in June, July, and August 2000 when NOx prices were highest.

[132] Id. at 22–33.

[133] SEVERIN BORENSTEIN ET AL., MEASURING MARKET INEFFICIENCIES IN CALIFORNIA'S RESTRUCTURED WHOLESALE ELECTRICITY MARKET (Feb. 2002 Working Paper), subsequently revised and replaced by BORENSTEIN ET AL., MEASURING MARKET INEFFICIENCIES IN CALIFORNIA'S RESTRUCTURED WHOLESALE ELECTRICITY MARKET (CSEM WP 102, June 2002) (concluding that increased market power accounted for 59 percent of the increased cost of electricity) The General Accounting Office summarized five studies, all of which found the exercise of substantial market power causing uncompetitive prices in California, in U.S. GENERAL ACCOUNTING OFFICE, RESTRUCTURED ELECTRICITY MARKETS: CALIFORNIA MARKET DESIGN ENABLED EXERCISE OF MARKET POWER 36-37, app. III (2002) (GAO-02-828).

[134] Robert McCullough, Revisiting California: Market Power after Two Years, PUB. UTIL. FORTNIGHTLY, April 1, 2002, at 28.

FERC for its "appalling indecision,"[135] and the WSCC for its failure to release data that could have helped analyze the markets. The ISO had no good log of plant outages and did not know if electricity was being exported out-of-state (to avoid price caps) or if generating units were experiencing abnormal bouts of maintenance shutdowns. New data showed that plants in the ISO control area were operating far below the levels of similar plants elsewhere in the western region. While some commentators blamed cutbacks in generating units on local air pollution rules, the air control authorities had acted quickly and aggressively to allow diesel generators into the market. The data indicated that Duke, Dynegy, Mirant, Reliant, and AES had operated at about 50 percent of capacity from May 2000 to June 2001.[136] Their plants were not dispatched at peak, even during ISO-called emergencies. Whistleblowers from the plants' staff found instructions from management inexplicable. FERC's preliminary investigation in February 2001 of the abnormal plant outages of these five generators was done by inexperienced staff with little expertise and without access to information on individual plants.

The clarity of the evidence led McCullough to one striking conclusion: If FERC had intervened knowledgably in the California markets in May 2000 and imposed a western-wide price cap and a "must offer" rule to counter the generators' strategic withholding of bids and supplies, the entire California energy crisis would have been avoided. While some of the analysis and conclusions of McCullough's report may well be overstated, its "big picture" view of the market power of generators and the lagging role of regulators is supported by many other reports.[137]

When the Enron memos were released a month later, in May 2002, it appeared that no regulators at either the state or federal level had been ready, willing, or able to monitor the California power markets in a way that merited the public trust. Private consultants and academics seemed far ahead of the regulators in their understanding

---

[135] *Id.* at 29.

[136] *Id.* at 31.

[137] The issue of widespread physical withholding of generating supplies has proved difficult to document. A report by the California Public Utility Commission on withheld power concluded that if Duke, Dynegy, Mirant, Reliant, and AES/Williams had operated all of their plants at available capacity, all four days of blackouts would have been avoided in Southern California and 65 percent of blackout hours would not have occurred in Northern California. CALIFORNIA PUBLIC UTILITY COMM'N, REPORT ON WHOLESALE ELECTRICITY GENERATION INVESTIGATION (Sept. 17, 2002). The California ISO, its reputation under attack, disagreed with aspects of the CPUC report, although it admitted that the power plant operators routinely ignored ISO instructions and sometimes "feigned" pollution limits to justify shutdowns. Rick Jurgens, *California Electricity Grid Operators Dispute Regulator's Report Methodology*, CONTRA COSTA TIMES, Oct. 29, 2002 (Energy Central Professional online). Dynegy, Duke, and AES/Williams continued to assert that they had not withheld power. John M. Browder, *California Power Failures Linked to Energy Companies,* N.Y. TIMES, Sept. 18, 2002, at A16. At the request of California Senator Barbara Boxer, FERC reviewed the data in the CPUC report and concluded that it was inaccurate. *See* text *infra* accompanying notes 185–88.

of the power markets. However, even the academics had not discovered a pervasive strategy used by marketers to manipulate power prices during the California meltdown. In attempting to confirm some of McCullough's statements, a newly energized FERC discovered that natural gas prices, the key input in the cost of generating electricity, had been misreported and manipulated to favor the trading positions of traders in the gas markets. This stunning development surfaced in FERC's initial staff report on Western price manipulation, released in August 2002, and is discussed *infra* in Part E of this essay.

D. Affiliate Abuse in the Gas Pipeline Sector

When FERC required unbundling of natural gas pipelines, separating their merchant function (of buying and selling gas) from their transportation function, FERC did not require the physical divestiture of pipeline assets, but only the "functional" divestiture of separating the operations of the two different activities with a "firewall." Most pipeline companies established marketing affiliates. FERC's task then was to enforce rules of nondiscrimination that prevented a pipeline company from favoring its own marketing affiliate with sweetheart deals that gave its affiliate's gas an advantage in securing pipeline space, especially during shortages, or which gave price discounts to its affiliate that were not also available to others.

Natural gas now plays a crucial role in electric markets. Much of the new generating capacity built in the past decade uses natural gas rather than coal or nuclear power because of recent technological efficiencies in combined-cycle gas turbines and because of the clean air benefits of burning gas rather than coal. Thus, nondiscriminatory, open access to pipeline capacity to transport natural gas to power plants is essential for competitive markets in both gas and electricity to work.

In April 2000, a month before the California energy crisis began, the California Public Utility Commission ("CPUC") filed a complaint with FERC charging that El Paso Pipeline and its merchant affiliate had engaged in anticompetitive practices and affiliate abuse, in violation of FERC's Standards of Conduct for pipeline operations. This episode is a case study of the difficulties of using behavioral rules to police large, diversified energy holding companies in deregulated markets.[138]

In February 2000, El Paso Pipeline put a large block of capacity on its pipeline up for auction. Two of its own merchant affiliates outbid other bidders and won all 1.22 billion cubic feet of capacity, even though the rates that they offered to pay for the service were below the level set in El Paso Pipeline's tariff published with FERC. The CPUC's complaint to FERC charged that this auction allowed El Paso Merchant, as the largest holder of pipeline capacity (one-sixth of the pipeline capacity into California),

---

[138] This account of El Paso's actions is taken from AMERICAN BAR ASS'N, SECTION ON ENV'T, ENERGY & RESOURCES, ELECTRIC & NATURAL GAS MARKETING COMMITTEE, THE YEAR IN REVIEW 2001 REPORT Tab A, 6-10 (2001) [hereinafter ABA 2001 REPORT].

to exercise market power and raise the price of gas brought into the state, with a projected financial impact of $100 million on gas and electric consumers.

No sooner was the complaint filed than the energy crisis began in May 2000. On March 28, 2001, FERC found no evidence of affiliate misconduct in the award of capacity or the grant of discounts. However, FERC stated that it was concerned about the high gas prices because it had seen certain internal El Paso memos, protected by confidentiality during discovery, that allegedly showed an intent by the pipeline company and its merchant affiliate to manipulate California's gas and electricity markets. FERC ordered an expedited hearing on this issue.[139]

The case proved to be much more complex than the Chief Administrative Law Judge Curtis Wagner had anticipated. After months of hearings and media attention, Judge Wagner issued his initial decision in October 2001, concluding that El Paso Pipeline and El Paso Merchant had the ability to exercise market power, but it was unclear whether they had actually done so. He recommended that this part of the complaint be dismissed. However, he did find clear evidence that the El Paso companies were guilty of affiliate abuse and had violated FERC's Standards of Conduct prohibiting communications between the two affiliates. He saw "hanky panky" and "blatant collusion" in the transcript of a phone conversation between El Paso Merchant and El Paso Pipeline personnel to keep the discounts secret until the open season for bidding for the block of capacity had ended.[140] Indeed, the firewall that was to keep the two companies functionally "unbundled" seemed nonexistent. Also, sitting at the very top of the firewalled companies was William Wise, the president of El Paso Corporation, the parent holding company, and he had approved El Paso Merchant's bid to acquire the capacity from El Paso Pipeline.

FERC's Market Oversight and Enforcement Section filed post-hearing comments asserting that the record suggested possible violations of FERC's open access regulations. The FERC commissioners ordered additional hearings on the issue of whether El Paso Pipeline had made all its capacity available to California from November 1, 2000 to March 31, 2001. The spot price for natural gas delivered at the Southern California border during this time had skyrocketed to $20–30 per million BTUs, with spikes as high as $60 per million BTUs.[141] Moreover, when the contract between El Paso Pipeline and El Paso Merchant ended on May 31, 2001, natural gas prices dropped in California almost immediately.[142]

---

[139] *Id.* at 7.

[140] *Id.* at 8–9.

[141] Natural gas prices had been in the $2–3 dollar per million BTU range. A study by the Brattle Group, energy consultants for Southern California Edison, estimated that El Paso boosted natural gas and electric prices by $3.7 billion from March 2000 to March 2001. Alexei Barrionuevo, *Hearing Could Shape Future of Energy Company El Paso*, WALL ST. J., Dec. 2, 2002 (online).

[142] Ken Silverstein, *El Paso Energy in Crisis Mode*, SCIENTECH ISSUEALERT, Sept. 26, 2002, at 2.

The subsequent March 2002 hearings resulted in 14 volumes of transcripts of evidence. The Chief Judge concluded that El Paso Pipeline had failed to schedule all of the pipeline capacity that it posted and failed to post all of the capacity that it had available to transport gas into California, as required by FERC's open access rules. El Paso's pipeline had operated at only 79 percent of its capacity, after accounting for the Carlsbad explosion[143] and El Paso's claim of "sick compressors." Therefore, the Chief Judge modified his 2001 Initial Decision and found that El Paso had exercised market power by withholding gas.[144]

Evidence released at this hearing made media headlines, countered by full-page ads purchased by El Paso in nationwide newspapers. Some of the released transcripts, for example, showed that in a February 2000 presentation to Chair and CEO William Wise, an official of the merchant energy unit discussed the "ability to influence the physical market to the benefit of any financial hedge/position."[145] Another document described a February 2000 presentation to El Paso's risk management committee that discussed ways to boost profits by "idling large blocks of transport."[146] In defending his company at the hearings, Wise dismissed the documents as "just part of the day-to-day business planning of a large corporation," and then stated that "no inappropriate information ever gets communicated in our company between those two segregated segments of our business."[147] El Paso also pursued a massive public media campaign, complete with full-page ads in newspapers across the nation and letters to legislators and policymakers, asserting that its pipeline to California had to run at lower pressure for safety reasons after the explosion. Indeed, the Office of Pipeline Safety of the Department of Transportation confirmed, after the hearings had concluded, that it had imposed an order setting pressure limits on the pipeline.[148] It is not clear why this information was not presented at the hearing.

---

[143] This is the same pipeline explosion that is reported to have resulted in trading profits to Enron of almost $500 million dollars in one day. Federal regulators in the Office of Pipeline Safety proposed a $2.52 million fine against El Paso Pipeline for violating safety regulations related to the accident. El Paso failed to use X-ray or sonar equipment on the outside of the pipeline to look for corrosion, even though a company investigator had recommended this practice following a similar, but not deadly, 1996 accident. Alexei Barrionuevo & Stephen Power, *El Paso Corp. Is Focus of Probe into Fatal Pipeline Rupture*, WALL ST. J., Nov. 15, 2002, at B4.

[144] Public Utilities Comm'n of California, Docket No. RP00-241-006 (FERC Sept. 23, 2002) (Initial Decision by Judge Curtis L. Wagner, Jr.).

[145] *FERC Releases El Paso's Calif Strategy Documents*, REUTERS, Dec. 2, 2002 (Energy Central Professional online).

[146] *Id.*

[147] *Id.* An El Paso attorney said there was no evidence that Wise violated FERC rules against sharing information between its merchant and its pipeline affiliates in an attempt to influence the physical market to benefit El Paso's trading position. Meanwhile, El Paso and the pipeline industry engaged in a huge lobbying effort to defeat new affiliate abuse rules proposed by FERC.

[148] Michael Davis, *Investors Bid El Paso Shares Up*, HOUS. CHRON., Nov. 22, 2002, at 1C.

Just days before FERC was expected to issue a final order in the El Paso pipeline case, El Paso agreed to a $1.7 billion payment to the state of California to settle the charges of withholding pipeline capacity to that state.[149] If approved by FERC, this settlement payment, the largest ever made by a regulated energy company, will remove these issues from FERC's agenda.

As an ABA Energy Committee Report concluded, the lengthy hearings in the El Paso case show the difficulty of detecting and proving the exercise of market power.[150] More troublesome, the FERC affiliate rules at issue in these hearings were enacted before large mergers in the gas industry created holding companies like El Paso Corporation. In the report's view, the hearings speak to the need for more control over affiliates of holding companies, especially when the magnitude of the transactions between them is so large.[151]

FERC has proposed changes in the standards of conduct for pipeline companies in an effort to curb affiliate abuse.[152] However, industry trade groups assert that the proposed reforms (which would automatically impute unlawful disclosure of confidential information upon its receipt by a shared employee who works for both the pipeline and the marketing affiliate) are irreconcilable with the dictates of the Sarbanes-Oxley Act.[153] This act generally requires that senior management be fully informed about the financial position of their companies and affiliates. The final rule will have to be a complicated one, because a transmission provider must communicate some crucial operational information to its merchant sales and generation affiliates in order to assure reliability of the transmission systems, especially in power markets.

---

[149] Laura Goldberg, *El Paso to Pay $1.7 Billion in Calif. Scheme*, HOUS. CHRON., Mar. 21, 2003 (online). Investors considered a settlement crucial to El Paso's survival. The company was in a proxy battle with dissident shareholders seeking to oust the existing management.

[150] ABA 2001 REPORT, *supra* note 138, at 10.

[151] In a less publicized case of pipeline affiliate abuse, FERC found that Enron's Transwestern Pipeline Company gave preferential treatment to two of its customers to allow them to ship gas into California at the height of the California crisis. David Ivanovich, *Enron Subsidiary Cited for Abuses*, HOUS. CHRON., July 18, 2002, at 1A. Also, just before the El Paso settlement was announced, Williams agreed to pay a $20 million civil fine to FERC to resolve allegations that its Transco pipeline had given preferential treatment to its energy-trading affiliate between 1999 and 2002. David Ivanovich, *Hefty Fine by FERC Seals Deal*, HOUS. CHRON., Mar. 17, 2003 (online).

[152] FERC Docket No. RM01-10-000, Notice of Staff Conference on Standards of Conduct for Transmission Providers, Staff Analysis of Major Issues Raised in Comments (Apr. 25, 2002).

[153] *Energy Groups, Southern Company Say FERC Proposal Conflicts with Sarbanes-Oxley*, DAILY REP. FOR EXECUTIVES, Apr. 15, 2003, at A-19.

E. Manipulating Gas and Electric Price Indices

The process [of reporting gas and electricity prices], based on trust, is a potential minefield for manipulation.[154]

The erosion of confidence in the gas indices that has taken place . . . may well impede the benefits that customers get from this industry.[155]

—FERC Chair Pat Wood, 2003

With the release of the Enron trading memos in May 2002, FERC stepped up its efforts to police the industry and to rid it of any more scandals so that it could be rebuilt on a firm foundation. In June 2002, FERC Commissioner Nora Brownell invited industry participants to come forward and admit their involvement in manipulative trading schemes by "visiting the confessional" in FERC's headquarters, where its new Office of Market Oversight and Investigation ("OMOI") was located.[156] Both she and FERC Chairman Pat Wood began visits to Wall Street to encourage investment in energy infrastructure despite the plunging credit ratings of energy trading and merchant generating companies, pledging an "end to the series of surprises" that had been revealed throughout 2002.

Yet, a fourth bombshell exploded just a few short months later. In August 2002, the FERC staff released a preliminary report finding that substantial evidence existed that the published prices for natural gas sold into the spot market at the California border might have been manipulated.[157] This new scandal went far beyond price manipulation by any one pipeline owner and its affiliated marketer. Rather, it implicated the very heart of all effective markets: the transparency of price data that allows buyers and sellers to know whether a deal is a good one. Literally billions of dollars of natural gas and electricity contracts have been priced in reliance on the accuracy of published spot prices in industry publications such as *Inside FERC* and *Gas Daily*. If these price data had been manipulated, contracting parties who had thought they were buying at a price set by competitive market forces would be incorrect.[158] These prices in the published

---

[154] *AEP Cracks Down on Traders in Bid for Credibility*, REUTERS, Oct 9, 2002 (Energy Central Professional online).

[155] *FERC Staff Urge Strict Standards for Natgas Indices*, REUTERS, Jan. 15, 2003 (Energy Central Professional online).

[156] Stephanie M. Ingersoll, *Brownell Urges Confessions for Power Industry; Sees End to Industry Surprises*, DAILY REP. FOR EXECUTIVES, June 21, 2002, at A-38.

[157] FERC INITIAL REPORT 2002, *supra* note 112, at 33–57 (Docket No. PA02-2-000).

[158] *See* Craig R. Carver, *Natural Gas Price Indices: Do They Provide a Sound Basis for Sales and Royalty Payments?*, 42 ROCKY MTN. MIN. L. INST. 10–15 (1996) (describing problems with bias and coverage in these indices several years before the scope and reality of the problems surfaced).

indices are gathered by reporters for trade publications (such as Platts and Bloomberg) who phone traders daily, soliciting the prices at which gas sales were actually transacted that day. If traders lie, and the reporting services do not catch the lies, then the published prices will not reflect the market. As the FERC staff concluded:

> Certainly, there is a significant incentive on the part of certain market participants to deliberately misreport prices, given that natural gas is the fuel input for the electricity generators that set the market price in California and the rest of the West. Unscrupulous traders could manipulate natural gas price indexes in order to increase the profitability of their electricity positions. The means by which this misreporting could occur is actually quite simple. Traders overstate prices to the reporting firms, which in turn publish price data that incorporate the overstated prices. Buyers and sellers cannot verify those prices. . . .[but they] assume that the published prices are accurate.[159]

Data presented at an April 2002 Congressional hearing showed that Enron had traded significant volumes of electricity among five of its own subsidiaries, four of which had the same board of directors and executives and were staffed in some cases by the same employees.[160] By trading back and forth between each other, the traders inflated the price, which would then get reported as a market price in published indices. This "wash" trading, round-trip trading, or "megawatt laundering" is deceptive because it gives the illusion of a deep market that leads buyers to assume they are getting a competitive price in a liquid market, when this is not true. Loretta Lynch, Chair of the California PUC, testified that Enron's trades among its subsidiaries led to increased revenues being reported on EnronOnline at artificially high prices, which were then used by other buyers and sellers as benchmark prices, inflating the published

---

[159] FERC INITIAL REPORT 2002, *supra* note 112, at 47. FERC's inquiry into the price indices was triggered by Robert McCullough, the private energy consultant who had written widely publicized studies on generator withholding and regulatory failures in data gathering and marketing, discussed in the text *supra* accompanying notes 125–29. In early January 2002, McCullough testified that the day after Enron filed for bankruptcy protection, prices in the futures market for West Coast energy fell by 30 percent. He believed that Enron had been using its market dominance to set the forward price, which collapsed when Enron toppled. Stephanie M. Ingersoll, *Enron Rate Investigation Requested by Davis*, DAILY REP. FOR EXECUTIVES, Feb. 1, 2002, at A-24. FERC Chair Pat Wood initiated an investigation. Jeanne Cummings, *U.S. Probes Enron's Effect on Power Prices*, WALL ST. J., Jan. 30, 2002 (online). The FERC Staff Report showed that McCullough's 30 percent number was incorrect and that much of the price drop was attributable to seasonal factors. However, the staff could not explain the discrepancies in price data between that reported by Platts and that reported by Bloomberg, meaning that the staff could not ascertain what the actual price of electricity was during the days after Enron declared bankruptcy. FERC INITIAL REPORT 2002, *supra* note 112, at 37–41.

[160] Stephanie M. Ingersoll, DAILY REP. FOR EXECUTIVES, *California Claims Enron Manipulated Prices, Doctored E-Mails Given to State*, Apr. 12, 2002, at A-35.

indices. The Securities and Exchange Commission ("SEC") was already heavily involved in investigating allegations of round-trip trading that boosted companies reported trading volumes and revenues (thanks to mark-to-mark accounting). A new Task Force of FERC, SEC, CFTC (the Commodity Futures Trading Commission), and Department of Justice officials began investigations centered on the effect of wash trading on market prices of energy.[161]

The inaccuracy of the reported price indices for gas and electricity strongly impacted FERC's docket devoted to determining whether generators and gas suppliers should refund money to California consumers. California officials seek about $9 billion in refunds to consumers based on unjust and unreasonable rates paid to generators during the energy crisis. The reported spot prices for gas at California delivery points would not be appropriate for use in computing the mitigated market clearing price of electricity in the refund proceedings. Since such a high percentage of California's power plants ran on natural gas, if gas prices were artificially inflated, then the price of electricity would also be artificially raised.

The August 2002 FERC staff report found that the spot price for natural gas at the California border published in trade publications differed enormously from the spot price of gas at producing basins (largely in Texas) or from the spot price at the large market and transport center for gas, called the Henry Hub, in Louisiana.[162] The abnormal spread between these numbers suggested that natural gas prices were manipulated between October 2000 and July 2001. FERC could not verify that the reported prices in the widely used industry publications for gas sold on the spot market during this time were based on actual, real trades between arms-length parties. Thus, the published prices could not be used to determine refunds to California purchasers. Instead, the FERC staff recommended a redefinition of the benchmark price for electricity sales for refund purposes. The new proposed benchmark price would equal the actual cost of gas in producing basins like the Texas Permian Basin, plus the transportation tariff to ship the gas to the California border.[163]

The FERC staff also questioned the prices that had been posted on EnronOnline's e-commerce trading platform.[164] Many participants closely watched the prices listed there assuming that those prices reflected the market. An obvious circularity existed in

[161] A Senate Governmental Affairs Committee report found that Enron successfully exploited regulatory voids among FERC, the SEC, and the CFTC because none of the agencies communicated with each other about developments in the quick-moving, deregulated power markets. John J. Fialka, *Jurisdiction Issues Put Off Regulatory Action on Enron*, WALL ST. J., Nov. 12, 2002 (online).

[162] FERC INITIAL REPORT 2002, *supra* note 112, at 63–74.

[163] *Id.* at 61–72. The different methodology would produce a tremendous difference in the imputed market clearing price for electricity for refund purposes. The market price would fall from $497 per megawatt-hour (using published spot prices) to $153 per megawatt-hour (using the new formula). *Id.* at 72.

[164] *Id.* at 48–54.

this arrangement: Traders relied on EnronOnline prices, which they then reported to the publishers of the price indices as market prices. EnronOnline used the Southern California border as its exclusive hub for California gas trading. Because EnronOnline was a proprietary platform, Enron made all the rules and was a party to every deal traded on its boards. With Enron's market dominance in trading and superior information, the system was ripe for abuse. Internal Enron training exercises indicated that Enron knew of the potential to influence published price data in order to profit in its related derivative positions.[165] The empirical evidence from EnronOnline's databases suggested that EnronOnline was a significant part of the price formation process and that Enron took large positions in the markets using its own trading platform.

Within a month of the April hearings, Dynegy and AEP disclosed that some of their traders had provided inaccurate data for energy prices indices. In some cases, the volume of round-trip trading had accounted for astounding growth in revenues. During one hour on November 15, 2001, Dynegy and CMS simultaneously traded megawatts with each other to create a deal "worth" $1.68 billion in revenues. Dynegy explained that it was "stress testing" its Dynegy Direct trading platform that had been "having problems with large transactions."[166] Analysts saw the trades as "competing for brag-a-watts": attempting to build volume to show the public that their trading platforms had captured a large share of EnronOnline's shrinking business.[167] In another case, a trader engaged in repeated back and forth trades with Enron simply to win a TV set, the award for highest trading volume that day.[168] More seriously, the practice seems to have been institutionalized in several companies. A gas trader described the standard practice thus: Company analysts circulated on the trading floor each month and calculated the price that would most benefit each trading desk at each market hub. The analyst would then create trades and work the prices to arrive at the weighted average that would most favor the company. These trades were then reported to the publications.[169]

The disclosures of false data to index publishers vindicated the outspoken views of the head of a large, independent natural gas producing company, Raymond Plank of

---

[165] *Id.* at 53.

[166] Mitchell Benson et al., *Trade Disclosures Shake Faith in Damaged Electricity Market*, WALL ST. J., May 13, 2002, at A1. Round-tripping or wash trading is not illegal on these unregulated, over-the-counter exchanges. On the stock exchange and futures exchanges like NYMEX, such conduct is illegal, and regulators have prosecuted traders who inflated trading in a security to affect its price or to give the illusion that the security is trading in a liquid market. However, round-trip trading may ultimately violate securities regulations if the trades are materially misleading to the investing public.

[167] *Id.*

[168] Richard A. Oppel, Jr., *Report Voices Suspicions on Energy Crisis*, N.Y. TIMES, Aug. 14, 2002, at C1.

[169] Michael Davis, *Energy Traders Say Giving Out False Information Was Common*, HOUS. CHRON., Dec. 16, 2002, at 1A, 11A.

Apache, who had been saying for years that the indices were not accurate.[170] He and others have called for an index published by a government agency with standardized reporting rules and the power to impose penalties for false submissions.

Five companies, Dynegy, AEP, CMS, El Paso, and Williams, admitted that some of their traders had done round-trip trades.[171] Many companies fired traders for passing false data, in an attempt to self-regulate and regain credibility.[172] Criminal indictments and arrests of traders punctuated the headlines in December 2002 and early 2003.[173] Some companies instructed employees to suspend reporting any information to publications, making price transparency in these markets even more problematic.[174] An editorial in the *Houston Chronicle*, the hometown newspaper of many of these traders, read:

> Apparently, it has been common practice for energy trading firms to pass around phony energy price information to publications that track energy markets. . . .
>
> A small number of key newsletters use [this] price information to determine prices on gas contracts that are worth billions of dollars. Utility companies can end up overcharging millions of customers . . . if traders are lying about trade prices. . . . [D]eregulation is not supposed to be a way for companies to use fraud to benefit their own bottom line at everyone else's expense.[175]

---

[170] The former director of gas research at *Gas Daily* testified that the prevalence of false price information supplied to that publication was so blatant that she received permission to contract with PriceWaterhouseCoopers to conduct an audit. The audit never occurred because Platt, a competing publisher, purchased *Gas Daily*. Enron was Platt's largest customer. Harvey Rice, *Gas Price Fudging Detailed*, HOUS. CHRON., Nov. 19, 2002, at 5B.

[171] Dynegy was the first company to settle with the CFTC over the practice of submitting false data to publications, paying a $5 million fine. Michael Davis, *$5 Million Settlement for Dynegy*, HOUS. CHRON., Dec. 20, 2002, at C1.

[172] *AEP Cracks Down on Traders in Bid for Credibility*, REUTERS, Oct. 9, 2002 (Energy Central Professional online). Laura Goldberg, *Dynegy Dismisses 6 Workers*, HOUS. CHRON., Oct. 19, 2002, at 1C.

[173] Todd Geiger, a former vice president at El Paso, was indicted on December 4, 2002 for submitting 48 false gas trades to *Inside FERC*, which did not use the trades in its index because the prices were outliers, too far from normal. Laura Goldberg, *El Paso ex-VP Indicted*, HOUS. CHRON., Dec. 5, 2002, at 1A, 6A. Michelle Valencia, a former trader with Dynegy, was indicted in January 2003. Laura Goldberg, *Former Dynegy Trader Charged in Pricing Case*, HOUS. CHRON., Jan. 27, 2003 (online). In February 2003, another Enron trader (the first was Timothy Belden) pleaded guilty to criminal charges of attempting to manipulate the California energy market. Rebecca Smith, *Former Enron Trader Pleads Guilty on Conspiracy Count*, WALL ST. J., Feb. 4, 2003 (online).

[174] *Fear Clouds Pricing in U.S. Power, Gas Markets*, REUTERS, Nov. 21, 2002 (Energy Central Professional online). Chip Cummins, *Natural-Gas Prices Thrown in Doubt*, WALL ST. J., Nov. 12, 2002, at C1, C12.

[175] Editorial, *Phony Baloney*, HOUS. CHRON., Dec. 18, 2002, at 25A.

F. The FERC Staff's Final Report on Western Price Manipulation, March 2003

[P]rice index manipulation was part of the price formation process.[176]

—FERC Final Report on Western Price Manipulation, 2003

This long-awaited final report by FERC tests both the ability and resolve of this agency to prove that it can fairly and effectively police market participants and assure that gas and electric markets operate in the public interest. Its 350 pages of analysis, explanation, econometric studies and data conclude that many participants in the California market did indeed exercise market power, illegally game the California system, and manipulate gas and electric prices in very significant ways. Enron's business model is revealed as being more predatory than anyone had yet claimed.[177] In fact, it is impossible to read the report without being both riveted and appalled by what transpired in California and by the many market participants—not just Enron—identified as profiteers in this out-of-control market.

The core objective of the Final Report was to analyze whether spot power prices in the West were just and reasonable in 2000–2001 and whether spot power prices adversely affected long-term power prices in the bilateral contracts that California signed in spring 2001 as the state attempted to escape the spot market gone awry. The answers are: no, spot prices were not just and reasonable; and yes—spot prices affected forward prices. The report looks backwards at past events with sharply keener eyes than FERC once had, and it looks forward, searching for ways to rebuild trading markets that can be trusted. The report contains known truths and new surprises. One chapter alone names 37 entities—private enterprises and public entities like municipalities and the Los Angeles Department of Water and Power—and recommends that they be subject to show-cause hearings to disgorge profits from illegal gaming of the California market protocols.[178]

The report will clearly be used in litigation, in policy debates in many state, regional, and federal forums, and, hopefully, as a training guide to market monitors in regulatory agencies and to those market participants that wish to avoid a future show-cause order. Despite its many charts and graphs of dry data and econometric studies, large sections of the report read as a *Who's Who of Market Rogues* and a reverse-engineered guide on *How to Be a Millionaire by Manipulating the Physical and Financial Gas and Electric Power Markets,* on a par with Fagin's instructions to Oliver Twist on

---

[176] FERC FINAL REPORT 2003, *supra* note 112, at III-16.

[177] *Id.* at VI-37 to VI-40. Enron formed "strategic business alliances" with small municipal utilities and QFs (the qualifying facilities promoted by PURPA in geothermal, wind, and cogeneration) and effectively gained control over the assets of these smaller parties, without filing any information with FERC that it controlled significant generation by using these entities as "sleeves" over Enron's muscled arm.

[178] *Id.* at VI-35 to VI-36.

how to be a good pickpocket. A brief summary of the Final Report's major findings follows, in the same order as the four major problem areas identified and discussed in the preceding section:

Gaming a Flawed Deregulatory Plan. The FERC report concluded that almost all of the colorfully named Enron trading schemes violated the FERC-approved rules of California's Market Monitoring and Information Protocol ("MMIP"), which prohibited "gaming" and "anomolous market behavior."[179] The schemes thereby violated FERC's tariff provisions. The protocol's broad anti-gaming prohibitions, while not prohibiting any specific behavior, gave market participants ample notice that misconduct that adversely affected the efficient operation of the California ISO and Power Exchange markets was illegal. Inflated bidding and economic withholding of generation violated the protocol. Moreover, a FERC order issued in April 2001 forbad "hockey stick" bidding, in which the last megawatts bid from a unit are bid at an excessively high price relative to the bids on the other output from the same unit.[180]

This part of the report is likely to be quite controversial, at least to economists. The power generators argued that no protocol required that they bid only at their marginal cost of production (reflecting actual supply cost conditions of their own units, as FERC interpreted the rules). They argued that FERC's interpretation did not recognize market uncertainty, scarcity rents, and opportunity costs that are the foundation of micro-economic pricing in competitive markets with supply shortages.[181] FERC staff found their arguments unpersuasive and an inadequate explanation of the timing of many of the dramatic price spikes. The staff recommended that the companies involved be ordered to show cause why they should not be made to disgorge their unjust and illegal profits.

The response of many of the companies named in the report was immediate and loud: the protocol rules were too vague to provide adequate notice of illegal behavior, some of the amounts at issue were trivial, and some of the suggested remedies, such as revoking certain companies' power to trade at market-based rates, were too harsh and would destroy investment in the trading sector.[182]

Physically Withholding Generating Power. The allegation that generators physically withheld power is probably the most damaging of all the charges against market participants. The allegation is easy for the public to understand (compared to phantom

---

[179] *Id.* at VI-6 to VI-10.

[180] *Id.* at VI-45 to VI-54.

[181] *Id.* at VI-52 to VI-54.

[182] *See, e.g.,* Mark Golden, *Calif Power Sellers Say FERC Charges Rest on Vague Rules,* WALL ST. J., Apr. 14, 2003 (online); Mark Golden, *Power Points: Second Thoughts on FERC's California D-Day,* WALL ST. J., Mar. 31, 2003 (online). Duke Energy countered that the market monitors themselves did not know the purpose, meaning, or scope of the protocol's provisions. *Duke: CA Monitoring Rules Lack "Clarity" to Justify FERC Retroactive Sanctions,* NGI's POWER MARKET TODAY, Apr. 7, 2003 (Energy Central Professional online).

congestion and load shifts) and easy to link to real health and safety dangers caused by blackouts. Here, the FERC report is only a few paragraphs long, citing to the $13.8 million fee paid by Reliant to settle the charges that it withheld power for two days in June 2000.[183] The report states that other entities have submitted evidence of additional alleged incidents of feigned maintenance, but a separate investigation was addressing these allegations.

The issue of physical withholding seems to be a particularly difficult one to resolve. As noted in a report by the General Accounting Office, it is practically impossible to tell when a unit is down for bona fide, rather than feigned, repairs.[184] Strangely, however, this FERC report does not even mention a second report that FERC released on the same day in March 2003. The second staff report analyzed a prior California PUC ("CPUC") report, dated September 17, 2002, which had concluded that five merchant generators (the quintet of Duke, Dynegy, Mirant, Reliant, and Williams) had withheld significant amounts of power on the 38 days that Californians experienced interrupted electricity service.[185] The CPUC report charged that most blackouts could have been avoided had these generators not curtailed their plant's output.

The second FERC report concluded that the CPUC study was inaccurate. After reviewing reams of data, FERC could account for almost all the power that the CPUC report had identified as withheld power.[186] However, the FERC report itself cautioned that its conclusions were very narrow. FERC staff only looked at six days when firm service customers experienced actual blackouts, and FERC assumed that all reported plant outages were legitimate. The report noted that the analysis that the CPUC tried to do was "extremely difficult and complex given the variables and the recordkeeping systems in place" at the California ISO during the crisis.[187] Errors in the log and outage database accounted for 31 percent of the power allegedly withheld.[188] Perhaps similar difficulties are slowing the thorough investigation of physical withholding on a broader scale in California markets. The number of hours required to do this type of detailed analysis is enormous. The data errors of the magnitude found by FERC show the need for much better systems of data collection and analysis and much better training of market monitors.

Affiliate Abuse in the Gas Pipeline Sector. Shortly before the Final Report was released, El Paso agreed to a $1.7 billion settlement of charges that its pipeline affiliate

---

[183] *Id.* at VI-54 to VI-55.

[184] U.S. GENERAL ACCOUNTING OFFICE, ENERGY MARKETS: RESULTS OF STUDIES ASSESSING HIGH ELECTRICITY PRICES IN CALIFORNIA (GAO-01-857) (June 2001).

[185] STAFF OF FEDERAL ENERGY REGULATORY COMMISSION, REVIEW OF CALIFORNIA PUBLIC UTILITY COMMISSION'S SEPTEMBER 17, 2002 INVESTIGATIVE REPORT ON WHOLESALE ELECTRIC GENERATION, Mar. 26, 2003.

[186] *Id.* at 4–5.

[187] *Id.* at 8.

[188] *Id.* at 22–23.

had withheld natural gas supplies to California so that its marketing affiliate could profit from selling scarce gas into the market during the crisis. Thus, the final report does not discuss this issue.

Manipulating Gas and Electric Price Indices. About half of the FERC Final Report analyzes the pervasive dysfunctions in gas price reporting that then fed into the spot prices for electricity. The data show that the spot gas prices in California reflected extraordinary differentials that far exceeded the price of gas produced in states like Texas and then shipped at regulated rates. Three chapters of the report document with great detail the behavior that led to these extraordinary spot gas prices. One chapter is devoted to the "churning" trades of a single Reliant trader at Topock, a major delivery point for gas shipped on El Paso's interstate pipeline.[189] Churning is the rapid, high-volume buying and selling of physical gas in quick bursts designed to significantly increase its price. Reliant profited from its churning by selling gas at the top of the price climb that it created.

Reliant was such a large presence at Topock, where EnronOnline traded gas, that its churning inflated the entire market price. FERC's econometric studies showed that the price of gas would have been more than $8 dollars per MMBTUs lower in December 2000 if Reliant had not churned.[190] (For comparison, the spot price of gas averaged about $3 dollars per MMBTUs in Southern California for most of 1999.) Incredibly, Reliant's churning did not violate FERC's blanket certificate under which it sold gas. Therefore, no illegal profits could be disgorged.

Because Reliant's churned trades took place on EnronOnline's real-time screen, all gas traders everywhere could see these sudden surges in buying and selling large volumes. Only Enron and Reliant would know why the screen price was moving up. The EnronOnline spot gas prices were fed into the published trade indices for spot gas. Indeed, the correlation between the EnronOnline price and the *Gas Daily* index price was virtually perfect.[191]

Reliant profited handsomely from the churning whenever it was a net buyer of physical gas. In addition, Reliant's financial derivatives trader made millions of dollars on the price churning in the physical gas market.[192] Enron also earned lucrative returns from the huge information advantage that EnronOnline gave it over competitors. Only Enron traders knew both sides of the market trades. Enron leveraged its information advantage about the physical gas market into large speculative positions in the financial markets, earning more than $500 million in 2000 and 2001.[193] The staff report estimated that California gas buyers paid excessive gas costs of as much as

---

[189] FERC FINAL REPORT 2003, *supra* note 112, at Ch. II.

[190] *Id.* at II-60.

[191] *Id.* at II-6.

[192] *Id.* at II-32 to II-43; II-50 to II-57.

[193] *Id.* at VIII-1 to VIII-6.

$1.15 billion for the refund period of October 2000 through June 20, 2001. These excess costs then would have inflated electric spot prices by some $1.2 billion for December 2000 alone.[194]

Another chapter of the Final Report reviewed the evidence that companies manipulated the gas price indices to benefit their own positions in the power markets. The report found that false data reporting was not limited to California markets. For example, El Paso Merchant's trades in the Northeast, mid-Continent, and Gulf Coast failed to match actual trades 99 percent of the time.[195] El Paso systematically reported data according to its "book bias," that is, its trading position. Some traders reported EnronOnline prices as their own, again indicating Enron's influence on the published indices. In a stunning disclosure, the final report found that Enron traders used EnronOnline to manipulate the Henry Hub market price in order to make huge profits in financial derivatives by selling short when the price was rising, knowing that the price would soon fall.[196] Few participants in the industry would have believed that a trader could influence the largest and most liquid trading hub for natural gas in the United States.

Because of the overwhelming evidence that spot gas prices were artificially high, the FERC report concluded that these inflated prices should not be used in the California Refund Proceeding to compute the just and reasonable clearing prices for the spot power market. Instead, FERC should use a mitigated price based on the producing-area gas price plus transportation to California, which would reduce gas costs used in the refund formula by more than $7 per MMBTU's in southern California.

The FERC report then linked the dysfunctions in the spot gas and electric markets to the forward price for electricity sold under long-term contracts entered into during the spring of 2000. With the help of a highly respected academic economist, Robert Pindyck, the FERC staff analyzed whether the inflated prices in the spot markets tainted the forward contracting market for electricity.[197] Because electricity cannot be stored, one would expect to see little or no relationship between the spot price today and the forward price for electricity sold, say, two years from today. However, the study found that a "statistically significant and economically important"[198] relationship existed, especially for contracts of one-to-two years' duration. To illustrate, such contracts had actual prices averaging $153 per megawatt-hour. An undistorted, competitive price would be expected to average about $100 per megawatt-hour, or one-third less.[199] The

---

[194] *Id.* at II-59 to II-60.

[195] *Id.* at III-3.

[196] *Id.* at III-36 and IX-12 to IX-24. In another instance, Enron moved the price of gas in the physical market by only ten cents per million BTUs, but this earned it a $3 million profit in the financial markets. *Id.* at IX-9 to IX-11. *Id.* at IX-9 to IX-11.

[197] *Id.* at V-1 to V-5.

[198] *Id.* at V-12.

[199] *Id.* at V-17.

staff recommended that FERC send its analysis to the Administrative Law Judge hearing the complaints seeking to modify the long-term contracts.

Shortly after the Final Report was released in March 2003, Commissioners Pat Wood and Nora Brownell indicated that they were unlikely to modify any long-term contracts, saying that modification would impose more harm on the market than would leaving them intact. The principle of sanctity of contract was necessary to provide stability in the energy markets and to attract capital investment back into the industry. The commissioners' comments raised a storm of protest from California officials who were pressing for $9 billion in additional refunds, largely from modifications of the price in the long-term contracts for electric power. As one California consumer group declared: "[F]or FERC to say 'Oh, they robbed you,' affirms what we already know. The question is what FERC is going to do about it, and the answer so far is not much."[200]

The FERC commissioners have unanimously found that prices in the spot market for electricity were not just and reasonable. With the finding that these dysfunctional prices flowed through to the forward markets, FERC will have a difficult task arguing that the forward prices were nonetheless just and reasonable such that the contracts should be upheld. In this regard, the standard to be used in determining the modification issue is likely to make all the difference. FERC will have to justify its refusal to modify the contracts by raising the bar in suits brought to abrogate unjust contracts: Even though prices are unjust and unreasonable, the higher "public interest" standard of review will allow the contracts to stand, as real signals of the sanctity of contract.[201]

The public may well ask what "public interest" is served by preserving contracts that reflect the extensive manipulation of market forces by participants acting deceitfully and in violation of market rules. The industry's abysmal conduct in the energy markets has put FERC in a no-win position on this issue.

IV. CAN ENERGY MARKETS BE TRUSTED?[202]

Mainstream economics still stumbles because the market's dazzling benefits half blind it to the defects. On the other hand, many critics perceive the benefits only through the smoke of their burning disapprobation. . . . There is not much intellectual interchange on the market system between

---

[200] Stephanie M. Ingersoll et al, *FERC Ups California Refunds by $1.5 Billion: Officials Disappointed with Likely Increase*, DAILY REP. FOR EXECUTIVES, Mar. 27, 2003, at A-40 to A-41.

[201] The difference in standards of review under the "public interest" standard and the "unjust and unreasonable" standard is discussed in FERC Docket No. PL02-7-000, *Standard of Review for Proposed Changes to Market-Based Contracts*, Aug. 1, 2002.

[202] Section IV of this essay is a revised form of Section VIII of the lengthier article appearing in Weaver, *supra* note 93, 3 HOUS. BUS & TAX L. J. (forthcoming 2004). The omitted sections of the article include: Section IV, titled *Where Was FERC?*; Section V, titled *Reforms—Actual and Proposed* (discussing reforms in Congress, at FERC, and industry self-reform of codes of conduct; Part VI, titled *The Fallout* (describing the effect of the disclosures of market manipulation, affiliate abuse, and gaming on the companies,

economists, most of whom admire it, and scholars of history and philosophy who judge its consequences for values like freedom, rationality and
morality.[203]

—Charles E. Lindblom, *The Market System,* 2001

[T]here is no substitute for seeing whether competition does in fact succeed rather than assuming it will not.[204]

—Alfred E. Kahn, 1998

So, should we plunge forward, as Alfred Kahn suggests, or engage in dialogue first
about the morality and rationality of markets? How many of you read the transcripts
of the energy trader's voices captured in this essay—giddy with delight at the prospect
of gaming the California system—without a sense of outrage at the market ethic embodied in the profit and bonus incentives underlying their decisions? Did no trader
contemplate the chaos caused by blackouts—the possibility of serious injuries and
deaths from failed traffic lights, elevators, or medical equipment? What were the traders thinking as California's dairy and agricultural businesses threw out large quantities
of milk and other perishables; as pumping stations for gasoline and jet fuel pipelines
shut down, leaving San Francisco airport and motorists in peril; as breweries laid off
workers and Silicon Valley businesses paid punitively high prices for electricity rather
than shut down?[205] Here is the reaction of energy traders when one of their own stars,
Timothy Belden, pled guilty to criminal fraud for submitting false information to the
California ISO: "What law did he break? Wire fraud—that's a joke, that's Mafia stuff."[206]

---

on energy policy, and on the national economy); and Section VII titled *The Future* (discussing the decline
in energy trading and the prospects of further energy restructuring, especially through demand-side response innovations).

[203] CHARLES E. LINDBLOM, THE MARKET SYSTEM: WHAT IT IS, HOW IT WORKS, AND WHAT TO
MAKE OF IT 3 (2001).

[204] Vicky A. Bailey, *Reassessing the Role of Regulators of Competitive Energy Markets, or: Walking the Walk
of Competition*, 20 ENERGY L.J. 1 (1999) (quoting ALFRED E. KAHN, INSTITUTE OF PUBLIC UTILITIES
AND NETWORK INDUSTRIES, LETTING GO: DEREGULATING THE PROCESS OF DEREGULATION 43
(1998)). Alfred Kahn is the towering economist who headed the Civil Aeronautics Board and initiated the
deregulation of the airline industry over two decades ago.

[205] Tapan Munroe & Leslie Baroody, *California's Flawed Deregulation—Implications for the State and
the Nation*, 26 J. ENERGY & DEV. 159, 167–171 (2001).

[206] Mark Golden, *Power Points: Politics Show in Pursuit of Ex-Enron Trader, Special Report on Enron
Corporation*, DOW JONES NEWSLETTERS, Oct. 31, 2002, at 10. The traders interviewed at an energy
traders' conference wanted to know specifically what Belden had done wrong, as if giving false information to the California ISO was not enough. The executive director of the Western Power Trading Forum,
who once considered Belden a friend, now appeared to view him as a traitor. A second Enron trader,
Jeffrey Richter, subsequently pleaded guilty to manipulating prices during the California energy crisis by
submitting false information about energy schedules and emergency backup power to the California ISO.
Mary Flood, *Ex-Trader Pleads Guilty to Schemes*, HOUS. CHRON., Feb. 5, 2003 (online).

To many traders, the politics of "megawatt McCarthyism" was unfairly focusing too many government investigations on the merchant energy sector.[207]

If these voices bother you, then join the great debate that Charles Lindblom posits as his thesis: "[T]here are great unsettled issues about a place for the market system in the future of any society."[208]

To Lindblom, an economist, the marvels of the market abound—in its ability to coordinate, induce cooperation, and promote the freedom of individual choice. But its darker side is also all too apparent. In his view, two power elites exist in the market system: the elected political elite and the managerial elite that controls business enterprises. But, between the two, corporations have the upper hand because they must be induced with incentives to produce and provide jobs and tax revenues to society. The corporate elite have a privileged position of power in the political system, and political leaders will act to provide business with whatever its says it needs to do its job. In Lindblom's view, the enormous influence of the business elite on legislative policies at all levels of government seriously distorts the democratic nature of our society.

Lindblom's thesis finds considerable support in other studies tracing the reasons behind the great transformation in regulated industries law in the transportation, telecommunications, and energy sectors over the last few decades. The original paradigm of regulation charged an administrative agency with strong regulatory oversight of particular industries. The new paradigm views the goals of regulation as the promotion of competition and consumer choice. Once in place, competition and choice will police the markets without much need for a regulatory bureaucracy.[209] "Light-handed" regulation will suffice. The reasons for this paradigm shift have been found to be twofold: First, key interest groups, notably large business interests, discovered that deregulation was to their advantage;[210] and second, economists and other policy elites reached an ideological consensus that the risks of regulatory failure under the original paradigm exceeded the risk of market failure under the new paradigm.[211] To date, large industrial and commercial users have been the chief recipients of benefits from competition in electricity and natural gas.[212] And there is so much money being spent on

---

[207] Golden, *Power Points, supra* note 206, at 10; *see also* Peter Rosenthal, Outlook Opinion, *Too Much Heat on Energy Trade Costs Consumers*, HOUS. CHRON., Jan. 10, 2003, at 20A (regulatory agencies are making energy trading hazardous to a company's financial well-being and to traders' personal liberty by arresting traders for reporting false prices. Consumers will end up paying a higher cost as trading volume falls and markets become less liquid.).

[208] LINDBLOM, *supra* note 203, at 14.

[209] Joseph D. Kearney & Thomas W. Merrill, *The Great Transformation of Regulated Industries Law*, 98 COLUM. L. REV. 1323 (1998).

[210] Lindblom's sweeping view probably overstates industry's embrace of deregulation. In some cases, such as airlines and trucking, industry had to be dragged into deregulation. *See generally*, SAM PELTZMAN & CLIFFORD WINSTON (eds.), DEREGULATION OF NETWORK INDUSTRIES: WHAT'S NEXT? (2000).

[211] *See generally,* Kearney & Merrill, *supra* note 209.

[212] *Id.* at 1393–97. Of course, lower industrial and commercial prices should ultimately trickle through to lower-priced products and services for consumers.

political lobbying by every major group within the electricity industry that cynics say that Congress has little incentive to resolve energy issues quickly.

As to the ideological consensus, strongly fostered by economists, that markets are superior to regulation, there is little doubt that this ideology has been a major factor in electricity restructuring. This ideology explains FERC's long reluctance to intervene in the chaos of California and California's own embrace of a Power Exchange as the ultimate market of all power markets. The California crisis precipitated an extraordinary round of competing "manifestos" by prominent economists. The true believers urged officials to resist any form of price cap, while those who recognized the reality of dysfunctional markets urged regulatory intervention.[213] Another manifesto was issued in January 2003, urging California to create commodity market institutions, to implement real-time pricing, and to "rely on markets whenever possible."[214]

But when are markets "possible"? Here are the words of a former FERC commissioner, inspired by Alfred Kahn's words, describing her goal of speeding up merger applications in the energy industry to enhance efficiency and competition:

> In a concurring statement attached to a recent merger order, I expressed concern that the Commission, in setting a merger application for hearing on its competitive effects, deemed itself unable to assess the adequacy of the applicants' various commitments to alleviate any potential adverse merger-related effects on competition.[215]

Admitting that she tended to err on the side of competition versus regulation, she then wrote:

> . . . I felt compelled to concur separately in a recent order . . . in which the utility decided—for no reason other than to avoid immediately reporting price information—to divide up a three-year power sale transaction into three separate, identical one-year power sales. . . . I am discouraged to see deals structured in a manner simply to defeat Commission information requirements.[216]

One of the lessons of California is that this type of light-handed regulation combined with the entrepreneurial, profit-maximizing behavior of private participants does not serve the public well.

---

[213] *See, e.g.,* Carolyn Whetzel, *Bush Turns Aside Davis Request for Wholesale Electric Power Relief*, DAILY REP. FOR EXECUTIVES, May 30, 2001, at A-38. Alfred Kahn, the inspirational mentor of deregulation, signed the manifesto advocating regulatory intervention.

[214] The January 2003 manifesto was posted at www.haas.berkeley.edu/news/manifesto.

[215] Vicky A. Bailey, *Reassessing the Role of Regulators of Competitive Energy Markets, or: Walking the Walk of Competition*, 20 ENERGY L.J. 1 at 6–7 (2001).

[216] *Id.* at 13.

So, can electricity markets be trusted? Here again is Fukuyama's definition of trust as "the expectation that arises within a community of regular, honest, and cooperative behavior."[217] I think the easy answer is: No. They cannot be trusted to work without a high degree of government intervention that true believers will continue to find "offensive"[218] and continue to criticize as retarding the "dazzling benefits" that markets can provide. In this conclusion, I have the company of others:

> [T]he process of deregulation is more corruptible than the process of regulation. . . .[I]t is absolutely clear that if we are to pursue "deregulation," then we must be willing to regulate deregulation.[219]

> —Alan Richardson, American Public Power
> Association President, June 2002

> The curious paradox of a market-based regulatory reform [in electricity] is that we may end up with more rather than less regulation.[220]

> —Joseph P. Tomain, Dean and Professor of Law, 2002

And will the government intervention be well-designed even when it incorporates lessons learned from experience? FERC has learned this lesson from its study of market problems in California and the Northeast:

> Small details of market design can turn out to have major effects on market performance."[221]

> —FERC's proposal for Standard Market Design, July 2002

---

[217] FUKUYAMA, *supra* note 4, at 26.

[218] In November 2000, then-FERC Commissioner Curt L. Hebert stated that he found the concept of government-imposed price mitigation to be an "offensive one." Rather, energy suppliers and consumers should be "entrusted with the ability and the responsibility to mitigate their price exposures as they deem best." San Diego Gas & Elec. Co. v. Sellers of Energy & Ancillary Services, 93 FERC ¶ 61,121 (Nov. 1, 2000), Docket No. EL00-95-000, Order Proposing Remedies for California Wholesale Electric Markets, concurring opinion.

[219] *Richardson: Corruption, Deregulation Go Hand in Hand*, PUBLIC POWER WEEKLY, June 17, 2002 (Energy Central Professional online).

[220] Joseph P. Tomain, *2002 Energy Law Symposium: The Past and Future of Electricity Regulation*, 32 ENVTL. LAW 435, 474 (2002).

[221] Notice of Proposed Rulemaking, *Remedying Undue Discrimination Through Open Access Transmission Service and Standard Market Design*, App. E at 8, available at 67 Fed. Reg. 55,451 (proposed Aug. 29, 2002). True believers in privatized utility markets often use "the devil was in the details" as justification for proceeding with privatization as a goal, despite its spectacular failure in particular instances. *See, e.g.*, the Reason Foundation's response to Atlanta, Georgia's, failed water privatization in Rick Brooks, *A Deal All Wet: Atlanta's Plan for Water Privatization Failed*, WALL ST. J., Jan. 31, 2003, at C4.

If the "devil is in the details," but the details are so difficult to get right because electricity has such unique attributes compared to any other commodity, then it is time to say that markets have met their match in this arena.[222] Certainly, electricity markets can and will be designed to avoid the more obvious flaws in California's noble, but failed, experiment. For example, a "churn alarm" in the monitoring programs can be devised to detect extraordinary trading volumes.[223] But the real question is whether deregulated energy markets will produce a better grade than the C+ that Pat Wood gave to traditional utility regulation. The FERC chairman is hoping for a grade of B for restructured markets.[224] In my mind, the mid-term grade to date for deregulation is a U for "unsatisfactory." Residential consumers have, for too long, been wooed with hyperbolic promises of great benefits from electricity deregulation—lower rates, more reliability, and greater choice.[225] There is little evidence that restructured markets will reduce electricity rates in any meaningful amount for the residential consumer.[226]

Reliability becomes more precarious as the industry "de-integrates" into competitive rather than coordinated units. And no one in these new markets—except traders, and then only sometimes—appears to like the volatility that has accompanied deregulation.[227] The dreaded Averch-Johnson inefficiency of regulated utilities does not seem

---

[222] Even in simpler markets, such as auctions for the telecommunications spectrum, "disastrous" results have occurred because "superficially trivial" distinctions between policy proposals were actually quite important and because the economic consultants' market design, while sound in theory, could not translate into good policy, given real-world political pressures, including lobbying from the regulated industry. Paul Klemperer, *Using and Abusing Economic Theory*, Discussion Paper No. 3813, Centre for Economic Policy Research, Mar. 2003, *available at* www.cepr.org/pubs. Dr. Klemperer delivered this paper as the 2002 Alfred Marshall Lecture to the Annual Congress of the European Economic Association.

[223] The FERC staff recommended a churn alarm, even though it might generate a large proportion of false positives. FERC FINAL REPORT 2003, *supra* note 112, at IX-40.

[224] *Enron Had No Apparent Impact on Markets, Delivery to Consumers, FERC's Wood Says*, DAILY REP. FOR EXECUTIVES, Jan. 29, 2002, at A-27. Pat Wood's comments on the grades were made before the May 2002 release of the memos detailing Enron's trading schemes in California and before the FERC Staff reports on Western price manipulation.

[225] In 1994, Jeff Skilling, then Chief Executive Officer at Enron, told the California Public Utilities Commission that annual savings to California voter-citizens from electricity deregulation would be $9 billion, an amount that could pay off the interest on the state's debt and fund new teachers and police in all the major cities of the state. *Lawmaker Says Enron Duped California*, UNITED PRESS INT'L, Apr. 11, 2002 (Energy Central Professional online).

[226] See Weaver, *supra* note 93 (forthcoming 2003); and Paul L. Joskow, *The Difficult Transition to Competitive Electricity Markets in the U.S.*, Mar. 24, 2003 draft prepared for "Electricity Deregulation: Where to From Here?" conference, Bush Presidential Center, Texas A&M Univ., Apr. 4, 2003.

[227] Traders are not so happy when they are "fooled" by prices that move in the "wrong" direction. *See, e.g.,* Laura Goldberg, *Bad Deals Cost Reliant $80 Million*, HOUS. CHRON., Mar. 8, 2003, at 1C. Reliant, Houston's largest electricity provider, lost $80 million in speculative trading at a time that it was working with banks to restructure $5.9 billion in debt. The CEO of Reliant said the trading loss resulted from "unprecedented market volatility."

to be so large that deregulation will capture significant gains that regulators were not already capturing through incentive-based performance standards, mandatory competitive bidding by utilities for new generation supplies, and other mechanisms that were lowering electricity rates before restructuring began.[228] Increasingly, proponents of continuing deregulation point to "innovation" rather than price as the benefit that markets will most likely provide.[229] There is little evidence that these innovations are economic for the small consumer at this time.

In an overview of regulatory concepts and doctrines that have either survived or died out with the great transformation in regulated industries law, Professor Douglass Jones has found that "fairness" in both process and outcome still ranks as the central test of sound regulation, trumping efficiency even in this era of pro-market ideology.[230] The one unassailable lesson of California is that people expect electricity prices to be just and reasonable and that government will intervene—sooner or later, for better or for worse—to assure such an outcome. To date, restructuring in all the implementing states is a gerry-rigged, managed system of prices to beat, price caps, must-run orders, market monitors, and regulatory investigations—all designed to assure fairness. Electricity markets are being tried—but they are not trusted. These "managed-market" mechanisms are supposed to be temporary: a transitional phase necessary to allow real competition to gain a firm ground. But I agree with a long-time observer, practitioner, and scholar of energy markets, Judge Richard Cudahy:

> [I]t seems this prospect of an electricity regime "half slave and half free" makes it dubious that a market approach can work at all. Orthodox supporters of deregulation would be very skeptical that markets could ever work at all, if they are subject to suspension for what many would perceive as short-term or trivial reasons.[231]

---

[228] Douglass N. Jones, *Regulatory Concepts, Propositions, and Doctrines: Casualties, Survivors, Additions*, 22 ENERGY L.J. 41, 60 (about four-fifths of the states had authorized some form of incentive regulation which decoupled rates and costs as a kind of "halfway house" to full deregulation).

[229] *See, e.g.*, Clifford Winston, *U.S. Industry Adjustment to Economic Deregulation*, 12 J. ECON. PERSPECTIVES 89 (1998) (describing many innovations in the deregulated transport sector—rail, trucking, and air travel—that have benefited consumers and lowered prices). Real-time metering of electricity is the most often mentioned innovation, followed by a growth in distributed generation. Distributed generation uses new, small-scale technologies, such as mini-natural gas turbines, placed onsite at the user's home or place of business, to self-generate electricity, allowing users to escape dependence on the transmission grid (but not on the natural gas market). *See* AMORY B. LOVINS ET AL., SMALL IS PROFITABLE (2002). Innovations in distributed generation may well be driven by higher electricity prices, congested transmission lines, and less reliability in electric services—hardly a bright selling point for deregulation if these types of problems are themselves the result of a rocky transition to deregulated markets.

[230] Jones, *supra* note 228, at 54.

[231] Richard D. Cudahy, *Electric Deregulation After California: Down But Not Out*, 54 ADMIN. L. REV. 333, 355 (2002).

So, the question is: Can we trust government to intervene and design restructuring rules that allow competition, consumer choice, and fair and reasonable rates to co-exist in a hybrid system that is more regulated (albeit differently regulated) than the traditional utility model? Can market-based rates co-exist with price caps that have become a rather permanent part of the regulatory landscape of deregulation?[232] Can regulators stay one step ahead of market participants who, under a competitive regime, will naturally seek to test loopholes in market protocols to maximize profits—in ways that consumers will consider fundamentally unfair? In competitive electricity markets, participants can exploit legal loopholes or use market power to make millions of dollars in profits in a very short time.[233] And there is every reason to expect them to do so; it is the very nature of a profit-based capitalist system.

In Texas, a cold wave hit on February 24 and 25, 2003, and unusually high bids for power resulted in $17 million in additional power costs to users, due to the "hockey stick" bidding curve that prevails in electricity markets under scarcity conditions. While legal, the Texas Public Utility Commission's market monitor had not expected that this type of bidding would result in price jumps for certain services that were 45 to 80 times higher than those of the previous week.[234] The Texas commission has proposed new rules to limit the danger of a repeat of such a spike. Has the commission got it right? Dynegy Power Marketing, the company with the high bid, says that natural gas curtailments and higher electricity demand caused market-clearing prices. Does anyone really know what the "right price" should have been, or what it should be in the future, to serve as an efficient market signal? If not, how can this system be efficient? More importantly, how can it be fair—to either the consumer or to Dynegy?

The new restructured Texas electricity markets may not be a worse system than the traditional ratemaking we once had, but it certainly does not appear to be much better—or much different. Yet, it is the best "restructuring" that has been achieved to date in the United States.[235] Maybe this is Enron's dying gift to its home state and to the energy trading business that it began in Houston, Texas in the 1980s: We have done better than other states, even while the trading industry lies in shambles around us.

QUESTIONS

1. Why are competitive electricity markets so much more difficult to create and monitor than markets for other commodities?

---

[232] Jones, *supra* note 228, at 49 (2001). Price caps are often reviewed every few years in proceedings that do not differ that much from traditional cost-of-service ratemaking. *Id.* at 54.

[233] U.S. General Accounting Office, Concerted Actions Needed by FERC to Confront Challenges That Impede Effective Oversight 48–49 (2002) (GAO-02-656).

[234] Bill Hensel, Jr., *Price Spikes Not Going Unnoticed*, Hous. Chron., Mar. 8, 2003, at 1C.

[235] The Center for the Advancement of Energy Markets (CAEM) keeps a scorecard called the Red Index, rating progress on retail energy competition in the United States and various countries. Texas is ranked first among the states. See www.caem.org.

2. What parallels can you draw between the light-handed regulation by FERC of energy markets and the SEC's regulation of securities markets before Enron and other corporate scandals came to light? Congress passed the Sarbanes-Oxley Act to prevent future Enrons. Congress has not acted to strengthen federal control over energy markets. Why do you think this is so?

3. If you were a state legislator voting on a proposal to deregulate retail energy markets, what questions would you ask and what information would you demand before you voted?

4. Do you trust "firewalls" to be effective among a gas producing affiliate, pipeline affiliate, and marketing affiliate of a parent corporation? Or between an electric generator and its transmission or marketing affiliate? If not, should energy restructuring require real "restructuring" through the forced divestiture of assets?

5. If your state has adopted retail electricity restructuring, have you chosen a competitive supplier to provide your household electricity or have you stayed with your regulated utility? Did you trust one more than the other? Why?

Chapter 3

Enron and the Legal Environment

In Chapter 2, we linked Enron's downfall in part to a lack of integration of the work of the accountants and lawyers. The accountants gave advice and conducted audits, and the lawyers structured transactions, but their relationships with Enron were triangulated. Each gave advice to Enron, but they didn't seem to communicate with each other.

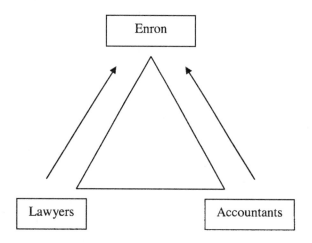

We believe that one way of preventing future Enrons is to make sure that lawyers know more about business concepts and that executives and accountants know more about legal issues. This chapter gives you the opportunity to explore the complexity of some of Enron's legal issues: bankruptcy issues, pension issues, criminal law issues, and corporate governance issues. The best executives don't try to supplant the advice of their professionals, but they do know a little about the various areas so that they can better evaluate that advice.

The Enron Bankruptcy

Charles J. Tabb[*]

1. INTRODUCTION

On Sunday, December 2, 2001, Enron Corp. and 13 affiliates[1] filed for Chapter 11 bankruptcy protection in the Southern District of New York. Thereafter, numerous other Enron affiliates filed. At the time, Enron was the largest bankruptcy filing in history; the affiliated entities listed over $63 *billion* in assets and debts of close to $50 billion.[2] To date, it has been one of the most complex bankruptcies in history. Indeed, it may be the most complex.[3] After eighteen months, over 10,000 documents have been filed in the case, and the lawyers in the case have received professional fees of over $400 million—a rate of $20 million per month—and the case is far from over.[4] After all this, it appears that Enron may be broken up and sold off piecemeal, rather than

---

[*] Alice Curtis Campbell Professor of Law, University of Illinois College of Law. I want to thank the following students from the University of Illinois College of Law, all of whom provided invaluable research assistance: James Antonopoulos; Jason Bohm; Jeffrey Davis; David Deschler; Joseph DiRago; Kristen Jacobsen; Mi-Seon (Tina) Kim; Christopher Leasor; Tyler Mertes; Linda Salfisberg; Peter Sgro; Cynthia Stencel; Jeffrey Stotler; Erin Sylvester; Aaron VanGetson; Kevin Van Hout; and Andrew Wool. Matthew Sostrin must be singled out for extraordinary contributions.

[1] The initial filing entities were: Enron Metals & Commodity; Enron Corp.; Enron North America Corp.; Enron Power Marketing, Inc.; PBOG Corp.; Smith Street Land Company; Enron Broadband Services, Inc.; Enron Energy Services Operations, Inc.; Enron Energy Marketing Corp.; Enron Energy Services, Inc.; Enron Energy Services L.L.C.; Enron Transportation Services Company; BAM Leasing Company; and ENA Asset Holdings, L.P. In addition, Enron stated in court documents that the affiliated group had more than 4,000 direct and indirect subsidiaries.

[2] Six months later, WorldCom surpassed this record. Its bankruptcy filing in July 2002 listed $107 billion in assets and $41 billion in debt. Simon Rivero & Riva D. Atlas, *WorldCom's Collapse: The Overview; Extra Level of Scrutiny in WorldCom Bankruptcy*, N.Y. TIMES, July 23, 2002, at C1.

[3] Mary Flood et al., *Far From Finished: Eighteen Months After Enron's Bankruptcy Filing, $400 Million Has Been Spent on Legal Bills, 20 People Have Been Charged and Loose Ends are Everywhere*, HOUS. CHRON., June 22, 2003, at Business 1.

[4] *Id.* (noting the amount is more than double any other bankruptcy on record).

being reorganized.[5] So, is this case the modern-day equivalent of Dickens' *Bleak House* tale of legal bilking in an endless case? Or is it, as the Bard observed in another context, "a tale told by an idiot, full of sound and fury, signifying nothing?"[6] Or is there a method to all this madness? This essay tells the tale of the Enron bankruptcy—so far.[7] By necessity of space, the essay presents but snippets from an extraordinarily complex landscape; a full treatment might rival Tolkien's massive *Lord of the Rings* (perhaps an apt analogy!).

The filing by Enron—the "crooked E"—marked its official fall from grace as the seventh largest *Fortune 500* company—a company that had employed 25,000 individuals, and in the prior year had generated revenues of over $100 billion.[8] Enron's filing followed close on the heels of the late November collapse of a proposed merger agreement with Dynegy, Inc. Enron's downfall was triggered in part by Enron's revelation that its stated balance sheet debt of $13 billion did *not* include another $25 billion in "off balance sheet" liabilities, meaning that the true debt picture was a bit higher—*viz.,* $38 billion. Much of that additional "debt" was generated by structured finance transactions with related parties. In the wake of that startling disclosure, additional "allegations surfaced of securities fraud, accounting irregularities, energy market price manipulation, money laundering, breach of fiduciary duties, misleading financial information, ERISA violations, insider trading, excessive compensation and wrongdoing by certain of Enron's bankers."[9]

In one swift public relations downdraft, Enron went from the poster child of the 1990s' economic boom to the premier symbol of corporate fraud, greed, and malfeasance marking the recession of the new millennium. Indeed, Enron's "evil ways" have even been dramatically portrayed in a made-for-television movie.[10] What better forum in our bankruptcy-happy culture to sort out the doings of such a financial misadventure than in the bankruptcy court?

2. VENUE[11]

Everyone knows that Enron is headquartered in Houston, Texas—it even had its own high-rise office building there, with the huge "crooked E" logo out front. So the

---

[5] Andrew Hill, *Bankrupt Enron Likely to be Broken Up*, FIN. TIMES, Feb. 17, 2003, at 1.

[6] WILLIAM SHAKESPEARE, MACBETH, act 5, sc. 5.

[7] A shameless borrowing from the title of the 1994 "greatest hits" album by rock group Crosby, Stills & Nash. This essay discusses most developments through June 22, 2003. Subsequent developments, such as the Second Examiner's Report, are discussed in the following essay.

[8] Useful background on the events leading up to Enron's filing may be found in the First Interim Report of Neal Batson, Court-Appointed Examiner, *In re* Enron Corp., No. 01-16034 (Bankr. S.D.N.Y. Sept. 21, 2002) [hereinafter First Interim Report], *available at* http://www.elaw4enron.com, docket entry no. 6615.

[9] *Id.* at 9.

[10] *The Crooked E: The Unshredded Truth About Enron* (CBS television broadcast, Jan. 5, 2003).

[11] I thank Cynthia Stencel for her excellent work on this section.

natural venue for the bankruptcy case would be in Houston, in the Southern District of Texas, right? Alas, no. Enron filed in New York City, in the Southern District of New York. How did it do that? Is Enron a New York corporation? No, it is an Oregon corporation. Did Enron have substantial business operations in New York? Not really. So what was the trick?

Simple, really. Just prior to Enron Corp.'s filing, an Enron *affiliated* company— Enron Metals & Commodity Corp. ("EMC")—filed a voluntary bankruptcy petition in the Southern District of New York. EMC did have its principal place of business in New York. This is known as the "venue hook."[12] Under section 1408(2) of the Bankruptcy Code, a debtor may file for bankruptcy protection in any jurisdiction where an affiliate already has a pending bankruptcy proceeding,[13] which gave Enron Corp. the green light to file in a jurisdiction away from its corporate headquarters or state of incorporation. In short, Enron was able to "forum shop" to a desired court.

Why New York? An Enron attorney justified the decision by pointing to New York's experience with complex cases and the availability of court time.[14] Indeed, Enron's choice of venue was not unusual. The Southern District of New York was a popular choice for bankruptcy filings in the 1980s, and four of the next five major corporate bankruptcy filings after Enron also were filed there.[15] Commentators have suggested that New York is attractive to corporate debtors (and their counsel!) not only because of supposed big-case expertise, but also because of convenience to the lawyers and generous grants of attorneys' fees.[16] Enron's chief bankruptcy counsel, the New York City firm of Weil, Gotshal & Manges, likes to "stay home" and likes the fees routinely awarded in bankruptcy cases in the Southern District of New York. For its work in the first four months of the case alone, Weil Gotshal received fees of over $23 million! Fees awarded in Texas, by contrast, likely would have been much lower. Furthermore, the New York court is known for its solicitude for corporate debtors, exemplified by lenient extensions of the debtor's 120-day "exclusive" right to file a reorganization plan, under 11 U.S.C. § 1121. Maintaining exclusivity is seen as a *sine qua non* of effective large corporate Chapter 11 practice. To date, Enron's strategy has worked on that front as well, as it has retained exclusivity fifteen months into the case.

---

[12] Lynn M. LoPucki & William C. Whitford, *Venue Choice and Forum Shopping in the Bankruptcy Reorganization of Large, Publicly Held Companies*, 1991 WIS. L. REV. 11, 22 (1991).

[13] 28 U.S.C. § 1408(2) (2002); *see also* 11 U.S.C. § 101(2) (2002) (defining affiliate broadly as any entity that owns 20% or more of debtor's securities and any entity whose securities are 20% or more owned by the debtor).

[14] *See* Rebecca Smith, *Enron Files for Chapter 11 Bankruptcy, Sues Dynegy*, WALL ST. J., Dec. 3, 2001, at A3.

[15] Gary Young, *Major Bankruptcies Filed in New York City*, N.Y.L.J., Aug. 1, 2002, at 5 (noting WorldCom, Global Crossing, Adelphia Communications, and NTL, Inc. also filed bankruptcy in the S.D.N.Y. court).

[16] LoPucki & Whitford, *supra* note 12, at 30–31, 36; *see also* Marcus Cole, *"Delaware is Not a State": Are We Witnessing Jurisdictional Competition in Bankruptcy?*, 55 VAND. L. REV. 1845 (2002).

Note that Enron could have filed in Delaware, because it had an affiliate incorporated there. Beginning in the 1990s, Delaware became a big-case venue favorite.[17] Like New York, the Delaware court was viewed as favorably inclined to the interests of corporate debtors and their counsel, and the court soon accumulated considerable experience in managing big cases. Ironically, though, the rush to Delaware eventually caused congestion there. Since Enron's counsel anticipated that the case would require considerable court time, they returned to the equally debtor-friendly confines of New York.

Despite the validity of Enron's venue choice under section 1408(2), Dynegy, Inc., other creditors, and groups of employees sought to transfer the venue to the Southern District of Texas pursuant to 28 U.S.C. § 1412 and Federal Rule of Bankruptcy Procedure 1014(a)(1), which, together, permit transfer in the interests of justice and for the convenience of parties. The Official Committee of Unsecured Creditors (several of whose members are located in New York) opposed the transfer motion. Bankruptcy Judge Arthur Gonzalez denied the motion on January 11, 2002.[18]

Judge Gonzalez considered "the efficient administration of the bankruptcy estate and matters of judicial economy, timeliness and fairness based upon the unique . . . complex corporate structure."[19] He noted that, where venue is proper, the debtor's choice of venue is entitled to great weight. The court reviewed the multiple parties involved in the Enron case and their locations, and pointed to the significant New York ties of those groups having an interest in the outcome of the bankruptcy plan or involved in its implementation.[20] While the judge considered the fact that thousands of Enron employees resided in Houston, he discounted the significance of that fact because many of the issues the employees sought to resolve would not be addressed in the bankruptcy. Furthermore, other individuals, such as Enron officers, would not be required for all hearings. Therefore, after an exhaustive review of the "convenience of parties," the court found that "Texas provides no better venue, and perhaps may be

---

[17] *See generally* Cole, *supra* note 16; Theodore Eisenberg & Lynn M. LoPucki, *Shopping for Judges: An Empirical Analysis of Venue Choice in Large Chapter 11 Reorganizations*, 84 CORNELL L. REV. 967 (1999); Lynn M. LoPucki & Sara D. Kalin, *The Failure of Public Company Bankruptcies in Delaware and New York: Empirical Evidence of a "Race to the Bottom,"* 54 VAND. L. REV. 231 (2001); Robert K. Rasmussen & Randall S. Thomas, *Whither the Race? A Comment on the Delawarization of Corporate Reorganizations*, 54 VAND. L. REV. 283 (2001); Robert K. Rasmussen & Randall S. Thomas, *Timing Matters: Promoting Forum Shopping by Insolvent Corporations*, 94 NW. U. L. REV. 1357 (2000); David A. Skeel, Jr., *What's So Bad About Delaware?*, 54 VAND. L. REV. 309 (2001); David A. Skeel, Jr., *Bankruptcy Judges and Bankruptcy Venue: Some Thoughts on Delaware*, 1 DEL. L. REV. 1 (1998).

[18] Memorandum Decision Regarding Movant's Request to Transfer Venue to the Southern District of Texas, *In re* Enron Corp., 274 B.R. 327 (Bankr. S.D.N.Y. 2002).

[19] *Id.* at 345.

[20] Six of the fifteen members of the Official Committee of Unsecured Creditors are in New York, compared with three in Texas. *Id.* at 335. Ten of the largest seventeen unsecured creditors are in New York; none are in Texas. *Id.* at 337. The professional legal advisors of the Enron debtors have main offices in New York. *Id.* at 339.

more inconvenient, than New York."[21] The judge observed, "The Debtors' multifaceted business enterprises affect parties throughout the nation and world. New York's accessibility for all creditors . . . weighs in favor of a New York venue."[22]

The judge's analysis with respect to the "interests of justice" prong seemed a bit self-rationalizing: he emphasized the court's experience with cases like Enron. He also relied on the availability of resources in New York to address complex financial matters in the case, and pointed to the "learning curve" already undertaken by the court.[23]

There is a widespread belief that one reason transfer of venue is difficult to achieve in large cases is due to the judge's own motives. Presiding over a high-profile bankruptcy case can be a "career opportunity," making judges reluctant to transfer the case from their district.[24] The filing of a high-profile case like Enron has been called a "prize" and commentators talk of the "competition" between the courts for these cases, which bring prestige and publicity to the court.[25]

At the end of the day, the moral of the story in large cases like Enron is: forget change of venue; it is not going to happen. The only solution would be a legislative one. The 1997 report of the National Bankruptcy Review Commission recommended amending section 1408 to limit forum shopping, and recent bankruptcy reform bills considered by Congress have adopted those recommendations. Until such legislation is enacted, however, expect Enron to be a venue exemplar.

3. WHO'S IN CHARGE?[26]

An issue that often raises concerns is who is in charge of the reorganization effort. Under the old Bankruptcy Act, the norm was for a trustee to be appointed in Chapter X cases and for the debtor to remain in possession in Chapter XI cases. The benefits of appointing an independent trustee included ferreting out fraud and ending mismanagement; the detriments were that the managers of corporate debtors resisted filing, fearing replacement, and that the debtor's business might founder while the newly appointed trustee got up to speed.[27]

---

[21] *Id.* at 345.

[22] *Id.*

[23] *Id.* at 350.

[24] LoPucki & Whitford, *supra* note 12, at 25–26 (discussing the unlikelihood of success of a motion to transfer venue); *see also id.* at 37–38 (describing the pressure on judges to attract large reorganization cases to their district for their own careers as well as for the local bar and local attorneys); Richard B. Schmitt & Michael Orey, *Courts Compete for High-Profile Bankruptcies*, WALL ST. J., Dec. 5, 2001, at B1 ("[It is] a point of pride that large companies have filed in [a particular] court.").

[25] Schmitt & Orey, *supra* note 24.

[26] Christopher Leasor did excellent work on this section.

[27] Charles J. Tabb, *The Future of Chapter 11*, 44 S.C. L. REV. 791, 854–861 (1993).

In the 1978 reform, which unified business reorganizations into a single chapter, Congress compromised: the strongly preferred norm is for the debtor to remain in possession, but in exceptional circumstances an independent trustee may be appointed for "cause" or in the "interests of creditors, any equity security holders, and other interests of the estate."[28] "Cause" includes "fraud, dishonesty, incompetence, or gross mismanagement of the affairs of the debtor by current management."[29] Enron's managers, by all accounts, had the singular "honor" of satisfying *all* of the statutory criteria for "cause" to appoint a trustee. So, has a trustee been appointed in the case? Perhaps surprisingly, the answer is "no." How can that be?

The answer lies in a two-part strategy. First, the old, corrupt management *was* all removed—but not for a trustee. Instead, Enron's Board of Directors appointed new management to run the company and shepherd the reorganization process. Second, as discussed in the next section, the Bankruptcy Court appointed an examiner to investigate Enron's questionable pre-bankruptcy financial transactions.

Some key managers were eased out even before the bankruptcy filing, the most notable being Andrew Fastow, Enron's Chief Financial Officer, who was placed on leave of absence on October 24, 2001. After the bankruptcy filing, the first of the old guard to go was Chief Executive Officer Kenneth Lay, who resigned that post on January 23, 2002. He then resigned from the company's Board of Directors on February 4, 2002. On February 12, 2002, the company announced that it was restructuring its Board of Directors. As part of this plan, six Board members announced their resignations, effective on March 14, 2002. By June 6, 2002, all of Enron's pre-bankruptcy Board members had resigned, with the exception of Raymond S. Troubh, who had been appointed to the Board on November 28, 2001, less than one week prior to Enron's bankruptcy filing.

On January 29, 2002, Enron appointed Stephen F. Cooper as its interim CEO and Chief Restructuring Officer. Mr. Cooper has 25 years' experience rehabilitating financially troubled companies. Enron elected two eminent, highly qualified independent directors on May 30, 2002, John W. Ballantine and Corbin A. McNeill, Jr., and its last new Board member, Ron W. Haddock, on July 25, 2002. Mr. Haddock's credentials typify the "new" Enron Board member model: he served as president and CEO of FINA, Inc. for eleven years and had 23 years of experience working for Exxon. This complete turnover in management was brought about by the previous Board's resolution to "reconstitute the Board in a prompt and orderly manner to a Board composed, at a minimum, of a majority of new independent Directors and, preferably, composed entirely of new independent Directors."[30]

---

[28] 11 U.S.C. § 1104(a) (2002).

[29] *Id.* at § 1104(a)(1).

[30] *Resolutions Unanimously Approved by the Board of Directors of Enron Corp. at a Meeting held on June 6, 2002, available at* http://www.enron.com/corp/pressroom/releases/2002/ene/docs/26-060602Release.pdf (last visited May 29, 2003).

The Enron Board decided to hire Mr. Cooper and to replace itself partly in order to avoid the appointment of a Chapter 11 trustee in the bankruptcy case.[31] By quickly replacing all of its management, especially with experienced turnaround expert Stephen Cooper at the helm, Enron can say that its "current management" had nothing to do with the alleged frauds of the previous management.[32] Indeed, "As a reorganization expert brought in to steer Enron through Chapter 11, Mr. Cooper essentially is already playing the role a trustee appointed by the bankruptcy court would fill."[33]

However, in the wake of the scandalous allegations surrounding Enron's downfall, several parties in interest filed motions to appoint a Chapter 11 trustee to oversee Enron's affairs.[34] The hearing on these motions was held on April 4, 2002. As a result of this hearing, Judge Gonzalez issued a stipulation and consent order that stated, "the parties have met and agree that the appointment of an Examiner for Enron Corp. with expanded powers is a more appropriate remedy" and that "the parties recognize that it is in their best interests to adjourn the hearing of these motions."[35] On April 8, 2002, Judge Gonzalez issued an order that authorized the U.S. Trustee to appoint an examiner instead of a trustee.[36] The U.S. Trustee selected Neal Batson on May 22, 2002 to be the examiner for Enron.[37] Judge Gonzalez approved his selection two days later.[38]

---

[31] David Ivanovich, *Enron Choice Known for Charisma; Interim CEO Brings Proven Record*, HOUS. CHRON., Jan. 30, 2002, at B1.

[32] *See* Siobhan Roth, *Independent Trustee Sought by Parties in Enron Bankruptcy*, N.Y.L.J., Feb. 14, 2002, at 1 ("The fact that Kenneth Lay, Enron's one-time CEO, no longer has any connection to the company and that well-respected workout specialist Stephen Cooper has replaced him as interim CEO makes the appointment of a trustee less likely, they say, though not unimaginable.").

[33] *Id.*

[34] *In re* Enron Corp., No. 01-16034 (Bankr. S.D.N.Y. 2002), *available at* http://www.elaw4enron.com, docket entry nos. 1028, 1125, 1136, 1472.

[35] Stipulation and Consent Order Adjourning Hearing of Motions For an Order to Appoint a Chapter 11 Trustee for Enron Corp. Pursuant to 11 U.S.C. § 1104(a), Direct Debtors to Produce Documents and Related Relief Pursuant to 11 U.S.C. § 2004 and Preserve, Account For and Segregate Documents Pursuant to 11 U.S.C. § 105, *In re* Enron Corp., No. 01-16034 (Bankr. S.D.N.Y. Apr. 8, 2002), *available at* http://www.elaw4enron.com, docket entry no. 2836.

[36] Order Pursuant to 11 U.S.C. §§ 1104(c) and 1106(b) Directing Appointment of Enron Corp. Examiner, *In re* Enron Corp., No. 01-16034 (Bankr. S.D.N.Y. 2002) [hereinafter Appointment Order], *available at* http://www.elaw4enron.com, docket entry no. 2838.

[37] Application of the United States Trustee For Order Approving the Appointment of the Examiner For Enron Corp., *In re* Enron Corp., No. 01-16034 (Bankr. S.D.N.Y. 2002), *available at* http://www.elaw4enron.com, docket entry no. 3924.

[38] Order Approving the Appointment of Neal Batson As the Examiner For Enron Corp., *In re* Enron Corp., No. 01-16034 (Bankr. S.D.N.Y. 2002), *available at* http://www.elaw4enron.com, docket entry no. 7003.

4. THE EXAMINER[39]

As just noted, Neal Batson was named the examiner in the Enron case in May 2002. This appointment is part of the clear trend in recent cases involving allegations of corporate wrongdoing to appoint examiners for investigative purposes. Batson is an experienced Atlanta bankruptcy lawyer, a partner in the firm of Alston & Bird, chair of the American College of Bankruptcy, member of the National Bankruptcy Conference, former member of the Advisory Committee on the Federal Rules of Bankruptcy Procedure—the list of his credentials goes on and on.[40] Batson previously had served as examiner in the complex and highly publicized Chapter 11 case of Dallas real estate and financial services conglomerate Southmark Corporation.

In the 1978 bankruptcy law revision, Congress provided two grounds for the appointment of an examiner as an alternative to a trustee. One ground is discretionary: the court may appoint an examiner if "such appointment is in the interests of creditors, any equity security holders, and other interests of the estate."[41] The other ground is mandatory and is triggered if "the debtor's fixed, liquidated, unsecured debts, other than debts for goods, services, or taxes, or owing to an insider, exceed $5,000,000."[42] Congress intended that a "trustee would not be needed in any case where the protection afforded by a trustee could equally be afforded by an examiner."[43] The protection afforded by the examiner was primarily to conduct an investigation of the debtor's financial condition and report the results of such an investigation. Section 1104(c) directs the court to appoint an "examiner to conduct such an investigation of the debtor as is appropriate, including an investigation of any allegations of fraud, dishonesty, incompetence, misconduct, mismanagement, or irregularity in the management of the affairs of the debtor of or by current or former management of the debtor." The language, "as is appropriate," allows the court flexibility to tailor the examiner's investigation to match the needs of the specific bankruptcy case.

Judge Gonzalez delineated the scope of the examiner's investigation in his April 8th order:

> [T]he Enron Examiner shall have the authority and power to investigate all transactions (as well as all entities as defined in the Bankruptcy Code and

---

[39] My thanks go out to Andrew Wool for his outstanding assistance on this section.

[40] In the interest of full disclosure, the author of this essay should note that he served on the Advisory Committee on the Federal Rules of Bankruptcy Procedure for six years with Batson, and that he holds Batson in the highest personal and professional regard.

[41] 11 U.S.C. § 1104(c)(1) (2002). The legislative history explained that the court should make the appointment if "protection . . . is needed and the costs and expenses . . . would not be disproportionately high[] . . . ." H.R. REP. NO. 95-595, 402 (1977), *reprinted in* 1978 U.S.C.C.A.N. 5963, 6358.

[42] 11 U.S.C. § 1104(c)(2) (2002). Some courts have held that the language in § 1104 (c) allowing the court to tailor the investigation of the debtor "as is appropriate" qualifies this mandatory language and renders it discretionary. *See* CHARLES JORDAN TABB, THE LAW OF BANKRUPTCY 780-82 (1997).

[43] H.R. Rep. No. 95-595, 402-403 (1977), *reprinted in* 1978 U.S.C.C.A.N. 5963, 6358.

pre-petition professionals involved therein): (i) involving special purpose vehicles or entities created or structured by the Debtors or at the behest of the Debtors (the "SPEs"), that are (ii) not reflected on the Enron Corp. balance sheets, or that (iii) involve hedging using the Enron Corp. stock, or (iv) as to which the Enron Examiner has the reasonable belief are reflected, reported or omitted in the relevant entity's financial statements not in accordance with generally accepted accounting principles, or that (v) involve potential avoidance actions against any pre-petition insider or professional of the Debtors.[44]

In pursuit of this directive, Batson filed a lengthy (185 pages) motion on August 1, 2002, seeking permission to subpoena documents from over 200 financial institutions and law firms.[45] Batson requested documents from 45 law firms that were involved in various transactions with Enron or the SPEs. In December 2002, Batson filed a second motion for the production documents, bringing the total number of subpoenaed law firms to 46. The subpoenas were issued in an attempt to "determine the scope of the matters concerning the Debtors' SPEs and related pre-petition transactions, and most importantly, who was involved in such transactions and to what extent."[46] Judge Gonzalez authorized the subpoenas on September 13, 2002, ordering Batson and the Creditors' Committee to coordinate their requests, with one group issuing the subpoena and receiving the documents.[47]

As one might have guessed, Batson's subpoenas were met with considerable opposition from banks and law firms. These targets argued that the requests were overly broad and burdensome and would breach the attorney-client privilege.[48] Batson, citing *Commodities Futures Trading Commission v. Weintraub*,[49] argued that the "[e]xaminer has the right, just as any of the Debtors would, to obtain such documents."[50] The Supreme Court held in *Weintraub* that a trustee had the authority to waive the attorney-client privilege for a corporate debtor,[51] but it does not necessarily follow that an

[44] Appointment Order, *supra* note 36.

[45] Notice of Motion of Neal Batson, the Examiner, Pursuant to Federal Rule of Bankruptcy Procedure 2004 For an Order Directing the Production of Documents, *In re* Enron Corp., No. 01-16034 (Bankr. S.D.N.Y. Aug. 1, 2002) [hereinafter Production of Documents], *available at* http://www.elaw4enron.com, docket entry no. 5522.

[46] *Id.* at 10.

[47] *See Bankruptcy Judge Approves Subpoenas for Bank, Legal and Insurance Records,* 1 No. 18 ANDREWS ENRON LITIG. REP. 1 (Sept. 23, 2002).

[48] *See* Eric Berger, *The Fall of Enron; Banks Leery of Data Release,* HOUS. CHRON., Oct. 13, 2002, at B1; *Banks, Lawyers Top List of Objections to Subpoena Motion in Enron Case,* 1 No. 17 ANDREWS ENRON LITIG. REP. 1 (Sept. 9, 2002).

[49] 471 U.S. 343 (1985).

[50] Production of Documents, *supra* note 45, at 6.

[51] *Weintraub,* 471 U.S. at 352–354.

examiner possesses this power.[52] In response to these objections, Judge Gonzalez ordered a procedure for the production of confidential information,[53] but otherwise required the law firms to comply with the subpoenas[54]—much to their chagrin.

Batson issued his First Interim Report ("First Report"),[55] an impressive 158-page document, on September 21, 2002, a short eight days after the grant of subpoena power. That first report therefore does not analyze law firm behavior. The focus of the First Report instead "provides . . . preliminary conclusions regarding six Enron transactions involving special purpose entities . . . . These transactions . . . are representative of some of the types of transactions employed by Enron."[56] His tentative conclusion, discussed in more detail in the next section on "Recharacterization," was that the transactions appeared to be loans, not sales, thus opening the door for the recovery of hundreds of millions of dollars in assets for the Enron estate.

The First Report also provides some insight into the probable focuses of Batson's Second Interim Report ("Second Report").[57] His investigation is zeroing in on the SPEs and their legitimacy, and the roles of and possible liability of law firms and accountants pertinent thereto. As one expert commentator noted, "You can't have structured finance without lawyers at the table. They're there every step of the way."[58] She further observed, "It takes a lot of little pieces of paper for an Enron to happen—and lawyers wrote a lot of those little pieces of paper."[59]

Issues that Batson in the First Report specifically identified as the subject of ongoing investigation include:

---

[52] *See* Leonard L. Gumport, *The Bankruptcy Examiner*, 20 CAL. BANKR. J. 71, 125–26 (1992) (noting that the examiner doesn't inherently have the power, but can compel debtor to waive the privilege with threat of recommending appointment of trustee to investigate and displace debtor).

[53] Order Governing the Production and Use of Confidential Material Among the Examiner, the Official Committee of Unsecured Creditors, the Debtors and Non-Parties, *In re* Enron Corp., No. 01-16034 (Bankr. S.D.N.Y. Oct. 11, 2002), *available at* http://www.elaw4enron.com, docket entry no. 7122; *see Bankr. Judge Issues Order for Production of Confidential Material*, 8 No. 23 ANDREWS DERIVATIVE LITIG. REP. 9 (Oct. 21, 2002) (explaining that the order defines confidential information and what may be called "highly classified" information, and that Batson will be allowed to release confidential information to the public in his interim report, so long as the subpoenaed company is given five business days to seek a protective order barring publication of the information).

[54] *See* Berger, *Banks Leery, supra* note 48 (noting that Judge Gonzalez told the parties that he would not tolerate delays in their efforts to seek a compromise on keeping information collected by Batson confidential, and to work all night if they had to).

[55] First Interim Report, *supra* note 8.

[56] *Id.* at 13.

[57] The Second Report was filed with the court on January 21, 2003. The next essay addresses this report in depth.

[58] Peter Berh & Carrie Johnson, *Enron Probes Now Focus on Tax Deals; Bankruptcy Examiner to File Report Today; Congressional Investigation Nears Completion*, WASH. POST, Jan. 21, 2003 at E01 (quoting Professor Susan Koniak).

[59] Mike France, *What About the Lawyers*, BUS. WK, Dec. 23, 2002, at 58 (quoting Susan Koniak).

- Are the SPE structures subject to legal challenge? Are there any assets that were purportedly transferred from the Debtors' estates that should be considered part of the Debtors' estates?
- What was the role of SPEs in the collapse of Enron?
- Did Enron use SPEs to manipulate its financial statements in violation of GAAP or applicable laws?
- Was there proper disclosure to the public of these SPE transactions under applicable disclosure standards?
- If it is determined that wrongful acts were committed in connection with the SPE transactions (including manipulation of Enron's financial statements in violation of GAAP or applicable laws), are the officers, directors, professionals, or other third parties involved in such transactions liable under applicable legal standards?[60]

The conclusions in the Second Report may be the single most significant component of the entire Chapter 11 case, dictating the likelihood of recapturing enormous sums of money for the estate that had been placed "off balance sheet" in SPEs.[61]

5. RECHARACTERIZATION AND "SPECIAL PURPOSE ENTITIES"[62]

So what about the SPEs? The collapse of Enron was in large part caused by the improper use of Special Purpose Entities ("SPEs") to hide losses and inflate earnings. As a general rule,

> [a] company that does business with an SPE may treat that SPE as if it were an independent, outside entity for accounting purposes if two conditions are met: (1) an owner independent of the company must make a substantive equity investment of at least 3% of the SPE's assets, and that 3% must remain at risk throughout the transaction; and (2) the independent owner must exercise control of the SPE.[63]

However, because these requirements were not met for many of Enron's partnerships, the company was required to consolidate financial statements and restate its earnings in the fall of 2001, leading to the company's downfall.

---

[60] First Interim Report, *supra* note 8, at 19–20.

[61] See following essay discussing the Second Report. *Editors' note:* In fact, the Third Examiner's Report, filed July 28, 2003, and the Final Report, filed November 24, 2003, were also extremely detailed in sorting out Enron's financial activities and in suggesting possible causes of action.

[62] My thanks go out to David Deschler, Matthew Sostrin, and Andrew Wool for their excellent work on this section.

[63] WILLIAM C. POWERS, JR. ET AL., REPORT OF INVESTIGATION BY THE SPECIAL INVESTIGATIVE COMMITTEE OF THE BOARD OF DIRECTORS OF ENRON CORP. 4 (Feb. 1, 2002), *available at* 2002 WL 198018.

The first major report to examine the SPEs was submitted to the board of directors by the Special Investigations Committee, headed by William Powers, Jr., on February 1, 2002. The report addressed basic transactions between Enron and the flawed SPEs (primarily Chewco, LJM1, and LJM2). In many cases, Enron was unable to attract outside investors for these vehicles and had to be the sole contributor to the SPE's assets, often in the form of Enron stock (in exchange for notes). Even though the non-consolidation rules were not met, Enron continued to treat these SPEs as independent for accounting purposes.

The report concluded that many of the most significant transactions with the SPEs "apparently were designed to accomplish favorable financial statement results, not to achieve *bona fide* economic objectives or to transfer risk."[64] These typically took the form of purported asset sales and hedging transactions. Most of the purported asset sales were mere accounting manipulations. For example, five of the seven asset sales to LJM1 and LJM2 were made at the end of an earnings period, and the assets were repurchased by Enron shortly thereafter.[65] The partnerships profited in each instance, even though in some cases, the asset had declined in value. There was some evidence that in at least three of those transactions, Enron had agreed in advance to protect the SPE against any loss, thus retaining all risk.[66]

The purported hedging transactions likewise failed to transfer risk from Enron. In a typical hedging transaction, an outside party takes on the economic risk of an investment for a price. Here, the SPEs were to pay Enron if certain merchant investments declined in value. But remember, Enron provided the sole capital to fund the SPEs in the first place. And since this was often in the form of Enron stock, once that began its decline in value, the SPEs could not even cover their hedges. Thus, by using the SPEs, Enron conveyed the misleading impression that some of its investments were effectively hedged. Certain Enron employees improperly profited from these dealings as well, led by Andrew Fastow taking in an estimated $30 million from the partnership arrangements.[67]

Batson's First Report focused on six[68] of thousands of partnerships allegedly used by Enron to inflate financial results. These six partnerships, all characterized by Enron as a sale of the asset to the SPE, had raised approximately $1.383 billion in cash for Enron.[69] Batson preliminarily concluded that "each of the Selected Transactions . . . appears to be, from both an economic and risk allocation perspective, a loan rather than a sale of an asset," and "[i]f all of these purported sales are recharacterized as

---

[64] *Id.* at 3.

[65] *Id.* at 7.

[66] *Id.*

[67] *Id.* at 3.

[68] Cerberus, Nikita, Hawaii, Backbone, SO_2, and Destec.

[69] First Interim Report, *supra* note 8, at 13–14.

loans, then the assets, currently valued in the range of $500 million, would be added to the debtor's estates."[70] Thus, the First Report raises the possibility of unwinding many of these partnerships to recover assets—perhaps even billions of dollars—for creditors. The "lenders" would be left with an unsecured claim, unless they perfected an unavoidable security interest in the assets, which was seldom done.[71]

According to the First Report, "Enron was prolific in its use of highly complex structured finance transactions using SPEs, with the result that billions of dollars of recourse obligations were not disclosed as debt on Enron's balance sheet, and the proceeds of these recourse obligations were reported as revenue and cash flow."[72] What did these transactions look like? Batson explains:

> In most of these transactions, an Enron entity purported to sell an asset to an SPE in exchange for cash and other consideration. That cash was most often obtained through a loan to the SPE or an affiliated SPE. However, unlike most transactions in which a person sells an asset, in most of the Selected Transactions Enron or its affiliate agreed to repay the amount of debt the SPE incurred to finance the purchase price. Furthermore, Enron or its affiliate would continue to control the "sold" asset and would receive the upside benefit if the asset ultimately generated proceeds in excess of the costs of financing.[73]

The lenders typically did not seek collateral for their loans (as many of the assets produced insufficient cash flow), but instead relied merely on Enron's creditworthiness. Enron would enter into a financial arrangement with the SPE referred to as a "Total Return Swap."[74] Enron would agree to make payments to the SPE in amounts equal to scheduled payments on the borrowed funds, and Enron would maintain control of the asset and entitled to all revenues it generated (essentially making the transaction an economic wash).[75]

In short, "Enron would have one unit sell an asset to another unit, allowing the company to retain ownership of the asset while booking the gain."[76] In each case, however, as noted above, Enron documents characterize the transaction as a sale.[77] The

---

[70] *Id.* at 17 (citation omitted).

[71] *Id.* at 38.

[72] *Id.* at 22.

[73] *Id.* at 14.

[74] *Id.*

[75] *Id.* at 14–15.

[76] *Enron First Examiner's Report Questions Financial Dealings, Banks*, BCD NEWS & COMMENT, Oct. 11, 2002.

[77] First Interim Report, *supra* note 8, at 16.

party seeking to recharacterize the purported sale as a loan would have the burden of proof.[78]

For bankruptcy purposes, the relevant question that Batson asked is, "Are there any assets that were purportedly transferred from the Debtors' estates that should properly be considered part of the Debtors' estates?"[79] The answer to this question rests on whether the Enron transactions were "true sales." In his Report, Batson summarizes the law of "true sales." "The key to a true sale analysis is 'the substance of the relationship' between the parties to the transaction, 'and not simply the label attached to the transaction.'"[80] Furthermore, the *intent* of the parties is critical. Intent is determined by looking at "contents of the document[s], the testimony of the contracting parties, and the circumstances surrounding the transaction."[81]

Batson explains, "Where the risk of ownership of an asset is not transferred to a buyer, and the seller retains the benefits of the appreciation of the asset, then the transaction is likely to be viewed as a loan, rather than a sale."[82] Also, "if the seller has an ability to re-acquire the asset transferred, then courts are more likely to call the transaction a loan."[83]

So, how do these factors impact the recharacterization issue in Enron? Batson analyzes whether the Enron transactions were "true sales"—and finds that the evidence tilts heavily otherwise.

The first factor is "control over asset." Batson notes that Enron usually "continued to exercise significant control over the transferred asset."[84] One strike against Enron.

Second, Batson discusses "benefits and risks" of the transactions. He notes that "Enron continued to have the risks of the performance of the assets, as well as the true economic benefits of the underlying asset."[85] Strike two.

Third, Batson looks at the lenders' intent. He believes it was Enron's status as a good credit risk, rather than the value of the transacted asset, that lenders were interested in. This would tend to support the characterization of the transaction as a loan. Batson notes that "these transactions could not have occurred without Enron's credit. Enron's credit was necessary because the assets . . . produced insufficient cash flow to support the financing or may have been difficult to sell to third parties on acceptable terms."[86] Batson also finds it telling that lenders did not take a back-up security inter-

---

[78] *Id.* at 43.

[79] *Id.* at 19.

[80] *Id.* at 39 n.101 (quoting Endico Potatoes, Inc. v. CIT Group/Factoring, Inc., 67 F.3d 1063, 1069 (2d Cir. 1995)).

[81] *Id.* at 40 n.102 (quoting People v. Serv. Inst. Inc., 421 N.Y.S.2d 325, 327 (Sup. Ct. 1979)).

[82] *Id.* at 45 (citation omitted).

[83] *Id.* at 46 (citation omitted).

[84] *Id.* at 48 (citation omitted).

[85] *Id.*

[86] *Id.* at 15–16; *see also id.* at 39.

est in these transactions, which a lender would normally do when making a loan.[87] Nor did they always require a "true sale" opinion from counsel as a condition of closing the deals[88]—a noteworthy omission. All in all, "intent" looks like strike three.

Enron may argue that the characterization be determined by "the intent of the parties to the transaction as determined by the language of the transaction documents."[89] That language, of course, purports to support "sale" status. Ball one for Enron.

Batson also looks at loan pricing, Enron's intent, and tax treatment when trying to characterize the transactions. Each suggests "something less than final sales" and supports treatment as loans.[90] Strikes four, five, and six.

In sum, Batson says that the economic realities of the transaction control the sale versus loan issue; and as noted earlier, Batson's preliminary conclusion is that "the economic consequences to Enron of these transactions were substantially similar to loans."[91] If he is right, then a major cornerstone of the bankruptcy case will involve recovery of assets for the estate. The Examiner's Second Report should probe more deeply into the possibility of recharacterizing SPEs and recapturing assets for the estate.

However, there already have been some attempts to unwind certain transactions to recover additional assets. These have primarily focused on the SPE (Whitewing Associates) and its affiliate (Osprey trust).[92] Much like the transactions analyzed in the Examiner's First Interim Report, Enron often "sold" assets to Whitewing in exchange for cash, but also gave Whitewing a promissory note obligating Enron to make payments back, in this case totaling $1.7 billion. In the year before its bankruptcy filing, Enron paid a total of $957 million to Whitewing under these arrangements. The contemplated litigation by the Official Committee of Unsecured Creditors seeks to recover these payments through the substantive consolidation of Whitewing, challenges based on lack of true sale, and avoidance actions.[93]

6. THE OFFICIAL COMMITTEE OF UNSECURED CREDITORS: COMPOSITION AND CONFLICTS[94]

The composition of Enron's Official Committee of Unsecured Creditors has been an issue of significant concern for many of Enron's creditors. The committee, ap-

---

[87] *Id.* at 48 n.125.

[88] *Id.* at 38–39 n.98.

[89] *Id.* at 42 n.108.

[90] *Id.* at 49–50.

[91] *Id.* at 39.

[92] Eric Berger, *Suit Seeks $1 Billion From Former Partner; Enron Wants Cash From Off-Books Deal*, HOUS. CHRON., Feb. 22, 2003, at B2.

[93] Motion of Official Committee of Unsecured Creditors For Order Under 11 U.S.C. §§ 105(a), 1103(c) and 1109(b) Authorizing Committee to Commence Litigation Against Whitewing LP, Whitewing Management, Osprey and Other Related Entities, *In re* Enron Corp., No. 01-16034 (Bankr. S.D.N.Y. Jan. 28, 2003), *available at* http://www.elaw4enron.com, docket entry no. 8959.

[94] Kristen Jacobsen made superb contributions to this section.

pointed by the United States Trustee on December 12, 2001, originally included 15 members: five banks, five bondholders, three energy traders, one holder of surety bonds, and one former Enron employee.[95]

The controversy revolves around the appointment of two of the bank creditors: Citigroup and J.P. Morgan Chase. Each is under investigation for its role in structuring many of the partnerships that led to Enron's collapse. Both banks have been accused of helping Enron conceal its deteriorating financial condition by structuring, investing, and promoting the "off balance sheet" partnerships.[96] Thus the seeming conflict: Creditors' Committee members have a fiduciary duty to maximize assets and contest doubtful claims, and thereby to seek recovery from or the equitable subordination of the claims of such inside contributors to the collapse, but the involved banks on the committee are unlikely to vote to sue themselves![97] Indeed, shareholders have sued Citigroup and J.P. Morgan Chase over their involvement in Enron's financial crisis.[98]

A. Creditors' Committee—Role and Functions

The United States Trustee appoints an Official Committee of Unsecured Creditors in most reorganization cases.[99] The Committee is typically composed of the creditors holding the seven (or more) largest claims against the debtor who are willing to serve.[100] Because the debtor is often left in control of the reorganization, the Committee plays an important role in representing the interests of other creditors.[101]

The main functions of the Committee are to oversee the progress of the reorganization and negotiate with the debtor over the plan.[102] The Committee is granted broad powers in order to ensure fairness in the proceedings; these powers include the ability to investigate the acts, conduct, and liabilities of the debtor, and "perform such other ser-

---

[95] Leslie Wayne, *At Center of Enron Bankruptcy, Dispute Over Big Bank Creditors*, N.Y. TIMES, Apr. 30, 2002, at C1. The banks: J.P. Morgan Chase; Citigroup; Credit Lyonnais; ABN/AMRO; and Credit Suisse First Boston. The bondholders: Bank of New York; National City Bank; Oaktree Capital Management; Silvercreek Management; and Wells Fargo. The energy traders: Duke Energy Trading & Marketing; National Energy Group; and Williams Companies. The surety bond holder is St. Paul Fire & Marine, and the former Enron employee is Michael Moran.

[96] Wayne, *supra* note 95.

[97] Patrick Oster & Jeff St. Onge, *Citigroup, J.P. Morgan Role on Enron Panel Reviewed*, BLOOMBERG NEWS, Apr. 18, 2002.

[98] George Stein, *Citigroup, Rivals May Pay $6 BLN Fines, Report Says*, BLOOMBERG NEWS, Aug. 7, 2002; Christopher Mumma & Michael Nol, *J.P. Morgan's Harrison, Other Directors Sued Over Enron Deals*, BLOOMBERG NEWS, Nov. 27, 2002.

[99] 11 U.S.C. § 1102(a)(1) (2002).

[100] *Id.* at § 1102(b)(1).

[101] TABB, *supra* note 42, at 782.

[102] *Id.* at 783.

vices as are in the interest of those represented."[103] Members of the Creditors' Committee serve as fiduciaries to other members in their respective class of creditors.[104] As a fiduciary, a member must act in and promote the best interests of all the members in the class. In other words, a Committee member should not use its position to further its own self-interest in the reorganization.[105] Although Committee members are not required to have the same interests and concerns as each other, they are expected not to have any conflicts between their own interests and those of the constituents they represent.[106]

B. Apparent Conflicts in the Appointment of Enron's Major Bank Creditors to the Creditors' Committee

Soon after Enron's Official Committee of Unsecured Creditors was appointed, Enron's creditors questioned how Citigroup and J.P. Morgan Chase would be able to serve as Committee members while their roles in the Enron bankruptcy were under scrutiny.[107] The propriety of Citigroup's and J.P. Morgan Chase's actions has been the subject of lawsuits and investigations. Lawsuits against the banks include those by Enron investors and employees, as well as the banks' own shareholders; the lawsuits seek approximately $36 billion in damages. These suits allege that the banks assisted Enron in hiding its debt from investors by structuring the "off balance sheet" partnerships and SPEs, and further deceived investors by issuing positive reports on the company.[108]

Both banks have also been under investigation by the Securities and Exchange Commission and Congress. The SEC is pursuing the allegations of fraud by shareholders, specifically targeting the banks' culpability in structuring loans to look like sales in order to disguise the debt as cash flow.[109] The House Energy and Commerce Committee and Senate Governmental Affairs Permanent Subcommittee on Investigations each have conducted separate inquiries into the banks' involvement. The Senate Subcommittee has found that both Citigroup and J.P. Morgan Chase aided Enron in misleading investors.[110]

---

[103] 11 U.S.C. § 1103(c)(2)–(5) (2002).

[104] *In re* SPM Mfg. Corp., 984 F.2d 1305, 1315 (1st Cir. 1993).

[105] *In re* Nationwide Sports Distrib., Inc., 227 B.R. 455, 464 (Bankr. E.D. Pa. 1998).

[106] *See In re* Daig Corp., 17 B.R. 41, 43 (Bankr. D. Minn. 1981); *In re* Microboard Processing, Inc., 95 B.R. 283, 285 (Bankr. D. Conn. 1989); *see also In re* Johns-Manville Corp., 26 B.R. 919, 925 (Bankr. S.D.N.Y. 1983).

[107] Wayne, *supra* note 95; Oster & St. Onge, *supra* note 97.

[108] Stein, *supra* note 98; Mumma & Nol, *supra* note 98.

[109] William Roberts et al., *Citigroup, J.P. Morgan Probed On Enron, Person Says*, BLOOMBERG NEWS, July 25, 2002.

[110] Jeff Bliss, *House Panel Investigates Citigroup Deals With Enron*, BLOOMBERG NEWS, May 2, 2002; William Roberts et al., *Citigroup, J.P. Morgan Shares Tumble On Enron Probe*, BLOOMBERG NEWS, July 23, 2002; Robert Schmidt & Helen Stock, *Investment Banks Aided Enron "Deceptions," Senate Report Says*, BLOOMBERG NEWS, Jan. 2, 2003.

The Enron Creditors' Committee will be searching for potential lawsuits to bring against bankers, brokers, and other individuals who participated in the creation of Enron's off balance sheet entities.[111] The Creditors' Committee has begun investigations of many of Enron's affiliated partnerships, subpoenaing Enron's financial institutions, including Citigroup and J.P. Morgan Chase, for the production of documents in connection with Enron's financial matters.[112] Many creditors doubt that Citigroup and J.P. Morgan Chase would bring lawsuits against themselves in connection with Enron's downfall.[113] Because the banks are clearly conflicted between their fiduciary role of maximizing returns to the creditors *and* protecting themselves in subsequent litigation, creditors fear that the banks do not fairly represent their constituents and may hinder the Committee's progress in investigating and negotiating the reorganization.[114]

The creditors' concern was exemplified by the Committee's investigation of Mahonia Ltd., a bank entity created by J.P. Morgan Chase for Enron.[115] In its investigation, the Committee sought to obtain documents from J.P. Morgan that were produced in a lawsuit brought by the bank against 11 surety companies (the "Surety Group"). Because the Surety Group alleged that the Mahonia transactions constituted fraudulent conduct by J.P. Morgan, the Creditors' Committee requested access to the documents to further its review of Mahonia's financial transactions, as well as to minimize the Committee's investigative costs.[116] Although the Committee reached an agreement with the Surety Group regarding the requested documents, J.P. Morgan sought to limit the scope of the Committee's discovery, requiring the Committee to expend further efforts to seek a judicial order compelling the bank to cooperate with its investigation.[117]

---

[111] Jeff St. Onge & Jef Feeley, *Enron Creditors Seek to Investigate Partnerships*, BLOOMBERG NEWS, Feb. 8, 2002.

[112] *Id.*; Motion of Official Committee of Unsecured Creditors For Order, Pursuant to 11 U.S.C. § 1103(c) and Rule 2004 of the Federal Rules of Bankruptcy Procedure, Authorizing Issuance of Subpoenas for the Production of Documents and Oral Examination of Financial Institutions at 3–4, *In re* Enron Corp., No. 01-16034 (Bankr. S.D.N.Y. Aug. 1, 2002), *available at* http://www.elaw4enron.com, docket entry no. 5520.

[113] Wayne, *supra* note 95.

[114] *Id.*; Oster & St. Onge, *supra* note 97.

[115] Christopher Mumma, *Enron Creditors Say J.P. Morgan is Hampering Mahonia Probe*, BLOOMBERG NEWS, July 31, 2002.

[116] Motion of Official Committee of Unsecured Creditors for Order, Pursuant to 11 U.S.C. § 1103(c) and Rule 2004 of the Federal Rules of Bankruptcy Procedure, Authorizing Issuance of Subpoenas for the Production of Documents and Oral Examination of JP Morgan Chase Bank, *In re* Enron Corp., No. 01-16034 (Bankr. S.D.N.Y. July 30, 2002), *available at* http://www.elaw4enron.com, docket entry no. 5453.

[117] *Id.*; Notice of Presentment of Stipulation and Order Governing the Production and Use of Confidential Information, *In re* Enron Corp., No. 01-16034 (Bankr. S.D.N.Y. Aug. 26, 2002), *available at* http://www.elaw4enron.com, docket entry no. 6035.

C. Removal from the Creditors' Committee

The creditors' challenges to the banks' appointments have caused both the bankruptcy court and the United States Trustee to take action to determine the banks' involvements with Enron and any potential conflicts of interest. Upon the urging of several of Enron's creditors, the trustee agreed to review whether the banks were fulfilling their fiduciary obligations to their constituent creditors.[118] The bankruptcy judge also ordered the trustee to appoint an independent examiner to further investigate and issue a report on the banks' respective roles in Enron's bankruptcy.[119] Possibly as a result of pressure from creditors and critics, Citigroup voluntarily withdrew from the Creditors' Committee in June 2002.[120]

With regards to the possibility of revoking J.P. Morgan Chase's membership, courts are currently split as to whether a court may remove a member of an existing creditors' committee.[121] Prior to 1986, the Bankruptcy Code specifically provided courts with this authority under § 1102(c). That section was repealed, however, in order to expand the role of the United States Trustee.[122] Courts that do believe they retain the authority to change the membership of the Creditors' Committee premise their ability to do so on the general powers of the court under § 105(a).[123] Under that section, the court may review the trustee's actions to ensure that the trustee did not abuse his discretion or otherwise act "arbitrarily or capriciously."[124]

However, until J.P. Morgan Chase's full role and involvement in Enron's bankruptcy is revealed, showing that the trustee acted arbitrarily or capriciously in appointing the bank to the Creditors' Committee may be a difficult burden to meet. The creditors must show that the trustee's decision was patently unreasonable, arbitrary, or otherwise not based on any factual evidence.[125] Further, an appointed member will not be removed due to mere speculation that the member will further his own interest, but the moving party must provide evidence that the member "has, will, or is about to act in a manner inconsistent with his fiduciary duty."[126]

---

[118] Oster & St. Onge, *supra* note 97.

[119] *Id.*; Jeff St. Onge & Christopher Mumma, *Enron Judge Orders Examiner to Probe Transactions*, BLOOMBERG NEWS, Apr. 9, 2002.

[120] *See* Memorandum Decision Regarding Motions to Appoint an Enron North America Committee and an Energy Traders' Committee and Alternative Motion of Upstream Energy Services to Require Enron North America as Debtor In Possession to Obtain Separate Counsel at 10, *In re* Enron Corp., No. 01-16034 (Bankr. S.D.N.Y. June 21, 2002), *available at* http://www.elaw4enron.com, docket entry no. 4658.

[121] TABB, *supra* note 42, at 785; *see also In re* Pierce, 237 B.R. 748 (Bankr. E.D. Cal. 1999).

[122] TABB, *supra* note 42, at 785.

[123] 11 U.S.C. § 105(a) (2002); *In re* Barney's, Inc., 197 B.R. 431, 438–39 (Bankr. S.D.N.Y. 1996).

[124] *Barney's*, 197 B.R. at 439.

[125] *Id.*

[126] *In re* First Republic Bank Corp., 95 B.R. 58, 61 (Bankr. N.D. Tex 1988); *In re* Enduro Stainless, Inc., 59 B.R. 603, 605 (Bankr. N.D. Ohio 1986).

7. CREDITORS' COMMITTEE COUNSEL[127]

On December 12, 2001, ten days after Enron filed Chapter 11, the United States Trustee appointed the Official Committee of Unsecured Creditors for Enron Corp. (the "Committee").[128] On January 15, 2002, the Committee submitted an application for the Bankruptcy Court to authorize the New York City law firm of Milbank, Tweed, Hadley & McCloy ("Milbank") to serve as official counsel for the Committee.[129] The Committee requested Milbank's representation due to the firm's extensive prior experience with large, complex bankruptcies, as well as its expertise in structured finance and derivatives transactions.[130] In addition, Milbank submitted an 80-page Affidavit, which disclosed all of its contacts with the debtors, creditors, and other parties in interest over the past five years.[131]

Two items in Milbank's Affidavit require careful scrutiny. The first item concerns the *fees* that Milbank had received from Enron and its affiliated debtors prior to the bankruptcy filing. Milbank disclosed that it had received nearly $450,000 in fees from the Debtors within 90 days prior to Enron's Chapter 11 filing—transfers that may be voidable under bankruptcy preference law.[132] Additionally, Milbank disclosed that its largest Enron client for the preceding five years was Enron Wind Corp., a subsidiary of Enron, from which Milbank collected roughly $1.3 million in fees in 2001 alone.[133]

The second item concerns Milbank's *contacts* prior to Enron's filing. Milbank disclosed that it never directly represented Enron in structured finance transactions. However, Milbank did represent arrangers and initial purchasers of structured finance offerings involving Enron Corp. from 1998 through 2001; Milbank also advised, and continues to advise, Citibank regarding six "credit-linked note transactions" that Enron Corp. used to purchase investments prior to bankruptcy.[134]

On January 28, 2002, Judge Gonzalez approved the Committee's application and authorized Milbank's representation.[135] However, Milbank could not represent the

---

[127] My thanks to Kevin Van Hout for excellent work on this section.

[128] Application of Official Committee of Unsecured Creditors of Enron Corp., et al., Under 11 U.S.C. § 1103 and Fed. R. Bank. P. 2014 and 5002, For Order Authorizing and Approving Retention and Employment Nunc Pro Tunc of Milbank, Tweed, Hadley and McCloy, LLP as Counsel at 2, *In re* Enron Corp., No. 01-16034 (Bankr. S.D.N.Y. Jan. 15, 2002) [hereinafter Application], *available at* http://www.elaw4enron.com, docket entry no. 933.

[129] *Id.*

[130] *Id.* at 4–5; Affidavit of Stephen J. Blauner In Support of Application [hereinafter Affidavit].

[131] Affidavit, *supra* note 130; FED. R. BANKR. P. 2014 (2002).

[132] 11 U.S.C. § 547 (2002).

[133] Affidavit, *supra* note 130, at 10.

[134] *Id.* at 17–18.

[135] Order Authorizing and Approving Retention and Employment of Milbank, Tweed, Hadley & McCloy, LLP, Nunc Pro Tunc, as Counsel To Official Committee of Unsecured Creditors of Enron Corp. et al., *In re* Enron Corp., No. 01-16034 (Bankr. S.D.N.Y. Jan. 28, 2002), *available at* http://www.elaw4enron.com, docket entry no. 1146.

Committee regarding the firm's prior transactions with Enron; those duties fell to the law firm of Squire, Sanders & Dempsey, engaged and approved as "conflicts counsel" on January 29, 2002.[136] Additionally, the Court appointed an independent examiner to review Enron's partnerships and accounting irregularities.[137] As Committee counsel, Milbank submitted to the Bankruptcy Court a request for payment of fees and expenses for approximately $580,000 on March 11, 2002.[138] On March 19, 2002, Exco, a creditor of an Enron subsidiary, filed a motion objecting to payment and requesting Milbank's disqualification as Committee counsel.[139]

A bankruptcy court generally will give a Committee considerable latitude in choosing its counsel, and will intervene only if that choice is prohibited by statute. Thus, Exco had the burden of producing evidence to support Milbank's disqualification.[140] The Committee may employ an attorney who does not "simultaneously represent[] another entity in a Chapter 11 case with an interest adverse to the bankruptcy estate."[141] It is generally acceptable for Committee counsel to represent creditors in matters (1) outside bankruptcy, (2) not adverse to Committee's interests, or (3) predating Committee representation.[142] Milbank argued it was subject only to this standard.[143]

When an attorney requests compensation from the Bankruptcy Court, the relevant Bankruptcy Code provision speaks both to professionals retained by the Committee, as well as those retained by the trustee or debtor in possession.[144] This compensation provision invites confusion because the Code employs a stricter standard for professionals employed by the trustee or debtor in possession.[145] In addition to the above standard, the stricter standard prohibits the attorney from holding an interest adverse to the estate or creditors *and* requires the attorney to be a "disinterested person."[146] Although the term is not defined in the Code, Milbank would have an "adverse inter-

---

[136] Bench Decision and Order at 2 n.1, 20, *In re* Enron Corp., No. 01-16034 (Bankr. S.D.N.Y. May 23, 2002) (denying Motion to Disqualify Milbank as Counsel) [hereinafter Denial Order], *available at* http://www.elaw4enron.com, docket entry no. 3980.

[137] Appointment Order, *supra* note 36; *see supra* section 4 of this Essay.

[138] Monthly Fee Statement of Milbank, Tweed, Hadley & McCloy, LLP, *In re* Enron Corp., No. 01-16034 (Bankr. S.D.N.Y. 2002), *available at* http://www.elaw4enron.com, docket entry no. 2037.

[139] Objection of Exco Resources, Inc. To Monthly Fee Statement of Milbank, Tweed, Hadley, & McCloy LLP For Services Rendered and Expenses Incurred From December 12, 2001 Through December 31, 2001 and Motion to Disqualify Milbank, Tweed, Hadley & McCloy LLP As Counsel for Official Committee of Unsecured Creditors, *In re* Enron Corp., No. 01-16034 (Bankr. S.D.N.Y. 2002) [hereinafter Motion to Disqualify], *available at* http://www.elaw4enron.com, docket entry no. 2243.

[140] Denial Order, *supra* note 136, at 9.

[141] *Id.* at 12 (citing 7 COLLIER ON BANKRUPTCY 1103.04, 1103–17 (15th ed. rev. 2002)).

[142] *Id.* at 12–13.

[143] *Id.* at 12.

[144] 11 U.S.C. §§ 328, 1107(a) (2002).

[145] Denial Order, *supra* note 136, at 13; 11 U.S.C. § 327(a) (2002).

[146] 11 U.S.C. §§ 101(14)(E), 327(a).

est" if its representation of another interest could cause the firm to act differently than if the other interest did not exist.[147] The Code defines a "disinterested person" as, *inter alia,* a person who has not been an attorney for an investment banker within three years before the petition.[148] Exco argued that this stricter standard applied to and required the disqualification of Milbank.[149] In any event, the Bankruptcy Court concluded that Milbank satisfied the stricter standard.[150]

Exco argued that Milbank was not a "disinterested person" under the Code because the firm had acted as an attorney to an investment banker within three years of Enron's filing. Further, Exco asserted that the transactions in which Milbank represented the arrangers and initial purchasers of structured finance transactions from 1998 through 2001 constituted disguised sales of shares through trust vehicles. These "sham transactions" allegedly were intended to disguise Enron's debt as the sale of preferred stock. As a result, Milbank acted as counsel to an investment banker insofar as Milbank represented the investment banks for the sale of Enron preferred stock from 1998 through 2001 and, thus, was not a "disinterested person."[151]

The Court rejected Exco's argument. Some of the materials on which Milbank based its response, and the Court its opinion, were sealed from public scrutiny.[152] Nevertheless, the Court reviewed the sealed documents and agreed with Milbank's position. Further, the Court characterized Exco's arguments regarding these transactions as "speculation" and "conjecture."[153] Although the independent examiner (or Squire Sanders, as conflicts counsel) has a duty to investigate these allegations, the court took the view that there was insufficient evidence to conclude that Milbank was not a "disinterested person."[154]

Regarding whether Milbank possessed an interest adverse to the estate or the unsecured creditors, Exco submitted three examples: (1) the Debtors' pre-petition preferential transfers to Milbank, (2) Milbank's extensive pre-petition relationship with the Debtors, and (3) Milbank's pre-petition representation of individual creditors.[155] First, Exco argued that the roughly $450,000 in fees which Enron paid Milbank within 90 days prior to Enron's filing, as well as the roughly $830,000 in fees which Exco claimed Enron Wind paid Milbank in December 2001 and January 2002, constituted poten-

---

[147] Denial Order, *supra* note 136, at 15 (citing *In re* Leslie Fay Cos., Inc., 175 B.R. 525, 533 (Bankr. S.D.N.Y. 1994)).

[148] *Id.* at 15; 11 U.S.C. § 101(14)(C) (2002).

[149] Motion to Disqualify, *supra* note 139.

[150] Denial Order, *supra* note 136, at 16–25.

[151] *Id.* at 17.

[152] *Id.*

[153] *Id.* at 17–18.

[154] *Id.* at 18.

[155] Motion to Disqualify, *supra* note 139.

tial voidable transfers.[156] Although Enron Wind, Milbank's largest single Enron client, filed for Chapter 11 protection in February 2002, the Court ultimately found the payments to Milbank were not made by Enron Wind or any debtor; therefore, the $830,000 in fees could not constitute potential preferences.[157] Further, the Court concluded that the $450,000 in fees from Enron would not disqualify Milbank's representation so long as Milbank agreed to the Examiner's determination concerning these fees and withheld this amount from the fees it sought to collect for Committee representation.[158]

Exco then argued that Milbank's pre-petition relationship with Enron disqualified Milbank's Committee representation.[159] Exco asserted that no other firm, other than debtor's pre-bankruptcy counsel, Vinson & Elkins, had more connections with Enron than Milbank.[160] Exco suggested that Milbank overstated its specialized expertise in representing the Committee because the very attorneys with expertise in structured finance transactions could not share their knowledge from the restricted side of the Court-imposed "firewall."[161] Again, the Court found no evidence to support Exco's arguments and dismissed Exco's contentions.[162]

Finally, Exco argued that Milbank's pre-petition representation of J.P. Morgan Chase, as well as its continuing representation of Citibank, two individual unsecured creditors on the Committee,[163] disqualified Milbank.[164] According to Exco, Milbank has an interest adverse to the estate with respect to Chase because Milbank helped Chase structure "sham loans" on which Enron later defaulted.[165] With respect to Citibank, Milbank's interest is equally adverse to the estate because Milbank continues to advise Citibank regarding the six "credit-linked note transactions."[166] Additionally, Exco characterizes Chase and Citibank as "some of the most active participants in Enron's structured

---

[156] *Id.* at 2–3.

[157] Denial Order, *supra* note 136, at 18.

[158] *Id.* at 19.

[159] Motion to Disqualify, *supra* note 139, at 7.

[160] *Id.* at 9.

[161] *Id.* at 10–11.

[162] Denial Order, *supra* note 136, at 21.

[163] Citibank resigned from the Committee in June 2002.

[164] Motion to Disqualify, *supra* note 139, at 15–17. Interestingly, Milbank took a leading roll in the 2001 bankruptcy filed by PG&E. Enron and PG&E are major creditors of each other. Ethical walls were put in place to prevent attorneys on the cases from exchanging information. Nathan Koppel, *Milbank's Second Helping of Enron Pie; Law Firm Once Did Work for the Energy Giant, Now It Represents Some of Enron's Biggest Creditors in Bankruptcy*, LEGAL TIMES, Mar. 11, 2002, at 20.

[165] Motion to Disqualify, *supra* note 139, at 16.

[166] *Id.* at 17.

finance transactions."[167] However, the Court rejected Exco's reasoning because no evidence suggested that the entire Committee would allow its counsel to benefit two of its members and the Debtors at the creditors' expense.[168]

Furthermore, Milbank's representation was limited by retained conflicts counsel (Squire Sanders).[169] Therefore, the Court denied Exco's motion to disqualify because Milbank possessed no interest adverse to the estate or creditors. The Court also expressed the points that Milbank had fully disclosed all conflicts in its initial application, and that Exco had delayed in challenging Milbank's representation.

Exco appealed the bankruptcy court's ruling, but the district court affirmed the decision.[170] The Examiner indicated in his First Report that he will probe Milbank's disinterestedness in future reports.[171] Thus, the final chapter has not been written on this topic. Whatever the ultimate outcome, one cannot escape a nagging sense of concern about the impropriety—or at least the appearance thereof—of one of the leading law firm architects of Enron's structured finance system being brought in to represent the unsecured creditors to challenge those very schemes. The old adage of "the fox guarding the henhouse" naggingly comes to mind.

8. EQUITABLE SUBORDINATION[172]

An interesting question is whether claims brought by J.P. Morgan Chase & Co. and Citigroup in Enron's bankruptcy case should be equitably subordinated pursuant to § 510(c)(1) of the Bankruptcy Code. Section 6, *supra,* explored issues regarding the propriety of those banks' membership on the Creditors' Committee, due to possible conflicts, including the threat of subordination. It is to that threat that we now turn for a more detailed examination.

Section 510(c)(1) of the Bankruptcy Code permits a bankruptcy court to "subordinate for purposes of distribution all or part of an allowed interest to all or part of another allowed interest." "The statutory distribution scheme thus may be overridden in part by the bankruptcy court to prevent inequitable results."[173] Furthermore, § 510(c)(1) refers simply to "principles of equitable subordination," but does not define the term.[174] The legislative history indicates that Congress's intent in using this

---

[167] *Id.* at 17–18.

[168] Denial Order, *supra* note 136, at 4–5.

[169] *Id.* at 20.

[170] *In re* Enron Corp., 2003 WL 223455 (S.D.N.Y. Feb. 3, 2003).

[171] First Interim Report, *supra* note 8, at 20 n.48.

[172] Aaron VanGetson did a tremendous job on this section, for which I thank him.

[173] TABB, *supra* note 42, at 527.

[174] *Id.; see* 11 U.S.C. § 510(c)(1) (2002).

term was to "follow existing case law and leave to the courts development of this principle."[175] "Thus, while the starting point in identifying the parameters of equitable subordination doctrine is the state of the law as of 1978, Congress also wanted to give the courts some flexibility."[176]

The Fifth Circuit, in *In re Mobile Steel Co.*,[177] identified three conditions necessary to establish equitable subordination: (1) the claimant must have engaged in some type of inequitable conduct; (2) the misconduct must have resulted in injury to the creditors of the bankrupt or conferred an unfair advantage on the claimant; and (3) equitable subordination of the claim must not be inconsistent with the provisions of the Bankruptcy Act.[178] Furthermore, "[i]nequitable conduct sufficient to support a finding of equitable subordination is much easier to establish in the case of a creditor who is an *insider* or an *alter ego* of the debtor," and more difficult to subordinate the claim of a non-insider creditor.[179]

Insider status is important because it determines the standard the court will apply to determine if equitable subordination is appropriate. Where the creditor is a non-insider, the trustee must show that the creditor's conduct was "egregious and severely unfair in relation to other creditors."[180] Where the creditor is an insider, however, the trustee must only show "unfairness" to justify the subordination of the insider-creditor's claims.[181] "The reason that the transactions of insiders will be closely studied is because such parties usually have greater opportunities for . . . inequitable conduct, not because the relationship itself is somehow a ground for subordination."[182] Section 101(31)(B) of the Bankruptcy Code defines the term "insider" when the debtor is a corporation.[183]

---

[175] 124 CONG. REC. S17, 412 (daily ed. Oct. 6, 1978) (statement of Sen. DeConcini); 124 CONG. REC. H11, 95 (daily ed. Sept. 28, 1978) (statement of Rep. Edwards).

[176] TABB, *supra* note 42, at 527.

[177] 563 F.2d 692 (5th Cir. 1977); *see also In re* Missionary Baptist Found. of America, Inc., 712 F.2d 206, 212 (5th Cir. 1983).

[178] 563 F.2d at 700. Although decided before the enactment of the current Code, *Mobile Steel* continues to command a devoted following. *See In re* Herby's Foods, Inc., 2 F.3d 128, 130 (5th Cir. 1993). The Supreme Court noted the continuing influence in 1996 in *United States v. Noland*, 116 S.Ct. 1524, 1526 (1996).

[179] TABB, *supra* note 42, at 528.

[180] *In re* Hyperion Enterprises, Inc. 158 B.R. 555, 563 (D.R.I. 1993) (quoting *In re* Giorgio, 862 F.2d 933, 939).

[181] *Id.*

[182] *Id.* at 562 (citing *In re* Fabricators, 926 F.2d 1458, 1465 (5th Cir. 1991) (quoting *In re* Missionary Baptist Foundation, Inc., 818 F.2d 1135, 1144 n.8 (5th Cir. 1987))).

[183] 11 U.S.C. § 101(31)(B)(i)–(vi) (2002). The term "insider" includes: director of the debtor; officer of the debtor; person in control of the debtor; partnership in which the debtor is a general partner; general partner of the debtor; or relative of a general partner, director, officer, or person in control of the debtor.

A lender may be an insider if it "generally acted as a joint venturer or prospective partner with the debtor rather than an armslength creditor."[184] The legislative history to § 101(31) states that the term "insider" covers "one who has a sufficiently close relationship with the debtor that his conduct is made subject to closer scrutiny than those dealing at arms length with the debtor."[185]

In determining whether a creditor is an "insider" of the debtor under this flexible approach, courts have considered a wide variety of factors, including whether the creditor:

(i)   received information from the debtor that was not available to other creditors, shareholders and the general public;

(ii) attempted to influence decisions made by the debtor;

(iii) selected new management for the debtor;

(iv) had special access to debtor's premises and personnel;

(v)   was the debtor's sole source of financial support; and

(vi) generally acted as a joint venturer or prospective partner with the debtor rather than an armslength creditor.[186]

In other words, the operative question is whether the non-insider creditor so assumed control over the debtor's affairs so as to create a fiduciary duty owed by the non-insider to the debtor or to other creditors in the collection of the non-insider creditor's claim.[187]

A. J.P. Morgan Chase & Co.—Mahonia Transactions

"[A] decade ago, Chase Manhattan Bank (now merged with J.P. Morgan [& Co.]) set up a special purpose entity" in the British Channel Islands named Mahonia Ltd.[188] According to records from the Jersey Financial Services Commission, Mahonia Ltd. was incorporated on December 16, 1992, and has two nominee shareholders, Lively Ltd. and Juris Ltd., who represent undisclosed owners.[189] The Jersey-based business

---

[184] Pan Am Corp. v. Delta Air Lines, Inc., 175 B.R. 438, 500 (S.D.N.Y. 1994).

[185] S. REP. NO. 95-989, at 25 (1978).

[186] Pan Am, 175 B.R. at 500 (citations omitted).

[187] See In re W.T. Grant Co., 699 F.2d 599, 609–10 (2d Cir. 1983).

[188] Review & Outlook: Enron's Enablers, WALL ST. J., July 29, 2002, at A14 [hereinafter Enron's Enablers].

[189] Jathon Sapsford & Anita Raghavan, Trading Charges: Lawsuit Spotlights J.P. Morgan's Ties To the Enron Debacle, WALL ST. J., Jan. 25, 2002, at A1 [hereinafter Trading Charges]; see also Financial Institutions and Collapse of Enron: Hearing Before the Perm. Subcomm. On Investigations of the Senate Comm. On Gov'tal Affairs, 107th Cong. (2002) (statement of Jeffrey Dellapina, Managing Director, J.P. Morgan Chase & Co.) [hereinafter Dellapina], available at 2002 WL 1613799:

Neither Chase nor Enron has any ownership interest in Mahonia. No employee or officer of Chase or Enron served as an officer or director or held shares in Mahonia. The directors and officers of Mahonia make the ultimate determination as to whether or not to enter into a transaction.

has been the subject of investigations by the Securities and Exchange Commission, Manhattan District Attorney Robert Morgenthau, the Federal Reserve Bank of New York, and the Justice Department. The heart of the investigations is whether J.P. Morgan used an offshore special purpose entity to help Enron "hide debt and artificially boost cash flow."[190]

The Mahonia transactions were structured such that "J.P. Morgan would pay Enron between $150 million and $250 million for the future delivery of natural gas or crude oil."[191] The transaction "was constructed as a 'trade,' not a loan. So Enron would report [the transaction] as earnings that would cancel out, temporarily, losses on Enron['s] books."[192] To hedge against the risk of loss in the event that Enron defaulted before delivery, J.P. Morgan paid a portion of its earnings to other banks, such as ABN Amro Holding NV and West LB, in exchange for their guaranteeing portions of the arrangement.[193]

But Enron had to eventually deliver the oil or gas, usually in regular installments with the value of $10 million to $20 million, the people familiar with Mahonia say. With each delivery, the losses began to appear on Enron's ledger. These deliveries would begin the following year, so the losses were carried from one year to the next, without showing up clearly on Enron's books.

> [As a result,] Enron kept those losses in reserve in case Enron had any profit windfall on which it might pay tax. . . . If it did, it would use those losses to cancel out profits, and thus lower its tax burden. Or if Enron didn't have big profits to hide, it would just roll the losses over again to the next fiscal year—by going back to J.P. Morgan and selling it another gas contract. . . . As one Wall Street banker put it, the arrangements "practically guaranteed" Enron would come back to J.P. Morgan for more.[194]

The deals generated "fees and interest measuring as much as $100 million."[195] J.P. Morgan also "often [received] a small fee for arranging the financing."[196] J.P. Morgan has said that, besides Enron, seven other companies, including "Columbia Natural Resources, Inc., now part of NiSource, Inc.; Occidental Petroleum Co.; Ocean Energy Inc.; Santa Fe Synder Corp., which is now part of Devon Energy Corp.; and Tom

---

[190] Jathon Sapsford & Paul Beckett, *Citigroup Deals helped Enron Disguise Its Debts as Trades*, WALL ST. J., July 22, 2002, at A1 [hereinafter *Citigroup Deals*].

[191] *Trading Charges, supra* note 189.

[192] *Id.*

[193] *Id.*

[194] *Id.*

[195] *Id.*

[196] *Id.*

Brown Inc.," all engaged in similar transactions with Mahonia Ltd.[197] "Yet by far Mahonia's biggest customer was Enron, accounting for roughly 60% of its business, people familiar with the matter say."[198]

On July 23, 2002, Jeffrey Dellapina, Managing Director of J.P. Morgan Chase & Co.'s Credit and Rates Group, testified to the Committee on Senate Governmental Affair's Permanent Subcommittee on Investigations that, "[f]rom 1994 through 2001, Enron entered into a total of 10 more prepaid transactions involving Chase. Nine of these transactions were with Mahonia Limited and one was with Mahonia Natural Gas Limited, both Jersey Channel Islands SPEs."[199] While the Mahonia-Enron transactions were originally for $150 to $250 million per transaction, in the summer of 1999, when "oil prices were weak" and there were "concerns over the future profitability of the energy industry," Enron officials sought to do even larger deals.[200] "Enron officials contacted [J.P.] Morgan with requests to do bigger and bigger trades, including a large arrangement of $650 million in one trade."[201] The bank, which had shouldered a portion of the risk, was not willing to handle such large risk.

> Enron turned to 11 insurance companies . . . to issue "surety bonds." . . . Enron arranged these contracts for J.P. Morgan—and paid the insurance companies for it—so that the bank would feel more comfortable making increasingly large trades with the energy company."[202]

The arrangement among Enron, Mahonia, and J.P. Morgan continued even as Enron's problems worsened. "On September 10, 2001, Enron and [J.P.] Morgan arranged to obtain a $165 million letter of credit from West LB to guarantee derivatives trades between Mahonia and Enron North America."[203] If the letter of credit transaction was truly between Mahonia and Enron North America, then why did Philip Levy, J.P. Morgan's associate general counsel, review the legal documentation? After the bankruptcy filing on December 2, 2001, "[J.P.] Morgan requested to be paid under the letter of credit."[204] West LB refused to pay, "depositing the $165 million in an escrow account, which it says it will make available when the Mahonia transactions underlying the lending facility are proved proper."[205]

---

[197] Paul Beckett & Jathon Sapsford, *Energy Deals made $200 Million in Fees for Citigroup, J.P. Morgan,* WALL ST. J., July 24, 2002, at A1.

[198] *Trading Charges, supra* note 189.

[199] Dellapina, *supra* note 189.

[200] *Trading Charges, supra* note 189.

[201] *Id.*

[202] *Id.*

[203] *Id.*

[204] *Id.*

[205] *Id.*

On January 2, 2003, J.P. Morgan settled its dispute with insurers over its role in the Enron debacle. J.P. Morgan "agreed to accept only about 52 cents on the dollar—60% on the [surety] bonds, plus a pledge to buy out the insurers' claims against Enron's bankruptcy corpse for 13 cents on the dollar."[206] The eleven insurance companies that issued surety bonds at Enron's request so as to reduce the risk exposure to J.P. Morgan had filed suit on June 21, 2002, alleging that J.P. Morgan "knew that unless something was done to bolster or otherwise support Enron's precarious financial condition, of which [J.P. Morgan] had knowledge, it would never be able to recover those loans."[207]

B. Citigroup—Yosemite Transactions

Like its competitor, J.P. Morgan Chase & Co., Citigroup, Inc. also set up commodity "prepay" deals for Enron.

> Citigroup set up a trust that raised money from investors in Europe or the [United States]. Then the money moved to a Citigroup-sponsored special purpose vehicle in the Cayman Islands known as Delta. Delta then sent the money in a circle through a series of oil trades, first to Enron, then to Citigroup, and then back to Delta, each time moving the money through oil prepay contracts.[208]

As commentators later explained: "Oil never actually exchanged hands [between the parties discussed above], and the trades effectively canceled each other out. Cash settlement [of trades] is common in commodity transactions, but the round-trip nature of the trades is one uncommon aspect" of the Delta transactions.[209] The series of deals, known collectively as Yosemite, "helped Enron borrow money over the past three years that was booked as coming from trades instead of loans . . . [and] helped boost the company's weak cash flow to match its growth in paper profits, at a time when the gap between the two had grown to as much as $1 billion a year, according to one Enron memo."[210]

Other banks, such as FleetBoston Financial Corp. and Credit Suisse First Boston, structured Enron prepay transactions totaling a little more than $1 billion. J.P. Morgan arranged roughly $3.7 billion, according to Congressional investigators. Citigroup, however, topped them all, "providing Enron with $4.8 billion in fourteen separate

---

[206] *Review and Outlook: Morgan's Costly Virtue*, WALL ST. J., Jan. 3, 2003, at A10 [hereinafter *Morgan's Costly Virtue*].

[207] Jathon Sapsford, *Insurers' Filing Says J.P. Morgan Burnished Enron Financial Status*, WALL ST. J., June 24, 2002, at C14.

[208] *Citigroup Deals, supra* note 190.

[209] *Id.*

[210] *Id.*

transactions through prepays in just the last three years before Enron filed for bank-ruptcy protection [on December 2, 2001]."[211]

C. Were J.P. Morgan and Citigroup Insiders?

A strong argument could be made that the two banks were insiders because the banks acted as joint venturers with Enron, rather than as arm's-length creditors. As several commentators later observed:

> The Wall Street firms are tied to Enron in a variety of ways: They partici-pated in the underwriting of Enron shares over the years and the selling of Enron bonds. Their analysts almost universally recommended the pur-chase of Enron shares. They also marketed investments in Enron-related partnerships.[212]
>
> J.P. Morgan Chase & Co. was deeply involved in Enron Corp.'s finances, simultaneously investing in the company, buying Enron stock for funds it managed and recommending the energy company's stock to investors. . . . J.P. Morgan's Enron investments meant that the bank would benefit if the Houston company's stock price rose. Its purchases of Enron's stock and "strong buy" recommendations boosted share prices. At the time J.P. Mor-gan analysts recommended Enron stock, other bank officials knew that the energy company had major off-balance-sheet debts. The bank also was a major investor in one of Enron's largest outside partnerships, LJM.[213]

As a result, Enron and the major banks benefited substantially from multi-faceted relationships between the financiers and the energy-trading company. For example, in the case of the stock analysts' recommendations,[214] the value of the major banks' eq-uity investments in Enron increased as the stock price appreciated, as a result of buy-ing based on those recommendations. Enron, meanwhile, benefited in the sense that the company's cost of capital decreased as the stock price rose—making it easier for the company to secure additional financing underwritten by the major banks.

---

[211] *Id.*

[212] Dan Ackman, *Enron Probe Widens on Two Fronts*, Forbes, Apr. 4, 2002, *available at* http://www.forbes.com/2002/04/04/0404topnews.html.

[213] Peter Behr & Ben White, *J.P. Morgan Had Many Ties With Enron*, Wash. Post, Feb. 23, 2002, at E1.

[214] "[N]early every . . . analyst reached the same conclusions about Enron in 2001. . . . As of Oct. 18, [2001,] all 15 analysts tracked by Thomson Financial/First Call rated Enron a 'buy'—12 of the 15 called it a 'strong buy.' Even as late as Nov. 8, [2001,] the date of Enron's disclosure that nearly five years of earnings would have to be recalculated, 11 of the 15 recommended buying the stock." Dan Ackman, *Enron Analysts: We Was Duped*, Forbes, Feb. 27, 2002, *at* http://forbes.com/2002/02/27/0227analysts.html.

D. Inequitable Conduct

In two 1996 decisions, *U.S. v. Nolan*[215] and *U.S. v. Reorganized CF&I Fabricators of Utah, Inc.,*[216] the Supreme Court virtually eliminated subordination absent proof of inequitable conduct.[217] The inequitable conduct may arise out of any unfair act by the creditor so long as the conduct affects the bankruptcy results of the other creditors.[218] Three categories of conduct have been recognized as sufficient to qualify as "inequitable conduct," thereby satisfying the first prong of the *Mobile Steel* test:

1. Fraud, illegality, or breach of fiduciary duties;
2. Undercapitalization; and
3. A claimant's use of the debtor as a mere instrumentality or alter ego.[219]

Furthermore,

> [t]he inequity which will entitle a bankruptcy court to regulate the distribution to a creditor, by subordination or other equitable means, need not therefore be specifically related to the creditor's claim, either in its origin or in its acquisition, but it may equally arise out of any unfair act on the part of the creditor, which affects the bankruptcy results to other creditors and so makes it inequitable that he should assert a parity with them in the distribution of the estate.[220]

E. Fraud, Illegality, or Breach of Fiduciary Duties

As a scholar recently explained,

> In order for equitable subordination to be imposed based on fraud or breach of fiduciary duties, the bankruptcy court need not find actual fraud. . . . Examples of fraudulent conduct demanding subordination of claims include a creditor knowingly making false statements regarding the debtor's

---

[215] 517 U.S. 535 (1996).

[216] 518 U.S. 213 (1996).

[217] Jo Ann J. Brighton, *Capital Contribution or a Loan? A Practical Guide to Analyzing Recharacterization Claims (or, when is Equitable Subordination the Appropriate Analysis?)*, 21 AM. BANKR. INST. J. 41, 45 (2002).

[218] *In re* Mobile Steel, 563 F.2d 692, 700 (5th Cir. 1977).

[219] *In re* Clark Pipe and Supply Co., 893 F.2d 693, 699 (5th Cir. 1990) (citing *In re* Missionary Baptist Foundation, Inc., 712 F.2d 206, 212 (5th Cir. 1983)).

[220] *Mobile Steel,* 563 F.2d at 700 (quoting *In re* Kansas City Journal-Post Co., 144 F.2d 791, 804 (8th Cir. 1944)).

financial condition, and when a creditor colludes with a debtor using its claim to defraud other creditors.[221]

Other examples of fraudulent conduct include "misrepresentation of credit status, misuse of judgment claims, concealment and overt misrepresentation."[222]

A number of documents uncovered in the Congressional investigation into the Enron scandal suggest that Enron and Citigroup tried actively to conceal the substance of the Yosemite transactions from rating agencies and investors.[223] Enron documents suggest that "[o]nly two parties would know the precise details [of the Yosemite transactions]: Enron and Citigroup."[224] As one Enron document states, "[t]he use of prepays as a monetization tool is a sensitive topic for both ratings agencies and institutional investors," while other Enron documents "commonly refer[] to the Yosemite transactions as keeping details in a 'black box.'"[225] One February 1999 e-mail from Adam Kulick, a Citigroup vice president, told the working group for the Yosemite transactions that "the client does not wish to have to explain the details of many of the assets to investors or rating agencies."[226] "On Nov[ember] 14, 2001, Enron executive Doug McDowell sent an e-mail to Richard Caplan, co-head of credit derivatives at Citigroup's Salomon Smith Barney investment banking unit, saying: 'Apparently an investor spoke to someone at citi and received info on delta . . . . We need to shut this down.'"[227]

Similarly, a J.P. Morgan executive, in a 1998 e-mail to colleagues, stated that Enron "loves these deals as they are able to hide funded debt from their equity analysts because they (at the very least) book it as deferred rev or (better yet) bury it in their trading liabilities."[228] In a 1999 review of internal accounting, J.P. Morgan Vice Chairman Donald Layton wrote, "We are making disguised loans, usually buried in commodities or equities derivatives."[229]

These documents suggest that Citigroup and J.P. Morgan actively concealed information concerning the Yosemite and Mahonia transactions, respectively, from shareholders, rating agencies, and the general public. Third parties continued to do business with Enron in reliance on Enron's *apparent* financial condition. This alone may justify the subordination of the banks' claims.

---

[221] Brighton, *supra* note 217, at 45 (citing Heiser v. Woodruff, 327 U.S. 726, 732–33 (1946)).

[222] *Id.* (citing Asa S. Herzog & Joel B. Zweibel, *The Equitable Subordination of Claims in Bankruptcy*, 15 VAND. L. REV. 83, 99 (1961)).

[223] Beckett & Sapsford, *supra* note 197.

[224] *Citigroup Deals, supra* note 190.

[225] *Id.*

[226] Beckett & Sapsford, *supra* note 197.

[227] *Id.*

[228] Paul Beckett & Laurie P. Cohen, *J.P. Morgan is Still Shadowed By Enron Links*, WALL ST. J., Jan. 16, 2003, at C1.

[229] *Morgan's Costly Virtue, supra* note 206.

Claims of fraudulent conduct on the part of J.P. Morgan and Citigroup appear to have traction in the securities fraud litigation already levied against the two banks. In a memorandum and order issued on December 20, 2002, District Judge Melinda Harmon refused to dismiss claims of violations of the anti-fraud provisions contained in § 10(b) of the Securities Exchange Act of 1934 asserted against J.P. Morgan and Citigroup, saying that the Enron SPE transactions were utilized to deceive investors in a "regular pattern of related and repeated conduct."[230] The Judge added that the SPE transactions "were not isolated, one-of-a-kind instances of violations of the statutes, but deliberate, repeated actions with shared characteristics that were part of an alleged common scheme through which defendants all profited handsomely, many exorbitantly."[231]

F. Undercapitalization

For purposes of determining when the claims held by organizers or shareholders should be equitably subordinated on the grounds of undercapitalization, the amount of undercapitalization that is appropriate is "what reasonably prudent men with a general background knowledge of the particular type of business and its hazards would determine was reasonable capitalization in light of any special circumstances which existed at the time of the incorporation of the now defunct enterprise."[232] The adequacy of capitalization is to be judged at the time of organization. Enron, formed in 1985 after the merger of Houston Natural Gas and InterNorth of Omaha, Nebraska,[233] had been in operation for a number of years before entering into the Yosemite and Mahonia transactions, without obvious capitalization issues. Therefore, the undercapitalization inquiry is not relevant for the purposes of determining whether the major banks' claims should be equitably subordinated.

G. Control

"It is clear that domination and control, accompanied by fraud, will lead courts to equitably subordinate a claim."[234] "Control means 'the actual exercise of managerial discretion,' or 'usurping the power of the debtors' directors and officers to make busi-

---

[230] Phyllis Lipka Skupien & Robert Woodman McSherry, *Houston Court Says Enron Defendants Missed Red Flags*, 1 No. 26 ANDREWS ENRON LITIG. REP. 1 (Jan. 13, 2003) (quoting Memorandum and Order Issued, Newby v. Enron Corp., No. 01-3624 (S.D. Tex., Dec. 20, 2002)).

[231] *Id.*

[232] *In re* Mobile Steel, 563 F.2d 692, 703 (5th Cir. 1977) (quoting N. LATTIN, THE LAW OF CORPORATIONS §§ 15, 77 (1971)).

[233] Company Snapshot, *available at* http://www.enron.com/corp/pressroom/factsheets/company.html (last visited June 3, 2003).

[234] Brighton, *supra* note 217, at 45.

ness decisions."[235] The creditor must, in effect, exercise such "total control over the [debtor] as to have essentially replaced its decision making capacity with that of [the debtor]."[236] "There must be, 'to some extent, a merger of identity.'"[237]

It is not clear that either J.P. Morgan or Citigroup exercised the requisite level of control over Enron. In fact, it was Enron who "had a reputation for brow-beating its bankers," and "put some pressure on Citigroup to carry out elements of the deals."[238] Similarly, it was Enron who arranged surety bonds for J.P. Morgan so as to increase the size of the Mahonia transactions from $150 million per deal to $650 million per deal.[239] Most of the evidence seems to point to a close relationship between Enron and the major banks in which all parties benefited, but not to a relationship dominated or controlled by the financiers.

H. Unfair Advantage

One court recently explained, "In [the Second] Circuit, the second requirement for equitable subordination involves a conjunctive test, requiring a showing of both unfair advantage to one creditor and harm to the debtor or its other creditors."[240] Thus, "[t]he court must determine if the misconduct affected the bankruptcy proceedings—specifically, if the creditors lost something that they had an equitable right to receive in bankruptcy."[241]

Although it is by no means clear precisely to what extent the banks may have benefited vis-à-vis other creditors in bankruptcy as a result of their arrangements with Enron, certain events seem to suggest that the banks may have improved their status as Enron creditors in the days and months immediately preceding the bankruptcy filing. For example, in October 2001, "Enron owed Citigroup $250 million in unsecured debt that was coming due in early December [2001]. . . . Citigroup told Enron it would provide $600 million of a new $1 billion secured loan—as long as $250 million was used to pay back existing Citigroup debt. . . ."[242] Other creditors claim that the

---

[235] *In re* Kids Creek Partners, L.P., 212 B.R. 898, 929 (Bankr. N.D. Ill. 1997) (quoting *In re* Kids Creek Partners, L.P., 200 B.R. 996, 1016 (Bankr. N.D. Ill. 1996)).

[236] *In re* Abatement Corp., 157 B.R. 590, 592 (E.D. La. 1993) (quoting *In re* Clark Pipe & Supply Co., 893 F.2d 693, 699, 701 (5th Cir. 1990)).

[237] *In re* Kids Creek Partners, L.P., 212 B.R. at 929 (quoting *In re* Ludwig Honold Mfg. Co., Inc., 46 B.R. 125, 128 (Bankr. E.D. Pa. 1985)).

[238] *Citigroup Deals, supra* note 190.

[239] *Trading Charges, supra* note 189.

[240] *In re* Mr. R's Prepared Foods, Inc., 251 B.R. 24, 29 (Bankr. D. Conn. 2000) (quoting *In re* W.T. Grant Co., 699 F.2d 599, 611 (2d Cir. 1983)).

[241] Brighton, *supra* note 217, at 46.

[242] Jathon Sapsford & Mitchell Pacelle, *Citigroup's Enron Financing Stirs Controversy*, WALL ST. J., Jan. 16, 2002, at C1.

deal "effectively reduced the pool of collateral available to all of Enron's other creditors in the bankruptcy proceedings."[243] Also, J.P. Morgan "contributed the remaining $400 million to the $1 billion credit line," but "[u]nlike Citigroup, it made no demands that its own existing loans be rolled into the new credit facility."[244]

Such evidence is undoubtedly damaging to any argument put forth by Citigroup that it was not acting to secure a stronger position among Enron creditors. Although J.P. Morgan did not follow suit with Citigroup for this particular method of protecting its interest vis-à-vis other creditors, that does not imply that J.P. Morgan did not engage in any related conduct.

I. Equitable Subordination of the Claim Is Not Inconsistent with the Provisions of the Code

"This element of the test is a reminder to bankruptcy courts that they cannot adjust valid claims by good-faith creditors simply because the courts sense inequitable results."[245] Whether a court will see J.P. Morgan and Citigroup as "good faith" creditors and thus saved by this final test is open to question, to put it mildly. In other words, it would not behoove either bank to rest its hopes on this prong of the subordination test.

J. Examiner's Report

As discussed earlier, Examiner Neal Batson filed his Second Report on January 21, 2003. Although the contents of the Second Report had not been made public as of the time of this writing, Ted Janger's essay (following this essay) discusses this report in depth. The Second Report was "expected to be much more detailed, and play a significant role in deciding if any of Enron's creditors should have their claims reduced for playing a part in its downfall."[246] Unquestionably, whatever the eventual outcome, it seems quite likely that the issue of equitable subordination of the enormous claims of Citigroup and J.P. Morgan will be thoroughly investigated and is likely to be of considerable importance and visibility in the Enron bankruptcy.

9. SUBSTANTIVE CONSOLIDATION[247]

Enron North America ("ENA"), Enron's largest affiliate, has filed for bankruptcy as well. ENA ran the energy-trading operation and generated over 90 percent of Enron's

---

[243] *Id.*

[244] *Id.*

[245] Brighton, *supra* note 217, at 46 (citation omitted).

[246] Eric Berger, *The Fall of Enron: Initial Report to Stay Sealed Until Feb. 14*, HOUS. CHRON., Jan. 22, 2003, at 3.

[247] Thank you to James Antonopoulos for his very fine help on this section. Matthew Sostrin also contributed excellent work.

$100.7 billion of revenue in 2000.[248] In its schedules, ENA reported "assets of $13.7 billion and debts of $8.8 billion."[249] Thus, creditors of ENA are potentially far better off than other creditors of Enron Corp., and, not surprisingly, have been fighting to keep ENA separated from Enron Corp. and the clutches of Enron's creditors.

ENA's trading creditors also have been concerned about "cash sweeps," which have allegedly transferred assets from ENA to Enron Corp. since the bankruptcy filings. Judge Gonzalez responded to these concerns by appointing an independent examiner, Harrison Goldin, in the ENA case to review the finances and cash flow of ENA to ensure against improper transfers.[250] Goldin's initial and subsequent reports indicated that no improper transfers had occurred.[251]

Bondholders of Enron Corp. have pushed for "substantive consolidation" to combine ENA and Enron Corp. under a single reorganization plan to treat creditors more fairly.[252] However, if substantive consolidation occurs, Enron Corp.'s massive debt will dilute recoveries by creditors of ENA.[253] Thus far, Enron Corp. and ENA have been treated separately. Judge Gonzalez established separate timetables for each to file a reorganization plan.[254] Batson's First Report reserves any recommendation on substantive consolidation for future reports.[255]

Let us now turn to a more detailed examination of whether ENA's bankruptcy case should be substantively consolidated with the other Enron cases. Preliminarily, a decisive factor is whether Judge Gonzalez will deem substantive consolidation to be fair to *all* creditors—considering that ENA generated 90% of Enron's revenue and *appears* to have enough to repay its creditors.[256]

---

[248] Jeff St. Onge, *Enron Creditors' Panel to Explore Combining Company and Units*, BLOOMBERG NEWS, May 16, 2002.

[249] *Id.*

[250] Order Approving the Appointment of Harrison J. Goldin as the Examiner in Enron North America Corp., *In re* Enron, No. 01-16034 (Bankr. S.D.N.Y. Mar. 12, 2002), *available at* http://www.elaw4enron .com, docket entry no. 2066.

[251] Weekly Report of Harrison J. Goldin, the Court-Appointed Examiner In the Enron North America Corp. Bankruptcy Proceeding, Listing Deposits and Disbursements Made Into and Out of the ENA Consolidation Account for the Period April 1, 2002 Through April 5, 2002, *In re* Enron, No. 01-16034 (Bankr. S.D.N.Y. Apr. 25, 2002), *available at* http://www.elaw4enron.com, docket entry no. 3667; *Enron Examiner Releases Interim Report*, BCD NEWS & COMMENT, Apr. 24, 2002.

[252] St. Onge, *supra* note 249.

[253] Jeff St. Onge et al., *Enron Creditors are Vying for Energy Trader's Remains*, BLOOMBERG NEWS, May 7, 2002.

[254] Christopher Mumma, *Enron's Trading Creditors Won't Get Own Committee, Judge Says*, BLOOMBERG NEWS, June 24, 2002.

[255] First Interim Report, *supra* note 8, at 157.

[256] St. Onge et al., *supra* note 254; *see also* Lingling Wei, *Enron Examiner Wants Plan Extension*, ASSOCIATED PRESS, July 28, 2002 (ENA's financial statements are incomplete, because they do not take into account money transfers within Enron or transactions involving off-balance-sheet partnerships).

Substantive consolidation is not expressly provided for in the Bankruptcy Code.[257] Instead, courts have used their general equitable powers under § 105(a) to substantively consolidate assets and claims of certain debtors and satisfy liabilities from the resultant pool. Because substantive consolidation forces creditors of one debtor to share in this consolidated pool with creditors of a less solvent debtor, courts view substantive consolidation not as a "mere instrument of procedural convenience . . . but a measure vitally affecting substantive rights."[258] Because of its dramatic effect on the potential recovery of creditors, substantive consolidation should be used sparingly. The purpose of substantive consolidation is to treat all creditors equitably. In deciding whether to invoke the doctrine of substantive consolidation, the following factors are decisive:

1. whether creditors dealt with the entities as a single economic unit and did not rely on their separate identity in extending credit; *or*
2. whether the affairs of the debtors are so entangled that consolidation will benefit all creditors.[259]

Baupost Group, L.L.C. and Racepoint Partners, L.P. ("Bondholders") are holders of $1 billion of senior unsecured indebtedness of Enron. The Bondholders filed a motion requesting the court to expand the scope of the duties of the ENA Examiner, to include an analysis of whether Enron and its debtor subsidiaries should be substantively consolidated.[260] The Bondholders argued that both factors determinative of the substantive consolidation analysis, as set forth in *In re Augie/Restivo Banking Co.*,[261] are satisfied in the Enron bankruptcy, and that accordingly substantive consolidation should be ordered.

First, the Bondholders argued that creditors dealt with Enron and its subsidiaries as a single economic unit and did not rely on their separate identity in extending credit. The creditors of ENA treated Enron and ENA as a single economic unit and relied on

---

[257] *See* TABB, *supra* note 42, at 133–38.

[258] *In re* Augie/Restivo Banking Co., 860 F.2d 515, 518 (2d Cir. 1988) (quoting Flora Mir Candy Corp. v. R.S. Dickson & Co., 432 F.2d 1060, 1062 (2d Cir. 1970)).

[259] *Id.* Regarding the second factor, all creditors will be benefited if untangling the debtors' affairs is either impossible or so costly as to consume assets.

[260] Motion of Certain Holders of Enron Debt for Order, Pursuant to 11 U.S.C. Sections 105 and 1106, Expanding the Scope of the Duties of the Enron North America Examiner or the Enron Examiner to Include an Investigation and Report as to (i) Whether The Cases Of Enron And Its Debtor Subsidiaries (Including Enron North America And Its Debtor Subsidiaries) Should Be Substantively Consolidated; (ii) Whether Certain Prepetition Transfers By Enron To Or For The Benefit Of Enron North America Or Its Creditors Constituted Fraudulent Conveyances; And (iii) Related Matters, *In re* Enron, No. 01-16034 (Bankr. S.D.N.Y. Apr. 16, 2002) [hereinafter Motion of Certain Holders], *available at* http://www.elaw4enron.com, docket entry no. 3189.

[261] 860 F.2d at 515.

the credit of *Enron*, not on the assets and liabilities of *ENA*, in doing business with ENA.[262] Additionally, they asserted that ENA was dependent on Enron's credit rating in order to function—not on the financial health or creditworthiness of ENA itself.[263] Next, the Bondholders argued that Enron routinely guaranteed the debts of ENA.[264] Finally, Enron regularly issued consolidated financial statements. The Bondholders thus argued that evidence that creditors of ENA sought, received, or relied upon any stand-alone financial statements of ENA is lacking.[265]

Second, the Bondholders asserted that the affairs of the various Enron subsidiaries were so entangled that consolidation would benefit all creditors. The various Enron subsidiaries functioned as a financially integrated economic unit, without regard to corporate lines.[266] Specifically, the Enron subsidiaries utilized a centralized cash management system, under which each Enron subsidiary transferred all monetary receipts to an account controlled by Enron.[267] From this account, Enron would make disbursements to or for the benefit of each subsidiary without regard to the original source of the funds.[268] Further, corporate services were provided across corporate lines and paid out of the centralized cash management system, without a complete or consistent allocation of corporate overhead among the Enron subsidiaries.[269] These corporate services included the cost of office space, data processing, and management of information systems, insurance and payroll costs. The Bondholders claim that the affairs of the Enron subsidiaries would be impossible to unwind, because records would not accurately and fairly reflect the inter-company indebtedness. To support this statement, the Bondholders used a previous report of the Examiner, where he stated that Enron's method for allocating overhead to its subsidiaries was not always complete or consistent. Therefore, Bondholders assert, determining the accuracy of the historical allocation would be a difficult and complex task that would deplete assets that could otherwise be used to pay creditors.[270] To prevent this costly process, the bankruptcies of the subsidiaries should be consolidated with Enron's bankruptcy.

To date, arguments *against* substantive consolidation have not been publicly articulated. In ENA's August 13, 2002 motion requesting extension of the exclusive period to file a reorganization plan, ENA stated that it had conducted an initial investigation with the Official Committee of Unsecured Creditors, looking into whether substan-

---

[262] Motion of Certain Holders, *supra* note 261, at 2.

[263] *Id.* at 14.

[264] *Id.* at 9.

[265] *Id.* at 2.

[266] *Id.*

[267] *Id.* at 6.

[268] *Id.*

[269] *Id.* at 2.

[270] *Id.* at 7–8.

tive consolidation of ENA and Enron should be pursued.[271] But in that motion, ENA did not disclose the findings of the initial investigation. Further, on September 17, 2002, the Committee stated, in its response to ENA's motion, that it had taken "significant strides" and made "substantial progress" in its analysis of whether ENA's bankruptcy should be substantively consolidated with Enron's bankruptcy.[272] But again, the Committee did not disclose any specific findings or take a position on the issue. The Committee concluded by stating that its factual investigation is nearly complete and that it awaits additional information from the Debtors in order to evaluate the overall impact that consolidation would have on creditors.[273]

Clearly, creditors of ENA desire a stand-alone reorganization, because then ENA's assets would be used only to pay its own claims, and not the claims against Enron (which, if included in a substantively consolidated case, would greatly dilute any recovery for ENA creditors).

On October 30, 2002, the ENA Examiner filed a report that recommended granting ENA yet another extension, to January 31, 2003, of the exclusive period to file a reorganization plan.[274] The ENA Examiner supported extension of ENA's exclusivity period, because the Enron Debtors had shifted their focus from a *separate* plan of reorganization for ENA to cooperation with the Committee on the formulation of a *joint* plan of reorganization for all Enron Debtors (including ENA).[275] The joint plan will not necessarily be a "consolidated" plan that treats the creditors of Enron and its affiliates the same.[276] In making his recommendation, the ENA Examiner applauded the shift in focus to a joint plan of reorganization plan and requested the court to allow him to review the fairness and equity of any such joint plan proposed.[277] The ENA Examiner concluded by stating that, in order to evaluate a proposed joint reorganiza-

---

[271] Enron North America Inc.'s Motion For an Order Extending Exclusive Periods For It to File a Chapter 11 Plan and Solicit Acceptances Thereof at 7, *In re* Enron, No. 01-16034 (Bankr. S.D.N.Y. 2002), *available at* http://www.elaw4enron.com, docket entry no. 5754.

[272] Response of Official Committee of Unsecured Creditors to Motion of Enron North America Inc. for Order Extending Exclusive Periods to File Chapter 11 Plan and Solicit Acceptances Thereof at 4–5, *In re* Enron, No. 01-16034 (Bankr. S.D.N.Y. 2002), *available at* http://www.elaw4enron.com, docket entry no. 6499.

[273] *Id.* at 5.

[274] Report of Harrison J. Goldin, the Court-Appointed Examiner in the Enron North America Corp. Bankruptcy Proceeding, Regarding His Recommendation As To Any Further Extension of the Exclusive Period for ENA to File A Plan of Reorganization and Solicit Acceptances Thereof, *In re* Enron, No. 01-16034 (Bankr. S.D.N.Y. 2002) [hereinafter Report Regarding Recommendation], *available at* http://www.elaw4enron.com, docket entry no. 7539.

[275] *Id.* at 6.

[276] Jeff St. Onge, *Enron and Units Will File Single Reorganization Plan*, BLOOMBERG NEWS, Oct. 31, 2002.

[277] Report Regarding Recommendation, *supra* note 275, at 8.

tion plan, he would need the Committee's findings from its investigation on the substantive consolidation issue (which had not yet been disclosed).[278]

On November 26, 2002, ENA filed a motion requesting extension of the exclusivity period, then due to be terminated on November 30, 2002.[279] As part of its request for the extension, ENA stated that it is working with the Committee in conducting an analysis as to whether substantive consolidation should be pursued. ENA stated that its investigation to date had focused on whether ENA should be substantively consolidated with Enron. In the motion, it requested an extension to investigate and analyze whether ENA should be consolidated with other subsidiaries.[280] Again, at that time, ENA did not disclose any findings or conclusions made with respect to the substantive consolidation of ENA and Enron.

On January 27, 2003, ENA again filed a motion requesting extension of the exclusivity period.[281] In requesting an extension, ENA stated that the issue of substantive consolidation must be resolved before Enron could know "whether it needs one plan or multiple plans."[282] Although not disclosing specific findings or conclusions made, ENA stated that it, along with the Committee, had investigated the "net effect of the elimination of inter-company claims and of guaranties which would result from consolidation," and had analyzed the intangible benefits and burdens from such consolidation.[283] As of March 1, 2003, neither ENA nor the Committee has disclosed any findings or taken a position on the substantive consolidation issue. Obviously, though, the issue is of central importance in determining the core question of "who gets paid what" under the eventual plan. The continued extensions of exclusivity, predicated in large part on the as-yet unresolved investigation into the propriety of substantive consolidation, reflect that this critical question is still very much on the table.

10. THE CHANGING (AND CONTINUALLY DELAYED) SHAPE OF THE PLAN: FROM DOWNSIZING TO BREAKUP?[284]

The ultimate question in the bankruptcy case, of course, is what sort of plan (if any) will be confirmed. At a minimum, it would seem safe to say that one facet of any plan

---

[278] *Id.* at 10. The Examiner is foregoing an individual investigation, choosing to rely instead on the Committee's findings in its investigation of substantive consolidation, in order to conserve estate assets. *Id.* at 10 n.8.

[279] Motion of Enron North America Corp. for Order Extending Exclusive Periods to File Chapter 11 Plan and Solicit Acceptances Thereof, *In re* Enron, No. 01-16034 (Bankr. S.D.N.Y. 2002) (extension was granted to Jan. 31, 2003), *available at* http://www.elaw4enron.com, docket entry no. 8084.

[280] *Id.* at 10.

[281] Motion of Debtors for Order Extending Exclusive Periods To File Chapter 11 Plan and Solicit Acceptances Thereof, *In re* Enron, No. 01-16034 (Bankr. S.D.N.Y. 2003), *available at* http://www.elaw4enron.com, docket entry no. 8921.

[282] *Id.* at 2.

[283] *Id.* at 16.

[284] Linda Salfisberg, Joseph DiRago, and Matthew Sostrin did outstanding work on this section.

would include a trust vehicle or similar device into which realized funds could be deposited, either for operational use of a new company or for distribution to creditors. The sources of possible funds include recoveries against the beneficiaries of any "recharacterized" SPEs; recoveries from avoidance actions; monies recovered in lawsuits against various targets, including Dynegy, Arthur Andersen, former Enron officers, law firms, and banks; and major asset sales.

Will any operating company survive? At this juncture, that is not clear. At one time, as discussed below, the debtor was favoring restructuring and continuing operations as a "slimmed down" company. As of March 2003, though, the suggestion is being taken more seriously that the Enron empire might instead be broken up and sold off in pieces.[285] The staggering professional fees, already running into the hundreds of millions of dollars, are inspiring many creditors to think more fondly of a speedier resolution to the case.

Either way, significant asset sales have been and will continue to be affected. Indeed, "reorganization" and "liquidation" are not "either-or" options; many Chapter 11 cases involve aspects of both, and Enron has proven to be no exception. Assets already sold include the former EnronOnline, Enron's energy trading business, for a projected gross of up to $2 billion in ensuing years; Enron Oil & Gas India Ltd., for $350 million; Enron Wind, for $358 million; Wessex Water, for $1.77 billion; and Enron's Houston skyscraper, for $102 million (which cost Enron about $200 million *more* to build, alas!). The most coveted asset on the sale block is the Portland General Electric utility, which Enron had a contract to sell to Northwest Natural Gas Company for $2.98 billion, but then Northwest backed out due to complications from the bankruptcy case. Several valuable pipelines could also be sold, including the Transwestern pipeline, which runs from Texas to California and can carry 2 billion cubic feet of gas a day.

The first question of interest regarding the plan, though, is: whither the delay? Enron filed for bankruptcy on December 2, 2001, with the stated goal of filing a plan within a year.[286] Well over a year later, Enron still does not have a plan; its CEO now hopes the company can submit one by the end of 2003.[287]

A. The Exclusivity Period

Under the Bankruptcy Code, a debtor has an exclusive period of 120 days to file a reorganization plan.[288] After the expiration of that date, other interested parties are permitted to file plans and solicit support. However, § 1121(d) allows for the extension or reduction of this exclusivity period for cause.

While the statute does not define what "cause" is sufficient to extend the exclusivity period, the legislative history indicates that courts should be flexible when deciding

---

[285] *See* Hill, *supra* note 5.

[286] Eric Berger, *Enron Seeks Deal With Its Creditors*, HOUS. CHRON., Nov. 1, 2002, at A5.

[287] Eric Berger, *Enron Deciding What to Do With Assets, Procedure for Claims*, HOUS. CHRON., Jan. 17, 2003, at B3. *Editors' note:* Enron filed its Plan of Reorganization on July 11, 2003. The various parties in interest are still working on the resolution of several objections to a second version of that plan.

[288] 11 U.S.C. § 1121(b) (2002).

whether to grant extensions.[289] Courts will consider the size and complexity of the bankruptcy case, whether there is a good-faith progress towards reorganization, whether the debtor uses the extension to put pressure on creditors, the existence of contingencies, and whether the debtor is paying its bills on time.[290] In addition, courts will extend the exclusivity period to allow the unsecured creditor's committee "to review and negotiate an acceptable plan" and to ensure the creditors receive "substantial financial information with respect to the ramifications of any proposed plan" so as to make "an informed decision concerning the acceptance or rejection of a proposed plan."[291] On those considerations, Enron seems a likely candidate for multiple extensions: when filed, it was the largest case ever, and as this essay has shown, is full of extraordinarily complex problems. The Examiner's Second Report weighed in at several hundred pages. If this case is not a candidate for extensions, what would be?

And in fact, Enron has petitioned the court for and has been granted several extensions of the exclusivity period since filing for bankruptcy. Judge Gonzalez granted an extension on April 24, 2002,[292] and another one on October 31, 2002.[293] That exclusivity period was to expire on January 31, 2003, but Enron once again filed for an extension.[294] On February 20, 2003, the Court extended the exclusivity period to April 30, 2003.[295] Although Judge Gonzalez granted one final extension to June 30, 2003,[296] Enron will test the finality of this date in seeking to squeeze out a few more weeks in an appearance before Judge Gonzalez on that day.[297]

---

[289] *In re* McLean Indus., 87 B.R. 830, 833 (Bankr. S.D.N.Y. 1987) (citing H.R. REP. NO. 95-595, 231 (1978)).

[290] *Id.* at 834.

[291] *In re* Texaco, Inc., 76 B.R. 322, 327 (Bankr. S.D.N.Y. 1987).

[292] Order, Pursuant to Section 1121(d) of the Bankruptcy Code and Bankruptcy Rule 1007, Extending Exclusive Periods During Which Debtors May File Chapter 11 Plans and Solicit Acceptances Thereof, *In re* Enron, No. 01-16034 (Bankr. S.D.N.Y. 2002), *available at* http://www.elaw4enron.com, docket entry no. 3302.

[293] Order Pursuant to Section 1121(d) of the Bankruptcy Code Extending the Exclusive Periods for Debtors to File Chapter 11 Plans and Solicit Acceptances Thereof, *In re* Enron, No. 01-16034 (Bankr. S.D.N.Y. 2002), *available at* http://www.elaw4enron.com, docket entry no. 7562.

[294] Motion of Debtors For Order Extending Exclusive Periods to File Chapter 11 Plan and Solicit Acceptances Thereof, *In re* Enron, No. 01-16034 (Bankr. S.D.N.Y. Jan. 27, 2003) [hereinafter January Extension], *available at* http://www.elaw4enron.com, docket entry no. 8921.

[295] Order Pursuant to Section 1121(d) of the Bankruptcy Code Extending the Exclusive Periods for Debtors to File Chapter 11 Plans and Solicit Acceptances Thereof, *In re* Enron, No. 01-16034 (Bankr. S.D.N.Y. 2003), *available at* http://www.elaw4enron.com, docket entry no. 9319.

[296] *Enron Reorganization Plan Now Has Deadline, November; Company Plans to Pursue PGE Sale*, ELECTRIC UTIL. WK., May 19, 2002, at 2.

[297] Jonathan Berke, *Enron, Creditors Reach Tentative Pact*, DAILY DEAL, June 30, 2003, *available at* 2003 WL 4170074 ("Enron is expected to go before Judge Arthur Gonzalez . . . on Monday, June 30, [2003,] to seek an extension on its exclusivity period until July 11.")

These extensions are to be expected. Enron meets many of the criteria to extend the exclusivity period. As noted, at the time of the filing, Enron was the biggest bankruptcy in history. While WorldCom later surpassed it in size, Enron will likely remain the most expensive bankruptcy in history and one of the most complex.[298] Investigators have struggled to unravel the twisted, possibly fraudulent transactions in which Enron engaged prior to filing.[299]

Since the petition date Enron has made some progress towards reorganization. Enron's bankruptcy lawyers have had to unscramble the company's complicated structure of subsidiaries, partnerships, and deals.[300] Furthermore, they have been busy selling assets worth hundreds of millions and even billions of dollars, and have filed many lawsuits to recover other assets.[301] The company continues to solicit bids on its remaining major assets.[302] While getting its financial statements in order, Enron has made progress on formulating a plan. In November, the company presented the Creditors' Committee with a preliminary plan of reorganization.[303] Enron's financial advisors created a model to predict recoveries for creditors under various scenarios.[304]

While Enron has made progress, it asserts (correctly) that there is much more yet to do. The deadline for filing claims was October 15, 2002,[305] and creditors filed thousands of claims worth hundreds of billions of dollars.[306] Enron continues to sift through these claims while it seeks to sell its remaining assets. Furthermore, much litigation regarding Enron's estate remains unsettled.[307] Finally, the subject of substantive consolidation remains unresolved. Enron still needs to negotiate with creditors over whether it will consolidate all of Enron's subsidiaries into one company to file a plan and pay claims.[308] Enron asserts that filing a reorganization plan before resolving these issues would be fruitless.[309]

---

[298] David Barboza, *The Meter Runs In Enron Case, As the Lawyers Retain Lawyers*, N.Y. TIMES, Dec. 25, 2002, at C1.

[299] Eric Berger, *The Fall of Enron; A Year Later, Survival is Greatest Milestone; Fees Pile Up As Fast As Assets Liquidated*, HOUS. CHRON., Dec. 2, 2002, at A1.

[300] Barboza, *supra* note 299.

[301] Berger, *A Year Later, supra* note 300.

[302] Berger, *Enron Deciding, supra* note 288.

[303] Berger, *A Year Later, supra* note 300.

[304] January Extension, *supra* note 295, at 10.

[305] Eric Berger, *The Fall of Enron; Enron Asks Judge For Still More Time*, HOUS. CHRON., Sept. 27, 2002, at B1.

[306] Berger, *Enron Deciding, supra* note 288.

[307] January Extension, *supra* note 295, at 12–13.

[308] Berger, *Enron Asks Judge, supra* note 306.

[309] January Extension, *supra* note 295, at 17.

B. The Reorganization Plan

When it filed for bankruptcy, Enron claimed it had $49.8 billion in assets; however, $10 to $20 billion is now considered the more realistic figure.[310] With billions of dollars in claims filed, creditors likely will receive only cents on the dollar, whatever the plan.[311] In May 2002, the company presented a plan to creditors that outlined a new, shrunken company (perhaps "lean and mean" sounds better) with a new name that would elicit no mental connections to the old Enron—"OpCo Energy." The post-bankruptcy company "would include 15,000 miles of natural gas pipeline assets, 75,000 miles of primarily electricity distribution assets, 6,700 megawatts of electricity generation, and 12,000 employees,"[312] with about $10 billion in assets. This plan called for Enron to transfer some of its major assets to OpCo free of liability.[313] Any revenues that OpCo generated would be put in a trust to be divided between creditors. Enron estimated that this new company could generate $3 billion in revenue and $350 million in profits the first year. Enron would sell its remaining assets and complete the bankruptcy process once the new company was operating on its own. Some criticize this approach because it reduces the creditors' oversight function; Enron would merely sell assets rather than submit a detailed reorganization plan. However, others note that this approach may put money into the creditors' hands sooner.[314]

While Enron may want a new corporation to emerge from the bankruptcy process, liquidation is still a distinct possibility. The plan that finally emerges will depend on the sale of Enron's final assets. These include pipelines and power plants, as noted earlier. The prices that these assets generate will determine whether Enron liquidates or forms a smaller natural-gas pipeline company. If Enron receives strong bids, the CEO has promised to sell the assets,[315] but if the bids are below market value, Enron will repackage them to form a liability-free company.[316] Those close to the auction indicate that the assets in North America likely will sell at market value, while the South American assets are not receiving much interest. Enron may decide to reorganize the South American assets into a small company and sell it to the creditors.[317]

---

[310] Berger, *A Year Later*, *supra* note 300.

[311] Berger, *Enron Deciding*, *supra* note 288.

[312] *Enron Submits Salvage Plan*, OIL DAILY, May 6, 2002.

[313] Berger, *The Fall of Enron*, *supra* note 300.

[314] This proposed plan seems to have the same problems that numerous courts have struck down as in *In re Braniff Airways, Inc.*, 700 F.2d 935 (5th Cir. 1983), in which the Fifth Circuit reversed a § 363(b) sale authorization on the ground that the transaction was "much more than the 'use, sale, or lease' of Braniff's property authorized by § 363(b)." *Id.* at 939. Plan confirmation rules cannot be evaded by calling a plan a sale. The Fifth Circuit concluded in *Braniff*, "The debtor and the Bankruptcy Court should not be able to short circuit the requirements of Chapter 11 for confirmation of a reorganization plan by establishing terms of the plan *sub rosa* in connection with a sale of assets." *Id.* at 940.

[315] Peter Behr, *Bankruptcy Tangles Enron's Future*, WASH. POST, Dec. 3, 2002, at E1.

[316] Berger, *Enron Deciding*, *supra* note 288.

[317] Berger, *A Year Later*, *supra* note 300.

Others, however, are calling for Enron to liquidate, claiming that legal fees are consuming assets that otherwise would be available to creditors.[318] Enron pays $20 to $30 million *a month* on professional services, and may end up spending a half a *billion* dollars in administrative costs to keep Enron running.[319] A creditor for Enron North America said, "Spending money in the hopes that a phoenix will rise from the ashes . . . doesn't make much sense."[320] Some of a more cynical bent describe Enron's approach of selling its major assets as a liquidation while keeping Enron's officers and lawyers in charge, and more than gainfully employed.

Whatever happens, the old "Enron" that we loved to hate will be dead and gone, relegated to the dustbin of great historical scams.

11. OTHER TARGETS[321]

Enron is a notable bankruptcy case if for no other reason than the extraordinary plenitude of litigation targets. At the very least, those with a "bulls-eye" painted squarely on their backs include the ill-fated and apparently complicitous accounting firm Arthur Andersen; Enron's former officers, who led them on the road to perdition; and Dynegy, Inc., which effectively turned off Enron's life support when it backed out of the proposed merger with Enron in the fall of 2001. Part of the Dynegy litigation has already been settled. Entire chapters could (and probably will) be written about each of those affairs. Space permits but short mention here, and coverage of the Andersen fiasco is omitted. Monies recovered from any of these targets would be added to the general pool of assets for distribution to Enron's creditors.

A. Enron's Officers

Every grand fraud requires architects; Enron has its share. Probably the most notorious (in all senses of the word) are Kenneth Lay, the former CEO; Jeffrey Skilling, former COO and CEO prior to Lay; and Andrew Fastow, the CFO. Each of these three, and perhaps others, is likely to take his rightful place in corporate American history's "hall of shame."

Enron's creditors recently won approval to sue former Enron officers in Texas state court. These suits claim that Skilling, Fastow, Lay, and others engaged in fraud, conspiracy, gross negligence, and other violations in creating the partnerships which led to Enron's downfall. Former executive Michael Kopper has already turned over $8 million to the SEC, which will be paid to senior Enron bondholders.

Currently, there are numerous civil suits filed against former Enron top executives and officials. A class action lawsuit led by the University of California alleges that

---

[318] Barboza, *supra* note 299.

[319] Berger, *A Year Later*, *supra* note 300.

[320] *Id.*

[321] Tyler Mertes, Jeffrey Davis, Tina Kim, and Erin Sylvester all did fabulous work on this section.

Enron's directors and officers profited by almost $1.2 billion by selling their Enron stock between October 1998 and November 2001.[322] In addition, there are various shareholder derivative suits as well as fiduciary liability claims brought by participants of Enron's 401(k) plan. These civil suits are as yet unresolved.

There are also numerous federal investigations and cases pending against former Enron executives. Prosecutors have indicted Fastow on 78 counts, "including charges of fraud, money laundering and obstruction of justice."[323] A superseding indictment, unsealed on May 1, 2003, expanded the charges to include a total of 109 counts, also naming Ben F. Glisan, Jr., the former Enron treasurer, and Dan Boyle, a former finance executive.[324] Contemporaneously, federal prosecutors revealed indictments against Fastow's wife, Lea, a former Enron assistant treasurer, and seven other ex-Enron officials.[325]

The government is currently seeking to seize $28 million in assets from Fastow and several other former Enron employees on the grounds that those assets are proceeds of fraudulent activity. Glisan recently agreed to turn over approximately $625,000 he received from one of the off book partnerships.

The ex-Enron officers don't have it all bad, however. The bankruptcy judge entered an order lifting the stay on May 17, 2002, to permit Associated Electric & Gas Insurance Services Limited ("AEGIS") to advance defense costs to current and former Enron officers and directors.[326] The proceeds paid out for defense costs could reduce the available monies for paying creditors, as the Oregon General Attorney's Office noted in its objections.

Whatever litigation fate befalls these executives, though, some of them can rest comfortably in their large, *exempt* homes. The Texas Constitution provides an unlimited homestead exemption. These executives have availed themselves of same.

---

[322] Press Release, University of California, *University of California Joins Federal Class Action Suit Against Senior Enron Management and Arthur Anderson LLP* (Dec. 21, 2001), *available at* http://www.ucop.edu/news/archives/2001/dec21art1.htm. For example, Kenneth Lay, CEO, sold 1.8 million shares for $101 million; Jeffrey Skilling, former CEO, sold 1.1 million shares for $66.9 million, and Andrew Fastow, former CFO, sold 561,423 shares for $30.4 million between October 1998 and November 2001. *Defendants in Lawsuit against Enron*, Dec. 17, 2002, *at* http://abclocal.go.com/ktrk/business/120701_news_defendants.html (last visited June 3, 2003). Cases currently pending include *In re* Enron Corporation Securities, Derivative & ERISA Litigation, 235 F. Supp. 2d 549 (S.D. Tex. 2002), led by Mark Newby against former Enron executives, alleging securities fraud violations in connection with insider trading, and artificially inflating the corporation's earnings as well as concealing debt.

[323] *The Fall of Enron; Business Briefs: Pursuit of Fastow Assets on Hold*, HOUS. CHRON., Jan. 16, 2003, at B2.

[324] Brenda Sapino Jeffreys, *Enron Corp. Defendants and Their Lawyers*, TEX. LAW., June 2, 2003, at 9.

[325] Rebecca Smith, *New Charges Added Against Fastow*, WALL ST. J., May 2, 2003, at A3.

[326] Order Lifting Automatic Stay, To the Extent Applicable, To Permit Parties To the Debtors' Directors and Officers Liability Insurance and ERISA Fiduciary Liability Insurance Policies to Exercise Contractual Rights Thereunder, *In re* Enron Corp., 2002 WL 1008240 (Bankr. S.D.N.Y. 2002).

First, consider Lay. Prior to Enron filing for bankruptcy, Lay and his wife Linda owned four homes in Aspen, Colorado. One home sold for $10 million, and a vacant lot sold for $2.15 million.[327] In May 2003, a third home sold for $4.7 million—less than what the Lays paid for it in 1999—and the last of the Lays' Aspen home was under contract for an undisclosed amount.[328]

The Colorado properties were not the only ones that the Lays owned, and it appears that the Lays intend to maintain their primary residence, a penthouse in Houston worth $8 million. They live on the 33rd floor of the Huntington building, "a lone luxury apartment block in the mansion-rich, elite neighborhood of River Oaks . . . [where] the Lays had an entire floor and a house nearby for the servants."[329] It is reported that the Lays own 10 more properties in Texas, the status of which is unknown. Linda Lay has opened a second-hand store, Jus' Stuff, in order to sell their furnishings.

Fastow finds himself in a less enviable situation than the Lays. His aide, Michael Kopper, entered a plea, which caused the federal judge to freeze Fastow's $23 million in the bank, brokerage accounts, his family foundation, and two holding companies, alleging that the accounts contain money from illegal Enron deals. As mentioned above, Fastow faces over 100 counts of fraud and money laundering. In addition to his financial assets being frozen, the $3.9 million he received for his new Tudor mansion in River Oaks was turned over to the U.S. Marshals. The Fastows' other home, worth $700,000, in the Houston subdivision of Southampton, cannot be taken by the federal government.

Finally, consider Jeffrey Skilling. "According to friends and former colleagues, Skilling, 48, spends most days here secluded in his 9,000-square-foot, Mediterranean-style mansion, a trophy home that he tells people he wishes had never been built."[330] Skilling's home in River Oaks is valued at $4.2 million. Skilling and Lay are yet to be charged in connection with the Enron collapse.[331]

B. Dynegy

Prior to Enron's bankruptcy filing, the company entered into a merger agreement with Dynegy, Inc. and Dynegy Holdings, Inc. ("Dynegy"). The Merger Agreement was entered into in November 2001, and provided, *inter alia*, that Dynegy would assume Enron's debts. Further, Dynegy agreed to invest $1.5 billion in preferred stock

---

[327] Danielle Reed, *Private Properties: Lay Takes a Loss*, WALL ST. J., Apr. 25, 2003, at W1.

[328] *Former Enron Chief Sells Aspen Site*, CHI. TRIB., May 4, 2003, at 2 (noting selling price of final home was less than the $6 million asking price).

[329] James Meek, *Houston, We Have a Problem*, GUARDIAN, Jan. 30, 2002, at 2.

[330] David Barboza, *Enron's Ex-CEO Wallows in Pain*, DESERET NEWS, Aug. 22, 2002, at D10.

[331] Flood et al., *supra* note 3.

350 ENRON: CORPORATE FIASCOS AND THEIR IMPLICATIONS

issued by an Enron subsidiary.[332] Finally, the Merger Agreement contemplated that Dynegy would issue Enron's shareholders stock in Dynegy equivalent to 36 percent ownership in the new entity.[333]

In late November 2001, Dynegy pulled out of the Merger Agreement with Enron. Before pulling out, however, Dynegy exercised an option that gave the company control of Enron's Northern Natural Gas Pipeline (the "Pipeline"). The Pipeline was considered one of Enron's most valuable assets and was worth approximately $2.7 billion.[334]

On December 2, 2001, Enron filed for protection under Chapter 11. The very same day, Enron filed a lawsuit against Dynegy for breach of contract, seeking damages in the amount of $10 billion.[335] In response, the day after Enron filed its suit, Dynegy filed a suit of its own against Enron in Texas state court, seeking control of the Pipeline. The Enron bankruptcy did not stay this action because the Enron subsidiary that held the Pipeline was not part of the bankruptcy filing. Ultimately, Enron agreed to cede control of the Pipeline, and Dynegy agreed to drop its Texas lawsuit. However, the agreement regarding the Pipeline did not affect the parties' rights as to the original Enron suit against Dynegy.

Dynegy and Enron ultimately settled that dispute out of court as well. In August 2002, Dynegy agreed to pay Enron approximately $25 million, and released $62.9 million to Enron from an escrow account for the Pipeline that Enron ceded to Dynegy.[336] The Bankruptcy Court approved this settlement "as in the best interests" of Enron and its creditors. The settlement agreement provided that Enron release all claims against Dynegy. However, no mention was made of the Enron shareholders' rights.[337]

Less than a month after Enron petitioned for bankruptcy and filed suit against Dynegy, Enron shareholders brought two class action lawsuits against Dynegy. The first suit, *Pearl v. Dynegy, Inc.*, was filed on December 20, 2001, in the Southern District of New York. The second suit, *Shapiro v. Dynegy, Inc.*, was filed on January 3, 2002, in Texas state court. Both suits were filed against Dynegy seeking damages as

---

[332] *In re* Enron Corp., 292 B.R. 507, 509 (S.D.N.Y. 2002) This $1.5 billion was given to Enron to continue operations of the Northern Natural Gas pipeline. In return, Dynegy received the preferred stock. In this opinion, Judge Hellerstein discusses some of the history and dealings between Enron and Dynegy.

[333] *Enron Shareholders Allowed to Sue Dynegy Over Failed Merger*, 8 No. 12 ANDREWS SEC. LITIG. & REG. REP. 6 (Nov. 2002).

[334] Paul Brenman, *Bankruptcy and Class Action: An Important Decision in Enron*, LEGAL INTELLIGENCER Dec. 20, 2002, at 6; Margot Habiby et al., *Enron to Cede Pipeline to Dynegy, Retain $10 Bln Suit*, BLOOMBERG NEWS, Jan. 4, 2002. The Pipeline was eventually acquired by Dynegy for $2.45 billion. Dynegy later sold the Pipeline to Berkshire Hathaway, Inc. for $1.88 billion.

[335] Jeff St. Onge & Jef Feeley, *Enron Wins Approval to Settle Suit Over Dynegy Matter*, BLOOMBERG NEWS, Aug. 29, 2002.

[336] *Id.*

[337] *In re Enron Corp.*, 292 B.R. at 510.

third-party beneficiaries of the agreement.[338] On February 25, 2002, Enron filed a motion in Bankruptcy Court to enjoin further prosecution of the shareholders' suits as a violation of the § 362(a) automatic stay. On April 29, 2002, the Bankruptcy Court enjoined further prosecution of the shareholders' suits. This order prompted a shareholder' appeal to the District Court.[339] The District Court decided the case and determined that, under relevant Texas law, the shareholders' right of action was "distinct and separate" from the rights and injuries of Enron itself. The District Court determined, therefore, that the shareholders' rights were not a part of the bankruptcy estate. Reversing the decision of the Bankruptcy Court, the court held that the shareholders' actions could proceed without violating the automatic stay.[340]

12. WHAT ABOUT THE POOR EMPLOYEES?[341]

No one got a worse deal than Enron's employees. The shocking collapse of Enron had profound effects on the plight of Enron employees, both rank and file workers and executives, and has drawn the attention of judges, legislators, and the business community. Several bills have been proposed that would amend the Bankruptcy Code in response to the alleged unfair treatment of employees in the Enron collapse.

Many Enron employees saw their retirement benefits nearly wiped out when Enron stock fell from a peak of over 90 dollars a share to approximately 50 cents a share. Their employer-sponsored 401(k) had over sixty percent of the assets invested in Enron stock. Employees also felt betrayed by regulations that prevented them from selling company stock during its precipitous decline, while Enron executives were able to unload their shares.

Another development that infuriated many Enron employees related to retention payments made to "key" Enron employees. Immediately after filing bankruptcy, Enron paid $55 million to retain 500 key employees.[342] By the end of March 2002, Enron had filed a plan for a third round of retention bonuses seeking to hang on to employees for a bit longer.[343] For the "rank and file" employees who had been left out in the cold, Judge Gonzalez *did* approve a $28.8 million severance package from Enron on August 28, 2002. The package caps payments at $13,500 per worker. This plan also permits

---

[338] *Enron Shareholders, supra* note 334.

[339] *Enron Shareholders Allowed to Sue Dynegy Over Failed Merger*, 13 No. 4 ANDREWS MERGERS & ACQUISITIONS LITIG. REP. 6 (Nov. 2002).

[340] *In re Enron Corp.*, 292 B.R. at 515.

[341] Peter Sgro did a superb job on this section, and I thank him.

[342] Margot Habiby et al., *Fired Enron Workers Irate at $55 MLN Bonus for 500 Employees*, BLOOMBERG NEWS, Dec. 7, 2001.

[343] Laura Goldberg, *Enron Says It Must Pay Bonuses: Company Seeks Permission to Spend Millions More on Retaining Employees*, HOUS. CHRON., Mar. 30, 2002, at A1.

employees to challenge $80 million in retention bonuses paid to Enron executives before the bankruptcy filing.

Retention bonuses illustrate a tension common in Chapter 11 reorganizations. Fired employees and other creditors want to get what they are owed. However, key employees are still needed to run the company during the reorganization. "The premise of giving these people bonuses is that their presence is more valuable than their departure," noted Professor David Gray Carlson.[344] Still others question the validity of paying bonuses to executives who oversaw the decline of a company. "Why are we going to pay these people big bonuses and expect them to turn a company around after it filed for bankruptcy when they worked there before it filed?" asked Bill Coleman, Senior Vice President for compensation at Salary.com, in Wellesley, Massachusetts.[345] That being said, the practice of paying retention bonuses is common in large reorganization cases.

There is also the question of bonuses paid to the Enron executives immediately *before* bankruptcy. On November 21, 2002, Judge Gonzalez approved the request of the Enron Employment-Related Issues Committee to hire legal counsel to seek to recover millions of dollars in bonuses paid to Enron executives immediately prior to the bankruptcy filing.[346]

Several lawsuits have been filed by, or on behalf, of Enron employees. The Severed Enron Employees Coalition, a group of more than 400 present and former workers, seeks the return of money lost in their retirement plans. Kenneth Lay and other Enron executives also face a federal racketeering lawsuit. The lawsuit, filed on behalf of 21,000 Enron workers, alleges that top executives violated the RICO Act when they encouraged workers to invest in the company's 401(k) plan and accept stock as bonuses.

A. Bankruptcy Reform?

The Employee Abuse Prevention Act of 2002 (S. 2798), introduced last session by Senator Dick Durbin of Illinois, attempts to address the unfair treatment of workers in Enron-like bankruptcies. Currently, § 1114 prevents a Chapter 11 debtor from modifying certain retiree benefits. The bill would amend § 1114 to stop debtors from terminating retiree benefit plans in contemplation of bankruptcy. It would mandate reinstatement of benefits that were modified "in contemplation of bankruptcy" within 180 days before the filing, unless the modification was necessary for the continuation of the debtor's business.

---

[344] Rachel Beck, *Are Big Bonuses During Bankruptcy Greed or Need*, Associated Press, Jan. 21, 2003.

[345] *Id.*

[346] Order Authorizing the Joint Employment of McClain & Leppert, P.C. and Wynne & Maney LLP as Special Litigation Counsel for the Employment-Related Issues Committee, *In re* Enron, No. 01-16034 (Bankr. S.D.N.Y. 2001), *available at* http://www.elaw4enron.com, docket entry no. 7983.

The bill would also enhance employees' recovery on wage claims by increasing §
507(a)(3) priority for unpaid wages from $4650 to $13,500, and would extend the
time period where wages qualify for priority from 90 days to 180 days. It would also
deem severance payments to have been earned in full on the date of the termination.
Employees fired within 180 days before the filing would have the entire severance
obligation subject to a § 507(a)(3) priority, instead of having just the portion earned in
the final 180 days as a priority claim. The bill also would change § 503(b) to give
administrative expense priority for the first $13,500 of severance obligations to em-
ployees terminated post-petition.

Senate Bill 2798 also proposes new standards for the approval of retention and
severance payments to officers and directors. Retention payments to insiders would
only be allowed if the retention benefit were "essential" to the retention of such person
and "essential to the survival of the business." The retention benefit could not be more
than ten times the average similar benefit given to non-management employees during
the same calendar year. If no similar benefits were given to non-management employees, the benefit could not exceed 125 percent of any similar benefit given to the insider
during the prior calendar year.

The bill would also provide for heightened scrutiny of post-petition employment
of officers or consultants. The bill would not allow post-petition transfers and obligations that are outside the ordinary course of business unless justified by the facts and
circumstances of the case. Transfers to officers, managers, or consultants hired post-
petition would be considered outside the ordinary course of business. The bill also
expands § 548 to provide for the recovery of excessive benefit transfers and obligations
made to insiders during the four years prior to bankruptcy if the debtor was insolvent
or rendered insolvent by the transaction. The payments would be considered excessive
if they were equal to or greater than ten times the average similar benefit given to non-
management during the same calendar year. If no benefits were given to non-management employees, the benefit will be deemed excessive if it was equal to or greater than
125 percent of any similar benefit provided in the calendar year prior to the year of the
transaction. The entire transaction would be avoided, not just the portion deemed
excessive.

There are several other bills with similar provisions seeking to protect employees.
All of these bills are currently stalled on Capitol Hill.[347] Some observers considered
these proposals too controversial to get widespread support.[348]

---

[347] *Corporate Financial Scandals Inspire New Proposal in Congress*, AM. BANKR. INST. J., Sept. 21, 2002,
at 3.

[348] *See* William M. Burke, Esq. et al., *Report on Avoidance, Subordination, Super Priority and Recharacterization Provisions of the Employee Abuse Prevention Act of 2002*, Sept. 3, 2002, *available at*
www.brownwelsh.com/UCC9/Durbin-Delahunt_Bill_Report.pdf.

13. PLAY BALL? NOT.[349]

Take me out to the ball park, buy me some peanuts and Cracker Jacks, and let's root, root, root for the home team in . . . "Enron Field?" In April 1999, Enron Corp. and the Houston Astros baseball club entered into a licensing agreement whereby Enron would pay the Astros $100 million over the next 30 years for the naming rights to the field that would replace the Astrodome.[350] In explaining why the Astros contracted with Enron, the Astros owner, Drayton McLane, explained "Enron was by far the No. 1 corporate citizen in Houston and probably in all of Texas."[351] Over the next two and a half years, Enron satisfied the agreement by staying current on its annual payments. Each annual payment was approximately $3.3 million. Enron, through December of 2001, had paid about $10.2 million to the Astros.[352]

However, in December of 2001, of course, Enron filed for Chapter 11 bankruptcy protection. Following the bankruptcy filing, the relationship between the Astros and Enron began to deteriorate. There is some discrepancy as to what transpired between them. The Astros claim that they "sought to terminate" the agreement immediately after Enron filed, but Enron claims that it was "constantly pressured" to buy tickets from the team.[353] Whether because of pressure from the Astros or because of expectations that Enron would continue to hold the naming rights to the field, Enron paid $108,000 for a 14-person luxury suite on January 22, 2002, and another $90,000 for 35 season box seats in early February 2002.[354] See, bankruptcy is not that rough on a company!

Apparently unsatisfied with the actions that Enron had taken, the Astros filed a motion on February 5, 2002, seeking to get out of the agreement. In the motion, the Astros asked the court to compel Enron to assume or reject the licensing agreement, a standard motion under § 365 but in a somewhat more interesting setting than usual.[355] The Astros argued that Enron was "wasting" its assets by continuing with the agreement. In addition, the Astros believed that they were being "materially and adversely affected by the negative publicity surrounding the company's bankruptcy."[356] No kid-

---

[349] Jason Bohm ably handled this section. Nice work. My thanks.

[350] Dan Feldstein & Kristen Mack, *Enron's Time Runs Out At Home Plate*, HOUS. CHRON., Feb. 28, 2002, at A1.

[351] Ann Hodges, *Juggling "Other People's Money,"* HOUS. CHRON., Jan. 27, 2003, at Houston 6.

[352] Eric Berger, *The Fall of Enron; Astros Go To Court Today Over Naming-Rights Deal*, HOUS. CHRON., Feb. 27, 2002, at A16.

[353] *Id.*

[354] Dale Robertson, *Astros Must Sever All Ties With Enron*, HOUS. CHRON., Feb. 14, 2002, at Sports 1.

[355] Notice of Presentment and Hearing On Motion By Houston Astros For Order Compelling Enron Corp. to Assume or Reject License Agreement, *In re* Enron Corp., No. 01-16034 (Bankr. S.D.N.Y. 2002), *available at* http://www.elaw4enron.com, docket entry no. 1289.

[356] *Enron Asks for More Time on Field*, ASSOCIATED PRESS, Feb. 26, 2002.

ding—to the layperson baseball fan (including the author), the Astros were the subject of endless jokes due to their Enron ties. Thus, the Astros sought to terminate their relationship with Enron.

Enron, on the other hand, wanted to keep the agreement in order to possibly transfer it to a reorganized Enron entity, or sell the naming rights to another organization.[357] It is unclear, however, whether such a license would be assignable under § 365(c) without the Astros' consent. Enron claimed, in its written objection to the Astros' motion dated February 26, 2002, that the Astros were trying to "have [their] cake and eat it too" and that there were insufficient grounds for compelling Enron to "immediately decide whether to assume or reject the Naming Rights Agreement."[358] Thus, invoking the usual patter in responding to a motion to compel assumption or rejection, Enron believed that it was "entitled to a reasonable time to decide whether to assume or reject" the agreement.[359]

A hearing was set for February 27, 2002. However, that day, the parties announced that they had reached a settlement agreement on the issue. In the settlement, the Astros agreed to pay Enron $2.1 million in order to end the licensing agreement.[360] This "buyback" also included the suite and box seats that Enron had purchased in early 2002. However, the deal would not be finalized until approved by Enron creditors and Judge Arthur Gonzalez. Perhaps in an attempt to sway some creditors to approve the settlement, the Astros contributed $150,000 to the Enron Employee Transition Fund in March 2002.[361] On April 25, 2002, Judge Gonzalez approved the settlement by terminating the licensing agreement.[362]

Postscript: the Astros called the team's stadium "Astros Field" until June of 2002, when Coca Cola subsidiary Minute Maid agreed to pay "an estimated $170 million over 28 years."[363] The Houston Astros now play at Minute Maid Field (also known in Houston as the "Juice Box"). If Enron had been able to assign the licensing rights, it apparently could have reaped a profit of $70 million (the difference in the $170 million that Minute Maid had agreed to pay and Enron's $100 million obligation).

---

[357] Berger, *Astros Go to Court*, *supra* note 353.

[358] Objection to Motion By Houston Astros For Order Compelling Enron Corp. To Assume or Reject License Agreement, *In re* Enron Corp., No. 01-16034 (Bankr. S.D.N.Y. 2002), *available at* http://www.elaw4enron.com, docket entry no. 1692.

[359] *Id.* at 16.

[360] Kristen Hays, *Astros Will Pay to Eliminate Enron Name; Taking Firm's Moniker Off the Ballpark Will Cost Team $2.1 Million*, CHARLOTTE OBSERVER, Feb. 28, 2002, at 2D.

[361] Frank Ahrens, *Former Enron Workers Turn to Relief Funds; Distributions Pay Bills For Laid-Off Employees*, WASH. POST, Mar. 21, 2002, at E04.

[362] Eric Berger, *Judge Approves Deal Ending Enron Field*, HOUS. CHRON., Apr. 26, 2002, at B3.

[363] Joseph Duarte, *Astros Get A New Squeeze; $170 Million Name Deal Turns Home Into Minute Maid Park*, HOUS. CHRON., June 6, 2002, at A1.

14. CONCLUSION

So much could be said about the Enron saga. Bright promise, hot stock, fraud, greed, collapse, finger-pointing, stern promises of "never again." But nothing is really new under the sun. Consider the following excerpt from the classic novel, *César Birotteau*, by the famous nineteenth century French writer Honoré de Balzac. Balzac captures beautifully the rise and fall of a Parisian perfumer, resulting ultimately in the ignominy of bankruptcy. Balzac's words seem almost prescient for a close follower of the Enron drama:

> Bankruptcy brings with it a more or less hermetic closing of a business in which the looters have still left some money. He is a lucky man who can slip through the roof or cellar with an empty sack over his back and bring it out loaded. Under these catastrophic circumstances, people feel entitled to behave like Napoleon's army crossing the Beresina river, where every soldier was desperately intent on saving his own skin. All standards of true and false, honest and dishonest, are broken down.[364]

---

[364] HONORÉ DE BALZAC, CÉSAR BIROTTEAU 276 (Frances Frenaye trans., Juniper Press 1955).

The Enron Bankruptcy: Financial Engineering, Recharacterization, Substantive Consolidation, and Avoidance

Edward J. Janger*

As Charles Tabb noted in the previous essay, Neal Batson, was appointed the Examiner (the "Examiner") in the Enron case in May 2002. In September 2002, he filed his First Interim Report, examining six of the Enron SPEs. In that report, he concluded that assets on the order of $500 million could be recovered for the Enron estate by unwinding just those transactions alone. On January 21, 2003, the Examiner finished his Second Interim Report ("Second Report" or "Report"), and the Report was filed (i.e., made publicly available) in March of 2003. In the Second Report, the Examiner analyzed another 11 broad sets of transactions and concluded that under "true sale" or "substantive consolidation" theories, "assets having an estimated aggregate value between $1.7 billion and $2.1 billion" could be restored to the Enron estate. In addition, the Examiner identified a number of potential "avoidable transfers" in the face amount of $2.9 billion.[1]

The Second Report itself is 134 pages long, and it includes over 4,000 pages of Appendix, detailing the various transactions examined. My essay can therefore only skim the surface. It is divided into three parts. The first part will explore why the Examiner concluded that Enron felt the need to use aggressive financial engineering techniques. The second part will describe the six broad accounting abuses that the Examiner found that Enron used. The third part will sketch the Examiner's theories of liability for recovering funds for the estate.

* Professor, Brooklyn Law School. My profound thanks to Nancy Rapoport for giving me the opportunity to participate in this project, and to Dean Joan Wexler, and the Dean's Research Fund at Brooklyn Law School, for generous financial support.

[1] Neal Batson, Second Interim Report of Neal Batson, Court-Appointed Examiner, *In re* Enron Corp., No. 01-16034 (Bankr. S.D.N.Y. Jan. 21, 2003), *available at* 2003 Extra Lexis 4, 2003 WL 1917445 [hereinafter Second Report].

I. WHY DID ENRON DO WHAT IT DID?

The Second Report begins with a striking statement: "The Examiner has concluded that, through pervasive use of structured finance techniques involving [Special Purpose Entities] and aggressive accounting practices, Enron so engineered its reported financial position and results that its financial statements bore little resemblance to its actual financial position and performance."[2]

The Examiner concluded that "[t]wo key factors drove Enron's management of its financial statements: (i) its need for cash and (ii) its need to maintain an investment grade credit rating."[3] In short, Enron's business strategy during the mid and late 1990s placed it between a rock and a financial hard place. Although Enron started as a humble oil pipeline company, by 2000, its business depended on energy trading and investment activities.[4] This expansion and investment activity created a tremendous need for cash. However, in 1999, 66% of Enron's revenues came from one of its businesses, Enron Wholesale Services ("EWS"). EWS was in the business of energy trading, and the Examiner notes, "In order to continue the growth of this business, Enron needed to trade with other market participants without being required to post collateral."[5] As the 1999 Enron Annual Report put it: "Enron's continued investment grade status is critical to the success of its wholesale business as well as its ability to maintain adequate liquidity."[6] This need to maintain its credit rating placed a severe constraint on Enron's ability to raise cash by borrowing money.

This profound need not to borrow arose because, in order to maintain its credit rating, Enron had to keep five key credit ratios within certain boundaries. Those ratios were: (1) funds flow interest coverage, (2) pre-tax interest coverage, (3) funds flow from operations to total obligations, (4) total obligations to total obligations plus shareholders' equity and certain other items, and (5) debt to total capital.[7] The ratios can be described intuitively:

- Both "funds flow interest coverage" and "pre-tax interest coverage" seek to determine whether a company (in this case, Enron) is generating sufficient cash to pay the interest on its debt.
- "Funds flow from operations to total obligations," helps determine whether a company's cash flow from operations—over time—will be sufficient to amortize its debt obligations.
- Finally, the last two ratios seek to determine a company's balance sheet solvency, comparing its total debt to the value of its assets.

---

[2] *Id.* at 15.

[3] *Id.*

[4] *Id.* at 16.

[5] *Id.* at 18–19.

[6] *Id.* at 18 (*quoting* "Financial Review—Management's Discussion and analysis of Financial Condition and Results of Operations—Capitalization," Enron 1999 Annual Report, at 37) (emphasis omitted).

[7] *Id.* at 19–20.

The need to manage these ratios gave rise to two competing imperatives. First, Enron needed to raise money in order to fund operations. Second, it could not book debt without running afoul of some or all of those ratios. Any cash raised by borrowing money would adversely affect its credit ratios. To solve this problem, cash had to be generated (or at least appear to be generated) through "operating activities." Enron turned to financial engineering to try to accomplish this seemingly impossible task.[8]

The tension between these two prime imperatives was exacerbated by the manner in which Enron "earned" money. Even when Enron entered into a transaction that appeared to generate significant earnings, the transaction did not always lead to immediate generation of cash, thanks to Enron's extensive use of a device called "mark to market" ("MTM") accounting. Under MTM accounting, Enron entered assets on its books at their market value, rather than at cost. Thus, if Enron entered into a transaction that would produce income over period of a number of years, Enron would discount the income stream to present value and book that value as "earnings" in the year in which the transaction began, rather than booking the earnings as they came in. While this made Enron's "earnings" look good, and helped with the ratios that turned on earnings (particularly the second ratio), MTM accounting did not actually produce cash with which to run the company.[9]

This is not necessarily a problem. If appropriate valuations are used, MTM accounting, in many cases presents a *more* accurate picture of a company's finances than traditional "cost based" accounting. Also, the transaction, which will produce cash over time, can form the basis for borrowing, and thus be "monetized" or turned into cash before the money actually turns up. The *quid pro quo* for this early appearance of cash is that a debt is created, which prevents the double-counting of the assets on the books. The Report argues that Enron violated these cardinal principles in two ways. First, as the Blockbuster transaction (discussed below) demonstrates, the valuations used by Enron did not necessarily reflect reality, and second, in the Examiner's view, many of the transactions studied were driven by the desire to raise money to fund operations without booking debt.[10] Thus, by listing a deal as an asset along with the cash raised by borrowing against it, Enron double-counted and overstated the value of the company.

II. WHAT DID ENRON DO?

According to the Examiner, Enron both abused MTM accounting to overstate the value of certain transactions *and* used six other distinct transactional strategies to make borrowed money look like cash from operations or otherwise inflate earnings: (1) FAS

---

[8] *Id.* at 15.

[9] *Id.* at 15 ("Enron's use of mark-to-market ("MTM") accounting created a large gap between net income and funds flow from operations. This "quality of earnings" problem made it particularly challenging for Enron to raise cash without issuing equity while maintaining its credit rating.")

[10] *Id.*

140 Transactions, (2) Tax Transactions, (3) Non-Economic Hedges, (4) Share Trust Transactions, (5) Minority Interest Transactions, and (6) Prepay Transactions.[11] This section describes Enron's abuse of MTM accounting, and each of the six other techniques used by Enron to massage its balance sheet.

A. Abuse of MTM Accounting—Braveheart

An example of how Enron abused MTM accounting can be seen through the "Braveheart" transaction. In July of 2000, Enron entered into a "20 year-exclusive agreement" with Blockbuster "to deliver . . . movies-on-demand, via the Enron Intelligent Network."[12] Enron then sold the contract to a subsidiary for $57 million and recognized a "$53 million gain, and $57 million in funds flow from operations." As the Examiner noted, "In order to recognize this gain, applicable GAAP required that it be practical to measure the fair value of the asset."[13] Andersen appraised the value of the contract at "between $120 million and $150 million." This valuation was based on a number of assumptions, including that the company would begin commercial operations within 12 months in 10 metropolitan areas, would add 8 more cities each year, and so on.[14] The problem with these assumptions (as a basis for a balance sheet valuation) was that at the time, "Enron did not have the technology to deliver [video-on-demand] on a commercially viable basis and Blockbuster did not have the rights to the movies to be delivered."[15] As the Examiner said, in what can only be read as a tone of ironic understatement:

> [T]he Examiner questions whether it was appropriate for a public company to transfer this contract to a structured finance vehicle, assign it a speculative value and recognize that amount currently as income and cash flow from operating activities.[16]

B. The FAS 140 Transactions

MTM accounting was a way of accelerating, and sometimes manufacturing, earnings and funds flow. The problem was that Enron still needed money to fund operations. The FAS 140 Transactions were the first of a number of techniques that Enron used to raise cash without admitting that it was borrowing money. This technique turned on Enron's ability to describe[17] a "loan" as a "sale." To accomplish this Enron

---

[11] *Id.* at 36–37.

[12] *Id.* at 29.

[13] *Id.* at 29–30.

[14] *Id.* at 30–31.

[15] *Id.* at 29.

[16] *Id.* at 31.

[17] *Id.* at 37–38.

would create a corporation for the sole purpose of purchasing assets from Enron (a "Special Purpose Entity" or "SPE"). The SPE (instead of Enron) would then borrow money to pay for the assets purchased.

Such transactions are common, and unproblematic, so long as the SPE's "purchase" of the asset can be characterized as a "true sale" to a "separate entity." FAS 140[18] is the statement of the Financial Accounting Standards Board that governs whether it is appropriate under generally accepted accounting principles ("GAAP") to account for a transaction as a "true sale" to an "unconsolidated" (or "separate") entity, and when it must be treated as a loan. The key to "true sale" treatment is that, when a given asset is "sold" the economic risks and benefits of ownership should be transferred to the purchaser. The difficulty presented by many modern financial transactions is that the line between a sale and a loan can be quite blurry. Even though an asset is "sold," the buyer may retain an option to sell the asset back for a certain price (a "put"), or the seller may retain an option to purchase the asset back (a "call") for a certain price. Similarly, the purchaser may have some common ownership with the seller. Thus, FAS 140 was written in order to specify when the asset has or has not truly been transferred, and whether the purchaser is a separate entity.

The transactions that the Examiner studied were known respectively as Cerberus, Nikita, Hawaii 125-0, and Backbone. According to the examiner, the FAS 140 transactions were designed to comply with the "letter" of FAS 140, while violating its spirit. The typical way in which Enron structured these transactions was as follows: (1) Enron would create a subsidiary (the "Sponsor"), which would hold a financial asset; (2) the Sponsor would sell the asset to a special purpose entity ("SPE"), in the form of a trust (the "Trust"); (3) the Trust would then issue equity and borrow money in order to pay for the asset.[19] Note that, so long as the risks of ownership of the asset are indeed transferred to a separate entity, then the sales price can be booked as earnings and no debt is incurred.

This is where Enron pushed—indeed exploded—the envelope. In these transactions, Enron transferred none of the risk to the purchaser. The Examiner concluded:

> Enron (i) had the obligation to repay substantially all of the financing regardless of the value of the underlying assets and (ii) retained substantially all of the future appreciation in value and cash flows from the underlying asset.[20]

The device through which Enron accomplished this prestidigitation was known as a "Total Return Swap." Under such a swap:

---

[18] ACCOUNTING FOR TRANSFERS AND SERVICING OF FINANCIAL ASSETS AND EXTINGUISHMENTS OF LIABILITY—A REPLACEMENT OF FASB STATEMENT NO. 125, Statement of Financial Accounting Standards No. 140 (Financial Accounting Standards Bd. 2000) (articulating rules and standards for accounting for SPEs).

[19] Second Report at 37–38.

[20] *Id.* at 38.

> [T]he Enron entity: (i) agreed to make payments to its counterparty (usually an SPE created for the transaction or the lenders to the SPE) equal to the scheduled payments (and interest thereon) on the amounts borrowed by the SPE under its credit facility (which was usually equal to 97% of the purchase price of the transferred asset) and (ii) remained entitled to all amounts produced by the transferred asset (whether by the sale of the asset or otherwise), except, in some transactions, for amounts used to satisfy the small portion of the purchase price that the SPE funded through the sale of equity rather than borrowings (typically at least 3% of the purchase price of the asset) and a specified return on equity. In . . . transactions where there was an equity investor, the Total Return Swap typically provided that any proceeds of the underlying asset were distributed first to the Enron entity in amounts up to the amounts payable on the related debt financing, then to the equity holder up to the specified return and, finally, all remaining amounts to the Enron entity.[21]

While this structure appeared complicated on paper, in practice, it was not. The so called "sale" existed on paper alone. Instead of borrowing money, Enron created an SPE, which would borrow the money. To gain access to this borrowed money, Enron would "sell" an asset to the SPE (but would undertake to collect the money and "service" the contract). The SPE would purchase the asset with the borrowed money. Then when the asset (still in Enron's hands) produced income, Enron would use that income to pay its obligations under the Swap, which would then be used by the SPE to pay the debt. If the income from the asset was insufficient to pay the SPE's debt (and the specified return to the equity holders), Enron would make up the difference. If Enron received more than the amount required, Enron kept the difference. In practice, the asset never left Enron's hands, and Enron's only obligation was to repay the "purchase price" plus interest. In short, the Examiner concluded, "loans" were being disguised as sales.

Through this technique:

> Enron: (i) increased its reported net income by $351.6 million (36% of its total reported net income); (ii) increased its reported funds flow from operations by $1.2 billion (38% of its total reported funds flow from operations); and (iii) kept $1.4 billion of debt off its balance sheet.[22]

Moreover, the Examiner concluded that—if these transactions were recharacterized as loans—the estate would recover assets with a value of $500,000,000. In the wake of

---

[21] *Id.* at 38 n.102.

[22] *Id.* at 38.

Enron, the FASB has proposed to revise FAS 140 to expressly preclude the practices (like "total return swaps") that Enron used.[23]

C. The Tax Transactions

Enron used certain tax transactions in order to improve Enron's reported current net income (by "'generating' accounting income from projections of future tax savings"). For example, in one type of transaction, Enron would transfer assets to an SPE in order to increase the tax basis (the value) of a depreciable asset (in one instance, Enron's corporate headquarters building). The depreciation of that asset could then be deducted from Enron's tax liability in future years. These transactions did not change Enron's tax liability during the year in which they occurred. However, through an extreme use of MTM accounting, Enron recorded the tax benefits (and the resulting increase in income) right away.[24] Through September 2001, these transactions allowed Enron to record an aggregate increase of net income of $460 million, even though it did not depreciate any of these assets during that period.[25] These techniques accounted for $269.1 million, or 27% of Enron's net income in 2000 alone.

D. The Non-Economic Hedges

The non-economic hedges included the Raptor SPEs that have been discussed elsewhere in this book (and in the Powers Report). The purpose of these transactions was to lock in the value of certain of its investments, by hedging those investments in transactions with unconsolidated or "off-book" entities that were not reported on Enron's balance sheet. The investments were placed in the Raptor SPEs, and Raptor entered into hedging transactions with other entities which, according to the Examiner, were also owned indirectly by Enron and LJM2. The problem with these transactions was that the counterparties to the hedges were Enron affiliates, so the risk associated with any fall in value in the investments was not shifted to another party: the risk stayed with Enron.[26] The effect of the hedges was to inflate Enron's net income for 2000 by $346 million (or 35% of its total net income).[27] Had the fact that Enron still bore the risk that these assets would decline in value been made clear, Enron's net income would have been much lower.

---

[23] PROPOSED STATEMENT OF FINANCIAL ACCOUNTING STANDARDS: QUALIFYING SPECIAL-PURPOSE ENTITIES AND ISOLATION OF TRANSFERRED ASSETS—AN AMENDMENT OF FASB STATEMENT NO. 140 (Exposure Draft) (Financial Accounting Standards Bd. June 10, 2003), *available at* http://accounting.rutgers.edu/raw/fasb/draft/ed_qspe.pdf.

[24] Second Report *supra* note 2, at 92.

[25] *Id.*

[26] *Id.* at 41.

[27] *Id.*

E. The Share Trusts

The share trust transactions, Marlin and Whitewing, were similar to the FAS 140 transactions in that they were used to transfer debt to entities that were treated as separate from Enron and were used to increase funds flow, while keeping debt off the balance sheet. As the Examiner described it:

> In each Share Trust Transaction, Enron created a Delaware statutory business trust (the "Issuer") that sold notes and certificates . . . to the institutional private placement market. The issuer then contributed the proceeds fro the sale of its securities to another entity (the "Holding Entity") and Enron (directly, or through subsidiaries) contributed other assets to the Holding Entity. The Holding Entity (i) used a portion of the cash received from the Issuer and the assets contributed by Enron to establish a reserve fund to support the payment of the Issuer's securities and (ii) used the remaining cash received to purchase assets or to repay existing financing.[28]

The cash to actually repay the securities issued by the Issuer were to come from Enron pursuant to its "Share Trust Obligations." Enron undertook to (i) issue preferred stock to a trust (the "Share Trust"); (ii) sell the stock in sufficient amounts to pay the Issuer's notes when due; (iii) if the stock in the Share Trust was not sufficient to pay the Issuer's notes, Enron would issue more stock to make up the shortfall; and (iv) if the increased issuance of stock was still insufficient to make up the shortfall, then Enron would pay the funds necessary to pay the Issuer's notes.[29] Neither the Issuers nor the Holding Entities nor Enron's contingent Share Trust Obligations were listed on Enron's financial statements.[30]

The Examiner took the view that at least one of these transactions (Whitewing) could be subjected to a successful "true sale" challenge or to substantive consolidation in bankruptcy.[31] In either case, the result would be recovery of assets for the Enron estate worth $700 million to $1 billion.[32] A second transaction (Marlin) was, in the Examiner's view subject to a substantive consolidation challenge, but not to a "true sale" challenge.[33]

F. Minority Interest Financings

Under these structures, Enron set up a holding company (the "Majority Owned Subsidiary"). Enron owned a majority of the company's stock, and a minority portion

---

[28] *Id.* at 68.

[29] *Id.* at 68–69.

[30] *Id.* at 69.

[31] For a discussion of "true sale" and "substantive consolidation," see text at note 38, *infra.*

[32] *Id.* at 67.

[33] *Id.*

of the company's stock was owned by another entity (the "Minority Shareholder"). The Minority Shareholder would then borrow money and contribute it to the Majority Owned Subsidiary as its capital contribution. Nominally, Enron also contributed assets to the Majority Owned Subsidiary, but it effectively retained control over those assets, even though the new company was supposed to be the owner (except to the extent necessary to repay the loan taken out by the Minority Shareholder). These Majority Owned Subsidiaries were carried on the Enron books, but the debt of these entities was not carried as Enron debt; instead, the debt was booked as a "minority interest" in the partnership.[34] This structure allowed Enron to characterize $1.74 billion in debt as "minority interests."[35]

G. Prepays

The prepay transactions, known as "Mahonia" and "Yosemite," were perhaps the most egregious device developed by Enron for concealing debt, and for disguising cash from financing activities as cash from operations. In these transactions Enron would disguise a loan as a commodities transaction. First, Enron would enter into a contract with an SPE. Under the contract, Enron would promise to deliver oil or gas to the SPE at a future date, at a specified price. The SPE would then prepay the present value of the contract. The SPE would then enter into a similar prepaid forward contract with a bank (Citibank or JPMorgan). Under this structure, standing alone, both Enron and the Bank faced risk associated with price fluctuations in the underlying commodity. However, Enron and the Bank would then enter into a contract under which the bank would agree to sell, and Enron would agree to purchase, the commodity at market price. As a result of this structure, neither Enron nor the Bank faced any risk as a result of price fluctuations on the underlying commodity. In fact, no one even expected the commodities ever to change hands. These transactions were simply paper transactions that disguised loans. But, instead of booking the loans as debt, Enron booked them as "liabilities from price risk management." As such these transactions accounted for $1.527 billion (50%) of Enron's funds flows from operations. Because the money coming in counted as fund flow from operations, while the liability was not booked as debt, this transaction significantly enhanced Enron's credit ratios.[36] In addition, Enron kept $5 billion in debt of its 2001 balance sheet.

H. Conclusion

According to the Examiner, 96% of Enron's income—and 105% of its funds flow— was generated by these accounting techniques. Moreover, $11.9 billion dollars in debt was kept off of Enron's balance sheet.

---

[34] *Id.* at 84.

[35] *Id.* at 44.

[36] *Id.* at 45.

III. RECHARACTERIZATION, SUBSTANTIVE CONSOLIDATION, AND AVOIDANCE

Having concluded that Enron's aggressive management of its balance sheet painted a misleading picture of the company, what are the consequences for the bankruptcy case? These financing structures had two distinct effects. First, they deceived both shareholders and creditors about the financial status of Enron. Second, they caused numerous assets, which might have been used to pay Enron's unsecured creditors, to be parked in special purpose entities, ostensibly beyond the reach of Enron's creditors.

The principal remedies discussed by the Examiner seek to fix the second of these evils directly, and only indirectly relate to the first. The Examiner discusses at length, three theories: recharacterization, substantive consolidation, and avoidance. Recharacterization and substantive consolidation provide a remedy for balkanization of assets. The trustee's avoidance powers may provide a mechanism for recovering payments actually made to the investors in the questionable transactions.

A. Recharacterization

The Examiner often refers to transactions as being subject to a "true sale" challenge. A "true sale" challenge turns on the power of the court to recharacterize a sale as a loan, and in so doing, recovering the "sold assets" for the estate. As noted above, many of these transactions turned on the sale of a financial asset from one Enron entity to another. Because the only creditors of the purchasing entity were the counterparties to the particular transaction, this structure had the effect of isolating the assets from the general Enron estate and leaving the assets subject only to the claims of the particular counterparty. If, by contrast, the transaction had been characterized as a loan and not as a sale, then the transaction would not be sufficient to transfer title in the asset to the SPE, and the asset would remain within the control of the selling entity (Enron). The effect of such recharacterization would be to sweep the sold asset back into the Enron estate. The effect would be doubly powerful, because, according to the Examiner, few of the counterparties took "backup security interests" in the conveyed assets.[37] Hence, after the assets came into Enron's bankruptcy estate, the value of those assets could be used to help pay Enron's unsecured creditors as part of a plan of reorganization.

The doctrine of true sale is governed by non-uniform state law, but as the Examiner notes:

> The principal factors considered by courts include: (i) whether the transferor continued to have the economic benefits of an increase in the value or performance of the asset, and the economic risks of a decrease in value or the non-performance of the asset, after the transfer ("Benefits and Risks"); (ii) the actions of the parties after the closing of the sale ("Post-Sale con-

---

[37] *Id.* at Appendix C at 3.

duct"), including whether the transferor continued to exercise significant control over the asset, or the proceeds of the asset, after the transfer ("Control over Asset"); (iii) the transferor's intent in entering into the transaction ("Enron's Intent"); (iv) the transferee's intent in entering into the transaction ("Lender's Intent"); (v) the basis for the pricing of financial obligations of the parties in connection with the transfer ("Loan Pricing"), including the amount of the proceeds "paid" to the transferor compared to the value of the asset transferred ("Proceeds vs. Value"); (vi) how the transaction was treated for tax purposes ("Tax Treatment"); (vii) how the transaction was treated for accounting purposes ("Accounting Treatment"); and (viii) the name, or label given to the transaction by the parties ("Nomenclature").[38]

The most important of these factors—both because it reflects the economic substance of the transaction and is indicative of intent—is the "Benefits and Risks" factor.[39] As discussed above, most of the six techniques that Enron used to structure its transactions share the fact that Enron retained both the risks and benefits of ownership of the assets conveyed. Similarly, Enron often retained control over the asset itself—another reason to recharacterize the transaction. Also, a common attribute of a number of the sales is that the purchase price far exceeded the economic value of the asset conveyed, and the entities that purchased the assets were closely related, through cross-guaranties, swaps, and so on, to Enron itself. To the extent that the Examiner can prove these facts with regard to each transaction, Enron's estate may be able to recover the assets allegedly sold to SPEs.

B. Substantive Consolidation

A related theory that the Examiner discusses is substantive consolidation. While the effect is similar to that of recharacterization, in that both assets and liabilities are swept back into the estate, the theory is slightly different. Instead of looking at the intent in the particular transaction, substantive consolidation looks to whether the corporate form that was used to remove the asset from the estate should be respected. It is related to, though not identical to the non-bankruptcy doctrines of corporate veil-piercing.[40] While the principles are similar, substantive consolidation is generally thought to arise from the general equitable powers contained in Section 105 of the Bankruptcy Code.[41]

The leading case on substantive consolidation is a Second Circuit case, *In re Augie/Restivo Baking Co.*[42] In that case, two bakeries, Augie's and Restivo, which had merged

---

[38] *Id.* at 9–10.

[39] *Id.*

[40] F.D.I.C. v. Colonial Realty Co., 966 F.2d 57, 60–61 (2d Cir. 1992).

[41] *Id.* at 59.

[42] *In re* Augie/Restivo Baking Co. Ltd., 860 F.2d 515 (2d Cir. 1988).

their businesses but not their corporate forms, sought substantive consolidation in order to prevent a creditor of one of the predecessors from blocking a bankruptcy sale. The Court focused on two main justifications for substantive consolidation: (1) creditors' expectations (did the creditors deal with the entities as a single unit or as two separate entities?); and (2) entanglement.

Taking those two requirements in reverse order, entanglement turns on whether the costs associated with disentangling the affairs of two debtors would be so great that the cost outweighs any benefit to creditors as a result of consolidation. The Court found that entanglement was not a factor in *Augie/Restivo*.[43] With regard to creditor expectations, the Court had to balance the expectations of two different sets of creditors. On the one hand, there were the creditors of Augie's, who lent funds to Augie's alone, before the merger, and on the other, there were the creditors of the consolidated entity, after the merger. These creditors further divided into two groups: the bank creditors and the trade creditors. The Court found that Augie's creditors expected to have recourse to the assets of Augie's alone.[44] The bank creditors of Restivo knew that the two entities had not been merged and therefore obtained a guaranty from Augie's before extending credit. The only creditors who were deceived by the existence of two separate corporations were thus the trade creditors of the consolidated business.[45]

The Examiner points out that the two factors discussed in *Augie/Restivo* (creditor expectation and entanglement) can turn on numerous other factors, many of which might arise in the various Enron cases. Indeed, as noted above, with regard to a number of the transactions, the Examiner recommended a substantive consolidation challenge.

C. Avoidance Actions

In addition to recharacterization and substantive consolidation theories, a number of the transfers made in connection with Enron's transactions may be subject to avoidance as either fraudulent conveyances or preferences under sections 547, 548, and 550 of the Bankruptcy Code. An important threshold point, however, is that, to the extent that the transactions are used to avoid transactions between and among Enron entities, substantive consolidation would cause many of the actions to disappear.

1. Preferences

Section 547 of the Bankruptcy Code permits the trustee to avoid those payments, made shortly before bankruptcy, that prefer one creditor over all others. To the extent that Enron made transfers to the various SPEs, or to investors or financial institutions, in connection with the total return swaps, or to the extent that Enron undertook other

---

[43] *Id.* at 519–520.

[44] *Id.* at 519.

[45] *Id.*

payment obligations arising out of the transactions described above, those payments might be subject to avoidance as preferences. The elements of a preference are (1) a transfer, (2) for or on account of antecedent debt, (3) made while the debtor was insolvent,[46] (4) made within 90 days before the bankruptcy (one year for insiders), and (5) that enables the creditor to receive more than it would have in a Chapter 7 case, if the transfer had not been made.[47] There are numerous defenses, which include arguing that the payment was a contemporaneous exchange for new value, that it was made in the ordinary course of business, or that it was followed by a subsequent advance that itself went unpaid.[48] Whether these defenses would apply would obviously be fact-specific.

A central issue as to how much might be avoided is whether the recipient of the payment could be considered an insider.[49] Obviously far more payments would be swept within the avoidance power (and back into Enron's bankruptcy estate), if the reach-back period were one year rather than 90 days. It seems likely, however, that many of the SPEs *would* be considered insiders of Enron. A second issue that would

---

[46] Insolvency is presumed within 90 days of the bankruptcy. 11 U.S.C. § 547(g) (2003).

[47] 11 U.S.C. § 547(b) (2003).

[48] 11 U.S.C. § 547(c) (2003).

[49] 11 U.S.C. § 101(31) (2003). Under the Bankruptcy Code an insider is defined as:
   "insider" includes—
   (A) if the debtor is an individual—
       (i)   relative of the debtor or of a general partner of the debtor;
       (ii) partnership in which the debtor is a general partner;
       (iii) general partner of the debtor; or
       (iv) corporation of which the debtor is a director, officer, or person in control;
   (B) if the debtor is a corporation—
       (i)   director of the debtor;
       (ii) officer of the debtor;
       (iii) person in control of the debtor;
       (iv) partnership in which the debtor is a general partner;
       (v)   general partner of the debtor; or
       (vi) relative of a general partner, director, officer, or person in control of the debtor;
   (C) if the debtor is a partnership—
       (i)   general partner in the debtor;
       (ii) relative of a general partner in, general partner of, or person in control of the debtor;
       (iii) partnership in which the debtor is a general partner;
       (iv) general partner of the debtor; or
       (v)   person in control of the debtor;
   (D) if the debtor is a municipality, elected official of the debtor or relative of an elected official of the debtor;
   (E) affiliate, or insider of an affiliate as if such affiliate were the debtor; and
   (F) managing agent of the debtor.

likely be subject to litigation, which the Examiner does not discuss,[50] is when Enron became insolvent. Given the lack of transparency in Enron's financial statements, it may be difficult to determine when Enron actually became insolvent; without such a determination, it may be difficult to recover any preferences.

2. Fraudulent Conveyances

There are two types of fraudulent conveyance actions that might be available to Enron in order to try to avoid transfers of assets to the SPEs, and to recover them for the estate. The first is an intentional fraudulent conveyance—a transaction made with the intent to hinder delay or defraud creditors.[51] The second is a constructive fraudulent conveyance—a transaction made while the debtor was insolvent in return for which the debtor did not receive reasonably equivalent value.[52] The intent element of *actual* fraud is often difficult to prove, but it can be established through circumstantial evidence.[53] It is possible to argue that various aspects of the SPE transactions were intended to defraud both creditors and shareholders. By overstating the value of assets conveyed, and by characterizing loans as sales, many creditors may have been fooled into lending money to Enron. As such, it might be possible to unwind a number of the SPEs on this theory. The constructive fraud theory may, paradoxically, be more difficult to use to avoid conveyances by Enron. In many of the cases, the problem was *not* that Enron received *too little* in return for the asset, but in fact that it received *too much* for the property, and that it had promised to make up the difference between the stated and true value. Thus, intentional fraud seems a more likely source of recovery than constructive fraud.

CONCLUSION

In sum, Enron turned to financial engineering as a remedy for the fact that it had an untenable business plan, which hinged simultaneously on boosting earnings through MTM accounting while generating cash without borrowing money. Unwinding these transactions will not remedy all the harm of the fraud, but it might alleviate some of the inequality of treatment suffered by the various creditors hurt by Enron's actions.

---

[50] The Examiner notes that the Debtor and/or the Creditors' Committee have stated that they will undertake an insolvency analysis, so he leaves the matter to them. Second Report, Appendix C, at 84.

[51] 11 U.S.C. § 548(a)(1) (2003), UFTA § 4(a)(1) (1999).

[52] 11 U.S.C. § 548(a)(2) (2003), UFTA § 5 (1999).

[53] UFTA § 4(b) (1999).

Four (or Five) Easy Lessons from Enron*

Douglas G. Baird** & Robert K. Rasmussen***

> Mr. Lay, I've concluded that you're perhaps the most accomplished confidence man since Charles Ponzi. I'd say you were a carnival barker, except that might not be fair to carnival barkers. A carny will at least tell you up front that he's running a shell game. You, Mr. Lay, were running what purported to be the seventh largest company in America.
>
> —Senator Peter Fitzgerald, addressing former Enron chief executive Kenneth Lay, February 13, 2002.

Temptation. It lies at the heart of financial swindles. The promise of 50% returns in three months can lure thousands of investors—so too can a stock that soars 500% in three years. To be sure, those who are tempted are often skeptical. Before they invest, they want to know how one can enjoy such supracompetitive returns. The answer usually is a facially plausible story, though with a bit of mystery attached. The mystery is often touted as the reason that the investment opportunity is exclusive to the entrepreneur who discovered it. It is what ensures that the gains are not competed away.

The classic case remains that of Charles Ponzi. While not a very adept con artist—he was caught several times—in a six-month period in 1920, Ponzi convinced ten thousand investors to part with an aggregate of $9.5 million.[1] He promised amazing returns—50% in ninety days.[2] As a testament to his financial wizardry, Ponzi often

* Originally published at 55 VAND. L. REV. 1787 (2002). Reprinted with permission.

** Harry A. Bigelow Distinguished Service Professor of Law, The University of Chicago Law School.

*** Associate Dean for Academic Affairs and Professor of Law, Vanderbilt Law School. We would like to thank Barry Adler, Steve Schwarcz, and the participants at the Vanderbilt Conference on the Delawarization of Bankruptcy Law for helpful comments on an earlier draft of this piece. We would also like to thank the John M. Olin Foundation, the Sarah Scaife Foundation, the Lynde and Harry Bradley Foundation, and the Dean's Fund at Vanderbilt University Law School for support.

[1] *See* Cunningham v. Brown, 265 U.S. 1, 7–8 (1923).

[2] *Id.*

paid off his investors in half the time he had initially promised.[3] How could he work such financial magic? Allegedly, Ponzi had discovered a lucrative arbitrage opportunity in postal reply coupons. Postal reply coupons allowed the sender of a letter to ensure that the recipient in another country would be able to obtain sufficient postage to respond.[4] For example, a letter writer in America would purchase a reply coupon here and send it along with a letter to a relative in another country, say, Spain. The Spanish relative could then redeem the coupon for Spanish stamps sufficient to send a reply.

Ponzi noticed a pricing discrepancy in the postal reply coupons. One could buy a coupon in one country for, say, one penny, and redeem it in another for six cents worth of stamps.[5] This opportunity existed because exchange rates had been set in a postal convention in 1906, well before the outbreak of the Great War. The Great War changed the relative value of many currencies, but the rates for postal exchange coupons remained fixed. The failure to adjust the exchange rates on postal reply coupons meant that a trader could buy a postal reply coupon in a country where the relative value of the currency had declined, redeem it in a country where the relative value of the currency had increased, and turn a profit. There were, in theory, gains to be had by exploiting government inertia.

But transaction costs limit any opportunity to profit from arbitrage. Consider the steps necessary to exploit this state of affairs. Money would be gathered in the United States. This money then had to be converted into a foreign currency and put in the hands of an agent in the appropriate foreign country. The agent would have to buy the postal reply coupons in large quantity, although there were limits on the number of coupons that could be bought at one time. The agent then had to send the coupons back to the United States. Another agent would have to redeem them. Given these elaborate requirements, it is hard to imagine how anyone could purchase a sufficient number of reply coupons to support the millions of dollars that Ponzi collected.

When pressed by potential investors on how he could overcome these costs, Ponzi resorted to a favorite theme of the con artist—that such information was a trade secret that could not be disclosed.[6] After all, letting the cat out of the bag would allow his

---

[3] *Id.*

[4] *See* Foreign Treaty Multilateral, 35 Stat. 1639 (1907–1909).

[5] *See* Francis Russell, *Bubble, Bubble—No Toil, No Trouble*, AM. HERITAGE 74, 75 (Feb. 1973) ("He had conceived his scheme, so he said, when he received a business letter from Spain enclosing a reply coupon . . . which was exchangeable at any United States post office for a six-cent stamp. Ponzi was struck by the fact that the coupon in Spain had cost the buyer only the equivalent of one cent."); *Ponzi to Start Back in New York: Boston 'Wizard' Says He Needs Larger Field and Will Come Here at Once*, N.Y. TIMES, July 30, 1920, at 1 (same).

[6] "My secret is how I cash the coupons. I do not tell it to anybody. Let the United States find it out if it can." *Ponzi to Start Back in New York: Boston 'Wizard' Says He Needs Larger Field and Will Come Here at Once*, N.Y. TIMES, July 30, 1920, at 2; *see also* Mark C. Knutson, *The "Ponzi Scheme," available at* http://www.mark-knutson.com (last visited Oct. 5, 2001).

competitors to come in and seize the opportunity he had discovered.[7] A 50% return based on a somewhat plausible story coupled with the allure of a trade secret proved irresistible to over ten thousand investors who willingly gave their money to Ponzi. At its high point, the "Ponzi Plan" as he called it, was taking in $200,000 a day.[8]

Of course, Ponzi's real trade secret was to never incur transaction costs at all. He was able to avoid them because he never bought a significant amount of postal reply coupons.[9] Rather, Ponzi was running a simple pyramid scheme, with the money from later investors being used to pay off earlier ones.[10] When the pyramid collapsed, panic ensued as investors' dreams of fantastic riches turned to fears of losing all that they had entrusted to Ponzi. Ponzi, of course, lacked sufficient funds to return the money to those who were the last to invest, let alone make good on his promised return. Ultimately, it fell to the bankruptcy court to sort out the mess.[11] All were clear, however, on what was and what was not at stake in the court's proceedings. The court's job was to apportion the loss among the disappointed investors in Ponzi's operations. It had to determine what assets were available and who had claims against these assets. These are not easy questions; it took a decision by the Supreme Court to decide exactly which funds belonged in the bankrupt estate.[12]

One thing the bankruptcy court did not have to do, however, was make any decision about how this group of assets should be deployed in the general economy. There was no firm to rescue. There was simply a pile of cash with too many claims against it. This particular aspect of Ponzi's failure would seem to distinguish it from current corporate bankruptcy practice. Chapter 11 today is often viewed as a forum where a decision has to be made as to how the assets of a financially distressed firm should be used. These are real firms with real assets. The goal of bankruptcy, in this view, is to preserve the firm's going-concern value.[13] In contrast, there were no assets in the Ponzi

---

[7] *See* DONALD H. DUNN, PONZI! THE BOSTON SWINDLER 52 (1975) (noting that Ponzi refuses to disclose his method because "the DuPonts and Vanderbilts and Astors could come charging in").

[8] *See* David Segal, *Money for Nothing; Forget the Work Ethic: Mr. Ponzi Showed Us the Real American Dream*, WASH. POST, June 2, 1996, at C1.

[9] *See id.* ("Charles quickly discovered that a welter of red tape was swallowing his profit margins. So he stopped buying coupons but sought out investors anyway.").

[10] *See* Lowell v. Brown, 280 F. 193, 196 (D. Mass. 1922) ("His scheme was simply the old fraud of paying the early comers profits out of the contributions of the later comers.").

[11] *See In re* Ponzi, 268 F. 997, 1002–03 (D. Mass. 1920) (refusing to dismiss involuntary bankruptcy petition against Ponzi).

[12] *See* Cunningham v. Brown, 265 U.S. 1, 7–14 (1923).

[13] This view can be found in court cases, see, e.g., United States v. Whiting Pools, Inc., 462 U.S. 198, 203 (1983); casebooks, see, e.g., ROBERT L. JORDAN ET AL., BANKRUPTCY 633 (5th ed. 1999); treatises, see, e.g., MARK S. SCARBERRY ET AL., BUSINESS REORGANIZATION IN BANKRUPTCY 1–2 (2d ed. 2001); and law review articles, see, e.g., Elizabeth Warren, *The Untenable Case for Repeal of Chapter 11*, 102 YALE L.J. 437, 467–68 (1992); Elizabeth Warren, *Bankruptcy Policymaking in an Imperfect World*, 92 MICH. L. REV. 336, 344–52 (1993).

case other than the remaining cash the court could collect. The major issue was whether earlier investors who had been paid off should be forced to return their proceeds to the kitty and settle for a pro rata share of the money they had originally turned over to Ponzi. There was no contention that the money was worth more if kept together rather than distributed to other parties. As such, it would be tempting to conclude that Ponzi is a colorful figure who reminds us of our tendency to be blinded by the prospect of easy money, but offers little by way of analogy to today's bankruptcy proceedings of publicly held firms.

As the quotation at the outset of this essay illustrates, the recent collapse of Enron has revived the memory of Charles Ponzi. It is easy to see why. Early investors in Enron who cashed out became rich. Enron told its investors that it would continue to enjoy above-market returns indefinitely and that it was a firm that would live up to the promise embedded in its high stock valuation relative to its reported earnings.[14] At its peak, it traded at a price-earnings ratio of fifty-five to one.[15] Similar energy and trading firms had a PE ratio of a quarter of this amount.[16]

This situation should have raised questions—the same questions raised by Ponzi's promise to increase an investor's money by half in a three-month period. Like Ponzi, Enron had answers. Enron presented itself to the world as a market-maker, a firm that excelled at creating new markets.[17] Market-makers, however, rarely enjoy spectacular returns in the long run. To be sure, the enterprise of creating new markets is a worthwhile endeavor. By organizing markets, one enables buyers and sellers to find each other at low cost, eliminating wasted resources through a reduction in transaction costs. The entrepreneur who creates such a market can capture as profit a fair portion of the benefit the initial buyers and sellers enjoy by finding each other. Creating a market for the first time offers the promise of a big one-time profit—the proverbial home run. Enron was no Charles Ponzi; it actually made markets. Indeed, in at least the energy markets where Enron first operated, they seem to have made a good deal of money. Billions of dollars changed hands across the various markets that Enron created.[18]

---

[14] *See* Enron Corp., ENRON ANNUAL REPORT 2000, at 5 (2001), *available at* http://www.enron.com/corp/investors/annuals/2000/ar2000.pdf (last visited Aug. 27, 2002) [hereinafter 2000 ANNUAL REPORT] ("Our performance and capabilities cannot be compared to a traditional energy peer group. . . . Taken together, [the] markets [in which Enron competes] present a $3.9 trillion opportunity for Enron, and we have just scratched the surface.").

[15] *See* Ronnie J. Clayton et al., *Enron: Market Exploitation and Correction,* FIN. DECISIONS, Spring 2002, at 13.

[16] Indeed, Enron assured its investors that such a comparison was not apt. *See* 2000 ANNUAL REPORT, *supra* note 14, at 5 ("Our performance and capabilities cannot be compared to a traditional energy peer group.").

[17] Enron's website stated, "It's difficult to define Enron in a sentence, but the closest we come is this: we make commodity markets so that we can deliver physical commodities to our customers at a predictable price." Enron Corp., *Who We Are, available at* http://www.enron.com/corp/whoweare.html (last visited Feb. 13, 2002).

[18] *See* 2000 ANNUAL REPORT, *supra* note 14, at 9.

Over the long-term, however, market-makers must be satisfied with making a small profit on each trade. One cannot create a market and keep it secret. Once the entrepreneur creates the market, others can follow the example at little cost. As soon as buyers and sellers can choose among a number of different market-makers, profits are competed away. Despite this, Enron was able to convince investors that it was special. It did not maintain that it would increase its returns in the energy markets that it developed. After all, basic economic principles suggest that, if anything, Enron could expect decreasing returns in this aspect of its business. Rather, Enron sold investors on the notion that it could translate its success to international energy markets and to all commodities alike.[19] After colonizing one market, Enron believed it could transport its expertise to other, undeveloped markets. What worked in North America would work in Europe, Asia, and South America. What worked in natural gas and electricity should work in water, broadband, newsprint, metals, coal, crude oil, and steel.[20] The firms that had worked in these areas for years simply had not seen the money that they were leaving on the table.

This concept, while plausible in theory, did not work in practice. Enron, however, endeavored to hide this truth from investors, and perhaps even from itself. As a result, Enron is currently best known as a company that cooked its books. In early October 2001, before disclosing its bookkeeping improprieties, Enron's stock sold for more than $30 a share.[21] Less than two months after these shenanigans came to light, Enron filed for bankruptcy.[22]

When Ponzi failed, there was no business to carry on. The only issue was allocating the few remaining assets. Enron presents a different sort of case. Unlike Ponzi's feigned use of postal reply coupons, Enron ran a real business. Indeed, it was an innovator in energy trading, a business that provided a valuable service and has spawned many imitators.

It might seem that the job of the bankruptcy judge is to preserve Enron's ongoing operations. Just as we would not tear apart a railroad that had dishonest managers, we would not want to allow Enron to be torn apart, either.[23] Enron offers what would

---

[19] For example, see Enron Corp., ENRON ANNUAL REPORT 1999, at 2 (2000), *available at* http://www.enron.com/corp/investors/annuals/annual99/pdfs/1999_Annual_Report.pdf (last visited Aug. 27, 2001) [hereinafter 1999 ANNUAL REPORT] ("What we've learned about natural gas pipelines in the United States helps us build new natural gas markets in South America and India. Our knowledge of optimizing capacity in energy networks will allow us to revolutionize the bandwidth market."); 2000 ANNUAL REPORT, *supra* note 14, at 5 ("We have a proven business concept that is eminently scalable in our existing businesses and adaptable enough to extend to new markets.").

[20] *See* 2000 ANNUAL REPORT, *supra* note 14, at 11–13.

[21] *See* PETER C. FUSARO & ROSS M. MILLER, WHAT WENT WRONG AT ENRON 119 (2002).

[22] *See* Voluntary Pet., *In re* Enron Corp., No. 01-16034, 2001 Extra LEXIS 159 (Bankr. S.D.N.Y. Dec. 2, 2001).

[23] Indeed, we can trace the origins of modern chapter 11 to the challenge of preserving such railroads in the nineteenth century. *See* DAVID A. SKEEL, JR., DEBT'S DOMINION 48–70 (2001); Douglas G. Baird & Robert K. Rasmussen, *Control Rights, Priority Rights, and the Conceptual Foundations of Corporate Reorganizations*, 87 VA. L. REV. 921, 925–33 (2001).

appear to be a paradigmatic case for an old-fashioned chapter 11. In this essay, we show that this view is mistaken. In the end, what the bankruptcy court can do for Enron (and, indeed, other firms in chapter 11)[24] is not much different from what it could do with the mess left by Charles Ponzi. The bankruptcy court is well suited to the task of penetrating the accounting miasma that enshrouds Enron. It may take years, but eventually the court will clear away the obfuscation created by Chewco, JEDI, the Raptors, and the other creatures of accounting imagination that encircled Enron. Other decisions, such as what to do with the assets that once comprised the nation's seventh largest company, are best left to others. Some of Enron's assets left the company prior to bankruptcy, others shortly after, and most of the rest will soon be gone. It will be the new owners, not the bankruptcy court nor Enron's erstwhile managers, who decide the future use of these assets. The market will decide what happens to Enron's business, not the bankruptcy judge.

I. ENRON'S BUSINESS PLAN AND THE IDEA OF THE GOING-CONCERN SURPLUS

Enron was nothing if not dynamic. Enron began in the mid-1980s as a gas pipeline company owning the largest gas pipeline in the United States.[25] It was formed by the merger of two natural gas pipeline companies, Houston Natural Gas and InterNorth. This merger left Enron with $4.2 billion in debt.[26] Using additional debt financing, Enron soon acquired other energy-related assets, including power plants.[27] In 1989, after deregulation of the gas industry, it opened GasBank—an energy trading operation that allowed consumers of natural gas to secure reliable sources of supply at a predictable price. Five years later, it created a market for electricity. These two markets operated at the wholesale level. By the late 1990s, most of Enron's earnings came from businesses in which it had not engaged ten years earlier.[28] In a decade and a half, Enron evolved from an old-economy firm centered on hard assets to a new-economy enterprise centered on a scalable strategy of creating markets where none had existed previ-

---

[24] We make this argument in Douglas G. Baird & Robert K. Rasmussen, *The End of Bankruptcy*, 55 STAN. L. REV. 751 (2002).

[25] *See* Loren Steffy & Adam Levy, *Enron's Original Sins: Lies Began Long Before Current Crisis*, BLOOMBERG NEWS, Mar. 20, 2002, *available at* LEXIS, Bloomberg-All Bloomberg News ("In 1986, . . . Enron . . . owned the largest U.S. gas pipeline.").

[26] *Id.*

[27] *See id.*

[28] *See* Report of Investigation by the *Special Investigative Committee of the Board of Directors of Enron Corp.* 36 (Feb. 1, 2002), *available at* No. 01-16034, 2002 Extra LEXIS 45, at *53 [hereinafter *Report of Investigation*].

ously.[29] In the year before its stunning collapse, Enron touted that its most valuable asset was its people and their ability to apply Enron's business strategy far and wide.[30]

In both the natural gas and electricity markets, Enron hit it big. Deregulation allowed the natural gas industry to change both the way in which natural gas was delivered and the structure of the contracts among the various market participants.[31] Enron was well positioned to take advantage of these changes. It knew where overcapacity existed and where it did not. Its computer system and highly skilled traders allowed it to identify and enter favorable transactions. At the same time, deregulation made utilities more sensitive to price fluctuations than they had been in the past and, hence, more willing to enter into transactions with Enron. In addition, deregulation naturally led to lower prices. Therefore, by locking customers into a fixed price for natural gas, Enron stood to gain as deregulation became more widespread. Enron's success in the natural gas market, coupled with its business in the wholesale electricity market, allowed it to capture a large share of the wholesale electricity trading market when that market was deregulated. By the mid-1990s, Enron dominated the domestic wholesale markets in natural gas and electricity. There were few other players in this field at the outset, and none possessed Enron's knowledge of the marketplace.

As the market for energy trading became thicker, Enron expected to ultimately reduce its commitment to capital-intensive assets such as power plants.[32] Indeed, in the fifteen years from 1985 to 2000, its pipeline capacity decreased from 37,000 miles to 25,000 miles.[33] Its ability to shed these assets, however, did not result in higher

---

[29] Not only did Enron expressly style itself as a "new-economy" firm, *see* 1999 ANNUAL REPORT, *supra* note 19, at 2 ("When you define a New Economy company, you define Enron."), but its annual reports draw heavily on the new-economy lexicon. *See, e.g.,* 2000 ANNUAL REPORT, *supra* note 14, at 2 ("[r]obust networks of strategic assets"); *id.* at 3 ("integrating EnronOnline into all our businesses as an accelerator"); *id.* at 4 ("network connectivity"); *id.* at 5 ("leverage"); 1999 ANNUAL REPORT, *supra* note 19, at 2 ("knowledge-based company," "global networks," "What you own is not as important as what you know," "constant innovation," "connectivity," and "strategic contractual relationships"); *id.* at 4 ("first mover advantage" and "leverage"); *id.* at 5 ("intellectual capital"); Enron Corp., ENRON ANNUAL REPORT 1998, at 3 (1999), *available at* http://www.enron.com/corp/inves-tors/annuals/annual98/pdfs/1998_Annual_Report.pdf (last visited Aug. 27, 2001) [hereinafter 1998 ANNUAL REPORT] ("business platform").

[30] *See* 2000 ANNUAL REPORT, *supra* note 14, at 5 ("We have metamorphosed from an asset-based pipeline and power generating company to a marketing and logistics company whose biggest assets are its well-established business approach and its innovative people.").

[31] *See generally* Regulation of Natural Gas Pipelines After Partial Wellhead Decontrol, 50 Fed. Reg. 42,408, FERC Order No. 436 (Oct. 18, 1985).

[32] *See* 2000 ANNUAL REPORT, *supra* note 14, at 9 ("We continually assess the necessity of adding or owning assets in a region. . . . [A]s liquidity increases, asset ownership may no longer be necessary. . . . The result is the same earnings power with less invested capital.").

[33] *Id.* at 18 (reporting interstate pipeline capacity to be 25,000 miles); Enron Corp., *Fast Facts for the Media: Company History & Milestones, available at* http://www.enron.com/corp/pressroom (last visited Aug. 28, 2002) (stating that Enron owned 37,000 miles of gas pipeline at the time of its formation in 1985).

profits. If Enron did not need hard assets, then neither did its competitors. The ability to maintain a trading operation without hard assets facilitates entry into the energy trading business. Deepening of a market lowers profits. Trading firms in mature markets simply do not receive the returns that Enron did when it first developed the electricity and natural gas markets. At this point, Enron could have simply accepted this steady flow of less spectacular profits.[34]

Enron's managers, however, were not content with standing pat. The lesson that they took from their success in energy markets was not that they were in the right place at the right time, but that they had discovered a strategy for reducing risks that could be transplanted to other areas. Enron sought to expand in two ways. It attempted to expand internationally on what it had done in the United States by acquiring assets in Asia, Europe, South America, and the Caribbean. Trading markets were to follow.[35] Enron envisioned itself dominating the wholesale market for energy worldwide in the same way that it towered over the domestic market.[36]

More provocatively, Enron believed that its success in wholesale energy could be replicated in other domestic markets, many of which were unrelated to energy. Enron's managers believed that what they had done for the wholesale energy market they could do for the retail market. In late 1996, they created Enron Energy Services to provide energy management services to business customers.[37] To illustrate the potential demand for this service, consider a department store chain. It competes with other chains based on selection and price of its merchandise. It does not want to have its success turn on its energy costs. Enron's trading operations would allow the chain to enter into a long-term contract for up to ten years where its supply of electricity was secured and its costs fixed.[38]

Enron's vision was to expand this model across all commodities and other risks that a firm must manage. Simply put, Enron decided to lead the way in solving a problem that entrepreneurs have faced for as long as commerce has existed: how to contend with fluctuating commodity prices and other risks over which they have no control. Retailers have to contend with fluctuating energy needs; farmers can do nothing about the weather; airlines can do nothing to change the price of jet fuel; and importers can do nothing about exchange rates. Businesses sometimes succeed and sometimes fail for reasons that have nothing to do with the competence of their managers. Firms often file for bankruptcy because their most important supplier or customer filed before

---

[34] Indeed, Enron itself predicted only "stable earnings and cash flows" from its most established business—the business on which it was founded—transportation of natural gas. 2000 ANNUAL REPORT, *supra* note 14, at 22.

[35] *See* 1998 ANNUAL REPORT, *supra* note 29, at 14–16.

[36] This theme dominates Enron's 1998 Letter to the Shareholders, which begins with three words: "Global energy franchise." *Id.* at 3.

[37] *See id.* at 34.

[38] *Id.* at 19.

them. Enron promised to change all this. As it boasted on its website, Enron would "make markets in . . . industries that need a more efficient way to deliver commodities and manage risk."[39]

To be sure, all entrepreneurs must take risks. As Chaucer observed: "Nothing ventured, nothing gained."[40] But entrepreneurs want to choose their risks and bear the ones they believe they can control. They want to focus on areas where they believe they have a comparative advantage. For example, Ford Motor Company lost a billion dollars in the market for palladium.[41] While Ford needed palladium to make cars, Ford had no comparative advantage in timing the market for this rare metal. Enron's dream was to prevent situations like this. Enron would make it possible for companies to eliminate such risks by supplying commodities, making markets in them, and strategically investing in the firms and resources needed to provide them. Ultimately, Enron might promise to protect the retail chain that wanted to fix its energy costs not merely if energy prices went up, but also if unusual weather increased its demand for energy. Weather derivatives and other exotic financial instruments allow an intermediary like Enron to make these promises and transfer risk to others.[42]

In creating these various markets, Enron attempted to mimic the strategy that it had used in the wholesale energy business.[43] The first step was to acquire assets. Just as they could assure liquidity in their energy contracts by buying power plants, they could acquire other hard assets to reinforce the other derivative contracts they created.[44] Enron became the seventh largest producer of newsprint. It built fiber-optic networks, acquired firms that dealt in precious metals, and bought a water company.[45] It made strategic investments in start-up ventures built around these commodities. The fiber-optic cable created a demand for routers and other pieces of hardware. Enron invested in these items, and invested big.[46] Similarly, the new capacity created a new

---

[39] Enron Corp., *Who We Are, available at* http://www.enron.com/corp/whoweare.html (last visited Feb. 13, 2002).

[40] *See* GREGORY Y. TITELMAN, RANDOM HOUSE DICTIONARY OF POPULAR PROVERBS AND SAYINGS 250 (2d ed. 2000).

[41] *See* Norihiko Shirouzo et al., *Driving Lessons: Beyond Explorer Woes, Ford Misses Key Turns in Buyers, Technology,* WALL ST. J., Jan. 14, 2002, at A1.

[42] Enron began its weather derivatives market in 1997. *See Enron Leads the Weather Pack,* TREASURY & RISK MGMT., Jan./Feb. 1999, at 17.

[43] *See* 1999 ANNUAL REPORT, *supra* note 19, at 2 (noting that "the skills and resources we used to transform the energy business are proving to be equally valuable in other businesses"); 2000 ANNUAL REPORT, *supra* note 14, at 3 (stating that "[w]e are extending Enron's proven business approach to other markets").

[44] *See* 1999 ANNUAL REPORT, *supra* note 19, at 2 ("Assets form the foundation of network businesses that sell up and down the value chain.").

[45] *See* 1998 ANNUAL REPORT, *supra* note 29, at 4.

[46] Enron's 2000 Annual Report listed the cost of its fiber-optic network and equipment at $839 million. *See supra* note 14, at 32.

outlet for movies. Enron took advantage of this opportunity to invest in a start-up venture that would supply movies on demand on the fiber-optic cables it was building and its trading operations were making accessible.[47]

Enron also created financial derivatives. Enron's bankruptcy contracts helped those whose business depended heavily on one of its customers staying out of chapter 11. To see the attraction of such a contract, consider a shopping center owner that leases its largest store to a retailer. The shopping center faces the risk that the retailer will file for bankruptcy and use the Code's inefficient rules to reject the lease and redistribute the nonbankruptcy rights of the lessor to the other creditors. A contract with Enron could provide for a payout in the event that such a bankruptcy petition took place.

As an example of Enron's vision, consider the following. During the summer of 2000, Enron helped a zinc producer in the Northwest shut down its operations for six weeks and sell the power it would otherwise have used to a buyer who needed it more.[48] Enron then provided a financial derivative to lock in the sale at a fixed price.[49] Enron also provided zinc from its metals subsidiary so that the zinc producer could meet preexisting obligations.[50] Such transactions make everyone better off and put resources to their highest valued use. Enron created value in situations such as these.

Enron's business plan rested on two crucial ideas. First, it assumed that creating markets that helped other firms eliminate risk required owning hard assets and strategically investing in these industries in addition to making a market in derivatives associated with the risk.[51] During the late 1990s, this idea had considerable currency. The great fortunes in cyberspace were to be won with the right combination of bricks and clicks. For instance, Webvan aspired to transform the world of grocery shopping by interconnecting warehouses and fleets of trucks with sophisticated software that allowed grocery delivery within the half-hour time slot the customer wanted.[52] The cost of the infrastructure created a barrier to entry, and the returns to scale were substantial. By becoming the first mover in such a market, the potential profits were enormous. The synergy between any particular combination of "bricks and clicks" might exist.[53] Or it might not.

---

[47] Rebecca Smith, *Blockbuster, Enron Agree to Movie Deal*, WALL ST. J., July 20, 2000, at A3, *available at* 2000 WL-WSJ 3037214.

[48] 2000 ANNUAL REPORT, *supra* note 14, at 12.

[49] *Id.*

[50] *Id.*

[51] Such ownership, however, need not last forever. As Enron created markets and learned how they operated, it eventually could shed assets, as it had done in its energy business.

[52] *See* RANDALL E. STROSS, EBOYS: THE FIRST INSIDE ACCOUNT OF VENTURE CAPITALISTS AT WORK 30–36 (2000). Immediately after Webvan's IPO, it had a market capitalization of more than $8 billion. *Id.* at 286.

[53] *See, e.g.*, MCKINSEY & COMPANY, BRICKS AND CLICKS: WINNING IN THE NEW ECONOMY (July 2000), *available at* http://retail.mckinsey.com/pdf/speech_internetworld.pdf (last visited Oct. 3, 2002); Stuart Elliott, *Technology Briefing: E-Commerce; Bricks and Clicks Convergence?*, N.Y. TIMES, Sept. 28, 2000, at C10.

Second, Enron assumed that its success in the natural gas and electricity markets gave it a comparative advantage in creating markets elsewhere,[54] but it turns out that Enron's success in energy may have been smaller than its managers thought. Enron marked its contracts to market in environments in which liquid markets did not exist. The computer models used to extrapolate a "market price" proved wildly optimistic. In addition to inflating its success in a way that affected the investors who bought the company's shares, Enron's financial modeling may have also misled managers.

Even if it had been successful in the energy market, Enron's success may have stemmed not from its ability to make markets, but rather from industry-specific expertise. For example, Enron's pipeline and power businesses gave it knowledge of where excess capacity lay. When it created markets in water, broadband, coal, and steel, it lacked similar knowledge. Finally, Enron's success came in two markets—natural gas and electricity—that were moving from regulation to deregulation.[55] Whether substantial opportunities existed in other markets not undergoing this transition was unclear.

To implement its business strategy, Enron, as it existed at the end of 2001, combined three separate types of businesses. First, it owned a variety of hard assets, including power plants and natural gas pipelines. Second, it ran trading operations in which it made markets in many different commodities and financial derivatives and advised businesses about how they could take advantage of these instruments. Third, it was a venture-capital investor in many high-technology and energy-related ventures, both in this country and abroad. Moreover, Enron viewed these separate businesses as part of a single plan. The venture-capital investments were designed to spur development of hard assets, which would then serve as the base on which it would build its trading operations.

Few companies attempt to combine such disparate activities. It would be as if Exxon combined with the New York Stock Exchange and a Silicon Valley venture capital fund such as Sequoia Capital. Running each of these units effectively tends to require different types of management strategies. Managing hard assets such as pipelines and utilities requires managers who know how to keep things running and minimize costs. Those who sell commodities at market prices get their profit from lowering costs. Market-makers require transparent operations—everything turns on counterparties believing that they are dealing with an entity that will honor its promises. Strategic investing requires industry-specific expertise and an ability to close deals and cut losses. Each of these businesses ordinarily operates under radically different governance and capital structures. Enron's strategy of putting all three operations under one roof makes sense only if a way could be found to manage them at a low cost.

---

[54] *See* 2000 Annual Report, *supra* note 14, at 5 ("We have a proven business concept that is eminently scalable in our existing businesses and adaptable enough to extend to new markets."); 1999 Annual Report, *supra* note 19, at 2 ("We are clearly a knowledge-based company, and the skills and resources we used to transform the energy business are proving to be equally valuable in other businesses."); *id.* at 5 ("The fundamental skills and expertise we use to develop energy and communications solutions can be applied to many situations that inhibit our customers' profits and growth.").

[55] *See* 1998 Annual Report, *supra* note 26, at 3.

In fact, such a mixture of business operations may be highly toxic. Market-makers can only make markets to the extent that their counterparties believe they will fulfill their promises. If any threat exists that the market-maker will not be able to come through on promises made, the market will evaporate. In Enron's case, its contracts stretched out for years. Some of its natural gas and electricity contracts committed Enron to supply these commodities for over two decades.[56] People enter into such long-term relationships only when they have reason to believe the other side will be there in the future.

Venture capitalists, in contrast, swing for the fences. In a good year, most of their investments will fail. To be sure, there is the promise of extraordinary returns, but there is also the specter of extraordinary losses. Successful venture capitalists depend on great returns in a handful of successes to counterbalance the losses they incur in most of their investments. In its venture investing, Enron was doing more than looking to score big in a handful of cases. It was looking to support its other operations. This self-interest in success could well cloud the decision about whether to fund a venture and when to terminate it. Combining venture activity and market-making activity, far from being a source of synergy, might reduce Enron's value as a going concern.

Enron identified its business model as a "network" where the trading operations allowed it to "leverage" its investments in assets. Enron believed that others could not compete with it because it was the only competitor able to combine trading operations with hard assets. Yet its own experience suggested that combining these two components was becoming less important. For example, Enron's 2000 Annual Report boasted that, over time, it would become less reliant on its own assets in servicing its customers.[57] But rather than a source of pride, this goal should have sounded an alarm. To the extent that owning the hard assets is less necessary, the less value Enron has as a going concern and the more plausible it becomes that others can compete with it in the market. There is no reason to believe that Enron had access to contracts with third parties that could not be replicated by others.[58]

---

[56] See 2000 Annual Report, *supra* note 14, at 38.

[57] See *id.* at 9 ("We continually assess the necessity of adding or owning assets in a region. . . . [A]s liquidity increases, asset ownership may no longer be necessary."); *id.* at 24 ("In North America, Enron expects to complete the sale of five of its peaking power plants located in the Midwest and its interstate natural gas pipeline. In each case, market conditions, such as increased liquidity, have diminished the need to own physical assets.").

[58] Here is where Enron comes perilously close to Ponzi's invocation of a trade secret. Enron's annual reports are replete with references to Enron's intellectual capital but are sketchy at best as to the exact nature of that capital. See, e.g., *id.* at 3 ("We are extending Enron's proven business approach to other markets, and integrating EnronOnline [its computer trading system] into all our businesses as an accelerator."); 1999 Annual Report, *supra* note 19, at 2 ("Enron has been and always will be the consummate innovator because of our extraordinary people. It is our intellectual capital—not only our physical assets—that makes us Enron. Move our assets to another company, and the results would be markedly

If transaction costs go down, a firm can stabilize its costs by entering into different contracts with a number of firms. It no longer needs a single firm such as Enron. Even if it wants to deal with one firm, a single intermediary who is neither a market-maker nor a supplier can bundle the appropriate contracts and sell them. The technological advance that Enron relied upon to create its markets was a dramatic decline in transaction costs, but such a decline also reduces any advantage Enron had over competitors. The easier it is for others to compete with Enron, the less value Enron has above and beyond the value of its assets.[59] The same force that made Enron possible also capped its value as a going concern.

When Enron filed for bankruptcy, it owned thousands of miles of gas pipelines and fiber-optic cable. It was one of the largest wholesalers of coal and the seventh largest producer of newsprint. It owned power plants all over the world, some completed, some still under development. Even if it had made astute investments in all these areas (and there is much to suggest that it did not),[60] there seems to have been little synergy between these assets. There is no reason to think that these assets have a greater value in Enron's hands than in the hands of some other party.[61] The ability to enter into contracts for any of these commodities and the ability to form networks through contracts made it less valuable to have a collection of physical assets under the control of any particular firm.

We come then to the first easy lesson of Enron. It is all too easy, inside of bankruptcy and out, to assume that any particular business has an enormous going-concern surplus. Much is lost if a firm is shut down and its assets are sold off piecemeal. But the extent to which a firm as a whole has value above and beyond the sum of the highest value of its discrete assets is easy to overestimate. In a world in which transaction costs are rapidly declining, the value created by simply bringing assets into the firm is likely to decrease over time. Enron may provide an especially vivid illustration. Indeed, as we have noted above, Enron's business plan was to make money by reducing transaction costs. Enron made it continuously cheaper for others to buy and sell all the things for

different."); *id.* at 5 ("We recognize that our intellectual capital is our most important asset, and we cherish it."); 1998 ANNUAL REPORT, *supra* note 29, at 4 ("We have the people and the skills in place to widen our strong competitive advantage, and we think it would be very difficult, if not impossible, for any other company to replicate our overall capabilities in the foreseeable future.").

[59] As we explain in detail elsewhere, this is a corollary of Ronald Coase's observation seventy years ago that transactions are brought inside a firm when it is cheaper for the firm to control the assets rather than contract for them. Ronald H. Coase, *The Nature of the Firm*, 4 ECONOMICA 386 (1937); *see* Baird & Rasmussen, *supra* note 23.

[60] Enron designed the Raptors and other similar instruments to ensure that, at least temporarily, declines in its investments would not be recognized on its bottom line. *See Report of Investigation, supra* note 28, at 97–99. The ultimate collapse of these structures was due in large part to the precipitous drop in the value of Enron's investments.

[61] As we discuss below, Enron's disparate groups are in the process of being sold off separately. *See infra* Parts III & IV. The market thus seems to value the sum of the parts as greater than the whole.

which it was a market-maker. But as these costs declined, Enron's own ability to profit as a market-maker declined as well. The benefits that arise when transaction costs decline and markets come into being are commonly called "consumer surplus." The name is no accident. When markets work correctly, it is the buyers who enjoy the benefits rather than the intermediaries that made the trade possible. The huge valuations the stock market placed upon Enron (and other similar intermediaries who brought us the "new economy") may reflect a failure to acknowledge this basic principle.

II. ENRON'S TRADING SYSTEM AND PRESERVING DEDICATED ASSETS

Enron's hard assets, such as its power plants and pipelines, appear to have no more value in Enron's hands than they would in the hands of another firm. The search for going-concern value must therefore begin elsewhere. Did Enron own other kinds of assets that did have their highest valued use inside of Enron? The most significant asset designed and dedicated to Enron's activities was its trading and information infrastructure. It provided real-time information on everything that affected the value of the goods and services in the markets it made, from the weather to the latest news. The system was operated and maintained by a group of several hundred highly talented traders and information specialists. Enron claimed that this group generated $2 billion in profits in the year 2000 alone.[62] Indeed, this group was responsible for 90% of the profits Enron reported for that year.[63]

We know now that Enron made less on its operations than it reported. How much less or indeed whether they generated any profit at all is now unclear. Enron marked to market its profits from the trading operations, even when the contracts (such as a contract with a single entity to provide power or electricity) were one of a kind and extended over a decade.[64] These contracts represented a discounted cash flow derived from financial modeling rather than hard numbers based on the same contracts in liquid markets. Moreover, Enron was a market-maker in many areas in which its employees were also the principal traders. Many contracts were executed between two Enron traders. By making each of its traders a stand-alone profit center, Enron's compensation system may have created an environment in which phantom profits appeared through trades that Enron traders made with each other. When the dust settles, it may well be that Enron's vaunted technology had little value.

Yet, even if we were to take Enron's profit numbers at face value, it is far from clear that Enron's trading system is a source of large going-concern surplus, given the emergence of other trading systems by competitors. Information systems like Enron's are

---

[62] *See* 2000 ANNUAL REPORT, *supra* note 14, at 21.

[63] *See id.* at 21 (reporting that in 2000, Wholesale Services had income of $2,260,000 and Enron as a whole had income of $2,482,000).

[64] *See id.* at 38 (listing a range from six to twenty-nine years as maximum terms of risk management contracts for various commodities and financial products).

public goods. The cost of providing additional consumers access to any system is quite small. Whether a particular system has value does not depend upon whether it provides valuable information, but whether it can compete effectively with other information and trading operations. A system may be very good, but in a competitive market, it may have little value if it is not quite as good as other systems, or if it offers a comparable product at a higher price.

One also has to identify the components that give any system value. Much of the information is real-time information that has value only because it is constantly updated. It may take a large investment in resources to maintain the system, but comparatively little to establish it at the outset. Knowing the price at the close of business the previous day is not at all difficult, but maintaining an information system that provides the price of a commodity in real time is costly. For the system to have value, the increased value one gets from constantly updated prices must be greater than the cost of gathering such information and making it available. Even if it is worthwhile to maintain a real-time system, there is no reason to believe that Enron's system could be run more cheaply than anyone else's. To the extent that Enron's system possessed the information by virtue of hiring a large number of individuals to acquire and enter this data into the system, others could do the same thing at the same cost.

Enron's computer system, of course, did not operate itself. Much of the value of Enron's operations is attributable to the traders and researchers who maintained the system. Few possess the skills needed to execute derivative contracts, to hedge risks, and to assess the overall risk of a portfolio. Those who worked at Enron may have possessed such skills and thus may have added value to its trading and information systems. Here again, however, these assets do not by themselves necessarily contribute to the value of this operation. First, we do not know whether the traders as a group created any value for Enron at all. The extent of Enron's liabilities is not known. Enron's traders may, in the end, have been able to enter into the number of transactions they did only because they could not estimate the value of these transactions properly. It is very easy for a trader to sell $100 dollar bills for $95, especially in an environment in which the internal control mechanisms allow the trader to book a $10 profit on the deal. Put simply, the enormous volume of Enron's trading operations may reflect no more than the ability of other traders to profit at Enron's expense.

Even if Enron's traders were in fact highly skilled, we are still left with the question of whether they added value to Enron. To retain such traders in a competitive environment, Enron needed to pay them. If the traders could employ their expertise in other firms as readily as at Enron, they—not Enron—would enjoy the value of their skills. What began as a firm-specific asset—the ability to trade on Enron's proprietary system—may have morphed into an industry-specific one—the ability to trade on any number of trading systems. Whereas Enron could garner much of the surplus of firm-specific skills, it would capture considerably less of industry-specific ones. For firm-specific skills, the surplus created is shared between the employee and the firm. For industry-specific skills, the surplus is up for bid, with the employee able to take her skills to the highest bidder.

Hence, the value of Enron's trading operation available to its creditors and other investors did not lie in the skill of individual traders. Instead, its value, if any exists, must be the unique combination of assets—the marriage of the traders and the proprietary trading system. If so, traders who moved to operations at other firms might not be able to do as much or be as successful, because their skills would not mesh as effectively with the system and people at the other firm. But such synergies tend to disappear as markets evolve anyway.

This is the second lesson of Enron. One should not assume that specialized assets generate going-concern value. In the case of cutting-edge markets, firm-specific assets often become industry-specific. The traders who created new markets at Enron can work anywhere. They have valuable skills, but these skills do not belong to Enron. Assets dedicated to a particular enterprise, such as Enron's computer system and the team that ran it, may lose their value in the wake of competition.

III. COHERENT CONTROL RIGHTS AND ENRON

Enron's basic business plan—combining contracting over commodities with supplying the physical asset itself—created a large network of interrelated entities.[65] Moreover, tax rules made it attractive to create elaborate vehicles to minimize corporate tax, while accounting rules created the temptation to use such vehicles to foist things off the balance sheet that investors did not like to see, like debt and losses. Although these vehicles minimized taxes and allowed the reporting of ever-increasing profits, they simultaneously made it more difficult for those in charge to assess exactly how any given Enron division was performing. As the old saying goes, one advantage of consistently telling the truth is that it is much easier to keep your story straight. One of the worst things a decisionmaker can do is pollute her own sources of information. The sheer complexity of understanding what Enron did and did not own undermined the business model premised upon the idea that a firm that combines the trading function with the delivery function enjoys a comparative advantage.

The transactions that ultimately precipitated Enron's collapse complicate the current reorganization proceeding. Consider, for example, the "Raptor III" transaction.[66] Enron created a subsidiary, The New Power Company ("TNPC"), in which it owned a 75% interest.[67] TNPC was to provide energy to retail customers. Enron then engaged in a set of transactions designed to allow it to report large gains from its invest-

---

[65] Enron had approximately four thousand subsidiaries. *See* Motion of the Debtors Pursuant to Rule 1015(B) of the Federal Rules of Bankruptcy Procedure for Joint Administration of the Cases, *In re* Enron, No. 01-16034, 2001 Extra LEXIS 304, at *2, (Bankr. S.D.N.Y. Dec. 10, 2001).

[66] Further details of the Raptors and other similar transactions can be found in the special master's report in Enron's bankruptcy case. *See* First Interim Report of Neal Batson, Court-Appointed Examiner, *In re* Enron Corp., No. 01-16034, at 3–4 (Bankr. S.D.N.Y. Sept. 21, 2002).

[67] *Report of Investigation, supra* note 28, at 114–18.

ment in TNPC. It sold a portion of its stock of TNPC to a special purpose entity, dubbed "Hawaii 125-0," that it created with an outside institutional investor.[68] At the same time, Enron entered into a series of swap arrangements with Hawaii 125-0 that left most of the economic risks and rewards associated with the TNPC stock with Enron itself. These transactions taken, as a whole, allowed Enron to book a large gain on the TNPC stock transferred to Hawaii 125-0.

Enron, however, sought to ensure that its future income statements would not have to account for any losses based on its promise to guard Hawaii 125-0 against a decrease in the value of the TNPC stock. Thus, it looked for a way to "lock in" its gain on the sale to Hawaii 125-0.

Enter Raptor III and LJM2, a limited partnership run by Enron's Chief Financial Officer. Enron used a limited liability company it had previously created—"Porcupine"—in which it was the principal shareholder.[69] LJM2 contributed $30 million in equity to Porcupine, but part of the deal was that LJM2 would receive $39.5 million from Porcupine before Porcupine could engage in any hedging transactions. The only other assets of Porcupine were 24 million shares of TNPC stock that came from Enron. Porcupine gave Enron a note for $259 million for these shares; the price for the shares was based on the price that Hawaii 125-0 had paid for its shares months earlier. Enron was in the final phase of readying for an IPO that would price the TNPC stock significantly higher than the price that Hawaii 125-0 had paid.

One week later, the IPO of TNPC took place.[70] On the same day, Porcupine paid LJM2 its promised $39.5 million. Porcupine then entered into a swap on 18 million shares of TNPC under which Porcupine, in essence, promised to reimburse Enron to the extent that the price of TNPC fell below $21 a share. But, the only asset that Porcupine had to back up this obligation was stock in TNPC itself. If the stock went down enough, Enron would take the fall. Porcupine would be unable to pay off the note that it had given to Enron for the 24 million shares, and it would not be able to honor its promise to reimburse Enron for the decline in price below $21 a share on the hedged 18 million shares. Enron gained nothing other than an ability to hide its finances from investors for losses over the short term, and for this facade it paid LJM2 $9.5 million.[71]

Numerous transactions such as this make it very hard to put a value on Enron. Enron may have claims against Porcupine, LJM2, and the principal owner of LJM2, its erstwhile Chief Financial Officer, but the legal status of these claims is uncertain. The economic value of these claims is also cloudy because it is unclear whether any of the affected parties have the resources to fully satisfy their obligations.

---

[68] *Id.* at 115.

[69] *Id.*

[70] *Id.* at 117.

[71] *Id.* at 118.

These transactions make it nearly impossible to ascertain the value of Enron's principal asset, its energy trading system. The value of the trading system depends on the ability of the market-maker to settle its contracts. Raptor III and its brethren made it impossible for any party to ascertain what Enron was really worth. This opacity sets Enron apart from the typical bankruptcy of publicly traded firms that we see today. Many large modern chapter 11 cases begin only after those in control have already decided to sell the firm's assets. Shortly after bankruptcy is filed, the bankruptcy judge oversees the sale of the firm's assets and ensures that the assets may be transferred free of contention among those who have competing claims.[72] For example, when American Airlines agreed to buy TWA last year, chapter 11 was initiated only to consummate the speedy sale.[73] TWA's principal assets ended up in American's hands roughly three months after TWA filed for bankruptcy.[74] Divvying up the cash took over a year.[75]

In many of these cases, control rights over assets have been parceled to ensure that all decisions about asset deployment are made outside of bankruptcy.[76] In the case of a large firm in bankruptcy, we find that, at the moment chapter 11 is filed, a revolving credit facility is already in place that entrusts decisionmaking authority to a single entity.[77] This entity will often step in and replace management. It will make the necessary operational decisions before chapter 11 begins. Where synergy among assets exists, they will be kept; where the market places as high or higher value on the assets than does the firm, they will be sold. By the time the firm enters bankruptcy, the process of shutting down or selling off operations is well underway. The bankruptcy process itself has little to do with making decisions about how the assets are used. Bankruptcy is used only because, as a legal matter, it provides a cheaper mechanism for assuring the buyer clean title than state law.[78]

Modern firms may have complicated and dynamic divisions of control rights. These rights are nevertheless coherent in the sense that they represent a bargained agreement among investors about who should exercise control over the firm's assets in any par-

---

[72] *See* Baird & Rasmussen, *supra* note 24, at 786–88.

[73] *See* Susan Carey, *American Airlines' TWA Financing Plan Is Approved, Although Rivals Cry Foul,* WALL ST. J., Jan. 29, 2001, at A3, *available at* 2001 WL-WSJ 2852465.

[74] *See* Susan Carey, *TWA's Sale to American Airlines Clears Hurdle, Is to Close Today,* WALL ST. J., Apr. 9, 2001, at B9, *available at* 2001 WL-WSJ 2859670.

[75] TWA's plan was confirmed in June 2002. *See In re* Trans World Airlines, Order Confirming Joint Liquidating Plan of Reorganization of the Debtors and the Official Committee of Unsecured Creditors Pursuant to Chapter 11 of the United States Bankruptcy Code, No. 01-00056 (Bankr. D. Del. June 14, 2002).

[76] *See* Baird & Rasmussen, *supra* note 24, at 778–85.

[77] *See id.* at 784–85.

[78] *See id.* at 787–86.

ticular state of the world.[79] Indeed, in the case of many modern, new-economy firms, the enterprise is designed so that the firm enters bankruptcy only after all the economic opportunities associated with the assets have been exhausted. Webvan is a recent example. It filed for chapter 11 only after its professional managers and venture capital backers concluded that it would never be able to maintain a positive cash flow.[80] Chapter 11 was only used as a way to ensure an orderly liquidation.[81]

Some cases can arise, particularly those where conditions can change rapidly or those that involve fraud, where the control rights are no longer allocated in a coherent manner. Enron is such a case. Assets were placed in various entities to avoid taxes or to make the books look favorable. Added to the maze of entities in the Enron family is the problem of fraud. The introduction of tortious conduct for which the firm is liable further compounds the problem, as claims against the assets may be both unliquidated and contingent. This lack of coherent control rights does create some work for the bankruptcy judge.

When the firm's assets are hard to identify and are locked in different related entities where individuals have different rights, matters are complicated. The appropriate disposition of assets may be unclear, and different dispositions may have different distributional consequences. Unwinding various derivative transactions can have the effect of terminating the option value of those who have an ownership interest in them. This possibility creates disparate incentives and controversy among investors, all of whom have an interest in recovering as much as possible individually.

With respect to many of Enron's traditional assets, however, the lack of coherent control rights may be of little moment. The revenue stream a utility will generate is largely independent of who controls it, at least during the initial months when the asset still resides inside the firm being reorganized. Control rights over the day-to-day operations of these assets will remain in the hands of employees who take care of them. Even if decisions need to be made (such as replacing the management team), those decisions usually do not create controversies among investors, who share a common interest in maximizing the value of the firm.

Here, then, is the third lesson of Enron. The basic decisions in a reorganization ought to begin with an examination of the way in which control rights are allocated. Their coherence, or lack of coherence, tells us how much work the bankruptcy judge

---

[79] WorldCom's capital structure was arranged so that, should the unthinkable happen and WorldCom be unable to pay its debts, the decision as whether to keep WorldCom's assets together or sell them off rested in the hands of its bankers. *See* Mitchell Pacelle & Carrick Mollenkamp, *WorldCom's Banks Face Big Choice*, WALL ST. J., June 27, 2002, at A3. Only when the banks could not find a ready buyer did the firm file for bankruptcy. *See* Simon Romero & Riva D. Atlas, *WorldCom's Collapse*, N.Y. TIMES, July 22, 2002, at A1.

[80] *See* Baird & Rasmussen, *supra* note 24 (manuscript at 50).

[81] *Id.*

must do. When the rights are coherently allocated, or the assets are conventional and easy to identify, there is little work for the bankruptcy judge. Often, the judge need only follow the lead of those who have bargained for control. These individuals have greater knowledge and incentives to ensure that assets are put to their highest valued use. In such cases, judicial work, to the extent it exists at all, involves allocating the assets among competing claimants and vindicating bankruptcy's prohibitions on preferences and fraudulent conveyances.

IV. MARKET SALES AND THE ENRON ASSETS

We come now to one more lesson of Enron. Modern chapter 11 practice, unlike that of twenty years ago, relies on the market. Even where dedicated assets exist and control rights are in disarray, modern bankruptcy judges often maintain control of the assets and take the necessary steps to preserve their value for only as long as it takes to find a buyer. For example, bankruptcy judges today have the ability to approve short-term contracts to keep a business together and the ability to sell the assets as soon as buyers can be found.[82] In Enron's case, the bankruptcy judge approved the retention of the traders and others for a period of weeks even though they were only coming to work to play poker with each other.[83] As those in control searched for a reliable counterparty to run the trading operation, Enron's traders needed to be kept on board.

A trading operation in a rapidly changing economy cannot remain dormant for long. The fate of the trading operation could not wait until Enron's financial affairs were sorted out. Within a few weeks of the bankruptcy petition, the bankruptcy judge conducted an auction in which the winning bidder promised to pay only a portion of the profits of the operation for some period of years.[84] In a different world, where the firm was not clouded by improprieties, a prevailing bidder would have been required to produce some amount of hard cash. But Enron no longer possessed the credibility needed to be a market-maker and could not engage in any transactions at all, rendering it considerably less valuable as an acquisition. Moreover, the sudden shutdown of the trading system made it unclear how many customers would return when the power went back on. In such a world, a bankruptcy judge must simply do the best she can. It is a testimony to the flexibility and creativity of the modern bankruptcy bench that the judges administering the Enron cases were able to orchestrate such sales and ensure that they took place within a few weeks.

Enron has already sold its main natural gas pipeline. Before entering into chapter 11, it tried to engineer a takeover by its competitor, Dynergy. As part of the transac-

---

[82] See Ann Davis, *Want Some Extra Cash? File for Chapter 11: 'Pay to Stay' Bonuses Are Common at Busted Tech Firms*, WALL ST. J., Oct. 31, 2001, at C1.

[83] See *In re* Enron Corp., No. 01-16034, 2001 Bankr. Lexis 1563, at *4, *7 (Bankr. S.D.N.Y. Dec. 3, 2001).

[84] See FUSARO & MILLER, *supra* note 21, at 178.

tion, Enron promised that, were the acquisition talks to collapse, it would sell its pipeline to Dynergy.[85] The talks did in fact collapse, and Dynergy took control of the pipeline.[86] Just before it filed for bankruptcy, Enron agreed to sell its wholly-owned subsidiary, Portland General Electric, to Northwest Natural Gas Company for $1.9 billion.[87] While this sale ultimately was not completed because of complications arising from the bankruptcy proceeding, this asset is currently on the block.[88] Eleven other Enron subsidiaries are also on the block.[89] Other assets have already found buyers. Enron's wind operations have been sold to General Electric.[90]

Enron's new CEO has proposed moving Enron's pipeline and energy business, the type of assets on which Enron was founded in 1985, out of bankruptcy and into a new company.[91] Enron's new managers and creditors apparently believe that Enron's disparate assets will fetch the highest price if sold separately. This conclusion should not be surprising. The new chief executive officer is a specialist in selling distressed assets, not in running a going concern. The large array of assets that came into the bankruptcy court when Enron filed its petition is systematically being turned into cash. Thus, the questions addressed in Enron's reorganization will focus largely upon dividing assets among many claimants.

Enron is the twenty-first century's parallel to the late nineteenth century railroads. They too had their share of fraud and corruption.[92] They also had capital structures that took years to unravel. Much of the railroad reorganization business, however, required judicial oversight of the railroad's operations and their restructuring. This aspect of the equity receivership was necessary only because the capital markets of the time

---

[85] *Dynergy to Pay Enron a $25 Million Settlement*, N.Y. TIMES, Aug. 16, 2002, at C4.

[86] Dynergy, which subsequently encountered its own financial troubles, sold the pipeline in the summer of 2002 to legendary investor Warren Buffett. *See* Kathryn Kranhold, *Enron Takes Bid on Major Assets, Adding to a Glut*, WALL ST. J., Aug. 28, 2002, at B3, *available at* 2002 WL-WSJ 3404659.

[87] *See* Robin Sidel, *Northwest Natural Buys Enron Unit for $1.9 Billion in Cash and Stock*, WALL ST. J., Oct. 9, 2001, at A4, *available at* 2001 WL-WSJ 2877908.

[88] *See* Press Release, Enron Corp., Enron Commences Auction Process to Maximize Value of Core Assets, (Aug. 27, 2002), *available at* http://www.enron.com/corp/pressroom/releases/-2002/ene/29-082702ReleaseLtr.html.

[89] *Id.*

[90] Jeff St. Onge & Christopher Mumma, *$358 Million Wind-Asset Sale to GE Is Approved*, BLOOMBERG NEWS, Apr. 11, 2002, *available at* LEXIS, Bloomberg-All Bloomberg News.

[91] *See* Press Release, *Enron Corp., Enron Presents Process to Creditors' Committee for Separating Power, Pipeline Company from Bankruptcy* (May 3, 2002), *available at* http://www.enron.com/corp/pressroom/releases/2002/ene/23-050302ReleaseLtr.html (last visited Aug. 21, 2002); *see also* Neela Banerjee, *Enron to Sell Major Units to Raise Cash for Settlements*, N.Y. TIMES, Aug. 28, 2002, at C1.

[92] For a description of the events surrounding nine of the largest railroad reorganizations, see STUART DAGGETT, RAILROAD REORGANIZATION (1908); *see also* WILLIAM Z. RIPLEY, RAILROADS: FINANCE & ORGANIZATION 390 (1920) (noting that in equity receiverships "the old management, particularly when held responsible for the failure, is [usually] excluded").

were insufficient to allow marketplace sales of the assets.[93] Today, however, firms can muster the billions needed to buy Enron's hard assets or serve as a reliable counterparty for its trading operations. The fourth lesson of Enron is again a simple one. Markets for the assets of large firms exist in a way they did not at the time the law of corporate reorganization came into being. Shortly before it filed for chapter 11, Enron controlled 25% of a trading volume that measured many billions of dollars.[94] Its working capital itself ran in the billions.[95] But it could cease its trading operations without creating even a ripple in the marketplace. When the trading operation that had purportedly generated billions in profits was put up for sale, no cash bidders appeared. The absence of a cash bid for its trading operations did not raise concern about the liquidity of markets, but rather new doubts about the underlying value of Enron's operation. With respect to large firms in reorganization, liquidity constraints and the inability to raise sufficient capital can no longer justify a law of corporate reorganizations.

V. CONCLUSION

Enron was not a Ponzi scheme. Money from late-arriving investors was not used to pay off those who arrived earlier. But Enron and Ponzi do have two features in common. First, the bankruptcy itself was precipitated by the failure of investors to understand that extraordinary profits from financial intermediation, to the extent they exist, disappear in competition. Second, the primary business of bankruptcy is not to save or rehabilitate firms, but to allocate losses after the assets are sold. The business of making such decisions, especially in the presence of fraud, is a hard business, but it is one in which our bankruptcy judges are especially skilled.

Enron's story has cast a shadow over nearly everyone associated with it, from politicians to accountants, but the bankruptcy bench and the modern chapter 11 process may be a striking exception. Judges in Delaware and elsewhere have transformed chapter 11 just as judges in the nineteenth century transformed the then-arcane equity receivership. Bankruptcy judges no longer pretend to possess the wisdom to chart the destiny of great corporations. Nor does chapter 11 provide a chance for investors to sit down and spend years pondering the fate of a large firm. But the new face of large-firm bankruptcy practice, one that began only a few years ago in Delaware, may give us something to celebrate. Judges and markets work hand-in-hand, each doing its work in the arena in which it operates best. This observation is another, and perhaps the most reassuring, lesson from Enron.[96]

---

[93] *See* Jerome N. Frank, *Some Realistic Reflections on Some Aspects of Corporate Reorganization*, 19 VA. L. REV. 541, 554 (1933).

[94] 2000 ANNUAL REPORT, *supra* note 14, at 9.

[95] *See id.* at 32.

[96] *See* Baird & Rasmussen, *supra* note 24 (manuscript at 43–61) (developing this theme at greater length).

Enron and the Long Shadow of Stat. 13 Eliz.*

Douglas G. Baird**

Two years ago, Enron was one of the most admired corporations in America. Today, its assets have been sold and its managers led off in handcuffs. Creditors have discovered that Enron's assets will give them only a few cents on the dollar. Those closest to fraud and other mischief are likely judgment-proof. But a number of entities just off stage have deep pockets and the creditors are in active pursuit of them. In this essay, I set out the challenges that await Enron's creditors and assess their prospects. The creditors have some reason for optimism. Often the best paths are the oldest and the most well-trodden, and this case is no exception. While the transactions in Enron involved full-return swaps, derivatives, and every variety of financial instrument, the best course for the creditors is set out in the Statute of 13 Elizabeth, as interpreted by Lord Coke in *Twyne's Case* in 1601.

I. ENRON'S BUSINESS PLAN

Financial analysts became smitten with Enron's business plan.[1] But we should not be too quick to ridicule them. Almost any innovative idea looks bad if it fails. In 1907,

* Originally published as Douglas Baird, *Enron and the Long Shadow of Stat. 13 Eliz., in* SARAH WORTHINGTON, COMMERCIAL LAW AND COMMERCIAL PRACTICE __ (forthcoming 2004). Reprinted with permission.

** Harry A. Bigelow Distinguished Service Professor, University of Chicago. An earlier version of this essay was presented at the Commercial Law and Commercial Practice Seminar at the London School of Economics in November 2002. Its participants and especially Kevin Davis provided helpful comments. Many of the ideas in this essay grow out of my long, fruitful, and continuing collaboration with my colleague Robert Rasmussen, to whom I am, as always, most indebted. For its support of this and many other projects, I am grateful to the John M. Olin Foundation.

[1] For a pre-lapsarian account of the analysts and Enron, see Brian O'Reilly, *The Power Merchant*, Fortune, Apr. 17, 2000, at 148 ("In January, before a room packed with Wall Street securities analysts, Enron "broke radio silence" on its plans. . . . It was like Jesus showing up at a tent revival. Analysts swooned; they cheered; one declared that Enron had "instant credibility" in the new endeavor.").

cars were a plaything for the rich and paved roads were the exception. Nevertheless, a car designer who had already failed twice bet millions on a radically new car. By using exotic vanadium steel alloys and stamped metal casings, he believed his car could be produced for $500 and that millions of average Americans would buy it at that price, even though $500 at the time was the better part of a year's wages. In the 1950, the Haloid Company risked all on a machine that made copies of documents on plain paper, even after the experts at IBM and General Electric had established that there was no market for such a machine, as carbon paper was a cheaper and simpler way of making duplicates. In 1986, an entrepreneur in Seattle bet every penny that ordinary Americans would spend several dollars a day on espresso and cappuccino. All these ideas seemed far-fetched in their time. But Henry Ford's Model T changed the world. Haloid thrived (and changed its name to Xerox). Starbucks has become a fixture on every street corner.

The analysts who looked at Enron found a business plan that seemed more plausible, and the potential payoff was enormous. Moreover, those who had bet against Enron over the previous decade had been wrong. Enron was once a sleepy, debt-ridden pipeline that provided point-to-point transport of natural gas. It worked in a heavily regulated environment that placed few demands on its managers. Enron's world changed in the late 1980s when the regulations were lifted. Its managers suddenly realized that Enron's pipeline did not have to work as a discrete link between one gas well and a given end user. Instead, deregulation allowed Enron to use its pipeline as a network. It could reallocate natural gas from where there was excess capacity to where there was excess demand.

Enron also discovered that, once free of regulation, it was able to refashion contracts to purchase and sell natural gas according to the needs of its buyers and sellers. Its network protected it from liquidity shocks that can unseat market makers. In short order, Enron created a "gas bank" that allowed buyers and sellers to lock in the prices for natural gas.[2] Enron went quickly from being a company that transported natural gas to a nimble market maker that allowed everyone from Owens Corning to the Archdiocese of Chicago to control energy costs.

As the market for electricity became deregulated, Enron again recognized that, once deregulated, the power grid was another network that allowed market makers to match buyers and sellers. Soon Enron was making a market in electricity. It was an intermediary that could use its network to exploit the gains from trade. A utility in Boston that had more natural gas than it needed and a utility in California that wanted additional electricity cannot trade with each other directly. Enron, however, could create a series of transactions, using its network and its ability as a market maker to effect such a trade.

After proving itself as a successful maker of markets in gas and electricity, the analysts who once doubted that markets could be made in gas or electricity now believed

---

[2] *See* PETER C. FUSARO & ROSS M. MILLER, WHAT WENT WRONG AT ENRON 29–34 (John Wiley & Sons 2002).

Enron as it tried to establish markets in other commodities. Enron had something to offer any business that was subject to risks that it had no skill in managing. Before Enron filled the niche, a newspaper's profits would turn on the changing price of newsprint. The publisher had no way to lock in a reliable supply of newsprint for an extended period. Enron's managers created markets for newsprint, water, weather, and many other commodities.[3] Enron, by its account, had a comparative advantage in creating markets acquired from its years in the energy business.[4]

Enron prided itself on its ability to spot opportunities. During the summer of 2000, Enron helped a zinc producer in the Northwest shut down its operations for 6 weeks and sell the power it would otherwise have used to a buyer who needed it more. Enron helped the zinc producer find the buyer and provided a financial derivative to ensure the sale at a fixed price. Enron also supplied zinc from its metals subsidiary so that the producer could meet pre-existing obligations.[5] These transactions made everyone better off.

Enron's managers believed its ability to match sellers and buyers of energy would allow it to create exotic new markets. Internet traffic was growing geometrically. Some believed that it was doubling every 100 days.[6] But the Internet itself was not well-managed. At times, people would overload parts of the system and at other times it would remain largely unused. Enron could create a market in broadband, just as it created one in gas and electricity. Its pipelines gave it the ability to lay fiber-optic cable cheaply, and it formed alliances with other firms that would allow easy shifting of the cable from one user to another. Just as it acquired natural gas to put through its pipelines, it could also acquire content to pump through the fiber-optic cable. It reached a deal with Blockbuster to provide video on demand.[7]

The ultimate vision Enron put to the rest of the world was one in which a single firm (Enron) would be where everyone turned to ensure reliable sources of supply and avoid risks that they had no particular ability to manage. A carmaker's profits would turn on the cars it made, not on what happened to the price of palladium.[8] The man-

---

[3] *See* O'Reilly, *supra* note 1, FORTUNE, Apr. 17, 2000, at 148.

[4] *See* Enron Annual Report 1999, at 2 (2000) ("We are clearly a knowledge-based company, and the skills and resources we used to transform the energy business are proving to be equally valuable in other businesses."); *id.* at 5 ("The fundamental skills and expertise we use to develop energy and communications solutions can be applied to many situations that inhibit our customers' profits and growth."); Enron Annual Report 2000, at 5 (2001) ("We have a proven business concept that is eminently scalable in our existing businesses and adaptable enough to extend to new markets.").

[5] *See* Enron Annual Report 2000, at 12 (2001).

[6] *See* Yochi J. Dreazen, *Wildly Optimistic Data Drove Telecoms to Build Fiber Glut*, WALL ST. J., Sept. 26, 2002, at A1.

[7] *See* Robert Preston & Mike Koller, *Enron Broadens into Broadband*, INFORMATIONWEEK, Nov. 6, 2000.

[8] Ford Motor Company took a $1 billion charge to its earnings to reflect the loss in value of the palladium it had stockpiled for its catalytic converters. *See* Norihiko Shirouzo, Gregory L. White & Joseph B. White, *Driving Lessons: Beyond Explorer Woes, Ford Misses Key Turns in Buyers, Technology*, WALL ST. J., Jan. 14, 2002, at A1.

ager of an office building would know in advance how much it would cost to heat during the winter and cool during the summer.

Enron could exploit economies of scale and enjoy the liquidity that comes from having its own supplies of the gas, electricity, paper, precious metals, and much else. Others could try to imitate Enron, but Enron had a first-mover advantage. The expertise it had gained in making markets ensured it would be better than anyone else. In a winner-take-all market, the firm that is even a little bit better flourishes and the others disappear. Standard Oil became dominant because it could refine and sell oil at a profit even when it sold the oil for less than its competitors' costs. Jeffery Skilling boasted that Enron was in the same position as Standard Oil in 1890.[9]

In short, Enron was a new economy company with a long track record. While the dot.coms never had any earnings, Enron had a solid record of earnings. It had outperformed the market for the better part of a decade. Anyone looking at Enron, of course, could see risks. It had taken a huge one-time write-off in 1997 because of a bad deal involving North Sea natural gas. Its managers were arrogant, and its financials were opaque. But if Enron succeeded as it had in the past, it would play a central role in the new economy.[10]

A large part of Enron's failure can be traced not to any misdeeds, but simply to the failure of its business plan. The analysts who believed in a bright future for Enron made a systematic mistake about the opportunities in the information industry.[11] Analysts misjudged the growth in Internet traffic. While the growth was large, it was far short of 100% every 100 days. Moreover, new technologies dramatically expanded the capacity of the existing network. The effects of the deregulation of the telecommunications industry in 1996 were also poorly understood. Billions invested in hard assets proved worthless. Much of the fiber optic cable laid was "dark." It has never been used and never will be. Trillions in market valuations have disappeared. The valuation of Enron was premised in part upon its ability to take advantage of the shortage in broadband. When the shortage disappeared, a large component of Enron's value in the market disappeared as well.

---

[9] *See* Christopher Palmeri, *At the Heart of a Revolution*, FORBES, Jan. 12, 1998, at 48.

[10] *See* Erin Davies, *Enron: The Power's Back On: Rousing a $20 Billion Giant*, FORTUNE, April 13, 1998, at 24. Not only did Enron expressly style itself as a "new economy" firm, *see* 1999 ANNUAL REPORT, at 2 ("When you define a New Economy company, you define Enron."), but its annual reports draw heavily on the new economy lexicon. See, for example, Enron Annual Report 1998, at 3 (1999) ("business platform"), Enron Annual Report 1999, at 2 ("knowledge-based company," "global networks," "What you own is not as important as what you know," "constant innovation," "connectivity," "strategic contractual relationships"); *id.* at 4 ("first-mover advantage," "leverage"); *id.* at 5 ("intellectual capital"); Enron Annual Report 2000, at 2 ("[r]obust network of strategic assets"), *id.* at 3 ("integrating EnronOnline into all our businesses as an accelerator"), *id.* at 4 ("network connectivity"); *id.* at 5 ("leverage").

[11] *See* Dreazen, *supra* note 6.

Second, Enron's business plan required it to be too many things at the same time.[12] It had to be a supplier of basic commodities, it had to be a market maker in those commodities, and it had to make the alliances and strategic investments, all at the same time. It was as if a single firm was an oil refiner, a stock exchange, and a venture capitalist. Enron could not maintain its trading operations where it routinely entered into 10-year contracts unless it appeared to be financially sound. It needed to meet its earnings targets and maintain its credit-rating. Its crown jewel, its trading operation, would collapse without it. But Enron's business plan required it to make bold investments that might not bring returns for many years, if at all. Put differently, Enron was a firm that could maintain its high stock price only by making bold and risky moves, but it could maintain its on-going operations only if its earnings were reliable and steady. These two forces are fundamentally at odds.

Beginning in 1997, Enron began taking steps to ensure that outsiders believed that its operations were sound and that it was a reliable counterparty. Instead of insulating its trading activities and making sure that its fortunes were independent of the rest of the firm, Enron resorted to a series of increasingly elaborate transactions that gave the appearance of solid earnings and ensured that its bond rating would remain high enough to maintain itself as a reliable counterparty. These arrangements made it appear as if the dot.com collapse left it unaffected. As a result, its stock price continued to rise as other firms closely tied to the new economy fell.

The expertise Enron developed in managing its network and creating markets served it well in creating subsidiaries and Special Purpose Entities ("SPEs") that fooled investors, analysts, and rating agencies. Put in its simplest form, imagine (in a world in which the discount rate is 0%) that Enron wants to borrow $100 from Investor, but it wants to keep the loan hidden. Enron can sell $100 in stock to Investor. At the same time, one of Enron's 4,000 subsidiaries can enter into an arrangement with a subsidiary of Investor in which the Enron subsidiary acquires the right to buy the stock back for $100 at a specified time. Another subsidiary gives Investor the right to sell the share of stock to it for $100. When we view all these transactions together, we see that Investor has the same economic position vis á vis Enron as a creditor. It gave Enron $100 and returned in exchange a right to get back $100 at some time in the future. The amount it will receive from Enron is the same whether Enron fares well or poorly. It enjoys neither the upside nor the downside we associate with equity. But outsiders can know this only if they step these transactions together. In a world in which Enron itself is engaged in massive trading activities as its day-to-day business, outsiders have no way of doing this.

If the creditors are to recover anything from the third parties involved in Raptor III and other ventures, they must first find a legal theory that entitles them to hold these

---

[12] *See* Douglas G. Baird & Robert K. Rasmussen, *Four (or Five) Easy Lessons from Enron*, 55 VAND. L. REV. 1787 (2002), *reprinted in this book at* 371–392.

parties responsible. While these transactions involve the use of derivatives and other financial instruments, nothing about the legal theory available to Enron's creditors turns on their use. Indeed, the easiest way to understand the legal theories is to step away from transactions with such elaborate machinations and focus instead on mundane transactions in which a firm engages in transactions that have the same form.

II. RAPTORS AND OTHER BEASTS

One of the representative transactions that Enron used is Raptor III. Enron created a subsidiary (The New Power Company) in which it owned a 75% interest. TNPC was designed to provide energy to retail customers in deregulated markets. Enron then engaged in a set of transactions designed to reflect currently future revenues from this business. Enron transferred TNPC stock to a special purpose entity (Hawaii 125-0) and booked large gains as it marked the value of the stock to market. But along with this transfer, Enron also engaged in transactions involving total return swaps that exposed it to risks of subsequent changes in the value of the TNPC stock, and mark-to-market accounting would also require it to incorporate any subsequent decline in the value of TNPC stock in its earnings. The purpose of the Raptor III was to be able to show income that would offset these losses.

Enron used Raptor III to avoid showing a loss if TNPC fell in value. To do this, Enron used a limited partnership (LJM2) run by its Chief Financial Officer (Andrew Fastow) to "hedge" (at least from the perspective of its income statement) the losses it might incur from declines in the value of TNPC stock. LJM2 became the principal shareholder of a limited liability company (Porcupine). Porcupine acquired TNPC stock (through yet another entity) from Enron and gave it a promissory note in return. Porcupine then engaged in a hedging transaction with Enron that obliged it to pay Enron in the event that TNPC stock went down. Within a week, Porcupine also made a distribution to LJM2 that returned to it the entire amount it had invested in Porcupine. Porcupine had no assets other than TNPC stock.

Porcupine would be unable to repay its note to Enron if the stock went down. Moreover, if the stock went down, it would have no ability to honor its obligations under the hedge. The transaction would allow Enron to prevent declines in the value of TNPC from affecting its earnings over the short term, but over the long term, the transaction would bring Enron no benefit. Indeed, the transaction is affirmatively costly. Not only are there fees to lawyers and accountants, but the investors in LJM2 earned extraordinary returns. In Chapter 11, the creditors of Enron now need to figure out Enron's claims against Porcupine, its rights to whatever assets Porcupine still has, and its rights against LJM2 and any others who invested in Porcupine or transacted with it. The bankruptcy questions raised by Raptor III replicates itself in many different guises in Enron.

The transactions used elaborate hedges and derivatives and were motivated by arcane accounting rules, but the legal problem can be separated from them. We can focus on them by using the following hypothetical. OfficeCo builds and manages office buildings. It has shown impressive growth and consistent earnings in a highly volatile real estate market. Much of OfficeCo's success is attributed to, in the financial press's words, its "ingenious and creative" CFO. One of OfficeCo's recent projects was carried out by its wholly owned subsidiary, White Elephant Enterprises. Its sole asset is White Elephant Plaza, a large office building that cost $800 to build, much more than anyone expected. OfficeCo manages the building. The managers of OfficeCo believe that the Plaza is worth at least $1,000, but they fear that it may decline in value. To protect OfficeCo's track record, they decide to sell the Plaza. To their surprise, they cannot find anyone willing to buy the property for $1,000. Indeed, they cannot find anyone willing to buy it from them for $800.

The CFO, however, finds a way to ensure that the uncertain fortunes of the Plaza do not jeopardize OfficeCo's solid reputation among investors. With the approval of the Board, the CFO creates CFOPartners, a limited partnership. The general partner of CFOPartners is the CFO and the limited partners are a group of outside investors. The CFO contributes $2 and the limited partners put in $198.

CFOPartners then forms WhiteElephantCo, a wholly owned subsidiary of CFOPartners. WhiteElephantCo buys OfficeCo's equity stake in White Elephant Enterprises for $1,000 ($200 in cash and a long-term unsecured note for $800). WhiteElephantCo also enters into a long-term contract with OfficeCo that gives OfficeCo the right to manage the building. Soon after the purchase of the Plaza, WhiteElephantCo borrows $250 from Bank and gives it a first mortgage on the Plaza. A little later, WhiteElephantCo declares a dividend of $250. CFOPartners distributes the cash to the partners.

OfficeCo reports record profits for the year, and its CFO continues to be highly praised for his astute and aggressive management. Three years pass, but then OfficeCo's fortunes take a turn for the worse. OfficeCo defaults on its loans. The CEO and CFO are fired. The firm files for bankruptcy. The assets of OfficeCo are only enough to give its general creditors a return of 10 cents on the dollar. The creditors of OfficeCo would like to bring White Elephant Plaza into the bankruptcy estate free of Bank's security interest. They would also like to recapture the $250 paid out to the investors in CFOPartners.

The creditors of OfficeCo are fundamentally in the same position as the creditors of Enron. Enron took an illiquid asset (TNPC stock) and transferred it to a Special Purpose Entity (Porcupine) in a way that protected it from the risk that its value would fall. OfficeCo took an illiquid asset (White Elephant Plaza) and transferred it to a Special Purpose Entity (WhiteElephantCo) in a way that also allowed it to lock in the value of the asset. In both cases, the outside investors that made the transaction possible (LJM2 and CFOPartners) enjoyed substantial returns while putting nothing at risk. The general legal theories that are relevant to solving these problems are the same in both cases. We explore these in the next part of this paper.

III. AVENUES OF RECOURSE

When we take several steps back from this hypothetical, we can see that something is amiss in what OfficeCo has done. When we look at the various discrete transactions as a single deal, we can see that OfficeCo is spending real resources merely to give outsiders the illusion of financial stability.

Because WhiteElephantCo has no assets of its own, the transaction does nothing to protect OfficeCo if Plaza declines in value (or simply turns out to be worth less than the amount of the note, an amount that exceeded what any third party was willing to pay for the property). By selling the asset to WhiteElephantCo, any upside will be enjoyed by CFOPartners. OfficeCo has given up its right to enjoy the upside in the event that the real estate market improved.[13] The principal beneficiary of this transaction is CFOPartners. When the transactions are stepped together, we see that it put nothing at risk, and ended up with $50 in cash and all the upside in the event that Plaza ever is worth more than $1,000. Though not couched in these terms, CFOPartners ends up, in addition to the cash with the equivalent of an option to buy Plaza for $1,000.

Anglo-American debtor-creditor law relies in large measure on creditors to protect themselves. Many loan agreements would prohibit the sale of Plaza without the creditor's blessing. Our concern, however, is with the background protections that creditors as a group enjoy in bankruptcy. Such protections are necessary because not all creditors enjoy written loan agreements.[14] Moreover, even the most elaborate loan agreements cannot enumerate all the ways in which a debtor set upon mischief can compromise their rights. We need basic principles that work in simple cases (such as ours) and in more elaborate ones (such as those we see in Enron).

A. Caplin's Legacy and Piercing the Corporate Veil

Individual creditors may be able to bring actions based upon nonbankruptcy law, such as a violation of the securities laws, against CFOPartners, Bank, and the investors. Such causes of action are not sure-fire, even if the transactions, when viewed as a whole, seem suspect. For example, the Supreme Court has held that private plaintiffs cannot bring Rule 10b-5 actions against those who merely aided and abetted violations of the securities law.[15] Showing that the various third parties were themselves directly responsible is harder. State law theories of liability exist as well. In addition to state blue sky laws, various common law theories of recovery are available. Transac-

---

[13] In some Enron transactions, an entity related to Enron engaged in a total return swap with the special purpose entity that would ensure that Enron would enjoy the upside in the event that the asset rose in value. In the context of the hypothetical, such an arrangement would have the effect of OfficeCo acquiring, as part of the deal, an option to buy White Elephant Plaza for $1,000. OfficeCo's acquisition of this option is as troubling as giving the upside to CFOPartners. If OfficeCo has such an option, then the transaction is utterly without economic substance. If OfficeCo gives it up, it is parting with some of the economic value of the asset and receiving nothing in return. As discussed below, each is a different, but equally compelling, "badge of fraud" that makes the transaction suspect.

[14] For example, tort victims are necessarily creditors without written loan agreements.

[15] Central Bank of Denver v. First Interstate Bank of Denver, 511 U.S. 164 (1994).

tions less conventional than OfficeCo and WhiteElephantCo might be *ultra vires* or illegal.[16]

Our focus, however, is not on the discrete actions that might be available, but rather on those that can be asserted on behalf of the creditors in bankruptcy. It might seem that CFOPartners and WhiteElephantCo are merely empty shells that are impermissible manipulations of the corporate form. Nonbankruptcy law sometimes authorizes creditors to disregard the corporate form and "pierce the corporate veil" in such situations. These entities are not truly separate, but rather merely "alter egos" of OfficeCo. All of the power over White Elephant Plaza resides in the CFO of OfficeCo. OfficeCo makes all decisions about the Plaza and continues to manage it as it did before the sale. WhiteElephantCo is nothing more than a set of bookkeeping entries. To go beyond mere form, one should ignore WhiteElephantCo and treat the Plaza just like all of OfficeCo's other assets.

This theory, however, immediately runs up against a well-established doctrine of U.S. bankruptcy law, the inability of the bankruptcy trustee to bring damage actions on behalf of creditors.[17] The trustee can avoid only *transfers* that the debtor made or obligations the debtor incurred. The trustee lacks the power to bring *damage actions*. The trustee can bring damage actions only if the debtor itself would have been able to bring the action outside of bankruptcy and that are therefore property of the estate within the meaning of § 541.[18] Hence, the estate can bring a veil-piercing action on behalf of the creditors only if the debtor would be able to bring the cause of action under nonbankruptcy law.

In our example, the *Caplin* principle limits the ability of the trustee to bring this transaction in the bankruptcy case. The estate can bring a veil-piercing action, like any other damage action, only if the debtor could have maintained the action outside of bankruptcy. Some federal courts have found that the debtor can bring veil-piercing actions against its own shareholders, and hence the trustee can as well because of § 541.[19]

---

[16] *See* In re Adler Coleman Clearing Corp., 263 Bankr. 406 (S.D.N.Y. 2001).

[17] Section 544(b) of the Bankruptcy Code was written in the shadow of Caplin v. Marine Midland Grace Trust Company, 406 U.S. 416 (1972). It provides, "the trustee may avoid any transfer of an interest of the debtor in property . . . that is voidable under applicable law by a creditor holding an unsecured claim." The focus on transactions that are voidable outside of bankruptcy was deliberate.

[18] Section 541(a)(1) includes in the bankruptcy estate "all legal or equitable interests of the debtor in property as of the commencement of the case." An action that the debtor could bring outside of bankruptcy is such an "interest of the debtor in property." An action that only a creditor could bring is not. *See, e.g.,* Mediators, Inc. v. Manney, 105 F.3d 822 (2d Cir. 1997); Steinberg v. Buczynski, 40 F.3d 890 (7th Cir. 1994); Schertz-Cibolo-Universal City Independent School District v. Wright, 25 F.3d 1281 (5th Cir. 1994); Williams v. California First Bank, 859 F.2d 664 (9th Cir. 1988).

[19] *See, e.g.,* St. Paul Fire & Marine Insurance Co. v. Pepsico, Inc., 884 F.2d 688 (2d Cir. 1989); Steyr-Daimler-Puch of America Corp. v. Pappas, 852 F.2d 132 (4th Cir. 1988); S.I. Acquisition, Inc. v. Eastern Delivery Service, 817 F.2d 1142 (5th Cir. 1987); *see also* Koch Rening v. Farmers Union Central Exchange, 831 F.2d 1339, 1347 n.11 (7th Cir. 1987).

State law authority for this proposition, however, is not easy to find. Indeed, the gravamen of the action—that the firm and the shareholders are one and the same—is inconsistent with the idea that the firm can sue the shareholders. At least one state supreme court has repudiated a federal circuit court's opinion that the debtor did possess such a cause of action against its shareholders.[20]

Even if we overcome this obstacle, veil piercing in our example (or in the case of Enron) does not fit comfortably within traditional notions of veil piercing. The shareholder of WhiteElephantCo is not in fact related to OfficeCo. When the alter ego doctrine is invoked, it is usually between a subsidiary and a parent that holds all of its equity. Here, WhiteElephantCo is owned by CFOPartners. OfficeCo has no ownership interest in it. The former CFO may run CFOPartners, but it is a distinct entity and it has substantive economic rights (the upside in the event that the Plaza goes up in value).

Even if we could ignore the lack of a formal relationship between the two firms, other problems remain. The typical state veil-piercing action takes three forms: (1) Individuals wholly neglect the formalities of corporate form in running their affairs and those of their sole proprietorship; (2) An entrepreneur sets up a parent corporation with many subsidiaries whose operations are hopelessly intertwined; or (3) A business takes the form of a shell parent corporation with multiple, thinly capitalized operating subsidiaries (e.g., a taxicab company in which a separate subsidiary exists for each cab) designed to limit any tort victim to the assets of a single subsidiary. Veil-piercing actions in which creditors of a *parent* (OfficeCo in our case) reach assets in the hands of a subsidiary, however, tend to be less successful.[21]

In assessing the strength of a veil-piercing action, the law of the specific state matters.[22] Under Oregon law, for example, the test seems to focus on "improper conduct" by the party seeking to take advantage of the legal separateness of the entities.[23] Under New York law, the corporate veil can be pierced in the absence of fraud when the "corporation has been so dominated by an individual or corporate parent that the subsidiary is relegated to the status of a mere shell, instrumentality, or alter ego."[24]

---

[20] *See* In re Rehabilitation of Centaur Insurance Co., 632 N.E.2d 1015 (Ill. 1994).

[21] *See* Robert B. Thompson, *Piercing the Corporate Veil*, 76 CORNELL L. REV. 1036, 1055 (1991).

[22] Traditional conflicts rules suggest that the forum jurisdiction will look to the conflict rules of the state of incorporation. *See* Fletcher v. Atex, Inc., 68 F.3d 1451, 1458 (2d Cir. 1995); Wausau Business Insurance Co. v. Turner Construction Co., 141 F. Supp. 2d 412 (S.D.N.Y. 2001). But we do see cases in which courts apply the law of the forum. *See, e.g.,* Vuylsteke v. Broan, 17 P.3d 1072, 1074 n.2 (Oregon App. 2001).

[23] *See* Amfac Foods, Inc. v. International Systems & Controls Corp., 654 P.2d 1092 (Oregon 1982). Enron is incorporated in Oregon.

[24] *See* Wausau Business Insurance Co. v. Turner Construction Co., 141 F. Supp. 2d 412, 417 (S.D.N.Y. 2001). Enron's bankruptcy is taking place in New York, and a federal court sometimes looks to the law of the forum state. Moreover, many of Enron's transactions with investors took place in New York and would ordinarily be governed by New York law outside of bankruptcy.

Under Texas law, with respect to contract claims, actual fraud must be shown. Constructive fraud is insufficient.[25]

If veil-piercing actions are unavailable, the trustee might still seem to be able to ask the bankruptcy court to invoke its equitable power to achieve much the same end. The doctrine of substantive consolidation does in bankruptcy what veil-piercing does outside.[26] When two bankruptcy estates are substantively consolidated, we combine the assets and liabilities of both.[27] The affairs of the two firms may be so closely entwined that each lacks a separate existence. Substantive consolidation avoids the hard conflict of laws and standing questions that state veil-piercing brings:

The consolidated assets create a single fund from which all claims against the consolidated debtors are satisfied; duplicate and inter-company claims are extinguished; and the creditors of the consolidated entities are combined for purposes of voting on reorganization plans.[28]

There is, however, a threshold problem in using substantive consolidation in this context. Substantive consolidation usually involves two estates that are in bankruptcy. In our example, WhiteElephantCo has not filed.[29] Substantive consolidation of a debtor and nondebtor is precedented.[30] Nevertheless, courts are more reluctant to invoke the bankruptcy court's equitable power in such cases, as it involves property that is not yet within its control.

Even if this problem could be surmounted, the creditors are ill-advised to rely too heavily on veil-piercing or substantive consolidation. These actions merge the assets of OfficeCo and WhiteElephantCo, but leave Bank's security interest untouched.[31] Moreover, they do nothing to recover the dividend paid out to the investors.

---

[25] See Harco Energy, Inc. v. The Re-Entry People, Inc., 23 S.W.3d 389 (Tex. App. 2000); Western Horizontal Drilling, Inc. v. Jonnet Energy Corp., 11 F.3d 65 (5th Cir. 1994). Enron's principal place of business is in Texas.

[26] Substantive consolidation is also used for a purpose altogether different from the issues raised here. Sometimes, the affairs of the two firms may have become so entangled and their assets so meager that unscrambling the mess may simply not be worth the cost. When the administrative costs of sorting out the obligations of the two firms dwarf the benefits to any group of creditors from keeping the firms separate, it is in everyone's interest to consolidate the two. See In re The Leslie Fay Companies, 207 Bankr. 764 (Bankr. S.D.N.Y. 1997).

[27] The leading discussion of substantive consolidation can be found in Union Savings Bank v. Augie/Restivo Baking Company, Ltd, 860 F.2d 515, 518–19 (2d Cir. 1988). The D.C. Circuit put forward a slightly different formulation of substantive consolidation in Drabkin v. Midland-Ross Corp. (In re Auto-Train Corp.), 810 F.2d 270 (D.C. Cir. 1987), but there is consensus on the doctrine's basic contours.

[28] In re Bonham, 229 F.3d 750, 764 (9th Cir. 2000).

[29] Similarly, the SPEs, such as LJM2, in Enron have not filed for bankruptcy, either.

[30] See In re Bonham, 229 F.3d 750, 765 (9th Cir. 2000); Munford, Inc. v. TOC Retail, Inc., 115 Bankr. 390, 397–98 (Bankr. N.D. Ga. 1990).

[31] In Enron, there seem to be a number of transactions in which the investor in the position of Bank failed to take and perfect a security interest in the assets. In these cases, the veil-piercing action would bring about the desired result, but the problem of retrieving assets now in the hands of investors would remain. It seems odd to hold Bank liable, but not the investors.

B. Form, Substance, and True Sales

A firm's transfer of an asset to a special purpose entity is sufficient to remove it from the bankruptcy estate only if the transfer is a "true sale" that terminates all of the debtor's rights to the asset. OfficeCo may be able to bring Plaza into its bankruptcy estate without invoking theories of veil piercing or substantive consolidation if it can show that the transfer to WhiteElephantCo was not a "true sale."

The standards by which one measures whether a "true sale" takes place are massively undeveloped. Bankruptcy courts will not, of course, accept the parties' characterization of the transaction. Conventional black-letter doctrine suggests that bankruptcy courts should look to substantive nonbankruptcy law to discover whether an asset is "property of the estate" within the meaning of § 541.[32] Whether the transfer of White Elephant Plaza (or more precisely OfficeCo's transfer of its equity interest in the firm that owned White Elephant Plaza) was a "true sale" turns on substantive nonbankruptcy law where even the threshold choice of law questions are hard.[33]

Some bankruptcy courts have shown a willingness to derive the answer to the question of whether a transfer is a true sale from the bankruptcy court's equitable powers.[34] A debtor's ongoing control over its accounts receivable may be sufficient to make them property of the estate and hence subject the third party to the automatic stay. Using such a test, one could argue that WhiteElephantCo is close enough to OfficeCo that the bankruptcy court should have jurisdiction over the asset. Once OfficeCo is in bankruptcy, CFOPartners is no longer free to sell White Elephant Plaza. OfficeCo may have enough of an interest in the property such that the automatic stay prevents its sale and prevents CFOPartners from taking unilateral action.

Much of the concerns raised about special purpose entities revolve around the question of whether assets transferred to the SPEs are removed from the bankruptcy process. (Indeed, the purpose of many of these transactions is to make the assets in the SPE "bankruptcy remote.") It can make an important difference whether a firm's property that has been conveyed to the SPE is part of the bankruptcy estate. If the property is part of the bankruptcy estate, it can be used in the firm's ongoing operations, provided the third party's rights are adequately protected.[35] If the property has been transferred outright, the debtor must reorganize without it. An outright nonrecourse sale of accounts is likely a true sale, but other transactions are more problematic. It is not obvious, for example, that a debtor should be able to convey its raw materials to a third

---

[32] See Chicago Board of Trade v. Johnson, 264 U.S. 1 (1924).

[33] Traditional conflicts rules suggest that the forum jurisdiction will look to the conflict rules of the state of incorporation. See Fletcher v. Atex, Inc., 68 F.3d 1451, 1458 (2d Cir. 1995); Wausau Business Insurance Co. v. Turner Construction Co., 141 F. Supp. 2d 412 (S.D.N.Y. 2001). But we do see cases in which courts apply the law of the forum. See, e.g., Vuylsteke v. Broan, 17 P.3d 1072, 1074 n.2 (Oregon App. 2001).

[34] See, e.g., In re LTV Steel Co., 274 Bankr. 278 (Bankr. N.D. Ohio 2001).

[35] See 11 U.S.C. § 364.

party and thus remove them from the bankruptcy estate, even if it continues to possess them and process them in its ongoing business.[36]

Existing debates over SPEs, however, are largely useless where a creditor such as Bank has a perfected security interest in the assets. Bank will prevail in the end even if White Elephant Plaza becomes part of the bankruptcy estate. But even if Bank's claim against White Elephant Plaza were unsecured and the investors had not received a dividend, the idea that the sale can be disregarded must be rooted in some established legal doctrine. The body of law that has emerged over whether a transaction is a true sale is quite limited. Bankruptcy law does not establish whether a transaction is a true sale. Instead, bankruptcy law looks to nonbankruptcy law. In this case, the relevant law is the law governing security interests. That law, however, allows parties in the position of Bank to prevail as long as they jump through the right hoops. Moreover, states have tried to make it easier to keep assets out of the bankruptcy estate.[37] The transaction here between OfficeCo and CFOPartners seems quite suspect even apart from whether the actors complied with whatever formalities were put in their path. Focusing on a true sale, however much it might work under the facts of a particular case, does not squarely focus upon whether transactions of this nature are, as a general matter, suspect. To do this, we must turn to fraudulent conveyance law.

IV. FRAUDULENT CONVEYANCES IN THE POST-MODERN ERA

Fraudulent conveyance law is built on the same principles as substantive consolidation and true sales. Indeed, these doctrines are best understood as being specific elaborations of more general legal principles.[38] Fraudulent conveyance is the most direct way of attacking the various transactions involving OfficeCo and Plaza. Fraudulent conveyance law provides that transfers made and obligations incurred with the intent to "delay, hinder, or defraud" creditors are fraudulent and void as against creditors. To fall within the reach of fraudulent conveyance law, it is not necessary to prove actual fraud. It is sufficient if the transaction bears "badges of fraud."

---

[36] An example of such a case is In re LTV Steel Co., 274 Bankr. 278 (Bankr. N.D. Ohio 2001). In that case, the debtor conveyed its inventory, including steel in the process of being fabricated, to an SPE. The legal basis for disregarding such a transaction, however, is unclear, at least if the hurdles of Article 9 have been complied with.

[37] Delaware recently enacted the "Asset-Backed Securities Facilitation Act." Without actually defining a "securitization transaction," it provides that "[a]ny property, assets, or rights purported to be transferred, in whole or in part, in the securitization transaction shall be deemed to no longer be the property, assets or rights of the transferor." These provisions were designed to provide a safe harbor to securitization transactions. For example, if this provision were effective in bankruptcy, a firm could establish a Special Purpose Entity into which it transferred its accounts receivable, and investors would be able to acquire interests in the Special Purpose Entity, confident that they would be insulated from any bankruptcy involving the parent. Texas, Alabama, and Ohio enacted non-uniform provisions of Revised Article 9 intended to have a similar effect.

[38] See Robert C. Clark, The Duties of the Corporate Debtor to its Creditors, 90 HARV. L. REV. 505 (1977).

The most often invoked "badge of fraud" is a transfer an insolvent debtor makes without reasonably equivalent value. Creditors can avoid an insolvent debtor's birthday present to her mother. The motivations of the debtor are irrelevant, and the mother's love and gratitude are not worth anything from the perspective of the debtor's creditors. When a debtor is insolvent, he is no longer giving away his own assets. A dividend or a stock repurchase is the corporate analog to a gift. These transactions are so likely to injure creditors and bring no corresponding benefit to the firm that it makes sense to ban them whenever they leave the debtor insolvent or with unreasonably small capital.

In our example, the $250 dividend to CFOPartners may well have been a fraudulent conveyance. WhiteElephantCo had nothing other than the income that the Plaza generated to meet its obligations. Assuming that the Plaza was worth no more than $1,000, the firm lacked the resources to repay Bank and OfficeCo at the time it made its dividend. OfficeCo, a creditor of WhiteElephantCo, can seek to set aside the transfer as a fraudulent conveyance. But CFOPartners may be able to argue that White Elephant Plaza was worth more than its purchase price and that therefore the dividend did not leave the firm insolvent. The more volatile the value of the underlying asset, the harder it will be to show insolvency at the moment that the dividend is made.[39]

Many suspect transactions that compromise the rights of creditors leave the debtor insolvent and without reasonably equivalent value. We can find, however, other "badges of fraud" (that similarly require no showing of "fraud" as traditionally understood) in the case law. Hence, the creditors of OfficeCo do not necessarily need to show insolvency, as long as they can show that some other "badge of fraud" is present.[40] "Badge of fraud" is a term of art and does not track the meaning of "fraud" as used elsewhere. It identifies behavior that reasonable creditors would prohibit if they could, regardless of whether it is actionable as "fraud" at common law.

A transaction is not voidable merely because it contains a single badge of fraud, but transactions that contain a sufficient number of badges of fraud are voidable. "Badges of fraud" are not clearly defined. Unlike the familiar "without reasonably equivalent value while insolvent" badge that has taken on a rule-like character, the other badges require traditional common law reasoning and resist easy categorization. They can be found in part in the case law and in statutes.

---

[39] Recall that, in the Raptor III transaction, the asset was TNPC stock. Indeed, it was the volatility of the stock price that motivated the transaction in the first place.

[40] In his excellent comment on this essay, Kevin Davis points out that there may be significant costs associated with a fraudulent conveyance law that embraces "badges of fraud" beyond an insolvent debtor's transfer of assets for less than reasonably equivalent value. *See* Kevin E. Davis, *Does the Proper Domain of Fraudulent Conveyance Law Include Deceptive but Fair Transactions? in* Sarah Worthington, Commercial Law and Commercial Practice __ (forthcoming 2004). In his view, the familiar test picks up the vast majority of suspect transactions, and other doctrines, such as those involving breach of fiduciary duty, pick up many more. *See, e.g.,* Geyer v. Ingersoll Publications Co., 621 A.2d 784, 787 (Del. Ch. 1992). Hence, in Professor Davis's view, the uncertainties of a more expansive fraudulent conveyance regime make it a game not worth the candle.

The basic ideas are clear. A transfer can be found to "hinder, delay, or defraud" if it has enough of the following sorts of characteristics:

(1) A close relationship between the parties;[41]
(2) A questionable transfer not in the usual course of business;[42]
(3) The retention of control of the property by the transferor after the conveyance;[43]
(4) The concealment of the transfer.[44]

A fraudulent conveyance law can exist even when the debtor is solvent. If a transaction serves no function other than to lull creditors into inactivity, it is a fraudulent conveyance.

We can take several steps back from OfficeCo's transaction and see that it exhibits many of these traditional "badges of fraud." The transaction between OfficeCo and CFOPartners took the form of a sale of stock. There was no public record of the transfer. The acquiring entity was controlled by an insider of OfficeCo. From the perspective of creditors, the transaction was invisible. The day-to-day operations of White Elephant Plaza continued. The owner of record (White Elephant Enterprises) remained unchanged. Debtors, of course, routinely engage in transactions that have, as a side effect, making its balance sheet look healthy and robust. But these transactions offer some collateral benefit, such as favorable tax treatment. The transaction served no purpose other than to make OfficeCo's earnings appear more stable than they actually were and to prevent creditors from seeing that the capital spent on Plaza was more at risk than it appeared. Here, we have a transaction that served no purpose other than to make it hard for creditors to understand what their debtor was doing. The absence of a business justification for a transaction has long been a common hallmark of those that are ultimately found to have sufficient "badges of fraud" to make them fraudulent conveyances.[45]

The OfficeCo transaction involved a number of steps, but these do not matter, as fraudulent conveyance law looks to substance rather than form. A debtor cannot escape the reach of fraudulent conveyance law merely by respecting the niceties of legal forms and generally accepted accounting principles. The step-transaction doctrine is an essential feature of fraudulent conveyance law.[46] Courts can recharacterize transactions, treat discrete transactions as part of a larger scheme, and otherwise ensure that the substance of the transaction is the focus rather than the form. Indeed, this idea

---

[41] *See* Wall Street Associates v. Brodsky, 684 N.Y.S.2d 244 (App. Div. 1999).

[42] *Id.*

[43] *Id.*

[44] UFTA § 4(b)(7).

[45] *See, e.g.,* Clow v. Woods, 5 Sergeant & Rawle 275 (Pa. 1819).

[46] *See, e.g.,* Orr v. Kinderhill Corp., 991 F.2d 31 (2d Cir. 1993).

embedded in fraudulent conveyance law is what generates specific doctrines, such as the power of a court to recharacterize, as a secured transaction, a deal that purports to be an outright sale.

The availability of the fraudulent conveyance remedy can be put more simply. It matters not at all how elaborate the transaction or the nature of the underlying assets. Just as Enron is no different from our hypothetical, our hypothetical would be no different if, instead of equity in a firm that owned an office building, the debtor had transferred sheep to some third party, but continued to possess the sheep, shear them, and mark them as his own. If such a transaction falls within the reach of fraudulent conveyance law even in the absence of actual fraud, then OfficeCo's transaction (and Enron's) should as well. And there is no doubt about the outcome of the case involving sheep. Indeed, the voidability of such a transaction has been one of the foundational principles of Anglo-American law for over 400 years.[47]

It might seem that Bank's security interest should be respected. It parted with $250 and hence gave value in turn for its security interest. All is not so simple, however. We can recharacterize Bank's transaction as a transfer to CFOPartners for which Bank received a security interest from WhiteElephantCo. Bank's security interest is vulnerable in exactly the same way it would have been had it facilitated a leveraged buyout, in which the proceeds of a loan to a firm are immediately transferred to its shareholders. In such cases, courts are empowered to recharacterize the transaction and treat it as one in which the firm gave the lender a security interest, but received nothing in return.[48] Bank will undoubtedly argue that its lien on White Elephant Plaza should be respected at least to the extent that it gave value. But the trustee can argue that, in substance, though not in form, the transaction was one in which Bank made a transfer to the investors in CFOPartners and gave nothing to WhiteElephantCo itself.

Bank might be able to resist this argument on the ground that it acted in good faith and engaged in an arms' length transaction according to ordinary business terms. Courts, however, have been quick to question the bona fides of Bank in such a case as this.[49] While a leveraged buyout can serve important aims, a transaction such as this one has no legitimate purpose. In any event, there are few cases in which a fraudulent conveyance is found, but in which courts have nevertheless refused to void the security interest of the party in the position of Bank. Bank's position would be even less tenable if it or an entity related to it also participated as an investor in CFOPartners, as occurred in some of the Enron transactions.

The strength of the fraudulent conveyance attack in cases like Enron may ultimately depend upon the willingness of courts to look to the basic ideas of "badges of fraud." The drafters of the Bankruptcy Code and the Uniform Fraudulent Transfer Act slighted their importance. In the vast majority of cases, the badge of fraud that has

---

[47] *See* Twyne's Case, 3 Coke 80b, 76 Eng. Rep. 809 (Star Chamber 1601).

[48] *See* Lippi v. Citibank, 955 F.2d 599 (9th Cir. 1992).

[49] *See, e.g.,* United States v. Tabor Court Realty Corp., 803 F.2d 1288 (3d Cir. 1986).

received explicit codification (transfers by an insolvent for less than reasonably equiva-lent value) applies with full force. Most suspect transactions are done within a year of bankruptcy by an insolvent debtor for less than reasonably equivalent value. There is no need to look further for other badges of fraud. Similarly, badges of fraud rarely accompany transfers for reasonably equivalent value or fair consideration. Hence, courts too often assume that, absent such a transaction, actual fraud is required. One can doubt, however, that the bankruptcy court will make this mistake in Enron. New York is one of the few jurisdictions that still has Uniform Fraudulent Conveyance Act (the predecessor to the modern Uniform Fraudulent Transfers Act). State courts in New York have invoked the idea of "badges of fraud" even where actual fraud has not been proved and reasonably equivalent value exists.[50] The creditors' lawyers are most un-likely to overlook this body of law.

V. CONCLUSION

One can doubt whether we have done enough to craft laws and regulations that prevent the gaming of the system such as we have seen in Enron. Existing legal rules rely too heavily on categories that are rapidly losing significance in the world of com-merce. A legal regime that depends upon a fundamental difference between debt and equity is useless in a world in which actors are free to exploit the lessons of Black-Scholes and put-call parity.[51]

By the same measure, legal rules that are focused upon discrete legal entities may prove similarly ineffective. As Coase taught us long ago,[52] transactions that can be done inside a firm can be done outside as well. The only differences are the transaction costs associated with the two. In a world in which transaction costs are collapsing both inside the firm and in the market, the difference between the two ways of engaging in the same economic enterprise becomes less important.[53] A computer maker may own a factory or sit in a rented office and control everything with a single laptop.[54] In such a world, preventing those bent upon mischief before the fact becomes increasingly hard.

Nevertheless, the failure of legal rules before the fact should not obscure the ability of common law principles to right the score after the fact. Those who participated in lucrative deals with Enron will likely suffer the consequences of being too clever by half. Debtors cannot undermine the rights of their creditors by manipulating legal

---

[50] *See, e.g.,* Wall Street Associates v. Brodsky, 684 N.Y.S.2d 244 (App. Div. 1999).

[51] *See* Fischer Black & Myron Scholes, *The Pricing of Options and Corporate Liabilities,* 81 J. POL. ECON. 637 (1973). For a discussion of how these ideas undermine corporate taxation, see Alvin C. Warren, *Financial Contract Innovation and Income Tax Policy,* 107 HARV. L. REV. 460 (1993).

[52] *See* R.H. Coase, *The Nature of the Firm,* 4 ECONOMICA 386 (1937).

[53] *See* Douglas G. Baird & Robert K. Rasmussen, *The End of Bankruptcy,* 55 STAN. L. REV. 751 (2002).

[54] *See Incredible Shrinking Plants,* ECONOMIST, Feb. 23, 2002, at 71.

forms and accounting conventions. This was the lesson of *Twyne's Case* in 1601, and it has remained the lodestar of bankruptcy law ever since. Those who delight in artifice and contrivance in structuring a debtor's affairs forget it at their peril.

The Enron Story and Environmental Policy*

Victor B. Flatt**

There are many aspects of the Enron saga that would give pause to someone who thinks about the environment and its problems. One of the most obvious is the concern that allowing unregulated energy trading likely does not account for the costs of environmental externalities that are concurrent with energy production and usage.[1] Another concern is that reducing the cost of energy may increase consumption and accelerate environmental degradation. However, these are concerns with the concept of energy trading itself, and they would be problematic even if (*especially* if) Enron had been a well-run and well-managed company that traded and delivered electricity and natural gas exactly as promised. As such, these policy questions exist notwithstanding the demise of Enron. The policy questions present important issues that still need to be examined with respect to the restructuring of the wholesale and retail power delivery markets ("deregulation").

Beyond the basic energy trading policy concerns, the demise of Enron presents a more fundamental question about the ability of government regulators to curb harmful or illegal behaviors in the face of structural incentives to commit such behaviors. More pointedly, can the regulated entities ever be trusted to police themselves, and if so, under what circumstances? This question is germane to environmental protection because two different strands of environmental regulatory theory may depend on it: the issue of whether polluters will voluntarily comply with the law and control their own pollutants, and the issue of how market-based pollutant trading regimes depend on this voluntary compliance mechanism, which eliminated the previously established command and control regimes.

---

* Originally published at 33 ENVTL. L. REP. 10485 (2003). Reprinted with permission.

[1] By deregulating energy and increasing competition among companies, we encourage them to produce power by the least expensive means. If environmental externalities, such as dirty air or impacts on animal habitats, are not part of that cost equation process, those that have major externalities will be the lowest cost producers, encouraging further environmental degradation.

In order to understand the lesson that Enron teaches about the practicalities of voluntary environmental compliance and enforcement, this essay first reviews the collapse of Enron and its relation to problems inherent in a regulatory scheme that purposefully relies upon self-policing for compliance. Then this essay will examine why Enron engaged in certain policies in the newly deregulated California energy market in 2000, and why complex trading schemes are difficult to monitor. Finally, this essay examines what these occurrences suggest about the future of using environmental policies that depend on complex trading regimes and purposefully rely (or—because of the complexity of the trading regime or the elimination of command and control equipment—must rely) upon self-policing for compliance.

A. THE COLLAPSE OF ENRON

Though the rise and fall of Enron has been detailed elsewhere in the book, there are some aspects that should be examined further. First, how did problems with Enron's finances occur, and what does this discussion have to do with regulation in general and environmental regulation in particular? The answer is that these problems would not have occurred if regulation were effective and had worked properly. With the continual growth of Enron and its stock price, the company became infallible in the mind of its officers.[2] Enron believed it would work better without regulation, and it exemplified that internally by setting minimal administrative controls, such as plans of organization, procedures, and records that would lead to management's approval of transactions.[3] Internal controls are only effective when those bearing responsibility for developing, implementing, and overseeing those controls stress the need to adhere to all policies and procedures and actually follow them themselves.

An example of the lack of internal controls occurred in 1999, when Enron's board waived conflict of interest rules three times by allowing Andrew Fastow, the Chief Financial Officer, to create private partnerships to do business with the firm.[4] This poor internal oversight allowed illegal concealment of debts and losses that would have a significant effect on Enron's reported profits.[5]

Not only did self-regulation fail, but also Enron's auditors were compromised. An auditor examining these transactions should have been able to correctly interpret and understand what had occurred, required the proper reporting of such transactions, and ordered Enron to change its practices for future transactions. That did not hap-

---

[2] Peter C. Fusaro & Ross M. Miller, What Went Wrong at Enron: Everyone's Guide to the Largest Bankruptcy in U.S. History (2002).

[3] Id.

[4] Robert K. Herdman, Testimony: Are Current Financial Accounting Standards Protecting Investors?, 1324 Prac. L. Inst. Corp. L. & Prac. Course Handbook Series 695, 779 (2002).

[5] Enron Collapse, available at http://fpc.state.gov/documents/organization/9110.pdf.

pen. The Securities Exchange Commission ("SEC") uses auditing as its primary method of regulation of information and financial documents for large publicly traded companies. The failure of the audits to reveal the problems, therefore, hampered any possible SEC enforcement actions.

But why did the audits fail to disclose these problems? The answer seems to be related to the fact that Enron's auditors also sold Enron some very creative financial structuring advice. For instance, in addition to the use of Special Purpose Entities ("SPEs"), Enron also purchased advice from its accounting firms and several large investment banks—advice that allowed it to book losses sufficient to prevent Enron from having to pay much income tax for many years, despite the vast profits that Enron was simultaneously reporting to shareholders and the SEC.[6]

The use of large accounting firms simultaneously to perform auditing and non-auditing services created a huge conflict of interest between auditor independence and company pressures. During 2000, Enron paid a total of $52 million to Arthur Andersen: $25 million for auditing services and $27 million for non-auditing (consulting) services. The consulting services provided Enron with advice for structuring its business deals. Andersen estimated that keeping Enron as a client would generate $100 million a year in revenues.[7] In order to satisfy auditing standards, auditors must remain independent. The $27 million that Andersen received from Enron in 2000 could easily have compromised Andersen's incentive to audit independently.[8] Andersen's extensive consulting work for Enron may well have compromised its independence and its judgment in determining the nature, timing, and extent of audit procedures. Further, these sums may also have deterred Andersen from asking Enron to make revisions to its financial statements.[9]

Even if Enron and its accountants' internal controls were lacking, why were applicable laws and regulations not enforced? Where were the governmental watchdogs? In Enron's case, the accounting and regulatory standard setting model established by the SEC, which relied on the accounting firms themselves to report and correct problems, was, at best, ineffective in addressing accounting oversight and auditor controls.[10] Notwithstanding the SEC's rules requiring periodic audits of the companions under its regulatory control, the SEC had not audited Enron's books since 1996.

---

[6] David Cay Johnston, *Wall St. Banks Said to Help Enron Devise Its Tax Shelters*, N.Y. TIMES, Feb. 14, 2003, at C1.

[7] *Id.*

[8] On occasion, Fastow used fury and tantrums to push through deals for Enron; he could be heard from his office yelling at bankers that they would not be dealing with Enron in the future unless they were willing to close the deal on the table. MIMI SWARTZ WITH SHERRON WATKINS, POWER FAILURE: THE INSIDE STORY OF THE COLLAPSE OF ENRON 73–74 (2003).

[9] *Id.*

[10] Manuel A. Rodriguez, *The Numbers Game: Manipulation of Financial Reporting by Corporations and Their Executives*, 10 U. MIAMI BUS. L. REV. 451 (2002).

The SEC has the statutory authority to set accounting principles,[11] but for over 60 years it has relied on the accounting industry to police and regulate itself.[12] The SEC has generally acquiesced to the rules and standards adopted by the FASB ("GAAP"). But when the accounting industry was allowed to begin offering other financial services, the SEC failed to recognize the inherent incentive problems in the industry, such as the conflict in auditing and consulting functions. Such clear conflicts of interest should suggest problems with self-enforcement. After the Andersen debacle, the public has acknowledged that accounting regulation is inadequate and that the industry needs stronger and more independent oversight. Prior to Enron's collapse, the FASB sought to address concerns about timeliness, transparency, and complexity in financial standards.[13] But when the FASB tried to implement regulations to more tightly monitor the energy-trading industry, substantial lobbying efforts by the accounting community guaranteed the failure of the FASB's efforts.[14]

Deregulation of the accounting industry, coupled with the complexity of the energy markets that the accounting industry was auditing, created a complex system that was extremely difficult to monitor (and which, in fact, largely remained unmonitored).[15] Even though a complicated system might suggest a need for stringent government oversight, as a result of Enron's political influence, the government failed to employ its enforcement powers to prevent corporate abuses of market power.[16] Throughout Enron's lifespan, Enron aggressively lobbied for less regulation and oversight by Congress, the Commodity Futures Trading Commission ("CFTC"), the SEC, and the Federal Energy Regulatory Commission ("FERC").

Enron's lobbying success can be traced historically. The complexity of the deregulated energy system began emerging in the late 1980s and 1990s. Through a series of decisions, FERC authorized "power marketers" like Enron to operate with little oversight in its energy markets.[17] Following FERC's decisions freeing Enron from regulatory oversight, Enron petitioned the chairwoman of CFTC, Wendy Gramm, to exempt energy derivatives from regulation. Ms. Gramm initiated two actions in 1993 and granted Enron's petition to be exempt from CFTC oversight.[18] Five weeks after stepping down from her governmental position, Ms. Gramm was named to Enron's board of directors.[19]

---

[11] *Id.*

[12] MINORITY STAFF COMM. OF GOV'T REFORM, FACT SHEET: HOW LAX REGULATION AND INADEQUATE OVERSIGHT CONTRIBUTED TO THE ENRON COLLAPSE (2002) [hereinafter FACT SHEET].

[13] Herdman, *supra* note 4, at 698.

[14] *Firms Campaign To Soften FASB Stock Option Rule,* Corporate Accounting International (May 1, 1995); *see also* Rodriguez, *supra* note 10, at 481.

[15] *Id.*

[16] *Id.*

[17] FACT SHEET, *supra* note 12, at 1.

[18] 7 U.S.C. § 6b (2003).

[19] FACT SHEET, *supra* note 12, at 2.

Enron's lobbying efforts continued and were so aggressive and successful that staff members of one Congressional committee asked a lobbyist for an Enron-led industry group to negotiate a bill directly with regulators.[20] In 2000, the CFTC was further removed from regulating energy traders when Congress passed the Commodity Futures Modernization Act. That bill codified the CFTC's decision exempting energy contracts from regulatory oversight.[21]

There were also problems caused by legislative changes. According to Richard Walker of the SEC, "[I]ncreases in financial fraud . . . [are] partially attributable to court rulings limiting corporate liability for financial fraud [as well as] the Private Securities Reform Act of 1995, which removed joint and several liability. . . ."[22] With such limitations on a shareholder's ability to sue companies, financial frauds increased.[23]

Financial accounting scandals occurred at Enron and other companies as a result of increasing incentives for self-regulated entities to act illegally, the lessening presence of watchdog organizations, and an increasing dependence on self-regulation. Enron is a result of the complete breakdown of corporate governance and professional gatekeeping systems. This breakdown is an important lesson for environmental regulation because it indicates that the reliance on self-regulation alone, when there are incentives to cheat, is, at best, a dangerous proposition.

B. ENRON AND CALIFORNIA'S ENERGY DEREGULATION

The misplaced reliance on self-regulation was not the only lesson of Enron. Enron's practices in California's energy market provide an example of how difficult it is to regulate a complex trading system even if companies follow the letter of the law. Unlike the regulation of its financial and accounting documents, which failed to pick up explicitly illegal behavior, Enron simply took advantage of legal loopholes in the California energy trading regulatory scheme.[24]

So what went wrong in California? Primarily, there was a failure to effectively regulate a complex trading system. Several key features of the California system helped to

---

[20] *Out of Reach: The Enron Debacle Spotlights Huge Void in Financial Regulation*, WALL ST. J., Dec. 13, 2001, at A1.

[21] Private Securities Reform Act of 1995, Pub. L. No. 106-554, § 1(a)(5), 114 Stat. 2763 (1995).

[22] William S. Lerach, *"The Chickens Have Come Home to Roost," How Wall Street, the Big Accounting Firms and Corporate Interests Chloroformed Congress and Cost America's Investors Trillions,* 1324 PRAC. L. INST. CORP. L. & PRAC. COURSE HANDBOOK SERIES 759 (2002).

[23] *Id.*

[24] It should be noted that the "schemes" Enron put to use in the California market were not clearly legal. Indeed, Enron's counsel advised the company that the trading strategies might be illegal. *See* Harvey Rice, *Enron Was Told Strategy in California Could be Illegal,* HOUS. CHRON., Dec. 12, 2002, at A1. The ambiguous nature of these schemes is a result of a complex system in which "legal" and "illegal" could not be easily defined.

create the 2000–2001 crisis: (1) the Power Exchange's ("PX") market structure flaws, (2) the Independent System Operators' ("ISO") market structure flaws, (3) CPUC's prohibition on long-term contracts and other risk-reducing tools, (4) CPUC's forced divestiture of the Investor Owned Utilities' ("IOU") generation, and (5) FERC's failure to timely respond to the crisis.[25]

Both the PX and the ISO were designed in ways that failed to address the underlying technology and economics of the electric industry and marketplace.[26] The PX day-ahead and hour-ahead markets are considered "spot markets," meaning that purchases are based on each day's price for electricity.[27] Day-ahead and hour-ahead pricing effectively creates individual markets for each hour and day of the year. Spot pricing in any market creates the risk of volatile prices, subjecting both the buyer and the seller to increased risk. In the PX market, however, structural flaws resulted in the majority of the price volatility risk being borne by California's IOUs.[28]

The PX buying and selling mechanisms, fueled by CPUC's requirement for all IOUs to purchase all their power from the PX, functioned like an auction house.[29] Power generators would bid their next day's power output in the PX at various prices, and purchasing IOUs would submit bids on a daily basis.[30] The "clearing price" was equivalent to the most expensive megawatt price paid by any purchaser from the PX.[31] If a supplier submitted a selling bid *higher* than the clearing price, it could not sell anything into the market; however, those bidding *under* the clearing price received the clearing price bid anyway.[32] In other words, even if a supplier submitted a lower-priced bid to the PX for that day, California's IOUs were required to pay the highest possible price that was bid into the PX for that day.[33] This market structure proved to be a fatal flaw, because the IOUs could not enter into long-term contracts or other price hedging products to reduce the price volatility incumbent with the spot market.[34]

Believing that transmission-owning utilities would manipulate the transmission of power through and across the state, the CPUC also required the utilities to give up control of their transmission facilities to the ISO.[35] The ISO was responsible for ensur-

[25] *Id.*

[26] Timothy P. Duane, *Regulation's Rationale: Learning from the California Energy Crisis,* 19 YALE J. ON REG. 471, 496 (2002).

[27] Darren Bush & Carrie Mayne, *In (Reluctant) Defense of Enron: Why Bad Regulation is to Blame for California's Power Woes (or Why Antitrust Law Fails to Protect Against Market Power When the Market Rules Encourage its Use),* 83 OREGON L. REV. __ (2004).

[28] Mike Stenglein, *The Causes of California's Energy Crisis,* 16 NAT. RESOURCE & ENV'T. 237 (2002).

[29] *Id.*

[30] *Id.*

[31] *Id.*

[32] *Id.*

[33] *Id.* at 237–238.

[34] *Id.*

[35] *Id.*

ing that all electricity demand was met.[36] If the PX had insufficient supply to meet the state's demand, the ISO was required to purchase and provide electricity from outside the PX market to make up for the shortfall.[37] The ISO charged the PX for this imported power, which, in turn, passed the cost of this imported power on to the IOUs.[38]

This structure created a significant flaw in the market system: it left the IOUs with no ability to protect themselves from these unexpected prices and created a huge incentive to game the system. Sellers learned to use this structure to their financial advantage once they realized that the ISO would pay any price for power to meet this shortfall. Indeed, the ISO was, by law, required to pay any price necessary to keep the transmission grid operating.[39] Therefore, on days when the forecast weather was likely to demand all of the available power, the power producers knew that they did not have to participate in the PX, because the ISO would call in the next day and offer higher prices.[40] This tactic reduced the amount of power available in the grid and forced the ISO to act as a buyer of high-cost spot power, in effect buying power at higher prices that was kept off of the market in order to require "premium" buying at higher prices.

The role of FERC has been correctly criticized in light of the deregulation disaster, because major suppliers came from out of state and were thus under FERC's regulatory jurisdiction. FERC allegedly adhered too strongly to the free market ideology despite mounting evidence that the free market was not working.[41] Most important, FERC failed miserably in its duty to discipline the anticompetitive behavior by the sellers who were driving the increases.[42] Starting at the genesis of California's deregulation efforts, FERC was advised about the potential problems that might accompany deregulation.[43] It obtained reports as early as 1996 commenting on the potential for price manipulation and weakness in California's deregulation scheme.[44] FERC ignored all of these reports and signed off on California's deregulation plan. Critics have charged that "FERC's failure to act has forced California into this energy crisis of unprecedented proportions."[45]

There appear to be two reasons behind FERC's lack of involvement: (1) It misunderstood and misdiagnosed California's problem as being a supply and demand imbalance, and (2) its entire program of promoting competitive wholesale market would have been threatened by any other interpretation of the cause of the California crisis.[46]

---

[36] *Id.*

[37] *Id.*

[38] *Id.*

[39] Duane, *supra* note 26, at 499.

[40] *Id.*

[41] Stenglein, *supra* note 28, at 241.

[42] Duane, *supra* note 26, at 516.

[43] Stenglein, *supra* note 28, at 271.

[44] *Id.* at 241.

[45] *Id.*

[46] Duane, *supra* note 26, at 516.

A recent report notes how few resources FERC then spent and currently spends on controlling anti-competitive behavior in the energy market.[47] Understandably, then, FERC laid the blame on all of the flaws in the design of the California system at the feet of the California CPUC, California PX, and California ISOs, thus deflecting attention from its own deficiencies and culpability.[48] Notwithstanding FERC's review and approval of the California restructuring scheme, FERC claimed no responsibility for the crisis,[49] even though there was ample evidence that structural features specific to electricity markets limited a regulator's ability to rely upon the traditional aspects of competitive markets.[50]

Perhaps FERC's greatest failure occurred when it initially refused to enforce the Federal Power Act[51] and issue the requested refunds from the obscenely high charges that were imposed upon the wholesale market from May to October 2000.[52] Generators profited exponentially from overcharges, yet FERC initially did nothing to sanction those who had gamed the system and caused the "unjust and unreasonable" wholesale rates.[53] Had FERC acted in a timely manner, it could have saved Californians an estimated $9+ billion dollars.[54] At the most critical moment of the California crisis, FERC abandoned its role as a regulator, leaving the market wide open for massive profiteering at California's expense.[55] In hindsight, it is not at all clear that FERC would have pursued the California energy market profiteering had Enron managed to avoid filing for bankruptcy. FERC chose to investigate the various ploys and schemes being used to game the California energy market only after the disclosure of an internal memo at an Enron subsidiary that was leaked to FERC.[56] Prior to the Enron memo's roadmap on how to scheme the California energy market, FERC was convinced that California's problems were merely the result of poor design and a supply and demand imbalance.[57]

The central feature of the 2000–2001 California energy crisis was the failure of the state and federal regulators to properly supervise and control market behavior by gen-

---

[47] David Ivanovich, *Report Raps FERC Over Enron Schemes*, HOUS. CHRON., Nov. 12, 2002, at 1B.

[48] *Id.*

[49] *Id.*

[50] Bush & Mayne, *supra* note 27, at 28.

[51] 16 U.S.C. § 824 (2000).

[52] Duane, *supra* note 26, at 517.

[53] Stenglein, *supra* note 28, at 242.

[54] *Id.*

[55] Duane, *supra* note 26, at 517.

[56] Richard Simon et al., *Enron Memos Prompt Calls for a Wider Investigation Electricity: Regulators order all energy trading companies to preserve documents on tactics*, L.A. TIMES, May 8, 2002, at A1.

[57] *Id.*

erators and traders. The market design had flaws, but the crisis was caused more precisely by a failure to understand the inherent rationale of regulation or to regulate despite those flaws.[58] The act of converting from a monopoly energy system to a market-based energy system will always have surprises. The power of such a conversion is that it allows companies to search for and exploit efficiencies. Enron and other out-of-state wholesale power suppliers did just that. What they did may not necessarily have been illegal, although one can certainly argue that the ISO rules against gaming the system were violated, clearly causing "unreasonable" wholesale rates. But the real problem was not with these companies. They were doing what they should have been expected to do—exploiting the system for their financial benefit. The problem was in failing to aggressively examine the newly deregulated system and correct the flaws that existed, so that the original goal of using efficiencies to lower prices for consumers would be met. Instead, the deregulation of California's energy market resulted in creating enormous profits for some aspects of the energy industry and bankruptcy for some of the others. FERC, in particular, depended upon the market to discipline the participants in the system and provide checks and balances toward the ultimate goal of increasing efficiencies and lowering prices. It failed to adequately examine and predict the ways that the proposed system could be gamed and the implementation of policies and rules to curb and control that behavior. When a system has vague rules, regulated entities will push the edge of the envelope as much as possible. Moreover, as with the accounting and financial documents strategy that relies upon self-regulation, there is considerable evidence that energy companies generally engaged in false reporting in those areas that used voluntary reporting, such as the reporting of trades used in setting market prices.[59] The dispute over whether the trading schemes used in California's energy market were illegal illustrates this point precisely.[60]

One could argue that close monitoring and correction was unreasonable in this case because it would have taken a considerable number of resources to do so. Expending huge resources to monitor and protect the system goes against the grain and the purposes of deregulation and calls into question a one-size-fits-all mantra. The fact that Enron's numerous profit-generating schemes were later shown to take advantage of the simplistic system indicates that these schemes would have been discovered earlier had there been sufficient staffing to monitor California's energy market. But appropriate staffing in such a complex market may be disproportionately large (perhaps hundreds of people) to monitor the 56,000 simultaneous markets that existed in the California system. As Darren Bush and Carrie Mayne have explained, regulation is an essential

---

[58] *Id* at 531.

[59] Laura Goldberg, *New Blows to Traders' Credibility,* HOUS. CHRON., Oct. 10, 2002, at 1C.

[60] Harvey Rice, *Enron Was Told Strategy in California Could Be Illegal,* HOUS. CHRON., Dec. 12, 2002, at A1.

protection against exercises of power manipulation.[61] Power manipulation, in turn, makes deregulation look less attractive or perhaps less efficient.

This lesson must not be ignored. Deregulation alone will not meet any particular goals—it is merely a method to reach those goals. To meet particular goals, deregulated systems, particularly complex ones with unclear boundaries, may require high monitoring costs. These costs must be considered in determining whether retail competition and deregulation, or one-size-fits-all market-based strategies, would be a more efficient system than the traditional command and control regulation.

C. THE ENRON DEBACLE AS AN EXAMPLE OF THE PROBLEMS WITH VOLUNTARY ENFORCEMENT AND LARGE-SCALE MARKET-BASED TRADING SCHEMES

What lessons can we learn from Enron's financial misstatements and its role in profiteering in the California energy markets? Although Enron's problem has been described as the work of greedy, corrupt individuals, Enron's market games in the California energy market, as well as the illegal and misleading accounting devices that helped overstate earnings, were inevitable, given the way that Enron's core businesses and accounting practices were monitored and regulated internally and the way that California's deregulation scheme was set up.

In the aggregate, human behavior will lead to personal wealth accumulation to the detriment of others, if such behavior is permitted. With Enron, a poorly developed oversight of the then-new energy trading industry and the lack of oversight by the accounting industry virtually insured that anything that was not explicitly forbidden would occur. Indeed, even things that *were* explicitly forbidden occurred when there was no system to prevent violations from happening. In the vernacular, we would say that Enron "took everything that was not nailed down." The lesson that unregulated human behavior leads to selfishness is likely the most important lesson that we can take from the Enron debacle—and the one that has the most implication for the future of environmental protection.

Because this assertion is central in forming the basis for the claim that environmental protection must—indeed, *can only*—occur in particular ways, it deserves further explication. I will start with a quote from the seminal piece by Carol Rose on why certain kinds of environmental protection are needed.[62] In explaining why cooperative systems of resource control do not generally work when many people have access to the resource, she states:

---

[61] Bush & Mayne, *supra* note 27, at 86.

[62] Carol Rose, *Rethinking Environmental Controls: Management Strategies for Common Resources*, 1991 DUKE L.J. 1, 3 (1991) (emphasis added); Bush & Mayne, *supra* note 27.

Why does everyone overfish, even to the detriment of the body of water and its living stocks? According to the economic account, everyone does so because each user knows that, even if any particular individual refrains from fishing so intensely, everyone else will continue to fish, and in fact the other might just fish a little bit more to take up the slack left by any moderate fisher. *The moderate fisher in short would just be a sucker.*[63]

This is, in fact, always the result when organisms compete for limited resources. Though some animal species cooperate in large groups, if members of that species (or other animals) are recognized as foreign, they are driven away. The law of animals operates in such a way that, unless cooperation has evolved as an evolutionary positive, most animals exist by taking what they need for support.[64] This taking occurs through grazing, attacking, killing, or stealing. When animals share a resource, such as a waterhole, the flourishing of one species or animal necessarily depends upon the lack of success for the other. The paradigmatic conception of survival is a zero-sum game because there are only so many resources.

The only reason we tend to forget this pre-eminent principle in looking at human interaction is because human ingenuity has allowed us to opt out of the zero-sum game and actually increase overall resources. Since the beginning of recorded history, this increase has been accompanied by laws and moral codes (such as property law and laws that prohibit the harming of another) that limit such zero-sum behavior in individual actions.[65] Unfortunately, we forget that these laws are in derogation of the basic animal rule and are not the norm. They only came into existence because humans were able, as a group, to perceive the universal advantages of protecting individual accumulations, having learned that an increase in overall resources is possible only if we protect individual incentives for accumulation and production.[66]

That this was the "legal" response that arose really should be no surprise, as it recognizes and respects the basic nature of survival among animals—it respects the concept of selfishness that is the basis of capitalism. And lest we forget that "property law" and its attendant enforcement mechanisms exist in derogation of what has evolved naturally for humans and all animals, one need only look back at Professor Rose's example.[67] When there is no property system, the old adage still reigns supreme. Despite vast increases in knowledge and technology, the fishermen of today's lakes are no more

---

[63] Rose, *supra* note 62, at 3.

[64] For example, wolves hunt in packs to the betterment of all.

[65] Robert C. Ellickson & Charles D. Thorland, *Ancient Land Law: Mesopotamia, Egypt, and Israel,* 71 CHI. K. L. REV. 321, 337 (1995).

[66] *Id.* at 332.

[67] *See* text accompanying note 62 *supra*.

likely to control their selfish impulses to over-fish than were the fishermen of eight thousand years ago.[68]

In order to understand why Enron's actions and subsequent collapse were inevitable, we must focus on the basic primal principle of "taking" what is available. Property rights and accompanying moral codes must be seen as a derogation of what occurs "naturally," and what exists in most animal species. That is, humans take whatever they can, in any way they can, without restraint, at least from non-cooperating family or tribal units. This observation suggests that humans will work around any prohibition that is not clear, or will be tempted to take anything of value if the taking is not explicitly prohibited.

An example from the common law is instructive. We would never seek to protect private property from those who would appropriate it by simply saying we will "work with those that are stealing property to make sure they don't steal so much." Nor would we say that we do not need deeds and ownership concepts because everyone will leave everyone else's valuable property alone. Similarly, we do not try to protect property rights by putting forth vague, unclear legal norms or principles. Instead, we have specific, strict rules and punishments that are enforced. Without clear requirements and/or enforcement of these requirements, humans revert to "taking" whatever is available.

No one seriously proposes that all property rights could be protected simply by exhortation and cooperation, or that we could protect property with an incomplete system that does not make clear who has what property right and how all of those rights interact. The reason that we do not propose such solutions is that they clearly do not work. Absent an enforceable mandate to the contrary, human behavior defaults to taking that which is available.[69] Human behavior will also fill in any interstices of ambiguity. Vague and unclear mandates present a great possibility of non-compliance. Indeed, human ingenuity in exploiting whatever situation is presented is recognized as the efficiency of capitalism. The evolution of common law is designed to curb this tendency by protecting rights necessary for capital generation.

Despite this truism, the Enron debacle shows that our state and federal governments have attempted to protect valuable commodities by clearly ineffective methods. Energy trading, as a system of creating wealth (or accumulating property), has only been possible since the deregulation of certain energy markets. Yet instead of taking steps to clearly protect this newly created "property," the regulators imposed few rules

---

[68] Carol Kaesik Yoon, *Scientist at Work, David Pauly, Iconoclast, Looks for Fish and Finds Disaster*, N.Y. TIMES, Jan. 21, 2003, at F1.

[69] This is not to discount the role that morality has come to play in our society and its ability to control certain behavior. However, I posit that morality alone can rarely enforce the right; there must be occasional enforcement of transgressors, or the whole system collapses as everyone realizes the commons are being taken to their detriment. *See* Rose, *supra* note 62, at 1. Indeed, what we call "morality" may be another enforcement mechanism crafted by human evolution to coincide with the evolution of common law.

and showed no appreciation for all of the conflicts that might occur. That companies abused this system should be no surprise.

Similarly, our accounting and auditing system is designed to protect the "property" of equal access to information for investment purposes—a right that is recognized as necessary for the efficient functioning of our stock market and the wealth that can be produced by the access to capital that it provides. Yet oversight of this system was, by and large, protected only by self-regulation. Again, when the law deregulating much of our financial system was changed to permit accounting firms to profit by shifting their focus from auditing to making a profit with consulting, it should be no surprise that accounting firms sacrificed their auditor's role and "took" this profit as soon as it was available.[70]

It appears now that Enron was able to combine the abuses of financial misreporting with the lack of clear rules in California's deregulated energy market. Enron not only exploited loopholes in California's energy trading regulations, but it also speculated on energy prices, which in turn was not reported to shareholders, thanks to shoddy accounting practices.[71]

Arguably, such complex systems are inherently hard to regulate, because it is too difficult to craft clear rules that address all of the possibilities of the new system. However, in such a case, it may be that the system should otherwise not exist. As Professor Rose notes, market-based enforcement systems are the most expensive systems to monitor and enforce.[72] Some property systems simply should not be protected in this manner. Any advantages gained through trading schemes seeking to capture efficiencies of individual initiative might be swallowed up by the costs of enforcing those schemes. This may well be the case with energy deregulation. If you cannot create a system to police how energy trades are occurring and at what advantage to whom, it may be cheaper and more efficient to have fixed energy sources with fixed costs. Indeed, from California's perspective, the people of that state are likely sick unto death of deregulation.

D. SUGGESTIONS FOR CERTAIN ENVIRONMENTAL POLICY INITIATIVES

The protection of our environment in a "cooperative" enforcement scheme or by using market controls while eliminating the command and control system is exactly what is being proposed by commentators in many areas of environmental regulation. Indeed, this premise was the cornerstone of the Bush administration in Texas and now in Washington, D.C.[73] One of the new centerpieces of the Bush administration is the

---

[70] See part D infra.

[71] Records and Interviews Show that Enron Was Speculating on Trades, N.Y. TIMES, Dec. 12, 2002, at A1.

[72] Rose, supra note 62, at 21–23.

[73] Business Group Readies Voluntary Initiative on Climate Change, 23 INSIDE 2 (Nov. 15, 2002); EPA Administration Expects New Guidelines For Voluntary Emissions Reporting by 2004, 33 BNA ENV'L REP. 2077 (Sept. 27, 2002) (detailing the Bush administration's approach to voluntary trading and reporting of global warming emissions).

heavily touted idea that greenhouse gases responsible for global warming can be controlled voluntarily, and that air pollution will be better controlled by trading systems.[74]

As noted above, "cooperative" strategies that depend entirely upon self-regulation simply will not work if human nature holds true. Indeed, anecdotal evidence bears this out.[75] Significantly, the Bush administration was so concerned that its "voluntary" greenhouse gas controls might not work that it is being accused of coercive tactics from the industry in order to demonstrate the ease and effectiveness of "volunteerism."[76]

Situations in which there is to be pollution trading are more nuanced. If such trading schemes are accompanied by effective enforcement systems, they should work well and, indeed, may provide important efficiencies. But, as we have seen, some trading systems may simply be too complex for any cost-effective enforcement mechanism. Thus, the advisability of environmental trading schemes should be dependent on the complexity of enforcement. Where enforcement includes adequate resources, contains an easily identifiable mechanism (such as the requirement of certain equipment), and does not have to depend entirely upon self-regulation, it should work.

The application of alternative administration regimes to the environment has been studied. The primary goal of using laws to protect the environment is to internalize the negative environmental externalities attributable to human existence and activities. For this goal to function properly, there must be a determination of the optimal level of environmental protection and the employment of the proper tools to achieve that optimal level.[77]

Carol Rose categorized the tools used in the implementation of environmental policies.[78] These implementation devices are entitled "do nothing," "keepout," "rightway," or "property."[79] These last strategies are more commonly known as "grandfathering," "command and control," and "market-based" strategy.[80] To these, I would also add "education and exhortation." Our current environmental controls use all of these,

---

[74] S. Bill No. 2815, 107 Cong., 2d Sess. (2002), 148 Cong. Rec. S7473-98 (daily ed. July 29, 2002); *see also* H.R. Bill No. 5266, 107 Cong., 2d. Sess. (2002) ('Clear Skies Bill').

[75] Barnaby J. Feder, *Dialogue on Pollution is Allowed to Trail Off,* N.Y. TIMES, Nov. 23, 2002, at B1 (noting that Dow Chemical's cooperative environmental program went away with the death of its major company proponent).

[76] Andrew Revkin, *U.S. is Pressuring Industry to Cut Greenhouse Gases,* N.Y. TIMES, Jan. 20, 2003, at A1.

[77] Victor B. Flatt, *Saving the Lost Sheep: Bringing Environmental Values Back into The Fold With a New EPA Decisionmaking Paradigm,* 74 WASH. L. REV. 1, 2 (1999). Though there are disagreements about where acceptable levels of environmental harm should be set, there is little dispute that subsequent action must be taken to get there.

[78] Rose, *supra* note 62, at 1.

[79] *Id.*

[80] *Id.*

either singly or in combination.[81] However, all of these controls are not created equally. They have different effectiveness and different costs.

Professor Rose's great contribution is to recognize what variables might affect the changing cost structure of each of these strategies and to explore what those variables suggest about the employment of these various strategies.[82] She characterized the variables as "system and administrative costs," "user costs," and "overuse or failure of strategy" cost.[83] The first cost is generally the cost to the government or regulated entity of the regulation itself—in other words, the cost to monitor and enforce. The second cost is the cost of equipment or other requirements, which is usually borne by the regulated party. The third is the cost that comes from the ineffectiveness of a strategy, or the loss due to commons overuse.

In examining the various strategies, Professor Rose noted in particular that market-based trading strategies, while significantly reducing costs to users, might significantly increase the costs of monitoring or enforcement.[84] In a market-based system, each source must be individually monitored, and, in order to achieve actual efficiencies, each individual must be able to change and trade "outputs" instantaneously.[85] Professor Rose speculated that a market-based control strategy might be an effective control of an environmental externality under extreme pressure, because it could provide reductions at a lower cost to the polluter and with little loss due to failure of the program. But she also noted that, in order to get effective reductions, enforcement is important, but that this cost could be high. Thus, she concluded that market-based control strategies would be best used only in situations in which there is pressure to massively overuse resources, because only control of such an extreme problem could provide enough of a benefit to justify the high cost of administration. This approach mirrors the lessons learned about Enron and the necessity to adequately monitor and police the California energy deregulation.

Similarly, enforcement schemes that depend on an administration to monitor an overall "level" of desired environmental quality, which can be degraded from various and dispersed sources, also presents the difficulty of monitoring multiple sources simultaneously. Both the Clean Water Act ("CWA") and the Clean Air Act ("CAA") originally only required the maintenance of an ideal standard of environmental pro-

---

[81] For instance the Clean Air Act has "grandfather" provisions regarding existing stationary sources, "command and control" in the New Source Performance Standards, and "market based strategies" in the Sulfur Dioxide trading system, designed to control acid deposition. See generally 42 U.S.C. Sec. 7401 et seq. (one could also note that with respect to climate change gases, the strategy appears to be "do-nothing").

[82] Rose, *supra* note 62, at 1.

[83] *Id.* at 12.

[84] *Id.* at 21.

[85] *Id.* at 21–22.

tection without requiring any particular command and control system to get there.[86] The individual states were supposed to ensure that this level was met. But without any mechanisms for compliance, any capacity to monitor companies suspected of violating the standards, or any enforcement standards, both laws[87] failed miserably.[88] The part of the modern CWA that still requires the maintenance of overall water quality, whether technological or process controls work or not—the Total Maximum Daily Load program (TMDL)—lay unenforced by regulators for decades.[89]

Congress recognized the failure of this strategy as recently as 1990. Part of the 1990 CAA amendments altered the requirements for regulating hazardous air pollutants.[90] Prior to 1990, the EPA administrator was supposed to set emissions limitations at the place that would adequately protect public health.[91] But in the case of hazardous air pollutants, many of which are carcinogenic, this setting of emissions limitations was difficult to do in any principled manner. The administration was bogged down and only listed eight pollutants in a twenty-year period, even though thousands more were clearly at issue.[92] In 1990, Congress recognized that the certainty that came along with command and control regulation outweighed the supposed efficiencies that could come from a standard that allowed maximum flexibility but contained no mechanism or resources to enforce it.

In such cases, it is not that inefficient regulation is eliminated, but that there is no regulation at all—not because such regulation is not necessary or required by law, but that it is impractical and difficult. This theory of environmental regulation and history of the success or failure of programs might suggest that our administrators would be wary of enforcement schemes that rely on monitoring of divergent, multiple sources simultaneously or that depend heavily on self-regulation. Sadly, this is not the case.

The current administration, pointing to the success of market-based regulation in controlling acid rain,[93] suggests that market-based regulation can be replicated in many, if not all, areas, and that command and control regulation or direct emissions controls may be unnecessary.[94] A superficial glance at *only* the acid rain trading provision might support this theory.

---

[86] Fredrick R. Andersen et al., Environmental Protection: Law and Policy 1, 375–76, 589–90 (3d ed. 1999).

[87] 33 U.S.C. § 1251 (2003); 42 U.S.C. §§ 1857–18571 (2003).

[88] Andersen, *supra* note 86.

[89] *See generally Sierra Club v. Hankinson*, 939 F. Supp. 865 (N.D. Ga. 1996).

[90] 42 U.S.C. § 7651(a) (2002).

[91] Andersen, *supra* note 86, at 1.

[92] *Id.*

[93] 42 U.S.C. § 7651(a) (2002).

[94] Under the Acid Deposition Control Provision compliance has been an "unprecedented success (over 99%)." *Emissions Cap and Trade: A Basic Explanation & Results Under the Acid Rain Program, available at* http://www.epa.gov/clearskies/emissions_cap_and_trade_3_14.pdf.

The acid rain provisions that went into effect in 1990 allowed fossil-fueled power plants to control emissions of sulfur dioxide not just by installing particular required equipment, but also by allowing the plants to try other control methods, and to purchase and sell the right to pollute.[95] As a result of this change, some companies chose to invest in expensive pollution control equipment because they could sell the additional "control" to other polluters. Similarly, some polluters could avoid installing expensive technology by purchasing the right to pollute from others who had installed higher-than-needed capacity, due to the incremental nature of pollution control.[96] In terms of lowering the costs to the regulated parties, this program has worked remarkably well.[97]

Significantly, this program has functioned without enormous administrative cost.[98] However, the acid rain program alone does not provide sufficient evidence that we should eliminate command and control to rely completely on market-based control strategies. The acid rain sulfur dioxide trading program is somewhat unique among market-based schemes, and unique in such a way that it would work well. The number of sulfur dioxide emitters in the program is fairly small, there are generally similar types of production facilities, the trades are for relatively long time periods, the sources are already regulated by the federal EPA and the individual states' environmental protection agencies, and the cost of ensuring that the trades are complied with is small.[99] Only a few hundred reports have to be examined each year. The acid rain program does not require an enormous expense and thus does not require that the government depend on self-regulation for compliance.[100]

Of greater applicability might be the situation of states that have attempted to create trading programs for many, if not all, pollution sources. So far, these programs have been disastrous. According to the EPA's Inspector General, "state emissions programs to control air pollution are hobbled by a lack of adequate oversight from the EPA, lax enforcement, and bad emissions data."[101] The California RECLAIM program, which attempted to trade nitrogen oxide emissions between stationary and mobile sources, has failed to meet its predicted pollution reductions, and was characterized by EPA's Region IX as having serious compliance problems.[102]

---

[95] *Id.*

[96] 42 U.S.C. §7651(a).

[97] Andersen, *supra* note 86, at 1.

[98] *See Emissions Cap and Trade: A Basic Explanation & Results Under the Acid Rain Program, available at* http://www.epa.gov/clearskies/emissions_cap_and_trade_3_14.pdf.

[99] Andersen, *supra* note 86, at 1.

[100] *Id.*

[101] EPA Inspector General Calls on Agency to Improve Oversight of State Programs, 33 BNA ENV'T. REP. 2142 (Oct. 4, 2002).

[102] Trading Foes Hail EPA Region IX Report Criticizing RECLAIM Program, *Inside EPA,* Nov. 22, 2002, at 7.

Moreover, there is mounting evidence that compliance, backed by actual data supplied by the regulated industry, may be suspect. The number of cases of falsified pollution data reported to regulatory agencies is increasing.[103] An article chronicling this problem notes that "lab fraud hampers an environmental protection system that frequently relies on voluntary compliance . . . ."[104]

Thus, the only lesson that can truly be drawn from the success of the acid rain trading program is that we can assume that market-based strategies are more likely to be efficient when there is an opportunity for innovation or when there are economies of scales in the control of that pollutant—and when these efficiencies are not squandered either by enormous administrative costs or through regulatory failure because of lack of compliance and effective enforcement. Without market efficiencies, the preferred method of control could simply be mandated at no loss of efficiency, and there would not be the additional costs of administration of the market mechanism. Similarly, the efficiencies produced by market-based controls are more useful if they can be achieved without significantly increasing the cost of enforcement. Thus, we would expect that easily enforced individual polluter systems, due either to their limited number or other regulations, would be better suited to market-based control strategies, because greater efficiencies (such as lower pollution control costs to the regulated entity) would not be consumed by the additional costs of administration.

Although the one large-scale market trading mechanism in environmental policy works, it does not justify wholesale changes in environmental policy. The market-trading principle is based on a unique set of circumstances that are limited to particular types of control. The result of broad-based national market-based regulation and the reliance on self-regulation is more appropriately found in the Enron debacle. Enron's activities were subject to mature regulatory regimes at the SEC and FERC. The SEC relied upon accountant self-regulation, notwithstanding the introduction of a new incentive that encouraged accountants to abandon their self-regulation obligations. The FERC assumed that the market would regulate itself, even in the absence of clear information or requirements for the selling of wholesale electricity into the California markets. Of course, effective FERC regulation of the California market would have been very costly.

Notwithstanding the problems incumbent in this type of regulatory scheme, the proposals to alter environmental policy in this same manner march on. Several commentators have repeatedly suggested that the flaws with state regulation in the 1960s, before the advent of the strict command and control regime, have been remedied and that the states now have the capacity to regulate complex ambient air programs with

---

[103] Larry Margasak, *Labs Falsifying Environmental Tests*, HOUS. CHRON., Jan. 22, 2003, at 3A.

[104] *Id.*

multiple sources and/or trading schemes.[105] President Bush has indicated a preference for "cooperative" enforcement, and he actively pursued such mechanisms as Governor of Texas.[106] Parts of the Clean Skies Initiative, a series of legislative changes proposed by the Bush administration and introduced in both houses of Congress, represent this change in focus. Though the most publicized part of the program deals with expanding the fossil-fuel utility cap and trade program for sulfur dioxide to include nitrogen oxides and mercury (which face some of the similar "market" advantages of the acid rain deposition program), other parts are more problematic.

In addition to the cap and trade program, the Clear Skies proposal seeks to alter the Hazardous Air Pollutant program by eliminating the requirement for Maximum Achievable Control Technology.[107] This provision was added in 1990 precisely because the EPA administrator was not effective in determining what levels might be unhealthy and thus be able to require appropriate regulation. But this is all of the Hazardous Air Pollutant Program that would remain under the Bush initiative.[108] Moreover, the program would eliminate new source review for power plants, eliminating any incentive for plant equipment upgrades that would ultimately result in cleaner-burning plants.[109] Plants will now expand without upgrading their equipment, instead simply buying and selling pollutants.[110] Although total pollutants may be reduced over all, it is not clear that they will provide greater reductions over time when compared to the current alternatives. The Bush administration has already moved to alter the new source review program to eliminate some situations that would require more stringent pollution control equipment.[111] One study noted that this proposal would increase pollution over current controls.[112] Note that the current acid rain provisions work in tandem with new source review and other portions of the CAA.[113] One of the reasons that power plants are easy to monitor is that they utilize similar equipment and are already regulated. A completely unfettered market across numerous pollutants will present a much more difficult administration picture.

---

[105] *See* Currie, *State Pollution Statutes*, 48 U. CHI. L. REV. 27 (1981); Jody Freeman, *Collaborative Governance and the Administrative State*, 45 UCLA L. REV. 1 (1997); C. Foster Knight, *Voluntary Environmental Standards versus Mandatory Environmental Regulation and Enforcement in the NAFTA Market*, 12 ARIZ. J. INT'L & COMP. L. 619 (2001).

[106] Jim Yardley, *Governor Bush and the Environment: Bush Approach to Pollution: Preference for Self-Policing*, N.Y. TIMES, Nov. 9, 1999, at A1.

[107] S. Bill No. 2815, 107 Cong., 2d Sess. (2002), 148 Cong. Rec. S7473-98 (daily ed. July 29, 2002); *see also* H.R. Bill No. 5266, 107 Cong., 2d Sess. (2002) ('Clear Skies Bill').

[108] *Id.*

[109] *Id.*

[110] *Id.*

[111] N.Y. TIMES, Nov. 23, 2002, at A1.

[112] *Studies: New Rules Would Add Pollution*, HOUS. CHRON., Oct. 24, 2002, at 2A.

[113] 42 U.S.C. §§ 7651(a) (2002).

The Enron debacle illustrates that there is no panacea in self-regulation, market-trading, market controls, and market efficiencies. Some examples of energy deregulation have been notably efficient, and the large-scale market mechanism of the acid rain deposition program has been successful. But that success is not attributable solely to the fact that "market" mechanisms are used. The Enron financial collapse shows that, when self-regulation is undermined by strong incentives to cheat, as it was in Enron's financial reporting, self-regulation does not work. The Enron story in California also shows that the trades that can generate great profit for some may not meet the market's goals of lower costs. If the goal of deregulation includes lower costs, then the program must have enforcement mechanisms to control the schemes that participating companies will employ for their own self-benefit. After all, the only reason that they are participating in the market is to make a profit. Monitoring every participant's trades and potential trading schemes can be very expensive. Therefore, if there are to be trading schemes that allow for rent-seeking behavior by participants (which is necessary to capture efficiencies), these must be controlled in order to preserve other goals. Self-regulation cannot be counted on in a vacuum, and if government regulation is too expensive or difficult to be effective, the potential savings of the "market" program likely will be illusory. Enron's story gives us a preview of what happens in a complex trading scheme and self-regulation in the face of strong opposing incentives. It is the story of human behavior itself. Our own large-scale market-based strategy, acid rain deposition, has worked, but it is the exception, not the rule. Enron is the rule. This is the legacy for environmental policy of the collapse of Enron.

QUESTIONS

1. Under what circumstances would voluntary compliance be an effective and efficient method for enforcing environmental policy?
2. Does the technical complexity of environmental law militate for or against market enforcement mechanisms?
3. In what way does the article suggest that accounting advice should be regulated?

An Enron Lesson: The Modest Role of Criminal Law In Preventing Corporate Crime*

Geraldine Szott Moohr**

As the Enron scandal unfolded, government and industry officials, editorial writers, Enron employees and retirees, and the general public spoke with one voice: those responsible should be punished. In the months that followed Enron's disclosures, a flood of reports about executive malfeasance at other corporations—WorldCom, Adelphia, Tyco, and others—increased the demand for criminal sanctions.[1]

After some initial hesitation, the Bush administration wholeheartedly embraced a criminal response to the crisis.[2] Early in 2002, the Department of Justice indicted David Duncan, the chief auditor at Arthur Andersen on the Enron account, for obstructing justice when he directed subordinates to destroy accounting documents. Prosecutors secured his plea agreement and promise to testify, and only months later won conviction of Enron's auditor, Arthur Andersen LLP, for obstruction of justice.[3]

---

* Originally published at 55 Fla. L. Rev. 937 (2003). Reprinted with permission.

** Associate Professor of Law, University of Houston Law Center; B.S., University of Illinois; M.S., Bucknell University; J.D., American University. I would like to thank Roger Sherman for his guidance on the work of economists and Eric Bentley for his excellent research assistance.

[1] By one count, fifty-four firms were being investigated by prosecutors and regulatory agencies for accounting frauds and other financial misdeeds as of October 2002. *See* Gary Stoller, *Funny Numbers*, USA Today, Oct. 21, 2002, at 3B (listing other firms such as ImClone, Intel, Sunbeam, Waste Management, Xerox, Global Crossing, Qwest, RiteAid, Duke Energy, and Merck).

[2] *See* Robert H. Frank, *The Case for Sanctions*, N.Y. Times, Aug. 24, 2002, at A25 (noting that the Bush administration at first resisted criminal initiatives); Stephen Labaton, *Seemingly Close to Nominee, S.E.C. Search is Back to Start*, N.Y. Times, Nov. 15, 2002, at A1 (stating that the administration's use of vigorous prosecution was a tool to blunt calls for tougher regulations).

[3] Andersen, which would not survive the investigation, trial, and verdict, was ultimately fined $500,000. *See* Mary Flood & Tom Fowler, *Enron's Auditor Is Given the Max*, Hous. Chron., Oct. 17, 2002, at A1. At the time of this writing, Duncan has not been sentenced.

In mid-July, the Bush administration created a "corporate crime task force" to coordinate the growing number of criminal investigations,[4] and newspapers began to headline arrests with photographs of suited executives in handcuffs doing the "perp walk."[5] Congress moved in tandem, holding various congressional hearings at which executives asserted their Fifth Amendment rights.[6] In July 2002, Congress enacted the Sarbanes-Oxley Act, which, among other initiatives, created new offenses and mandated severe penalties for violating criminal laws.[7] In October 2002, prosecutors reached Enron executives, charging Michael Kopper and Andrew Fastow with multiple offenses.[8] As this essay is being written, there are almost daily reports of investigations and arrests.[9]

Empathy with employees, investors, and creditors readily explains the public's demand for punishment. One can also understand the political expediency of a tough-on-crime response.[10] Yet this rather reflexive turn to criminal law may be premature and is almost certainly incomplete. The catastrophic events at Enron and other companies point to the need for a careful analysis to determine how criminal law can contribute most effectively to the prevention of future Enrons.

With this goal in mind, the first section of this essay reviews the chief criminal laws implicated by conduct at Enron and notes changes wrought by the Sarbanes-Oxley Act. The review indicates that, despite the failure of the criminal law to deter corporate misconduct, there was no shortage of criminal laws *and* substantial sanctions already "on the books." The evaluation of the criminal provisions of the Sarbanes-Oxley Act in

---

[4] *See* John R. Wilke, *President Praises Work of Task Force on Business Crime*, WALL ST. J., Sept. 27, 2002, at A4 (reporting that the task force includes law enforcement personnel from the FBI, Treasury, and the SEC).

[5] David Duncan of Andersen, Andrew Fastow of Enron, Samuel Waksal of ImClone, Scott Sullivan of WorldCom, Dennis Kozlowski of Tyco International, and John Rigas of Adelphia Communications were among those photographed doing the "perp walk."

[6] Floyd Norris, *Capital Scorn: Communists to Accountants*, N.Y. TIMES, Jan. 25, 2002, at C1.

[7] *See* Sarbanes-Oxley Act of 2002, Pub. L. No. 107-204, 116 Stat. 745 (2002); *infra* Part I (detailing the Act's criminal provisions).

[8] *See* David Barboza, *From Enron Fast Track to Total Derailment*, N.Y. TIMES, Oct. 3, 2002, at C3.
In March 2003, federal prosecutors charged Kevin Howard and Michael Krautz with securities fraud, wire fraud, and lying to investigators. *See* Kurt Eichenwald, *Fraud Charges Filed Against 2 Employees of Enron Unit*, N.Y. TIMES, March 13, 2003, at C1 (reporting indictment of two midlevel Enron employees).

[9] *See* Rebecca Smith and John Wilke, *Enron Ex-Trader Admits to Fraud in California Crisis*, WALL ST. J., Oct. 18, 2002, at A3 (reporting that prosecutors had reached Enron's electricity dealings and that Timothy Belden, former head of Enron's energy-trading desk, had pleaded guilty to wire fraud for submitting false data to California's grid operator); Kurt Eichenwald, *Second Enron Energy Trader Pleads Guilty*, N.Y. TIMES, Feb. 5, 2003, at C2; Rebecca Smith and John R. Emshwiller, *Prosecutors Probe Skilling's Role in Enron's Failed Telecom Venture*, WALL ST. J., Dec. 13, 2002, at A1 (reporting that federal prosecutors are investigating fraud in connection with Enron's high-speed communications business).

[10] *See* David Stout, *Washington Talk: For Candidates, Crimes Are Now Wearing White*, N.Y. TIMES, Sept. 5, 2002, at A15 (noting that politicians of both parties agreed on what to do: punish the wrongdoers).

Part II reveals that their most significant feature is severe prison terms. Will enhanced criminal penalties be any more effective in preventing corporate crime than were the previously existing sanctions?

In an effort to answer that question, Part III presents the two primary theories of law-abiding behavior, the rational choice and the unconscious instinct models, and discusses their inherent limitations. The rational choice model is limited because biased judgment can impair the calculation that measures risk of punishment. The unconscious instinct model is limited because competing social values of subgroups, such as a corporate culture, can subvert an instinct to obey the law. The Enron experience illustrates the limitations of each model. The experience demonstrates that, standing alone, criminal law is not a particularly effective means of creating a law-abiding business community.

But the criminal law does not stand alone. In Part IV, I suggest that criminal laws are only one method of monitoring business conduct; private civil suits and government regulatory enforcement actions are also important deterrent mechanisms. Although the criminal law can and should be part of the effort to prevent future Enrons, it is no panacea. For maximum effectiveness, the criminal law is better viewed as one part of a comprehensive scheme that includes private enforcement and government regulation. Each of these enforcement mechanisms should deliver a single, consistent message to the corporate sector that expresses the community's conception of law-abiding behavior in the corporate world.

I. THE CRIMINAL LAW LANDSCAPE BEFORE AND AFTER THE SARBANES-OXLEY ACT

Published reports and criminal indictments indicate that at least some of the misconduct at Enron and other firms violated existing federal criminal laws. These laws carried substantial prison terms and fines. Thus far, the indictments indicate that prosecutors are relying on familiar criminal laws that are often applied to white-collar crimes. For instance, Andrew Fastow, the former Chief Financial Officer of Enron, is charged with committing wire fraud, money laundering, and obstruction of justice, as well as conspiracy to commit wire fraud, securities fraud, and money laundering.[11]

These offenses trace a typical trajectory that centers on providing misleading and material information to others with intent to defraud them. This conduct motivates a course of other criminal violations. For instance, when a fraudulent scheme is undertaken by more than one person, it is often preceded by an agreement to defraud, which implicates the conspiracy statute.[12] The fraud may be followed by attempts to conceal

---

[11] *See* Indictment of Andrew S. Fastow, filed in the U.S. District Court, Southern District of Texas, Oct. 31, 2002 (listing charges of 18 U.S.C. § 371 (2001) (conspiracy); 18 U.S.C. § 1343 (2001) (wire fraud); 18 U.S.C. §§ 1956 & 1957 (2001) (money laundering); 18 U.S.C. § 1512(b) (2001) (obstruction of justice)).

[12] *See* 18 U.S.C. § 371 (2001).

evidence from investigators, leading to violations of obstruction of justice statutes.[13] Finally, the offense of money laundering follows completion of the fraud, when actors conceal their proceeds by using or transferring profits gained from the fraud.[14]

Each of the criminal laws just mentioned specifies a maximum term of imprisonment. In addition, convicted felons who obtained pecuniary gain or caused pecuniary loss are subject to criminal fines that are authorized by a separate provision.[15] The amount of the criminal fine depends upon the defendant's gain or the victim's loss; the fine is twice the gain or loss, whichever is greater.[16]

It is commonly assumed that white-collar offenders are not subject to significant penalties.[17] Troubling disparities in sentences between "crimes in the suites" and "crime in the streets" undoubtedly exist.[18] Nevertheless, punishment of white-collar offenders is significantly harsher than the prison terms that were the focus of Edwin Sutherland's critique.[19] Accordingly, a few comments about the federal sentencing scheme for white-collar crimes are instructive before turning to a more detailed discussion of the existing fraud and obstruction statutes.

Penalties for federal crimes are a function of both the particular criminal offense and the Sentencing Guidelines.[20] Although each criminal law specifies maximum punishment, in most cases, the Guidelines largely determine the actual sentence.[21] Since

---

[13] See 18 U.S.C. §§ 1503, 1505, 1512 (2001).

[14] See 18 U.S.C. §§ 1956, 1957 (2001).

Mail and wire fraud, obstruction, and money laundering are predicate acts for Racketeer Influenced and Corrupt Organizations ("RICO") Act charges. See 18 U.S.C. §§ 1961–1968 (2001). Under RICO, forfeiture of real property and financial accounts follow conviction, and in the meantime, defendants' assets are placed in escrow. See 18 U.S.C. § 1963(a).

[15] 18 U.S.C. § 3571(d) (2001). In nonpecuniary crimes, the maximum fine is $250,000 for individuals and $500,000 for corporations. 18 U.S.C. § 3571(b), (c) (2001).

Unless a specific provision indicates otherwise, all Title 18 felonies are subject to this fine provision. 18 U.S.C. § 3571.

[16] 18 U.S.C. § 3571(d).

[17] See Clifton Leaf, White-Collar Criminals: Enough Is Enough, FORTUNE, March 18, 2002, at 60. But see Russ Mitchell, White-Collar Criminal? Pack Lightly for Prison, N.Y. TIMES, Aug. 11, 2002, at BU4 (disputing the notion that major-league white-collar offenders do not face heavy prison time).

[18] For analyses of this discrepancy, see Daryl K. Brown, Street Crime, Corporate Crime, and the Contingency of Criminal Liability, 149 U. PA. L. REV. 1295 (2001); Joseph E. Kennedy, Making the Crime Fit the Punishment, 51 EMORY L.J. 753 (2002).

[19] Sutherland is credited with identifying white-collar crime in 1939. See EDWIN H. SUTHERLAND, WHITE COLLAR CRIME: THE UNCUT VERSION (1983).

[20] See Sentencing Reform Act of 1984, Pub. L. No. 98-473, 98 Stat. 1987 (codified at 18 U.S.C. §§ 3551–3742 (2001) and 28 U.S.C. §§ 991–998 (2001); U.S. SENTENCING GUIDELINES MANUAL, ch. 1, pt. A(3) (2002) (explaining that the Guidelines were formulated to provide greater honesty, uniformity, and proportionality in federal sentencing).

[21] See Mistretta v. United States, 488 U.S. 361 (1989) (upholding constitutionality of guidelines).

the advent of the Guidelines, punishment of federal white-collar offenses has become more serious and more certain.[22] From their inception, the Guidelines took a tough approach to white-collar crime. For example, the Guidelines immediately reduced the possibility of probationary sentences for white-collar offenders.[23] They also increased prison time served by white-collar offenders by ensuring that guideline sentences exceeded the average prison time imposed in the pre-Guideline era.[24]

Moreover, under the Guidelines, judges have far less sentencing discretion,[25] which may have led in the past to lighter sentences for middle class offenders. Certain factors that would normally operate to reduce the prison terms of white-collar offenders, such as community service and family responsibilities, are considered irrelevant in determining the Guideline sentence.[26] Although judges may depart from that sentence,[27] they may not use an offender characteristic, such as age or family responsibility, unless it "is present to an unusual degree."[28] In 2001, the sentencing scheme was modified to

---

[22] *See generally* Frank O. Bowman, III, *The Quality of Mercy Must Be Restrained, and Other Lessons in Learning to Love the Federal Sentencing Guidelines,* 1996 WIS. L. REV. 679; Stephen Breyer, *The Federal Sentencing Guidelines and the Key Compromises Upon Which They Rest,* 17 HOFSTRA L. REV. 1 (1998); Kate Stith & Steve Y. Koh, *The Politics of Sentencing Reform: The Legislative History of the Federal Sentencing Guidelines,* 28 WAKE FOREST L. REV. 223 (1993).

[23] *See* U.S. SENTENCING GUIDELINES MANUAL, § 1A(4)(d) (2002) (noting in the policy statement that the Commission purposely wrote guidelines that treat white collar offenses, such as tax evasion, antitrust violations, insider trading, and fraud, as serious offenses that justify prison terms rather than probation).

[24] To arrive at its initial sentencing scheme, the Commission surveyed existing sentencing practices and used average sentences to compile new guideline sentences. *See* Bowman, *supra* note 22, at 733–34 (noting that the Commission attempted to discover the federal common law of sentencing and to codify it, rather than to determine what the penalty for an offense should be). White-collar crimes were treated differently. Instead of basing sentences on past practices, for white-collar crimes the Commission prescribed substantial increases over average prior sentences. *See* Mistretta v. United States, 488 U.S. 361, 413–424 (1989) (Scalia, J., dissenting) (providing examples of public corruption, antitrust violations, and tax evasion).

[25] The discretion of prosecutors, however, is enhanced by the Guidelines. Prosecutors decide what charges will be brought and also play a role in recommending a prison sentence. *See* Gerard Lynch, *The Role of Criminal Law in Policing Corporate Misconduct,* 60 LAW & CONTEMP. PROBS. 23, 56 (1997) (discussing current role of prosecutors).

[26] *See* U.S. SENTENCING GUIDELINES MANUAL § 5H1.1 (2002) (stating that age may not be considered); *id.* at § 5H2.1 (educational skills); *id.* at § 5H1.5 (employment record); *id.* at § 5H1.6 (family ties and responsibilities and community ties); *id.* at § 5H1.10 (socio-economic status); *id.* at § 5H1.11 (2002) (military, civic, charitable, or public service; employment-related contributions; record of prior good works).

[27] *See, e.g., id.* at § 5K2.0 (2002) (Grounds for Departure); *see also* Koon v. United States, 518 U.S. 81, 110–11 (1996) (providing guidance on when departure from the Guideline range of punishment is appropriate).

[28] *See* U.S. SENTENCING GUIDELINES MANUAL § 5K2.0 (2002) (policy statement); *see also Koon,* 518 U.S. at 98.

increase sentences of white-collar offenders who cause great pecuniary harm.[29] Thus, before passage of the Sarbanes-Oxley Act, those who committed federal white-collar crimes faced significant prison sentences and criminal fines. The failure of these penalties to deter business misconduct raises the issue of whether increasing criminal penalties is an effective mechanism for preventing corporate crimes.

To begin that analysis, the following discussion reviews three of the crimes implicated in recent scandals: mail fraud, securities fraud, and obstruction of justice. It also notes how the Sarbanes-Oxley Act changes the white-collar crime landscape. The discussion ends with an evaluation of the criminal provisions of Sarbanes-Oxley.

A. Mail and Wire Fraud

Fraud, which courts have historically regarded as particularly iniquitous,[30] is the heart of most white-collar offenses. Fraud is synonymous with dishonesty, disloyalty, and a disregard for ethical standards of conduct; it is inherently dishonorable, marked as it is by secrecy, lies, and betrayal.[31] In both the civil and criminal context, the main component of fraud is a deceit.[32] Two federal criminal laws generally prohibit fraud in the private sector.

1. Mail Fraud Before the Sarbanes-Oxley Act

The mail and wire fraud statutes apply to fraudulent schemes that involve a mailing or an electronic transmission and that are intended to harm another person or entity.[33]

---

[29] Among other changes, the Commission modified the loss table, which is the major determinant of the offense level and thus the ultimate prison term. *See* U.S. SENTENCING GUIDELINES MANUAL § 2B1.1 (2002).

The new guidelines provide a more comprehensive definition of monetary loss: all losses that the defendant knew or reasonably should have known were a potential result of the offense in the loss calculation. *See* U.S. SENTENCING GUIDELINES MANUAL § 2B1.1, cmt n. 2 (2002).

[30] *See* Geraldine Szott Moohr, *Federal Fraud and the Development of Intangible Property Rights in Information*, 2000 U. ILL. L. REV. 683, 689 n.31 (2000) (presenting judicial characterization of fraud).

[31] *See id.* at 689 (noting that fraud often requires the victim's participation).

[32] *See* MELVILLE M. BIGELOW, THE LAW OF FRAUD AND THE PROCEDURE PERTAINING TO THE REDRESS THEREOF 92 (1887) ("All fraud, properly speaking, involves something of deceit. A truly fraudulent act cannot be committed without the practice of deception.").

[33] 18 U.S.C. §§ 1341, 1343, 1346 (2001).

The mail and wire fraud statutes are interpreted jointly, so decisions under one statute apply to the other. *See* United States v. Fermin Castillo, 829 F.2d 1194, 1198 (1st Cir. 1987). If a fraud involves mailing by the post office or through an interstate private carrier, mail fraud is charged; if it involves the use of wire or electronic transmission, wire fraud is charged. For convenience, the term "mail fraud" as used herein includes both offenses.

Reflecting its breadth and power, mail fraud has attracted a significant body of commentary. For a useful bibliography, see Ellen S. Podgor, *Mail Fraud: Redefining the Boundaries*, 10 ST. THOMAS L. REV. 557 (1998).

Victims may sustain a loss of money, property, or honest services that are owed by the offending actor.[34] Mail fraud is written broadly and has been expansively interpreted so the offense now encompasses an extraordinarily wide range of deceptive conduct.[35] As one would expect, the statute is a favorite and much-used tool of federal prosecutors.[36]

The elements of the federal fraud offense are (1) devising or participating in a scheme to defraud; (2) commission of the act with intent to defraud; and (3) use of the mails or wires in furtherance of the fraudulent scheme.[37] Although use of the mails or wires would seem to limit applicability of the offense, that is not the case. It is not difficult to establish that the defendant mailed or caused a mailing, wire, or electronic transmission for the purposes of executing the fraud.[38]

The statute prohibits "devising" a scheme to defraud, so the government need not prove that the victim actually sustained a loss. The prosecution must prove, however, that the defendant intended to harm the victim by depriving the victim of money, property, or honest services. Thus, participation in a fraudulent scheme is not a crime unless it was devised with the specific purpose of defrauding another person. An aggressive business deal is not criminal even if a person recklessly disregarded the risk that the scheme will deprive another of money or property. Nor is taking advantage of accounting standards, or even gaming those standards, a crime unless undertaken with intent to defraud another person or entity. Although the intent element is often cited as a significant hurdle to conviction, this is not necessarily the case. Factfinders may use circumstantial evidence to infer culpability.[39] The task is made easier when actual

---

[34] 18 U.S.C. § 1346.

[35] *See* United States v. Handakas, 286 F.3d 92, 101–03 (2d Cir. 2002) (tracing development of the mail fraud statute); Roger J. Miner, *Federal Court, Federal Crimes, and Federalism,* 101 HARV. J. L. & PUB. POL'Y 117, 121 (1987) (stating that the mail fraud statute is a "vehicle for the prosecution of an almost unlimited number of offenses").

[36] *See Handakas,* 286 F. 3d at 108 (describing mail fraud as an "all purpose prosecutorial expedient"); John C. Coffee, Jr., *From Tort to Crime: Some Reflections on the Criminalization of Fiduciary Breaches and the Problematic Line Between Law and Ethics,* 19 AM. CRIM. L. REV. 117, 126 (1981) (quoting prosecutor's maxim, "when in doubt, charge mail fraud"); John C. Coffee, Jr., *The Metastasis of Mail Fraud: The Continuing Story of the "Evolution" of a White-Collar Crime,* 21 AM. CRIM. L. REV. 1, 3 (1983) (arguing that mail fraud statute "seems to provide the federal prosecutor with what Archimedes long sought—a simple fulcrum from which one can move the world"); Jed S. Rakoff, *The Federal Mail Fraud Statute (Part I),* 18 DUQ. L. REV. 771, 771 (1980) (noting prosecutors' reference to the statute as "our Stradivarius, our Colt 45, our Louisville Slugger, our Cuisinart").

[37] *See* Emery v. American General Finance, Inc., 71 F.3d 1343, 1349 (7th Cir. 1995); *see also* United States v. Altman, 48 F.3d 96, 101 (2d Cir. 1995); United States v. Walker, 9 F.3d 1245, 1249 (7th Cir. 1993).

[38] *See* Schmuck v. United States, 489 U.S. 705, 715 (1989) (stating the issue is whether the mailing is part of the execution of the scheme as conceived by the perpetrator); Peter J. Henning, *Maybe it Should Just Be Called Federal Fraud: The Changing Nature of the Mail Fraud Statute,* 36 B.C. L. REV. 435 (1995).

[39] *See* United States v. Berndt, 86 F.3d 803, 809 (8th Cir. 1996); United States v. Behr, 33 F.3d 1033, 1035 (8th Cir. 1994); United States v. Hatch, 926 F.2d 387, 396 (5th Cir. 1991).

loss occurs because evidence of loss or gain creates an inference of a specific intent to defraud.[40] On the other hand, proving intent is more problematic when an attempted scheme would not necessarily result in loss.[41]

2. Mail Fraud After the Sarbanes-Oxley Act

In testament to the effectiveness of the mail and wire fraud statutes, Congress did not alter the substantive elements of mail and wire fraud. The Sarbanes-Oxley Act does, however, drastically increase penalties of these crimes. It increases by four times the maximum penalty for mail and wire fraud, from five to twenty years in prison.[42] The Sarbanes-Oxley Act also makes clear that the penalty for conspiracy to and attempt to commit fraud is the same as the penalty for the fraud that is the object of the conspiracy.[43]

B. Securities Fraud

Securities fraud is a specialized kind of fraud that applies to misrepresentations made when issuing or trading securities. After the stock market crash of 1929, the securities laws were enacted in an effort to restore confidence in the stock market and thereby to encourage investment. The type of securities fraud dealt with here is prohibited by the Securities Exchange Act of 1934, which governs trades in secondary markets and sales of already-issued securities.[44] The law is enforced through government regulatory actions, implied private causes of action, and the criminal law.

1. Insider Trading Before the Sarbanes-Oxley Act

The Exchange Act prohibits the use of manipulative and deceptive devices in connection with the purchase or sale of a security.[45] Rule 10b-5, authorized by the Act,

---

[40] *See* United States v. D'Amato, 39 F.3d 1249, 1257 (2d Cir. 1994); *see generally* Geraldine Szott Moohr, *Mail Fraud Meets Criminal Theory*, 67 U. CIN. L. REV. 1 (1998).

[41] *See D'Amato*, 39 F.3d at 1257.

[42] *See* Sarbanes-Oxley Act of 2002 § 903 (codified at 18 U.S.C. §§ 1341, 1343 (West Supp. 2002)). The maximum penalty for these fraud offenses was five years.

[43] *See* Sarbanes-Oxley Act of 2002 § 902(a) (codified at 18 U.S.C. § 1349 (West Supp. 2002)). The provision applies to all Chapter 63 frauds, which include bank fraud, health care fraud, and the new securities fraud provision, as well as mail and wire fraud. *See* 18 U.S.C. § 1344 (2001) (bank fraud); *id.* at § 1347 (health care fraud); *id.* at § 1348 (securities fraud).

[44] *See* Securities Exchange Act of 1934, 15 U.S.C. §§ 78a–78ll (2001). The Securities Act of 1933 regulates registering and issuing securities in the primary market and requires full disclosure by companies that sell securities and also contains a criminal provision. *See* Securities Act of 1933, 15 U.S.C. §§ 77a– 77aa (2001).

[45] *See* 15 U.S.C. § 78j(b) (2001). Section 10(b) of the Act provides:

It shall be unlawful for any person, directly or indirectly, by the use of any means or instrumentality of interstate commerce or of the mails, or of any facility of any national securities exchange—

provides more specific prohibitions, such as making any untrue statement of a material fact in connection with a securities trade.[46] Actors who willfully violate the statute or the rules adopted pursuant to it are subject to criminal penalties.[47] The Department of Justice has sole authority to bring criminal charges,[48] but depends on the Securities Exchange Commission ("SEC") for referrals.

Perhaps the most common type of criminal securities fraud involves insider trading.[49] Classic insider trading occurs when an insider, such as an executive of the company, uses information that is not available to the public to buy or sell a security of that company. Acting in breach of a fiduciary duty to shareholders, the failure to disclose that material information to buyers or sellers is considered a "deceptive device."[50] Under a recent Supreme Court decision, those who do not have a fiduciary obligation that runs to the buyers or sellers in the trade may also violate insider trading rules.[51] Insider trading now applies to a person who violates a duty that he or she owes to the source of the nonpublic information and thus includes "outsiders."[52]

In addition to identifying a proper defendant and establishing that the conduct at issue involved interstate commerce, the government must prove that the accused possessed and used material, nonpublic information in a securities trade, and that he acted willfully. Willfulness has been defined as a deliberate and intentional act that

(b) To use or employ, in connection with the purchase or sale of any security registered on a national securities exchange or any security not so registered, any manipulative or deceptive device or contrivance in contravention of such rules and regulations as the Commission may prescribe as necessary or appropriate in the public interest or for the protection of investors.

15 U.S.C. § 78j(b).

[46] Rule 10b-6 provides:

It shall be unlawful for any person, directly or indirectly, by the use of any means or instrumentality of interstate commerce, or of the mails or any facility of any national securities exchange,
(a) To employ any device, scheme, or artifice to defraud,
(b) To make any untrue statement of a material fact or to omit to state any such fact to make the statement not misleading, or
(c) To engage in any act, practice, or course of business which operates or would operate as a fraud or deceit upon any person, in connection with the purchase or sale of any security.

17 C.F.R. § 240.10b-5 (2002).

[47] 15 U.S.C. § 78ff(a) (2001).

[48] Criminal actions are within the exclusive control of the Justice Department. *See* 17 C.F.R. § 202.5(f) (2002). The SEC may bring civil or administrative actions. *See* Securities Exchange Act of 1934 , 15 U.S.C. § 78u-3 (2001).

[49] *See* Lynch, *supra* note 25, at 33 n.31 (remarking on the number of insider trading prosecutions).

[50] *See* Chiarella v. United States, 445 U.S. 222, 228 (1980).

Courts have held that fiduciary duties run to buyers as well as to sellers of stock on the ground that buyers are prospective shareholders. *See* United States v. Chestman, 947 F.2d 551, 565 n.2 (2d Cir. 1991). Tippees of insiders and temporary insiders, such as attorneys, may also violate insider trading rules. *Id.* at 565.

[51] *See* United States v. O'Hagan, 521 U.S. 642 (1997).

[52] *Id.*

encompasses fraudulent intent.[53] Violators are subject to fines and a maximum penalty of ten years in prison.[54]

2. Insider Trading After the Sarbanes-Oxley Act

Without otherwise disturbing this prohibition, Sarbanes-Oxley altered the penalty scheme of the Exchange Act crime: the maximum penalty of ten years in prison was doubled to twenty years; maximum fines for individuals were increased from one million to five million dollars.[55]

In a more significant change, the Act inserted a securities fraud provision into the federal criminal code.[56] The provision prohibits the knowing execution (or attempt to execute) of "a scheme or artifice to defraud any person in connection with any security" of a registered or reporting company.[57] The maximum prison term is twenty-five years. The new provision provides prosecutors with greater flexibility and allows them to operate independently of the SEC.[58] It applies to frauds that are merely in "connection with any security," rather than being restricted to frauds in sales or purchases.[59] The culpability element of the new securities fraud offense requires knowledge, as opposed to the higher standard of willfulness of the securities laws.[60] Finally, the new provision is intended to have a broader application than those offenses, signaled by its text that mirrors the language of expansively interpreted fraud statutes.

C. Obstruction of Justice

The federal criminal code addresses obstruction of justice in several independent and overlapping provisions.[61] The common purpose of the obstruction statutes is to

---

[53] *See* Ernst & Ernst v. Hochfelder, 425 U.S. 185 (1976).

The definition varies somewhat between circuits. *See* United States v. Weiner, 578 F.2d 757 (9th Cir. 1978) (defining willfulness as reckless indifference to or disregard for truth); United States v. Langford, 946 F.2d 798 (11th Cir. 1991) (defining willfulness as deliberate ignorance of truth); *see also* William H. Kuehnle, *On Scienter, Knowledge, and Recklessness Under the Federal Securities Laws*, 34 HOUS. L. REV. 121 (1997).

[54] 15 U.S.C. § 78ff(a) (2001).

[55] *See* Sarbanes-Oxley Act of 2002 § 1106 (codified at 15 U.S.C. § 78ff (West Supp. 2002)) (authorizing maximum fine for corporations of $25 million).

[56] *See* Sarbanes-Oxley Act of 2002 § 807 (codified at 18 U.S.C. § 1348 (West Supp. 2002)).

[57] 15 U.S.C. § 1348(1) (2001). The provision also includes a "false pretense" subsection that bars obtaining money or property by means of false pretenses in connection with the purchase or sale of a registered or reporting company. 15 U.S.C. § 1348(2).

[58] *See* 148 CONG. REC. S7421 (daily ed. July 26, 2002) (statement of Sen. Leahy that the bill creates a "more general and less technical provision" that is "intended to provide needed enforcement flexibility").

[59] Note that the new provision is somewhat narrower in that it applies only to registered securities or those of issuers required to file reports with the SEC. 18 U.S.C. § 1348 (2001).

[60] This standard may be the operational equivalent of willfulness in some circuits. *See supra* note 53.

[61] *See e.g.*, 18 U.S.C. §§ 1503, 1505, 1510, 1512 (2001).

protect the integrity of judicial, administrative, and legislative proceedings. Accordingly, the provisions ban altering or destroying documents, offering or promoting false testimony, and threatening or influencing witnesses, jurors, and court officials.[62] Like perjury and false statements, obstruction is a "cover-up" crime that arises from an attempt to conceal evidence of earlier illegal activity.

1. Obstructing Justice Before the Sarbanes-Oxley Act

The obstruction offense of which the firm Arthur Andersen was convicted generally prohibits interfering or tampering with witnesses, victims, or informants.[63] Among other acts, section 1512(b) prohibits "corruptly persuading" another person to alter, destroy, mutilate or conceal an object with intent to impair the object's integrity or availability for use in an official proceeding.[64] The culpability element, "corruptly persuading," exists when the actor is motivated by an inappropriate or improper purpose to convince someone else to obstruct justice.[65] An "official proceeding" is any proceeding before a federal court or grand jury, Congressional hearing, or federal agency.[66] In Andersen's case, the proceeding was an announced SEC investigation. The maximum punishment authorized by section 1512(b) was, until passage of Sarbanes-Oxley, ten years in prison and/or statutory fines.

2. Obstructing Justice After the Sarbanes-Oxley Act

In reaction to the wholesale shredding at Enron by the Andersen auditors, Congress added three new laws prohibiting conduct that undermines government investigations. First, Sarbanes-Oxley amends the obstruction statute under which Duncan and Andersen were convicted so that it now applies to those individuals who actually destroyed documents. This provision thus moves beyond witness tampering and corruptly persuading. Specifically applying to documents, the new provision makes it a crime for anyone to corruptly alter, destroy, mutilate, or conceal a record or document with intent to impair its use in an official proceeding.[67] In the Duncan/Andersen scenario, those employees who corruptly shredded documents would now be liable for criminal punishment. Violators are subject to statutory fines and a maximum term of twenty years in prison—twice the term of the Duncan/Andersen offense.

---

[62] In addition to banning specific obstructive conduct, the statutes contain broad omnibus clauses that bar any endeavor to interfere with the judicial system. *See* 18 U.S.C. §§ 1503, 1505; United States v. Aguilar, 515 U.S. 593, 598 (1995) (noting that the omnibus clause of section 1503 "serves as a catchall, prohibiting persons from endeavoring to influence, obstruct, or impede the due administration of justice").

[63] *See* 18 U.S.C. § 1512.

[64] *See* 18 U.S.C. § 1512(b)(2)(B). Subsection (b) also applies to witness testimony. *Id.*

[65] *See* United States v. Khatami, 280 F.3d 907, 911–12 (9th Cir. 2001).

[66] *See* 18 U.S.C. § 1515(a)(1) (2001).

[67] *See* Sarbanes-Oxley Act of 2002 § 1102 (codified at 18 U.S.C. § 1512(c) (West Supp. 2002)). The provision also contains an omnibus provision. 18 U.S.C. § 1512(c)(2).

Sarbanes-Oxley also adds two independent obstruction provisions to the federal criminal code. One new provision creates the crime of obstructing a federal investigation of "any matter" and specifically includes bankruptcy proceedings.[68] Prosecutors must establish two culpability elements, that the accused knowingly acted—altered, destroyed, etc.—and acted with an intent to impede, obstruct, or influence a federal investigation. Violators are subject to fines and a maximum of twenty years in prison. Its application to *any* kind of document and *any* matter in a greater range of investigations adds considerably more breadth to the document provisions.

Finally, a second independent obstruction provision requires "any accountant" to maintain audit documents and workpapers for five years.[69] Knowing and willful violations of this obligation subject the actor to fines and/or up to ten years in prison.[70] The prohibition is not contingent on an investigation or official proceeding, but is a flat directive to maintain documents, and is enforced through criminal sanctions.

The new obstruction statutes differ from one another and from existing provisions in their culpability elements, the inclusion of attempts, and character of the proceeding. Nevertheless, there is significant overlap between these offenses, and their ultimate usefulness is uncertain.

D. Sarbanes-Oxley's New Obligations

The criminal provisions discussed thus far cannot be characterized as "new" in the sense of imposing different obligations on businesspersons and corporations. The Sarbanes-Oxley Act does, however, create two obligations that have not been directly subject to criminal enforcement. First, chief executives and chief financial officers must personally certify that reports filed with the SEC comply with regulatory requirements.[71] An executive who knowingly certifies financial statements that do not fairly

---

[68] Sarbanes-Oxley Act of 2002 § 802 (codified at 18 U.S.C. § 1519 (West Supp. 2002)).

Whoever knowingly alters, destroys, mutilates, conceals, covers up, falsifies, or makes a false entry in any record, document, or tangible object with the intent to impede, obstruct, or influence the investigation or proper administration of any matter within the jurisdiction of any department or agency of the United States or any case filed under title 11, or in relation to or contemplation of any matter or case, shall be fined under this title, imprisoned not more than 20 years, or both.

18 U.S.C. § 1519 (2001).

[69] *See* Sarbanes-Oxley Act of 2002 § 802 (codified at 18 U.S.C. § 1520 (West Supp. 2002)).

[70] *Id.* The criminal provision includes violating rules promulgated by the SEC to implement the obligation. 18 U.S.C. § 1520(a)(2) (2001).

[71] *See* Sarbanes-Oxley Act of 2002 § 906 (codified at 18 U.S.C. § 1350 (West Supp. 2002)).

Before passage of Sarbanes-Oxley, executives could be liable for inaccurate financial reports under a fraud theory. *See* Howard v. Everex Corp., 228 F.3d 1057 (9th Cir. 2000) (holding that CEO who signed an inaccurate SEC filing was liable under § 10(b)). The Securities Act of 1933 also requires corporate officers to sign registration statements and provides a cause of action if the statements are misleading. Securities Act of 1933, 15 U.S.C. §§ 77f–77h (2001).

present the firm's financial condition is subject to maximum fines of one million dollars and prison terms of ten years, or both. When the executive acts willfully, maximum penalties are increased to five million dollars and twenty years in prison.

The second new obligation created by Sarbanes-Oxley protects employees who report wrongful conduct internally or to external investigators.[72] Under the Act, whistleblowers may file civil suits for damages resulting from retaliatory acts.[73] Moreover, executives who knowingly and intentionally retaliate against whistleblowers are subject to criminal fines and a maximum of ten years in prison.[74] This provision is intended to encourage employees to inform federal agencies and internal gatekeepers about suspected wrongful conduct. Accordingly, it provides attorneys' fees to informers to aid in enforcing the new right.

Nevertheless, the new provision may not be as effective at encouraging whistleblowing as it might have been.[75] Congress provided no incentive, such as a financial reward or punitive damages, that would stimulate reporting.[76] Moreover, claims must be brought within a short ninety days of the retaliatory act.[77]

II. AN EVALUATION OF SARBANES-OXLEY'S CRIMINAL PROVISIONS

The Sarbanes-Oxley Act was enacted to protect investors by improving the accuracy and reliability of corporate disclosures relating to securities laws.[78] Enacted in

---

[72] See Sarbanes-Oxley Act of 2002 §§ 806, 1107 (codified at 18 U.S.C. § 1514A, 1513 (West Supp. 2002)).

[73] See 15 U.S.C. § 1514A (providing cause of action for wage-related damages and special damages such as attorneys fees).

[74] See 18 U.S.C. § 1513(e).

[75] Early reports were not encouraging. See Fawn H. Johnson, *Lawmakers Decry Bush's Interpretation of Whistleblower Protections in New Law*, 34 BNA 1326 (Aug. 12, 2002) (reporting Bush administration's decision to limit applicability of the provision).

[76] In contrast, qui tam actions brought under the False Claims Act provide substantial monetary rewards for whistleblowing. See 31 U.S.C. § 3730 (2001); *see generally* Joan H. Krause, *Health Care Providers and the Public Fisc: Paradigms of Government Harm under the Civil False Claims Act*, 36 GA. L. REV. 121 (2001).

The federal government has recovered $8.7 billion from fraudulent contractors since 1986. See Jack Meyer & Stephanie E. Anthony, *Reducing Health Care Fraud: Assessment of the Impact of the False Claims Act*, *available at* www.taf.org/publications/PDF/reducing.pdf (Taxpayers Against Fraud website).

Following misconduct at savings and loan institutions in the 1980s, rewards for whistleblowers rather than mere protection were recommended. See Maria S. Boss & Barbara Crutchfield George, *Challenging Conventional Views of White Collar Crime*, 28 CRIM. L. BULL. 32, 34 (1992).

[77] See 18 U.S.C. § 1514A.

[78] See Preface, Sarbanes Oxley Act of 2002, Pub. L. No. 107-204, Preface, 116 Stat. 745, 745 (2002).

President Bush characterized the Act as embodying "the most far-reaching reforms of American business practices since the time of Franklin Delano Roosevelt." See Signing Statement of George W. Bush, July 30, 2002, *available at* http://www.whitehouse.gov/news/releases/2002.

haste and out of political expediency,[79] it was an effort to restore confidence in securities markets in a sagging economy. Although the Act focuses on the administrative regulatory scheme, especially as to accounting standards, the criminal law is to play a major role in the effort to eradicate corporate fraud. President Bush emphasized the law's strong criminal component at the signing ceremony: "[There is n]o more easy money for corporate criminals, just hard time."[80] He later reinforced that characterization: "If you're a CEO and you think you can fudge the books in order to make yourselves look better, we're going to find you, we're going to arrest you and we're going to hold you to account."[81]

A. Substantive Criminal Laws and Enforcement

Sarbanes-Oxley did not create radically new substantive offenses or realize genuine change in existing legal standards. Thus one of the more interesting points about Sarbanes-Oxley is what Congress did *not* do.

The standards embodied in the federal fraud statutes were not disturbed; their broad proscription against devising a scheme to defraud already captured a wide range of fraudulent conduct, making it unnecessary to define a new type of fraud. The new securities fraud provision also does not add new substantive law; it is best viewed as codifying the practice endorsed by federal courts that treats securities fraud as a variant of mail or wire fraud offenses. Similarly, the new obstruction provisions refine existing statutes that have been used successfully by prosecutors, as evidenced by the convictions of David Duncan and Arthur Andersen. The new obligations that relate to certification and retaliation against whistleblowers do not address underlying criminal behavior, but deal instead with its aftermath. Thus, Sarbanes-Oxley does not fundamentally change the substantive criminal standards that govern corporate insiders.

Having said that, it would be unwise to underestimate the significance of the criminal provisions. The Act strengthens the enforcement power of Justice Department prosecutors and SEC regulators, and thereby increases the exposure of corporate managers and directors to criminal sanctions. To the extent that the new crimes utilize the lower culpability element of "knowing" conduct rather than "willful" conduct, criminality

---

[79] *See* Robert W. Hamilton, *The Crisis in Corporate Governance: 2002 Style*, 40 HOUS. L. REV. 1, 46 (2003) (noting that neither publicly held corporations, the political parties, nor organizations and individuals interested in matters of corporate governance were able to study or seriously consider the bill).

The administration resisted reform legislation, but in the end supported it in response to reports that the business scandals were eroding the administration's political support. *See* Stephen Labaton, *Handcuffs Make Strange Politics, You Say? But Not in Washington*, N.Y. TIMES, Aug. 2, 2002, at C1 (noting that a public backlash prompted a sharp about-face at the White House).

[80] *See* Signing Statement, *supra* note 78.

[81] *See* Mike Allen, *Bush Pledges More Corporate Fraud Arrests*, WASH. POST, July 30, 2002, at A10.

will be easier to establish at trial.[82] Similarly, the executive certification requirement will make it easier to establish fraudulent conduct if its effect is to eliminate the defenses of lack of knowledge or good faith. Requiring officer certification and encouraging whistleblowers, along with other provisions,[83] should result in an increased flow of information to investigating agencies. Nevertheless, although buttressing enforcement efforts is an important initiative, the major function of the criminal law under Sarbanes-Oxley is to deter future crime through the threat of severe punishment.

B. The Penalty Provisions

The overwhelming characteristic of Sarbanes-Oxley's new criminal provisions is the severity of its prison terms.[84] For the individuals involved, the certification offense has a twenty-year penalty and the whistleblower statute has a ten-year penalty. Similarly, the new obstruction provisions carry ten- and twenty-year terms, an increase of 200% in the offense for which Arthur Andersen was convicted. The penalties for mail and wire fraud were increased by 400%.[85] The maximum prison term for insider trading was increased from ten- to twenty-five years, a 250% increase. Conspiracy to commit such fraud carries twenty and twenty-five year penalties, an increase of at least 400%. In cases of fraud involving pensions, penalties were increased 1000%, the maximum term of imprisonment rising from one year to ten years.[86] These punishment schemes

---

[82] Compare the culpability element of the new securities fraud provision, 18 U.S.C. § 1348, which is acting with knowledge, with the element of willfulness in 15 U.S.C. §§ 18j(b), 78ff.

[83] These criminal provisions work in concert with other sections of the bill. For instance, in addition to the leverage provided by severe penalties, the SEC may also extract cooperation by its authority to order disgorgement and to bar employment opportunities. *See* Sarbanes-Oxley Act of 2002 §§ 305, 306, 307 (2002)).

The goal of information gathering and reporting is also achieved in section 307, which obliges attorneys to disclose suspected wrongdoing. *See* Leslie Griffin, *Whistleblowing in the Business World, in* NANCY B. RAPOPORT & BALA G. DHARAN, ENRON: CORPORATE FIASCOS AND THEIR IMPLICATIONS (2003) (explaining attorney's obligations under Sarbanes-Oxley and SEC rules).

[84] The approach contrasts markedly with amendments to the mail and wire fraud statutes that followed the savings and loan scandals of the 1980s, which increased penalties only for frauds that involved financial institutions. 18 U.S.C. § 1341 (2001) (providing maximum of thirty years in prison and/or fines of up to $1,000,000 for frauds involving a financial institution).

[85] One report sheds light on the fourfold increase in maximum prison terms for mail and wire fraud. In April 2002, the House refused to increase prison sentences for mail and wire fraud. By July, as the scandal and public outrage peaked, the White House successfully urged the Senate to double the maximum sentence to ten years. The House, not to be outdone, then doubled that penalty, resulting in the maximum twenty-year prison term. *See* Joseph F. Savage, Jr., & Stephanie R. Pratt, *Sarbanes-Oxley: New Ways to Solve Old Crimes*, 9 BUS. CRIMES BULL. 1 (Dec. 2002)

[86] *See* Sarbanes-Oxley Act of 2002 § 904 (codified at 29 U.S.C. § 1131 (West Supp. 2002)) (Employee Retirement Income Security Act). Criminal fines are increased from $5,000 to $100,000 and, in the case of organizations, from $100,000 to $500,000. *Id.*

are comparable to such heinous crimes as attempted murder, which carries a maximum of twenty years in prison; torture, which carries a maximum punishment of twenty years, and sexual abuse of a minor, which carries a maximum punishment of fifteen years.[87]

The extraordinarily severe penalties of Sarbanes-Oxley are a telling indication of the depth of public outrage and the seriousness with which the community regards fraud and other corporate misconduct. But how likely is it that more severe penalties will deter similar conduct in the future? Raising prison terms by 400% is unlikely to result in a 400% increase in deterrence; at best, it will result in some marginal degree of deterrence.[88] Moreover, raising prison terms may have no effect at all. As a former SEC official remarked, "[i]f they're willing to risk five years, they're going to risk 10 years."[89]

The criminal charges brought thus far against Enron executives demonstrate that there was no scarcity of criminal laws "on the books." The federal fraud statutes are universally recognized as flexible tools that offer inclusive and comprehensive application. Penalties for fraud and obstruction, while not as draconian as sanctions under Sarbanes-Oxley, were already significant, especially when coupled with money laundering and RICO charges. Finally, the Sentencing Guidelines ensure a certain term of imprisonment.[90]

---

[87] 18 U.S.C. § 1113 (2001) (attempted murder, maximum of twenty years in prison); 18 U.S.C. § 2340A (2001) (torture, twenty years); 18 U.S.C. § 2243 (2001) (sexual abuse of a minor, fifteen years). *See also* 18 U.S.C. § 111 (2001) (assault of certain officers or government employees with a deadly weapon, ten years) and 18 U.S.C. § 1112 (2001) (voluntary manslaughter, ten years).

As Ira Lee Sorkin, former federal prosecutor and director of the New York office of the SEC, put it: "If a CEO commits a willful fraud, he can get 25 years. If he commits manslaughter, he's going to get 15." *See* Alex Berenson, *A U.S. Push on Accounting Fraud*, N.Y. TIMES, April 9, 2003, at C1.

[88] The magnitude of effect is measured not only by time in jail, but also by other factors such as age. Consider a thirty-year-old felon who is expected to live to age eighty. With a 5-year sentence, the thirty year old will have 45 free years of life. With a 20-year sentence, our felon can expect 30 free years, or two-thirds as much. In contrast, a fifty-year old serving a five-year sentence would have 25 free years, while a 20-year sentence would allow only 10 free years. I am grateful to Roger Sherman, Professor of Economics, University of Houston, who provided this example. *See also* A. Mitchell Polinsky & Steven Shavell, *On the Disutility and Discounting of Imprisonment and the Theory of Deterrence*, 28 J. LEG. STUD. 1 (1999) (explaining that cost of imprisonment to the offender declines over time).

[89] Marcia Coyle, *Tough New Laws—Substance or Show?*, NAT'L L. J., July 22, 2002, at A1; *see also* Floyd Norris, *How Pitt Could Make Fraud Less Tempting*, N.Y. TIMES, July 7, 2002, at C1 (writing that "the possibility of long prison terms won't end corporate fraud any more than it has halted the sale of heroin").

These common sense notions are corroborated by research. *See* Erling Eide, *Economics of Criminal Behavior*, *in* V ENCYCLOPEDIA OF LAW AND ECONOMICS 345, 352–55 (Boudewijn Bouckaert & Gerrit De Geest, eds. 2000) (presenting various explanations of criminal behavior).

[90] *See supra* text accompanying notes 20–29 (discussing Guidelines).

The Sentencing Commission has issued temporary guidelines and called for comments before permanently adopting them in November 2003. *See* Press Release, U.S. Sentencing Commission, Sentencing Commission Stiffens Penalties for White Collar Criminals (Jan. 8, 2003), *available at* http://www.ussc.gov/PRESS/re1010803.htm.

To avoid an unintended result of skewing penalties for those frauds that do not result in widespread harm, the temporary guidelines resist an overall increase in penalties for fraud. See Eric Lichtblau, *Panel*

Yet longstanding federal criminal laws, substantial penalties, and increased certainty of punishment did not deter serious business misconduct at an astonishing number of corporations. Wrongdoers were not deterred by the possibility of contact with the criminal justice system's enforcement agents and mechanisms—judges, prosecutors, police officers, courtrooms, fingerprinting, perp walks, and bail hearings. Nor were they deterred by the stigma and societal condemnation that attaches to a felony conviction or even to an indictment.[91] Instead, they forfeited their reputations and their standing in the local and national business community. This evidence suggests that penal sanctions alone will not prevent future Enrons. With these considerations in place, the following discussion surveys the role of criminal law in encouraging law-abiding behavior and applies those models of law-abiding behavior to the corporate setting.

III. USING CRIMINAL LAW TO ENCOURAGE LAW-ABIDING BUSINESS CONDUCT

Criminal law is thought to encourage law-abiding behavior in two ways: people either comply with the law after a conscious evaluation of the risks of disobeying it, or they comply out of an unconscious instinct to obey the law. The two models are counterposed as external or internal control mechanisms, as instrumental or normative, and as based on self-interest or on moral values. In the case of Enron, neither conscious calculation nor unconscious instinct appears to have operated to prevent harmful and immoral conduct.

A. A Conscious Choice to Obey the Law

The rational choice theory of law-abiding behavior suggests that people comply with the law because they decide, after a calculation of the likely costs and benefits of the crime, to forego the criminal conduct.[92] This calculation of risk includes the like-

---

Clears Harsher Terms in Corporate Crime Cases, N.Y. TIMES, Jan. 9, 2003, at C1 (noting that the measures raise penalties for frauds involving great sums of money).

This approach has been criticized by the Justice Department, which is aggressively lobbying for a more comprehensive overall increase in the penalty scheme for fraud. *See* Eric Lichtblau, *U.S. Is Seeking Stern Penalties in White-Collar Criminal Cases*, N.Y. TIMES, Dec. 19, 2002, at C1.

[91] As a colleague wryly remarked on the day the *Houston Chronicle*'s front page featured a picture of Andrew Fastow in handcuffs, "How much would it be worth to keep your son from seeing that?"

Reputations are not always destroyed by felony convictions. *See* John Markoff, *Poindexter's Still a Technocrat, Still a Lightning Rod*, N.Y. TIMES, Jan. 20, 2003, at C1 (reporting that Poindexter, convicted on five felony counts that were overturned on procedural grounds, is currently heading the Pentagon's Total Information Awareness project).

[92] This utilitarian theory rests on the work of Jeremy Bentham and is associated with law and economics scholars. *See generally* Gary S. Becker, *Crime and Punishment: An Economic Approach*, 76 J. POL. ECON. 169 (1968); Kenneth G. Dau-Schmidt, *An Economic Analysis of Criminal Law as a Preference-Shaping Policy*, 1990 DUKE L.J. 1; Richard A. Posner, *An Economic Theory of the Criminal Law*, 85 COLUM. L. REV. 1193 (1985); Steven Shavell, *Criminal Law and the Optimal Use of Nonmonetary Sanctions as a Deterrent*, 85 COLUM. L. REV. 1232 (1985).

lihood of being caught and the severity of punishment. To achieve an optimal level of deterrence, the community could increase enforcement efforts, thus increasing the likelihood of detection. Or the community could theoretically achieve the same level of prevention by increasing penalties of those who were caught and convicted.[93] Although it may be less expensive to choose severe penalties over enforcement, this strategy is less than fair because it intends that only some offenders will be punished. The severe penalties of the Sarbanes-Oxley criminal provisions appear to reflect the core proposition that increasing the severity of the penalty is an efficient and effective way to deter future crime.

The role played by the criminal law in this model is frankly coercive: law-abiding behavior is achieved through threats of punishment and disgrace. Research supports the suggestion that behavior may be shaped to some degree by estimates of the likelihood and severity of punishment.[94] Other studies suggest, however, that the calculation has only a minor influence, and that law-abiding behavior is only weakly linked to the risk of punishment.[95] The following discussion reviews refinements to the rational choice theory and certain characteristics of white-collar crime, both of which reveal that increasing the severity of criminal penalties may not deter business misconduct.

1. A More Complete Rational Choice Model

The rational choice theory of law-abiding behavior has some resonance in the area of business crime.[96] Crimes such as fraud typically require advance planning, which provides an opportunity for reflection and an assessment of the risk of detection and punishment.[97] Yet the individuals at Enron apparently never made that calculation or,

---

[93] See A. Mitchell Polinsky & Steven Shavell, *Public Enforcement of Law*, in V ENCYCLOPEDIA OF LAW & ECONOMICS 307 (Boudewijn Bouckaert & Gerrit De Geest, eds. 2000).

[94] See, e.g., Michael K. Block & Robert C. Lind, *An Economic Analysis of Crimes Punishable by Imprisonment*, 4 J. LEGAL STUD. 479 (1975).

[95] See Tom R. Tyler & John M. Darley, *Building a Law-Abiding Society: Taking Public Views About Morality and the Legitimacy of Legal Authorities into Account When Formulating Substantive Law*, 28 HOFSTRA L. REV. 707, 712–13 (2000) (summarizing research results).

[96] See Sally S. Simpson & Nicole Leper Piquero, *Low Self-Control, Organizational Theory, and Corporate Crime*, 36 LAW & SOC'Y REV. 509, 539–43 (2002) (providing extensive bibliography of studies applying the theory to white collar and corporate crime).

For other articles that focus on punishment of white-collar criminals, see generally Dan M. Kahan & Eric A. Posner, *Shaming White-Collar Criminals: A Proposal for Reform of the Federal Sentencing Guidelines*, 42 J.L. & ECON. 365 (1999); John R. Lott, Jr., *Do We Punish High Income Criminals Too Heavily?*, 30 ECON. INQUIRY 583 (1992); Richard A. Posner, *Optimal Sentences for White-Collar Criminals*, 17 AM. CRIM. L. REV. 409 (1980); Joel Waldfogel, *Are Fines and Prison Terms Used Efficiently? Evidence on Federal Fraud Offenders*, 38 J.L. & ECON. 107 (1995).

[97] See Brown, *supra* note 18, at 1325 (noting that deterrence theory seems appropriate in context of corporate wrongdoing); Lynch, *supra* note 25, at 45 (noting probability that rational calculation is more common in white-collar context than in others).

if they did, grossly underestimated the risk that their business dealings implicated criminal laws and punishment. Behavioral economists and psychologists offer insights that explain such behavior and that identify limitations of the rational-choice theory of deterrence.[98]

Individuals differ in their tendencies to be optimistic and confident in their ability to control future events. A few are so optimistic and confident that their ability to assess reality becomes impaired and amounts to a judgment bias.[99] Such individuals may also operate from an inflated sense of self-esteem that assigns success to skill and failure to bad luck.[100] Biased judgment, over-confidence, and an inflated sense of self-esteem interfere with the capacity to perceive risk. Yet the rational choice theory of motivation for law-abiding behavior depends upon the actor's realization that planned conduct might result in punishment. Whether characterized as self-deception, hubris, or biased judgment, some individuals may not recognize that their behavior is approaching, or even crossing, the line that separates lawful from unlawful conduct. Thus, they either do not calculate the risks of their behavior or, if they do balance costs and benefits, they may not assess the risk accurately.

Overconfidence, optimism, and resulting misjudgments may also postpone the timing of a rational calculation so that it comes too late. Market situations change constantly, and the environment that presented a modest risk yesterday may turn to catastrophe today. By the time an executive understands the full implications of risky or aggressive dealings, the situation is precarious.[101] Unless the deception is continued, the firm will fail to meet investor and market expectations. The alternate course of

---

[98] *See, e.g.,* JUDGMENT UNDER UNCERTAINTY: HEURISTICS AND BIASES (Daniel Kahneman, et al. eds., 1982) (presenting essays by economists and psychologists on how people make decisions); Colin Camerer & Dan Lovallo, *Overconfidence and Excess Entry: An Experimental Approach,* 89 AM. ECON. R. 306 (1999); Craig R. Fox & Amos Tversky, *Ambiguity Aversion and Comparative Ignorance,* 110 Q. J. OF ECON. 585 (1995); *see also* Donald C. Langevoort, *Behavioral Theories of Judgment and Decision Making in Legal Scholarship: A Literature Review,* 51 VAND. L. REV. 1499, 1500–02 (1998) (providing summary of recent scholarship in the field).

Daniel Kahneman received a Nobel Prize in economics in 2002.

[99] *See generally* Donald C. Langevoort, *The Organizational Psychology of Hyper-Competition: Corporate Irresponsibility and the Lesson of Enron,* 70 GEO. WASH. L. REV. 968 (2002) [hereinafter *Organizational Psychology*] (applying psychological research to competitive firms); Donald C. Langevoort, *Organized Illusions: A Behavioral Theory of Why Corporations Mislead Stock Market Investors (and Cause Other Social Harms),* 146 U. PA. L. REV. 101 (1997) (suggesting that some executives may be more confident about their ability to control future events than an objective evaluation of the situation calls for).

[100] *See Organizational Psychology, supra* note 99, at 969–71; Larry E. Ribstein, *Market vs. Regulatory Responses to Corporate Fraud: A Critique of the Sarbanes-Oxley Act of 2002,* 28 J. CORP. L. 1, 19–22 (2002).

[101] *See* Ribstein, *supra* note 100, at 21 (suggesting that hyper-motivated and super-optimistic insiders could persuade themselves that any setbacks were temporary and that cover-ups need only work for a short time).

action, disclosure, brings certain disgrace. In an excess of confidence, the executive may embark on a third option, to continue in the same course of conduct.[102]

Biased judgment does not justify or excuse criminal conduct, but it may explain why the deterrence model of criminal law does not always prevent criminal behavior. In the case of Enron, observers note that optimism, self-confidence, and risk-taking were hallmarks of the corporate culture and were rewarded.[103] The point for our purposes is that realization and thus a calculation of risk can be totally absent or come well after harmful conduct begins. When realization comes, the overconfident actor may rationally decide to continue the deception in the hope that the crisis will pass.

2. An Impediment From White-Collar Crime Itself

The second impediment that stands in the way of the operation of the rational choice model lies in the nature of white-collar crime. Compared to other forms of criminal activity, white-collar crime, such as fraud, is famously written in shades of gray.[104] In this realm, conduct that is immoral or harmful is not always criminal fraud,[105] while conduct that is not obviously immoral or harmful may be criminal fraud.[106]

One of the chief distinctions between white-collar crime and other crimes is that often neither the accused nor the prosecutor knows whether a criminal act has oc-

---

[102] *See id.* (suggesting also that views about the accuracy of stock price play a role in a decision to "ride out" a stock price that is considered inaccurately low).

[103] *See infra* text accompanying notes 132–140.

[104] *Cf.* United States v. United States Gypsum Co., 438 U.S. 422, 440–41 (1978) (Burger, J., writing) ("[T]he behavior proscribed by the [Sherman] Act is often difficult to distinguish from the gray zone of socially acceptable and economically justifiable business conduct.") (citation omitted).

In the context of bribery, see Daniel H. Lowenstein, *Political Bribery and the Intermediate Theory of Politics,* 32 UCLA L. REV. 784 (1985) (noting that corruption blurs into accepted practice). For an historical perspective, *see* JOHN T. NOONAN, BRIBES (1984); *see also* United States v. Sawyer, 85 F.3d 713, 741–42 (1st Cir. 1996) (stating in fraud case involving bribery that the line between "unattractive and actually criminal conduct [i]s blurred.")

In the context of federal conspiracy law, see the classic treatment by Abraham S. Goldstein, *Conspiracy to Defraud the United States,* 68 YALE L.J. 405 (1959).

[105] For instance, executives with sensitive corporate information who sold stock according to pre-arranged trading plans probably do not violate insider trading laws—even when they possess information about the falling value of the company. *See* 17 C.F.R. 10b5-1 (2002); *see also* United States v. Cochran, 109 F.3d 660, 662 (10th Cir. 1997) (stating that, in fraud cases, "greed and criminal liability are not necessarily synonymous").

[106] Consider the extensive literature that seeks to explain why insider trading is a crime. *See, e.g.,* LEO KATZ, ILL-GOTTEN GAINS: EVASION, BLACKMAIL, FRAUD, AND KINDRED PUZZLES OF THE LAW (1996); Kim Lane Scheppele, *"It's Just Not Right": The Ethics of Insider Trading,* 56 LAW & CONTEMP. PROBS. 123 (1993).

curred, even after conduct has been identified.[107] Laws are broadly written in nonspecific, general terms in order to capture a wide range of conduct. One result is that such laws fail to provide notice that certain conduct is criminal. In the context of fraud, ambiguous and vague statutory prohibitions can reach such proportions as to implicate the constitutional requirement of fair notice.[108] What we deal with here is a pragmatic effect of vague prohibitions: if individuals do not realize that their conduct is criminal or even borders on it, they will not engage in the rational calculation.

These observations are not offered to justify or excuse criminal conduct. It has long been established that the community may subject those who work within certain industries to proscriptions whose moral content is not written in black ink.[109] Nevertheless, the ambiguous nature of many white-collar offenses may explain the failure of criminal penalties to deter the recent examples of business misconduct. Unless individuals recognize that proposed conduct triggers criminal sanctions, they will not pause to evaluate the risk of detection and punishment. Even if they do pause to calculate such risks, judgment biases may impair that evaluation.

Another limitation of the rational choice model lies in the difficulty of enforcing white-collar crimes like fraud. In addition to the ambiguity of conduct that can confuse prosecutors as well as the accused,[110] it simply is difficult to ferret out fraud. Fraud occurs in secret, often by those who are able to control and conceal information

---

[107] See Pamela H. Bucy, *Corporate Ethos: A Standard for Imposing Corporate Criminal Liability*, 75 MINN. L. REV. 1095, 1147 (1991) (providing examples). Immoral and harmful conduct, even when all facts are established, may not constitute mail or wire fraud. *See, e.g.,* United States v. Cleveland, 531 U.S. 12 (2000); United States v. Handakas, 286 F.3d 92 (2d Cir. 2002); United States v. Brown, 79 F.3d 1550 (11th Cir. 1996).

[108] See Geraldine Szott Moohr, *Mail Fraud and the Intangible Rights Doctrine: Someone to Watch over Us*, 31 HARV. J. ON LEGIS. 153, 190–97 (1994) (discussing legality, notice, and vagueness in context of honest services fraud).

Recent opinions have reconsidered the issue of vagueness in mail and wire fraud. *See* United States v. Handakas, 286 F.3d 92, 96 (2d Cir. 2002) (stating that if it were the first panel to address the issue, it would find "honest services" mail fraud (§ 1346) unconstitutionally facially vague, and finding its application in present case was void for vagueness); United States v. Rybicki, 287 F.3d 257 (2d Cir. 2002) (agreeing fully with the Handakas panel's observations concerning the vagueness of the term "honest services," but finding statute was not unconstitutionally vague as applied) (currently under en banc consideration); United States v. Brumley, 116 F.3d 728, 733 (5th Cir. 1997) (conceding that some defendants "on the outer reaches of the [wire fraud] statute" may be without notice); United States v. Czubinski, 106 F.3d 1069, 1077 (1st Cir. 1997) (noting defendant in wire fraud case was without notice that his actions could lead to criminal sanctions).

[109] See United States v. Park, 421 U.S. 658 (1975) (affirming conviction of chief executive officer of supermarket chain for the strict liability offense of food adulteration); United States v. Dotterweich, 320 U.S. 277 (1943).

[110] See United States v. Walters, 997 F.2d 1219, 1226–27 (7th Cir. 1993) (stating that government had indicted the wrong party to the fraud).

that might lead to detection. The inherent difficulty of identifying fraudulent conduct affects the rational calculation made by corporate actors, who may accurately assess the chances of detection as slim. Yet if criminal penalties are increased enough to account for a low probability of detection, they are likely to reach unacceptable levels.[111] The point is not to debate here the fairness issues inherent in increasing punishment as opposed to enforcement efforts, but merely to note another impediment to the rational-choice model. Taken together, the new behavioral theories and the problems regarding enforcement of white-collar crimes suggest greater attention be paid to the second theory of law-abiding behavior.

B. An Unconscious Instinct to Obey the Law

The second theory that explains how criminal law supports law-abiding behavior suggests that people obey the law without conscious reflection because of an instinct to do the right thing.[112] The role of the criminal law in this model is to embody and communicate the social norm of the community that defines "the right thing." This model posits that law-abiding behavior results when individuals have internalized the prevailing social norms and are, in effect, self-regulators.[113] In contrast to the model of external social control, this model is based on an internal control system.[114]

Individuals gradually develop personal codes of conduct at a young age through interactions with other individuals in their family, school, and social circles.[115] A person has internalized a social norm when it has become part of the internal motivation system that guides individual behavior even in the absence of external authority.[116]

---

[111] See Paul H. Robinson & John M. Darley, *The Utility of Desert*, 91 Nw. U. L. Rev. 453, 463 (1997) [hereinafter *The Utility of Desert*] (calculating a 250-year sentence is necessary to deter burglary when only 1.6% of burglars go to prison and four year sentence is desired).

[112] See generally PAUL H. ROBINSON & JOHN M. DARLEY, JUSTICE, LIABILITY & BLAME (1995); TOM R. TYLER, WHY PEOPLE OBEY THE LAW (1990); Robinson & Darley, *The Utility of Desert, supra* note 111; Dan M. Kahan, *Social Influence, Social Meaning, and Deterrence*, 83 VA. L. REV. 349 (1997); Richard H. McAdams, *The Origin, Development, and Regulation of Norms*, 96 MICH. L. REV. 338 (1997); Tyler & Darley, *supra* note 95.

[113] A related theory suggests that people obey the law because they fear the disapproval of their social group. See Robinson & Darley, *The Utility of Desert, supra* note 111, at 468 (noting that social scientists categorize compliance as produced by social influence or internalized morals standards). This model seems to be inherent in both the rational choice and internalized value theories. As to rational choice, individuals would consider disgrace and stigmatization as a cost of criminal conduct. As to the self-regulated, internalized norm theory, individuals have internalized the external social control of the community.

[114] See Tyler & Darley, *supra* note 95, at 714 (stating that behavior is determined by a set of internal values about the morality of behavior).

[115] See id. at 718 (noting that children are trained by a powerful socialization process into internalizing the beliefs represented in the culture to which they belong).

[116] See id. at 715 (quoting Martin L. Hoffman, *Moral Internalization: Current Theory and Research, in* 10 ADVANCES IN EXPERIMENTAL SOCIAL PSYCHOLOGY 85, 85–86 (L. Berkowitz ed. 1977)).

Individuals then unconsciously regulate their behavior so that it is consistent with the internal principles and values by which they define themselves.[117]

In this model, criminal laws and their enforcement communicate societal standards. Criminal law expresses the community's shared moral standards, and violations trigger universal condemnation; it thus has an educative function that influences the development of norms.[118]

1. The Limitations of the Social Norm Model

The social norm model, like the rational choice model, has inherent limitations that impede its effectiveness in encouraging law-abiding behavior. The commonly-held notion that it is difficult to instill moral values and ethical codes solely through law[119] is supported by studies indicating that criminal law does not directly influence individual behavior.[120] The effect of criminal law on individuals seems to be indirect and attenuated; at best, it influences and strengthens the norms of the social group, which individuals then internalize.[121] In the end, criminal laws may have a greater impact on reinforcing behavior of the good citizen than changing behavior of the bad citizen.[122]

The criminal law is not, however, without influence on people. Criminal laws may indirectly influence individuals by confirming and maintaining existing values.[123] Fur-

---

[117] See id. at 714 (contrasting internalized social values with the contemporaneous, self-interested calculations of the rational choice model). It has been suggested that external directives, such as legal prohibitions through criminal law, are not as effective in guiding conduct as internalized moral codes. Id. at 717.

[118] See Johannes Andenaes, General Prevention—Illusion or Reality, 43 J. CRIM. L. & CRIMINOLOGY 176, 179–80 (1952) (noting secondary effects of punishment include forming and strengthening the public's moral code); Harry V. Ball & Lawrence M. Friedman, The Use of Criminal Sanctions in the Enforcement of Economic Legislation: A Sociological View, 17 STAN. L. REV. 197, 220 (1965) (claiming that "social sanctions can be used to change beliefs, attitudes, and personal values and goals"); John C. Coffee, Jr., Does "Unlawful" Mean "Criminal"?: Reflections on the Disappearing Tort/Crime Distinction in American Law, 71 B.U. L. REV. 193, 200 (1991) ("[T]he public learns what is blameworthy in large part from what is punished.").

[119] See Robert Prentice, An Ethics Lesson for Business Schools, N.Y. TIMES, Aug. 20, 2002 at A19 (stating that if students did not get a sense of right and wrong from their families or their faith, it is unlikely that a business school professor can instill it); Jeffrey L. Seglin, Will More Rules Yield Better Corporate Behavior?, N.Y. TIMES, Nov. 17, 2002, at BU4 (quoting David A. Nadler, chairman of a New York consulting firm: "You don't legislate morality.").

[120] Robinson & Darley, The Utility of Desert, supra note 111, at 470–71 (citing research by Harold Grasmick & Donald Green, Harold Grasmick & Robert Bursik, Raymond Paternoster & Lee Ann Iovanni, Robert Meir & Weldon Johnson, and Tom R. Tyler).

[121] See id. at 471–77 (explaining influence of criminal law on social forces that produce compliance).

[122] See Lynch, supra note 25, at 46 (noting the need for occasional reminders that society at large continues to abide by shared norms, which provide respect for the good and shame for the bad).

[123] See Michael C. Harper, Comment on The Tort/Crime Distinction: A Generation Later, 76 B.U. L. REV. 23, 24–25 (1996) (stating that the "more significant" educative force of criminal law "operates not to change morals or values, but rather to confirm them in such a way as to insure that they become more deeply internalized or inculcated in the public psyche").

ther, values are not frozen in childhood experience; encounters with the law in adult-hood probably have some influence, albeit reduced, on the formation of individual norms.[124] This notion emphasizes the significance of even-handed enforcement and interest-free, transparent legislation. If the system is viewed as morally credible and legitimate, individuals tend to obey the law in marginal situations when conduct is ambiguous or of borderline criminality.[125] If people respect the criminal law system, they are likely to defer to the authority of the law even in the absence of a strong internalized norm. But of course, criminal laws, or for that matter laws in general, are not the only influences on behavior.

2. The Influence of Subgroups

The public outrage that followed disclosure of Enron's true financial condition demonstrates general community views about the conduct of Enron's officers. The alleged conduct at Enron—insider trading, misleading investors, misstating financial results—is viewed as immoral, harmful, and blameworthy. Yet the conduct of the Enron actors suggests that they had not internalized this community norm against self-deal-ing and manipulative behavior. Even when a person understands that others would condemn certain conduct, or knows that certain behavior is prohibited, he or she may not have internalized the underlying value in a way that changes behavior.[126] Then those individuals will not instinctively constrain themselves and may even adopt val-ues that are contrary to those of the greater community.

Although we speak of the "community" to mean the entire citizenry, that "commu-nity" is actually made up of various groups, rather than isolated individuals.[127] Opin-ions about wrongdoing can vary with positions of individuals in the social structure of the community. Thus, general social norms may not be shared by specific subgroups, and corporate cultures, like juvenile gangs, may form a localized culture. Individuals, whether executives or ordinary employees, may be influenced by a specific corporate culture.

Companies may develop distinctive characteristics that set them apart from their counterparts.[128] Indeed, a specific business culture may embrace values that are inimi-cal to those of the greater community and may even encourage its members to break

---

[124] Tyler & Darley, *supra* note 95, at 717–18 (noting that people are also influenced by their adult experiences).

[125] *See* Robinson & Darley, *The Utility of Desert, supra* note 111, at 468.

[126] *See* Coffee, *supra* note 118, at 232 (noting distinction between knowing what the public morality is and internalizing that morality).

[127] *See* Ball & Friedman, *supra note* 118, at 207 (commenting on various conceptions of the "public" and pointing out the infirmity of relying on notions of "prevailing morality").

[128] *See* Bucy, *supra* note 107, at 1123–25 (providing research of organizational theorists to this effect).

the law.[129] Loyal individuals may also be motivated by a conviction that their actions are good for the company. In that case, they are even less likely to consider those acts as dangerously close to unlawful.[130] Moreover, when the subgroup is strong and cohesive, efforts to stigmatize certain conduct by applying criminal law may even be counterproductive.[131]

C. The Enron Experience

Reports indicate that, like many other corporations, Enron had developed a localized subculture.[132] The Enron culture is reminiscent of Tom Wolfe's fictionalized account, in which securities traders, or "Masters of the Universe," produced amazing profits in a single morning.[133] Enron's "masters" seem to have produced profits out of fictional trades in sometimes nonexistent products.[134] In order to reach its profit goals, Enron management encouraged aggressive competitive behavior where success was measured by contributions to corporate wealth. Reports characterize Enron as a corporate culture that disdained regulation and pressured middle managers to produce profit.[135] As in the fiction, executives were rewarded extremely well for this work.

---

[129] See id. at 1127–50 (providing factors that define corporate ethos). For an example from current events, see Floyd Norris & Diana B. Henriques, 3 Admit Guilt in Falsifying CUC's Books, N.Y. TIMES, June 15, 2000, at C1 (explaining that fraud at Cendant was a result of "a culture that had been developing over many years" that was ingrained in employees by superiors).

The demand of shareholders for high profit may also encourage aggressive dealings that border on negligent or criminal conduct. The effect of American companies' emphasis on maximizing shareholder profits also poses other dilemmas. See generally LAWRENCE E. MITCHELL, CORPORATE IRRESPONSIBILITY: AMERICA'S NEWEST EXPORT 30–48 (2001).

[130] See Ribstein, supra note 100, at 21 (noting that actors who are convinced they "are doing the right thing" in maintaining their company's value may not be subject to moral constraints).

[131] See Kahan, supra note 112, at 374–377 (recounting experience of authorities with juvenile gangs); Robinson & Darley, The Utility of Desert, supra note 111, at 481 (stating that use of stigmatization in absence of consensus about morality of the conduct is likely to be ineffective because "it offends rather than educates the moral code of the community").

[132] See ROBERT BRYCE, PIPE DREAMS: GREED, EGO, AND THE DEATH OF ENRON 12 (2002) (stating that reason Enron failed "was the culture, stupid"); PETER C. FUSARO AND ROSS M. MILLER, WHAT WENT WRONG AT ENRON 43 (2002) (noting Enron was an "extremely dysfunctional organization"); MIMI SWARTZ WITH SHERRON WATKINS, POWER FAILURE: THE INSIDE STORY OF THE COLLAPSE OF ENRON 56 (2003).

A similar story is told about Arthur Andersen. See BARBARA LEY TOFFLER & JENNIFER REINGOLD, FINAL ACCOUNTING: AMBITION, GREED AND THE FALL OF ARTHUR ANDERSEN (2003).

[133] TOM WOLFE, THE BONFIRE OF THE VANITIES (1987).

[134] One deal involving video on demand and the Blockbuster video chain has been described as "absurd," "a sham from its inception," and, most damning, "Not only did the emperor have no clothes, there was no emperor." See Floyd Norris, Maybe the Most Dubious of the Deals, N.Y. TIMES, March 13, 2003 at C6 (quoting sources).

[135] See BRYCE, supra note 132, at 12; FUSARO & MILLER, supra note 132, at 43.

The extraordinary sums paid to executives in salary and stock options are now generally viewed as misplaced incentives that skewed the loyalty of executives.[136] Instead of aligning their interest with those of investors, stock option awards seem to have encouraged aggressive tactics that enhanced the company's stock price in order to increase the personal wealth of executives. Although this debate continues,[137] at a minimum such extraordinary rewards communicate a not-so-subtle message that a result favorable to the company justifies any method used to achieve it.

The Enron culture was also marked by the use of a Darwinian market discipline to evaluate employees. Enron's policy was to replace each year all employees who were ranked in the lowest 15% of their group.[138] This system contributed to an environment in which employees were afraid to express their opinions or to question unethical and potentially illegal business practices.[139] The incentives in this system led to acquiescence and compliance as junior executives avoided encounters that could negatively affect their semi-annual evaluation, and may have discouraged employees from reporting misgivings about borderline deals. Enron's end shows that rewarding aggressive tactics invites fraud in; squelching employees' misgivings shuts the door behind it.

The Enron culture probably influenced the behavior of its executives and employees. One commentator has charged the Enron culture with creating a "Machiavellian, narcissistic, prevaricating, pathologically optimistic, free from self-doubt and moral distractions," and risk-taking business executive.[140] If the individuals who engaged in wrongdoing were influenced by this socially-destructive corporate culture, then relying only on criminal sanctions may not be effective in containing its effects. Punishing those caught up in such cultures, without changing the environment that influenced them, will not prevent other individuals from being similarly influenced. Remedying an environment that encourages law-breaking is one reason for levying criminal sanctions against the corporate entity itself.

IV. A COMPREHENSIVE APPROACH TO ENCOURAGE LAWFUL BUSINESS CONDUCT

The current embrace of criminal penalties seems to rest on the proposition that the Enron experience is the product of a few "bad apples" who were not deterred by exist-

---

[136] *See generally* JOSEPH BLASE, DOUGLAS KRUSE, & AARON BERNSTEIN, IN THE COMPANY OF OWNERS: THE TRUTH ABOUT STOCK OPTIONS (2003).

[137] *See* Gretchen Morgenson, *When Options Rise to Top, Guess Who Pays*, N.Y. TIMES, Nov. 10, 2002, sec. 3, at 1.

[138] *See* FUSARO & MILLER, *supra* note 132, at 51–52 (explaining Enron's "rank-and-yank" evaluation system, in which the lowest 15% of employees were replaced every six months); SWARTZ & WATKINS, *supra* note 132, at 160–62 (describing the review system as the star chamber combined with fraternity rush). Enron hired ambitious, aggressive self-starters who were intelligent and had a capacity for hard work. *See* BRYCE, *supra* note 132, at 121–22; FUSARO & MILLER, *supra* note 132, at 48–50.

[139] *See* BRYCE, *supra* note 132, at 128 (stating that the review system "perverted Enron's internal risk management systems").

[140] *See* Ribstein, *supra* note 100, at 9.

ing criminal sanctions when tempted by an opportunity to enrich themselves.[141] The "bad apple" assumption, however, is unsatisfactory. Rather than being confined to a few individuals, the criminal conduct at Enron appears to have involved many people in a wide range of fraudulent activity. Evidence disclosed thus far indicates that the conduct was prevalent, and indeed, may have been endemic to the firm. As is now known, the wrongdoing extended to Enron's accountants, auditors, and bankers.

Moreover, such misconduct was not confined to Enron. Although Enron stands out because of its serious and dramatic consequences, what happened there was not an isolated case. Investigators have uncovered unlawful conduct at a plethora of firms, including Intel, Adelphia, World Com, Sunbeam, Waste Management, Xerox, and Global Crossing.[142] The Enron saga has not yet completely unfolded, as investigators uncover evidence of fraud in the California energy market and in Enron's telecommunication division.[143]

Finally, the view of Enron as an exception wrought by bad actors ignores a rich history of fraud and misconduct in American business. The major frauds of the South Sea Bubble in the early 1700s and those that contributed to the market crash of 1929 are well-known.[144] Recent incarnations involve price fixing in the electrical equipment industry, fraud in the savings and loan and banking industries, and a massive insider trading episode.[145] More recently, criminal antitrust violations occurred in the international commodities markets and in a prestigious auction house.[146] The evidence of widespread misconduct at Enron and other companies and the historical record of corporate frauds indicates that a systemic failure, rather than bad apples, is at work.

The "bad apple" interpretation of events at Enron suggests that it is a simple story of purposeful criminal conduct based on greed. Although there is no doubt some truth

---

[141] See Adam Cohen, *Before WorldCom, the Funeral Industry Set the Standard for Venality,* N.Y. TIMES, Sept. 13, 2002, at A23 (recounting President Bush's argument that the executive misdeeds were ethical lapses of a few bad actors, and that the solution was criminal prosecutions).

[142] See supra note 1 (noting that 54 firms were under investigation in October 2002).

[143] See supra note 9 (noting continuing prosecutorial efforts).

[144] These have been characterized as inevitable results of boom-to-bust business cycles. Kurt Eichenwald, *After a Boom, There Will Be Scandal, Count On It,* N.Y. TIMES, Dec. 16, 2002, at C3 (quoting John C. Coffee, Jr.: "[C]onstant re-emergence of scandal . . . goes back at least 300 years. It's just part of capitalism.").

[145] See JAMES B. STEWART, DEN OF THIEVES (1991) (recounting insider trading and junk bond scandals); Ball & Friedman, *supra* note 118, at 219 (discussing public outrage directed at trusts that led to passage of the Sherman Act and the price-fixing scandal in the electricity industry); Boss & George, *supra* note 76 (reacting to the savings and loan scandal of the 1980s).

In a similar episode, increased penalties failed to deter insider trading by Milken, Boesky, Drexel Burnham, and others. See Boss & George, *supra* note 76, at 42–49 (providing legislative history that chronicled legislators' surprise).

[146] See KURT EICHENWALD, THE INFORMANT (2000) (chronicling the price-fixing scheme of Archer Daniels Midland); JAMES B. LIEBER, RATS IN THE GRAIN (2000) (same); Carol Vogel, *Court Accepts Sotheby's Guilty Plea in Price Fixing,* N.Y. TIMES, Feb. 3, 2001, at C14.

in the greed hypothesis,[147] an alternate account provides a more complete explanation. The alternate theory, based on evidence from the firm's practices and research on rational behavior and social norms, suggests a more complex narrative that has implications for the role of criminal penalties in encouraging law-abiding conduct in the business world. The expression of public values through criminal law does not necessarily lead to law-abiding behavior when powerful subgroups create opposing values. Criminal law is not particularly effective against such subgroups and may not create the internalized social norms that are necessary for compliance. Nor does the threat of stigmatization or punishment always trigger the rational calculation that might deter wrongdoers. Conduct that is perilously unlawful may not be recognized or the risk of punishment may not be accurately assessed. And even when the danger is recognized, it may be too late to change behavior.

A broader, more inclusive strategy would utilize a greater range of enforcement mechanisms than that provided by criminal law. After all, criminal law exists within an enforcement structure that also includes government administrative regulation, market incentives, and private actions.[148] A comprehensive strategy should include all of these tools. They provide several sources of intervention and many opportunities to signal the possibility of unlawful conduct and to maintain and strengthen the social norms that lead to law-abiding behavior.

A. Market Incentives and Private Actions

Private actors, such as gatekeepers and investors, can encourage law-abiding business conduct. The wholesale failure of every monitor of corporate conduct to identify and report wrongful or suspicious business dealings is a prominent feature of what we know about Enron.[149] The failure of its board, its bankers, its accountants, and its

---

[147] The self-dealing aspect of Enron's special purpose entities, which concealed the firm's true financial condition while directing windfall profits to executives, certainly speaks of greed. Yet, the greed narrative does not explain the absence of Swiss bank accounts and a flight plan. Both Fastow and Kopper had involved their families and friends in the special purpose entities. These factors speak of hubris, as well as greed.

[148] *See* Brown, *supra* note 18, at 1325 (noting corporate criminal law is part of an elaborate regulatory regime governing firms and commercial activity).

[149] Judge Sporkin's question, following the Lincoln Savings & Loan fraud, echoes in the aftermath of Enron.

> Where were these professionals . . . when these clearly improper transactions were being consummated? . . . With all the professional talent involved (both accounting and legal), why [didn't] at least one professional . . . blow[] the whistle to stop the overreaching that took place in this case?

Lincoln Sav. & Loan Ass'n v. Wall, 743 F. Supp. 901, 920 (D.D.C. 1990). Before being appointed to the federal bench in 1985, Judge Sporkin served as Director of the Division of Enforcement at the SEC for many years.

The failure of gatekeepers may provide a defense for wrongdoers. To the extent that gatekeepers, lawyers, accountants, and analysts blessed the creation of Enron's special purpose entities and other deals, executives may colorably claim a lack of intent to defraud. *See supra* text accompanying notes 38–41 (discussing culpability element in criminal fraud).

lawyers to identify misrepresentations or to inform regulatory agencies and the public was exacerbated by the failure of outside gatekeepers, such as securities analysts and credit rating agencies, to alert investors of Enron's true financial condition. Professor Coffee has remarked on the wholesale failure of market monitors to alert investors of the true financial condition of Enron.[150] My reason for focusing on gatekeepers is to credit their significant function: they can encourage law-abiding behavior.

Effective gatekeepers provide a counterweight to the norms that may develop in corporate subcultures and to the judgment biases that lead to inaccurate assessments of the risks of criminal sanctions. Monitors provide an important measure of outside control, if only because they can increase the chances of "getting caught" in civil or criminal actions. Thus, they may deter those who engage in a rational calculation of risk and benefit. Market monitors may also sound a timely warning that can signal corporate actors that they are treading treacherously close to the line, leading them to make the rational calculation in time to avoid or abandon potentially harmful acts. At a minimum, early warnings by outside gatekeepers signal that the company is the subject of a scrutiny that has market implications. Finally, gatekeepers insert a countervailing pressure of community norms into the firm's local culture.

A second private enforcement mechanism is the civil lawsuit brought by investors who seek damages for negligence and civil fraud. Private suits also express community norms, and the threat of civil litigation enhances the risks of engaging in marginally lawful conduct. Congress generally handicapped the use of private lawsuits in the 1990s, however, and reduced the incentive of gatekeepers to monitor firms aggressively.[151] Perhaps because of the focus on criminal penalties after Enron, there has been little interest in or hope of reversing this weakening of the civil lawsuit remedy for corporate malfeasance.[152]

In 1995, Congress passed the Private Securities Litigation Reform Act ("PSLRA").[153] One provision of the PSLRA eliminated the practice of using securities fraud as the

---

[150] *See* John C. Coffee, Jr., *Understanding Enron: It's All About the Gatekeepers, Stupid, in* NANCY B. RAPOPORT & BALA G. DHARAN, ENRON: CORPORATE FIASCOS AND THEIR IMPLICATIONS (2004); John C. Coffee, Jr., *What Caused Enron?: A Capsule Social and Economic History of the 1990's* (2003), *available at* http://ssrn.com/abstract_id=373581.

[151] *See* Michael H. Granof and Stephen A. Zeff, *Unaccountable in Washington*, N.Y. TIMES, Jan. 23, 2000, at A23; Stephen Labaton, *Now Who Exactly Got Us Into This*, N.Y. TIMES, Feb. 3, 2002, at C1; Don Van Natta, Jr., *Bipartisan Outrage But Few Mea Culpas in Capital*, N.Y. TIMES, Jan. 25, 2002, at C11.

[152] *See* John C. Coffee Jr., Testimony Before the Senate Committee on Commerce, Science, and Transportation (Dec. 18, 2001), *available at* http://www.senate.gov/~commerce/hearings/121801Coffee.pdf (noting that the Private Securities Litigation Reform Act was an intensely lobbied statute that Congress would not wish to repeal or modify); Melissa Harrison, *The Assault on the Liability of Outside Professionals: Are Lawyers and Accountants Off the Hook?*, 65 U. CIN. L. REV. 473 (1997); Hamilton, *supra* note 79, at 72–73 (suggesting repeal or modification of the Private Securities Litigations Reform Act (PSLRA) and the Securities Litigation Uniform Standards Act).

[153] See Pub. L. No. 104-67, tit. I, § 107, 109 Stat. 737. The controversial bill was enacted over President Clinton's veto. *See* Harrison, *supra* note 152, at 518.

basis for civil RICO actions.[154] Plaintiffs who won such suits had been entitled to triple damages,[155] and these were thought to encourage frivolous suits and coercive settlements.[156] By protecting businesses from coercive settlements, the PSLRA also eliminated a significant deterrent mechanism. In addition to Congress's action, the Supreme Court reduced the deterrent element of civil RICO actions when, in 1993, it restricted plaintiff's use of civil RICO suits against consulting, auditing, and legal firms that had advised corporations accused of fraud.[157]

The PSLRA also discouraged investor lawsuits that do not involve RICO. It made it more difficult to bring class action suits, limited joint and several liability, expanded safe harbors for certain company statements, and toughened pleading requirements for fraud.[158] The Supreme Court took similar action when, in 1994, it eliminated civil liability for aiding and abetting fraudulent conduct involving securities laws.[159] By narrowing civil lawsuits against accountants and attorneys to cases of actual participation, the Court reduced the incentive of such gatekeepers to monitor their clients closely.

Congress also restricted plaintiffs' ability to file securities fraud cases in state courts.[160] The Securities Litigation Uniform Standards Act ("SLUSA"), enacted in 1998, re-

---

[154] *See* Private Securities Litigation Reform Act of 1995 §§ 107, 108 (1995) (codified at 18 U.S.C. § 1964(c)).

[155] *See* 18 U.S.C. § 1964(c) (providing civil cause of action). The purpose of the triple damages was not only to compensate those injured by racketeering activity, but also to discourage such activity. *See* Sedima, S.P.R.L. v. Imrex Co., 473 U.S. 479 (1985).

[156] 141 CONG. REC. 42, H2770–H2773 (daily ed. March 7, 1995) (statement of Rep. Cox) (also available at 1995 WL 91687).

[157] *See* Reves v. Ernst & Young, 507 U.S. 170 (1993) (holding that civil RICO's "operation and management" test to determine whether defendant participated in a pattern of racketeering activity required proof of some level of operating or managing the enterprise).

In 1991, the Court announced a uniform statute of limitations for securities cases. *See* Lampf v. Gilbertson, 501 U.S. 350 (1991) (holding that limitations period for private actions was within one year of discovery but not more than three years after the transaction occurred).

To provide investors an expanded opportunity to bring suit, Sarbanes-Oxley extended the limitations period to two years after discovery of the violation. *See* Sarbanes-Oxley Act of 2002 § 807 (codified at 28 U.S.C. § 1658 (West Supp. 2002)).

[158] *See* Linda D. Fienberg, et al., *Safer Harbors: Securities Litigation After the Reform Act of 1995*, 5 BUS. LAW TODAY 24 (May/June 1996). *See also, e.g., In re* K-tel Intl. Inc., 300 F. 3d. 881 (8th Cir. 2002) (affirming dismissal of class action for failing to allege accounting violations with requisite particularity and failure to plead facts giving rise to a strong inference of culpability).

[159] *See* Central Bank of Denver, N.A. v. First Interstate Bank of Denver, N.A., 511 U.S. 164 (1994).

The PSLRA restored aiding and abetting liability in SEC enforcement actions. *See* Private Securities Litigation Reform Act of 1995 § 104(f) (1995), 15 U.S.C. § 78t (2003).

[160] Another obstacle to private suits is the arbitration agreement that investors must sign in order to do business with broker-dealers. Investor contracts typically mandate arbitration, rather than adjudication, of securities claims. *See* Rodriguez de Quijas v. Shearson American Express, Inc., 490 U.S. 477 (1989).

duced securities fraud litigation in state courts by making federal courts the exclusive venue for class actions involving securities fraud.[161] The combined effect of these actions was to make it more difficult for private plaintiffs to bring allegations of securities fraud against gatekeepers.

Although the long-term effect of these initiatives on the number and nature of securities suits is subject to debate,[162] their immediate effect was to raise substantive standards and to heighten procedural hurdles to investor civil suits against companies and gatekeepers. Two repercussions, related to encouraging law-abiding business behavior, may be registered. First, restricting the availability of a civil remedy expresses a counterproductive community norm to corporate actors. An executive might understandably reason that if conduct is not subject to suit in tort, it is not unlawful; if the conduct is not unlawful, then it could not be criminal. Second, the restrictive legislation may enter into the risk calculation of the rational decisionmaker. If the risk of civil liability is low, then there is even less risk of criminal action. Thus, on the enforcement level, reducing civil liability also removed an enforcement mechanism that had operated to deter wrongful conduct. On the whole, the message inherent in the restriction of civil fraud suits is inconsistent with, and thus undercuts the effectiveness of, parallel criminal laws.

B. Government Administrative Actions

A second type of enforcement comes from government regulatory actions.[163] Civil administrative penalties are problematic because they can implicate due process rights of individuals subject to civil punishment.[164] Notwithstanding the need to avoid that serious dilemma, administrative enforcement offers an effective way to induce law-

---

[161] See 17 U.S.C. §§ 77p, 78bb(f). See also Newby v. Enron, 302 F.3d 295 (5th Cir. 2002) (holding that defendant's attempts to avoid the SLUSA were not in themselves an abuse of the courts).

[162] See Harrison, supra note 152; James A. Kassis, The Private Securities Litigation Reform Act of 1995: A Review of its Key Provisions and an Assessment of its Effects at the Close of 2001, 26 SETON HALL LEGIS. J. 119, 148 (2001) (presenting data and concluding that the PSLRA has not curbed meritless class action suits).

[163] See Lynch, supra note 25, at 34–36 (presenting theoretical rationale for use of administrative remedies).

[164] Civil sanctions that are essentially punitive raise substantial due process concerns. See Mary M. Cheh, Constitutional Limits on Using Civil Remedies to Achieve Criminal Law Objectives: Understanding and Transcending the Criminal-Civil Law Distinction, 42 HASTINGS L.J. 1325 (1991); Susan R. Klein, Redrawing the Criminal-Civil Boundary, 2 BUFF. CRIM. L. REV. 679 (1999); Kenneth Mann, Punitive Civil Sanctions: The Middleground Between Criminal and Civil Law, 101 YALE L.J. 1795 (1992); Carol Steiker, Foreword: Punishment and Procedure: Punishment Theory and the Criminal-Civil Procedural Divide, 85 GEO. L.J. 775 (1997).

abiding behavior.[165] Less costly to the public fisc than are criminal trials, government regulation can reach more offenders in a way that achieves a degree of horizontal equality between them. In addition, administrative enforcement avoids the "psychology of resentment" that accompanies harsh punishment and, instead, fosters self-regulation, voluntary compliance, and a sense of social responsibility.[166]

On the regulatory front, Sarbanes-Oxley addresses weaknesses in the present administrative scheme, especially those that pertain to accountants and auditors. Those weaknesses were perceived as contributing to the fraud at Enron and other firms. In creating the Public Company Accounting Oversight Board, the Act strengthens the ability of government regulators to monitor and enforce administrative remedies.[167] It also reshapes executive incentives by limiting corporate loans. The Act encourages vigilant monitoring by limiting conflicts of interest in boards and by requiring lawyers to report evidence of securities law violations. Sarbanes-Oxley also expands the flow of information to the public by shortening the time that corporate insiders have to disclose stock trades. Thus the Act promises to use regulatory law to control corporate misconduct.

To be effective, however, administrative agencies must have adequate budgets and personnel. Several authorities have noted the declining rate of enforcement by the SEC, which has faced increased filings and decreased enforcement capability for a decade.[168] Budgetary concerns have been alleviated by increased funding for SEC enforcement,

---

[165] In order to buttress their effectiveness, most regulatory statutes include criminal sanctions. Securities laws are one example; another is environmental statutes that include criminal sanctions for air and water pollution. *See* 42 U.S.C. § 7413(c) (2001); 33 U.S.C. § 1319(c) (2001).

Imposing criminal sanctions for technical violations of regulatory statutes has met with significant criticism. *See* Henry M. Hart, Jr., *The Aims of the Criminal Law,* 23 LAW & CONTEMP. PROBS. 401 (1958); *see also* HERBERT L. PACKER, THE LIMITS OF THE CRIMINAL SANCTION (1968); Coffee, *supra* note 118; Sanford H. Kadish, *Some Observations on the Use of Criminal Sanctions in Enforcing Economic Regulations,* 30 U. CHI. L. REV. 423 (1963). *But see* Stuart P. Green, *Why It's a Crime to Tear the Tag Off a Mattress: Overcriminalization and the Moral Content of Regulatory Offenses,* 46 EMORY L. J. 1153 (1997) (rejecting one critique on the ground that engaging in conduct prohibited by the sovereign has a moral dimension).

[166] *See* Brown, *supra* note 18, at 1313 (citing IAN AYRES & JOHN BRAITHWAITE, RESPONSIVE REGULATION: TRANSCENDING THE DEREGULATION DEBATE 8, 49 (1992)).

[167] Congress mandated that the SEC complete the administrative restructuring by April 26, 2003. That process has gotten off to a slow and unpromising start. The first appointment to head the accounting board, which is to formulate accounting rules, was mired in conflict when one popular candidate, John H. Biggs, was bypassed. The selected candidate, William Webster, resigned after it became public that he had been the audit committee chairman of a company that had issued questionable financial statements. Shortly thereafter, Harvey Pitt, the SEC Chairman, also resigned. *See* Floyd Norris, *S.E.C. Picks Fed President to Lead Panel,* N.Y. TIMES, April 16, 2003, at C1.

[168] Filings grew by 61%, from 61,295 in 1991 to 98,745 in 2000; during that time, the SEC staff had grown from 125 to 161, an increase of only 29%. In the 1980s, the SEC gave in-depth review to company filings once every three years; by 2000 that level of review occurred only once in seven years. *See* Hamilton, *supra* note 79, at 6–7 n.16.

some $711.7 million for the current year.[169] Proper funding is important because the ultimate effectiveness of Sarbanes-Oxley in encouraging lawful business conduct largely depends upon implementation and enforcement of its regulatory reforms.

C. A Modest Role for Criminal Law

Depending solely upon criminal law to control corporate crime is misguided, at best. The threat of criminal penalties is not an adequate deterrent given the limitations of the rational choice model of law-abiding behavior.[170] Judgment biases, created by optimism and risk-taking, may impair an individual's decisions. The deterrent threat is also not effective when the risk of apprehension is slight and when it is aimed at actors who control information and who may discount the costs of incarceration. Changing the criminal law and increasing penalties does not directly lead to an unconscious instinct to comply.[171] Although the criminal law has an important expressive function, reliance on criminal law alone is not an effective way to create internalized norms. The criminal law can only influence, not form, individual norms. In a corporate setting, contrary values may have a greater influence on individuals than those of the community.

The punishment approach, which properly places blame on individual actors, has a tendency to mask the need for a more comprehensive solution. Criminal law's emphasis on personal accountability does not address systemic characteristics of business crime, such as judgment biases and corporate subcultures that might actually encourage illegal conduct. Moreover, reliance on criminal law may lead legislators to neglect initiatives that could be more productive in preventing future fraud. Recourse to the criminal law alone is not an effective response to the type of wrongdoing exemplified by the corporate scandals of 2002.

In the scheme endorsed here, enforcement through criminal law is one part of a comprehensive approach. Criminal laws are the ultimate expression of social norms that condemn immoral or harmful conduct. But civil enforcement through private suits and government regulatory actions similarly express the community's values. Moreover, using criminal law as a last resort, instead of as a primary mechanism, reinforces its legitimacy. Legitimacy is an important factor in encouraging law-abiding behavior because, when the system is viewed as morally credible, even those who have not internalized the social norm are inclined to obey the law.[172]

Constructing a viable structure in which these systems interact for maximum effectiveness and minimum intrusion upon due process rights of the accused requires fur-

---

[169] Following criticism of the administration's backpedaling on its commitment to fund the agency, Congress gave the SEC $170 million more than the White House had requested. The budget request for next year is $841.5 million, a 92% increase over last year's budget. *See* Stephen Labaton, *S.E.C. Chief Says Fixing the Agency Will Take Time*, N.Y. TIMES, March 14, 2003, at C1.

[170] *See supra* text accompanying notes 98–111 (discussing limitations of rational choice theory).

[171] *See supra* text accompanying notes 119–139 (discussing limitations of the social norm model).

[172] *See supra* text accompanying notes 123–125.

ther development and the participation of all stakeholders and enforcers, as well as Congress. My point here is to emphasize the importance of consistency in communicating a common standard. Each part of the comprehensive scheme should reinforce the message sent by the other enforcers. A consistent and forceful message is more likely to encourage law-abiding conduct under the rational choice or the unconscious instinct models of compliance with the law. It is counterproductive to include contrary messages, such as those arguably embodied in legislation that hamstrings plaintiffs or in inadequate funding for administrative enforcement. In the end, the regulatory provisions of the Sarbanes-Oxley Act may be more significant in controlling business misconduct than its criminal provisions.

In sum, Enron and related scandals demonstrate the need for structural reform that will encourage law-abiding behavior by corporations and those who serve them. Although the competitive impulse is the engine that drives a free market system, a strong regulatory structure is necessary "to prevent the ideal from consuming itself."[173] The ultimate challenge is to create systems within corporations to ensure that "fairly decent people cannot be put under these hidden pressures again."[174] The most effective way to encourage law-abiding conduct is through a combination of market-motivated gatekeepers, private remedial suits, government administrative actions, and finally, criminal punishment.

V. CONCLUSION

Recent cheating scandals at major educational institutions show that it is short-sighted to neglect the framework that makes cheating difficult and to rely instead on honor systems that impose harsh penalties.[175] Studies show that honor systems are more effective if supported by procedures such as monitoring of examinations, grading by professors, and warning students about plagiarism and cheating. In the absence of such devices, it is disingenuous for college administrators to express surprise and shock when widespread cheating is uncovered.

---

[173] See Kadish, supra note 165, at 425.

[174] Kurt Eichenwald, *Even if Heads Roll, Mistrust Will Live On*, N.Y. TIMES, Oct. 6, 2002, at BU1.

[175] See Stuart P. Green, *Plagiarism, Norms, and the Limits of Theft Law: Some Observations on the Use of Criminal Sanctions in Enforcing Intellectual Property Rights*, 54 HASTINGS L.J. 167, 191 (2002) (noting startling increase in student plagiarism).

Cheating scandals have caught officials at prestigious institutions by surprise. See Glenn C. Altschuler, *College Prep; Battling the Cheats;* N.Y. TIMES, Jan. 7, 2001, sec. A4 at 15 (Cornell University); Amy Argetsinger, *U-Md Says Students Use Phones to Cheat*, WASH. POST, Jan. 30, 2003, at B1; Elissa Gootman, *Columbia Students Charged in High-Tech Cheating*, N.Y. TIMES, Nov. 20, 2002, at B1; Diana Jean Schermo, *U. of Virginia Hit by Scandal Over Cheating*, N.Y. TIMES, May 10, 2001, at A1.

One college professor has linked the increase of corporate fraud with widespread academic dishonesty. See Miguel Roig, *Letters*, N.Y. TIMES, June 5, 2002, at A26 (stating that one way of reducing tomorrow's white-collar crime is to hold today's students to higher academic ethical standards).

Relying on criminal law as the chief means to prevent business misconduct is like relying on honor codes to prevent student cheating in college. Criminal laws, like harshly punished honor codes, are not sufficient in and of themselves to prevent bad conduct. Like a college, we need structural support for the values reflected in criminal laws. That support is provided when the law works in concert with other regulatory devices, namely private suits and government regulatory actions. Criminal law plays an important role in regulating business conduct, but it is not the only player.

NOTES AND QUESTIONS

1. Under federal law, the standard of respondeat superior is used to determine whether a corporation has committed a crime. A corporation may be subject to criminal penalties when an agent of the corporation, acting within the scope of his or her authority and on behalf of the corporation, violated the law. *See* Commonwealth v. Beneficial Finance Co., 275 N.E. 2d 33 (Mass. 1971). What are the advantages of this standard? Are there any disadvantages? Should the courts require that a high managerial agent of the firm committed or ratified the criminal act?

2. Firms that suspect wrongdoing often conduct an investigation in which officers and employees are questioned. When criminal conduct is discovered, the firm faces several difficult choices. Should it disclose that information to federal prosecutors? Advise implicated officers and employees to obtain counsel? Offer to pay for such counsel? Terminate the officers and employees? These questions become even more difficult when investigators only suspect that crimes were committed or when it is unclear that criminal acts occurred. Note that cooperation with prosecutors can expose the firm to civil suits.

3. One reason that the rational choice model may fail to prevent business crime is that character traits like over-optimism can bias a person's judgment. Can you think of any other impediments to the operation of the theory?

4. The criminal law may not be an effective means to create a law-abiding business community, especially when corporate cultures encourage contrary values. Can you think of any other impediments to the operation of the instinct to obey model of law-abiding behavior?

5. The criminal law functions to express societal values and thus communicates and educates citizens. Is this function more properly considered a by-product of the enforcement of criminal law or a purpose of the criminal law? Does it matter?

Enron and the Pension System

*Colleen E. Medill**

The collapse of Enron and the resulting consequences for participants in the Enron pension plan represent a watershed event for the future of the modern American pension system. In terms of national notoriety, this event is similar in magnitude to two prior public scandals in the history of the pension system. The first such scandal occurred during the decade of the 1960s: the closing of the Studebaker automobile plant and the termination of its underfunded pension plan. Shortly thereafter came the second scandal, heralded by Congressional hearings revealing the misuse of plan assets for personal gain by officials of the Teamsters union. These two landmark events raised public awareness of problems in the pension system and led to the enactment of the Employee Retirement Income Security Act of 1974 ("ERISA").[1] ERISA forms the underlying regulatory structure for the pension system today.

The Enron story challenges all of the stakeholders in the modern American pension system to reconsider ERISA's regulatory structure. This structure derives from a paradigm that no longer exists today—the workplace environment and the business market structure of the 1950s and 1960s. The fundamental public policy question raised by Enron is how to modernize ERISA so that the pension system remains viable for American businesses and their workers in the twenty-first century.

I. HISTORICAL PERSPECTIVE: ENRON AS A MODERN TWIST ON STUDEBAKER AND THE TEAMSTERS

Beginning in the late 1940s, pension plans first became widely available to unionized workers in the mining, steel, and automobile manufacturing industries through collective bargaining agreements. Although federal labor laws regulated the collective

---

* Professor of Law, University of Tennessee College of Law.

[1] Employee Retirement Income Security Act of 1974, Pub. L. No. 93-406, 88 Stat. 829 (1974) (codified as amended in scattered sections of 26 & 29 U.S.C.) ("ERISA").

468   ENRON: CORPORATE FIASCOS AND THEIR IMPLICATIONS

bargaining agreement process that led to the establishment of pension plans, the key features of pension plans themselves, such as vesting and adequate employer funding, were left unregulated by federal law. In essence, a worker's pension benefits were only as financially secure as the employer itself.

The problems associated with this lack of federal oversight over the pension system became national news in the early 1960s, when the Studebaker Corporation ("Studebaker") closed its automobile manufacturing plant in Indiana due to financial difficulties.[2] Since 1950, the workers at Studebaker had been covered by a pension plan negotiated on their behalf by the United Automobile Workers Union ("UAW"). When the plant closed, Studebaker and the UAW negotiated an agreement to terminate the pension plan. Under this termination agreement, of the approximately 10,500 retirees and active workers covered by the plan, only 3,600 individuals received their full benefits promised under the terms of the plan. Due to grossly inadequate funding, the remaining plan participants received little or nothing from the terminated pension plan. The plight of these plan participants, many of whom had long years of service with Studebaker, was well-publicized by the media. Studebaker became a public symbol of the insecurity of pension plan benefits, one of the focal points of subsequent Congressional hearings on the need for pension system reform.

While Congress and a Presidential committee[3] were investigating the Studebaker incident and reporting on the need for pension system reform, another Congressional investigation uncovered serious financial abuse concerning the management of assets held in employee benefit plans sponsored by the International Brotherhood of Teamsters ("Teamsters") for union members. Union officials responsible for administering the plans and investing plan assets were being personally enriched, sometimes by millions of dollars, through dubious and self-dealing transactions. Members of Congress were shocked to learn that, under existing federal law, such misuse of plan assets was not prohibited. These revelations emphasized the need for federal law to impose more stringent standards of fiduciary conduct upon the persons who administer pension plans and manage plan assets. In the words of one first-hand observer and participant in the formation of ERISA, "Federal fiduciary standards leaped to the top of the emerging pension reform agenda."[4]

[2] For a detailed, and fascinating, historical account of the Studebaker incident, see James A. Wooten, *"The Most Glorious Story of Failure in the Business": The Studebaker-Packard Corporation and the Origins of ERISA*, 49 BUFF. L. REV. 683–739 (2001).

[3] In 1962, President John F. Kennedy established the President's Committee on Corporate Pension Funds and Other Private Retirement and Welfare Programs to study the implications of the growing pension plan system for the national economy. The Committee's final report, issued in 1965, recommended that the system be reformed through mandatory minimum vesting and funding standards and a federal program of termination insurance that would guarantee pension benefits to plan participants. *See* PRESIDENT'S COMMITTEE ON CORPORATE PENSION FUNDS AND OTHER PRIVATE RETIREMENT AND WELFARE PROGRAMS, PUBLIC POLICY AND PRIVATE PENSION PROGRAMS: A REPORT TO THE PRESIDENT ON PRIVATE EMPLOYEE RETIREMENT PLANS (1965).

[4] S. PRT. 98-221, CHAP. 1, AT 10 (1984) (Michael Gordon's explanation of why ERISA was enacted).

The Studebaker incident and revelations of misuse of plan assets for personal gain by the Teamsters created the political atmosphere that, eventually, led to the enactment of ERISA and the creation of the modern American pension system. Viewed from this historical perspective, Enron presents a modern twist on the pension reform issues first raised by Studebaker and the Teamsters. In a single set of circumstances, Enron combines incredibly sympathetic stories by workers of ruined retirement dreams with equally incredible stories of greed and self-enrichment by company executives at the expense of the company's 401(k) retirement plan participants. It is this combination of factors that has made Enron such a powerful symbol in the public mind of the need to reform today's pension system.

As even the most casual observer of the legislative process knows, however, strong public opinion alone does not guarantee that Congress will act. Congress enacted ERISA in 1974 because, in addition to strong public opinion, the major stakeholders in the pension system (at that time, primarily employers and unions) perceived that they each had something to gain by supporting reform measures at the federal level.[5] Ultimately, Enron's long-term effect on the modern pension system will depend on whether the numerous stakeholders in the system perceive that it is in their own best interests to support reform measures.

II. STAKEHOLDER INTERESTS AND THE CHANGING STRUCTURE OF TODAY'S PENSION SYSTEM

There are five main categories of stakeholders in today's pension system. Broadly defined, these categories are: (1) employers; (2) labor unions; (3) workers; (4) persons who assist plan sponsors (employers and labor unions) in administering pension plans (known collectively as *plan service providers*); and (5) federal regulatory agencies. Within each category, there is a broad range of players and corresponding interests.

Employers vary in size from *Fortune 500* companies, who have tens of thousands of employees and operate throughout the United States and internationally, to local small businesses with at least one employee. Employers also represent the entire spectrum of the modern American economy. Their products range from the latest high-tech innovations to labor-intensive manufactured goods that must compete with imported products from abroad.

Labor unions vary according to the types of workers and industries they represent. *Workers* vary significantly in age, compensation, education and training, job mobility, and investment knowledge.

Plan service providers include virtually every major player in the financial services industry—mutual fund companies, securities firms, banks, trust companies, and in-

---

[5] For a discussion and analysis of the behind-the-scenes stakeholder motivations and politics that led to the enactment of ERISA, see STEVEN A. SASS, THE PROMISE OF PRIVATE PENSIONS, CHAPTER 8 (1997), and Wooten, *supra* note 2.

surance companies. Plan service providers also include professionals such as attorneys, accountants, actuaries, and independent financial asset managers.

Government regulators include four federal agencies. The *Department of Labor* has primary enforcement jurisdiction over the provisions of ERISA that regulate plan fiduciaries and protect plan participants and their pension benefits. The *Internal Revenue Service* has primary oversight over pension plan compliance with the Internal Revenue Code requirements that entitle the employer and plan participants to very favorable income tax treatment. The *Pension Benefit Guaranty Corporation* is an independent federal agency that insures the benefits provided through traditional defined benefit pension plans[6] in the event of employer insolvency. Finally, the *Securities and Exchange Commission* indirectly regulates the pension system through its oversight of the financial markets in which plan assets are invested.

The story of the modern pension system, and the evolving nature of stakeholder interests, is truly the story of the emergence of the 401(k) plan. When Congress enacted ERISA in 1974, the 401(k) plan did not exist. The 401(k) plan became possible when Congress later amended the pension tax rules of the Internal Revenue Code by adding Section 401(k).[7] The Department of Labor describes the dramatic effect on the pension system of this change as follows:

> The Revenue Act of 1978 permitted certain types of defined contribution plans to add a cash or deferred arrangement allowing employees to defer part of their pre-tax salaries to retirement. Plans established or modified to include this arrangement are known as 401(k) plans. This legislation has radically altered the structure of the U.S pension plan system over the last 20 years, shifting responsibility for the financing and investment of benefits from employers toward employees. Since the early and mid-1980s, the number of 401(k) plans has grown at a rate that in 15 years has led them to dominate the private pension system by providing primary or supplemental plan coverage to about 70 percent of all pension covered workers.
>
> With an overwhelming share of the growth in pension plan coverage over the last 15–20 years occurring under 401(k) type plans, the percentage of the pension covered work force participating in defined benefit plans (DB) has been in a slow but continuous decline. In 1998, an estimated 44% of all pension covered workers participated in a DB plan, down from 84% in 1978. In addition to the extremely low rate of new DB plan formation, the DB plan coverage rate has declined because of large numbers of terminations by small and medium sized plans and the lack of growth in employment among large unionized manufacturing firms maintaining their DB plans.

---

[6] The characteristics of defined benefit pension plans are described *infra* page 472.

[7] These amendments, part of the Revenue Act of 1978, became effective in 1980. *See* Revenue Act of 1978, Pub. L. No. 95-600, § 135, 92 Stat. 2763 (1987) (codified as amended at I.R.C. § 401(k)(2003)).

Paralleling the decline in DB plan coverage has been a decline in coverage under DC plans[8] without a 401(k) plan feature. Most of this decline resulted from the adoption of a 401(k) feature by ongoing DC plans. The DC plans initially adding a 401(k) feature were generally savings plans where the employer matched a portion of post-tax employee contributions. In more recent years many of the plans adopting a 401(k) feature have been profit sharing, and money purchase plans where employer contributions are made on a basis other than a match of employee contributions.

In 1998, the number of 401(k) plans topped the 300,000 mark. 401(k) type plans now make up 41% of all plans, cover 51% of all active participants, and hold 38% of all pension plan assets. A major consequence of the growth of 401(k) type plans has been the shift in the financing of plan benefits from employers to employees. In 1998, 47% of all contributions to pension plans were made by employees compared to only 11 % in 1978. In real dollars, employer contributions to all types of pension plans were 18% lower in 1998 than in 1978 while employee contributions were 480% higher.[9]

The most significant trend for the future of the pension system is the growing number of workers, primarily employed at smaller firms, whose only pension plan is a 401(k) plan. The Department of Labor reports that, of the 300,593 401(k) plans in existence in 1998, 90% of these plans (covering 19,219,000 active plan participants) were the only retirement plan sponsored by the employer for its workers.[10]

The reasons for this dramatic shift in the pension system are complex.[11] One explanation attributes this shift to underlying structural change in the United States economy and labor workforce away from traditional large firms and unionized manufacturing industries, where defined benefit plans are more common, toward smaller firms and non-unionized industries, particularly in the services sector, where defined contribution plans, and 401(k) plans in particular, are the most popular. Another explanation is that the relative cost of plan sponsorship and administration for the employer is higher for defined benefit plans than for defined contribution plans. This cost differ-

---

[8] A Defined Contribution ("DC") plan contains an individual account for each participant. The 401(k) plan is a type of DC plan where the individual participant funds his or her own account using his or her own wages or salary. In other types of DC plans, such as a profit sharing plan, the employer funds each individual worker's account through employer contributions to the plan.

[9] U.S. DEPT. OF LABOR, PRIVATE PENSION PLAN BULLETIN, ABSTRACT OF 1998 FORM 5500 ANNUAL REPORTS, 4 (Winter 2001–2002) (Highlights from the 1998 Form 5500 Reports). For historical data, *see* the Appendix to this essay, *infra*.

[10] *See id.* at Tables D.4 & D.5.

[11] For a discussion of these trends and a summary of the academic literature, see EMPLOYEE BENEFIT RESEARCH INST., AN EVOLVING PENSION SYSTEM: TRENDS IN DEFINED BENEFIT AND DEFINED CONTRIBUTION PLANS, ISSUE BRIEF NO. 249 (2002).

ential was exacerbated in the 1980s, when Congress enacted changes to the pension tax laws that reduced the tax incentives for small and medium-sized employers to sponsor defined benefit plans. A third explanation is that, as job insecurity and mobility increased, workers preferred the portability of retirement benefits provided by individual account plans. Finally, as the United States stock market experienced spectacular investment returns during the later half of the 1990s, workers increasingly demanded 401(k) plans to reap the benefits of a rising stock market.

Why are 401(k) plans attractive to the stakeholders in the pension system? This appeal is best understood by comparing and contrasting the fundamental features of the 401(k) plan with the traditional defined benefit pension plan.

In the traditional defined benefit pension plan, the plan provides that it will pay the participant a specific amount upon retirement, typically in the form of a monthly annuity for the life of the participant or the joint lives of the participant and the participant's spouse. These annuity payments terminate at death, leaving no opportunity for the intergenerational transfer of accumulated pension wealth. The plan typically provides this annuity benefit by using plan assets to purchase the annuity from an insurance company for the participant when the participant retires. The amount of the participant's monthly annuity benefit is determined by a formula contained in the plan, and is usually based on the participant's compensation and years of service with the employer. Under this formula mechanism, defined benefit plans provide the most generous annuity benefits to those workers with long years of service for a given employer.

The employer who sponsors a traditional defined benefit plan is responsible for funding the benefits promised by the plan at a minimum level specified under federal law. This funding obligation exists irrespective of the employer's profitability. Specialized pension tax law attorneys and actuaries are needed to assist the employer in determining and reporting to federal regulators the funding status of the plan and the amount of any additional employer contributions needed to satisfy the federal minimum funding requirements. The employer also is responsible for investing the plan's assets. Often, the employer hires a plan service provider with investment expertise to manage and invest the plan's assets for the employer. If the plan's investment returns are inadequate, the employer may be required to make additional contributions to the plan to ensure that the plan continues to meet the federal minimum funding requirements.

In contrast to defined benefit plans, 401(k) plans offer flexibility to both employers and workers. Although the employer is not required to make contributions to the 401(k) plan, many employers do make matching contributions as an incentive to encourage worker participation in the plan. In addition, 401(k) plans are often offered in conjunction with profit-sharing plans, where the employer has the option to make contributions to the individual accounts of participants in the profit-sharing plan.

The nature of the employer's business, its workforce demographics and characteristics, and market conditions often favor the flexibility offered by 401(k) plans. Businesses who want to attract a younger and potentially mobile workforce are likely to find that these employees prefer a 401(k) plan to a traditional defined benefit plan. Unlike the defined benefit plan, the 401(k) plan allows for a more flexible compensation system. The 401(k) plan allows individual workers to choose between deferring part of their earnings to save for retirement, or to receive all of their compensation as current income.

In contrast to defined benefit plans, 401(k) plans require individual workers to make several important decisions (and assume significant risks) concerning their future retirement benefits. Each worker initially must decide whether to participate in the plan at all. If the worker decides to participate, the worker must determine how much of his or her current compensation to contribute, and how to invest the assets in the account. At retirement, the worker's retirement benefit is the balance of the 401(k) plan account. This balance consists of worker contributions to the account plus accumulated investment earnings. In addition to assuming the investment risk, the worker also assumes the risk that she will outlive her retirement savings (known as the *risk of longevity*). The 401(k) plan account balance is usually distributed (or rolled over to an IRA) in the form of a lump sum at retirement. The retired worker must decide how much of this lump sum to consume for current living expenses, how much to save for future living expenses, and, possibly, how much to transfer to future generations at death.

Although the employer is not responsible for funding the 401(k) plan, the employer retains several other fiduciary responsibilities in sponsoring a 401(k). The most important fiduciary duty of the employer is selecting the menu of investment options for the 401(k) plan.[12] Most employers rely on a plan service provider in the financial services industry to assist them in this fiduciary task. The 401(k) plan's investment options usually consist of a variety of mutual funds, or, less commonly, a brokerage-type account that allows the participant to invest in individual stocks and bonds. Publicly-traded company stock of the employer also is a permissible investment option. The employer is responsible for deducting worker contributions to the 401(k) plan from current compensation and forwarding these sums to the plan's trustee in a timely fashion.

Many employers use plan service providers in the financial services industry to serve as plan trustees and plan administrators. These service providers hold the account assets and invest them pursuant to the directions of the 401(k) plan participants. A 401(k) plan service provider usually benefits financially whenever the provider's own mutual funds form part or all of the menu of investment alternatives for the 401(k) plan participants. When participants invest in these proprietary mutual funds, the service provider typically receives investment management and administrative fees. Service providers who provide brokerage services or facilitate transactions in company stock can receive commissions. The employer may, but is not required, to provide investment education or advice to 401(k) plan participants. Again, if investment education or advice is offered to the 401(k) plan participants, it is a service provider who typically provides this investment assistance to the participants.

---

[12] For a detailed discussion of the employer's fiduciary responsibilities under ERISA in selecting the 401(k) plan's menu of investment options, *see* Colleen E. Medill, *Stock Market Volatility and 401(k) Plans*, 34 U. MICH. J. L. REFORM, 469, 479–513 (2001).

The employer-controlled defined benefit and the participant-directed 401(k) plan represent two distinct models for the future of the pension system. The defined benefit plan represents a *paternalistic model.* Under this paternalistic model, employers bear the funding costs and market investment risk of providing retirement benefits to their workers. In contrast, the participant-directed 401(k) plan represents an *individual responsibility* model, where each worker is responsible for planning and providing for the worker's own retirement benefit.[13]

These two contrasting models lie at the heart of Enron's implications for the future of the pension system. Enron illustrates, in dramatic fashion, the potential retirement wealth polarization effect of the individual responsibility model. Some workers, particularly astute investors, will be retirement "winners." Others will be retirement "losers." Viewed from the broader perspective of the pension system as a whole, Enron raises the question of whether this polarization effect is an inevitable, and acceptable, byproduct of the individual responsibility model.

How policymakers respond to this question will profoundly affect the stakeholders in the pension system. More significantly, the answer to this fundamental question poses far-reaching consequences for the federal budget, the American taxpayer, and the future of American society. The tax subsidy that supports and promotes the pension system represents money that is not collected as tax revenue by the federal government. (In technical terms, this tax subsidy is known as a *tax expenditure.*[14]) For 2002, the tax expenditure for employer pension plans was $87.9 billion, the single largest tax expenditure in the entire federal budget.[15] The underlying public policy rationale for

---

[13] Although many employers offer a matching contribution to encourage participants to participate in the 401(k) plan, the modest levels of most employer matching contributions are insufficient to fund a significant portion of the worker's retirement benefit. Enron was an unusual situation because the employer matching contribution, made in company stock, greatly appreciated in value over a relatively brief period of time. Thus, the matching contribution account came to represent a significant percentage of each participant's total plan benefit. When the stock price fell sharply, so did the future retirement benefits of many of the 401(k) plan participants, because the Enron 401(k) plan prohibited them from selling the Enron stock held in their matching contribution accounts until age 50.

[14] STAFF OF THE JOINT COMMITTEE ON TAXATION, ESTIMATES OF FEDERAL TAX EXPENDITURES FOR FISCAL YEARS 2002–2006, 1–4 (Joint Comm. Print 2002) [hereinafter ESTIMATES OF FEDERAL TAX EXPENDITURES].

[15] ESTIMATES OF FEDERAL TAX EXPENDITURES, *supra* note 14, Table 1. This estimate is based on the provisions of the tax law as enacted through December 31, 2001. *See Id.* at 1. The estimate does not include the increased contribution and benefit limits for pension plans enacted by the Economic Growth and Tax Relief Reconciliation Act of 2001, Pub. L. No. 107-16, 115 Stat. 38, 41 (2001) (codified at scattered sections of 26 U.S.C.) ("EGTRRA"), which are effective for taxable years beginning after December 31, 2001. *See* ESTIMATES OF FEDERAL TAX EXPENDITURES, *supra* note 14, 10. To put the private pension system tax subsidy into perspective, the second and third largest tax expenditures in the federal budget for 2002 were for employer contributions for health care, health insurance premiums, and long-term care insurance ($69.1 billion) and the home mortgage interest deduction ($66.5 billion). *See* ESTIMATES OF FEDERAL TAX EXPENDITURES, Table 1.

the pension system tax expenditure is to encourage employers and workers to sponsor and participate in pension plans so that retirees will have an adequate income during retirement and not be dependent on their Social Security benefits as their sole source of retirement income. To the extent the pension system fails to achieve this public policy goal, the pension tax subsidy potentially represents forgone tax revenues that could have been used to fund other federal budget priorities.

If the pension system fails to provide adequate retirement income to future generations of retired workers, additional political and financial pressure will placed on maintaining and funding the traditional Social Security system. As the baby boomer generation attains age 65 (between 2010 and 2030), the traditional Social Security system is projected to place increasing fiscal pressure on the federal budget.[16] A few statistics illustrate the magnitude of the future demographic problem and the critical role of the pension system in resolving it. Persons age 65 and older represented 12.4% of the United States population in 2000.[17] By 2030, there will be about 70 million persons age 65 and older, or about twice the number in 2000.[18] The average annual income of persons age 65 and older in the United States in 2000 was $20,851. Of this amount, the average elderly person received $8,617 annually in Social Security benefits and $3,981 from pensions and annuities.[19] If the pension system is successful at generating retirement wealth for the baby boomer generation and beyond, it will lessen the current financial dependence of elderly Americans on the traditional Social Security system. If the pension system fails, there will be significant political pressure from retired elderly Americans (who vote in disproportionately high numbers for their demographic group) to increase the Social Security payroll tax to maintain the level of traditional Social Security benefits. In turn, an increase in the Social Security payroll tax will require younger workers to pay a greater percentage of their current income to fund the Social Security benefits of retirees. When placed in this demographic context, it becomes clear that every American taxpayer—young and old—has a personal financial stake in ensuring the future success of the pension system, not just for themselves as future retirees, but also for the system as a whole.

---

[16] *See* BOARD OF TRUSTEES, FED. OLD AGE AND SURVIVORS INS. AND DISABILITY INS. TRUST FUNDS, THE 2003 ANNUAL REPORT OF THE BOARD OF TRUSTEES OF THE FEDERAL OLD-AGE AND SURVIVORS INSURANCE AND DISABILITY INSURANCE TRUST FUNDS (2003). According to estimates by the board of trustees for the Social Security program, Social Security benefit expenditures are expected to exceed payroll tax revenues starting in 2018. It is at this point that Social Security will be in direct competition with other federal programs for annual funding in the federal budget. *Id.* at 2.

[17] Administration on Aging, U.S. DEPT. OF HEALTH AND HUMAN SERVICES, A PROFILE OF OLDER AMERICANS: 2002, 1 (based on 2000 Census data), *available at* http://www.aoa.gov/aoa/stats/profile/profile.pdf (last visited March 13, 2003).

[18] *Id.*

[19] EMPLOYEE BENEFIT RESEARCH INST., INCOME OF THE ELDERLY (2002), *available at* http://www.ebri.org/facts/0602fact.pdf (last visited March 13, 2003).

III. WHAT ARE THE "LESSONS" OF ENRON FOR THE PENSION SYSTEM?

As the materials by Professor John Langbein indicate,[20] the superficial problem that Enron represents and its solution both seem clear. When given a choice, publicly-traded employers who sponsor 401(k) plans will use company stock for matching contributions and as an investment option for plan participants. Plan participants, in turn, will choose to invest in company stock, a retirement investment strategy fraught with risk, rather than pursuing a diversified investment strategy. As Professor Langbein notes, one obvious solution to this problem is to limit the amount of company stock that participants can own through their retirement plan accounts.

At a deeper level, however, Enron represents a crossroads for the future of the pension system and its stakeholders. Should the pension system return to the employer-controlled paternalistic model? Or is it inevitable that the individual responsibility model will dominate the pension system of the twenty-first century? If the latter course is followed, is there an appropriate role for paternalism in the form of greater regulatory constraints on the behavior of the stakeholders in the system? These fundamental policy issues, and the ideological perspectives they represent, are likely to be the subject of vigorous and ongoing public debate. The following discussion and the notes and questions section highlight several of the most contentious issues in this debate. As you read the materials below, place yourself in the roles of the various stakeholders in the pension system. As a particular stakeholder, what would be your perspective on these issues?

A. Promoting Defined Benefit Plans

Advocates for the paternalistic model claim that the federal government needs to do more to promote defined benefit plans. Proposals to promote defined benefit plans vary. Some proponents of defined benefit plans claim that all employers should be required to sponsor defined benefit plans for their employees. Others claim that an employer who sponsors a 401(k) plan should be required to offer a defined benefit plan as the "primary" retirement plan for employees.[21] Still other proponents of the paternalistic model claim that greater tax incentives are needed to encourage employers voluntarily to sponsor more, and more generous, defined benefit plans.

These proposals can be seen as sharing a common philosophical approach, namely, that corporate decision-makers should consider the welfare of their workers and the interests of society as well as the interests of shareholders when determining whether and what type of retirement plan to offer to employees. This philosophical approach is

---

[20] *See* John. H. Langbein, *What's Wrong with Employer Stock Option Plans, this book* at 487–494.

[21] Under this approach, the alternatives for an employer who wanted to sponsor a retirement plan, but who did not want to sponsor a defined benefit plan, would be some other type of individual account plan that is funded by the employer, such as a profit-sharing plan, a money purchase pension plan, or an employee stock ownership plan.

sometimes framed as an argument that employers have a moral or ethical obligation to ensure that their workers enjoy a financially secure retirement. The implicit assumption underlying this argument is that a 401(k) plan cannot provide adequate retirement income security, particularly for low-wage workers.

Requiring employers to sponsor defined benefit plans is controversial for several reasons. Historically, the hallmark characteristic of the pension system established by ERISA has been that the employer's decision whether or not to sponsor a retirement plan, and if so, the type of plan to sponsor, is *voluntary*. This approach provides employers with the flexibility to tailor their retirement benefits (or lack thereof) to meet the demands of both a competitive market and the employer's workforce.

Defined benefit plans today typically are sponsored by large employers. Several provisions of the Economic Growth and Tax Relief and Recovery Act of 2001 ("EGTRRA")[22] are designed to encourage small employers voluntarily to sponsor defined benefit plans. EGTRRA increased the employer's maximum possible tax deduction for contributions to a defined benefit plan. EGTRRA also authorized a simplified defined benefit plan that reduces the administrative complexity (and related costs) of defined benefit plans for small employers.

Will such incentives promote the growth of defined benefit plans? Skeptics argue that the employer's assumption of investment risk for funding a defined benefit plan is simply too great a deterrent to be overcome by increased tax incentives and greater administrative simplicity. Particularly for smaller employers and less established companies with variable earnings, the financial unpredictability associated with defined benefit plans is a significant deterrent to sponsoring them Requiring employers to sponsor a defined benefit plan could cause fewer companies to go into, or stay in, business. The recent experience of *Fortune 500* companies who sponsor defined benefit plans illustrates the financial volatility associated with defined benefit plans. As of 2002, approximately 360 of the 500 companies comprising the Standard and Poor's Index ("S&P 500") sponsored a defined benefit plan for their workers. During the bull market of the 1990s, investment returns on defined benefit plan assets were sufficiently high that these employers were not required to make annual funding contributions to their defined benefit plans. Moreover, under the rules for pension plan accounting, these corporations were allowed to report projected investment earnings that exceeded minimum federal funding requirements as operating revenues.[23] Thus,

---

[22] Economic Growth and Tax Relief and Recovery Act of 2001, *supra* note 16.

[23] Even though these projected "excess" investment earnings are reported as operating revenue for the corporation, ERISA requires that the assets of the plan must remain inside the trust for the plan and cannot be withdrawn or otherwise used by the corporation for its operations or be distributed as dividends to shareholders. These pension accounting rules are the target of reform measures designed both to reduce the financial volatility associated with current pension accounting standards and to make the financial reporting and disclosure process concerning defined benefit pension funding liabilities more transparent to the investing public.

sponsoring a defined benefit plan during this period of a rising stock market served to boost reported corporate earnings and increase shareholder value.[24] Measured by book value, as of the end of 2000, these 360 companies reported a cumulative pension asset surplus of $263 billion.[25]

Over the next two years, the combination of a dismal stock market and low interest rates[26] resulted in a dramatic funding reversal for these companies. By the end of 2002, these 360 corporations reported a cumulative plan funding deficit of $216 billion, despite having voluntarily contributed almost $46 billion to their defined benefit pension plans during 2002.[27] This cumulative funding deficit, and lower projected rates of future investment returns for defined benefit plan assets, are likely to play a significant role in reducing reported corporate earnings for these companies in the future.[28]

Observers of the pension system predict that the stock market's decline is likely to result in fewer and fewer *Fortune 500* companies who continue to sponsor traditional defined benefit plans. For smaller employers who do not sponsor a defined benefit plan, the lesson from the *Fortune 500* experience is particularly sobering. The plan assets of defined benefit plans sponsored by *Fortune 500* companies typically are invested and managed by professional investment managers. This expertise is unavailable to most small employers, either because the assets of the plan are insufficient in size to attract the best investment managers, or because the price of professional investment services is cost-prohibitive. Despite this investment expertise, *Fortune 500* companies suffered significant funding deficiencies due to uncontrollable interest rate and investment risk. Given these circumstances, it seems unlikely that additional tax incentives for small employers to sponsor defined benefit plans will be sufficient to overcome employer concerns about the financial unpredictability and uncertainty associated with defined benefit plans.

B. Achieving Retirement Income Security Through 401(k) Plans

Researchers have begun to study whether participants in 401(k) plans can achieve a level of retirement income security comparable to participants in defined benefit plans. Some of these studies indicate that it may be possible for participants in 401(k) plans to achieve a level of income during retirement that is equal to or greater than the level

---

[24] Christine Dugas, *Pension Revenue Can Mislead Investors*, USA TODAY, Sept. 5, 2002, at 1B.

[25] Allen Sloan, *Pension Funds' Risky Business*, NEWSWEEK, Dec. 9, 2002, at 59.

[26] Interest rates play a crucial role in estimating future defined benefit plan liabilities and then discounting these future liabilities to present value to determine the current level of required minimum funding for the plan. The lower the interest rate, the higher the level of current funding required. As of the end of 2002, interest rates were at a 40-year low.

[27] CREDIT SUISSE FIRST BOSTON, THE QUARTERLY REPORT, 4 (April 14, 2003).

[28] *See id.* at 8–12.

of retirement income for participants in defined benefit plans.[29] These studies also confirm what stakeholders in the pension system have long known intuitively. There are two behavioral barriers that must be overcome for workers to achieve retirement income security through a 401(k) plan. First, beginning early in their careers, workers must regularly contribute sufficient amounts to the plan. Second, workers must invest their 401(k) plan accounts wisely.

Reform proposals concerning the individual responsibility model seek to encourage this type of desirable behavior among workers. Reform focuses primarily on two areas: investment education and investment advice for 401(k) plan participants, and greater government regulation of the investment options available to 401(k) plan participants. To fully appreciate the potential ramifications of these reform proposals for the stakeholders in the pension system, it is useful to have a basic understanding of the rules that currently govern these issues, as well as the findings of researchers who have studied the investment behavior of participants in 401(k) plans.

The rise to prominence of the 401(k) plan in the pension system began in 1992, when the Department of Labor issued final regulations governing 401(k) and other individual account plans for which the participants direct the investment of their own individual plan accounts.[30] These regulations are commonly known as the "404(c) Regulations."[31] The 404(c) Regulations provide that if the employer's plan was structured to comply with these regulations, the employer would not be liable for investment losses resulting from the participant's investment directions. There are two general requirements of the 404(c) Regulations that are relevant for this discussion. These requirements concern: (1) the information that the employer must provide to plan participants, and (2) the types of plan investment options that the employer must make available to plan participants.

The 404(c) Regulations require that participants must receive general information concerning the plan, and specific financial information concerning the plan's investment options.[32] This financial information concerning the plan's investment options

---

[29] *E.g.*, EMPLOYEE BENEFIT RESEARCH INST., CAN 401(K) ACCUMULATIONS GENERATE SIGNIFICANT INCOME FOR FUTURE RETIREES?, ISSUE BRIEF NO. 251 (2002), *available at* http://www.ebri.org/pdfs/1102ib.pdf (last visited March 13, 2003); Andrew A. Samwick & Jonathan Skinner, *How Will Defined Contribution Pension Plans Affect Retirement Income?* (Oct. 2001). For a contrary view, *see* EDWARD N. WOLFF, ECONOMIC POLICY INSTITUTE, RETIREMENT INSECURITY (2002), *available at* http://www.epinet.org/books/retirement.pdf (last visited March 13, 2003).

[30] *See* Colleen E. Medill, *The Individual Responsibility Model of Retirement Plans Today: Conforming ERISA Policy to Reality,* 49 EMORY L. J. 1, 33–35 (2000).

[31] The 404(c) Regulations are codified at 29 C.F.R. § 2550.404(c)-1. The 404(c) Regulations derive their popular name from ERISA Section 404(c), 29 U.S.C. § 1104(c)(2001), the statutory authority under which the regulations were promulgated.

[32] *See* Medill, *Individual Responsibility Model, supra* note 30, at 34–36 and accompanying footnotes.

is provided in the form of (and at the sophistication level of) a securities prospectus required under federal securities laws. Significantly, the 404(c) Regulations do *not* require the employer to provide investment education or investment advice to the 401(k) plan participants. Although many employers today do voluntarily offer some form of investment education to 401(k) plan participants, very few employers offer investment advice.

The 404(c) Regulations require that the plan must offer at least three investment options. The employer who sponsors the plan is responsible for selecting these investment options. In performing this task, the employer acts as a fiduciary and is subject to two ERISA fiduciary duties. These duties are the duty of prudence and the duty to act exclusively for the benefit of the plan participants (also known as the fiduciary duty of loyalty).[33]

The range of investment alternatives offered by the plan must offer materially different risk and return characteristics, and must provide participants, even those with small account balances, the opportunity to diversify their investments and minimize the risk of large investment losses. Most employers select a set of three core mutual funds—a stock fund, a bond fund, and a money market fund—to satisfy these requirements. Other investment options, such as more specialized industrial sector mutual funds, employer company stock, or even a brokerage feature allowing the participant to invest in the individual stock of other companies, can be added to this group of core funds. The average 401(k) plan today offers ten to twelve mutual fund investment alternatives.

If the company stock of the plan's sponsoring employer is publicly traded, the 404(c) Regulations expressly permit such company stock to be included as a permissible investment option in the employer's 401(k) plan. Although only 3% of 401(k) plans offer company stock as an investment option, these plans are sponsored by some of the nation's largest employers.[34] Consequently, plans where company stock is an employer matching contribution or an optional participant investment option represent 23 million plan participants.[35] To offer company stock as an investment option, the plan must provide for certain additional safeguards against improper employer influence over the participant's investment decisions concerning company stock.[36] The plan must have some procedures in place to protect the confidentiality of participants who buy and sell company stock. The plan also must designate a fiduciary to monitor compliance with these confidentiality procedures. If necessary, a third-party independent fiduciary must be appointed to handle 401(k) plan transactions in company stock. This situation typically arises when the company is engaged in a merger or acquisition, or when there is a contested election of company directors.

---

[33] 29 U.S.C. § 1104(a) (2001). For a detailed discussion and analysis of how these fiduciary duties apply in the context of 401(k) plans, *see* Medill, *Stock Market Volatility, supra* note 12, at 481–521.

[34] *See* Olivia S. Mitchell & Stephen P. Utkus, *The Role of Company Stock in Defined Contribution Plans*, 10–11, Pension Research Council (Working Paper 4, Aug. 2002) *available at* http://rider.wharton.upenn.edu/~prc/PRC/WP/WP2002-4b.pdf (last visited March 13, 2003).

[35] *See id.*

[36] *See* Medill, *Stock Market Volatility, supra* note 12, at 524–25.

Several research studies have examined the investment behavior of 401(k) plan participants. The largest ongoing empirical study to date has been conducted by the non-partisan Employee Benefit Research Institute ("EBRI Study").[37] The EBRI Study, which began in 1996, covers 35,367 401(k) plans, with 11.8 million active participants and $579.8 billion in plan assets. This study has consistently found that, when company stock is offered as an investment option, participants strongly tend to select company stock in lieu of a more diversified equity mutual fund. The EBRI Study also found that many 401(k) plan participants do not follow sound retirement investing principles. For example, the 2000 study results showed that, although the average 401(k) plan account was invested 51% in equity mutual funds, the accounts of individual 401(k) plan participants varied widely around this average. Of 401(k) plan participants in their 20s, 28.3% of this group of participants was *zero percent* invested in equity mutual funds.[38] Although this percentage dropped to 23.5% for participants in their 30s, it rose steadily thereafter, from 26.0% for participants in their 40s, to 29.9% for participants in their 50s, to 41.9% for participants in their 60s. The study results for prior years reported similar findings.

Researchers have identified several reasons why participants are strongly attracted to company stock as a 401(k) plan investment. First, participants *minimize the investment risk of company stock.*[39] Rather than breeding contempt, familiarity leads participants to underestimate the investment risk associated with company stock. Employees feel that they understand the company's business and that, by their labor, they have some degree of influence over the future financial fortunes of the company. Second, when the employer makes matching contributions in the form of company stock and also offers company stock as an elective investment option, participants *perceive that the employer is endorsing company stock* as a "good" investment option.[40] Participants view the employer's decision to make matching contribution in company stock as an implicit form of investment advice. Third, participants *simplify what they perceive to be a complex investment decision* by investing disproportionately in company stock.[41] If numerous other investment options are offered along with company stock, participants tend to simplify their decision-making process by investing heavily in the investment with which they are most familiar—company stock.

---

[37] EMPLOYEE BENEFIT RESEARCH INST., ISSUE BRIEF NO. 239, 401(K) PLAN ASSET ALLOCATION, ACCOUNT BALANCES, AND LOAN ACTIVITY IN 2000 (2001) *available at* http://www.ebri.org (last visited March 13, 2003).

[38] *See id.* at Table 7, p. 12.

[39] *See* Gur Huberman, *Familiarity Breeds Investment*, 14 REV. OF FIN. STUD. 659 (2001).

[40] *See* Nellie Liang & Scott Weisbenner, *Investor Behavior and the Purchase of Company Stock in 401(k) Plans—The Importance of Plan Design*, N.B.E.R., Research Working Paper 9131 (Sept. 2002); Shlomo Benartzi, *Excessive Extrapolation and the Allocation of 401(k) Accounts to Company Stock*, J. OF FIN., 1747 (Oct. 2001).

[41] *See* Shlomo Benartzi & Richard H. Thaler, *Naive Diversification Strategies in Defined Contribution Saving Plans*, THE AM. ECON. REV., March 2001, at 79.

Other researchers have explored the effect of providing investment "education"[42] to 401(k) plan participants on investment behavior. Recent research in this area has found that providing investment education to 401(k) plan participants may not be effective in influencing their investment behavior.[43] After receiving investment education, participants may *say* they are going to change their contribution amounts and investment allocations, but few 401(k) participants actually *implement* these changes. This research is consistent with earlier studies of investment behavior finding that, in general, *there is a strong bias among 401(k) plan participants in favor of maintaining the status quo.*[44] In other words, 401(k) plan participants are great procrastinators when it comes to changing their contribution amounts and investment allocations. Researchers attribute this status quo bias to two root causes—the high indirect cost of gathering and analyzing the information necessary to make an investment decision, and problems of self-control.[45]

As an alternative to investment education, reform proposals have focused on making technical amendments to ERISA's rules that financially deter plan service providers from providing investment advice to 401(k) plan participants.[46] Assuming for purposes of discussion that these technical amendments eventually are enacted, two unresolved, and controversial, issues remain. First, who should bear the cost of providing investment advice to plan participants: the employer who sponsors the plan, or the plan participants themselves? Second, should employers continue to have *discretion* to decide whether or not to offer investment advice to 401(k) plan participants? Or should federal law *require* employers to make investment advice available to 401(k) plan par-

---

[42] Investment "education" is a term of art in the ERISA field, and is often used as a contrast with another related term of art, investment "advice." In theory, the difference between these two legal concepts is that education involves general information concerning investment theory and plan investment options, whereas advice consists of specific investment recommendations tailored to the unique circumstances of the individual participant. *See* Medill, *Individual Responsibility Model; supra* note 30, at 28–30, 51–54. In practice, the difference between education and advice oftentimes is unclear, particularly from the perspective of the plan participants. The Department of Labor has issued guidance in the form of regulations attempting to clarify what types of information and methods of presentation will constitute investment "education." *See id.* at 51–54.

[43] *See* James J. Choi, David Laibson, Brigitte C. Madrian, & Andrew Metrick, *Defined Contribution Pensions: Plan Rules, Participant Decisions, and the Path of Least Resistance*, N.B.E.R., Working Paper 8655 (Dec. 2001).

[44] *See* Brigitte C. Madrian & Dennis F. Shea, *The Power of Suggestion: Inertia In 401(k) Participation and Savings Behavior*, Q. J. OF ECON., 1149–1187 (Nov. 2001); James J. Choi, David Laibson, Brigitte C. Madrian, & Andrew Metrick, *For Better or for Worse: Default Effects and 401(k) Savings Behavior*, N.B.E.R., Working Paper 8651 (Dec. 2001).

[45] *See* Madrian & Shea, *supra* note 44.

[46] How ERISA discourages plan service providers from rendering investment advice under current law is a highly technical subject, even for ERISA experts. For an introduction to this topic, see Medill, *Individual Responsibility Model, supra* note 30, at 38–46. In brief, participants do not receive investment advice because of the fiduciary prohibited transaction rules of ERISA. Reform proposals in Congress aim to exempt plan service providers who provide investment advice from ERISA's prohibited transaction rules, thereby encouraging them to provide investment advice to plan participants.

ticipants? Resolution of these contentious issues is likely to be the subject of a vigorous future debate among the stakeholders in the pension system.

Other reform proposals have focused on increased government regulation of the investment options available to participants in 401(k) plans. As a practical matter, the 404(c) Regulations impose a minimal level of constraint on the employer's fiduciary discretion in selecting the plan's investment options. To date, government regulation of 401(k) plan investment options primarily has been indirect, through enforcement of the employer's fiduciary duties of prudence and exclusive loyalty to the plan participants.

Interpretation and enforcement of these fiduciary standards by the federal courts and the Department of Labor are likely to change in the future as a result of Enron and the other corporate fiascoes that contributed to the general decline of the stock market. From 1992 through 1998, during the period that 401(k) plans were rapidly expanding throughout the workforce, the stock market also experienced significant gains, particularly in the later half of the 1990s. As a practical matter, this rising stock market made it unnecessary for employers to consider the prudence of their investment option selections, and in particular, the wisdom of including company stock as an investment option for 401(k) plan participants. Under these market conditions, almost any investment option (including company stock) generally made money, which in turn made for satisfied 401(k) plan participants.

Starting in 1999, however, the stock market began to fall. By the end of 2002, the stock market recorded its third consecutive year of losses, an extended period of decline unprecedented since before World War II. Although the investment losses experienced by the participants in the Enron 401(k) plan were the most dramatic, during this same period, millions of other 401(k) plan participants also experienced significant losses due to the general downturn in the stock market. Such losses, in turn, have led plan participants to scrutinize more closely the employer's selection of investment options for their 401(k) plan. In egregious cases such as Enron, such scrutiny has led to federal class action lawsuits where the 401(k) plan participants have alleged that the employer's choice of company stock as a 401(k) plan investment option constituted a breach of fiduciary duty under ERISA.

The primary focus of these cases to date has been on the employer's breach of the duty of loyalty to 401(k) plan participants in the context of company stock as an investment option. The underlying legal principles of fiduciary prudence and loyalty, however, are not unique to Enron-like circumstances. For example, many businesses fail honestly. Given this fact, and combined with the research evidence concerning participant investment behavior for 401(k) plans that offer company stock as an investment option, is it prudent for any employer today to include company stock as an investment option for its 401(k) plan? The fiduciary principle of prudence in selecting and monitoring the 401(k) plan's investment options also raises significant issues concerning the types of mutual funds offered by the plan. For example, is it prudent for the employer to include narrow industrial sector mutual funds, such as funds that invest solely in the stock of high-technology companies, as investment options? To select mutual funds with above-average investment management fees? To retain mutual funds that have consistently underperformed their peers?

These questions illustrate the difficulty of regulating 401(k) plan investment options indirectly through ERISA fiduciary litigation. In the final analysis, the most enduring lesson of Enron for the pension system may be that more direct government regulation of 401(k) plan investment options is necessary for sound retirement policy. The retirement income security of 401(k) plan participants is heavily dependent upon the investment earnings generated by their 401(k) plan accounts. Even with the best of investment advice, 401(k) plan participants cannot invest successfully unless they have the opportunity to choose from a menu of "good" investment options. Thus, the employer's choice of investment options is critical to the future success of the individual responsibility model, and ultimately the success of the modern American pension system.

Rather than opposing more direct government regulation of plan investment options, such reform measures eventually may be welcomed by the stakeholders in the pension system. Relying on expensive and time-consuming ERISA fiduciary litigation to indirectly regulate 401(k) plan investment options is inefficient for all of the stakeholders. Employers and other fiduciary plan service providers lack clear guidance concerning their fiduciary responsibilities in selecting plan investment options. This lack of clear guidance results in uncertainty at best and, at worst, ERISA fiduciary liability. Professional ERISA advisors are frustrated by their inability to give definitive compliance advice. Finally, as evidenced by Enron, 401(k) plan participants, the very group of stakeholders for ERISA was supposed to protect, clearly suffer under the current system. Perhaps it is only by passing through a post-Enron period of ERISA fiduciary litigation misery that the necessary stakeholder consensus can be forged to modernize the pension system for the twenty-first century.

APPENDIX

Table 1 below summarizes the extent of the fundamental shift in the structure of the pension system away from the defined benefit plan toward the defined contribution plan in general, and the 401(k) plan in particular.

Table 1. Number of Pension Plans[47]

Year	Total	DB Plans	DC Plans	401(k) Plans
1979	470,921	139,489	331,432	Not available
1985	632,135	170,172	461,963	29,869
1990	712,308	113,062	599,245	97,614
1995	693,404	69,492	623,912	200,813
1998	730,031	56,405	673,626	300,593
2001	758,000	51,000	707,000	361,000

---

[47] Data for years 1979–98 are from U.S. DEPT. OF LABOR, PRIVATE PENSION PLAN BULLETIN, ABSTRACT OF 1998 FORM 5500 ANNUAL REPORTS, Table E1, E23 (Winter 2001–2002). Data include both single- and multi-employer plans. The figures given for DC plans include 401(k) plans. Data for 2001 are estimates made by Olivia S. Mitchell and Stephen P. Utkus, *The Role of Company Stock in Defined Contribution Plans*, Table 1, Pension Research Council Working Paper 2002-4.

Table 2. Number of Active Plan Participants (thousands)[48]

Year	Total	DB Plans	DC Plans	401(k) Plans
1979	46,929	29,440	17,489	Not available
1985	62,268	29,024	33,244	10,339
1990	61,831	26,344	35,488	19,548
1995	66,193	25,531	42,662	28,061
1998	73,328	22,994	50,335	37,114
2001	78,000	22,500	55,500	43,800

Table 3. Plan Assets ($ millions)[49]

Year	Total	DB Plans	DC Plans	401(k) Plans
1979	445,430	319,595	125,835	Not available
1985	1,252,739	826,117	426,622	43,939
1990	1,674,139	961,904	712,236	384,854
1995	2,723,735	1,402,079	1,321,657	863,918
1998	4,021,849	1,936,600	2,085,250	1,540,975
2001	4,000,000	1,900,000	2,100,000	1,700,000

NOTES AND QUESTIONS

1. *Achieving Stakeholder Consensus on Reform Legislation.* Discuss the perspectives of the stakeholders for modernizing the pension system. Are they likely to agree or conflict? How likely is it that these groups will reach the level of consensus necessary to pass reform legislation in Congress?

2. *The Voluntary Nature of the Pension System.* Should the pension system continue to be voluntary? If you were a business owner, would you voluntarily sponsor a pension plan for your workers? If so, what type? What factors would you consider in making this decision?

3. *Providing Investment Assistance to 401(k) Plan Participants.* Numerous research studies have found that many workers are financially illiterate. Should the law require employers who sponsor 401(k) plans to provide investment education or investment advice to their workers? Does the employer have a moral or ethical obligation to go beyond the minimum legal requirements to assist financially illiterate workers in achieving retirement income security? Alternatively, should

---

[48] Data for years 1979–98 are from U.S. DEPT. OF LABOR, PRIVATE PENSION PLAN BULLETIN, ABSTRACT OF 1998 FORM 5500 ANNUAL REPORTS, Table E8, E23 (Winter 2001–2002). Data include both single and multi-employer plans. The figures given for DC plans include 401(k) plan participants. Data for 2001 are estimates made by Olivia S. Mitchell and Stephen P. Utkus, *The Role of Company Stock in Defined Contribution Plans*, Table 1, Pension Research Council Working Paper 2002-4.

[49] Data for years 1979–98 are from U.S. DEPT. OF LABOR, PRIVATE PENSION PLAN BULLETIN, ABSTRACT OF 1998 FORM 5500 ANNUAL REPORTS, Table E11, E23 (Winter 2001–2002). Data include both single and multi-employer plans. The figures given for DC plans include 401(k) plan assets. Data for 2001 are estimates made by Olivia S. Mitchell and Stephen P. Utkus, *The Role of Company Stock in Defined Contribution Plans*, Table 1, Pension Research Council Working Paper 2002-4.

the federal government assume this responsibility? If the federal government takes over the responsibility of educating employees, what might such an education program look like? How should such a program be funded?

4. *The Employer's Role in Selecting 401(k) Plan Investment Options.* The pension system's reliance on employer discretion in selecting 401(k) plan investment options stands in stark contrast to the regulatory approach advocated by President Bush's Commission to Strengthen Social Security ("Bush Commission") concerning personal Social Security accounts. The Bush Commission recommended that small accounts (under $5,000) be limited to a choice of nine indexed, low fee mutual funds. The assets of these nine mutual funds would be invested and managed by professional investment managers selected by government officials. Large accounts (over $5,000) could be invested in additional mutual funds offered by the private sector, but only if such funds were "balanced and diversified" across all industrial sectors of the economy. These additional mutual fund investment options would have to be approved by government officials before workers could invest their personal Social Security account assets. Under the Bush Commission's recommendations, industrial sector and firm investment risk are effectively eliminated. Workers would not be allowed to invest their personal Social Security account assets in the stock of individual companies, or in mutual funds that consist of the stock of companies in narrow industrial sectors. As an individual participant in a 401(k) plan, which approach to the selection and regulation of your plan's investment options would you prefer? Which approach is the better public policy?

5. *Prohibiting Company Stock As An Investment Option.* Is it sound public policy to prohibit 401(k) plans from offering company stock as an investment option? Or would prohibiting company stock as a 401(k) plan investment option merely exacerbate the differences between company executives who receive stock options and rank-and-file workers who, without access to company stock through a 401(k) plan, are less likely to share in large stock market gains if the company does extraordinarily well?

6. *Allocating Oversight Responsibility Among Competing Federal Regulatory Agencies.* When Congress originally enacted ERISA, Congress's focus was primarily on defined benefit pension plans for union workers. This original focus made the Department of Labor a natural fit for primary regulatory supervision of plan sponsors who managed pension plan assets and enforcement of the rights of 401(k) plan participants. In contrast, under today's individual responsibility model, the security of each participant's eventual retirement benefit is tied much more directly to the integrity of the financial markets, and, in the case of company stock, to the financial integrity of the employer itself. Given the paradigm shift in the pension system that has occurred since Congress enacted ERISA in 1974, should the Department of Labor continue to retain primary regulatory authority? Or would the Securities and Exchange Commission be better equipped for this task?

What's Wrong with Employer Stock Pension Plans

John H. Langbein *

I appreciate the invitation to speak with you about the pension investment aspects of the Enron Corporation bankruptcy.

I have been teaching and writing about pension law and pension policy for two decades. I coauthor the principal book on pension law that is used in American law schools.[1] I serve as a Uniform Law Commissioner from Connecticut, and I was the reporter (drafter) for the Uniform Prudent Investor Act (1994), which now governs fiduciary investing at the state level in most American states.

1. The Enron plan. Enron Corp. sponsored a 401(k) pension plan for its employees.[2] The plan permitted the employee to contribute up to 15 percent of his or her salary, subject to a ceiling.[3] Enron made a matching contribution of half of what the employee contributed.[4] The sums contributed by both employee and employer were tax deferred under Sections 401(a) and 401(k) of the Internal Revenue Code. The plan provided that Enron's contribution would be entirely in Enron stock.[5] The employee

---

* JOHN H. LANGBEIN, THE ENRON PENSION INVESTMENT CATASTROPHE: WHY IT HAPPENED & HOW CONGRESS SHOULD FIX IT (Jan. 24, 2002), *available at* http://www.law.yale.edu/outside/html/Public_Affairs/183/Langbein.pdf.

[1] JOHN H. LANGBEIN & BRUCE WOLK, PENSION AND EMPLOYEE BENEFIT LAW (3d ed. 2000 & 2001 Supp.).

[2] The plan document is titled "Enron Corp. Savings Plan As Amended and Restated Effective July 1, 1999" [hereafter cited as Enron Plan].

[3] *Id.*, § III.l.

[4] *Id.*, § III.4. (The matching contribution was subject to the limit that it could not exceed six percent of the employee's base pay.)

[5] *Id.* § V.16(a).

participant could choose to invest his or her contribution among a menu of options, including leading well-diversified mutual funds[6] or more Enron stock.

The plan required the employee-participant to hold the employer-contributed Enron shares until age fifty.[7] Only at that age could he or she direct that the Enron shares be sold and the proceeds redirected into other investments. With respect to these match shares, the plan made the employee-participants into involuntary Enron shareholders until age fifty.

As Enron's financial difficulties began to be revealed in the fall of 2001, the value of Enron shares, including those held in the pension plan accounts, declined precipitously. Shares that had traded above $80 per share at the apogee are now effectively worthless. As a result, many Enron employees have lost huge portions of their expected retirement funds—both the employer-match shares and those Enron shares that many employees elected to purchase with their own contributed funds.

Although some of the alleged financial skullduggery of Enron's managers, directors, and accountants may have violated ERISA fiduciary law, it is vital for Congress to understand that the key feature of the Enron plan that made it possible for these losses to occur—the large concentration of employer stock in the plan's investments—was permitted under ERISA, the federal pension regulatory law.

ERISA invited this mess, and unless you change ERISA, I can predict to you with utter certainty that such cases will happen again, as they have repeatedly in the past. What's new about the Enron calamity is simply the enormity of the losses.

2. DC plans. 401(k) plans such as Enron's are known as defined contribution (DC) plans, or in the language of ERISA, as "individual account plans." DC plans "provide[] for an individual account for each participant;" the participant's "benefits are based solely upon the amount contributed to the participant's account," plus the investment experience (dividends, gains or losses) of the account. ERISA § 3(34).

The distinctive feature of any DC plan is that investment risk rests entirely upon the account of each participating employee. The employee captures market gains, the employee suffers market declines.

By contrast, in a traditional defined benefit (DB) plan of the sort that prevails among large employers in manufacturing and transportation industries and utilities, the employer (or other sponsor) bears the investment risk. In a DB plan, the employer promises the employee a certain benefit on retirement, and if the investments in the pension fund don't produce enough to pay the benefit, the employer must make up the shortfall from company assets.

3. The DC or 401(k) structure is not the problem. As ERISA now stands, the high concentration of employer stock that allowed the catastrophic losses to the Enron

---

[6] Including the Vanguard 500 Index Trust, the Fidelity Magellan Fund, the Fidelity Growth and Income Fund, the PIMCO total Return II Fund, and the T. Rowe Price Small Cap Fund. *See* Enron Benefits Dept., *Money in Motion: Enron Corp. Savings Plan 401(k) Plan Details.*

[7] Enron Plan § IV-16(b).

employees could only have occurred in a DC plan, because ERISA's diversification requirements (discussed below) would have prevented these concentrations in a DB plan. It would be a fallacy, however, to conclude that the problem lies in the nature of DC plans. The truth is that it is as easy to avoid over-concentration in a single stock in a DC plan as in a DB plan. For example, most of us who are employed in academia participate in DC plans operated by TIAA-CREF. TIAA-CREF diversifies its stock and bond investments across literally thousands of issues.

The ERISA failure that allowed the Enron employees' loss to occur is that ERISA contains an exception to its diversification requirement. ERISA allows certain types of DC plans, including 401(k) plans, to permit and/or require employees to hold these large concentrations of employer stock in their plan accounts.

Over the past two decades that 401(k) plans have been allowed[8] there has been a huge increase in the use of DC plans, especially 401(k) plans. The Employee Benefits Research Institute (EBRI) reports that, as of the year 2000, there were more than 327 thousand 401(k) plans in effect, covering more than 43 million active participants, holding assets of $1.8 trillion. There are many reasons for this complex development.

DC plans do have disadvantages,[9] but they have two great advantages for employees that help explain their popularity.

First, DC plans offset the lack of portability in the private pension system. DC plans produce better results for the employee who works for several employers across his or her career than does a DB plan, because DB plans use career-average service formulas that favor long-service employees. DC plans are a response to the increasing mobility of the workforce.

Second, DC plans encourage employees to engage in more pension saving than usually occurs under DB plans,[10] both because the transparency of the individual account mechanism is easier for the employee to understand and to value than a distant benefit formula; and because there are ways to arrange that any money in a DC account that the employee and his or her spouse do not turn out to need for their retire-

---

[8] IRC § 401(k) originated in the Revenue Act of 1978, but 401(k) plans became attractive only when the IRS issued regulations in 1981 clarifying the salary reduction mechanism that allows the employee to contribute pretax dollars.

[9] The two most important: (1) DC plans require ordinary workers to make important investment management decisions, which in a DC plan are the work of investment professionals; (2) DB plans can deliver larger retirement benefits per dollar of savings, because they mandate annuitization as the mode of distribution, recapturing for other plan members the sums not needed to support short-lived participants and beneficiaries. *See* LANGBEIN & WOLK, *supra* note 1, at 51–61 (providing for further discussion of the pluses and minuses of DC plans).

[10] *See* James M. Poterba, Steven F. Venti & David Wise, *The Transition to Personal Accounts and Increasing Retirement Wealth: Macro and Micro Evidence*, (National Bureau of Economic Research Working Paper 8610) (2001), *available at* http://papers.nber.org/papers/w8610.pdf (providing evidence that "assets at retirement after lifetime employment under a 401(k) plan would typically be much higher than under a defined benefit plan").

ment will pass to their heirs. The ability to transfer the account balance on death encourages employees to make more ample provision for their retirement, secure in the knowledge that they will not forfeit the cushion.

Accordingly, the lesson to learn from the Enron debacle is not that DC plans should be restricted, but that the diversification standards that Congress wisely imposed on DB plans need to be extended to DC plans.

4. Diversification. The duty to diversify investments is a standard principle of good fiduciary investing practice, which was long ago[11] absorbed into the trust investment law.[12] ERISA has, from its enactment in 1974, imposed this duty to diversify pension fund investments. ERISA § 404(a)(1)(C).

ERISA's duty to diversify does not, however, apply to all pension plans. Rather, Congress allowed an exception for certain types of DC plans. ERISA §§ 404(a)(2), 407(d)(3). That exception is a major mistake of pension policy, and until Congress fixes it, I can predict to you with utter certainty that cases like Enron will continue to occur.

Let me say a quick word about the underlying economics of the duty to diversify. The importance of diversification is by far the most important finding in the entire field of financial economics. Over the past 40 years, we have had a stream of empirical and theoretical studies, which have led so far to six Nobel prizes in economics, conclusively showing that there are large and essentially costless gains to diversifying an investment portfolio thoroughly.

Investment risk has three distinct components: market risk, industry risk, and firm risk. Market risk is common to all securities; it reflects general economic and political conditions, interest rates, and so forth; hence, it cannot be eliminated. Industry risk, by contrast, is specific to all the firms in each industry or industry grouping. Firm risk refers to factors that affect the fortunes only of the particular firm. My favorite illustration is the example of the international oil companies. All of them suffered from the 1973 Arab embargo (industry risk). By contrast, only Exxon incurred the liabilities arising from the great Alaskan oil spill of March 1989 (firm risk). Holding shares in other industries helped prudent investors to offset the decline of the oils in 1973; holding shares of other oils helped offset the decline in Exxon.

Only about 30 percent of the risk of security ownership is market risk, that is, risk that cannot be eliminated by diversification. By contrast, industry risk amounts to about 50 percent of investment risk, and firm risk comprises the remaining 20 percent.[13] Thus, effective diversification can eliminate roughly 70 percent of investment risk.

---

[11] We have had the duty to diversify in American trust investment law for well over a century. *See, e.g.,* Dickinson, Appellant, 152 Mass. 184, 25 N.E. 99 (1890).

[12] RESTATEMENT (SECOND) OF TRUSTS § 228 (1959); RESTATEMENT (THIRD) OF TRUSTS: Prudent Investor Rule § 227(b) (1992).

[13] R.A. BREALEY, AN INTRODUCTION TO RISK AND RETURN FROM COMMON STOCKS 117 (2d ed. 1983). Brealey's actual numbers are 31 percent market risk; 12 percent industry risk; 37 percent other groupings; and 20 percent firm risk. I consolidate industry and other groupings as industry risk and round to 50 percent.

And that is why, from the standpoint of good investment practice, a portfolio such as the Enron pension fund, so heavily concentrated in a single stock, any stock, is pure folly. But there are many plans sitting out there with even more employer stock than Enron. For example, as of January 2000, Proctor and Gamble had a DC plan with 96 percent in employer stock, Pfizer has one with 88 percent, Abbott Laboratories with 87 percent.[14]

According to the most recent data reported by EBRI, employer stock comprises 19 percent of all 401(k) plan assets,[15] but that number, which averages plans with and without employer stock, understates the magnitude of the problem for the plans with the employer stock.[16]

5. What's wrong with employer stock. A pension fund portfolio holding a massive part of its assets in any one stock is bad; but holding such a concentration in the stock of the employer is worse. For the employees of any firm, diversification away from the stock of that employer is even more important. The simple reason is that the employee is already horrifically underdiversified by having his or her human capital tied up with the employer. The employee is necessarily exposed to the risks of the employer by virtue of the employment relationship. The last thing in the world that the employee needs is to magnify the intrinsic underdiversification of the employment relationship, by taking his or her diversifiable investment capital and tying that as well to the fate of the employer.

The Enron debacle illustrates this point poignantly. Just when many of the employees have lost their jobs, they have also lost their pension savings, which in a 401(k) plan they could have borrowed against (or with a penalty, withdrawn) in order to tide them over.

6. The incentives argument. What's the case for having employer stock in pension funds? The argument is that employers want to incentivize employees to identify with the stockholders of the firm. Making employees into stockholders will motivate them to care about the firm's profitability.

There's a simple answer to that argument: Don't do it in the pension fund. If you want to sell stock to your employees for such sound business reasons, go right ahead and do so (subject to adequate disclosure of the risks—a subject to which I shall return). But you should not be able to treat such a program as a pension fund, for two very good reasons: It abuses the pension tax subsidy and it misleads employee-participants.

Congress provides two huge tax subsidies for qualified pension plans: Employee and employer contributions to such plans are tax-deferred, and so is any investment buildup. Congress grants this subsidy in order to promote pension saving, hence to promote retirement income security. That policy is concerned to protect the employee

---

[14] PENSIONS & INVESTMENTS, Jan. 24, 2000, at 26.

[15] Sarah Holden & Jack VanDerhei, *401(k) Plan Asset Allocation, Account Balances, & Loan Activity in 2000*, EMPLOYEE BENEFIT RESEARCH INST., Issue Brief (Nov. 2001), at 1, 6 & Chart 3.

[16] *See id.* at 13 & Table 10.

and his spouse in their post-employment years. The policy has nothing to do with promoting employer interests. To the contrary, the most fundamental principle of ERISA fiduciary law is the so-called exclusive benefit rule, requiring that pension plan investing and administration must be done "solely in the interest of the participants and beneficiaries and . . . for the exclusive purpose of providing benefits" to them. ERISA § 404(a)(1)(A). Ordinarily, therefore, subordinating the interests of the employees to those of the employer is a breach of the fiduciary duty to avoid such conflicts of interest under ERISA. Apart from the statutory exception that allows employer stock in pension plans, the message of ERISA is: pension plans are for employees, not for employers. Congress provides the pension tax subsidy for employee interests.

Another way to make that point is to remind ourselves that the employee has earned the pension. Employers do not offer pension plans in order to be nice guys—indeed, employers have a fiduciary duty to their shareholders not to waste the company's assets by giving those assets away to people, even employees. These plans are not gratuities. Employers offer pension plans as part of the compensation package, as what we call deferred compensation.[17] Pensions are the employee's earnings, channeled into retirement saving at the source. We should not let supposed employer preferences interfere with the best interests of the employee.

As the Enron calamity shows, employees do not understand the risks involved in holding employer stock in their pension accounts. They rely on these accounts for their retirement. Many of the employees do not have enough years left in the workforce to be able to replace the losses in subsequent employment.

7. The plan formation argument. The other claim on behalf of the status quo is that in our voluntary private pension system, if you don't let employers stuff employer stock in these plans, they won't offer the plans at all. This is highly unlikely.

In competitive markets, if one employer won't offer a pension plan while others do, that employer will be at a disadvantage in competing for workers. The employers who offer pensions today do so in order to be competitive for workers who are pension-sensitive, and such employers will continue to want to be competitive for such workers by offering pensions even if the employers are forbidden to stuff the plans with company stock.

We heard the same argument when Congress imposed vesting rules in ERISA in 1974, and when congress mandated spousal shares in 1984. The truth is that sensible pension regulation does not discourage plan formation. To the contrary, by making pension promises more reliable, it increases the attractiveness of pension plans to employees, and causes firms to offer more of them.

As regards 401(k) plans, the argument is sometimes made that if employer stock investments were curtailed, employers might continue to offer 401(k) plans, but em-

---

[17] The claim that pensions were gifts, the so-called gratuity theory of pensions, has a long history. American law decisively rejected the gratuity theory in favor of the deferred compensation theory across the twentieth century. For discussion, see LANGBEIN & WOLK, *supra* note 1, at 16–17, 122–27. ERISA's vesting and benefit accrual rules implement the deferred compensation view.

ployers would not continue to offer matching contributions unless in employer stock. While I doubt that, there is an easy compromise: let the employer who wishes continue to contribute employer stock (and to get the tax deduction for doing so), but require that the plan fiduciary dispose of it on the open market within a short period and reinvest the proceeds in a diversified portfolio.

8. The solution is already in ERISA. If there is one bright spot for the future in the Enron pension catastrophe, it is that we know exactly how to prevent such cases from occurring again. We not only know the cause, we also know the cure.

The losses have been caused by allowing DC plans to be underdiversified. The cure is to require diversification. Congress has successfully insisted on diversifying plan investments in DB plans for a quarter century. What is needed is to extend that regime across the DC universe, to cover all tax-qualified plans.

Congress should not prohibit employer stock from pension plans altogether, because there are situations in which a prudent fiduciary investor may choose to hold some. For example, it is common for pension investment managers to buy index funds in fiduciary accounts. Index funds hold shares in all the companies in the index, and the employer may be one of those companies.

In ERISA § 407(a)(2), Congress set a ceiling on employer stock, saying that a plan may never hold more than ten percent,[18] but Congress then left it to the prudence and diversification rules of ERISA § 404(a) to govern the question of how much less than 10 percent is appropriate. The normal answer will be little or none. The one time a DB plan tried to approach the 10 percent limit, in the most famous of all ERISA investment cases, Donovan v. Bierwirth, the Second Circuit held that the investment in employer stock was imprudent. Bierwirth stands for the proposition that the prudence and diversification norms of ERISA § 404(a) govern the exercise of the up-to-ten-percent authority in ERISA § 407(a)(2).

The paradox of ERISA is that it contains both the problem and the solution to the Enron mess. ERISA contains a diversification regime that would prevent such cases form ever happening again if extended from DB to all DC plans. (Obviously, were Congress to take that step, it would be important to provide a transition period to assure orderly compliance.)

9. ESOPs. I must emphasize that everything I have said about the evils of employer stock in 401(k) plans applies equally to employee stock ownership plans (ESOPs). It has been known from the beginning in the specialist literature that ESOPs represent bad retirement policy.[19] They are tools of corporate finance masquerading as pension plans.

---

[18] ERISA § 407(a)(2), 29 U.S.C. § 1107(a) (2000).

[19] ESOPs have been trenchantly criticized on a variety of policy grounds. *See, e.g.,* Michael W. Melton, *Demythologizing ESOPs,* 45 TAX L. REV. 363 (1990); Richard L. Doernberg & Jonathan R. Macey, *ESOPs & Economic Distortion,* 23 HARV. J. LEGIS. 103 (1986); D. Bret Carlson, *ESOPs & Universal Capitalism,* 31 TAX L. REV. 289 (1976).

10. Disclosure. My main recommendation to you is to extend ERISA's diversification regime to all tax-qualified plans. If a plan gets the tax benefits of a pension plan, it should not hold material concentrations of employer stock.

If Congress lacks the political will to take that step, or to take it across the entirety of the DC plan universe, I would offer a weaker alternative: Congress should at least insist upon alerting employees about the risks of holding employer stock. My source of inspiration is the Surgeon General's warnings on cigarette packages. The thinking behind those warnings is that people need to be aware of the risks, so that they can alter their behavior. Transferred to the pension arena, the point is that, if employees were warned about the risks of employer stock, they would be in a better position (1) to avoid electing to buy more of it in plans that offer it as an employee option, and (2) to pressure employers to move away from ESOPs and to discontinue using employer stock in the match feature of 401(k) plans.

ERISA § 102 presently requires employers or other plan sponsors to send to employees annually a summary plan description ("SPD"), describing key features of each plan. I would recommend that Congress require that the SPD for any plan that contains an employer stock option or employer stock match contain a Surgeon General's warning, something like this:

WARNING

> Under commonly accepted principles of good investment practice, a retirement account should be invested in a broadly diversified portfolio of stocks and bonds. It is particularly unwise for employees, who are already subject to the risks incident to employment, to hold significant concentrations of employer stock in an account that is meant for retirement saving.

A disclosure solution of this sort is, I repeat, a second-best solution.

The best solution is for Congress to mandate diversification across the entire universe of pension plans, as a condition of the tax subsidy that Congress grants these plans. By taking that step, Congress could tell the American worker with confidence that Congress has done what is necessary to assure that there will never again be another Enron-type pension calamity.

Enron: The Board, Corporate Governance, and Some Thoughts on the Role of Congress

Troy A. Paredes*

I. INTRODUCTION

Enron and the scandals that followed in its wake at WorldCom, Tyco, Adelphia, and elsewhere teach us an important lesson: An effective board of directors is central to good corporate governance; and good corporate governance, in turn, is central to good corporate performance. Unfortunately, it took the recent wave of corporate corruption and abuses to focus our attention on the board of directors and on corporate governance more broadly. Having focused attention on the board, many people do not like what they see. Shareholders, employees, creditors, and others place broad trust, confidence, and authority in directors to ensure the corporation's success. But as the Enron board starkly demonstrated, boards often fail to live up to our expectations, and ineffectual boards cast doubt on the entire corporate governance system. Now that boards have gotten our attention, we need to ask the tough question: How do we ensure that boards of directors run and oversee their corporations effectively? One answer, including from Congress and the New York Stock Exchange, has been more regulation. However, as I argue in this essay, more regulation might do more harm than good.

The board of directors is granted expansive authority under state corporation codes around the country. Take Delaware, the most important state for purposes of corporate law, not only because the majority of public companies are incorporated there, but also because other states look to Delaware corporate law for guidance.[1] Section 141(a) of the Delaware General Corporation Law provides that the "business and affairs of every corporation . . . shall be managed by or under the direction of a board of directors."[2]

Associate Professor of Law, Washington University School of Law. I owe special thanks to Chris Bracey, Kathy Brickey, Dan Keating, Scott Kieff, Joel Seligman, and Peter Wiedenbeck for very helpful discussions and comments during the writing of this essay. All remaining errors are mine.

[1] *See* Lucian Arye Bebchuk & Assaf Hamdani, *Vigorous Race or Leisurely Walk: Reconsidering the Competition Over Corporate Charters,* 112 YALE L.J. 553 (2002) (collecting data).

[2] DEL. CODE ANN. tit. 8, § 141(a). This provision is typical of other states. *See, e.g.,* MODEL BUS. CORP. ACT § 8.01.

This is an expansive grant of authority. Shareholders, of course, have the right to sue directors for breach of fiduciary duty. But the right to sue is little comfort in most cases. Although boards are charged with running the business in good faith and in the best interests of the corporation and its shareholders, courts are reluctant to interfere with a board's exercise of its authority and generally defer to the board under the business judgment rule.[3] This, of course, assumes a suit for breach of fiduciary duty can even be brought. Shareholders face a number of procedural hurdles, most notably the demand requirement, before bringing a derivative action against directors (or officers) for breach of fiduciary duty.[4] In addition to the right to sue, shareholders have the right to vote, including the right to vote for the board,[5] and the right to sell their shares, both of which can influence board behavior.[6] But the rights to vote and sell only go so far in practice.[7] For example, for the most part, management controls the shareholder voting process and sets the agenda, and there are few things that shareholders have a right to

---

[3] The business judgment rule reflects the broad discretion that directors have to manage the corporation's business and affairs and the presumption that directors (and officers) are able to run the business better than are judges. Under the business judgment rule, courts generally will not second-guess the board's business judgment so long as the directors acted with requisite care, on an informed basis, in good faith, and loyally—in other words, so long as the directors did not breach their fiduciary duties of care or loyalty. If the directors are found to have breached their fiduciary duty, the burden shifts to the board to show that the transaction was entirely fair to the corporation. *See* ROBERT CHARLES CLARK, CORPORATE LAW §§ 3.4 & 3.5 (1986); CHARLES R.T. O'KELLEY & ROBERT B. THOMPSON, CORPORATIONS AND OTHER BUSINESS ASSOCIATIONS, CASES AND MATERIALS 295–395 (3d ed. 1999); *see also infra* notes 103, 112–113, and 140–42 and accompanying text.

[4] Before bringing a derivative action, shareholders are generally required to make a demand on the board of directors to initiate the suit on the corporation's behalf. If the board refuses to bring suit, the board's decision to reject the shareholder demand is subject to judicial review under the business judgment rule. Shareholders cannot pursue the litigation independently unless the business judgment rule does not protect the board's decision not to sue. In many jurisdictions, such as Delaware, pre-suit demand is excused if it would be futile for shareholders to make, such as when the directors are not independent from the defendants or suffer from a conflict of interest. However, in response to a claim of demand futility, the board can establish a special litigation committee comprising disinterested and independent directors to evaluate any pre-suit demand. For more on derivative litigation and the demand requirement, see CLARK, CORPORATE LAW, *supra* note 3, at §§ 15.1–15.3; O'KELLEY & THOMPSON, *supra* note 3, at 395–431.

[5] Shareholders also typically have the right to vote on certain fundamental changes, including mergers, amendments to the articles of incorporation and bylaws, and the sale of all or substantially all of the corporation's assets.

[6] Notably, non-shareholder constituencies, such as employees, have no legal authority over a corporation's internal affairs, unless they also happen to be shareholders. Non-shareholder constituencies, nonetheless, often exert a great deal of pressure on management. For an interesting discussion of the role of employees in corporate governance, see EMPLOYEES AND CORPORATE GOVERNANCE (Margaret M. Blair & Mark J. Roe eds., 1999).

[7] For a useful overview of the right of shareholders to vote, sell, and sue, see generally Robert B. Thompson, *Preemption and Federalism in Corporate Governance: Protecting Shareholder Rights to Vote, Sell, and Sue*, 62 LAW & CONTEMP. PROBS. 215 (1999).

vote on as a matter of corporate law.[8] The proxy rules under the federal securities laws[9] supplement shareholder voting rights under state corporate law by granting shareholders limited access to the company's proxy materials for the purpose of making proposals for a shareholder vote; but even here, the board of directors can omit many, if not most, shareholder proposals from the corporation's proxy materials and can ignore other proposals, even if they receive a majority shareholder vote.[10] Insofar as the right to sell is concerned, shareholders can always follow the "Wall Street Rule" and sell into the market; but boards can adopt defensive tactics to fend off a hostile bidder. In fact, boards can often "just say no" to a bid without giving shareholders a meaningful choice to sell when it can matter most—namely, when a premium offer is made for the company.[11]

In practice, directors typically do not manage the corporation's business directly, but delegate day-to-day control to officers. Directors do, however, retain important

---

[8] *See supra* note 5 and accompanying text.

[9] The proxy rules under the federal securities laws regulate shareholder communications, as well as communications between a corporation and its shareholders. The proxy rules, among other things, require extensive disclosures in connection with the "solicitation" of proxies. For an overview of the proxy rules, see LOUIS LOSS & JOEL SELIGMAN, FUNDAMENTALS OF SECURITIES REGULATION 488–561 (4th ed. 2001). The concern is that the cost of complying with the proxy rules, and the risk of liability for failure to comply, discourages shareholders from communicating. In order to facilitate shareholder communication, the SEC adopted a series of proxy reforms in 1992 that exempted certain shareholder communications from the proxy rules. For an interesting empirical analysis of the effect of the 1992 proxy reforms, see Stephen Choi, *Proxy Issue Proposals: Impact of the 1992 SEC Proxy Reforms*, 16 J. L. ECON. & ORG. 233 (2000).

[10] Rule 14a-8 under the Securities Exchange Act of 1934 affords shareholders limited access to their company's proxy materials. In general, a shareholder who, when submitting her proposal, has owned at least $2,000 worth or one percent of her company's voting stock for at least one year can include a proposal in management's proxy materials. The shareholder might, for example, want the company to stop doing business in Angola, adopt an anti-discrimination employment policy, redeem a poison pill, or expense stock options. The company, however, can omit shareholder proposals in several instances, such as when the shareholder proposal relates to the company's ordinary business or is not considered a proper subject of shareholder action under state law. To avoid this latter basis for omitting a shareholder proposal, shareholders can cast their proposals as non-binding recommendations or requests, which management is then free to follow or reject. For an overview of the shareholder proposal process, see LOSS & SELIGMAN, *supra* note 9, at 510–33.

[11] Boards can adopt a host of measures that, such as poison pills, staggered boards, and anti-takeover charter provisions, that can fend off a hostile bid that the board does not favor, even if the shareholders want to sell. An active market for corporate control—the market in which companies are bought and sold—is thought to discipline directors and officers to run their business profitably. Otherwise, the management team is subject to removal via a tender offer from a bidder who believes it can run the business better. Defensive tactics designed to defeat a hostile bid insulate directors and officers from the risk of removal. The literature on takeovers is extensive. For a sampling, see John C. Coffee, Jr., *Regulating the Market for Corporate Control: A Critical Assessment of the Tender Offer's Role in Corporate Governance*, 84 COLUM. L. REV. 1145 (1984); Frank H. Easterbrook & Daniel R. Fischel, *The Proper Role of a Target's Management in Responding to a Tender Offer*, 94 HARV. L. REV. 1161 (1981); Alan Schwartz, *Search*

managerial authority.[12] At the very least, boards retain authority over major corporate policy decisions and the company's overall business strategy, which might involve a significant acquisition, a corporate restructuring, a public offering, or a decision to enter a new line of business. Further, even if only on an informal basis, directors are available to consult company executives and to provide input and guidance on how the business should be run. Moreover, because directors ultimately have the power to hire and fire officers and to set their compensation, the board might have much more authority over the day-to-day business than the generic organizational chart of a company with numerous top executives might suggest.[13] Related to its managerial role, the board also serves an important resource function. Directors provide access to key resources, such as industry expertise, competitors, customers, labor, suppliers, capital, and government officials.

More recently, attention has focused less on the board's managerial or resource functions and more on its monitoring role, reflecting the fact that officers are the principal managers of the business. The charge of the "monitoring board" is to monitor the corporation's officers in running the business. Why are directors needed to monitor officers? Because of agency costs—the concern that officers are inclined to shirk or otherwise act in their own self-interest, at the expense of the corporation and its shareholders.[14] The board's monitoring duties include hiring and firing top executives, set-

---

Theory and the Tender Offer Auction, 2 J.L. ECON. & ORG. 229 (1986); Lucian Arye Bebchuk, *Toward Undistorted Choice and Equal Treatment in Corporate Takeovers*, 98 HARV. L. REV. 1693 (1985); David D. Haddock et al., *Property Rights in Assets and Resistance to Tender Offers*, 73 VA. L. REV. 701 (1987); Ronald J. Gilson, *Seeking Competitive Bids Versus Pure Passivity in Tender Offer Defense*, 35 STAN. L. REV. 51 (1982); Martin Lipton, *Takeover Bids in the Target's Boardroom: A Response to Professors Easterbrook and Fischel*, 55 N.Y.U. L. REV. 1231 (1980); Robert Daines & Michael Klausner, *Do IPO Charters Maximize Firm Value? Antitakeover Protection in IPOs*, 17 J.L. ECON. & ORG. 83 (2001); Lucian Arye Bebchuk, *The Case Against Board Veto in Takeovers*, 69 U. CHI. L. REV. 973 (2002); Robert B. Thompson & D. Gordon Smith, *Toward a New Theory of the Shareholder Role: "Sacred Space" in Corporate Takeovers*, 80 TEX. L. REV. 261, 272 (2001); Troy A. Paredes, *The Firm and the Nature of Control: Toward a Theory of Takeover Law*, __ J. CORP. LAW __ (forthcoming 2004).

[12] The following summary of the board's role draws from an extensive literature on the board of directors. *See infra* note 50.

[13] *Cf.* KENNETH J. ARROW, THE LIMITS OF ORGANIZATION 78 (1974) ("[I]f every decision of A is to be reviewed by B, then all we have really is a shift in the locus of authority from A to B and hence no solution to the original problem."). Of course, the board's authority might be diluted when the CEO also serves as the chairman of the board.

[14] To expand on this point, the concern is that those charged with managing the company might have a conflict of interest with the corporation's shareholders, in which case the managers have an incentive to serve their own interests. For example, managers might decide to shirk, line their own pockets, have fancy corporate jets and other perks, or build an empire by acquiring companies. Three of the classic articles discussing agency costs are Eugene F. Fama, *Agency Problems and the Theory of the Firm*, 88 J. POL. ECON. 288 (1980); Eugene F. Fama & Michael C. Jensen, *Separation of Ownership and Control*, 26 J.L. & ECON. 301 (1983); Michael C. Jensen & William H. Meckling, *Theory of the Firm: Managerial Behavior, Agency*

ting executive compensation, and otherwise overseeing the management team to ensure that the company is run well. The received wisdom is that independent directors—directors who are free from the undue influence of the CEO and other top managers (i.e., those being monitored)—are essential to an effective monitoring board.[15]

Recent scandals at Enron and elsewhere highlight a core concern about boards of directors that has preoccupied corporate law since Berle and Means ("B&M") wrote their 1932 classic, *The Modern Corporation and Private Property*.[16] The concern is that shareholders of public companies have little influence over the corporation, and that directors and officers are ultimately unaccountable, affording directors and officers broad discretion to favor themselves and other constituencies at the expense of shareholders; in other words, agency costs. The narrow concern is that boards are passive or, worse yet, dominated by management. B&M said that shareholders of public corporations have a hard time coordinating their activities because stock ownership is widely dispersed among shareholders in public corporations.[17] Moreover, dispersed stock ownership means that few shareholders have a large enough stake in the company to justify the cost of keeping up to speed about the business. As a result, B&M concluded, not only day-to-day control over the business, but also control over the board, ultimately resides in management, if not solely the chief executive, since management is able to control the election process and ensure that the management-sponsored di-

---

Costs and Ownership Structure, 3 J. FIN. ECON. 305 (1976). Shareholders are able to monitor the management team to some extent, although collective action problems and rational apathy make shareholder monitoring difficult; stock ownership is fragmented among shareholders, and few shareholders own enough stock to make it worthwhile to monitor the company actively. *See, e.g.*, Cynthia J. Campbell, Stuart L. Gillan, & Cathy M. Niden, *Current Perspectives on Shareholder Proposals: Lessons from the 1997 Proxy Season*, 28 FIN. MGMT. 89 (1999); Lilli A. Gordon & John Pound, *Information, Ownership Structure, and Shareholder Voting: Evidence from Shareholder-Sponsored Corporate Governance Proposals*, 48 J. FIN. 697 (1993); Bernard S. Black, *The Value of Institutional Investor Monitoring: The Empirical Evidence*, 39 UCLA L. REV. 895 (1992); John Pound, *Proxy Contests and the Efficiency of Shareholder Oversight*, 20 J. FIN. ECON. 237 (1988). After the recent scandals, institutional investors have begun to take a more active role in overseeing directors and officers. In recent years, various shareholder services, such as the Investor Responsibility Research Council and Institutional Shareholder Services, have made shareholder monitoring easier and more effective.

[15] A burgeoning theory of the firm, called team production, describes yet another role for the board of directors, a mediating role. In the view of team production, the board acts as an independent "mediating hierarch" that mediates conflicts among the various corporate constituencies. At bottom, the goal of the mediating board is to elicit the optimal level of firm-specific investments from all the constituencies that make up the corporation. It is worth noting that proponents of team production also challenge the shareholder primacy norm. *See, e.g.*, Margaret M. Blair & Lynn A. Stout, *A Team Production Theory of Corporate Law*, 85 VA. L. REV. 247 (1999).

[16] ADOLF A. BERLE, JR. & GARDINER C. MEANS, THE MODERN CORPORATION AND PRIVATE PROPERTY (1932).

[17] *Id.* at 47–68 (showing empirically the dispersion of stock ownership).

rectors are elected.[18] Control is thus separated from ownership, giving rise to agency costs as shareholders are further marginalized in the corporation's governance.

Notwithstanding the rise of institutional investors, the problems associated with the separation of ownership and control still resonate. The CEO, for example, has assumed an ever-more dominant role in the corporation, culminating in what people have begun to refer to as the "imperial CEO."[19] Needless to say, the CEO is particularly influential when he also serves as chairman of the board. (Not surprisingly, many influential individuals and organizations have recently urged that the roles of chairman and CEO be split and performed by separate people or at least that a lead director who is independent be appointed as a counterweight to the chairman/CEO.[20]) But even if management does not control the board, there is still reason to worry that directors will not perform their roles effectively and will create their own agency costs. Directors, like officers, presumably have a tendency to shirk or otherwise act in their own self-interest. In addition, many directors, even when acting in good faith, simply do not have the time, knowledge, or understanding of the business to effectively oversee corporate strategy or to monitor top executives.

Concerns about director accountability and independence are not new. What the disasters at Enron, WorldCom, Adelphia, Tyco, and elsewhere suggest, however, is that the problems relating to board structure and performance are more widespread—and the consequences of board failure are more serious—than people had thought. In short, there is a new realization that corporate governance really matters.

Clearly, there are many top-notch directors and boards. Nonetheless, the challenge is to make boards more effective overall. Put differently, how do we ensure that directors are accountable and act in the best interests of the corporation and its shareholders, especially given that shareholders' legal and practical influence over the corporation is limited?[21] As suggested above, shareholders have some ability to oversee and influence

---

[18] *Id.* at 69–70, 87–89. Institutional investor activism can mitigate the problem of the separation of ownership and control. For more on the role of institutional investors, see, e.g., John C. Coffee, Jr., *The SEC and the Institutional Investor: A Half-Time Report*, 15 Cardozo L. Rev. 837 (1994); Bernard S. Black, *Shareholder Passivity Reexamined*, 89 Mich. L. Rev. 520 (1990); Alfred F. Conard, *Beyond Managerialism: Investor Capitalism?*, 22 U. Mich. J.L. Reform 117 (1988); Ronald J. Gilson & Reinier Kraakman, *Reinventing the Outside Director: An Agenda for Institutional Investors*, 43 Stan. L. Rev. 863 (1991).

[19] For an interesting take on the role of the CEO, see Rakesh Khurana, Searching for a Corporate Savior: The Irrational Quest for Charismatic CEO's (2002).

[20] *See, e.g.*, The Conference Board, Commission on Public Trust and Private Enterprise, Findings and Recommendations (Part 2) (Jan. 9, 2003), at 6–9 [hereinafter the Conference Board Report]; *see also* Phyllis Plitch, *GE Will Let Shareholders Vote on Chairman Proposal*, Wall St. J., Feb. 11, 2003, *available at* http://online.wsj.com.

[21] For critiques of the shareholder primacy norm, see, e.g., Blair & Stout, *supra* note 15; Thomas A. Smith, *The Efficient Norm for Corporate Law: A Neotraditional Interpretation of Fiduciary Duty*, 98 Mich. L. Rev. 214 (1999); Progressive Corporate Law (Lawrence A. Mitchell ed., 1995). However, even critics of shareholder primacy would not countenance the recent corporate scandals or support a board's being beholden to management.

the board by voting, selling, or suing. In addition, institutional investors can influence the board in more informal ways, somewhat behind the scenes. Further, directors can be encouraged to internalize norms of good corporate conduct that can result in better board performance.[22] Moreover, directors can be given stock options and other equity stakes as a way of aligning the directors' and shareholders' interests in maximizing corporate profits, although recent experience suggests that large equity stakes in the company might create perverse incentives for directors.[23] Finally, markets, including product markets, capital markets, the market for directors, and the market for corporate control, can discipline directors to act in shareholders' best interests.[24]

Note, though, that all of these corporate governance devices were in place when the wave of corporate scandals, led by Enron, broke in 2001 and 2002. Not surprisingly, on the basis that something had to be done to ensure good board performance and the integrity of our corporate governance system, there has been a corresponding wave of regulatory and legislative reforms to remedy the types of corporate abuses that we have witnessed. (To be sure, politics, in addition to policy, partly motivated the regulatory response.) Of particular note are the Sarbanes-Oxley Act of 2002 ("Sarbanes-Oxley")[25] and the revised listing standards proposed by the New York Stock Exchange ("NYSE") that companies trading on the exchange must meet.[26]

---

[22] *See infra* notes 173–75 and accompanying text.

[23] Incentive-based compensation, such as stock options, were thought to ameliorate the agency costs arising from the separation of ownership and control by aligning the interests of directors and officers with the shareholders' interests. It turns out that the huge equity compensation packages might have also created pressures to manage earnings in order to meet quarterly earnings targets. *See infra* note 57–58 and accompanying text. The SEC has responded to concerns about earnings management by, among other things, requiring more disclosure regarding pro-forma financial measures and earnings announcements. *See* Conditions for Use of Non-GAAP Financial Measures, Release No. 33-8176 (Jan. 22, 2003).

[24] *See generally* O'KELLY & THOMPSON, *supra* note 3, at 51–52 (summarizing the role of markets in corporate law).

[25] Sarbanes-Oxley Act of 2002, Pub. L. No. 107-204, 116 Stat. 745 (2002) [hereinafter Sarbanes-Oxley].

[26] Corporate Governance Rule Proposals Reflecting Recommendations from the NYSE Corporate Accountability and Listing Standards Committee As Approved by the NYSE Board of Directors August 1, 2002 (No. SR-NYSE-2002-33 filed Aug. 16, 2002), as amended by Amendment No. 1 to the NYSE Corporate Governance Rule Proposals (filed April 4, 2003) [hereinafter NYSE Listing Standards Proposal]. The National Association of Securities Dealers, Inc. has also proposed revised listing standards for NASDAQ-listed companies. It is simply in the interest of space that I focus on the NYSE listing standards. The concerns expressed below about the approach adopted in Sarbanes-Oxley and the NYSE listing standards apply equally to the revised NASDAQ listing standards, to the extent that they reflect a mandatory approach to regulating corporate governance. For a good comparison of the NYSE and NASDAQ proposals, see William B. Chandler III & Leo E. Strine, Jr., *The New Federalism of the American Corporate Governance System: Preliminary Reflections of Two Residents of One Small State,* __ U. PA. L. REV. __ (forthcoming 2004).

Not to be forgotten, the SEC has adopted several new rules and regulations, some on its own initiative and some as mandated by Sarbanes-Oxley. For a sampling, see Standards Relating to Listed Company Audit Committees, Securities Act Release No. 33-8220 (April 9, 2003); Disclosure Required by Sections

It is too soon to tell whether the reforms will result in better corporate governance and performance. There are certainly reasons to be optimistic; indeed, some might say that corporate governance could not be much worse than in recent years. But there are also reasons to be skeptical. The mix of roles and functions that a board serves varies from company to company. Accordingly, the expertise and skills required for a board to be effective are not the same in each instance. The regulatory reforms, however, are mandatory in nature, adopting a "one-size-fits-all" approach to corporate governance.[27] Yet it is far from certain that these reforms, chief among them being the increased role played by independent directors and the stiffened definition of independence, are appropriate for all public or NYSE-listed companies. Furthermore, if these governance changes are appropriate, it is far from certain that new rules are needed to institute them. Capital markets have themselves put pressure on corporations to reconstitute their governance structures voluntarily along similar lines, while still affording a company the flexibility to tailor its governance structure to fit its particular needs.

In this brief essay, it is impossible to cover the entire range of corporate governance issues raised by Enron and the other scandals. My goals, therefore, are limited. The first is to consider the potential costs of the recent corporate governance reforms directed at the board of directors, focusing primarily on Sarbanes-Oxley and the NYSE listing standards. I am concerned that these reforms will do more harm than good by requiring companies to adopt a corporate governance structure that does not fit their business or governance needs. My second goal is to consider what role Congress should play in legislating corporate governance. I conclude that Congress should not engage in the substantive regulation of corporate governance, precisely because Congress is likely to adopt a one-size-fits-all mandatory approach.[28]

---

406 and 407 of the Sarbanes-Oxley Act of 2002, Securities Act Release No. 33-8177 (Jan. 1, 2003); Strengthening the Commission's Requirements Regarding Auditor Independence, Securities Act Release No. 33-8183 (Jan. 28, 2003); Regulation Analyst Certification, Securities Act Release No. 33-8193 (Feb. 20, 2003); Disclosure of Proxy Voting Policies and Proxy Voting Records by Registered Management Investment Companies, Securities Act Release No. 33-8188 (Jan. 31, 2003); Implementation of Standards of Professional Conduct for Attorneys, Securities Act Release No. 33-8185 (Jan. 29, 2003); Disclosure in Management's Discussion and Analysis about Off-Balance Sheet Arrangements and Aggregate Contractual Obligations, Securities Act Release No. 33-8182 (Jan. 28, 2003); Insider Trades During Pension Fund Blackout Periods, Exchange Act Release No. 34-47225 (Jan. 22, 2003); Certification of Disclosure in Companies' Quarterly and Annual Reports, Securities Act Release No. 33-8124 (Aug. 28, 2002); Ownership Reports and Trading by Officers, Directors and Principal Security Holders, Exchange Act Release No. 34-46421 (Aug. 27, 2002).

[27] For a critical look at the one-size-fits-all approach of the NYSE listing standards, see Stephen M. Bainbridge, *A Critique of the NYSE's Director Independence Listing Standards*, 30 SEC. REG. L.J. 370 (2002) [hereinafter Bainbridge, *Critique of NYSE's Listing Standards*].

[28] In this essay, I join the chorus of others critical of a one-size-fits-all mandatory approach to regulating corporate governance and the increased federalization of corporate law. *See, e.g.*, Larry E. Ribstein, *Market vs. Regulatory Responses to Corporate Fraud: A Critique of the Sarbanes-Oxley Act of 2002*, 28 J. CORP. L. 1 (2003) [hereinafter Ribstein, *Market vs. Regulatory Responses*]; Bainbridge, *Critique of the NYSE's Listing Standards*, *supra* note 27; Chandler & Strine, *supra* note 26; *see also* Silvia Ascarelli, *One*

II. ENRON'S COLLAPSE: WHERE WAS THE BOARD?

Enron's collapse was dramatic. It is also well-documented, so I can be brief here.[29] In short, Enron's collapse boiled down to massive accounting fraud and irregularities, a principal feature of which was the use of structured finance techniques designed to get debt off Enron's balance sheet and inflate Enron's profits. We have all heard about the special purpose entities ("SPEs") named "Chewco," "Raptors," "JEDI," and "LJM1" and "LJM2." In addition to, and perhaps motivating, the financial manipulations were a number of suspect conflict-of-interest transactions involving members of Enron's management. Most notable among the conflicts were those of Enron's Chief Financial Officer, Andrew Fastow. Fastow was on both sides of a number of the financing deals, serving as the general partner of the LJM special purpose entities, in which capacity Fastow stood to make millions by, essentially, negotiating against Enron. In October 2001, the "truth" came to light as the accounting errors and related party transactions were exposed. Enron was forced to take a $544 million after-tax charge against its earnings and announced a $1.2 billion reduction in shareholders' equity.[30] Less than a month later, Enron again restated its financials because of accounting errors, this time for the entire period from 1997 through 2001.[31] Clearly, Enron was not the successful business that had been portrayed, and the market lost all confidence in the company. Enron filed for bankruptcy in December 2001, capping a spectacular fall for a company that had recently been the seventh largest company in the United States, based on reported revenues.[32]

Many things contributed to Enron's demise. There were breakdowns all around—accountants, lawyers, securities analysts, and credit rating agencies (the "gatekeepers"); the SEC;[33] and the board of directors, not to mention the underlying corporate misconduct. Even the "victims"—the investors—bear some responsibility for seemingly,

---

Size Doesn't Fit All: In Europe, Corporate-Governance Rules Are Not in the Details, Wall St. J., Feb. 24, 2003, at R6. Here, I voice some of the same concerns expressed by Bainbridge, Ribstein, Chandler, and Strine about the approach that the recent regulatory reforms take. The interested reader is encouraged to read these other articles.

[29] *See* William C. Powers, Jr. et al., Report of Investigation by the Special Investigative Committee of the Board of Directors of Enron (2002) [hereinafter Powers Report]; Report of the Senate Permanent Subcommittee on Investigations of the Committee on Governmental Affairs, The Role of the Board of Directors in Enron's Collapse, Rep. No. 107-70, 107th Cong., 2nd Sess. (2002) [hereinafter Subcommittee on Investigations Report]; William W. Bratton, *Enron and the Dark Side of Shareholder Value*, 76 Tulane L. Rev. 1275 (2002); Joel Seligman, *No One Can Serve Two Masters: Corporate and Securities Law After Enron*, 80 Wash. U. L.Q. 449 (2002) [hereinafter Seligman, *No One Can Serve Two Masters*].

[30] Powers Report, *supra* note 29, at 2–3.

[31] Powers Report, *supra* note 29, at 2–3.

[32] *See Five-hundred Largest U.S. Corporations*, Fortune, Apr. 16, 2001, at F-1.

[33] The SEC, for example, had not reviewed thoroughly Enron's annual report filings since 1997, prompting the Senate Governmental Affairs Committee to be very critical of the SEC's regulation of Enron. *See* Report of the Staff to the Senate Committee on Governmental Affairs, *Financial Oversight of Enron: The SEC and Private-Sector Watchdogs* (Oct. 8, 2002) [hereinafter Committee on Governmental

perhaps understandably, becoming complacent after historic bull markets and failing to ask the tough questions of Enron's management that should have been asked. To be sure, the personal impact on investors and employees from Enron's collapse was devastating and made Enron worthy of front-page headlines and congressional hearings. But what makes Enron especially troubling from a corporate governance and capital markets perspective is that so many aspects of our corporate governance system and capital markets failed. No check or balance rooted out the misconduct until the damage was done, raising serious concerns about what appeared to be a deeply flawed system.[34] My focus in all this is the board.[35] Indeed, to the extent that other corporate governance devices fail, the board of directors becomes all the more important.

An obvious question is, "Where was Enron's board?" In some respects, I wish I could report that the board was nowhere to be found. To the contrary, the Enron board was on the scene and, for the most part, taking most of the steps we ask a board to take. However, as suggested below, it looks like the board was just going through the motions and checking the boxes. Perhaps most frustrating is that by all appearances, Enron's board looked great. Of Enron's 14 directors, only two (Kenneth Lay and Jeffrey Skilling) were insiders.[36] The directors reflected a wide range of business, finance, accounting, and government experience.[37] The board had all the committees one would

---

Affairs Report, *The SEC and Private-Sector Watchdogs*]; *see also* Jonathan Weil & John Wilke, *Senate Panel Chides SEC for Falling Short in Enron Regulation*, WALL ST. J., October 7, 2002, at C1. In response to a concern that the SEC's process for reviewing company filings was too lax, Section 408 of Sarbanes-Oxley was adopted. Section 408 requires the SEC to review filings required under the Securities Exchange Act of 1934 "on a regular and systematic basis" and in any event, no less than once every three years.

[34] Kurt Eichenwald, *Could Capitalists Actually Bring Down Capitalism?*, N.Y. TIMES, June 30, 2002, S4, at 1.

[35] For a good discussion of the potential impact of Enron on the future of boards of directors, see Jeffrey N. Gordon, *What Enron Means for the Management and Control of the Modern Business Corporation: Some Initial Reflections*, 69 U. CHI. L. REV. 1233 (2002); Leo E. Strine, Jr., *Derivative Impact? Some Early Reflections on the Corporation Law Implications of the Enron Debacle*, 57 BUS. LAW. 1371, 1377–85 (2002).

[36] ENRON CORP. PROXY STATEMENT PURSUANT TO SECTION 14(A) OF THE SECURITIES EXCHANGE ACT OF 1934 (2001) [hereinafter Enron Proxy Statement].

[37] As of 2001, Enron's directors, as described in Enron's 2001 proxy statement, included:

- Robert A. Belfer (Chairman and CEO of Belco Oil & Gas Corp.; director since 1983)
- Norman P. Blake, Jr. (Chairman, President, and CEO of Comdisco, Inc.; former CEO and Secretary General of the United States Olympic Committee; former Chairman, President, and CEO of the Promus Hotel Corporation and of USF&G Corporation; director of Owens-Corning Corporation; director since 1993)
- Ronnie C. Chan (Chairman of Hang Lung Group; co-founder and director of affiliates comprising the Morningside/Springfield Group; director of Standard Chartered PLC and Motorola, Inc.; director since 1996)
- John H. Duncan (private investor; director of EOTT Energy Corp. and Group I Automotive Inc.; director since 1985)

hope to see, including an executive committee, finance committee, audit and compliance committee, compensation committee, and nominating and corporate governance committee. Perhaps most important to the board's monitoring role, the Enron audit committee had a model charter and was chaired by a former accounting professor who had served as the Dean of the Stanford Graduate School of Business. Finally, the board regularly met five times a year, with special meetings called as needed.[38]

But the proof is in the pudding, not in appearances. Whether or not any Enron director violated his or her fiduciary duties or engaged in fraud, the board's conduct

---

- Wendy L. Gramm (economist and Director of the Regulatory Studies Program of the Mercatus Center, George Mason University; former Chairman of the Commodity Futures Trading Commission; director of IBP, Inc., State Farm Insurance Co., and Invesco Funds; former director of the Chicago Mercantile Exchange; director since 1993)
- Robert K. Jaedicke (Professor Emeritus of accounting and former Dean of the Stanford University Graduate School of Business; director of California Water Service Company and Boise Cascade Corporation; former director of GenCorp., Inc.; director since 1985)
- Kenneth L. Lay (Chairman of the Board of Enron; former CEO of Enron; director of Eli Lilly and Company, Compaq Computer Corporation, EOTT Energy Corp., i2 Technologies, Inc., and NewPower Holdings, Inc.; director since 1985)
- Charles A. Lemaistre (President Emeritus of the University of Texas M.D. Anderson Cancer Center; director since 1985)
- John Mendelsohn (President of the University of Texas M.D. Anderson Cancer Center; former Chairman of the Department of Medicine at Memorial Sloan-Kettering Cancer Center; director of ImClone Systems, Inc.; director since 1999)
- Paulo V. Ferraz Pereira (Executive Vice President of Group Bozano; former President and Chief Operating Officer of Meridional Financial Group and Managing Director of Group Bozano; former President and CEO of the State Bank of Rio de Janeiro; director since 1999)
- Frank Savage (Chairman of Alliance Capital Management International; director of Lockheed Martin Corporation, Alliance Capital Management L.P., and Qualcomm Corp.; director since 1999)
- Jeffrey K. Skilling (President and CEO of Enron; former Chief Operating Officer of Enron; former Chairman and CEO of Enron North America Corp.; director of the Houston Branch of the Federal Reserve Bank of Dallas; director since 1997)
- John Wakeham (Chairman of the Press Complaints Commission in the U.K.; former U.K. Secretary of State for Energy and Leader of the Houses of Commons and Lords; former Member of Parliament; chartered accountant; chairman or director of several publicly-traded U.K. companies; director since 1994)
- Herbert S. Winokur, Jr. (Chairman and CEO of Capricorn Holdings, Inc. and Managing General Partner of several affiliated investment funds; former Nonexecutive Chairman of Azurix Corp.; former Senior Executive Vice President and director of Penn Central Corporation; director of NATCO Group, Inc., Mrs. Fields' Holding Company, Inc., CCC Information Services Group, Inc., and DynCorp.; director since 1985).

ENRON PROXY STATEMENT, *supra* note 36. Other directors, who served earlier, were also implicated by the scandals at Enron.

[38] For an overview of Enron's board, see Subcommittee on Investigations Report, *supra* note 29, at 8–11; *see also* ENRON PROXY STATEMENT *supra* note 36.

fell far short of what is expected and what is required for good corporate governance.[39] For example, the board approved the conflicted transactions involving Fastow, and in

---

[39] The U.S. Senate Permanent Subcommittee on Investigations summarized the role of Enron's board in the company's demise as follows and made the following recommendations:

Based upon the evidence before it, including over one million pages of subpoenaed documents, interviews of thirteen Enron Board members, and the Subcommittee hearing on May 7, 2002, the U.S. Senate Permanent Subcommittee on Investigations makes the following findings with respect to the role of the Enron Board of Directors in Enron's collapse and bankruptcy.

(1) **Fiduciary Failure**. The Enron Board of Directors failed to safeguard Enron shareholders and contributed to the collapse of the seventh largest public company in the United States, by allowing Enron to engage in high risk accounting, inappropriate conflict of interest transactions, extensive undisclosed off-the-books activities, and excessive executive compensation. The Board witnessed numerous indications of questionable practices by Enron management over several years, but chose to ignore them to the detriment of Enron shareholders, employees and business associates.

(2) **High Risk Accounting**. The Enron Board of Directors knowingly allowed Enron to engage in high risk accounting practices.

(3) **Inappropriate Conflicts of Interest**. Despite clear conflicts of interest, the Enron Board of Directors approved an unprecedented arrangement allowing Enron's Chief Financial Officer to establish and operate the LJM private equity funds which transacted business with Enron and profited at Enron's expense. The Board exercised inadequate oversight of LJM transaction and compensation controls and failed to protect Enron shareholders from unfair dealing.

(4) **Extensive Undisclosed Off-The-Books Activity**. The Enron Board of Directors knowingly allowed Enron to conduct billions of dollars in off-the-books activity to make its financial condition appear better than it was and failed to ensure adequate public disclosure of material off-the-books liabilities that contributed to Enron's collapse.

(5) **Excessive Compensation**. The Enron Board of Directors approved excessive compensation for company executives, failed to monitor the cumulative cash drain caused by Enron's 2000 annual bonus and performance unit plans, and failed to monitor or halt abuse by Board Chairman and Chief Executive Officer Kenneth Lay of a company-financed, multi-million dollar personal credit line.

(6) **Lack of Independence**. The independence of the Enron Board of Directors was compromised by financial ties between the company and certain Board members. The Board also failed to ensure the independence of the company's auditor, allowing [Arthur Andersen LLP] to provide internal audit and consulting services while serving as Enron's outside auditor.

Based upon the evidence before it and the findings made in this report, the U.S. Senate Permanent Subcommittee on Investigations makes the following recommendations:

(1) **Strengthening Oversight**. Directors of publicly traded companies should take steps to:
   (a) prohibit accounting practices and transactions that put the company at high risk of non-compliance with generally accepted accounting principles and result in misleading and inaccurate financial statements;
   (b) prohibit conflict of interest arrangements that allow company transactions with a business owned or operated by senior company personnel;
   (c) prohibit off-the-books activity used to make the company's financial condition appear better than it is, and require full public disclosure of all assets, liabilities and activities that materially affect the company's financial condition;

fact waived Enron's code of conduct to allow the deals.[40] It is rare that the board of a public company would approve such transactions. To mitigate the risk of having Enron's CFO on the other side of transactions involving hundreds of millions of dollars, the board put in place a number of controls involving oversight by both the board and top members of management. However, the controls proved to be inadequate in design and were ineffectively implemented.[41] To be sure, management kept key information away from the board. The board, however, has been faulted for not carefully considering the information it did have and for not asking for more information. There is also concern that the board did not even understand the underlying financing transactions.[42] The Special Investigative Committee of Enron's board, led by William Powers, levied a particularly stinging criticism against the board's handling of various related party transactions. The Special Investigative Committee concluded that the very need

---

(d) prevent excessive executive compensation, including by—
    (i) exercising ongoing oversight of compensation plans and payments;
    (ii) barring the issuance of company-financed loans to directors and senior officers of the company; and
    (iii) prevent stock-based compensation plans that encourage company personnel to use improper accounting or other measures to improperly increase the company stock price for personal gain; and
(e) prohibit the company's outside auditor from also providing internal auditing or consulting services to the company and from auditing its own work for the company.
(2) **Strengthening Independence**. The Securities and Exchange Commission and the self-regulatory organizations, including the national stock exchanges, should:
(a) strengthen requirements for Director independence at publicly traded companies, including by requiring a majority of the outside Directors to be free of material financial ties to the company other than through Director compensation;
(b) strengthen requirements for Audit Committees at publicly traded companies, including by requiring the Audit Committee Chair to possess financial management or accounting expertise, and by requiring a written Audit Committee charter that obligates the Committee to oversee the company's financial statements and accounting practices and to hire and fire the outside auditor; and
(c) strengthen requirements for auditor independence, including by prohibiting the company's outside auditor from simultaneously providing the company with internal auditing or consulting services and from auditing its own work for the company.

Subcommittee on Investigations Report, *supra* note 29, at 3–4.

For an early indication of the extent to which Enron's outside directors might be held liable for securities law violations, see *In re* Enron Corp. Securities Derivative & ERISA Litigation, 2003 WL 1089307 (S.D. Tex. March 12, 2003) (considering motions to dismiss filed by Enron's outside directors).

[40] Subcommittee on Investigations Report, *supra* note 29, at 24–38; Powers Report, *supra* note 29, at 4, 8–10, 16–17, 22–23.

[41] Subcommittee on Investigations Report, *supra* note 29, at 24–38; Powers Report, *supra* note 29, at 9–10, 148–65.

[42] Powers Report, *supra* note 29, at 23.

to waive the company's code of conduct and establish extensive internal controls should have sent up red flags recommending against approving the transactions.[43]

Enron's board, especially the audit and compliance committee, also bears responsibility for Enron's inaccurate accounting treatment, most notably with respect to Enron's SPEs.[44] A board's audit committee is charged with overseeing the corporation's financial reporting, although management, with the support of the company's auditor, takes the lead in preparing financial statements. Enron's SPEs were not properly accounted for; they should have been reflected on Enron's balance sheet.[45] The board apparently was aware of the off-balance-sheet accounting treatment, but failed to exercise the kind of oversight required to ensure that Enron's financial statements were accurate and that proper disclosures were made.[46] Indeed, as I have mentioned earlier, questions remain as to whether the board even understood the financing transactions, let alone the accounting treatment.

Finally, the Senate Permanent Subcommittee on Investigations found that financial ties with the company compromised the independence of many outside directors, rendering a majority of the Enron board not independent in fact and reluctant to challenge management.[47]

The Special Investigative Committee of Enron's board summed up the failure at Enron simply: "In short, no one was minding the store."[48] If Enron were the only scandal, perhaps the breakdowns there could have been brushed aside as peculiar to Enron and some bad apples. Indeed, until the fraud at WorldCom broke in June 2002, it was unclear whether Congress would pass any corporate and accounting reform legislation, let alone final legislation in the form of Sarbanes-Oxley (which looked more like the original Sarbanes Bill than the original Oxley Bill).[49] But as more scan-

---

[43] Powers Report, *supra* note 29, at 156 ("At bottom, however, the need for such an extensive set of controls said something fundamental about the wisdom of permitting the CFO to take on this conflict of interest. The two members of the Special Committee participating in this review of the Board's actions believe that a conflict of this significance that could be managed only through so many controls and procedures should not have been approved in the first place.").

[44] *See* Subcommittee on Investigations Report, *supra* note 29, at 14–24, 38–52; Powers Report, *supra* note 29, at 5–16, 149–58; Committee on Governmental Affairs Report, *The SEC and Private-Sector Watchdogs, supra* note 33, at 24–26.

[45] For a description of Enron's off-balance-sheet transactions, see Subcommittee on Investigations Report, *supra* note 29, at 38–52; Powers Report, *supra* note 29, at 41–158.

[46] Subcommittee on Investigations Report, *supra* note 29, at 14–24, 38–52.

[47] Subcommittee on Investigations Report, *supra* note 29, at 54–57; *see also infra* notes 59–61 and accompanying text.

[48] Powers Report, *supra* note 29, at 166.

[49] For a brief overview of the legislative process leading to Sarbanes-Oxley, see Seligman, *No One Can Serve Two Masters, supra* note 29, at 474–82.

dals came to light, concern spread that our corporate governance system was systemically flawed and in need of reform. Boards have been the subject of scrutiny and reform talk for years, but they received renewed attention following the scandals. This time, there was a sense of urgency. Although not exhaustive, the following discussion highlights in brief some of the more important concerns about boards of directors that have troubled both the markets and regulators in the wake of Enron et al.[50]

First, questions have been raised about whether outside directors spend enough time, or have enough information and expertise about the company, to perform their roles effectively or challenge senior officers.[51] Were five regular board meetings really enough for Enron's board to effectively oversee such a complex business and its management team, especially when the meetings often only lasted a couple of hours?[52] Could any outside director really understand Enron's business?[53] In addition, outside directors typically have "day jobs" and other commitments that demand the bulk of their attention and effort. For example, directors often sit on multiple boards or are executives of other companies. It should come as no surprise, then, that outside directors often rely on insiders (*i.e.,* the very individuals the board is supposed to oversee) for information and guidance in performing their duties.

---

[50] The following discussion, as well as the discussion in Part III.B below, draws from an extensive literature on the role of the board and of independent directors in particular. For a sampling of the literature, see Sanjai Bhagat & Bernard Black, *The Uncertain Relationship Between Board Composition and Firm Performance*, 54 BUS. LAW. 921 (1999); Ira M. Millstein & Paul W. MacAvoy, *The Active Board of Directors and Performance of the Large Publicly-Traded Corporation*, 98 COLUM. L. REV. 1283 (1998); Victor Brudney, *The Independent Director—Heavenly City or Potemkin Village?*, 95 HARV. L. REV. 597 (1982); Martin Lipton & Jay W. Lorsch, *A Modest Proposal for Improved Corporate Governance*, 48 BUS. LAW. 59 (1992); Charles M. Elson, *Director Compensation and the Management-Captured Board—The History of a Symptom and a Cure*, 50 SMU L. REV. 127 (1996); Lynne L. Dallas, *Proposals for Reform of Corporate Boards of Directors: The Dual Board and Board Ombudsperson*, 54 WASH. & LEE L. REV. 91 (1997); Jonathan L. Johnson et al., *Boards of Directors: A Review and Research Agenda*, 22 J. MGMT. 409 (1996); Jill E. Fisch, *Taking Boards Seriously*, 19 CARDOZO L. REV. 265 (1997) [hereinafter Fisch, *Taking Boards Seriously*]; Donald C. Langevoort, *The Human Nature of Corporate Boards: Law, Norms, and the Unintended Consequences of Independence and Accountability*, 89 GEO. L.J. 797 (2001) [hereinafter Langevoort, *The Human Nature of Corporate Boards*]; Stephen M. Bainbridge, *Why a Board? Group Decisionmaking in Corporate Governance*, 55 VAND. L. REV. 1 (2002) [hereinafter Bainbridge, *Why a Board?*]; Bainbridge, *Critique of NYSE's Listing Standards, supra* note 27.

[51] *See* DIRECTORS & BOARDS 55, 2002 WL 20878497 (June 22, 2002) (explaining that boards of companies in the S&P 500 hold an average of eight meetings per year); Korn/Ferry International, KORN/FERRY'S 29TH ANNUAL BOARD OF DIRECTORS STUDY, at 14 (reporting that (a) nearly a majority (46%) of boards of companies in the *Fortune 1000* meets quarterly, (b) ten percent of the boards meet more than ten times annually, (d) fourteen percent of the boards meet between seven to nine times per year, and (d) directors spend an average of just over fifteen hours per month on board matters).

[52] *See* Subcommittee on Investigations Report, *supra* note 29, at 9.

[53] For an interesting explanation of Enron's business, see William B. Bratton, *Enron and the Dark Side of Shareholder Value*, 76 TULANE L. REV. 1275 (2002).

Second, director compensation has increased dramatically. As reported in 2001 proxy statements, for example, the average compensation package for directors at the 200 largest public industrial and service companies topped $150,000.[54] The total compensation package, including cash and equity, of Enron's outside directors was approximately $350,000 in 2000.[55] The concern here, of course, is that an outside director will be reluctant to oppose management, especially the CEO, because of the risk that the director will not be renominated to the board if she does, thereby undermining the director's independence.[56] Equity-based compensation for directors, such as stock options or restricted stock, raises additional concerns. On the one hand, equity-based compensation aligns the interests of directors and shareholders by encouraging the board to run the business profitably in order to increase the company's stock price, even if it means opposing the CEO and other senior executives. On the other hand, if a director has significant equity in the corporation, the director might be hesitant to take steps, such as pushing for certain disclosures or more conservative accounting practices, that might cause the stock price to fall. The director might even be more agreeable when it comes to "earnings management."[57] At the very least, directors with large equity stakes might focus too much on the short term in an effort to meet, if not beat, quarterly earnings targets at the expense of more effective long-term business planning and strategy.[58] Such efforts to "manage to the market" can compromise a company's performance over the long run.

Third, new concerns have been raised about "soft" conflicts of interest and "structural biases" that might compromise director independence. For example, is an outside director really independent when the corporation, at the direction of the CEO, makes significant charitable contributions to an institution with which the director is affiliated? Enron and its CEO and chairman, Kenneth Lay, had donated nearly $600,000 to the M.D. Anderson Cancer Center, where two of Enron's directors had served as

---

[54] *See* Pearl Meyers & Partners, *2001 Director Compensation, Boards in the Spotlight Study of the Top 200 Corporations, available at* http://www.execpay.com/PMP/2001DirectorsStudy.pdf; *see also* Subcommittee on Investigations Report, *supra* note 29, at 11 (citing study showing that the average total board compensation at top 200 U.S. public companies in 2000 was nearly $140,000).

[55] *See* Subcommittee on Investigations Report, *supra* note 29, at 11.

[56] Having said that, directors will have to be compensated commensurately if we want them to spend more time on their board duties.

[57] "Earnings management" refers to the process by which a company manipulates its earnings in order to meet certain earnings targets. Arthur Levitt was critical of earnings management and brought attention to this practice when he was Chairman of the SEC. *See* Arthur Levitt, *The Numbers Game*, Remarks at NYU Center for Law and Business (Sept. 28, 1998). For more on earnings management and the role it played in the recent corporate scandals, see John C. Coffee, Jr., *What Caused Enron?: A Capsule Social and Economic History of the 1990's, available at* http://ssrn.com/abstract_id=373581.

[58] Companies have begun to structure compensation packages so that they are tied to long-run performance. It is becoming increasingly popular, for example, to restrict directors and officers from selling shares they obtain upon the exercise of options until some period after they leave office.

president; these donations followed a 1993 pledge of $1.5 million by the Enron Foundation to the center.[59] A somewhat "harder" conflict arises from consulting arrangements and other business dealings between a company and its directors. In 2000, Enron paid one of its outside directors over $490,000 for his consulting work;[60] and the National Tank Company, on whose board an Enron director sat, recorded over $2.5 million in revenue from sales of equipment and services to Enron subsidiaries.[61] The risk is that a director will appease management in order to maintain a lucrative consulting or business relationship or to continue the flow of charitable donations.

Not just economic ties matter; social and personal ties also can compromise a director's independence. People are often asked to serve on boards precisely because they have a tie to the CEO or other senior officers or directors.[62] Moreover, a bias can develop among directors simply by virtue of the fact that they all serve together; not only might directors be less critical of one another, but they might also be less critical of the CEO and other officers with whom the directors work closely and serve. Whatever the ties might be at the start of a directorship, the very process of working closely for a number of years can create relationships that can cloud a director's independent judgment over time. At the very least, an outside director who herself is an executive at another company might be inclined to identify with and defer to management, just as she hopes her board will defer to her, or she might simply believe that CEOs generally know what is best for the business and should be afforded wide discretion. In addition, an outside director might feel indebted to the CEO who put her on the board and might therefore tend to give the chief executive the benefit of the doubt. More generally, the board might become committed to the management team it has decided to retain, if not actually selected, as part of a management transition.[63] At bottom, relationships affect board performance.[64] At Enron, four outside directors, including the chair of Enron's audit and compliance committee, had served on the board since 1985, and a fifth outside director had served since 1983.[65]

Fourth, is the risk of legal liability too low to ensure that directors are accountable for their conduct and act in the shareholders' long-term best interests? If directors are

---

[59] See Subcommittee on Investigations Report, supra note 29, at 55.

[60] Id.

[61] Id.

[62] See Gerald F. Davis et al., The Small World of the American Corporate Elite, 1982–2001, STRATEGIC ORGANIZATION (forthcoming 2003) (study showing a high degree of connectivity among boards of directors).

[63] See Jonathan R. Macey, A Pox on Both Your Houses: Enron, Sarbanes-Oxley and the Debate Concerning the Relative Efficacy of Mandatory Versus Enabling Rules, WASH. U. L.Q. (forthcoming 2004) (explaining that directors might become biased toward the executives they retain and select).

[64] For an interesting perspective on the importance of social and personal ties from a Vice Chancellor on the Delaware Chancery Court, see Strine, supra note 35, at 1377–85.

[65] See ENRON PROXY STATEMENT, supra note 36.

held liable too readily, there is a risk that innovation, entrepreneurism, and risk-taking will be chilled, ultimately at the shareholders' expense, or that people will simply refuse to sit on boards. On the other hand, it is possible for the risk of liability to be too low. Presently, directors are largely insulated from liability for breaching their duty of care by the business judgment rule,[66] a gross negligence standard of judicial review for determining whether the duty of care has been breached,[67] exculpatory charter provisions exonerating directors from monetary damages,[68] indemnification rights,[69] directors and officers ("D&O") insurance,[70] and procedural hurdles that make it difficult and costly for shareholders to bring derivative actions.[71] Cutting the other way, at least in Delaware, and potentially expanding the risk of liability, is the Delaware Chancery Court's 1996 opinion, *In re Caremark International Inc. Derivative Litigation*, in which Chancellor Allen said in dicta that boards, in satisfying their oversight duty, have an obligation to establish internal controls designed to root out misconduct.[72] The case suggests, though, that boards will only be liable if they fail to act in good faith.

The risk that directors will be held liable for fraud under the federal securities laws is also relatively low. For example, there is no private right of action for aiding and abetting fraud under Section 10(b) and Rule 10b-5 of the Securities Exchange Act of

---

[66] *See supra* note 3.

[67] The duty of care generally requires directors to exercise reasonable care in performing their duties. Courts are reluctant to find that a board has breached its duty of care. As Professor Eisenberg has pointed out, although directors are supposed to "act reasonably," courts generally have adopted a more lax standard of review. *See* Melvin Aron Eisenberg, *The Divergence of Standards of Conduct and Standards of Review in Corporate Law*, 62 FORDHAM L. REV. 437 (1993). Directors are rarely, if ever, held liable for simple negligence. Rather, in most cases, directors will not be held liable for breach of the duty of care unless they acted grossly negligent. *See* Smith v. Van Gorkom, 488 A.2d 858 (Del. 1985). Accordingly, Eisenberg has suggested that the duty of care reflects more of an aspiration or norm than a legal mandate. *See* Melvin A. Eisenberg, *Corporate Law and Social Norms*, 99 COLUM. L. REV. 1253, 1265–71 (1999 [hereinafter Eisenberg, *Corporate Law and Social Norms*]).

[68] Corporations often include in their articles of incorporation provisions exculpating directors from liability for breach of fiduciary duty. Delaware, for example, adopted § 102(b)(7) of the Delaware General Corporation Law in the aftermath of *Smith v. Van Gorkom*, in which directors were held liable for breach of the duty of care even though they acted loyally and in good faith. *See* Smith v. Van Gorkom, 488 A.2d 858 (Del. 1985). Under § 102(b)(7), a company can eliminate or limit a director's liability for monetary damages arising from the breach of the duty of care by including a provision to this effect in the company's articles of incorporation (called the certificate of incorporation in Delaware). DEL. CODE ANN. tit. 8, § 102(b)(7). Most states similarly allow corporations to limit director liability. *See, e.g.*, MODEL BUS. CORP. ACT § 2.02(b)(4). For more on exculpatory provisions, see O'KELLEY & THOMPSON, *supra* note 3, at 310–16.

[69] Companies often agree to indemnify a director for liability arising in connection with the discharge of her duties as a member of the board; indeed, corporation codes require indemnification in many cases. *See, e.g.*, DEL. CODE ANN. tit. 8, § 145; MODEL BUS. CORP. ACT §§ 8.50–8.59; *see generally* CLARK, CORPORATE LAW, *supra* note 3, at § 15.10; O'KELLEY & THOMPSON, *supra* note 3, at 432–50.

[70] Directors are also typically covered by D&O insurance policies that cover certain claims filed against directors and related litigation costs.

[71] *See supra* note 4.

[72] *In re* Caremark Int'l Inc. Derivative Litigation, 698 A.2d 959 (Del. Ch. 1996).

1934, and it is often difficult to show that an outside director had the requisite intent to defraud or was sufficiently involved in the alleged fraud so as to be a primary perpetrator of fraud.[73] Although it might be possible to hold a director liable for fraud as a "controlling person," a director will be exonerated from controlling person liability so long as he is found to have acted in good faith and did not induce the actual fraud.[74] In addition, the federal securities laws provide safe harbors for forward-looking statements;[75] there is now proportionate, instead of joint and several, liability for fraud in many instances;[76] and the heightened pleading standards, adopted as part of the Private Securities Litigation Reform Act of 1995, make it difficult for private plaintiffs to survive a motion to dismiss a fraud claim.[77]

Finally, cognitive biases can affect board behavior. The field of behavioral law and economics focuses on how people's decisions and conduct are influenced by various cognitive biases.[78] There is reason to believe that these biases affect directors, like everybody else.[79] While numerous biases have been catalogued, a few are of special note when it comes to the board.

---

[73] Central Bank of Denver, N.A. v. First Interstate Bank of Denver, N.A., 511 U.S. 164 (1994); *see generally* LOSS & SELIGMAN, *supra* note 9, at 1241–61; *see also In re* Enron Corp. Securities Derivative & ERISA Litigation, 2003 WL 1089307 (S.D. Tex. March 12, 2003).

[74] LOSS & SELIGMAN, *supra* note 9, at 1234–39.

[75] *Id.* at 145–55, 544–47.

[76] *Id.* at 1324–25.

[77] *Id.* at 1278–85.

[78] *See generally* Jennifer Arlen, *Comment: The Future of Behavioral Economic Analysis of Law*, 51 VAND. L. REV. 1765 (1998); Russell Korobkin, *A Multi-Disciplinary Approach to Legal Scholarship: Economics, Behavioral Economics, and Evolutional Psychology*, 41 JURIMETRICS J. 319 (2001); BEHAVIORAL LAW & ECONOMICS (Cass R. Sunstein ed., 2000); Russell Korobkin & Thomas Ulen, *Law and Behavioral Science: Removing the Rationality Assumption from Law and Economics*, 88 CAL. L. REV. 1051 (2000); Christine Jolls et al., *A Behavioral Approach to Law and Economics*, 50 STAN. L. REV. 1471 (1998).

[79] Behavioral law and economics is increasingly influential in the area of corporate and securities law. *See* Troy A. Paredes, *Blinded by the Light: Information Overload and Its Consequences for Securities Regulation*, __ WASH. U. L.Q. __ (forthcoming 2004) [hereinafter Paredes, *Blinded by the Light*]; Donald C. Langevoort, *Taming the Animal Spirits of the Stock Markets: A Behavioral Approach to Securities Regulation*, 97 NW. U. L. REV. 135 (2002); Donald C. Langevoort, *Organized Illusions: A Behavioral Theory of Why Corporations Mislead Stock Market Investors (and Cause Other Social Harm)*, 146 U. PA. L. REV. 101 (1997) [hereinafter Langevoort, *Organized Illusions*]; Donald C. Langevoort, *Selling Hope, Selling Risk: Some Lessons for Law from Behavioral Economics About Stockbrokers and Sophisticated Customers*, 84 CAL. L. REV. 627 (1996); Robert Thompson, *Securities Regulation in an Electronic Age: The Impact of Cognitive Psychology*, 75 WASH. U. L.Q. 779 (1997); Stephen M. Bainbridge, *Mandatory Disclosure: A Behavioral Analysis*, 68 U. CIN. L. REV. 1023 (2000); Kent Greenfield, *Using Behavioral Economics to Show the Power and Efficiency of Corporate Law as Regulatory Tool*, 35 U.C. DAVIS L. REV. 581 (2002); James A. Fanto, *Braking the Merger Momentum: Reforming Corporate Law Governing Mega-Mergers*, 49 BUFF. L. REV. 249 (2001); Bainbridge, *Why a Board?, supra* note 50; Langevoort, *The Human Nature of Corporate Boards, supra* note 50; Hillary A. Sale, *Judging Heuristics*, 35 UC DAVIS L. REV. 903 (2002); Robert A. Prentice, *The Case of the Irrational Auditor: A Behavioral Insight Into Securities Fraud Litigation*, 65 N.W. U. L. REV. 133 (2000).

For example, studies show that people tend to become committed to a course of conduct or outcome once it has been chosen and to search for evidence that confirms the decision.[80] In addition, people have been shown to be overly optimistic and overly self-confident about their own abilities.[81] Further, individuals often become subject to groupthink or herd behavior when they act as part of a larger cohesive group.[82] As a result of these and other biases, boards, even when acting in good faith, might tend to pursue some of their chosen paths too far and ignore, or at least discount, evidence that a mistake has been made; directors might defer too much to management and might not recognize ill-advised or ill-conceived, or even illegal, ideas or behavior. Even a director who is initially uneasy about some decision might ultimately be persuaded to go along with the rest of the group and might indeed convince himself that everybody else is right.

It is hard to know whether or not any of these biases influenced Enron's board and, if so, to what extent. It is, however, worth noting that the board generally acted unanimously[83] and that the Special Investigative Committee concluded that the board, in approving the related party transactions involving Fastow, "substantially underestimated the severity of the conflict and overestimated the degree to which management controls and procedures could contain the problem."[84] In any event, the directors apparently convinced themselves that there was a sufficient business justification to allow Fastow to be on the other side of Enron in connection with many of the SPE transactions, even though the arguments against allowing these transactions seem overwhelming, at least with the benefit of hindsight.

The existence of cognitive biases is particularly vexing for corporate law. It is very hard to monitor biased decision-making when there is no indication of bad faith or disloyalty or even procedural shortcomings. The law of fiduciary duty is nimble, but it is unlikely to account adequately for cognitive biases.

The corporate abuses and scandals at Enron and elsewhere challenged, in a fundamental way, how boards are structured and how directors conduct themselves. In short,

---

[80] *See, e.g.,* Langevoort, *Organized Illusions, supra* note 79, at 142–43; SCOTT PLOUS, THE PSYCHOLOGY OF JUDGMENT AND DECISION MAKING 231–34, 238–40 (1993); DANIEL KAHNEMAN ET AL., JUDGMENT UNDER UNCERTAINTY: HEURISTICS AND BIASES 149–50 (1982).

[81] *See, e.g.,* Arlen, *supra* note 78, at 1773–75, 1781–85; KAHNEMAN ET AL., *supra* note 80, at 287–93; Robert Prentice, *Whither Securities Regulation? Some Behavioral Observations Regarding Proposals for Its Future,* 51 DUKE L.J. 1397, 1457–59 (2002) [hereinafter Prentice, *Whither Securities Regulation?*].

[82] *See, e.g.,* Cass R. Sunstein, *Deliberative Trouble? Why Groups Go to Extremes,* 110 YALE L. J. 71 (2002): PLOUS, *supra* note 80, at 203–04; Bainbridge, *Why a Board?, supra* note 50, at 28–29; Marcel Kahan & Michael Klausner, *Path Dependence in Corporate Contracting: Increasing Returns, Herd Behavior and Cognitive Biases,* 74 WASH. U. L.Q. 347-59 (1996).

[83] Subcommittee on Investigations Report, *supra* note 29, at 8.

[84] Powers Report, *supra* note 29, at 22.

the scandals called into question our entire corporate governance system. As the scandals mounted after Enron, it became clear to most that this was not just the case of a few bad apples, but instead reflected several flaws in the system. Attention turned to how to fix the system.

III. THE REGULATORY RESPONSE: IS IT WORTH IT?

Only time will tell whether the regulatory response really was worth it. The scandals—and the headlines—prompted several bold legislative and regulatory responses. A number of reforms address the role of gatekeepers, including auditors, securities analysts, and lawyers. Gatekeepers serve an important monitoring role overseeing directors and officers and holding them accountable, and they facilitate investors in doing the same. A number of the reforms, however, attempt to regulate the substance of corporate governance—that is, the internal affairs of corporations—more directly by, for example, changing the structure and responsibilities of boards of directors, in effect easing the burden on gatekeepers and investors as checks on management. These board-oriented reforms, as well as other reforms that directly bear on a corporation's internal affairs, are my focus. Two sets of reforms are particularly important. The first is Sarbanes-Oxley, adopted by Congress in July 2002.[85] Sarbanes-Oxley is especially important because it signifies an expanded role for the federal government in regulating corporate governance, an area traditionally left to state corporate law, with the exception of disclosure-oriented regulation under the federal securities laws. The second is the revised listing standards the NYSE has proposed.[86]

A. Summarizing the Reforms

The reforms can be summarized briefly, beginning with Sarbanes-Oxley. Although the Public Company Accounting Oversight Board might be the central feature of Sarbanes-Oxley,[87] Sarbanes-Oxley contains a number of important provisions relating to boards of directors. Most notable is Section 301 and the expanded role of the audit committee. Section 301 of Sarbanes-Oxley requires the SEC to adopt rules directing national securities exchanges and associations (i.e., the NYSE and NASDAQ) to revise

---

[85] The SEC has since engaged in extensive rulemaking to implement Sarbanes-Oxley. *See supra* note 26. Indeed, the SEC had already initiated a number of reforms by the time Congress adopted Sarbanes-Oxley. A number of the SEC's early proposals found their way, in one form or another, into the final legislation. For an overview of the process leading to the adoption of Sarbanes-Oxley, see Seligman, *No One Can Serve Two Masters, supra* note 29.

[86] At the time of this writing, the proposed listing standards are awaiting SEC approval. Although the listing standards only apply to companies listed on the NYSE, they are generally understood to represent good corporate practice and provide a model for non-listed companies.

[87] Sarbanes-Oxley §§ 101–109.

their listing standards to require that the audit committee be responsible for appointing, compensating, and overseeing the company's auditor. Further, the audit committee is directed to establish procedures for the receipt, retention, and treatment of complaints regarding accounting, internal accounting control, or auditing matters and the confidential, anonymous submission by employees of concerns regarding "questionable accounting or auditing matters." Sarbanes-Oxley also grants the audit committee authority to engage its own outside advisors and gives a public company a choice of placing at least one "financial expert" on its audit committee or explaining in its SEC filings why it has no "financial expert."[88] Perhaps most important, Section 301 requires that NYSE- and NASDAQ-listed companies have an audit committee comprised solely of independent directors. In order for a director to be considered "independent," she may not receive any fees from the company, other than a director or committee fee, or otherwise be an affiliated person of the company or any of its subsidiaries. Given the central role of a board's audit committee, especially when it comes to the board's monitoring function, the requirement that all of its members be independent is of great significance.[89]

Sarbanes-Oxley contains several other provisions that regulate corporate governance. For example:

- Section 302 requires the SEC to adopt rules requiring the CEO and CFO of a public company, in each quarterly and annual report, to vouch for the accuracy of the report and to certify the accuracy of the company's financial statements and that the company has adopted adequate internal controls;[90]
- Section 304 requires the CEO and CFO to reimburse the company for any bonus or incentive- or equity-based compensation, or any profit from the sale of securities of the company, received during the twelve months prior to any earnings restatement resulting from the material noncompliance of the company as a result of "misconduct" with any financial reporting requirements under the federal securities laws;
- Section 305 expands the SEC's ability to remove directors and officers and to bar them from serving in similar capacities at other public companies by showing their "unfitness" (the prior standard required "substantial unfitness");

[88] Sarbanes-Oxley § 407; *see also* Disclosure Required by Sections 406 and 407 of the Sarbanes-Oxley Act of 2002, Securities Act Release No. 33-8177 (Jan. 23, 2003).

[89] *See also* Standards Relating to Listed Company Audit Committees, Securities Act Release No. 33-8220 (April 9, 2003); *infra* note 99 (discussing Rule 10A-3 implementing Sarbanes-Oxley § 301).

[90] *See also* Certification of Disclosure in Companies' Quarterly and Annual Reports, Securities Act Release No. 33-8124 (Aug. 29, 2002); Sarbanes-Oxley § 906 (providing for criminal sanctions for CEOs and CFOs who do not comply with certain financial certification requirements, in addition to those required by § 302).

- Section 306 generally prohibits directors and officers from trading in their company's stock during any pension fund "blackout periods";[91]
- Section 402 bars a public company from directly or indirectly making any loans to any director or executive officer, subject to certain limited exceptions; and
- Section 406 directs the SEC to adopt rules requiring a public company to disclose if it has adopted a code of ethics for senior financial officers or to explain why it has not done so and to disclose immediately any waiver of or change in the code of ethics.[92]

Unlike Congress, which generally has not attempted to regulate the internal affairs of corporations, the NYSE has been substantively regulating corporate governance through listing standards. The NYSE has proposed extensive amendments to its listing standards after Enron and the other corporate scandals.

The proposed NYSE listing standards require that companies listed on the NYSE have a majority of independent directors, and the standards also tighten the definition of "independent director."[93] To be "independent," a director cannot have any "material relationship" with the company, which includes commercial, industrial, banking, consulting, legal, accounting, charitable, and familial relationships.[94] In addition, a director will be presumed not independent if, at any time during the past five years, the director:[95]

- receives, or has an immediate family member who receives, more than $100,000 per year in compensation from the company, other than director and committee fees and pension or other forms of deferred compensation;
- is affiliated with or employed by, or has an immediate family member who is affiliated with or employed in a professional capacity by, a present or former internal or external auditor of the company;
- is employed, or has an immediate family member who is employed, as an executive officer of another company where any of the listed company's present executives serves on the other company's compensation committee; or
- is an executive officer or an employee, or has an immediate family member who is an executive officer, of another company (a) that accounts for at least two percent or $1 million, whichever is greater, of the listed company's

---

[91] *See also* Insider Trades During Pension Fund Blackout Periods, Exchange Act Release No. 34-47225 (Jan. 22, 2003).

[92] *See also* Disclosure Required by Sections 406 and 407 of the Sarbanes-Oxley Act of 2002, Securities Act Release No. 33-8177 (Jan. 23, 2003)

[93] NYSE Listing Standards Proposal § 303A(1).

[94] *Id.* § 303A(2). Ownership of stock by itself will not preclude a director from being independent.

[95] *Id.*

consolidated gross revenues or (b) for which the listed company accounts for at least two percent or $1 million, whichever is greater, of the other company's consolidated gross revenues.

In no event will a current employee of the company be considered independent.[96]

Other highlights of the proposed amendments are to require outside directors to meet regularly outside management's presence;[97] require listed companies to have a nominating or corporate governance committee, a compensation committee, and an audit committee, in each case comprised solely of independent directors;[98] require that the audit committee have at least three directors who, in addition to being independent in accordance with the definition of "independence" outlined above, satisfy the independence requirements mandated by the Securities and Exchange Commission, as directed by Sarbanes-Oxley, for listed company audit committee members;[99] expand the duties and authority of the audit committee, including granting the audit committee the sole authority to hire and fire the company's auditor;[100] require listed companies to adopt and disclose corporate governance guidelines covering, among other things, director qualification standards, director responsibilities, director access to management, director compensation, director education, management succession, and annual board evaluations;[101] and require listed companies to adopt and disclose a code of business conduct and ethics, as well as promptly disclose any waivers of the code for directors or executive officers.[102]

---

[96] *Id.* § 303A(2).

[97] *Id.* § 303A(3).

[98] *Id.* § 303A(4), 303A(5), 303A(7).

[99] *Id.* § 303A(6), (7). The SEC recently adopted Rule 10A-3, as directed by § 301 of Sarbanes-Oxley. Rule 10A-3, among other things, requires that the audit committee members of exchange-listed companies meet two specific independence criteria: audit committee members may not (1) accept directly or indirectly any consulting, advisory, or other compensatory fee from the company or its subsidiaries (other than board and committee fees) or (2) be an "affiliated person" of the company or its subsidiaries. Any person "that directly, or indirectly through one or more intermediaries, controls, or is controlled by, or is under common control with" the company or its subsidiaries is an "affiliated person." "Control" means "the possession, direct or indirect, of the power to direct or cause the direction of the management and policies of a person, whether through the ownership of voting securities, by contract, or otherwise." Rule 10A-3, however, creates a safe harbor from the definition of "affiliated person" for any person who is not the beneficial owner of at least ten percent of the voting securities and is not an executive officer of the company.

[100] *Id.* § 303A(7). Rule 10A-3 requires that the audit committee appoint, compensate, retain (and terminate), and oversee the company's independent auditor; have the authority to engage outside advisors, at the company's expense; and establish procedures for handling complaints regarding the company's accounting practices.

[101] *Id.* § 303A(9).

[102] *Id.* § 303A(10). The NYSE separately proposed requiring shareholder approval of equity-compensation plans. *See* Securities Exchange Act Release No. 46620 (October 8, 2002), 67 FR 63486 (October 11, 2002) (File No. SR-NYSE-2002-46). The SEC recently approved the new requirements.

A general theme of all of these reforms is that good process and board structure are likely to result in good decisions and outcomes. This focus on procedure is consistent with how courts review director and officer conduct. The fiduciary duty of care, for example, is about procedural due care and not substantive due care; courts review the decision-making process of directors and officers, but generally do not regulate the substance of their business decisions. The focus on the process of corporate decision-making, rather than its substance, reflects several concerns: first, with the benefit of hindsight, courts will tend to be too critical of management; second, judges lack the business expertise to challenge management's business judgment; and third, management might become too risk averse, to shareholders' detriment, if second-guessed by courts.[103] Indeed, judicial deference to the business decisions of directors and officers is the essence of the business judgment rule. As Enron suggests, however, (relatively) good process and (very) good board structure do not guarantee good results.

Sarbanes-Oxley and the proposed NYSE listing standard amendments are intended to prevent future corporate abuses and corruption. But the reforms served a more immediate purpose than promoting good corporate governance. Beyond the merits of the specific proposals, a strong regulatory response was needed to boost investor confidence. Simply by doing something, Congress and the NYSE showed that there was a cop on the beat and that fraud and corporate corruption would not be tolerated.[104]

---

[103] Bayless Manning captured these concerns well: "There is no agreed upon roster of functions of a director, analogous to driving the car. We do not have any common standard or experience as to what directors do; and what they do varies from company to company, from situation to situation, and from time to time. Abandoning all effort to state what directors do, the present law simply announces that they must do it 'carefully,' like a prudent person." Bayless Manning, *The Business Judgment Rule and the Director's Duty of Attention: Time for Reality*, 39 BUS. LAW. 1477, 1493–94 (1984); *see also infra* notes 112–113 and 140–142 and accompanying text.

[104] For a discussion of how regulation can promote confidence, see Prentice, *Whither Securities Regulation? supra* note 81, at 1500–01 (discussing the role of legal sanctions in bolstering trust in capital markets); Tamar Frankel, *Regulation and Investors' Trust in the Securities Markets, available at* http://ssrn.com/abstract_id=333340 (explaining that regulation can promote investor trust in capital markets); William W. Bratton, *Game Theory and the Restoration of Honor to Corporate Law's Duty of Loyalty, in* PROGRESSIVE CORPORATE LAW (Lawrence E. Mitchell ed., 1995); Paredes, *Blinded by the Light, supra* note 79. *But see* Larry E. Ribstein, *Law v. Trust*, 81 B.U. L. REV. 553, 576–84 (arguing that law can destroy trust). On the other hand, it has been suggested that at some point trust can turn into complacency. *See* Ribstein, *Market vs. Regulatory Responses, supra* note 28, at 24–25.

Sarbanes-Oxley and the NYSE listing standards might also serve an important expressive function. Above and beyond imposing sanctions, the law can make a statement about how people are supposed to behave—that is, the law can express certain social values—and thereby shape norms of conduct. Whatever else one might think about Sarbanes-Oxley and the listing standard reforms, they signal what counts as good corporate governance.

B. But at What Cost?

Regulation is a blunt tool. Sarbanes-Oxley and the NYSE listing standards, for example, treat all companies and all boards as if they were alike. These reforms are mandatory in nature, adopting a one-size-fits-all approach. The reality, however, is that business is complicated. Not all companies and boards are the same.[105]

Take a centerpiece of the corporate governance reforms: independent directors. There is no doubt that a more active board, with more independent directors, might well promote good corporate governance, but it does not follow that a more independent board is optimal for each corporation. Independence has its potential costs. Indeed, for some companies, a more active independent board might, on net, be counterproductive. Recall that boards are thought to serve three broad roles: a monitoring role, a managerial role, and a resource role.[106] Different companies have different needs. The mix of functions a board is asked to perform will vary from company to company and from time to time as a company's needs change. By way of example, the needs of a small company that recently went public might be very different from the needs of a well-established blue-chip like General Electric; and what Microsoft expected and needed out of its board twenty years ago is presumably different from what it expects and needs from its board today. Not only do companies have different needs, but they have different corporate cultures and ways of doing things and different people and personalities.[107] In other words, group dynamics vary from board to board.[108]

Even if a more independent board results in a better monitoring board—although I am not convinced that the same model of a monitoring board fits all companies[109]— it might well come at the expense of the board's other roles, especially its managerial role. For example, insiders typically have better information about the company and know the business better than outside directors. Furthermore, insiders can dedicate more time to the business and, because they typically have more at stake, have a greater incentive to ensure the company's success and to make investments in themselves as members of management.[110] Moreover, by requiring more independent directors, and by tightening the definition of independence and subjecting directors to a greater risk of legal liability, there is a risk that the reforms narrow the pool of potential directors in

---

[105] For other critiques of the one-size-fits-all approach, see Ribstein, *Market vs. Regulatory Responses, supra* note 28; Bainbridge, *Critique of NYSE's Listing Standards, supra* note 27; Chandler & Strine, *supra* note 26.

[106] *See supra* notes 12–15 and accompanying text.

[107] *See, e.g.,* Manning, *supra* note 103, at 1491–92.

[108] *See* Bainbridge, *Why a Board?, supra* note 50.

[109] *Cf.* Bainbridge, *Critique of NYSE's Listing Standards, supra* note 27, at 393–94 (explaining that "firms have a wide range of accountability mechanisms from which to choose," independent directors being only one option).

[110] On the other hand, because insiders have a greater stake in the company, it might create greater pressure to "cook the books." *See supra* notes 54–58 and accompanying text.

a way that compromises the board in all of its duties. The increased emphasis on independence might artificially preclude a number of good people, with varied experiences and expertise and with access to useful resources, from being able or willing to serve.[111]

In addition, there can be too much monitoring. A certain degree of collegiality, openness, and trust is important in the boardroom and between directors and officers.[112] As directors become more independent, they are likely to become more adversarial vis-à-vis top managers and each other. A healthy dose of skepticism from directors and some friction within a corporation—what one might call "constructive tension"—are good for business, but animosity and distrust are not. Too much suspicion and too little collegiality can spawn factions, cause people to play things too close to the vest, and impede the flow of information. It can undermine the cooperation that is needed for a business to thrive. Moreover, active board oversight can make management too risk averse.[113] Further, the presence of an aggressive monitoring board can deter good people from serving as officers of public companies. Although the "imperial CEO" might not be a good idea, a strong CEO that can lead the company is preferable to a company where the CEO and other senior executives are weakened or, at the very least, distracted from running the business because they are forced to spend more time tending to independent directors. Finally, if other monitoring devices—including gatekeepers, various market pressures, and an active (institutional) shareholder base— are effective, an active monitoring board becomes less important, and the board is freed to spend more time on its other roles, where independence loses its comparative advantage over other director qualities.

The data on the relationship between board independence and company performance bear out these concerns.[114] The data are mixed on whether a more independent board results in better corporate performance, whether measured in terms of stock price or financial performance or more discrete metrics, such as the likelihood of replacing the CEO, executive compensation, or the adoption of anti-takeover tactics.[115]

---

[111] See, e.g., Phyllis Plitch, *Ready and Able? Companies Say the List of Qualified Directors Is Depressingly Short. Critics Say That's Because Companies Are Looking in the Wrong Places*, WALL ST. J., Feb. 24, 2003, at R3; Dow Jones Newswires, *Nasdaq Chairman Suggests Forming Director Talent Pool.*, WALL ST. J., June 10, 2002, at C12; Kemba J. Dunham, *Reforms Turn Search for Directors into a Long, Tedious Task*, WALL ST. J., Aug. 29, 2002, at B1.

[112] See Langevoort, *The Human Nature of Corporate Boards, supra* note 50, at 810–14.

[113] See infra notes 140–42 and accompanying text.

[114] For a recent analysis of the data on independence as a basis for critiquing the proposed NYSE listing standards, see Bainbridge, *Critique of NYSE's Listing Standards, supra* note 27, at 386–88.

[115] See, e.g., April Klein, *Firm Performance and Board Committee Structure*, 41 J. L. & ECON. 275 (1998); Bhagat & Black, *supra* note 50; Sanjai Bhagat & Bernard Black, *The Non-Correlation Between Board Independence and Long-Term Firm Performance*, 27 J. CORP. L. 231 (2002); Bainbridge, *Critique of NYSE's Listing Standards, supra* note 27, at 14–21 (reviewing studies); Fisch, *Taking Boards Seriously, supra* note 50, at 276–80 (reviewing studies); Johnson et al., *supra* note 50 (reviewing studies).

The tradeoffs of a more independent board will vary for each company. The reform efforts could, and should, have done more to account for the cost of independence and the diverse needs of companies. Indeed, the fact that so many different board reforms have been suggested over the years, let alone in the wake of the recent corporate scandals, suggests that there is no one model of corporate governance that is optimal for every company.

Even if one is convinced that more independent boards are a worthwhile goal, there are still gaps in the tightened definition of independence in Sarbanes-Oxley and the proposed listing standards. The definition of independence has been expanded to cover certain financial and business ties that in the past generally were not understood as compromising a director's independence. However, with the reforms, a director will still be "independent" even if he has significant personal or social ties with the CEO or other senior executives, although it is possible that courts will close this gap as fiduciary duties continue to evolve, post-Enron.[116] Further, the definition of independence does not account for the array of cognitive factors that might bias a director in favor of the CEO or for what Vice Chancellor Strine calls the "acculturating power of the board room."[117] To be clear, I am not advocating an even stricter definition of independence, largely because I do not think it would do any good. Any definition of independence that relies on proxies for a person's judgment or for what a person will do when push comes to shove is necessarily going to be underinclusive, as well as overinclusive. At the end of the day, independence is about a director's state of mind and willingness to act; in particular, it is about a director's ability to engage issues objectively and to be willing to stand up to and challenge management. Indeed, some have said that the true test of a director's independence is whether she is willing to resign if need be. Admittedly, the stiffened definition of independence is likely to result in more directors who truly are more independent both on paper and in deed. But it is important for investors to realize the gaps in the definition of independence and not to view compliance with the stricter definition of independence as a cure-all for corporate corruption and mismanagement and as a guarantee of good corporate performance in the future.[118]

---

[116] *See* Strine, *supra* note 35, at 1374–95, *see also In re* Oracle Corp. Derivative Litigation, 2003 WL 21396449 (Del. Ch. July 17, 2003) (finding that a number of Stanford University colleagues serving on a special litigation committee of Oracle's board were not independent, given their social and professional connections to each other and to the defendants).

[117] *Id.* at 1375. One way to address some of these concerns might be to adopt term limits for directors.

[118] *Cf.* Ribstein, *Market vs. Regulatory Responses*, *supra* note 28, at 24–25 (cautioning that investor confidence and trust can turn into complacency); Donald C. Langevoort, *Managing the "Expectations Gap" in Investor Protection: The SEC and the Post-Enron Reform Agenda*, *available at* http://papers.ssrn.com/paper.taf?abstract_id=328080 (explaining that investors often expect that the federal securities laws provide more investor protection than they actually do).

C. Market-Based Alternatives

Regulation is only one way to shape conduct, in this case to root out fraud and prevent corporate corruption and mismanagement. Markets can also regulate conduct. Indeed, markets—including product markets, capital markets, the market for management, and the market for corporate control—have long been an important part of corporate governance. There are clearly downsides to the legislative and regulatory responses outlined above. Admittedly, markets are imperfect also. The policy question raised by the recent scandals, then, is which is preferable on net: market-based responses or more regulation.[119]

There have been a number of market-based responses following Enron.[120] For example, relatively early on, accounting firms began to separate their consulting and auditing businesses,[121] and investment banks instituted reforms to remedy securities analyst conflicts of interest, although admittedly facing regulatory pressure at the time.[122] On the investor front, institutional and other investors have stepped up the pressure on companies to adopt good corporate governance practices,[123] and the number of governance-related shareholder proposals is up.[124] In addition, several shareholder ad-

---

[119] For an extensive consideration of market-based responses to the corporate scandals, see Ribstein, *Market vs. Regulatory Responses, supra* note 28.

[120] Even if the capital markets did not push for corporate governance reforms, political pressure might have caused companies to change the way they do business. The public outcry over the scandals at Enron, WorldCom, Tyco, Adelphia, and elsewhere, together with attention-grabbing headlines, editorials vilifying management, and the "perp walks" by indicted executives, might have shamed companies into revamping their governance structures as companies and their executives sought to mute the public scorn. Appearing to be (if not actually being) a model of good corporate governance can be important to a company's business strategy, especially for high-profile companies whose reputations matter to their consumers, let alone their investors. For more on shaming as a means of influencing corporate behavior, see David A. Skeel, Jr., *Shaming in Corporate Law*, 149 U. PA. L. REV. 1811 (2001).

[121] *See, e.g.*, Raymond Hennessey, *IPO Outlook: Market May Be Key Tool to Elude Accounting Issues*, WALL ST. J., Feb. 11, 2002, at C15; Rachel Emma Silverman, *Questioning the Books: Deloitte to Separate Consulting Services from Audit Business*, WALL ST. J., Feb. 6, 2002, at A8; Seligman, *No One Can Serve Two Masters, supra* note 29, at 490–91 (quoting Accounting and Investor Protection Issues Raised in Enron and Other Public Companies: Hearing Before the S. Comm. On Banking, Housing, & Urban Affairs, 107th Cong. (2002) (testimony of David S Ruder)).

[122] *See, e.g.*, Charles Gasparino & Jeff D. Opdyke, *Merrill Alters a Policy on Analysts*, WALL ST. J., July 11, 2001, at C1; Dow Jones Newswires, *Merrill to Disclose Its Analysts' Holdings in Researched Entities*, WALL ST. J., June 19, 2001, *available at* 2001 WL-WSJ 2867026; Judith Burns, *Brokers' Group Has Mixed View of Rules Plan*, WALL ST. J., Apr. 17, 2002, *available at* 2002 WL-WSJ 3392073; Paul Beckett, *Outsider Aims to Restore Citigroup's Luster*, WALL ST. J., Oct. 31, 2002, at C1.

[123] *See, e.g.*, Claudia H, Deutsch, *Revolt of the Shareholders*, N.Y. TIMES, Feb. 23, 2003, at Section 3, 1.

[124] *See, e.g., id.*; 2003 SHAREHOLDER PROXY SEASON OVERVIEW: SOCIAL AND CORPORATE GOVERNANCE RESOLUTIONS TRENDS, Report from the Investor Responsibility Research Center and Interfaith Center on Corporate Responsibility (Feb. 12, 2003), *available at* http://www.hastingsgroup.com/021203_proxy_season_overview_FINAL.PDF.

vocacy groups, blue-ribbon panels, and other associations have recommended a series of "best practices" that they are exhorting boards to adopt.[125] Further, Institutional Shareholder Services, GovernanceMetrics International, Standard & Poor's, and others have started grading the corporate governance structures of companies, just as Standard & Poor's or Moody's grade their debt.[126] Finally, you can hardly watch CNBC or read the *Wall Street Journal* without hearing from investors, pundits, regulators, and others that corporate governance matters and is focused on more than ever. There are innumerable examples of companies of all sizes and across all industries responding to the market's call for reform. The fact that so many quarters are skeptical, indeed critical, of officers and directors and pressuring companies to adopt new governance regimes is reason to be optimistic that market-based responses would be effective, even without more corporate governance regulation. Indeed, the very fact that the gatekeepers are subject to extensive reforms, such as the new Public Company Accounting Oversight Board,[127] the new rules regulating lawyers practicing before the SEC,[128] and a $1.4 billion global settlement addressing securities analyst conflicts of interest[129] to name a few, lessens the need to regulate the internal affairs of corporations, since the gatekeepers are themselves a key part of the market response and help facilitate more direct investor monitoring of the company and management.

Perhaps the best indicator that markets work is the major selloff that occurred after Enron and the other scandals broke.[130] The stock market affects corporate behavior because it punishes poor corporate performance (and, sometimes, just the whiff of poor performance). Investors value not only a company's business model, but also its governance structure, at least post-Enron. Once the scandals broke, investors became skittish about all companies, good and bad, and sold off stocks across the board and

---

[125] *See, e.g.,* Jeffrey Sonnenfeld, *Meet Our Corporate Governance Watchdogs,* WALL ST. J., Mar. 11, 2003, at B4; CONFERENCE BOARD REPORT, *supra* note 20; Korn/Ferry International, *Twenty "Best Practices" to Improve Board Performance, available at* http://www.kornferry.com/Sources/PDF/PUB_015.pdf; Financial Executives International, *Improving Financial Management, Financial Reporting and Corporate Governance, available at* http://www.fei.org/download/ReformRecommendations.pdf; CalPERS, *Governance Principles, available at* http://www.calpers-governance.org/principles/default.asp.

[126] *See, e.g.,* http://governancemetrics.com/(gu3yaan4lw1ofd55tsqjxk55)/Default.aspx; http://www.isscgq.com/abouttheratings.htm; http://www.governance.standardandpoors.com.

[127] Sarbanes-Oxley §§ 101–109.

[128] *Implementation of Standards of Professional Conduct for Attorneys,* Securities Act Release No. 33-8185 (Jan. 29 2003).

[129] *See* Randall Smith et al., *Wall Street Firms to Pay $1.4 Billion to End Inquiry,* WALL ST. J., Apr. 29, 2003, at A1; Stephen Labaton, *10 Wall Street Firms Settle with U.S. in Analyst Inquiry,* N.Y. TIMES, Apr. 29, 2003, at A1.

[130] On the other hand, some have suggested that the very existence of the scandals, requiring the failure of so many redundant checks and balances in the corporate governance system, evidences the failure of markets. To be fair, the critics of market-based responses would have to admit that the scandals equally indict the efficacy of regulation.

began to sit on the sidelines, hording cash. While this indiscriminate response might have been overwrought, it gave "good" companies (i.e., those that are generally well-run and honest with good corporate governance) a chance to demonstrate that they were not "lemons"; otherwise, investors would assume the worst.[131] The CEO and CFO financial certifications required by the SEC in August 2002[132] helped companies signal that their financials were accurate and that they were not one of the other shoes about to drop; the market was able to begin self-correcting once it had better information to evaluate companies. Since then, companies have voluntarily adopted many of the best practices that have been urged upon them, in part to signal their commitment to good corporate governance and to avoid being punished by investors for having a suspect governance structure in place. When companies commit voluntarily to "do the right thing," that commitment can do more to restore investor confidence than can new legal requirements mandating that companies change their governance structures.

Some have suggested that those who favor market-based responses over regulation do so in order to go easy on boards and officers. It turns out, however, that the market-based responses to the scandals, which began before it was certain that any serious federal legislation would be enacted or the amended NYSE listing standards were proposed, are comparable in many respects to what Sarbanes-Oxley and the revised listing standards require, at least when it comes to boards of directors. In fact, a number of reforms advocated by investors are more stringent than what Congress and the NYSE have called for. Case in point: a number of institutional investors, shareholder watchdog groups, and blue-ribbon panels have urged that companies separate the CEO and chairman positions or, at the very least, appoint a lead director.

The reason for favoring market-based responses over regulation is straightforward: markets are more flexible than regulation, and market-based responses can be more narrowly tailored than regulation to the needs of a particular company, which might change over time. In short, market-based reforms are not one-size-fits-all and they are not mandatory. Further, if a company changes its corporate governance system under market pressure, it can always unwind the decision if it turns out to be unwise. This give-and-take allows a more efficient set of governance techniques to evolve over time and for each company and its investors to pick and choose the measures that work best for it. Regulation has much less play in the joints; for example, it will be difficult to revise the NYSE listing standards or to amend Sarbanes-Oxley as these regulation-based reforms ossify. Some argue that market-based reforms are too short-lived, that good corporate governance will go by the wayside during the next bull market. This is

---

[131] See George A. Akerlof, The Market for "Lemons": Quality Uncertainty and the Market Mechanism, 84 Q.J. ECON. 488 (1970). For a discussion of the lemons problem in the context of securities markets, see Paredes, Blinded by the Light, supra note 79.

[132] Commission Order No. 4-460, Order Requiring the Filing of Sworn Statements Pursuant to Section 21(a)(1) of the Securities Exchange Act of 1934 (June 27, 2002).

a fair concern. But on the other hand, regulation often overstays its welcome. This is a particular concern in the case of Sarbanes-Oxley, much of which was quickly adopted in a politically-charged atmosphere where each member of Congress wanted to be able to claim that he or she was "doing something" to protect investors.[133] In the haste to pass the bill, it appears as though the potential costs of the measures were not given due consideration and the drafting was, at the very least, clumsy in many instances.[134] Furthermore, there is no reason to believe that regulatory enforcement itself might not become lax during the next bull market, just as it did during the last one.[135] Who wants to upset the apple cart, even if there are some bad apples in it? It generally is not until the bears come out that regulators get tough, often in a fit of overreaction.

To be sure, there is a role for law. Indeed, markets could not function without the support of the law and of regulatory institutions. It is important, though, that those who advocate a more heavy-handed regulatory response recognize the costs of more rules when it comes to regulating corporate governance. Of course, it is equally important for proponents of markets to recognize that markets are also imperfect and can fail. In other words, the Nirvana fallacy cuts both ways. Whether markets or regulation are ultimately better at promoting good corporate performance is an empirical question. However, given the theory and available data, when it comes to regulating a corporation's internal affairs, I place my bet with the more flexible market-based approach.

But the choice between markets or regulation does not have to be an "either/or" proposition. A compromise solution would have regulators and policy makers propose a list of "best practices" for corporate governance, instead of mandatory rules.[136] Companies could then either comply with the recommendations or explain in their SEC filings why they have chosen not to. (A more paternalistic version of this approach would have Congress or the NYSE adopt the best practices as default rules, which companies could opt out of with a (super)majority shareholder vote.) The "com-

---

[133] From an historical perspective, the passage of Sarbanes-Oxley should come as no surprise. Stuart Banner has found that major changes in securities regulation over the past 300 years typically follow market collapses. *See* Stuart Banner, *What Causes New Securities Regulation?: 300 Years of Evidence*, 75 WASH. U. L.Q. 849 (1997). For an interesting analysis of causes contributing to the market bubble that set the stage for Enron and the other scandals, see John C. Coffee, Jr., *What Caused Enron?: A Capsule Social and Economic History of the 1990's, available at* http://ssrn.com/abstract_id=373581.

[134] Furthermore, as in any legislative or regulatory process, there is an array of public choice concerns. *See generally* PERSPECTIVES ON PUBLIC CHOICE (Dennis C. Mueller ed., 1997); PUBLIC CHOICE AND PUBLIC LAW READINGS AND COMMENTARY (Maxwell L. Stearns ed., 1997). For a discussion of the politics of reform in the context of Sarbanes-Oxley, see Ribstein, *Market vs. Regulatory Responses, supra* note 28, at 45–47; Seligman, *No One Can Serve Two Masters, supra* note 29.

[135] *See* Committee on Governmental Affairs, *The SEC and Private-Sector Watchdogs, supra* note 33.

[136] For a similar view, see Bainbridge, *Critique of NYSE's Listing Standards, supra* note 27, at 395–96 (endorsing a best-practices model, where "issuers would not be strapped into an ill-fitting 'one-size-fits-all' model" of corporate governance).

ply or explain" approach is popular in the United Kingdom[137] and is reflected in the approach taken in Sarbanes-Oxley when it comes to the audit committee's financial expert[138] and whether or not a public company has adopted a code of ethics for senior financial officers.[139] The "comply or explain" approach would provide investors with useful information about a company's governance system, and investors could then respond accordingly through their trading and voting. "Comply or explain" is consistent with the thrust of the federal securities laws, which are premised on a philosophy of empowering investors with information and then letting them make their own investment decisions.

At bottom, whatever the approach to reform, the key is accountability. Directors and officers need to be accountable for their conduct. Even a more independent board will not be effective if the directors are not accountable for their failures. But just as too little corporate accountability can be harmful, so can too much accountability.[140] As I suggested earlier,[141] if directors and officers feel that they are "under a microscope," and that serious consequences will follow if they make a mistake, an atmosphere of distrust and hesitancy might develop. Members of management might become less candid with each other and might spend too much time looking over their shoulders instead of concentrating on running the company. More important, managers might become risk-averse and refrain from taking prudent business risks, especially as the risk of legal liability increases. Business typically does not welcome such risk aversion. No company succeeded, at least not for very long, without taking some risks; and when risks are taken, failures will follow. Managers, for example, should not have to fear legal liability every time they are wrong, assuming that they acted in good faith. Through the business judgment rule, courts recognize that directors and officers, when readily second-guessed, can become too cautious to the detriment of shareholders and economic growth more broadly. Judge Winter put it this way:

> [C]ourts recognize that after-the-fact litigation is a most imperfect device to evaluate corporate business decisions. The circumstances surrounding a corporate decision are not easily reconstructed in a courtroom years later, since business imperatives often call for quick decisions, inevitably based

---

[137] *See, e.g.,* Special Study Group of the Committee on Federal Regulation of Securities of the Business Law Section of the American Bar Association, *Special Study on Market Structure, Listing Standards and Corporate Governance,* 57 Bus. Law. 1487, 1494–95 (2002); Silvia Ascarelli, *One Size Doesn't Fit All, In Europe, Corporate-Governance Rules Are Not in the Details,* Wall St. J., Feb. 24, 2003, at R6.

[138] Sarbanes-Oxley § 407.

[139] Sarbanes-Oxley § 406.

[140] For others highlighting the potential consequences of corporate accountability, see Langevoort, *The Human Nature of Corporate Boards, supra* note 50; Bainbridge, *Why a Board?, supra* note 50, at 48–54; Ribstein, *Market vs. Regulatory Responses, supra* note 28, at 35–47.

[141] *See supra* notes 3, 103, and 112–113 and accompanying text.

on less than perfect information. The entrepreneur's function is to encounter risks and to confront uncertainty, and a reasoned decision at the time made may seem a wild hunch viewed years later against a background of perfect knowledge. . . . [B]ecause potential profit often corresponds to the potential risk, it is very much in the interest of shareholders that the law not create incentives for overly cautious corporate decisions.[142]

The challenge is to strike the right balance between managerial discretion for directors and officers to run the business on the one hand and adequate shareholder protection on the other.[143] The real genius of U.S. corporate law[144] is its ability to strike this balance, notwithstanding that it might get out of whack from time to time, by adopting an enabling approach to corporate law. The enabling model of corporate law largely eschews bright-line mandatory rules and is flexible enough to re-equilibrate itself from time to time, whether in response to scandal or in the ordinary course as companies' needs evolve over time.[145]

Enron et al. do present strong evidence that corporate accountability had become too lax. But more can be done, short of adopting a series of rules regulating corporate governance, to enable markets to hold directors and officers more accountable. Indeed, corporate law expects shareholders to hold directors and officers accountable through their right to vote, their right to sell, and their right to sue for breach of fiduciary duty. First, the proxy rules could be revised under the federal securities laws to allow shareholders to communicate more freely.[146] If shareholders, especially institutional investors, are better able to coordinate, they can more effectively exercise their franchise and, if necessary, wage a proxy contest,[147] or simply bring informal pressures to bear on

---

[142] Joy v. North, 692 F.2d 880, 886 (2d Cir. 1982).

[143] *See also* Stephen M. Bainbridge, *The Board of Directors as Nexus of Contracts*, 88 IOWA L. REV. 1, 31–33 (2002) (discussing the tradeoff between managerial discretion and corporate accountability).

[144] The word "genius" is borrowed from Roberta Romano's influential book, *The Genius of American Corporate Law*, in which she argues that regulatory competition among the states is the genius of American corporate law. ROBERTA ROMANO, THE GENIUS OF AMERICAN CORPORATE LAW (1993).

[145] *See infra* notes 170–76 and accompanying text for more on the U.S. corporate law system. *Cf.* Edward B. Rock & Michael L. Wachter, *Islands of Conscious Power: Norms and the Self-Governing Corporation*, 149 U. PA. L. REV. 1619 (2001) (explaining that corporate law carves out a large swath of corporate conduct to be regulated by "nonlegally enforceable rules and standards" (i.e., norms)).

[146] *See supra* note 9. In particular, the SEC is currently considering a number of rule changes that would allow shareholders to include shareholder-nominated directors in the corporation's proxy statement. *See Staff Report: Review of the Proxy Process Regarding the Nomination and Election of Directors*, Division of Corporation Finance, July 15, 2003 [hereinafter *Staff Proxy Process Report*].

[147] "Proxy contests" refer to those instances where a shareholder or shareholder group opposes incumbent management by, for example, offering an insurgent slate of directors to replace the management-sponsored board. For more on proxy contests, see MEREDITH M. BROWN ET AL., TAKEOVERS: A STRATEGIC GUIDE TO MERGERS AND ACQUISITIONS 186–218 (2nd ed., 2001).

management. Further, the board's ability to omit shareholder proposals from the company's proxy materials could be limited; in particular, shareholders could be allowed to include shareholder-nominated directors in the corporation's proxy statement, a reform the SEC is considering,[148] and the company could be required to implement certain governance-related shareholder proposals that receive a (super)majority shareholder vote.[149] In addition, boards could be given less discretion to adopt defensive tactics that fend off, and in some cases defeat, a hostile takeover attempt, thereby spurring the market for corporate control, which is an important corporate governance device.[150] In short, corporate control could be made more contestable, whether through shareholder voting or takeovers.[151] Moreover, some of the procedural hurdles to derivative litigation, including the demand requirement and special litigation committees, might be lowered, without stiffening the substantive duties of care and loyalty or asking courts to second-guess management's business decisions more.[152] Even the media have a role to play in bringing pressure to bear on directors and officers who care about their reputations.[153] A final possibility is that directors and officers can be encouraged to internalize norms of good corporate conduct that are self-enforcing.[154] The internalization of "good corporate governance norms" requires that directors and officers become self-conscious of their duties and obligations to the corporation and its shareholders. Put differently, with encouragement, directors and officers might heed (even when nobody is watching) Judge Cardozo's statement that the measure of fiduciary conduct is whether it stands up to "the punctilio of an honor the most sensitive."[155]

Ultimately, the onus is on investors, especially institutional investors, to be more active and responsible overseers of the business and management if markets are going to be a powerful governance tool.[156] If investors are unwilling to shoulder the burden, they will have little room to complain if there is further regulation of corporate governance.

---

[148] *See Staff Proxy Process Report, supra* note 146.

[149] As I mentioned earlier, *see supra* note 10 and accompanying text, presently, management can ignore most shareholder proposals, even if they receive a majority shareholder vote.

[150] *See supra* note 11.

[151] *See* John C. Coates, *Measuring the Domain of Mediating Hierarchy: How Contestable Are U.S. Public Corporations?*, 24 J. CORP. L. 837 (1999) (developing a "contestability index").

[152] To overcome concerns that the risk of legal liability for directors and officers could become excessive, a cap on damages would be worth considering.

[153] *See* Skeel, *supra* note 120.

[154] *See infra* notes 173–75 and accompanying text.

[155] Meinhard v. Salmon, 249 N.Y. 458, 464 (1928).

[156] Two prominent members of the Delaware Chancery Court, Chancellor Chandler and Vice Chancellor Strine, have recently urged institutional investors to become more active in corporate governance by, among other things, nominating representatives to sit on boards. *See* Chandler & Strine, *supra* note 26.

IV. FEDERALISM AND SOME THOUGHTS ON THE ROLE OF CONGRESS

Corporate law has traditionally been left to the states. The states, not the federal government, have primary responsibility for regulating corporate governance, with Congress steering clear of the substantive regulation of corporate governance. The federal securities laws, for example, reflect a philosophy of disclosure—the federal mandatory disclosure system is designed to give investors adequate information to protect their own interests without the need for more substantive regulation of a corporation's internal affairs.[157] The Supreme Court and several lower federal courts have relied on federalism principles to limit the reach of the federal securities laws and the SEC's authority to regulate internal corporate affairs. For example, in *Santa Fe Industries, Inc. v. Green*,[158] the Supreme Court held that mere instances of corporate mismanagement or fiduciary duty breach fall outside the scope of the antifraud provisions of the federal securities laws and should be left to state corporate law to address.[159] Similarly, the Second Circuit held in *Business Roundtable v. Securities and Exchange Commission*[160] that the SEC did not have the authority to promulgate Rule 19c-4, the "one-share/one-vote" rule,[161] because the rule regulated the allocation of authority among shareholders and was unrelated to disclosure.[162]

To say that Congress and the SEC never regulate corporate governance would be an overstatement. Many aspects of the federal securities laws affect corporate governance and how managers run companies.[163] For example, the federal securities laws regulate proxies, shareholder proposals, and tender offer bids.[164] Moreover, disclosure itself can

---

[157] For an overview of the federal mandatory disclosure system, see Paredes, *Blinded by the Light, supra* note 79; Robert B. Thompson & Hillary A. Sale, *Securities Fraud as Corporate Governance: Reflections Upon Federalism*, 56 VAND. L. REV. 859 (2003).

[158] 430 U.S. 462 (1977).

[159] *Id.* at 1301–04; *see also* Schreiber v. Burlington Northern, Inc., 472 U.S. 1 (1985); Burks v. Lasker, 441 U.S. 471 (1979).

[160] 905 F.2d 406 (D.C. Cir. 1990).

[161] For a discussion of the "one-share/one-vote" controversy, see Joel Seligman, *Equal Protection in Shareholder Voting Rights: The One Common Share, One Vote Controversy*, 54 GEO. WASH. L. REV. 687 (1986).

[162] Generally, matters of disclosure fall to the federal government to regulate, largely through the SEC under the federal securities laws, and the substantive regulation of corporate governance is principally left to the states.

[163] *See generally* Robert B. Thompson, *Preemption and Federalism in Corporate Governance: Protecting Shareholder Rights to Vote, Sell, and Sue*, 62 LAW & CONTEMP. PROBS. 215 (1999); Thompson & Sale, *supra* note 157; Amir N. Licht, *International Diversity in Securities Regulation: Roadblocks on the Way to Convergence*, 20 CARDOZO L. REV. 227, 245–63 (1998); Mark J. Roe, *Delaware's Competition, available at* http://papers.ssrn.com/sol3/papers.cfm?abstract_id=354783.

[164] *See* LOSS & SELIGMAN, *supra* note 9, at 488–630.

indirectly affect corporate governance by deterring certain conduct or by empowering shareholders and other corporate constituencies by giving them information about the corporation and the performance of management.[165] As Professors Thompson and Sale reveal in an interesting study, securities fraud class actions often focus on how the business has been operated, in effect regulating corporate managers by subjecting them and their business decisions to greater scrutiny.[166] Furthermore, failure to disclose corporate misconduct or mismanagement might itself constitute fraud under the federal securities laws.[167] Nonetheless, the core of federal securities regulation is disclosure, albeit with an indirect impact on corporate governance; the substantive regulation of corporate governance is principally left to state corporate law.

Sarbanes-Oxley is an about-face. Aside from its substance, Sarbanes-Oxley is significant because it marks an expanded role for Congress in the substantive regulation of corporate governance. Sarbanes-Oxley veers from the federal securities laws' regulatory philosophy of disclosure and regulates the substance of corporate governance in ways that Congress has not before. The increased federalization of corporate law raises concerns,[168] and not surprisingly, has received the attention of the most important body making corporate law, the Delaware judiciary.[169]

States (again, focusing on Delaware) have largely opted for an enabling approach to corporate law that permits private ordering among corporate constituencies, primarily

---

[165] For an overview of how mandatory disclosure under the federal securities laws can influence corporate conduct and reduce agency costs, see Paredes, *Blinded by the Light*, supra note 79; Paul G. Mahoney, *Mandatory Disclosure as a Solution to Agency Problems*, 62 U. Chi. L. Rev. 1047 (1995); A.A. Sommer, Jr., *Therapeutic Disclosure*, 4 Sec. Reg. L.J. 263 (1976); Merritt B. Fox, *Required Disclosure and Corporate Governance*, 62-SUM Law & Contemp. Probs. 113 (1999); Louis Lowenstein, *Financial Transparency and Corporate Governance: You Manage What You Measure*, 96 Colum. L. Rev. 1335 (1996); Edmund W. Kitch, *The Theory and Practice of Securities Disclosure*, 61 Brook. L. Rev. 763 (1995).

[166] *See* Thompson & Sale, *supra* note 157. Thompson and Sale's study shows that state shareholder litigation primarily is brought for breach of the duty of loyalty by directors, whereas securities fraud class action litigation is directed primarily at how officers have operated the business.

[167] Donald C. Langevoort, *Seeking Sunlight in* Santa Fe's *Shadow: A Study of Law and Strategic Behavior*, 79 Wash. U. L.Q. 449 (2001).

[168] For other critiques of the federalization of corporate law post-Enron, see Ribstein, *supra* note 28, at 57–61; Bainbridge, *Critique of NYSE's Listing Standards*, *supra* note 27, at 396–99; Chandler & Strine, *supra* note 26. My focus here is on Congress. Many, however, see the stock exchanges, including the NYSE, as extensions of the SEC, and in turn the federal government, since the exchanges are subject to stringent SEC oversight and influence. For extensive analyses of the stock exchanges as regulators, beyond the concerns I express in this essay about the mandatory approach of the revised NYSE listing standards, see, e.g., Paul G. Mahoney, *The Exchange as Regulator*, 83 Va. L. Rev. 1453 (1997); A.C. Pritchard, *Markets as Monitors: A Proposal to Replace Class Actions with Exchanges as Securities Fraud Monitors*, A.C. Pritchard, 85 Va. L. Rev. 925 (1999); Marcel Kahan, *Some Problems with Stock Exchange-Based Securities Regulation*, 83 Va. L. Rev. 509 (1997).

[169] *See, e.g.*, Chandler & Strine, *supra* note 26.

the officers, directors, and shareholders.[170] The parties have wide discretion to organize their affairs as they see fit, although, as a practical matter, very little private ordering takes place in large public corporations. To be sure, Delaware does have a corporation code that contains a number of key provisions; but for the most part, Delaware has rejected a system of mandatory rules for regulating corporate governance. The most important aspect of state corporate law is not what is on the books, but rather the common law of fiduciary duties administered, in the case of Delaware at least, by a very sophisticated judiciary against the background norm of shareholder primacy.[171] But the law is only one component of the state corporate law system. Other important features include market pressures that discipline directors and officers to run the business profitably and in share-holders' best interests and contracts, such as equity-based compensation arrangements designed to align the interests of management with shareholders. The disclosure regime of the federal securities laws, along with numerous second-order institutions, such as accountants, investment bankers, lawyers, securities analysts, credit rating agencies, and, more recently, shareholder service and proxy solicitation firms, support the entire system of corporate law and are critical to the effectiveness of its enabling approach.[172]

Norms are another important extra-legal governance mechanism.[173] The Delaware judiciary, for example, often exhorts directors and officers through dicta or even speeches and articles to conduct themselves in accordance with good corporate practices; at the same time, the judges are hesitant to hold directors and officers liable, especially for breaching the duty of care.[174] Delaware Supreme Court Chief Justice E. Norman Veasey has time and again encouraged directors to adopt seven specific "aspirational norms for corporate practice" that he has offered.[175]

---

[170] *See, e.g.,* E. Norman Veasey, *Should Corporation Law Inform Aspirations for Good Corporate Governance Practices—Or Vice Versa?*, 149 U. PA. L. REV. 2179, 2179 (2001) (describing the enabling model as being "based on a few fundamental statutory guideposts and latitude for private ordering, with primary reliance on self-governance centered around judicial decisionmaking in applying fiduciary duties to fact-intensive settings") [hereinafter Veasey, *Aspirations*].

[171] For more on this standards-based approach to corporate law, see Leo E. Strine, Jr., *Delaware's Corporate Law System: Is Corporate America Buying an Exquisite Jewel or a Diamond in the Rough? A Response to Kahan & Kamar's Price Discrimination in the Market for Corporate Law*, 86 CORNELL L. REV. 1257 (2001) [hereinafter Strine, *Delaware's Corporate Law System*].

[172] *Cf.* Bernard S. Black, *The Legal and Institutional Preconditions for Strong Securities Markets*, 48 UCLA L. REV. 781 (2001). Troy A. Paredes, *A Systems Approach to Corporate Governance Reform: Why Improving U.S. Corporate Law isn't the Answer,* __ WILL. & MARY L. REV. __ (forthcoming 2004).

[173] *See, e.g., supra* note 67; Langevoort, *The Human Nature of Corporate Boards, supra* note 50; Edward B. Rock, *Saints and Sinners: How Does Delaware Corporate Law Work?*, 44 UCLA L. REV. 1009 (1997); Symposium on Norms and Corporate Law, 149 U. PA. L. REV. 1607 (2001). The role of trust in corporate law is also critical. *See* Margaret M. Blair & Lynn A. Stout, *Trust, Trustworthiness, and the Behavioral Foundations of Corporate Law*, 149 U. PA. L. REV. 1735 (2001).

[174] *See, e.g.,* Rock, *supra* note 173; Rock & Wachter, *supra* note 145.

[175] *See, e.g.,* E. Norman Veasey, *An Economic Rationale for Judicial Decisionmaking in Corporate Law*, 53 BUS. LAW. 681 (1998); Veasey, *Aspirations, supra* note 170; *see also* William T. Allen, *The Pride and the Hope of Delaware Corporate Law*, 25 DEL. J. CORP. L. 70 (2000).

The great virtue of the enabling approach is balance. The parts of the corporate law system work together in a way that achieves a healthy balance of managerial discretion and shareholder protection. Further, the system is flexible.[176] Because state corporate law is not made up of mandatory rules, a corporation and its constituencies can better adapt the company's governance structure as appropriate to fit its particular needs over time. In addition, the Delaware judges are able to develop corporate law incrementally and on a case-by-case basis through the law of fiduciary duties.

The rationale for leaving corporate law to the states has never been clear. When addressing the question, such as in the context of construing the scope of the federal securities laws, most courts simply assert that corporate law should be left to the states because "corporations are creatures of state law" and states have traditionally regulated in the area.[177] But this does not justify a federalism principle that limits the federal regulation of corporate governance. Today, corporations are not local in nature, even if they were in the early days of corporations when a charter had to be sought from the state legislature to incorporate.[178] Further, given Congress's broad authority under the Commerce Clause[179] and the Supremacy Clause,[180] no one seriously challenges Congress's authority to regulate corporate governance, as it has in Sarbanes-Oxley.

There is a sound reason to resist federalizing corporate law, however. That is, as described, state corporate law is enabling in nature, and federal corporate law is likely to be mandatory and one-size-fits-all in its approach, like Sarbanes-Oxley.[181] I have already described why an enabling approach to corporate law is preferable to a manda-

---

[176] See Strine, *Delaware's Corporate Law System, supra* note 171; Marcel Kahan & Ehud Kamar, *Price Discrimination in the Market for Corporate Law*, 86 CORNELL L. REV. 1205 (2001); Jill E. Fisch, *The Peculiar Role of the Delaware Courts in the Competition for Corporate Charters*, 68 U. CIN. L. REV. 1061 (2000) [hereinafter Fisch, *Peculiar Role of Delaware Courts*].

[177] *See, e.g.,* Santa Fe Inds., 430 U.S. at 479–80; Burks, 441 U.S. at 477–78; *see also* Alison Grey Anderson, *The Meaning of Federalism: Interpreting the Securities Exchange Act of 1934,* 70 VA. L. REV. 813 (1984); Richard M. Buxbaum, *The Threatened Constitutionalization of the Internal Affairs Doctrine in Corporation Law,* 75 CAL. L. REV. 29 (1987).

[178] *See* LAWRENCE M. FRIEDMAN, A HISTORY OF AMERICAN LAW 177–201, 511–25 (1985).

[179] U.S. CONST. art. I, § 8.

[180] U.S. CONST. art. VI.

[181] Along similar lines, although with a greater emphasis on state competition for corporate charters, Stephen Bainbridge has recently argued, in critiquing the NYSE listing standard reforms, that states should regulate corporate governance because states are more likely than the federal government (or even stock exchanges) to experiment with alternative solutions to the myriad problems corporate law must address. *See* Bainbridge, *Critique of NYSE's Listing Standards, supra* note 27, at 396–99. State competition, Bainbridge concludes, will result in more efficient corporate law, consistent with the "race-to-the-top" view of state competition for corporate charters. *Id.* at 397–98; *see also infra* note 185. Larry Ribstein, in critiquing Sarbanes-Oxley, has offered a similar view, explaining that the regulation of corporate governance is "best resolved in a market for regulation that would permit experimentation and flexibility." Ribstein, *Market vs. Regulatory Responses, supra* note 28, at 57.

tory approach.[182] Delaware, of course, has an added benefit. Its judiciary is very sophisticated in corporate matters and can tweak or update its decisions more readily than the Congress or an administrative agency such as the SEC can amend, let alone overturn, statutes, rules, and regulations.[183] The Delaware courts also have a history of deciding cases extraordinarily quickly, which is particularly important for fast-moving transactions where timing can be critical.[184]

Admittedly, state corporate law is far from being supplanted by Sarbanes-Oxley or other federal action. While I have concerns about Sarbanes-Oxley (as well as the NYSE listing standards), I am more troubled that Sarbanes-Oxley portends an even greater role for Congress in regulating corporate governance in the future. This is not to say that the enabling approach of Delaware or other states is perfect. There is a decades-long debate, for example, over whether regulatory competition among states for corporate charters had led to a "race to the top" or a "race to the bottom."[185] Over the

---

[182] *See supra* Parts III.B. & III.C. The concern can be made more concrete with a simple example, but one that has received a great deal of attention. Take § 402 of Sarbanes-Oxley, which bans most loans to directors and officers of public companies. Beyond the more fundamental concern that § 402 regulates executive compensation, which seems to fall squarely within a corporation's internal affairs, many worry that the ban sweeps too broadly, prohibiting many common business practices that appear to involve the extension of credit but that should not necessarily be discouraged as bad corporate conduct. *See* Alston & Bird LLP et al., *Sarbanes-Oxley Act: Interpretive Issues Under § 402—Prohibition on Certain Insider Loans* (2002); RICHARD W. JENNINGS ET AL., FEDERAL SECURITIES LAWS SELECTED STATUTES, RULES AND FORM, SARBANES-OXLEY ACT SPECIAL SUPPLEMENT 13–16 (2002).

[183] For a thorough analysis of the special role the Delaware judiciary plays in Delaware corporate law, see Fisch, *Peculiar Role of Delaware Courts, supra* note 176 (emphasizing the responsiveness and sophistication of the Delaware judiciary, including its ability to "fine tune" its case law in response to "business developments").

[184] As a practical matter, the SEC probably would bear primary responsibility for implementing any federal corporate law, just as it has been charged with promulgating a host of rules implementing key provisions of Sarbanes-Oxley. Although beyond this essay's scope, a comparative institutional analysis of the Delaware judiciary and the SEC would be interesting. Indeed, the Delaware Chancery Court is similar to an administrative agency tasked with making and enforcing corporate law. Undoubtedly, the sophistication advantage of the Delaware judiciary is less when the Delaware judges are compared to the commissioners and the staff at the SEC instead of to federal judges or members of Congress and their staffs. However, the SEC is a large bureaucracy that acts more slowly than the Delaware judges and is more likely to be subject to political pressures and the influence of special interest groups. Furthermore, with federal corporate law, the federal judiciary would ultimately get involved. Moreover, at least to date, SEC rulemaking has reflected a mandatory, rules-based approach to securities regulation, as opposed to a flexible, standards-based approach. Although interesting, any institutional comparison of the Delaware judiciary and the SEC is largely beside the point so long as the approach the SEC would implement is mandatory.

[185] Those arguing that there is a "race to the bottom" contend that states, in competition with one another for corporate charters and the fees and other benefits that go along with them, adopt a corporate law that is favorable to management, which decides where to incorporate, at the expense of shareholders. According to the "race to the top" view, because shareholders will require a premium (that is, discount the price they pay for shares) when investing in a company incorporated in a jurisdiction with an inferior corporate law from the shareholders' perspective, managers are encouraged to incorporate in jurisdictions

years, reasonable arguments have been made in favor of minimum federal standards for corporate behavior, focusing on the possibility of enacting minimum federal fiduciary duty standards, and even for federal incorporation.[186]

Understandably, many point to the scandals at Enron and elsewhere as a strong indictment of state corporate law. Mindful of these critiques, I nonetheless conclude that, as between a more enabling approach or a more mandatory approach to corporate law, the former is preferable, especially in light of the greater vigilance of the markets after Enron.[187] Moreover, if need be, steps can be taken to enhance corporate accountability without adopting more mandatory rules.[188]

V. CONCLUSION

Boards of directors should not simply rubber-stamp management's decisions and certainly should not fall asleep at the wheel. The board cannot perform any of its functions effectively if it is not meaningfully engaged in the business. To address shortcomings of boards of directors and other corporate governance failures raised by Enron's demise, Congress and the NYSE have adopted several rules, many of which restructure

---

where the corporate law maximizes shareholder wealth. Instead of racing to create lax rules that benefit management, states race to adopt rules that favor shareholders. The literature debating whether there has been a race to the bottom or to the top is extensive. *See, e.g.*, William L. Cary, *Federalism and Corporate Law: Reflections Upon Delaware*, 83 YALE L.J. 663 (1974); Ralph Winter, Jr., *State Law, Shareholder Protection, and the Theory of the Corporation*, 6 J. LEGAL STUD. 251 (1977); Lucian Bebchuk et al., *Does the Evidence Favor State Competition in Corporate Law*, 90 CAL. L. REV. 1775 (2002); Fisch, *Peculiar Role of Delaware Courts, supra* note 176; Lucian Arye Bebchuk & Allen Ferrell, *Federalism and Corporate Law: The Race to Protect Managers from Takeovers*, 99 COLUM. L. REV. 1168 (1999); Robert Daines, *Does Delaware Law Improve Firm Value?*, 62 J. FIN. ECON. 525 (2001); ROBERTA ROMANO, THE GENIUS OF AMERICAN CORPORATE LAW (1993); Marcel Kahan & Ehud Kamar, *The Myth of State Competition in Corporate Law*, 55 STAN. L. REV. 679 (2002). For an interesting article arguing that the real race is not among states, but between states (namely, Delaware) and the federal government, see Mark J. Roe, *Delaware's Competition, supra* note 163.

[186] *See, e.g.*, Cary, *supra* note 185; Joel Seligman, *The Case for Federal Minimum Corporate Law Standards*, 49 MD. L. REV. 947 (1990). The most recent iteration of the debate is over whether the federal government should provide an optional regime regulating takeovers that shareholders can opt in to. *See, e.g.*, Bebchuk & Ferrell, *supra* note 185; Lucian Arye Bebchuk & Allen Ferrell, *A New Approach to Takeover Law and Regulatory Competition*, 87 VA. L. REV. 111 (2001); Stephen J. Choi & Andrew T. Guzman, *Choice and Federal Intervention in Corporate Law*, 87 VA. L. REV. 961 (2000); Jonathan R. Macey, *Displacing Delaware: Can the Feds Do a Better Job Than the States in Regulating Takeovers*, 57 BUS. LAW. 1025 (2002). The concern is that managers have too much discretion under state corporate law to fend off hostile bids.

[187] Finally, it is worth noting that the critiques made here of mandatory corporate law are not intended to argue against mandatory disclosure. While the federal mandatory disclosure system could certainly be made more effective, mandatory disclosure can be seen as facilitating the enabling approach to corporate law and market-based responses by ensuring that investors and other corporate constituencies have access to key information to evaluate corporate performance.

[188] *See supra* notes 146–55 and accompanying text.

boards by requiring that boards become more independent and that independent directors assume more responsibility in governance.

But these reforms come at a cost. Independent directors, for example, can do a lot of good, and might ultimately be more important to good corporate performance than earlier data suggest. Nonetheless, it does not follow that all public companies (in the case of Sarbanes-Oxley), or even all NYSE-listed companies (in the case of the NYSE listing standards), should be required to have more independent directors who take a more active role in the corporation. Rather, corporations should be able to structure their boards as they see fit in light of each corporation's needs. Even if one thinks that most companies would, if given the option, voluntarily adopt the reform measures, it does not follow that the reforms should be mandatory. As an alternative to adopting a mandatory set of new requirements, Congress and the NYSE could have instead adopted a set of new default rules that corporations could opt out of, even if it took a supermajority vote of shareholders to opt out.[189] Some flexibility would be better than none. Further, to improve corporate accountability, regulatory reforms should have been directed toward empowering investors to hold directors and officers more accountable, as opposed to regulating the board directly.[190] Vice Chancellor Strine, of the Delaware Chancery Court, put it this way: "[Q]uite bluntly, it is questionable whether costly government policies ought be directed at placing crutches under well-heeled investors who can walk for themselves. The most vigorous enforcement of director fiduciary duties cannot hope to substitute for careful monitoring performed by rational and active investors . . . ."[191]

Although corporate governance needs reworking, a one-size-fits-all approach mandated by regulation, whether Sarbanes-Oxley or the NYSE listing standards, is not needed. A more flexible enabling approach that accounts for the differences among companies and that strikes a better balance between managerial discretion and shareholder protection is preferable. Although there is room for improvement, Delaware has the right model. I hope Congress recognizes this and that Sarbanes-Oxley is an aberration that does not mark a new trend toward the increased federalization of corporate law.

NOTES AND QUESTIONS

1. The board of directors is delegated broad authority to manage the corporation's business and affairs. This broad delegation of authority to the board reflects what Berle & Means ("B&M") observed—namely, that because share ownership is dispersed, shareholders are not able to run the business. Does the B&M corporation still exist? Recent data show that institutional investors—insurance compa-

---

[189] *See supra* notes 136–39 and accompanying text.

[190] *See supra* notes 146–55 and accompanying text.

[191] Strine, *supra* note 35, at 1402.

nies, pension funds, mutual funds, and the like—hold a substantial portion of U.S. equities. *See* 2001 NYSE FACT BOOK, *available at* http://www.nyse.com/pdfs/2001_factbook_06.pdf. In other words, control is not as separated from ownership as it once was. What is the significance of this convergence of ownership and control? Does it argue for granting shareholders more direct authority over the corporation's business, instead of relegating them to the rights to vote, sell, and sue? Does the broad grant of authority given to the board still make sense, especially in light of the recent scandals? On the other hand, do shareholders want more direct control over the business?

2. The contractarian theory of the firm views a corporation as a nexus of contracts among the various suppliers of inputs to the firm's production process—employees, creditors, suppliers, shareholders (providers of equity capital), and even local communities. *See, e.g.*, FRANK H. EASTERBROOK & DANIEL R. FISCHEL, THE ECONOMIC STRUCTURE OF CORPORATE LAW (1991); *Symposium—Contractual Freedom in Corporate Law*, 89 COLUM. L. REV. 1395 (1989). Some of these contracts are explicit, such as credit agreements and employment contracts, while others are implicit or informal, and might not even be enforceable. In the contractarian view, a corporation's governance structure is the product of a series of (hypothetical) contractual negotiations among the various corporate constituencies. Fiduciary duties, for example, are thought of as the protections that shareholders would be willing to negotiate for if actual bargaining took place. How might the hypothetical bargain approach explain Sarbanes-Oxley and the proposed NYSE listing requirements? Do Sarbanes-Oxley and the amended listing standards reflect governance changes that shareholders would negotiate for, at least in most instances? What else might shareholders negotiate for, if given the chance?

3. Sarbanes-Oxley helped boost investor confidence. How should the short-term need for an investor confidence boost have been balanced against what I claim are the needs for flexibility? Would a more moderate response from Congress have provided the needed confidence boost? How important was it for investors to watch handcuffed corporate executives be indicted and do "perp walks"? Does this do more to shore up investor confidence than any sort of congressional action?

4. How can we prevent capital markets and regulators from becoming lax during the next bull market?

5. Corporate corruption at relatively few companies can have dramatic consequences across capital markets and the economy as a whole. Over the course of the scandals, which occurred at relatively few publicly-traded companies, the public equity markets lost trillions of dollars in market capitalization, in part because of concerns about uncovered corruption—the proverbial other shoe that was yet to drop. In other words, negative externalities are associated with corporate corruption—the harm extends far beyond the particular companies where the abuses occur. Negative externalities are a classic example of a market failure. Do the

negative externalities of corporate corruption argue against relying on market-based responses? Do these negative externalities justify a stringent regulatory response such as Sarbanes-Oxley?

6. Are director term limits a good idea? If shareholders wanted to retain some directors beyond their stated terms, how might that be accomplished?

7. For markets to monitor directors and officers effectively, institutional investors need to be active. But does institutional investor activism give rise to its own agency costs? What are the motivations and incentives of large financial institutions? What are the motivations and incentives of individual portfolio managers? Who will monitor the institutional investors and portfolio managers? *See, e.g.,* Bernard S. Black, *Shareholder Passivity Reexamined*, 89 MICH. L. REV. 520 (1990); John C. Coffee, Jr., *Liquidity Versus Control: The Institutional Investor as Corporate Monitor*, 91 COLUM. L. REV. 1277 (1991). Does the recent opposition of many of the country's largest mutual funds to the new SEC rule requiring mutual funds to disclose their proxy votes help us answer these questions? *See Disclosure of Proxy Voting Policies and Proxy Voting Records by Registered Management Investment Companies,* Securities Act Release No. 33-8188 (Jan. 31, 2003).

8. Why do lawyers and certified public accountants have to get licensed, but not directors? Should there be a professional licensing system for directors? If so, who should administer it? The SEC? The Federal Reserve Board? The U.S. Treasury Department? Delaware? Should we instead establish a new oversight board charged with overseeing the directors of public companies, similar to the Public Company Accounting Oversight Board created by Sarbanes-Oxley to oversee accounting firms that audit public companies? What about a rating system for directors and officers? In addition to rating a company's overall corporate governance structure, should GovernanceMetrics International and other organizations rate boards of directors and senior executives?

General Counsel and the Shifting Sea of Change*

*Michele M. Hedges***

I. BEFORE THE STORM: LIFE AS A GENERAL COUNSEL

The practice of a general counsel[1] is flush with unique challenges and obstacles not present in the day-to-day work of outside counsel. Unlike a lawyer in a firm ("outside counsel") who juggles limited-scope projects for a myriad of clients, the general counsel is, in a manner of speaking, sleeping with the enemy. The company is the general counsel's only client. The "single client" scenario is further complicated by the multiplicity of the general counsel's roles as counsel to the entity and as a senior executive within the organization for which she works. Therefore, the general counsel assumes dual, sometimes contradictory, roles—one as gatekeeper and the champion of corporate compliance, the other as a businessperson with an interest in the financial success and longevity of the entity. Not surprisingly, if the general counsel function is properly executed, it may, at times, threaten the entity's very financial success and longevity.

Prior to Enron's[2] collapse, general counsel of both public and private companies encountered many gray areas and were forced to consider and balance their competing roles on a daily basis: the ethics of promoting the business from the inside, while

---

** Ms. Hedges is Senior Vice President and General Counsel at NextiraOne, LLC. NextiraOne is headquartered in Houston, Texas and Paris, France. Prior to joining NextiraOne, Ms. Hedges was General Counsel for Benchmark Electronics, Inc., Senior Commercial Counsel for Compaq Computer, and Vice President, General Counsel, and Corporate Secretary for Toshiba International Corporation. NextiraOne is owned by Platinum Equity, a global organization specializing in the acquisition and strategic management of mission-critical companies. I would like to thank Amber R. Lee, Senior Counsel at NextiraOne, and Jeff Van Niel, who provided substantial assistance in the preparation of this essay.

[1] As used in this essay, the term "general counsel" refers to the Chief Legal Officer of a company, and the term "in-house counsel" refers to a member of the general counsel's legal staff.

[2] Enron has come to be the poster-child for the series of corporate misdeeds, mismanagement, abuse, and events occurring in or before 2002 that have come to be referred to generically as the "Post-Enron era."

strictly adhering to ethical mandates, confidentiality obligations, and the ever-evolving regulatory, SEC, and common law guidelines. In the post-Enron world, this balancing has become even more treacherous, and the rendition of both legal and business advice to corporate representatives is subject to even greater scrutiny. With the threat of criminal indictment looming in the background, general counsel have cause to be more careful than ever in defining and executing their responsibilities. Surely Mark Belnick, the general counsel of Tyco, never anticipated being indicted for furtherance of Tyco's business objectives, or for accepting a substantial bonus from the CEO for resolving an SEC investigation.[3]

General counsel are uniquely positioned to affect the legal well-being of their corporate clients and the professional agenda of the state and local bars. Because of their increasing stature and visibility, there is a corresponding increase in public scrutiny of the role of general counsel, as well as of their functions and responsibilities in shaping the legal and ethical behavior of their clients. This presents wonderful opportunities for presenting our messages to others, as well as concurrent dangers if we do not adequately articulate our profession's perspective or if we allow others to manipulate issues for us.

This essay highlights the challenges facing general counsel in the post-Enron era, the effect of new and proposed regulations by the Securities and Exchange Commission ("SEC") that affect general counsel, the influence of both outside and independent counsel on general counsel, the importance of an effective document retention policy, and the market factors affecting general counsel's behavior.

A. Structure of the General Counsel's Office

The office of general counsel in a public or private entity is responsible for all of the legal affairs of the entity. Although individual general counsel may structure their offices differently, all offices are generally organized by legal specialty. See Figure 1. A large office of general counsel is typically broken down into a number of subspecialties, including: litigation, labor and employment, contract negotiation, tax, corporate, insurance and surety, merger and acquisitions, corporate compliance, and business transactional law groups. Large legal departments are also apt to assign lawyers to business units directly, with the reporting chain still connected to the legal department to insure the integrity and independence of the advice offered. Of course, the general counsel usually reports to a non-lawyer CEO. A smaller general counsel's office would deal

---

[3] Otis Bilodeau, *What Happened to Mark Belnick*, Tex. Law., Oct. 7, 2002, at 8; Nicholas Varchaver et al., *Fall From Grace; Mark Belnick's Indictment In the Tyco Scandal Has Left Friends In Shock and Colleagues Bewildered. What Went Wrong?*, Fortune, Oct. 28, 2002, at 112; Kara Scannell, *Charges Against Tyco Ex-Counsel Expand to Include Grand Larceny*, Wall St. J., Feb. 4, 2003, at A3; Miriam Rozen, *Losing It All*, Corp. Couns., Feb. 2002, at 66.

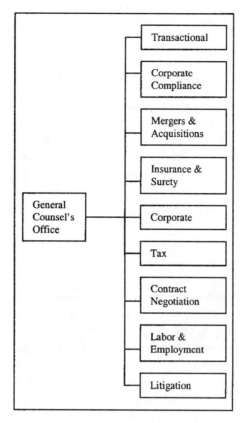

Figure 1

with the same substantive legal areas, but would have a few generalists who would rely on outside counsel for subject matter expertise when needed.[4]

The office of general counsel, as a non-revenue producing department, still experiences budgetary pressures and has substantial accountability for compliance and business practices, which ultimately bear on potential corporate criminal, civil, and regulatory exposure. Finally, all counsel operating in a corporate environment are at risk of delivering abstract legal advice if not finely attuned to the business and kept "in the loop" regarding significant business issues. Relevant advice delivered in the context and language of the business is essential for the function to be properly discharged and for the corporate culture to benefit from "lessons learned." The general counsel must keep the decision-makers apprised of material exposure issues related to the operation

---

[4] The small internal law department is often referred to as the "command control" model, as specialized legal projects are defined and managed by the in-house lawyer supervising outside counsel. Of course, it is possible that a Star Trek fanatic coined the term.

of the entity, and report to the independent auditors on material issues that may affect operations.

B. Who Is the Client—The Board of Directors or Senior Executives?

As a threshold matter, the general counsel must be clear to whom she owes her professional obligation of loyalty. Rule 1.13 of the Model Rules of Professional Conduct ("Model Rules") makes it clear that a lawyer who is employed by an organization represents the corporate entity itself and not the stockholders, directors, officers, or employees.[5] The Model Rules caution against non-client actors (owners, officers, and directors) believing that the lawyer is representing their interests as well as the entity's.[6] Although the concept of representing the entity seems simple in theory, how that representation plays out in the general counsel's day-to-day activities is far more complex. While the general counsel owes her ultimate fiduciary obligations to the entity, the agents or responsible decision-makers for the entity who may seek and rely upon advice of counsel are typically the executives. Therefore, it would seem that the general counsel owes her allegiance to the executive team. This is not problematic so long as the interests of the entity itself and those of its executives are aligned.

As we have seen in the past year of corporate scandals,[7] the senior executive officers' objectives and the implementation of their business plans to achieve such goals do not always align with the best interests of the entity and, in fact, may actually be adverse to the long-term interests of the entity. It is in these circumstances that the general counsel's dual roles within the company conflict. Model Rule 1.13 suggests that when the general counsel becomes aware that a senior executive intends an action that will be materially harmful to the entity, the general counsel is obligated to question that executive and ask the executive to consider alternatives.[8] If the executive refuses, the general counsel may then have to escalate her concerns to higher levels in the organization, even to a committee of the board or to the full board of directors, if necessary.[9] This escalating reporting process is often referred to as reporting up the corporate ladder. It goes without saying that a general counsel likely will incur the wrath of members of the executive team if forced to escalate material issues to the board of directors. If this final appeal to address injurious conduct is unsuccessful, then the last alternative is to

---

[5] MODEL RULES OF PROF'L CONDUCT R. 1.13(a) (2002).

[6] *Id.* R. 1.13(d).

[7] In addition to Enron, some of the nation's largest and most prominent corporations have filed for bankruptcy in the past year under a cloud of shame: WorldCom, July 2002; Adelphia, June 2002; Global Crossing, January 2002; and Kmart, January 2002.

[8] *See* MODEL RULES OF PROF'L CONDUCT R. 1.13(d) (2002).

[9] *Id.*

withdraw from representation of the entity.[10] Thus, as a practical matter, the general counsel may be forced to quit her job. If the injurious conduct is not a matter that must be disclosed under state or federal law, the general counsel should negotiate a severance package with a confidentiality clause to preserve her professional reputation. My experience is that entities that have been appraised of improper conduct and have declined to correct the conduct have an incentive to enter into such an agreement, since the confidentiality provision also inures to the benefit of the entity. However, the better approach is for the general counsel to negotiate an employment contract that includes such provisions at the inception of the relationship.

Historically, boards have followed the lead of management and been loath to challenge management decisions. Boards of directors have endured much public criticism in recent months regarding their lack of independence, and therefore, lack of objectivity or willingness to question the motives or actions of the executive management team.[11] The boards were, in essence, a fiefdom of the senior executive team. And the criticism is legitimate since, historically, board members have either been company insiders or appointed by the executive team, leaving a minority of board members independent from the direct influence of the executive team. As a result of the new SEC-imposed requirements that independent directors must constitute at least half of the corporate board and must run the nominating and audit committees,[12] general counsel should expect that directors will be far more proactive in questioning them regarding the legal and ethical ramifications of particular corporate activities. General counsel should also expect that board members will make greater efforts to fully understand not only the finer details of a company's accounting practices, but also each of the complex business deals that general counsel often help to engineer.

Compounding the lack of independence has been executive management's habit of providing insufficient information to board members to permit them to make informed decisions regarding corporate activities.[13] Of course, board members were often lax in demanding additional information or exercising their right of independent inquiry, which might involve hiring independent experts, such as independent board counsel. This is, in part, attributable to the lack of time that independent board members had available to discharge their duties, since most all of them had full-time, de-

---

[10] *Id.*

[11] Laurie P. Cohen, *Corporate-Governance Guru Millstein Defends Tyco Directors, In a Twist*, WALL ST. J., Nov. 6, 2002, at C1; Kurt Eichenwald, *Even if Heads Roll, Mistrust Will Live On*, N.Y. TIMES, Oct. 6, 2002, § 3, at 1; David Ivanovich, *Enron Revelations Prompt Examination in Many Business Areas*, HOUS. CHRON., Dec. 1, 2002, at A23; Jeffrey A. Sonnenfeld, *What Makes Great Boards Great*, HARV. BUS. REV., Sept. 2002, at 106.

[12] *See* Sarbanes-Oxley Act of 2002, Pub. L. No. 107-204, § 101, 116 Stat. 745, 750 (codified at 15 U.S.C. § 7211).

[13] *See* Sonnenfeld, *supra* note 11, at 109 n.14.

manding careers of their own, and may also sit on multiple boards. Under the new Sarbanes-Oxley legislation, being a board member, especially on the audit committee, is a full-time job.[14] The legislative ideal of having truly independent directors to oversee the corporation may backfire if director pay has to increase exponentially to address the intensity of the position (thereby excluding other work or board memberships, reducing the independent directors to veritable employees of the entity they are charged with overseeing).[15]

The pre-Enron era of corporate oversight is generally referred to in corporate law nomenclature as the era of "managerialism," where executives reigned supreme in their management and governance of the corporate entity. This post-corporate-scandal era is emerging as the era of "shareholder primacy," with heightened shareholder activism and attendant board activism on behalf of shareholders. Even in privately held corporations of any magnitude, which have equity or consortium lenders, oversight by stakeholders has increased significantly. Some of the manifestations of this increased scrutiny are stricter reporting requirements and closer monitoring of loan covenants. Of course, the new SEC-imposed requirements for public companies mandating a majority of truly independent directors, as well as the creation of board committees (e.g., accounting committee), are forcing management to be significantly more forthcoming with information while allocating more responsibility and exposure to board members for analyzing and understanding the business operations.

These developments are both a blessing and a curse for general counsel, who must now report more frequently to the board on both the legal and ethical ramifications of particular corporate activities. The blessing is that general counsel may no longer be the sole figure disclosing questionable corporate activities to the board. The general counsel may even be relieved of the necessity of a "noisy withdrawal" that requires disclosure to the SEC if the entity has established a qualified legal compliance committee ("QLCC").[16] The curse is the increased burden on the general counsel's office to learn and master the details of all of the company's undertakings, including accounting practices.

C. Who Reports To Whom?

The general counsel is a senior executive and typically reports directly to the CEO or president of the company. Many general counsel also serve as the corporate secre-

---

[14] *Id.*

[15] *Id.*

[16] The Proposed Rules under section 307 of the Sarbanes-Oxley Act provide that as an alternative to up the ladder reporting, an attorney can report evidence of material violation directly to a QLCC of the board.

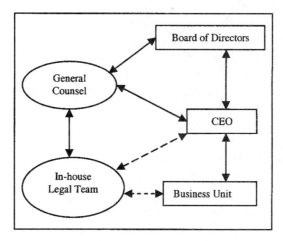

Figure 2

tary for the organization and can have the additional title of chief compliance officer. In daily business matters, the general counsel looks to the CEO and other senior executives to determine the organization's business strategy and objectives. Generally speaking, members of the general counsel's team are supervised directly by the general counsel and, sometimes, have a dotted-line reporting to business units or other members of senior management. See Figure 2. This reporting structure is not problematic so long as the interests of senior executives coincide with the best interests of the entity itself. Problems arise when the interests of the senior executives diverge from what is legally and ethically best for the entity.

D. The Balancing Act—Which Hat Am I Wearing?

Because the general counsel is both an officer in the company and the company's attorney, it is sometimes difficult to tell whether the advice given by the general counsel is legal and may be privileged, or whether the advice is business advice and, therefore, not privileged. This dual role creates problems for the general counsel; those problems arise when legal and compliance issues trigger an internal investigation.

The receipt of a Department of Justice subpoena, an SEC subpoena, an EEOC compliance audit, or the like should immediately trigger the general counsel to hire skilled outside counsel to assist. Such engagement is not premised on the office of the general counsel's inability to properly undertake such activities on the company's behalf. Rather, it is essential that the investigatory privilege, the work product privilege, and the attorney-client privilege remain intact. Because of the general counsel's dual role within the company, there is a very real threat that the investigating organization will allege that the general counsel was acting in a business capacity, not in a legal capacity, which could gut the privilege or create the risk that the general counsel will become a material fact witness.[17] Accordingly, prudence is mandatory. Providing a complete set of copies of all business documents likely to be tendered in response to a subpoena or discovery to outside counsel is wise. Should the risk of litigation or administrative proceedings become real, the general counsel must also have outside counsel hire and manage skillful public relations persons.[18] This will insure that the public relations professionals do not publish information that contradicts the investigation or the strategy of counsel.

Thus, regardless which hat the general counsel believes that she was wearing, the courts may disagree (to the great detriment of the company). Further, the general counsel is better postured as the bearer of objectively unpleasant findings, as corroborated by outside counsel and experts, versus serving as the actual papal legate advancing the cause of the inquisition against her own management brethren.

1. A Day in the Life of the General Counsel

Companies are as unique as DNA sequences. Accordingly, it is hard to generalize the day-to-day duties and obligations of general counsel from company to company. Having now given the obligatory disclaimer, there are some traditional duties that tend to fill the days of the general counsel and her legal team. It is perhaps easiest to understand the myriad of tasks that face the general counsel if the tasks are broken out into functional areas. Companies grow in one of two ways, through organic growth in market opportunity or market share, and through acquisition. When organic growth is accomplished through aggressive efforts to increase market share, competition issues arise, and the general counsel's office often addresses issues related to predatory pricing, price fixing, collaboration among competitors, or other antitrust-type issues.[19] Additionally,

---

[17] *See* United States v. KPMG, 237 F. Supp. 2d 35, 40 (D.D.C. 2002) ("[C]ommunications made by and to in-house lawyers in connection with representatives of the corporation seeking and obtaining legal advice may be protected by the **attorney-client privilege** just as much as communications with outside counsel. By contrast, communications made by and to the same in-house lawyer with respect to business matters, management decisions or *business advice* are not protected by the privilege") (quoting Boca Investerings Partnership v. United States, 31 F. Supp. 2d 9, 11–12 (D.D.C. 1998)) (emphasis in original).

[18] In response to allegations of sexual harassment at its plant in Normal, Illinois, Gary Schultz, Mitsubishi vice president and general counsel, publicly made inflammatory remarks that may have influenced the EEOC's ultimate decision against the company. *See* Kirstin Downey Grimsley, *EEOC Says Hundreds of Women Harassed at Auto Plant*, WASH. POST, Apr. 10, 1996, at A01 ("This is a mean streak. . . . It is more than unfair. . . . [D]iscrimination of any kind will never [be]—and has never been—tolerated at this plant. We find harassment in the workplace to be reprehensible and it has no place. . . .").

[19] *See* Hart-Scott-Rodino Act, Pub. L. No. 94-435, 90 Stat. 1383 (1976) (codified in scattered sections of 15, 18 and 28 U.S.C.); 15 U.S.C. § 18a (2003). For more on this topic, see Allan Van Fleet & Edward A. Carr, *Planning Conducting, and Protecting the Antitrust Audit: Selected Articles: Antitrust Audits: Ethical Considerations Upon Discovering a Violation*, 59 ANTITRUST L.J. 915 (1990).

marketing issues arise, requiring auditing of marketing and communications materials to insure that product and performance claims can be adequately substantiated.[20]

When a company elects to expand or grow through the acquisition of another business, in-house counsel are faced with a veritable buffet of legal tasks, including participating in due diligence,[21] negotiating non-disclosure agreements, drafting and reviewing letters of intent and sales and purchase agreements, setting up corporate structures for the combined entity, making changes in state registrations, evaluating intellectual property portfolios, negotiating finance agreements, preparing the novation of all contracts, evaluating litigation, claims, and warranty reserves, preparing for the post-acquisition consolidation of businesses, any necessary reductions in force, and overseeing the post-sale working capital adjustment. While there are other legal issues that arise in the acquisition context, these are some of the key areas with which general counsel must concern herself.

If an acquisition is financed, or if the company has outstanding commercial loans, the general counsel monitors compliance with the loan covenants and provides periodic reporting on exposure issues that could financially affect the company's performance. For purposes of the annual independent company audit, the general counsel must provide a detailed letter to the auditors in conformance with GAAP on the company's material exposures. Also in the financial area, the office of general counsel manages bankruptcies and the collection of substantial debts owed the company.

If the company is publicly traded, the general counsel manages all SEC filings and disclosures and usually works hand-in-hand with the executives to prepare for analyst telephone conferences. If the general counsel is also performing the tasks of the corporate secretary, she maintains all of the corporate books, prepares information for the board members, drafts all consents and unanimous resolutions, schedules all board meetings, and takes the minutes of the board meetings. She also certifies official corporate documents requested by government entities and customers.

The general counsel's office drafts, revises, and negotiates vendor and customer contracts. The general counsel also address all intellectual property issues, including filing patent, trademark, copyright applications, and the licensing of such intellectual property.

Labor and employment issues run the gamut from reviewing and negotiating employment contracts, crafting hiring documents, engaging in termination counseling, drafting policies and procedures, and managing ERISA issues related to qualified employee plans. General counsel will also address unionization efforts and the annual negotiation of union contracts.

---

[20] *See* the Lanham Act, 15 U.S.C. *See* §§ 1051-1129 (2003); *see also Guides Concerning Use of Endorsements and Testimonials in Advertising,* 16 C.F.R. § 225 et seq., pt. 255 (2003) (promulgated by the Federal Trade Commission).

[21] Due diligence is the process of evaluating all of the material facets of a business in anticipation of a potential acquisition to determine the viability of the business and to determine if buyer's representations regarding the business are accurate. Letters of intent to purchase a business usually leave an out for buyer if material misrepresentations are discovered during the due diligence.

Management of litigation and claims against the company are a constant. If the company manufactures products, then product liability issues, as well as field retrofits and recalls, also demand in-house counsel's expertise.

One of the most rewarding arenas is preventative maintenance and compliance. Preventative maintenance can include counseling a business client on a proposed transaction or debriefing corporate clients after a dispute in order to modify corporate conduct to avoid recurrence of the problem. The compliance task, in its elementary form, requires general counsel to draft, implement, and enforce a corporate code of ethics and business conduct. If the company operates in the international arena, then an export control policy, customs compliance policy, Foreign Corrupt Practices Act policy, and anti-boycott policy must also be created. All of these policies require reporting, training, periodic audit, and updating to be effective.

Unfortunately, the various issues referred to the general counsel's office do not come neatly packaged by the businesspersons, or in a systematic manner. In other words, the general counsel's office often gets an onslaught of issues in any number of substantive legal areas that need to be resolved contemporaneously.[22]

2. Matters Handled In-House

Having discussed some of the types of legal issues that face the general counsel and her legal team on a day-to-day basis, it is important to explain how the general counsel decides which issues to address entirely in-house and which issues to refer to outside counsel. Typically, the general counsel's office handles most, if not all, of the legal needs of the company if those needs are within the areas of expertise found within her legal team. Specialized projects are often addressed with the assistance of outside counsel, with the scope, budget, and management of the project managed by in-house counsel. Because of the volume and diversity of matters handled, opinions of counsel may take the informal approach of an email dialogue on a limited-scope inquiry posed to counsel. Post-Enron, in-house counsel are hesitant to offer opinions without detailed knowledge of all of the surrounding facts. While this may slow the rendering of legal services, the experience of Andersen's Nancy Temple has chastened the in-house bar. In-house counsel now fear the misapprehended intent of opinion letters may suggest indicia of wrongdoing or complicity with corporate misconduct.

3. Matters Referred To Outside Counsel

Corporate America long ago realized that it is uneconomic to build or maintain an in-house legal team that includes specialized skill sets that reach beyond the normal day-to-day activities of the company. Consequently, the general counsel's office will routinely refer specialized matters to outside counsel for assistance and resolution.

---

[22] The general counsel function is not for the faint of heart or the multitasking-impaired!

Depending on the size of the in-house legal staff, myriad specialized projects may also be referred to outside counsel, and the projects may encompass specialized tax advice, corporate financing, or crafting of compliance programs, just to name a few areas. In most in-house legal departments, one of the biggest budget line item expenses is outside counsel fees. As general counsel are asked to lower expenses and contribute cost-savings to the corporate bottom line, the new challenge is how to get the biggest bang for the buck from outside counsel without compromising the quality of professional service.[23]

Senior executive teams look to general counsel for guidance and instruction when engaging outside law firms. Accordingly, general counsel must be hyper-vigilant in insuring that the outside firms that the company retains are able to represent the best interests of the entity, consistent with such firms' professional obligations of competence and loyalty. Not only must general counsel be cognizant of conflicts of interest, she must also insure the outside counsel is truly masterful in the required legal specialty.

4. The Relationship Among the General Counsel and Other Senior Executives

No matter how effective a particular board is in terms of ferreting out misbehavior by senior executives, the general counsel may still fear retribution and loss of employment if she takes legal and ethical positions that conflict with senior executives' wishes. The general counsel's relationship with senior executives differs greatly from the relationship between the outside counsel and the senior executives.[24] As a member of the senior executive team, the general counsel often develops close personal and professional relationships with the other senior executives. Such relationships may sometimes make it difficult for general counsel to confront and oppose their colleagues. Furthermore, while outside attorneys are at liberty to take on multiple clients and can diversify their sources of income, the general counsel has a single client—the corporate entity—and thus the general counsel is economically dependent on that client. Additionally, senior executives readily communicate amongst themselves, and a general counsel who routinely fights her senior management on legal and ethical issues may well find herself ostracized from the executive management team, unable to gather the factual information necessary to execute on her responsibilities, and professionally blacklisted.

---

[23] Vinson & Elkins is probably going to argue that its response to Watkins's August 15, 2001 memo to Lay was appropriate, given the restrictions that Derrick gave to Vinson & Elkins ("don't look at the underlying transactions"). *See* Letter from Max Hendrick, III, Attorney, Vinson & Elkins, to James V. Derrick, Jr., Executive V.P. and General Counsel, Enron Corp. (Oct. 15, 2001), *available at* http://news.corporate.findlaw.com/hdocs/docs/enron/veenron101501ltr.pdf.

[24] Susanna M. Kim, *Dual Identities and Dueling Obligations: Preserving Independence in Corporate Representation*, 68 TENN. L. REV. 179, 201-02 (2001).

These risks and the accompanying fears are well founded, as the Model Rules provide clients an unfettered right to discharge counsel, including in-house counsel.[25] Moreover, the Model Rules also impose on counsel, including in-house counsel, the obligation to maintain client confidentiality even after the attorney-client relationship has ended, with limited exceptions.[26] Simply put, the general counsel, in contrast to the senior executives, may not only be unfairly discharged, but she is specifically precluded by the Model Rules from making certain disclosures in connection with that discharge. General counsel, therefore, may face disciplinary action as a result even of asserting a claim against their employers. This result is not unheard of, given that state bars differ on when a counsel may make certain disclosures. Accordingly, an SEC-imposed disclosure may result in the violation of an ethical or disciplinary rule imposed by the state bar. The possibility of conflict in this arena is increased when an attorney is admitted to more than one state bar, and the requirements of each bar differ regarding mandatory and permissive disclosures and the corresponding obligations of confidentiality. Although there has been movement toward allowing in-house counsel to sue for retaliatory discharge under certain limited circumstances,[27] there is still uncertainty surrounding the courts' willingness to allow a cause of action for in-house counsel who are terminated in retaliation for speaking out against executives or acting against executives' directives.[28]

Taking into consideration the inherent tensions and potential conflicts that are part of being a general counsel, it is clear that, although the duty of loyalty to the corporate entity is important, it is only one small piece of a much larger puzzle. After establishing, both for herself and executive management, the allegiance that the general counsel owes to the corporate client, she must then execute her duties in compliance not only with her state's ethics rules, but also in line with other guidelines governing in-house attorney conduct.

5. *The Relationship Between the General Counsel and Outside Counsel*

Outside counsel are practically indispensable to general counsel. Even large in-house legal departments engage outside law firms to assist in complex matters and to serve as

---

[25] *See* MODEL RULES OF PROF'L CONDUCT R. 1.16 (2002).

[26] *See id.* R. 1.6 (providing only limited exceptions for revealing confidential information without the client's consent).

[27] General Dynamics v. Rose, 876 P.2d 487, 490 (Cal. 1994) ("[W]e conclude that that there is no reason inherent in the nature of an attorney's role as house counsel to a corporation that in itself precludes the maintenance of a retaliatory discharge claim, *provided* it can be established without breaching the attorney-client privilege or unduly endangering the values lying at the heart of the professional relationship.").

[28] Balla v. Gambro, Inc., 584 N.E.2d 104, 110 (Ill. 1991) ("[W]e refuse to allow in-house counsel to sue their employer/client for damages because they obeyed their ethical obligations."). For more on this topic, see Brenda Marshall, *In Search of Clarity: When Should In-House Counsel Have the Right to Sue for Retaliatory Discharge?*, 14 GEO. J. LEGAL ETHICS 871 (2001).

independent experts to corporate counsel. As the Enron debacle unfolded, everyone asked the obvious question: where were the lawyers?[29] And the lawyers that everyone asked about were not only in-house counsel; outside counsel were also perceived to have been conspicuously absent as gatekeepers in the face of corporate misconduct. Outside counsel for both Enron and Andersen were criticized for failing to properly counsel or intercept their clients' misconduct.[30] In particular, one of the firms retained by Andersen was criticized for failing to stop Andersen from shredding the Enron documents.[31] One of Enron's firms was criticized for agreeing to investigate Enron's alleged misconduct during the course of that same firm's representation on a myriad of other matters.[32] The firm's investigation of Enron seemed to have been tempered, at least in part, by the magnitude of the other work that the firm was performing for Enron.[33]

In the future, general counsel will also have to more closely evaluate and consider the company's conflicts of interest with its own outside counsel and determine whether outside counsel's representation is truly independent from the company. The necessity of a thorough conflicts check is a given.[34] Additionally, the general counsel should consider several factors in determining whether any outside law firm is capable of providing objective and independent advice to the company: 1) whether the company's business represents a high percentage of that law firm's gross revenues, 2) whether the law firm is dependent upon the continuation of the engagement with the company for profitability, 3) and whether the attorneys involved in reviewing a prior matter are the same attorneys responsible for developing the matter being reviewed in the first place. One report suggests that this type of economic pressure can compromise the integrity of the outside counsel-client relationship.[35] Clearly, the old system of general counsels

---

[29] *Accountability Issues: Lessons Learned from Enron's Fall, Hearing Before the S. Comm. On the Judiciary,* 107th Cong. 830 (2002) (prepared statement of Susan P. Koniak, Professor of Law, Boston Univ. School of Law), *available at* http://www.access.gpo.gov/congress/senate/senate14ch107.html [hereinafter Koniak Statement]; *see also* WILLIAM C. POWERS, JR. ET AL., REPORT OF INVESTIGATION BY THE SPECIAL INVESTIGATIVE COMMITTEE OF THE BOARD OF DIRECTORS OF ENRON CORP. (Feb. 1, 2002), *available at* http://news.findlaw.com/hdocs/docs/enron/sicreport/index.html [hereinafter THE POWERS REPORT).

[30] Koniak Statement, *supra* note 31.

[31] *Id.*

[32] *Id.*

[33] *Id.*

[34] Before engaging outside counsel, the general counsel should provide the law firm with the full and proper spelling of the entity, its parent, and all of its subsidiaries and affiliates. A prudent general counsel would also provide a list of competitors. The law firm would then check its records to determine if it had ever been adverse to any of the listed entities or whether it had ever represented a key competitor. If no conflicts of interest are identified through this process, the general counsel should issue an engagement letter defining the scope of the engagement.

[35] Daniel J. Dilucchio & Marci M. Krufka, *The Impact of Recent Corporate Scandals on Corporate Counsel: Four Questions Every General Counsel Must Answer,* METROPOLITAN CORP. COUNS., Sept. 2002, at 37.

assigning all work to her prior firm is a grossly unacceptable model. The general counsel must not only locate competent outside counsel, she must also know enough about the legal issues under examination to question outside counsel's legal strategy, opinions, and monthly billings. Such dialogue is essential to the ethical discharge of the general counsel's duties.

Although subject to certain exceptions, the general counsel is normally responsible for coordinating the hiring of, defining the scope of work for, and managing outside counsel. Using the general counsel for this coordination function permits the general counsel to stay abreast of current developments in litigation and specialized matters and maintain direct control of outside counsel. While some organizations allow businesspersons to retain outside counsel directly, there are sound legal and business reasons for the general counsel to control the retention of outside counsel. Aside from the obvious necessity of performing conflicts checks, issuing engagement letters, and monitoring privilege issues, the general counsel is in a better position to frame the legal issues and garner the internal factual data in support of a germane legal analysis. And since the general counsel is ultimately responsible for all legal issues regarding the entity and is more familiar with the entity and its operations than is outside counsel, she should monitor the rendering of services to insure the work product is thorough and germane.[36] General counsel is also best positioned to translate legal advice into the practical business terms of the entity so that the businesspersons understand and follow it. Finally, since outside counsel fees are budgeted by the corporate legal department, the only effective means of managing the budget is to control and insure efficiency in the outside counsel's fees.

6. The Relationship Between the General Counsel and Independent (Investigative) Counsel

In addition to outside counsel, the general counsel needs to be able to coordinate with independent counsel. The concept of independent counsel recently came into high focus under the Sarbanes-Oxley Act. Pursuant to the Act, members of the board of directors are free to engage independent outside counsel for the purposes of answering and addressing questions that may arise in the governance of the company. Independent counsel is, as it connotes, independent from the corporate management and the general counsel and is retained by the board or an independent committee of the board. The board is thus the client and the independent counsel takes its assignments from, and reports exclusively to, the board. While the board may choose to involve the general counsel in an independent counsel project, especially if it results from an "up the ladder" disclosure presented to the board by the general counsel, the independent counsel's fiduciary obligation runs to the board and should be independent of managerial pressure. Because independent counsel are used to explore corporate issues, it is

---

[36] Entities that have recurring litigation regarding similar issues, such as product liability cases, need to insure that discovery responses in different venues are harmonized.

logical that corporate management not be involved in directing or influencing the work of independent counsel. The general counsel community anticipates that most audit committees of the board will retain independent counsel to aid them in discharging the expanded obligations that they will have under Sarbanes-Oxley.

II. RIDING OUT THE STORM: REFLECTIONS OF GENERAL COUNSEL ON THE REVELATIONS ABOUT ENRON'S BUSINESS PRACTICES

From my chair behind the general counsel's desk, I can tell you that the news stories and rumors surrounding Enron's various business practices were both horrifying and, sadly, predictable. My feeling is not unique. Other general counsel with whom I've spoken also feel that the Enron debacle further drives a stake into the heart of the collegial practice of law. That which is not governed by sound judgment and ethical behavior alas falls prey to legislation. This suggests a heightened level of diligence for general counsel. The concomitant result is higher costs for the entity; ergo, higher costs for the entity's goods and services. The sting of this reality is that the general counsel who are familiar with the Enron corporate culture considered it fast and loose with the goal of self-interested profiteering. Where was Enron's general counsel when executives were improperly setting up the special purpose entities to remove debt form the books? Where was the general counsel when the board was asked (much less permitted) to waive Enron's Code of Ethics and permit Andrew Fastow to have a stake in select special purpose entities? And where was the general counsel when the house of cards began collapsing? The consensus is that Enron's general counsel fell dramatically short of the mark in his fiduciary obligation to the entity and the marketplace at large, as well as to his colleagues, counsel of other companies. We all now get to pay the price.

III. AFTER THE STORM: CRIMINAL INDICTMENTS, SEC INVESTIGATIONS AND SANCTIONS, SARBANES-OXLEY—THE NEW MILLENNIUM AND LIABILITY FOR GENERAL COUNSEL

A. The Effect of Regulatory Guidelines on General Counsel

On July 30, 2002, Congress enacted the Sarbanes-Oxley Act of 2002 (the "Act"), in order to increase fiduciary obligations in publicly traded companies and address financial fraud injurious to the market, the public at large, and shareholders. The end game is to increase overt accountability and transparency in the corporate financial processes, which have historically been the domain of auditors and senior executives, in order to increase confidence in the financial data provided to the public, employees, investors and regulators. Although initially the Act appeared to apply only to companies that have registered securities and/or file reports with the SEC, there are cases where the Act applies to privately held companies as well.[37] The criminal provisions of

---

[37] Bradley S. Rodos, *Not Just For The Big Guys,* CORP. COUNS., Apr. 2003, at 51.

the Act cover all federally regulated businesses. The Act also addresses private companies that deal with federal agencies such as the Environmental Protection Agency, the Federal Communications Commission, and the Federal Trade Commission, to name a few. Even if your company falls outside of the Act, the Act still provides sound guidance for general counsel regarding disclosure and overall corporate compliance matters, such as document retention.[38] Moreover, in this new climate of public skepticism, all general counsel are wise to familiarize themselves with the Act's regulatory framework, which will no doubt shape the expectations not only of government agencies, but of the public, the courts, auditors, and (potentially) state bars.

After the initial passage of the Act, general counsel of public companies viewed with some trepidation the Act's promise that the SEC would establish minimum standards of professional conduct for all attorneys practicing before it.[39] Some in the legal profession feared that the SEC would impose more stringent professional obligations on attorneys than do state model rules of conduct, or that attorney conduct ultimately would be federalized. As discussed in more detail below, these concerns were well-founded.

B. Sarbanes-Oxley and Reporting Up the Ladder

On November 21, 2002, the SEC published its Proposed Rule regarding the standards of professional conduct for attorneys (the "Proposed Rule").[40] Among other things, the Proposed Rule contained an "up the ladder" reporting requirement[41] for all attorneys practicing or appearing before the SEC.[42] Because of the controversy of this provision, it drew significant opposition from the in-house bar, which prompted the SEC to give a sixty-day extension to seek comments and give additional consideration to the provision.[43] Specifically, Section 205.3 of the Proposed Rule obligates counsel first to report evidence of a material violation[44] to the chief legal officer of the com-

---

[38] Although the Act, by its terms, currently applies only to companies that have registered securities and/or file reports with the SEC, its reach likely will be expanded to include all companies.

[39] *See* Sarbanes-Oxley Act of 2002, Pub. L. No. 107-204, § 307, 116 Stat. 745, 784 (codified at 15 U.S.C. § 7245).

[40] Implementation of Standards of Professional Conduct for Attorneys, 67 Fed. Reg. 71,670 (proposed Dec. 2, 2002) (codified at 17 C.F.R. pt. 205) [hereinafter Proposed Rules].

[41] *Id.*

[42] *Id.*

[43] The "noisy withdrawal" provision of the Act conflicts with Model Rule 1.13, which does not mandate up-the-ladder reporting. Under the Model Rule, if a material violation is detected, the attorney is required to proceed as reasonably necessary in the best interest of the client. Up-the-ladder reporting is only one of the options contemplated.

[44] The definition of "material" is consistent with the meaning of the term in the Sarbanes-Oxley Act, i.e., violations about which a reasonable investor would want to know. *See* Proposed Rules, 67 Fed. Reg. at 71,679.

pany,[45] who, in most cases, will be the general counsel. No matter how the general counsel obtains the evidence of a material violation, her next step is to conduct an investigation to determine if the violation has already occurred, is occurring, or will occur—or if the allegations of a material violation are without merit.[46]

If the evidence came from a reporting attorney, then after the general counsel completes her investigation and determines that no violation exists, she must advise the reporting attorney of her conclusion.[47] On the other hand, if the general counsel determines from her investigation that a violation has occurred, is occurring, or will occur, she must take "reasonable steps" to effect remedial actions to correct the violation.[48] This means that she must insure that remedial measures are undertaken. Furthermore, she must then report to the CEO, the audit committee, or the full board and the reporting attorney her conclusions and her corrective actions.[49] The general counsel must also properly document the findings of the investigation.

Reporting to the CEO does not end the general counsel's obligations under the Proposed Rule. If the general counsel "reasonably believes" that the CEO has not responded appropriately to the report,[50] the general counsel is required to continue reporting "up the ladder" to the audit committee, or if there is none, to another appropriate committee of independent directors, or to the board of directors.[51] In certain cases, the Proposed Rule allows general counsel to bypass disclosure to the CEO altogether and go directly to the board when she believes reporting to the CEO will be futile.[52] If an appropriate response to the reporting is not received by the general counsel (or outside counsel, if they conduct the investigation), counsel must: withdraw from representation, notify the SEC of the withdrawal based upon "professional considerations'"; and disaffirm any SEC submissions that the attorney assisted in preparing and believes are false or misleading. This disclosure requirement is markedly different from a disclosure sanctioned by executive management for capping damages or protecting directors and officers, since it puts the general counsel directly at odds with company management.

As an alternative to the "up-the-ladder" reporting requirement, the Proposed Rule provides that counsel can report evidence of a material violation directly to a qualified

---

[45] As noted above, the Proposed Rules apply to all attorneys practicing or appearing before the SEC. However, for the purposes of this essay, the Proposed Rules will be discussed as they apply specifically to the general counsel and her legal team.

[46] *See* Proposed Rules, 67 Fed. Reg. at 71,685–86 (codified at 17 C.F.R. § 205.3(b)(2)).

[47] *Id.*

[48] *Id.*

[49] *Id.*

[50] Proposed Rules 67 Fed. Reg. at 71,686 (codified at 17 C.F.R. § 205.3(b)(3)).

[51] *Id.*

[52] Proposed Rules, 67 Fed. Reg. at 71,686–87 (codified at 17 C.F.R. 205.3(b)(4)) ("If an attorney reasonably believes that it would be futile to report . . . to the . . . chief executive officer . . . the attorney may report . . . as provided under paragraph (b)[(3)]. . . .").

legal compliance committee ("QLCC"). The establishment of such a committee is discretionary for the company. If a company does establish a QLCC, which it should, the QLCC would have the authority and responsibility to conduct an investigation of the alleged material violation and to require the company to adopt appropriate remedial measures.[53] If the company does not adopt the remedial measures, then the QLCC, the general counsel, and the CEO must each individually notify the SEC. As is clear, even if the general counsel reports a material violation to the QLCC, she retains an interest in the outcome of the investigation and any proposed remedial action.

The Proposed Rule permits counsel to use the records that she compiles in an internal investigation to defend against charges of attorney misconduct and further permits disclosure of confidential information to the SEC, if necessary, to prevent the commission of an illegal act she reasonably believes will work a fraud on the SEC or injure investors or the company. While the Proposed Rule states that internal disclosures within the corporate entity or the board are *not* considered to be a violation of the attorney-client privilege, the effect of the rule is not yet clear on the attorney-client privilege.[54]

In keeping with this principle, the American Bar Association Task Force on Corporate Responsibility (the "ABA Task Force") has recommended that reporting up the ladder within the organization be expressly incorporated into Model Rule 1.6,[55] and that Rule 1.13 be modified to explicitly mandate such reporting.[56] These changes to the Model Rules would require general counsel for both public and private organizations to adhere to up the ladder reporting requirements as part of discharging their professional obligations.[57]

Notwithstanding amendments to the Model Rules, and before the enactment of the Proposed Rule, prudent general counsel will create and follow a planned escalation procedure that is triggered when they become aware of evidence of wrongdoing by

---

[53] *See* Proposed Rules, 67 Fed. Reg. at 71,679–80 (codified at 17 C.F.R. § 205.2(k)).

[54] Proposed Rules, 67 Fed. Reg. at 71,681 (codified at 17 C.F.R. § 205.3(b)(1)). However, this provision does not provide general counsel or other in-house counsel with complete protection because the attorney-client privilege is a rule of evidence, not an ethics rule. Accordingly, the safe harbor provisions in the Proposed Rule do not protect attorneys in jurisdictions that forbid revealing some of these confidences, either directly or via noisy withdrawal. *See, e.g.*, CAL. BUS. & PROF. CODE § 6068(e) (Deering 2003) (setting forth the duty of an attorney "[t]o maintain inviolate the confidence, and at every peril to himself or herself, to preserve the secrets of his or her client").

[55] THE ABA PRESIDENTIAL TASK FORCE ON CORPORATE RESPONSIBILITY, PRELIMINARY REPORT 28 (2002), *available at* http://www.abanet.org/buslaw/corporateresponsibility/preliminary_report.pdf [hereinafter THE CHEEK REPORT].

[56] *Id.* at 29 ("The Task Force therefore recommends that Rule 1.13 be amended to make clear that it requires the lawyer to pursue the measures outlined in Rule 1.13(c)(1) through (3) (including referring the matter to higher corporate authority). . . .").

[57] *Id.* at 25 ("All of these recommendations address the role of counsel for all corporations, and not just those with publicly traded stock.").

their corporate clients. General counsel are obliged as part of their fiduciary duty to the entity to investigate credible reports of misconduct, institute remedial measures to rectify past and ongoing bad acts or to prevent future incidents, and report such activities to senior executives. In select cases, such reporting has even warranted disclosure to government agencies to mitigate any potential punishment and to protect directors and officers from vicarious liability, assuming their non-involvement.[58] Ideally, the general counsel would incorporate audit and policing skills into the law department. Historically, however, audit and policing functions and skills are rarely incorporated into the law department because of the high cost of acquiring and maintaining these skill sets.

C. Other Disclosure Requirements

Sarbanes-Oxley and the Proposed Rule were responses to the rise of widespread corporate and accounting fraud. Accordingly, the newly imposed SEC obligations on general counsel are directed primarily to prevent future types of financial misconduct. However, there are other contexts in which general counsel are required to make external disclosures regarding internal corporate conduct. For instance, general counsel is required to make disclosures outside of her client, an action that might otherwise breach the attorney-client privilege or violate client confidentiality, in order to prevent a crime or fraud that her services have helped to facilitate. General counsel is also required to make disclosures when she believes her client's conduct will result in substantial physical or financial harm either to the corporate entity or to third parties.[59] The Department of Justice requires general counsel to make external disclosures when her client is engaging in conduct that violates antitrust laws.[60] There are certain environment-related violations that require general counsel to make external disclosures.[61] Also, one extraordinarily bad act of an executive, such as material accounting fraud by a CFO, may have such far-reaching negative implications as to impose upon general counsel a duty to make disclosures outside of the entity. Looking at the issue of disclosure through a broader lens, it is clear that general counsel have an affirmative responsibility not only to know about but also to understand their corporate client's activities

---

[58] *See supra* note 18.

[59] Note: States differ on when lawyers can disclose potential future harm—some say only when there is imminent risk of serious physical harm, some say that lawyers can disclose for financial harm—but there's NO uniformity in the states, so a general counsel with more than one state bar card could be in a whole heap of trouble.

[60] *See supra* note 59.

[61] An attorney may have an obligation to report violations of the Comprehensive Environmental Response, Compensation and Liability Act ("CERCLA") when the violations could lead to imminent death or substantial bodily harm. *See* 42 U.S.C. §§ 9601–75 (2003).

in order to effectively discharge their duties to provide meaningful legal guidance and steer the corporate ship along the ever-narrowing path of compliance.

D. The Effect of Disclosure Requirements Upon the General Counsel and the Company

The potential loggerhead between general counsel and executive management created by the Act will likely have a chilling effect on the relationship between in-house counsel and senior executives. John H. McGuckin, Jr., Vice Chairman of the American Corporate Counsel Association (ACCA), voiced concerns that the consequence of greater mandatory disclosure obligations will be the "marginalization of lawyers" in corporate decision-making.[62] Bluntly stated, senior executives may respond to the general counsel's disclosure requirements by keeping her out of the loop. In turn, general counsel may find it more difficult to unearth and prevent misconduct and noncompliance, especially in the financial arena.[63] While there has been a push to increase penalties for white-collar crime, an executive must first be caught. If general counsel is excluded from the decision-making process, she will be incapable of providing the type of legal guidance that might steer senior executives and the entity out of troubled waters. The lack of preventative lawyering is apt to lead to more catastrophic consequences for the company down the road.

McGuckin asserts that, rather than constricting the general counsel's role, the counsel's "position and role must be expanded, protected and facilitated."[64] The challenge, then, is to find the delicate balance between encouraging and empowering general counsel to perform their duties as compliance champions, while preserving and enhancing their roles as full participants in, and informed members of, the senior executive team.

Even among the most collegial executive teams, there are circumstances in which the general counsel will find herself unable to represent the corporation. General counsel may make this determination as a result of the company's past, present, or future course of conduct and her recognition that her continued representation will result in her participation in a criminal or fraudulent act. However, the general counsel who finds herself in this situation is not without options.

Rule 1.16 of the Model Rules provides that counsel *may* terminate representation if she believes her client is engaging in criminal or fraudulent activities.[65] She may also withdraw from representation if her client "insists upon taking action that [she] con-

---

[62] John H. McGuckin, Jr., Vice Chairman, Am. Corp. Couns. Assoc., *Déjà Vu All Over Again: The Marginalization of Lawyers?* (Nov. 12, 2002) (testimony to the ABA Task Force on Corporate Responsibility), *available at* http://www.acca.com/advocacy/corpresponstestimony.pdf.

[63] *See id.* at 2.

[64] *Id.* at 8.

[65] MODEL RULES OF PROF'L CONDUCT R. 1.16(b)(1) (2002).

siders repugnant or with which [she] has a fundamental disagreement."[66] The SEC has codified a version of this rule in the form of a mandatory withdrawal requirement in the Proposed Rule.[67] Section 205.3(d)(1)(ii) of the Proposed Rules requires that the general counsel must, within one business day after she concludes the entity's response to her disclosures under Section 205.3(b)(1) is inappropriate or inadequate, advise the SEC in writing of her intention to disaffirm, and promptly thereafter disaffirm in writing, all or some part of a communication to which she was a party that was submitted to the SEC, which she "reasonably believes" to be "materially false or misleading."[68] The general counsel is then *mandated* to withdraw from her employment[69] and inform any replacement counsel that she withdrew for "professional considerations."[70]

Such withdrawal, either under the Model Rules or the Proposed Rule, is no small matter. The general counsel who resigns from her position forfeits not only her current employment; she may also be forfeiting her future employability.[71] The corporation may cast public aspersions on the departing general counsel in an effort to downplay the reasons she gives for her departure. Although it is unlikely that the corporation would publicly disparage counsel for fear of potentially exposing its own bad acts, such threats are real, and departing counsel faces the possibility that defending herself under these circumstances might result in a breach of her state-imposed ethical confidentiality obligations. The corporation may file complaints against exiting counsel for breach of the attorney-client privilege or breach of confidentiality to the extent that she has made impermissible external disclosures. Also, if she represents a public company, the general counsel faces discipline and penalties imposed by the SEC if the Commission finds that she violated any of the Proposed Rule's disclosure (or other) requirements, or otherwise finds that she engaged in "improper professional conduct,"[72] including "intentional," "knowing," "reckless," or "negligent"[73] conduct. The classifications and connotations of improper, reckless, or negligent conduct are far-reaching and empower third parties to retrospectively evaluate the general counsel's actions through the equivalent of a high-resolution magnifying glass.[74]

---

[66] *Id.* R. 1.16(b)(4).

[67] Proposed Rules, 67 Fed. Reg. 71,670, 71,688–90 (proposed Dec. 2, 2002).

[68] *Id.* at 71,688.

[69] *Id.* Even the SEC concedes that the requirement of counsel to resign under these circumstances "appears to be unreasonably harsh." *See supra* note 48.

[70] Proposed Rules, 67 Fed. Reg. at 71,688.

[71] *See* Kim, *supra* note 27.

[72] Proposed Rules, 67 Fed. Reg. at 71,696.

[73] *Id.* (Negligent conduct includes "[a] single instance of highly unreasonable conduct" or "repeated instances of unreasonable conduct.").

[74] Consider what happens to ants when they have a magnifying glass focused on them—they burst into flames.

Ultimately, the decision of whether to disclose and/or withdraw will be made by each individual general counsel on a case-by-case basis. And the determination will be informed not only by the potential consequences of *not* disclosing, but by the general counsel's ability to discern when disclosures are necessary and appropriate. For that reason, general counsel will be called upon to exercise more than her raw legal skills in her capacity as a compliance officer. She will also be expected to understand basic economic and finance principles,[75] as well as business practices and the legal ramifications of her corporate clients' business plans and strategies. As compliance leaders, general counsel must educate themselves on both legal and business requirements and best practices for their industries in light of the corporate cultures of their clients. Likewise, the general counsel arguably violates her duty of competence to her client if she is unable to comprehend the business and financial implications of the organization's charted course of action.[76]

Until the SEC establishes final rules for section 307 of Sarbanes-Oxley, and until the SEC begins enforcement actions under those rules, general counsel will not know exactly what behavior will get them into trouble. The best that general counsel can do, in the meantime, is to continue to walk that fine line between their duties to their respective employers and their duties under their state ethics rules.

E. The Importance of an Effective Document Retention Policy

Any discussion about general counsels' challenges in a post-Enron world is incomplete without mentioning document retention, especially after Arthur Andersen lawyer Nancy Temple became a household name.[77] To the extent that general counsel once believed that document retention policies were not *that* important, the Arthur Andersen document-shredding fiasco changed everything.

Ms. Temple is notorious not only due to her suggested changes to the Enron press release related to a restatement of earnings, but also because of her email reminding her Andersen colleagues of their document retention policy. Andersen employees destroyed thousands of Enron-related documents, notwithstanding the SEC's announcement of an investigation of Enron. Some interpret Ms. Temple's memo as demonstrating intent to

---

[75] Lawrence A. Cunningham, *Sharing Accounting's Burden: Business Lawyers in Enron's Dark Shadows*, 57 BUS. LAW. 1421, 1449 (2002) ("[A] business lawyer's professional ethics should command [him] to master accounting basics.").

[76] *See id.* at 1423 ("[L]awyers doing Enron-like deals better know enough accounting to credibly contribute the value of that knowledge to other members of the deal team.").

[77] Ms. Temple has been largely criticized for her October 12, 2001 memo to David Duncan regarding document retention and destruction. *See* E-mail from Michael C. Odom to David B. Duncan (Oct. 12, 2001, 10:55 AM) (forwarding message from Nancy Temple) ("It might be useful to consider reminding the [Enron] engagement team of our documentation and retention policy. It will be helpful to make sure that we have complied with the policy."), *available at* http://news.corporate.findlaw.com/hdocs/docs/enron/andersen101201email.pdf.

commit criminal conduct, namely, a company-known "code" that encouraged Andersen employees to destroy documents in disregard of the SEC investigation of Enron. The Justice Department's indictment of Andersen for obstruction of justice was primarily based on Andersen's shredding of Enron documents after it knew that such documents would likely be relevant to an investigation of certain of Enron's financial undertakings.[78]

Andersen was criminally charged and convicted for obstructing justice pursuant to 18 U.S.C. § 1512, a statute used to punish persons, both real and fictitious (i.e., corporate entities), who *knowingly* cause the destruction of documents intending to make them unavailable in an official proceeding.[79] Moreover, Ms. Temple's actions could be characterized in such a way as to make her personally indictable in connection with fraud and obstruction of justice. After Andersen's conviction, a House Committee urged the U.S. Department of Justice to investigate whether Ms. Temple's characterization of events surrounding her document retention email constituted perjury—specifically, whether she was truthful in asserting that her email was not sent in response to a probable SEC investigation.[80] Consequently, Ms. Temple may still face prosecution for her conduct.

Perhaps influenced at least in part by the Andersen matter, the SEC inserted a provision in the Proposed Rule requiring counsel, at every stage of disclosure, to create contemporaneous records (or, if not contemporaneous, as close in time as possible) about evidence of any material violation, her investigation of the evidence, any disclosures made as a result of her investigation, and senior executives' (or the board's, as the case may be) responses to the disclosure.[81] She must then preserve these records "for a reasonable time" to substantiate her actions.[82]

Although general counsel have been in the practice of implementing and enforcing document retention policies for years, the uproar over document shredding in the Arthur Andersen/Enron debacle has compelled some general counsel to revisit their policies.

---

[78] *See* Indictment at pt. III, United States v. Arthur Andersen, LLP, CR. No. H-02-121 (Mar. 7, 2001) ("By Friday, October 19, 2001, Enron alerted the ANDERSEN audit team that the SEC had begun an inquiry regarding the Enron 'special purpose entities' and the involvement of Enron's Chief Financial Officer. . . . ANDERSEN partners assigned to the Enron engagement team launched on October 23, 2001, a wholesale destruction of documents at ANDERSEN's offices in Houston, Texas. . . . [A] coordinated effort by ANDERSEN partners and others, similar to the initiative undertaken in Houston, was put in place to destroy Enron-related documents within days of notice of the SEC inquiry."), *available at* http://news.findlaw.com/wp/docs/enron/usandersen030702ind.pdf.

[79] 18 U.S.C. § 1512(b)(2)(B) (2003).

[80] David Ivanovich & Michael Hedges, *The Fall of Enron; Pressure Builds on Andersen Lawyer; Panel Urges Criminal Inquiry*, HOUS. CHRON., Dec. 18, 2002, at 1C.

[81] *See* Proposed Rules, 67 Fed. Reg. 71,670, 71,684-85 (proposed Dec. 2, 2002) (proposed rule § 205.3(b)(2)) ("Such contemporaneous records would typically include the date, time, location, manner, and substance of the report and the response and the identity of witnesses to either.").

[82] *Id.*

General counsel need document retention policies to facilitate their organizations' needs for identifying and retrieving (or quickly recognizing the irretrievability of) documents in the event of audits or litigation.[83] A properly drafted and implemented document retention policy creates uniform standards for storage and retrieval of records throughout an organization, taking the guesswork out of whether and when to destroy a record. And, in the face of litigation, the Federal Rules of Civil Procedure (the "Federal Rules") require general counsel to produce documents related to the litigation in response to discovery requests.[84] Absent a policy whereby such documents can be readily identified and produced, the general counsel faces not only potentially avoidable expenses in tracking down documents, but also the addition of a jury charge regarding spoliation and possible sanctions for failure to comply with the Federal Rules.

General counsel are obliged by the Federal Rules to protect and retain discoverable documents after they are made aware that such documents may be the subject of litigation.[85] This includes investigatory reports of potential material violations within the company which the proposed rule mandates that general counsel compile. Any general counsel who destroys discoverable information in the face of litigation runs the risk of being sanctioned by the court.[86] In a typical multi-tiered corporate entity, the ability to preserve, identify, and produce evidence is virtually impossible without a document retention policy that identifies, for *each* functioning department: (i) the documents to be preserved, (ii) the procedures for uniform identification and archiving, (iii) the time period over which documents must be preserved, and (iv) a regularly-observed schedule for purging and destroying documents.

A well-researched and drafted document retention policy is just one component of an effective corporate compliance program. Moreover, when a problem arises in which general counsel are aware that certain documents may be implicated, it is her responsibility to be as clear and unequivocal as possible in directing employees to preserve all documents regarding the matter. As general counsel continue to receive mounting pressure to be the legal and ethical leaders of corporations, general counsel serve themselves and their corporate clients well by learning from the Andersen disaster and making document retention policies enforced in their organizations.

F. The Effect of Market Volatility and Outsiders' Perceptions on General Counsel

Harvey Pitt resigned as chairman of the SEC on November 6, 2002. Even prior to his resignation, the stock market was volatile, unpredictable, and lacking any sign of

---

[83] Chris Wolfe & C.E. Rhodes, Jr., *Corporate Compliance in Document Retention in Today's Business Environment* (2002), *available at* http://www.haynesboone.com.

[84] FED. R. CIV. P. 26.

[85] FED. R. CIV. P. 26(b)(1) defines a broad scope of discoverable information: "Parties may obtain discovery regarding any matter . . . that is relevant . . . including . . . books, documents, or other tangible things. . . ."

[86] FED. R. CIV. P. 37.

stabilization in the immediate future. William Donaldson was confirmed as Pitt's replacement in early 2003. During this leadership transition, Roel Campos, who has been described in the Wall Street Journal as the "feisty Democratic Commissioner," was already making waves.[87] Campos takes a hard line on enforcement, and he seeks to limit executives' discretion on what information it discloses to research analysts.[88] Campos also voted against settlements into which the SEC entered with two companies accused of violating Regulation Fair Disclosure because the settlements did not include fines.[89] This hard-line enforcement approach, coming from a revitalized SEC, will increase general counsels' visibility and may promote even greater interest in their role as captains of corporate compliance within their organizations.

An uncertain and unstable employment market has accompanied the extended period of market volatility for general counsel. Although there are reports of many law firms laying off associates and encouraging partners to pursue other interests,[90] other reports indicate that attorneys in legal departments have been fairly secure in their employment.[91] In fact, some reports indicate that in-house attorneys enjoy their jobs now more than ever before, in no small part due to new challenges related to corporate governance and compliance.[92] But even general counsel with great job satisfaction have been affected by the economic downturn. General counsel hired with the promises of hefty stock option packages may never receive the huge dollar values that appeared to be present when they accepted their positions.[93] As a related matter, the opportunity for quick wealth through cashing in stock options might have served to hamper general counsels' objectivity in rendering advice to corporate clients during the dot-com boom. However, with the bursting of the economic bubble, the possibility of such internal conflicts may be significantly lessened. The collective effect of a tumbling economy and a tight job market creates a greater incentive for general counsel to discharge their duties at high levels to secure continued employment.

In addition to the precarious stock market and fewer alternative employment opportunities than in times past, the public perception of general counsel matters now more than ever. Discussion of general counsels' roles and responsibilities in promoting and insuring corporate compliance has reached the mainstream media:

---

[87] Michael Schroeder, *Campos Ruffles Feathers at the SEC*, WALL ST. J., Dec. 16, 2002, at A4.

[88] *Id.*

[89] *Id.*

[90] L.M. Sixel, *The Fall of Enron: Enron Fallout Bruises Lawyers; Vinson & Elkins Suffers, Regroups*, HOUS. CHRON., Nov. 3, 2002, at 1; Justin Pope, *Law Firms Firing With One Hand, Hiring With the Other*, ASSOC. PRESS, Dec. 20, 2002 (noting that Silicon Valley firm Cooley Godward laid off 27 attorneys, and Boston firm Brown Rudnick Berlack Israels laid off 17 lawyers, in late 2002).

[91] Sheryl Fred et al., *High Impact; The 20 Events, People & Stories That Shaped Your World in 2002*, CORP. LEGAL TIMES, Dec. 2002.

[92] Catherine Aman, *Love the Job You're With*, CORP. COUNS., Dec. 2002, at 60.

[93] *Id.*

- *U.S. News & World Report* raised questions regarding attorney accountability, that is, questioning the roles of attorneys in recent financial fraud cases, as well as pointing out perceived limitations in state bars' abilities to adequately police attorneys.[94]
- The *Houston Chronicle* has assured attorneys that there is no reason to fear, even in this time of extreme scrutiny of their conduct, if they simply advise their clients "to behave honestly and obey the law."[95]
- The *Miami Daily Business Review* reflected that general counsel have emerged virtually unscathed from corporate fraud investigations, and suggested that general counsel will likely have an expanded role in advising corporate leaders in this new era of accountability.[96]
- The *Boston Herald,* on the other hand, declared that corporate lawyers have endured their share of ignomy as the practices of scandal-plagued companies were brought to light.[97]

State bars are also reevaluating how they monitor general counsels' professional conduct. Many states currently allow general and other in-house counsel to practice in corporations without admission to the state in which they are practicing, so long as they are licensed in any state. The *Washington Business Journal* recently reported that the Virginia State Bar has proposed to the Virginia Supreme Court that corporate counsel admitted in other states be required to join the Virginia State Bar and be subject to its rules.[98] The incoming president of the Massachusetts Bar Association has indicated that he will use his platform to educate the bar and the public about the unique challenges that corporate counsel face in daily practice.[99] Other state bars will likely go public regarding their efforts at catalyzing greater corporate compliance through their regulation of general counsel.

Mainstream media and state bars are not the only ones keeping their eyes on general counsel. Senior executives within organizations served by general counsel also have heightened expectations of general counsels' ability to keep the company on the path of legal and ethical compliance. At a minimum, CEOs and other executives may seek

---

[94] Megan Barnett, *How to Account for Lawyers*, U.S. NEWS & WORLD REP., Dec. 9, 2002, at 26.

[95] *Legal Advice: Good Lawyers Advise their Clients to Obey the Law*, HOUS. CHRON., July 2, 2002, at A18.

[96] Ashby Jones, *Teflon Counsel—General Counsel Have Been Virtually Untouched During Recent Accounting Scandals, But New Laws May Change That*, MIAMI DAILY BUS. REV., Sept. 13, 2002, at A10.

[97] Maggie Mulvihill, *At the Bar; Leader Arrives with Aim to Fix Elite-Lawyer Image*, B. HERALD, Sept. 3, 2002, at 031.

[98] Tim Mazzucca, *Virginia State Bar Targets In-House Counsel Sign-Ups*, WASH. BUS. J., Nov. 1, 2002, at 6.

[99] *See* Mulvihill, *supra* note 97.

the advice of general counsel more often in their decision-making.[100] Nevertheless, as discussed above, there may still be instances in which executives freeze general counsel out in order to shield themselves from potential disclosures by counsel to outsiders.

In light of rising premiums for directors and officers ("D&O")[101] insurance, and high dollar claims against errors and omissions ("E&O") insurance,[102] senior executives have an even greater interest in treading carefully when embarking on unprecedented, innovative, or out-of-the-box business strategies and transactions. More and more, senior executives will be looking to general counsel as the beacons of corporate compliance on the dark and uncertain seas of economic and corporate change.

G. General Counsel as Champion of Corporate Compliance

[G]eneral counsel are not going to be pursued for being general counsel. They're going to be pursued for committing fraud, failure to disclose . . . [and for] being misleading.

—Harold F. Degenhardt, district administrator, Securities and Exchange Commission.[103]

The transaction or office lawyer, as distinguished from her trial colleagues, must understand what her client is doing and whether that is within or without the law. Otherwise, there is simply no reason for the lawyer being there.

—Susan P. Koniak, Professor of Law, Boston University School of Law.[104]

In this tumultuous sea of change, general counsel are called to be the captains of corporate compliance and the champions of corporate governance within their organizations. Failure to do so can mean unemployment and unemployability, civil and criminal charges, and even disbarment. The question, then, is not whether the general counsel should bolster efforts to promote and enforce compliance; rather, the inquiry should focus on determining the most efficient and effectual methods for general counsel

---

[100] *See* Jones, *supra* note 99.

[101] D&O premiums rose as high as 200 percent for some companies in 2001. *See* Alix Nyberg, *Your Move; Corporate Directorships; Board Games Turn Serious*, CFO Mag., Feb. 2002, at 70.

[102] E&O claims may be as high as seven figures. *See* Lynna Goch, *Cover Charge: Premiums for Professional Liability Insurance for Public Companies are Likely to Skyrocket Following Years of Escalating Claims and Recent High-Profile Cases*, Best's Rev., May 1, 2002, at 65.

[103] *Sarbanes-Oxley: GCS Under Scrutiny*, Tex. Law., Dec. 2, 2002, at S111.

[104] Koniak Statement, *supra* note 32.

to stimulate voluntary corporate reform within their organizations. The core corporate social responsibility is a corporate culture focused on compliance with law.

The first step must be the implementation of an effective corporate compliance program. To be effective, the compliance program must take into account the organization's culture and the organization's business objectives. Corporate compliance programs typically include precepts and requirements directed at the following areas: antitrust and fair trade, environmental issues, sexual harassment, intellectual property, workplace safety, government contracting, labor and employment relations, document retention and destruction, political contributions and lobbying, protection of company assets, accurate books and records, securities and insider trading, substance abuse, consumer protection/consumer fraud, money laundering, conflicts of interests and gifts, international issues, and consent decree compliance. The general counsel should determine which subject areas will be included in the corporate compliance program, based on the areas that typically affect the organization. Of course, standards of conduct will not protect the entity unless all employees are trained to understand the standard of conduct and the general counsel performs an ongoing audit program to insure compliance. Moreover, senior executives must "walk the walk." If the senior executives do not comply with their standards of conduct in day-to-day business, the corporate compliance program is guaranteed to fail. Employees will only buy into conduct and corporate compliance standards when they believe that senior executives don't fall into the trap of "do as I say, not as I do." The failure of senior executives to engage in appropriate standards of conduct undermines compliance initiatives and can result in widespread indifference (or worse) among employees.[105]

The role of general counsel has evolved over the last century. In the 1920s and 1930s, general counsel were highly regarded in organizations.[106] Many CEOs of that period were trained attorneys, and the ability to "think like a lawyer" was considered an invaluable business tool.[107] When business schools came to prominence as the premier corporate training ground between the 1940s and mid 1970s, the role and perception of corporate attorneys declined.[108] Consequently, law firms became the employers of choice for up-and-coming attorneys.[109] Beginning in the late 1970s and continuing through the mid 1990s, businesses developed renewed interest in corporate counsel, as marked by the creation and expansion of in-house legal departments.[110]

---

[105] *See, e.g.,* Stuart Gilman, *The Bottom Line Is Integrity,* 1 ETHICS TODAY ONLINE (Sept. 2002), *available at* http://www.ethics.org/resources/article_detail.cfm?ID=728.

[106] Carl D. Liggio, *The Randolph W. Thrower Symposium: The Role of the General Counsel: Perspective: The Changing Role of Corporate Counsel,* 46 EMORY L.J. 1201, 1202 (1997).

[107] *Id.*

[108] *Id.*

[109] *Id.*

[110] *Id.* at 1203.

Among the factors contributing to this boom in corporate counsel opportunities were the increase in business litigation, the growth in business regulation, and the high costs of outside legal counsel.[111] The late 1990s saw a movement toward general counsel playing a dominant role in corporate legal affairs, with outside counsel being called upon for transaction-specific or litigation-specific legal services.[112] Modern general counsel now perform bifurcated roles as managers of corporate legal affairs and active participants in corporate strategic planning.

Moving forward into the 21st century and beyond, general counsel's role as the manager of corporate compliance will continue to expand. To be effective in her role as compliance captain, general counsel must move from a reactive, incident-specific coach to a forward-looking, proactive corporate player. "The forward-looking corporate counsel who identifies trends, evaluates the likelihood of [a trend's] occurrence, devises legal solutions to probable changes, and alerts management to the changes for purposes of devising business strategies in response to them will make a key contribution to the future economic health and well-being of a business entity."[113]

General counsel will need to develop and refine skills that facilitate successful execution of their functional legal duties and corporate strategic responsibilities. David Meltzer identified four core competencies that he believes will enable corporate counsel along this path: (1) knowledge of the law, (2) analytical skills, (3) timeliness, and (4) clear communications.[114] Other attributes, such as knowledge of an industry, market factors affecting business, and research skills also contribute to the general counsel's ability to discharge her duties effectively. Ultimately, however, the general counsel's capacity to safeguard her organization through the implementation of compliance measures is dependent upon her understanding of the legal parameters within which the organization must operate, her ability to apply those parameters to specific matters that arise in the course of doing business, and her ability to accurately communicate meaningful information to the organization's constituents in a timely manner.

General counsel will continue to play leading roles in developing and maintaining the legal and ethical character of businesses. The general counsel's influence and effectiveness will be enhanced by the ability to partner with other senior executives for a team-based approach to corporate compliance. Enhanced regulations may provide a deterrent for misconduct; however, general counsel must assist in creating incentives for legal and ethical conduct that transcend fears of civil and criminal liability. General counsel must raise the level of standards of conduct and steer businesses toward legal and ethical best practices. The general counsel who can help her company take the high road while maintaining profitability may well be worth her weight in gold.

---

[111] *Id.* at 1204.

[112] *Id.* at 1207.

[113] *Id.* at 1209.

[114] David Meltzer, *Better Business Lawyering—Improving Skills Will Help You Become a Catalyst for Growth and Profitability*, LEGAL TIMES, Oct. 21, 2002, at 20.

QUESTIONS

1. Is public policy furthered by permitting a company to dismiss its in-house counsel without regard to claims for retaliatory dismissal or wrongful termination? Is your answer the same if the attorney is terminated for refusing to participate in breaking the law or violating regulatory constraints?

2. Identify the potential conflicts of interest that may occur between the general counsel and the CEO when the general counsel reports directly to the CEO. Are the conflicts that you identified eliminated when the general counsel reports directly to the board of directors?

3. Is the general counsel going to be immune from liability if she is unable to understand the intricacies of a deal that her company is about to enter? Is she required to get an MBA in finance, economics, or accounting to be able to understand virtually every nuance of every deal in which the company may engage?

4. Will the greater burdens placed on members of the board of directors, and on committees of the board, make recruiting board members more difficult? What is the incentive to serve on a board these days?

5. Did the Justice Department's prosecution of Andersen serve justice and the business community? Did the Justice Department target the correct wrongdoer in prosecuting Andersen?

Chapter 4

Enron and Ethics

You've now had an opportunity to view Enron from an historic perspective, from a business perspective, and from a legal perspective. In this chapter, we want you to view Enron from a perspective that crosses all boundaries: ethics. Admittedly, many of the essays in this chapter involve discussions of legal ethics (not surprising, considering that one of us—NBR—writes in that area). But the discussion of legal ethics often can open up broader questions about human behavior that go far beyond mere legal rules.

Many people, including some of the authors in this book, have asked two questions in reaction to the various corporate crises that have arisen in the first few years of the 21st century. After Enron (and WorldCom, and Global Crossing, and Tyco, and Health South, etc.), people asked, (1) "why didn't the auditors catch these mistakes?" and (2) "why didn't the lawyers catch these mistakes?"

Don't be fooled by the apparent simplicity of these two questions. Not only do the questions include the embedded assumption that the mistakes were "catchable" (and we want you to think carefully about that assumption), but they also include the embedded assumption that it was the role of the auditors and the lawyers to "catch" these mistakes. Be aware of your assumptions; then, after reading these essays, see if your assumptions were justified. When you discuss ethics, it is particularly important that you are aware of your own biases and assumptions.

It is also important that you remember that you're reviewing the behavior of humans, with all of their inherent internal contradictions and flaws. Someday, you will also be judged in retrospect, by strangers, based on your actions and decisions. When it comes to ethics, thinking about tough issues ahead of time can save you a lot of pain later.

Enron and the Corporate Lawyer: A Primer on Legal and Ethical Issues*

Roger C. Cramton * *

INTRODUCTION

For more than fifty years, numerous and massive corporate frauds (e.g., National Student Marketing in the 1970s,[1] OPM in the early 1980s,[2] Lincoln Savings & Loan during the S & L crisis of the 1980s,[3] and the huge BCCI bank failure and fraud of the

---

* Originally published at 58 BUS. LAW. 143 (2002). Reprinted with permission.

** Roger C. Cramton is the Robert S. Stevens Professor of Law Emeritus, Cornell Law School. Comments should be addressed to <rcc10cornell.edu>. This article was initially prepared for a Practicing Law Institute program, "The Impact of Enron: Regulatory, Ethical and Practice Issues for Counsel to Issuers, Underwriters and Financial Intermediaries," New York City, April 25–26, 2002. The Article has benefited from my continuing work with Susan Koniak on Enron-related topics. I am greatly indebted to Doug Branson, George Cohen, Chuck Davidow, Jim Hanks, Mark Sargent, and Chuck Wolfram for extremely helpful comments on earlier drafts.

[1] The spectacular rise and fall of National Student Marketing Corp. led to charges that lawyers in two elite firms (New York's White & Case and Chicago's Lord, Bissell & Brook) had aided and abetted the fraud. Both settled with investors, and two accountants were convicted. SEC v. Nat'l Student Mktg. Corp., 457 F. Supp. 682 (D.D.C. 1978); see GEOFFREY C. HAZARD, JR., SUSAN P. KONIAK & ROGER C. CRAMTON, THE LAW AND ETHICS OF LAWYERING 104–22, 739–43 (3d ed. 1999) [hereinafter HAZARD, KONIAK & CRAMTON] (reprinting and discussing National Student Marketing and discussing subsequent SEC proceedings against lawyers who learned that their client's agents violated securities laws); see also United States v. Natelli, 553 F.2d 5 (2d Cir. 1977) (reversing the conviction of one of the two accountants).

[2] See HAZARD, KONIAK & CRAMTON, supra note 1, at 304–10. OPM, the largest commercial fraud of its time, was the most discussed legal ethics case of the 1980s. Fraud claims against banks, accounting firms, and lawyers were subsequently settled for $65 million, of which Singer Hutner's share was $10 million. Id. at 308; In re O.P.M. Leasing Servs., Inc., 13 B.R. 64 (Bankr. S.D.N.Y. 1981), aff'd, 670 F.2d 383 (2d Cir. 1982); see also Stuart Taylor, Jr., Ethics and the Law: A Case History, N.Y. TIMES MAG., Jan. 9, 1983, at 31 (presenting a detailed exposé of the involvement of OPM's lawyers in seeing to it that their client's fraud went undiscovered until after the total collapse of the pyramid scheme).

[3] Jones Day, which resigned from a regulatory compliance representation of Lincoln Savings & Loan, later settled fraud and other claims of investors for $24 million and government claims against it for $51 million. See HAZARD, KONIAK & CRAMTON, supra note 1, at 743–56. Kaye Scholer, which succeeded Jones Day, later settled the government's claim against it for $41 million. Id. at 757. For discussion of the

1990s)[4] have raised questions concerning a lawyer's responsibilities when the lawyer learns, or has reason to know, that officers or other agents of the lawyer's corporate client are engaged in conduct that violates the law or their fiduciary duty to the corporation and is likely to result in harm to the corporation, shareholders, or other third parties. In each of these situations, and in hundreds of less-publicized frauds, outside law firms settled civil liability actions for substantial and sometimes huge sums, while denying that they had assisted or participated in the fraud. Similar lawsuits have already been brought against two law firms involved in the Enron affair, Vinson & Elkins ("V&E") and Kirkland & Ellis ("K&E")[5] and others are likely to follow.

The Enron affair and the flood of other recent corporate scandals (e.g., Adelphia, Arthur Andersen [hereinafter "Andersen"], Dynegy, Global Crossing, Tyco, WorldCom, Xerox) have led to a loss of investor and public confidence in the integrity of the securities and other markets that make American capitalism work. Investors have lost confidence in the reliability and honesty of corporate executives. Andersen's indictment and conviction for obstruction of justice highlighted the role of accountants in structuring and auditing corporate transactions that turned out to be fraudulent or illegal. But compliant lawyers as well as greedy executives, lazy directors, and malleable accountants are necessary for large corporate frauds to come to life and persist long enough to cause major harm.[6] The assistance of inside and outside lawyers is required to structure and report on corporate transactions. Other reforms will not suffice unless lawyers who violate legal and ethical rules are held accountable.

The premises of this article are well stated in the recent preliminary report of the American Bar Association (ABA) Task Force on Corporate Responsibility: Even if most corporate officers, directors, and professional advisers act honestly and in good faith, the interests of corporate managers are not fully aligned with those of shareholders.[7] As the Preliminary Report states:

---

savings and loan cases, see William H. Simon, *The Kaye Scholer Affair: The Lawyer's Duty of Candor and the Bar's Temptations of Evasion and Apology,* 23 LAW & SOC. INQUIRY 243 (1998); Symposium,: *The Attorney-Client Relationship in a Regulated Society,* 35 S. TEX. L. REV. 571 (1994); In the Matter of *Kaye, Scholer, Fierman, Hays & Handler: A Symposium on Government Regulation, Lawyer's Ethics, and the Rule of Law,* 66 S. CAL. L. REV. 977 (1993).

[4] *See, e.g.,* DOUGLAS FRANTZ & DAVID MCKEAN, FRIENDS IN HIGH PLACES 285–400 (1995) (discussing Clark Clifford's role in the BCCI failure); JONATHAN BEATY & S. C. GWYNNE, THE OUTLAW BANK: A WILD RIDE INTO THE SECRET HEART OF BCCI (1993).

[5] Amended Complaint, Newby v. Enron Corp., No. H-01-3624 (S.D. Tex. filed Apr. 8, 2002).

[6] *See* Susan P. Koniak, *Who Gave Lawyers a Pass? We Haven't Blamed the Real Culprits in Corporate Scandals,* FORBES, Aug. 12, 2002, at 58 ("The dirty secret of the mess is that without lawyers few scandals would exist, and fewer still would last long enough to cause any real harm.").

[7] ABA Task Force on Corporate Responsibility, *Preliminary Report of the American Bar Association Task Force on Corporate Responsibility,* 58 BUS. LAW. 189 (2002) [hereinafter ABA Preliminary Report]; *see also* Joan C. Rogers & Rachel McTague, *SEC Must Issue Attorney Conduct Rules Under New Federal Accounting Reform Law,* 18 LAW. MANUAL ON PROF'L. CONDUCT (ABA/BNA) 457–58 (July 31, 2002) (reporting and summarizing section 307 of the Sarbanes-Oxley Act).

[E]xecutive officers and other employees of public companies may succumb to the temptation to serve personal interests in maximizing their own wealth or control at the expense of long-term corporate well-being. . . . [I]ndependent participants in the corporate governance process, such as the outside directors, outside auditors, and outside counsel [are essential to check such temptation]. [E]videnced by recent failures of corporate responsibility, the exercise by such independent participants of active and informed stewardship of the best interests of the corporation has in too many instances fallen short. Unless the governance system is changed in ways designed to encourage such active and informed stewardship, . . . public trust and investor confidence in the corporate governance system will not be restored.[8]

Part I of this Article examines the current legal and ethical rules that govern lawyers in client-fraud situations. Part I concludes that these rules are controverted and often ambiguous, and they provide insufficient guidance to lawyers and inadequate protection to the public interest in preventing corporate frauds and illegalities.

Part II illustrates the theses of Part I by applying the current rules to three problems that regularly arise when managers breach their fiduciary duties to the corporation or embark on fraudulent conduct: (1) advising a corporate client concerning retention of documents and other relevant evidence when it becomes clear that litigation is likely or impending; (2) conducting an internal investigation of allegations that one or more corporate managers have engaged in misconduct; and (3) providing legal assistance in creating, documenting, and reporting client transactions that raise substantial legal problems (primarily securities fraud issues). The complexity and difficulty of these recurring problems are revealed by examining the known facts concerning (1) the advice given Andersen by its inside lawyers, (2) the conduct of V&E's "preliminary investigation" of Sherron Watkins's allegations of misconduct by some Enron managers, and (3) V&E's role in creating and reporting the corporate transactions that appear to be fraudulent and led to Enron's demise.

Part III argues that the problems we now face are systemic in character and not merely a problem of a few executives, auditors, and lawyers who are "bad apples." The inadequacy of the current rules governing lawyers requires that existing rules be clarified and some new ones created. The federal legislation that has already occurred, with its provision for a Securities and Exchange Commission ("SEC") rule requiring lawyers to report illegalities to superior officers and the corporate board, is a sound beginning,[9] but more is required, especially the overruling of the *Central Bank* decision eliminating any claim against professional advisers for aiding and abetting a securities

---

[8] *ABA Preliminary Report, supra* note 7, at 193–94 (emphasis in original).

[9] Sarbanes-Oxley Act of 2002, Pub. L. No. 107–204, § 307, 116 Stat. 745, 784. *See infra* discussion in text beginning *infra* note 145.

fraud.[10] In addition, state high courts should modify their ethics rules along the lines recommended in the ABA Task Force Preliminary Report.[11]

ANALYSIS OF THE FACTUAL AND LEGAL ISSUES

What is or should be the role of the corporate lawyer, inside or outside the client corporation, when faced with a client fraud situation? What ethics and liability rules should govern the situation?

The problems are complex ones that turn on factual and legal issues including the following: (1) When and what did the lawyer know at the time of action or non-action?; (2) What *scienter* (intent) standard should be applied to the lawyer's conduct?; (3) Does a lawyer who learns of facts or circumstances suggesting possible fraud have a duty to inquire further?; (4) When the lawyer knows, or has reason to know, that officers of his corporate client are pursuing a fraudulent course of conduct, should or must the lawyer take this information to the client's highest authority, the board of directors?; and (5) If the officers and the board refuse to cease or rectify what the lawyer believes is fraudulent conduct, may or must the lawyer disclose this information to defrauded third parties or a public officer?

Finding or Assuming the Relevant Facts

The initial problems are primarily factual in character.

First, what was the lawyer retained to do by the corporate client (including agreed-upon limits on the scope of representation) and what did the lawyer do? Are the limitations so severe that the lawyer is unable to provide the competent and adequate representation required by ethics rules?[12]

Second, what did the corporate agents do (a purely factual question), and did their actions constitute a breach of fiduciary duty to the organization, a crime or intentional tort that might be imputed to the corporation, or a fraud or other illegality harming third persons (investors, shareholders, creditors, etc.)?

Third, what did the lawyer know, or have reason to know, at the time the lawyer acted or failed to act? The lawyer's conduct should not be judged on the basis of facts learned at a later time. After the dust has settled, and with the benefit of hindsight, it

---

[10] Cent. Bank of Denver v. First Interstate Bank of Denver, 511 U.S. 164, 191 (1994). *See* discussion *infra* notes 44 and 121–23 and accompanying text.

[11] *See infra* notes 157–68 and accompanying text.

[12] A lawyer owes every client a duty of "competent representation," a requirement that can never be waived by the client. MODEL RULES OF PROF'L CONDUCT R. 1.1 (2002). Although Rule 1.2(c) of the Model Rules of Professional Conduct permits a lawyer to "limit the scope of the representation if the limitation is reasonable under the circumstances and the client gives informed consent[,]" the client may not be asked to agree to representation so limited in scope as to violate Rule 1.1. *Id.* R. 1.2 cmt. 7.

is easier to conclude that corporate managers were engaged in fraudulent conduct that was harmful to third persons and the corporate client. But a judgment based on later-discovered facts is unfair and unlawful.

In representing clients in the vicinity of fraudulent or suspected fraudulent activity, lawyers should bear in mind several fundamental cautions.

First, an innocent state of mind will not save a lawyer from responsibility or liability. Because lawyers convince themselves that they do not "know" that fraud is going on, often ignoring what is plain to see, they believe they are safe from liability. They will not, however, be judged by their recollection of their state of mind. The fact-finders who will judge lawyers cannot read their minds and are likely to be skeptical about what the lawyers say they believed and thought. Lawyers will be judged by the facts and circumstances known (or which they had reason to know) at the time, which surrounded their actions and what they did in response to those facts and circumstances.

Second, one of the grave risks professional advisers face is the "hindsight bias": the tendency of all human beings to exaggerate the extent to which an event that they know has happened could have been anticipated in advance.[13] Any subsequent fact-finding of whether a lawyer knew of and assisted a client's fraudulent conduct almost always arises after bankruptcy or other events have revealed that a fraud occurred. While a lawyer should not be held to have known at the time of action or inaction facts that only became known later, those facts will inevitably color a fact-finder's retrospective judgment. The hindsight bias, in the civil fraud context, makes defendants appear more culpable than they may be. Lawyers, knowing that this will happen, should exercise greater caution than they often do when dealing with a client that is pushing the law to its limits and perhaps beyond. Liability problems always start with clients whose managers are not trustworthy or who create a corporate culture in which short-term goals are the only goals. Caution in selecting and retaining such clients is essential, as well as healthy skepticism concerning their actions and motives.

Third, lawyers cannot rely on the attorney-client privilege to protect them. The privilege belongs to the entity client, not the lawyer. Major frauds that become publicly known usually result in bankruptcy or change in control of the client corporation. The trustee in bankruptcy or other successor in interest typically waives the attorney-client privilege and the professional duty of confidentiality. Every law firm document or communication relating to the representation becomes available to the corporation in a malpractice action against the law firm and to plaintiffs' lawyers in third-party liability actions. Even if the privilege is not waived, other doctrines usually lead to many or most documents becoming available. For example, under the crime-

---

[13] See Jeffrey J. Rachlinski, *A Positive Psychological Theory of Judging in Hindsight*, 65 U. CHI. L. REV. 571 (1998) (stating that the hindsight bias is one of the best-established findings of cognitive psychology and examining its implications on fact-finders' decisions). A lawyer's "level of care will be reviewed by a judge or jury who already knows that it proved inadequate to avoid the plaintiff's injury. . . . The bias, in general, makes defendants appear more culpable than they really are." *Id.* at 572 (footnotes omitted).

fraud exception to the privilege, a *prima facie* showing of client fraud penetrates the privilege;[14] under the *Garner* doctrine, a shareholder plaintiff in a derivative suit may obtain otherwise privileged material relating to a plausible derivative claim.[15]

A complete factual story of lawyer conduct in the Enron affair is not available as of November 2002 when this article was completed and may never be fully available. Consequently, my discussion of ethical and legal issues must be based on assumed facts. I will operate on a factual assumption, not yet established but clearly plausible, that Andrew Fastow and perhaps other managers of Enron were engaged in a course of conduct that was fraudulent and perhaps criminal: using unlawful means to make Enron's financial position appear much better than in fact it was, while violating their fiduciary duty to Enron by misappropriating for themselves huge sums of money from self-dealing transactions. This factual assumption is supported by the report of Enron's special board investigative committee headed by William Powers,[16] the guilty plea of Michael Kopper,[17] and the first interim report of the Examiner appointed by Enron's bankruptcy court.[18]

I also assume for purposes of this article that certain publicly available facts are true: first, the admissions concerning document destruction made by Andersen officials in

---

[14] *See* HAZARD, KONIAK & CRAMTON, *supra* note 1, at 244–54. As Justice Cardozo said, "[t]he privilege takes flight if the relation is abused. A client who consults an attorney for advice that will serve him in the commission of a fraud will have no help from the law." Clark v. United States, 289 U.S. 1, 15 (1933); *see also* Geoffrey C. Hazard, Jr., *An Historical Perspective on the Attorney-Client Privilege*, 66 CAL. L. REV. 1061, 1063–64 (1978).

[15] Garner v. Wolfinbarger, 430 F.2d 1093, 1103–04 (5th Cir. 1970).

[16] *See* WILLIAM C. POWERS, JR. ET AL., REPORT OF INVESTIGATION BY THE SPECIAL INVESTIGATIVE COMMITTEE OF THE BOARD OF DIRECTORS OF ENRON CORP. (2002) [hereinafter POWERS REPORT], *available at* 2002 WL 198018.

[17] On August 21, 2002, Kopper pled guilty to money laundering and wire fraud charges. His plea agreement described a criminal conspiracy running from 1997 through July 2001, in which Kopper, Fastow, and unnamed others used a series of Enron-related partnerships to conceal debt, falsify Enron's financial position, and make millions for the conspirators at Enron's expense. *See* Jonathan Weil et al., *Guilty Plea by Enron's Kopper Increases Scrutiny of Ex-CFO*, WALL ST. J., Aug. 22, 2002, at A1.

[18] *In re* Enron Corp., First Interim Report of Neal Batson, Court-Appointed Examiner, No. 01-16034 (AJG) (Bankr. S.D.N.Y. Sept. 21, 2002) [hereinafter Batson], *available at* 2002 WL 31113331. In the report, the examiner analyzes six series of Enron transactions involving special purpose entities (SPEs) selected for their representative character. In each of the transactions Enron purported to sell an asset to an SPE in exchange for cash provided almost entirely by a financial institution. In four of the six transactions Enron or its affiliate entered into a "total return swap" under which Enron was obligated to repay the investment plus a specified return on it. The transactions were supported by Enron's credit because the assets were difficult to sell and produced insufficient cash flow to support the financing. Enron retained control of the assets and the benefit or loss of their rise or fall in value. The examiner's interim conclusions were that: (1) although documented as sales and usually supported by "true sale opinions" provided by Enron's outside lawyers, the transactions were in fact loans, (2) Enron's obligations under the total return swaps were not properly disclosed in Enron's 2000 financial statements, as required by GAAP, and (3) the transactions and their reporting "had dramatic effects on both the balance sheet and income statement portions of Enron's financial statements." *Id.* at *7–*8.

congressional testimony and, as to his personal conduct, Duncan's guilty plea; second, the facts concerning V&E's representation of Enron included in the Powers Report[19] and, in connection with V&E's "preliminary investigation" of Enron, the facts stated in V&E's opinion letter to Enron of October 15, 2001,[20] and the firm's narrative summaries of interviews conducted.[21]

What *Scienter* (Intent) Standard Should be Applied to the Lawyer's Conduct?

Should the lawyer's conduct be judged by an "actual knowledge" standard or by the "recklessness" and "willful blindness" standards that are generally applicable to lay persons? This raises the question of why lawyers, who are supposedly experienced and knowledgeable about corporate transactions and the elements of illegality and fraud, should be afforded a less demanding *scienter* standard in professional discipline cases and SEC aiding and abetting proceedings than the standard that lay persons must meet to avoid criminal and civil liability.

The profession's ethics rules, designed for purposes of professional discipline, adopt an "actual knowledge" standard. Rule 1.2(d) of the American Bar Association's Model Rules of Professional Conduct,[22] dealing with prohibited assistance, states that the lawyer "shall not counsel a client to engage, or assist a client, in conduct that the lawyer knows is criminal or fraudulent. . . ."[23] "Knows" is defined in the terminology section as "actual knowledge of the fact in question[,]" but adds that "[a] person's knowledge may be inferred from circumstances."[24] "Fraud" is defined as "conduct . . . [having] a purpose to deceive" and not merely negligent misrepresentation or failure to apprise another of relevant information.[25] These definitions provide greater protection to lawyers in discipline proceedings than other law provides them in other contexts. The

---

[19] *See* Powers Report, *supra* note 16, at *15.

[20] Opinion Letter from Max Hendrick III, Vinson & Elkins, L.L.P., to James V. Derrick, Jr., Executive Vice President and General Counsel, Enron Corp. (Oct. 15, 2001) [hereinafter Hendrick Opinion Letter], *available at* 2001 WL 1764266.

[21] These interview summaries may be found at the Web site of the House Committee on Energy and Commerce [hereinafter V&E Interview Narratives], *available at* http://energycommerce.house.gov.

[22] The Model Rules of Professional Conduct, first adopted by the ABA in 1983, with subsequent amendments, provide the framework for the legal ethics rules of forty-three U.S. jurisdictions. The rules have also been influential in the eight states that base their rules on the 1969 ABA Model Code of Professional Responsibility. The Model Rules were substantially amended in February 2002, but the many changes have little effect on the issues discussed in this Article. For the amended rules, see the ABA Center for Professional Responsibility Web site, *available at* http://www.abanet.org/cpr/mrpc/mrpc_toc.html (last visited Oct. 17, 2002).

[23] Model Rules of Prof'l Conduct R. 1.2(d) (2002) (emphasis added).

[24] *Id.* at R. 1.0(f).

[25] *Id.* at R. 1.0(d).

definitions create a risk of misleading lawyers concerning the standards by which they will be judged in client fraud situations.[26]

Federal and state laws dealing with fraud and various deceptive practices generally adopt or are interpreted as embodying a less demanding standard of knowledge of culpable conduct than that of the ABA Model Rules: a lawyer cannot state facts with reckless disregard of their truth or falsity; nor can the lawyer turn a blind eye to facts and circumstances that indicate fraud or illegality—conduct that falls within the "willful blindness" rubric.

Scienter under the federal securities acts may be summarized as follows:

(1) Criminal liability. The defendant must be proven to have acted "willfully," that is, with a culpable state of mind.[27] The defendant's knowledge of false statements, however, may be inferred "from the actor's special situation and continuity of conduct"[28] and "the cumulation of instances, each explicable only by extreme credulity or professional inexpertness, may have a probative force immensely greater than any one of them alone."[29] The court in *United States v. Benjamin* stated, "the Government can meet its burden [in a securities fraud prosecution] by proving that a defendant deliberately closed his eyes to facts he had a duty to see or recklessly stated as facts things of which he was ignorant."[30] As Judge Friendly put it:

> In our complex society the accountant's certificate and the lawyer's opinion can be instruments for inflicting pecuniary loss more potent than the chisel or the crowbar. Of course, Congress did not mean that any mistake of law or misstatement of fact should subject an attorney or an accountant to criminal liability simply because more skillful practitioners would not have made them. But Congress equally could not have intended that men holding themselves out as members of these ancient professions should be able to escape criminal liability on a plea of ignorance when they have shut their eyes to what was plainly to be seen or have represented a knowledge they knew they did not possess.[31]

---

[26] The *ABA Preliminary Report, supra* note 7, at 207, recognizes that the Model Rules' restriction to a lawyer's "knowing" conduct "presumably does not reach conduct covered by the term 'reasonably should know.'" The Report recommends revision of Rules 1.2(d), 1.13, and 4.1 "to reach beyond actual knowledge to circumstances in which the lawyer reasonably should know of the crime or fraud." *Id.* at 214. These changes, if adopted, would conform the Rules' definition of fraudulent intent to federal and state law governing the subject.

[27] United States v. Benjamin, 328 F.2d 854, 861 (2d Cir. 1964) (affirming the criminal convictions of an accountant and a lawyer for securities and mail fraud).

[28] *Id.* (quoting Bentel v. United States, 13 F.2d 327, 329 (2d Cir. 1926)).

[29] *Id.* at 862 (quoting United States v. White, 124 F.2d 181, 185 (2d Cir. 1941)).

[30] *Id.* at 862 (citations omitted) (summarizing the holding of two prior decisions) (citations omitted).

[31] *Id.* at 863.

(2) Civil liability under securities acts. In *Ernst & Ernst v. Hochfelder,*[32] the Supreme Court found that "[e]ach of the provisions of the 1934 Act that expressly create civil liability [including § 10(b)] . . . contains a state-of-mind condition requiring something more than negligence."[33] The required *scienter* includes a mental state embracing "intent to deceive, manipulate, or defraud"[34] and may be shown by "knowing or intentional misconduct."[35] The *Hochfelder* case was extended in *Santa Fe Industries v. Green*[36] and *Cort v. Ash,*[37] which held that state law governs questions involving the fairness of transactions or internal corporate mismanagement "except where federal law expressly requires certain responsibilities of directors with respect to stockholders. . . ."[38] Thus, allegations of breach of fiduciary duty alone will not suffice; fraudulent or deceptive conduct must be alleged.

Hochfelder and *Aaron* left open the question whether allegations of "recklessness" satisfy the *scienter* requirement. The federal courts of appeals, however, have almost uniformly concluded that the recklessness and "willful blindness" sufficient for criminal liability also suffice for civil liability. Under the most common standard, recklessness means conduct that is "highly unreasonable" and that represents "an extreme departure from the standards of ordinary care . . . [to the extent that the] danger . . . [was] either known to the defendant or [was] so obvious that the [defendant] must have been aware of it."[39]

The Private Securities Litigation Reform Act of 1995 ("1995 Act") imposes special pleading requirements on civil plaintiffs in securities fraud actions.[40] The complaint

---

[32] 425 U.S. 185 (1976).

[33] *Id.* at 209 n.28. In Aaron v. SEC, 446 U.S. 680, 691 (1980), in which the SEC sought injunctive relief for a securities violation, the Court held that "scienter is an element of a violation of § 10(b) and Rule 10b-5, regardless of the identity of the plaintiff or the nature of the relief sought."

[34] Hochfelder, 425 U.S. at 193.

[35] *Id.* at 197.

[36] 430 U.S. 462, 473 (1977) (stating that a shareholder's claim under section 10(b) that his shares were undervalued in a merger transaction, but not alleging a misrepresentation, was insufficient because the statutory language and legislative history gave "no indication that Congress meant to prohibit any conduct not involving manipulation or deception").

[37] 422 U.S. 66 (1975).

[38] *Id.* at 84 (emphasis added).

[39] Hollinger v. Titan Capital Corp., 914 F.2d 1564, 1569 (9th Cir. 1990) (en banc decision frequently cited in other circuits). Decisions in a few circuits support an arguably more relaxed standard of something more than negligence. *See, e.g.,* Lanza v. Drexel & Co., 479 F.2d 1277, 1306 n.98 (2d Cir. 1973) (en banc) (finding that reckless conduct exists if the defendant, knowing that material facts were omitted or misstated, failed to obtain and disclose such facts when doing so could be done without extraordinary effort); *see generally* Kevin R. Johnson, *Liability for Reckless Misrepresentations and Omissions Under Section 10(b) of the Securities Exchange Act of 1934,* 59 U. CIN. L. REV. 667 (1991).

[40] Pub. L. No. 104-67, § 21D(b), 109 Stat. 737 (codified as amended at 15 U.S.C. §§ 77–78 and 18 U.S.C. § 1964).

must "specify each statement alleged to have been misleading," provide "reasons why the statement is misleading," and "state with particularity all facts on which [a belief that a statement is misleading] is formed."[41] Concerning proof of the required state of mind, the complaint must, with respect to each act or omission, "state with particularity facts giving rise to a strong inference that the defendant acted with the required state of mind."[42]

(3) Assisting a client's crime or fraud. A lawyer's duty under criminal and civil law to refrain from "assisting" (aiding or abetting) a client in conduct that is "criminal" or "fraudulent" is violated if:

(1) The client is engaged in a course of conduct that violates the criminal law or is an intentional violation of a civil obligation, other than failure to perform a contract or failure to sustain a good faith claim to property;

(2) The lawyer has knowledge of the facts sufficient to reasonably discern that the client's course of conduct is such a violation; and

(3) The lawyer facilitates the client's course of conduct either by giving advice that encourages the client to pursue the conduct or indicates how to reduce the risks of detection, or by performing an act that substantially furthers the course of conduct.[43]

The effect of the holding in *Central Bank of Denver v. First Interstate Bank of Denver*,[44] eliminating private causes of action for aiding and abetting federal securities laws violations, is to force private plaintiffs to charge defendants as primary violators (principals), rather than secondary ones. In some situations, an alternative course of action is to proceed under state securities or fraud laws that permit aiding and abetting claims.[45]

(4) SEC aiding and abetting actions against professional advisers. The 1995 Act authorizes the SEC to bring actions for injunctions and monetary penalties against any person, including a professional adviser, who "knowingly provides substantial assistance to another person in violation" of federal securities laws.[46] The statute substi-

---

[41] *Id.* at § 21D(b)(1)(B), 109 Stat. at 737, 747.

[42] *Id.* at § 21D(b)(2), 109 Stat. 737, at 747.

[43] Geoffrey C. Hazard, Jr., *How Far May a Lawyer Go in Assisting a Client in Legally Wrongful Conduct?*, 35 U. MIAMI L. REV. 669, 682–83 (1981).

[44] 511 U.S. 164 (1994). The Central Bank case is discussed *infra* at notes 121–23 and accompanying text.

[45] A plaintiff's resort to state securities laws must take account of the Securities Litigation Uniform Standards Act of 1998, Pub. L. No. 105-353, 112 Stat. 3227, which "preempted state statutory and common law securities fraud claims by requiring class actions involving nationally traded securities to be brought exclusively in federal court under uniform federal standards." Jill E. Fisch, *The Scope of Private Securities Litigation: In Search of Liability Standards for Secondary Defendants*, 99 COLUM. L. REV. 1293, 1295–96 (1999).

[46] 15 U.S.C. § 78t(e) (2000).

tutes an actual knowledge standard for the "recklessness" standard that governs civil liability of primary offenders under Section 10(b) and criminal liability of all actors for aiding and abetting.[47]

A Duty of Inquiry?

When the lawyer learns facts that, if true, strongly suggest that a corporate officer has engaged in illegal or fraudulent conduct, what should or must the lawyer do? Probably the most unsettled and controverted question is whether a lawyer must investigate suspicious circumstances that suggest fraud or follow up on specific allegations of fraud. There is very little direct precedent. A few federal cases hold that inquiry is required under some circumstances:

The *O'Melveny* case. In *FDIC v. O'Melveny & Myers*,[48] the receiver of a failed thrift was held to have stated a claim for relief against a law firm that had assisted the thrift in two real estate syndications offered to investors. When the private placement was made, the thrift was in unsound financial condition; its officers had fraudulently overvalued assets, embezzled funds, and generally "cooked the books." The complaint alleged that O'Melveny, knowing of the recent resignations of the thrift's prior auditors and outside law firm, did not question the auditors, the law firm, federal or state regulators, or the thrift's financial officer about the thrift's financial status before giving legal opinions and doing other work that assisted the thrift in soliciting investors. After the thrift failed, the Federal Deposit Insurance Corporation ("FDIC"), acting as conservator, rescinded the investments and was assigned the investors' claims against O'Melveny. The receiver then brought suit against O'Melveny for professional negligence (malpractice) and negligent misrepresentation (third-party liability). The U.S. Court of Appeals for the Ninth Circuit, reversing the trial court's dismissal of the complaint, held that these allegations stated claims for relief.[49] *O'Melveny* holds that the recent resignations of the issuer's prior auditor and lawyer were suspicious circumstances, known to the lawyer, that required further inquiry.[50] The duty of due care owed to both the investors and the client required a "reasonable, independent investigation" of the client's financial status before giving legal opinions and assisting the client in soliciting investors.[51]

---

[47] *See supra* note 42 and accompanying text.

[48] 969 F.2d 744 (9th Cir. 1992), *rev'd and remanded on other grounds,* 512 U.S. 79 (1994), *reaffirmed on remand,* 61 F.3d 17 (9th Cir. 1995). The Supreme Court based its reversal on a concern that the initial decision was grounded on a federal common law ruling that the FDIC was not bound by certain equitable defenses that could have been raised by the bank, O'Melveny & Meyers, 969 F.2d at 752; on remand, the U.S. Court of Appeals for the Ninth Circuit held that its initial decision was based, as it should have been, on California and not federal law, O'Melveny & Meyers, 512 U.S. at 89.

[49] O'Melveny & Meyers, 969 F.2d at 752.

[50] *Id.* at 749.

[51] *Id.* (quoting Felts v. Nat'l Account Sys. Ass'n, 469 F. Supp. 54, 67 (N.D. Miss. 1978)).

The *Clark* case. In *FDIC v. Clark,*[52] the receiver of a failed bank sued the bank's outside counsel for failing to investigate claims made in a civil lawsuit against the bank that alleged that the bank's president had conspired to defraud the bank of several million dollars through a fraudulent loan scheme. The lawyers accepted the president's explanation of the situation and failed to inquire further or to inform the board of directors of the allegations. The court upheld a jury verdict against the lawyers, stating that "there was ample proof for the jury to find that defendants were negligent in their professional duties to the bank, and that their negligence was a cause of loss" to the bank.[53]

The *Schatz* case. Some decisions, however, take a "no duty" approach in the third-party liability context, as distinct from the malpractice context. *Schatz v. Rosenberg*[54] is the most vivid and notorious example of a case holding that a lawyer has no duty to correct client misrepresentations to third persons before closing a transaction with the defrauded person.[55] The plaintiffs alleged that the lawyer, aware that the client's financial situation had deteriorated, forwarded the client's false financial statement to the person buying the client's business and taking in return an unsecured note for a portion of the purchase price. When the client filed for bankruptcy, the purchasers suffered financial loss. The court affirmed dismissal of counts charging the firm with liability as an aider and abettor under federal securities law and Maryland tort law. The court held, agreeing with the U.S. Court of Appeals for the Seventh Circuit, that "lawyers have no duty to disclose information about clients to third party purchasers or investors in the absence of a confidential relationship between the attorney and the third party."[56] When the lawyer merely documents the transaction and does not himself make representations to the third party or provide a legal opinion that does so, the lawyer is not liable even though ordinary agency law (applicable to agents of sellers generally) would impose liability.[57] *Schatz* and other cases apply a lower standard of conduct to lawyers negotiating and preparing documents for a client transaction than would be applied to a used-car salesman acting as agent for his principal.

Some ethics opinions discuss situations in which a lawyer must either make further inquiry or decline to provide an opinion or service. The ABA Preliminary Report states that a lawyer who uncritically accepts management's instructions and limits advice or services to a narrowly defined scope, "ignoring the context or implications of

---

[52] 978 F.2d 1541 (10th Cir. 1992).

[53] *Id.* at 1551.

[54] 943 F.2d 485 (4th Cir. 1991).

[55] *Id.* at 492.

[56] *Id.* at 490 (footnote omitted).

[57] See RESTATEMENT (SECOND) OF AGENCY § 348 (1958). "An agent who fraudulently makes representations, . . . or knowingly assists in the commission of tortious fraud . . . by his principal . . . is subject to liability in tort to the injured person although the fraud . . . occurs in a transaction on behalf of the principal." *Id.*

the advice they are giving [,]" may violate obligations owed to the corporate client and the public.[58] The Report also states: "The ABA has long advised that lawyers providing transactional opinions that may be relied upon by third parties cannot blindly accept facts posited by the client; they must question and investigate the factual predicate for their advice, at least to some extent and in some circumstances."[59]

Climbing the Corporate Ladder

If a lawyer learns, or has reason to know, of prospective or ongoing fraud on the part of the corporation's managers and the managers refuse to cease or rectify their course of conduct, should the lawyer take the problem to the corporation's highest authority, usually the board of directors? Is "loyal disclosure," that is, disclosure of client confidences within the client entity, different from disclosure outside the organization (e.g., whistleblowing to the SEC, persons thought to be harmed, or the press)?

Model Rule 1.13(b), addressing the situation in which an organization's lawyer "knows" that an agent is engaged in conduct in violation of fiduciary duties to the organization or in law violations harmful to the organization, states that a lawyer "shall

---

[58] *ABA Preliminary Report, supra* note 7, at 207 (citing and quoting from ABA ethics opinions directed at lawyers who provide tax opinions "on hypothetical facts in circumstances in which the opinions served to facilitate fraudulent transactions"). *E.g.,* ABA Comm. on Ethics and Prof'l Responsibility, Formal Op. 346, 68 A.B.A. J. 471 (1982).

[59] *ABA Preliminary Report, supra* note 7, at 208 n.49. ABA Comm. on Ethics and Prof'l Responsibility, Formal Op. 335 (1974) (quoted in ABA Formal Op. No. 346, *supra* note 58, at 472) explains the lawyer's duty to investigate:

[T]he lawyer should, in the first instance, make inquiry of his client as to the relevant facts and receive answers. If any of the alleged facts, or the alleged facts taken as a whole, are incomplete in a material respect, or are suspect, or are inconsistent, or either on their face or on the basis of other known facts are open to question, the lawyer should make further inquiry. The extent of this inquiry will depend in each case upon the circumstances. For example, it would be less where the lawyer's past relationship with the client is sufficient to give him a basis for trusting the client's probity than where the client has recently engaged the lawyer, and less where the lawyer's inquiries are answered fully than when there appears a reluctance to disclose information.

Where the lawyer concludes that further inquiry of a reasonable nature would not give him sufficient confidence as to all the relevant facts, or for any other reason he does not make the appropriate further inquiries, he should refuse to give an opinion. However, assuming that the alleged facts are not incomplete in a material respect, or suspect, or in any way inherently inconsistent, or on their face or on the basis of other known facts open to question, the lawyer may properly assume that the facts as related to him by his client, and checked by him by reviewing such appropriate documents as are available, are accurate. . . .

The essence of this opinion . . . is that, while a lawyer should make adequate preparation including inquiry into the relevant facts that is consistent with the above guidelines, and while he should not accept as true that which he should not reasonably believe to be true, he does not have the responsibility to "audit" the affairs of his client or to assume, without reasonable cause, that a client's statement of the facts cannot be relied upon.

proceed as is reasonably necessary in the best interest of the organization."[60] Although the Rule does not explicitly require an organization's lawyer to take a problem up the corporate ladder, that response, I believe, is required in circumstances in which that action is the only one that is in the "best interest of the organization." The Rule, however, is ambiguous. It recites a number of factors a lawyer should consider and then lists three measures, including going up the corporate ladder to the board of directors, that the lawyer "may" take, along with other unspecified measures. Many lawyers view the provision only as giving the lawyer discretion to choose among a number of options, including doing nothing at all, an interpretation that creates a clear risk of liability.[61]

The uncertainty on this question is a continuing problem. Many lawyers may not realize that a lawyer who fails to take effective steps to prevent the harm is exposed to the risk of civil liability. In the case against Jones Day arising out of its representation of Lincoln Savings & Loan, the court, denying the law firm's motion for summary judgment, stated that "where a law firm believes the management of a corporate client is committing serious regulatory violations, the firm has an obligation to . . . urge cessation of the activity."[62] Failure to go to the board of directors could not be excused simply because such action is thought to be "futile."

Why isn't it always in the best interests of the corporation for fraud to be reported up the ladder as high as necessary?[63] "Loyal disclosure" within the hierarchy of an entity client protects the client from disloyal managers and furthers the diligence and loyalty of the lawyer to the interests of the organization itself. As one commentator noted, "[h]onest corporate officers intent on complying with legal requirements, who are certainly the vast majority, should welcome the enhanced vigilance and protection from their legal counsel."[64]

---

[60] MODEL RULES OF PROF'L CONDUCT R. 1.13(b) (2002).

[61] The ABA Preliminary Report criticizes the current text of Model Rule 1.13 and its comments on additional grounds. The tone of the Rule and its comments "tends to discourage action by the lawyer to prevent or rectify corporate misconduct" by giving large emphasis to the avoidance of "disruption" of the organization and requiring the lawyer to have "[c]lear justification . . . for seeking review over the head of the constituent normally responsible. . . ." *ABA Preliminary Report, supra* note 7, at 203–04. In addition, the current rule requires that the matter be "related to the lawyer's representation," while it should also include any matter "that has come to the lawyer's attention through the representation." *Id.*

[62] *In re* Am. Cont'l/Lincoln Sav. & Loan Sec. Litig., 794 F. Supp. 1424, 1453 (D. Ariz. 1992); *see also* FDIC v. Clark, 978 F.2d 1541 (10th Cir. 1992) (dismissing law firm's motion for summary judgment when lawyer failed to take allegations of officer misconduct to the board of directors).

[63] *See* Richard W. Painter, *Obliging Lawyers to Report Acts of Organizational Clients,* PROF. LAW., Spring 1998, at 10 (arguing that lawyers should be required by ethics rules and SEC regulations to climb the corporate ladder to prevent a prospective or ongoing fraud by managers of the corporate client).

[64] George C. Harris, *Taking the Entity Theory Seriously: Lawyer Liability for Failure to Prevent Harm to Organizational Clients Through Disclosure of Constituent Wrongdoing,* 11 GEO. J. L. ETHICS 597, 653 (1998); *see also* 1 GEOFFREY C. HAZARD, JR. & W. WILLIAM HODES, THE LAW OF LAWYERING: A

The ABA Preliminary Report reaches the same conclusion: "When the lawyer knows or reasonably should know [that a corporate 'officer or employee is acting illegally or fraudulently, or in breach of a duty to the corporation,'] the lawyer should be encouraged to act promptly to protect the interests of the corporation."[65] The Preliminary Report recommends that Rule 1.13

> be amended to make clear that it requires the lawyer to pursue the measures outlined in Rule 1.13(c)(1) through (3) (including referring the matter to higher corporate authority), in a matter either related to the lawyer's representation (as currently provided) or that has come to the lawyer's attention through the representation, where the misconduct by a corporate officer, employee or agent involves crime or fraud, including violations of federal securities laws and regulations.[66]

Section 307 of the Sarbanes-Oxley Act[67] has changed the legal landscape on this question. Lawyers representing public companies will be required to report to higher authority within the organization when they have credible evidence of a material violation of the federal securities laws or of a breach of fiduciary duty by the company or any of its agents. The recommendations of Richard Painter and the ABA Task Force will have been put in place in somewhat different form by an SEC rule promulgated as required by the Act.

The practical problem, especially for inside counsel, is that of angering the person within the organization with the power to fire the lawyer. That person may be part of the problem. Tough choices, but who said that being an honorable lawyer was an easy job? Corporate lawyers are paid $200 to $700 per hour for a good reason—they deal with difficult and complex matters that require specialized knowledge, excellent professional skills and, most of all, good judgment.

Disclosure Adverse to a Client's Interest

As a last resort, when a client's officers and board have refused to cease or rectify a corporate fraud on third parties, should the corporation's lawyer become a whistleblower? Should rules of professional ethics or regulatory law permit (or require) the lawyer to disclose confidential information outside the organization when the managers and the

---

HANDBOOK ON THE MODEL RULES OF PROFESSIONAL CONDUCT § 1.13.111 (2d ed., 1998 Supp. 1998) (arguing that the present form of Model Rule 1.13 provides less protection to clients than it would if it required resort to the entity's highest authority).

[65] *ABA Preliminary Report, supra* note 7, at 204.

[66] *Id.*

[67] *See infra* notes 143–52 and accompanying text.

board refuse to cease or rectify the ongoing fraud? If the black letter of ABA Model Rule 1.6 is taken to mean what it says, a lawyer is forbidden from disclosing confidential information either to prevent or rectify client fraud on a third person, even when the lawyer learns of the fraud and it involves the use of the lawyer's services. Buried in the comments, and inconsistent with the black-letter text of the Rule, is language permitting a lawyer to "disaffirm documents"—such as legal opinions prepared for a client—"that are being, or will be, used in furtherance of the fraud, even though such a 'noisy' withdrawal may have the collateral effect of inferentially revealing client confidences."[68] The ABA opinion just quoted infers this permission to reveal confidential information from Rule 1.2(d), prohibiting a lawyer from assisting a client in criminal or fraudulent conduct, and Rule 1.16(a)(1), requiring a lawyer to withdraw when the client will use the lawyer's services to further a crime or fraud. In addition, the self-defense exception of Rule 1.6(b)(2) permits disclosure when a lawyer's representation is attacked. In the few jurisdictions which have followed the ABA's lead on exceptions to the professional duty of confidentiality, a "noisy" withdrawal in some client fraud situations is possible despite its omission in the black-letter text of the Rule—and may be necessary to avoid civil liability.

The vast majority of U.S. jurisdictions, however, have not adopted Model Rule 1.6 as recommended by the ABA. Forty-one states permit a lawyer to disclose confidential information to prevent a client's criminal fraud; four of those states require a lawyer to make such a disclosure; and only nine states and the District of Columbia may be viewed as forbidding a lawyer to reveal such information.[69] In the forty-one states that permit or require a lawyer to reveal information to prevent a criminal fraud, Rule 4.1(b) has additional bite. Because disclosure is not prohibited, a lawyer must "not knowingly . . . fail to disclose a material [fact to a third person] when disclosure is necessary to avoid assisting a criminal or fraudulent act by a client . . . [,]" effectively creating an affirmative duty of disclosure in those situations.[70]

During the 1970s, the SEC made some noises suggesting that it might adopt a rule or decisional standard that would require a lawyer to disclose a client's securities violations to the SEC. In *SEC v. National Student Marketing Corp.*,[71] the SEC took the

---

[68] ABA Comm. on Ethics and Prof'l Responsibility, Formal Op. 366 (1992) (discussing a lawyer's duties in client fraud situations, including the possibility of a "noisy" withdrawal).

[69] *See* ATTORNEYS' LIABILITY ASSURANCE SOCIETY, INC., ETHICS RULES ON CLIENT CONFIDENCES (2001), *reprinted in* THOMAS D. MORGAN & RONALD D. ROTUNDA, MODEL CODE OF PROFESSIONAL RESPONSIBILITY, MODEL RULES OF PROFESSIONAL CONDUCT AND OTHER SELECTED STANDARDS 134–144 (2002) 134–144 (tabulating the current law of all U.S. jurisdictions on disclosure of confidential information to prevent harm to third persons).

[70] MODEL RULES OF PROF'L CONDUCT R. 4.1(b) (2002).

[71] 457 F. Supp. 682 (D.D.C. 1978).

position that lawyers, knowing that their client had gone ahead with a merger on the basis of materially misleading financial information in the shareholder proxy statements, had a duty to prevent the merger from taking place; the court agreed that the lawyers had aided and abetted the securities fraud but was much more vague about what the lawyers should have done, and imposed no sanction on them. Faced by a storm of professional outrage, the SEC took a considerably more modest position in *In re Carter & Johnson*:[72]

> When a lawyer with significant responsibilities in the effectuation of a company's compliance with the disclosure requirements of the federal securities laws becomes aware that his client is engaged in a substantial and continuing failure to satisfy those disclosure requirements, his continued participation violates professional standards unless he takes prompt steps to end [his] client's noncompliance.[73]

In a later case, *In re Gutfreund*,[74] the SEC held that Feuerstein, Salomon's chief legal officer, knowing that a Salomon trader had submitted false bids on Treasury securities, was "obligated to take affirmative steps to ensure" that the misconduct was adequately addressed.[75] Those steps might include "disclosure of the matter to the entity's board of directors, resignation from [the representation], or disclosure to regulatory authorities."[76] Having raised the specter of disclosure of client wrongdoing to a public officer, the SEC added that applicable state ethics rules "may bear upon what course of conduct [the] individual may properly pursue."[77]

Under *Carter & Johnson and Gutfreund*, the lawyer must do something, but what? The decisions, by their reference to "professional standards" and their emphasis on the obligation to withdraw if the client does not cease or rectify the violation, reflect the ambiguity of the states' ethics rules, which generally give the lawyer choices but no mandates (other than remonstrating with the client and then required withdrawal if the client persists in the wrongdoing). At least until Enron, the SEC, aware of the legal profession's bitter opposition to SEC regulation and discipline of lawyers, has shown little interest in taking a more aggressive position.

---

[72] SEC Release No. 34-17597, [1981 Transfer Binder] Fed. Sec. L. Rep. (CCH) ¶ 82,847, at 84,145 (Feb. 28, 1981).

[73] *Id.* at 84,172 (emphasis added).

[74] Exchange Act Release No. 34-31554, [1992 Transfer Binder] Fed. Sec. L. Rep. (CCH) ¶ 85,067, at 83,597 (Dec. 3, 1992).

[75] *Id.* at 83,609.

[76] *Id.*

[77] *Id.* at 83,609 n.26.

LAWYER CONDUCT IN THE ENRON AFFAIR

Andersen's Document Destruction

The testimony of Andersen officials to congressional committees, supplemented by documents that have subsequently been published and Duncan's guilty plea, indicates that a massive shredding of Andersen documents relating to its Enron engagement began on October 23, 2001 and continued for eighteen days until terminated on November 9, 2001. The shredding damaged Andersen's reputation, placed it in a disastrous liability situation, and led to a criminal indictment charging the firm with obstruction of justice. The indictment itself doomed Andersen, and the subsequent conviction sealed its fate.[78] It is extraordinary that such a massive shredding could have occurred without inside or outside lawyers providing clear directions that all Enron-related material should be preserved and establishing procedures to ensure that that occurred. This single event led to Andersen's disintegration, with horrendous results for its retired and current employees.

Factual Summary[79]

After being fined by the SEC and settling a damage action for its conduct relating to Waste Management's failure and bankruptcy, Andersen revised its "document retention policy." The government offered evidence that the policy statement was motivated at least in part by a desire to ensure that, in a future situation, damaging work papers would not be available to regulators and plaintiffs' lawyers.[80] In September and early October 2001, as concern increased within Andersen about impending scrutiny of its work for Enron, a group of high-level Andersen partners in Houston and Chicago discussed matters relating to the Enron account in meetings and teleconferences. The group included Nancy Temple, an in-house lawyer in Chicago; Michael Odom, the audit practice director; and David Duncan, the Houston partner in charge of the Enron engagement. During those conferences, Temple says she asked Duncan, per-

---

[78] *See* Kurt Eichenwald, *Andersen Guilty in Effort to Block Inquiry on Enron,* N.Y. TIMES, June 16, 2002, at A1 (reporting Andersen's conviction on June 15, 2002, of one count of obstructing justice).

[79] As indicated earlier, this brief summary of facts relating to Andersen's destruction of Enron-related documents relies on: (1) testimony of top Andersen officials and Nancy Temple to Congressional committees, especially the hearing of the House Energy & Commerce Committee on January 24, 2002, DESTRUCTION OF ENRON-RELATED DOCUMENTS BY ANDERSEN PERSONNEL: HEARING BEFORE THE SUBCOMM. ON OVERSIGHT AND INVESTIGATIONS OF THE COMM. ON ENERGY AND COMMERCE, 107th Cong. 30-183 (2002) [hereinafter DESTRUCTION OF ENRON-RELATED DOCUMENTS], *available at* http://energycommerce.house.gov/107/action/107-80.pdf; and (2) David Duncan's guilty plea, United States v. Duncan, 2002 WL 534544 (S.D. Tex. 2002). It is confirmed by newspaper reports of the first seven days of the criminal trial against Andersen. *See* Jonathan Weil & Alexei Barrioneuvo, *In the Balance: As Trial Nears End, Andersen Case Proves Surprisingly Tough,* WALL ST. J., June 4, 2002, at A1 (summarizing the first two weeks of the trial).

[80] *See* DESTRUCTION OF ENRON-RELATED DOCUMENTS, *supra* note 79.

haps on more than one occasion, whether he was in compliance with Andersen's policy dealing with retention and destruction of documents ("retention/destruction policy"). On October 12, Temple sent an e-mail to Odom, which he then forwarded to Duncan. The e-mail said: "It might be useful to consider reminding the engagement team of our documentation and retention policy. It [would] be helpful to make sure that we have complied with the policy. Let me know if you have any questions. Nancy."[81]

Temple also attached a copy of Andersen's retention/destruction policy with her e-mail. That policy covered systematic destruction of documents, not just "documentation and retention." When Odom forwarded the e-mail and the policy to Duncan, he included a note saying, "more help."[82] Duncan told the House committee staff that never before, during his lengthy tenure at Andersen, had he been asked about compliance with the firm's retention/destruction policy. He viewed the communications from Temple as inviting him to destroy documents.

On October 21, 2001, Duncan learned that the SEC had, on October 16, opened an informal inquiry into Enron's financial dealings, particularly the elaborate partnership transactions and Enron's fuzzy disclosures of those deals. On October 22, Duncan and other engagement team members met with Rick Causey, Enron's chief accounting officer, to discuss the SEC inquiry. The following day, Duncan called an urgent meeting of the Enron engagement team, at which, according to an Andersen executive, "he organized an expedited effort to shred, or otherwise dispose of, Enron-related documents."[83] During the next two and one-half weeks (eighteen days), "a very substantial volume of documents and e-mails were disposed of by the Enron engagement team."[84]

On November 8, 2001, Andersen received an SEC subpoena for Enron-related documents. Temple, the following day, left a message with Duncan's assistant that all Enron documents should be preserved. The shredding activity stopped on November 9 when the assistant sent an e-mail to secretaries telling them, "no more shredding."[85]

Legal Analysis

What were Andersen's lawyers (in-house and outside counsel) doing while Andersen's accountants and staff were shredding documents? The facts disclosed thus far suggest three possibilities, none of them good. Andersen's lawyers were either: (1) encouraging this destruction through none-too-subtle hints; (2) recklessly ignoring the very real possibility that documents might be destroyed by employees seeking to protect themselves or Andersen; or (3) acting carelessly in relation to whether the Enron files were preserved

---

[81] *Id.* at 45.

[82] *Id.* at 148.

[83] *Id.* at 32.

[84] *Id.*

[85] *Id.*

or not. Any of these explanations exposed Andersen to civil liability to Enron and its shareholders and resulted in Andersen's criminal indictment.

While there is some doubt whether or not knowledge of an SEC investigation satisfies one element of the general obstruction of justice act,[86] it is reasonably clear that 18 U.S.C. § 1512, discussed below, was violated by Andersen's destruction of documents. Section 1512 does not require that a proceeding be pending or imminent, but only that the defendant has some reasonable basis for understanding that a future proceeding is likely or probable.[87]

Duncan was the partner in charge of the Enron account, and federal criminal law often imputes any wrongdoing on the part of an agent to an entity such as Andersen. Duncan's plea of guilt satisfies the requirements of 18 U.S.C. § 1512: he "knowingly . . . engage[d] in misleading conduct toward another person [employees working under him on the Enron account], with intent to . . . cause or induce [that] person to—(A) withhold . . . a record, document, or other object, from an official proceeding; [or] (B) alter, destroy, mutilate, or conceal an object with intent to impair the object's integrity or availability for use in an official proceeding[.]"[88] In addition to the imputed liability for Duncan's conduct, the government presented evidence in the criminal trial that high-level officials of Andersen, in its Chicago headquarters, were worried about the availability of harmful Enron documents to the SEC and plaintiffs' lawyers, and that the requests to Duncan that his team follow Andersen's retention/destruction policy were an indirect way to communicate a desire that harmful working papers and e-mails be destroyed.

---

[86] 18 U.S.C. §§ 1503, 1505, 1512 (1994). The case law requires that some form of official proceeding be pending and that the defendant have notice of the proceeding. *See* United States v. Aguilar, 515 U.S. 593, 599 (1995). An SEC informal inquiry initiated on October 16, 2001, which became a formal inquiry on October 30, 2001, may or may not meet this standard. *See* United States v. Kelly, 36 F.3d 1118, 1127 (D.C. Cir. 1994) (summarizing an earlier case dealing with an informal SEC investigation as holding that "the SEC's authority to issue subpoenas and administer oaths in conjunction with its investigations made an SEC investigation a § 1505 proceeding").

[87] *See* 18 U.S.C. § 1512; *see also* C. Evan Stewart, *Andersen: Reviewing Ethics of Document Shredding*, N.Y. L.J., Apr. 15, 2002, at 1, 6 (discussing application of ethics rules). *See generally* John C. Coffee, Jr., *Criminal Law: The Andersen Fiasco*, NAT'L L.J., Feb. 11, 2001, at A19 (concluding that the Andersen situation meets any of the lower court tests for when a proceeding is sufficient under 18 U.S.C. § 1512, including the strict one expressed by United States v. Shively, 927 F.2d 804, 812 (5th Cir. 1991)). The Sarbanes-Oxley Act of 2002, Pub. L. No. 107-204, 116 Stat. 745, created additional penalties for document destruction. 18 U.S.C. § 1505 makes it a crime, punishable by a fine and up to five years imprisonment, to alter, destroy, mutilate, or conceal a document with the intent to make it unavailable in an official proceeding or otherwise obstruct any official proceeding. The Act also creates an additional crime, 18 U.S.C. § 1519, with the same penalties, to alter, destroy, mutilate, conceal, falsify, or make a false entry in any document with the intent to obstruct a federal investigation or bankruptcy case "or in relation to or contemplation of any such matter or case." Corporate and Criminal Fraud Accountability Act of 2002, Pub. L. No. 107-204, § 802, 116 Stat. 800.

[88] 18 U.S.C. § 1512(b).

In-house lawyer Temple appears to have failed in her duty to advise Andersen employees that, under these circumstances, any destruction of Enron documents would be a federal (and perhaps state) crime. Andersen's retention/destruction policy was ambiguous and Duncan, a non-lawyer, was left to decipher its competing provisions that, on the one hand, documents that were not essential in proving that audits were done properly should be destroyed and, on the other, that documents should not be destroyed in situations involving "litigation" or perhaps also "threatened litigation."[89] The clear application of the latter statement was surely indicated, but that direction never occurred until November 10, 2001, after the shredding was over.

An outside law firm, Davis, Polk & Wardwell ("Davis Polk"), was also looking after Andersen's interests during most of the document destruction period. Davis Polk was retained by Andersen on October 9, 2001, and began work on October 16. Temple has testified that on October 16, 2001, she consulted with Davis Polk lawyers concerning document retention. We do not know the scope of Davis Polk's representation of Andersen other than public statements that the firm was advising Andersen concerning its legal problems relating to the Enron engagement. If in-house counsel had told Davis Polk that it had already taken care of requiring the preservation of documents, the firm could reasonably rely on that assurance and devote itself to other matters. Under other scenarios, the firm's advice or lack thereof may raise questions of adequacy of representation.

This recital makes one thing clear: Some lawyer or lawyers failed to protect Andersen's interest in preserving all of its Enron-related documents. One of the initial steps in any internal investigation is the preservation of relevant documents. There is always a danger that some employees may believe that destruction of troublesome documents will serve their or the company's interest. Preventing such actions is essential to the company's reputation and, in this case, its very survival. How could Andersen demonstrate its innocence of participation in Enron's fraud, assuming it was innocent, when many files had been destroyed after an SEC inquiry had begun? Without its files, how could

---

[89] The executive summary of Andersen's policy statement stated: "[i]n cases of threatened litigation, no related information will be destroyed." ARTHUR ANDERSEN BUSINESS UNIT, ENRON CORP., PRACTICE ADMINISTRATION: CLIENT ENGAGEMENT INFORMATION—ORGANIZATION, RETENTION AND DESTRUCTION, STATEMENT NO. 760, at *2 (2000), *available at* 2000 WL 33680396. But the section to which the summary refers, section 4.5.4, provides for document retention when the responsible accountant "is advised of litigation or subpoenas regarding a particular engagement." *Id.* at *10. It is unclear whether the omission of "threatened" in the text of the policy statement was an inadvertent omission or intentional obfuscation. In any event, the policy statement had to be viewed in the light of state and federal criminal laws, which often prohibit destruction of relevant documents when litigation is reasonably foreseeable or imminent. Lawyer Temple claimed in her congressional testimony that her statements were intended to invite Duncan to read and follow the firm's policy. The policy, however, was ambiguous on its face and a careful lawyer should have applied it to the particular context in the light of applicable criminal prohibitions (e.g., federal law and Illinois and Texas law). Application of this relevant law, a matter for a lawyer rather than an accountant, clearly required the retention of all relevant documents as of October 21.

it reestablish its reputation by convincing the public that it had gotten to the bottom of any problem and made the necessary changes? Why would it want to risk being criminally charged? Many failures contributed to Andersen's disintegration, but lawyer failure was surely one of them.

V&E'S "Preliminary Investigation" of Watkins's Allegations

Factual Background and Assumptions[90]

Sherron Watkins's anonymous letter of August 14, 2001, supplemented by several later communications in which she identified herself, stated that "Enron has been very aggressive in its accounting."[91] Watkins's allegations raised serious questions concerning the accounting treatment and economic substance of the LJM and Raptor transactions and Andrew Fastow's conflicts of interest, and correctly predicted that negative publicity and litigation would occur when the public learned about the transactions.

Enron's CEO, Kenneth Lay, met with Watkins on August 22, 2001. After agreeing to initiate an investigation, Lay discussed the situation with James V. Derrick, Jr., Enron's general counsel. Lay and Derrick agreed that Enron should retain an outside law firm to investigate and that V&E, if it could do so ethically, should conduct the investigation. Lay and Derrick recognized that V&E had done legal work creating some of the limited partnerships at issue and had advised on the securities disclosures concerning them. Nevertheless, they concluded that V&E was in the best position to help Enron determine whether a full-scale investigation by independent lawyers and accountants was necessary. According to Enron and V&E, the firm's familiarity with Enron and the transactions would allow it to do the job quickly, and that explains why V&E was chosen. V&E agreed to do the investigation and two V&E lawyers (the partner responsible for the Enron relationship and a litigation partner who had done no prior work for Enron) began work on the matter on August 23 or 24, 2001.

The scope of V&E's investigation was limited in significant respects. It was a "preliminary investigation" to determine "whether the [Watkins allegations] . . . presented any new information . . . that may warrant further independent investigation."[92] V&E had also agreed with Enron's Derrick and Lay that "our initial approach would not involve the second guessing of the accounting advice and treatment provided by [Andersen]" and "that there would be no detailed analysis of each and every transaction."[93] In fact, there does not appear to have been a detailed analysis of any transaction.

---

[90] The documents relied on for this summary of assumed facts are cited *supra* in notes 16, 20, and 21.

[91] Letter (originally anonymous) from Sherron Watkins to Kenneth L. Lay, Chief Executive Officer, Enron Corp. 1 (Aug. 14, 2001), *available at* http://news.findlaw.com/hdocs/docs/enron/empltr2lay82001.pdf.

[92] Hendrick Opinion Letter, *supra* note 20, at *2.

[93] *Id.* at *1.

During late August and early September 2001, V&E interviewed eight high-level Enron officials and two Andersen partners (Duncan and Cash), studied documents relating to the LJM partnerships, met informally with V&E lawyers who had worked on these matters, and, finally, met with Watkins.[94] On September 21, 2001, they reported orally to Lay and Derrick; the same conclusions were later embodied in V&E's October 15 opinion letter.[95]

V&E's opinion concluded that "the facts disclosed through our preliminary investigation do not, in our judgment, warrant a further widespread investigation by independent counsel and auditors."[96] This statement was accompanied by a statement that "the bad cosmetics involving the LJM entities and Raptor transactions, coupled with the poor performance of the merchant investment assets placed in those vehicles and the decline in the value of Enron stock" created "a serious risk of adverse publicity and litigation."[97]

The following day Enron announced that it was taking a nearly $600 million charge against earnings and a reduction of shareholders' equity of $1.2 billion related to Raptor transactions. Investor confidence was undermined, Enron stock plummeted, credit triggers were set off, and, some six weeks later, Enron sought bankruptcy protection.

ETHICAL AND LEGAL ISSUES CONCERNING V&E'S INVESTIGATION

Should V&E have undertaken an investigation the scope and purpose of which were unclear? Should V&E have accepted limits on its investigation that restricted whom it should interview and what it should accept, such as Andersen's resolution of accounting matters, without further review? Did the investigation require V&E to evaluate its own prior work? Did V&E provide adequate representation to Enron in conducting its investigation?

The scope of the intended investigation remains unclear. On its face it was a very narrow one: to determine whether Watkins's communications advanced any "new facts" that would justify a full investigation, with all accounting issues left unexamined. But Watkins raised disclosure and conflicts issues as well as accounting issues; and the investigation actually carried out considered much broader questions, such as the "bad cosmetics" of the accounting actions, the likelihood of shareholder litigation, and the conflicts of interest raised by the LJM transactions. While a client's regular lawyer can undertake a narrow investigation whether "new facts" have been raised, the broader one ("Do we have a problem here?") suggested by the inquiry actually made, and by the report itself, did involve disclosure issues and V&E's prior work. Moreover, the context suggests that Lay and Derrick wanted and got an opinion that would be read

---

[94] POWERS REPORT, *supra* note 16, at *80.

[95] *Id.*

[96] Hendrick Opinion Letter, *supra* note 20, at *7.

[97] *Id.*

to provide cover on the broader question: "There is no problem that deserves a full investigation."

Under the profession's conflict of interest rules, a lawyer may not represent a client if there is a substantial risk that the lawyer's representation of the client would be materially and adversely affected by the lawyer's own interest, unless the client gives a fully informed and valid consent.[98] Model Rule 1.7, either in its 1983 form or as recently revised, contains the same prohibition in different language, as does Rule 1.06 of the Texas Rules of Professional Conduct.[99] But there is more. A client's consent is not effective if, "in the circumstances, it is not reasonably likely that the lawyer will be able to provide adequate representation . . . ."[100]

It is clear that V&E could not undertake the investigation without Enron's informed consent. Enron was V&E's largest client and it had done extensive legal work in structuring and documenting the transactions in question and approving financial disclosures concerning them. The investigation required V&E to assess objectively, as if it had not been there at all, the soundness and propriety of its prior representation. Thus, the situation presented a serious conflict between Enron's presumed interest in an objective investigation and V&E's own interests.

Normally, a client experienced in the use of legal services who is advised by in-house counsel concerning an actual or potential conflict of interest may give a valid consent if fully informed of the risks and implications of the conflict of interest. I assume that Enron was fully informed and consulted. Nevertheless, there is a question whether the consent was a valid one, and, even if it was, whether the second requirement—the objective standard that the lawyer reasonably believe the representation will not be adversely affected by the lawyer's conflict of interest—was satisfied.

The situation is analogous to ones arising when a derivative suit charges a corporate manager with wrongful conduct harmful to the corporation.[101] The manager's consent to a lawyer's conflict is insufficient under these circumstances; the consent must be given by an officer or by board members who are not charged with misconduct. In the V&E situation, general counsel Derrick and CEO Lay were high-level officials impli-

---

[98] *See* RESTATEMENT (THIRD) OF THE LAW GOVERNING LAWYERS §§ 121, 122 (2000).

[99] *Compare* MODEL RULES OF PROF'L CONDUCT R. 1.7 (2002), *with* TEXAS RULES OF PROF'L CONDUCT R. 1.06 (1989).

[100] RESTATEMENT (THIRD) OF THE LAW GOVERNING LAWYERS § 122(2)(c) (2000).

[101] *See, e.g.,* Yablonski v. United Mine Workers of Am., 448 F.2d 1175 (D.C. Cir. 1971); Cannon v. U.S. Acoustics Corp., 398 F. Supp. 209 (N.D. Ill. 1975), *aff'd in relevant part,* 532 F.2d 1118 (7th Cir. 1976); HAZARD, KONIAK & CRAMTON, *supra* note 1, at 726–31. Consent to a lawyer's conflict of interest cannot be given under those circumstances by the corporate managers who may be involved in the wrongdoing, but only by disinterested officers or board members. *See* RESTATEMENT (THIRD) OF THE LAW GOVERNING LAWYERS § 122 cmt. c(ii) (2000), (dealing with the capacity of the consenting person: "When the person who normally would make the decision whether or not to give consent . . . is otherwise self-interested in the decision whether to consent, special requirements apply to consent.").

cated in the misconduct alleged by Watkins. The explanation that V&E was familiar with the transactions and therefore could provide the report quickly is a dubious basis for waiver of V&E's serious conflict.

Corporate law requires, in some instances, that internal investigations be conducted by "independent counsel."[102] Moreover, the standard advice for internal investigations dealing with a wide range of issues (e.g., illegal foreign payments, illegal campaign contributions, special litigation committees in derivative suit situations, and indemnification decisions) is that "independent counsel" be used.[103]

In any event, there remains a serious question as to whether V&E's own conflict of interest would not "adversely affect" its performance of the investigation. V&E's opinion letter stated that the Enron transactions it facilitated and documented were "creative and aggressive," suggesting that they went to the outer edge of legality.[104] Transactions may be within the bounds of the law even though they entail legal risks. But a course of action that involves pushing things to the edge in an effort every quarter to increase the reported earnings creates enormous risk that some of the many transactions and devices will turn out to be illegal or fraudulent. The bounds of the law are always indeterminate and fuzzy. As Brandeis said, lawyers should advise conduct that is a safe distance from the uncertain precipice of illegality rather than attempt to tread the edge of the precipice.[105]

V&E's letter also concluded that "because of the bad cosmetics involving the LJM entities and Raptor transactions, coupled with the poor performance of the merchant investment assets placed in those vehicles and the decline in the value of Enron stock, there is a serious risk of adverse publicity and litigation."[106] It was reasonably foreseeable, as has happened, that that litigation would include V&E as a defendant and that

---

[102] For example, the MODEL BUS. CORP. ACT § 8.55(b)(2) (1998–99 Supp.) requires that "special legal counsel" be used to make decisions whether to indemnify officers and directors. Some states, in the indemnification context, phrase the requirement in terms of "independent counsel"—defined in Ohio as a law firm that has not represented the corporation or any person to be indemnified within the past five years. *See, e.g.,* OHIO REV. CODE ANN. § 1701.13(E)(4) (Anderson 2001).

[103] *See* Arthur F. Matthews, *Internal Corporate Investigations,* 45 OHIO ST. L.J. 655 (1984).

[104] Hendrick Opinion Letter, *supra* note 20, at *6.

[105] When lawyers habitually push the envelope of the permissible, their actions will occasionally involve illegality. As Louis Brandeis put it in replying to claims of business executives that antitrust law was intolerably fuzzy:

"[Y]our lawyers . . . can tell you where a fairly safe course lies. If you are walking along a precipice no human being can tell you how near you can go to that precipice without falling over, because you may stumble on a loose stone . . . ; but anybody can tell you where you can walk perfectly safe within convenient distance of that precipice." The difficulty which men have felt . . . has been rather that they wanted to go to the limit rather than they wanted to go safely.

Hearings Before Sen. Comm. on Interstate Commerce, S. Res. No. 98, 62nd Cong. 1161 (1911) (statement of Louis D. Brandeis), *quoted in* HAZARD, KONIAK & CRAMTON, *supra* note 1, at 62.

[106] Hendrick Opinion Letter, *supra* note 20, at *7.

Enron officers, directors, and other co-defendants would defend themselves by blaming V&E for giving poor advice. Under these circumstances, the conflict appears to be too severe to be undertaken: a reasonable lawyer would not believe that his representation would not be adversely affected.

The adequacy of the investigation is also questionable. Aside from two investor relations officers, V&E interviewed only seven high-level officials, most of whom were directly implicated in the self-dealing and fiduciary violations raised by the Watkins allegations and corroborated by McMahon. V&E relied on the denials of wrongdoing by those officers and on the fact that none of the persons interviewed could identify a specific transaction that was illegal. Although McMahon, one of those interviewed, mentioned ten lower-level employees who might be good sources of information concerning Fastow's self-dealing, V&E failed to interview any of them. V&E was informed by Causey of the "mistake" that was made concerning accounting failures on the LJM2 transactions (resulting in the October 16, 2001 restatement of shareholder equity), but never pursued how and why this occurred. The investigation as a whole, when compared to the subsequent investigation by the board's special committee, using the services of Wilmer, Cutler & Pickering, appears perfunctory. As the Powers Report stated, the result of the V&E investigation "was largely predetermined by the scope and nature of the investigation and the process employed."[107] It was performed with insufficient skepticism.[108] Did V&E give some thought to why Enron's managers wanted V&E to investigate matters related to its own prior work and what opinion they wanted the firm to provide? There is a serious question of whether adequate representation was provided to the entity client, as distinct from satisfying the managers' apparent desire to have a protective document.

V&E, supported by two opinions of legal ethics experts, relies on the characterization of its investigation as "preliminary" and concludes that there was no conflict of interest because its own prior work was not involved and "no new facts" were produced by its inquiry.[109]

First, it is a truism that a corporation's regular counsel may inquire whether allegations of manager misconduct warrant a full-scale investigation. The issue here is whether the "preliminary" investigation was structured at the managers' request in a way that made it a final investigation, a conclusion not based on an adequate inquiry of whether a full-scale investigation by independent counsel was necessary.

Second, V&E and its experts argue that no independent investigation was necessary. That argument can be made only if legal issues are totally subsumed in the ac-

---

[107] POWERS REPORT, *supra* note 16, at *81.

[108] *Id.*

[109] Opinion letter from Charles W. Wolfram, Professor of Law Emeritus, Cornell Law School, to John K. Villa, Esq., Williams & Connolly LLP (Mar. 13, 2002); Opinion letter from Geoffrey C. Hazard, Jr., Trustee Professor of Law, University of Pennsylvania, to John K. Villa, Esq., Williams & Connolly LLP (Mar. 13, 2002).

counting issues left to Andersen and the "economic substance" questions left to Enron's managers and board.[110] But legal as well as factual questions were involved and, if they were not, why would Enron be interested in V&E's advice and legal opinion? The extraordinary nature of many of the related-party transactions raised issues of their legality and whether the financial disclosures concerning them met legal requirements. If the transactions were merely accounting gimmicks designed to artificially inflate Enron's profits and conceal its debts, they were illegal and fraudulent transactions.

Lawyers cannot absolve themselves from legal responsibility by pretending that only accounting issues are involved, just as accountants cannot relieve themselves of responsibility by relying on the judgments of lawyers. If a series of transactions have no substantial business purpose (i.e., no property or risk is transferred to a third party) and the facts and circumstances suggest that their sole function is to give the balance sheet a false boost, legal questions are raised that are not resolved by an accountant's approval.[111] If representations are repeatedly made in financial disclosure documents to the effect that related-party transactions were "at arms' length," meaning that the managers have reason to believe that comparable market transactions involving independent parties would be made on the same terms, the lawyers must ask for some factual verification other than the mere assertion of interested managers. Legal questions do not evaporate because accountants and managers are also making judgments.

Finally, V&E's conclusion that "no new facts" emerged from its "preliminary" inquiry is incorrect.[112] Watkins and McMahon both identified serious conflicts of interest on the part of Fastow that had been communicated to Skilling, Buy, and Causey—allegations those executives had ignored. Although Fastow's dual role was not new information (it had been approved by the board), the way the conflicts had played out, and the failure of the controls to mitigate the conflicts, were new information. Watkins and McMahon, cumulatively, identified twelve Enron employees and

---

[110] A statement of V&E's senior partner, responding to criticism of the firm's role in Enron's failure, apparently takes that position: "[outside counsel has] 'no role in determining whether, or what, accounting treatment was appropriate' for a client." John Schwartz, *Enron's Many Strands: The Lawyers; Troubling Questions Ahead for Enron's Law Firm,* N.Y. TIMES, Mar. 12, 2002, at C1. Lawrence Cunningham criticizes this artificial separation of "legal" and "accounting" issues, arguing that related party transactions invariably create legal and accounting issues. *See* Lawrence A. Cunningham, *Sharing Accounting's Burden: Business Lawyers in Enron's Dark Shadows,* 57 BUS. LAW. 1421, 1454 (2002). A lawyer's characterization of the legality of the transaction as a "sale" and the financial disclosures required concerning it are legal questions that have to be decided with knowledge and understanding of the related accounting principles. The interim conclusions of Enron's court-appointed bankruptcy examiner are that the appropriate legal characterization of many of Enron's SPE transactions was "loan" rather than "sale," and that the financial disclosures concerning the transactions were false and misleading. *See* Batson, *supra* note 18, at *7–*8.

[111] Documenting a transaction as a "sale" and issuing a "true sale opinion" to the lender present legal questions. The First Interim Report of the Bankruptcy Examiner, Batson, *supra* note 18, at *7–*8, after studying six representative Enron transactions, concluded that, as a matter of law, most or all of them were disguised loans rather than sales.

[112] *See supra* note 109 and accompanying text.

three former employees who they said were knowledgeable about Fastow's conflicts; none of those individuals was interviewed by V&E. The identities of persons who could provide more detailed information about possible breaches of fiduciary duty by corporate managers were themselves "new facts" warranting further inquiry.

Common Law Claims Against Lawyers

Under the common law, a lawyer was liable for negligence only to those in privity of contract with the lawyer, typically clients. Although the privity doctrine has been abolished in negligence cases involving physical harm, it retains considerable vigor in negligence suits claiming purely economic harm, such as a negligent misrepresentation case brought against a lawyer by a non-client. Today, however, many jurisdictions have adopted exceptions to privity of contract in situations in which (1) the purpose of the lawyer-client relationship was to benefit or influence a third person[113] or, alternatively, (2) where someone in the business of supplying information for others "supplie[d] false information for the guidance of others [on which they have reasonably relied] in their business transactions."[114] The resulting duty of care is most commonly found in situations in which the lawyer, in handling a transaction for a client, is dealing directly with the injured third person or the representation seeks to benefit that person.[115]

Texas law would probably govern any claims brought against V&E other than those arising under federal securities laws. In Texas, the privity of contract doctrine bars a non-client from bringing a negligence action against a lawyer except in a few special situations. In *McCamish, Martin, Brown & Loeffler v. F.E. Appling Interests*,[116] the Texas Supreme Court followed Restatement (Second) of Torts Section 552 in a situation in which a lawyer gave negligent legal advice concerning the legality of a settlement that harmed both the client and the other settling party.[117] The latter was permitted to recover for the lawyer's negligent misrepresentation when information falsely supplied for the guidance of others was given to "a limited group of persons" to whom the law firm knew or should have known his client would give the information.[118] Does a shareholder have standing to bring a negligent misrepresentation claim against a pro-

---

[113] *See, e.g.,* Greycas, Inc. v. Proud, 826 F.2d 1560 (7th Cir. 1987) (upholding a negligent misrepresentation claim against a lawyer under Illinois law).

[114] RESTATEMENT (SECOND) OF TORTS § 552 (1977).

[115] *See* RESTATEMENT (THIRD) OF THE LAW GOVERNING LAWYERS § 51 (2000) (recognizing three exceptions to the privity requirement: (1) when the lawyer's client invites the non-client to rely on the lawyer's opinion or provision of legal services and the non-client so relies; (2) when one of the primary objectives of the representation is to benefit the non-client; and (3) when the lawyer's client is a fiduciary acting primarily to perform fiduciary duties owed to a non-client beneficiary).

[116] 991 S.W.2d 787 (Tex. 1999).

[117] *Id.* at 791–93.

[118] RESTATEMENT (SECOND) OF TORTS § 552 (1977).

fessional adviser? The answer may depend upon whether the adviser merely gave legal advice concerning a transaction or, in addition, prepared a disclosure document intended to provide information to shareholders and others.

Intentional torts, such as fraud, are not subject to the privity doctrine and may be brought by non-clients. A fraudulent misrepresentation claim under Restatement (Second) of Torts section 531 may be brought for economic damages if the injured parties reasonably relied on the fraudulent misrepresentations and if they belong to a "class of persons" whom the defendant "has reason to expect" would rely on the misrepresentation.[119] State law governing the scope of reliance on fraudulent misrepresentations, however, is not shaped by the "fraud on the market" legal fiction applied in federal securities cases, a fiction that permits any investor to be included in the "class of persons" who has relied on the misrepresentation. In Texas, a prospective purchaser of shares who relied upon a fraudulent misrepresentation contained in an accountant's report is not within the persons protected by that section.[120] The purchaser does not belong within the class of persons whom the defendant had reason to expect would rely on the misrepresentation. How this decision applies to those who own shares when the misrepresentation is made is unclear. Another uncertainty is whether the repeated statements of Enron executives addressed to Enron employees concerning the value of Enron stock had the effect of putting those employees within the protected class.

Claims Against Lawyers Under Federal Securities Laws

1. Elimination of Accessory Liability

Central Bank's elimination of accessory liability requires that claims under section 10(b) of the Securities Exchange Act of 1934 be framed as primary violations. *Central Bank*[121] held that a secondary actor in a securities transaction (e.g., an accountant or a lawyer) is not liable for damages for aiding and abetting a securities law violation.[122] Criminal liability, however, is still a possibility, and the SEC has authority to bring administrative proceedings against professional advisers. Civil liability actions against solvent and well-insured accounting and law firms in a fraud situation now must cast them as primary violators of section 10(b). Under *Central Bank,* the plaintiffs must show that a defendant actually engaged in manipulative or deceptive acts or made

---

[119] *Id.* § 531.

[120] *See* Ernst & Young, LLP v. Pac. Mut. Life Ins. Co., 51 S.W.3d 573, 581–83 (Tex. 2001).

[121] Cent. Bank of Denver v. First Interstate Bank of Denver, 511 U.S. 164 (1994). For a discussion of the effect of Central Bank on secondary actors, see Fisch, *supra* note 45; Melissa Harrison, *The Assault on the Liability of Outside Professionals: Are Lawyers and Accountants Off the Hook?*, 65 U. CIN. L. REV. 473 (1996); Douglas M. Branson, *Chasing the Rogue Professional After the Private Securities Litigation Reform Act of 1995,* 50 SMU L. REV. 91 (1996).

[122] Central Bank, 511 U.S. at 191.

fraudulent representations. As the *Central Bank* decision put it: "Any person or entity, including a lawyer, accountant, or bank, who employs a manipulative device or makes a material misstatement (or omission) on which a purchaser or seller of securities relies may be liable . . . ."[123]

The federal courts of appeals are divided on whether primary liability reaches a professional adviser who stays in the background, writing and approving the fraudulent financial statement or solicitation, but who does not make a misrepresentation in person, provide a legal opinion, or whose name is not included in the document. Several courts of appeals have upheld primary liability when the complaint alleges that the lawyer, aware of their falsity, anonymously drafted false representations that were relied on by investors;[124] on the other hand, other circuits have struck down such complaints.[125]

My own view is that it is wrong to make liability turn on whether or not the substantial participation of the professional adviser is concealed. Why should an anonymous draftsman escape responsibility for fraudulent representations merely because his identity is concealed? My position does push the margins of primary liability, and the uncertainty on this question provides a strong argument for the statutory overruling of *Central Bank* to permit aiding and abetting claims to be brought against lawyers and accountants. The lawyer, present at the time the fraud is committed and having reason to know about it, who substantially participates in facilitating the fraud should be accountable to those who are harmed.

2. Securities Fraud Issues

Securities fraud issues relating to Enron's inside or outside lawyers raise legal issues that are difficult, controverted, and uncertain.

Lawyer liability for misleading audited financial statements contained in filings under the Securities Exchange Act of 1934. The extent to which lawyers may rely, without further inquiry, on what the auditors tell them is a controverted and uncertain issue. Uncertainty also exists about whether Andersen's application of generally accepted accounting principles ("GAAP") was proper and, even if so, whether liability still exists when the actor knows that the financial statements as a whole do not fairly present the financial position of the company.

---

[123] *Id.*

[124] *See* Klein v. Boyd, [1998 Transfer Binder] Fed. Sec. L. Rep. (CCH) ¶ 90,136, at 90,317, 90,325 (3d Cir. Feb. 12, 1998) (holding that a lawyer "spoke" to the investors by drafting the solicitation documents, even though his identity was unknown to those solicited); Dannenberg v. Painewebber Inc. (In re Software Tools, Inc.), 50 F.3d 615, 619 (9th Cir. 1994) (holding that substantial participation in drafting is sufficient if there is "a reasonable inference that [the firm] knew or recklessly disregarded this falsehood").

[125] Anixter v. Home-States Prod. Co., 77 F.3d 1215, 1226 (10th Cir. 1996) (finding no primary liability for representations made by others); Ziemba v. Cascade Int'l, Inc., 256 F.3d 1194, 1204 (11th Cir. 2001) (holding that the complaint must include an allegation that the law firm made misrepresentations or omissions upon which the investors relied).

Lawyers and accountants often talk as if compliance with GAAP and generally accepted accounting standards ("GAAS"), or with an SEC guideline, such as the 3% outside equity participation required of special purpose entities, is conclusive. The case law is to the contrary. In *United States v. Simon,*[126] the U.S. Court of Appeals for the Second Circuit, in a lengthy opinion by Judge Friendly, affirmed the convictions of three accountants for securities and wire fraud even though seven eminent accounting experts testified that the accountants' certification of the client's financial statements was in full compliance with generally accepted auditing principles and standards (GAAP and GAAS). The accountants, knowing that the manager of a vending machine company had diverted millions of dollars from the company for personal investments in the stock market, included a footnote in the financial statement that referred obliquely to the obligation owed to the company by the manager, but did not disclose either the manager's diversion of funds or the unsatisfactory collateral that supposedly secured it. The decision, affirming the trial court's instructions and the sufficiency of the evidence, holds that technical compliance with the standards established by accountants' organizations is relevant but not conclusive evidence of the accountants' good faith; the crucial question for the trier of fact is whether the accountants' statement was or was not "materially false or misleading."[127]

But there is more. Judge Friendly states that general accounting principles:

> instruct an accountant what to do in the usual case where he has no reason to doubt that the affairs of the corporation are being honestly conducted. Once he has reason to believe that this basic assumption is false, an entirely different situation confronts him. Then . . . he must "extend his procedures to determine whether or not such suspicions are justified." If as a result [of further inquiry] he finds his suspicions to be confirmed, full disclosure must be the rule, unless he has made sure the wrong has been righted and procedures to avoid a repetition have been established.[128]

Judge Friendly also stated that:

> it simply cannot be true that an accountant is under no duty to disclose what he knows when he ha[s] reason to believe that, to a material extent, a corporation is being operated not to carry out its business in the interest of all [shareholders] but for the private benefit of its president . . . .[129]

---

[126] 425 F.2d 796 (2d Cir. 1969).

[127] *Id.* at 806.

[128] *Id.* at 806–07.

[129] *Id.* at 806. Subsequent decisions follow *Simon. See, e.g., In re* Haw. Corp., 567 F. Supp. 609, 617 (D. Haw. 1983) ("Compliance with GAAP and GAAS . . . will not immunize an accountant when he consciously chooses not to disclose on a financial statement a known material fact."); Siemens Info. Sys., Inc. v. TPI Enters., Inc., [1991–1992 Transfer Binder] Fed. Sec. L. Rep. (CCH) ¶ 96,573, at 92,659,

It is an open question whether a lawyer may be charged and convicted as a principal in a securities action under Section 10(b) for conduct similar to that in *Simon*. But *Simon* surely states standards that should also apply to lawyers.

Disclosure of derivatives transactions. Enron's financial disclosures did not reveal the magnitude of the risks associated with the huge derivatives business in which Enron was engaged. Did the auditors comply with SEC guidelines? Did the lawyers know that the disclosures failed to reveal their substantial effect on Enron's balance sheet, the risks involved, and other material facts? Are the lawyers responsible for a failure to disclose the underlying realities in a non-misleading manner?

Insider trading. Sales of Enron stock by Enron executives (and perhaps some in-house lawyers) while Enron's financial condition was deteriorating may present some insider-trading issues. What did Enron's lawyers know about these sales? Should they have done something? If so, what? A further complication is that some of the executives' selling may have been appropriate as part of a planned program of divestiture of stock held as compensation.

Conflict of interest problems. The conflicts of interest arising from Fastow's (and later Kopper's) dual roles in the LJM transactions pose serious problems for everyone who assisted or participated in those transactions. The conflicts were extraordinary; their effect on Enron's reported financial position was very large; enormous effort and casuistry was employed to conceal the compensation that Fastow, Kopper, and other LJM partners received; and the failure to comply with equity participation or other accounting requirements on some of the transactions ultimately led to public exposure of Enron's financial situation and its precipitous collapse. What did the inside and outside lawyers know about the details of the related-party transactions?[130] Did those

---

92,662 (S.D.N.Y. 1992), *available at* 1992 U.S. Dist. LEXIS 3018, at *14 (finding that conformity to GAAP is not enough; moreover, to avoid liability, full disclosure of any suspicions that are well founded is required); Fund of Funds, Ltd. v. Arthur Andersen & Co., 545 F. Supp. 1314, 1366 (S.D.N.Y. 1982) (rejecting accounting firm's argument that compliance with GAAP was "highly persuasive"; "the consensual, self-regulating accounting standards were not a substitute for the substantive standards under the securities laws," which require the accountant "to present a full and fair picture of its client's financial conduct"); United States v. Colasurdo, 453 F.2d 585, 594 (2d Cir. 1971) (finding that the fundamental question is not compliance with GAAP but one of "honesty and good faith").

[130] Information concerning the extensive participation of V&E in creating Enron's special purpose partnerships, providing true sale opinions concerning some of them, and advising and approving Enron's financial disclosures concerning them is contained in the POWERS REPORT, *supra* note 16, and Ellen Joan Pollock, *Limited Partners: Lawyers for Enron Faulted Its Deals, Didn't Force Issue*, WALL ST. J., May 22, 2002, at A1. The Pollock article provides the following details: one of the partners, Ronald Astin, raised conflict of interest objections to the participation of Enron employees (Fastow and Kopper) in managing and profiting from the JEDI and Chewco partnerships in 1997, but did not pursue the matter when Enron went ahead anyway. V&E also represented Enron in a series of off-balance-sheet transactions with the LJM partnerships in 1999, providing "true sale" opinions in some of them but declining to do so in others. For the latter, Enron had no difficulty in obtaining opinions from another firm, Andrews & Kurth. V&E also prepared the documents for Raptor transactions with LJM2, but Astin

lawyers give adequate advice concerning the transactions and the financial disclosures concerning them to top executives and to the board? Did the lawyers advise the adoption of procedures adequate to prevent breaches of fiduciary duty and subsequently monitor whether the procedures were being followed? Did they know that some of the procedures (such as Skilling's approval and signature) were not followed? Did the failure of inside and outside lawyers to pursue concerns or allegations of an inside lawyer (Mintz), Enron's treasurer (McMahon), and an accountant (Watkins) constitute negligence or worse?

3. The Newby Complaint

The lawsuit brought by Enron shareholders now includes most of the major participants in Enron's failure: officers, directors, law firms (V&E and K&E), accountants (Andersen), and seven investment banks.[131] The complaint charges that the two law firms were active participants in an ongoing fraud in which manipulative and deceptive devices that they created and approved were a central component. V&E, the complaint alleges, *inter alia,* participated in the fraudulent scheme by assisting in the structuring and documenting of fraudulent transactions that had no purpose other than to falsely misstate Enron's earnings; V&E also provided "true sale" opinions that enabled the related-party transactions to take place even though in some of them no property changed hands; and its "preliminary investigation" was part of the cover-up of the fraudulent scheme. K&E, the complaint alleges, participated in the fraudulent scheme by structuring the related-party transactions "to falsify Enron's financial condition."[132] V&E spoke directly to creditors and investors in the LJM transactions through legal opinions and to shareholders and investors by approval of financial statements concerning those transactions.

4. Conclusion

More guidance is needed concerning a lawyer's responsibilities under the securities laws. The continuing controversy, confusion, and uncertainty concerning a lawyer's duties in the various situations that arise in securities and client fraud situations such as Enron need clarification. Bar organizations tend to support the present state of

---

communicated his concerns about some of the deals to an Enron in-house lawyer, Rex Rogers; Astin was concerned because risks and rewards were not shifted from Enron to the partnerships. Opinions on some of those transactions were also obtained from Andrews & Kurth. V&E's concerns were not communicated to Enron's CEO, Lay, even though Reasoner, V&E's managing partner, had a close personal relationship with him, nor were the firm's concerns communicated to the Enron board. V&E also advised and approved Enron's decisions not to disclose in its 2001 proxy statement the compensation Fastow received from managing the partnerships. *Id.*

[131] Amended Compliant, Newby v. Enron Corp., No. H-01-3624 (S.D. Tex. filed Apr. 8, 2002).

[132] *Id.* at 447.

affairs because it permits them to maintain that lawyers have extremely limited or no obligations under current law in situations not subject to the "due diligence" requirement applicable to new offerings. The bar's position does not reflect the uncertainty of present law, which frequently results in large settlements and reputation loss whenever lawyers rely on it. The current situation is both unfair to lawyers and fails to give sufficient protection to the public interest in corporate integrity and honest markets.

PERSONAL OBSERVATIONS AND SUGGESTED REFORMS

The conduct of the inside and outside lawyers who represented Enron, Arthur Andersen, and the many financial institutions involved in the Enron scandal tell the same story that has been told to us by a long string of major financial frauds for fifty years: the professional ideal of "independent professional judgment" does not inform the behavior of some lawyers who represent large corporations in major transactions and high-stakes litigation. These lawyers take the position that they must do everything for the client that the client's managers want them to do, providing the conduct is permitted by law. The problem is that, by constantly going to the edge of the law and taking a very permissive view of what the law permits, these lawyers gradually adopt a mindset that ignores and may eventually assist the client's managers in illegality that harms third persons and the client entity.[133] These lawyers have confused the role of advocate in litigation or adversary negotiation with the need of corporate clients for independent, objective advice in the course of corporate decision-making. Current practices have resulted in a widespread problem, not just a failure of individual law firms.[134]

---

[133] *See, e.g.,* Geoffrey C. Hazard, Jr., *Lawyers and Client Fraud: They Still Don't Get It,* 6 GEO. J. L. ETHICS 701, 720 (1993) ("Responsible law-giving require[s] recognition . . . that honest lawyers can suffer the misfortune of having dishonest clients."). Lawyers representing such clients risk civil and criminal sanctions for aiding and abetting client fraud if the lawyers protect client confidences too zealously. Thus an honest lawyer "is at risk of being drawn into a transaction which is tainted with fraud . . . [and] can be charged with being an accessory to the client's wrongdoing . . . [Responsible law-giving] requires having no tears for clients who draw their lawyers into fraudulent schemes." *Id.* Responsible law-giving also involves heeding Brandeis's advice that lawyers in counseling clients and facilitating transactions should channel client conduct away from the precipice of illegality onto ground that is solid. *See supra* note 105.

[134] Law firms involved in major client fraud situations are identified by name in this Article to make it clear that many prestigious law firms have been the victims (and perhaps the aiders and abettors) of client fraud. It is not a "bad apples" problem, requiring greater vigilance on the part of prosecutors or regulators. There are systemic problems that require broader and more meaningful reforms. *See also* John C. Coffee, Jr., *Understanding Enron: "It's About the Gatekeepers, Stupid,"* 57 BUS. LAW. 1403 (2002) (arguing that the verification and certification functions of gatekeepers—accountants, analysts, and lawyers—failed to operate effectively because legal risks declined during the 1990s and changes in the provision of professional services created conflicts of interest that affected independent judgment). Implicit in Coffee's argument is the conclusion drawn here: professional advisers should be made more accountable to the law to deter them from acquiescing in managers' unlawful requests.

Lawyers rationalize their behavior by viewing others (the managers, the accountants, etc.) as responsible for the decisions that are made, largely ignoring their own responsibility. As potential disaster looms, those involved (managers, accountants, and lawyers) are faced with only bad choices and, cognitive psychology tells us, there is a strong tendency to take even greater risks in what turns out to be an unsuccessful effort to avoid financial failure and disclosure of the prior fraud.[135] A "circle of blame"—a classic form of deflection of responsibility—results when things predictably go wrong and each group of participants places the blame on the others.[136] When that occurs, it becomes likely that many of the major participants who are solvent and have assets (e.g., the outside law firm with substantial liability insurance coverage) will be forced eventually to make large settlements that partially recompense some of those who were harmed. This scenario played itself out hundreds of times during the savings and loan crisis and is already underway in the Enron affair.

For a variety of reasons, too many lawyers tend to believe that they are largely immune from legal liability when they turn a blind eye to signs that those who are in control of the client corporation are engaged in fraudulent conduct.[137] Applicable ethics rules, especially the exceptions to the professional duty of confidentiality and the rule dealing with steps to be taken when insiders themselves refuse to take steps to rectify a prospective or ongoing fraud, are controverted, ambiguous, and often discre-

---

[135] "Prospect theory" in cognitive psychology finds that decision-makers tend to be risk-averse when deciding between two choices that result in a gain, but risk-preferring when faced with two choices that result in a loss. Jeffrey Rachlinski has applied this theory to the framing of choices in litigation. *See* Jeffrey J. Rachlinski, *Gains, Losses, and the Psychology of Litigation,* 70 S. CAL. L. REV. 113 (1996). He and Richard Painter have applied the same approach to managers and lawyers faced with a decision whether to disclose or conceal information that, whatever they do, involves large risks of loss. Business and legal literature tend to confirm the hypothesis that managers and lawyers will be risk-preferring in this situation, opting for concealment of information rather than disclosure. *See* Richard W. Painter, *Lawyers' Rules, Auditors' Rules and the Psychology of Concealment,* 84 MINN. L. REV. 1399, 1413–24 (2000) (stating the theory and the literature and events that support it).

[136] The "circle of blame" among those involved in Enron transactions is also characteristic of lawyers' and judges' views concerning discovery abuse in high-stakes litigation. *See* Lawrence J. Fox et al., *Report: Ethics Beyond the Rules: Historical Preface,* 67 FORDHAM L. REV. 691, 695 (1998) ("each participant justifies his or her conduct, but savages the conduct of others"). Studies of business organizations reflect many of the same themes of diffused responsibility leading to no one accepting responsibility while attempting to maintain secrecy and then blaming others when secrecy is lost. *See, e.g.,* ROBERT JACKALL, MORAL MAZES: THE WORLD OF CORPORATE MANAGERS 17–22 (1988). Other studies reflect a theme found in the POWERS REPORT, *supra* note 16, that the ethical climate of an organization is set by the conduct of those in authority. *See* DIANE VAUGHAN, THE CHALLENGER LAUNCH DECISION: RISKY TECHNOLOGY, CULTURE, AND DEVIANCE AT NASA 405–09 (1996) (concluding that an organizational culture established at high levels and emphasizing production goals, often develops a normative environment that conflicts with that of the outside world, becoming a deviant culture).

[137] For discussion of the reasons why lawyers tend to believe they are immune from liability, see Susan P. Koniak, *Corporate Fraud: See, Lawyers,* 26 HARVARD J. PUB. POLICY 195 (2003).

tionary. Although courts have held that a lawyer is required to take some meaningful steps to prevent a future or ongoing fraud, the decisions are few, and only rarely apply effective sanctions to lawyers. Confused by the barrister's rule that the lawyer is not supposed to displace the judge or jury by "judging the client," lawyers apply the same approach to corporate actions in which one of their major functions is to determine whether the action meets legal standards. The managers, who hire and fire lawyers, rather than the corporate entity itself, become the client. The *Central Bank* case and the Private Securities Litigation Reform Act also give lawyers a false sense of security by suggesting that they are not accountable for assisting a securities fraud.

Preaching to lawyers and bar groups about their moral and public responsibilities has proven to be ineffective. Professional discipline, for a variety of reasons, provides virtually no control over the failure of law firms to monitor the partners who are bringing in juicy fees from corporate clients.[138] The spread of limited liability partnerships accentuates the willingness of partners to ignore the risks that other partners are taking. Today's emphasis on "the bottom line" both in corporations and law firms gives rise to a culture valuing the false sense of prestige and status that flows from being among the leaders in the annual listings of profits per partner. From the vantage point of respect for law and the public responsibilities of lawyers, the current scene runs the risk of being "a race to the bottom." As stated above, there is a systemic problem that requires systemic solutions.[139]

The ABA and major state bar organizations speak with divergent voices when engaged in formulating the ethics rules that should govern a lawyer in client fraud situations. Many lawyers, especially business and securities lawyers, argue that a lawyer should be at least permitted to disclose confidential information to prevent or rectify a

---

[138] Discipline of large firm corporate lawyers rarely occurs even in situations in which lawyers have been sanctioned by a court for misconduct or found civilly liable for assisting a client's fraud. As indicated previously, ethics rules applicable in client fraud are controverted, ambiguous, and often discretionary. Moreover, disciplinary authorities lack the resources and the will to charge large law firm lawyers with misconduct in matters that are complex and would require large effort. The occasional efforts to do so are attacked vigorously by the organized bar. For other reasons why professional discipline plays virtually no role in the regulation of lawyers engaged in specialized corporate practice in extensively regulated fields such as securities law, see Ted Schneyer, *From Self-Regulation to Bar Corporatism: What the S&L Crisis Means for the Regulation of Lawyers,* 35 S. TEX. L. REV. 639, 643–50 (1994); *see also* Koniak & Cramton, *supra* note 137.

[139] The blizzard of accounting and related scandals following Enron and Andersen suggests the breadth of the problem: Adelphia, CMS Energy, Dynegy, Merrill Lynch, Tyco, WorldCom, Xerox. "'Everybody did this,' says economic historian Peter Temin . . . 'The people who got in trouble are those who are most at the edge. Enron didn't get caught. Enron got so far out on the edge that it fell off.'" David Wessel, *Venal Sins: Why the Bad Guys of the Boardroom Emerged en Masse,* WALL ST. J., June 20, 2002, at, A1. Treasury Secretary O'Neill "recalls a parade of Wall Street professionals who came to his office with plans for 'new and exotic' financial maneuvers to reduce his company's tax bill or report debt levels in ways 'not clearly prohibited by the tax code or law,' but not designed to illuminate corporate operations, either." *Id.* "The remnants of a professional ethos in accounting, law and securities analysis gave way to getting the maximum revenue per partner." *Id.*

client fraud. They argue that the professional duty of confidentiality should include the same policy that the law has always applied to the attorney-client privilege: confidentiality evaporates when a client attempts to use the privilege to further a crime or fraud. This balance of confidentiality and the public interest in preventing crimes and frauds has been persuasive to most state courts in promulgating ethics rules.

But the ABA House of Delegates and some major jurisdictions (e.g., California and District of Columbia) have differed, concluding that client candor and adversary representation would suffer if a lawyer were permitted to disclose information to prevent or rectify crimes or frauds.[140] These voices oppose attempts to clarify the duties of lawyers who find themselves in client fraud situations. Some of the bar's apologies and evasions are:

- Lawyer liability will grow. (Why shouldn't lawyers be liable to third persons when they aid or assist a client in defrauding third persons?)
- The rules governing lawyers aren't clear. (Why should lawyers be entitled to more clarity than is provided to non-lawyers, who must deal all the time with uncertain rules in law, accounting, and elsewhere?)
- The lawyer's job is to provide zealous advocacy. (They are not acting as courtroom advocates but as office counselors who can assist only lawful transactions)
- "Everybody [is] doing it." (That may well be the case but since when does that excuse wrongdoing?)[141]

Many informed and able commentators argue that the Enron collapse should not provide the basis for any "reforms" that would affect lawyers and the legal profession. Some tinkering with the accounting rules may be desirable, but in all other respects things are just fine as they are.[142] The savings and loan crisis also led to some cries for reform, but the accounting and legal professions, usually supported by the corporate community, opposed the reforms. The result was legislation designed to deal with too much litigation against corporations and their advisers: enactment of limited-liability partnership statutes in virtually every state, and on the federal level, passage of the 1995 Act and other follow-up securities legislation. Professional advisers were given more protection from being accountable for their legal wrongs.

---

[140] The *ABA Preliminary Report, supra* note 7, is a happy exception. The Report treats the current scene as one requiring substantial improvements in the corporate governance process and major changes in the ethics rules governing lawyers.

[141] *See* William H. Simon, *The Kaye Scholer Affair: The Lawyer's Duty of Candor and the Bar's Temptations of Evasion and Apology,* 23 LAW & SOC. INQUIRY 243, 268–74 (1998) (discussing these and other apologies and evasions).

[142] *See, e.g.,* Thomas J. Donahue, Let the Market Do Its Work, NAT'L L.J., May 6, 2002, at A20, C. Evan Stewart, *Caveat "Reformers": Lessons Not To Be Learned from Enron's Collapse,* 34 SEC. REG. & L. REP. (BNA) 310 (Feb. 25, 2002).

I believe that the following reforms are needed to make lawyers more accountable guardians of the public trust, a goal that depends upon lawyers channeling conduct along lawful paths rather than looking the other way as their clients violate the law. We need more respect for the law on the part of all lawyers, not gradually accelerating disrespect.

Changes in Federal Law and Regulation

When the first draft of this Article was prepared in April 2002, one of its principal recommendations was that legislation should be adopted to give the SEC clear authority to regulate and discipline lawyers who assist clients in securities laws violations. At that time, I could not anticipate that such legislation would in fact be enacted. For many years, the accounting and legal professions, usually joined by the business community, have managed to block federal legislation that would provide the SEC with greater authority to regulate accountants and lawyers. The SEC, recognizing that political opposition to such regulation was affecting its staffing and funding, abandoned its earlier efforts to set some minimal standards for lawyers. In view of this background, I believed that a political whirlwind would be necessary to produce legislation explicitly authorizing the SEC to create standards of professional conduct applicable to lawyers engaged in securities law practice.

However unlikely it seemed in April 2002, that whirlwind came about some three months later. The storm aroused by Enron's collapse became a hurricane after the WorldCom bankruptcy and the corporate responsibility scandals at a number of other major companies. The political fallout of the public's concern resulted in the Sarbanes-Oxley Act ("Corporate Reform Act"),[143] which became law on July 30, 2002. The Corporate Reform Act made two major changes in the law governing lawyers. Section 307 of the Act, first, conferred a broad power on the SEC to establish rules of professional conduct for securities lawyers and, second, directed the SEC to issue a specific rule requiring a lawyer for a public company to climb the ladder of authority within the company, to the board of directors, if necessary, "to report evidence of a material violation of securities law or breach of fiduciary duty or similar violation by the company or any agent thereof . . . if the [chief legal] counsel or [chief executive] officer does not appropriately respond to the evidence [by] adopting, as necessary, appropriate remedial measures or sanctions with respect to the violation."[144]

---

[143] Pub. L. No. 107-204, 116 Stat. 745 (2002). The legislation was supported by a unanimous vote in the Senate and an overwhelming vote in the House. My discussion of section 307 of the Act has benefited from unpublished letters and e-mails of George Cohen, Richard Painter, and John Steele.

[144] Pub. L. No. 107-204 § 307, 116 Stat. at 745, 784. Section 307 of the Corporate Reform Act, entitled "Rules of Professional Responsibility for Attorneys," reads as follows:

Not later than 180 days after the date of enactment of this Act, the Commission shall issue rules, in the public interest and for the protection of investors, setting forth minimum standards of professional conduct for attorneys appearing and practicing before the Commission in any way in the representation of issuers, including a rule—

SEC AUTHORITY TO PROMULGATE RULES OF PROFESSIONAL CONDUCT FOR SECURITIES LAWYERS

The initial clause of Section 307 gives the SEC 180 days to "issue rules, in the public interest and for the protection of investors, setting forth minimum standards of professional conduct for attorneys appearing and practicing before the Commission in any way in the representation of [public companies]. . . ."[145] This grant of general rulemaking authority in the professional responsibility area is broad and mandatory. The phrase "minimum standards of professional conduct" characterizes all professional rules of conduct. The only constraints are the limitation to lawyers practicing federal securities law and the requirements that the rules serve the public interest and protect investors.

The provision transfers primary regulatory authority in this area of practice from the state courts that now promulgate the profession's ethics rules to the SEC. Securities lawyers will now be subject to discipline by the SEC for violations of the rules of conduct the Commission adopts. Because no preemptive intent is indicated, securities lawyers will remain subject to state disciplinary proceedings that are not inconsistent with the rules of professional conduct adopted by the SEC. The many questions that will arise concerning the scope of SEC authority, the manner in which the SEC promulgates and enforces the conduct rules, the effect of the new rules on state authority under the Supremacy Clause, and the like are important matters, but they are beyond the scope of this article.

How should the SEC approach this broad task during the limited time available (i.e., prior to January 26, 2003)? I believe that the SEC would be well-advised to start with a review of the ABA Model Rules of Professional Conduct, as amended in February 2002 in response to the recommendations of the Ethics 2000 Commission. That review should then determine which rules and topics should be made applicable to securities lawyers. The SEC's long experience in enforcing the securities laws in the interest of investors can inform judgments whether a particular aspect of securities law practice should lead to an SEC rule defining minimum professional conduct for securities lawyers. The rules relating to prohibited assistance, the professional duty of confidentiality, conflicts of interest, representing an entity, withdrawal, and probably other subjects should be studied and modified as necessary to meet the special require-

---

(1) requiring an attorney to report evidence of a material violation of securities law or breach of fiduciary duty or similar violation by the company or any agent thereof, to the chief legal counsel or the chief executive officer of the company (or the equivalent thereof); and

(2) if the counsel or officer does not appropriately respond to the evidence (adopting, as necessary, appropriate remedial measures or sanctions with respect to the violation), requiring the attorney to report the evidence to the audit committee of the board of directors . . . or to another committee of the board of directors comprised solely of directors not employed directly or indirectly by the issuer, or to the board of directors.

Id.

[145] *Id.*

ments of securities law practice. Rules having to do with subjects that do not directly relate to the special circumstances of securities practice (e.g., rules dealing with the economic regulation of the profession, unauthorized practice, and the provision of information about legal services) should be omitted from consideration.

In several important areas, the SEC should substitute its own judgment and that of the ABA Task Force on Corporate Responsibility for those of the ABA House of Delegates. The Corporate Reform Act requires that it do so with respect to Rule 1.13, representing an entity.[146] With respect to the rules relating to disclosure of confidential information to prevent or rectify a client's prospective or ongoing crime or fraud, the Task Force's recommendations, formed in the light of current problems and informed by broad knowledge of corporate and securities practice, should be substituted for the rules adopted by the House of Delegates in February 2002.

SEC RULE REQUIRING LAWYERS TO CLIMB THE CORPORATE LADDER

In addition to the required general rulemaking with respect to the professional conduct of securities lawyers, the SEC is directed to establish a rule within 180 days that will require securities lawyers to climb the ladder of authority within a public company "to report evidence of a material violation of securities law or breach of fiduciary duty or similar violation by the company or any agent thereof to the chief legal counsel or the chief executive officer of the company," and to the board or board committees if those officers do not take "appropriate remedial measures or sanctions."[147]

---

[146] *See id.;* MODEL RULES OF PROF'L CONDUCT R. 1.13 (2002).

[147] Pub. L. No. 107-204 § 307, 116 Stat. at 745, 784. The prior work and advocacy of two academic lawyers contributed substantially to the enactment of the Corporate Reform Act. Richard Painter initiated the matter by asking the ABA Ethics 2000 Commission to amend Rule 1.13 to require a lawyer to inform senior officers of the corporation of illegal acts for which the corporation could be held responsible. If those officers failed to take appropriate preventive measures, the lawyer should be required to report the matter to the board of directors or to an appropriate organ of the board, for example, the outside directors or the audit committee. *See* Painter, *supra* note 63, at 10–11 (discussing his proposed amendment to Rule 1.13). In 2001, Painter revised his proposal as an SEC regulation and obtained the support of about forty academic lawyers (including the author). *See* letter from Richard W. Painter, College of Law, University of Illinois at Urbana–Champaign, to Harvey Pitt, SEC, Chairman (Mar. 7, 2002) and response letter from David Becker, SEC, General Counsel, to Richard W. Painter, College of Law, University of Illinois at Urbana–Champaign (Mar. 28, 2002) (declining to consider the matter because of the legal profession's heated opposition to it and the SEC's lack of express legislative authority), *available at* http://www.abanet.org/buslaw/corporateresponsibility/responsibility_relatedmat.html.

Susan Koniak, who testified before a Senate committee considering the role of lawyers in the Enron affair, later worked with Senator Edwards and his staff on the rulemaking proposal that became section 307 of the Senate bill in mid-July. Senator Edwards, with Ms. Koniak's assistance, defended the provision in the Senate and in the conference committee against opposition fueled by the ABA. The provision survived, becoming law on July 30, 2002.

The breadth of the provision is notable: it applies to any "breach of fiduciary duty," issues that generally are viewed as matters of state corporate law unless federal law creates a fiduciary duty. The major qualification is that the violation must be a "material" one. Until the SEC provides more guidance, securities lawyers will have to make difficult judgment calls: When does a lawyer have sufficient "evidence" of a violation? What constitutes a "securities law violation," a "breach of fiduciary duty," or a "similar violation"? When is a violation "material"?[148]

The statutorily-prescribed rule clearly draws on the prior actions and decisions of the SEC. In essence, it is a version of the standard that the SEC has been pushing for years: in-house and outside counsel who become aware of facts strongly suggesting that an agent of a corporation is involved in securities fraud must take steps, designed to be effective, to ensure that the board understands what the lawyer has discovered and must take steps to encourage the board to take action to disclose to the SEC and investing public what it has discovered.[149]

Moreover, the new law clearly draws on the ethics rule now in effect in all or virtually all states. Model Rule 1.13 requires a corporate lawyer to act in the best interests of the corporation.[150] Many commentators interpret the rule as requiring a lawyer to climb the ladder of authority in the organization when the lawyer knows that the organization's managers are harming the organization (and third persons) by engaging in criminal or fraudulent conduct. The difference is that the new law clearly requires the lawyer to act in these extreme circumstances, while Rule 1.13 is ambiguous and can be construed as discretionary and permissive. In short, the new law provides clear and helpful guidance to lawyers.

Several objections to the new law should be discussed. First, the ABA and state bar organizations argue that the formulation of rules of professional conduct for lawyers has been and should be carried out by the high courts of the states and not by federal

---

[148] The generality of the statutory terms outlining the report requirement can be taken care of by good drafting on the part of the SEC. The major problems are the vagueness of "evidence" of a "material violation" and the absence of an intent standard. The SEC should make it clear that "evidence" does not refer to evidence rules concerning admissibility, but to "facts or circumstances that a lawyer, acting with reasonable care, knows or reasonably should know are credible and substantial evidence of a violation of federal securities law or breach of fiduciary duty or similar violation by the company or any agent thereof." Comments to the text of the report rule should make it clear that a duty of inquiry exists under some circumstances. The *ABA Preliminary Report, supra* note 7, at 208 n.49, relying on ABA ethics opinions, provides a useful statement of the facts or circumstances that give rise to a duty to investigate. *See supra* notes 58–59 and accompanying text.

[149] The court in the *National Student Marketing* case stated that the lawyers had a duty to take steps that would prevent the securities violation, which in that case might require informing shareholders if the officers and directors refused to act. 457 F. Supp. 682, 713 (D.D.C. 1978); *see In re* Carter & Johnson, SEC Release No. 34-17597, [1981 Transfer Binder] Fed. Sec. L. Rep. (CCH) ¶ 82,847, at 84,145 (Feb. 28, 1981); *In re* Gutfreund, Exchange Act Release No. 34-31554, [1992 Transfer Binder] Fed. Sec. L. Rep. (CCH) ¶ 85,067, at 83,597 (Dec. 3, 1992).

[150] MODEL RULES OF PROF'L CONDUCT R. 1.13 (2002).

regulation. The exclusion of the legislative process, both state and federal, leaves lawyers and their organizations more in control, resulting in more self-regulation than is given to any other profession. Self-regulation has many advantages, but falls short when the interests of the profession are put above those of the public. On the fundamental question of a lawyer's duty to prevent or rectify criminal or fraudulent conduct by a client or a client's agent, the ABA and a number of state bars have put the interests of the profession above those of the public. Federal legislation and regulation provide the best vehicle for needed change.

Moreover, the dispersion of authority to the high courts of the fifty states and the District of Columbia results in rules that are often conflicting and inevitably different. The ABA makes recommendations that are then filtered through bar groups in each state. The result, at least in every state with a large lawyer population, is a separate set of rules with some common characteristics but differing language. Conflicting requirements and lack of uniformity are especially frequent and most troublesome on the vital subject of a lawyer's obligations in dealing with the prevention and rectification of criminal and fraudulent client conduct, which is precisely the problem that Congress and the public are most concerned about.

The federal government has a strong interest in assuring the integrity of securities markets, and the role and conduct of accountants and lawyers are important components. Moreover, there is a long history of federal involvement in specialized areas of law, including patent law, tax law, securities law, and other fields. The further development of distinctive rules of professional conduct in various areas of practice may well be a desirable development in departing from the "one size fits all" approach of state ethics rules. The Commerce Clause clearly supports this federal involvement, which has the great benefit of providing lawyers in those areas of practice with clearer and more uniform standards.

The ABA, in opposing Section 307, urged that Congress should allow the process begun by the ABA Task Force to continue. But consider the problems. The Task Force arrived at a "preliminary" recommendation that Model Rule 1.13 be amended by the ABA to require lawyers to report to superior authority within the organization in situations similar to those dealt with in the federal legislation.[151] Even if the Task Force

---

[151] The ABA Task Force proposal would require the lawyer to report "that the officer or employee is acting illegally or fraudulently, or in breach of a duty to the corporation . . . [w]hen the lawyer knows or reasonably should know" of such activity. *ABA Preliminary Report, supra* note 7, at 204. The federal rule is triggered by the lawyer's possession of credible "evidence of a material violation of securities law or breach of fiduciary duty or similar violation by the company or any agent thereof. . . ." Sarbanes-Oxley Act of 2002, Pub. L. No. 107-204, § 307(1), 116 Stat. 745, 784. Both rules appear to reach all serious violations of law and the required element of knowledge or intent is similar. The major difference is that the federal rule is applicable only to "public companies" (about 17,000 corporations who are subject to SEC financial disclosure obligations) while the Task Force proposal would reach all entity organizations, public or private, profit or nonprofit.

persists in the recommendation, it is unclear whether the ABA House of Delegates will adopt the Task Force's sweeping recommendations concerning exceptions to confidentiality (Rules 1.6 and 4.1) and reporting within an organization (Rule 1.13). Similar recommendations were rejected by the House of Delegates during the past year as well as in 1991 and 1983. Even if the ABA adopted the Task Force's proposed amendments, that action would only begin a long and uncertain process in which fifty-one U.S. jurisdictions would consider whether and in what form to adopt the changes. The process would take years, and the results would probably be uneven and non-uniform. Federal regulation, on the other hand, will produce a uniform national rule by the end of this year.

Nor does the new "climb the ladder" rule involve a breach of confidentiality (i.e., disclosure not authorized by current ethics rules). The new rule is limited to disclosure within the client organization. The rule merely ensures that the superior officers or board of a public company will learn of information that is of vital importance to the company and be in a position to take corrective action. In short, the new rule overcomes the tendency of lawyers to treat the managers, with whom the lawyer deals day-to-day, as if they were "the client," rather than to follow the law in treating the corporate entity as the client. In short, the rule protects the interests of the real client.

Another objection is that the new rule will expose lawyers to greater civil liability and that the threat of liability will distort the lawyer-client relationship. Section 307 does not create any new private cause of action against lawyers who participate in corporate fraud. Existing law providing for malpractice liability to a client and, in some situations, liability to non-clients, will be unaffected. It is true that any new standard of professional conduct provides an opportunity in a malpractice or third-party liability situation for a showing that a lawyer has departed from customary standards. That would be true of the ABA Task Force recommendations as well as the new federal rule. But this risk must be weighed against the uncertainties of current law, which lead some lawyers to remain silent while corporate managers commit illegal acts that harm the corporation and third persons. Greater clarity about a lawyer's duties in these troublesome situations may well reduce the frequency of claims, rather than increase them, while protecting important interests of the economy and the public. And even if lawyer exposure to liability claims is increased somewhat, the trade-off in prevention of serious frauds on the public justifies that risk.

Whether the new rule will substantially affect the lawyer-client relationship is also highly speculative.[152] Some lawyers worry that corporate lawyers will be too self-protective and, as a result, will prematurely "jump the queue" straight to the board, thus undermining the chief legal officer or manager to whom the lawyer regularly reports. If so, candor and trust between outside counsel and those officers would be adversely affected. It seems more likely, however, that inside and outside counsel will allow the issue to percolate within the corporation in the customary manner until it is properly

---

[152] I am indebted to John Steele for the ideas in this paragraph.

resolved. The informal norms by which sensitive issues are handled within a corporation are extremely powerful; corporate lawyers will continue to respect them and will not go up the ladder prematurely. The report provision merely gives the outside lawyer some last-resort leverage that may ensure that the problem is properly resolved at an earlier stage without going to the board.

In sum, the new federal rule is a welcome, meaningful, prudent, and timely reform. The bar should embrace it rather than resist it. Thus, I am very pleased that Congressional action has deprived me of one of the reform recommendations for federal action that I included in my initial draft. Several other important matters, however, are left untouched by the Corporate Reform Act, and I now turn to them.

OTHER DESIRABLE CHANGES IN FEDERAL LAW AND REGULATION[153]

Restore a private right of action for aiding and abetting liability of professionals who assist a client in a securities fraud. The *Central Bank* case should be overruled by legislative action.[154] Congress should restore private causes of action against lawyers and accountants for aiding and abetting federal securities law violations. Since 1994, professional advisers can be held civilly liable for securities fraud only if they are central participants in a client's fraudulent scheme, that is, primary violators. Ethics rules placing limits on what a lawyer may do for a client are phrased in terms of a prohibition of "assisting" fraudulent or illegal conduct and state and federal law routinely provide for civil and criminal liability for someone who assists another in wrongdoing. The absence of civil liability for aiding and abetting the federal securities law puts pressure on courts to stretch the meaning of what constitutes a primary violation. The absence of a private cause of action for aiding and abetting securities fraud is an anomaly that should be corrected.

Apply the "recklessness" and "willful blindness" standards to govern intent (*scienter*) in proceedings against lawyers and accountants under the federal securities laws. Legislation overruling the *Central Bank* case should also provide that a uniform *scienter* standard of "recklessness" and "willful blindness" applies in all securities actions, whether they are civil or criminal, public or private. The standards that govern those who aid and abet a fraud in nearly all other contexts under federal and state law should apply also to lawyers and accountants, whether the action is brought by a federal prosecutor, the SEC, or by private plaintiffs.

Give the SEC clear authority to regulate and discipline lawyers who assist clients in securities laws violations. Section 307 of the Corporate Reform Act appears to remove the legal cloud that has long surrounded Rule 102(e), promulgated by the SEC to

---

[153] This section draws on conversations with Susan Koniak.

[154] *See supra* notes 121–23 and accompanying text.

discipline securities lawyers and accountants.[155] Its enactment, by giving the SEC express rulemaking authority to promulgate "minimum standards of professional conduct" for securities lawyers should make it clear that the SEC need not first secure a ruling from a federal district court affirming that the lawyer has violated the securities laws before proceeding against that lawyer via Rule 102(e).[156]

Provide the SEC with adequate funding to carry out existing and new responsibilities. The SEC has been underfunded for many years. Salaries of its professionals are much lower than those paid to professionals performing similar work in the private sector. Moreover, SEC professionals have been paid at a lower rate than that provided to federal government professionals who perform similar tasks. Finally, the SEC has been woefully understaffed in relation to current duties and cannot handle new ones without increased funding. The SEC should be provided with sufficient funds for all of its current responsibilities. In addition, funds should be provided to enforce the rules required under the Corporate Reform Act and enough funds to bring enforcement actions against lawyers and accountants who aid and abet securities fraud. The Department of Justice will also need additional funding if the new criminal provisions of the Act are to be anything other than window dressing.

Recent actions at the federal level have alleviated some of these concerns by increasing modestly the staffing and funding of the SEC. The long-term concern is whether political support for the SEC will continue several years from now when public attention will have shifted from issues of corporate responsibility.

---

[155] Rule 102(e) has been upheld as a valid exercise of the SEC's rule-making authority as to accountants, *see, e.g.,* Touche Ross & Co. v. SEC, 609 F.2d 570 (2d Cir. 1979), but I know of no similarly definitive rulings when it comes to the rule's application to lawyers. Moreover, the fact that, prior to the enactment of section 307, it was a rule and not a clear statutory mandate led courts to withhold deference from the SEC's interpretation of the rule and application. *Cf.* Checkosky v. SEC (In re Checkosky), 23 F.3d 452 (D.C. Cir. 1994); and especially, Checkosky v. SEC, 139 F.3d 221, 225 (D.C. Cir. 1998) (criticizing the SEC's straddling of the fence on whether negligence sufficed in a Rule 102(e) proceeding or whether recklessness was the standard for discipline). That matter, too, should be decided. Moreover, some modest discipline, a reprimand but not disbarment or suspension, should be provided on a finding of negligence. By definition, negligence is the first step on the road to recklessness, and it should be discouraged, at least when it comes to accountants, by the threat of SEC censure or reprimand.

[156] *See* Ann Maxey, *SEC Enforcement Actions Against Securities Lawyers: New Remedies vs. Old Policies,* 22 DEL. J. CORP. L. 537 (1997) (discussing the SEC's declaration that it would not use Rule 102(e) against lawyers without first seeking a court ruling that the lawyers had violated the securities laws). This declaration was one of many retreats the SEC has had to make over the years from its efforts to see to it that securities lawyers were not recklessly assisting fraud. For a description of some of that history of retreat and how aggressively the bar reacts to any attempt by the SEC to rein in reckless securities lawyers, see HAZARD, KONIAK & CRAMTON, *supra* note 1, at 117–39, 739–43; *see also* Susan P. Koniak, *The Law Between the Bar and the State,* 70 N.C. L. REV. 1389 (1992); Susan P. Koniak, *When Courts Refuse To Frame the Law and Others Frame It To Their Will,* 66 S. CAL. L. REV. 1075 (1993).

Changes in State Ethics Rules

In addition to reforms at the federal level, the high courts of the states need to amend their ethics codes to achieve the following goals: (1) provide nationwide uniformity on the important issue of exceptions to confidentiality, and (2) bring about conformity of state ethics rules with the emerging federal law on a corporate lawyer's duty to report law violations within a client organization.

Adoption by all states of an ethics rule providing an exception to the professional duty of confidentiality to prevent and rectify client fraud. As of 2001, forty-one U.S. jurisdictions permit or require a lawyer to disclose confidential information to prevent a client's proposed or ongoing criminal fraud. Most of these states, however, do not have provisions permitting the rectification of a fraud that involved the use of the lawyer's services. Despite its rejection in August 2001 by the ABA House of Delegates, the Ethics 2000 proposal contains a model that is worthy of adoption in all states. Proposed Model Rule 1.6(b) provides for both prevention and rectification:

> (b) A lawyer may reveal information relating to the representation of a client to the extent the lawyer reasonably believes necessary: . . .
> (2) to prevent the client from committing a crime or fraud that is reasonably certain to result in substantial injury to the financial interests or property of another and in furtherance of which the client has used or is using the lawyer's services;
> (3) to prevent, mitigate or rectify substantial injury to the financial interests or property of another that is reasonably certain to result or has resulted from the client's commission of a crime or fraud in furtherance of which the client has used the lawyer's service . . . .[157]

The ABA Task Force Preliminary Report "recommends that the House of Delegates reconsider and adopt these Ethics 2000 proposals[,]" quoting the rationale contained in the Ethics 2000 recommendation.[158] When a client seriously abuses the lawyer-client relationship by using the lawyer's services in furtherance of a crime or fraud, a lawyer should be permitted to reveal information to the extent necessary to prevent the client from committing a crime or fraud reasonably certain to result in substantial economic loss. "The client's entitlement [to confidentiality] must be balanced against the prevention of the injury that would otherwise be suffered and the interest of the lawyer in being able to prevent the misuse of the lawyer's services."[159]

---

[157] Proposed Model Rule 1.6(b), *available at* http:// www.abanet.org/cpr/e2k-rule16.htm (last visited Oct. 8, 2002).

[158] *ABA Preliminary Report, supra* note 7, at 205.

[159] *Id.*

The Task Force, however, goes further than did the Ethics 2000 Commission in recommending that the disclosure under Rule 1.6 be mandatory, rather than permissive, in order to prevent client conduct known to the lawyer to involve a crime, including violations of federal securities laws and regulations, in furtherance of which the client has used or is using the lawyer's services, and which is reasonably certain to result in substantial injury to the financial interests or property of another.[160]

The Preliminary Report also makes desirable recommendations for changes in the text or comments of Rules 1.2 and 4.1, which prohibit active participation in a client's criminal or fraudulent conduct. The Report argues that these provisions are overly restrictive in applying only if the lawyer "knows" that a person associated with an organization is engaging in or intends to engage in criminal or fraudulent conduct. Lawyers are encouraged to avoid knowing by "accepting management's instructions and limiting their advice and/or services to a narrowly defined scope, ignoring the context or implications of the advice they are giving."[161] Because some lawyers may "turn[] a blind eye to the natural consequences of what they observe and claim[] that they did not 'know' that the corporate officers they were advising were engaged in misconduct,"[162] Rules 1.2(d) and 4.1 should be amended to provide an intent standard of "knows or reasonably should know," which is defined in the Model Rules as denoting "that a lawyer of reasonable prudence and competence would ascertain the matter in question."[163] This recommendation should be adopted wholly apart from the question of whether disclosure to prevent crime and fraud is permissive or mandatory.

I prefer the stronger position of the ABA Preliminary Report on mandatory disclosure in certain instances,[164] but would be delighted if ABA support for either proposal would lead the ten holdout jurisdictions (including California, Delaware, and District of Columbia) to adopt a crime-fraud exception to confidentiality.[165] The more moderate permissive measure may have a better chance of adoption at the state level.

---

[160] *Id.* at 206.

[161] *Id.* at 207.

[162] *Id.*

[163] *Id.*

[164] The text of the ABA Task Force's preliminary recommendation concerning Rule 1.6 reads as follows:

Extend permissible disclosure under Rule 1.6 to reach conduct that has resulted or is reasonably certain to result in substantial injury to the financial interests or property of another [as recommended by the Ethics 2000 Commission], and [in addition] require disclosure under Rule 1.6 to prevent felonies or other serious crimes, including violations of the federal securities laws, where such misconduct is known to the lawyer.

Id. at 214.

[165] In California, despite many assertions that the duty of confidentiality is "absolute," the law is unclear. In the few states that have followed Rule 1.6 as recommended by the ABA (such as Delaware), a "noisy withdrawal" is permitted when the lawyer has issued an opinion or other document that may be withdrawn, providing a lawyer with an indirect opportunity to disclose confidential information.

Keeping a client's secrets is among the most important duties of a lawyer—a sacred trust. But the duty is not and has never been an absolute one. Historically, and in the vast majority of American states, the duty of confidentiality evaporates when a client abuses the attorney-client relationship by using the lawyer's services to further criminal or fraudulent activity. Disclosure to prevent future client fraud on a third person or rectify a past one involving use of the lawyer's services reflects the historic position of the legal profession, the prevailing rule in most states, and properly balances the lawyer's duty to the client with responsibilities owed to third persons and the public. The same principle limits the attorney-client privilege, which evaporates when the client is using the lawyer's services to further a crime or fraud. Moreover, it is shamelessly inconsistent for the profession to permit lawyers to disclose information to protect their own financial interests (e.g., collect a fee) while prohibiting them from doing so when clients, abusing the relationship, are defrauding third parties. The growing balkanization of American ethics rules would be stemmed by universal adoption of a single rule on this critical subject, which is vital to public trust in the legal profession's integrity and public responsibility.

Adoption by the states of an ethics rule requiring a lawyer for an organization to inform the organization's highest authority of the organization's pending or ongoing involvement in illegal conduct. As a general matter, the power to direct the management of the business and affairs of a corporation or other organization is vested in the board of directors, who can be held personally liable to the corporation for failing to prevent illegal conduct by the corporation's agents.[166] Given the potential risks to the corporation and to those responsible for its management, a lawyer should inform senior officers of the corporation of illegal acts for which the corporation could be held responsible. If those officers fail to take appropriate preventive measures, the lawyer should report the matter to the board of directors or to an appropriate organ of the board, for example, the outside directors or the audit committee. This course of conduct may be mandated by corporate law and is permissible under Model Rule 1.13. Moreover, as Richard Painter has said, "informing a client about the client's past or future violations of the law goes to the heart of the purpose of legal representation."[167] Consequently, lawyers should be required to climb the corporate ladder to protect the corporation from harm caused by its wrongdoing agents.

Model Rule 1.13, which is generally included in state ethics codes, should be amended in each state to require that a lawyer representing an organization report a prospective or ongoing illegal act that is likely to be committed by the organization or one of its agents to the board of directors or other highest authority authorized to act on behalf of the organization, once the appropriate official within the organization has been informed of the illegal act and has failed to take preventive measure.[168] Corporations

---

[166] *See, e.g., In re* Caremark Int'l Inc. Derivative Litig., 698 A.2d 959 (Del. Ch. 1996).

[167] Painter, *supra* note 63, at 10.

[168] *See ABA Preliminary Report, supra* note 7, at 214 (stating the ABA Task Force's recommendations).

would thus be provided greater protection and corporate directors would be given the information they need to protect themselves from personal liability. The proposed rule would also provide guidance to lawyers as to how, in a difficult situation, to uphold both the law and the entity client's interest.

In revising current Rule 1.13, the ABA and state high courts should give high priority to providing lawyers with language and substance that mirror the requirements the SEC will have in place in January 2003. Lawyers should not be faced with conflicting obligations even though the Supremacy Clause demands that the federal one be respected. Maximum guidance will come from national uniformity.

CONCLUSION

The stunning collapse of Enron, coupled with the large number of accounting irregularities and apparent corporate fraud, has created a climate in which reform and improvement of the law governing corporate lawyers is underway. The ABA Task Force on Corporate Responsibility has issued a preliminary report that recommends promising changes in the rules of professional conduct. And the Corporate Reform Act of 2002 has changed the landscape by authorizing the SEC to promulgate rules of professional conduct for securities lawyers and directing the SEC to issue a rule requiring securities lawyers to climb the corporate ladder to prevent or rectify a securities law violation by the corporation or a breach of fiduciary duty by a corporate employee. Some other reforms are also needed, especially a statutory overruling of the *Central Bank* decision, which eliminated private causes of action for aiding and abetting a securities fraud.

NOTES AND QUESTIONS

1. The SEC has called for a shift from rules-based accounting standards to principles-based accounting standards. Theoretically, with principles-based accounting standards, there would be many fewer "principles," phrased more broadly, and accountants would have to comply with the spirit of the principles, rather than the letter of the rules. Assume that you're an accountant who is faced with a situation in a grey area of one of these accounting principles. How would you go about determining whether you were in compliance with the spirit of the principles?

2. For lawyers, who are governed by the ethics rules of the state(s) in which they are licensed (and sometimes by other, special courts or agencies before which they appear), the "rules vs. standards" debate has played out, at least in part, by the shift from the Model Code of Professional Responsibility to the Model Rules of Professional Conduct. The Model Code had three components: the Canons (broad principles), the Disciplinary Rules (the part of the Model Code that was enforceable; the DRs set forth a minimum acceptable standard of conduct), and the Ethical Considerations (not enforceable in attorney discipline actions, the ECs

instead set forth aspirational goals). The tripartite structure of the Model Code—seen by some as too complex and disorganized—led to the Model Rules revision. The Model Rules had just two parts: the Rules themselves, which were enforceable, and comments to the Rules, which provided interpretations and explanations of the Rules. Most states have adopted a form of the Model Rules; a few states have hewed to the Model Code; and still other states have their own codes, which are based on neither model format.

Take a look at Canon 7 of the Model Code of Professional Responsibility: "A Lawyer Should Represent a Client Zealously Within the Bounds of the Law." Ignore the rather emphatic nature of the "initial caps" in the Canon, which *are* a bit distracting. Canon 7 is a classic example of a standard, rather than a rule. Standing alone—without either the ten accompanying DRs or thirty-nine accompanying ECs to flesh it out, how useful is Canon 7 as a guide? One of the ten DRs fleshing out Canon 7 is DR 7-102:

(A) In his representation of a client, a lawyer shall not:

     (1) File a suit, assert a position, conduct a defense, delay a trial, or take other action on behalf of his client when he knows or when it is obvious that such action would serve merely to harass or maliciously injure another.

     (2) Knowingly advance a claim or defense that is unwarranted under existing law, except that he may advance such claim or defense if it can be supported by good faith argument for an extension, modification, or reversal of existing law.

     (3) Conceal or knowingly fail to disclose that which he is required by law to reveal.

     (4) Knowingly use perjured testimony of false evidence.

     (5) Knowingly make a false statement of law or fact.

     (6) Participate in the creation or preservation of evidence when he knows or it is obvious that the evidence is false.

     (7) Counsel or assist his client in conduct that the lawyer knows to be illegal or fraudulent.

     (8) Knowingly engage in other illegal conduct or conduct contrary to a Disciplinary Rule.

(B) A lawyer who receives information clearly establishing that:

     (1) His client has, in the course of the representation, perpetrated a fraud upon a person or tribunal shall promptly call upon his client to rectify the same, and if his client refuses or is unable to do so, he shall reveal the fraud to the affected person or tribunal, except when the information is protected as a privileged communication.

     (2) A person other than his client has perpetrated a fraud upon a tribunal shall promptly reveal the fraud to the tribunal.

Brings the difference between a standard and a rule into rather sharp contrast, doesn't it? Now take a look at MRPC 3.1:

> A lawyer shall not bring or defend a proceeding, or assert or controvert an issue therein, unless there is a basis for doing so that is not frivolous, which includes a good faith argument for an extension, modification, or reversal of existing law. A lawyer for the defendant in a criminal proceeding, or the respondent in a proceeding that could result in incarceration, may nevertheless so defend the proceeding as to require that every element of the case be established.

If you're a transactional lawyer, how helpful is MCPR DR 7-102 to you? How might you rephrase it to cover transactions? What about MRPC 3.1? Which of the two rules—MCPR DR 7-102 or MRPC 3.1—is more helpful for a transactional lawyer? Is Canon 7 more helpful, or less helpful, than either of these rules?

3. At its August 2003 annual meeting, the American Bar Association adopted some changes to its Model Rules of Professional Conduct. The ABA amended Rule 1.6 (confidentiality) to permit, but not require, the lawyer to

> [r]eveal information relating to the representation of a client to the extent the lawyer reasonably believes necessary:
> . . . .
> (2) to prevent the client from committing a crime or fraud that is reasonably certain to result in *substantial injury to the financial interests or property of another* and in furtherance of which the client has used or is using the lawyer's services;
> (3) to prevent, mitigate or rectify *substantial injury to the financial interests or property of another* that is reasonably certain to result or has resulted from the client's commission of a crime or fraud in furtherance of which the client has used the lawyer's services . . . .[169]

This revision to Rule 1.6 marks the first time that the ABA was willing to extend the exceptions to confidentiality to include "substantial injury to the financial interests or property of another." Of course, Rule 1.6 only permits, and doesn't require, the lawyer to reveal this information.

The ABA also amended Rule 1.13 (organization as client) to require "up the ladder" reporting, "[u]nless the lawyer reasonably believes that it is not necessary in the best interest of the organization to do so." Furthermore, if the lawyer goes

---

[169] Model R. Prof'l Conduct R 1.6, *available at* http://www.abanet.org/cpr/ethics.html (last visited on Aug. 28, 2003) (emphasis added).

all the way "up the ladder" inside the organization (e.g., to a company's board of directors) and the organization doesn't address the problem, *and*

> (2) the lawyer reasonably believes that the violation is reasonably certain to result in injury to the organization, then the lawyer *may* reveal information relating to the representation whether or not Rule 1.6 permits such disclosure, but only if and to the extent the lawyer reasonably believes necessary to prevent substantial injury to the organization.[170]

Note that amended Rule 1.13(c)(2) is permissive, not mandatory.

What happens if the SEC decides to enact its original proposal, which would require "reporting out" to the SEC if the "up the ladder" reporting doesn't prevent or rectify a company's fraud?[171] Things could get downright ugly for those lawyers who hold law licenses in states that don't permit "noisy withdrawal" or other forms of "outside the organization" reporting. If the lawyer *doesn't* "report out" the appropriate information to the SEC, then she violates the SEC's rules and can find herself barred from practice before the SEC. If, however, she *does* comply with the SEC's rules, then she has violated her own state's ethics rules and can be subject to discipline by her state. Take a look at the diagram below to see this "rock and a hard place" dilemma:

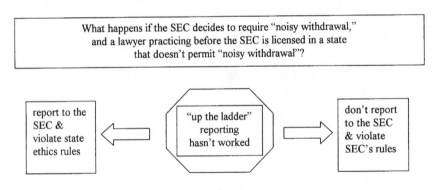

---

[170] *Id.* 1.13(c) (emphasis added).

[171] Currently, the SEC is not proposing such a rule. *See* SECURITIES AND EXCHANGE COMMISSION, PROPOSED RULE, IMPLEMENTATION OF STANDARDS OF PROFESSIONAL CONDUCT FOR ATTORNEYS, 17 C.F.R. Part 205, 240 and 249, Release Nos. 33-8186; 34-47282; IC-25920; File No. S7-45-02, *available at* http://www.sec.gov/rules/proposed/33-8186.htm (visited 8/29/03); *see also* SECURITIES AND EXCHANGE COMMISSION, FINAL RULE, IMPLEMENTATION OF STANDARDS OF PROFESSIONAL CONDUCT FOR ATTORNEYS, 17 C.F.R. Part 205, Release Nos. 33-8185; 34-47276; IC-25919; File No. S7-45-02, *available at* http://www.sec.gov/rules/proposed/33-8186.htm (visited 8/29/03) ("[W]e are also proposing and soliciting comment on an alternative procedure to the "noisy withdrawal" provisions. Under this proposed alternative, in the event that an attorney withdraws from representation of an issuer after failing to receive an appropriate response to reported evidence of a material violation, the issuer would be required to disclose its counsel's withdrawal to the Commission as a material event.").

Lest you think that we're making mountains out of molehills, we're not the only ones thinking about possible conflicts between SEC rules and state ethics rules. For example, the Washington State Bar Association "is warning its corporate lawyers not to disclose client information allowed by new Securities and Exchange Commission regulations unless such disclosures are also permitted by the state's own professional conduct rules."[172] This interim opinion by the Washington State Bar Board of Governors refers to permissive disclosures to the SEC, and not to mandatory disclosures.

What would happen to lawyers with a "national practice" if the SEC were to require certain disclosures that a state's ethics rules prohibit?[173] Let's assume that the lawyer holds a bar card in state *A*, which doesn't permit the lawyer to reveal "financial fraud," and in state *B*, which will discipline a lawyer for violating another state's ethics rules. A violation of state *A*'s rules may well create a chain-reaction of state discipline in state *B*, whether or not state *B*'s own ethics rules might have permitted the attorney to reveal financial fraud.

On the one hand, maybe we're making too much of this possibility. Lawyers aren't supposed to be complicit in crimes planned or committed by the client, and they may be able to withdraw before the situation becomes truly awful. On the other hand, there are still real ethics issues for lawyers. For instance, what about lawyers who are employed by the company (as "in-house" or "inside" counsel)? For them, "withdrawal" means "quitting."

In any event, the ABA's recent amendments to the Model Rules will give those states that want to adopt rules relating to financial fraud some guidelines for how they could draft those rules.

---

[172] Mark Hansen, ABA JOURNAL eREPORT, August 29, 2003, *available at* http://www.abanet.org/journal/ereport/au29sec.html (last visited Aug. 29, 2003). The Washington State Bar's Board of Governors said, in an interim informal opinion issued on July 26, 2003, that "'[i]t is the opinion of the board that, to the extent that this SEC regulation authorizes but does not require revelation of [a] client's confidences and secrets, the Washington lawyer cannot reveal such confidences and secrets unless authorized to do so under the Washington [rules of professional conduct].'" *Id.* (quoting *Interim Formal Ethics Opinion Re: The Effect of the SEC's Sarbanes-Oxley Regulations on Washington Attorneys' Obligations Under the RPCs*).

[173] Roger Cramton believes that a federal ethics rule, such as the one the SEC is implementing, will trump any state rule that conflicts with it. *See* email from Roger Cramton to Nancy Rapoport, dated Sept. 26, 2003 (on file with author). I (NBR) hate to disagree with such a talented colleague, but I'm not so sure that what Congress intended to have happen (with the SEC's rule trumping, per Sarbanes-Oxley) is necessarily what will happen. *infra.* Given some recent confusion in the United States Supreme Court's jurisprudence, it's possible that, even though the SEC may determine the rules for practice before it, a lawyer could still be disciplined for doing the "right" thing in front of the SEC but the "wrong" thing in terms of her state bar license. That's one of the reasons I'm in favor of specific "trumping" language in federal statutes that give lawyers a true safe harbor. *See, e.g.,* Nancy B. Rapoport, *The Intractable Problem of Bankruptcy Ethics: Square Peg, Round Hole*, 30 HOFSTRA L. REV. 977 (2002).

Lawyers, Ethics, and Enron

Deborah L. Rhode* & Paul D. Paton**

I. INTRODUCTION

The fall of Enron, once the seventh largest corporation in America, is more than the story of individual misconduct, greed, and deceit. As Senator Fred Thompson has rightly noted, "the real scandal here may be from not what is illegal, but what is totally permissible. . . . The system is clearly not designed with the interest of the general public or the investor in mind."[1] Enron and the other corporate scandals that have followed in its wake have focused new attention on longstanding problems, including inadequate disclosure obligations, conflicts of interest, offshore tax havens, and insider trading. All of these inquiries are essential for creating greater awareness of the structural features that permitted Enron and similar debacles to take place, and to ensure meaningful reform.[2]

Scrutiny of lawyers' conduct is equally critical. Too many members of the legal profession were part of the problem, rather than the solution. This essay seeks to understand why, and what might be done to address it. Only by more clearly identifying the limitations of the American bar's formal rules and informal practices can we develop an appropriate agenda for reform.

The stakes in clarifying these issues are self-evident. With the collapse of the former energy giant, more than 4,000 employees lost their jobs; thousands of investors also

---

* Ernest W. McFarland Professor of Law and Director, Keck Center on Legal Ethics and the Legal Profession, Stanford Law School. B.A. (Yale University), J.D. (Yale Law School).

** Fellow, Keck Center on Legal Ethics and the Legal Profession, and J.S.D Candidate, Stanford Law School. He is also a lawyer with PricewaterhouseCoopers LLP in Toronto, Canada. B.A. (University of Toronto), M.Phil (Cambridge), LL.B (Toronto), J.S.M (Stanford).

[1] *The Fall of Enron: How Could This Have Happened: Hearing Before the Committee on Governmental Affairs*, 107th Cong. (Jan. 24, 2002), (Statement of Sen. Fred Thompson, Senate Governmental Affairs Committee), *available at* http://www.senate.gov/~gov_affairs/012402thompson.htm (last accessed July 29, 2002).

[2] This chapter is adapted and updated from Deborah L. Rhode and Paul D. Paton, *Lawyers, Ethics and Enron*, 8 STAN. J. L. BUS. & FIN. 9 (2002).

lost their life savings, as "$70 billion in wealth vanished."[3] Confidence in corporate America plunged, and the stock market has yet to recover from the aftershock.[4] Arthur Andersen LLP ("Andersen"), one of the world's "Big Five" accounting firms, derived less than 1% of its business from Enron-related matters.[5] Yet the accounting firm imploded in less than a year when its other clients fled after public exposure of the firm's alleged role in the creation and misleading public reports of Enron investment structures. While Andersen's complicity in other corporate misconduct may have played a role, the firm's work for Enron was clearly a decisive factor. Any lingering doubts about its involvement dissipated following its June 2002 criminal conviction.[6] The wholescale abandonment of Andersen by its clients, though, occurred even before the Department of Justice successfully prosecuted Andersen for obstructing justice in the Securities and Exchange Commission's investigation of Enron.[7]

Given these events, it is not surprising that regulators, legislators, and commentators have focused most of their attention on accountants, managers, and boards of directors.[8] President Bush captured widespread sentiment in calling for "a new ethic of personal responsibility in the business community"; greater transparency in corporate accounting and corporate conduct; more accountability for chief executive officers and directors; and stricter enforcement of securities laws.[9]

Yet lawyers' roles and rules have received too little emphasis in the public debate. An otherwise comprehensive PBS website on Enron omits any discussion of attorneys in its identification of the story's "key players."[10] When Harvey Pitt, former Chairman of

---

[3] *Destruction of Enron-Related Documents by Andersen Personnel: Hearing Before the House of Representatives Committee on Energy*, 107th Cong. 1 (Jan. 24, 2002) (statement by James C. Greenwood, Chairman, House of Representatives Committee on Energy and Commerce, Subcommittee on Oversight and Investigations), *available at* http://www.access.gpo.gov/congress/house (last accessed July 30, 2002) [hereinafter *Andersen Hearing*] (the reference to $70 billion is to Enron's market capitalization in Aug. 2000).

[4] *See* CBS News, *Poll: Little Faith in Big Business*, (July 10, 2002), *available at* http://www.cbsnews.com/stories/2002/07/10/opinion/polls/main514732.shtml (last accessed Oct. 24, 2002).

[5] Floyd Norris, *Execution Before Trial for Andersen*, N.Y. TIMES, Mar. 15, 2002, at C1, C7.

[6] *See* BARBARA LEY TOFFLER WITH JENNIFER REINGOLD, FINAL ACCOUNTING: AMBITION, GREED AND THE FALL OF ARTHUR ANDERSEN (2003); Nancy B. Rapoport, *Enron, Titanic, and The Perfect Storm,* 71 FORDHAM L. REV. 1373 (2003)

[7] United States v. Arthur Andersen LLP, No. H-02-12 (S.D. Tex. March 7, 2002).

[8] Peronet Despeignes, *Enron's directors 'contributed to collapse',* FIN. TIMES, July 7, 2002, *available at* http://news.ft.com (last accessed July 12, 2002); *see also* Jeffrey N. Gordon, *What Enron Means for the Management and Control of the Modern Business Corporation: Some Initial Reflections,* 69 U. CHI. L. REV. 1233 (2002).

[9] President George W. Bush, *President Announces Tough New Enforcement Initiatives for Reform, Remarks on Corporate Responsibility* (July 9, 2002) (transcript available at http://www.whitehouse.gov/news/releases/2002/07/print/20020709-4.html) (last accessed July 12, 2002); *see also* Richard W. Stevenson & Elisabeth Bumiller, *Parties Jousting Over Wrongdoing by U.S. Businesses*, N.Y. TIMES, July 8, 2002, at A1, A14.

[10] *See* http://www.pbs.org/newshour/bb/business/enron/players.html (last accessed March 4, 2003).

the Securities and Exchange Commission, offered the *Wall Street Journal* an op-ed optimistically titled "How to Prevent Future Enrons" two months after the scandal first erupted, he made no mention of the legal profession. His critique of self-regulation referred only to accountants.[11] Although some of his later comments focused on lawyers, they have assumed only a walk-on role in much of the policy discussion.[12] Such marginal coverage is a missed opportunity. Meaningful reform requires a better understanding of lawyers' contributions to recent corporate misconduct and the structural incentives that affected their actions.[13]

In our view, Enron and the corporate scandals that have followed present an occasion for lawyers to profit from experience, and not just in the extraordinarily handsome financial way that many have already done. In the first four months of the Enron bankruptcy, one dozen law firms reportedly pocketed nearly $64 million in fees and expenses, with hourly rates as high as $900; one firm, Weil Gotshal, billed more than 50,000 attorney hours.[14] Eight months later, estimates put professional fees at $1 million or more *per day*.[15] This essay is a step in another, and more necessary, direction. Although its focus is on the roles played by in-house counsel for Enron and Andersen, as well as Enron's largest outside legal advisor, the law firm of Vinson & Elkins LLP ("Vinson & Elkins"), the point is not to pass judgment on whether these lawyers violated any statutory requirements or ethical rules. The facts have not yet been fully

---

[11] Harvey L. Pitt, *How to Prevent Future Enrons*, WALL ST. J., Dec. 11, 2001, *available at* http://www.sec.gov/news/speech/spch530.htm (last accessed July 29, 2002).

[12] Harvey L. Pitt, *Remarks Before the Annual Meeting of the American Bar Association's Business Law Section* (Aug. 12, 2002) (transcript available at http://www.sec.gov/news/speech/spch579.htm.)

[13] Select reports in the *Wall Street Journal,* the *New York Times,* and the *Washington Post* paid increasing attention to lawyers: *see* John Schwartz, *Questions From Congress for Enron's Law Firm*, N.Y. TIMES, March 12, 2002, at C1; John Schwartz, *Enron's Many Strands: The Lawyers, Troubling Questions Ahead for Enron's Law Firm*, N.Y. TIMES, March 12, 2002, at C1; Michael Orey and Richard B. Schmitt, *Enron Entangles Lawyers*, WALL ST. J., May 8, 2002, at B1, B4; Michael Orey, *Launching Broadsides at the Bar*, WALL ST. J., May 8, 2002, at B1; and a five-part series in the *Washington Post,* particularly Peter Behr and April Witt, *Concerns Grow Amid Conflicts*, WASH. POST, July 30, 2002, at A01; April Witt & Peter Behr, *Losses, Conflicts Threaten Survival*, WASH. POST, July 31, 2002, at A01; and the various reports on Nancy Temple of Arthur Andersen, and on Vinson & Elkins LLP, *infra* text accompanying notes 44–47, 67, 72–75; *see also* Susan Koniak, *Who Gave Lawyers a Pass? We Haven't Blamed the Real Culprits in Corporate Scandals,* FORBES, August 12, 2002, at S8. Later revelations brought lawyer conduct increasing attention, *see* Otis Bilodeau, *Enron Report Casts Harsh Light on Lawyers*, LEGAL TIMES, Sept. 30, 2002, *available at* www.law.com; Kurt Eichenwald, *The Findings Against Enron*, N.Y. TIMES, Sept. 23, 2002, *available at* www.nytimes.com; Mike France, *What About the Lawyers?*, BUS. WEEK, December 23, 2002, at 58. See also the discussion of Section 307 of Sarbanes-Oxley and the subsequent SEC rule-making on attorney conduct, *infra*, Part IV-B.

[14] Lisa Stansky, *Enron Fees: $64 Million—So Far*, NAT'L L.J., July 8, 2002, at A1, A12.

[15] Andrew Hill, *Creditors angry over errors in Enron fees: U.S. $1M a day 'outrageous': Committee wants legal, accounting bills slashed*, FIN. POST, December 2, 2002, at FP2.

established, and many other opportunities will be available to evaluate liability.[16] But enough information is now part of the public record to assess whether the rules and incentives governing lawyer behavior were up to the task. Vinson & Elkins senior partner, Harry M. Reasoner, maintains that his firm "honored its professional obligations."[17] If that proves to be so, or if many lawyers share such assessments, such views of themselves suggest problems in bar standards and the legal culture that sustains them.

So, too, the Enron case history is an opportunity to consider signposts in what should be a broader debate over professional accountability. One key question often overlooked is whether self-regulation is part of the problem.[18] Greater attention should focus on the structure, as well as the substance of, bar oversight. Where should the balance be struck between candor and confidentiality? And who should decide?

Some significant progress on that issue is already apparent. The Sarbanes-Oxley Act of 2002 ("Sarbanes-Oxley"), which cleared the House of Representatives by a vote of 423-3 and which cleared the Senate by a 99-0 vote a few hours later, included a provision that obligates lawyers to report corporate fraud, and new rules that would require the SEC to establish "minimum standards of professional conduct" for the lawyers who practice before the Commission.[19] These features of the legislation aroused little public debate or controversy at the time and passed despite strong opposition from the American Bar Association ("ABA").[20] Sarbanes-Oxley also obligates lawyers to report "evidence of a material violation of securities law or breach of fiduciary duty," first to a company's general counsel, then to its CEO, and ultimately to its board of directors.[21] The statute also provides greater protection for whistleblowers and directs the SEC to adopt rules to interpret and implement this legislation. The bar's resistance to

---

[16] Civil lawsuits in Texas with respect to the liability of Vinson & Elkins LLP allege civil conspiracy and fraudulent conduct by the law firm. *See*, inter alia, the pleadings in *In re* Enron Corp. Securities Litigation, Newby v. Enron Corp., No. 01-3624, (S.D. Tex. 2002); Wilt v. Fastow, No. H-02-576 (U.S. District Court, S.D. Tex.).

[17] Schwartz, *supra* note 13.

[18] That possibility has been raised for well over two decades. *See* DEBORAH L. RHODE, IN THE INTERESTS OF JUSTICE: REFORMING THE LEGAL PROFESSION (2000) [hereinafter RHODE, REFORMING THE LEGAL PROFESSION]; Deborah L. Rhode, *Why the ABA Bothers: A Functional Perspective on Professional Codes*, 59 TEX. L. REV. 689 (1981).

[19] Sarbanes-Oxley Act of 2002, H.R. 3763, 107th Cong. (2002); These features originally appeared in a Senate bill, Public Company Accounting Reform and Investor Protection Act of 2002 (S. 2673); the counterpart reform bill approved by the House of Representatives in April 2002 (H.R. 3763) contained no comparable provision. *See also Senate Passes Amendment to Accounting Bill Requiring Corporate Lawyers to Report Fraud*, 18 (15) ABA/BNA LAWYERS' MANUAL ON PROFESSIONAL CONDUCT 433, July 17, 2002; Richard B. Schmitt, *Lawyers Pressed To Report Fraud Under New Law*, WALL ST. J., July 25, 2002, at B1, B4.

[20] Lisa Girion, *Corporate Reform Bill A Defeat for Bar Assn.*, L.A. TIMES, July 26, 2002, C1, C4; Stephanie Francis Cahill, *Task Force Has Take on Lawyers' Responsibility*, ABA JOURNAL EREPORT, Aug. 2, 2002, *available at* http://www.abanet.org/journal/ereport/au2task.html (last accessed Aug. 6, 2002).

[21] Jonathan D. Glater, *Round Up the Usual Suspects. Lawyers Too?* N.Y. TIMES, Aug. 4, 2002, 3.4; Stephanie Francis Cahill, *Corporate-Fraud Law Forces Lawyers to be Whistle-Blowers*, ABA JOURNAL EREPORT, Aug. 2, 2002, *available at* http://www.abanet.org/journal/ereport/au2corp.html.

these regulatory initiatives reflects a disturbing gap between professional interests and societal values.[22]

The following discussion explores the need for greater public accountability for professional conduct, and key areas for reform. After a brief overview of the relevant facts, analysis focuses on the role of lawyers working for Enron, for its outside law firms, and for Arthur Andersen. Discussion then turns to the formal rules and informal structures that shaped the attorneys' conduct, and the regulatory strategies necessary to address it. A final section focuses on the role of professional education across the disciplines in promoting higher ethical standards and the structures needed to sustain them.

II. THE FACTUAL BACKDROP

Despite the risks of oversimplifying an extraordinarily complex saga, a brief summary of key facts is necessary to understand the role of lawyers involved with Enron.[23] The company was formed in 1985 from a merger of Houston Natural Gas and Internorth. This merger created America's first nationwide natural gas pipeline network. Over time, the firm's business focus shifted from regulated transportation of natural gas to energy trading in an increasingly deregulated environment. During this evolution, top management ventured away from traditional approaches to the core business in order to generate higher financial returns.[24] According to a Congressional Research Service Report, "[t]he guiding principle seems to have been that there was more money to be made in buying and selling financial contracts linked to the value of energy assets (and to other economic variables) than in the actual ownership of physical assets."[25]

A Special Investigation Committee of Enron's Board of Directors (the "Powers Committee") was established in late October 2001 as the scandal was nearing the height of public exposure. Chaired by University of Texas School of Law Dean William Powers, Jr., the Committee concluded in its February 2002 report (the "Powers Report") that as financial problems arose in operations outside its core energy business, Enron had used Special Purpose Entities ("SPEs") or Special Purpose Vehicles ("SPVs") and off-balance-sheet partnerships to enter into transactions generally considered too risky or controversial for ordinary commercial entities. These SPEs and partnerships were not

---

[22] See the discussion of Section 307 of Sarbanes Oxley and the SEC Rule "Implementation of Standards of Professional Conduct for Attorneys," in Part IV-B, *infra*.

[23] *See* J. Michael Anderson, *Enron: A Select Chronology of Congressional, Corporate and Government Activities*, C.R.S. Report for Congress, Apr. 9, 2002 [hereinafter *CRS Chronology*].

[24] William C. Powers, *Report of Investigation by the Special Investigative Committee of the Board of Directors of Enron Corp.*, Feb. 1, 2002, at 36 [hereinafter *Powers Report*].

[25] Mark Jickling, CONGRESSIONAL RESEARCH SERVICE, THE ENRON COLLAPSE: AN OVERVIEW OF FINANCIAL ISSUES 1 (March 28, 2002).

consolidated with Enron's other activities on Enron's financial statements; as a result, Enron's significant losses and debts could be concealed from public disclosure.[26]

In hindsight, the rules governing accounting treatment of SPEs have become a key issue, underscoring the need for unbiased professional judgment by lawyers as well as by accountants.[27] For certain SPE partnerships, Financial Accounting Standards Board ("FASB") rules did not require consolidation of the SPE's financial statements with the financial statements of the corporation that established it as long as an independent third party invested as little as 3% of the SPE's capital and the third-party investment was genuinely at risk.[28] There was also no generally accepted definition of SPEs; they could take any legal form, including that of partnership, corporation, or trust. In determining whether an entity was an SPE, FASB staff focused on whether the entity's power and activities were significantly limited by its charter or other contractual arrangement.[29] This determination was important because the accounts for a properly constituted SPE would not have to be consolidated on Enron's balance sheet. On the other hand, if the entity was not an SPE, the accounts would need to be included in the corporation's financial statements.

Public corporations like Enron must comply not only with FASB requirements for generally accepted accounting practices, but also with SEC disclosure rules.[30] Whether

---

[26] *Powers Report, supra,* note 24, at 4–5, 15–16, 37.

[27] For a lengthy and detailed discussion of selected SPE transactions, see Neal Batson, Court-Appointed Examiner, First Interim Report: *In re* Enron Corp., Case No. 01-16034 (Bankr. S.D.N.Y. Filed Sept. 21, 2002) [hereinafter Batson Report] at 22–156.

[28] Jickling, *supra* note 25, at 3; *see also* United States v. Kopper, No. H-02-0560, at paragraphs 3–6 (S.D. Tex., filed Aug. 20, 2002) (discussing Enron's use of SPEs); Kurt Eichenwald, *The Findings Against Enron,* N.Y. TIMES, Sept. 23, 2002. For a more general discussion of off-balance-sheet accounting principles, see Peter Jeffrey, *International Harmonization of Accounting Standards, and the Question of Off-Balance Sheet Treatment,* 12 DUKE J. COMP. & INT'L. L. 341 nn. 1–2 (2002). On the role of F.A.S.B., see Edmund L. Jenkins, Chairman, Financial Accounting Standards Board, Prepared Remarks, Testimony before the Subcommittee on Commerce, Trade and Consumer Protection of the Committee on Energy and Commerce (Feb. 14, 2002) (available at http://www.fasb.org/news/remarks.pdf); *see also* Edmund L. Jenkins, Chairman, Financial Accounting Standards Board, Testimony Before the Subcommittee on Commerce, Trade and Consumer Protection of the Committee on Energy and Commerce (June 26, 2002) (*available at* http://www.fasb.org/news/6-26-02_testimony.pdf).

[29] *Powers Report, supra* note 24, at 20.

[30] *See, e.g.,* 17 C.F.R. §§ 210.2, 210.3, 210.4–08, 240.10b-5 (2001). For a recent discussion of SEC disclosure requirements, see William F. Dietrich, *Legal and Ethical Issues for Attorneys Dealing with Financial Data: Heightened Scrutiny after the Enron and Andersen Debacle,* 1325 PRACTISING L. INST. 925, at 940–944 (2002); *see also* Press Release, SEC, Proposed Rule: Disclosure in Management's Discussion and Analysis about the Application of Critical Accounting Policies (*available at* http://www.sec.gov/rules/proposed/33-8098.htm). For a consideration of the relationship between SEC and F.A.S.B. Rules, see Robert K. Herdman, Chief Accountant, SEC, *Testimony Before the Subcommittee on Commerce, Trade and Consumer Protection, Committee on Energy and Commerce: Are Current Financial Accounting Standards Protecting Investors?* (2002) *in* 1324 PRACTISING L. INST. 695.

Enron's SPEs should have been consolidated, and whether they ought to have been disclosed, were not only accounting issues but also key legal questions. For answers, Enron relied on assistance not only from accountants and auditors at Andersen, but also from its in-house lawyers and outside counsel at Vinson & Elkins. These attorneys all played an important role in the process of drafting and certifying disclosure statements, and in advising whether the legal and accounting requirements governing SPEs and SPVs had been met.[31]

The Powers Report noted that, in some cases, transactions were designed specifically for the results they would produce on financial statements, not for legitimate economic objectives. Nor were the transactions adequately disclosed. Further, even though Enron's public filings revealed the existence of Enron's transactions with the partnerships, "the disclosures were obtuse, did not communicate the essence of the transactions completely or clearly, and failed to convey the substance of what was going on between Enron and the partnerships."[32] Other transactions were used to offset investment losses and to create the appearance that the investments had been "hedged" against risk of loss by a third party, even though Enron was the only investor with a significant financial stake in the third party. In effect, it was "hedging" against itself and thus still liable for the losses. As the Powers Report later concluded, these transactions "appear to have been designed to circumvent accounting rules by recording hedging gains to offset losses . . . in the value of merchant investments on Enron's quarterly and annual income statements. The economic reality of these transactions was that Enron never escaped the risk of loss, because it had provided the bulk of the capital with which the SPEs would pay Enron."[33] As the value of the merchant investments continued to fall in 2001, credit problems in SPE entities meant that they could no longer pay Enron on the "hedges." The SPEs were terminated in September 2001, resulting in a surprise announcement that was the first public disclosure even hinting at the severity of the problems.[34]

This announcement came on October 16, 2001, and marked the beginning of formal confirmations that matters had gone awry. Enron confirmed that it was taking a $544 million after-tax charge against earnings related to transactions with an investment partnership created and managed by Andrew Fastow, Enron's former Executive Vice President and Chief Financial Officer, and by other Enron employees who worked with Fastow. About a month later, on November 8, 2001, Enron announced in an SEC filing that it was restating its financial statements for the years 1997 through 2001 because of "accounting errors relating to transactions with a different Fastow partnership . . . and an additional related-party entity." The restatements reduced Enron's reported net income by a total of $1.5 billion, reduced reported shareholder equity by

---

[31] *Powers Report, supra*, note 24, at 17, 25–26.

[32] *Id.* at 17.

[33] *Id.* at 14.

[34] *Id.* at 13–14.

over \$2 billion, and shattered the confidence of the market and investors in the company. In November, Enron also revealed for the first time that it had learned that Fastow had received more than \$30 million from two of the partnerships; other Enron employees involved in the partnerships had been enriched at Enron's expense "in the aggregate, by tens of millions of dollars they should not have received."[35] On November 28, 2001, major bond rating agencies downgraded Enron's debt to junk bond status. The company filed for chapter 11 bankruptcy on December 2, 2001.

In the year following the collapse, investigations of Enron-related criminal conduct resulted in three criminal indictments. In June 2002, a Texas jury convicted Andersen of federal charges of obstruction of justice.[36] In August 2002, Michael Kopper, an Enron employee working for the company's Chief Financial Officer between 1994 and July 2001, pled guilty to conspiracy to commit wire fraud and money laundering.[37] Under the terms of a Cooperation Agreement, Kopper admitted participating in a scheme to secretly use the SPEs to defraud Enron for his own financial benefit. On October 1, 2002, the Justice Department charged Enron's former Chief Financial Officer, Andrew Fastow, with securities fraud, money laundering, mail fraud, wire fraud, bank fraud, and conspiracy related to secret deals he allegedly made with the company for his own financial benefit.[38] Press reports have suggested that the First Interim Report of the Court-Appointed Examiner in Enron's bankruptcy proceedings, filed on September 21, 2002, provides "possible signals" for further criminal charges.[39] And in December 2002, a Congressional Committee urged federal prosecutors to pursue charges against Nancy Temple, Andersen's in-house counsel, based on her allegedly false testimony before Congress concerning Andersen's conduct in Enron matters.[40]

---

[35] *Id.* at 16.

[36] United States v. Andersen, Indictment No. H-02-121 (S.D. Tex., filed March 7, 2002). See the discussion of the jury's findings, *infra* text accompanying notes 80–84; *see also Arthur Andersen Verdict Upheld*, AP ONLINE, Sept. 13, 2002; Michael Hedges, *The Fall of Enron*, HOUS. CHRON., Aug. 1, 2002 at 3 (discussing generally the Andersen appeal).

[37] United States v. Kopper, No. H-02-0560 (S.D. Tex., filed Aug. 20, 2002); United States v. Kopper, Cooperation Agreement, No. H-02-0560 (S.D. Tex., filed Aug. 21, 2002).

[38] United States v. Fastow, No. H-02-0889-M (S.D. Tex. Filed Oct. 1, 2002); *see also* Securities and Exchange Commission v. Fastow (S.D. Tex. Filed Oct. 2, 2002), *available at* http://news.findlaw.com/hdocs/docs/enron/secfastow100202cmp.pdf. Larry Thompson, Dep. Att'y Gen., U.S. D.O.J., News Conference (Oct. 2, 2002) (transcript *available at* http://www.usdoj.gov/dag/speech/2002/100202dagnewsconferencefastow.htm) (last accessed Oct. 3, 2002); Kurt Eichenwald, *An Ex-Official Faces Charges in Enron Deals*, N.Y. TIMES, Oct. 3, 2002, *available at* http://www.nytimes.com/2002/10/03/business/03ENRO.html.

[39] *See* Batson Report, *supra* note 27; Kurt Eichenwald, *The Findings Against Enron*, N.Y. TIMES, Sept. 23, 2002 at 1; *see also* Eric Berger and Tom Fowler, *Enron Masked Loans As Sales, Report Says*, HOUS. CHRON., Sept. 22, 2002, *available at* http://www.chron.com/cs/CDA/printstory.hts/special/enron/158546 (last accessed Oct. 4, 2002).

[40] Greg Burns, *Panel says Andersen lawyer lied*, CHI. TRIB., Dec. 18, 2002 at 1; *see also* the discussion of Temple's actions in Part III-C, *infra*.

III. THE ROLE OF THE LAWYERS

On the basis of the facts now publicly available, lawyers' activities in three contexts merit particular attention. The actions of Enron's in-house counsel, Enron's primary outside counsel, Vinson & Elkins, and Andersen's in-house counsel all raise important concerns.

A. Enron's In-House Counsel

The role of Enron's in-house counsel in structuring critical transactions and advising the firm on disclosure requirements reflects longstanding issues about conflicts of interest and professional independence. The Powers Report's detailed references to these lawyers make clear their integral contribution to the creation and operation of the various partnerships and SPEs; to the negotiations between Enron and the partnership entities; and to the preparation of related-party proxy disclosure statements. In assessing that conduct, the Report criticized "an absence of forceful and effective oversight by Senior Enron Management and in-house counsel" in the failure to disclose meaningful information about the SPEs and the essential nature of the transactions in issue.[41]

Of still greater concern was the Powers Report's finding that one of the company's in-house lawyers, Kristina Mordaunt, not only gave advice on the SPE transactions, but also invested her own money in one of the entities. She did so without obtaining the consent of Enron's Chairman and CEO, in violation of Enron's Code of Conduct.[42] Mordaunt reportedly received $1 million in return for a $5,800 investment.[43] That investment may also have violated bar disciplinary rules concerning conflicts of interest.[44] The Powers Report itself notes, though, that Mordaunt later admitted that her participation in the SPE was an error in judgment and that "she did not consider the issue carefully enough at the time."[45]

By contrast, at least two Enron attorneys had serious concerns about the company's financial conduct, but were stymied by other Enron lawyers or managers in efforts to respond. A case in point involves a September 2000 memo by an Enron North America attorney expressing concern about the possibility that "the financial books at Enron are being 'cooked' in order to eliminate a drag on earnings that would otherwise occur under fair value accounting."[46] More senior attorneys who received the memo did not

---

[41] *Powers Report, supra* note 24, at 17.

[42] *Id.* at 92–96.

[43] Witt & Behr, *supra* note 13; *see also* Mike France, *supra* note 13, at 59.

[44] *See* AMERICAN BAR ASSOCIATION, MODEL RULES OF PROFESSIONAL CONDUCT Rule 1.7(b), Comment 6; Rule 1.8(a) (2001).

[45] *Powers Report, supra* note 24, at 94.

[46] *Powers Report, supra* note 24, at 109; *see also* April Witt & Peter Behr, *Dream Job Turns Into a Nightmare*, WASH. POST, July 29, 2002, at A01.

believe the factual assertions on which the memo's conclusions were based, but conducted no investigation to verify their belief and took no further action. A second example involves an Enron attorney who reportedly asked the law firm of Fried Frank Harris Shriver & Jacobsen to review the legality of the partnerships and SPEs. After Fried Frank recommended that Enron halt the practice of using such structures, the Enron attorney sent written internal memoranda to company executives to the same effect.[47] The failure by more senior counsel and by Enron executives to follow such advice, or to investigate its factual basis, suggests greater problems with the corporate culture—one that prized aggressive behavior, put a premium on risk, and "valued appealing lies over inconvenient truths."[48]

B. Enron's Outside Counsel: Vinson & Elkins

Of equal concern is the role of Vinson & Elkins's lawyers, Enron's primary outside legal counsel, in structuring transactions and providing legal advice on public disclosure documents. While questions about the law firm's exposure to malpractice suits remain open, the facts available to date suggest that the firm was more than a bystander to corporate misconduct.[49] The failure of Vinson & Elkins motion to dismiss the major shareholder lawsuit filed against the firm suggests some credible evidence of complicity in fraud.[50] Indeed, the Powers Report concludes that Vinson & Elkins

> provided advice and prepared documentation in connection with many of the [problematic] transactions. . . . It also assisted Enron with the preparation of its disclosures of related-party transactions in the proxy statements and the footnotes to the financial statements in Enron's periodic SEC filings. Management and the Board relied heavily on the perceived approval by Vinson & Elkins of the structure and disclosure of the transactions.

---

[47] Press Release, Committee on Energy and Commerce, *Tauzin, Greenwood Want Law Firm Review of Enron's Related-Party Transactions* (Jan. 29, 2002), *available at* http://energycommerce.house.gov/107/ news/01292002_478print.htm (last accessed July 27, 2002); *see also* Richard A. Oppel, Jr., *Enron's Many Strands: Early Warnings; Lawyer at Enron Warned Officials of Dubious Deals*, N.Y. TIMES, Feb. 7, 2002, at A1; Peter Behr & April Witt, *Visionary's Dream Led to Risky Business*, WASH. POST, July 28, 2002, at A01.

[48] *See* James Larnder, *Why Should Anyone Believe You?*, BUS. 2.0, March 2002, at 40 (discussion of Enron's culture).

[49] Riva D. Atlas, *A Law Firm's 2 Roles Risk Suit by Enron, Experts Say*, N.Y. TIMES, Jan. 29, 2002, at C1, C7.

[50] The suit was brought in late 2001 by large investors in Enron, led by the University of California, which lost millions of dollars when Enron failed. Eight investment banks and two law firms, including Vinson & Elkins, were added as defendants in April 2001. The decision by the judge on the motion to dismiss failed except for two defendants, Deutsche Bank and Kirkland & Ellis, the other law firm. See Kristen Hays, *Judge upholds case against defendants in massive Enron shareholder lawsuit*, GLOBE & MAIL, Dec. 23, 2002, at B9; *see also* Kurt Eichenwald, *A Higher Standard For Corporate Advice*, N.Y. TIMES, Dec. 23, 2002, at A1.

Enron's Audit and Compliance Committee, as well as in-house counsel, looked to it for assurance that Enron's public disclosures were legally sufficient. It would be inappropriate to fault Vinson & Elkins for accounting matters, which are not within its expertise. However, Vinson & Elkins should have brought a stronger, more objective and more critical voice to the disclosure process.[51]

Vinson & Elkins's leaders have denied that the firm acted improperly. In their view, outside lawyers may assist in a transaction that is not illegal and that has been approved by company management. In so doing, "the lawyers are not approving the business decisions made by the clients."[52] Yet not only is that an unduly circumscribed understanding of the lawyer's ethical responsibilities, it also begs the question of who is the "client." As our subsequent discussion notes, the firm's response also raises a question that has become central to debates over regulatory reform: when do lawyers have an obligation to bring dubious conduct to the attention of more senior management or the board of directors?[53]

A related issue involves the responsibility of Vinson & Elkins when it was asked to investigate initially anonymous allegations by Sherron Watkins.[54] In August 2001, Watkins, Enron's vice president of corporate development, wrote an anonymous six-page memo to Kenneth Lay, Enron's Chairman and CEO, detailing her concerns about the propriety of Enron's disclosure statements and accounting treatment of the SPE and partnership transactions. Watkins recommended that Enron's Chief General Counsel hire an independent law firm to investigate the transactions, and specifically advised against using Vinson & Elkins. As she noted, "(Can't use V&E due to conflict—they provided some true sale opinions on some of the deals)."[55] In agreeing

---

[51] *Powers Report, supra* note 24, at 25–26; *see also id.* at 44, 51, 65, 72, 100, 115, 158,178, 181,183, 187,190 for further discussions of Vinson & Elkins's involvement, particularly with respect to the structuring of the transactions and decisions about and preparations for disclosure. For a discussion of whether the fiduciary duties of business lawyers require accounting knowledge, see Lawrence A. Cunningham, *Sharing Accounting's Burden: Business Lawyers in Enron's Dark Shadows,* 57 BUS. LAW. 1421 (2002).

[52] Ellen Joan Pollock, *Limited Partners: Lawyers for Enron Faulted Its Deals, Didn't Force Issue* WALL ST. J. May 22, 2002, at A1.

[53] See the discussion of disclosure obligations in Part III-B, *infra.*

[54] *See* Dan Ackman, *Sherron Watkins Had Whistle, But Blew It,* FORBES.COM, Feb. 14, 2002, for a profile of Sherron Watkins, *available at* http://www.forbes.com/2002/02/14/0214watkins.html (last accessed Oct. 4, 2002); Frank Pellegrini, *Person of the Week: 'Enron Whistleblower' Sherron Watkins,* TIME.COM, Jan. 18, 2002, *available at* http://www.tie.com/time/pow/printout/0,8816,194927,00.html (last accessed Oct. 4, 2002); *see also* Roger C. Cramton, *Enron and the Corporate Lawyer: A Primer on Legal and Ethical Issues* 58 BUS. LAW. 143, 162–67 (2002), *reprinted in this book at* 571–623.

[55] A copy of the memo is reprinted in *Andersen Hearing, supra* note 3, at 39, 44; also *available at* http:// www.itmweb.com/f012002.htm (last accessed Oct, 4, 2002). *See* Witt & Behr, *supra* note 13 for a discussion of Watkins's goals in writing the memo, and a further discussion of the retainer of Vinson & Elkins.

to take on this investigation, Vinson & Elkins placed itself in the position of evaluating its own work. The firm also agreed to highly restrictive limitations on the scope of its review, which further circumscribed the value of its advice.[56] At a minimum, as most legal ethics experts have suggested, Vinson & Elkins's lawyers should have discussed the possible conflict with Enron executives and directors and secured a written conflicts waiver.[57] It is, however, by no means clear that a waiver would have solved the problem. Prevailing bar ethical rules prohibit lawyers from representation that would be "materially and adversely affected" by the lawyers' own interests, unless the client gives informed consent and the lawyer reasonably believes the representation will not be adversely affected.[58] According to the Restatement of the Law Governing Lawyers, client consent is not effective if, "in the circumstances, it is not reasonably likely that the lawyer will be able to provide adequate representation."[59] Whether it was reasonable for Vinson & Elkins's lawyers to believe that they could have provided disinterested representation is open to doubt.

As it was, the nine-page report that the firm provided to Enron's General Counsel on October 15, 2001 left much to be desired. Although Vinson & Elkins characterized its investigation as "preliminary," the report recommended no additional scrutiny. After a notably inadequate review of the facts, the law firm's report concluded that they did not "warrant a further widespread investigation by independent counsel and auditors."[60] Without meaningful discussion of the substance of the transactions at issue, the report primarily focused on their "bad cosmetics," namely "a serious risk of adverse publicity and litigation."[61] To that end, Vinson & Elkins recommended "some response should be provided to Ms. Watkins to assure her that her concerns were thoroughly reviewed, analysed, and although not found to raise new or undisclosed information, were given serious consideration."[62]

Despite that recommendation, the Powers Committee was established just two weeks later to undertake precisely the sort of detailed investigation that Vinson & Elkins had found unnecessary. The Powers Committee retained a different law firm for assistance,

---

[56] *See Powers Report, supra* note 24, at 173–77, for its discussion of the investigation leading up to the Vinson & Elkins Oct. 15 reporting letter.

[57] David Hechler, *Report criticizes V&E's Enron work*, NAT'L L. J., Feb. 11, 2002, at A1, A11.

[58] *See* TEX. DISCIPLINARY R. PROF. CONDUCT (1989) § 1.06, *reprinted in* TEX. GOVT. CODE ANN., tit.2, subtit.G, app. (Vernon Supp. 1995) (State Bar Rules art X [1.06]9).

[59] RESTATEMENT (THIRD) OF THE LAW GOVERNING LAWYERS § 122(2)(c) (2000). For a more detailed discussion of the point, see Cramton, *supra* note 54, at 164–67.

[60] Letter from Max Hendrick, III, Vinson & Elkins L.L.P., to Mr. James V. Derrick, Executive Vice President and General Counsel, Enron Corp. (Oct. 15, 2001) (*reprinted in Andersen Hearing, supra* note 3, at 46–54).

[61] Peter Behr & April Witt, *Concerns Grow Amid Conflicts*, WASH. POST, July 30, 2002, at A1 (quoting letter); letter to James V. Derrick, *supra* note 60, at 54.

[62] Letter to James Derrick, *supra* note 60, at 9.

and in February 2002 released a report of some 200 pages. That report criticizes Vinson & Elkins's actions with respect to many aspects of the investigation. Because Enron's General Counsel had instructed Vinson & Elkins that a detailed examination of the relevant transactions and discussions with accounting advisors need not be part of the law firm's review, the "result of the V&E review was largely predetermined by the scope and nature of the investigation and the process employed."[63] By contrast, the Powers Report notes that its own investigation was able to identify the most serious problems at Enron only after making the detailed inquiries that Vinson & Elkins had agreed were unnecessary. In reaching that conclusion, Vinson & Elkins lawyers had interviewed only "very senior people" at Enron and Andersen, who "with few exceptions, had substantial professional and personal stakes in the matters under review."[64] So did Vinson & Elkins, given its advice on the events under scrutiny and its ties to the key players. The firm's willingness to undertake a review, given this conflict of interest, is emblematic of the broader concerns about professional accountability discussed in Part IV below.

C. Andersen's In-House Counsel

Nancy Temple, in-house counsel at Andersen, emerged as a key figure in Andersen's demise, and her actions have been a controversial centerpiece in discussions of lawyers' social responsibilities. As noted earlier, Andersen played a crucial role in creating and auditing questionable investment vehicles, and in certifying Enron's financial statements and public disclosures. Accordingly, Andersen's documents regarding those matters could be critical to government investigators and civil litigants. The firm's detailed document retention policies called for the destruction of all nonessential draft documents or conflicting documentation relating to an audit, including the e-mails, voicemail messages, and desk files of Andersen personnel working on the audit.[65] The policy itself was not unusual; what created problems was the timing and manner of Temple's calls for compliance with the policy.[66]

Temple's actions became the subject of a highly unflattering congressional hearing in January 2002.[67] Committee members were left incredulous by her characterization of actions concerning Andersen's document retention and destruction as customary housekeeping duties. She admitted awareness, prior to October 8, of allegations by an

---

[63] *Powers Report, supra* note 24, at 176.

[64] *Powers Report, supra* note 24, at 176–77. For example, Andrew Fastow, Enron's Chief Financial Officer, reportedly gained $45 million from the limited partnerships. Peter Behr & April Witt, *Hidden Debts, Deals, Scuttle Last Chance,* WASH. POST, Aug. 1, 2002, at A1.

[65] A complete copy of the Andersen policy, *Client Engagement Information—Organization, Retention and Destruction,* Feb. 1, 2000, is *reprinted in Andersen Hearing, supra* note 3, at 79–105.

[66] *See* Cramton, *supra* note 54, at 158–162.

[67] *See Andersen Hearing, supra* note 3.

Enron employee of inappropriate accounting procedures, as well as an investigation by Vinson & Elkins. She also admitted that between September 28 and October 12, she provided legal advice about specific documentation and retention issues.[68] The SEC placed Enron under investigation in early October, and it confirmed that fact publicly in an October 22 press release. Temple's notes from a conference call on October 8 anticipated that outcome: "Highly probable some SEC investigation."[69]

Despite her knowledge, Temple sent an e-mail on October 12 to Andersen's Houston practice director making reference to the firm's document retention and destruction policy: "It might be useful to consider reminding the engagement team of our documentation and retention policy. It will be helpful to make sure that we have complied with that policy."[70] On October 23, David Duncan, Andersen's lead engagement partner on the Enron audit, ordered his team to comply with Andersen's policy and gathered all of the documents relating to Enron. Andersen officials later admitted that significant numbers of documents were shredded between this time and November 10. Media reports chronicled the accumulation of more than eighteen trunks and thirty boxes of documentary debris on only one of the days at one of the offices.[71] Not until November 10, after the SEC had subpoenaed documents from Andersen concerning its Enron investigation and after Andersen had received a second subpoena in a related lawsuit, did Temple instruct the Enron engagement team "to preserve documents, computer files and other information relating to Enron."[72]

Andersen officers were clearly alert to problems with Enron in September 2001. By October 9, the accounting firm had retained lawyers at Davis, Polk & Wardwell ("Davis, Polk") to "help with the complex issues that were going on in the third quarter."[73] Temple admitted that she had discussed documentation and retention issues with Davis, Polk as early as October 16.[74] In testimony during a congressional subcommittee hearing, Andersen's Senior Executive, C.E. Andrews, initially disclaimed any expectation of litigation on October 9.[75] However, a few minutes later, in response to a different

---

[68] *Andersen Hearing, supra* note 3, at 120, 122.

[69] Witt & Behr, *supra* note 13, at A1.

[70] Andersen internal e-mail message from Nancy Temple to Michael C. Odom, Oct. 12, 2001, *reprinted in Andersen Hearing, supra* note 3, at 45.

[71] Witt & Behr, *supra* note 13, at A1.

[72] Andersen internal e-mail memorandum from Nancy Temple to David Duncan, et al, *re: Enron—Procedures for Responding to Subpoenas and Litigation*, Nov. 10, 2001, *reprinted in Andersen Hearing, supra* note 3, at 63; *see also* Witt & Behr, *supra* note 13.

[73] C.E. Andrews, Senior Executive, Andersen LLP, Testimony before the House of Representatives Committee on Energy, 107th Cong. 1 (Jan. 24, 2002) (*reprinted in Andersen Hearing, supra* note 3, at 119).

[74] *Andersen Hearing, supra* note 3, at 118–120.

[75] *Id.* at 119: "We had no reason at that particular time to expect litigation, no."

question, Temple acknowledged that as soon as she was aware that Enron would be restating its prior financials, she concluded that Andersen "would likely be sued."[76] Almost immediately thereafter, Andrews conceded that Davis, Polk had been hired "for purposes to help [Andersen] with the financial reporting and possible litigation."[77] Accordingly, a "reminder" about the audit firm's document shredding policies in early October 2001 could plausibly be interpreted as encouraging destruction of background papers that might be relevant to its liability or to the regulatory investigation of its client.

In a televised interview on *Meet the Press,* Andersen's CEO Joseph Berardino attempted to discount this possibility: "Nancy just told people to use their judgment. She did not instruct them to do anything, to my knowledge."[78] Yet, despite the insistence that Temple had made no error, legally or ethically, Andersen fired David Duncan, its Enron team leader, for similar conduct. According to Andersen's CEO in the same interview, Duncan "displayed extremely poor judgment in the destruction of documents' issue" after he learned of the SEC investigation.[79] The attempt to scapegoat Duncan while exonerating Temple did not sit well with congressional investigation. As the Subcommittee Chairman noted, "common sense gets a little lost here."[80]

The jury that convicted Andersen of obstructing the SEC's Enron investigation took a similar view, but paid closer attention to Temple's other activities. Jurors reportedly were less concerned with Temple's "shredding memo" than with one of her e-mails to Duncan and the Enron team. The e-mail suggested changes to a draft memo that Duncan had prepared about a forthcoming Enron press release concerning its third quarter financial results. Temple's modifications deleted references in the memo to Andersen's legal counsel, herself included, in order to protect the attorney-client privilege and to minimize "the chances that I might be [called as] a witness, which I prefer to avoid."[81] Temple's note also recommended "deleting some language that might suggest we have concluded [Enron's] release is misleading."[82] The jury interpreted this

---

[76] *Id.* at 119.

[77] *Id.* at 122.

[78] *Meet the Press* (NBC television broadcast, Jan. 20, 2002) (interview of Joseph Berardino, CEO, Arthur Andersen) (*reprinted in Andersen Hearing, supra* note 3, at 74).

[79] *Id.* at 74. Berardino made no accusation that Duncan failed to respond to the Nov. 10 instruction from Temple about the subpoenas, just that he displayed "extremely poor judgment" in the period between his receipt on Oct. 23 of an SEC letter concerning the investigation and Temple's Nov. 10 direction. *See also Andersen Hearing, supra* note 3, at 120.

[80] *Andersen Hearing, supra* note 3, at 134.

[81] Internal Andersen E-mail memorandum from Nancy A. Temple, to David B. Duncan, *Re: Press Release draft* (Oct. 16, 2001) (available in *Andersen Hearing, supra* note 3, at 58). For a copy of Duncan's revised memo to file, see *Andersen Hearing, supra* note 3, at 60.

[82] Internal Andersen E-Mail from Temple, available in *Andersen Hearing, supra* note 3, at 58.

language as evidence of criminal intent to withhold information from SEC investigators.[83] The jury's comments to reporters after the conviction explaining their rationale became a primary basis of Andersen's appeal.[84]

In a *New York Times* article after the verdict, Stephen Gillers, a prominent legal ethics expert, defended Temple's actions as "the kind of advice that lawyers routinely give."[85] Other ethics experts take a different view.[86] Under the statutes and ethics rules of most jurisdictions, it is unethical to destroy documents if they are subject to discovery or relevant to a "clearly foreseeable" legal action.[87] The facts currently available permit the inference that Temple knew or should have known that a proceeding was clearly foreseeable at the time that she reminded Andersen partners and employees about document retention policy. Her failure to clarify the need to preserve critical Enron-related materials was highly problematic. Her instructions on revising a characterization of financial disclosure was problematic as well, particularly if part of the motivation was her own self-interest in avoiding involvement in the government's investigation.[88] In any event, whether or not Temple violated bar ethical rules, it is troubling that so many lawyers, including ethics experts like Gillers, assumed that such actions are "routine." If current norms and standards of conduct permit complicity in frustrating federal investigation, then reform initiatives are clearly appropriate.[89]

IV. RETHINKING LAWYERS' ROLES AND RULES

This complex case history provides the backdrop for consideration of an equally complex set of issues concerning lawyers' conduct. Addressing these issues will, in turn, require attention to the forces that influence such conduct and the regulatory norms

---

[83] Cathy Booth Thomas, *Called to Account,* TIME, June 24, 2002, at 52; *see also The Newshour with Jim Lehrer* (PBS television broadcast, June 20, 2002) (*available at* http://www.pbs.org/newshour/bb/law/jan-june02/andersen_6-17.html) (last accessed July 10, 2002).

[84] *See also* Carrie Johnson, *Judge Urged to Uphold Andersen Verdict,* WASH. POST, Aug. 1, 2002, at E03; *supra* note 36.

[85] Stephen Gillers, *The Flaw in the Andersen Verdict,* N.Y. TIMES, June 18, 2002, at A25.

[86] *See* Joan C. Rodgers, *Lawyers Debate Best Way to Advise Clients on Editing, Shredding Records Post-Andersen,* 18 ABA/BNA LAWYERS' MANUAL ON PROFESSIONAL CONDUCT 484 (2002); e-mail letter from William H. Simon, Professor, Stanford Law School, to Deborah L. Rhode, Stanford Law School (Aug. 20, 2002) (on file with the authors).

[87] *See* DEBORAH L. RHODE & DAVID LUBAN, LEGAL ETHICS, 359–365 (3d ed. 2001). For a discussion of in-house counsel concerns about shredding policies post-Enron, see David Hechler, *Shred Smarts,* NAT'L L.J., May 20–27, 2002, at A23.

[88] For similar views, see Rodgers, *supra* note 86, at 485 (quoting Robert Hinerfeld).

[89] *See* David Hechler, *Lawyers see lessons in trial of Andersen,* NAT'L L.J., June 24–July 1, 2002, at A1.

and standards that permit it. As many experts have noted, new rules will not address the root causes of the Enron problem if they fail to alter underlying reward structures. The key challenge is to alter any "incentives built into the financial system that encourage deception and fraud."[90] Jeffrey Garten, Dean of the Yale School of Management, has rightly noted that one of the risks of regulatory responses is that they "create a kind of 'audit' society in which there is the illusion that if there are enough [rules] and if you check off enough boxes, everything will be fine. . . . [Y]ou begin to gear the system to comply with the regulations in such a way that you're adhering to the letter of the law but the actual spirit of it has totally evaporated."[91] Any adequate response to the problems illustrated in Enron will require not simply a few more rules, but also a fundamental reassessment of professional roles and the culture that sustains them.

A. Professional Independence

For lawyers, a place to start is with conditions that compromise independent professional judgment. A case in point involves the financial incentives created by Vinson & Elkins's dependence on Enron-related work and employment opportunities. In 2001, Enron was Vinson & Elkins largest client, accounting for more than 7% of the law firm's revenues.[92] Both Enron's general counsel and deputy general counsel at the time were former Vinson & Elkins partners; an additional twenty or so Vinson & Elkins attorneys reportedly had taken jobs at Enron since 1991.[93] Firm lawyers' personal investments in Enron created further risks to independent judgment. While none of these relationships are of themselves unethical, they together created a context that should be of concern. Under such circumstances, firms need internal structures to prevent conflicts of interest and ensure independent judgment. Specific standards should also be in place governing ethical investments in clients.[94]

It bears noting that the SEC made the independence of accountants a priority well prior to the Enron affair. A November 2000 overhaul of SEC rules dealt with whether and how accountants could invest in the shares of the firms they audited, and the ability of accounting firm partners and employees to accept employment with audit

---

[90] Jeff Madrick, *Economic Scene*, N.Y. TIMES, July 11, 2002, at C2.

[91] Jeffrey L. Seglin, *The Right Thing: Will More Rules Yield Better Corporate Behavior?*, N.Y. TIMES, November 17, 2002, at § 3-4.

[92] *See* Schwartz, *supra* note 13 at C8; Mike France, *One Big Client, One Big Hassle*, BUS. WEEK ONLINE, Jan. 28, 2002, *available at* http://www.businessweek.com:/print/magazine/content/02_04/b3767706.htm?mainwindow (last accessed July 29, 2002).

[93] *See* France, *supra* note 92 (quoting estimates by Vinson & Elkins's managing partner).

[94] *See* RHODE & LUBAN, *supra* note 87, at 556–558; *see also* Poonam Puri, *Taking Stock of Taking Stock*, 87 CORNELL L. REV. 99 (2001).

clients.[95] The Enron debacle should also prompt a reconsideration of the circumstances under which lawyers may take equity interests in their clients.[96]

Although close linkages between accounting firms and the clients they audit have been the subject of intense scrutiny and reform proposals in the wake of Enron, far less attention has focused on law firms. Yet some of the same concerns are present in legal as well as accounting contexts. Increased competition from within and outside the bar has led to increased pressure on firms to favor responsiveness to client demands over broader societal concerns. Allegiance to management's short-term financial interests may compromise obligations to the broader public, as well as to the entity itself, which is, at least in theory, the lawyer's client.[97]

The challenges of maintaining independent judgment are compounded in a competitive market where powerful clients can shop for expedient advice. Yet while resisting client pressures can carry financial risks, so, too, can satisfying their demands. In the long run, firms' reputational interests are not well served by assisting conduct that cuts ethical corners. The prudent objective for both lawyers and clients should be to identify a course of action that is legally sound, financially practical, and ethically defensible.[98] To that end, attorneys may need to refuse a retainer, withdraw from representation, or deliver an unwelcome message about what the governing rules require.[99] Some circumstances may also demand disclosure, or threats of disclosure of client misconduct.[100]

B. Disclosure Obligations

Such disclosure obligations have figured prominently in recent legislative responses to corporate misconduct.[101] Experts have long sought to have the SEC take a more

---

[95] SEC, *Final Rule: Revision of the Commission's Auditor Independence Requirements* [Release Nos. 33-7919; 33-43602; 35-27279; IC-24744; IA-1911; FR-56; File No S7-13-00; *available at* http://www.sec.gov/rules/final/33-7919.htm] (Nov. 15, 2000) (amending Rule 2-01 of Regulation S-X (17 C.F.R. § 210.2-01) and Item 9 of Schedule 14A (17 C.F.R. § 240.14a-101) under the Securities Exchange Act of 1934 (15 U.S.C. § 78a)).

[96] For general discussion, see RHODE & LUBAN, *supra* note 87, at 556–558; Richard W. Painter, *Lawyers' Rules, Auditors' Rules and the Psychology of Concealment*, 84 MINN. L. REV. 1399 (2000); Audrey I. Benison, *The Sophisticated Client: A Proposal for the Reconciliation of Conflicts of Interest Standards for Attorneys and Accountants*, 13 GEO. J. L. ETHICS 699, 715, 738 (2000).

[97] *See* RHODE, REFORMING THE LEGAL PROFESSION, *supra* note 18, at 33–38, 40; *see also* Milton C. Regan, Jr., *Professional Responsibility and the Corporate Lawyer*, 13 GEO. J. L. ETHICS 197, 202–203 (2000); Pitt, *supra* note 11.

[98] For a discussion of Enron's "opinion-shopping," see France, *supra* note 92; Julie Hilden, *Scummery Judgment. Why Enron's sleazy lawyers walked while their accountants fried*, SLATE.COM, June 21, 2002, *available at* http://slate.msn.com/?id=2067206 (last accessed July 1, 2002).

[99] *See* RHODE, REFORMING THE LEGAL PROFESSION, *supra* note 18, at 298–299.

[100] *See* Lisa Girion, *Calls for Lawyers to Blow the Whistle*, L.A. TIMES, Mar. 24, 2002, at Part 3, Page 1.

[101] Jonathan D. Glater, *A Legal Uproar Over Proposals to Regulate the Profession*, N.Y. TIMES, Dec. 17, 2002 at C1; Stephanie Francis Cahill, *Corporate Fraud Forces Lawyers to be Whistle-Blowers*, ABA J. EREPORT, August 2, 2002, *available at* http://www.abanet.org/journal/ereport/au2corp.html; Richard B. Schmit, *Lawyers Pressed to Report Fraud Under New Law*, WALL ST. J., July 25, 2002, at B1.

active role in the regulation of lawyer conduct and in disclosure of fraudulent conduct.[102] The recent legislative focus is, in turn, a product of the bar's own failure to impose adequate requirements. Just before the Enron scandal broke, the ABA voted twice against a recommendation by its Ethics 2000 Commission to amend the bar's Model Rules of Professional Conduct governing disclosure obligations. The proposed reform would have required lawyers to reveal information when necessary to prevent or rectify substantial economic harm, as well as preserve life.[103]

Section 307 of Sarbanes-Oxley, and the rule the SEC originally proposed to implement it would have provided the ethical safeguards that the bar has not.[104] Section 307 has two dimensions. First, it instructs the SEC to adopt a rule of practice establishing "minimum standards of professional conduct" for lawyers "appearing or practising before the Commission." Second, Section 307 specifically directs the SEC to include a rule requiring all such lawyers to report "evidence of a material violation" of fraud and other corporate misconduct to the company's senior management and, if necessary, to its board of directors. The Proposed Rule that the SEC designed to implement these requirements attracted a barrage of criticism from the ABA and corporate lawyers, and pitted the corporate bar against some fifty law professors who argued that it was long overdue.[105] The end result of this dispute was a much less demanding SEC Final Rule, and a deferred decision on its most significant disclosure provision.

In its initial form, the Rule took an expansive approach to coverage. It defined those "appearing and practising before the Commission" to include individuals "preparing, or participating in the process of preparing" any document filed with the Commission or incorporated into any communication with the SEC. The proposed definition also included someone who advised a party against filing a document. The ABA criticized

---

[102] *See* RHODE & LUBAN, *supra* note 87, at 231–232 for discussion of the 1972 complaint filed in SEC v. National Student Marketing, 457 F. Supp. 682 (D.D.C. 1978); *see also* Richard W. Painter & Jennifer E. Duggan, *Lawyer Disclosure of Corporate fraud: Establishing a Firm Foundation*, 50 SMU L. REV. 225 (1996) (suggesting amendments to the 1934 Securities and Exchange Act to provide for lawyer disclosure of known illegal acts first to senior management and then, if those acts were not rectified, to the client's board of directors).

[103] *See* RHODE & LUBAN, *supra* note 87.

[104] For a more detailed discussion of the effect of Section 307, see Robert D. Brown and Paul D. Paton, *Public Interest, Public Accountability and Canadian Tax Professionals After Sarbanes-Oxley*, Report of the Proceedings of the 54th Tax Conference [2002], CANADIAN TAX FOUNDATION (2002) at 35:1.

[105] Mitchell Cacelle and Michael Schroeder, *Proposed SEC Rules Could Turn Lawyers into Whistle-Blowers* WALL ST. J. January 9, 2003, at A1; Terry Carter, *Going Before the SEC—ABA, Others Criticize Proposed Lawyer Regs*, ABA J., Dec. 20, 2002, *available at* http://www.abanet.org/journal/ereport/d20sec.html. For some professors' perspective, see letter from Professor Richard Painter to Jonathan G. Katz, SEC, December 18, 2002, *available at* http://www.sec.gov/rules/proposed/rwpainter1.htm [hereinafter Painter Submission]; letter from Professors Susan Koniak, Boston University School of Law, Roger Cramton, Cornell Law School, & George Cohen, University of Virginia School of Law to Jonathan G. Katz, SEC, December 18, 2002, *available at* http://www.sec.gov/rules/proposed/s74502.htm/spkoniak1.htm. This last letter was also signed by fifty other law professors who, in signing, indicated their accord with the letter's general direction and approach, though not necessarily its detail [hereinafter Koniak Submission].

this approach as overly broad because it "inappropriately encompassed" foreign lawyers subject to different rules and "non-securities specialists who do no more than prepare or review limited portions of a filing, lawyers who respond to auditors' letters or prepare work product in the ordinary course unrelated to securities matters that may be used for that purpose, and lawyers preparing documents that eventually may be filed as exhibits."[106] By contrast, some legal academics criticized the proposed Rule as overly narrow, by not including law firms as well as individual lawyers within its disciplinary ambit.[107]

Proposals for mandatory disclosure and "noisy withdrawal" were, however, the primary focus of criticism. Section 307 of Sarbanes-Oxley directed the Commission to promulgate rules "requiring an attorney to report evidence of a material violation of securities law or breach of fiduciary duty or similar violation by the company or any agent thereof, to the chief legal counsel or the chief executive officer of the company (or the equivalent thereof)."[108] In its initial form, the SEC's Proposed Rule implementing this requirement defined evidence of material violation to include "information that would lead an attorney reasonably to believe that a material violation has occurred, is occurring, or is about to occur," and defined reasonable belief as what "an attorney, acting reasonably, would believe."[109] Under the initially proposed rule, if a lawyer believed that the company had not "adequately responded" to reports of misconduct, the lawyer must then 1) withdraw from representation; 2) notify the SEC of the withdrawal, indicating that it was based on professional considerations; and 3) disaffirm any filing with the SEC the attorney has prepared or assisted in preparing that the attorney believes is or may be materially false or misleading.[110]

Alternatively, an organization could avoid having lawyers subject to external disclosure obligations by establishing a Qualified Legal Compliance Committee ("QLCC"). Such a panel would include at least one member of the organization's audit committee, and two other independent board members, who would investigate reports of material violations. If the organization did not take remedial actions requested by the QLCC, its members would be responsible for notifying the SEC. The rule further provided that any sharing of confidential information with the Commission would not waive the applicable lawyer-client privilege.[111]

---

[106] See the 40-page American Bar Association submission to the SEC on *Section 307 and Minimum Standards of Professional Conduct for Attorneys*, at 12, Dec. 18, 2002, *available at* http://www.abanet.org/poladv/factsheet.html; *see also* Bart Schwartz, *Lawyer rules go too far*, NAT'L LAW J., Dec. 16, 2002, at A13.

[107] Koniak et al. submission, *supra* note 105, at 4, 28–33; Painter submission, *supra* note 105, at 11–12.

[108] Sarbanes-Oxley Act of 2002, § 307(1).

[109] Securities and Exchange Commission, *Proposed Rule: Implementation of Standards of Professional Conduct for Attorneys*, 17 CFR Part 205 [Release Nos. 33-8150; 34-46868; IC-25829; File No. S7-45-02] *available at* http://www.sec.gov/rules/proposed/33-8150.htm, ss. 205.2(5)(e) and (l).

[110] *Id.* § 205.3(d)(i).

[111] *Id.* § 205(3)(c); *see also supra* 79, discussion at pages 31–32.

Comments from the practicing bar vehemently opposed these "noisy withdrawal" provisions. The arguments echoed those that bar leaders have traditionally voiced against disclosure obligations. Lawyers would become involuntary "auditors," "regulators," "whistleblowers," and "adversaries" of these clients.[112] Such a rule, commentators warned, would threaten a "Bill of Rights enshrined value" of lawyers being "independent of government agencies and unburdened by concern over self-protection when engaged in the vindication of the client's rights."[113] Under the SEC's proposed rule, corporate employees would reportedly become less candid and less willing to seek legal advice; the result would be fewer opportunities for the lawyer to prevent or rectify misconduct.[114]

Many academic experts were skeptical. Geoffrey Hazard, former Director of the American Law Institute and Reporter for the Model Rules of Professional Conduct, saw the bar's reaction as another instance of lawyers being "allergic to regulation of any kind" that could expose them to liability or disciplinary action.[115] As other commentators noted, the ethical rules of over forty states already permitted noisy withdrawal, and the Bill of Rights had not yet crumbled. Nor did any evidence suggest that lawyers' representation had been impaired in the minority of states that required disclosure to prevent financial fraud in which the lawyer's services had been used.[116] Moreover, as law professor Richard Painter pointed out in his comments to the Commission, "it is no secret that the most pervasive argument" against disclosure requirements is that it reduces lawyers' risk of liability to defrauded parties. But, as Painter noted, "professional responsibility rules should not be designed with defense of malpractice claims as their primary objective, but with a view toward minimizing lawyer complicity in fraud that gives rise to malpractice claims to begin with. The [Commission's] Proposed Rule furthers this objective."[117] Other ethics experts emphasized the value in having a single SEC rule on noisy withdrawal, rather than subjecting attorneys in multijurisdictional practice to the inconsistent ethical codes of different states. University of Houston Law Center Dean and Professor Nancy Rapoport urged the SEC to address directly whether the Proposed Rules could or should preempt state ethics rules.[118] As Law

---

[112] Alison Frankel, *No Confidence*, AM. LAWYER, Dec. 2002, 79, 101; Michael Pacelle and Michael Schroeder, *Proposed SEC Rules Could Turn Lawyers Into Whistleblowers*, WALL ST. J. MAG., Jan. 9, 2003, at A1 (quoting Lawrence Fox); Bart Schwartz, *Lawyer Rules Go Too Far* Nat'l Law J., Dec. 16, 2002, at A15.

[113] Pacelle and Schroeder, *supra* note 112, at A2 (quoting Edward Fleischmann).

[114] See sources cited in note 112. For similar arguments by opponents to earlier disclosure proposals, *see* Rhode & Luban, *supra* note 87, at 226, 233–239.

[115] Glater, *Legal Uproar, supra* note 101 (quoting Geoffrey Hazard, Jr.).

[116] Painter Submission, *supra* note 105.

[117] *Id.*

[118] Letter from Dean and Professor Nancy Rapoport, University of Houston Law Center, to Jonathan G. Katz, Secretary, Securities and Exchange Commission, December 18, 2002, *available at* http://www.sec.gov/rules/proposed/s74502/nbrapoport1.htm (last accessed June 3, 2003).

Professor William Simon maintained, "[i]t doesn't make sense to have 51 state processes in what is basically a unified, federal securities system."[119]

The disinterested view of academic experts was not, however, sufficient to offset the powerful opposition of the organized bar. The Final Rule that the SEC released in January 2003 deferred or diluted the most controversial requirements. In essence, the Final Rule maintained the "up the ladder" reporting requirement for evidence of material violations of securities laws, but narrowed the definition of what would trigger the obligation.[120] Under the Final Rule, "evidence of a material violation means credible evidence, based upon which it would be unreasonable, under the circumstances, for a prudent and competent attorney not to conclude that it is reasonably likely that a material violation has occurred, is occurring, or is about to occur." This new "double negative" definition was, in the view of many experts, both confusing and toothless, particularly since the Commission added a provision absolving the lawyer of reporting responsibilities if another lawyer finds that the company has a "colorable defense" for the company's actions.[121] Moreover, as other commentators have noted, since the Rule imposes no obligation to investigate, a lawyer could often avoid reporting obligations through wilful blindness. As a practical matter, this new standard seems likely to cover only such obvious and egregious misconduct that current bar ethical rules would already mandate withdrawal.[122]

The Final Rule also modified the earlier draft in other significant ways. The proposed Rule's expansive scope was narrowed to exempt foreign attorneys not advising directly on U.S. securities laws or the Commission's rules and regulations.[123] The Commission extended the comment period on the "noisy withdrawal" requirement, and suggested a possible alternative. Under that alternative, the responsibility for disclosure would shift from the lawyer to the client. If an attorney withdrew from representation of an issuer after failing to receive an appropriate response concerning evidence of a material violation, the company would be required to disclose its counsel's withdrawal to the Commission as a "material event."[124]

---

[119] Renee Deger, *Law Professors Led Fight for New SEC Rules,* THE RECORDER, Dec. 2, 2002.

[120] Securities and Exchange Commission, *Final Rule: Implementation of Standards of Professional Conduct for Attorneys,* 17 CFR Part 205 [Release Nos. 33-8185; 34-47276; IC-25929; File No. S7-45-02] Jan. 29, 2003, *available at* http://www.sec.gov/rules/final/33-8185.htm ["SEC Attorney Conduct Final Rule"]; *see also* Securities and Exchange Commission, *SEC Adopts Attorney Conduct Rule Under Sarbanes-Oxley Act,* Press Release 2003-13, Jan. 23, 2003, *available at* http://www.sec.gov/news/press/2003-13.htm.

[121] SEC Attorney Conduct Final Rule, *supra* note 119, §§ 205.3(b)(6)(ii) and (7)(ii); Floyd Norris, *No Positives in this Legal Double Negative,* N.Y. TIMES, Jan. 24, 2003, at C1.

[122] See the discussion in Floyd Norris, *No Positives in this Legal Double Negative,* N.Y. TIMES, Jan. 24, 2003, at C1.

[123] SEC Attorney Conduct Final Rule, *supra* note 120, at 3–6 of 74; *see also* § 1 205.2(a)(2)(ii) (definition of "appearing and practicing") and § 205.2(j) (definition of non-appearing foreign attorney).

[124] SEC Attorney Conduct Final Rule, *supra* note 120, at 3 of 74, *see also* U.S. Securities and Exchange Commission, *Proposed Rule: Implementation of Standards of Professional Conduct for Attorneys,* 17 CFR Parts 205, 240 and 249 [Release Nos. 33-8186, 34-47282; IC-25920; File No. S7-45-02], at 10–16 of 37, *available at* http://www.sec.gov/rules/proposed/33-8186.htm.

Whatever requirements the SEC ultimately adopts are likely to be the subject of ongoing controversy and challenge. As the process to date makes abundantly clear, the organized bar's involvement in regulatory reform has been compromised by its own self-interest in maintaining client relationships and minimizing professional liability. Significant progress in checking corporate misconduct is likely to require a greater public role in establishing and enforcing lawyers' ethical requirements.

C. Professional Accountability

Different voices can provide different perspectives on the need to balance client loyalty with broader societal responsibilities.[125] Models for such external oversight are readily available. One is the "Public Company Accounting Oversight Board" created by the Sarbanes-Oxley Act, with responsibility to register public accounting firms, and to establish quality control, ethics and independence standards for auditors. The Act also directed the Board to "perform such other duties or functions . . . necessary or appropriate to promote high professional standards among, and improve the quality of audit services . . . in order to protect investors or to further the public interest."[126] The Board's five members could include only two current or former certified public accountants and its Chair could not be a CPA who had practised within the past five years prior to appointment to the Board.

Alternative models are available from other nations as well. For example, a new Canadian Public Accountability Board ("CPAB") began operating in October 2002. It performs a function comparable to that of its U.S. counterpart. With eleven members, seven of whom are not accountants, the CPAB oversees firms performing audits of Canadian public companies. That oversight includes independent inspection of accounting firm behavior, supplementing, if not supplanting, the work of self-regulatory bodies.[127]

While these models are not in all respects a direct fit for the legal profession, their direction is worth exploring. Adding a role for public representation in formulating and enforcing lawyers' ethical responsibilities would provide a critical perspective on rules designed primarily by and for the profession.[128] Moving away from bar selection of token public representatives on various regulatory committees is another important step.[129]

---

[125] RHODE, REFORMING THE LEGAL PROFESSION, *supra* note 18, at 200.

[126] Sarbanes-Oxley Act of 2002, *supra* note 20, § 101(c). The appointment of board members has proven controversial; *see* Stephen Labaton, *S.E.C. Appears Split on Board to Oversee Accountants*, N.Y. TIMES, Oct. 8, 2002 at C1; Adrian Michaels, *White House Steps in Over Furore at SEC*, FIN. TIMES, Oct. 5, 2002 at C1; Michael Schroeder, *SEC Widens Hunt for Audit Board*, WALL ST. J., Oct. 8, 2002, at A8.

[127] Richard Blackwell, *Auditing firms get tighter rules*, GLOBE & MAIL, online edition, July 18, 2002, *available at* http://www.globeandmail.com/servlet/RTGAMArticleHTMLTemplate?tf=gam/realtime/f... (last accessed July 18, 2002); Press Release, Canadian Ministry of Finance, *Manley Welcomes Auditor Oversight Body as Part of Actions Needed to Strengthen Public Confidence in Canada's Financial Markets* (July 17, 2002) (on file with the authors).

[128] RHODE, REFORMING THE LEGAL PROFESSION, *supra* note 18, at 208.

[129] *Id.* at 146.

The legal profession has traditionally opposed such oversight structures on the grounds that they would risk government domination, threaten courts' inherent power to regulate the practice of law, and jeopardize the separation of powers.[130] As the preamble to the ABA's Model Rules emphasizes: "An independent legal profession is an important force in preserving government under law, for abuse of legal authority is more readily challenged by a profession whose members are not dependent on government for the right to practice."[131] But governmental control and regulatory autonomy are not the only alternatives. Nor is preserving professional independence the only value. Some measure of public accountability is also necessary as a check on self-interest. The models that other nations and other professions have developed could be adapted in ways that provide safeguards against state retaliation.[132] While this is not the occasion for a detailed blueprint of alternative regulatory structures, it is an opportunity to emphasize their importance for any post-Enron reform agenda. Greater public accountability would be the best strategy for avoiding undue public control, and ensuring some of the professional independence necessary for a well-functioning legal system.

D. Liability Standards

With or without such structural changes in bar regulatory processes, it would be possible, and desirable, to reconsider certain specific ethical rules that contribute to debacles like Enron. One is the absence of appropriate standards of third-party liability for lawyers who passively acquiesce in client fraud. In some states, including Texas, privity requirements now bar non-clients from suing attorneys for "wilful blindness" to client misconduct.[133] At least under state law, Vinson & Elkins attorneys would be exempt from liability to third parties if a court found that they acted in good faith and

---

[130] *See id.* at 14–15; Charles Wolfram, Modern Legal Ethics (1986); *see also* Carroll Seron, *Is "In the Interests of Justice" In the Interests of Lawyers? A Question of Power and Politics,* 70 Fordham L. Rev. 1849, 1851–52 (2002).

[131] American Bar Association, Model Rules of Professional Conduct, Preamble, para. 10 (2001).

[132] *See* Rhode, Reforming the Legal Profession, *supra* note 18, at 145–146.

[133] McCamish v. F.E. Appling Interests, 991 S.W. 2d 787, 792 (Tex. 1999). Federal law may impose liability more broadly; see Securities Exchange Act of 1934, § 15 U.S.C.S. § 78j, and Securities and Exchange Commission Rule 10b-5 promulgated thereunder, 17 C.F.R. § 240.10b-5. *But see* Central Bank of Denver v. First Interstate Bank of Denver, 511 U.S. 164 (1994) (holding that a private cause of action could not be sustained against a defendant that had not been the "primary violator" of a statutory prohibition, assuming "all of the requirements for primary liability," and that had not engaged in any directly manipulative or deceptive acts). Courts of Appeal have split on the proper interpretation of *Central Bank, see In re* Software Tools, 50 F. 3d 1215 (9th Cir. 1996); Anixter v. Home-Stake Production Co., 77 F. 3d 1215 (10th Cir. 1996); David E. Rovella, *Milberg Guns for Enron's Lawyers,* Nat'l Law J., April 15, 2002, at A1; *see also* Jenny B. Davis, *The Enron Factor,* A.B.A. J., April 2002, at 40, 44.

that their activities did not constitute "conduct in furtherance of a fraud."[134] Given the important role that malpractice proceedings play in enforcing ethical standards, such liability restrictions require rethinking.[135]

Limited Liability Partnerships ("LLPs") are another example of rules designed by and for the profession that deserve a closer look. Texas was the first state to enact legislation creating LLPs for lawyers in the wake of the Savings and Loan scandals, and now such structures are permissible with variations in almost every state.[136] These structures largely eliminate personal financial exposure for partners in firms implicated in malpractice proceedings. LLPs absolve non-supervising lawyers of any financial responsibility for their colleagues' ethical violations, and deprive victims of remedies if those who commit the violations lack adequate assets or insurance coverage.[137] In essence, LLPs privilege professional over public interests. Moreover, the benefits of this system flow disproportionately to the largest law firms, which could most readily prevent and spread the costs of misconduct.[138] Reducing this insulation from accountability could give lawyers greater incentives to address collegial misconduct and to establish the internal oversight structures that can check abuses.[139]

E. Substantive Standards and Professional Norms

Of course, reforming professional rules will not of itself transform professional culture. Indeed, many commentators have highlighted the limitations of doctrinal tinkering in their assessment of new criminal prohibitions proposed in the wake of Enron. According to some critics, these new provisions are "as likely to make things worse as make them better. The reason is both too simple and all too easily ignored: Criminal laws lead people to focus on what is legal instead of what is right."[140] Similar

---

[134] Central Bank of Denver, 511 U.S. 164 (1994); *see also* Davis, *supra* note 133, at 40, 44.

[135] For a more detailed discussion of third party liability for malpractice and options for reform, see RHODE, REFORMING THE LEGAL PROFESSION, *supra* note 18, at 165–168.

[136] Martha Neil, *Partners at Risk*, A.B.A. J., Aug. 2002, at 45–46; Charles W. Wolfram, *Inherent Powers in the Crucible of Lawyer Self-Protection: Reflections on the LLP Campaign*, 39 S. TEX. L. REV 359, 359, 364 n.10 & 11, 365 (1998), citing John S. Dzienkowski, *Legal Malpractice and the Multistate Law Firm: Supervision of Multistate Offices; Firms as Limited Liability Partnerships; and Predispute Agreements to Arbitrate Client Malpractice Claims*, 36 S. TEX. L. REV. 967, 981–982 (1995); *see also* Robert W. Hamilton, *Registered Limited Liability Partnerships: Present at the Birth (Nearly)*, 66 U. COLO. L. REV. 1065 (1995).

[137] RHODE, REFORMING THE LEGAL PROFESSION, *supra* note 18, at 167.

[138] Poonam Puri, *Judgment Proofing the Profession*, 15 GEO. J. L. ETHICS 1 (2001).

[139] Neil, *supra* note 136, at 47 (quoting Robert Hillman); Cramton, *supra* note 54, at 175; Ted Schneyer, *A Tale of Four Systems: Reflections on How Law Influences the "Ethical Infrastructure" of Law Firms*, 39 S. TEX. L. REV. 245, at 273, 276 (1998).

[140] David Steel & William Stuntz, *Another Attempt to Legislate Corporate Honesty*, N.Y. TIMES, July 10, 2002, at A25.

claims are often made about a rule-bound approach to professional ethics. But at least some of the problems involved in Enron and subsequent corporate scandals involved a failure to focus on what was legal or on gaps in what the law required.[141] Moreover, good rules can prescribe as well as prohibit; they can encourage individuals to behave in socially defensible ways by framing the interests at issue in terms of accepted moral values.[142] Regulation is no substitute for internalized norms, but it can foster their development and reinforce their exercise.[143]

Efforts to rethink professional regulatory standards could also profit from international comparisons. In an era of increasing globalization in legal practice, it makes sense to consider how other nations deal with similar issues.[144] For example, although American lawyers generally view client loyalty and adversarial practices as pre-eminent values, other common law systems function effectively without such norms. The English and Canadian legal professions recognize greater obligations as officers of the court than does their American counterpart.[145]

American lawyers' tendency to privilege client interests over other values is not, of course, readily challenged. The current norm is rooted not only in practitioners' bottom-line concerns, as Vinson & Elkins alleged conduct amply demonstrates, but also in cognitive psychological processes. As many legal ethics experts note, in cases of client misconduct, lawyers' professional norms of client loyalty often conflict with personal norms of honesty and integrity. To reduce the cognitive dissonance, lawyers will often unconsciously dismiss or discount evidence of misconduct and its impact on third parties.[146] The risks of such dissonance are exacerbated when lawyers bond socially and professionally with the client's management team. The more that counsel

---

[141] For lack of attention to legal compliance, see Robert Prentice, *An Ethics Lesson for Business Schools*, N.Y. TIMES, Aug. 20, 2002, at A21. For gaps in the law, see the discussion of SPEs and accounting practices, at text accompanying *supra* notes 26–34.

[142] W. Bradley Wendel, *Public Values and Professional Responsibility*, 75 NOTRE DAME L. REV. 1, 22 (1999).

[143] RHODE, REFORMING THE LEGAL PROFESSION, *supra* note 18, at 18; *see also* Ted Schneyer, *supra*, note 139, at 1839–1840; Tanina Rostain, *Ethics Lost: Limitations of Current Approaches to Lawyer Regulation*, 71 S. CAL. L. REV. 1273, 1277, (1998).

[144] *See* Mary C. Daly, *The Dichotomy Between Standards and Rules: A New Way of Understanding the Differences in Perceptions of Lawyer Codes of Conduct by U.S. and Foreign Lawyers*, 32 VAND. J. TRANSNAT'L L. 1117, 1157–1161 (1999); Paul D. Paton, *Legal Services and The GATS: Norms as Barriers to Trade*, 9 NEW ENGL. J. INT'L & COMP. L. 361 (2003).

[145] Christopher J. Whelan, *Ethical Conflicts in Legal Practice: Creating Professional Responsibility*, 52 S.C. L. Rev 697, 700–702 (2001); *see also,* LEGAL PROFESSION ACT, S.B.C., ch. 9, § 3 (1998) (British Columbia, Can.) ("Public interest paramount"); LAW SOCIETY OF BRITISH COLUMBIA, PROFESSIONAL CONDUCT HANDBOOK, CANONS OF LEGAL ETHICS, ch. 1; LAW SOCIETY OF UPPER CANADA, RULES OF PROFESSIONAL CONDUCT, Rule 4.01(1)(2), 4.06(1); CHRISTINE PARKER, JUST LAWYERS 88–95(1999).

[146] Donald C. Langevoort, *The Epistemology of Corporate-Securities Lawyering: Beliefs, Biases and Organizational Behavior*, 63 BROOK. L. REV. 629, 650 (1997).

blends into the culture of corporate insiders, the greater the pressures of conformity to group norms. That, in turn, encourages lawyers to underestimate risk and to suppress compromising information in order to preserve internal solidarity.[147] Yet in the long run, this dynamic may ill serve all concerned. Clients lose access to disinterested advice; lawyers lose capacity for independent judgment and moral autonomy; and the public loses protection from organizational misconduct. Enron is a case history of all those costs.

The problems in maintaining independence are especially challenging for in-house counsel, who generally face the greatest pressures to maintain group cohesion. Although outside lawyers can risk substantial losses in power and profits from walking away from a major client, the results are seldom devastating. For in-house counsel, the stakes are higher; their position involves "maximum information, maximum responsibility, and minimum job security."[148] Rules requiring these lawyers to report misconduct can provide a much-needed counterweight against pressures to remain team players. The Sarbanes-Oxley legislation is a step in the right direction, by requiring disclosure of evidence of misconduct in at least some circumstances. Further reforms are equally necessary in state bar ethical rules and rules governing whistleblowers.[149]

The organized bar's resistance to such federal regulation is troubling on several counts. According to then-ABA President Robert Hirshon, "We don't need the S.E.C. to be drafting new codes of ethics."[150] A.P. Carlton, Hirshon's successor as President, agreed, noting, "I've never seen the practicing bar—all the different lawyers' organizations—so unified."[151] Carlton vigorously defended the status quo: "We have a very fine system of lawyer regulation in this country. . . . If lawyers have transgressed, they will be called into account."[152] Would that it were true. But legislators, regulators, and the general public have understandably taken a different view, well-supported by the recent record of regulatory failures. Lawyers have been involved in most of the leading corporate scandals in recent memory, and the bar's own regulatory responses have been demonstrably inadequate. While lawyers have justifiable concerns about potential conflicts between federal and state ethical rules, the answer is not to pre-empt

---

[147] *Id.* at 637, 647–648, 655–656. For a discussion of irrational risk taking to cover up problems, *see* Richard W. Painter, *Irrationality and Cognitive Bias at a Closing in Arthur Solmssen's The Comfort Letter,* 69 FORDHAM L. REV. 1111 (2000).

[148] DEBORAH L. RHODE & GEOFFREY HAZARD, ON PROFESSIONAL RESPONSIBILITY AND REGULATION 128 (2002).

[149] RHODE, REFORMING THE LEGAL PROFESSION, *supra* note 18, at 109–115; Cramton, *supra* note 54, at 184–86; Leonard M. Baynes, *Just Pucker and Blow?: An Analysis of Corporate Whistleblowers, The Duty of Care, The Duty of Loyalty, and the Sarbanes-Oxley Act,* 76 ST. JOHN'S L. REV. 875, 891–96 (2002).

[150] Jonathan D. Glater, *Round Up the Usual Suspects. Lawyers, Too?,* N.Y. TIMES, Aug. 4, 2002, at 3, 4.

[151] Jonathan Peterson, *SEC Wants Attorneys to Stand Up to Companies' Misconduct,* L.A. TIMES, May 19, 2003, at C1, C5.

[152] Glater, *Legal Uproar, supra* note 101 , at C2 (quoting Carlton).

needed reforms. It is rather for the bar to cooperate with other regulatory entities in establishing socially responsible rules and a professional culture that reinforces them. That will require the best efforts, not only of lawyers and government officials, but also of professional schools.

V. PROFESSIONAL EDUCATION AFTER ENRON

In a publication targeted to students and faculties, it is appropriate to close with a few observations about the professional responsibilities of professional schools. One of the few welcome by-products of recent scandals is likely to be increased curricular attention to legal and business ethics. It was, after all, Watergate that inspired the first systematic coverage of such topics a quarter-century ago, and recent scandals are a necessary reminder of progress yet to be made.[153]

Before the mid-1970s, professional responsibility education was noticeable for its absence. Many schools offered only anecdotal lectures, for which no credit and no grade were given. And in some schools, neither were the lectures.[154] The curricular coverage that did occur was usually short on content and long on platitudes. "General piffle" was the description offered by one of the few early twentieth century scholars in the field.[155]

Watergate was a much needed watershed in professional education. The sheer number of lawyers and business executives involved in illegal activities under the Nixon administration contributed to a sharp dip in public standing. Popular opinion surveys found that respect for the legal profession, never high to begin with, sunk to new lows, with lawyers narrowly edging out used-car salesmen.[156] American Bar Association leaders, in search of some visible and easily implemented response, decided to require that all accredited law schools provide mandatory instruction in professional responsibility.[157] Many business schools imposed similar ethics requirements.[158]

The adequacy of this response was open to challenge. At least initially, many law schools made only token efforts at compliance and offered minimal coverage of bar disciplinary codes. Many of these offerings constituted the functional equivalent of

---

[153] For the evolution of legal ethics curricula, see Deborah L. Rhode, *Legal Ethics by the Pervasive Method*, 42 J. LEGAL EDUC. 31, 33–39 (1972) [hereinafter Rhode, *Legal Ethics by the Pervasive Method*]. For the ethics curricula in business schools, see *id.* at 37–39; Jeff Gottlieb, *Enron Ethics—The Business Course*, L. A. TIMES, July 9, 2002, at B1, B4; Charles Powers & David Vogel, *Ethics in the Education of Business Managers*, HASTINGS CENTER REPORT (1980). For the evolution of ethics curricula generally, see Derek C. Bok, *Can Ethics Be Taught?*, CHANGE, Oct. 1976, at 26. For a discussion of the effect of Watergate, see also Paul R. Tremblay, *Shared Norms, Bad Lawyers, and the Virtues of Casuistry*, 36 U.S.F. L. REV. 659, 673 (2002).

[154] Rhode, *Legal Ethics by the Pervasive Method*, *supra* note 153, at 35.

[155] George P. Costigan, Jr., *The Teaching of Legal Ethics*, 4 AM. U. L. REV. 290, 295 (1917).

[156] Rhode, *Legal Ethics by the Pervasive Method*, *supra* note 153, at 39.

[157] *Id.* at 39; A.B.A., STANDARDS FOR THE APPROVAL OF LAW SCHOOLS, Standard 302(a)(iii)(1974).

[158] Gottlieb, *supra* note 153, at B4.

legal ethics without the ethics.[159] Cartoonist Garry Trudeau captured widespread reactions to this form of moral fiber. As presented in his Doonesbury comic strip, the new professional responsibility requirement appeared little more than "trendy lip service to our better selves."[160] Most observers found it ludicrous to suppose that the massive misconduct among Nixon appointees and campaign contributors stemmed from their lack of familiarity with bar codes of conduct.[161] On the rare occasions when anyone asked, Watergate defendants acknowledged as much. As John Dean once put it, "I knew the things I was doing were wrong and one learns the difference between right and wrong long before they enter law school. A course in legal ethics would not have changed anything."[162]

It seems equally implausible that today's hue and cry for more ethics courses in business schools will of itself ensure more ethics in business.[163] Yet President Bush, in a recent Wall Street address, joined countless other commentators in demanding that "Our schools of business must be principled teachers of right and wrong and not surrender to moral confusion and relativism."[164]

If that is, in fact, the mission of the academy, most observers believe that our current efforts fall well short.[165] According to a recent survey by the National Association of Scholars, only a quarter of business students believed that the most common statement about ethics transmitted by professors was that there were "clear and uniform standards of right and wrong by which everyone should be judged." About three-

---

[159] See Rhode, *Legal Ethics by the Pervasive Method*, supra note 153, at 40; see also RHODE, REFORMING THE LEGAL PROFESSION, supra note 18.

[160] Garry Trudeau, *Doonesbury*, reprinted in THOMAS D. MORGAN & RONALD D. ROTUNDA, PROFESSIONAL RESPONSIBILITY: PROBLEMS AND MATERIALS (7th ed. 2000).

[161] See Rhode, *Legal Ethics by the Pervasive Method*, supra note 153, at 39; Hart Jones, *Lawyers and Justice, The Uneasy Ethics of Partisanship*, 23 VILL. L. REV. 957 (1978).

[162] John Dean, *quoted in* Thomas Lickona, *What Does Moral Psychology Have to Say to the Teacher of Ethics*, in ETHICS TEACHING IN HIGHER EDUCATION 129 (Daniel Callahan & Sissela Bok, eds., 1980).

[163] See Tremblay, supra note 153, at 673–674, (commenting on the $20 million donation in 1987 by then-SEC Chair John Shad to Harvard Business School for business ethics education, at the time of insider trading and junk bond scandals involving Ivan Boesky and Michael Milken: "Did John Shad really believe that Ivan Boesky's criminal activities were the result of inadequate instruction in business school classes? It does seem fair to draw a distinction between brazenly illegal behavior and worrisome but borderline unethical behavior, and it then seems not a little naïve to suggest that felons and law breakers just need a good does of compulsory chapel."). For similar scepticism, see business school faculty members interviewed in Lynley Browning, *M.B.A. Programs Now Screen for Integrity, Too*, N.Y. TIMES, Sept. 15, 2002, at B4; Penelope Patsuris, *Can Integrity be Taught?*, FORBES.COM, Oct. 4, 2002, *available at* http://www.forbes.com/2002/10/04/1004virtue.html (last accessed Oct. 4, 2002).

[164] Press Release, *Bush Announces Tough New Enforcement Initiatives for Reform* (July 9, 2002), *available at* http://www.whitehouse/gov/news/releases/2002/07. *See also* Browning, *Money, Ethics and the M.B.A.*, N.Y. TIMES, Aug. 25, 2002, Letters to the Editor, at A16; Charles Duhigg, *Ethicists at the Gate: Can Harvard Make Its Graduates Behave?*, BOSTON GLOBE, Dec. 8, 2002 at D5.

[165] See sources cited in *supra* notes 162 and 163, and *infra* note 168.

quarters believed that the message conveyed was that "what is right and wrong depends on differences in individual values and cultural diversity."[166] Although almost all of those surveyed felt that their studies were helpful in preparing them to behave ethically in business life, "most were cynical about the moral culture they would confront there." Over half believed that the "only real difference between executives at Enron and those at most other big companies is that those at Enron got caught."[167] If the message to students is that the morality of conduct depends on culture, and the culture of business values money over morality, there is surely cause for concern.

Our own view is that better ethics coverage is necessary in undergraduate and professional schools, but not for the reason that President Bush and other commentators have offered. The basic responsibility for "teaching right and wrong" cannot rest with universities. For that mission, courses on legal and business ethics offer too little too late. A few hours of classroom discussion is unlikely to alter the values that individuals have acquired over a lifetime from families, churches, schools, peers, and the culture generally.[168] As one Harvard Business School student put it, "the real causes of the recent business scandals lie not in our classrooms, but in ourselves. Put simply, Enron and WorldCom and Tyco didn't happen because CEOs ignored their Aristotle. . . . They happened because they—like you and I—really wanted to get rich."[169]

Yet, while the contributions of professional responsibility education should not be overstated, neither should they be undervalued. Most research indicates that strategies for dealing with ethical issues change significantly during early adulthood, and that well-designed curricular coverage can improve capacities for moral reasoning.[170] Such coverage can increase students' understanding of ethical dilemmas, as well as the analytic approaches and regulatory responses that can assist in solutions. Rather than abstract sermonizing on "right and wrong," ethics curricula can focus on concrete cases, as well as on professional codes, organizational policies, and legal requirements. So, too, well-designed courses can explore the structural conditions underlying moral dilemmas and the most promising regulatory responses.

Measured by this more modest goal, current professional ethics instruction still leaves much to be desired. In most law schools, it is relegated to a single required

---

[166] *Report on Ethics, Enron, and American Higher Education: An NAS/Zogby Poll of College Seniors,* National Association of Scholars, *available at* http://www.nas.org/reports/zogethics_poll/zogby _ethics_report.htm.

[167] *Id.*

[168] *See* Rhode, *Legal Ethics by the Pervasive Method, supra* note 153, at 44–46; James S. Leming, *Curricular Effectiveness in Moral Values Education: A Review of Research,* 10 J. MORAL EDUC. 147 (1981); Ann Colby & Thomas Ehrlich, *Higher Education and the Development of Civic Responsibility, in* THOMAS EHRLICH, CIVIC RESPONSIBILITY AND HIGHER EDUCATION (2000).

[169] Dunhigg, *supra,* note 164, at D5.

[170] Rhode, *Legal Ethics by the Pervasive Method, supra* note 153, at 45–46; Deborah L. Rhode, *The Professional Responsibility of Professors,* 51 J. LEGAL EDUC. 158, 165 (2001) [hereinafter Rhode, *Professional Responsibility of Professors*].

course that ranks low on the academic pecking order. Although ethical issues arise in every subject, that would not be apparent from the core curriculum, or from leading casebooks, which devote less than 2% of their total coverage to professional responsibility concerns.[171] With a few notable exceptions, business schools do no better.[172] Such marginalized treatment of professional responsibility topics undercut the message they intend to convey. Ethics need to be the focus not only of specialized courses but also of coverage throughout the curricula. Students learn from subtexts as well as texts, and silence is a powerful socializing force.

The point of such integrated approaches to professional responsibility is not for faculty members to use the podium as a bully pulpit. It is rather to help students develop their own capacities for moral reasoning, to heighten their understanding of legal and ethical boundaries, and to learn what imposes pressure to cross them. Although many faculty members are uncomfortable with explicit discussion of moral values, their failure to initiate such discussion is not value-neutral. And the implicit content of current curricula has disquieting dimensions. For example, recent surveys find that as students go through business school, their priorities shift from consumer needs and product quality to shareholder value and stock prices.[173] Many individuals accordingly believe that they will have to act contrary to their values in corporate culture.[174] The prevailing image is that portrayed in a recent *New Yorker* caricature of a corporate boardroom. There, a well-heeled chair solemnly reminds his colleagues, "we are gathered here today, gentlemen, to make money."[175]

So, too, many students who enter law school talking of justice leave talking of jobs, and client loyalty becomes a pre-eminent priority. As new lawyers quickly discover, firms are generally ranked on profits per partner, not on broader criteria of social responsibility such as pro bono service, adequate internal ethics structures, and the incidence of malpractice, disciplinary, or discovery sanctions.[176] Overemphasizing short-term financial performance has paved the way for much of the misconduct that now belatedly attracts our attention.

Enron et al. should serve as a wake up call to improve both teaching and research on professional ethics. More interdisciplinary approaches should be crucial priorities. The ethical challenges that confront those in professional roles cut across subject-matter boundaries. An effective response to corporate abuses requires collaboration among professionals from diverse backgrounds, such as law, management, economics, organizational behavior, and public policy. Professional schools could play a central role in

---

[171] Rhode, *Professional Responsibility of Professors, supra* note 170, at 164.

[172] Gottlieb, *supra* note 153; Browning, *supra* note 163.

[173] Gottlieb, *supra* note 153; Browning, *supra* note 163.

[174] Gottlieb, *supra* note 153; Browning, *supra* note 163.

[175] Cartoon, NEW YORKER, Aug. 12, 2002, at 64.

[176] *See, e.g, The Global 100,* AMERICAN LAWYER, Nov. 2001, *available at* http://www.americanlawyer.com/newcontents11.html (last accessed Nov. 5, 2002).

identifying the structural causes of misconduct and the strategies most effective in addressing them.

VI. THE END OF THE BEGINNING

Debacles like Enron have all the makings of medieval morality plays. The challenge is to ensure that a more enduring legacy from the lessons they impart. Part of that challenge involves building stronger coalitions among stakeholders. The corporate misconduct still unfolding involves failures of multiple regulatory institutions.[177] Accountants, politicians, lawyers, government regulators, corporate officers, and financial advisors all need to work together to devise solutions. It should not take the loss of billions of dollars to remind the professions of progress yet to be made and our personal responsibility to make that progress possible.

QUESTIONS

1. What should a lawyer's obligation be when he or she has reservations about the morality or legality of a company's conduct, even though that conduct might not constitute "material violations" of securities laws? Does your answer change if the lawyer is acting as in-house counsel, rather than as an attorney from an outside law firm?

2. Is "noisy withdrawal" by lawyers ever appropriate or necessary? If auditor resignations serve to protect the public by signalling to the market that corporate conduct is awry, why should lawyers be exempted from similar requirements? Do the steps in the SEC's Proposed Rule on Minimum Standards of Attorney Conduct go too far, as most bar leaders suggest? Do they go far enough?

3. Should Vinson & Elkins have accepted the retainer to investigate the allegations Sherron Watkins raised? Was Enron's waiver of any conflict of interest enough to permit Vinson & Elkins to take on that representation?

4. On at least two different occasions, junior in-house counsel at Enron raised concerns about firm conduct, only to have those concerns dismissed by senior lawyers. Other in-house counsel raised misgivings with outside firms but not with senior firm management or the board. What strategies would be most likely to encourage reporting by subordinate lawyers? Is the SEC's proposed approach sufficient? Should firms be responsible for establishing formal channels for addressing ethical concerns and protecting internal whistleblowers? Consider Rule 5.2 of the ABA's Model Rules of Professional Conduct, which provides that a "subordinate lawyer does not violate the rules of professional conduct if that lawyer acts in

---

[177] For more recent illustrations, see Kurt Eichenwald, *Charges Against Ex-Enron Official Unveil Some Ugly Truths*, N.Y. TIMES at A1, Oct. 3, 2002; Batson Report, *supra* note 27.

accordance with a supervisory lawyer's reasonable resolution of an arguable question of professional duty." Is this Rule adequate to deal with situations like Enron?

5. Are the American Bar Association objections to SEC regulation of lawyer conduct warranted? Who should regulate lawyers? Who should be able to decide?

Business Ethics at "The Crooked E"

Duane Windsor*

On December 2, 2001, Enron filed the then-largest corporate bankruptcy in U.S. history, measured by reported assets.[1] (WorldCom filed a larger bankruptcy in 2002.)[2] Enron reported recently that it is the object of some 22,000 claims by various injured stakeholders, totaling $400 billion.[3] This essay assesses what (sadly) passed for "business ethics" at Enron and at other firms associated with Enron; and also examines key public policy and corporate governance reforms for fostering responsible management in the wake of multiple corporate scandals.[4] At Enron, "business ethics" *was* an

---

* Lynette S. Autrey Professor of Management, Jesse H. Jones Graduate School of Management, Rice University.

[1] *In re Enron Corp.*, No. 01-16034 (Bankr. S.D.N.Y. 2001).

[2] *In re WorldCom, Inc.*, No. 02-13533 (Bankr. S.D.N.Y. 2002).

[3] Darren Fonda, *Enron: Picking over the carcass*, TIME, Dec. 30, 2001–Jan. 6, 2002 (double issue), at 56. The Enron bankruptcy occurred in declining economic conditions and following on the 9-11 (2001) terrorist attacks on the World Trade Center and the Pentagon, so that tracing the bankruptcy's effects and repercussions are difficult. Economic weakness and accounting irregularities in 2002 resulted in a record bankruptcy year measured as $368 billion in assets. *The year of the falling companies*, HOUS. CHRON., Jan. 2, 2003, at 1B (citing BankruptcyData.com). There were 257 Chapter 11 bankruptcy filings in 2001 by public companies, versus 186 in 2002. *Id.* Over those two years, Chapter 11 filings involved $626 billion in assets. *Id.* Year 2003 may be at least as bad. *Id.*

[4] Martha Stewart, then a member of the NYSE governing board, allegedly engaged in insider trading in ImClone Systems stock. Stewart was indicted, as was her former stockbroker Peter Bacanovic, in early June 2003. Five counts were alleged against Stewart, including obstruction of justice, conspiracy, lying to investigators, and securities fraud. Both defendants pleaded innocent. The SEC filed a civil action for insider trading that would bar Stewart from ever leading a public company. (There was no criminal charge of insider trading.) *See* Erin McClam (Associated Press), *Stewart's denial now part of case: Prosecutors call it securities fraud*, Hous. Chron., June 6, 2003, at 1C, 2C. In late May 2003, NBC televised a film, *Martha Inc.: The Story of Martha Stewart,* based on the book by CHRISTOPHER M. BYRON, MARTHA INC.: THE INCREDIBLE STORY OF MARTHA STEWART LIVING OMNIMEDIA (Wheeler Pub., 2002). Of course, scandals and stock markets go back a long way. In the 1930s, Richard Whitney, a former NYSE president (and apparent confidant of J.P. Morgan), went to prison for theft.

oxymoron.[5] It may be, however, that the board of directors was duped, as well as negligent, and that corruption and misconduct were restricted to a handful of key executives.[6] (Ongoing investigations may reveal the truth.) There is no reason on any present evidence to suspect the vast majority of Enron employees—who lost jobs, pensions, and reputations—of any legal or moral indiscretions. In keeping with Machiavelli's advice to *The Prince* to appear honorable always,[7] Enron leadership made a public display of professed ethical standards, corporate citizenship, and consumer welfare innovations having nothing to do with actual motives or conduct.[8] The public display marched with imprudent disregard or perhaps even contempt for customary business morality, fiduciary responsibility, stakeholder responsibility, and in at least some proven instances, law.[9]

The Enron debacle reveals lessons about business leadership, corporate governance, and government regulation. What happened is reasonably clear—in rough outline, if not yet in full detail. Greed and opportunism at the top were, of course, the motive

---

[5] *Cf.* Norman Augustine, *Foreword* to JEFFREY SEGLIN, THE GOOD, THE BAD, AND YOUR BUSINESS: CHOOSING RIGHT WHEN ETHICAL DILEMMAS PULL YOU APART, at vii (2000).

[6] In testimony before the House Committee on Energy and Commerce, Subcommittee on Oversight and Investigations, Robert K. Jaedicke rejected the conclusions concerning the Enron board of the Powers Committee. He argued that a board must rely on cross-checking controls and "the full and complete reporting of information to it" (by management and outside advisors). *See The Role of the Board of Directors in Enron's Collapse: Hearing Before the House Comm. on Energy and Commerce, Subcomm. on Oversight and Investigation,* 107th Cong. 511 (2002) (testimony of Robert K. Jaedicke, Enron Bd. of Dir., Chairman Audit and Compliance Comm.). In Jaedicke's view, the board received regular assurances of legality and appropriateness of transactions and adequacy of internal controls. *Id.* The board may have been overwhelmed by "systemic failure" and had no direct interest in any of the transactions. *Id.* "We could not have predicted that all the controls would fail." *Id.* Jaedicke's view cannot be rejected out of hand. On the contrary, it raises the difficulty that a very stringent standard of vigilance must be defined for the board in ways that mean concretely an utter lack of trust in management and external advisors. By prevailing standards of the time, anything less than a very vigilant board might have been duped; by the same token, the board may also have been negligent.

[7] NICCOLÒ MACHIAVELLI, THE PRINCE 109 (Leo P.S. de Alvarez trans., 1980) (1515).

[8] Steve Salbu, *Foreword* to BRIAN CRUVER, ANATOMY OF GREED: THE UNSHREDDED TRUTH FROM AN ENRON INSIDER, at xii (2002) (noting that *Fortune* surveys for 1996 through 2001 identified Enron as the most innovative U.S. firm).

[9] LARRY A. ELLIOTT & RICHARD J. SCHROTH, HOW COMPANIES LIE: WHY ENRON IS JUST THE TIP OF THE ICEBERG 25 (2002). Salbu calls the effect "bone-chilling." Salbu, *supra* note 8. Enron emphasized principles of "respect, integrity, communications, and excellence." *Id.* These principles were nicknamed RICE internally. CRUVER, *supra* note 8, at 43. Chairman Kenneth L. Lay's letter to the shareholders in the 2001 annual report "contained a lengthy and heady sermon about the integrity and high standards of the Enron culture" and social responsibility and stakeholder protection activities. ELLIOTT & SCHROTH, *supra* at 24. CFO Andrew S. Fastow was named CFO of the Year by *CFO* magazine for innovative financial engineering. *Id.* at 31. Jeffrey K. Skilling was introduced at one conference as the number one CEO in America. D. QUINN MILLS, BUY, LIE, AND SELL HIGH: HOW INVESTORS LOST OUT ON ENRON AND THE INTERNET BUBBLE 48 (2002). Fastow is quoted as stating: "We're going to do the right

and the modus operandi, respectively.[10] "Enron failed because its leadership was morally, ethically, and financially corrupt."[11] But greed and opportunism are expected of all market actors (if not, strictly speaking, socially encouraged). "Shirking" by managers is at the heart of agency theory. Given shirking, a board can trust management only where trust can be personally confirmed in moral integrity or reasonably reliable (and hence costly) contracts and controls.[12] Why greed and opportunism got so wildly, and widely, out of hand, has not yet been well studied.[13] The interesting possibility is that not only did key actors lack any effective internal moral compass and believe (as must all "Machiavels") that some end justifies any means (and some undoubtedly violated laws), but they may have substituted other values for fiduciary, moral, and legal responsibilities. It is not necessary to dwell on distinctions here—Enron flagrantly violated all of these responsibilities.[14] The Enron value set apparently included an extreme laissez-faire ideology of absolutely "free" (i.e., absolutely unregulated) markets[15]—conceptualized as purely price-volume mechanisms;[16] and a cynical (if arguably valid)

---

thing and make money without having to do anything but the right thing." *Id.* at 47 (citing Shaila K. Dewan, *Enron's Many Strands: A Case Study; A Video Study of Enron Offers A Picture of Life Before the Fall*, N.Y. TIMES, Jan. 31, 2002, at C7 (quoting Robert F. Bruner & Samuel E. Bodily, Darden Graduate School of Business Administration, U. of Virginia, *A Video Study of Enron Officers, A Picture of Life Before the Fall* (2002))).

[10] "Greed is good," proclaimed the character Gordon Gekko (played by Michael Douglas) in the film *Wall Street*. Salbu, *supra* note 9, at xiv (quoting *Wall Street* (20th Century-Fox 1987)).

[11] ROBERT BRYCE, PIPE DREAMS: GREED, EGO, AND THE DEATH OF ENRON 12 (2002).

[12] It is possible to model morally sensitive agents. Douglas E. Stevens & Alex Thevaranjan, *Ethics and Agency Theory: Incorporating a Standard for Effort and an Ethically Sensitive Agent* (Syracuse University Working Paper, Oct. 18, 2002). Carroll suggests that the supply of moral managers could prove thin. Archie B. Carroll, *The Pyramid of Corporate Social Responsibility: Toward the Moral Management of Organizational Stakeholders*, 34.4 BUS. HORIZONS 39, 39–48 (1991).

[13] *Cf.* BRYCE, *supra* note 11, at 8.

[14] *See* Terry L. Price, *The Ethics of Authentic Transformational Leadership*, 14.1 LEADERSHIP QUARTERLY 67, 67–81 (2003) (arguing that leaders may sometimes behave immorally because they are blinded by their own values).

[15] PETER C. FUSARO & ROSS M. MILLER, WHAT WENT WRONG AT ENRON: EVERYONE'S GUIDE TO THE LARGEST BANKRUPTCY IN U.S. HISTORY 2, 20, 28 (2002).

[16] This extreme ideology (by no means unique to Enron) is a profound distortion of the liberal market economy tradition. Adam Smith in THE THEORY OF MORAL SENTIMENTS (1759) and THE WEALTH OF NATIONS (1776) argued that (workably) competitive markets will outperform (unsound) government monopolies and excessive regulation, so that economic self-interest should be free to innovate. *See* James Q. Wilson, *Adam Smith on Business Ethics*, 32.1 CAL. MGMT. REV. 59, 59–71 (1989). But Smith also made important assumptions about the cooperative nature of society, moral education, and moral sympathy for others. Alfred Marshall, in his neoclassical PRINCIPLES OF ECONOMICS (various editions), emphasized ethics in economic behavior. Milton Friedman argued for profit maximization—but with (appropriate) legal and moral "rules of the game" and an early stakeholder conception of the firm. *See* Milton Friedman, *The Social Responsibility of Business*, N.Y. TIMES MAG., Sept. 13, 1970, at 32–33, 122, 126.

view of purchase of influence in government.[17] The Enron organizational history apparently evolved a financial and moral corruption machine, something akin to "victory disease," denying the possibility of failure, and a corporate culture and moral climate ultimately hostile to business ethics. The evidence lies unavoidably in detailed study of individuals, corporate culture, and ethical climate.

The Enron debacle is the story of two self-destructing firms, Enron and Arthur Andersen—the latter being a supplier of both external and internal auditing[18] and of consulting services also.[19] All the usual suspects were involved: senior management, the board of directors, their accounting advisors (Arthur Andersen) and legal advisors (Vinson & Elkins),[20] and, albeit more distantly, investment banks, commercial banks, and brokerage firms. Professional codes of conduct for accountants and attorneys did not suffice. Although even more distantly, one must also add Congress (which killed a proposed stock option expensing rule), the White House (which had political linkages with Lay), and various regulators (e.g., the SEC, the NYSE, the evidently highly vulnerable California energy framework) as considerations in what turned out to be defective corporate governance and weak regulation. Enron was a political scandal as well as a business failure,[21] and the revelations helped propel sudden passage of the Bipartisan Campaign Reform Act of 2002. Something like a financial and moral corruption machine, commencing with the top management, evolved progressively—almost logically or compellingly as a series of "missteps"[22]—out of the constellation of circumstances at work, both internal and external to Enron. While likely not the most

---

[17] Duane Windsor, *Public Affairs, Issues, Management, and Political Strategy: Opportunities, Obstacles, and Caveats*, 1.4 J. OF PUB. AFF. 382, 382–415 (2002).

[18] CRUVER, *supra* note 8, at 181.

[19] Arthur Andersen was the auditor for WorldCom and also Freddie Mac. The second largest U.S. mortgage finance company announced on June 9, 2003, that it had fired its president (and chief operating officer) for failing to cooperate fully with counsel to the board of directors' audit committee in reviewing earnings statements for 2000, 2001, and 2002. The chairman (and chief executive officer) "retired," and the chief financial officer "resigned." *See* Philip Klein, *Freddie Mac fires president, replaces top executives,* REUTERS (June 9, 2003, 2:06 p.m. ET), *accessed at* http://biz.yahoo.com/rb/030609/financial_freddiemac .12.html (document expired subsequently).

[20] For a discussion of attorneys' roles and duties, see Megan Barnett, *How to account for lawyers: Attorneys are facing more scrutiny in cases of corporate financial fraud*, U.S. NEWS & WORLD REP., Dec. 9, 2002, at 26, 28. The Sarbanes-Oxley Act of 2002 requires the SEC to introduce a rule requiring corporate attorneys to report wrongdoing to superiors. Sarbanes-Oxley Act of 2002, Pub. L. No.107-204, 116 Stat. 745 (codified in scattered sections of 15 U.S.C. & 18 U.S.C.). A Congressional committee recommended criminal charges against Arthur Andersen attorney Nancy Temple. *See* David Ivanovich & Michael Hedges, *Pressure builds on Andersen lawyer, available at* HoustonChronicle.com, http://www.chron.com/cs/CDA/ story.hts/special/andersen/1706699 (Dec. 18, 2002).

[21] BRYCE, *supra* note 11, at 6.

[22] FUSARO & MILLER, *supra* note 15, at xi.

economically important bankruptcy among recent filings, Enron may prove the most interesting—in terms of complexity, sophistication, and breadth of corruption.[23]

The title of this essay draws on a sadly appropriate internal nickname, "The Crooked E"—reportedly passed to a new Enron employee, Brian Cruver, by a friend also working there.[24] This characterization may endure as the symbol both of how Enron came to be bankrupt, and of a whole era of shameless corporate scandal uncovered in 2001–2002 and involving a number of other large companies (e.g., Adelphia, Global Crossing, ImClone, Merrill Lynch, Tyco, WorldCom), with Cendant, Sunbeam, and Waste Management being earlier harbingers, and not just in the U.S. (e.g., Allied Irish Bank, and the Korean unit of Lernout & Hauspie Speech Products NV).[25] Xerox improperly recognized some $6 billion in revenues over 1997–2001; and Halliburton was investigated by the SEC for cost overruns when it was headed by now-U.S. Vice President Dick Cheney.[26] The registered mark or corporate logo of Enron was a capital E, with ENRON as the base—the logo tilted 45 degrees leftward of vertical. This logo appeared on business cards as well as a simple tilted E situated outside the Enron headquarters in Houston, Texas.[27] The Enron logo was adapted as a mark for a continuing *Houston Chronicle* newspaper series on "The Fall of Enron" (in Enron red, green, blue) for each article, with the addition of "The Fall of" at the top of the tilted E. The CBS Network[28] premiered (on January 5, 2003) the first made-for-TV movie based ("loosely" would be a polite term) on Cruver's book and titled *The Crooked E: The Unshredded Truth about Enron*—drawing on the subtitle of Cruver's book.[29]

---

[23] U.S. NEWS & WORLD REPORT'S "Rogue of the Year" was Tyco's former CEO Dennis Kozlowski, not Enron's former Chairman Lay. *See* Marianne Lavelle et al., *Rogues of the Year*, U.S. NEWS & WORLD REP., Dec. 30, 2002, at 33 (published in parallel with Jodie Morse & Amanda Bower, *Persons of the Year/Coleen Rowley/Cynthia Cooper/Sherron Watkins*, TIME MAG., Dec. 30, 2002, at 52). Prosecutors charge that Kozlowski obtained $600 million through theft, misuse of loans, and selling of Tyco shares. *Id.*

[24] CRUVER, *supra* note 8, at 9. A University of Texas at Austin MBA, Cruver joined Enron as a risk trader nine months before its bankruptcy.

[25] ELLIOTT & SCHROTH, *supra* note 9, at 41 (citing a WALL STREET JOURNAL report of April 2001); *see* John Carreyrou, *Lernout Unit Engaged in Massive Fraud to Fool Auditors, New Inquiry Concludes*, WALL ST. J., Apr. 6, 2001, at A3; John Carreyrou, *Lernout Files Complaint with Prosecutors in Seoul*, WALL ST. J., Apr. 26, 2001, at A17.

[26] LOREN FOX, ENRON: THE RISE AND FALL 305 (2003).

[27] The sign was sold at bankruptcy auction for $44,000. Jodie Morse & Amanda Bower, *The Party Crasher*, TIME, Dec. 30, 2002, at 52, 53.

[28] *See* Bill Murphy, *CBS flick shows difficulty of making drama out of Enron*, HOUS. CHRON., Dec. 23, 2002, at 1A.

[29] Lay's attorney, who had warned CBS about misportraying his client, dismissed the film because "[t]he production values were so bad on the thing that it's largely meaningless." *Lay lawyer says movie no big deal*, HOUS. CHRON., Jan. 10, 2003, at Business-4. A number of ex-Enron women employees criticized the depiction of women in the film. Murphy, *supra* note 28, at A1. Arthur Andersen stood convicted on June 15, 2002, of obstruction of justice. Its responsible partner, David Duncan, had pleaded guilty in

This essay makes a preliminary moral assessment and examines public policy reform proposals. It makes no specific judgments concerning criminal culpability or civil liability. Criminal investigations, civil litigation, and the bankruptcy proceedings are still ongoing and may continue for years. A basic guide for moral responsibility is to avoid harming others (defined here as various stakeholders, including investors) and to meet obvious moral and legal rules of conduct (prohibiting mendacity, fraud, and so on). Enron creditors, employees, investors, and other stakeholders have been badly harmed. Thousands of employees lost their jobs; all employees lost pensions to the degree held in Enron stock; and, as Sherron Watkins cautioned in her one-page anonymous memo (August 15, 2001) to Chairman Kenneth L. Lay, an Enron resume may prove worthless.[30] A bad business model and self-destructive culture, as appear to have prevailed at Enron, can reflect poor judgment, but not necessarily legal accountability. Long-Term Capital Management self-destructed in 1998 due to bad investment decisions involving Nobel Prize laureates in (financial) economics.[31] There is, however, a vital difference between bad judgment and recklessly gambling with corporate destiny while self-dealing for profit. Moral responsibility occurs at two distinct levels in business leadership. One level is broadly defined: the senior executives of Enron had the same general responsibility of prudent concern for corporate and stakeholder safety as the officers of any ship at sea. At Enron, everything that could go wrong by and large did go wrong. The senior executives of Enron bear the moral responsibility of such blatant negligence.[32] The other level is more narrowly defined: particular individuals at Enron engaged in specific commissions or omissions of moral duty, such as self-dealing and intimidation, or failing to caution employees about sound diversification of pension risk. The sciences of mendacity, deception, hype, fraud, and hypocrisy[33] seem to have become highly developed at Enron's upper levels.

The facts for a systematic and definitive assessment are not completely available in the public record. Congress conducted hearings in February 2002, at which Chairman Kenneth L. Lay, CFO Andrew S. Fastow, Rick Causey (Chief Accounting Officer), Michael Kopper (a key figure in the Chewco arrangement organized by Fastow, and who later pleaded guilty), and Rick Buy (Chief Risk Officer) took Fifth Amendment protection,[34] while former President and CEO Jeffrey K. Skilling, Sherron Watkins,

---

April 2002 in connection with the shredding of Enron-related documents. Arthur Andersen closed its auditing business in August 2002.

[30] MIMI SWARTZ WITH SHERRON WATKINS, POWER FAILURE: THE INSIDE STORY OF THE COLLAPSE OF ENRON at 362 (2003). The same caution logically applies by extension to an Arthur Andersen resume.

[31] FUSARO & MILLER, *supra* note 15, at 36, 43, 118–19.

[32] Henry (Lord) Acton urged that moral responsibility (historically if not legally) must march with power. ACTON, letter to Mandell Creighton, April 5, 1887; *in* ESSAYS ON FREEDOM AND POWER 364 (Gertrude Himmelfarb, ed., 1948). I argue that Acton's principle applies directly to Enron's top leadership.

[33] *Cf.* ELLIOTT & SCHROTH, *supra* note 9, at 12.

[34] BRYCE, *supra* note 11, at 358–59.

and Robert K. Jaedicke (Chairman, Audit and Compliance Committee) testified. Available are *Houston Chronicle* coverage and a number of books[35] that collectively draw on SEC filings and the Powers Committee report (published February 2, 2002),[36] and a revealing book by an Enron insider.[37] Bryce and Fox conducted interviews with former Enron employees. Watkins has just participated in publishing a book with Mimi Swartz.[38] For purposes of this essay, I have relied on the facts set forth in these books: in general, the basic facts seem well-published at this point. There is some range of differing opinions about aspects of the Enron story. There have been criticisms as well as defenses, for example, of Watkins. The ethics of Watkins's whistleblowing will be treated as a separable matter.

A recommended methodology for business ethics diagnosis and action planning comprises four steps or phases in sequence: (1) determine objectively the key facts of a situation; (2) delineate the important issues, principles, and/or stakes involved in the situation; (3) identify options or alternatives for concrete action; and (4) make a decision from among those options, and design and implement a practical action plan.[39] The remainder of the essay following this introduction is accordingly organized into three sections. The immediately following "facts" section marshals the morally relevant information. What happened inside Enron (and, by extension, Arthur Andersen, Vinson & Elkins, and banking partners and brokerages)? Senior executives and directors, and their accounting and legal and financial advisors, faced and apparently disregarded plain moral (and some legal) considerations. The subsequent "issues" section examines issues, principles, and stakes and emphasizes assessment of the constellation of causes (i.e., the etiology) resulting in Enron's bankruptcy. How widespread within Enron was an apparent culture or climate of corruption and misconduct involving fraudulent misrepresentation, self-dealing, and contempt for moral values and Enron's stakeholders? How and why did such corruption occur? In the "reforms" section following the "issues" section, I summarize various reform proposals. How widespread is the phenomenon of corporate corruption in U.S. public companies? A brief concluding section addresses the nature of moral responsibility and business ethics education for managers. What are the implications for corporate governance and government regulation reforms to moderate future repetitions?

---

[35] *E.g.*, BRYCE, *supra* note 11; ELLIOTT & SCHROTH, *supra* note 9; FOX, *supra* note 26; FUSARO & MILLER, *supra* note 15; MILLS, *supra* note 9.

[36] In mid-October 2001, the Board established a special investigation committee chaired by William C. Powers, Jr., Dean of the University of Texas Law School (Austin), who joined the board temporarily for that purpose. The inquiry was conducted with independent counsel (Wilmer, Cutler & Pickering) and accountants (Deloitte & Touche). The lengthy committee report was filed February 2, 2002.

[37] CRUVER, *supra* note 8.

[38] SWARTZ WITH WATKINS, *supra* note 30.

[39] Kenneth E. Goodpaster, *Illustrative Case Analysis for Consolidated Foods Corporation (A)*, *in* POLICIES AND PERSONS: A CASEBOOK IN BUSINESS ETHICS 500–503 (John B. Matthews et al. eds., 1985).

SOME MORALLY KEY FACTS

The Enron debacle involves a business judgment story, a legal story, a public policy story, and a blatantly irresponsible business ethics story of moral bankruptcy. Despite an enormous welter of complex details (still being unraveled), the business and moral basics of the Enron debacle seem now reasonably clear in general outline (if not full detail) sufficient to a preliminary assessment.[40] Kenneth L. Lay was head of Enron from November 1985. Jeffrey K. Skilling was President and COO from January 10, 1997, and CEO from February 1, 2001. The senior executives were highly experienced and professionally trained.[41] The head of a public company has a broad responsibility for sound business judgment and selection of reliable subordinates, and a parallel moral responsibility for stakeholders' welfare.[42] The senior executives did not even meet a reasonable standard for prudence and fiduciary responsibility to investors, but focused instead on self-dealing (as predicted by agency theory), and some, at least, engaged in illegal actions. When Skilling took over as COO in 1997, Enron's stock price was about $19.[43] At July 31, 1998, Enron's stock price was about $25.[44] It rose to range around $40 during the second half of 1999. It then jumped during 2000 to a high of about $90 in August 2000, generally sliding thereafter. Both the desire to increase stock price and the desire to restore falling stock price would have been powerful motives for increasingly risky courses of action, from which some number of senior executives and directors personally benefited—even if indirectly.[45] In 2000, Enron became the seventh largest company in the U.S., measured by (apparently inflated) revenues.[46] Between end 1996 and end 2000, employment nearly tripled, from 7,500 to 20,600.[47] The Enron stock price growth strategy followed a reasonable business-judgment path: from pipeline firm to online energy trading to varied trading and online services for a

---

[40] FOX, *supra* note 26, at vii–xiii (provides a detailed chronology).

[41] Lay was a Ph.D. economist with prior regulatory and executive experience; Skilling was a Harvard MBA (graduating a George F. Baker Scholar, top 5% of his class). *See* BRYCE, *supra* note 11, at 49; Fastow was a Northwestern MBA. Skilling brought Fastow to Enron in 1990. FUSARO & MILLER, *supra* note 15, at 37. The long-serving chair of the audit and compliance committee was Robert K. Jaedicke, a distinguished accounting professor and former dean of the Stanford business school. The chair of the finance committee was Herbert Winokur, a member in 2001 of the Harvard Corporation—that university's governing body. BRYCE, *supra* note 11, at 268. In addition to an accounting professor, the 2001 board had two former energy regulators and four executives of financial or investment firms. FOX, *supra* note 26, at 309.

[42] If grounded in economic reality, long-run stock price increase arguably could be a win-win outcome for most of the key stakeholders.

[43] BRYCE, *supra* note 11, at 137.

[44] BRYCE, *supra* note 11; FUSARO & MILLER, *supra* note 15, at xiv.

[45] Expansion of shares outstanding would increase the pressure.

[46] Morse & Bower, *supra* note 27, at 55

[47] BRYCE, *supra* note 11, at 134.

large range of commodities and risks. The result was to make markets in risks; but then, effectively, Enron assumed rather than reduced the risks; the underlying driver was signaled when, in late March 2001, the lobby banner became "From the World's Leading Energy Company—To the World's Leading Company."[48]

In retrospect, the apparent success of Enron was not grounded in economic reality. Skilling's sudden resignation on August 14, 2001, was a key signal of coming difficulties. Key features of the business model were exotic "financial engineering" schemes, aggressive hyping of stock value "stories" to analysts, aggressive accounting manipulations, and apparently unprofitable expansions into trading of more types of commodities and risks.[49] "A videotape of a 1997 party has surfaced, showing Skilling joking that Enron could make 'a kazillion dollars' through an exotic new accounting technique."[50] Flood and Fowler amplify that Skilling was reading from a script; the authors do not report who prepared the script.[51] Skilling's reading from the script mentioned moving "from mark-to-market accounting to something I call HFV, or hypothetical future value accounting" as the basis for "a kazillion dollars." Enron used thousands of special purpose entities ("SPEs") to place debt off the balance sheet. Some SPEs may have been legitimate, with corrupt practices restricted to a few; but some apparently included "material adverse change" clauses that would precipitate Enron's resumption of obligations under conditions involving, for example, bond status and stock price.[52]

On July 13, 2001, Skilling unexpectedly informed Lay of his intention to resign from Enron as President and CEO.[53] That resignation was effective August 14, 2001, when announced, and Lay resumed the post of President and CEO, in addition to chairmanship. Skilling cited personal (i.e., family) reasons, and Lay publicly described the voluntary departure in these terms. Bryce reports that Skilling conceded to Lay at the July meeting that he was not sleeping, out of his concern for the falling stock price.[54] If the allegation is true, then Lay omitted vital information in his public statement. Moreover, if the allegation is true, then Skilling's resignation marks a dividing line between lying and omitting to tell the whole, unvarnished truth.[55]

On October 15, 2001, there was a surprise restatement involving a $618 million loss for third quarter 2001, $1.01 billion in non-recurring charges (including $287

---

[48] CRUVER, *supra* note 8, at 20–21, 26, 3.

[49] Fayez Sarofim, one of Houston's top money managers, declined to invest because he did not understand how Enron made money. *See* BRYCE, *supra* note 11, at 267–269.

[50] Fonda, *supra* note 3, at 56.

[51] Tom Fowler & Mary Flood, *Broadband claims investigated as fraud*, HOUS. CHRON., Dec. 29, 2002, at 1A, 24A.

[52] BRYCE, *supra* note 11, at 332.

[53] BRYCE, *supra* note 11, at 285.

[54] *Id.*

[55] Naturally to reveal concerns about stock price is to precipitate a decline.

million for Azurix water operations and $180 million for Enron Broadband Services), and a $1.6 billion reduction of equity.[56] Of the non-recurring charges, $544 million were for various bad investments and early termination of arrangements "with a previously discussed entity"—the latter in fact being entities controlled by CFO Fastow, called LJM (initials for Fastow's wife and children), involving only $35 million in Enron losses but from which Fastow had profited.[57] On October 23, 2001, Fastow went on a leave of absence, replaced as CFO by Jeff McMahon (Enron treasurer, 1998–2000).[58] The October revelation sent Enron sliding down into eventual bankruptcy.[59] A November 8, 2001 restatement reduced earnings of the prior four years by nearly $600 million (by $96 million for 1997, $113 million for 1998, $250 million for 1999, and $132 million for 2000) and disclosed an additional $3 billion in debt obligations. This second restatement also revealed that Fastow had made $30 million from two dozen deals with LJMs (actually $45 million).[60] The November 19, 2001 restatement (the third in just over a month) further increased the third quarter 2001 losses from $618 million,[61] already raised to $635 million in the November 8, 2001 restatement, to $664 million.[62] It was revealed in the November 19, 2001 restatement that the November 12 downgrade of debt by Standard & Poor's to just above junk status shifted a $690 million note payable into a cash demand obligation due on November 27. Moreover, if debt was downgraded further to junk status and stock price fell below an unspecified price, then Enron would face obligations of $3.9 billion; nearly a fourth would be due to Marlin—an SPE removing debt from Azurix water company.[63] There were looming $18.7 billion in liabilities from derivatives and commodities futures contracts.[64] On November 20 (the next day), Enron stock fell by almost 25% to $6.99.[65] On November 28, Standard & Poor's reduced Enron debt to junk, followed by Moody's and Fitch.[66] Stock price fell that day from $4.11 at the previous close to 60 cents, with 342 million shares changing hands—a record to that point.[67]

Federal investigations have been conducted in Houston and New York (into the role of banks and brokerages), and San Francisco (into the role of Enron and other

---

[56] CRUVER, *supra* note 8, at 116, 117. *See also* Sen. Rep. No. 107-146, at 3 (2002).

[57] CRUVER, *supra* note 8, at 120.

[58] *Id.* at 138.

[59] Rosanna Ruiz, *Watkins, 2 others share Time honor*, HOUS. CHRON., Dec. 23, 2002, at 12A.

[60] BRYCE, *supra* note 11, at 328.

[61] October 16 10-Q filing with the SEC.

[62] BRYCE, *supra* note 11, at 329.

[63] *Id.* at 330.

[64] *Id.* at 332.

[65] *Id.* at 331.

[66] BRYCE, *supra* note 11, at 337.

[67] *Id.*

energy firms in the California energy crisis of 2000 and 2001), as well as by the SEC and the Commodity Futures Trading Commission ("CFTC"). On March 12, 2003, the CFTC filed charges that Enron and Hunter Shively, previously the supervisor of the Enron natural gas trading desk for the central U.S., had manipulated natural gas prices in 2001 and that Enron Online had functioned as an "illegal futures exchange" between September and December 2001 by way of failing to register or inform the CFTC of a change in its approach.[68] As of early January 2003, no sentences had been handed down, as criminal investigations continued.[69] Michael Kopper had pleaded guilty to fraud and money laundering (in connection with Chewco, a SPE organized by Fastow); Timothy Belden (an energy trader working in Portland, Oregon) had pleaded guilty to wire fraud and conspiracy (in connection with California energy trading);[70] Lawrence Lawyer (a finance employee) had pleaded guilty to a false tax report (in not reporting personal earnings from a SPE, allegedly on advice by Kopper).[71] Fastow was indicted in October 2002 on 78, counts including fraud and money laundering. (A superseding indictment followed in May 2003.) In relation to Kopper's guilty plea, indictments were issued against three former British bankers (of National Westminster Bank) for mail fraud. Rick Causey, former Chief Accounting Officer of Enron, was cited (by job title) in a criminal complaint against Fastow for a secret agreement allegedly guaranteeing no loss to Fastow from LJM. Ben Glisan, former treasurer of Enron, was cited (by job title) in a Fastow indictment; and subsequently informed that he is a subject of inquiry by federal prosecutors.[72] Glisan had been an investor in a SPE and had announced he would return huge profits made on a $5,800 investment in Southampton;[73] such profits are a powerful incentive. It was speculated in two newspaper

---

[68] Laura Goldberg, *Gas price charges are filed: Agency alleges manipulation*, HOUS. CHRON., Mar. 13, 2003, at 1B, 4B.

[69] Tom Fowler & Mary Flood, *Task force moving at steady pace: With indictments and guilty pleases in hand, Enron prosecutors expect more charges in second year,* HOUS. CHRON., Jan. 6, 2003, at 1A, 4A.

[70] A report by the California Independent Systems Operator ("ISO") complains that 21 energy companies and publicly owned utilities (including Enron) *"may* [emphasis added here] have engaged in a trading practice known as Death Star, an Enron strategy that earns a profit without selling power." *See* Harvey Rice, *Report cites others in Enronlike trades*, HOUS. CHRON., Jan. 7, 2003, at 1B. ISO is trying to get the Federal Energy Regulatory Commission ("FERC") to compel return of about $9 billion to California ratepayers, and the claims have not been established conclusively. In May 2002, Enron memos outlined "Death Star, Fat Boy and other questionable—and possibly illegal—strategies." *Id.* at 4B.

[71] Tom Fowler & Mary Flood, *Sentencing delayed on partnership tax charges*, HOUS. CHRON., Jan. 24, 2003, at 3C.

[72] Bill Murphy & Tom Fowler, *Pressure on Glisan builds up: Former treasurer may see criminal case*, HOUS. CHRON., Dec. 28, 2002, at 1C, 4C.

[73] Glisan received about $1.04 million, but paid $412,000 in taxes—he will repay $628,000. Tom Fowler, *Enron treasurer to repay $628,000 from shady deal*, HOUS. CHRON., Dec. 18, 2002, at 1A, 25A. Former Enron lawyer Kristina Mordaunt, in contrast, has claimed she is entitled to earnings on a similar investment. *Id. Editor's note:* On September 10, 2003, Glisan was sentenced to five years in prison, apparently as a result of a plea bargain.

articles that insider trading charges might be brought against Lay (on the basis that his stock sales exceeded requirements for repaying various loans).[74]

Skilling might prove very difficult to prosecute on the perjury charge, as he had voluntarily testified before Congress (albeit without immunity), or about Enron's broadband hyping.[75] Skilling was explicit in his congressional testimony that he had not lied to anyone.[76] In 1997, Enron had acquired Portland General (an electric utility), which had a fiber-optic network along its utility rights of way. A Houston federal grand jury has been investigating whether broadband hype (at January 2000, January 2001, and February 2001 meetings with analysts) by then-Enron Broadband Services ("EBS") CEO Ken Rice and CFO Kevin Howard, and CEO Skilling involved fraud (selling shares while hyping broadband and a proposed deal with Blockbuster that never came to fruition).[77] Following the January 2000 meeting, Enron stock price rose 25% that day. (Such price movements are powerful incentives.) In July 2000, Enron announced a twenty-year deal with Blockbuster for video on demand delivered across the Enron fiber-optic network. In August 2000, Enron stock price reached a high of $90.56, after which the price began to decline. On January 2, 2001, stock price was valued at $79.88. At the January 2001 presentation, Skilling told analysts that the Enron stock price should be $126 per share, with EBS having added about $40. In March 2001, the deal with Blockbuster was cancelled.[78] However, defense attorneys have argued that such hype was widespread throughout the market, and prosecution would be difficult.[79] If

---

[74] Fowler & Flood, *supra* note 69, at 4A; Fonda, *supra* note 3, at 56.

[75] Fonda, *supra* note 3, at 56.

[76] FUSARO & MILLER, *supra* note 15, at 27.

[77] Murphy & Fowler, *supra* note 72. During late April and early May 2003, a Houston federal grand jury issued a six-count indictment against Lea Fastow ("conspiracy to commit wire fraud, money laundering, and making false tax returns") and two reindictments: a 218-count reindictment superseded the March 2003 indictment of Kevin Howard and Michael Krautz (*see infra* note 79) and added Kenneth Rice, Joseph Hirko, Kevin Hannon, Scott Yeager, and Rex Shelby ("securities fraud, wire fraud and money laundering" in connection with Enron Broadband Services); a 109-count reindictment superseded the October 2002 indictment of Andrew Fastow and added Ben Glisan and Dan Boyle (for conspiracy to manipulate Enron's financial reports). *See Summary of charges in latest 3 indictments filed in the Enron case*, HOUS. CHRON., May 2, 2003, at 17A.

[78] The Braveheart partnership with a Canadian bank CIBC paid for rights to future earnings of the Blockbuster deal, and Enron recorded a $110.8 million gain. *See* BRYCE, *supra* note 11, at 282. On March 12, 2003, this so-called gain resulted in the arrest for fraud of former CFO Kevin Howard and the former senior director of accounting Michael Krautz, both still working at Enron in different positions. (*See supra* note 77 concerning reindictment.) The SEC filed additional civil charges. Howard and Krautz were also charged with conspiring to keep information from Andersen auditors. *See* Kurt Eichenwald, *Fraud Charges Filed Against 2 Employees of Enron Unit*, N.Y. TIMES, Mar. 13, 2003, at C1.

[79] Enron Broadband Services ("EBS") reflected an Enron strategy of becoming a trader of anything. Fowler & Flood, *supra* note 69, at 4A. Enron was being portrayed as the epitome of the "new economy"— the dot.com bubble world that burst. *See* JOEL KURTZMAN & GLEN RIFKIN, RADICAL E: FROM GE TO ENRON—LESSONS ON HOW TO RULE THE WEB (2001).

the defense is correct, then a widespread pattern of puffery can be protection against prosecution (e.g., the dot.com phenomenon).

In December 2002, a dozen New York banks and brokerages agreed to a "global settlement" with the New York Attorney General, the SEC, and other regulatory bodies.[80] The settlement involved some $1.4 billion in fines and another nearly $1 billion over five years to fund independent stock research. About half the fines would go to an investor restitution fund. Investigations concerned improperly bullish research reports to generate investment banking business, with e-mails, for example, revealing that analysts privately derided stocks they publicly recommended, and improper distribution of IPOs to favored executives at companies that were investment banking clients. Merrill Lynch had agreed earlier to pay $100 million to avoid criminal charges.[81]

A brief review of Enron's financial history is highly revealing. Rich Kinder (subsequently a co-founder of Kinder Morgan) was President and COO during 1990–1996 (being succeeded by Skilling). In 1990, Enron revenues were $5.336 billion and net income $202 million (a profit rate of 3.8%, calculated here).[82] In 1996, revenues were $13.289 billion and net income $584 million (a calculated profit rate of 4.4%).[83] Long-term debt rose from $2.982 billion to $3.3 billion, an increase of just over 10%.[84] In 1997, revenues were $20.273 billion (up substantially) and reported net income (before restatement) $105 million (down substantially, and a calculated profit rate of only 0.5%).[85] The actual net income (per the November 8, 2001 restatement) was just $9 million (effectively a zero rate of profit).[86] The continuing low profit rate may have been a driver of aggressive financial engineering and accounting and stock value hype.[87] In 2000, revenues were $100.789 billion (a quintupling of the 1997 turnover), and reported net income (later reduced on restatement) $979 million (a calculated profit rate of just under 1%).[88] Long-term debt rose from $6.254 billion in 1997 (almost

---

[80] Ben White, *Wall St. agrees to $1 billion in fines*, HOUS. CHRON., Dec. 20, 2002, at 1A, 14A.

[81] The SEC filed charges on March 17, 2003 (in Federal District Court in Houston) alleging that Merrill Lynch and four former Merrill executives had aided securities fraud at Enron. FOX, *supra* note 26, at 305. Merrill announced that day the finalization of a previously announced agreement with the SEC to pay $80 million in settlements. *See* Kurt Eichenwald, *4 at Merrill Accused of an Enron Fraud*, N.Y. TIMES, Mar. 18, 2003, at C1.

[82] BRYCE, *supra* note 11, at 287 (based on Enron SEC filings).

[83] *Id.*

[84] *Id.*

[85] *Id.*

[86] BRYCE, *supra* note 11, at 287.

[87] *Id.*

[88] *Id.* In early 2002, Petroleum Finance Co. recalculated the 2000 revenue down from $100.8 billion to about $9 billion, doing recalculations for several other trading firms as well. *See* MILLS, *supra* note 9, at 49 (citing *The Ship That Sank Quietly*, THE ECONOMIST, February 16, 2002, at 57).

doubled over 1996) to $9.763 billion in first quarter 2001.[89] When the material adverse change provisions kicked in, the firm could not obtain enough cash to meet obligations. Skilling stated that there was a "run on the bank," or a liquidity crisis that destroyed trading, the heart of the firm.[90] While this statement is true technically, it does not address causes and responsibilities.

Revenues ballooned in 2001, at $50.129 billion for first quarter, $100.189 billion for second quarter, and $138.718 billion for third quarter.[91] Long-term debt fell to $6.544 billion in 3rd quarter 2001, but short-term debt ballooned from $1.67 billion (end of 2000) to $6.4 billion in November 2001.[92] Net cash from operating activities fell from $4.779 billion in 2000 (basically quadrupled over 1999) to $2.554 billion through the first three quarters of 2001.[93] (Net cash from operating activities had been, with a minor exception in 1995, positive since 1990.) Bryce reports that Enron was taking losses on repurchasing the shares of the failed water company Azurix, buying paper mills, buying into and operating in the metals trading business, and operating Enron Broadband Services ("EBS").[94] It should be noted that, even as restated at November 8, 2001, net income rose from $590 million in 1998 (reported at $703 million) to $643 million in 1999 (reported at $893 million) to $847 million in 2000 (reported at $979 million).[95] It is the low profit rate (on revenues) that is dramatic information. Restatements did not particularly affect 2001 net income (the changes were minor). Net income (restated) was $442 million for first quarter 2001 (up a little from original report) and $409 million for second quarter 2001 (also up a little from original report).[96] But net income (restated) was negative $635 million for third quarter 2001 (a modest improvement over the original report).[97]

SOME ISSUES, PRINCIPLES, AND STAKES

The moral and public policy interest in Enron lies in the relative sophistication of the schemes created by CFO Fastow (with key details allegedly concealed from the directors and even upper management), the moral and business failings of the senior leadership, the systematic failure of virtually all the conventional checks-and-balances of corporate governance (the board of directors, the accounting and legal advisors,

---

[89] BRYCE, *supra* note 11, at 287.

[90] FOX, *supra* note 26, at 308; FUSARO & MILLER, *supra* note 15, at 141.

[91] Bryce, *supra* note 11, at 287.

[92] *Id.*

[93] *Id.*

[94] BRYCE, *supra* note 11, at 286.

[95] *Id.* at 287, 328.

[96] *Id.* at 287.

[97] *Id.*

bankers, and brokerages), the apparent promotion or at least toleration of a self-destructive business culture and ethical climate, and the weakness of external political and regulatory checks. It must be borne in mind that Fastow, although indicted, has not been convicted of any charge.

Powers blames senior management (Lay, Skilling, and Fastow by name), the board of directors, Enron's outside advisors, and "a flawed idea, self-enrichment by employees, inadequately-designed controls, poor implementation, inattentive oversight, simple (and not-so-simple) accounting mistakes, and overreaching in a culture that appears to have encouraged pushing the limits."[98]

The report (May 6, 2002) from the Chairman of the Senate Committee on the Judiciary, Senator Leahy, recommending the proposed Corporate and Criminal Fraud Accountability Act of 2002 (S. 2010), stated:

> According to a Report of Investigation commissioned by a Special Investigative Committee of Enron's Board of Directors ("the Powers Report"), Enron apparently, with the approval or advice of its accountants, auditors and lawyers, used thousands of off-the-book [special purpose] entities [or vehicles] to overstate corporate profits, understate corporate debts and inflate Enron's stock price.
>
> The alleged activity Enron used to mislead investors was not the work of novices. It was the work of highly educated professionals, spinning an intricate spider's web of deceit. The partnerships—with names like Jedi, Chewco, Rawhide, Ponderosa and Sundance—were used essentially to cook the books and trick both the public and federal regulators about how well Enron was doing financially. The actions of Enron's executives, accountants, and lawyers exhibit a 'Wild West' attitude which valued profit over honesty.
>
> . . . [T]he few at Enron who profited appear to be senior officers and directors who cashed out while they and professionals from accounting firms, law firms and business consulting firms, who were paid millions to advise Enron on these practices, assured others that Enron was a solid investment.[99]

In my view, a number of considerations reveal the profound absence of business ethics and fiduciary responsibility within management at Enron. The available evidence reveals imprudent behavior, self-dealing, defects of moral character, company code of

---

[98] *See Enron Bankruptcy: Hearing Before the Comm. on Commerce, Sci., and Transp.*, 107th Cong. 2, 5 (2002) (statement of William C. Powers, Jr., Chairman, the Special Investigative Comm. of the Bd. of Dir. of Enron Corp.).

[99] Sen. Rep. No. 107-146, at 2–4 (2002).

conduct relaxation or violation, defects of corporate culture, and defects of corporate governance. Each consideration is addressed in more detail immediately below.

Imprudent Behavior. This book's cover features, appropriately, an image of the sinking *Titanic;* and the introduction by the editors makes reference to the *Titanic.* Like the captain of the *Titanic* steaming a poorly designed and ill-equipped vessel at high speed at night in iceberg waters to achieve a time record for economic gain, Enron's senior management hazarded investors' equity and other stakeholders' welfare by imprudent behavior for personal gain while profiting personally (so far, pending future legal outcomes). A fatally wrong assumption in both instances was that the "ship" was unsinkable. There was no contingency planning for failure of that assumption. Fundamentally, it now appears that the Enron business model was ill-considered and ill-executed, that it functioned in conjunction with deliberately concealed financing manipulations carried out by some managers who profited personally, and that this business model marched with corrupt leadership, hardball tactics applied to stakeholders and regulators, and a dominating culture of aggressive and opportunistic self-dealing. There are now proven instances of illegalities.[100]

Self-Dealing. During the period October 19, 1998 to November 27, 2001, gross proceeds from Enron stock sales were over $270 million for Lou Pai (head, Enron Energy Services), over $184 million for Lay, nearly $112 million for Robert Belfer (a director), over $76.8 million for Ken Rice (CEO, Enron Broadband Services), nearly $70.7 million for Skilling, and nearly $33.7 million for Fastow.[101] The chair of the audit committee, Robert Jaedicke, sold a little over $840,000; Bryce does not report on stock sales by Winokur (chair of the finance committee). Bryce estimates that for this period, some two dozen Enron executives and directors sold stock for more than $1.1 billion.[102] During the Enron debacle, a change in pension plan administrator caused a blackout period during which employees could not sell holdings for several weeks.[103] The Sarbanes-Oxley Act of 2002 tries to fix this matter.[104]

Defects of Moral Character. Following the Clinton presidential sex scandal, there has been a prevailing view that private behavior is separate from the conduct of high office. Enron revisits the matter of moral character. The Greek historian Plutarch considered that character is exactly to be judged by small details and not great achieve-

---

[100] "Literal" compliance with accounting principles may not be a sufficient defense against criminal prosecution if creating "a fraudulent or misleading impression." *See* MILLS, *supra* note 9, at 53 (citing Floyd Norris, *An Old Case Is Returning to Haunt Auditors*, N.Y. TIMES, February 4, 2002, at 1).

[101] BRYCE, *supra* note 11, at ix; CRUVER, *supra* note 8, at 131–132.

[102] BRYCE, *supra* note 11, at 7.

[103] FUSARO & MILLER, *supra* note 15, at 115.

[104] Sarbanes-Oxley Act of 2002, Pub. L. No. 107-204, 116 Stat. 745 (codified at scattered sections of 15 U.S.C. & 18 U.S.C.).

ments.[105] Cruver characterizes Lay as a politician[106] and Skilling as a risk-taker.[107] The London Metal Exchange levied a fine of $264,000 against Enron for "seriously inadequate" compliance with the exchange's trading rules that "jeopardized confidence" in the exchange.[108] Skilling publicly rebuked an analyst with foul language during a conference call.[109] There have been reported (apparently well-known) office adulteries of Lay (before joining Enron), Skilling, Rice, and Pai.[110] An Enron executive told Bryce: "I knew Enron was corrupt when Jeff [Skilling] made his mistress [Rebecca Carter, subsequently Mrs. Skilling] the corporate secretary and the board never said a word about it."[111]

Relaxation or Violation of Codes of Conduct. On two known occasions, Enron faced (in principle) company code of conduct issues concerning Fastow's financial engineering. Chewco, managed by Kopper,[112] was formed in November 1997.[113] There is suspicion that Fastow and/or Kopper may have concealed key information from the directors (or even from Lay and Skilling) or did not receive desirable permissions before embarking on the orgy of perverse SPEs.[114] Chewco was subsequently a signifi-

---

[105] JOHN HETHERINGTON, BLAMEY x (The Australian War Memorial and The Australian Government Publishing Service, 1973) (citing Plutarch, *Life of Alexander, in* PLUTARCH'S LIVES (Aubrey Stewart trans., G. Bell & Sons vol. 3 1924)).

[106] CRUVER, *supra* note 8, at 22, 24. John Biggs, the retired chairman, President, and CEO of TIAA-CREF pension funds (TIAA-CREF does *not* separate the positions), and erstwhile candidate for chairmanship of the new Public Company Accounting Oversight Board, has commented: ". . . Enron's Ken Lay, when asked for a $100,000 donation [to an accounting standards foundation], was bold enough to ask his corporate counsel if it would buy any influence." Scott Burns, *Biggs' loss was no gain for investors,* DALLAS MORNING NEWS, Dec. 1, 2002, at 1H.

[107] CRUVER, *supra* note 8, at 22, 24. It has been reported by a Harvard Business School professor that, in an MBA class, then-student Skilling supported the position that he would keep selling a harmful (even fatal) product for profit maximization unless the government prohibited such conduct. *See* FUSARO & MILLER, *supra* note 15, at 28. I hold such a position to be defective: the role of moral responsibility is to stand between market opportunity and lag in public policy action. But it is also not strictly fair (in isolation) to hold the student's class comment against the later manager: positions may be defended in class for pedagogical purposes (the student was asked the question by the professor in a class setting) without automatically telling against moral character. No known later evidence reverses the initial inference, however.

[108] BRYCE, *supra* note 11, at 286. While small, the amount was the second-largest such fine after that levied against a group of banks involved in the earlier Sumitomo Corporation copper-trading scandal. *Id.*

[109] BRYCE, *supra* note 11, at 268–269; CRUVER, *supra* note 8, at 53–54.

[110] BRYCE, *supra* note 11, at 11.

[111] BRYCE, *supra* note 11, at 145.

[112] Evidently to avoid disclosure requirements. FOX, *supra* note 26, at 123.

[113] *Id.* at viii.

[114] BRYCE, *supra* note 11, at 141; FOX, *supra* note 26, at 124; FUSARO & MILLER, *supra* note 15, at 132 (citing the Powers report).

cant portion of Enron losses.[115] In June 1999, Fastow's role as manager of LJM received specific waiver of the code of ethics by the board.[116] LJM also passed "scrutiny" by Arthur Andersen and Vinson & Elkins.[117] A reasonable perspective here is what should have concerned a prudent director. It is conceivable that officers and directors were deceived by early signals of success, and that they understood at some later point that a continuation of growth by any possible means was the only path away from potential disaster.

Defects of Corporate Culture. "It was the culture, stupid."[118] Dallas defines "corporate culture" as the set of beliefs and expectations held in common by employees based on shared values, assumptions, attitudes, and norms.[119] Dallas defines "ethical climate" as the manifestation of corporate culture that characterizes the ethical meaning attached by employees to corporate policies, practices, and procedures.[120] Enron has been characterized as "a culture that valued only deal-making and money."[121] Skilling has allegedly said: "Relationships don't matter. Trust doesn't matter."[122] There was hardball intimidation (inside and outside the company), as revealed, for instance, in the California energy crisis; the treatment of external analysts and banks;[123] and the internal performance review system. Such pressure tends to erode anyone's moral compass. The Peer Review Committee ("PRC") process—nicknamed internally "rank and yank"—in effect deliberately drove out the bottom 15% of employees every six months and put others on notice that their careers were in jeopardy.[124] And the "rank and yank" system was itself reportedly corrupt:[125] it was not strictly peer evaluation of performance, but

---

[115] FUSARO & MILLER, *supra* note 15, at 133.

[116] FOX, *supra* note 26, at ix; FUSARO & MILLER, *supra* note 15, at 41; 135.

[117] FUSARO AND MILLER, *supra* note 15, at 135.

[118] BRYCE, *supra* note 11, at 12.

[119] Lynne Dallas, *A Preliminary Inquiry into the Responsibility of Corporations and Their Directors and Officers for Corporate Climate: The Psychology of Enron's Demise*, ST. JOHN'S L. REV. (forthcoming October 2002), *available at* http://papers.ssrn.com/paper.taf?abstract_id=350341.

[120] *Id.*

[121] Murphy, *supra* note 24, at 15A; *see also* Juin-Jen Chang & Ching-Chong Lai, *Is the Efficiency Wage Efficient? The Social Norm and Organizational Corruption*, 104.1 SCANDINAVIAN J. OF ECON. 27, 27–47 (2002) (arguing that pandemic organizational corruption has a snowballing effect that can overwhelm the expected efficiency incentive effect of wages), *available at* http://papers.ssrn.com/taf?abstract_id=312931.

[122] BRYCE, *supra* note 11, at 124.

[123] *Id.* at 224.

[124] CRUVER, *supra* note 8, at xv, 61–64; *see also* Kim Clark, *Judgment day: It's survival of the fittest as companies tighten the screws on employee performance reviews*, U.S. NEWS & WORLD REP., Jan. 13, 2003, at 31 (noting that General Electric, under Jack Welch, used a bottom 10%).

[125] FUSARO & MILLER, *supra* note 15, at 52.

who you knew, accompanied by "horse trading" among managers.[126] "The PRC created a culture within Enron that replaced cooperation with competition."[127]

Defects of Corporate Governance. Corporate governance is a fundamentally weak checks and balances approach, in that it has historically relied on reasonably honest and honorable managers and directors (in the face of agency theory to the contrary). A financial and moral corruption machine emanating from senior management, ensnaring a trusting or negligent board, shaped the corporate culture and ethical climate, and ensnared the auditors, the external attorneys, and to some degree, the politicians and regulators. This machine was built around specific elements: (1) a shared ideology[128] of free markets, deregulation, and innovation; (2) systematic attempts at political influence of legislation and regulation; (3) Lay's philanthropic activities as (perhaps genuine) evidence of corporate citizenship and community leadership;[129] (4) a cynical view that greed is good, personally and for society; (5) strong financial incentives for suborning checks and balances; and (6) hardball tactics. There was a constellation of interlinking elements at work.

The etiology of Enron's stock price bubble and subsequent collapse is gradually coming to light through the multiple investigations underway. Enron began running on a rising stock price treadmill that must steadily accelerate on management and the board[130]—and that ran into adverse economic conditions. Skilling came over to Enron from a partnership at McKinsey, in 1990, when that firm recommended that Enron go into financial products and services.[131] The shift to mark-to-market accounting began with Skilling at Enron Gas Services Group ("EGSG") and spread to the whole company when he became COO.[132] This accounting in effect simply booked Enron's own internal estimates of what markets were worth, virtually unregulated pro forma estimates.[133] Bryce[134] cites Skilling's employment contract from the 1990 Enron proxy

---

[126] BRYCE, *supra* note 11, at 128; CRUVER, *supra* note 8, at 64.

[127] BRYCE, *supra* note 11, at 129.

[128] Lay, in Spring 1997, was quoted: "We believe in markets. Sometimes there's an aberration. But over time, markets figure out value." *See* BRYCE, supra note 11, at 1 (citing Gary McWilliams, *The quiet man who's jolting utilities*, BUS. WK., June 9, 1997, at 84. The thesis applies, of course, to market valuation of a firm, whether built on economic reality or trickery (the latter presumably delaying discovery).

[129] Lay brokered the deal to keep the Astros baseball team in Houston, reflected in the new Enron Field ballpark (later renamed). He was co-chairman of the Houston host committee for the 1990 Economic Summit of Industrialized Nations, held at Rice University; he was head of the Houston host committee for the 1992 Republican national convention in Houston. BRYCE, *supra* note 11, at 87–88. There has been an Enron Prize for Distinguished Public Service given through Rice University's Baker Institute. BRYCE, *supra* note 11, at 323–324.

[130] *Cf.* FUSARO & MILLER, *supra* note 15, at 73, 78.

[131] MILLS, *supra* note 9, at 48.

[132] BRYCE, *supra* note 11, at 64–66.

[133] *Cf.* ELLIOTT & SCHROTH, *supra* note 9, at 39.

[134] BRYCE, *supra* note 11, at 64.

statement: he received cash bonuses ("phantom equity rights") as a percentage of the increase in market value of Enron Finance Corp.[135] These bonuses were worth $10 million at $200 million value and $17 million at $400 million value, relative to his salary of $275,000 (and loan of $950,000).[136] Bryce cites the 1997 proxy statement as revealing additional stock options.[137] Bryce argues that Skilling convinced Lay, the audit committee, and the board of the worth of mark-to-market accounting.[138] The strategic emphasis shifted to revenue growth.[139] On May 17, 1991, the audit committee adopted mark-to-market accounting for EGSG on a motion by the chair (Jaedicke).[140] Enron and Arthur Andersen lobbied the SEC, which granted permission by letter of January 30, 1992, for EGSG only.[141] Enron then introduced the approach a full year earlier than previously discussed with the SEC; Bryce reports that an anonymous auditor told him that, otherwise, the last quarter of 1991 would have been negative.[142] The Commodity Futures Trading Commission ("CFTC"), operating with only three of its five members, approved in late 1992, on recommendation by the chair, a rule exempting energy derivatives contracts from federal regulation.[143] The chair, Wendy Lee Gramm (wife of Senator Gramm of Texas), became a director of Enron in early 1993, shortly after stepping down from the CFTC. Derivatives thus involved no licensing or regulation by the SEC or the NYSE.[144]

It appears that these arrangements were only vaguely disclosed to analysts and investors. The Enron 2000 Annual Report[145] disclosed that there were limited partnerships whose general managing member was an Enron senior officer, but the report did not specifically name the officer involved.[146] The report stated that the transactions were regarded as comparable to what could have been negotiated with unrelated third parties.[147] If that were in fact the case, of course, the question should arise as to why unrelated third parties were not being used.

---

[135] *Id.*

[136] *Id.*

[137] *Id.* at 64–65.

[138] *Id.* at 65.

[139] *Id.* at 66.

[140] Bryce, *supra* note 11, at 66–67.

[141] Bryce, *supra* note 11, at 67.

[142] *Id.*

[143] *Id.* at 81.

[144] *Id.* at 83; *see also* Fusaro & Miller, *supra* note 15, at 20 (noting that hedging operations may necessitate secrecy for success, so off-shore operation and non-regulation might be viewed as logical steps).

[145] Cruver, *supra* note 8, at 59–60.

[146] *Enron Annual Report 2000*, 48 *available at* http://www.enron.com/corp/investors/annuals/2000/ar2000.pdf.

[147] *Id.*

In testimony before Congress, Powers summarized findings concerning transactions between Enron and partnerships controlled by CFO Fastow as follows: "What we found was appalling."[148] Fastow earned at least $30 million, Kopper earned at least $10 million, two others earned $1 million each, and two others earned some hundreds of thousands of dollars each.[149] There were *some* failures to follow accounting rules in these relationships. "We found a systematic and pervasive attempt by Enron's Management to misrepresent the Company's financial condition. Enron Management used these partnerships to enter into transactions that it could not, or would not, do with unrelated commercial entities. Many of the most significant transactions apparently were not designed to achieve bona fide economic objectives. They were designed to affect how Enron reported its earnings."[150] "Essentially, Enron was hedging with itself" through the Raptors, in which—despite appearances of being Fastow-organized partnerships—"only Enron had a real economic stake and . . . [the] main assets were Enron's own stock."[151] Powers cites notes by Enron's corporate secretary of a Finance Committee meeting on the Raptors: "Does not transfer economic risk [away from Enron] but transfers P+L volatility [away from Enron]."[152] The Powers report concludes that the purpose was to allow Enron to avoid reporting losses on investments: "there is no question that virtually everyone, from the Board of Directors on down, understood that the company was seeking to offset its investment losses with its own stock. That is not the way it is supposed to work. Real earnings are supposed to be compared to real losses."[153] Over the period from third quarter of 2002 through third quarter of 2001 (fifteen months), reported earnings were improperly inflated by over $1 billion, and more than 70% of reported earnings for the period were not real.[154]

The moral status of Watkins's whistleblowing at Enron is a separable matter, and is treated below as such. Three women whistleblowers were the 2002 *Time* magazine "Persons of the Year": WorldCom auditor Cynthia Cooper; FBI agent Coleen Rowley;

---

[148] *See Enron Bankruptcy: Hearing Before the Comm. on Commerce, Sci., and Transp.*, 107th Cong. 2 (2002) (statement of William C. Powers, Jr., Chairman, the Special Investigative Comm. of the Bd. of Dir. of Enron Corp.).

[149] *See id.*

[150] *Id.* at 3.

[151] *Id.* at 4. An Enron attorney sent an e-mail (September 1, 2000) to his superiors in the legal department questioning the Raptors as possibly generating a perception of cooking the books, while Arthur Andersen signed off. BRYCE, *supra* note 11, at 231.

[152] *See Enron Bankruptcy: Hearing Before the Comm. on Commerce, Sci., and Transp.*, 107th Cong. 4 (2002) (statement of William C. Powers, Jr.).

[153] *Id.* at 4–5.

[154] *See id.* at 5.

and former Enron vice president for corporate development Sherron Watkins.[155] *Time* states: "They took huge professional and personal risks to blow the whistle on what went wrong at WorldCom, the FBI and Enron—and in so doing helped remind Americans what courage and values are all about."[156]

Watkins came to public notice first, in January 2002, when it was leaked that she had communicated with Lay about suspected accounting manipulations at Enron.[157] She had gone to work for Fastow in June 2001, and was assigned to selling assets.[158] In the course of her duties, she discovered off-the-books irregularities.[159] It appears that she began looking for a job, planning to confront Skilling on her last day.[160] Skilling unexpectedly resigned on August 14, 2001.[161]

On August 15, 2001, the day after Skilling's resignation, she sent an anonymous one-page memo to Lay—a memo precipitated by the Raptors.[162] Watkins then saw Cindy Olson, head of Enron Human Resources, who advised her to go to Lay.[163] On August 20, in an interview with *Business Week*, Lay stated there were no issues, "no other shoe to fall."[164] On August 22, 2001, she met with Lay by appointment and gave him a second, detailed seven-page memo and an annotated document concerning a suspect partnership.[165] She advised Lay against using Vinson & Elkins for the inquiry. Lay had Vinson & Elkins look into the issues; the firm reported that SPEs were not a problem.[166] Two days after this meeting, an e-mail from a Vinson & Elkins attorney

---

[155] *See* Ruiz, *supra* note 59; *see also* Michael J. Gundlach, Scott C. Douglas, & Mark J. Martinko, *The decision to blow the whistle: A social information processing framework*, 28.1 THE ACAD. OF MGMT. REV. 107, 107–123 (2003) (examining decisions to blow the whistle).

[156] TIME 5 (Dec. 30, 2002–Jan. 6, 2003, double issue, vol. 160, no. 27). In June 2002, Cooper had informed the WorldCom board of accounting manipulations inflating 2001 and 2002 profits by $3.8 billion (wildly exceeding Enron manipulations with respect to profits). Ruiz, *supra* note 59, at 1A. Rowley had written the FBI director in May 2002 criticizing bureau failure to act on alleged warning signs received before the 9-11 (2001) terrorist attacks. *Id.*

[157] Morse & Bower, *supra* note 27.

[158] *Id.*

[159] *Id.*

[160] *Id.*

[161] *Id.*

[162] FUSARO & MILLER, *supra* note 15, at 135 (noting that Lay, in addressing Skilling's departure, had invited communications from employees). *See* SWARTZ WITH WATKINS, *supra* note 30, for this short memo.

[163] BRYCE, *supra* note 11, at 294.

[164] CRUVER, *supra* note 8, at 94 (quoting Stephanie Forest's interview of Kenneth Lay in *Business Week*, August 20, 2001).

[165] This action violated the chain of command, as Fastow was Watkins's superior. *See* SWARTZ WITH WATKINS, *supra* note 30.

[166] BRYCE, *supra* note 11, at 298.

stated: "Texas law does not currently protect corporate whistle-blowers."[167] Fastow reportedly seized Watkins's office hard drive.[168] She was moved down thirty-three floors from executive level and assigned (in effect) to "special projects" (notoriously the place where people on the way out of a firm are parked temporarily).[169] Cruver reports that Watkins asked for and received a transfer.[170] The attorney's e-mail was brought to Watkins's attention on February 13, 2002. She testified before Congress on February 14.[171] In her testimony, she characterized Lay as a "man of integrity."[172] "Watkins claimed that Lay had been 'duped' by Skilling and Fastow."[173]

Watkins left Enron in November 2002, reportedly to set up a global consulting firm to advise boards on governance and ethics; she reportedly receives up to $25,000 per speaking engagement, and she contracted for half of a $500,000 advance with Houston writer Mimi Swartz to prepare a book entitled *Power Failure.*[174]

Watkins's nomination for anything approaching decent business ethics at Enron is reportedly controversial for some ex-Enron employees. To some Watkins is a hero;[175] to others, she is a villain.[176] Some employees have criticized Watkins for not going to the SEC,[177] and for selling $47,000 in Enron stock in late August and in October[178]— as if anyone who could get out of the stock should have held it. Morse and Bower observe, correctly, in response, that Watkins was the only one to speak up (even internally) at Enron.[179] It is not clear that subordinate managers have strong duties to go public—at high personal cost. New SEC rules for attorneys specifically restricted (under great pressure by attorneys) the duty to report concerns about securities laws violations to management and the board, and excluded the SEC, contrary to what the agency had initially proposed.[180]

---

[167] E-mail from Carl Jordan, Vinson & Elkins Associate, to Joe Dilg (August 24, 2001, 07:02 PM), *available at* http://energycommerce.house.gov/107/hearings/02142002Hearing489/tab18.pdf.

[168] Morse & Bower, *supra* note 27, at 53.

[169] *Id.*

[170] CRUVER, *supra* note 8, at 95–96.

[171] *The Financial Collapse of Enron—Part 3: Hearing Before the Subcomm. on Oversight & Investigations of the Comm. on Energy and Commerce*, 107th Cong. 14 (2002) (testimony of Sherron Watkins, Vice President of Corporate Development, Enron Corp.).

[172] Morse & Bower, *supra* note 27, at 53.

[173] FUSARO & MILLER, *supra* note 15, at 142

[174] Morse & Bower, *supra* note 27, at 53, 54.

[175] *Id.* at 52.

[176] *See* BRYCE, *supra* note 11, at 295 (quoting half a dozen Enron employees saying Watkins was "calculating, vindictive . . . facing almost certain firing by Fastow . . .").

[177] Her role was apparently internal only and was leaked to the outside.

[178] Morse & Bower, *supra* note 27, at 56.

[179] *Id.*

[180] *SEC lays down rules for lawyers: Agency tells how to report violations.* HOUS. CHRON., Jan. 24, 2003, at 1C, 3C.

The reader should bear in mind that, arguably, under Texas law (and, in my view, in practice virtually everywhere, regardless of law), a whistleblower is not protected (certainly not well-protected), and should study a classic Harvard Business School case on whistleblowing, "Tony Santino."[181] The classic strategy for dealing with a corporate whistleblower is portrayal as a "disgruntled employee" in order to shift attention and blame. "Santino" (the disguised name of a Harvard MBA graduate), a former Navy aviator, had high standards of courage and values.[182] These standards caused him to lose one job at a defense contractor (what a surprise!), and to have to take a less attractive job at a manufacturing firm—where he was asked basically to falsify a pricing list to customers by faking product specifications with the firm's lab engineers. The case concerns not only courage and values, but equally important practical (or pragmatic) action planning—how to avoid being destroyed while doing the right thing. Ultimately "Santino" resigns while informing his superiors that they are violating the law; his wife (a CPA) divorces him; he winds up working at a third firm after six months without employment. In the case, "Santino" asks a lawyer for advice, and learns that the government is unlikely to prosecute such a minor case; he asks a business school professor (a consultant), who wonders why "Santino" is so impractical. Watkins (who has a husband and children) arguably played her cards very carefully (cards dealt to her by superiors and events), and, in effect, prospered. Her actions will make for a very useful case study of whistleblowing duties and tactics. Temporizing is not automatically a failure of duty or of moral integrity.

REFORM PROPOSALS

Norman Augustine, the ex-CEO of Lockheed Martin, comments in his foreword to Seglin: "Public confidence surveys invariably show [big] business . . . enjoying little public respect—ranking right in there with politicians, the media, and axe murderers."[183] One can point to a long history of executive and corporate misconduct in the U.S.;[184] and, regrettably, this tradition may be expected to recur in both refurbished and exotic new forms.[185]

---

[181] Jeffrey A. Sonnenfeld, *Tony Santino (A)* (October 1, 1981) (field study of a "recent MBA without a stable work history in the private sector who feels that he is being forced to compromise his personal convictions and professional integrity through a violation of the Robinson-Patman Act"), *available for purchase at* http://harvardbusinessonline.hbsp.harvard.edu/b02/en/common/item_detail.jhtml?id=482045.

[182] To draw on *Time's* theme for its "Persons of the Year." *See* Morse & Bower, *supra* note 23, at 52.

[183] SEGLIN, *supra* note 6, at vii.

[184] Michael Satchell, *Scandal as usual: America's economic history is riddled with tales of fraud, swindles, and get-rich-quick schemes*, U.S. NEWS & WORLD REP., Dec. 30, 2002–Jan. 6, 2003 (double issue), at 49.

[185] Barry Minkow's ZZZZ Best Company allegedly would obtain huge profits from insurance repairs of fire and water damage in large buildings. The market valuation rose to $200 million; when the bubble collapsed, the assets were auctioned for $64,000. Minkow was convicted in Dec. 1988 of fraud. *See* Satchell, *supra* note 184, at 49.

There are over 14,000 registered public companies in the U.S.[186] The U.S. economy produces annual output at a value of roughly $10 trillion. In the aftermath of corporate misconduct revelations, the SEC, in summer 2002, required the CEOs and CFOs of the 945 largest U.S. public companies (with greater than $1.2 billion revenues) to sign statements attesting to the accuracy of their firm's financial statements.[187] The strong majority of such officers evidently faced no serious difficulties in doing so.[188] Understandably, investor confidence has been badly shaken—but capital market effects involved a broader context of recession, terrorist sneak attacks and continuing threat, and diplomatic confrontations with Iraq and then North Korea.

Various doubtless useful reform measures have been proposed by the President, the Congress, SEC, NYSE, The Conference Board, and others. Additionally, pursuant to the Sarbanes-Oxley Act of 2002, the U.S. Sentencing Commission is strengthening white-collar crime penalties.[189] These reform measures are necessary (particularly to set standards and penalties and to restore investor confidence), but likely not sufficient to deter all future misconduct. The measures are necessary because there is an inherent conflict of interest between management (and their advisors) and investors and other stakeholders. This conflict of interest is the essence of the agency model,[190] in which amoral actors maximize self-interest. Amoral actors compute cost-benefit estimates of what to do.[191] The problem is not that so many executives and directors are bad; most of them probably calculate that misconduct is not worthwhile (even before Sarbanes-Oxley), and the summer 2002 CEO and CFO signatures attest so. The problem is that, given the sciences of deception and mendacity that can be practiced by executives, it is difficult to know which relatively few apples are bad; and that relaxation of standards or development of exotic new opportunities will entice additional violators into making rational calculations. Regulation is ever caught between the necessity of control to hamper deception and mendacity and the desirability of freedom to innovate, which in turn drives economic development.

Senior executives, directors, and their accounting, consulting, and legal advisors face enormous incentives for corruption and misreporting of performance. These incentives come in three general forms: (1) employment, salary, and bonuses tied (unavoidably) to perceived performance; (2) unnoticed selling of shares at gain, with shares typically in the form of stock options; and (3) ability to issue equity to finance new

---

[186] ELLIOT & SCHROTH, *supra* note 9, at 20.

[187] FOX, *supra* note 26, at 305.

[188] The proportion involving serious restatements might be a rough index of prior concealments and other difficulties. A detailed study would be necessary.

[189] Sarbanes-Oxley Act of 2002, Pub. L. No. 107-204, 116 Stat. 745 (codified at scattered sections of 15 U.S.C. & 18 U.S.C.).

[190] Prominent in financial economics literature.

[191] EDWARD C. BANFIELD, HERE THE PEOPLE RULE: SELECTED ESSAYS 337 (1985).

projects or acquisitions.[192] These incentives encourage efforts directed at rising stock prices, through both fair and foul means (i.e., any undetected means will serve).[193] The fatal conceit at Enron was that stock prices would rise and that foul means would remain undetected. Significant blame must attach to stock options for senior executives[194]—which Congress strongly resisted prior to recent revelations.[195] Such incentives encourage greater risk taking than is prudent.[196] Biggs notes that, at Intel, only 2% of options go to senior executives; it is younger personnel who should be so motivated.[197] Perhaps straight salary should suffice for senior executives.

President Bush (a Harvard MBA) in statements of March and July 2002 made several proposals for corporate governance reform: (1) Improving financial transparency and disclosure by quarterly investor access to data (which was already supposed to happen) and prompt access to critical data (concealed at Enron). (2) Strengthening of officer responsibilities and penalties as follows: CEO must vouch for disclosures subject to criminal penalties (one could add the CFO); officers cannot profit from errors; officers can lose the right to serve in any corporate leadership positions; officers must report stock activities. (3) Strengthening of auditor independence and oversight as follows: There must be auditor independence and integrity; the authors of accounting standards must be responsive to the needs of investors; and accounting systems should be best practices rather than minimum standards.[198]

The Sarbanes-Oxley Act of 2002 addressed a wide range of matters.[199] Much of the Act involves instructions to the SEC. Other than Title I, the Act is essentially a laundry list of monitoring and control enhancements. Title I established a Public Company Accounting Oversight Board, as a nonprofit corporation (District of Columbia), appointed by and reporting to the SEC, for registration and supervision of public accounting firms engaged in auditing services.[200] Title II addresses measures for auditor

---

[192] Lucian A. Bebchuk & Oren Bar-Gill, *Misreporting Corporate Performance, available at* http://papers.ssrn.com/paper.taf?abstract_id=354141 (Dec. 7, 2002).

[193] As soon as stock prices fell over the past few years, companies began asking investors to approve repricing of options (downward). *See* Timothy G. Pollock, Harald M. Fischer, & James B. Wade, *The role of power and politics in the repricing of executive options,* 45.6 THE ACAD. OF MGMT. J. 1172, 1172–1182 (2002). There might as well be no incentive strategy, if employees win whether stock price rises or falls.

[194] Burns, *supra* note 106, at 1H.

[195] Representative Oxley reportedly opposed stock option expensing rules proposed by the International Accounting Standards Board. *See* ELLIOT & SCHROTH, *supra* note 9, at 36.

[196] Burns, *supra* note 106, at 1H.

[197] *Id.*

[198] President Bush (a Harvard MBA) in statements of March and July 2002.

[199] Sarbanes-Oxley Act of 2002, Pub. L. No. 107-204, 116 Stat. 745 (codified at scattered sections of 15 U.S.C. & 18 U.S.C.).

[200] *Id.* § 7211–7219.

independence.[201] Title III ("Corporate Responsibility") addresses audit committees, corporate responsibility for financial reports, improper influence on conduct of audits, conditions for forfeiture of bonuses and profits, bars and penalties for officers and directors, prohibition of insider trades during pension fund blackout periods and rules for blackout notices (a feature of the Enron story), rules of professional responsibility for attorneys (to be issued by the SEC), redirection of civil penalties (and donations) to disgorgement funds for investors.[202] Title IV seeks ways to enhance financial disclosures, such as for special purpose entities or transactions involving directors, officers and principal stockholders, to reduce conflicts of interest for executives, to emphasize adequate internal controls, to require corporate code of ethics for senior financial officers, to encourage audit committees to contain at least one financial expert, to enhance SEC review of periodic disclosures, and disclosure of material changes "in plain English."[203] Title V seeks to reduce conflicts of interest for analysts.[204] Title VI directs additional resources and authority to the SEC.[205] Title VII requires certain studies and reports by the GAO (into public accounting industry consolidation and investment banks and financial advisers) and SEC (into credit rating agencies and recent violations of securities laws).[206] Title VIII, the Corporate and Criminal Fraud Accountability Act of 2002, addresses enhancements of various criminal penalties and related matters—directing a review of sentencing guidelines for obstruction of justice and "extensive criminal fraud" by the U.S. Sentencing Commission, and addressing whistleblower protection.[207] Title IX addresses white-collar crime penalty enhancements.[208] Title X is a sense of the Senate that CEOs should sign a firm's federal income tax return.[209] Title XI addresses criminal responsibility for obstruction of justice, and additional authority for the SEC, such as prohibiting individuals from serving as officers or directors.[210]

The Conference Board's Blue Ribbon Commission on Public Trust and Private Enterprise issued its final report on recommended corporate governance approaches.[211] The report recommended (rather than required) as alternatives formal separation of

---

[201] *Id..* § 7231.

[202] *Id.* § 7241.

[203] *Id.* § 7261.

[204] *Id.* § 78o-6.

[205] *Id.* § 78kk..

[206] *Id.* § 7201.

[207] 18 U.S.C. § 1501 (2003).

[208] *Id.* § 1341.

[209] *Id.*

[210] *Id.* § 1512.

[211] The Conference Bd., Comm'n on Pub. Trust & Private Enter., *available at* http://www.conference-board.org/pdf_free/758.pdf (last modified January 9, 2003).

Chairman and CEO roles[212] or a "Lead Independent Director" or a "Presiding Director" to control information flow, board agenda, and board schedule, with the non-management directors[213] encouraged to meet frequently.[214] John Biggs, the now-retired chairman, president, and CEO of TIAA-CREF, dissented from the separation recommendation.[215] The NYSE recommends only that a majority of directors be independent. Generally speaking, Enron's board met these standards. There are no real tests or standards for independence, any more than professional codes affected the conduct of accountants and attorneys in the Enron situation.

CONCLUSION

There is a philosophy holding that moral values are private choices and that markets, in combination with democratic public policy process, will resolve all important matters. The Enron debacle should be an object lesson that such philosophy may have its practical limits. Enron leadership substituted private choices for moral and legal responsibilities and strove to suborn public policy process. We may expect new methods of evading laws and regulations after some period of time has passed and new opportunities for wealth pursuit by any means arise.[216] The pressures and opportunities are organic to a dynamic marketplace.[217] Recent events occurred mostly (not exclusively) in the new frontier industries of energy trading and telecommunications. It is infeasible fully to regulate a complex economy. The reform proposals noted in the previous section are perfectly obvious—leading to the question of why they were not in place before the recent scandals. In the long run, ultimate reliance must be placed on the moral character of executives and directors.[218] External regulation is penultimate only. There are always pressures of various types to relax vigilance and concern. The purpose of voluntary morality—truly professional conduct, properly conceived—is to separate the marketplace and public policy so that economic actors regulate themselves. At Enron, it appears that key actors regarded public policy as just another kind of marketplace for dealmaking and markets as amoral machinery.[219] The view of Adam

---

[212] *Id.* at 15. Note that Chairman and CEO roles had been separated at Enron for years between Lay and Skilling.

[213] *Id.* A substantial majority of the board must be independent directors.

[214] *Id.*

[215] *Id.* at 35. The positions of Chairman and CEO are combined at TIAA-CREF.

[216] Elliot & Schroth, *supra* note 9, at 15.

[217] The Italian offices of Sotheby's (London auctioneers) reportedly were smuggling old masters out of Italy. *See* Peter Watson, Sotheby's: The Inside Story (1997).

[218] *Cf.* Elliot & Schroth, *supra* note 9, at 49.

[219] Wilson, *supra* note 16, at 59–71 (arguing that market capitalism is an amoral mechanism: its chief virtue, and not a negligible one, is that, on balance, it alleviates over time widespread poverty more effectively than other alternative social arrangements).

Smith is significant: he felt that natural moral sympathy for others could be improved more rapidly by moral education.[220] Even today, some significant proportion of business schools cannot show that they require ethics education of newly minted MBAs.[221] The response to recent corporate scandals by the American Association of Collegiate Schools of Business ("AACSB"), the key accrediting body (comprised of business school deans acting collectively), has been to consider moving ethics to the top of a list of important topics, while declining to endorse any necessity of a required course in business ethics and fostering development of school codes of conduct for faculty and students. The question arises as to why ethics was not at the top before recent corporate scandals. The AACSB prefers to let business schools choose between a required course and the "infusion" of ethics education into other courses—e.g., strategy, finance, marketing—without specifying who should handle such instruction.[222] The infusion approach is already suspect: "B-school assurances that ethics are examined throughout the curriculum sound hollow, if not downright laughable, to most students and recent M.B.A. graduates."[223]

---

[220] *Id.*; *see also supra* text accompanying note 12.

[221] Salbu, *supra* note 9, at xiii.

[222] See e-mail from author to AACSB & The Academy of Management, *An Open Letter on Business School Responsibility* (Oct. 8, 2002) (on file with author and available to the reader via e-mail at odw@rice.edu.)

[223] Salbu, *supra* note 8, at xiii.

Reexamining the Role of In-House Lawyers After the Conviction of Arthur Andersen*

Amon Burton** & John S. Dzienkowski***

> Sherron never liked the smell on the forty-eighth floor. It had been home to Enron's legal department for too many years. It was permeated with the odor of rotting paper . . . .

—MIMI SWARTZ WITH SHERRON WATKINS,
POWER FAILURE: THE INSIDE STORY OF THE
COLLAPSE OF ENRON 282 (2003)

I. INTRODUCTION

Recent media coverage of the massive corporate fraud scandals of the past two years has focused primarily on the conduct or misconduct of corporate officers and directors, and of the outside professional firms hired by their corporate entities. A significant part of the reform has focused on changing the roles of directors, increasing disclosure obligations to the regulators, and strengthening the independence of the public accounting firms. Very little attention has been focused on the role that in-house corporate lawyers played in these scandals.[1]

---

* © 2003 by Amon Burton and John S. Dzienkowski. We thank Loftus Carson and Robert Peroni for their comments on earlier drafts of this chapter. We also gratefully acknowledge the able work of our research assistants, Holly Eddington, Tran Nguyen, Brad Thompson, and especially Alexandra Chirinos.

** Adjunct Professor, University of Texas School of Law.

*** John Redditt Professor of State and Local Government, University of Texas School of Law.

[1] Although our point is made with reference to the recent scandals, the lack of attention on the ethical behavior of in-house counsel is not a new phenomenon. *See* Mary C. Daly, *The Cultural, Ethical, and Legal Challenges in Lawyering for a Global Organization: The Role of the General Counsel*, 46 EMORY L.J. 1057, 1067 (1997).

This lack of attention to the role of in-house counsel has occurred despite the fact that in-house legal departments have grown dramatically in the last quarter of a century.[2] And it is logical to conclude that many of these questionable corporate transactions were initially examined by—and involved the participation of—in-house lawyers.[3] Just as the savings and loan crisis of the 1980s generated the infamous question, "[w]here . . . were the outside . . . attorneys, when these transactions were effectuated?,"[4] the corporate fraud scandals of the early 2000s might also raise the question, where were the in-house lawyers who represented these corporations?[5]

During the 1990s, large corporations in the United States restructured the manner in which they obtained legal services. The notion that outside law firms perform all or most of a *Fortune 500* company's legal work is no longer the case in this country's large corporations.[6] Many corporations employ large numbers of in-house lawyers to represent them throughout the world.[7] This trend has caused significant changes in the role of in-house counsel.[8] They no longer merely prepare and file routine documents and draft corporate minutes. Enron had over 250 lawyers employed in its legal department to handle its transactions and litigation matters.[9] Wal-Mart's general counsel allegedly managed its highly aggressive litigation strategy against customer tort lawsuits.[10] The use of in-house lawyers may have begun as a means of controlling costs,[11] but many corporations believe that they receive superior work from lawyers who are more knowl-

---

[2] *See* Abram Chayes & Antonia Chayes, *Corporate Counsel and the Elite Law Firm*, 37 STAN. L. REV. 277 (1985) (in-house lawyers are involved in corporate planning and prevention of situations that may expose the entity to legal consequences as well as the management of outside counsel.).

[3] *See* Richard W. Painter, *The Moral Interdependence of Corporate Lawyers and Their Clients*, 67 S. CAL. L. REV. 507, 511, 544–45 (1994).

[4] Lincoln Savings & Loan Ass'n v. Wall, 743 F. Supp. 901, 920 (D.D.C. 1990) (Sporkin, Judge).

[5] For a report on initial reactions to this type of question, see Jonathan D. Glater, *Round Up the Usual Suspects. Lawyers, Too?*, N.Y. TIMES, Aug. 4, 2002, at C4 (quoting Senator Michael Enzi as saying, "in almost every transaction there was a lawyer who drew up the documents involved . . . .").

[6] *See* DALY, *supra* note 1, at 1058 (citing statistics of growth of in-house counsel offices). One impetus for this change was to reduce or control the corporations' budget for legal fees.

[7] *See* Eduardo J. Benitez, et al., *Telecommunication Reforms in the Americas: New Legislation and the Regulatory Framework*, 13 AM. U. INT'L L. REV. 971, 1014 (1988) (presentation by Ronald E. Pump) (noting that companies in the telecommunications industry employ large numbers of lawyers). A good starting point for researching members of corporate legal staffs is Martindale Hubbell's volume on Corporate Law Departments.

[8] Geoffrey C. Hazard, Jr., *Ethical Dilemmas of Corporate Counsel*, 46 EMORY L.J. 1011 (1997); Carl D. Liggio, *The Changing Role of Corporate Counsel*, 46 EMORY L.J. 1201 (1997); *see also* Robert Eli Rosen, *The Inside Counsel Movement, Professional Judgment and Organizational Representation*, 64 IND. L.J. 479 (1989) (examining the change in status of in-house counsel).

[9] *See* Mike France, *What About the Lawyers?*, BUS. WEEK, Dec. 22, 2002, at 58.

[10] *See* Catherine Aman & Gary Young, *Wal-Mart Shifting Litigation Strategy*, NAT'L L.J., Sept. 30, 2002, at A29.

[11] *See* DALY, *supra* note 1, at 1060 (examining the changing role of in-house lawyers, including comments on the shift of power from outside to in-house counsel).

edgeable about the business affairs of the corporation[12] and can help make corporate decisions on business and legal matters.[13] This trend has been accentuated in the recent downturn in the United States economy.[14]

Although the role of in-house lawyers has not occupied a central part of the debate on how to better address corporate fraud in the future, recent criminal litigation efforts by the government have highlighted the importance of in-house counsel to the outcome for the corporation. In 2002, Arthur Andersen L.L.P. was convicted for obstruction of justice for its participation in the Enron audit representation. The jury's foreman commented after the trial that an email written by an Andersen in-house attorney was the crucial evidence that led a deadlocked jury to find the corporation criminally responsible. Current efforts to examine other corporate frauds, such as Tyco, have included a very careful scrutiny of the conduct of in-house lawyers. And, it is likely that, in the civil litigation that will ensue for the next several years, the conduct of in-house lawyers will similarly affect a corporation's litigation posture.

This essay examines the standards for the regulation of in-house corporate lawyers. In Part II, we present the criminal trial of Arthur Andersen, L.L.P., as a short case study on the effect of in-house counsel on a corporation's compliance with the law.[15] Part III provides a brief introduction into the unique role of in-house lawyers and how their

---

[12] *Id.* at 1060–61.

[13] *See* Abram Chayes & Antonia Chayes, *Corporate Counsel and the Elite Law Firm*, 37 STAN. L. REV. 277, 282 (1985) ("[I]nside counsel generally participate in the structural planning process that results in a short-range annual budget, a mid- or long-range strategic plan, and long-term capital planning.").

[14] Daniel J. DiLucchio, *Law Firms on the Chopping Block?*, IN-HOUSE PRAC. & MGMT., June 2002, at 1 (discussing a survey showing that 62% of chief legal officers are considering firing one or more of their outside firms), *available at* http://www.altmanweil.com/about/articles/pdf/LawFirmsOnChopping BlockDJD.pdf.

[15] We have chosen to highlight the criminal prosecution of Arthur Andersen because it was the government's first effort to hold professionals responsible for corporate fraud related to Enron and, thus far, it has the most complete factual record of the conduct of professionals. There have been many allegations made against the in-house lawyers at Enron, Tyco, and other corporations, but as of late spring of 2003, the facts are still not fully known with respect to those allegations. However, in April 2003, Judge Harmon dismissed James V. Derrick, Jr., the former General Counsel of Enron, from the class action securities litigation filed by the Regents of the University of California et al. Memorandum and Order Re Remaining Enron Insider Defendants, Newby et al. v. Enron Corporation et al, Civil Action No. H-01-3624, United States District Court, Southern District of Texas, Houston Division (April 23, 2003). The reasons stated by Judge Harmon for dismissing Enron's in-house counsel were that the claims made against Mr. Derrick by the plaintiffs under Section 10(b) of the Securities Exchange Act of 1934 did not adequately plead specific factual information regarding *scienter* on the part of Mr. Derrick. The court noted that there were no allegations of false statements made against Mr. Derrick; likewise, there were no specific allegations in the Complaint—other than the fact that Derrick served for a period of time on Enron's management committee—showing that Derrick personally was involved in the day-to-day business decisions of Enron. The allegations did not indicate he had any background in accounting or personally was involved in preparing Enron's financial statements. With respect to the alleged failure by Derrick and other defendants to make adequate disclosures in the proxy statements sent to investors, Judge Harmon stated there were "no specifics about each's role, or how, when, where, why and what was not disclosed."

perspective differs from outside counsel. Part IV examines the legal profession's ethics rules on the representation of entities as clients. Part V provides a brief sketch of the response by the regulators and the legal profession on how future situations involving corporate fraud should be controlled. It includes a discussion of the newly promulgated Securities and Exchange Commission ("SEC") rules on the professional conduct of attorneys and the standards proposed by the ABA Task Force on Corporate Responsibility. Part VI offers two brief examples of the expanding reach of the criminal laws to the conduct of in-house lawyers.

The legal profession and society have presumed that the same rules apply to in-house and outside lawyers. However, this assumption has proven not to be the case in practice. Many in-house lawyers have failed to follow the professional norms and consequently frauds against their client, the corporation, have been allowed to continue for long periods of time. The regulators and the legal profession must recognize the inherent differences between in-house and outside lawyers. And, when such differences are taken into account, the rules of professional conduct must be strengthened to prevent the types of corporate fraud that have taken place over the last few years.

II. THE CRIMINAL TRIAL OF ARTHUR ANDERSEN LLP

A. Introduction

As Enron collapsed in late 2001 and its accounting and financial reporting problems were vetted in the media and in congressional hearings, Arthur Andersen LLP ("Andersen") stood at the epicenter of a brewing storm. How could a corporate fraud of this magnitude possibly have occurred? It was Andersen, a "Big Five"[16] international accounting firm with annual revenues of $9.3 billion in 2001 and 85,000 employees[17] that, after all, had audited Enron's consolidated financial statements and had certified *each year* that its financial reports complied with generally accepted accounting principles ("GAAP").

Andersen's role merely as Enron's auditor, however, was eclipsed when management of Andersen disclosed in January 2002 that some of its Houston partners had ordered employees to destroy some of the firm's documents related to Enron. And this document destruction occurred when federal investigations of Enron were commencing in the fall of 2001. Prior to that shocking announcement, Andersen did disclose this information to the SEC, the Department of Justice ("DOJ"), and Congress. At that

---

[16] For a brief history of the origin of the "Big Five," see Greg Billhartz, *Can't We All Just Get Along? Competing for Client Confidences: Integration of the Accounting and Legal Professions*, 17 ST. LOUIS U. PUB. L. REV. 427, 434 (1998) (noting that initially the accounting profession was controlled by the "Big Eight," later by the "Big Six," and finally in 1997 with the merger of Price Waterhouse and Coopers & Lybrand, the number shrunk to the "Big Five").

[17] Jonathan Galter, *Audit Firms Await Fallout and Windfall*, N.Y. TIMES, Mar. 14, 2002, at C1. Approximately 28,000 of Andersen's total employees worked in the United States.

point, the DOJ was presented with a silver-plated opportunity to pursue criminal charges against one of the central players in the Enron scandal without having to confront complex accounting issues dealing with special purpose entities and the esoteric treatment of hedging transactions under GAAP.

On March 7, 2002, a federal grand jury in Houston, Texas, indicted Andersen for obstructing the Securities and Exchange Commission's investigation of Enron.[18] The charge of obstruction of justice read:

> On or about and between October 10, 2001, and November 9, 2001, within the Southern District of Texas and elsewhere, including Chicago, Illinois, Portland, Oregon, and London, England, ANDERSEN, through its partners and others, did knowingly, intentionally and corruptly persuade and attempt to persuade other persons, to wit: ANDERSEN employees, with intent to cause and induce such persons to (a) withhold records, documents and other objects from official proceedings, namely: regulatory and criminal proceedings and investigations, and (b) alter, destroy, mutilate and conceal objects with intent to impair the objects' integrity and availability for use in such official proceedings. (Title 18, United States Code, Sections 1512(b)(2) and 3551 *et seq.*)[19]

---

[18] United States of America v. Arthur Andersen, LLP, Indictment CRH-02-121 filed on March 7, 2002, in United States District Court for the Southern District of Texas. The indictment was not made public until March 14, 2002.

[19] Judge Harmon's instructions to the jury stated: "18 U.S.C. § 1512(b)(2) provides: 'Whoever knowingly . . . [and] corruptly persuades another person, or attempts to do so, with intent . . . to cause or induce any person to withhold . . . a record, document, or other object from an official proceeding, [or] alter, destroy, mutilate, or conceal an object with intent to impair the object's integrity or availability for use in an official proceeding . . . [shall be guilty of a crime]'." Court's Instructions to the Jury, at 9, attached as Appendix C to this essay. The unedited language of § 1512(b)(2) provides:

"(b) Whoever knowingly uses intimidation, threatens or corruptly persuades another person, or attempts to do so, or engages in misleading conduct toward another person, with intent to

. . .

(2) cause or induce any person to

(A) withhold testimony, or withhold a record, document, or other object, from an official proceeding;

(B) alter, destroy, mutilate, or conceal an object with intent to impair the object's integrity or availability for use in an official proceeding;

(C) evade legal process summoning that person to appear as a witness, or to produce a record, document, or other object, in an official proceeding; or

(D) be absent from an official proceeding to which such person has been summoned by legal process;

. . .

shall be fined under this title or imprisoned not more than ten years, or both." 18 U.S.C. § 1512(b)(2) (2003).

The DOJ did not charge any individual officer or employee of Andersen; only the partnership was charged with violating federal criminal laws. United States District Court Judge Melinda Harmon gave the case expedited treatment, and the trial began a short two months following the issuance of the indictment.

On June 15, 2002, after deliberating for almost ten days, the jury found Andersen guilty of obstruction of justice.[20] The rapid demise of Andersen as a viable institution following its conviction for obstruction of justice is a stark reminder of the expanding demands and hidden dangers that in-house attorneys face.

In fact, one of the surprises in the Andersen trial was that, in interviews with jurors immediately after the verdict, several members of the jury revealed that, instead of focusing on document destruction, the jurors basically fashioned their own theory of the case and unanimously agreed that it was an e-mail from Andersen's in-house counsel, Nancy Temple, that convinced the holdout jurors to convict Andersen.[21] Ms. Temple had sent an e-mail to David Duncan,[22] the Andersen audit partner who was in charge of the Enron account, suggesting that he alter some language in a draft memorandum to the files so that it did not indicate that Andersen believed an important Enron press release was misleading to investors. The jury concluded that this advice caused Temple to be a "corrupt persuader," which satisfied a crucial element of the federal offense prohibiting the obstruction of an official proceeding.

The *Andersen* case raises many important issues about the role and responsibilities of in-house attorneys. For example, was Temple's advice in the October 16th email significantly different from advice that corporate counsel routinely give to their clients? Must corporate counsel now also become specialists in the intricacies of criminal law? After *Andersen*, what advice should in-house counsel give to employees about the destruction of documents? Does the conviction of Andersen change how an in-house counsel should perceive her role in representing a business entity? What lessons can in-house and outside corporate counsel learn from the *Andersen* case?

An assessment of the *Andersen* case should begin with an understanding of the events leading up to the trial and what both the prosecutors and defense attorneys argued to the jury. A timeline of events as they unfolded in the *Andersen* case appears as Appendix A to this essay.

---

[20] Kurt Eichenwald, *Andersen Guilty in Effort to Block Inquiry on Enron*, N.Y. TIMES, June 16, 2002, at A1.

[21] Mary Flood, *The Andersen Verdict; Decision by Jurors Hinged on Memo*, HOUS. CHRON., Jun. 16, 2002, at 1; Tom Fowler, *Andersen Guilty*, HOUS. CHRON., June 16, 2002, at 1; Kristen Hays, *Enron's Auditor Convicted*, THE SALT LAKE TRIBUNE, July 16, 2002, *available at* www.sltrib.com/2002/jun/06162002/nation_w/nation_w.htm; *One Angry Man: Inside the Andersen Jury*, THE DAILY ENRON, June 17, 2002, *available at* www.thedailyenron.com/documents/20020617084026-96760.asp.

[22] The text of Nancy Temple's e-mail is attached as Appendix B at the end of this essay. Hearing Before the Subcommittee on Oversight and Investigations of the Committee on Energy and Commerce, House of Representatives, *Destruction of Enron-Related Documents by Andersen Personnel*, One Hundred Seventh Congress, Second Session, January 24, 2002, Serial No. 107-80 (U.S. Government Printing Office 2002) [hereinafter Congressional Hearing Transcript], at 58.

B. Andersen's Reaction to the Developing Financial Crisis at Enron

On August 20, 2001, an Andersen audit partner[23] received a telephone call from Sherron Watkins, who was a former business colleague at Andersen now working at Enron. Watkins expressed her concerns about the propriety of how Enron had accounted for its transactions with third-party special purpose entities in prior financial statements. The special purpose entities, with provocative names like Raptor and Chewco, were "off balance sheet" partnerships that Enron had used to inflate its earnings and keep indebtedness off of its consolidated financial statements.[24] Watkins also mentioned that she intended to discuss these problems with Enron's chairman, Kenneth Lay.[25]

After that telephone conversation, the Andersen partner wrote a memo to the files and forwarded it to David Duncan, who was in charge of Andersen's audit engagement team at Enron. Andersen quickly established a special internal consultation group to coordinate the handling of concerns about Enron accounting issues. One member of this special group was Nancy Temple, an in-house attorney in Andersen's Chicago office. Temple had been a partner in the Chicago law firm of Sidley & Austin and was experienced in accounting firm litigation matters. During the first two weeks in October 2001, Andersen learned that Enron would report charges against income in its third quarter financial statements in the amount of $1.2 billion on an after-tax basis. This would surprise investors and likely have an adverse effect upon the price of Enron's stock. On October 9, before Enron publicly announced this adverse financial information, Nancy Temple wrote in her notes: "highly probable some SEC investigation."

Andersen and Enron had intensive discussions about how those losses would be described. On Friday evening, October 12, David Duncan received from Enron a draft of its proposed press release announcing this adverse information. Enron's draft described these huge charges again income as "non-recurring." In a draft memorandum

---

[23] Sherron Watkins has stated that her telephone call was to Jim Hecker, an Andersen partner who was not on the Enron engagement team. According to Watkins, after she talked to him for about forty-five minutes, his response was: "I hope you're not right, because this firm can't handle another scandal." *See* Mimi Swartz with Sherron Watkins, POWER FAILURE: THE INSIDE STORY OF THE COLLAPSE OF ENRON 285 (2003). Ironically, it was Mr. Hecker who, in 1995, had written a parody of the lyrics to the popular song "Hotel California," which the prosecution entered into evidence in the trial. The parody entitled "Hotel Kenneth-Lay-a" did not paint a favorable image of Andersen's relationship with Enron. One part read: "Welcome to the Hotel Mark to Market, Such a lovely face, Such a fragile place, They livin' it up at the Hotel Cram it Down Ya, When the [law] suits arrive, bring your alibis." The lyrics are available at http://money.cnn.com/2002/05/08/news/companies/andersen_song/ and reprinted here in Appendix D.

[24] Enron's special purpose entity transactions are described in the Report of the Special Investigation Committee of the Board of Directors of Enron Corp., commonly known as "The Powers Report." Report of Investigation by the Special Investigative Committee of the Board of Directors of Enron Corp. (Feb. 1, 2002), *available at* http://news.findlaw.com/hdocs/docs/enron/sicreport/index.html.

[25] A copy of the letter that Sherron Watkins wrote and delivered at her meeting on August 15, 2001, with Kenneth Lay appears in the Congressional Hearing Transcript, *supra* note 22, at 39–44.

to the files dated October 15, Duncan wrote that he had advised Enron against using the term "non-recurring" because those charges against income are included in normal operating earnings in GAAP financial statements.[26] In particular, Duncan's memorandum indicated that he told Enron officials about his concerns that presenting the charges as non-recurring could be "misconstrued or misunderstood by investors." Duncan emailed a copy of his draft memorandum to Nancy Temple with a request for her comments.

On the following day, October 16, Temple sent an e-mail to Duncan setting forth her "suggested comments for consideration" regarding his memorandum to the files.[27] Temple's now famous e-mail made the following suggestions:

- deleting any reference to "consulting with the legal group and deleting [Temple's] name on the memo to avoid any waiver of the attorney-client privilege" and noting that if her name was mentioned it would increase the chances that she "might be a witness, which I prefer to avoid."
- deleting language "that might suggest we [Andersen] have concluded the release is misleading"; and in light of the use of the term "non-recurring," the lack of any suggestion that this characterization was not in accordance with GAAP; and
- stating that she would consult further within the legal group about whether Andersen should do anything more to protect itself from potential liability under the securities laws.

Enron ignored Andersen's advice[28] and used the term "non-recurring" in its press release.

Andersen documents reflect that only a few days earlier, on October 12, Nancy Temple had sent another email to an Andersen partner, Mike Odum, advising him that it might be useful "to consider reminding the Engagement Team of our document and retention policy. It will be helpful to make sure that we have complied with the policy."[29] Prosecutors would later argue that this e-mail was Andersen "code" for "shred

---

[26] Memorandum to The Files dated October 15, 2001 from David B. Duncan, Re: Enron Press Release Discussions. Congressional Hearing Transcript, *supra* note 22, at 56.

[27] Email dated October 16, 2001, to David B. Duncan from Nancy A. Temple, Subject: Press Release draft. This email is available in Congressional Hearing Transcript, *supra* note 22, at 58.

[28] During the Andersen trial, witnesses testified that Andersen's normal pattern of dealing with Enron was that, if Enron objected to advice or a particular accounting treatment, partners working on the Enron account in Andersen's Houston office would often ignore the advice of Andersen's own technical experts and capitulate to Enron's position. *See* Kurt Eichenwald & Floyd Norris, *Early Verdict on Audit: Procedures Ignored*, N.Y. TIMES, June 6, 2002, at C6.

[29] Congressional Hearing Transcript, *supra* note 22, at 45.

every document that you can."[30] Temple also e-mailed copies of Andersen's document retention policy to other Andersen employees working on Enron matters. The actions by Andersen employees in response to the e-mail about "document retention" placed Andersen on a collision course with federal prosecutors.

Prosecutors presented evidence during the Andersen trial that, during the period from October 12 to November 9, Andersen employees shredded and destroyed tons of documents in its files related to Enron. The document destruction stopped only when Andersen received a subpoena on November 8 from the SEC requesting documents relating to its work for Enron. On the day after the subpoena was received, David Duncan instructed his assistant to send out an e-mail to Andersen employees working on Enron matters. The subject line of the e-mail stated: "No more shredding."

C. Andersen Seeks to Avoid an Indictment

Kurt Eichenwald published in *The New York Times* an in-depth investigative report on what happened inside Andersen as the firm began to confront the magnitude of its Enron problems.[31] When the outside legal team hired by Andersen[32] began efforts in early January 2002 to assemble documents, e-mails, and other Andersen information related to Enron, they discovered that many of the e-mails, records, and other documents sought by federal investigators were missing and apparently no longer existed.

After Andersen's in-house general counsel, Andrew J. Pincus, conducted interviews with Andersen employees in Houston, he learned about the widespread and suspicious shredding of Enron documents and deletion of e-mails from computers. With that information, Andersen's outside legal counsel recommended that Andersen promptly inform the DOJ, the SEC, and Congressional committees of the document destruction. On January 10, Andersen issued a press release acknowledging that a significant number of Enron documents had been destroyed.[33] Five days later, Andersen announced that it had fired David Duncan for his role in "the destruction of thousands of documents and e-mail messages after learning that the Securities and Exchange Commission

---

[30] *See* Sheila McNulty, *Andersen Sought Legal Counsel Before Shredding Began*, FIN. TIMES, May 25, 2002, at 17.

[31] Kurt Eichenwald, *Enron's Many Strands: The Accountants; Miscues, Missteps, and the Fall of Andersen*, N.Y. TIMES, May 8, 2002, at C1. Most of the information in this section has been derived from this excellent piece of investigative journalism by Mr. Eichenwald.

[32] The outside law firms hired by Andersen were Davis Polk & Wardwell of New York ("Davis Polk") and Mayer, Brown, Rowe & Maw of Chicago ("Mayer, Brown").

[33] Kurt Eichenwald & Floyd Norris, *Enron's Collapse: The Auditor; Enron's Auditor Says it Destroyed Documents*, N.Y. TIMES, Jan. 11, 2002, at C1.

had begun an investigation of Enron's accounting."[34] Prior to Duncan's termination, he was interviewed by telephone for less than twenty minutes by Andersen's legal team.

These revelations by Andersen generated a firestorm of media coverage, and a parade of Andersen's long-standing clients began leaving the firm. Surviving became Andersen's primary concern.

Andersen's legal team initially discounted the possibility that Andersen as an entity would be indicted by the DOJ, most likely based on prior experience that federal agencies typically do not indict large companies that self-disclose wrongdoing. Andersen had gone directly to the DOJ and SEC in January to disclose the document destruction; therefore, individuals might be subject to criminal prosecution, but not the company. Moreover, the consequences of indicting an accounting firm of Andersen's size under these circumstances would be very damaging. An indictment could doom the firm and reduce competition when there were, at the time, only five large accounting firms. Furthermore, an indictment would likely also result in the unemployment of tens of thousands of Andersen employees.

Time was not on Andersen's side. The firm apparently took an aggressive and risky gambit in dealing with federal prosecutors. In Andersen's early contacts with the DOJ, it supposedly told the DOJ to either prosecute the firm or let the public know that the DOJ would not seek criminal charges against Andersen. That aggressive approach by Andersen limited DOJ's options. Subsequent efforts to reach an agreement in which Andersen would sign a plea agreement, with deferred prosecution and with probation, collapsed.[35] Davis Polk, one of Andersen's outside law firms, eventually urged Andersen to consider a plea agreement. Following that advice, Davis Polk was replaced as lead counsel and Mayer, Brown was given the task of negotiating with the DOJ.

Finally, when Andersen realized that it faced an imminent indictment, Mayer, Brown wrote a final appeal on behalf of Andersen to Michael Chertoff, head of the DOJ's criminal division.[36] This letter stated that the government had demanded that Andersen plead guilty to obstruction of justice charges by the next day or face immediate indictment. The appeal claimed that an indictment of Andersen would be an extraordinary exercise of prosecutorial discretion and would place the survival of the firm "in grave jeopardy."

This appeal by Mayer, Brown admitted that several Andersen partners "unquestionably exercised poor judgment," but stated that responsibility for the document de-

---

[34] Richard A. Oppel, Jr. with Kurt Eichenwald, *Arthur Andersen Fires an Executive for Enron Orders*, N.Y. Times, Jan. 16, 2002, at A1.

[35] *See* Jonathan Weil, Devon Spurgeon, & Cassell Bryan-Low, *Arthur Andersen Breaks Off Talks to Settle Criminal Case*, Wall St. J., April 19, 2002, at A1 (describing the breakdown of settlement talks between the Justice Department and Andersen).

[36] Letter dated March 13, 2002, from Richard J. Favretto of Mayer, Brown, Rowe & Maw to Michael Chertoff, Assistant Attorney General, U.S. Justice Department.

struction was confined to a few partners and employees of the firm and was "almost entirely limited to the Houston office." The letter argued that there were other ways for the government to achieve its objectives without harming innocent employees.

As an alternative, Andersen offered, in Mayer, Brown's letter, to take the following steps: it would undertake all of the comprehensive reforms and reorganization plans proposed by former Federal Reserve Chairman Paul Volcker; it would agree to deferred prosecution (presumably without pleading guilty) and the appointment of a special monitor to oversee compliance; it would terminate all individuals who were responsible for the document destruction; and it would adopt a remedy by the SEC directed at the firm's Houston office. The last item was a sensitive subject at the DOJ because Andersen had reportedly said at one of its meetings with DOJ officials that SEC sanctions were just a risk of doing business.

In fact, a week earlier, on March 7, 2002, a federal grand jury in Houston had issued an indictment of Andersen that had been placed under seal. The indictment was announced on March 14. Negotiations continued between Andersen and the DOJ in an attempt to reach a settlement, but a proposed plea agreement collapsed on April 6 when David Duncan, the Andersen partner in charge of the Enron account who had been fired, reached an agreement with the government to plead guilty to a felony. As late as two weeks before the scheduled trial date, the DOJ and Andersen's lawyers made another attempt to settle the criminal claims against the firm, but that also fell apart. At that point, there was no turning back. Andersen and the DOJ were headed to a trial before a jury in the federal courthouse in Houston.

D. The Trial

In his opening statement to the jury on May 7, 2002, DOJ prosecutor Matthew Friedrich told the jurors that, when Enron was collapsing and Andersen realized that "the law was coming," some Andersen partners made a choice to do what they could to help the firm avoid liability by corruptly causing Andersen employees to shred files, delete e-mails, and destroy and alter boxes of documents relating to the firm's work for Enron so that information would unavailable to SEC investigators.[37] According to Friedrich, Andersen knew that the SEC would be investigating "because Nancy Temple [an in-house attorney] wrote it down." In a note drafted by Temple during a conference call with Andersen partners on October 9, 2002, she wrote "Highly probable some SEC investigation" referring to the possible repercussions arising from the Enron audit.[38] It was also Temple who sent the e-mail on October 12, 2001, to certain Andersen

[37] Transcript of Proceedings before the Honorable Melinda Harmon and a Jury, May 7, 2002, Crim. Action H-02-121, *United States of America v. Arthur Andersen, LLP*, U.S. District Court, Southern District of Texas, Houston Division, at 337 [hereinafter Transcript].

[38] Tom Fowler & Mary Flood, *Feds Launch Haymaker at Andersen*, HOUS. CHRON., May 21, 2001, at A1.

partners reminding them to follow the firm's document retention policy. Friedrich argued that Temple's e-mail was just a code for the instruction to start shredding documents in the firm's Enron files.

The government argued that Andersen had many reasons to try to cover its tracks. Enron was its second largest client (Enron paid Andersen fees of $50 million in 2000). Enron was an aggressive client that pushed the edges of the accounting envelope, and the relationship between Andersen and Enron had become too close. The accountants who made up the Enron engagement team often took Enron's side in accounting disputes, to the dismay of in-house professional standards experts at Andersen who disagreed. Andersen became incapable of being the "watchdog" that auditors are supposed to be when examining a client's accounting practices. What was the motive for destroying documents? The prosecutors argued that Andersen knew that there had been a series of massive accounting errors at Enron that were about to be revealed to the financial community. Moreover, Andersen had recently entered into a settlement agreement with the SEC relating to accounting fraud involving another client, Waste Management.[39] In the Waste Management settlement, Andersen had agreed to an injunction to avoid any future wrongdoing. If the SEC uncovered improper conduct by Andersen in the Enron case, Andersen's right to practice accounting before the SEC could be terminated.

Andersen's trial attorney, Rusty Hardin, argued to the jurors that the indictment against Andersen was a tragedy for thousands of Andersen employees.[40] He said that the employees of this Big Five accounting firm had merely followed an established document retention policy that allowed files to be purged of unnecessary documents. "This is a document-destruction charge by the government," Hardin stated, "based on evidence and documents that we [Andersen] preserved and we gave them. Is there some irony in that?"[41]

The government's main witness in the case was David Duncan, the former Andersen audit partner who had headed up the Andersen engagement team for the Enron account and who previously had pleaded guilty to participating in obstruction of justice. Duncan testified that he instructed employees to follow Andersen's document retention policy, knowing that his instruction would result in the destruction of records relating to Enron. However, his testimony proved to be a double-edged sword.

Duncan also testified that, when he encouraged employees on the Enron engagement team to destroy documents, he did not believe that he was committing a crime. He thought that he was allowed to destroy documents under the firm's document retention policy until Andersen received a subpoena from the SEC. Moreover, Duncan said that he told employees to follow the firm's document retention policy, which

[39] Kurt Eichenwald, *Enron's Many Strands: The Trial; Judge Says Andersen's Past can be Evidence*, N.Y. TIMES, May 8, 2002, at C6.

[40] Transcript, *supra* note 37, at 356.

[41] *Id.* at 360.

permitted destruction only of records that were not part of primary work-papers used to explain accounting decisions. He said he told employees to go no further than the retention policy allowed.[42]

This testimony was damaging to the government's case because it indicated that, during the critical time when Duncan was encouraging the destruction of documents, he may not have had the requisite criminal intent, and arguably could not be the "corrupt persuader" necessary to prove that all elements of the obstruction of justice statute had been satisfied. It is important to recognize that the destruction or alteration of documents is not a crime unless it is done with an intent to impede an official proceeding. However, the term "official proceeding" does not mean only a court proceeding or a formal investigation. It also includes an informal investigation by a governmental agency and can commence before receipt of a subpoena for documents. In effect, Duncan's testimony created an unlikely scenario where Andersen's lawyer was arguing that Duncan never actually committed a crime, even though he had in fact already pleaded guilty to a crime. On the other hand, the government found itself in the uncomfortable position of assuring the jury that its primary witness was in fact a criminal.

Perhaps the most damaging evidence against Andersen was Andersen's billing records, which indicated that, during October and November 2001, Andersen charged Enron over $700,000 for dealing with the informal investigation of Enron. This time was reflected by Andersen employees as being charged to "S.E.C. Inquiry." The billing records were damaging in two respects. These were official partnership documents that reflected that Andersen employees knew about the SEC's informal investigation of Enron. These billing records also demonstrated that, while a large number of Andersen partners knew about the informal investigation being conducted by the SEC, some Andersen employees were destroying Enron documents.

E. Judge Harmon's Instructions to the Jury

The trial court's written instructions to the jury explain the law applicable to the case. It describes what the government must prove to convict Andersen of obstruction of justice. The instructions also explain to the jury what the government is not required to prove in order to obtain a conviction. Judge Harmon's explanation of what is *not* required to convict Andersen may come as a surprise to corporate lawyers who are unfamiliar with the contours of federal criminal law.

The essential elements of § 1512(b)(2)[43] that the government had to prove in order for the jury to convict Andersen of obstruction of justice are that Andersen (through an agent or employee):

---

[42] Kurt Eichenwald, *Andersen Auditors Knew About Federal Inquiry*, N.Y. TIMES, May 15, 2002, at C10.

[43] *Supra* note 19.

- acted knowingly with a corrupt intent
- to cause or persuade one of Andersen's employees
- to withhold a document from an official proceeding;
- or alter, destroy or conceal an object
- with intent to impair its availability in an official proceeding.

However, the instructions explained that it was *not* necessary for the prosecution to prove any of the following in order for the jury to convict Andersen:

- It was not necessary to prove that the acts of an employee or agent of Andersen were approved by the partnership or were in accordance with its policies. A partnership is responsible for an agent's action taken within the scope of employment, even if the agent's conduct was illegal, contrary to the partnership's instructions, or against the policies of the partnership.[44]
- It was not necessary to prove that Andersen or its agents knew that their conduct violated federal law prohibiting the obstruction of justice. In other words, violating the obstruction of justice statute did not require a "willful" violation, which would have required the prosecution to prove *scienter*— that the violator knew and intended to violate the law.[45]
- It was not necessary to prove that Andersen actually succeeded in destroying or altering any document or even that Andersen was likely to succeed in subverting or undermining an official proceeding. It is an agent's purpose and intent to impede an official proceeding that matters, not whether the agent is successful or likely to succeed.[46]
- It was not necessary to prove that an official proceeding was pending, or even about to be initiated, at the time the obstructive conduct occurred.[47] An "official proceeding" includes an investigation by a government agency and does not require formal action by the agency or issuance of a subpoena for documents.[48]
- It was not necessary even to prove that Andersen destroyed any documents. Destruction of documents is not the only conduct prohibited in the federal obstruction of justice statute. Andersen could be convicted if its agents sought to cause another person to alter, mutilate, or conceal an "object" with intent to prevent the object from being available for use in a government investigation.[49]

---

[44] See Appendix C, *Court's Instructions to the Jury,* at 5.

[45] *Id.* at 12.

[46] *Id.* at 12.

[47] *Id.* at 11.

[48] *Id.* at 10.

[49] *Id.* at 12.

F. The Jury's Verdict

Following four weeks of hearing testimony and final arguments, the jury of nine men and three women received instructions and was sent off to decide the fate of an international accounting firm. After seven days, the jurors informed Judge Harmon that they were deadlocked. Judge Harmon then gave the jury an "*Allen* charge," which encouraged the jurors to continue deliberations because so much time and money had been spent on the trial and another group of jurors would be no more competent or conscientious in making a decision.[50]

After the jurors resumed their deliberations, they sent a note to Judge Harmon asking a clarification on a legal issue. The jurors asked: "If each of us believes that one Andersen agent acted knowingly and with corrupt intent, is it [necessary] for all of us to believe it was the same agent? Can one believe it was Agent A, another one believe it was Agent B, and another one believe it was Agent C?"[51]

This was not a question of law that could be answered easily. And it certainly came as a surprise to both the prosecutors and defense attorneys. Because the obstruction of justice statute requires an agent of the entity to corruptly persuade another person in the entity to destroy, alter, mutilate, or conceal a document so that the document was unavailable in a government investigation, the jury indicated it was not sure that it could convict Andersen if some of the jurors believed, for example, that the corrupt persuader was David Duncan while other jurors believed that Nancy Temple was the corrupt persuader. Because the jury had been deadlocked, Judge Harmon's decision was crucial. Moreover, there was no clear law on this issue.

The government argued for the lower standard that it was unnecessary for the jurors to agree upon the same actor.[52] A prosecutor compared the situation to a crime in which police found multiple guns, but only one suspect. It would not matter which gun was used. Andersen, on the other hand, argued that all jurors must agree upon the same actor:[53] If the government's theory was correct, it was conceivable that Andersen as an entity could be held to have committed a crime, even if a majority of jurors would not vote to convict any of its partners or employees individually for committing a crime. Stated bluntly from Andersen's perspective: "Under the government's theory, you could have criminal liability if no one committed a crime."

---

[50] Kurt Eichenwald, *Andersen Jury Tells the Judge It's Deadlocked*, N.Y. TIMES, June 13, 2002, at A1.

[51] Jonathan Well, Alexel Barrionuevo and Kathryn Kranhold, *Dramatic Question From Jury Could Shape Andersen's Fate*, WALL ST. J., June 14, 2002.

[52] Government's Memorandum of Law Regarding Jury Note 9, Crim. Action H-02-121, *United States of America v. Arthur Andersen, LLP*, U.S. District Court, Southern District of Texas, Houston Division.

[53] Andersen's Memorandum of Law Regarding Jury Note No. 9, Crim. Action H-02-121, *United States of America v. Arthur Andersen, LLP*, U.S. District Court, Southern District of Texas, Houston Division.

After considering the jurors' question overnight, Judge Harmon ruled in favor of the government's position and instructed the jurors that, to convict Andersen, they were not required unanimously to agree upon a single "corrupt persuader."[54] On the day following this decision by Judge Harmon, the jury unanimously agreed that Andersen was guilty of obstruction of justice.

G. The Missing Witness

When the trial was over, Judge Harmon allowed both parties and the media to speak with the jurors. The jury foreman told reporters that the jurors could not agree that the shredding of documents by Andersen employees constituted obstruction of justice.[55] Moreover, some jurors did not believe that David Duncan had committed a crime, even though he had already pleaded guilty to committing a crime. In effect, it appears that the jury rejected much of what the lawyers on both sides had argued throughout much of the trial.

Rather than focusing on Andersen's destruction of documents, some of the jurors developed their own theory of the case. Namely, that Nancy Temple's email to David Duncan on October 16, 2001, was the crucial fact that eventually convinced all members of the jury that Andersen should be convicted of obstruction of justice. Temple's one sentence—" I suggested deleting some language that might suggest we have concluded the [press] release is misleading"—was the proverbial smoking gun that caused jurors to believe she was the "corrupt persuader."

After the trial, Andersen's trial attorney commented that he could not get before the jury the one person he needed to testify—Nancy Temple. She was *in absentia*. Ms. Temple had exercised her Fifth Amendment privilege against self-incrimination and refused to appear and testify at the Andersen trial.

If Nancy Temple had testified, what information could she have provided to jurors that might have helped Andersen? What information might she have provided that could shed light her actions in the fall of 2001 as in-house counsel for Andersen? Nancy Temple did testify on one occasion before the Andersen trial. She testified, along with other Andersen officials, at a hearing in January 2002 before the Subcommittee on Energy and Commerce of the United States House of Representatives, which was investigating the Enron debacle:[56] At this Congressional hearing, Ms. Temple provided information relevant to those questions, and she indicated that her first involvement in the Enron matter was on September 28 when she participated in a telephone conference call.

First, Ms. Temple was adamant that she never counseled Andersen partners to destroy or shred documents. At the Congressional hearing she was asked about her email

---

[54] Kurt Eichenwald, *Judge's Ruling on Andersen Hurts Defense*, N.Y. TIMES, June 15, 2002, at C1.

[55] *Supra* note 19.

[56] *Supra* note 22.

on October 12 to Michael Odom, Andersen's practice director in Houston, stating: "It might be useful to consider reminding the engagement team of our documentation and retention policy. It will be helpful to make sure we have complied with the policy."[57] Temple testified that when she sent this email she was "concerned about making sure that we [Andersen] had accurate and complete documentation."[58]

Ms. Temple revealed that, by October 12, she knew about Sherron Watkins's allegations of accounting irregularities at Enron. Ms. Temple also said that she understood that Andersen had raised these allegations with the highest levels at Enron and that the Andersen engagement team had assured the legal group that the allegations had been addressed with the general counsel of Enron. Temple also knew that Enron had engaged Vinson & Elkins to conduct an independent investigation of Watkins's allegations.

Second, new information was revealed at the hearing about the role of Andersen's outside law firm. On October 9, 2002, the law firm of Davis, Polk & Wardwell was hired by Andersen to consult on the complex issues at Enron, including "financial reporting issues and with possible litigation."[59] Ms. Temple revealed that she consulted extensively with Davis, Polk beginning on October 16, which is the day she sent her famous email to David Duncan with suggestions about his memorandum to the file.

In response to a question about why she wrote the e-mail suggesting that Mr. Duncan delete any reference to consulting with the legal group, deleting her name in his memo, and deleting language that might suggest Andersen had concluded that the press release was misleading, Ms Temple stated: "I wrote that after reviewing the draft and consulting with Davis, Polk, our outside legal counsel."[60]

Ms. Temple was also asked: "If Mr. Duncan was concerned about misleading the public with this nonrecurring charge, why did you suggest deleting that?" Ms. Temple responded, "There's only one sentence they suggested deleting for two reasons, because it was inaccurate factually. . . . Andersen had not concluded that the press release was misleading."[61] She was not clear about who "they" were, but she did state, "And as an extra precaution, I sent these documents to Davis, Polk and asked them to review them to see if they had any suggested advice for additional steps that Arthur

---

[57] A copy of Ms. Temple's e-mail dated October 12, 2001, appears in Congressional Hearing Transcript, *supra* note 22, at 45.

[58] Congressional Hearing Transcript, *supra* note 22, at 148. Consistent with that testimony, in response to a related question, Ms. Temple revealed that a question had arisen during the crisis about whether the engagement team could delete a sentence in a memo that acknowledged that the firm had given incorrect accounting advice to Enron in the first quarter of 2001. Ms. Temple testified, "And I said absolutely not." *Id.* at 123.

[59] Testimony of C.E. Andrews, Senior Executive, Arthur Andersen L.L.P. at Congressional Hearing Transcript, p. 119. *See* Sheila McNulty, *Andersen Sought Legal Counsel Before Shredding Began*, FINANCIAL TIMES (LONDON), May 25, 2002, Section: Companies & Finance: International, at 17.

[60] Congressional Hearing Transcript, *supra* note 22, p. 143.

[61] *Id.* at p. 143.

Andersen should take in these circumstances. And the advice was, no, we were doing the right thing."[62] Moreover, Ms. Temple said that, after consulting with Davis, Polk, she advised the Andersen engagement team ". . . it is our standard practice in the legal group [at Andersen] to advise the engagement team not to write down and discuss in their memos legal advice that the legal group might give, because it may be a waiver down the road of attorney-client privilege."[63]

On the issue of what Ms. Temple knew by October 23rd, when the shredding of Enron documents began in earnest at Andersen's office in Houston, she stated that she knew that the SEC had begun an informal inquiry into Enron and that the SEC had written a letter to Enron asking for documents about related-party transactions. She also knew that Andersen was assisting Enron in preparing its response to the SEC. She had a copy of Vinson & Elkin's letter to Enron's general counsel, James V. Derrick, Jr. dated October 15, 2002, reporting on its investigation of Sherron Watkins's allegations,[64] and she knew that a class action securities lawsuit was filed against Enron on that date by certain investors.

Ms. Temple testified in her defense that David Duncan had assured her that "the [Andersen] team was trying to gather all documents"[65] regarding transactions from around the world and to have it in one place so they were available. When Andersen received a subpoena from the SEC at the end of business on November 8, Ms. Temple sent a voice mail on the next day to Andersen's audit engagement team working on Enron matters to preserve all documents related to Enron, which was confirmed the following day by an e-mail stating: "Effective immediately, all existing Enron-related documents and materials must be preserved and nothing should be destroyed or discarded."[66] Ms. Temple's testimony was that "it was drafted by our outside counsel, a law firm—Davis, Polk & Wardwell."[67]

One can only speculate about how this testimony might have affected the jury had Nancy Temple testified in person at the Andersen trial. The fact that she consulted extensively with outside counsel beginning on April 16 and, in particular, discussed with Davis, Polk the advice contained in her email to David Duncan would certainly have been used by Andersen's trial counsel to counter prosecution arguments that

---

[62] *Id.* at p. 143.

[63] *Id.* at p. 124.

[64] *Id.* at 46. A copy of Vinson & Elkins's letter, dated October 15, 2001, to James V. Derrick, Jr., reporting on its internal investigation at Enron appears at Congressional Hearing Transcript, *supra* note 22, at 46–54. It is interesting that this letter is dated the day before Nancy Temple sent her famous October 16th email to David Duncan.

[65] Congressional Hearing Transcript, supra note 22, at 132. A copy of a memo about the "Core Consultation Team Conference Call on 10/23/01" appears *id.* at 61.

[66] A copy of Ms. Temple's email and memorandum sent on November 10, 2001, to "All U.S. Enron Engagement Team" appears at Congressional Hearing Transcript, supra note 22, at 63–64.

[67] Congressional Hearing Transcript, supra note 22, at 118.

Nancy Temple was part of a conspiracy within Andersen to impede the SEC's investigation. After the trial, Andersen's attorney, Rusty Hardin, stated, "If I could have called Nancy Temple to the stand, Andersen would never have been convicted. The jury had to make a character judgment about someone—worst of all, a lawyer they'd never seen before."[68]

H. Temple's 'Smoking Gun' E-mail

Since some of the jurors stated that Nancy Temple's e-mail on October 16, 2002, was the proverbial "smoking gun" evidence that led them to conclude she was the "corrupt persuader" at Andersen, this particular e-mail has become probably the most widely circulated e-mail ever sent by a lawyer, as well as the subject of intense scrutiny.

In summary, Temple's e-mail included the following advice: (i) deleting reference to the fact that Duncan had consulted with the legal group, (ii) deleting her name from the memorandum, (iii) deleting language that might suggest that Andersen had concluded that Enron's press release was misleading, and (iv) indicating that she would consult further with the legal group to determine if Andersen should do anything more to protect itself from potential liability under the securities laws.

From the perspective of a general counsel's daily practice, the advice given by Nancy Temple's in her October 16 e-mail seems unremarkable. Professor Stephen Gillers wrote an op-ed article that appeared in *The New York Times* arguing that Temple's e-mail was merely giving her employer "routine legal advice."[69] As Gillers pointed out, lawyers routinely advise their clients not to put something in writing: "'Don't put it in writing' is advice lawyers give every day—to protect clients from creating documents that may be used, or often misused, to their detriment." Editing client documents, including recommending that a sentence be deleted, is often a valuable legal service that lawyers provide to clients. Moreover, Professor Gillers stated that lawyers are obligated to advise clients to protect the attorney-client privilege, and lawyers should generally avoid becoming witnesses. On the other hand, another commentator has argued at a legal conference that, in a post-Enron environment, advising a client to change, edit, or destroy documents is risky because "[t]oday, documents never really go away."[70]

So why was Ms. Temple's October 16 e-mail so damaging in the Andersen trial? In one word: context. A lawyer's advice to a client should always be given in the context of

---

[68] Pamela Colloff, *The Trick is Not to Act Like a Lawyer,* TEXAS MONTHLY, Sept. 2002, at 157, 218.

[69] Stephen Gillers, *The Flaw in the Andersen Verdict,* N.Y. TIMES, June 18, 2002, at 23. The view that Nancy Temple email "did what lawyers do" is shared by Professor Sandra L. DeGraw, in a written presentation, *Post-Enron and Andersen Ethics Issues,* presented at South Texas College of Law, Energy Law Institute, August 15–16, 2002.

[70] Comments by Robert E. Hinerfeld at a legal conference entitled *Aching for Andersen: How to Avoid Giving Advice That a Jury May Misconstrue,* reported in CURRENT REPORTS, ABA/BNA LEGAL MANUAL OF PROFESSIONAL CONDUCT, Aug. 14, 2002, at 484.

the surrounding facts and circumstances at the time the advice is given. The draft memorandum to the file written by David Duncan and sent to Ms. Temple for her review dealt with highly adverse financial news that Enron was about to reveal. And that information was perceived as a bombshell in the financial markets. Ms. Temple's notes also reflect that an SEC investigation of Enron was likely. During the trial, jurors learned that, only a few days earlier, Ms. Temple had advised another Andersen partner "to consider reminding the Engagement Team of our document and retention policy. It will be helpful to make sure that we have complied with the policy." Regardless of intent or motive, the document destruction that occurred at Andersen after her October 12 and October 16 e-mails put Andersen on a collision course with federal prosecutors. Viewed in that context, this "routine" legal advice was not perceived by the DOJ and twelve jurors as within the boundaries of legal conduct.

Another important factor is the nature of e-mail communications. When a person drafts an e-mail, it tends to be written informally. And the mere speed of e-mail communications may result in legal advice being sent without the reflection a lawyer typically gives before sending a written opinion to a client. E-mails are usually archived in a central server; and thus deleting an e-mail from a lawyer's personal computer does not typically erase the e-mail from a law firm's archived computer files. And as the Andersen trial dramatically illustrated, e-mails can be used as evidence in ways the author would ever have anticipated. As a state prosecutor wryly commented, "We view the 'e' in e-mail to mean evidence."[71]

I. Was Temple's Advice Consistent with Andersen's Document Retention and Destruction Policies?

Andersen had two policy memoranda related to retaining and destroying documents. One pertained to notification to the legal department about any litigation, investigations, and subpoenas. It provided:

> "2.8 Government Investigations-Notification to . . . the AA Legal Group should be made promptly when AA personnel become aware of investigations involving a client or former client and AA or any AA personnel (e.g., investigations by a federal or state grand jury, the FBI, the Justice Department, the SEC or the IRS in the United States. . . ."[72]

The other policy specifically addressed the retention and destruction of documents. It generally provided that client files would be purged annually of non-relevant docu-

---

[71] Statement of Ronnie Earle, District Attorney of Travis County, Texas, Jan. 29, 2003.

[72] Andersen Policy Statement, entitled *Practice Administration: Notification of Threatened or Actual Litigation, Governmental or Professional Investigations, Receipt of a Subpoena, or Other Requests for Documents or Testimony (Formal or Informal)*, Statement No. 780, October 1999, section 2.8, *available at* http://news.findlaw.com/legalnews/lit/enron (visited June 9, 2003).

ments. This was summarized in the Policy Statement as: "Only final documents will be retained; drafts and preliminary versions of information will be destroyed currently. (Section 3.5)"[73] There were, however, exceptions in the event of litigation or governmental investigations:

> "In the event . . . AA . . . is advised of litigation or subpoenas regarding a particular engagement, the related information should not be destroyed."[74]

> "4.7 Delay of Destruction. 4.7.1 . . . Reasons for extended retention might include regulatory agency investigations (e.g., by the SEC), pending tax cases, or other legal action in connection with which the files would be necessary or useful. In such cases, material in our files cannot be altered or deleted (See Policy Statement No. 789 regarding notification of litigation). Other reasons might include litigation involving AA or the client. . . ."[75]

David Duncan testified at the trial that he instructed Andersen employees to follow Andersen's document retention policy and he knew that this instruction would result in the destruction of records related to Enron. The destruction and shredding of Enron document began in earnest on October 23, 2001. Was this destruction of Enron related documents by Andersen employees done in compliance with the company's retention and destruction policies? During the trial, Andersen's attorney argued that Andersen employees were simply getting rid of extraneous documents as provided for under existing company policies and that no organized effort was made to get rid of any specific documents.

The terms of Andersen's document retention and destruction policies in effect at that time, however, reflect that routine purging of client files were to be suspended in the event of litigation or a government investigation involving Andersen or a client. The evidence presented at the trial indicated that, certainly by October 23, members of Andersen's special committee dealing with Enron problems knew that serious issues existed with the accounting treatment of Enron transactions, the SEC had informed Enron that it had begun an informal inquiry and had requested documents, and civil lawsuits had been already filed by investors against Enron. In view of these facts, it is difficult to make a credible argument that the destruction of Enron-related documents beginning on or after October 23 was consistent with the company's document retention and destruction policy.

---

[73] Andersen Policy Statement, entitled *Practice Administration: Client Engagement Information—Organization, Retention and Destruction, Statement No. 760, February 2000,* Section 2.0(4), *available at* http://news.findlaw.com/legalnews/lit/enron (visited June 9, 2003).

[74] *Id.* at 4.5.4.

[75] *Id.,* at 4.7.1.

Nancy Temple testified at the Congressional hearing that she never counseled an employee of Andersen to destroy or shred documents.[76] We know, however, that on October 9, 2001, she wrote in her notes that an SEC investigation of Enron was "highly probable." Likewise, on that same day, Andersen hired outside counsel to assist with possible litigation arising from Enron. On the next day, October 10, 2001, Ms. Temple advised a partner in Andersen's Houston office "to consider reminding the engagement team of our documentation and retention policy." Copies of the retention and destruction policies were circulated to other Andersen employees. On October 23, David Duncan instructed Andersen employees to begin shredding Enron-related documents. It was only after Andersen received a subpoena from the SEC—on November 8—that Ms. Temple expressly told Andersen employees to preserve all Enron related documents.

Although most attention has centered on Nancy Temple's October 16 e-mail suggesting that Mr. Duncan modify his memorandum to the files, her advice with regard to document preservation and destruction issues during the Enron crisis at Andersen raise equally difficult questions. What did her "reminder to follow the policy" mean? Was the advice ambiguous? If her communication was intended to remind employees to preserve Enron-related documents, why not simply make that statement? If she believed that it was permissible to destroy certain documents, why did she not provide a short memorandum with examples explaining what could and could not be destroyed? Was it reasonable for an attorney to assume that officers or partners of her client would understand how to apply the document retention and destruction policy under the circumstances that existed in October 2001? Did Ms. Temple perhaps believe that documents could be destroyed until an official or formal investigation had been announced by a government agency or until Andersen was sued? Do attorneys have a tendency in a crisis to get hyper-technical in interpreting a policy, a statute, or a regulation? If Ms. Temple was consulting on these issues with Andersen's outside legal counsel, why did outside counsel not recommend that Ms. Temple inform members of the Enron engagement team to preserve documents—at least after the SEC notified Enron on October 17 that it had begun an informal inquiry into the special purpose entities and had requested documents?[77]

Before the Andersen conviction, corporate lawyers dealing with document destruction policies may not have anticipated that the obstruction of justice statutes were relevant to their conduct and advice. One lesson of the Andersen case—particularly after recent amendments strengthening the federal obstruction of justice statute—is that in-house lawyers who are asked to advise employees about document retention issues should provide unambiguous information. There are no "routine" issues in this area when litigation or a government investigation is imminent.

[76] Congressional Hearing Transcript, *supra* note 22, at 134.

[77] For comparison purposes, Enron's general counsel, James V. Derrick, Jr., sent a memorandum to all Enron employees on October 25, 2001, advising them to preserve all Enron documents. A copy of this memorandum is available at http://news.findlaw.com/legalnews/lit/enron.

J. Why Did "Document Destruction" Not Convict Andersen?

In analyzing the trial, there are several reasons why the jury may not have been able to agree unanimously that Andersen's extensive destruction of documents satisfied the statutory elements of obstruction of justice.

First, there was no Andersen e-mail or other document expressly asking or instructing employees to destroy documents. Nancy Temple's e-mails to Andersen partners calling attention to the firm's document retention policy did not state use the words "destroy" or "shred" documents. The government was placed in the position of arguing that encouraging employees to "follow the document retention policy" was code for "destroy documents."

Second, David Duncan, who had entered a plea of guilty prior to the Andersen trial testified, on cross-examination that at the time he encouraged Andersen employees to destroy documents, he did not believe that he was acting illegally. He testified that it was only later that he concluded that his conduct had been illegal.

Third, Andersen's attorney, Rusty Hardin, repeatedly asked the jury the question: How could Andersen have committed obstruction of justice of an SEC investigation when Andersen preserved the e-mails and other documents that the government is relying upon in the trial to prove obstruction of justice? While that begs the question in the sense that destruction of only one document could legally constitute obstruction of justice, Hardin's question implicitly created doubt that what was destroyed was material enough to convict and put a large company out of business.

III. IN-HOUSE LAWYERS AND ENTITIES AS CLIENTS

Since the inception of the modern regulation of the legal profession, lawyers have represented business entities as clients, including trusts, partnerships, and corporations. Conceptually, this type of representation has required the legal profession to examine several issues unique to representing fictional "persons" as clients. The legal profession, however, did not address these issues in detail until the Model Code of Professional Conduct was promulgated in the 1960s. The ethics rules apply equally to in-house and outside lawyers; however, many differences exist between these two groups and the manner in which they perform legal services for the organizational client.

A. The Unique Role of In-House Lawyers

As we mentioned briefly in the introduction to this article, in the last twenty years, many corporations have developed large staffs of in-house lawyers to represent the entity. The American Corporate Counsel Association boasts a membership of over 14,000 lawyers and 6,500 corporations.[78] These attorneys are integral in the manner

---

[78] See About ACCA, *available at* http://www.acca.com/about/ (discussing the goals of ACCA).

in which corporations receive legal services in this country. And, with this development, the status and power of in-house lawyers has been significantly enhanced.[79]

Despite significant changes in the number and role of in-house counsel in providing legal services to corporate America,[80] the organized legal profession has largely refused to shape its ethics rules or offer special guidance to the special problems encountered by lawyers who are full-time employees of corporations or other business entities.[81] In-house lawyers are subject to the same state ethics rules that govern outside lawyers for an organization.[82] And relatively few court opinions address the unique issues confronted by in-house counsel. Moreover, the common law generally continues to characterize in-house lawyers as employees-at-will that can be fired despite the efforts of such counsel to comply with professional ethics rules and their attempts to make the employer operate within the boundaries of the law.[83]

Some very important practical differences exist between in-house counsel and outside counsel. First, in-house lawyers have only one client (and, in some cases, affiliates of that one client) and thus their livelihood depends upon the continued representation of the client in a manner acceptable to the individuals who control and manage the client. Outside lawyers and law firms have many clients and typically make efforts to ensure that their practices are diversified.[84] The economic pressure on an individual's ability to earn a living in a job clearly creates the potential to influence behavior.[85] Second, the in-house lawyer is an employee of the organization. This statement has several implications. In-house lawyers receive all their compensation from one client,

---

[79] *See* Daly, *supra* note 1, at 1059–67.

[80] *See* ROSEN, *supra* note 8, at n.7.

[81] We do acknowledge that much attention has been devoted to the conflicts of interest presented by the use of in-house lawyers in the insurance context. *See, e.g.,* CHARLES W. WOLFRAM, MODERN LEGAL ETHICS § 8.4 428-33 (1986); Ted Schneyer, *Professionalism and Public Policy: The Case of the House Counsel,* 2 GEO. J. LEG. ETHICS 449, 463–68 (1988) (discussing "recent cases on an insurance company's use of house counsel to represent insureds").

[82] *See* MODEL RULES OF PROF'L CONDUCT R. 1.13 (2002) ("Organization as Client").

[83] *See* Balla v. Gambro, Inc., 584 N.E.2d 104 (Ill. 1991) (rejecting an attempt to establish a wrongful discharge action when an in-house lawyer is fired for complying with the rules of ethics); *but see* Nordling v. Northern States Power Co., 478 N.W.2d 498 (Minn. 1991) (establishing a limited right of a lawyer to claim wrongful discharge in the corporate context); General Dynamics Corp. v. Superior Court, 876 P.2d 487 (Cal. 1994) (establishing a similar right of a lawyer to claim wrongful discharge in the corporate context).

[84] The need for outside law firms to diversify has been pointed out in the context of client fraud in the past. *See* PHILIP B. HEYMANN & LANCE LIEBMAN, THE SOCIAL RESPONSIBILITIES OF LAWYERS 186 (1988) (discussing the OPM Leasing case and the fact that the Singer Hutner law firm had relied upon OPM for 60% of its billings during the period of time from 1976–1980).

[85] Sarbanes-Oxley Act of 2002, Pub. L. No. 107-204, § 406116 Stat. 745 (2002) (requiring a company to have a code of ethics).

and they are organizationally monitored by non-lawyers. Also, the officers and managers of the organization may view the in-house lawyer differently from the outside lawyers. The officers and managers often consider their in-house lawyers to be "team players" and not like outside counsel, whose time and loyalties are shared by many other clients, some of whom might even be the client's competitors. In-house lawyers are often expected to make business as well as legal decisions. During the dot.com boom years, the compensation of an in-house lawyer often included options to acquire shares of stock in the corporation, and thus the lawyer might have had a more direct financial stake in the stock price of the client organization.[86]

In-house lawyers represent a significant exception to the principle that only lawyers should be allowed to control the practice of law. The legal profession generally acquiesced in the notion that lawyers could join a corporation as employees and continue to deliver legal services.[87] State ethics opinions have approved a corporation charging a subsidiary for legal services provided by in-house counsel.[88] Although this point was recently exposed in the debate over multidisciplinary practice of law, the legal profession was unlikely to prevail in taking the position that corporations could not hire lawyers in-house to represent the interests of the entity or that such work by in-house lawyers constituted the unauthorized practice of law.[89]

Other important differences exist between in-house and outside counsel. Interpersonal relationships often make a significant difference in how professionals interact with clients. When a lawyer works in the same office, walks the halls, and interacts with the constituents of an organization every day (and develops personal and social friendships with the managers of a business entity), those interpersonal relationships clearly influence the legal representation. Of course, outside lawyers presumably could have the identical situation. However, outside lawyers often have larger circles of professional acquaintances and certainly have the opportunity to be more detached from their client's constituents. Finally, in theory, in-house lawyers have much more information about the client than do the outside lawyers. They have access to business and legal information, as well as informal sources of information about the individuals who run the organization. This knowledge presents a unique opportunity to influence

---

[86] *See* John S. Dzienkowski & Robert J. Peroni, *The Decline in Lawyer Independence: Lawyer Equity Investments in Clients*, 81 TEXAS L. REV. 405, 516–19 (2002) (examining the propriety of the practice of in-house lawyers receiving stock in the corporation).

[87] *See* John S. Dzienkowski & Robert J. Peroni, *Multidisciplinary Practice and the American Legal Profession: A Market Approach to Regulating the Delivery of Legal Services in the Twenty-First Century*, 69 FORDHAM L. REV. 83 (2000).

[88] *See, e.g.*, Michael D. Morrison & James R. Old, Jr., *Economics, Exigencies and Ethics: Whose Choice? Emerging Trends and Issues in Texas Insurance Defense Practice*, 53 BAYLOR L. REV. 349, 400 (2001) (discussing Tex. Comm. On Prof'l Ethics, Op. 531, 62 TEX. B.J. 1123 (1999)).

[89] *See* Charles W. Wolfram, *In-house MDPs?*, NAT'L LAW J., Mar. 6, 2000, at B6.

the corporate decision-makers, including officers, employees, and directors, to avoid a risk of substantial injury to the client.

B. Lawyer for the Entity

In the Model Code, the American Bar Association adopted the position that lawyers for entities represent the entity as the client, even though the entity was not a real person.[90] This view was largely driven by the conclusion that no other position could be workable in the representation of entities without giving overdue emphasis to those who managed or directed the entities. Thus, the Model Code provided that lawyers should be careful not to allow other actors to conflict with the interests of representing the entity.[91] It was evident from the rule that having conflicting interests when representing entities is a major concern.

One of the major changes in the Model Rules of Professional Conduct, which was drafted in the early 1980s, was adding more explicit rules dealing with a lawyer's role in representing entities and handling non-litigation matters. Model Rule 1.13(a) sets forth the basic rule that lawyers for an organization represent the entity as it acts through its constituents. A specific provision under Rule 1.13(d) requires that a lawyer be on guard for non-client actors (officers, directors, and owners) who may believe that the lawyer is representing their interests as well as the interests of the entity. In such a situation, the lawyer who "knows or reasonably should know that the organization's interests are adverse to" the constituent's interests must inform that person that the lawyer represents the entity and not the constituent.[92] The drafters of the Model Rules elaborated upon this situation because it is natural for the agents of an entity to believe that a lawyer for the entity may also be watching out for their interests.[93] Model Rule 1.13(e) also expressly addresses multiple client representation in the corporate entity context. Situations will arise where it may be in the interests of the entity and one of its constituents for the lawyer to represent both as clients. When such a case arises, the

---

[90] MODEL CODE OF PROF'L RESPONSIBILITY EC 5-18 (1977) ("A lawyer employed or retained by a corporation or similar entity owes his allegiance to the entity and not to a stockholder, director, officer, employee, representative, or other person connected with the entity.").

[91] This cautionary rule included the possibility of even representing multiple clients when one of them may be an entity, but only if the lawyer properly evaluates the conflict of interest. For an examination of multiple client representations of the entity and other constituents of the entity, see Nancy J. Moore, *Conflicts of Interest for In-House Counsel: Issues Emerging from the Expanding Role of the Attorney-Employee*, 39 S. TEX. L. REV. 497, 501–508 (1998).

[92] MODEL RULES OF PROF'L CONDUCT R. 1.13(d) (2002).

[93] Of course, the lawyer's failure to properly identify the client or clients can lead to malpractice liability as well as disciplinary liability. *See* RONALD E. MALLEN & JEFFREY M. SMITH, LEGAL MALPRACTICE § 25.6 (2002).

lawyer must examine the conflict of interest under the present client conflicts rules[94] and should obtain the proper consent from the properly authorized individuals who can make a decision for the entity.[95]

The Restatement of Law Governing Lawyers similarly adopts the entity view of representation; however, it embraces the need of the lawyer to follow the instructions of the proper agents of the entity.[96] Under Section 96(1)(a), "the lawyer represents the interests of the organization as defined by its responsible agents acting pursuant to the organization's decision-making procedures."[97] The language goes on to require a lawyer to follow the instructions of those who are authorized to make decisions for the entity.[98] The comments to this section state that this "universally recognized" view describes the beneficiary of the lawyer's services and clarifies that the lawyer does not normally owe any duties to the other constituents.[99]

Although the entity theory of representation has evolved from a viewpoint that no other perspective could be workable,[100] commentators have made some valid criticisms of this model. The major criticism is that corporate lawyers are "selected and retained by, and report[ ] to and may be fired by, the principal officers and directors of the corporation—who are not his clients."[101] And commentators have criticized the concept as not reflecting the evolution of corporate and entity theories, especially those relating to law and economics.

One significant assumption made by the drafters of the various codes of professional responsibility and the Restatement is the application of the entity rule to all entities. In other words, the rule applies to public corporations, private corporations, closely held corporations, partnerships, limited liability companies, trusts, and government entities. Although the comments to the entity rule briefly explore the different considerations that may apply, depending on the type of entity, lawyers are often governed only by the text of the rule and not by the comments. This approach has

---

[94] *See* MODEL RULES OF PROF'L CONDUCT R. 1.7 (2002).

[95] MODEL RULES OF PROF'L CONDUCT R. 1.13(e) (2002). Note that when the represented constituent is also the person who is authorized to consent on behalf of the entity, the lawyer should obtain the consent of someone other than the represented agent of the entity.

[96] RESTATEMENT (THIRD) OF LAW GOVERNING LAW. § 96(1) (2002).

[97] *Id.* at § 96(1)(a).

[98] *Id.* at § 96(1)(b).

[99] *Id.* at § 96 cmt. b.

[100] This viewpoint has had implications for areas of law relating to entity representation. For example, shareholders have generally been unable to sue the entity's attorney in malpractice. *See* Palmer v. Software, Inc., 107 F.3d 415 (6th Cir. 1997).

[101] Ralph Jonas, *Who is the Client?: The Corporate Lawyer's Dilemma*, 39 HASTINGS L.J. 617 (1988).

resulted in the ABA issuing ethics opinions addressing potential differences when representing different types of entities.[102] However, the courts have often gone further, effectuating results that are not consistent with the entity theory of representation.[103]

C. Addressing Fraud on the Entity

The issue of fraud is addressed directly in the ethics rule defining the lawyer's representation of an organizational client. This rule is presented as a fundamental aspect of representing an entity—namely, dealing with constituents who are likely to cause material injury to the entity. The drafters of the Model Rules added a level of specificity highly unusual in the text of the ethics rules. This specificity is warranted because the conflicting interests that may arise between a client entity and its constituents can harm the client entity and also pose troublesome issues for the lawyer.

Under Model Rule 1.13(b), a lawyer who represents an entity and obtains knowledge that a person is acting or is intends to act in a manner "that is a violation of a legal obligation to the organization, or a violation of law which might be imputed to the organization, and is likely to result in substantial injury to the organization" must take action to protect the best interests of the client.[104] What action a lawyer for an entity should take depends upon many variables.

Is the lawyer's representation related to the fraud on the entity? Is the actor who is endangering the entity motivated by self-interest? How does the internal structure of the client address such situations? How serious is the violation, and how much injury is likely to result to the entity client? Model Rule 1.13 embraces the concept that the lawyer should go up the ladder to the highest authority that can act on behalf of the client.[105] If the efforts of counsel do not cause a change in the threat to the client, the lawyer may resign from the representation.

---

[102] *See* ABA Comm. on Ethics and Prof'l Responsibility, *Lawyer Serving as Fiduciary for an Estate or Trust*, Formal Op. 02-426, May 31, 2002; ABA Comm. on Ethics and Prof'l Responsibility, *Conflicts of Interest in the Corporate Family Context*, Formal Op. 95-390, Jan. 25, 1995; ABA Comm. on Ethics and Prof'l Responsibility, *Trade Associations as Clients*, Formal Op. 92-365, July 6, 1992; ABA Comm. on Ethics and Prof'l Responsibility, *Representation of a Partnership*, Formal Op. 91-361, July 12, 1991. For an examination of representation of entity issues in both the public and closely held corporate context, see Note, *An Expectations Approach to Client Identity*, 106 HARV. L. REV. 687 (1993).

[103] *See* Upjohn Co. v. United States, 449 U.S. 383 (1981) (attorney-client privilege in the context of the corporate representation); Fassihi v. Sommers, Schwartz, Silver, Schwartz & Tyler, 309 N.W.2d 645, 648 (Mich. Ct. App. 1981) (a lawyer who represents a closely held entity may owe fiduciary duties to a 50% shareholder or partner, even if that person is not a client); Good Old Days Tavern v. Zwirn, 686 N.Y.S2d 414 (N.Y. App. Div. 1999) (discussing third-party beneficiaries).

[104] MODEL RULES OF PROF'L CONDUCT R. 1.13(b) (2002).

[105] Some commentators have referred to this as "internal whistleblowing." DEBORAH L. RHODE, PROFESSIONAL RESPONSIBILITY: ETHICS BY THE PERVASIVE METHOD 280–82 (1998).

As mentioned, the ABA applies this rule equally to in-house and outside counsel. The general counsel of a corporation is customarily responsible for all legal matters affecting the entity. Thus, it would be difficult to argue that the scope of representation should alleviate a general counsel's obligation to the client. Similarly, subordinate lawyers who report to the general counsel should fall under the ambit of this broad rule. It is the general counsel's responsibility to establish procedures to ensure that the ethics rules are followed in all aspects of lawyering provided to the client.[106] Thus, when a lawyer in a legal department discovers a situation that threatens injury to the client, that lawyer should be obligated to bring this situation to the attention of those other members of the legal department who are responsible for the matter. The officers and directors of a corporation should demand that their general counsel establish such systems for monitoring the legal problems of the client. In-house lawyers do not have an excuse that the matter is beyond the scope of their representation.

In-house lawyers are likely to possess much more information about the officers and directors and the motivations underlying their decisions. In-house lawyers typically have more information about a corporate agent's past conduct (or they should be able to obtain it more readily than would outside counsel). Further, in-house lawyers should know the organizational structure of the corporation. So moving a sensitive decision up the ladder should be—at least in theory—easier, because the in-house lawyers should know who within the entity has the authority or power to act quickly to change any conduct that threatens the welfare of the entity. Further, based upon their past experience, in-house lawyers can work to change internal policies of the entity to prevent similar recurrences.

That explains the *theoretical* view of the role of the in-house lawyer. The problem is that in-house lawyers have often ignored the guidance of Model Rule 1.13. What reasons exist for this incongruence between theory and practice? On the one hand, in-house lawyers seldom have the professional risks that have become common when practicing at a private firm. Corporations rarely report in-house lawyers to state bar disciplinary authorities. And there is little threat of civil liability from the client entity.[107]

The major problem with Model Rule 1.13 from the perspective of in-house counsel is that if, despite efforts by an in-house lawyer to prevent conduct injurious to the entity, one or more officers or directors of the entity insist upon action or refuse to follow recommended legal advice, the lawyer's last alternative under ABA Model Rule 1.13 is to withdraw from representing the client. Withdrawal has consequences to an in-house lawyer quite different from lawyers in private law firms. If an in-house lawyer withdraws, he no longer has *any* client. Moreover, he no longer has a job or a monthly income. Outside lawyers, on the other hand, can withdraw from representing one

---

[106] *See* MODEL RULES OF PROF'L CONDUCT R. 5.1 (2002).

[107] *See* Scott L. Olson, *The Potential Liabilities Faced by In-House Counsel*, 7 U. MIAMI BUS. L. REV. 1 (1998).

client and still retain their other clients. And law firms that have a diversified client base can withdraw from representing one client and not be adversely affected from a financial standpoint. The bottom line is that an in-house lawyer who has one client and who faces the prospect of having to withdraw is asked to sacrifice a career to maintain the ethical norm.

Model Rule 1.13 does offer in-house counsel one avenue to fulfill their ethical responsibilities—reliance on the opinion of outside counsel. When in-house lawyers are confronted with a situation that may materially injure the client, they often ask management to obtain a legal opinion from outside independent counsel. In fact, this avenue is expressly endorsed by Model Rule 1.13. The implication is that Model Rule 1.13 contemplates an in-house attorney using outside attorneys to bolster the in-house lawyer's position that the corporation's management should choose another course of conduct. In corporate scandals, however, in-house lawyers have often relied upon outside law firms that had conflicts of interest, that had the scope of their investigation limited, or that ultimately gave opinions that stated that the conduct in question was not illegal.

In-house lawyers should be aware that reliance on an outside legal opinion to circumvent the in-house lawyer's obligations is not an automatic release of liability. In-house lawyers have significant input into choosing the outside law firm for an independent outside opinion and into how the legal questions are framed to those outside lawyers. An in-house lawyer who selects a firm that has no experience in the issue's subject matter, or a lawyer who may have a conflict or bias on the merits of the opinion has denied the client the opportunity of a truly independent opinion.[108] Of course, if the in-house general counsel is currently a partner in the outside law firm,[109] using that firm does not provide an independent legal opinion.[110] An in-house lawyer who fails to fully inform the outside counsel of all factual information similarly ren-

---

[108] Many in-house lawyers are hired from the outside firm used by the corporation. In some cases, the personal relationships that the in-house lawyers have developed with the outside firm may threaten the independence of the legal opinion. That may be accentuated if the conduct in question relates to other advice or work that the outside firm has done for the client.

[109] This dual employment situation was more common several decades ago; however, there still are situations where clients ask an outside law firm lawyer to serve as general counsel of the corporation. *Cf.* John K. Wells, *Multiple Directorships: The Fiduciary Duties and Conflicts of Interests that Arise When One Individual Serves More Than One Corporation*, 33 J. MARSHALL L. REV. 561, 565 (2000) (individuals commonly serve on three, four, or five corporate boards.).

[110] In Simpson Thatcher's representation of Global Crossing, there is some indication that the firm had placed one of its partners into the corporation to act as its general counsel. That practice, which was common in the oil industry, raises many ethical and liability concerns and should not be done except in the most unusual of circumstances. *See* Joseph Menn, *Global Crossing Case Figure Not Questioned*, L.A. TIMES, Feb. 22, 2002, at 3-1.

ders worthless any opinion provided. Additionally, even if outside counsel provides an opinion that the conduct is not improper, in-house counsel still needs to make an independent determination whether the conduct is a violation of the law or an obligation to the client that would be likely to cause material injury to the client. If the in-house lawyer believes that an injury is likely, the outside opinion does not relieve the lawyer from making the concerns known to the highest authorities within the entity. If, despite the lawyer's efforts to effect a change in corporate policy, the highest authority insists on pursuing the course of conduct that could materially injure the corporation, the lawyer may withdraw. However, the lawyer is instructed by the Model Rules to "minimize disruption of the organization and the risk of revealing information to persons outside the organization."[111]

Of course, this rule must be read in light of the general confidentiality rule in the jurisdiction, as well as the federal and state statutes applicable to the matter in question. These sources of professional standards or statutory law may permit or require disclosure, depending upon the circumstances. Many states permit lawyers to disclose ongoing financial crimes or frauds.[112] Additionally, federal and state statutes impose disclosure requirements upon entities and responsible parties for matters involving the public interest. Issues involving environmental, food and drug, endangered species, and toxic waste often have corresponding disclosure requirements. However, in the absence of such ethical rules or statutes permitting or requiring disclosure, in-house counsel is not permitted to breach client confidentiality to persons outside the entity.

E. Client Fraud and the Confidentiality Rules

The client fraud problem customarily arises when a lawyer undertakes representation in a transaction that he assumes is non-fraudulent but then, in undertaking legal work to carry out the transaction, discovers that the transaction involves fraud against the other party to the transaction or to some other person. The problem is usually *not* one of initial complicity in the fraud. If a lawyer knows at the outset that the transaction is fraudulent or illegal, the law is clear that he or she may not implement the transaction. If the lawyer assists in implementing the transaction, the lawyer is a joint tortfeasor in the tort of fraud; if the conduct is criminally proscribed, as will generally be the case given the operation of the mail fraud laws, the lawyer is an accessory to the crime of fraud; in addition, the lawyer is guilty of professional misconduct under the disciplinary rules.

---

[111] MODEL RULES OF PROF'L CONDUCT R. 1.13(b) (2002).

[112] For example, the Texas Disciplinary Rules authorize a lawyer to "reveal confidential information . . . [w]hen the lawyer has reason to believe it is necessary to do so in order to prevent the client from committing a criminal or fraudulent act." TEX. DISCIPLINARY R. PROF. CONDUCT R. 1.05(c)(7) (1995).

The problem usually is the "midpoint" discovery: when the lawyer's ignorance of the fraud ends, i.e., when he first becomes aware of the fraudulent nature of the transaction.[113] At that point, the lawyer has the mental state to be an accessory. Any act in furtherance of the transaction then becomes assisting or abetting fraud. Some lawyers, of course, stay on the sidelines and simply do not actively participate in the client fraud.

The client fraud problem is a complex interplay of conflicting duties: a lawyer should not assist criminal or fraudulent client conduct, and a lawyer should not reveal a client's confidential information. During the past decade, this debate has focused on

---

[113] The concept of a lawyer's "knowledge" about a client's fraud was the subject of the *Wuliger* decision. United States v. Wuliger, 981 F.2d 1497 (6th Cir. 1992). That case involved a lawyer who had been convicted after he used, in a divorce trial, the taped telephone conversations between his client's wife and her lawyer, her friends, and her marriage counselor. The lawyer was convicted for knowingly using recordings made in violation of the wiretap law. The wife did not know that the husband was intercepting the conversations. On appeal, the lawyer succeeded in his argument that the trial judge's instructions on "knowledge" were wrong. The trial judge had said that knowledge is established if a person (a) knows or (b) has reason to know a fact or (c) if the fact is reasonably foreseeable. The Court of Appeals said that (c) was wrong, but that (a) and (b) were proper definitions for the *mens rea* required for conviction. The Court of Appeals decision stated the following on what a lawyer is deemed to know:

> [D]efendant argues that due to an attorney's professional obligations, attorneys are entitled to a special instruction on the "reason to know" standard. The defendant asserts that as an advocate his role is not to pre-judge the merits of his client's factual allegations. [Husband represented that the tapes were made with the wife's knowledge.] Defendant points to his professional duty to present any evidence or theory which is arguably viable, subject to standards of good faith and reasonableness. Because he proceeded on the belief his client was telling the truth, the defendant contends he had "no reason to know" [wife] did not consent.

The Court concluded that the lawyer was not entitled to a special instruction. It also said:

> However, an attorney's professional duties may be a factor in determining whether there is reason to know that recorded information, given by the client, was illegally obtained. Although an attorney must not turn a blind eye to the obvious, he should be able to give his clients the benefit of the doubt. This countervailing duty is one the jury may take into account in deciding whether defendant had reason to know.

Stephen Gillers has discussed the *Wuliger* case on Lexis Counsel Connect (May 17, 1994). Gillers concluded:

> Did [the lawyer] really believe that his client's wife would let her husband tape her conversations with her own lawyer and her marriage counselor? I'd bet the contents of the tapes would undermine that contention. . . . At the very least, this means lawyers can't take their client's assertion of the facts, even facts particularly within the client's knowledge, at face value when the client's claim is dubious. Here, the claim surely was dubious. I don't know what happened on remand, but I doubt that a jury would find that this lawyer believed his client in good faith.

Geoffrey C. Hazard has written the following in an important law review article about when a lawyer is deemed to "know" about a client's fraudulent acts:

> The decisions say that a lawyer cannot "close his eyes" to facts that are readily apparent. The lawyer will be taken as having seen such facts. They also say that a lawyer must apprehend the significance, considered as a whole, of facts that may be innocuous when considered in isolation. The cases also say that a lawyer must gauge the significance of a fact, or set of facts, with the comprehension of one familiar with the type of transaction involved. In contrast to the criminal defense advocate's license to pretend ignorance of the truth about his client, the legal counselor, for

whether a lawyer may, must, or cannot disclose to third parties information revealing that the lawyer's client has used or is in the process of using the lawyer's services to facilitate fraudulent or criminal conduct. Within the legal profession, this has involved a debate between the ethics of advocacy, primarily promoted by litigators, and the ethics of transaction practice, where business lawyers are exposed to significant risks of liability if a transaction turns out to have involved fraud. Even more relevant to securities lawyers is that, with enhanced powers granted by Congress since 1989, federal regulators have argued that banking and securities lawyers should protect the investing public by being "gatekeepers" to prevent their clients from consummating illegal transactions or being "whistleblowers" to report their clients' violations of federal law.[114] One might also raise the question why lawyers have repeatedly been involved in representing clients who engage in fraud.[115]

---

the purposes of the crime/fraud rule, may be taken as knowing what an alert lawyer would know upon looking with a professional eye at the totality of circumstances there to be seen.

Geoffrey C. Hazard, *Rectification of Client Fraud: Death and Revival of a Professional Norm*, 33 EMORY L.J. 271 (1984).

In many of the recent corporate fraud scandals, the lawyers and executives have argued that they were unaware of the extent of the fraudulent transactions. The decision-makers at Arthur Andersen seemed to act with literal interpretations of the law despite the broader knowledge that they possessed. A key aspect of professional responsibility of the accountants and the lawyers is the extent to which they will be held to "know" about the fraudulent acts of others.

[114] *See Developments in the Law: Lawyers' Responsibilities and Lawyers' Responses*, 107 HARV. L. REV. 1547, 1605 (1994).

[115] In 1993, Professor Donald C. Langevoort published a behavioral inquiry into lawyers' attitudes and responsibilities for client fraud. *See* Donald C. Langevoort, *Where Were the Lawyers? A Behavioral Inquiry Into Lawyers' Responsibility for Client Fraud*, 46 VAND. L. REV. 75 (1993). This article does not make any claims about the extent of complicity by securities lawyers in client fraud. Professor Langevoort says, "In all fairness, of course, we do not know whether a serious problem really exists. . . . We lack actual base-rate data establishing the incident of complicity, or documentation of the offsetting events when attorney involvement has somehow deterred client misconduct. Still, the apparent incidence of complicity must trouble both the public and the profession." *Id.* What Langevoort does is to probe the obvious question that, no doubt, most of us have considered when reflecting on cases such as OPM, National Student Marketing, Vernon Savings, Lincoln Savings, and BCCI. Apart from the complex legal issues, a practical question that is seldom asked by lawyers is why competent and respected general counsel and lawyers in private law firms continue to represent a client when, in retrospect, objective signals existed that clearly indicated that the client was engaged in fraudulent conduct.

Langevoort focuses on the behavioral issue of why lawyer involvement in client fraud might be so extensive, rather than on the normative issue (what rules should govern lawyer conduct?). Langevoort suggests that "venality [greed, moral corruption, wealth, power] competes not so much with stupidity as with honest, even good faith behavior that only in hindsight seems incredible." *Id.* Drawing upon recent research in the field of social cognition, he raises the possibility that, because of the loyalty and commitment that lawyers have to their clients, coupled with normal to high levels of self-esteem exhibited by lawyers that function in a working environment dominated by stress, lawyers handling a transaction are prone to a diminished cognitive awareness (blind spots or self-deception) and thus do not recognize readily the likely harm flowing from a client's actions. This article is an excellent starting point for further analysis that needs to be done to explain why lawyers continued to represent clients when the objective signals pointed to fraudulent actions by corporate actors.

1. Client Fraud under the ABA Model Rules

The ABA Model Rules have been criticized often for establishing standards of conduct in the area of client misconduct that create an untenable dilemma for a lawyer struggling to deal with client fraud. On the one hand, Model Rule 1.2(d) provides that a "lawyer shall not counsel a client to engage, or assist a client, in conduct that the lawyer knows is criminal or fraudulent. . . . ."[116] On the other hand, the confidentiality provisions of Model Rule 1.6 and Model Rule 4.1(b) place severe restrictions on a lawyer's ability to reveal damaging confidential information of a client, even if that information involves on-going fraudulent conduct by the client that will cause financial injury to third parties.

Model Rule 1.6 permits a lawyer (a "may," not a "shall") to reveal confidential information relating to the representation of a client only under the following circumstances:

- to prevent reasonably certain death or substantial bodily harm;
- to secure legal advice about the lawyer's compliance with the ethics rules;
- to establish a claim or defense on behalf of the lawyer in a controversy between the lawyer and the client;
- to establish a defense to a criminal charge or civil claim against the lawyer, based upon conduct in which the client was involved, or to respond to allegations in any proceeding concerning the lawyer's representation of the client; or
- to comply with other law or a court order.

Revealing confidential information is not permitted in situations where the client has committed or plans to commit a fraud that causes financial injury to third persons. An effort to give lawyers more latitude under the Model Rules to disclose information preventing client fraud was voted down by the ABA House of Delegates in 2002.[117]

Model Rule 4.1(b) dealing with "Truthfulness in Statements to Others" provides that, in representing a client, a lawyer shall not knowingly "fail to disclose a material fact to a third person when disclosure is necessary to avoid assisting a criminal or fraudulent act by a client, *unless disclosure is prohibited by rule 1.6.*"[118] Because most information learned by a lawyer during the course of a representation is confidential information, the last clause effectively prevents disclosure when a lawyer learns during a representation that her client is engaged in fraud. These minimal standards that, in

---

[116] MODEL RULES OF PROF'L CONDUCT R. 1.2 (2002) ("Scope of the Representation").

[117] *See* PROFESSIONAL RESPONSIBILITY: STANDARDS, RULES, AND STATUTES (J. Dzienkowski ed. 2002).

[118] MODEL RULES OF PROF'L CONDUCT R. 4.1 (2002) (emphasis added).

effect, result in protection of client wrongdoing have been severely criticized as being inconsistent with the law governing lawyers as interpreted by judges.[119]

As discussed above, Model Rule 1.13 permits a lawyer to withdraw from the representation when all other efforts to protect an entity from a violation of a legal obligation or of law have failed. The ABA elaborated upon these withdrawal possibilities in a formal opinion:

> First, the lawyer must withdraw from any representation that, directly or indirectly, would have the effect of assisting the client's continuing or intended future fraud. Secondly the lawyer may withdraw from all representation of the client, and must withdraw from all representation if the fact of such representation is likely to be known to and relied upon by third persons to whom the continuing fraud is directed, and which the representation is therefore likely to assist. Third, the lawyer may disavow any of her work product to prevent its use in the client's continuing or intended future fraud. . . . In some circumstances, such a disavowal of work product (a "noisy" withdrawal) may be necessary in order to effectuate the lawyer's withdrawal. Fourth, if the fraud is completed, and the lawyer does not know or reasonably believe that the client intends to continue the fraud or commit a future fraud by use of the lawyer's services or work product, the lawyer may withdraw from the representation of the client but may not disavow any work product.[120]

This Opinion has been debated by scholars and lawyers in the profession, particularly with respect to its conclusions on issues one, two, and four.[121]

Under three applicable Model Rules: Rule 3.3 ("Candor Toward the Tribunal"), Rule 3.9 ("Advocate in Nonadjudicative Proceedings"), and Rule 4.1 ("Truthfulness in Statements to Others"), it is clear that a lawyer may not tell a lie, whether or not it might be considered necessary to protect client confidences. Beyond outright falsehood, however, the obligation to disclose information necessary to avoid assisting a

---

[119] Geoffrey C. Hazard, *Lawyers and Client Fraud: They Still Don't Get It*, 6 GEO. J. LEGAL ETHICS 701 (1993). The "they" referred to in Hazard's article is the ABA House of Delegates, which in 1991 rejected a proposal to amend Model Rule 1.6 by including another exception permitting disclosure "to rectify the consequences of a client's fraudulent act in the commission of which the lawyer's services had been used." The proposal was opposed by the American College of Trial Lawyers. A similar proposal was recently rejected by the ABA.

[120] ABA FORMAL OPINION 92-366 (Aug. 1992) (Withdrawal When a Lawyer's Services Will Otherwise Be Used to Perpetrate a Fraud).

[121] Professor Hazard argues that conclusions one, two, and four in Formal Opinion 92-366, indicating that those conclusions "are seriously erroneous in important respects." Hazard, *supra* note 119. This generated a response in a subsequent issue of the *Georgetown Journal of Legal Ethics* by two members of the ABA's Standing Committee on Ethics and Professional Responsibility. The response was sarcastically entitled, *Letter to Professor Hazard: Maybe Now He'll Get It*, 7 GEO. J. LEGAL ETHICS 145 (1993).

criminal or fraudulent act by a client overrides the lawyer's duty of confidentiality *only* under Model Rule 3.3 and 3.9. However, corporate lawyers in transactions have not had much opportunity under the ABA confidentiality rules to disclose client confidences when fraud is involved.

2. Client Fraud under the Texas Disciplinary Rules: A Different Approach

Texas Disciplinary Rule 1.02(c) states that a lawyer "shall not assist or counsel a client to engage in conduct that the lawyer knows is criminal or fraudulent."[122] From that point, the Texas Rules diverge significantly from the ABA Model Rules with respect to a lawyer's responsibilities in dealing with client fraud. There are two major differences. First, Texas Disciplinary Rule 1.05(c) *permits* a lawyer (grants discretion) to disclose confidential client information in the following circumstances:

> (7) When the lawyer has reason to believe it is necessary to do so in order to prevent the client from committing a criminal or fraudulent act.[123] [Rule 1.05(c)(7)]
> (8) To the extent revelation reasonably appears necessary to rectify the consequences of a client's criminal or fraudulent act in the commission of which the lawyer's services had been used. [Rule 1.05(c)(8)]

Second, Texas Disciplinary Rule 1.05(f) creates a duty and obligation upon a lawyer to reveal information if required by Texas Disciplinary Rule 4.01(b). Rule 4.01(b) states that a lawyer shall not knowingly "fail to disclose a material fact to a third person when disclosure is necessary to avoid making the lawyer a party to a criminal act or knowingly assisting a fraudulent act perpetrated by a client."[124] What is noticeably absent in Texas Rule 4.01(b) is the confidentiality exception at the end of ABA Model Rule 4.1(b): to wit: "unless disclosure is prohibited by rule 1.6."[125]

It is important for Texas lawyers to realize that an analysis under the ABA Model Rules rests on the fact that Model Rule 4.1(b) concludes with the words: "unless disclosure is prohibited by Rule 1.6."[126] Since that qualification does not exist in Texas Disciplinary Rule 4.01(b), it does not matter that the particular representation involves an adjudicative or a nonadjudicative proceeding. Texas Disciplinary Rule 4.1(b) places a higher duty on the Texas lawyer, and he or she does not have the luxury of

---

[122] TEXAS DISCIPLINARY RULES OF PROF'L CONDUCT, R. 1.02 (2002).

[123] *Id.* R. 1.05(c)(7).

[124] *Id.* R. 4.01.

[125] MODEL RULES OF PROF'L CONDUCT R. 4.1(b) (2002).

[126] *Id.*

saying that "the Rules of Ethics prohibit my disclosure in this client fraud circumstance."[127] In Texas, a lawyer is *obligated* to disclose a material fact to a third person when disclosure is necessary for the lawyer to avoid assisting a criminal or fraudulent act by his client. In Texas, the minimum standard of conduct *requires* a lawyer to disclose known material facts to a third person when disclosure is necessary to avoid making the lawyer a party to a criminal act or knowingly assisting a fraudulent act perpetrated by a client.

D. Addressing Entity Conflicts of Interest

The expansion in the number of in-house lawyers and their role within the organization has created the potential for many intra-entity conflicts of interests. These problems have not been extensively examined in the literature of professional responsibility; however, they do have the potential to create significant harm within the entity and to the relationships that it may have with other individuals or entities.[128]

Some of these problems involve the participation of corporations in contractual joint ventures. For example, assume that a corporation has acquired an entity and has paid the original owner with minority shares in the subsidiary. (A similar result may be reached if the original owner is paid based upon the performance of the subsidiary over a future period of time.) Vertically and horizontally integrated companies enter into contractual relationships among the various related companies. In-house lawyers are often asked to negotiate and draft those contracts. What typically would be arms-length negotiated contracts become more suspect when the entities are related or controlled by one holding or parent company. Non-lawyer decision-makers might demand that the in-house lawyers shift profits from a partially owned entity with a minority shareholder to a wholly owned entity. May a lawyer draft such an agreement? Does the lawyer have any obligations to the minority shareholders? Who does the in-house lawyer represent? The identity of the client may be easy—*if* the lawyer works for the parent or for the subsidiary. However, identifying the identity of the client only begins the analysis, because it does not solve the dilemma where an in-house lawyer is asked to shift profits from one company to another.

A similar problem arises when a corporation enters into a joint venture with three other companies. The corporation may be designated by contract to be the general partner in the venture and, thus, its in-house lawyer may become the lawyer for the joint venture, thereby moving into a dual-employment role. The lawyer is an in-house

---

[127] Of course, despite the ABA position, plaintiffs have sued lawyers who maintained their obligation of confidentiality based upon the ABA position.

[128] A recent article highlights such conflicts with Enron's relationships to their special purpose entities and other partnerships. *See* Deborah L. Rhode & Paul D. Paton, *Lawyers, Ethics, and Enron*, 8 STAN. J.L. BUS. & FIN. 9, 17 (2002) (citing the Powers Report as blaming in-house counsel and the Board on a failure to monitor conflicts within the company).

lawyer for the general partner corporation as well as the general counsel for the joint venture. What should the lawyer do when the president of the corporation asks the lawyer for the client lists of the joint venture? What should the lawyer do when the corporation makes a decision to compete with the joint venture? What if this decision is in violation of the terms of the joint venture?[129]

The legal answers may be clear if there is a board of directors of the joint venture and the lawyer answers to that board. Any disclosure would need to be cleared by that board and, with any luck, the other co-venturers would have representation on that board. But the legal answer may be unclear if the governance of the joint venture has been left to an informal structure. If the governance is unclear, the pressure on the lawyer who decides not to provide access to records of the joint venture to the president of the lawyer's main employer client is significant.

The purpose of raising intra-corporate conflicts of interest issues in this section is to highlight the possibility that in-house lawyers had some role in the corporate structures of companies like Enron, which hid losses in joint ventures and related companies. These lawyers may have structured these schemes or they may have continued to represent these co-owned or spun-off entities while they were in-house lawyers of the primary corporation. These lawyers may have violated obligations to the primary corporate client or they may have recommended the very structures that hid losses or accelerated gains. Nothing in the factual investigation to date has clarified the lawyers' roles. Nonetheless, even the potential problems that could ensue suggest that the organized bar needs to reassess its rules as they apply to in-house lawyers and to offer practical ways to regulate their conduct.

V. REGULATORY AND PROFESSIONAL REFORM AFTER ENRON

The bankruptcies of several of this country's largest corporations and the discovery of widespread fraud in corporate disclosures to the SEC led to hundreds of investigations on the federal, state, and private organizational levels. Congress enacted legislation requiring that the SEC adopt rules governing professionals and corporations. The SEC has held hearings and invited comment on the shaping of these standards. Federal agencies and state legislatures have similarly held hearings on how to reshape legal and professional standards to avoid similar frauds in the future. The ABA formed a commission to study the problem and to propose changes to the House of Delegates.

---

[129] A similar conflict could arise if the joint venture is sued by a third person and the in-house lawyer begins to represent the joint venture. The agreement may specify when and how the various partners are responsible for third-party lawsuits. The general partner corporation may have an incentive to limit information to the outside co-venturers. The general partner corporation may settle the case to hide the facts that could expose it to individual liability instead of the settlement, which would be shared by all. The lawyer is likely to be a necessary actor to this conduct; yet, the conflict of interest rules would seem to prohibit the lawyer's participation in such a scheme.

The following sections examine the SEC's promulgated rules under Sarbanes Oxley and the ABA's proposed changes to lawyers' professional standards.

A. SEC Rules on Professional Conduct for Attorneys

Following the recent corporate scandals and the staggering financial losses incurred by investors, it was difficult for Congress to ignore the loss of investor confidence in the securities markets and the growing awareness of systemic deficiencies in corporate responsibility and the governance of public companies. These deficiencies encompassed not only inaction by the boards of directors of these companies, but the contribution of various professional groups such as attorneys, accountants, and investment banking firms that assisted these companies in structuring and facilitating fraudulent transactions. Even a representative of the American Bar Association acknowledged that attorneys representing and advising corporate clients bear some share of the blame for this failure of the corporate governance system.[130]

In response to this crisis, Congress passed the Sarbanes-Oxley Act of 2002 ("Sarbanes-Oxley"), which was signed into law on July 30, 2002.[131] Section 307 of Sarbanes-Oxley mandated that the SEC establish minimum standards of professional conduct for attorneys appearing and practicing before the SEC.[132] It expressly provided that the SEC adopt rules requiring a lawyer to report evidence of a material violation of the securities laws or of a breach of fiduciary duty or similar violation to the chief legal counsel or executive officer of a public company. Moreover, if the chief legal counsel or chief executive officer fails to respond appropriately within a reasonable period of time, then the reporting lawyer must report the evidence of misconduct up the corporate ladder to a committee composed of independent members of the board of directors or the entire board of directors.

---

[130] In a press release issued in July 2002 by the American Bar Association regarding the ABA's Task Force on Corporate Responsibility, President Robert Hirshon of the ABA stated that ". . . [corporate] counsel have in too many instances fallen short of providing active, informed and independent stewardship." ABA Press Release, *ABA Corporate Responsibility Task Force Recommends New Corporate Governance Standards, Lawyer Ethics Rules* (July 24, 2002). Likewise the SEC's Proposed Rule: Implementation of Standards of Professional Conduct for Attorneys, Release Nos. 33-8186; 34-47282; IC-25920; File No. S7-45-02, Jan. 29, 2003, *available at* http://www.sec.gov/rules/proposed/33-8186.htm, stated that: "Indeed the Cheek Report Release [the Preliminary Report of the American Bar Association Task Force on Corporate Responsibility, dated July 16, 2002] concluded that 'the system of corporate governance at many public companies has failed dramatically.' Moreover, the Cheek Report acknowledges that attorneys representing and advising corporate clients bear some share of the blame for this failure."

[131] Sarbanes-Oxley Act of 2002, Pub. L. No. 107-204, 116 Stat. 745 (2002).

[132] *Id.* § 307.

The SEC adopted attorney conduct rules implementing Section 307 (the "SEC Rules") of Sarbanes-Oxley in late January 2003.[133] These rules represent an attempt by the SEC to balance the public interest in protecting investors from fraud while preserving client-attorney relationships and maintaining confidential client information. The SEC Rules established institutional procedures outlining the process by which in-house and outside attorneys are to report evidence of any material misconduct up the corporate ladder. The SEC Rules also imposed substantial obligations on the chief legal officer (normally the in-house general counsel) of a public company to investigate any reports of corporate misconduct.[134]

Reporting "up the ladder" under the SEC Rules means that any credible evidence of a material violation of law must be reported by either an in-house or outside lawyer (specifically including a subordinate lawyer[135] and his or her supervising lawyer[136]) for the entity to the chief legal officer or chief executive officer of the entity. The chief legal officer is then required to conduct an investigation and, unless he or she reasonably believes that no material violation has occurred, is ongoing, or is about to occur, the chief legal officer must take action to cause the company to adopt measures to stop the wrongdoing or prevent any material violations that have not yet occurred.[137] If the reporting lawyer does not reasonably believe that an appropriate response has been made, then he is obligated to report the evidence to a committee of independent members of the board of directors or to the entire board of directors.[138] As an alternative, if a public company has created a qualified legal compliance committee ("QLCC") consisting of independent directors not employed by the company, then a lawyer can report any evidence of misconduct to the QLCC.[139]

The concept of reporting "up the ladder" within an organization is not new. Most state lawyer ethics rules already include an "up the ladder" reporting requirement based on Model Rule 1.13.[140] However, Model Rule 1.13 and comparable state rules contain only general principles and provide that the lawyer for an entity simply must "proceed

---

[133] Securities and Exchange Commission, Final Rule: Implementation of Standards of Professional Conduct for Attorneys, Release Nos. 33-8185; 34-47276, *available at* http://www.sec.gov/rules/final/33-8185.htm, 17 CFR Part 205, 68 Fed. Reg. 6296. *See generally* Stephanie R.E. Patterson, *Professional Responsibility and Liability in a Post-Enron World: Section 307 of the Sarbanes-Oxley Act: Eroding the Legal Profession's System of Self-Governance?*, 7 N.C. BANKING INST. 155 (Apr. 2003).

[134] 17 C.F.R. at §205.3(b)(2), 68 Fed. Reg. 6321. The chief legal officer may refer a report of a material violation to a previously established qualified legal compliance committee, pursuant to § 205.3(c)(2).

[135] *Id.* at § 205.5, 68 Fed. Reg. 6323.

[136] *Id.* at § 205.4, 68 Fed. Reg. 6323.

[137] *Id.* at § 205.3(b)(2), 68 Fed. Reg. 6321.

[137] *Id.* at § 205.3(b)(3), 68 Fed. Reg. 6321.

[139] *Id.* at § 205.3(c), 68 Fed. Reg. 6322.

[140] MODEL RULES OF PROF'L CONDUCT R. 1.13 (2002).

as is reasonably necessary" in the best interests of the client if the lawyer knows that an officer or employee is engaged in conduct harmful to the entity.[141] These lawyer ethics rules do not *require* an attorney to report corporate misconduct to a higher authority within the organization; they merely suggest it as an option.[142] The recent wave of corporate scandals that wiped out billions of shareholders' equity in public companies and undermined investor confidence in United States securities markets laid to rest any illusions that existing lawyer ethics rules, such as ABA Model Rule 1.13, can realistically be expected to address and prevent client fraud.

The SEC Rules apply to all attorneys, whether in-house or outside counsel, who appear and practice before the SEC in representing public companies on securities related matters. The term "appearing and practicing" includes: transacting business with the SEC; representing an issuer in an SEC administrative proceeding or investigation; providing securities law advice regarding the preparing, or participating in preparing, documents that the attorney has notice will be filed with, or incorporated into, a filing for the issuer with the SEC; or advising an issuer regarding SEC filings, including whether information must be disclosed or filed or incorporated into documents that will be filed with the SEC.[143]

The scope of what misconduct must be reported "up the ladder" is quite broad. An attorney subject to the SEC Rules who *becomes aware of* evidence of a material violation by the entity or any of its officers, directors, employees or agents is required to report any evidence of a material violation of federal or state securities laws, or a material breach of a fiduciary or similar duty existing under state or federal laws.[144] The fact that Sarbanes-Oxley included a breach of "fiduciary or similar duty" substantially expanded the scope of misconduct covered under the SEC Rules.

This language, however, presents two questions. What level of knowledge is required to constitute awareness of credible evidence, and what constitutes material evidence? The SEC's interpretive discussion that accompanied issuance of the SEC Rules makes it clear that an attorney's obligation to report evidence of a material violation is based on an objective standard, not the attorney's subjective beliefs.[145] The threshold of knowledge required to invoke the reporting obligation requires only that evidence of material wrongdoing be "reasonably likely."[146] This is in contrast to the standard under Model Rule 1.13 and most state ethics rules, which require actual knowledge of

---

[141] *Id.* at § 1.13(b) (emphasis added).

[142] *Id.; see, e.g.,* TEXAS DISCIPLINARY RULES OF PROFESSIONAL CONDUCT, Rule 1.12.

[143] Securities and Exchange Commission, Final Rule: Implementation of Standards of Professional Conduct for Attorneys, 17 CFR Part 205.2(a), 68 Fed. Reg. 6297.

[144] *Id.* at § 205.2(i).

[145] Securities and Exchange Commission, Final Rule: Implementation of Standards of Professional Conduct for Attorneys, 17 CFR Part 205, 68 Fed. Reg. 6296, 6323.

[146] *Id.* at § 205.2(e), Fed. Reg. 6301.

a material violation.[147] Under the SEC Rules, a material violation must be more than a mere possibility, but it need not be "more likely than not."[148]

The critical question about the SEC Rules is: will these new rules alter how attorneys address potential client fraud and prevent future scandals similar to those at Enron, Global Crossing, Tyco, and WorldCom?"[149] A critical assessment of the SEC Rules raises serious doubts about whether they will be effective in causing lawyers to report corporate fraud up the ladder within an organization. In response to complaints from lawyers, some of the proposed rules and definitions submitted for public comment were diluted and weakened.

For example, the triggering standard for "evidence of a material violation," as originally proposed, was simply defined as "information that would lead an attorney reasonably to believe that a material violation has occurred, is occurring, or is about to occur."[150] Unfortunately, this term was transformed in the final SEC Rules into garbled legalese that may limit enforcement. This important standard, as finally adopted by the SEC, became: "credible evidence, based upon which it would be unreasonable, under the circumstances, for a prudent and competent attorney not to conclude that it is reasonably likely that a material violation has occurred, is ongoing, or is about to occur."[151] This change drew immediate criticism because defining this term by using a double negative may make it difficult for the SEC to prove that a lawyer failed to comply with his or her reporting obligation.[152] A group of legal ethics experts criticized this change in written comments to the SEC, stating, "Not only does the Commission's [triggering] standard invite inaction, it fails another critical test of sound

---

[147] MODEL RULES OF PROF'L CONDUCT R. 1.13(b) begins: "If a lawyer for an organization knows that an officer, employee or other person associated with the organization is engaged in action, intends to act or refuses to act in a matter related to the representation that is a violation of a legal obligation to the organization, or a violation of law. . . ." The definition of "knowingly," "known," or "knows" in the ABA Model Rules is ". . . actual knowledge of the fact in question. A person's knowledge may be inferred from circumstances." Terminology § 4, MODEL RULES OF PROF'L CONDUCT (2002).

[148] Securities and Exchange Commission, Final Rule: Implementation of Standards of Professional Conduct for Attorneys, 17 CFR Part 205.2(e), 68 Fed. Reg. 6302.

[149] As stated more bluntly in one of the public comment letters to the SEC: "Will the [SEC's] rules help ensure that the 'see no evil, report no evil' behavior of Enron's lawyers, of Global Crossing's lawyers, and of the lawyers at many other companies changes?" Letter dated April 7, 2003, to Jonathan G. Katz from Professors Susan P. Koniak, Roger C. Cramton, and George M. Cohen (together with a list of 38 law professors who were in general agreement with the comments and recommendations expressed in the letter), *available at* http://www.sec.gov/rules/proposed/s74502/lawprofs040703.htm [hereinafter Koniak Letter].

[150] Securities and Exchange Commission, Proposed Rule: Implementation of Standards of Professional Conduct for Attorneys, Release Nos. 33-8150; 34-46868; IC-25829 (November 21, 2002).

[151] Securities and Exchange Commission, Final Rule: Implementation of Standards of Professional Conduct for Attorneys, 17 CFR Part 205.2(e), 68 Fed. Reg. 6296.

[152] Jonathan Glater, *SEC Adopts New Rules for Lawyers and Funds,* N.Y. TIMES, Jan. 24, 2003, at C1.

rulemaking. It would be a nightmare to enforce. The Commission has asked its staff to assume the burden of proving not just one negative, but two. To enforce this rule, the Commission would have to show that it was unreasonable for a lawyer not to conclude that a violation was reasonably likely."[153] In addition, the terms "reasonable"[154] and "reasonably believes"[155] in the final SEC Rules are also defined using a double negative ("not unreasonable").

Another serious problem evident in the SEC Rules is they permit a company to assert a "colorable defense" to a material violation of law and treat that as an "appropriate response" to a lawyer's report of illegal corporate conduct. Hence, as an alternative to a company taking steps to rectify an ongoing fraud or stop a transaction or plan that involved fraud or illegal conduct, the SEC Rules permit a company to retain (with the consent of the audit committee, the board of directors, or a QLCC) an attorney to review the reported evidence of misconduct.[156] If that attorney advises the company that he can assert a colorable defense on behalf of the company in any investigation or proceeding, then that constitutes an "appropriate response."[157] As public comments to this provision have pointed out, "[t]he fact that a lawyer can concoct arguments that would meet a minimum level of plausibility sufficient to avoid sanction in an adversary proceeding does not mean that the conduct is likely legal."[158] Furthermore, under securities laws and the law governing lawyers, the fact that a lawyer can properly assert a nonfrivolous defense to a claim does not excuse the lawyer from advising his client that it must cease or avoid illegal conduct. The "colorable defense" alternative in the final SEC Rules seems entirely inconsistent with the underlying purposes of Sarbanes-Oxley.

Regardless of these problems, the SEC Rules do provide a safety valve that permits a lawyer to disclose confidential information to the SEC relating to a representation, even without the client's consent.[159] This is available to a lawyer if he reasonably believes that public disclosure is necessary to prevent a public company from committing a material violation likely to cause substantial injury to the financial interest of the issuer or investors, or to prevent fraud upon the SEC or perjury in an investigative or administrative proceeding, or to rectify a material violation in furtherance of which the attorney's services had been used and which caused or may cause a substantial injury to the issuer or investors.

---

[153] *See* Koniak Letter, *supra* note 149.

[154] *Id.*

[155] *Id.*

[156] Securities and Exchange Commission, Final Rule: Implementation of Standards of Professional Conduct for Attorneys, 17 CFR Part 205.2(b)(3), 68 Fed. Reg. 6298.

[157] *Id.* § 205.2(b)(3)(ii), 68 Fed. Reg. 6320.

[158] Koniak Letter, *supra* note 149.

[159] 17 CFR Part 205.3(c)(3), 68 Fed. Reg. 6321.

The most controversial provision in the rules initially proposed by the SEC required lawyers under certain circumstances to make a "noisy withdrawal" by notifying the SEC if they terminated their representation of a public company that had failed to make an appropriate response to a report of a material violation of law. This provision was not included in the SEC Rules issued in January 2003, but rather was deferred by the SEC pursuant to a separate Proposing Release issued on January 29, 2003[160] requesting additional public comments.

The new SEC Release proposed adding a new section 2.05.3(d) to the SEC Rules that would address the situation in which a lawyer reasonably believes a public company has made either no response within a reasonable time or had not made an appropriate response to reported evidence of a material violation. Because withdrawing from a representation of a company has substantially different consequences to in-house attorneys, section 205.3(d) would treat outside retained attorneys and in-house attorneys differently.[161]

If an outside (retained) attorney does not receive an appropriate response, or no response within a reasonable time, the outside attorney must withdraw from the representation and, within one business day, give written notice to the SEC of the attorney's withdrawal, indicating that the withdrawal was based on professional considerations.[162] Furthermore, the outside attorney must promptly disaffirm to the SEC "any opinion, document, affirmation, representation, characterization, or the like in a document filed with or submitted to the SEC that the attorney prepared or assisted in preparing and that the attorney reasonably believes is or may be materially false or misleading."[163]

Under the same circumstances, an in-house counsel who failed to receive an appropriate response would need only to notify the SEC within one business day that he or she intends to disaffirm any such similar document and promptly disaffirm to the SEC such document. The chief legal officer must then inform any new attorney who is retained or employed to replace the in-house attorney that the withdrawal was based on professional considerations.[164] The in-house attorney would not be required to resign his employment with the company. This is an acknowledgment of the reality that in-house attorneys effectively have only one client, and requiring them to withdraw means forcing them to quit a job and have no income. Hence, requiring an in-house counsel to resign would likely impede the disclosure of wrongdoing, which is the opposite of what the SEC Rules seek to accomplish.

---

[160] Securities and Exchange Commission, Proposed Rule: Implementation of Standards of Professional Conduct for Attorneys, Release Nos. 33-8186; 34-47282; IC-25920; File No. S7-45-02, January 29, 2003, *available at* http://www.sec.gov/rules/proposed/33-8186.htm, 67 Fed. Reg. 71,669.

[161] *Id.* at 71,688.

[162] *Id.* at 71,688.

[163] *Id.* at 71,688.

[164] *Id.* at 71,689.

Instead of having the lawyer or law firm required to make a noisy withdrawal, the SEC submitted an alternative proposal for public comment that would require the issuer or public company to report to the SEC in the event it receives a lawyer's notice of withdrawal for failure to receive an appropriate response.[165]

The public comments submitted to the SEC[166] on its noisy withdrawal proposals dramatically reflect how corporate law firms and bar associations perceive the issue of addressing client fraud. In a comment letter sent under the simple letterhead "79 Law Firms," a large group of large law firms stated that the noisy withdrawal proposals were contrary to the best interests of investors because of the "chilling effect" it would have on the attorney-client relationship.[167] This view is shared by the American Bar Association and other bar associations, which have lobbied to prevent the adoption of any such rule.[168]

The premise underlying the position of the 79 Law Firms is that a lawyer is considered to be a counselor and advocate for a client, rather than an independent gatekeeper such as an auditor. Accordingly, a rule requiring lawyers to notify the SEC about client misconduct would adversely affect the free exchange of information between a lawyer and client. The argument is: "if clients are afraid to confide candidly and completely in their counsel and instead proceed without the advice of counsel, the public will inevitably be harmed . . . ."[169] Finally, the 79 Law Firms proposed that if lawyers are required under the SEC Rules to withdraw because a client does not make an appropriate response to evidence of illegal conduct, the withdrawal should be limited to that par-

---

[165] *Id.* at 71,684.

[166] The public comments are available at http://www.sec.gov/rules/proposed/s74502.shtml.

[167] Letter dated April 7, 2003 to Jonathan G. Katz submitted by 79 Law Firms, *available at* http://www.sec.gov/rules/proposed/s74502/79lawfirms1.htm.

[168] American Bar Association News Release, *ABA Continues to Oppose SEC "Noisy Withdrawal" Proposals; Believes "Up the Ladder" Reporting Strikes Right Balance,* Apr. 2, 3003, *available at* http://www.abanet.org/media/apr03/noisy_withdrawl.html; the ABA's letter of comments to the SEC opposing noisy withdrawal, whether by lawyers or public companies, are *available at* http://www.abanet.org/poladv/new/307.pdf; examples of other bar associations opposed to noisy withdrawal include the District of Columbia Bar, *available at* http://www.dcbar.org/for_lawyers/sections/corporation_finance_and_securities_law/statement/part7.cfm; The Association of the Bar of the City of New York, *available at* http://www.sec.gov/rules/proposed/s74502/abcny040703.htm; the Florida Bar, *available at* http://www.sec.gov/rules/proposed/s74502/flbar040703.htm (discussing conflict of "noisy withdrawal" with current Florida Rules of Professional Conduct and requesting SEC to adopt "the Florida and majority rule that limits reporting requirements of in house attorneys regarding past conduct of their clients, to reporting up the chain of command within the client corporation, ultimately to the board of directors of the client.").

[169] *Supra* note 35. The comment letter submitted by the law firm of Jones Day is more critical. It states there is a "complete lack of evidence of lawyer misconduct the areas the proposed rule purports to regulate," and the actual purpose of the rules "is not to regulate lawyer conduct, but to achieve greater regulatory leverage over the lawyer's clients by conscripting lawyers to further the enforcement goals of the Commission." Letter dated April 7, 2003 to Securities and Exchange Commission submitted by Jones Day, *available at* http://www.sec.gov/rules/proposed/s74502/jonesday040703.htm.

ticular matter. In other words, if the client wishes to continue using the lawyer or law firm on other matters not involving fraud, the law firm would be entitled to continue representing that client.

Although the vast majority of public comments to the SEC about the proposed rule on "noisy withdrawal" came from lawyers and law firms opposed to the proposed SEC Rules, numerous law professors, lawyers, and investors submitted comments to the SEC reflecting an entirely different perspective. A comment letter to the SEC endorsed by forty-one law professors argued that the noisy withdrawal provisions were essential to the proper working of "up the ladder" reporting requirements.[170] They pointed out that, under existing securities laws and lawyer ethics rules, a lawyer cannot make material misrepresentations in documents that he authored—and that alone may necessitate the lawyer's withdrawal from the representation and disaffirmance of previously authored documents. They pointed out that corporate officers engaged in illegal conduct do not have an evidentiary privilege or a legitimate claim of confidentiality. The entity is the lawyer's client, not its officers or directors, and the attorney-client privilege is held by the entity. Moreover, the crime-fraud exception to the attorney-client privilege leaves unprivileged all communications in furtherance of illegality. Moreover, the law professors dismissed the notion that adoption of a "noisy withdrawal" requirement would cause clients to cease confiding in their lawyers.[171] In an increasingly complex and regulated business environment, corporate clients need lawyers to plan, structure, and draft documents to implement business transactions and to satisfy an increasing number of statutory and regulatory requirements. According to these law professors, ". . . the idea that 'noisy withdrawal' . . . would suddenly result in clients not talking to their lawyers seems untenable."[172]

The intensity of the opposition to "noisy withdrawal" reflected in the letters of comments by certain lawyer groups to the SEC is an extension of a long-simmering debate about addressing lawyer complicity—whether inadvertent, unknowingly, or simply disregarding signals evident in a transaction or series of transactions—involving client fraud. To date, the American Bar Association has steadfastly opposed any efforts to permit exceptions in the Model Rules on confidentiality of client information when confronted with client crime or fraud, except to prevent client conduct likely to result in the imminent death or substantial bodily harm of a person. In that situation, the Model Rules permit, but do not require, a lawyer to reveal what the client plans to do. In contrast, the Model Rules adopted by the ABA do permit a

---

[170] Koniak Letter, *supra* note 149.

[171] Professor William H. Simon also pointed out, in a separate letter to the SEC, that corporate agents have "powerful incentives to seek legal advice even without confidentiality." If they fail to seek advice, they lose the "advice of counsel" defense for claims of intentional wrongdoing, and they risk losing the protections of the business judgment rule. Letter dated December 13, 2002, from William H. Simon to Joseph G. Katz, *available at* http://www.sec.gov/rules/proposed/s74502/simon121302.htm.

[172] *Id.*

lawyer to reveal client confidential information to establish a claim to recover a legal fee or to defend themselves in a dispute between a lawyer and client.

The public comments by lawyers opposing "noisy withdrawal" are certainly correct in asserting that adoption of such a rule would alter the attorney-client relationship. Section 307 of Sarbanes-Oxley and the promulgated SEC Rules were intended to change lawyer conduct when confronted with credible evidence that a client is engaged in illegal conduct. The public interest in having public companies not engage in illegal and fraudulent conduct is compelling, particularly since public investors lost billions of dollars as a result of recent frauds. And it is obvious that Enron and many other companies involved in recent corporate scandals could not have accomplished their illegal transactions without the assistance of lawyers. What is often overlooked is that, for in-house lawyers, issues related to corporate culture are as important as technical issues about the language of the SEC Rules. A general counsel for a large public company recently articulated his major concern relating to Sarbanes-Oxley as: what attitude and approach do I, as the general counsel of a public company, want the lawyers who work for me to have when they encounter any evidence of potentially illegal conduct within the organization?

B. The Report of the ABA Task Force on Corporate Responsibility

In March 2002, the president of the ABA formed a Task Force on Corporate Responsibility to "examine systemic issues relating to corporate responsibility arising out of the unexpected and traumatic bankruptcy of Enron and other Enron-like situations[,] which have shaken confidence in the effectiveness of the governance and disclosure systems applicable to public companies."[173] The Task Force held public hearings and in March 2003 issued a final report with specific recommendations to the ABA House of Delegates.[174] These recommendations will be presented to the ABA at its annual meeting in August 2003.

The Task Force's mission was not confined only to examining only the role of lawyers in the corporate fraud scandals; instead, it was charged with examining all systemic issues including those involving corporate governance and the role of accountants. Thus, only part of its proposals relate to the regulation of lawyers. There are many recommendations relating to securities law, auditing law, corporate governance law, and corporate organizational theory. The changes proposed to the Model Rules, however, do attempt to place more responsibility on lawyers who represent corporations and other business entities.

---

[173] *See* AMERICAN BAR ASSOCIATION, REPORT OF THE AMERICAN BAR ASSOCIATION TASK FORCE ON CORPORATE RESPONSIBILITY 2 (2003) [hereinafter ABA CORPORATE RESPONSIBILITY TASK FORCE REPORT].

[174] *Id.* at 2–3 (chronicling activities of the Task Force).

Generally, the Task Force rejected the theory that lawyers for corporations should act as "gatekeepers" for the enforcement of the law.[175] However, the report advocates procedural and substantive changes for corporate attorneys. The procedural changes focused on how corporate entities should restructure lines of communication to facilitate improved communications with lawyers to ensure an entity's compliance with the law. The proposed substantive changes in the ethics rules clarify issues regarding Model Rule 1.13 and, more important, they advocate changing the confidentiality rule (Model Rule 1.6) to permit lawyers to disclose, in limited situations, client confidential information, which would make the Model Rules more consistent with the confidentiality rules in a majority of the states.[176]

On the issue of corporate structure, the Task Force focused on the manner in which communications between in-house and outside lawyers, on the one hand, and officers and directors, on the other hand, could be improved:

> First, the board of directors should establish a practice of regular, executive session meetings between the general counsel and a committee of independent directors. Second, each retention of outside counsel to the corporation, should establish two things at the outside of the engagement: (1) a direct line of communication between outside counsel and the corporation's general counsel; and (2) the understanding that outside counsel are obligated to apprise the general counsel, though that direct line of communication, of material violations or potential violations of law by the corporation or of material violations or potential violations of duties to the corporation.[177]

These recommendations were designed to remove impediments to frequent and frank communication between lawyers and corporate directors. Frequent meetings between independent directors and in-house counsel will foster the interpersonal relationships, trust, and frankness necessary to implement an effective "up the ladder" strategy. The requirement that outside counsel establish a line of communication with in-house counsel is designed to give outside lawyers access to a person with similar obligations to the entity—the in-house counsel—who may be able to implement corporate compliance with the law.

---

[175] A gap clearly exists between the profession and the academic and regulatory community. *National Student Marketing* was viewed to establish the "lawyer as gatekeeper" model. *See* SEC v. National Student Marketing Corp., 457 F. Supp. 682 (D.D.C. 1978). *See generally* Reinier H. Kraakman, *Gatekeepers: The Anatomy of a Third-Party Enforcement Strategy*, 2 J. L. Econ. & Org. 53 (1986). However, few in practice advocate this role for those lawyers who represent corporate clients.

[176] *See* Larry P. Scriggins, *Legal Ethics, Confidentiality, and the Organizational Client*, 58 Bus. Law. 123 (2002).

[177] ABA Corporate Responsibility Task Force Report, *supra* note 173, at 36 (footnotes omitted).

On the substantive rules that govern lawyer conduct, the Task Force recommended four changes to Model Rule 1.13. First, Model Rule 1.13 should be modified to apply an objective standard to the issue of when a lawyer should go "up the ladder." Instead of just requiring lawyer action when a lawyer "knows" about material injury to the entity, the lawyer would need to act when that lawyer "knows facts from which a reasonable lawyer, under the circumstances, would conclude that" the entity may be subjected to material harm.[178] Second, the Task Force recommended that the rule be changed to require more active "up the ladder" involvement by a lawyer for the entity. Third, when a lawyer withdraws from a representation or is fired by the client, the lawyer may inform the highest authority about the fact that the lawyer has withdrawn or has been fired.[179] Finally, the Task Force recommended that the rule be modified to permit a lawyer to disclose confidential information when corporate action or inaction would involve a clear violation of the law that is reasonably likely to result in substantial injury to the entity.[180]

The most important aspect of the Task Force recommendations is the suggestion that Model Rule 1.6 on confidentiality be modified to permit disclosure by a lawyer in two circumstances:

> (2) to prevent the client from committing a crime or fraud that is reasonably certain to result in substantial injury to the financial interests or property of another and in furtherance of which the client has used or is using the lawyer's services;
> (3) to prevent, mitigate or rectify substantial injury to the financial interests or property of another that is reasonably certain to result or has resulted from the client's commission of a crime or fraud in furtherance of which the client has used the lawyer's services;[181]

Similar proposals have been presented to the ABA House of Delegates, and all have been voted down repeatedly. The proponents of a broad confidentiality rule argue that any exception to the rule weakens the attorney-client relationship. The opponents of the current confidentiality standard point to the fact that a large majority of the states have rules similar to the one proposed.

The ABA Task Force's proposals represent a very important step in the right direction. The wave of recent corporate frauds demonstrate that in-house and outside lawyers did not have crucial access to management and higher authorities within the

---

[178] *Id.* at 82.

[179] *Id.* at 83–84.

[180] *Id.* at 83.

[181] *Id.* at 77.

organization. The defense used by some law firms has been that the ABA confidentiality rule prohibited them from disclosing information to the regulators or investors. If the ABA adopts these proposals, in-house lawyers are likely to be more prepared to meaningfully "go up the ladder" as a means of addressing to reveal corporate fraud and other illegal corporate conduct.

VI. THE EXPANDING REACH OF THE CRIMINAL LAWS TO THE CONDUCT OF IN-HOUSE COUNSEL

In the past, it was unusual for any in-house counsel to be a party to or the subject of any criminal or civil actions.[182] That principle has dramatically changed in the last few years. To illustrate, we have selected two brief examples (Koch Industries and Tyco) and one in-depth example (Arthur Andersen) where the conduct of an in-house attorney was deemed by prosecutors to be partly responsible for the decision to bring criminal charges against an entity.

A. General Discussion

Although criminal laws have always been applicable to the conduct of lawyers, exposure to any criminal sanction usually could be avoided merely by foregoing any direct involvement or participation in a crime. In the last twenty-five years, however, there have been substantial changes in the scope and types of criminal laws enacted by legislatures. Many criminal laws were drafted to reach patterns of conduct, such as the racketeering laws. Other criminal laws were directed towards corporations that used a cost-benefit analysis when deciding whether to comply with the law.[183] Some of these laws have created criminal entity liability with significant fines for corporations. Other laws have sought to reach "responsible parties" within or involved with entities and have threatened those parties with incarceration if they participate in the proscribed behavior.

These two types of laws have been enacted in areas of public concern, such as health and safety or environmental crimes. Often in these statutes, the traditional "intent" or *mens rea* requirement that is an element of traditional criminal laws has been relaxed significantly or eliminated entirely. Thus, a lawyer's conduct in representing a client under circumstances in which the lawyer did not intend to violate the laws may still subject the lawyer to criminal penalties. Additionally, prosecutors have expanded their

---

[182] *See* Ashby Jones, *Teflon Counsel: General Counsel Have Been Virtually Untouched During Recent Accounting Scandals, But New Laws May Change That,* BROWARD DAILY BUS. REV., Sept. 13, 2002, at 10. This article says that, under current law, in-house lawyers can plead ignorance and they have no legal obligation to scrutinize the underlying accounting transactions.

[183] *Cf.* Thomas Koenig & Michael Rustad, *"Crimtorts" as Corporate Just Deserts,* 31 U. MICH. J.L. REF. 289, 313 (1998) (noting that the "Ford Pinto litigation produced the only case in American history in which a corporation was criminally prosecuted for knowingly marketing a dangerously defective product").

use of accessorial crimes to reach responsible parties. Hence, the crimes of aiding and abetting, conspiracy, accessory before and after the fact, and wire and mail fraud are more commonly used to charge responsible parties such as lawyers when a crime was committed by their clients.

A focus on corporate criminal responsibility must also take into account the federal sentencing guidelines and the manner in which they address corporate actions.[184] Under the guidelines, a federal judge can consider the corporation's efforts before the offense to "prevent and detect" criminal conduct in the "culpability score."[185] Thus, corporations are rewarded for maintaining strict and regular legal compliance programs, and they are punished for failing to identify and correct potential violations of a criminal law.[186] Some commentators have argued that the organizational sentencing guidelines place significant burdens upon in-house counsel that could lead to professional disciplinary actions.[187]

B. Criminal Indictment of Koch Industries and Its In-House Lawyer[188]

In the late 1970s, the Environmental Protection Agency adopted regulations that added benzene to its list of hazardous pollutants. The Clean Air Act prohibited the operation of any facility that violated these regulations. These regulations, commonly referred to as NESHAP,[189] required companies to limit benzene emissions and to file an annual report that certified that their facilities complied with statutory and regulatory environmental emissions requirements.

Koch Industries, Inc., which is one of the largest privately owned companies in the United States, operated a petroleum refinery near Corpus Christi, Texas, that was subject to the requirements of the Clean Air Act. Under the Clean Air Act and NESHAP regulations, Koch had until 1993 to comply with the new benzene limitations, but the company asked for and received an extension of time to comply until 1995.

In 1995, Koch installed a pollution control device at its Corpus Christi refinery that allegedly could not handle the benzene routed to it and thus allegedly would shut down the facility for periods of time. This shut-down apparently led to several periods when the benzene emissions exceeded ten pounds per twenty-four-hour period, which

---

[184] *See* U.S. SENTENCING GUIDELINES MANUAL § 8 (2002) (codified at 18 U.S.C.).

[185] *Id.*, at § 8C2.5(f).

[186] *See* Harry S. Hardin, III & Andrew R. Lee, *Pitfalls for In-House Counsel*, 25 WTR BRIEF 32 (1996).

[187] *See* Joseph J. Fleischman et al., *The Organizational Sentencing Guidelines and the Employment At-Will Rules Applied to In-House Counsel*, 48 BUS. LAW. 611 (1993) (explaining in detail the operation of the culpability score).

[188] This fact pattern is derived from Press Release, Department of Justice, *Koch Industries Indicted for Environmental Crimes at Refinery, available at* www.usdoj.gov/opa/pr/2000/September/573enrd.htm.

[189] National Emissions Standards for Hazardous Air Pollutants, 40 CFR § 61.340–359 (2002).

---

would have required Koch Industries to file immediately a report to the Emergency Response Center under the Federal Environmental Response, Compensation, and Liability Act. Koch allegedly ignored information that benzene at the refinery exceeded permissible limits by a factor of fifteen.[190]

Moreover, even though the in-house lawyer at Koch's facility in Corpus Christi caused the company to self-report to the Texas Natural Resources Conservation Commission ("TNRCC"), which was responsible for enforcing the NESHAP regulations, that the company was in violation of benzene emission requirements, prosecutors sought an indictment of Koch and its in-house lawyer. The prosecutors alleged that, in 1995 and 1996, Koch made false and misleading statements to regulators about the extent of benzene violations at its Corpus Christi refinery and, in addition, made false statements in the annual environmental report that Koch filed pursuant to the NESHAP regulations.

Following a complaint to the EPA by a Koch employee, the Department of Justice presented charges to a federal grand jury that eventually indicted Koch Industries, Inc., Koch Petroleum Group, LP, and four corporate employees[191] for knowingly operating the facility in violation of environmental laws and regulations.[192] Two of the individuals were plant managers at the refinery in question. One individual was the environmental engineer at the plant. The fourth individual was an in-house lawyer for Koch who had worked on environmental compliance issues and, for a period of time, served as environmental manager of the facility. The in-house attorney was charged with "conspiracy to violate the Clean Air Act, and conspiracy to make false statements to Texas environmental officials; with operating the West Plant in violation of the Clean Air Act; and with two counts of making false statements to Texas environmental officials." If convicted, these charges against the in-house attorney carried a maximum jail term of thirty-five years and a fine of $1.75 million.

The charges against Koch's in-house lawyer stemmed from his direct participation in the company's attempt to comply with the benzene NESHAP regulations. Prosecutors alleged that, in meetings with the TNRCC, the lawyer misrepresented and concealed the extent to which the facility was out of compliance with the benzene NESHAP regulations. Moreover, prosecutors alleged that the company's annual report, which the lawyer had assisted in preparing and filing, was false and misleading.

The criminal indictment brought charges based on the very first time that Koch was required to file an annual report under the new benzene NESHAP regulations, even

---

[190] This information was provided to the authorities by a whistleblower. *See* John Tedesco, *Tipster Saw Koch Case to End*, SAN ANTONIO EXPRESS-NEWS, Apr. 11, 2001, at 8B.

[191] Because the charges brought by the government against the individuals were ultimately dropped, we will not identify these people by name. *Id.*

[192] There were actually two indictments in this case: one in 2000, and a revised indictment in 2001. The original indictment brought 97 charges against Koch and its 4 employees. The revised indictment reduced the number of charges to 11. *See* Dan Parker, *Prosecutors Move to Drop All but 11 Charges Against Koch*, Jan. 3, 2001, at A1. These charges were reduced to 8 by the time of trial. *See* James Pinkerton, *Koch Slapped with Big Penalty*, HOUS. CHRON., Apr. 10, 2001, at A1.

though the language of these regulations was unclear as to whether the report was to be based on historical data for emissions during the past year or only on current conditions at the facility as of the date of the report. The in-house lawyer interpreted the new regulations to permit reporting of benzene emissions on a current basis, which was most advantageous to the company. However, prosecutors used the aggressive interpretation of the benzene emissions stated in the annual report against the lawyer by alleging that he misled the regulators, knowing that Koch would not have to report the prior year's benzene violations if the state agency adopted his view of the regulations.

What was unusual about the indictment of the in-house attorney at Koch is that information indicated that he had actively worked to remedy the company's noncompliance under the benzene regulations, had caused the company to self-report to the TNRCC that the facility was in violation of its permit, and prepared a letter that accompanied the annual report explaining the basis upon which that report was prepared. Was this permissible zealous advocacy or crossing the line on what is permissible in preparing a regulatory report for a corporate entity?

In 2002, on the eve of trial, Koch pled guilty to "covering up environmental violations" at its Texas refinery. The plea required Koch to pay $10 million in criminal penalties and $10 million for environmental projects in the Corpus Christi area. The company also agreed to be on probation for five years in a strict environmental compliance program. According to the government's press release:

> In the plea agreement Koch admitted that it concealed its noncompliance with the requirements of the Clean Air Act in 1995, by among other things, failing to control emissions from certain waste management units at the refinery. Specifically, in January 1995, Koch certified that it had installed equipment necessary to control benzene-contaminated wastewater, and then without notifying the State of Texas or the U.S. EPA, disconnected a critical oil water separator used to control benzene emissions. Koch then constructed a line to bypass the control equipment and built a stack to vent benzene vapors to the oil-water separator into the atmosphere. In addition, in April 1995, Koch filed a report that concealed the fact that the separator was venting benzene vapors to the atmosphere and falsely stated that the company had tested for benzene in certain waste streams.

The company's in-house lawyer, as well as other individual corporate officials who had been indicted, were dismissed from any charges in connection with Koch's plea agreement.[193]

---

[193] In exchange for the dropped charges, the four individuals had to agree not to sue the federal government for its conduct in the case. News Release, Koch Industries, Inc. (April 9, 2001), *available at* http://www.kochnews.com/corpus/documents/KII_KPG.pdf. Throughout the case, Koch had maintained that the criminal charges were brought by a Democratic administration in retaliation for supporting Republican candidates in election contributions. *See* Dan Eggen, *Oil Company Agrees to Pay $20 Million in Fines,* WASH. POST, Apr. 10, 2001, at A03.

The *Koch Industries* case illustrates the manner in which prosecutors can use accesso-rial liability against corporate employees, including in-house lawyers. Moreover, it re-veals that, under certain statutes, traditional *mens rea* or intent to commit the crime may not be an element that the government must prove in order to obtain a conviction of environmental crimes. The government in *Koch Industries* argued that a defendant accused of violating the benzene NESHAP regulations need only know the operative facts of a violation, not the fact that his or its conduct constituted a violation of a crime. But how under these circumstances could the in-house lawyer have avoided the allega-tions of criminal conduct? Could the lawyer avoid the allegation if he knew that the company could not comply with the Clean Air Act? Would an outside environmental lawyer representing Koch have been subject to the same exposure to criminal liability?

C. The Indictment of a General Counsel Who Accepted a Bonus for Allegedly Resolving a Corporate SEC Problem

In the landscape of recent corporate scandals, Tyco Industries stands out as a tabloid example of corporate extravagance and greed by corporate officials. To date, three of its executives have been charged with crimes and forced to leave the company. Most media focus has been on Tyco's president and CEO, Dennis Kozlowski, and his flam-boyant lifestyle.[194] It is ironic that his downfall seems to revolve around the alleged non-payment of state taxes, rather than the mismanagement and waste of assets of a highly successful company.[195] However, the relevant Tyco story for the purposes of this essay is the pending criminal charges against its general counsel, Mark Belnick.[196]

The revised indictment against Tyco's former general counsel involves the following alleged conduct. Belnick faces nine counts, including grand larceny, plotting to de-fraud, and falsifying corporate documents to conceal $14 million dollars in loans that he received from Tyco.[197] He, along with many other Tyco executives, apparently au-

---

[194] *See e.g.*, James B. Stewart, *Spend! Spend! Spend!: Where Did Tyco's Money Go?*, NEW YORKER, Feb. 17, 2003, at 132 [hereinafter Stewart].

[195] However, consider the similar fates of Al Capone, Heidi Fleiss, and William Aramory as discussed in Pamela H. Bucy, *Criminal Tax Fraud: The Downfall of Murderers, Madams and Thieves*, 29 ARIZ. ST. L.J. 639 (1997).

[196] Mark Belnick was a lead investigator in the Iran-Contra proceedings and one who was considered to embody high ethical principles. *See* James Grimaldi, *Tyco Counsel is Embodiment of Lawyers' Fall*, SALT LAKE TRIB., Dec. 31, 2002, *available at* www.sltrib.com/2002/Dec/12312002/Business/16050.asp. For an in-depth story about Mark Belnick's rise and fall, see Nicholas Varchaver, *Fall from Grace*, FORTUNE, Oct. 28, 2002, at 112.

[197] *See* Andrew Ross Sorkin, *New Charges In Tyco Case Involve Bonus for Ex-Counsel*, N.Y. TIMES, Feb. 4, 2003, at C1. Apparently, some of these "loans" were obtained under a Tyco corporate relocation pro-gram, yet it is alleged that the general counsel did not qualify because he had not moved from the required locations to a new location. These loans allegedly were not disclosed to the SEC when the general counsel filled out executive questionnaires. However, for one of these loan programs, Belnick's hiring agreement had included a right to participate in the loan relocation program to move 25 miles. For a second reloca-tion program, Tyco alleges that Belnick did not complete the required paperwork. *See* GRIMALDI, *supra* note 196.

thorized significant loans from the company to themselves. A recent article reports that these executives viewed the loans from the perspective of how much they meant to each individual shareholder and, since they involved only pennies a share, they thought that such loans were justified.[198]

Prosecutors have also charged Belnick with failing to disclose a $2.5 million dollar related-party transaction with a Tyco director. He is also accused of conduct that obtained favorable proxies from Tyco shareholders, so as to keep existing management in control of the company. During this time, Belnick allegedly sold millions of dollars of Tyco stock, much of which was not reported in accordance with SEC rules. The final set of charges alleges grand larceny. Prosecutors allege that Belnick took a $2 million bonus plus $200,000 in Tyco shares when he resolved an SEC investigation into Tyco's practices. Belnick took the bonus because he claimed he had done an outstanding job in resolving the investigation.[199]

Recent events have shown that Tyco made significant misrepresentations to the SEC in that investigation. Tyco has conceded that the SEC was correct in its initial allegations. The grand larceny charges are premised upon the fact that Belnick's bonus was obtained under false pretenses to Tyco and to Tyco's board of directors.

Mark Belnick's response is that "he broke no laws, disclosed what was required, kept the Tyco officials in the loop, told auditors from PriceWaterhouseCoopers about the transactions and sought prior approval for the loans."[200] Apart from the criminal prosecution, Belnick faces civil enforcement actions from the SEC[201] and a lawsuit by Tyco alleging that he received $14 million in inappropriate loans and breached his fiduciary duty by helping Kozlowski hide $95 million of loan forgiveness. Belnick's response to the Tyco lawsuit is that he did not know about or approve any of Kozlowski's actions.[202] At the time that Tyco fired Belnick, Belnick had begun an internal investigation of the corporate fraud issues at his company. He has stated that his firing was due to a turf war between the new management and his efforts to complete the investigation.[203]

Regardless of whether the allegations are actually proven at trial, it is difficult to look past the flagrant greed in these transactions. It remains to be determined whether the board of directors approved of these transactions and whether the transactions were legal.

---

[198] *See* Stewart, *supra* note 194. This is an excellent exposition of the behind the scene corporate fraud at Tyco.

[199] *See* Alex Berenson, *Now, Questions Turn to Why Tyco's Lawyer Received Bonus*, N.Y. TIMES, June 12, 2002, at C1.

[200] GRIMALDI, *supra* note 196.

[201] *See TYCO Former Executives L. Dennis Kozlowski, Mark H. Swartz and Mark A. Belnick Sued for Fraud, reprinted at* http://www.sec.gov/litigation/litreleases/lr17722.htm.

[202] *See* VARCHAVER, *supra* note 196. This article reports that Belnick's lawyer claims that he informed the Board of Directors' compensation committee and he was told that he did not have to make disclosures on the SEC questionnaires.

[203] *See Ex-Tyco Lawyer Takes Offense*, CNN/MONEY, June 10, 2002, *available at* http://money.cnn.com/2002/06/10/news/companies/tyco/.

We use this narrative to illustrate an important point for in-house lawyers. An in-house lawyer's conduct will always be judged *as if* the lawyer knew all of the company's policies and rules and *as if* the lawyer was aware of relevant state and federal laws. Thus, a defense that an executive or auditor "told me that I could do this," must be viewed with much less weight when the lawyer is deemed to know that the conduct violated company policy or other law. The Tyco case also illustrates what often happens when control of a company changes from one group of executives to another. As long as Kozlowski and his selected executives controlled the company, information about large expenditures and loans to management largely remained private. However, when media attention focuses on widespread executive misconduct, reporters invariably ask why the company's general counsel did not take action to stop the fraudulent conduct by management or why she did not advise the outside members of the board of directors.

A broader issue is how in-house counsel should protect the client—in other words, the entity? Tyco was clearly the client, not Kozlowski. When Kozlowski decided to extend loans to tens of other executives, did that trigger obligations on Belnick's part? How could Kozlowski justify his decision to give Belnick a bonus because he resolved a 1999 SEC investigation? Wasn't Belnick being paid a salary to resolve SEC complaints? When does the granting of a bonus amount to larceny?

Tyco can only act through its duly authorized agents. As long as the Board of Directors of Tyco gave its President and CEO free rein, the only remaining constraints would be internal policies and external legal norms. At a minimum, it would seem that an in-house lawyer would need to make sure that officers and board members complied with company rules. But if they did not comply with the rules, would the general counsel have any further obligations? What about the fiduciary obligations that the officers and directors themselves owed to Tyco?

From one perspective, tens of millions of dollars in loans could cause material injury to the client—the magnitude of the loans represents expenditures of significant funds and a threat to the worth of the company. The self-dealing nature of the loans is troubling, especially if the in-house lawyer benefits from the loans personally. From the perspective of the Tyco executives who benefited from the loans, those funds represented a mere drop in the bucket compared to what they believed was superior management of a company whose stock value remained high in the face of a declining stock market. If the violation was only of internal policies, under the current Model Rules, the general counsel could stay silent or could possibly withdraw from performing the legal work on the specific loans. Of course, other counsel would need to be engaged. And it is dubious whether a general counsel could ever disclaim responsibility from part of a corporate client's legal work when the very nature of the general counsel position in a corporation is supervision over its legal affairs.

The primary constraints on an in-house lawyer's conduct are external legal norms. If the conduct of the president and CEO is criminal or fraudulent, the harm to the entity client requires the general counsel to go up the ladder, in this case to independent members of the Board of Directors. In other words, if the loan programs at Tyco were not disclosed in SEC documents and such disclosures were required, the in-house lawyer needed to inform the officers and eventually the directors at Tyco. The failure to do so would have violated the Model Rules.[204] After Sarbanes Oxley, the Legal Compliance Officer or the Qualified Legal Compliance Committee would have specific obligations here. Obviously, criminal laws directed at the in-house counsel (such as responsible party laws or accessorial liability) help to deter lawyer complicity with client fraud.[205] However, recent corporate frauds point to a need for redefining substantive corporate law.[206] New rules adopted by the SEC applicable to the conduct of attorneys under the Sarbanes-Oxley Act are a start, but the SEC must actively enforce the existing legal obligations of professionals who represent public companies if equity markets are to have a chance of working.

VI. CONCLUSION

The ethics rules have largely assumed that corporate in-house lawyers are subject to the same rules that govern outside counsel. In-house lawyers are not immune from discipline simply because they act at the direction of corporate employees. Therefore, little attempt has been made by the organized bar to elaborate upon the specific problems that in-house lawyers may face.

The organized bar's failure to address the particular problems faced by in-house counsel ignores the substantive context in which in-house lawyers work and the economic pressures that they may face which may cause them to act in a given manner. The failure to address these issues also ignores the developments that have been advanced in the application of criminal laws to in-house lawyers. Moreover, the failure to address these issues assumes that in-house and outside lawyers will act similarly in similar situations.

---

[204] Lawyers in the securities area have always needed to be mindful of the laws. *See* Harry S. Hardin, III & Andrew R. Lee, *Pitfalls for In-House Counsel*, 25 BRIEF 33 (1996). This article highlights an SEC investigation of a Solomon Brothers Treasury auction and the role of its general counsel. *See* In re Gutfreund, Exchange Act Release No. 34-31554 [1992 Transfer Binder] Fed. Sec. L. Rep. (CCH) ¶ 85,067, at 83,597, 83,604-608 (Dec. 3, 1993). The SEC argued that, even though the general counsel of Solomon Brothers had discovered the fraud and tried to get his client to report it to the SEC, he had an obligation to ensure that the client took the proper action. It is interesting to note that the SEC in this case argued that the lawyer had failed to conduct the proper work within the client organization structure to get the client to report; but the SEC did not argue that the lawyer had an independent duty to report. *See* Larry Smith, *In-House Counsel: New Targets for Malpractice Actions?*, 12 OF COUNSEL 5 (1993) (discussing the claims of the SEC that the in-house counsel had obligations to initiate an in-house investigation once he had discovered the violations of the law).

[205] It is interesting that many recent corporate hires for general counsel have included lawyers with past prosecutorial or government experience. *See* Joseph A. Slobodzian, *GCs for Tough Times*, NAT'L L.J., Nov. 25, 2002, at A15.

[206] *See* Steven Andersen, *Wave of Corporate Scandals Puts In-House Attorneys in the Hot Seat*, CORP. LEGAL TIMES, Sept. 2002, at 1.

This essay has used the context of the recent corporate scandals to illustrate the need for reform of the law governing in-house lawyers. Whether that reform should come from the legal profession's rules of conduct, from changes in substantive corporate and securities law, or from advances in criminal law is subject to debate. However, in our opinion, it is a mistake to impose rules that provide little practical guidance to lawyers who provide legal services to modern American corporations.

QUESTIONS

1. Is it realistic to apply the same ethics rules to in-house lawyers and to lawyers in private law firms? If specific rule changes were made to address the problems of in-house counsel, what changes would you suggest be made to the ABA Model Rules and state ethics rules?

2. Why was Model Rule 1.13 basically ineffective to prevent any of the recent corporate frauds such as at Enron, Global Crossing, and Tyco? Does Model Rule 1.13 adequately address the problems that in-house lawyers face when representing the entity? Do you think the new attorney conduct rules adopted by the SEC pursuant to the Sarbanes-Oxley Act will likely result in lawyers preventing client fraud? If current ethics rules dealing with entity representation have failed to prevent client fraud, can changing lawyer ethics rules be expected to make a difference in the behavior of in-house lawyers? Or should those changes come from substantive corporate and securities law?

3. In the *Andersen* case, examine and analyze Nancy Temple's e-mail to David Duncan. In view of the crisis that existed at the time, what would you have advised her to state in her e-mail to David Duncan? Do you think some members of the jury in the *Andersen* case implied too much or did they correctly interpret this e-mail?

4. Since Nancy Temple did not testify in the *Andersen* trial, do you think her absence at the trial prejudiced the representation of Andersen? How can a corporation defend itself when a significant actor relies on the Fifth Amendment and refuses to testify? In hindsight, what advice would you have given as in-house counsel to Andersen in October 2001? What should Ms. Temple have done when she learned that some Andersen employees were engaged in destroying documents?

5. The jury in the *Andersen* case asked Judge Harmon whether all members of the jury needed to believe that the same corporate actor met the requisite legal standard to violate the criminal law to convict the entity, or whether some of the members of the jury could believe that it was one employee of Andersen when other members of the jury believed it was another employee. Does Judge Harmon's instruction satisfy traditional notions of due process or the burden of proof needed to obtain a criminal conviction under the Constitution?

6. Read the material contained in the appendix to this chapter. Are you surprised by any of the instructions that Judge Harmon gave to the jury in the "Court's Instructions to the Jury?" Should the court have allowed the prosecution to intro-

duce the "Hotel California" lyrics to the jury? What probative value does it have, compared to the prejudice that it might create with the jurors?

7. Why has the American Bar Association resisted, for two decades, allowing lawyers to disclose client confidential information to any third party when the client is engaged in fraudulent or criminal conduct that will cause economic damages? Specifically, what is the justification for this position? Compare how this issue is addressed in the ABA Model Rules, the Texas Disciplinary Rule, and the new SEC rules governing attorney conduct?

8. Why might transaction lawyers have a propensity for blind spots or not recognizing signals indicating fraudulent conduct when it comes to misconduct by the lawyer's client? Read the Langevoort article in footnote 115 and articulate his explanation for why lawyers may unintentionally engage in complicity with client fraud. Do you know of other lawyers who represented a client that was involved in the recent corporate scandals who chose to withdraw from representing the client? What made these lawyers choose to decline the representation or withdraw early in the matter?

9. Does the SEC regulation implementing the Sarbanes-Oxley Act accomplish Congress's intent? Does it go far enough or too far in imposing obligations upon lawyers to disclose fraud? What are the arguments pro and con for lawyers being "gatekeepers" under the securities law to protect public investors? Should Congress or the SEC enlist other actors, such as auditors or corporate executives, to be the gatekeepers?

10. Did the ABA Task Force on Corporate Governance issue meaningful guidelines that change a lawyer's duty to disclose information about a client's fraudulent or criminal conduct? Or are the Task Force proposals essentially the same as what the ABA's policy has been in the past? How would you change the Task Force's proposals to the ABA House of Delegates?

11. Should the criminal law extend to lawyers' conduct through the accessorial crimes of aiding and abetting? In the *Koch Industries* case, was it proper under the facts to seek criminal penalties against general counsel? What did Mr. Belnick do that exposed him to criminal liability?

VII. APPENDIX

A. Timeline: The Demise of Arthur Andersen LLP[207]

6/19/01   Andersen agrees to pay $7 million fine to SEC for "knowingly or recklessly certifying incorrect financial statements" in Waste Management, Inc. case.

8/14/01   Enron Chief Executive Officer, Jeffrey Skilling, unexpectedly resigns.

8/20/01   Andersen partner, Jim Hecker, receives telephone call from Enron whistleblower, Sherron Watkins (formerly of Andersen), questioning Enron's structured third-party transactions and stating she intended to express her concerns to Kenneth Lay on August 23rd.

8/28/01   SEC quietly opens an informal inquiry into Enron's off-balance sheet partnerships. (This was revealed when an SEC lawyer testified at the *Andersen* trial.) This inquiry began shortly after the sudden and unexpected resignation of Enron's CEO, Jeffrey Skilling.

9/28/01   In-house attorney, Nancy Temple, joins Andersen special consultation group on Enron accounting problems

10/9/01   Nancy Temple's notes mention "highly probable some SEC investigation"

10/10/01   Andersen partner, Michael Odom, stresses at Andersen training conference the need to get rid of Enron documents. Andersen videotape made of Odom's comments.

10/12/01   Nancy Temple e-mail to Mike Odom: "It might be useful to consider reminding the Engagement Team of our document and retention policy. It will be helpful to make sure that we have complied with the policy. Let me know if you have any questions." Odom later tells AA employees: "If you're destroying records and then you get a subpoena the next day, that's great."

10/15/01   Calls and draft memo to file by Duncan about Enron's proposed Press Release announcing third-quarter financial statements, which included losses of $600+ million and a reduction in shareholder equity of $1.2 billion related to special purpose partnerships. Duncan advises Enron not to use term "non-recurring" to describe losses; says using that term "could be misconstrued or misunderstood by investors." Enron indicates to Duncan it has raised the issue internally and that the press release had gone through "normal legal review."

10/16/01   Enron issues its third-quarter financial statements. Temple's now famous e-mail to Duncan conveying "a few suggested comments for consideration"

---

[207] This timeline was prepared from various sources, including Def. Andersen Exhibit 864, entitled "Andersen-Enron Events June through November 2001," introduced by Andersen into evidence at the Andersen trial; "Timeline of Andersen Events," *available at* http://www.chron.com/cs/CDA/story.hts/special/enron/1452911; "Timeline of Events Surrounding Andersen Document Destruction," *available at* Findlaw.com *available at* http://lawcrawler.findlaw.com/scripts/lc.pl?entry=timeline &submit2=search& sites=findlaw.com.

regarding Duncan's memorandum to file, including deleting reference to consultation with legal group and Temple's name from memo; "deleting some language that might suggest we have concluded the [press] release is misleading"; and "the lack of any suggestion that this characterization ["non-recurring"] is not in accordance with GAAP. . . ."

10/17/01   SEC informal inquiry letter to Enron requesting information and documents.

10/19/01   Nancy Temple sends document retention and destruction policy to two Andersen partners. Andersen learns about SEC informal inquiry of Enron.

10/22/01   Enron makes public announcement of SEC informal inquiry. David Duncan meets with Enron to discuss helping Enron respond to SEC inquiry.

10/23/01   David Duncan reminds Andersen engagement partners to comply with document retention policy. Destruction of Enron documents continues at Andersen.

10/31/01   Enron announces SEC inquiry is upgraded to a formal investigation.

11/8/01   Enron announces restatement of financial statements for past five years; Andersen receives subpoena from SEC for documents relating to Enron.

11/9/01   David Duncan authorizes an e-mail informing Andersen employees: "no more shredding."

11/10/01   Nancy Temple e-mails memorandum to all U.S. Enron engagement personnel about subpoenas and litigation requesting that employees ". . . take all necessary steps to preserve all documents and other materials . . . ."

3/7/02   Grand Jury Indictment of Arthur Andersen LLP filed under seal in the U.S. District Court in the Southern District of Texas.

3/13/02   Letter to Department of Justice from Andersen's attorneys, Mayer, Brown, Rowe & Maw, rejecting proposed plea agreement and urging DOJ not to indict Andersen.

3/14/02   Criminal Indictment unsealed against Arthur Andersen LLP, alleging Andersen altered and destroyed documents to impair the documents' availability for use in SEC investigation of Enron.

5/7/02   Opening Statements to Jury in Andersen trial by DOJ prosecutor Matthew Friedrich and defense attorney Rusty Hardin.

6/15/02   Jury verdict finding Arthur Andersen guilty of obstruction of justice; jurors unanimously agree that Nancy Temple was the "corrupt persuader" in case.

8/16/02   Arthur Andersen's license to practice public accounting revoked by Texas State Board of Public Accountancy.

8/31/02   Arthur Andersen ceases to be an auditor of public companies.

10/16/02   Arthur Andersen sentenced by Judge Harmon to maximum five years' probation and fine of $500,000.

B. Nancy Temple E-mail

To:	David B. Duncan
CC:	Michael C. Odom@ANDERSEN WO; Richard Corgel@ANDERSEN WO; Gary B. Goolsby@ANDERSEN WO
BCC:	
Date:	10/16/2001 08:39 PM
From:	Nancy A. Temple
Subject:	Re: Press Release draft
Attachments:	ATT8ICIQ; 3rd qtr press release memo.doc

Dave—Here are a few suggested comments for consideration.

—I recommend deleting reference to consultation with the legal group and deleting my name on the memo. Reference to the legal group consultation arguably is a waiver of attorney-client privileged advice and if my name is mentioned it increases the changes that I might be a witness, which I prefer to avoid.

—I suggested deleting some language that might suggest we have concluded the release is misleading.

—In light of the "non-recurring" characterization, the lack of any suggestion that this characterization is not in accordance with GAAP, and the lack of income statements in accordance with GAAP, I will consult further within the legal group as to whether we should do anything more to protect ourselves from potential Section 10A issues.

Nancy

To:	Michael C. Odom@ANDERSEN WO, Richard Corgel@ANDERSEN WO, Nancy A. Temple@ANDERSEN WO, Gary B. Goolsby@ANDERSEN WO
cc:	
Date:	10/16/2001 05:00 PM
From:	David B. Duncan (Mailed by: Shannon D. Adlong)
Subject:	Press Release draft

First draft of memo regarding press release discussion for your comments.

C. The Charge to the Jury in the Arthur Andersen Case

IN THE UNITED STATES DISTRICT COURT
FOR THE SOUTHERN DISTRICT OF TEXAS
HOUSTON DIVISION

UNITED STATES OF AMERICA	}
	}
vs.	} CRIMINAL NO. H-02-121
	}
ARTHUR ANDERSEN, LLP	}

COURT'S INSTRUCTIONS TO THE JURY
GENERAL INSTRUCTIONS

Members of the Jury:

In any jury trial there are, in effect, two judges. I am one of the judges; the other is the jury. It is my duty to preside over the trial and to determine what evidence is proper for your consideration. It is also my duty at the end of the trial to explain to you the rules of law that you must follow and apply in arriving at your verdict:

First, I will give you some general instructions which apply in every case, for example, instructions about burden of proof and how to judge the believability of witnesses. Then I will give you some specific rules of law about this particular case, and finally I will explain to you the procedures you should follow in your deliberations.

You, as jurors, are the judges of the facts. But in determining what actually happened, that is, in reaching your decision as to the facts, it is your sworn duty to follow all of the rules of law as I explain them to you.

You have no right to disregard or give special attention to any one instruction, or to question the wisdom or correctness of any rule I may state to you. You must not substitute or follow your own notion or opinion as to what the law is or ought to be. It is your duty to apply the law as I give it to you, regardless of the consequences.

It is also your duty to base your verdict solely upon the testimony and evidence, without prejudice or sympathy. That was the promise you made and the oath you took before being accepted by the parties as jurors, and they have the right to expect nothing less.

The indictment or formal charge against a defendant is not evidence of guilt. The law presumes the defendant innocent. The presumption of innocence means that the defendant starts the trial with a clean slate. In other words, the defendant is presumed by you to be innocent throughout your deliberations until such time, if ever, you as a jury are satisfied that the government has proven the defendant guilty beyond a reasonable doubt. Unless you are satisfied beyond a reasonable doubt that the defendant is guilty, the presumption alone is sufficient to find the defendant not guilty. The law does not require a defendant to prove his or her innocence or produce any evidence at all. The government has the burden of proving the defendant guilty beyond a reasonable doubt, and, if it fails to do so, you must acquit the defendant.

While the government's burden of proof is a strict or heavy burden, it is not necessary that the defendant's guilt be proved beyond all possible doubt. It is only required that the government's proof exclude any "reasonable doubt" concerning the defendant's guilt.

A "reasonable doubt" is a doubt based upon reason and common sense after careful and impartial consideration of all the evidence in the case. Proof beyond a reasonable doubt, therefore, is proof of such a convincing character that you would be willing to rely and act upon it without hesitation in the most important of your own affairs. If you are convinced that the accused has been proved guilty beyond a reasonable doubt, say so. If you are not convinced, say so.

Evidence has been introduced as to the involvement of various individuals in the offenses charged. That these individuals are not on trial before you is not a matter of concern to you. You should not speculate as to the reason these individuals are not on trial before you, nor should you allow this to control or influence your verdict. Your duty is to determine the appropriate verdict with respect to Andersen only. You may not draw any inference, favorable or unfavorable towards the government or the defendant on trial, from the fact that certain persons were not named as defendants in the indictment. The circumstances that these persons were not indicted must play no part in your deliberations.

Whether a person should be indicted as a defendant is a matter within the sole discretion of the United States Attorney and the grand jury. Therefore, you may not consider it in any way in reaching your verdict as to the defendant on trial.

As I told you earlier, it is your duty to determine the facts. In doing so, you must consider only the evidence presented during the trial, including the sworn testimony of the witnesses and the exhibits. Remember that any statements, objections or arguments made by the lawyers are not evidence. The function of the lawyers is to point out those things that are most significant or most helpful to their side of the case, and in so doing, to call your attention to certain facts or inferences that might otherwise escape your notice. In the final analysis, however, it is your own recollection and interpretation of the evidence that controls in the case. What the lawyers say is not binding upon you. The attorneys for the government and the attorneys for Arthur Andersen, LLP (Andersen) have entered into stipulations concerning facts which are relevant to this case. When the attorneys on both sides stipulate and agree as to the existence of a fact, you must, unless otherwise instructed, accept the stipulation as evidence, and regard that fact as proved.

Do not assume from anything I may have done or said during the trial that I have any opinion concerning any of the issues in this case. Except for my instructions to you on the law or for my rulings and instructions to you regarding the evidence, you should disregard anything I may have said during the trial in arriving at your own findings as to the facts.

While you should consider only the evidence, you are permitted to draw such reasonable inferences from the testimony and exhibits as you feel are justified in the light of common experience. In other words, you may make deductions and reach conclusions which reason and common sense lead you to draw from the facts which have been established by the evidence.

You should not be concerned about whether the evidence is direct or circumstantial. "Direct evidence" is the testimony of one who asserts actual knowledge of a fact, such as an eye witness. "Circumstantial evidence" is proof of a chain of facts and circumstances indicating that the defendant is either guilty or not guilty. The law makes no distinction between the weight you may give to either direct or circumstantial evidence. It requires only that you weigh all of the evidence and that you not convict the defendant unless you are convinced of the defendant's guilt beyond a reasonable doubt.

The defendant in this case is a partnership rather than an individual. Under the law, a partnership is a person and may be liable for violating the criminal laws. However, as an entity, a partnership can only act through its agents—such as its officers, partners, and employees—and a partnership is legally bound by the acts and statements its agents do or make within the scope of their employment. Thus, in order to establish that Andersen is guilty as charged in the indictment, the government must prove, beyond a reasonable doubt, that each of the elements of the offense, as I will later explain them to you, was committed by one or more agents of Andersen acting within the scope of their employment with the firm.

In order for a partnership agent to be acting within the scope of his or her employment, the agent must be acting with the intent, at least in part, to benefit the partnership. It is not necessary, however, for the government to prove that the agent's sole or even primary motive was to benefit the partnership. Furthermore, the government need not prove that the partnership was actually benefited by the agent's actions. You may consider the presence or absence of actual benefit to the firm from the agent's actions in determining whether the agent acted with an intent to benefit the firm. But ultimately the question you must answer is whether the agent intended, in part, that the partnership benefit from his or her actions, whether or not any benefit actually resulted.

An agent must also be acting in line with his or her duties as an agent of the partnership in order to be acting within the scope of his or her employment. An agent is acting in line with his or her duties when the agent's acts deal with a matter the performance of which is generally entrusted to the agent. Stated another way, an act is in line with an agent's duties if it relates directly to the performance of the agent's general duties for the partnership. It is not, however, necessary for the particular act itself to have been authorized by the partnership.

If an agent was acting within the scope of his or her employment, the fact that the agent's act was illegal, contrary to the partnership's instructions, or against the partnership's policies does not relieve the partnership of responsibility for the agent's acts. A partnership may be held responsible for the acts its agents perform within the scope of their employment even though the agent's conduct may be contrary to the partnership's actual instructions or contrary to the partnership's stated policies. You may, however, consider the existence of Andersen's policies and instructions, and the diligence of its efforts to enforce any such policies and instructions, in determining whether the firm's agents were acting within the scope of their employment. The fact that some agents of the partnership may not have committed any improper acts or possessed any improper intent does not relieve the partnership of responsibility for the improper acts or intents of other agents of the firm. Finally, the agent of a partnership who commits an act need not be a high-level or managerial agent in order for the act to be attributable to the firm. A partnership may be held responsible for the acts of agents who are subordinate or low-level employees.

During this trial, you have heard evidence relating to an SEC enforcement action and sanctions against Andersen arising out of Andersen's audit work for Waste Management Incorporated, as well as evidence of an SEC enforcement action against an Andersen partner arising out of Andersen's audit work for Sunbeam Corporation. This evidence was admitted by the Court for limited purposes. You may not use such evidence to conclude that Andersen committed the crime charged in the indictment simply because Andersen had prior involvement with the SEC in the Waste Management and Sunbeam matters. However, you may consider this evidence for other purposes, which I will now explain to you.

You may consider evidence of the defendant's prior involvement with the SEC in the Waste Management and Sunbeam matters to determine whether the defendant acted with the state of mind necessary to commit the crime charged in the indictment. In other words, you may consider such evidence to determine whether the defendant acted knowingly and with a corrupt intent to cause or induce another person to withhold a document from an official proceeding, or to alter, destroy, mutilate, or conceal an object with the intent to impair the object's availability for use in an official proceeding. In addition, you may consider this evidence to determine whether the defendant had knowledge of SEC procedures, whether the defendant had a motive or opportunity to commit the crime charged in the indictment, and whether the defendant acted according to a plan or in preparation for commission of a crime. These are the purposes for which evidence relating to SEC enforcement actions arising out of Andersen's audit work for Andersen clients Waste Management and Sunbeam may be considered.

I remind you that it is your job to decide whether the government has proved the guilt of the defendant beyond a reasonable doubt. In doing so, you must consider all of the evidence. This does not mean, however, that you must accept all of the evidence as true or accurate. You are the sole judges of the credibility or "believability" of each witness and the weight to be given the witness's testimony. An important part of your job will be making judgments about the testimony of the witnesses who testified in this case. You should decide whether you believe what each person had to say, and how important that testimony was. In making that decision I suggest that you ask yourself a few questions: Did the person impress you as honest? Did the witness have any particular reason not to tell the truth? Did the witness have a personal interest in the outcome of the case? Did the witness have any relationship with either the government or the defense? Did the witness seem to have a good memory? Did the witness have the opportunity and ability to understand the questions clearly and to answer them directly? Did the witness's testimony differ from the testimony of other witnesses? These are a few of the considerations that will help you determine the accuracy of what each witness said.

In making up your mind and reaching a verdict, do not make any decisions simply because there were more witnesses on one side than on the other. Do not reach a conclusion on a particular point just because there were more witnesses testifying for one side on that point. Your job is to think about the testimony of each witness you have heard and to decide how much you believe of what each witness had to say.

David Duncan has pleaded guilty to a crime and entered into an agreement with the government. David Duncan also testified about conduct allegedly engaged in by Andersen, which testimony you may consider in your deliberations. You will have to assess David Duncan's testimony and decide whether or not you credit the testimony given. I have already given you general instructions about factors you should consider in evaluating the testimony of any witness. I wish to give you further instructions relevant to your evaluation of David Duncan's testimony.

The government argues, as it is permitted to do, that it must take its witnesses as it finds them. For that very reason, the law allows the use of such testimony. Indeed, it is the law in federal courts that such testimony maybe enough, by itself, to support a conviction, if the jury finds that the testimony establishes guilt beyond a reasonable doubt. The fact that David Duncan pleaded guilty is not evidence of the guilt of Andersen, but you may consider it in evaluating David Duncan's testimony.

Because of the very nature of testimony from a witness who has entered into a cooperation agreement with the government, it must be scrutinized with great care and viewed with particular caution when you decide how much of that testimony to believe. You should, for example, ask yourselves whether such a witness would benefit more by lying or by telling the truth.

In this case, you have heard that the cooperating witness David Duncan entered into a plea agreement with the government. Plea bargaining, as it is called, has been approved as lawful and proper, and is expressly provided for in the rules of this court. David Duncan's plea agreement provides for the possibility of a lesser sentence than he would otherwise be exposed to for the offense to which he pleaded guilty or any other conduct which he revealed to the government at the time he entered into the plea agreement. The plea agreement also provides, in part, that he would give testimony in any proceeding in which he is called. The government is permitted to enter into such agreements. But a witness who testifies pursuant to such an agreement does have an interest in this case different from that of an ordinary witness. You must carefully scrutinize whether the testimony of such a witness was made up in any way because the witness believed or hoped that he would receive favorable treatment by testifying falsely. Or, ask yourselves, did the witness believe that his interests would be best served by testifying truthfully? If you believe that the witness was motivated by hopes of personal gain, was the motivation one that would cause the witness to lie, or was it one that would cause the witness to tell the truth? Did this motivation color the witness's testimony? You should look at all of the evidence in deciding whether you believe such a witness and what weight, if any, his testimony deserves.

The testimony of any witness may be discredited or "impeached" by showing that the witness testified falsely concerning a material matter, or by evidence that at some other time the witness said or did something, or failed to say or do something, which is inconsistent with the testimony the witness gave at this trial. If you believe that any witness has been discredited in this manner, then it is your exclusive right to give the testimony of that witness whatever weight, if any, you think it deserves.

There was testimony at trial that the attorneys interviewed witnesses when preparing for and during the course of the trial. You should not draw any unfavorable inference from that conduct. To the contrary, the attorneys were obliged to prepare this case as thoroughly as possible.

Although the government is required to prove the defendant's guilt beyond a reasonable doubt, the law does not require the government to call as witnesses all persons who may have been present at any time or place involved in the case, or who may appear to have some knowledge of the matters in issue at this trial. Nor does the law require the government to produce as exhibits all documents mentioned during the course of the trial. You will recall that the defense is not required to put on any evidence at all.

You may remember Nancy Temple, Kate Agnew, and Thomas Bauer were mentioned frequently during the course of the trial. They were described as partners or an employee of Andersen and persons who made a number of statements concerning the facts of this case. This may have caused you to wonder why Nancy Temple, Kate Agnew, and Thomas Baur were not called as witnesses to answer questions in this trial. For reasons which are not relevant here and with which you need not concern yourself, Nancy Temple, Kate Agnew, and Thomas Bauer were unavailable to testify, and you should draw no conclusion; either for or against either the government or the defendant, from the failure of Nancy Temple, Kate Agnew, and Thomas Bauer to testify as witnesses in the trial.

You may have heard reference, in the arguments of defense counsel in this case, to the fact that certain investigative techniques were' not used by the government. There is no legal requirement, however, that the government prove its case through any particular means. While you are to consider carefully the evidence adduced by the government, you are not to speculate as to why they used the techniques they did or why they did not use other techniques.

SPECIFIC INSTRUCTIONS
The indictment charges in relevant part

> On or about and between October 1.0, 2001, and November 9, 2001, within the Southern District of Texas and elsewhere, including Chicago, Illinois, Portland, Oregon, and London; England, ANDERSEN, through its partners and others, did knowingly, intentionally and corruptly persuade and attempt to persuade other persons, to wit: ANDERSEN employees, with intent to cause and induce such persons to (a) withhold records,

documents, and other objects from official proceedings, namely: regulatory and criminal proceedings and investigations, and (b) alter, destroy, mutilate and conceal objects with intent to impair the :objects' integrity and availability for use in such official proceedings.

(Title 18, United States Code, Sections 1512(b)(2) and 3551 *et seq.*)

Title 18 U.S.C. § 1512(b) provides that:

Whoever knowingly . . . [and] corruptly persuades another person, or attempts to do so, with intent . . . to cause or induce any person to withhold . . . a record, document, or other object from an official proceeding, [or] alter, destroy, mutilate, or conceal an object with intent to impair the object's integrity or availability for use in an official proceeding . . . [shall be guilty of a crime].

In order to prove Andersen guilty of violating this provision, the government must prove each of the following two elements beyond a reasonable doubt:

First: That on or about the dates charged, the Andersen firm, through its agents, corruptly persuaded or attempted to corruptly persuade another person or persons; and

Second: That Andersen, through its agents, acted knowingly and with intent to cause or induce another person or persons to (a) withhold a record or document from an official proceeding, or (b) alter, destroy, mutilate, or conceal an object with intent to impair the object's availability for use in an official proceeding.

An "official proceeding" is a proceeding before a federal court, judge, or agency. In this regard, you are instructed that the Securities and Exchange Commission, otherwise known as the "SEC," is a federal agency, and that an "official proceeding," for this case, is a proceeding before a federal agency, such as the SEC. A proceeding before a federal agency includes all of the steps and stages in the agency's performance of its governmental functions, and it extends to administrative as well as investigative functions, both formal and informal. For purposes of this case a civil law suit brought by private litigants is not an official proceeding.

For the first element, to determine whether Andersen corruptly persuaded "another person," an employee or partner of Andersen is considered "another person." To "persuade" is to engage in any non-coercive attempt to induce another person to engage in certain conduct. The word "corruptly" means having an improper purpose. An improper purpose, for this case, is an intent to subvert, undermine, or impede the fact-finding ability of an official proceeding. In order to establish this corrupt persuasion element, the government must prove that the agent of Andersen who engaged in the persuasion, not the other person persuaded, possessed the improper purpose. The improper purpose need not be the sole motivation for the defendant's conduct so long as the defendant acted, at least in part, with that improper purpose.

Thus, if you find beyond a reasonable doubt that an agent, such as a partner of Andersen acting within the scope of his or her employment, induced or attempted to induce another employee or partner of the firm or some other person to withhold, alter, destroy, mutilate, or conceal an object, and that the agent did so with the intent, at least in part, to subvert, undermine, or impede the fact-finding ability of an official proceeding, then you may find that Andersen committed the first element of the charged offense.

The second element of the charged obstruction offense is that Andersen, through its agents, acted knowingly and with the intent to cause or induce another person to withhold a record or a document from an official proceeding, or to alter, destroy, mutilate, or conceal an object with intent to impair the object's integrity or availability for use in an official proceeding.

An act is done with the intent to impair the integrity or availability of a document or object only if it is undertaken with the specific purpose of making the document or object unavailable for use in an official proceeding. However, the government is not required to prove that Andersen's sole or even primary intent was to cause another person to make a document or object unavailable for use in an official proceeding. You may find that this intent element has been established if you conclude that Andersen acted, at least in part, with the intent to cause another person to make a document or object unavailable for use in an official proceeding.

In order to establish that Andersen committed the charged offense, it is not necessary for the government to prove that an official proceeding was pending, or even about to be initiated at the time the obstructive conduct occurred. Nor is it necessary for the government to prove that a subpoena had been served on Andersen or any other party at the time of the offense. The government need only prove that Andersen acted corruptly and with the intent to withhold an object or impair an object's availability for use in an official proceeding, that is, a regulatory proceeding or investigation whether or not that proceeding had begun or whether or not a subpoena had been served.

Furthermore, it is not necessary for the government to prove that Andersen knew that its conduct violated the criminal law. Thus, even if Andersen honestly and sincerely believed that its conduct was lawful, you may find Andersen guilty if you conclude that Andersen acted corruptly and with the intent to make documents unavailable for an official proceeding.

Moreover, the government is not required to prove that Andersen was successful or likely to succeed in subverting or undermining the fact-finding ability of an official proceeding. Nor is the government required to prove that Andersen was successful or likely to succeed in making documents unavailable for that proceeding. It is Andersen's purpose and intent, not the success of its effort, that the government must prove as elements of the charged offense.

The indictment charges the defendant with committing the offense in two different ways. The first is that the defendant sought to withhold a record or a document from an official proceeding. The second is that the defendant sought to alter, destroy, mutilate, or conceal an object with intent to impair the object's availability for use in an official proceeding.

The government does not have to prove both of these methods for you to return a guilty verdict on this charge. Proof beyond a reasonable doubt on one method or the other is enough. But in order to return a guilty verdict, all twelve of you must agree that the same method has been proved. All of you must agree that the government proved, beyond a reasonable doubt that the defendant sought to cause another person to withhold a record or a document from an official proceeding; or all of you must agree that the government proved beyond a reasonable doubt that the defendant sought to cause another person to alter, destroy, mutilate, or conceal an object with intent to impair the object's availability for use in an official proceeding. Of course, you may unanimously agree that the government did or did not prove beyond a reasonable doubt both methods.

It is a crime for anyone to attempt to commit a violation of certain specified laws of the United States. In this case, Andersen is charged with both obstructing an official proceeding and with attempting to do so. You may find Andersen guilty if the government proves beyond a reasonable doubt that Andersen either attempted to obstruct an official proceeding or that it actually did so.

For you to find Andersen guilty of attempting to obstruct an official proceeding, you must be convinced that the government has proved each of the following beyond a reasonable doubt:

First: That Andersen, through its agents, intended to obstruct an official proceeding; and

Second: That Andersen, through its agents, did an act constituting a substantial step toward the commission of that crime that strongly corroborates the defendant's criminal intent.

You will note that the indictment charges that the offense was committed "on or about" a specified date. The law only requires a substantial similarity between the dates charged in the indictment and the proof in the case. Thus, it does not matter if the indictment charges that a specific act occurred on or about a certain date, and the evidence indicates that, in fact, it was on another date. The law only requires substantial similarity between the dates alleged in the indictment and the dates established by testimony or exhibits. Accordingly, the government need only prove beyond a reasonable doubt that the defendant committed the crime on or about and between October 10, 2001 and November 9, 2001—the dates stated in the indictment.

You are here to decide whether the government has proved beyond a reasonable doubt that the defendant is guilty of the crime charged. The defendant is not on trial for any act, conduct, or offense not alleged in the indictment.

If a defendant is found guilty, it is my duty to decide what the punishment will be. You should not be concerned with punishment in any way. It should not enter into your consideration or discussion.

THE VERDICT

To reach a verdict, all of you must agree. Your verdict must be unanimous. Your deliberations will be secret. You will never have to explain your verdict to anyone.

It is your duty to consult with one another and to deliberate in an effort to reach agreement if you can do so. Each of you must decide the case for yourself, but only after an impartial consideration of the evidence in the case with your fellow jurors. In the course of your deliberations, do not hesitate to re-examine your own opinions and change your mind if convinced that you were wrong. But do not give up your honest beliefs as to the weight or effect of the evidence solely because of the opinions of your fellow jurors, or for the mere purpose of returning a verdict.

Remember at all times, you are judges, judges of the facts. Your sole interest is to seek the truth from the evidence in the case, to decide whether the government has proved the accused guilty beyond a reasonable doubt.

When you go to the jury room, the first thing that you should do is select one of your number as your foreman, who will help to guide your deliberations and who will speak for you here in the courtroom. A form of verdict has been prepared for your convenience.

The foreman will write the unanimous answer of the jury in the space provided, either guilty or not guilty, and should date and sign his name on the verdict form.

If you need to communicate with me during your deliberations, the foreman should write the message and give it to the marshal. I will either reply in writing or bring you back into the courtroom to answer your message.

Bear in mind that you are never to reveal to any person, not even to the Court, how the jury stands, numerically or otherwise, until after you have reached a unanimous verdict.

SIGNED at Houston, Texas, thus _____ day of June, 2002.

MELINDA HARMON
UNITED STATES DISTRICT JUDGE

D. The Hotel California Song Introduced into Evidence at the Andersen Trial

The following lyrics were written by Jim Hecker, an Andersen partner.

Hotel Kenneth-Lay-a (based upon the Eagles song, *Hotel California*)

On a sidewalk on Smith street, *Current Text* in my hand
Warm smell of kolaches, aren't Saturdays grand
Up ahead on my schedule nothing else was in sight
My head grew heavy and my hair grew thin
I knew I'd work through the night

Managers in the doorway
Thinking out of the box
And I was thinking to myself
I'll bust my butt and then I'll bust rocks
Then they burned up my schedule
And they threw it away
Then I found out what I thought before
Smith Street was a one-way.

"Welcome to the
HOTEL CAN'T AFFORD YA
Such a gravy train C-A-S or main
Plenty of work at the HOTEL CAN'T RECORD YA
Any time of year, you can charge it here"

Her mind is Black & Scholes twisted
Though her margins are thin
She got a lot of pretty, pretty spread
That she takes in
How we work in the bullpen, no budget sweat
Big hours on the summary, but nothing much net

So I called up the partner
I said, "Please book this entry"
He said, "We haven't had a debit here since 1993"
And still the gurus are calling from far away
Worry wart to the middle of the night
Just to hear them say

"Welcome to the
HOTEL MARK TO MARKET
Such a lovely face
Such a fragile place
They livin' it up at the
HOTEL CRAM IT DOWN YA
When the suits arrive, bring your alibis

Mirrors on the 10-K, makes it look real nice
And she said, We only make disclosures here
Of our own device"
And in the partners' chambers
Cooking up a new deal
Three percent in an S-P-E
But they just can't make it real

Last thing I remember I was running for the doors
I had to find the entries back
To the GAAP we had before
"Relax", said the client
"We are programmed to succeed
You can audit any time you like
But we will never bleed."

A New Role for Lawyers?: The Corporate Counselor After Enron*

*Robert W. Gordon***

Lawyers seem to have played a relatively minor part in the theater of deception and self-dealing that has led to the collapse of Enron Corp. ("Enron") and other corporate titans of the 1990s. The spotlight has been on the grasping managers at the heart of the drama, debased accounting standards and practices, corrupt politicians pressing to abolish or weaken regulations and cripple enforcement, opportunistic investment bankers, conflicted stock analysts, and a credulous business press. But lawyers—both in-house lawyers and outside law firms—were participants in many of the central transactions that ultimately brought about the companies' ruin.

SOME PROBLEMS WITH WHAT LAWYERS DID

A. Non-Disclosure by Technical Disclosure

Securities laws require accurate and transparent financial statements, so that investors can know the financial condition of the company. Enron arranged to borrow money from banks through transactions disguised as sales of real assets.[1] No real assets ever changed hands, nor were they going to; Enron was going to repay the money with interest and cancel the sales. The purpose was to show the debt on the company's books as earnings. Another purpose was to make it possible for Enron to borrow money on the security of assets without relinquishing any control, or any benefits from the pro-

---

* Originally published at 35 CONN. L. REV. 1185 (2003). Reprinted with permission.

** Chancellor Kent Professor of Law and Legal History, Yale University. Thanks to Susan Koniak, Robert Eli Rosen, and William Simon for useful insights for this piece, and to Erin Conroy and Dixie Lee Rodgers for research assistance.

[1] First Interim Report of Neal Batson, Court-Appointed Examiner, U.S. Bankr. Court, S.D.N.Y., *In re* Enron, No. 01-16034 (Bankr. S.D.N.Y. Sept. 21, 2002), at 7 n.26 [hereinafter Batson Report], *available at* http://www.entwistle-law.com/news/institutional/worldcom/rep_enron_exam.htm (last visited Feb. 22, 2003).

ceeds, of those assets.[2] Lawyers wrote opinions certifying the disguised loans as "true sales." Enron moved other debt off of its own books by creating sham transactions with limited-partner-entities. By law, these transactions must be "independent,"—i.e., conform to the (incredibly lax) requirement that a minimum of investors (3%) must be from "outside" the parent firm. In some cases, even the outside investors were invented by Andrew Fastow, Enron's CFO. Lawyers—both inside the company and outside counsel—approved all of these transactions. More generally, lawyers repeatedly facilitated Enron's strategy of structuring dubious transactions so that nobody could understand them, by using language to describe them in proxy and financial statements that, although literally and technically correct, was in practice completely opaque.

B. Approval of Insider Dealings

It is elementary that some of the main abuses that the Securities Acts of 1933 and 1934 were designed to prevent were those of insiders trading on information not available to the public. One of Enron's practices now most sharply challenged was that of offering select groups of rich investors special opportunities, through Enron's off-the-books partnerships, to profit from confidential information not available to ordinary shareholders. What made Enron's offerings possible were rules requiring investment bankers to set up Chinese walls prohibiting disclosure of confidential information. The purpose of those rules is to prevent bankers from profiting on inside information on deals they are financing. Enron used those rules for the reverse purpose, to create investment vehicles giving an information advantage to insiders. Also, since the partnerships were managed by Enron's CFO, and created gross potential conflicts between his roles as general partner and CFO, Enron obtained a waiver of the conflicts from the Enron Board.[3]

C. Facilitating Self-Dealing

Special Purpose Entities ("SPEs") paid enormous sums to managers (again, Enron officers—Fastow's subordinates and designates) for managing them. Fastow personally received over $30 million in management fees from one set of these SPEs.[4] Under Enron's own conflict-of-interest policy, such arrangements had to be approved in advance by the board of directors.[5] SEC rules require that disclosure is required "where practicable" of the amount of compensation being paid to interested parties.[6] Fastow

---

[2] *Id.* at 48.

[3] For a description of these transactions, see Diana B. Henriques & Kurt Eichenwald, *A Fog Over Enron, and the Legal Landscape*, N.Y. TIMES, Jan. 27, 2002, § 3, at 1, col. 3.

[4] William C. Powers, Jr., et al., Report of Investigation by the Special Investigative Committee of the Board of Directors of Enron Corp., at 3 (2002) [hereinafter Powers Report], *available at* http://news.findlaw.com/hdocs/docs/enron/sicreport (last visited Feb. 21, 2003).

[5] *Id.* at 194.

[6] 17 C.F.R. § 229.404 (2000) (codification of SEC Reg. S-K, item 404).

had a "strong desire" to avoid disclosure of his compensation,[7] and, apparently, was accustomed to treating the lawyers as his own personal vassals. The lawyers—in this case, Vinson & Elkins ("V&E")—obliged, by reasoning that, since it was uncertain how much Fastow would eventually earn from all the transactions, Enron did not have to disclose even what he had already earned.[8] In their SEC filings, the lawyers also asserted, as required by law, that these "related-party" transactions were negotiated at "arm's-length" and on "comparable terms" to deals with non-related parties, but apparently the lawyers did not look for any factual support for these assertions, although the deals seemed questionable on their face.[9]

D. The Investigation That Wasn't

Sherron Watkins, a vice president for corporate development at Enron, warned company chairman Kenneth Lay that the company was about to "implode in a wave of accounting scandals" because of dubious accounting by Enron's auditors, Arthur Andersen, for the many limited-partnership investment deals it had used to keep debt off the parent company's books and inflate Enron's earnings.[10] Watkins said that many senior executives had complained loudly about these practices, that the company was "crooked," and that the side deals either had to be undone (if it was not too late to escape detection) or disclosed.[11] She advised the chairman to ask an independent outside law firm to investigate, noting that Enron's regular law firm of V&E should be disqualified because it had signed off (i.e., given "true sale" opinions) on some of the deals and had a conflict of interest.[12] Contrary to her advice, Lay did ask V&E to review the transactions, but to stop short of looking into Andersen's treatment of them. V&E, overlooking its own conflict and the patent contradiction in Lay's instructions to avoid looking at the very source the whistleblower had identified as the cause of the problem, duly reported back that the transactions seemed fine—because Andersen had, after all, approved them. The lawyers interviewed only eight senior executives, each of whom denied knowledge of any problems, and failed to interview any of the lower-level employees who had been identified as people who might provide helpful information.[13] The lawyers then warned that "the bad cosmetics" of the partnerships

---

[7] Powers Report, *supra* note 4, at 187.

[8] *Id.* at 178–208.

[9] *Id.* at 198.

[10] *Text of Letter [by Sherron Watkins] to Enron's Chairman After Departure of Chief Executive*, N.Y. TIMES, Jan. 16, 2002, at C6 (reprinting a letter from Sherron S. Watkins, Enron's vice president of corporate development, to company chairman Kenneth L. Lay, Enron's chairman).

[11] *Id.*

[12] *Id.*

[13] *See* Roger Cramton, *Enron and the Corporate Lawyer: A Primer on Legal and Ethical Issues*, 58 BUSI-NESS LAW, 143, 163–67 (2002), *reprinted in this book at* 571–623.

could result in "a serious risk of adverse publicity and litigation," but concluded with the advice that no further investigation was necessary.[14]

Was there anything illegal or unethical about what these lawyers did? Many scholars who have studied these transactions in detail have argued that there was, that the lawyers' conduct subjects them to potential liability for criminal fraud, civil fraud, and violation of the securities laws. In addition, they could face discipline under state ethical codes for facilitating fraud, or malpractice liability for failing to competently represent their actual clients, the corporate entities.[15] Of course, the lawyers themselves vigorously deny any wrongdoing or ethical lapses, some even going so far as to say they would do it all over again.[16] Even if lawyers did step over any of these lines, however, it is difficult and exceedingly rare to hold corporate lawyers and law firms liable for frauds committed by their clients' managers. According to Susan Koniak, state bars and state prosecutors do not go after corporate law firms; neither do federal prosecutors, except in very rare cases. Even agencies like the SEC rarely try to regulate lawyers.[17] In addition, the Supreme Court and Congress have eviscerated private actions against lawyers for aiding and abetting under the securities laws.[18]

The organized bar is determined to keep things that way. After every wave of business failures resulting from corporate fraud, pressures mount to revise the rules to make lawyers and accountants better monitors—or at least less amiably cooperative enablers—of managers' misconduct. The lawyers and accountants sometimes lose a point or two, but their professional organizations and lobbies usually succeed in thwarting the reforms.[19] As I write, the SEC has just retreated in its efforts to write rules to enforce the Sarbanes-Oxley Act's attempts to reform corporate conduct, by making

---

[14] Jim Yardley & John Schwartz, *Legal Counsel in Many Ways Mirrors Client*, N.Y. TIMES, Jan 16, 2002, at C6.

[15] *See* especially Cramton, *supra* note 13, at 149–52; Susan P. Koniak, *Corporate Fraud: See, Lawyers*, 26 HARV. J.L. & PUB. POL'Y (forthcoming 2003).

[16] *See supra* note 13.

[17] *See* Koniak, *supra* note 15, at 118–31; Richard Painter & Jennifer E. Duggan, *Lawyer Disclosure of Corporate Fraud: Establishing a Firm Foundation*, 50 SMU L. REV. 225, 238–39 (1996).

[18] *See, e.g.*, Private Securities Litigation Reform Act of 1995, Pub. L. No. 104-67, 109 Stat. 757 (codified at 15 U.S.C. § 78t (2000)); Central Bank of Denver v. First Interstate Bank of Denver, 511 U.S. 164, 191 (1994).

[19] One of the most dramatic pre-Enron examples of this pattern of resistance to reforms comes from the organized bar's response to attempts to regulate lawyers of the Office of Thrift Supervision ("OTS"), the federal agency set up to handle the collapse of the savings-and-loan industry in the 1980s. The collapse ended up costing taxpayers around $500 billion. OTS brought actions to hold accountable law firms whose work had helped failing S&Ls conceal the riskiness of federally-insured loans and their precarious financial condition from banking regulators. The organized bar defended the law firms to the hilt and denounced the OTS's attempts to hold them accountable. *See* William H. Simon, *The Kaye Scholer Affair: The Lawyer's Duty of Candor and the Bar's Temptations of Evasion and Apology*, 23 LAW & SOC. INQUIRY 243, 248–49 (1998).

accountants more independent of the companies they audit,[20] and by requiring that lawyers report evidence of possible manager misconduct up the corporate ladder, to the board of directors if necessary.[21] Prior to Sarbanes-Oxley, the corporate bar had long strenuously resisted adding an "up-the-ladder" reporting requirement to its ethics rules; although, in the wake of the Enron scandal, and seeing the writing on the wall, an ABA Task Force actually did recommend this modest but important reform in 2002.[22] In December 2002, the SEC proposed rules that would put teeth into up-the-ladder reporting by requiring lawyers whose client's boards failed to take any action to make a "noisy withdrawal" from representing that client—i.e., to inform the SEC that they were withdrawing for professional reasons.[23] The ABA and many other bar organizations and law firms conducted a saturation bombing attack on the proposed rules and have succeeded, at least for the present, in getting the SEC to suspend the "noisy withdrawal" rule, pending more comments. Even more ominously, they pushed the SEC to rephrase the wording of what lawyers must know or suspect to trigger the new reporting requirements as to threaten to render the requirements meaningless.[24]

It is likely that some of these lawyers engaged in conduct that may expose them to civil liability.[25] Some may even face criminal liability for fraud or obstruction of justice (such as the lawyer who, on the eve of receiving subpoenas from the SEC, sent messages to Arthur Andersen accountants advising them to comply with "document retention policies," which the accountants reasonably interpreted as instructions to destroy documents).[26] Some may have violated state ethics rules; though, if past practice is any guide, no state bar counsel will have the will or resources to pursue such a case. The big problem, as I see it, is not so much that lawyers who actually crossed the line may get away with it. It is that lawyers can assist corporate managers to inflict enormous damage

---

[20] Sarbanes-Oxley Act of 2002, § 307 Pub L. No. 107-204, § 201, 116 Stat. 771 (2002) (to be codified at 15 U.S.C. § 78j-1).

[21] *Id.* § 307 (to be codified at 15 U.S.C. § 7245).

[22] Preliminary Report of ABA Task Force on Corporate Responsibility 26–30 (proposing amendments to ABA Model Rule 1.13), *available at* http://www.abanet.org/buslaw/corporateresponsibility/preliminary_report.pdf (last visited Feb. 5, 2003).

[23] SEC Release No. 8150 (discussing Proposed Rule § 205.3(d) in "Past Material Violations"), *available at* http://www.sec.gov/rules/proposed/33-8150.htm (last visited Feb. 22, 2003).

[24] Press Release, Sec. & Exch. Comm'n, *SEC Adopts Attorney Conduct Rule Under Sarbanes-Oxley Act* (Jan. 23, 2003), *available at* http://www.sec.gov/news/press/2003-13.htm (last visited Feb. 22, 2003) (on file with the *Connecticut Law Review*).

[25] *See* Kurt Eichenwald, *A Higher Standard for Corporate Advice*, N.Y. TIMES, Dec. 23, 2002, at A1 (reporting a recent decision by Judge Melinda Harmon of the federal district court in Houston that held that corporate advisers may be civilly liable to investors as primary participants in a fraud "if they constructed corporate transactions with the knowledge that such deals would mislead investors about a company's finances").

[26] *Excerpts from a House Hearing on Destruction of Enron Documents*, N.Y. TIMES, Jan. 25, 2002, at C8 (statements of Rep. James C. Greenwood and Arthur Andersen official partner Dorsey L. Baskin).

and then argue, often plausibly, that they are only doing the job they are supposed to do. If they are right, might there not be something seriously amiss with the way our profession defines that job?

II. SOME EXCUSES FOR WHAT THE LAWYERS DID

It is clear that the advice both in-house lawyers and outside law firms gave to the managers of Enron and other companies like it was instrumental in enabling those managers to cream off huge profits for themselves while bringing economic ruin to investors, employees, and the taxpaying public. Although the lawyers were not principally responsible for these acts of waste and fraud, their advice was a contributing (and often necessary) cause of those acts. Such fraud could not have been carried out without the lawyers' active approval, passive acquiescence, or failure to inquire and investigate. Nonetheless, not only the lawyers involved, but large numbers of practitioners and bar committees, have few or no regrets about the part they played. They vigorously justify their conduct as consistent with the highest conceptions of legal, ethical, and professional propriety, and just as vigorously resist all attempts to change the legal and ethical rules so as to increase their obligations as gatekeepers and monitors of managers' conduct. This attitude is not universal—there are prominent corporate lawyers who dissent from it, and who think the profession is failing to live up to its responsibilities; but the attitude is pervasive.

How are we to understand why the lawyers acted as they did, and why they are justifying their actions now? Observers from outside the profession (and even some from within the profession) are tempted to say that the lawyers were simply weak and corrupt, or, for those who prefer to talk this way, that the lawyers were rational economic actors. "Bad" lawyers want the client's business, in an intensely competitive market, and so they will wish to approve anything that senior management of the client firm asks, averting their eyes from signs of trouble and their noses from the smell of fish. Asking too many questions and (horrors) refusing to bless a transaction risks losing the client to another firm across town. Demonstrating ingenuity in giving the managers the results they want despite apparent legal obstacles wins praise and repeat business. Sailing close to or even over the line of illegal conduct is not unduly risky, because lawyers who advise on complex transactions for corporate clients almost never face sanctions.

But this is the amoral rational calculator's perspective, and professionals in high-status jobs at respectable blue-chip institutions do not like to think of themselves as amoral maximizers. Like human beings everywhere who want to enjoy self-respect and the esteem of others, they tell stories about how what they do is all right, even admirable.

A. Law as the Enemy: Libertarian Antinomianism

In recent years, many lawyers have taken on the values of, and completely identified with, their business clients, some of whom see law as an enemy or a pesky nuisance.

Such lawyers say things like, "Helping our clients is good because they create wealth, innovation, and jobs; while their adversaries, the people we help them fight, small-minded vindictive bureaucrats and greedy plaintiffs' lawyers, create nothing and destroy innovation and enterprise. We help our clients work around the constraints on their autonomy and wealth-maximizing activities."

I call this the viewpoint of the libertarian antinomian, because it rests on an express contempt for, and disapproval of, law and regulation. Tax law, products liability tort law, drug law, health and safety law, environmental law, employment discrimination law, toxic waste cleanup law, foreign corrupt payments law, SEC disclosure regulation, and the like are all shackles on risk-taking initiative. Such laws interfere with maximizing profits, and anything that does that must be bad. As the chairman of the American Institute of Certified Public Accountants recently put it, "Minimization of taxes maximizes profit for the company. That is a benefit to the company, therefore a benefit to the shareholders."[27] Companies that view law as nothing but a negative drag on profits naturally want professionals to minimize its effects. They are good customers for "creative" and "aggressive" lawyering and accounting services—for example, for the "tax products" (complex and ingenious tax-shelter schemes) that tax specialists from law and accounting firms like to devise and sell to attract clients. The IRS would most likely disapprove of most of these schemes if its agents had the resources and ingenuity to unravel them; but they do not—and even if they did, the savings realized even from illegal schemes exceed the penalties for adopting them.[28]

B. Law as Neutral Constraint: The Lawyer as Risk-Manager

This viewpoint is much like the first, but without the negative normative spin. Adverse legal consequences are not an evil, they are just a fact. In this view, law is simply a source of "risk" to the business firm; it is the lawyers' task to assess and, to the extent possible, reduce that risk. These lawyers do not feel a moral imperative, as libertarians do, to defy or undercut the law; but neither do they feel one to comply with the law.

> [Corporate] [m]anagers have no general obligation to avoid violating regulatory laws, when violations are profitable to the firm. . . . We put to one side laws concerning violence or other acts thought to be *malum in se*. . . . [M]anagers do not have an ethical duty to obey economic regulatory laws just because the laws exist. They must determine the importance of these laws. The penalties Congress names for disobedience are a measure of how much it wants firms to sacrifice in order to adhere to the rules; the idea of

---

[27] William F. Ezzell, *quoted in* Kathleen Day, *SEC Staff Urges Limits to Reforms*, WASH. POST, Jan. 22, 2003, at E1.

[28] Joseph Bankman, *The New Market in Corporate Tax Shelters*, TAX NOTES, June 21, 1999, at 1775.

optimal sanctions is based on the supposition that managers not only may but also should violate the rules when it is profitable to do so.[29]

This quotation restates what Holmes called the "bad man's" view of legal rules as prices discounted by sanctions—or, to reduce it still further, by the probability of enforcement of sanctions. The outputs of law in the regulatory state are not norms that express views of right conduct or desirable states of the world, but simply tariffs on conduct. The lawyer objectively assesses the risks, then games the rules to work around the constraints and lower the tariffs as much as possible. If some constraints are unavoidable he "not only may but should" advise breaking the rules and paying the penalty if the client can still make a profit.

These two story lines were not available in the case of Enron, for the obvious reasons that managers were looting the companies for their own benefit while concealing debts and losses from workers and investors. When the lawyers and accountants outwitted the pesky regulators—who, had they known what was happening, might have put a stop to it—they were not helping heroic outlaws add value to the economy and society by defying timid convention, but enabling, if not abetting, frauds and thieves. Nor were the professionals objectively, if amorally, assessing risks and weighing benefits against costs of efficient breach. It seems not to have occurred to them that outsiders might find out that the many-sided transactions with special entities were not actually earning any real returns, but merely concealing debts and losses, and that when that happened, Enron's stock price would tumble, and with it, all the houses of cards secured by that stock. The company they advised is now facing at least seventy-seven lawsuits as a result of its conduct. At best, the lawyers were closing their eyes to the risk of disaster; at worst, they were helping to bring it on.

The lawyers have been relying instead on different stories, somewhat in conflict with one another.

C. "We Din' Know Nothin'": The Lawyer as Myopic or Limited-Function Bureaucrat

These are claims that the lawyers were not at fault because their role was limited: We didn't know, we weren't informed;[30] the accountants said the numbers were okay;[31]

---

[29] Frank H. Easterbrook & Daniel R. Fischel, *Antitrust Suits by Targets of Tender Offers*, 80 MICH. L. REV. 1155, 1168 n.36, 1177 n.57 (1982). For an exceptionally penetrating critique of this view of law, see Cynthia A. Williams, *Corporate Compliance with the Law in the Era of Efficiency*, 76 N.C. L. REV. 1265, 1385 (1998) (asserting that the "law-as-price" theory weakens social and political relationships through its subjugation of the moral component of law in favor of an exclusively economic construction).

[30] This was the position taken by most of the Enron in-house and outside counsel, like Jordan Mintz, Vice President and General Counsel for Corporate Development at Enron Corp., who testified before a House subcommittee investigating the role of lawyers in the Enron collapse. *See* THE FINANCIAL COLLAPSE OF ENRON—PART 2: HEARING BEFORE THE SUBCOMM. ON OVERSIGHT AND INVESTIGATIONS OF THE HOUSE COMM. ON ENERGY AND COMMERCE, 107th Cong. 36, 42–43, 45, 73, 77, 82, 85 (2002).

[31] *Id.* at 42–43.

management made the decisions;[32] our representation was restricted to problems on the face of the documents or to information submitted to us.

Many of these claims of innocent ignorance now look pretty dubious. Some of the outside law firms, such as V&E and Andrews & Kurth, in fact worked closely with Andersen accountants in structuring many of the transactions. Sometimes, lawyers made notes that they needed further information or managers' or the board's approval to certify a deal, but they signed opinions and proxy statements even if they never got the needed information or requisite approval. Sometimes they expressed doubts about the deals. An in-house lawyer, Jordan Mintz, once even hired an outside law firm to look more closely into some of Fastow's deals. Ronald Astin of V&E repeatedly objected to some of Fastow's deals, saying they posed conflicts or weren't in Enron's best interests; but when Fastow persisted, Astin expressed unease to in-house attorneys or executives but not to the board. Moreover, in V&E's report on the whistleblower Watkins's allegations, Astin minimized suspected problems. In the end, the doubting lawyers never pressed the issues.[33]

Some of their claims of limited knowledge are plausible, however, because Enron never trusted any one set of lawyers with extensive information about its operations— it spread legal work out to over 100 law firms. If one firm balked at approving a deal, as V&E occasionally did, Enron managers would go across town to another, more compliant firm, such as Andrews & Kurth.[34] Even Enron's General Counsel, James Derrick, had no means of controlling or supervising all of the legal advice that the company was receiving, because the different divisions all had their own lawyers and outside firms. It is this layering of authority, fragmentation of responsibility, and decentralization that has made it possible for the chairman, CEO, and board of directors of Enron, as well as the lawyers, to claim that they did not know much about what was going on in their own company. One question for lawyers—as well as for senior managers and board members—is whether they can conscientiously and ethically do their jobs and exercise their functions as fiduciaries in organizations structured so as to diffuse responsibility and prevent their access to the big picture.

D. The Lawyer as Advocate

The classic defense of the corporate lawyer's role, both most often advanced and held in reserve if other defenses fail, is of course that we are advocates, whose primary duty is the zealous representation of clients. We are not like auditors, who have duties to the public; our duties are only to our clients. Our job is to help them pursue their interests and put the best construction on their conduct that the law and facts will

---

[32] *Id.* at 42–43, 45, 48, 50, 58.

[33] The transactions were detailed in two fine journalistic analyses of the Enron lawyers' role. *See* Mike France, *What About the Lawyers?*, BUS. WK., Dec. 23, 2002, at 58; Ellen Joan Pollock, *Limited Partners: Lawyers for Enron Faulted Its Deals, Didn't Force Issue*, WALL ST. J., May 22, 2002, at A1.

[34] *See* Pollock, *supra* note 33.

support without intolerable strain, so as to enable them to pursue any arguably legal ends by any arguably legal means. The paradigmatic exercise of the adversary-advocate's role is the criminal defense lawyer's; and the role is a noble role, both because it furthers the client's freedom of action and protects his rights against an overbearing state, and because it facilitates the proper determination of his claims and defenses.

For the advocate, the law is a medium of action and discursive moves, an arsenal of procedures, and a field of argumentation and negotiation. Ultimate responsibility for determining the facts and interpreting the law rests with other actors and institutions: the authoritative decision-makers, especially the courts. The lawyer does not look for truth or justice, although, of course, to play his role he needs to know what courts are likely to say, and how far he can get them to see the facts and bend the rules his client's way. As one of Enron's tax advisors put it recently, speaking of the company's complex tax-avoidance transactions, "The government is not going to like these deals. People can disagree on what works within the written rules. . . . If you know the rules you don't have to break the rules, you just use them. That's what lawyers and accountants do."[35] The lawyer is a specialist playing a differentiated role in an overall process (the adversary system) that will, if it functions property, approximate (we hope) truth and justice in the aggregate.

The advocate is subtly different from the other lawyer-types I have mentioned. Unlike the antinomian and the neutral risk-assessor, the advocate is not hostile or indifferent to law. Law, to the advocate, is binding if the rules and facts are clear and there is no plausible basis for spinning them. To put this another way, the advocate is loyal to the law seen as the outer boundaries of the arguably legal, the point beyond which facts and law can no longer be stretched. He will push up to the boundaries, and even to creative plausible extensions of the boundaries, but not beyond. And unlike the myopic bureaucrat, the advocate wants to know everything relevant to representing the client.

What is less clear and more debated about the corporate lawyer-as-advocate is whether he has any obligation to try to induce his clients to comply with the law. It is clear that the lawyer may not actively help clients engage in what he knows to be a crime or a fraud. It is not at all clear what steps lawyers should take to prevent the client's misbehavior, to encourage the client to walk in the paths of legality, or to respond if the client strays off the paths. Most state ethics codes impose stricter requirements on lawyers than do the ABA's Model Rules—they say that lawyers who become aware of fraud, especially if it has been accomplished through lawyers' efforts, must try to get clients to correct the wrong, and that if the client does not comply, the lawyer may or must withdraw and, often, also disaffirm any documents that he has helped to prepare; and if serious (physical, or sometimes merely financial) harm is

---

[35] Peter Behr & Carrie Johnson, *Enron Probe Now Focuses on Tax Deals*, WASH. POST, Jan. 21, 2003, at E1 (quoting Robert J. Hermann).

likely to result, the lawyer may or must disclose that impending harm to relevant parties or authorities.[36]

In the post-Enron debates—as in the wake of past corporate scandals—the view of the lawyer-as-advocate has most often been invoked to resist rule-changes that would give corporate lawyers positive obligations as monitors or gatekeepers of the legality of corporate conduct, especially by requiring them to report, if all else fails, managers' violations of law to authorities. Law firms and bar associations almost always take the position that such reporting requirements would turn lawyers into "cops," "snitches," or "informers," and thus pervert their function as confidential advisors and advocates.[37] If clients do not trust their lawyers, they will not be candid and forthcoming with the information that the lawyers need to do their job.

But what is their job? One view is that the lawyer needs the information simply so that he can present the best case for his client as an effective adversary-advocate, so as not to be sandbagged by prosecutors, regulators, or other adversaries who know more than he does and so that he can have access to facts more exculpatory than the client may suspect. But another view—which one hears just as often, or more so, from the corporate bar—is that the lawyer needs his client's trust so that he can learn about possibly illegal plans and take steps to stop them.[38] The argument for confidentiality here recognizes that one of the lawyer's functions is to monitor compliance and head off wrongdoing—not just to put the best face on things if the client goes ahead and breaks the law. This function is (weakly) recognized in the Comments to the ABA's Model Rules of Professional Conduct:

> The lawyer is part of a judicial system charged with upholding the law. One of the lawyer's functions is to advise clients so that they avoid any violation of the law in the proper exercise of their rights. . . . Almost without exception, clients come to lawyers in order to determine what their rights are and what is, in the maze of laws and regulations, deemed to be legal and correct. . . . Based upon experience, lawyers know that almost all clients follow the advice given, and the law is upheld.[39]

---

[36] *See, e.g.*, MODEL RULES OF PROF'L CONDUCT R. 1.6(b) (2003) (stating that "a lawyer may reveal [confidential] information . . . to the extent the lawyer reasonably believes necessary"); CONN. RULES OF PROF'L CONDUCT R. 1.6(b) (2003) (stating that "a lawyer shall reveal such information to the extent the lawyer reasonably believes necessary").

[37] For a rich sample of such arguments (some of them invoking the inspiring example of John Adams acting as counsel to the British soldiers who fired on the local crowd in the Boston Massacre), see the great majority of comments on the SEC's proposed "noisy withdrawal" rules regulating attorneys. Sec. & Exch. Comm'n, *Comments on Proposed Rule: Implementation of Standards of Professional Conduct for Attorneys, available at* http://www.sec.gov/rules/proposed/s74502.shtml (last visited Feb. 4, 2003).

[38] *See id.* (commenting on the need for confidentiality).

[39] MODEL RULES OF PROF'L CONDUCT R. 1.6 cmt. 1, 3 (1983) (requiring the confidentiality of information).

This Comment and the policy arguments against allowing lawyers to breach client confidences seem, however, to be among the few contexts in which the bar officially recognizes some sort of duty of lawyers to advise compliance with the law. The bar does not prescribe giving such advice as a duty, or suggest any sanction for failing to provide it. It fiercely resists attempts by legislatures or regulators to impose any such obligations:

> Efforts by the government to impose responsibility upon lawyers to assure the quality of their clients' compliance with the law or to compel lawyers to give advice resolving all doubts in favor of regulatory restrictions would evoke serious and far-reaching disruption in the role of lawyer as counselor, which would be detrimental to the public, clients and the legal profession.[40]

And the bar does not help at all to clarify what would seem to be the crucial issue, which is what view of "the law," or "the bounds of the law," the zealous advocate should take when giving a client legal advice about a prospective course of action. Should "the law" in this context be the same as the "law" in adversary proceedings charging the client with misconduct, i.e., a construction of the applicable legal regime as any arguably legal, even if strained, interpretation of facts and law that favors the client? The strong advocacy view of the lawyer's role says, yes: In advising the client, the lawyer may look forward to the defenses of the client's conduct that an advocate might raise in future adversary proceedings (i.e., a regulatory action, criminal prosecution, or civil lawsuit) down the road. As long as those defenses of the conduct are colorable, the lawyer-advocate may properly advise the client to engage in the conduct. Of course, if the client is likely to lose despite the availability of a colorable defense, the lawyer as neutral risk-assessor must also inform the client of that risk.

III. INADEQUACY OF THE EXCUSES

The Enron and similar scandals illustrate the limits of all these standard stories as adequate accounts of the corporate lawyer's proper role.

Despite their increasing popularity among practicing and some academic lawyers, the profession surely has to reject out of hand libertarian-antinomian and neutral-risk-assessment theories of its appropriate role and ethics. Both construe the client's interests and autonomously-chosen goals as supreme goods, and law as a set of obstacles that the lawyer helps to clear out of the way. The antinomian ranges the lawyer alongside his client as an opponent of law, someone who sees law as merely an imposition and a nuisance. The lawyer as risk-assessor also views legal norms, rules, institutions,

---

[40] Donald J. Evans et al., *Statement of Policy Adopted by the American Bar Association Regarding Responsibilities and Liabilities of Lawyers in Advising with Respect to the Compliance by Clients with Laws Administered by the Securities and Exchange Commission*, 31 BUS. LAW. 543, 545 (1975).

and procedures in a wholly alienated fashion from the outside, as a source of opportunity and risk to his client.

Some might dispute whether even ordinary citizens of a liberal-democratic republic may, consistent with their enjoyment of its privileges and protections, legitimately adopt such a hostile or alienated attitude toward its laws. People who participate in self-rule through the representatives they elect—constrained by the constitutional limits their ancestors have adopted in conventions or by amendments—and whose lives are mostly benefited from the restraints law puts on private predation and public oppression, should generally internalize the norms and purposes of their legal system and voluntarily respect and obey even the laws they do not particularly like.[41]

Others might reply that so long as they outwardly conform to its commands, citizens may adopt whatever attitude toward law they please. This response comes from our admirable liberal respect for individual dignity and autonomy, and consequent reluctance to coerce the inner souls of the unwilling. Fair enough; but the pragmatic limits of this position derive from the sociological fact that, unless people in fact internalize the norms and respect the general obligation to obey the law, they will tend to violate it when they can get away with it. That is a recipe for anarchy, because all law depends on voluntary compliance, on my willingness to keep my hands off of your property even when nobody can see me stealing it, and to report my taxable income honestly even though I know only 1% of returns are audited. Societies whose leaders and institutions have conditioned their members into contempt for law and its norms and its purposes are plagued by theft, fraud, crime, unenforceable contracts, uncollectible taxes, valueless currencies, and general civil strife. Evidently, this does not mean that society will fall apart unless everyone feels that he must obey every law all the time. In all societies, people obey some laws instinctually, some willingly, and others grudgingly; and they ignore or routinely violate others that they think do not matter all that much.[42] But a general disposition in most people to respect the laws and the purposes behind them really does seem to be a precondition to peaceful, prosperous, cooperative, and orderly social life, which is why good societies put a lot of effort into socializing their citizens into dispositions of general law-abidingness.

However one comes out on this broader argument does not, it seems to me, really much affect the question at issue here: Whether lawyers representing *public corporations* may confront the legal system as alienated outsiders, determined to work around the law and minimize its effects to the extent that the law gets in the way of the client's

---

[41] To be sure, the obligations to internalize, respect, and obey the law less convincingly bind groups who have been left out of the legal system's privileges and protections, such as African-Americans in the South in the ages of slavery and Jim Crow; or pariahs, dissenters, and the poor, whose main experience of law is as imposition rather than protection. Such groups may legitimately feel a privilege to defy and dishonor laws that they have had no share in making and whose purpose is to subordinate them.

[42] This is the subject of an enormous amount of literature. For a general treatment, see TOM R. TYLER, WHY PEOPLE OBEY THE LAW (1990).

projects. To this proposition, the right answer ought to be, unequivocally, no. I will discuss first the corporate clients, then their lawyers.

People who defend corporations' taking a "bad man's" approach to law sometimes seem to suggest that business entities should have special privileges—more leeway than individual persons—to game and evade regulations they do not like, because, as engines of growth, job-creation, innovation, and shareholder wealth, they are heroic actors on the social scene, a breed of Nietzschean supermen, beyond good and evil. The taxes, regulations, and liabilities that government pygmies and plaintiffs' lawyers keep trying to impose on them, on the other hand, are often foolish and inefficient, the product of ignorant populism or envy or special-interest rent-seeking. This attitude plays well in boom periods, but it sounds a lot less convincing when defrauded and impoverished employees and investors are licking the wounds from their losses and looking to more, not less, regulation to protect them in the future. Anyway, it is basically an incoherent position. A strong state and effective legal system are preconditions, not obstructions, to successful capitalism—preconditions capable of legislating and enforcing an adequate infrastructure of ground-rules creating stable currencies, defining and enforcing property rights, contracts, and rules for the transparent and fair operation of markets, and deterring frauds, thefts, torts, discrimination, abuses of labor and harms to competition, health, safety, and the environment.

Of course, the laws in force are not always those businesses would prefer, nor are all regulations anywhere near optimally efficient. But though businessmen running large public corporations love to grumble about the SEC, the EPA, and OSHA—and products-liability class-action suits—they are hardly in a position to claim that they are like Jim Crow southern blacks, or vagrants picked up and accused of crimes: powerless outcasts and victims. Big American business firms are not discrete and insular minorities. They have exceptional access to influence in legislatures, administrative agencies, and the courts through government advisory commissions, trade associations, lobbies, and lawyers.

Indeed, it is precisely because of their exceptional power to collectivize and command resources and employees, and to influence governments, that American legal tradition and popular opinion have usually concluded that corporations need to be more, and not less, constrained by law than ordinary citizens. If corporations cheat on or evade their taxes, the treasury loses billions; if corporations bribe politicians or officials, whole governments may be corrupted; and if corporations ignore environmental restraints, entire ecosystems may be wiped out. When it became clear that the financial statements of Enron, WorldCom, Tyco, Adelphia, and Global Crossing could no longer be trusted, investors fled the markets en masse.

It may be that a natural person cannot be compelled to internalize the values promoted by law, or to feel an obligation to obey the law, without violating his or her dignity or freedom of conscience. But a company has no soul to coerce, dignity to offend, or natural freedom to restrain. Nor can it be schooled by parents, educators, and peers into a general disposition toward sociability or law-abidingness. It can only have the character that its managers, contracts, and organizational incentives and the legal system build into it. It is a creature of law made to serve limited social purposes. Since we are free to construct the character of these artificial persons, we should construct them for legal purposes as good citizens, persons who have internalized the public values expressed in law and the obligation to obey even laws they do not like, for the sake of the privileges of the law, which generally benefits them as well as the rest of us.

Nothing in this conception prevents the good corporate citizen from challenging taxes and laws he thinks are unfairly or improperly applied to him; or trying to change them through political action. But it does foreclose the amoralist's argument, that the corporation should be free to ignore, subvert, or nullify the laws because the value it contributes to society justifies its obeying the higher-law imperatives of profit-seeking and shareholder-wealth-creation. If the artificial person is constructed as a good and law-abiding person, it follows that the manager who ignores or tries to nullify the valid objectives of law and regulation is not acting as a responsible or faithful agent of his principal, the good corporate citizen.

If the corporation should be constructed and presumed to have the interests of a good, law-respecting, citizen, so should its lawyers (even more so). Lawyers are not simply agents of clients—they are also licensed fiduciaries of the legal system, "part of a judicial system charged with upholding the law," to use the ABA's words.[43] They do not have, as the dissenting citizen does, the option of taking up a position outside the legal order, rejecting the norms and public purposes of the legal system and limiting themselves to a grudging and alienated outward compliance with such of its rules as they think they cannot safely or profitably violate when their interest or inclination is to do so.[44] The lawyer is, by vocation, committed to the law.[45]

Now, of course, the "norms and purposes and public values" of law are not something fixed and definite and certain; rather, they are contested and dynamic and alterable—by, among other people, corporate clients and their lawyers. But there is a difference between trying to game and manipulate a system as a resistance movement or alienated outsider would, and to engage in a committed and good faith struggle within the system to influence it to fulfill what a good faith interpreter would construe as its best values and purposes.

Applying these general standards to many of the Enron transactions seems in some ways pretty simple. The purpose of the securities laws is to make public companies' financial condition transparent to investors. Agents of Enron had an interest in making

---

[43] MODEL RULES OF PROF'L CONDUCT R. 1.6 cmt. 1 (1983).

[44] Again, I would partially except lawyers for the excluded, marginalized, and disinherited, who ought to have exceptional latitude to help their clients resist the imposition of unjust laws.

[45] For an interesting debate on this issue, see William H. Simon, *Should Lawyers Obey the Law?*, 38 WM. & MARY L. REV. 217 (1996) (noting that whether lawyers should obey the law turns on what is meant by the law); David B. Wilkins, *In Defense of Law and Morality: Why Lawyers Should Have a Prima Facie Duty to Obey the Law*, 38 WM. & MARY L. REV. 269 (1996).

their finances opaque, in order to boost the stock price of the company and with it their compensation in options, and to conceal the management fees they were paying themselves. They asked lawyers to manipulate the rules so that they would appear to be disclosing without actually disclosing. The lawyers obliged—and by so doing effectively thwarted the valid purposes of the laws.

How about the claims that the lawyers did not know the extent of the company's misrepresentations and frauds, relied on information given them by accountants or managers, saw only small pieces of the puzzle, and took on assignments validly narrowed and specialized in scope? These claims would really have to be analyzed in detail, case by case, to see if they are any good; and I do not find many of them very convincing—for example, the arguments of V&E that the firm acted reasonably in: (1) accepting the assignment to investigate Sherron Watkins's complaints, notwithstanding the firm's involvement in some of the complained-of deals; (2) accepting the limits excluding the accounting issues from the firm's inquiry, although that was where Watkins had located the problem; (3) failing to interview any but a handful of top managers, accepting without question the denials of those managers that anything was wrong, failing to follow up further leads; and (4) above all, given the limited scope of their own inquiry, concluding that no further investigation was necessary.[46] But I would make some general points about these claims.

One point is that, although lawyers may take on an assignment that limits the scope of their representation or asks them to accept some facts as given, they may not agree to such limits as will preclude them from competent and ethical representation. They should not, for example, agree to write an opinion certifying the legality of a deal to third parties if they have some reason to be suspicious of the facts or numbers reported to them, without first doing some digging to ensure that the facts are accurate. Nor should they give assurances that certain facts are true if they have no independent means of verifying them.[47] If the client's agents are given unrestricted discretion to limit the scope of the lawyer's work, it becomes all too easy for them to use lawyers to paint a gloss of respectability (sprinkle holy water, as it were) on dubious transactions. Lawyers like to say that they have to assume and hope that their clients are not lying to them. But they should not passively cooperate in a corporate strategy to attach a respectable law firm's name to a scam, even if they are not dead certain that it is a scam.

More generally, the ways in which many corporations structure their legal services operate to prevent their receiving appropriately independent law-respecting advice.

---

[46] See Cramton, *supra* note 13, at 162–67, for a particularly astute dissection of V&E's investigation; *see also* Wilkins, *supra* note 45.

[47] See Comm. on Legal Opinions, *Third Party Legal Opinion Report, Including the Legal Opinion Accord, of the Section of Business Law, American Bar Association*, 47 BUS. LAW. 167, 190 (1991) (reporting the "Silverado Accord"). The Silverado Accord "prohibit[s] such practices as rendering a literally accurate opinion on the basis of dubious factual assumptions or in circumstances where the opinion could further an illegal or fraudulent objective." Richard W. Painter, *Rules Lawyers Play By*, 76 N.Y.U. L. REV. 665, 718 (2001).

The practice of spreading fragments of business around to different outside firms, and different lawyers' offices within the company, makes it easy for managers to shop around for compliant lawyers, thus inducing races to the bottom, in which law firms or in-house counsel determined to give independent and conservative advice either lose out to their cross-town rivals or gradually acquiesce in the corrosion of their standards. That practice of "spreading the wealth around" also eliminates responsibility, since no one set of lawyers ever knows enough about the business decisions to know the likely purpose or effect of their advice, and how their advice fits into the company's plans as a whole. If you believe the testimony of Enron's general counsel and principal outside law firm partners, for example, their ignorance of what their client's senior managers were up to is astonishing. Enron also relied extensively on cut-outs: Its outside lawyers "interfaced" with and reported to in-house lawyers; as did in-house legal staff with other in-house lawyers. The lawyers could not sit down with managers and directly press them for information about the purposes and underlying facts of the transactions they were being asked to bless. And, for the most part, they did not try to do so.

Big companies used to have a single outside law firm on which they would rely for most of their legal advice. The firm's senior partners were personally close to the company CEO and senior managers. At its best (which may overly romanticize the practice), the system allowed lawyers to learn the business they were advising and, since they were not easily replaced, to give independent and critical advice. When, in the 1970s, companies began to move most of their legal business in-house—using outside firms only for specialized business and making those firms compete for their business—some established high-powered general counsel's offices (inside law firms, in effect), also with close ties to the CEO, to provide independent advice.[48] But in recent years, as Robert Rosen's recent research shows, the replacement systems in many companies have fallen apart. Lawyers are scattered over and outside the organization, usually working as legal consultants to project teams, providing legal risk analysis. There is no entity inside or outside the organization with the overall knowledge and prestige to give independent advice. In fact, independent advice is not valued—only occasionally is the appearance of independent advice.[49]

---

[48] *See generally*, Ronald J. Gilson, *The Devolution of the Legal Profession: A Demand Side Perspective*, 49 MD. L. REV. 869 (1990) (arguing that professional standards serve to cast lawyers in the role of enforcers, reducing information asymmetry and changing the nature of the relationship between client and counsel); Robert Eli Rosen, *The Inside Counsel Movement, Professional Judgment and Organizational Representation*, 64 IND. L.J. 479 (1989) (exploring inside counsel's "newfound success" and addressing the question of whether the legal profession should limit the corporate power lawyers may have).

[49] *See* Robert Eli Rosen, *"We're All Consultants Now": How Change in Client Organizational Strategies Influences Change in the Organization of Corporate Legal Services*, 44 ARIZ. L. REV. 637 (2002) (examining the ways in which the corporate bar has changed how companies use lawyers, and mapping out a possible future for corporate legal services); *see also* Robert Eli Rosen, *Risk Management and Corporate Governance: The Case of Enron*, 35 CONN. L. REV. 1157 (2003).

The pervasiveness of lawyers' "we din' know nothin'" defenses to critiques of what went wrong at Enron has to make one skeptical about another set of lawyers' claims. As mentioned earlier, lawyers resist all proposals for changes in the rules requiring them to disclose client wrongdoing, if clients persist in it, by saying that their advocate-adviser's role depends on a free flow of information from their clients, which in turn depends on the lawyers' being able to give an absolute assurance of confidentiality. The Enron lawyers, however, seemed mostly content with a system structured so that they were given very limited information and assignments of very limited scope, because the managers were determined to disclose as little as possible about their questionable transactions. If the lawyers had questions about some of the deals, they were discouraged from probing for answers, and by and large they did not try. Joseph Dilg, the lead V&E partner acting for Enron, told an investigating congressional committee that:

> With regard to the related party transactions, it is important to consider the role of legal counsel. If a transaction is not illegal and has been approved by the appropriate levels of corporation's management, lawyers, whether inside corporate counsel or with an outside firm, may appropriately provide the requisite legal advice and opinions about legal issues relating to the transactions.
>
> In doing so, the lawyers are not approving of the business decisions that were made by their clients. Likewise, lawyers are not passing on the accounting treatment of the transactions.[50]

The problem with this formulation is that whether a transaction is legal, or even "not illegal," depends on underlying facts. If a deal between Enron and one of its many special-purpose entities is to be reported as a "true sale," it must, in economic substance, actually have the characteristics of a sale. In analyzing such deals, courts put substance over form, disregarding the labels the parties have put on the transaction, and disregarding the accounting treatment they have given it.[51] The documents that Enron lawyers were given, however, on their face seemed to indicate that the deals were loans so thinly disguised as sales that, as the Bankruptcy Examiner has put it, "the *only* common characteristics in most of the Selected Transactions that support a sale characterization are the express terms of the documents that, among other things, state that the relevant transfers are sales, and that in some cases Enron accounted for most of these transactions as sales."[52]

These would seem to be situations in which legal and ethical rules—giving lawyers a duty to ascertain relevant facts, and a duty to refuse approval, where their approval is necessary, if those facts are not forthcoming—would be much more effective in induc-

---

[50] *Hearing, supra* note 16, at 20 (testimony of Joseph C. Dilg).

[51] Batson Report, *supra* note 1, at 41–42.

[52] *Id.* at 50–51 (emphasis added).

ing client candor than rules prohibiting disclosure of information that the client does not want to disclose and the lawyer finds it more convenient not to know.

The most important lessons of Enron, et al., for lawyers are the additional clouds of doubt they cast on the most common defense of the corporate lawyer's role, and the one most often invoked by the profession in the current debates over reform. That is the corporate lawyer as adversary-advocate. The usual way in which this role is framed is that the lawyer's loyalty runs to the client and only to the client. The lawyer must help the client realize its goals and desires, recognizing as hard limits only such legal constraints, the "bounds of the law," as the most ingenious interpretations he can construct of fact and law that are most favorable to his client's position. Even if the lawyer is advising the client not in an adversary proceeding, but in an office, and with respect to future rather than past conduct, the lawyer is entitled to make use of any colorable justification for the client's conduct that he could use to defend it in future adversary proceedings, however unlikely such proceedings may be.[53] Of course, the lawyer must advise the client of the risks of adventurous interpretations of law and fact, that decision-makers (if they ever find out) may not accept them and will find the client in violation of the law. But if the client is willing to take the risks, the lawyer may ethically assist the client beyond the merely conventional limits, all the way up to the arguable limits, exploiting all conceivable loopholes and ambiguities of the existing law.

This idea that the role of the corporate lawyer is really just like the role of the criminal defense lawyer has been criticized so often and so effectively that it always surprises me to see the idea still walking around, hale and hearty, as if nobody had ever laid a glove on it. I will quickly run through some of the strong objections to the analogy and then add another objection: The bar's standard construction of the corporate lawyer's role is deficient in part because it does not take the analogy seriously enough.

The most obvious objection is that legal advice given outside of adversary proceedings is not subject to any of the constraints of such proceedings. The reasons that the lawyer is given so much latitude to fight for his client in court is that the proceedings are open and public, effective mechanisms such as compelled discovery and testimony exist to bring to light suppressed inconvenient facts and make them known to adversaries and adjudicators, adversaries are present to challenge the advocate's arguments of law and his witnesses' and documents' view of facts, and there is an impartial umpire or judge to rule on the evidence's sufficiency and validity. Absent any of these bothersome conditions, lawyers can stretch the rules and facts very extravagantly in their clients' favor without risking contradiction by adversaries or the annoyed reactions of judges or regulators to far-fetched positions.

---

[53] For a nice account with many examples of this projection-back into office advice of arguable claims in hypothetical future adversary proceedings, see Bruce A. Green, *Thoughts About Corporate Lawyers After Reading The Cigarette Papers: Has the "Wise Counselor" Given Way to the "Hired Gun"?*, 51 DePaul L. Rev. 407, 422–24 (2001).

In the trial setting, aggressive advocacy (at least in theory) supposedly operates to bring out the truth, by testing one-sided proof and argument against counter-proof and counter-argument. Ideally, aggressive advocacy facilitates decisions of the legal validity of the parties' claims on the merits. Outside of such settings, one-sided advocacy is more likely to help parties overstep the line to violate the law, and to do so in such ways as are likely to evade detection and sanction, and thus frustrate the purposes of law and regulation.

Look at Enron for obvious examples. The legal system prescribes many rules calling for transparency of corporate activities: Disclosure of a company's financial condition to securities markets; disclosure to the IRS of the economic purpose and substance of tax-shelter schemes; and disclosure for potential bankruptcy purposes of whether assets have been actually transferred from one entity to another, so that they may properly be considered as part of the transferor's or transferee's estate. Corporations in short are, for many legal purposes, supposed to disclose material facts about their financial situations. The Enron lawyers apparently treated this injunction as: Corporations may actually conceal material facts so long as we help them do it in such a way that we can later argue that, technically, they did disclose in the sense of meeting the literal requirements of disclosure laws. The purpose of their advice was to facilitate effective non-disclosure under a cover of arguably lawful action. The lawyers looked forward to a hypothetical role as counsel in adversary proceedings and the arguments they would make in that role. But the main object and real point of the help they gave to clients was to prevent anyone from ever finding out what the client was actually doing, and a fig leaf of cover in case anyone ever did find out and challenge the non-disclosure disclosures.

The advocacy ideology regularly and persistently confuses the managers, who ask for lawyers' advice, with the lawyers' actual client, the corporate entity. Admittedly, much corporate-law doctrine makes this easy for them because corporate law doctrine is excessively permissive in allowing lawyers to treat the incumbent managers who consult them as the embodiment of the entity.[54] At least until the adoption last year of the Sarbanes-Oxley's Act's "up the ladder" reporting requirement, the bar's ethical rules also facilitated this conflation of the corporate client with management, by waffling over whether a corporate counsel who becomes aware that a corporate agent has engaged in conduct that is a "violation of law" and is "likely to result in substantial injury to the organization" must report the misconduct up to or, if necessary, even beyond the board of directors.[55] But the general principle is clear: A corporate agent acting unlawfully no longer represents the corporation, and the corporation's lawyer therefore owes him no loyalty, and no duty of zealous representation.[56] On the contrary, if

---

[54] *See* William H. Simon, *Whom (Or What) Does the Organization's Lawyer Represent?: An Anatomy of Intraclient Conflict*, 91 CAL. L. REV. 57, 65 (2003) (noting that courts "conflat[e] the interests of the corporation with those of incumbent management").

[55] MODEL RULES OF PROF'L CONDUCT R. 1.13 & cmt. (2003).

[56] *Id.*

the agent's illegal acts are harming the actual client, the lawyer should not help him out at all.[57] And that, obviously, is a huge difference between representing a company and representing the criminally accused.

The point I want to add to these standard, but valuable, points is a simple one. Corporate lawyers could actually learn something useful from the role of the criminal defense lawyer. And that is that the adversary-advocate's role—like that of all lawyers—is in large part a public role, designed to fulfill public purposes: The ascertainment of truth and the doing of justice; the protection of the autonomy, dignity, and rights of witnesses and especially of the accused; and the monitoring and disciplining of police and prosecutorial conduct. The defense lawyer is not merely or even mostly a private agent of his client, whose function is to zealously further the client's interest (which is usually to evade just punishment for his past conduct or to continue to engage in such bad behavior in the future). The criminal defense lawyer is assigned a specialized role in a public process in which his zealous advocacy is instrumental to the service of various public objectives. He is encouraged to make the best possible arguments for suppressing unlawfully seized evidence, not for the purpose of furthering his client's interest in freedom or getting away with crimes, but to protect third parties who are not his clients, i.e., other citizens whose freedom and security will be put at risk unless police misconduct is deterred. He is allowed to present a very one-sided, partial, and selective version of the evidence favoring the defense, in part because resourceful adversaries can poke holes in his story and present a counter-story, but even more to fulfill a public purpose—that of keeping prosecutors up to the mark, making sure they know that they have to put together a defense-proof case, deterring them from indicting where they do not have the evidence. Defense counsel's zeal is restricted precisely at the points where it might help the client at the risk of damage to the performance of his public functions and the integrity of the procedural framework that those functions are designed to serve. He may not, for example, lie to judges, suppress or manufacture real evidence, pose questions on cross-examination that he has no basis in fact for asking, or suborn or knowingly put on perjured testimony.

If you extend this analysis of the public functions of the defense bar to the corporate bar, what might you conclude? That, like the defense lawyer's role, the corporate lawyer's role has to be constructed so that it serves and does not disserve its public functions, as well as its private ones. I have explained the public benefits of allowing defense lawyers to suppress unlawfully seized evidence, or to refrain from volunteering inconvenient facts pointing to their clients' guilt.[58] But what are the benefits of allowing lawyers to

---

[57] *Id.* What the lawyer should do, unfortunately, is a hopeless muddle under present ethical rules, which try as hard as they can to avoid forcing lawyers into unpleasant confrontations with the corporate agents who hire and fire them.

[58] I do not think that these supposed benefits of an adversarial process and the exclusionary rule are actually as valuable as they are made out to be. They are clumsy devices for achieving goals that could be achieved in more straightforward ways, such as effective judicial supervision, under defense-side monitoring, of police and prosecutorial behavior. And their obvious downside is that they interfere with the search for truth and reliable fact-finding. But there is at least a plausible case for their public benefits.

conceal—or hide in a maze of fine print—facts from regulators and investors that would be highly relevant to determining what the companies' real earnings were, or whether its tax shelters had some economic purpose beyond avoidance, or that managers were setting up side deals paying themselves and their cronies huge bonuses? What is the virtue of allowing lawyers to pull the wool over the eyes of the understaffed bureaucrats who monitor their transactions and try to enforce the laws? Even if all of these schemes should turn out to be (at least arguably) technically legal, what values of overall human happiness, individual self-fulfillment, or economic efficiency are served by helping clients promote them? The autonomy of clients generally is a good thing, to be sure; but there is no virtue per se in action, any old action, that is freely chosen, if it is likely to bring destruction in its wake—including, in these examples, harm to the real clients themselves, not their incumbent managements, but the long-term corporate entities and their constituent stake-holders.

The real lesson from the defense lawyer's or advocate's role is simply that the lawyer is, in addition to being a private agent of his clients, a public agent of the legal system, whose job is to help clients steer their way through the maze of the law, to bring clients' conduct and behavior into conformity with the law—to get the client as much as possible of what the client wants without damaging the framework of the law. He may not act in furtherance of his client's interest in ways that ultimately frustrate, sabotage, or nullify the public purposes of the laws—or that injure the interests of clients, which are hypothetically constructed, as all public corporations should be, as good citizens who internalize legal norms and wish to act in furtherance of the public values they express.

IV. TOWARDS AN ALTERNATIVE CONCEPTION OF THE CORPORATE COUNSELOR'S ROLE

The view that I am pressing here of the corporate counselor's role is neither new nor unorthodox. It is, in fact, one of the traditional conceptions of the counselor's role in our legal culture, with a pedigree quite as venerable and considerably more respectable than the rival notion of the lawyer as zealous advocate or hired gun. It was regularly invoked by leading lawyers throughout the nineteenth century and surfaced as an express ethical standard in the ABA's first Canons of Ethics, promulgated in 1908:

> Canon § 32: No client, corporate or individual, however powerful, nor any cause, civil or political, however important, is entitled to receive, nor should any lawyer render, any service or advice involving disloyalty to the law, whose ministers we are . . . or deception or betrayal of the public. . . . [T]he lawyer . . . advances the honor of his profession and the best interests of his client when he renders service or gives advice tending to impress upon the client and his undertaking exact compliance with the strictest principles of moral law. He must also observe and advise his client to observe the statute law, though until a statute shall have been construed and interpreted by

competent adjudication, he is free and entitled to advise as to its validity and as to what he conscientiously believes to be its just meaning and extent.[59]

In the post World War II era, a group of lawyers and legal academics—including Lon Fuller, Willard Hurst, Hart and Sacks, and Beryl Harold Levy—theorized, from hints dropped by such Progressive lawyers as Brandeis and Adolf Berle (who disagreed on everything else but concurred on this), on the role of the new corporate legal counselor as a "statesman-advisor." The counselor represents his client's interest "with an eye to securing not only the client's immediate benefit but his long-range social benefit." In negotiating and drafting contracts, collective bargaining agreements, or reorganization plans, the lawyer is a lawmaker of "private legislation" and "private constitutions," a "prophylactic avoider of troubles, as well as pilot through anticipated difficulties."[60] The emphasis is on creative compliance with government regulators and labor unions, and on harmonious stable compromises with contract partners and the workforce. It is a vision founded on a very particular model of corporate leadership as the ideal business client, what we now call the "managerialist" model (Berle named the lawyer-executive Owen D. Young of General Electric as the exemplar of vanguard corporate leadership)—business leaders who had made their peace with the New Deal, accepted unions as the price of stability, and whose lawyers moved in and out of government and co-drafted regulations in semi-captured regulatory agencies. The vision also assumed the model of stable corporate law-firm relations that prevailed until the 1970s: A single firm composed of partners for life, who did virtually all of the legal work for companies that retained them indefinitely, rarely questioned their bills, and formed ties of trust and confidence with the senior partners. The "wise-counselor" vision of the lawyer's role found its way into the Joint Report prefacing the ABA's 1969 Model Code of Professional Responsibility and into portions of the Code itself;[61] and according to Erwin Smigel's 1964 study of Wall Street law firms, that vision had been completely internalized by the partners of those firms.[62]

Since the 1970s, this conception of the wise-counselor-lawyer-statesman has been in decay. It is no longer recognized by most corporate lawyers as a norm. It has almost

---

[59] AMERICAN BAR ASSOCIATION, CODE OF PROF'L ETHICS Canon 32 (1908). Notice that the lawyer's advice on the statute is not to be the construction that most favors the client, but the lawyer's independent view. *See* Susan D. Carle, *Lawyers' Duty to Do Justice: A New Look at the History of the 1908 Canons*, 24 LAW & SOC. INQUIRY 1, 2, 18–26 (1999) (on the debate among elite lawyers over the appropriate relative scope of client and public-regarding norms in the drafting of the Canons).

[60] BERYL HAROLD LEVY, CORPORATION LAWYER: SAINT OR SINNER? 151, 153 (1961).

[61] *See, e.g.*, MODEL CODE OF PROF'L RESPONSIBILITY EC 7-3, EC 7-4 (1969) (clearly distinguishing the lawyer's roles of advocate and counselor and suggesting that, in the counselor's role, the lawyer has far less latitude to exploit uncertainties and ambiguities in the law for his client's benefit than in adversary proceedings).

[62] ERWIN O. SMIGEL, THE WALL STREET LAWYER: PROFESSIONAL ORGANIZATION MAN? 341–54 (1969).

no institutional support in the rules and disciplinary bodies that regulate the profession. Some academic lawyers still support some version of the wise-counselor-lawyer-statesman; and so too do some judges and regulators. That conception resurfaces on occasion after business disasters such as the savings-and-loan and Enron scandals. The SEC, IRS, banking regulators, and the courts have sporadically revived it and brought enforcement actions in its spirit. Bar commissions on professionalism sometimes nostalgically evoke it. Yet, even where it still has some residual influence, there are no effective sanctions behind it.

The decline of the counselor's ethic has many causes: The collapse of the state-corporate-labor concords; the rise of the new social regulation and, with it, a newly adversary stance of companies toward regulation and regulators; the sharp rise in inter-corporate and mass-tort litigation; the consequent escalation of legal costs, which caused companies to bring operations in-house and make outside firms compete for specialized business; the reordering of law firms' priorities towards attracting business and maximizing profits-per-partner; the increased pressure on law firm economics caused by ever-escalating associate salaries; the reorientation of professional ethics from complying with aspirational standards to following rules; the displacement of the vocation of public-regarding lawyering onto a specialized "public-interest" bar, academics, and government lawyers; the rise of the cults of market economism and shareholder-wealth-maximization as supreme goods; and the vogue of contempt for government and regulation. All of these tendencies have resulted in lawyers' recharacterizing their calling as the wholly privatized business of providing consulting services aimed at legal-risk-reduction and creative law-arbitrage and law-avoidance schemes, rather than the professional service of public values and the rule of law.[63]

We cannot hope to revive the counselor's role as the profession's dominant role or self-conception or practical way of life. But events like the Enron collapse make one realize that the corporate counselor would still have a useful role to play, if one could revive it as one of the legal profession's many roles, to be deployed on occasions where clients and society would be best served by independent, public-regarding legal advice.

My idea is this: that there be established a separate professional role for a distinct type of lawyer, the Independent Counselor, with a distinct ethical orientation, institutionalized in a distinct governance regime of ethical codes, liability and malpractice rules, special statutory duties and privileges, and judicial rules of practice. Clients could, for most purposes, decide whether they wished to be represented by counselors or ordinary attorneys, making clear by contract and representations to the outside world which role they wanted the lawyer to occupy. For some legal purposes, however, clients would be required to act through counselors. "Counselor" would be primarily an elective role that lawyers could move in and out of, could assume for particular

---

[63] This and the preceding paragraph present, in compressed form, some of the narratives and arguments in another paper. *See* Robert W. Gordon, *The Privatizing of the American Legal Profession,* delivered at the Annual Meeting of the American Society for Legal History (Nov. 9, 2001) (unpublished manuscript, on file with author).

representations or transactions or purposes, and then resume the more common role and function of regular lawyer.[64] But it might also be a role regularly institutionalized in practice settings. Lawyers could organize law firms, branches, or offices within client organizations, consisting only of counselors. The counselor's role might eventually evolve into a distinct profession, one organized into separate law firms, or counselors' offices within firms or within client organizations.

This idea is only in an embryonic stage of its development. If it ever caught on as a practical possibility, there would, of course, be many, many details to be worked out. Before that day comes, it hardly seems worthwhile to try to fill out the fine points of what is only at present a hypothetical and possibly completely utopian scheme. So I will limit my job here to trying to spell out what I think would be the essential elements of the counselor's role.

The most basic element is this: That the lawyer engaged as a counselor adopt an independent, objective view of the corporate agents' conduct and plans and their legal validity. This emphatically does not mean that the counselor must take up an adversary stance to the client, or an attitude of indifference toward its welfare; indeed, as its lawyer, she ought to view the company's legitimate aims and objectives sympathetically and to give advice that will generally further those aims. Nor does it mean that her advice must be invariably conservative and obstructive, that she must be the unhelpful kind of lawyer who constantly tells managers that they cannot do what they want to do; counselors can and should be as creative as any other good lawyers in devising means to accomplish clients' objectives that will overcome and work around legal objections, and in devising innovative arguments that will alter and expand the boundaries of the existing law. But whatever advice the counselor gives, she should: (a) Construe the facts and law of the client's situation as a sympathetic but objective observer such as a judge, committed to serving the law's spirit and furthering its public purposes, would construe them; (b) impute to the corporate client the character of the good citizen, who has internalized legal norms and wishes to comply with the law's legitimate commands and purposes while pursuing its own interests and goals; and (c) be based on an interpretation and practical application of the law to the client's situation that helps the client, so constructed, to satisfy rather than subvert the purposes of the law.

When the counselor asserts facts or makes a legal claim or argument to authorities or third parties—outside the context of fully adversary proceedings, where all interested parties have effective access to relevant facts and legal knowledge necessary to forming the opinion—they should generally be facts and arguments that a fair-minded and fully-informed observer could accept as plausible and correct. For example, if the counselor is giving a legal opinion on the validity of a client's proposed conduct or transaction, she cannot leave out important facts that might cast doubt on her conclusions, or slant the facts so as to obscure difficulties with the conclusions. If she is not

---

[64] The role might be particularly attractive to older lawyers retiring from careers as law firm partners or in-house counsel.

sure that her client's agents have been giving her the important facts, or reporting them accurately, she has to ask questions until she is satisfied or she should refuse to give the opinion. In other words, she should give the kind of report that a lawyer hired to be an independent investigator and analyst of a client's situation would be expected to give. Unlike the Enron lawyers, she may not accept limits on the scope of her representation that would effectively prevent her from doing the counselor's job; nor may she permit her opinion or conclusions to be used to give cover or respectability to actions she has not really had a chance to examine.

The notion that the counselor's role has to be consistent with the law's public purposes, and should further rather than frustrate those purposes—and that she should give candid, truthful, and undistorted reports to authorities and third parties—does not mean that she must become an informer or enforcement officer. Nor does it mean that the lawyer has to accept regulators' or adversaries' constructions of the law, or an ultra-conservative and risk-averse construction of the law's purposes: She is perfectly entitled to present an innovative view of the law and facts that favor what her client wants to do, so long as it is a view that she thinks a judge or other competent lawmaker would actually be likely to accept. But the conception of the role does pretty clearly imply that, if a counselor wants to press on a client's behalf an adventurous, strained, or ingenious interpretation of existing law, or a construction of fact that an objective observer might reasonably think partial and one-sided and potentially misleading, she must do so in a way that flags the contentious nature of what she is proposing and thus permits its adequate testing and evaluation. If no effective adversary process and independent adjudicator is available to test it—not in the hypothetical distant future, but in the here and now—the counselor has either to refrain from pushing the envelope or give intended audiences signals sufficient to inform them of the legal riskiness of getting involved with the plan. Technical, cosmetic, or literal disclosure or compliance that, in practical effect, is non-disclosure or non-compliance is ruled out under this conception. So is tax-evasion parading as tax-minimization. So is trying to sneak a legally dubious transaction under the noses of regulators or third parties whom the lawyers know are too overburdened or unsophisticated or uninformed to discover the potential problems with it.

Maybe what most of the Enron lawyers did was permissible under current legal regimes and ethics codes. I doubt it, for all the reasons that Cramton, Koniak, and the Bankruptcy Examiner have given. Under the obligations of the counselor's role as I am trying to construct it, almost all of the doubtful advice they gave would be impermissible.

In advising clients contemplating litigation, the counselor takes into account the merits or justice of the claim. She seeks to dissuade plaintiffs from pursuing plainly meritless claims and encourages defendants toward fair settlement, and away from invalid defenses, of just claims. In conducting litigation or similar adversary proceedings, the public-minded lawyer regards herself as an "officer of the court," that is, a trustee for the integrity and fair operation of the basic procedures of the adversary system, the rules of the game and their underlying purposes. She fights aggressively for her client, but in ways respectful of the fair and effective operation of the framework.

In discovery, she frames requests to elicit useful information rather than to harass and inflict costs, and responds to reasonable requests rather than obstructing or delaying. She claims privilege or work-product protection only when she thinks that a fair-minded judge would be likely to support the claim independently. In deciding how ferociously to attack the credibility of a witness on cross-examination, she takes into account the likely truthfulness of the witness and the underlying merits of the case.

If the counselor perceives that her services have been or are being used to further, or even just to facilitate by providing plausible cover for, corporate strategies that could not be justified to a fully-informed objective observer as conforming to the letter, spirit, and public purposes of the law, she has to take steps to correct the problem and to try to bring the client's agents back into compliance. This element means that, if she has suspicions, she should investigate them; if she is still not satisfied, she should bring the problem to the general counsel, CEO, and, if necessary, the board of directors to insist on compliance; and if corrective steps are not taken, she must resign. Finally, if serious damage to outside interests may result from the agents' misconduct, she must signal the problem to people such as regulatory authorities, who could prevent it.

I can already hear the cries of protest: "But this is not the lawyer's role!" The obvious answer to that is, yes, I know that it is not the lawyer's role as most corporate lawyers and the bar now see that role; but that is precisely the problem that the savings-and-loan and Enron, etc., scandals have suggested needs to be solved. The legal profession already recognizes differentiated roles with special obligations. The prosecutor is supposed to be a minister of justice, with "special obligations to see that the defendant is accorded procedural justice and that guilt is decided on the basis of sufficient evidence."[65] Government lawyers are supposed to respect the public interest, not just the position of the agency that employs them.[66] Even private lawyers are not always expected to act as hardball adversary-advocates and strategic manipulators of the legal system. For many purposes, companies already want their lawyers to act more like counselors to get the benefits of their perceived independence as reputational intermediaries—for example, to reassure regulators or prosecutors that an errant company has cleaned up its act, to reassure potential transaction partners or investors that a deal is legally safe, or to reassure governments or regulators or local communities that a proposed action is environmentally safe or a proposed reorganization is fair to the labor force. Companies mired in scandal, fraud, and mismanagement often hire law firms as independent counsel to conduct sweeping investigations and house-cleanings and recommend reforms. Companies (like divorcing couples) who want to minimize the strains

---

[65] MODEL RULES OF PROF'L CONDUCT R. 3.8 cmt. (2003).

[66] See id. R. 1.13 cmt. (2002) (stating that "when the client is a governmental organization, a different balance may be appropriate between maintaining confidentiality and assuring that the wrongful official act is prevented or rectified, for public business is involved. . . . Moreover, in a matter involving the conduct of government officials, a government lawyer may have authority under applicable law to question such conduct more extensively than that of a lawyer for a private organization in similar circumstances.").

and expenses of litigation hire law firms with reputations for cooperative behavior, candor, and fair play in discovery, and for openness and a disposition to get to mutually beneficial solutions in negotiating settlements.[67] Sometimes, corporate law actually requires the use of independent counsel—for example, to assess whether the corporation should support or oppose a shareholder's derivative suit.[68]

If the counselor's role is already available by contract, why do we need a new type of professional (the counselor)? The reason is that the counselor's role is too weakly supported by current institutional structures, incentives, statutes, and ethical rules. Ethically, the default master norm of the bar is zealous partisan representation of client interests, rather than the counselor's norm of guidance of the client's desires to bring them into alignment with an objective and fair-minded construction of the public purposes of the law. Lawyers may face malpractice or disciplinary complaints if their advice is perceived as more public-regarding than client-regarding. Even if they are retained as counselors, they may face pressures to moderate their independence from clients' agents unhappy with their advice. Current ethical rules would preclude, or make optional, disclosures to outsiders of corporate agents' violations of law.[69] In short, the counselor may be impeded by ethical rules regarding zeal, confidentiality and conflicts, which are not always waivable by contract.

At the very least, such obligations of partisanship and secrecy should be waivable by contract. Corporations who want to commit themselves *ex ante* to having their business dealings structured, approved, and monitored by independent counselors, with the obligation to report up and even outside the organization if they cannot get managers to comply, should be able to do so, in order to get the benefits of independent advice and objective controls on misconduct.[70]

---

[67] *See* Ronald J. Gilson & Robert H. Mnookin, *Disputing Through Agents: Cooperation and Conflict Between Lawyers in Litigation*, 94 COLUM. L. REV. 509, 512–13, 525 (1994) (arguing that lawyers and law firms can gain benefits by developing reputations for cooperative approaches to dispute resolution).

[68] Model Rule 1.13(b) outlines a lawyer's options when her organizational client is "engaged in action, intends to act or refuses to act in a matter related to the representation that is a violation of a legal obligation to the organization, or a violation of law which reasonably might be imputed to the organization, and is likely to result in substantial injury to the organization." MODEL RULES OF PROF'L CONDUCT R. 1.13(b) (2003). In such event, the lawyer is afforded discretion in deciding whether to seek "a separate legal opinion . . . for presentation to appropriate authority in the organization." *Id.* R. 1.13(b)(2). The Comment to Rule 1.13 specifically addresses derivative suits and suggests that outside counsel may be required when conflicts arise between "the lawyer's duty to the organization and the lawyer's relationship with the board." *Id.* R. 1.13 cmt.

[69] All lawyers are subject to strict confidentiality duties; the Model Rules *permit* disclosure of confidences when necessary to prevent serious physical harm to third persons. *Id.* R. 1.6(b). And while Rule 1.13 permits a lawyer in some circumstances to advocate for an outside legal opinion on her client's conduct, it "does not limit or expand" the lawyer's duties under Rule 1.6. *Id.* R. 1.13(b) &and cmt.

[70] Richard Painter offers a detailed elaboration of the advantages of contracting *ex ante* for lawyer-monitors with the discretion to blow the whistle, and the change in ethics rules that might be required to permit this. *See generally* Richard W. Painter, *Toward a Market for Lawyer Disclosure Services: In Search of Optimal Whistleblowing Rules*, 63 GEO. WASH. L. REV. 221 (1995).

Giving clients the choice to hire counselors by contract would be a useful reform in itself. If the counselor-by-contract alternative were widely available and known about, there could be costs to clients for not choosing lawyers committed to act as counselors in situations where the clients wanted to assure third parties and regulators of good-faith and cooperative conduct. "If you're such good guys, how come your lawyers are hired-gun advocates?"

But counseling-by-contract is not enough. It does not ensure that lawyers will continue to give independent public-regarding advice, or candor and cooperation in bargaining and conflict situations, when the pressure is on to keep the client and prevent it from going over to more complaisant competitors. And it does not give clients enough incentives to hire counselors where—for the protection of third parties or the public—they are most needed.

So I think that the full-scale version of my proposal would have to contain at least two more components. First, there should be government mandates that, for some representations and transactions, corporations must hire lawyers who have undertaken the role and accompanying obligations of counselors. For example: Lawyers certifying compliance with laws, regulations, orders, consent decrees, or reporting requirements of official agencies; lawyers giving opinions to satisfy disclosure requirements or filing proxy statements under the securities laws; and lawyers giving opinions on conformity with tax laws on tax-minimization devices. In other words, when lawyers are hired to fulfill gatekeeper obligations for the protection of third parties, investors, or the public, or to certify conformity with taxing or regulatory laws, or with official orders or decrees, they are not entitled to act as advocates, and not entitled to exploit ambiguities or loopholes in existing laws—at least not without very clearly signaling that they are doing so. Moreover, lawyers in these capacities must not conceal inconvenient material facts, must not uncritically accept facially implausible assertions of fact from their client's agents, and must inquire when a reasonable attorney would suspect material lies or violations of law and try to correct them.

Second, there should be effective institutionalization of and support for the counselor's role, incentives to perform it, and sanctions for breaches. As I picture things, counselors, like lawyers, would be largely self-regulating, but with more effective monitoring and sanctions than most lawyers currently face. Counselors in each specialty (tax, securities, banking, litigation, structured-finance, etc.) would have to develop codes of best practices defining the specifics of the counselor's role for that practice. Then they would have to establish the procedures to inculcate novices into the role, and to monitor performance of it. Some law firms have already set up internal machinery to promulgate and enforce ethical standards; this type of internal machinery could be adapted for counselors. Obviously, they would be subject to special regimes of judicial enforcement, civil liability, and malpractice; and, where practicing before agencies such as the SEC or IRS, to administrative discipline. Counselors probably should not be allowed to take equity positions in client companies, or agree to fee arrangements conditioning compensation on results. But they also need incentives to take on the role of counselor and perform it faithfully. The most effective incentives would be ones where potential counselors would receive special privileges that would benefit clients—for example, expedited and presumptively favorable regulatory action, less scrutiny and more rapid approval by courts of discovery plans, settlements of class actions, terms of consent decrees, and safe harbors from malpractice or other liability for conscientious good faith advice.

Is this idea for reviving the counselor's role an idle dream? Perhaps it is. But the status quo—a situation in which lawyers effectively facilitate, or passively acquiesce in and enable, corporate frauds in the name of a noble idea of advocacy that has been ludicrously misapplied to the context of corporate advice-giving—is not tolerable. At least, some corporate lawyers may wish to revive the ideal of independent counseling, which has, until very recent times, been one of the most inspiring regulative ideals of their profession. And even if they do not, a society that wants its corporations to be good citizens, as well as efficient profit-maximizers, may insist on reviving it, or something like it, against their opposition, in order to preserve the underpinnings of the society itself.

QUESTIONS

1. Can you find justifications for Professor Gordon's "counselor" role in any current ethics rules, such as the Model Rules of Professional Conduct? Can you find any justifications for the "counselor" role in any comments to those rules? If you can find some justifications in current rules, why do you think lawyers aren't performing the "counselor" role already?

2. If you had a choice between joining a law firm composed of "regular" lawyers and a law firm composed of "counselors," which would you choose? What if "counselors" were paid a little less than "regular" lawyers? What if they were paid significantly less?

3. Do you think that government lawyers tend to act more like "counselors" or more like "regular lawyers"? Should the government be in charge of creating a system of "counselor-lawyers" separate from the lawyers already serving in various governmental capacities, such as the Department of Justice, the Securities and Exchange Commission, or the Internal Revenue Service?

Why Lawyers Can't Just Be Hired Guns*

*Robert W. Gordon***

My theme in this essay is the public responsibilities of lawyers—their obligations to help maintain and improve the legal system: the framework of laws, procedures, and institutions that structures their roles and work.

Ordinarily, this is a theme for ceremonial occasions, like Law Day sermons or bar association dinners or memorial eulogies—when we are given license to rise on the wings of rhetorical inspiration far above the realities of day-to-day practice. I want to try to approach the subject in a different spirit, as a workaday practical necessity for the legal profession. My argument is simple: that lawyers' work on behalf of clients positively requires—both for its justification and its successful functioning for the benefit of those same clients in the long run—that lawyers also help maintain and refresh the public sphere, the infrastructure of law and cultural convention that constitutes the cement of society.

The way we usually discuss the subject of lawyers' public obligations—outside ceremonial rhetoric—is as a problem in legal "ethics." We often hear things like, "Lawyers must be zealous advocates for their clients, but of course lawyers are also 'officers of the court'; and sometimes the duties mandated by these different roles come into conflict and must be appropriately balanced." And, indeed, some of the most contentious disputes about "ethics" in the legal profession concern such conflicts between the "private" interests of lawyers and clients and their "public" obligations to adversaries, third parties, and the justice system itself—issues like: When, if ever, should lawyers have to disclose client fraud or wrongdoing or withdraw from representing clients who persist in it? When, if ever, should they refuse to pursue client claims they believe legally frivolous? Or act to prevent clients or their witnesses from giving perjured or seriously misleading testimony or responses to discovery requests?

---

* Originally published in DEBORAH L. RHODE (ed.), ETHICS IN PRACTICE (Oxford University Press, 2000). Reprinted with permission.

** An early version of this essay was given as a Daniel Meador Lecture at the University of Alabama School of Law. Thanks to Deborah Rhode for helpful comments.

These are important issues, no doubt about it, but in this essay I want to look at them in a larger and slightly different perspective than we can usually get from the "legal-ethics" debates. For one thing, "ethics" isn't quite what I want to talk about. I suspect that most lawyers, when they hear "ethics," think, first, that something cosmically boring is about to be said, which one would only listen to in order to satisfy a bar admission or Continuing Legal Education requirement; or else that they are about to hear some unwelcome news about a conflict of interest disqualifying them from taking on a client. "Ethics" has come to mean either: (1) the detailed technical rules in the professional-ethical codes; or, alternatively, (2) a strictly personal morality, the morality of individual conscience, an aspect of personal character which people just have or don't have, and if they have it, acquired it, if not in kindergarten, at least well before they became lawyers. The responsibilities of lawyers I'm talking about in this essay are of a different order; and I'll call them "public responsibilities" instead of ethics, to emphasize that they are responsibilities that attach to lawyers both in their functions as lawyers and as "citizens" who benefit, and whose clients benefit, from participation in the political, legal, social, and cultural order of a capitalist constitutional democracy, and who thereby owe that order some obligations to respect and help maintain its basic ground rules.

The order is **capitalist**: that is, constituted by the basic ground rules of a system of private property and market exchange; this is not, contrary to the anti-government rhetoric we hear a lot of these days, a state of nature, but an order created and maintained by both coercive and facilitative government actions—the enforcement of rules of property, contract, tort, commercial law, employment law, and the law of unfair competition; the facilitation of collective action through corporations, cooperatives, partnerships, and collective bargaining.

The order is also **democratic**: meaning that the ground rules that constitute the "private" economy and society are subject to revision and modification by democratically elected representative institutions and by the administrative bureaucracies that these legislatures create to carry out legislation; and, finally,

The order is **constitutional**: in that its exercises of collective power are supposed to be limited by a set of fundamental substantive and procedural constraints—enforced in our system in the last instance by courts, but supposedly respected by all power-wielding bodies, private as well as public.

The general premise of a liberal polity in short is that freely-chosen goals (or "self-interest," if one prefers that reductive way of speaking) are to be pursued within a framework of constraints—established by norms, customary practices, rules, institutions, and procedures and maintained by systems of culture and morals backed by social sanctions and, selectively, by law.

Let's focus first on capitalism. Even the most libertarian theorists of capitalism, like Milton Friedman for example, would stipulate that capitalism only works if there are strong conventions maintaining the framework of order within which, supposedly, self-interested behavior will add up to the general welfare. If individual players resort to theft, trespass, corruption, force, fraud, and monopoly; if they regularly inflict uncompensated harms upon others, and consistently get away with it, the order will collapse. The order of law, it has come to be pretty clear, is not enough in itself to sustain a market economy: a capitalist system also requires what might be called an order of custom—a cultural infrastructure of norms—learned dispositions to respect property and keep promises and pay taxes and refrain from private violence to settle disputes, and of a certain degree of mutual trust—confidence that others will, within limits, for the most part, also respect the norms. The law without the custom supporting it doesn't work, because no legal system can maintain order against persistent and pervasive violations or evasions; without social conventions in place to maintain the framework, no state can be legitimate or strong enough to supply one. There will be no reliable system of contract enforcement, no effective safeguards against theft, fraud, and violence, no protection of consumers or labor against being cheated or abused, no effective protection of the environment, no way of extracting taxes to pay for public goods like law enforcement. Yet custom also needs the support of law. Norms of cooperation and mutual trust create openings for opportunists and free riders to abuse them, and outside of close-knit communities, non-legal social sanctions will not adequately police against such abuses. Although compliance with the framework norms has to be largely voluntary, you need coercive law to demonstrate the costs of abuse, and also to reaffirm the norms against the moral "outsiders," the amoral calculators who would otherwise profit from everyone else's trusting law-abidingness.

Readers will recognize here an exaggerated—but only slightly exaggerated—description of the current Russian scene. The Russians are trying to run a market economy with no customs or traditions supporting a private framework of constraints on opportunistic behavior in those markets; and also without the legitimacy and support for the state authority to supplement and supply the deficiencies of the private framework. Framework functions that we take for granted—like routine security for personal safety and business assets, and routine contract enforcement—since they are not being supplied by custom or law enforcement, are hired out instead to private purveyors of violence, Mafiosi, or ex-KGB thugs.

To return now to the developed capitalist economies such as ours. Such an economy depends, in short, as much on common agreement to abide by its ground rules as it does on competition and innovation; on the substructures of trust, cooperation and law that maintain that agreement. These frameworks are public goods or common property; they are like the air we breathe.

Now where do lawyers come into the picture? Lawyers have a dual role. They are agents of clients, and in that role help clients to pursue their self-interest—to manipulate the rules and procedures of the legal system on their behalf, to negotiate through bureaucratic labyrinths, to repel assaults on persons or property or liberty.

But lawyers must also be agents of the common framework of institutions, customs, and norms within which their clients' interests must be pursued if the premises underlying all these individual exercises of freedom are to be made good. Let me try to develop this argument for the "public" side of lawyers' obligations.

The dominant ideology of the legal profession, the norm of zealous advocacy or adversary ideal, tends to obscure the public side of the ledger. But that side is always present, and is not adequately described by the ritualistic phrase, "officer of the court." Much of the lawyer's role that is usually thought of as simply zealous representation is actually also designed to carry out the public-framework-regarding aims of the legal system. The obvious example is criminal defense. Our own painful history and the experience of most other nations today teach that the criminal justice system is prone to systematic abuses. Police will break down doors at night, detain suspects in secret, and coerce confessions; prosecutors will fabricate evidence or suborn perjury of witnesses. Against such abuses, legal reformers over time have enacted both substantive and procedural safeguards. The defense counsel's primary role is to act as the outside monitor; he is the gadfly who keeps the system honest and ensures that the police and prosecution go by the book in their treatment of suspects' collection of evidence. In this sense, defense counsel is a public agent of the framework.

So too in the civil justice system. Lawyers serve as public agents in helping clients to vindicate claims given by the substantive law; and in preventing government agents or adversaries from abusing the law, or from gaining advantages that are not permitted by law. In short, the lawyer's role is part of the foundations of a capitalist democratic system.

The term "ethics" doesn't really capture these public functions of the lawyer. These are functions of "citizenship" in the broad sense, of obligations to the framework of law and custom that makes the overall social system—a market economy within the rule of law—work.

Well, what obligations can be derived from the role? At minimum, one would think, a set of negative obligations: in the words of the Hippocratic oath: "First, do no harm," meaning, in this context, what the philosopher Jon Elster calls "everyday Kantianism"— refrain from actions, which if multiplied and generalized, would weaken or erode the essential framework norms and customs.[1] Why are these specially obligations of lawyers? In part, of course, they are not, they are obligations on all citizens. (By citizens, incidentally, I don't mean technically born or naturalized citizens, but all people who benefit from participation in the framework; so a foreign company doing business in the U.S.A. or a lawyer for that company would both be "citizens" in this expanded sense.) But lawyers do have special obligations: they are in a unique position to safeguard framework arrangements, because they are also in a unique position both to ensure that they are carried into effect and to sabotage them. All procedures that exist to vindicate claims given by the substantive law, especially complex and expensive ones like litigation or administrative rule-making, also deliver resources for strategic behavior—delay, obstruction, confusion of the record, raising costs to adversaries. The resources of law, in unscrupulous hands, can be used to nullify law. This is why we are told that outlaw organizations like the Mafia reportedly offer a key role to the

---

[1] *See* JON ELSTER, THE CEMENT OF SOCIETY: A STUDY OF SOCIAL ORDER 192–95 (1989).

consigliere—the lawyer who keeps the law at bay—so that the organization can operate outside the law.

But let us take a less extreme example. Suppose that the lawyer does not represent a persistently outlaw client—the enterprise that lurks at the margins of organized society, taking advantage of its rules and customs to rip off a surplus for itself—but the more usual client, like the ordinary business firm, whose interest is sometimes in vindicating, but also sometimes in avoiding, requirements of the substantive law: in enforcing some contracts but evading obligations under others, in protecting itself against employee theft or sabotage, but in circumventing labor law to forestall union organizing campaigns, in seeking compensation for torts committed against it, but immunity for its own torts. If lawyers employ every strategy to defeat the claims they don't like, they will erode the process's value for its good uses as well as its bad ones. Outcomes become expensive, time-consuming, and arbitrary. They reward wealth and cunning, and bear less and less relationship to judgment on the merits. Without controls, the system can rapidly deteriorate to a tool of oppression and extortion. By raising the enforcement costs of regulation, lawyers can encourage defiance of regulation by their competitors, as well as themselves, and begin a race for the bottom in which nice guys finish last, and the law-observing client is an innocent simpleton, a loser in the Darwinian struggle.

The legal-social framework is a common good; and self-interested individual behavior can destroy its value for everyone. Extreme adversariness in litigation or regulatory compliance settings is not just problematic because everyone—virtually all clients and all but the most predatory and ruthless lawyers—finds it incredibly unpleasant and because it is full of posturing and bad manners; but because it erodes the conditions of the economy and social order. Repeated lying in negotiations can destroy fragile networks of trust and cooperation that alone make negotiation—especially between relative strangers—possible. Strategic contract-breaking reduces the value of all contracts everywhere that are not already backed by strong customary sanctions.

Many lawyers at this point are tempted to say: We admit all this, but enforcing the framework norms isn't our business; it's the specialized role of public enforcement agents—judges, prosecutors, agency bureaucrats, and other officials. But if you accept any of the argument so far, this just has to be wrong. A legal system, like a social system, depends on largely voluntary compliance with its norms. When compliance is replaced by underground resistance—or only nominal compliance—when drivers stop at the red lights only when they think a cop is looking, or are prepared to exhaust the traffic court's limited resources by arguing that the light was green—the system has broken down. Suppose that, as happens in many of the world's societies, individuals and business began serious cheating on their taxes. In a world in which there are resources to audit only 1% of returns, the result is total system breakdown. Taxes that depend on self-reporting can no longer be collected. Some people are not very frightened by this particular prospect; but they might be if other enforcement mechanisms broke down—if, for instance, gangs of the physically strong, financed by the wealthy, started preying on their families and businesses, and counted on lawyers to stall enforcement of the legal controls on their predation.

In any case, lawyers, especially lawyers for powerful clients, are rarely just passive law-takers: they are active law-makers, designers of contractual and associational arrangements that create or limit rights and duties and dispute-settlement modes, and that are binding on trading partners, employees, suppliers or customers. The employment lawyers who draft contracts requiring employees to waive rights given by state labor law and submit all disputes to arbitrators chosen by the employer, the HMO lawyers who draft clauses forbidding doctors under contract to the organization from disclosing to patients that the organization policies will not authorize certain treatments, are engaged in what the "legal process" scholars Hart and Sacks called "private legislation."[2]

Lawyers have to help preserve the commons—to help clients comply with the letter and purpose of the frameworks of law and custom that sustain them all; and their obligation is clearly strongest where there is no adversary with access to the same body of facts to keep them honest, and no umpire or monitor to ensure conformity to legal norms and adequate protection of the interests of third parties and the integrity of the legal system.

Of course I realize that the view that I'm putting forward, a view that assigns to lawyers a major role as curators of the public frameworks that sustain our common existence, is drastically at odds with a view that is widespread in the legal profession, indeed is probably the dominant view. This view, which I'll call the libertarian-positivist view, holds that the lawyer owes only the most minimal duties to the legal framework—the duties not to violate plain unambiguous commands of law, procedure, or ethics, not to tell plain lies to magistrates, and perhaps also not to offer such outrageously strained interpretations of facts or law to tribunals as to amount to outright misrepresentations—and owes no duties to the social framework at all, if performing them would conflict with his client's immediate interests. In this view, the lawyer and client are alone together in a world where there are some positive rules: the lawyer's job is to help the client get what he wants without breaking the rules—or at least without breaking them when anyone's likely to notice—though it's all right to bend them.[3]

The problem I have with using the libertarian-positivist starting point is that, in a democratic society, it seems wrong to conceive of the law and the state wholly as adversaries, the "other," a bureaucratic maze to be adroitly negotiated on behalf of one's clients—and especially wrong if one's clients are members of groups who do in fact have some access to political power. We are, after all, members of a common

---

[2] HENRY HART AND ALBERT SACKS, JR., THE LEGAL PROCESS: BASIC PROBLEMS IN THE MAKING AND APPLICATION OF LAW 183–339 (William N. Eskridge, Jr. & Philip P. Frickey, eds. 1994).

[3] The best account and critique I know of this "dominant view" is in WILLIAM H. SIMON, THE PRACTICE OF JUSTICE: A THEORY OF LAWYERS' ETHICS 30–46 (1998).

political community, with agreed-upon procedures for establishing and changing its common frameworks. I would argue for the lawyer's starting from an opposite presumption from the libertarian one—though also rebuttable in particular contexts—a presumption that the law very imperfectly sets forth an approximately agreed-upon minimal framework of common purposes, a social contract. I don't mean a framework of "thick" moral norms, such as a communitarian or civic republican would imagine, but neither do I mean just a "thin" obligation to obey only the plainest unambiguous commands in circumstances where violations are likely to be detected. The domain of these obligations lies somewhere between morality and resentful minimal compliance with rules. The metaphor I'd suggest is that of relational contract—the long-term contract calling for repeated occasions for performance, a contract structured by norms of trust, reciprocity, and fair dealing. A contract partner is not expected to sacrifice her self-interest to the other party's, but does have a duty of good-faith observance of the principles and purposes of the contractual framework that has been set up to serve their mutual advantage. With most clients, including business clients, the lawyer could start with the presumption that many good lawyers do indeed begin with—that the client is not out to get away with anything he can in pursuit of its objectives, but wants to abide by the spirit of the framework and be a good citizen; and only face the more difficult dilemma of whether to advise him how to get around the rules if he makes the intention to evade them manifest, after being advised to comply.

I readily acknowledge that there's nothing simple or straightforward about complying with framework norms in the modern regulatory state—often just figuring out what they are is a considerable undertaking. Regulatory regimes tend to be appallingly complex and technical, crammed with loopholes and ambiguities, sometimes put there by regulated interests, often inadvertent. Regulatory statutes are often utopian; full compliance is impossible. They are often in part only symbolic—sweeping commands considerably qualified or even retracted in practice by a large discretion or ridiculously low budget for enforcement. Nonetheless, I think in most contexts lawyers can fairly readily tell the difference between making good faith efforts to comply with a plausible interpretation of the purposes of a legal regime, and using every ingenuity of his or her trade to resist or evade compliance.

And just as clearly, I'd maintain, lawyers have another obligation as well—though this is an obligation that they can discharge through collective action, through organizations, surrogates, or representatives as well as personally: and that is the obligation to work outside the context of representing clients to improve, reform, and maintain the framework of justice. One thing this obligation unmistakably calls for is helping to remedy the maldistribution—really, the "non-distribution" of legal services—to people with serious legal problems but without much money. But another is to help fix legal processes that waste everyone's money in administrative costs or otherwise systematically produce unfair results. Again, I would guess that many lawyers see this kind of framework-repair and reform work as a kind of *pro bono* philanthropy: they are glad that some prominent lawyers are doing it, but they see it as an optional task for the private bar. From this view, working on the framework is only in the actual job description of public officials—legislators, administrators, judges. And again, I would argue, that view can't be right—for reasons of both history and principle.

As a matter of tradition, in America private lawyers have assumed a large share of the public role—sufficiently long-standing and ingrained into customary practice so that you could reasonably call it a *constitutional* role—of safeguarding the framework and adapting it to changing conditions. This role devolved on lawyers at the founding of the republic, when private lawyers assumed the major share of responsibility for making the legal case for the Revolution and in drafting the basic charters of government, the State and Federal Constitutions. In the early decades of the republic, private lawyers undertook the task of producing an Americanized common law to serve as the basic ground rules for commercial life. In the Progressive era, the creation of the modern state, government through administrative commissions and professional associations, was also largely the work of practicing lawyers—though academic lawyers also got into the act as well in a big way in drafting the legislation of the New Deal and staffing its agencies. Lawyers have, of course, dominated the legislative bodies of the country, especially at the federal level, for its entire history. Lawyers temporarily on leave from practice have run the foreign policy of this country for most years of its existence.[4] Private lawyers don't play this role in every society; they have played it in America, primarily because, with our Revolution, we rejected the European model of government through a centralized bureaucracy staffed by an elite career civil service: our senior levels of statecraft have had to come from part-time volunteers—more often than not lawyers—like Alexander Hamilton, Thomas Jefferson, John Adams, Daniel Webster, John Quincy Adams, Charles Evans Hughes, Elihu Root, Henry Stimson, Dean Acheson, John J. McCloy, John Foster Dulles, Cyrus Vance, Warren Christopher, just for a short list.

But there is more to this story than the conspicuous lawyer-statesmen on the commanding heights of government. It's no accident that most of the names I've just mentioned were primarily active in foreign policy. In the domestic field, after the basic institutions of government had been established, Americans of the Jeffersonian persuasion turned away from Hamilton's aristocratic model of "energetic government" managed by elites drawn from professional classes.[5] Under the new ethos, America was to be dominantly a commercial republic, one in which happiness was to be pursued by those free to pursue it (which at the time meant mostly white males) through labor, trade, manufactures, land cultivation, and speculation. From an early date, the market economy, the sphere of "free enterprise," was naturalized, made to appear as if it were

---

[4] JAMES WILLARD HURST, THE GROWTH OF AMERICAN LAW: THE LAW MAKERS 352–56 (1950); MARK C. MILLER, THE HIGH PRIESTS OF AMERICAN POLITICS: THE ROLE OF LAWYERS IN AMERICAN POLITICAL INSTITUTIONS 57–75 (1995).

[5] JOYCE APPLEBY, LIBERALISM AND REPUBLICANISM IN THE HISTORICAL IMAGINATION 271–76, 304–19, 326–39 (1992).

a machine that would run of itself. The background frameworks that it presupposed and helped make it run, the infrastructures of law and government and custom, because they were relegated to the background, became invisible to many of the entrepreneurs who depended on them without realizing it.

In fact, of course, those networks of law and government and custom were everywhere: the U.S.A. was, even at the outset, a thoroughly "well-regulated society"[6]—every aspect of social life was criss-crossed with legal and customary regulations of family and employment relations; of land use and common resources; of nuisances, contracts, and debt-collection. Much of this regulation was decentralized and localized—government by local commissions and juries, by public enforcement actions brought by private informers and prosecutors, by county courts, and the case-by-case governance of the common law; or by special bodies like corporations, created by government to serve public purposes.[7] In a country lacking strong centralized bureaucracies, the operation of these regulatory bodies and processes was, to a large extent, by default, given over to lawyers. Tocqueville commented on this fact, that lawyers were the *de facto* governing class, and shrewdly guessed the reason for it: in a commercial society, as Adam Smith had warned, most people's energy and attention turns inward upon their private ambitions—getting ahead, making money; in such a society, people are likely to turn away from public life, to neglect or ignore (what I have been calling) the frameworks of law, government, and public custom on which a successfully functioning system of market exchange ultimately must depend. Enter lawyers—a professional class by training and usage devoted to the legal framework and to assuming a natural leadership role in civic life.[8]

Now obviously there's a lot of disagreement about how well lawyers have discharged the public stewardship that fell into their hands at the founding of the republic. There is nothing new in complaints about lawyers—that they exact a heavy monopolists' rent for running the public machinery, that they are excessively devoted to clumsy, cumbersome, expensive procedures, that they sow complexity, confusion, and ambiguity wherever they go, that they gratuitously stir up trouble, all for their own interest and profit. Some critics persistently charge that the regulatory frameworks they have built and interpret to clients tend to shackle and overburden enterprise; while others charge to the contrary, that lawyers have managed the framework far too often to the particular benefit of their principal business clients. These are complex debates that I

---

[6] This phrase, and the content of the sentence that follows, is taken from WILLIAM J. NOVAK, THE PEOPLE'S WELFARE: LAW AND REGULATION IN NINETEENTH CENTURY AMERICA 19–50 (1996).

[7] *See generally* NOVAK, PEOPLE'S WELFARE, *supra* note 6. OSCAR HANDLIN AND MARY FLUG HANDLIN, COMMONWEALTH: A STUDY OF THE ROLE OF GOVERNMENT IN THE AMERICAN ECONOMY: MASSACHUSETTS, 1774–1861 (1969).

[8] ALEXIS DE TOCQUEVILLE, DEMOCRACY IN AMERICA I:208, 272–280; II: 98–99 (Phillips Bradley, ed., Henry Reeve, trans. 1946).

clearly can't try to resolve here. The point I want to make is that, whatever you think of how lawyers have taken care of their civic responsibilities, those responsibilities, in our political-economic structure, are inescapable. If lawyers do not perform them, no one else can fully substitute for them.[9]

So it's absurd to pretend, as libertarian lawyers often like to do, that private lawyers just take care of their clients while relinquishing the public realm to officials. In fact, of course, lawyers are anything but inactive towards the public sphere. The public framework is dynamic, malleable, negotiable. Lawyers don't just passively follow framework rules: they take on active political roles—trying to change the ground rules in their clients' favor.

Here it seems to me is the area where the lawyers have to do the most complex balancing of their roles as agents for clients and agents of the general long-term welfare of the legal system and the public sphere. Adversary practice at the individual case or transactional level is relatively cabined and contained. At the policy level, where clients are pushing for major legislative change or alteration in basic doctrine, zealous representation of immediate client interests with no regard for anything or anyone else has the potential to turn political life into an uncontained war of all against all—litigation writ large, a Darwinian zero-sum struggle among social groups for their share of the pie—at the expense of the institutions of restraint, cooperation, and social bargaining that link the fates of the fortunate elites to those of the middling ranks and lower orders and thus promote the general welfare. The classical fears are of "rent-seeking" politics, of groups seeking public favors that milk the government for spending levels that threaten either fiscal crisis or confiscatory levels of taxation that destroy incentives to save and produce. The opposite, and in the U.S. more likely, danger is of public paralysis, brought about by groups that so successfully resist taxation or regulation that they exercise a practical veto on the government's being able to provide the public goods of defense, justice, order, ecosystem protection, health and safety, and the conditions of equal opportunity that most people in fact want provided; or simply of the capture of the legal system by the powerful, who use it to grab the largest shares of income, wealth, and public resources for themselves, and to neutralize and repress any other groups who might try to challenge their claims. An example of such wasteful struggle from our own history would be labor-capital relations in the U.S. between 1877 and 1935, relations of fairly constant zero-sum warfare, interrupted by intermittent truces and periods of exhaustion, polarizing public opinion, sharpening class con-

---

[9] In this century, lawyers have been displaced from their once near-total dominance of legislative and appointive positions, policy elites, and reform vanguards. They now share these roles with other public actors, such as economists, think-tank intellectuals, issue and area specialists, lobbyists, and grass-roots organizers. Nonetheless the role of lawyers, as public officials, public-interest advocates, and private lawyers advising clients, remains critical, especially as translators of public initiatives into legislative form, administrative rule and procedure, and practical enforcement.

flict, leading to enormous losses through work stoppages and, just as important, to enduring legacies of bitterness and mutual distrust whose effects are still being felt in some industries today.[10]

How to reconcile these interests? What should a lawyer do whose client wants the public framework altered in its favor, when the lawyer has reason to believe that the change may do serious damage to the commons, the public sphere? Louis Brandeis, one of the earliest lawyers to address this problem, believed that in his own time most of the country's top legal talent had been recruited to the service of a single faction of civil society, that of large corporate interests. He believed that on issues of major framework change, lawyers had sometimes to take a completely independent view from their clients—that they ought not to be partisan at all.[11]

Perhaps unfortunately, the Brandeis view has never taken hold and is probably no longer a practical option, if it ever was. My own view is that, in the policy arena, as in ordinary transactional and litigation work, the lawyer is entitled to pursue the client's interests but without risking sabotage of the general public-regarding norms of the framework that link the client's interest with that of other social groups in a long-term relational bargain. Any number of examples would serve, but since it's a hot topic, let's take tort reform. Companies and their insurers want to minimize liability; plaintiffs want to ensure that they are compensated. To some extent these interests conflict; though the parties have common interests, even if it's sometimes hard for them to see this, in making products safer, while reducing the costs of products and the transaction costs of the injury compensation system. What are the lawyers involved in tort litigation actually doing? Very little that's constructive. The plaintiffs' bar fights to hold on to the current system, remarkably unconcerned with the problems that the vast majority of victims of personal injury, other than auto accident victims, are unable to reach the justice system to obtain any compensation at all; and that the tort system is so expensive that half or more of its recoveries are eaten up in administrative costs, including payments to lawyers.[12] The defendants' bar has, if anything, been even less constructive in its public positions. Corporate and insurance counsel help to propagate the wildly exaggerated myths that the U.S. is in the midst of a personal-injury "litigation explosion" and "liability crisis" that add billions to the costs of products and seriously injure American competitiveness. (These are, by the way, clearly myths: filings for individual personal-injury tort claims have fallen, not risen, in the last decade; the big increases in federal civil suits are mostly increases in inter-corporate contract claims. The myths also tend to include in the count of the greatest "costs" of the

---

[10] For an epic history, see David Montgomery, The Fall of the House of Labor (1987).

[11] See Louis Brandeis, The Opportunity in the Law, in Louis Brandeis, Business: A Profession 329, 340–41 (1914).

[12] See Deborah R. Hensler, et al., Compensation for Accidental Injuries in the United States (1991).

system—the *benefits* that victims receive in compensation for injuries.[13]) These interests promote political "reforms" of the process that would limit liability and reduce damages without substituting alternative proposals for ensuring that the system will in fact adequately compensate injuries and keep in place incentives to make safer products; or for universalizing access to medical care so that treating accident victims could be financed outside the tort and workers-compensation systems. (In my view, corporate counsel are more at fault in this debate than the plaintiffs' bar, because their own livelihoods would not be jeopardized by sensible and just reforms. One cannot expect complete objectivity from parties under threat of extinction.)

In my model, the lawyers ought to see the parties to policy conflicts like the conflict over the tort system much as one would see parties to a long-term relational contract. The aim is to make a good deal for one's clients *in the context of an ongoing relation with other interests*, not to extract everything possible for one's own side; and to build long-term collaborative relationships. The kind of negotiation I have in mind resembles that undertaken towards the beginning of this century by the National Civic Federation, a sort of private-corporatist institution that brought together (relatively) progressive employers and (relatively) conservative unions and had their lawyers try to work out institutional solutions for social disputes. The NCF was one of the main backers of the first Worker's Compensation systems that moved industrial accidents out of the tort system that was expensive and risky for both employers and employees.[14]

I think it will be apparent that what I have been mainly arguing for so far is a remarkably conservative view of the legal framework, and a very conservative role for the legal profession: oriented towards maintenance and improvement of existing frameworks. I should make clear that I think the current set of rules, procedures, institutions, and conventions of democratic capitalism is a very long distance away from a legal/social framework that would effectively realize the promise of American life. Nothing I've said should be taken as designed to restrain lawyers from working to revise the framework's ground rules, especially if they fight for revision openly rather than through surreptitious undermining of the system. And I certainly don't want to exclude the possibility that at any time, including our own time, aspects of the framework may be fundamentally unjust or unsound, and thus in need of radical revision; and that in such times, lawyers may legitimately feel a calling to a morally activist,

[13] The literature on the tort "crisis" is enormous. For useful surveys of the data and assessment of the various positions, see Marc Galanter, Real World Torts: An Antidote to Anecdote, 55 MARYLAND L. REV. 1093 (1996); Deborah Rhode, *Too Much Law, Too Little Justice, Too Much Rhetoric, Too Little Reform*, GEORGETOWN J. L. ETHICS 989 (1998).

[14] The NCF has been sharply criticized, with reason, as a basically conservative organization that promoted Workers' Compensation schemes in large part to co-opt and blunt the edge of movements for more generous industrial-accident compensation schemes. *See, e.g.,* JAMES WEINSTEIN, THE CORPORATE IDEAL IN THE LIBERAL STATE, 1900–1918 (1968). It takes something like the partisan posturing of belligerents in the current battle over the tort system to make the NCF look good.

framework-transforming politics. There are times when the lawyers' most demanding conceptions of their calling may demand principled resistance to public norms they believe to be unwise or unjust. There are times when fire must be fought with fire, unscrupulous tactics met with fierce counter-tactics—though lawyers use this justification far too often as an excuse for anti-social behavior, which might be avoided by collaborative efforts to reform unjust systems. There are times when whole segments of society must be mobilized to overturn an unjust order. Lawyers have played important parts in such movements—like the movements to abolish slavery and racial segregation—and will, one hopes, do so again.

But in our time, even the most conservative view of the lawyer's public functions, that he is to respect the integrity and aid the functioning of the existing system and its purposes, has become controversial—in a way that would really have astonished the lawyers of the early republic, the lawyers of the Progressive period, and leading lawyers generally up until around 1970 or so, who took the idea of their public functions completely for granted.[15] The dominant view of most lawyers today—not all, but seemingly most—is one that denies the public role altogether if it seems to conflict with the job of aggressively representing clients' interests the way the client perceives them.

Yet, as I've said, a legal system that depends for its ordinary enforcement on information and advice transmitted by the private bar, that depends for its maintenance and reform on the voluntary activities of the private bar, and that relies on lawyers to design the architecture of private legislation, cannot survive the repeated, relentless battering and ad hoc under-the-counter nullification of lawyers who are wholly uncommitted to their own legal system's basic purposes. Lawyers, in fact, probably do serve the civic frameworks better than they occasionally like to pretend; they refrain from pushing every client's case, in every representation, up to just short of the point where no plausible construction of law or facts could support it. But it seems clear that, like many other groups in American social life, the legal profession in the last twenty years or so has adopted an increasingly privatized view of its role and functions. The upper bar, in particular, has come to see itself simply as a branch of the legal-and-financial services industry, selling bundles of technical "deliverables" to clients. There

---

[15] One of the best statements to be found anywhere of the lawyer's public functions appeared in the report that launched the American Bar Association's 1969 Model Code of Ethics. *Professional Responsibility: Report of the Joint Conference [on Professional Responsibility of the American Bar Association and Association of American Law Schools], * Lon L. Fuller and John D. Randall as co-chairs], 44 ABA J. 1159 (1958):

> Thus partisan advocacy is a form of public service so long as it aids the process of adjudication: it ceases to be when it hinders that process, when it misleads, distorts and obfuscates, when it renders the task of the deciding tribunal not easier, but more difficult. . . . [The lawyer as negotiator and draftsman] works against the public interests when he obstructs the channels of collaborative effort, when he seeks petty advantages to the detriment of the larger processes in which he participates. . . . *Private legal practice, properly pursued, is, then, itself a public service.*

Id. at 1162 (emphasis added).

are many reasons for this trend, chief among which is the increasing competition among lawyers (and in European markets, between lawyers and accountants) for the favor of business clients. That competition has brought many benefits with it in more efficient delivery of services, but one of those benefits cannot be said to be incentives to high-minded public counseling or the expenditure of time on legal and civic reform.

Our legal culture, in short, has mostly fallen out of the habit of thinking about its public obligations (with the significant exception of the obligation of *pro bono* practice, which has gained increasing attention from bar associations and large law firms). I expect, therefore, that if the idea of lawyers as trustees for the public good—the framework norms and long-term social contracts that keep our enterprise afloat—is going to stage a comeback, the impulse will have to come from some set of external shocks, such as legislation or administrative rules or rules of court that explicitly impose gatekeeper obligations on lawyers as independent auditors of clients' conduct. We have seen some steps taken in that direction already, in rules regulating tax shelter lawyers, securities lawyers, and the banking bar.

It would be much better, however, if the impulse were to come from the legal profession itself—especially to build and to finance organizations in which lawyers can carry out their public function of recommending improvements in the legal framework that will reduce the danger of their clients' and their own subversion of that framework. Many of the existing bar organizations, unfortunately, are losing their capacity to fulfill that function. Even the august American Law Institute has become a place which lawyers, instead of checking their clients at its door, treat as just one more forum for advancement of narrow client interests.[16]

Think of lawyers as having the job of taking care of a tank of fish. The fish are their clients, in this metaphor. As lawyers, we have to feed the fish. But the fish, as they feed, also pollute the tank. It is not enough to feed the fish. We also have to help change the water.

---

[16] On politics within the American Law Institute, see Alan Schwartz and Robert E. Scott, *The Political Economy of Private Legislation*, 143 U. PA. L. REV. 595 (1995).

When the Hurlyburly's Done:
The Bar's Struggle with the SEC*

*Susan P. Koniak***

INTRODUCTION

Enron went bust. Global Crossing went bust. WorldCom went bust. And underneath all their apparent gold we found, not mere mistakes, but rot and more rot and more rot still. And the rot had to be named, and it was: accounting scandal. The name stuck, and names matter. Arthur Andersen knows.

As I write this in February 2003, nearly a year after the Enron avalanche, the public's attention has moved past corporate scandal to matters of war and terrorism. Congress has grown tired of financial corruption hearings. Harvey Pitt's long exit from the Securities and Exchange Commission ("SEC") is finally complete. The overworked staff presses on, issuing regulation after regulation, as the agency was directed to do by Sarbanes-Oxley,[1] the reform bill, once thought dead, that got its second wind when WorldCom came tumbling down in Enron's wake. But SEC regulations cannot compete with the matters of life and death that now consume our nation. And so it should be.

Nonetheless, someone has to be minding the store. Some of our biggest companies have not just gone bankrupt; we found out they were made of papier mâché. And for years no one noticed, or no one who noticed told. The two largest banks, not just in this country, but in the world (yes, the world), were hauled before Congress and, in a set of remarkable hearings, were exposed to be carnival barkers, shell game aficionados, hawkers of snake oil, and only the slightest bit ashamed. All this trouble is not the

---

* Originally published at 103 COLUM. L. REV. 1236 (2003). Reprinted with permission.

** Professor of Law, Boston University School of Law. I owe a great debt of gratitude to Brad Meissner and Pankaj Venugopal of the *Columbia Law Review* for their tireless efforts in getting this manuscript in shape in a short period of time, for their patience and their good cheer throughout the process, and for their astute and helpful comments on the text. I also want to thank my colleague Professor Roger C. Cramton, with whom I wrote an article on Enron that unfortunately went unpublished because of scheduling problems and timeliness concerns. His diligence and insight are a constant source of support to me, but here they played a special role because of our earlier joint effort.

[1] Sarbanes-Oxley Act of 2002, Pub. L. No. 107-204, 116 Stat. 745 (codified in scattered sections of 11, 15, 18, 28, and 29 U.S.C).

work of the lone Arthur Andersen or any other accounting firm or all of them put together, either.

People and institutions broke the law. They lied to get the money of others, which is to say they committed fraud. Of those whom I believe committed crimes, few have been charged with crimes, and from all appearances, few will be. But just as I was convinced—before the jury began its deliberations—that O.J. Simpson was guilty of murder based on the evidence available, and remained convinced after the jury came back with its verdict of not guilty, I am convinced, based on the evidence available, that many (who may never be charged) have committed crimes in connection with the financial scams that came to light last year. In court, assuming these cases were brought and got to court, the charges might be difficult to prove. The schemes were complicated; the defendants would be well-heeled and would mount the best defenses that money could buy. But facts are stubborn things. So with or without trials, the legal judgment that I have made about those facts will abide (as long, that is, as my confidence in those facts remains). I repeat, people and institutions broke the laws: lots of people, lots of institutions, lots of laws.

And they did it with help. Sure, sure, the accountants pitched in. And some corporate executives, some analysts, and some traders showed entrepreneurial spirit and struck out to break laws on their own or with just a few of their fellows. But others, a good many others, had lawyers showing them the way. Lawyers structuring bogus deals, vouching for nonexistent "sales," writing whitewash reports to keep the law enforcers fooled and away. Lawyers going all out for, they would say, their "clients." As a technical matter, though, the lawyers were not going all out for "their clients" but for the reckless and dishonest cowboys in control of their clients. The clients of these lawyers were, after all, not corporate executives, but the corporations (some now bankrupt, for all their lawyers' tender care)—entities owned by all those duped shareholders.

Unlike their accountant cousins, the lawyers have, however, largely escaped responsibility for their role in this nation's latest spate of corporate fraud. Law firms were not hauled before Congress to face tough and detailed questions on their practices. Some of Enron's lawyers testified, but relatively early on, before most of the documents and other material necessary for a thorough examination of the practices of these lawyers was available to the Congressional investigators (or, at least, before that material had been assimilated by members of Congress and their staffs). I watched the testimony of Vinson & Elkins, one of Enron's lead law firms, and the testimony of (the now late) Brobeck, Phleger & Harrison (and assorted other firms), who had worked on Enron's energy trading schemes. The questioning of the law firms was softball compared to the serious grilling that the banks had to endure at the hands of Senator Levin.[2] More

---

[2] *See Lessons Learned from Enron: Hearing Before the S. Permanent Subcomm. On Investigations, Gov'tal Affairs Comm.*, 107th Cong. (2002), *available at* 2002 WL 31781071; *The Role of Financial Institutions In the Enron Collapse: Hearing Before the S. Permanent Subcomm. On Investigations, Gov'tal Affairs Comm.*, 107th Cong. (2002), *available at* 2002 WL 1767468; *Financial Institutions and the Collapse of Enron: Hearing Before the S. Permanent Subcomm. On Investigations, Gov'tal Affairs Comm.*, 107th Cong. (2002), *available at* 2002 WL 1722723.

telling, as more and more information emerged about the role that law firms played in the financial wheeling and dealing that ended up fleecing Enron investors, Vinson & Elkins was not recalled, nor were any of the other law firms—some named, some not—that now seemed to have been involved in Enron's shady transactions. The SEC announced no investigations of law firms, or even of individual lawyers, for their role in Enron's scams. Somewhat late in the game, the Justice Department issued a statement saying that its efforts to address corporate fraud would include scrutiny of the conduct of lawyers, among other professional advisors. But, since then, nothing more has been heard from the Justice Department about potential lawyer prosecutions, and, if something is in the offing, the press has yet to have ferreted it out.

But I'm leaving something out. Congress acted. The Sarbanes-Oxley Act, the bill designed to address Enron and the other blockbuster frauds so recently exposed, required the SEC to issue rules governing the conduct of securities lawyers. The relevant provision, Section 307 of the Act, further states that those rules should include a rule requiring lawyers to report, to the company's chief legal officer or CEO, evidence that company employees are violating the securities laws (or otherwise breaching their fiduciary duties).[3] If the reporting lawyer does not receive an appropriate response to the presentation of such evidence, the lawyer is to continue "up the ladder" and report the evidence to the company's board of directors or an appropriate committee of that board. That's something. Or is it?

When I worked with Senator Edwards's staff to draft the amendment that became Section 307, I certainly hoped so. But knowing, as I did, the history of the bar's battles with the SEC, battles that the government always seemed to end up losing, I was not confident that the amendment, even if it eventually passed, would end up changing anything. It did pass. The SEC issued its proposed rules. The bar fought back. The SEC retreated; the SEC would say that it retreated "a little," but retreating is surely not a sign of impending victory. This saga is not yet over; that much is true. But there is a history, and that history foretells an ending here, an ending that maintains the status quo. That ending leaves lawyers free to continue helping major corporations to deceive the investing public. That ending guarantees us more Enrons—lots more.

Whatever else more extraordinary is going on in the world as you read this, take a break to think about the ordinary and consider with me that prospect. Am I right? And, if so, why isn't anything being done about it? Will that change?

I. LAWYER PARTICIPATION IN CORPORATE FRAUD

Once upon a time, Enron had a legitimate special purpose entity ("SPE") called JEDI.[4] I say "legitimate" because, originally, JEDI had a real and independent outside investor that held a 50% interest in the SPE, and that was more than sufficient, under the relevant accounting rules, for Enron to report JEDI's profits on its books, but not

---

[3] Pub. L. No. 107-204 § 307 (codified at 15 U.S.C. § 7245 (2002)).

[4] *In re* Enron Corp. Sec., Derivative & ERISA Litig., 235 F. Supp. 2d 549, 614 (S.D. Tex. 2002).

list its debts. JEDI was apparently responsible for a hefty share of Enron's profits in 1997, maybe as much as 40%.[5] Near the end of 1997, the outside investors wanted out of the deal. If Enron could not find another outside investor to hold at least a 3% equity interest in JEDI, Enron would have to "consolidate" JEDI on its balance sheet, which would mean including JEDI's debts—wiping out all the profit that JEDI had been contributing to Enron's financial statements in 1997 and depriving Enron of the healthy-looking JEDI profits for future financial statements.

Enron could not find an independent outside investor for JEDI. Instead, it formed Chewco, which was totally controlled by Enron. Enron got Barclays Bank to lend Chewco $240 million to buy a 3% interest in JEDI.[6] But Chewco, allegedly the complete creation and instrument of Enron, also needed a 3% equity holder. Enron got "Barclays Bank to lend $11.4 million to two 'straw' parties, Little River and Big River," which served as the supposed "independent" three percent investors in Chewco and which were created specifically for that purpose.[7] Chewco also needed a manager.

If a senior manager of Enron had been put in control of Chewco, that fact would have to be disclosed by Enron to the SEC and investors. Apparently to avoid that disclosure, Michael Kopper, an employee who worked for Enron's CFO, Andrew Fastow, was put in charge of Chewco. For playing this role, Kopper was apparently given an interest in Chewco. Kopper transferred that interest to his life partner, again, allegedly as part of the scheme to hide Enron's control of Chewco.[8]

What did the lawyers do to facilitate this transaction? First, it should be apparent from what has been said thus far that the involvement of lawyers was necessary to implement these machinations. Indeed, it seems obvious that lawyers must have "structured" the various steps in this scheme. The point of the scheme was to create the impression of compliance with rules of law and accounting that would justify keeping JEDI's profits on Enron's books and its debts off those books. Yes, accountants can be helpful for these tasks, but all in all, creating the impression of compliance with rules is work that lawyers are especially "qualified" to do. And the complaint in the Enron securities litigation alleges that lawyers did just that in this case with Chewco.

According to the complaint, two large and prestigious firms, Vinson & Elkins ("Vinson") and Kirkland & Ellis ("Kirkland"), were involved in this scheme and in many of Enron's later, similarly fraudulent, transactions. Vinson represented Enron,

---

[5] That is the percent alleged in the plaintiffs' consolidated complaint. *Id.*

[6] *Id.*

[7] *Id.* at 615.

[8] In August 2002, Mr. Kopper pled guilty on counts of conspiracy to commit wire fraud and money laundering arising out of his activities while managing the partnership. Kurt Eichenwald, *Enron's Many Strands: The Overview; Ex-Enron Official Admits Payments to Finance Chief,* N.Y. TIMES, Aug. 22, 2002, at A1.

and Kirkland represented both Chewco and JEDI,[9] as well as later other Enron-related partnerships or entities.[10] Together, the two law firms allegedly set up Chewco and advised Enron and its management that putting Kopper in charge would avoid the senior manager disclosure problem. Presumably, both firms had knowledge of and helped paper the loans that funded Chewco and Little and Big River and were then funneled to JEDI as its 3% equity interest—loans backed by documents that were titled with obscuring names, like "investment certificate," but which the court said in fact resembled promissory notes.[11] Kopper allegedly was concerned that managing Chewco, serving as the "owner of [its] general partner," and having an equity interest in Chewco's limited partner Big River,[12] all while serving as an Enron employee, was improper. Both law firms allegedly said it was fine. "Neither law firm insisted on disclosure of the [Kopper] arrangement in Enron's SEC filings even though the impropriety was obvious."[13] The Chewco/JEDI scam, allowing Enron to book JEDI's profits and not its losses, continued from the end of 1997 to 2001. Moreover, this deal provided a basic structure for many of Enron's later scams.[14]

According to the complaint, Enron's use of SPEs became more and more aggressive as the years rolled by. The complaint alleges that both law firms understood quite clearly that Enron's stock was backing these SPEs and that, if the value of the stock dropped, the SPEs would fail, leaving Enron without any of its make-believe profits.[15]

---

[9] From the facts thus far related on the relationship between Chewco and JEDI, it does not appear that either received independent or sound legal advice. If we take seriously the idea of entity-representation, which lawyers are required to do, *see, e.g.,* MODEL RULES OF PROF'L CONDUCT R. 1.13 (2002), JEDI's lawyers (and Chewco's) would and should have been concerned with whether either met, at a minimum, the three percent investment rule, as not meeting it might mean one's client was nothing more than a pawn in another's (here, Enron's) fraud and/or had managers using the entity to break the law. Instead, the allegations in the complaint suggest that Kirkland treated Enron and its managers as its de facto clients, ignoring the interests of the paper-thin clients that their responsibilities as lawyers required them to take seriously. Making the conflict problem worse, Kirkland apparently also served as Andrew Fastow's personal counsel. *In re* Enron, 235 F. Supp. 2d at 672. According to the complaint, Fastow, currently facing criminal charges for his waist-deep involvement in Enron's schemes, *see* Kurt Eichenwald, *Ex-Enron Finance Chief Is Indicted on 78 Counts,* N.Y. TIMES, Nov. 1, 2002, at C2, was the person whom the firm treated as a real client. *In re* Enron, 235 F. Supp. 2d at 669. That client seems to have been the architect of massive fraud. Would Kirkland have it that it was Fastow's innocent dupe? In any event, the court granted Kirkland's motion to dismiss. *See infra* note 26 and accompanying text.

[10] *In re* Enron, 235 F. Supp. 2d at 669–73.

[11] *Id.* at 615, 658, 670.

[12] The opinion is unclear on whether Kopper "owned" Big River outright or whether his equity interest was controlling (or less than that). *See id.* at 670.

[13] *Id.* at 659.

[14] *Id.* at 616. And the law firms were allegedly around to paper a good number of those deals, too. *See id.* at 656–58, 669–70.

[15] *See id.* at 659–60, 672.

When, at the end of 2000, that "death spiral" seemed imminent, "Kirkland & Ellis helped restructure and capitalize the Raptor SPEs . . . by transferring even more shares of Enron stock to them."[16] The firm allegedly did the same thing the next year, arranging to transfer even more Enron stock to prevent the SPEs from failing. The now-famous Sherron Watkins memo, warning Enron's management that the company was engaged in massive wrongdoing that would likely lead to its demise, used the financing of the Raptors with Enron stock as exhibit one.[17]

The above cursory description just begins to scratch the surface of Enron's scandalous conduct. Thus far, it might appear that only two law firms were involved in this mess, but that is not true. Another aspect of Enron's conduct must be described to provide even a hint of how many lawyers and law firms were part of these schemes. Here, Enron made money and other assets go round in circles to inflate its profits. For example, J.P. Morgan (which was by no means the only bank to engage in this kind of behavior with Enron), set up an SPE of its own, Mahonia. Mahonia was controlled by J.P. Morgan (as was, for example, Delta, Citigroup's version of Mahonia), and its purpose was to engage in money-go-round deals.[18] J.P. Morgan would arrange to "pre-pay" Mahonia for oil or gas; Mahonia would arrange to "pre-pay" Enron for the designated commodity; and finally, Enron would arrange to "buy" the commodity from J.P. Morgan in the future for a price that appeared to be the amount that J.P. Morgan had originally laid out (to Mahonia, which ended up at Enron via the Mahonia-Enron leg of the deal), plus interest. In other words, J.P. Morgan was lending Enron money through Mahonia and calling it something else, so that Enron would not have to disclose this debt on its balance sheets. Instead, Enron would book as trading profit the money transferred to it from Mahonia and list as a trading liability the money it was due to pay back to J.P. Morgan.

The court in Texas found that the description of this scheme sufficed to justify denying J.P. Morgan's motion to dismiss the claim brought by Enron's shareholders against the bank that it had defrauded them (in cahoots with Enron).[19] Merrill Lynch and Citigroup, to name just two other banks, apparently engaged in similar money-go-round deals: loans to Enron that were disguised as trades or sales.[20]

These money-go-round deals are especially important to my claim that lawyers were central, even more central than accountants, to the corporate fraud at Enron.

---

[16] *Id.* at 672.

[17] *See id.* at 657 n. 92 (quoting Watkins memo).

[18] *See id.* at 627–28; *The Role of Financial Institutions in Enron's Collapse: Hearing before the Senate Permanent Subcomm. on Investigations*, 107th Cong. 14–16, 22–23 (2002) (statement of Robert L. Roach, Counsel and Chief Investigator, Senate Permanent Subcommittee on Investigations) [hereinafter Roach Statement], *available at* 2002 WL 1613793.

[19] *In re* Enron, 235 F. Supp. 2d at 697.

[20] *Id.* at 628–29, 651 n. 87; Roach Statement, *supra* note 18, at 16; Kurt Eichenwald, *4 at Merrill Accused of an Enron Fraud*, N.Y. TIMES, Mar. 18, 2003, at C1.

Accountants cannot book such circles as "sales" instead of "loans" without two legal opinions: a "true sale" opinion and a "nonconsolidation" opinion. The accountants, in other words, could not act without the lawyers vouching for these deals—not the other way around, as many lawyers would have people believe. Vinson apparently issued "true sales" opinions in a number of these transactions,[21] although it was surely not the only firm to do so.[22] More important, each of the banks had lawyers who helped the banks with their part of the sham. The banks' lawyers set up puppet SPEs to allow the banks to funnel loans to Enron disguised as trades or sales. The lawyers also helped the banks to protect themselves from the prospect that Enron would go belly-up from the weight of all this undisclosed debt by helping the banks to sell off or insure against their exposure to Enron if Enron defaulted on its promise to "buy" its own oil or gas back from the bank—that is, to repay the loan.[23]

How many major law firms were helping banks in what appear to be fraudulent transactions? The Texas court denied motions to dismiss charges of securities fraud in connection with Enron's shady deals against Citigroup, J.P. Morgan, Credit Suisse First Boston, and Merrill Lynch. I have no doubt that those banks were represented by the "best" legal talent in this country—law firms considered to be of the highest caliber. And none of those lawyers noticed anything amiss? We are not just to believe that the banks are all innocent, something I personally do not believe, having watched every single minute of the testimony given by Citigroup's and J.P. Morgan's managers before the Senate Permanent Subcommittee on Investigations.[24] Are we also to believe that all the lawyers who worked on these deals were incapable of grasping just what it was they were doing? I rest my case.[25]

It should be noted that the court in Texas denied Vinson's motion to dismiss fraud charges against it, but granted Kirkland's motion. Does that mean Kirkland did no

---

[21] *In re* Enron, 235 F. Supp. 2d at 704; Mike France, *What About the Lawyers?*, BUS. WK., Dec. 23, 2002, at 58, 61.

[22] *See* France, *supra* note 21, at 61–62.

[23] *In re* Enron, 235 F. Supp. 2d at 628, 636.

[24] Senator Levin's questioning of these witnesses was masterful. The documents, which demonstrated that the banks knew precisely how bogus these deals were, were devastating. The amount of legal work that went into constructing these deals was apparent and disgraceful.

[25] I rest only because of space limitations, not because I have run out of specific and concrete examples of wrongdoing. Vinson went on to conduct a "preliminary investigation" of the Sherron Watkins memo for Enron, something that was improper for it to do, given how involved it was in the very schemes it was supposedly investigating. *See In re* Enron, 235 F. Supp. 2d at 668 n.103 (discussing Vinson's conflict of interest). It conducted only the most cursory kind of "investigation" and then issued a report to Enron's management saying that nothing further had to be done to follow up on the Watkins charges. Simpson Thacher & Bartlett did a similar service for Global Crossing, except that its "investigation" was even more cursory. *See* Joseph Menn, *Global Crossing Case Figure Not Questioned*, L.A. TIMES, Feb. 22, 2002, at C1. For an excellent discussion of some of these matters, see Roger C. Cramton, *Enron and the Corporate Lawyer: A Primer on Legal and Ethical Issues*, 58 BUS. LAW. 143, 162–67 (2002), and *reprinted in this book* at 571–623.

wrong? No. It means that the court found the allegations against the firm insufficient to hold it liable as a primary violator of the securities laws' prohibitions against fraud. You see, Kirkland did not represent Enron, at least not technically. As a result, the opinions and documents that Kirkland issued were not issued directly to Enron's investors, but rather were issued to Enron itself or others.[26]

II. WHY THE REGULATION OF LAWYERS FAILS

A. Two Laws

The first article I wrote as a legal academic described two laws of lawyering: one maintained by the bar, the other maintained by the state.[27] I described how these two laws diverged.[28] I explained how the bar's law treated confidentiality as a constitutional norm[29] to which other norms must be subordinated. Loyalty to clients (some-

---

[26] As the court explained:

> Any documents that [Kirkland & Ellis] drafted were for private transactions between Enron and the SPEs and the partnerships and were not included in or drafted for any public disclosure or shareholder solicitation. Any opinion letters that the firm wrote are not alleged to have reached the plaintiffs nor been drafted for the benefit of the plaintiffs.

In re Enron, 235 F. Supp. 2d at 706. Those opinions helped Enron's schemes, but helping is no longer enough. Private parties may no longer sue anyone for aiding and abetting securities fraud. *See infra* text accompanying notes 112–16. I am convinced that the allegations discussed by the court would have been sufficient to sustain claims for aiding and abetting liability against the firm, but the plaintiffs had to show more. The SEC, as opposed to private parties, can still bring civil charges against law firms or anyone else for aiding and abetting securities fraud, although in 1995 Congress changed the SEC's burden from having to show "reckless" aiding of fraud to "knowing" aiding. *See* Private Securities Litigation Reform Act of 1995, Pub. L. No. 104-67 § 104, 109 Stat. 737, 757 (codified as amended at 15 U.S.C. § 78t (2000)). Nonetheless, the SEC still can bring these charges.

Aiding and abetting securities fraud is also still a crime. *See* Cent. Bank of Denver v. First Interstate Bank of Denver, 511 U.S. 164, 190 (1994) (noting criminal prohibition against aiding or abetting a criminal violation of the securities laws). The SEC has not brought such charges against Kirkland, or any other law firm for that matter.

[27] Susan P. Koniak, *The Law Between the Bar and the State*, 70 N.C. L. REV. 1389, 1409–27 (1992).

[28] "Two" is a simplification. There are some segments of the bar, lawyers at the SEC or with other branches of the government, whose "law" is closer to state law than to the law maintained by most of the bar. Similarly, there are certain states whose law (or some of it) is closer to that articulated by the bar than that articulated by most of the other states or the federal government. For example, California's law of confidentiality is closer to the bar's law in expressing a near absolute view of confidentiality than the law of almost any other state or the federal government. Nonetheless, the law maintained by almost all subgroups of the bar is more akin to that of other bar subgroups than it is to the law maintained by almost all government units, and the reverse is true as well. What I call "bar law" in this essay should be understood as a restatement of the majority position expressed by most bar groups as their law, and, similarly, the "state law" I describe is an ideal type of the law as expressed by most, albeit not all, government entities.

[29] By "constitutional norm," I mean a norm so central to group definition that it helps constitute the group itself. To be a lawyer is to embrace, celebrate, live by, and protect the norm of client confidentiality.

times referred to by lawyers as the duty of "zealous advocacy"), a norm connected to confidentiality, is also constitutional for the bar. It shapes the bar's understanding of the other norms that address lawyer conduct and is capable of trumping those norms, if necessary—i.e., if those other norms are resistant to interpretations that render them consistent with the constitutional norm.

The state's law, I explained, did not reflect the same hierarchy of norms.[30] In the state's law, the ethics rules, including the duties of confidentiality and loyalty to clients, are to be read as subordinate to other state law, not the other way around. Tax laws requiring lawyers to disclose cash payments of more than a certain amount, for example, trump the duty of confidentiality, according to the state.[31] The bar maintains that this is not so.[32] Moreover, by example after example, I demonstrated that the divergence obvious in the tax example just given is pervasive and predictable in other areas of law.[33]

How can there be two laws? Isn't the state's law real "law," and what I am calling the bar's law nothing more than advocacy about law—a legal understanding put forth by a private group to be accepted or rejected by the state?

The seemingly simple question I have just posed is simple only if we agree on a definition of the word "law." If we agree that the word "law" means that which the state says is law and nothing else, then "right" is the correct response to the question. But defining "law" is no simple task, and there are strong reasons, particularly salient to the subject matter of this essay—the involvement of lawyers in corporate fraud—to challenge what has become the standard understanding of the word "law," i.e., that law is simply what the state says it is.

Why is defining "law" so difficult? In *The Folktales of Justice: Tales of Jurisdiction*,[34] Robert Cover reminded us that H.L.A. Hart began his great work, *The Concept of Law*,[35] with a discussion of why the definition of law, so basic a question, has plagued jurisprudence for so long, when analogous questions, such as "what is chemistry?" have not proven particularly problematic. Hart's book is his answer: Law is a complex social institution, whose richness is not easily captured by the analytic tools and categories we use to describe it. But Cover wrote that there was a more direct answer to Hart's puzzle, a political and historical answer, as opposed to Hart's analytic response.

If we ask "what is science?," as opposed to "what is chemistry?" the debate over meaning is much closer to what we perceive in the debate over what counts as "law." That is so because the word "science," unlike the word "chemistry," but like the word

---

[30] *See* Koniak, *supra* note 27, at 1411–13.

[31] *Id.* at 1405.

[32] *Id.* at 1405–07.

[33] *Id.* at 1422–24.

[34] Robert M. Cover, *The Folktales of Justice: Tales of Jurisdiction*, 14 CAP. U. L. REV. 179 (1985).

[35] H.L.A. HART, THE CONCEPT OF LAW (1961).

"law," is a powerful normative commodity.[36] Whether one is doing science is normatively significant. If yes, then one's activity qualifies as a method of deriving a form of
truth—a specially privileged method of deriving truth, one with a powerful claim to
legitimacy. If not, then one is denied that kind of legitimacy (although one may be
participating in other legitimate activities). To affirm or deny that something is chemistry, as opposed to biochemistry or physics, does not involve similar stakes. To label
something "law" or not is at least as normatively charged a naming as proclaiming
something "science" or not. As Cover explained:

> The struggle over what is "law" is . . . a struggle over which social patterns
> can plausibly be coated with a veneer which changes the very nature of that
> which it covers up. There is not automatic legitimation of an institution by
> calling it or what it produces "law," but the label is a move, the staking out
> of a position in the complex social game of legitimation.[37]

I am often asked whether I am accusing lawyers of getting up in the morning intent
on breaking the law, and helping their clients to do so, too. I am not. I think that
lawyers believe what they are doing is lawful, that advising their clients in a manner
that I believe ends up undermining state law[38] is their job. I think that they believe, at
the end of the day, that they have done the right thing, acted not just as law permits,
but as it commands them to act. In other words, the bar's legal vision functions as law;
it operates not just plausibly, but also convincingly, to coat lawyer behavior, at least in
the minds of those acting (lawyers), with a veneer that changes the nature of the activity itself, making it "right." The bar's legal vision functions as law thoroughly enough
to render state law that is contrary to it at best ambiguous and at worst illegitimate—
the bar's vision functions in the day-to-day life of a substantial segment of the bar to
nullify state law. Something with that power is not a plea for law; it is law.

How could private groups have law at odds with the law of the state, when the state,
has force at its disposal to insist that its law be obeyed? And how could lawyers, expert
by definition at finding the state's law, not recognize that their actions were at odds with
it and that the state would be likely to call those actions "unlawful?" Assuming, as I do,
that you, my reader, are a lawyer (or, at least, a law student), you know that the clarity of
state law is not a constant. Some matters of state law are more debatable than others.
Now, what makes some state law more unclear than other state law? Sometimes it is the
sparsity (or perceived sparsity) of examples (stamped official by the state, as in court
opinions) of what a legal rule means in action. That might be either a function of the
real number of opinions being low or the proliferation of permutations of actions, each

---

[36] Cover, *supra* note 34, at 179–80.

[37] *Id.* at 181.

[38] I mean to refer here particularly to state law designed to prevent fraud, and to a lesser degree, state
law designed to prevent obstruction of justice.

slightly different from those encompassed by existing case law, even when the total number of cases is large. Notice that the second possibility, action-proliferation, is likely to be correlated with lawyer involvement in crafting behavior—behavior designed specifically to be outside (if only by a bit) the behavior designated as illegal by the state.

This "example gap" is not, however, the only variable affecting the clarity of state law. There is also "enforcement gap." By that, I mean state law whose meaning is clouded by the fact that the state demonstrates continued uncertainty about whether to hold anyone to the meaning that it has articulated as "law." Is it illegal or not for consenting adults to engage in oral sex in those states where the statutes still declare such conduct a crime? Is a contract to keep silent about criminal behavior illegal, as most state codes still declare, or does the open toleration by the state of settlement contracts to keep secret, for example, sexual abuse by priests, mean that these contracts are legal?[39]

Both example gaps and enforcement gaps may be (and perhaps always are) manifestations of a struggle over law, demonstrations of the existence of alternative legal understandings prepared to resist whatever it is the state is perceived to be saying (or trying to say). Unless the state is firmly committed to its vision of law, when faced with a private group committed to an alternative legal vision (with any chance of mustering the support of others in the larger community), the state is likely to make room, if not give in completely. One way to make room, to avoid unseemly and costly battles, is to create a gap in enforcement. Another is to cede ground to the proliferation of examples, allowing that law already articulated may not apply here or there, or, in the end, anywhere.

In short, the less committed the state is to its law and the more committed a private group is to a competing legal vision, the more likely we are to see significant example and enforcement gaps—in other words, the more likely we are to see unclear state law. In the battle between the bar and the state, the bar is very committed, but the state is weakly committed. Example and enforcement gaps abound, which means that it is easy for lawyers to continue to understand their law as "the law," without having to imagine themselves as lawbreakers.

From the perspective of the state, the ethics rules acknowledge the centrality and superiority of state law by insisting that lawyers not aid clients in unlawful activity.[40]

---

[39] For a more extensive discussion of this issue, see Susan P. Koniak, *Conference on Legal Ethics: "What Needs Fixing?": Are Agreements to Keep Secret Information Learned in Discovery Legal, Illegal or Something in Between?*, 30 HOFSTRA L. REV. 783 (2002).

[40] *See* MODEL RULES OF PROF'L CONDUCT R. 1.2(d) (2002). Additionally, the newly adopted Model Rule 1.6(b)(4) allows a lawyer to reveal confidences to comply with "other law or a court order." *Id.* R. 1.6(b)(4). The Model Code of Professional Responsibility included such an exception to confidentiality, but it was omitted from the Model Rules of Professional Conduct when they were adopted in 1983. *Cf. infra* notes 91–96 and accompanying text (discussing the American Bar Association's debate on the confidentiality provision in the Model Rules). The fact that the Model Code's "other law" exception to confidentiality was deleted from the Model Rules and remained out for over a decade demonstrates just how contingent the obligation to obey other law is, according to the bar's law.

But from the bar's perspective, ethical precepts that require lawyers to obey the law and to refrain from helping clients to break the law are contingent obligations, not constitutional norms. Example gaps and enforcement gaps are important here too. What does it mean to obey the law when the meaning of law is never certain? The ethics rules prohibit "knowing" assistance of illegality. Can lawyers ever "know" that X behavior will violate the law?[41]

In law schools, it is common to hear professors speak about training each student to "think like a lawyer," by which they mean to refer to analytic thinking, the ability to parse and critique an argument. But there is something much more central to lawyer thinking than that: the ability to envision the client's behavior as legal. Every lawyer understands, no matter what words she uses for it, that example and enforcement gaps are inherent in the nature of law. Moreover, we are not just trained to see them. The constitutional norm of client loyalty, as understood by lawyers, demands that we find them, demands that we use all our skill to imagine as legal, what our clients did, do, and want to do. Those who drafted rules demanding that a lawyer stop helping the client when the lawyer "knows" that she is assisting a crime or fraud understood that. In the bar's normative universe, lawyers never "know." State law, on the other hand, asserts that lawyers know before others are expected to know (however loath the state is to hold lawyers to that principle).[42] To the state, it is our job to know; to the bar, it is our job not to know. We have two laws, centered on two very different world views.

B. Divergence

1. *National Student Marketing Corporation.* In the early 1970s, the SEC took on the bar.[43] It filed a complaint against two major law firms, Lord, Bissell & Brook ("LBB") and White & Case ("W&C"), stating that the firms, as well as individual lawyers within those firms, had aided and abetted securities fraud by sitting passively by while directors of their client companies committed securities fraud. The companies, National Student Marketing Corp. ("NSMC") and Interstate Corp., had planned a merger and had solicited shareholder approval of the deal by disseminating information to

---

[41] In addition to the problem of "knowing," the obligation to obey the law is rendered contingent by bar attempts to limit what counts as "law" for purposes of the duty to obey. *See infra* notes 61–69 and accompanying text.

[42] "In view of the obvious materiality of the information, *especially to attorneys learned in securities law*, the attorneys' responsibilities to their corporate client required them to take steps to ensure that the information would be disclosed to the shareholders." SEC v. Nat'l Student Mktg. Corp., 457 F. Supp. 682, 713 (D.D.C. 1978) (emphasis added); *see also* U.S. v. Benjamin, 328 F.2d 854, 861–63 (2d Cir. 1964) (stating that the "actor's *special situation* and continuity of conduct" may allow an inference of knowledge where it might otherwise not be appropriate; referring to a lawyer and an accountant, and making clear that their "special situation" was as "members of these ancient professions") (emphasis added).

[43] The following factual description relies upon the opinion in SEC v. Nat'l Student Mktg. Corp., 457 F. Supp. 682, 687–99 (D.D.C. 1978).

shareholders that showed that the purchasing company, NSMC, was expected to have a $700,000 profit for the first nine months of that year. On the morning of the closing, however, the accountants had still not delivered a "comfort letter," required by the terms of the agreement, confirming that the $700,000 figure was legitimate (i.e., was arrived at in accordance with Generally Accepted Accounting Principles). A dictated letter finally arrived, listing various adjustments that would have to be made to the nine-month projected financial statement—adjustments that would transform the $700,000 expected profit into a projected loss of approximately $184,000.[44] The directors decided to close the deal anyway and did so with at least the tacit acquiescence of the lawyers present.

The SEC filed an enforcement action against NSMC, the directors of both companies, the lawyers who had been present at the meeting, and their law firms. The company and directors were charged with securities fraud for having closed the deal without disclosing material information to the shareholders—the significant change in NSMC's financial picture. The lawyers were charged with aiding and abetting that fraud. The SEC's complaint said that the lawyers had a duty to their client companies not to sit silently by while the companies' agents (here, the directors) committed fraud. According to the SEC, the law demanded that lawyers, plainly aware that material information was being withheld, had to speak up and demand that the directors comply with the law by disclosing the information to the shareholders and the SEC. If the directors had nonetheless persisted in going forward, the lawyers should have resigned and told the shareholders or the SEC themselves. The SEC's complaint was a statement that the law required lawyers to behave this way.

The bar was incensed. According to the securities bar, the lawyers had acted in accordance with the law. They had discussed the matter with their clients, acknowledged the right of the directors to make decisions on behalf of their respective companies, and, most important, kept their mouths shut about their clients' business, respecting the paramount duty of confidentiality. To the bar, the SEC's position was outrageous. The SEC was seeking to change lawyers from client-defenders into whistleblowers and policemen, thereby interfering with a central premise of our republic—the existence of an independent bar to stand between an individual (or company) and the all-powerful state. It is difficult to overstate the vehemence of the bar's reaction to the SEC complaint; references to the return of King George were commonplace, and the rhetoric suggested that the liberty of all Americans was at stake.

Where on earth had the SEC gotten the subversive ideas it put forth in its complaint? From the law extant in virtually every jurisdiction in the country, the ethics rules adopted or accepted by the states and the federal courts. In the early 1970s, virtually every jurisdiction in this country used as law a version of either the American Bar Association's Model Code of Professional Responsibility ("Model Code"), written in

---

[44] A later version of the comfort letter showed a change in the required adjustments and stated that the projected loss would be approximately $80,000.

1969, or its predecessor, the Canons of Professional Ethics ("the Canons"), first written in 1908 and revised from time to time thereafter. The Canons said: "The announced intention of a client to commit a crime is not included within the confidence [a lawyer] is bound to respect."[45] Securities fraud is a crime. The Canons also said:

> When a lawyer discovers some fraud or deception has been practiced, which has unjustly imposed upon . . . a party, he should endeavor to rectify it; at first by advising his client, and if his client refuses to forego the advantage thus unjustly gained, he should promptly inform the injured person or his counsel, so that they may take appropriate steps.[46]

This precept was not changed when the Model Code was written to replace the Canons; in fact, it was reiterated.[47]

However clear the Model Code and the Canons may appear to be, as every lawyer knows (or should know), rules alone are not enough to constitute law. We must ask how those rules are interpreted. The SEC, here representing the state's understanding of the law, interpreted those rules in what might be called the more straightforward fashion, although that should not be read to mean "the right way."[48]

The bar's contrary interpretation, however, was not invented to defeat the SEC's claim. The bar had long maintained that the words in the Canons and the Model Code (about disclosing client fraud when the client refused to rectify it) were subordinate to the duty of confidentiality. A norm that defines a group and its purpose—a constitutional norm—does not yield to other interests, however noble, such as protecting third parties from harm. However troubling the result may be in any individual case, the nonconstitutional interest must be the one to yield. This is a coherent legal position. It is not disingenuous or legal gibberish. It is, however, at odds with the law of the state, here exemplified by the SEC's complaint.

Just as the bar's law follows naturally from its understanding of the constitutional nature of the norm of confidentiality, the state's law is similarly rooted in a world view that orders norms. If we concentrate on lawyers as champions for clients, particularly in battles against the state, it is easy to understand how confidentiality and client loyalty are the constitutional norms. But, if instead, we see the primary function of

---

[45] ABA Canons of Professional Ethics, Canon 37 (1908).

[46] *Id.*, Canon 41.

[47] Model Code of Prof'l Responsibility DR 7-102(B)(1) (1969).

[48] I am not just saying this to appear fair. For example, it might equally be said (indeed, the Supreme Court seems to have said this) that the plain language of the securities laws does not provide for a private cause of action for aiding and abetting liability, and, therefore, there is none. *See* Cent. Bank of Denver v. First Interstate Bank of Denver, 511 U.S. 164, 175–78 (1994). But I believe that such a "straightforward" reading is wrong. Later, I explain what I mean when I assert that a legal interpretation is valid or invalid. *See infra* note 137. Here, suffice it to say that I reject the idea that the words of a rule are sufficient to decide the matter.

lawyers to be counseling others on the requirements of state law, the duty to ensure that one's services are not used to pervert state law becomes the constitutional touchstone. The law set out by the SEC emerges from this constitutional perspective and not just from the words quoted above from the Canons or the Model Code. Lawyers see themselves as champions; the state views them as keepers of the flame. Two distinct laws emerge from these competing visions.

Faced with the SEC's exposition of what state law required and the bar's version of what lawyers faced with clients who decide to withhold material information should do, the court had to choose between these competing visions. Its choice would, according to the state, stand as state law (at least within the jurisdiction of that court), unless and until overruled by a higher court.

The court, in *SEC v. National Student Marketing Corp.* (*"NSMC"*), said the lawyers had aided and abetted securities fraud.[49] But how? What should they have done differently? What does state law mean in action, according to the court? The court was quite shy to say. It said state law demanded that lawyers for corporations "at the very least" speak out to the agents of the company who are about to break the law, telling them clearly (and presumably forcefully) not to do it.[50] But what if the directors do not listen? The court refused to affirm the SEC's view of the law's demands at that point. At the same time, it refused to affirm the bar's view. Acknowledging in its opinion that the bar and the SEC were at odds on this question, and noting just how strongly the bar was protesting the SEC's view, the court said it trusted that the SEC's complaint had started a healthy debate that might well lead to the bar's reexamination of its view of lawyers' responsibilities.[51] Things did not turn out that way, but before getting to that, there is more to say about the court's opinion.

First, the opinion is parsimonious. The court justified its refusal to address whether lawyers should ever disclose client fraud to the state or affected parties by suggesting that the issue was best left to the bar and the SEC. It did not even make clear, as the SEC argued, that a lawyer whose services have been used or are about to be used to commit a fraud or crime must withdraw from the representation, a position again supported by language in extant ethics rules.[52] One might say that, having found some basis to hold that the lawyers aided and abetted securities fraud, the court had no need to say any more. But the issue before the court was whether to issue an injunction to prevent future lawbreaking by these lawyers. Nothing is more critical to that question

---

[49] Nat'l Student Mktg. Corp., 457 F. Supp. at 712–15.

[50] *Id.* at 713.

[51] *Id.* at 714.

[52] *See* MODEL CODE OF PROF'L RESPONSIBILITY DR 2-110(B)(2) (1969) (providing that a lawyer must withdraw from representation if his continued employment would violate the ethics rules). This duty to withdraw is clearly triggered where continued employment would result in aiding a client to commit fraud. *See id.* DR 7-102(A)(7) (stating that a lawyer shall not assist a client in illegal or fraudulent conduct).

than an assessment of just how bad the behavior of the defendants was in the past, including an accounting of just how many ways they had violated the law—here, how many ways they had helped the directors commit fraud. Thus, the court's failure to say whether it constituted unlawful assistance of a fraud for the lawyers not to have told the SEC of the fraud after the directors went through with the closing was not a natural legal move. The court was stretching not to discuss this point. It did not want to get in the middle of this fight over law. Of course, this is precisely the function of courts: to hear competing interpretations of what the law requires and to stamp one as official state law and disavow the other.

But the court's abdication of responsibility is even starker than this. Having held that the lawyers aided securities fraud, the court explained that no sanction was necessary.[53] Why? Well, the conduct was not that serious or persistent, the court said—although having failed to examine all the conduct that the SEC said was illegal, it is difficult to take this justification seriously. The court's second reason must bear more weight. The court explained that the defendants were lawyers and thus could be trusted in the future to abide by the law articulated by the court, at least now that that law had been set forth in the court's opinion.[54]

Elsewhere I have provided a more thorough analysis of the court's opinion, but something I have not previously discussed is the court's refusal to hold the lawyers accountable for what they did do, as opposed to what they failed to do—i.e., speak up at the closing or tell the SEC, the issue the court ducked. As I have watched the debate over lawyer responsibility unfold during the recent wave of corporate scandals, I have come to see the *NSMC* court's refusal to address the acts, as opposed to the omissions, of the lawyers involved as significant in a manner that I had previously neglected.

The SEC had alleged not just acts of omission but acts of commission. After the directors decided to proceed with the closing, notwithstanding the $884,000 discrepancy in NSMC's financial statement, the lawyers exchanged opinion letters stating that transactions in connection with the merger were in accordance with all applicable laws; and later LBB issued another opinion letter stating that the former directors of Interstate could sell their shares without violating an SEC rule on the sale of stock by insiders. The court held that the first opinion letter was not enough help to the fraud to constitute "substantial" assistance, which is required for aiding and abetting liability.[55] But that reasoning conflicts with the court's sole holding that silence during the meeting constitutes substantial assistance.

The court suggested that LBB's letter could be read, if only in small part, to state that Interstate had complied with the antifraud provisions of the securities laws.[56]

---

[53] Nat'l Student Mktg. Corp., 457 F. Supp. at 716.

[54] *Id.* at 716–17.

[55] *Id.* at 715.

[56] *Id.* at 714–15.

That means that the letter provided some evidence that the lawyers did not just remain silent, but rather acted in a manner that could have been read by the participants as blessing their actions as lawful. Indeed, the technicalities of the opinion letter's actual language notwithstanding, the overarching point of the exchange of such opinion letters is to signal that the lawyers have stamped the activity—at least that activity of which they were aware—as legal. But at the moment the letters were exchanged, any securities lawyer worth her salt, according to the court, would have known that the deal was not legal. To put it plainly, if silence was substantial assistance, how could an implicit signal that all was legal (the exchange of opinion letters) not be?

As to the opinion letter issued by LBB after the merger—the opinion letter blessing as legal the sale of shares by Interstate directors—the court's reasoning is, if anything, more confusing. The question was whether this opinion substantially assisted the sale of shares by Interstate directors after the merger when those directors were in possession of material information about the true value of those shares that they had acted to keep from the investing public (the buyers of those shares). The court pointed out that the content of the letter was primarily factual, but, of course, whether the letter was true or not, or whether the letter was itself fraudulent, was not the question; the question was whether the letter substantially assisted fraud. The court next mentioned that the letter was not intended for the investing public but was provided only to help NSMC and its counsel write up a more "formal, independent opinion" on the validity of the insider sales.[57] But again, one can substantially assist fraud (or any other illegal activity) through otherwise lawful acts; the fact that the letter was not itself a fraud on the public was simply not the issue. The only question was whether stating that the sale of shares was in compliance with X bit of law was a substantial help to the directors who were breaking Y bit of law, and the answer would appear to be "yes." Any blessing by a lawyer of an act as legal in some important aspect would seem to be a big help in facilitating the act. But not according to the court.

Why do I now see the *NSMC* court's active avoidance of the lawyers' acts of commission as significant in a manner that I did not earlier? As will become clearer when we get to the present debate over lawyer responsibility for the current wave of corporate frauds, one of the central tenets of the debate is the myth that lawyers are, at most, passive participants in the wrongdoing. They do not create the fraud. Others do that. Consider one of the bar's strongest and most constantly pressed arguments: Requiring lawyers to disclose corporate fraud (or, as many argue, even requiring them to take any strong actions to stop it, such as resigning) will only discourage corporate managers (or directors) from telling lawyers what they are doing, which will make it impossible for lawyers to have any influence in forestalling the wrongdoing. That argument presumes that most of the frauds could proceed without lawyer involvement, that lawyers are not part of the creation of the fraudulent schemes nor part of their implementation—at least not in a manner that would presume the lawyers understood what was

---

[57] *Id.* at 715.

going on. But the facts suggest otherwise.[58] And they suggested otherwise in *NSMC* as well.[59]

In the terms I introduced earlier, the court's opinion in *NSMC* seems designed to generate example gap with its refusal to tie the legal principle it enunciated to the activities of the lawyers in the case before it. It is also a stark demonstration of enforcement gap. The case set forth some law. It labeled some actions (more precisely, inactions) illegal. It just stated very little law (as little as possible). It avoided discussing most of the examples of conduct before it. And it rendered whatever little it said ambiguous, at best, by failing to attach any consequences to its holding that the lawyers had aided conduct that was not just a civil wrong, but also a felony. The court's commitment to the state law it was charged with articulating and enforcing was weak.

On the other hand, the bar's commitment to its defense of the activities of the *NSMC* lawyers and others like them was and remains strong. While the *NSMC* complaint was pending, the bar was busy. For example, the American Bar Association ("ABA") adopted a "Statement of Policy Regarding Responsibilities and Liabilities of Lawyers in Advising with Respect to the Compliance by Clients with Laws Administered by the Securities and Exchange Commission."[60] It states:

> [A]ny principle of law which, except as permitted or required by the [Model Code of Professional Responsibility], permits or obliges a lawyer to disclose to the SEC otherwise confidential information should be established only by statute after full and careful consideration of the public interests involved, and should be resisted unless clearly mandated by law.[61]

This is a remarkable bit of text. It has at least three audiences in mind. First, the *NSMC* court, to which the message is, "Lay off. It is illegitimate for you, as opposed to Con-

---

[58] *See* Part I of this essay (describing the actions of the lawyers in the Enron affair).

[59] W&C settled with the SEC, so its activities and those of its partner-in-charge were not before the court. Nonetheless, the court's description of that lawyer's activities demonstrates just how active lawyers can be. For example, unbeknownst to the Interstate lawyers, the W&C partner had a series of conversations with the accountants on the day of the closing that apparently involved considerable debate over just how forthright the comfort letter would be. Nat'l Student Mktg. Corp., 457 F. Supp. at 695. Presumably, the partner did everything he could to convince the accountants to downplay the discrepancy and portray it as an unextraordinary series of adjustments. After dictating the first version of the comfort letter (the most innocuous version), the accountants dictated two other versions to the W&C lawyer, each time with language increasingly strong on the significance of the adjustments to be made. The lawyer did not deliver either of those versions to the other participants at the meeting, at least not to Interstate or its lawyers. *Id.*

[60] *Statement of Policy Adopted by American Bar Association Regarding Responsibilities and Liabilities of Lawyers in Advising with Respect to the Compliance by Clients with Laws Administered by the Securities and Exchange Commission*, 31 BUS. LAW. 543, 543 (1975) [hereinafter *ABA Policy Statement*]. I put the name of the policy in the text for a reason. Notice the implicit separation of the SEC from the law the agency "administers" in this awkward and thus obviously consciously drafted title. The message is that the SEC's statements (certainly including its complaint) are a far cry from the law. The agency and the lawyers (advising on "compliance") are rendered equals by this artful phrasing.

[61] *Id.* at 544–45.

gress, to agree with the SEC that the law, under any circumstances, requires or even permits a lawyer to disclose client confidences to the agency." To bring home that point, the last paragraph of the policy statement worries about the possibility that some lawyers might be deterred from performing their duties (keeping confidences and maintaining their loyalty to the client) by either an "erroneous position of the SEC *or a questionable lower court decision.*"[62]

The second audience is Congress, to which the policy says, "We will vehemently oppose any such legislation before its passage and afterwards as well." The text does not, after all, content itself with stating that any statutory disclosure requirement (or even a statute purporting to give lawyers the discretion to disclose) should be adopted only after a lengthy period for consideration (and, of course, lobbying). More startling, it warns of resistance to any statutory command not "clearly mandated by law."[63] Here, we get a forewarning of the bar's intent to make the most of example gaps. It says, "We will limit the meaning of any law passed and any court interpretation holding that the law requires (or allows) disclosure by construing it for ourselves as narrowly as possible. Changing us with law will not be as easy as you think."[64]

Lawyers make up the third audience. To them, the policy is a text of resistance. Any community that maintains law at odds with the state must anticipate that the state will insist (with force) that its law must reign. How then are members of the group to react? Here, the policy states that even a statute, and thus by implication any lower court ruling, or rule or action by the SEC, "*should* be resisted unless clearly mandated by law."[65] This statement indicates that there is a limit to how far the bar expects its members to go in support of the bar's law when that law is inconsistent with the state's law; the bar expects resistance, but does not demand that its members martyr themselves.[66]

The policy statement was but one of the bar's preemptive and quite aggressive moves, while the *NSMC* complaint was pending, to stave off state law at variance with its own.[67] It also rewrote the ethics rule upon which the SEC was relying, DR 7-102(B)(1).

---

[62] *Id.* at 545 (emphasis added).

[63] *Id.*

[64] In testifying before Congress on efforts by the federal government to get criminal defense lawyers to testify about, *inter alia,* fees paid by clients, the then President-Elect of the National Association of Criminal Defense Lawyers put it this way: "Our members will litigate these issues at every turn." *Exercise of Federal Prosecutorial Authority in a Changing Legal Environment: Hearing Before the Subcomm. on Gov't Info., Justice, and Agric. of the House Comm. on Gov't Operations,* 101st Cong. 218 (1990) (statement of Alan Ellis, President-Elect, National Association of Criminal Defense Lawyers).

[65] *ABA Policy Statement, supra* note 60, at 545 (emphasis added).

[66] *See* Koniak, *supra* note 27, at 1422–26.

[67] *See* Junius Hoffman, *On Learning of a Corporate Client's Crime or Fraud—The Lawyer's Dilemma,* 33 BUS. LAW. 1389, 1406–08 (1978) (describing some of the other efforts by the ABA and state and local bars to restrict the obligations of securities lawyers in light of the SEC's *Nat'l Student Marketing* complaint). One particularly noteworthy example, because of its source—the heart of the securities bar—and its breadth, is *Association of the Bar of the City of New York, Report by Special Committee on Lawyers' Role in Securities Transactions,* 32 BUS. LAW. 1879, 1882–83, 1886–98 (1977) (setting forth guidelines for

In 1974, as a direct response to the filing of the *NSMC* complaint, the ABA House of Delegates adopted an amendment to this rule that effectively changed the meaning of the rule from "[a] lawyer shall disclose client fraud when the client refuses to rectify" to "a lawyer shall not disclose."[68] Of course, no provision of the ABA's Model Code (or its Model Rules of Professional Conduct ("Model Rules"), the ABA's current version of a model ethics code) is law, according to the state, until it is adopted by a state, and even then, it is only law in the form in which it is adopted. Notice the implicit assumption, evident too in the Policy Statement quoted above, that an ethics rule (state law, assuming the particular rule is adopted by some state) could or should trump federal securities law as interpreted by a court—here the court in mind was obviously the *NSMC* court. Official state law does not recognize that possibility; federal law would trump the state law, assuming that the federal law was in accordance with the United States Constitution (and the bar had no serious argument that requiring civil lawyers to disclose client fraud to the SEC would violate the Constitution). But in the bar's law, ethics rules are presumed to have the power to trump all other law.[69]

Is it possible that I am making too much of the SEC's position in *NSMC* or the court's admittedly weak siding with the SEC? How, in other words, can I maintain that state law actually diverges from the bar's, particularly given my concession that the state's weak commitment to its law renders (through example and enforcement gaps) the state's law in this area relatively unclear? As we continue with this history, my assertion that state law is at odds with that affirmed by the bar will become clearer, but one powerful demonstration of the state's position is apparent in the reaction to the ABA's new version of DR 7-102(B)(1). Despite years of lobbying by the ABA, no more than fourteen of the fifty states adopted the ABA's new "shall not" version of the rule.[70]

2. *In re Carter & Johnson.* Having ignited a firestorm with its complaint in *NSMC* and having received only lukewarm support from the court, the SEC might have been expected to take a rest, but by 1981 it was back in the thick of it.[71] This time, the SEC

---

securities lawyers rendering legal opinions and preparing registration statements, and stating belief that "as to the situations covered in these guidelines, a lawyer complying with the guidelines should not be subject to discipline or liability by the SEC or the courts").

[68] *Compare* MODEL CODE OF PROF'L RESPONSIBILITY DR 7-102(B)(1) (1969) (stating that a lawyer must reveal unrectified client fraud to the tribunal or the person affected) with MODEL CODE OF PROF'L RESPONSIBILITY DR 7-102(B)(1) (1974) (setting aside disclosure requirement "when the information is protected as a privileged communication"). For a full discussion of this change and how it was accomplished, see GEOFFREY C. HAZARD, JR. ET AL., THE LAW AND ETHICS OF LAWYERING 283–85 (3d ed. 1999) (arguing that "[t]o effectively repeal the duty to rectify fraud, while nominally preserving it, is surely disingenuous").

[69] For other examples of the bar's assumption that ethics rules trump (or at least are capable of trumping) contrary state and federal laws, see Koniak, *supra* note 27, at 1413–27.

[70] Geoffrey C. Hazard, Jr., *Rectification of Client Fraud: Death and Revival of a Professional Norm*, 33 EMORY L.J. 271, 294 (1984).

[71] The following factual description relies upon the opinion in *In re* Carter & Johnson, [1981 Transfer Binder] Fed. Sec. L. Rep. (CCH) ¶ 82,847, at 84,146–64 (Mar. 25, 1981).

decided to forego the courts. Instead of instituting a civil enforcement action, as in *NSMC*, it proceeded against two lawyers using Rule 2(e), now Rule 102(e), which gives the agency authority to discipline professionals who, *inter alia*, "have engaged in unethical or improper . . . conduct," or have "willfully aided and abetted the violation of any provision of the Federal securities laws."[72]

Like the undisclosed $884,000 change in NSMC's fortunes, the securities law violation by the client in this case was far from subtle. Lawyers Carter and Johnson represented National Telephone Company, a telephone leasing company, which was effectively run by one man: Sheldon Hart, who founded the company, was the controlling shareholder and served as CEO, chairman of the board, company president, and treasurer. The company had big financial troubles. The company arranged for a $15 million loan from a consortium of banks. But even before the loan was finalized, Hart had the company taking short-term advances against the loan. In a matter of months, he had gone through almost the entire line of credit. To prevent the banks from calling the loan due immediately as a response to this irresponsible behavior, Hart, on behalf of the company, agreed that if National's financial picture did not brighten, National would wind down its business, essentially restricting its operations to old business (maintaining existing leases).

During all this, National continued to issue optimistic reports on the company's financial condition and prospects to shareholders and the investing public. Lawyers Carter and Johnson, who were in "close and continuing contact with the company," obviously knew these reports were not true.[73] In December 1974, Hart, with the help of Carter and Johnson, prepared a press release and a Form 8-K to be filed with the SEC, but these documents failed to disclose that the loan provided for a wind-down plan to be implemented if the company's fortunes worsened. By March 1975, National's deteriorating financial condition triggered the company's obligation to the banks to wind down. The lawyers advised Hart that he had to disclose this fact to the public and the SEC, but he didn't. The lawyers did not resign, and they took no other effective steps to insist that the company make the required disclosures. The terms of the loan agreement were not disclosed until the end of May, three days after Hart resigned as National's president. A month later, National filed for bankruptcy.

The SEC staff charged Carter and Johnson with unethical conduct under Rule 2(e). Its position was that sitting around passively while a client committed securities fraud constituted unethical conduct.[74] This should not have been a hard case to make. If sitting passively by while the client committed securities fraud was aiding and abetting fraud, as *NSMC* seemed to say, then it surely was also unethical. The Administrative Law Judge ("ALJ") apparently saw it that way, sustaining the staff's charges and suspending Carter from appearing before the Commission for one year and Johnson

---

[72] 17 C.F.R. § 201.102(e) (2002).

[73] *In re* Carter & Johnson, [1981 Transfer Binder] Fed. Sec. L. Rep. (CCH) at 84,153.

[74] *Id.* at 84,165.

for nine months.[75] This was hardly the strongest discipline that might have been issued for conduct that might have been called aiding a felony, but, on the other hand, it was draconian given the *NSMC* court's "dressing down" solution.

Now the story gets interesting. The Commissioners agreed with the ALJ that lawyers should not behave this way; they too considered passivity in the face of obvious client fraud to be unethical. But they reversed the ALJ's ruling.[76] Why? Because, as the Commission put it, the ethical responsibilities of lawyers had "not been so firmly and unambiguously established that . . . all practicing lawyers . . . [could] be held to an awareness of . . . [the] norms."[77]

The state, here personified by the Commission members, repeated the same legal rule articulated three years earlier by the court in *NSMC*. At the same time, again like the *NSMC* court, it demonstrated a weak commitment to the rule that it announced. And what was the excuse this time? Well, it could hardly have used the *NSMC* judge's excuse: Having been told the law, lawyers will obey without the need for any sanctions. Instead, its enforcement gap was explained by a supposed example gap. The law was not "so firmly and unambiguously established."[78] And no wonder. The bar had spent years, both before and after the *NSMC* ruling, doing what it could to render the law on this subject unclear—passing resolutions, policy statements, and new "model" ethics rules. Meanwhile, the courts, and now the Commission, by refusing to enforce the law they were articulating, were contributing to the very ambiguity that the Commission described.

But there was hope. The Commission would now make the law clear. Carter and Johnson would not be punished, but the Commission would take this opportunity to articulate, without ambiguity, what the law demanded of lawyers whose clients were engaged in obvious violations of the securities laws. The Commission would use the *Carter & Johnson* case to articulate standards to govern lawyer conduct in such situations. The heart of those standards was this:

> When a lawyer with significant responsibilities in the effectuation of a company's compliance with the disclosure requirements of the federal securities laws becomes aware that his client is engaged in substantial and continuing failure to satisfy those disclosure requirements, his continued participation violates professional standards unless he takes prompt steps to end the client's noncompliance.[79]

Notice that this statement is arguably much narrower than the *NSMC* standard for aiding and abetting. There is no argument that it is broader. It adds that the lawyer has to have "significant responsibilities" for a company's required disclosures, and, even

---

[75] *Id.* at 84,146.

[76] *Id.* at 84,169–70.

[77] *Id.* at 84,170.

[78] *Id.*

[79] *Id.* at 84,172.

more important, it is triggered only by a client's "substantial and continuing" violation of the law.[80] With that addition, it seems to me that LBB's aiding and abetting in the *NSMC* case would not be labeled unethical—at least not by this rule.

The rule was also much milder than the law advocated by the SEC staff in the *NSMC* complaint. According to the SEC's proposed rule in *Carter & Johnson*, so long as the client's failure to make required disclosure was not part of a continuing pattern of nondisclosure, "counseling accurate disclosure" would suffice to keep a lawyer from being disciplined. This marked an obvious retreat from the SEC's *NSMC* position that it was aiding and abetting fraud to fail to disclose the client's fraud (even a single instance of fraud), if the client refused to make the requisite disclosure despite the lawyer's advice. If, on the other hand, the client's nondisclosure was part of a continuing pattern of nondisclosure sufficient to lead a reasonable lawyer to believe that his advice would be ignored, the lawyer had to take "more affirmative steps . . . to avoid the inference that he has been co-opted willingly or unwillingly into the scheme of nondisclosure."[81] The lawyer should, at that point, consider going to the board of directors to report the nondisclosures (known colloquially as going up the ladder) and/or resigning. The Commission refused to say which (or even whether some alternative) course of conduct might be an adequate substitute for the two possibilities mentioned. The Commission explained that this vagueness (one might say, this continuing ambiguity) was justified because the lawyer in the actual situation was in the best position to judge what steps to take.[82] The SEC summarized its rule this way: "What is required, in short, is some prompt action that leads to the conclusion that the lawyer is engaged in efforts to correct the underlying problem, rather than having capitulated to the desires of a strong-willed, but misguided client."[83]

Considering that the *NSMC* court had held that sitting passively by while the client committed fraud was aiding securities fraud, the SEC's proposed rule hardly seems onerous. The little law of *NSMC* had been made a little littler. Nonetheless, the trajectory of the state's law was intact, which meant that it was also still at odds with the bar's law. The bar's reaction to the SEC's proposed rule removed any remaining doubt about that. *NSMC*'s articulation of state law seemed, if anything, to have stiffened the bar's resolve.

The SEC was besieged with objections from the bar to its proposed rule.[84] The bar had not incorporated the state view, articulated by *NSMC*, that lawyers with clients

---

[80] *Id.*

[81] *Id.*

[82] *Id.* This reluctance to tie precepts to concrete actions in the world (or to many of them) mirrors the reluctance of the *Nat'l Student Marketing* court.

[83] *Id.*

[84] *See, e.g., ABA Section of Corporation, Banking and Business Law, SEC Standard of Conduct for Lawyers: Comments on the SEC Rule Proposal (Release No. 33-6344)*, 37 BUS. LAW. 915, 916–24 (1982) (questioning the SEC's authority to promulgate, and criticizing the substance of, the proposed rule, and concluding that "it is not advisable for the Commission to adopt or further consider this or any related proposal").

who commit fraud had to act affirmatively to stop the fraud or risk being held to account. The SEC's proposed rule was greeted as if it were foreign law, an unheard-of norm that an agency out of control[85] was bent on substituting a new law for what lawyers had long understood to be the law—their law, which held that the state had no business imposing restrictions on how lawyers handled "misguided" clients.

The SEC let the proposed *Carter & Johnson* rule die a quiet death. Once the comment period was over, the agency took no further action on the rule.

3. *O.P.M. and the Model Rules of Professional Conduct.* The scandals of recent years make the O.P.M. fraud look penny-ante, but at the time, the estimated toll of O.P.M.'s fraud, $210 million, was reported to be the largest in American history.[86] O.P.M. was created in 1970 by two old friends, Goodman and Weismann. It was a computer-leasing company.

Almost from the start, the company was basically insolvent and survived by means of fraud and bribery. A single computer would be used as collateral for two or three loans with different banks; the value of a given piece of equipment would be inflated to obtain larger loans.[87]

It was a form of pyramid scheme. O.P.M. would obtain a new bank loan through fraud to pay back money owed on an earlier bank loan obtained by fraud. To get sizable loans, O.P.M. would lie about whatever it had to: the duration of the leases that supposedly guaranteed repayment of the loan, the size of the payments due under the leases, or the existence of the leases themselves. The fraud went undetected, growing larger and larger, throughout the 1970s.

For the entire span of the fraud, the law firm of Singer, Hutner, Levine & Seeman ("Singer Hutner") handled O.P.M.'s transactions, papering and closing lease deals and

---

[85] The ABA not only challenged the content of the SEC's rule, but the validity of Rule 2(e) itself, arguing that the SEC had no legitimate power to regulate the conduct of lawyers. *See id.* at 917–19. In the years since *Carter & Johnson*, the bar has continued to press the argument that the Rule 2(e), as applied to lawyers, is beyond the agency's legitimate powers. Courts have consistently sustained the legitimacy of Rule 2(e) (although generally in cases involving accountants, to whom the rule also applies), but their commitment to the rule's legitimacy has been underwhelming. *See, e.g.*, Sheldon v. SEC, 45 F.3d 1515, 1518 (11th Cir. 1995) (rejecting the claim that Rule 2(e) "taints the fairness of proceedings before the SEC"); Checkosky v. SEC, 23 F.3d 452, 455–56 (D.C. Cir. 1994) (upholding SEC's authority to promulgate Rule 2(e)); Davy v. SEC, 792 F.2d 1418, 1421–22 (9th Cir. 1986) (same); Touche Ross & Co. v. SEC, 609 F.2d 570, 577–82 (2d Cir. 1979) (holding that Rule 2(e) is a "necessary adjunct to the Commission's power to protect the integrity of its administrative procedures and the public in general"). The position that federal regulation of lawyers is per se illegitimate has resurfaced with force in the aftermath of Sarbanes-Oxley. The bar's law is remarkably stable.

[86] The following factual description relies upon Stuart Taylor, Jr., *Ethics and the Law: A Case History*, N.Y. TIMES, Jan. 9, 1983, § 6 (Magazine), at 31, as well as a report issued by O.P.M.'s bankruptcy trustee. Report of the Trustee Concerning Fraud and Other Misconduct in the Management of the Affairs of the Debtor, *In re* O.P.M. Leasing Servs., Inc., No. 81 B 10533 (Bankr. S.D.N.Y. Apr. 25, 1983), *reprinted in part in* GEOFFREY C. HAZARD, JR. & SUSAN P. KONIAK, THE LAW AND ETHICS OF LAWYERING 255–71 (1st ed. 1990).

[87] Taylor, *supra* note 86, at 32.

providing legal opinions to lenders vouching for the soundness of the security for the loans—the underlying leases. By early 1979, if not earlier, the law firm had plenty of reasons to suspect that fraud was afoot, and those reasons multiplied in 1980. The lawyers at Singer Hutner working on O.P.M. business knew that O.P.M. had pled guilty to charges of check-kiting; they knew that O.P.M. was chronically cash-poor; they were told by their client not to send papers documenting lease transactions to the lessee, to whom such papers would normally be sent; they knew O.P.M. was paying insurance on computers when the terms of the supposed leases called for the lessee to make those payments; they knew O.P.M. was making payments on some leases (payments to be forwarded to the bank) when the lessee was supposed to make the payments; and they noticed other irregularities in the documentation for O.P.M. transactions. Then, in June 1980, O.P.M.'s chief financial officer resigned and sent the law firm a letter stating that he had discovered that a substantial number of O.P.M.'s loans had been obtained through fraud. Lawyer Hutner, of Singer Hutner, who received that letter, later claimed that O.P.M.'s Goodman had snatched the letter away from him before he had a chance to read it. Nothing terribly suspicious about that!

Later, however, Hutner met with the chief financial officer's lawyer, who told him that his client, Clifton, had evidence of a "multimillion-dollar fraud," "that [Singer Hutner's] opinion letters . . . had been based upon false documents," and that O.P.M. could only survive by continuing to engage in fraud.[88] Clifton's lawyer later said of his meetings with Hutner, "I had visions of [Hutner] clamping his hands over his ears and running out of the office."[89]

Faced with the near certainty that their work had been used (and was still being used) by their clients to defraud O.P.M.'s lenders, and that their client had no intention of rectifying its ongoing crimes or refraining from committing new ones, Singer Hutner was apparently unsure about what, if anything, the law required the firm to do.[90] Did Singer Hutner consult the criminal laws of the state of New York? No, the firm hired two experts to advise them on legal ethics: Joseph McLaughlin, who was later to become a federal judge, and still later to play a leading role in opposing the rules proposed by the SEC under Sarbanes-Oxley, and Henry Putzel. The consultants analyzed the problem under New York's ethics rules. Unfortunately for Singer Hutner, New York was one of the fourteen states to have adopted the ABA's amended version of DR 7-102(B)(1), purporting to bar lawyers from disclosing client fraud. Despite the fact that such disclosure might be the only effective way of demonstrating one's withdrawal from a conspiracy or lack of involvement in any wrongdoing in the first place, the experts told Singer Hutner it must not disclose its client's fraud. Further, their reading of the rules encouraged Singer Hutner to remain on the job, continuing to

---

[88] *Id.* at 33.

[89] *Id.*

[90] This is a perfect example of the real world costs of the ambiguity fostered by the unresolved struggle between the bar and the state over the law that governs lawyers.

close O.P.M. deals. The lawyers could do this, the experts said, so long as they received Goodman's word in writing, before each deal, that the deal was legitimate. That is an interesting twist: clients giving lawyers opinion letters.

The experts did tell Singer Hutner that it should try to find out just how bad their client's "past" conduct had been—conduct that the state, by the way, would classify as "ongoing," which is how the state's law classifies unrectified fraud. Nonetheless, the experts classified the conduct as past conduct. This classification turned information about O.P.M.'s conduct into information about a client's past crimes, thus triggering the lawyer's strongest duty of confidentiality. Apparently, the experts gave Singer Hutner the impression that a lawyer's obligation to trust his client allows the written word of a party who commits fraud to wipe out any suggestion that a lawyer is willfully aiding new fraud, other evidence that fraud is present notwithstanding. I say that because Singer Hutner continued to close deals for OPM on the basis of Goodman's written assurances of legitimacy, after there was no real doubt that the firm's past work had been employed to commit fraud, and even though the new deals bore traits as suspicious as the former deals.

In late September 1980, Goodman finally confessed just how much (or almost how much) fraud he had committed under Singer Hutner's nose and with its work, estimating the fraud at about $90 million dollars. The law firm finally resigned but kept quiet about what it knew. Kaye, Scholer, Fierman, Hays, & Handler ("Kaye Scholer") was hired by O.P.M. to take up where Singer Hutner had left off. O.P.M. continued to commit fraud until sometime in 1981, when one of its victims, a bank, noticed something funny about a lease, called the lessee to ask about it, and the lessee said it had no such lease arrangement. The whole house of cards soon came tumbling down. Goodman and Weismann went to prison. The prosecutor apparently considered bringing charges against lawyer Hutner but ultimately did not. The law firm paid out millions of dollars to settle civil litigation brought against it for willfully or recklessly aiding its client's fraud. Neither McLaughlin nor Putzel suffered any known ill effects for having provided such appallingly bad advice—not anticipating how Singer Hutner's conduct would be viewed under state, as opposed to bar, law.

In 1983, a mere month after the *New York Times Magazine* published a thorough exposé of Singer Hutner's involvement in the O.P.M. fraud, the ABA House of Delegates met to debate the adoption of a new model ethics code, which would become the Model Rules of Professional Conduct.[91] The Kutak Commission, as it was known, which had been charged with drafting the new rules, recommended that the ABA abandon the hard-line position on never disclosing client fraud that had been written into the Model Code while the *NSMC* case was pending. The Kutak Commission did not propose that the ABA mandate disclosure of client fraud, as the original version of the Model Code had seemed to require (at least when the lawyer's services had been

---

[91] *See generally* Hazard, *supra* note 70, at 296–303 (describing adoption of the Model Rules).

used to accomplish the fraud). Instead, the Commission recommended that lawyers be given discretion to disclose client fraud when their services had been employed to accomplish it.

The ABA would have none of that. The House of Delegates adopted a "never disclose client fraud" rule. The relevant Model Rule, Rule 1.6, did not say "do not disclose client fraud." It just provided no exception to the duty of client confidentiality that would allow a lawyer to make such a revelation.[92] Geoffrey Hazard, who served as the reporter for the Kutak Commission, notes that, after the vote rejecting discretionary disclosure of client fraud, several fellow lawyers called one of the lawyers at Singer Hutner to tell him that the ABA had vindicated his behavior.[93] State law had not; Singer Hutner's multi-million-dollar settlement payments attest to that.

The ABA's position was dangerous for lawyers and potentially quite expensive. Once a lawyer discovers ongoing client fraud that his services have furthered, keeping mum about it invites civil and possibly criminal charges for having knowingly aided the wrongdoing, at least when the lawyer knows that his work product—for example, an opinion letter—may be relied on tomorrow by a new victim of the fraud—say, the next day's purchasers of the client's stock. Lawyers needed an escape hatch, the ability to disclose before an accusation of wrongdoing, in case they were convinced that someone might be able to show that opinions of theirs, upon which purchasers were still relying, could have been issued when the lawyers really should have known better.[94] When the ABA met again, this time to adopt official comments to the Model Rules, they included in the Comment to Model Rule 1.6 just such an escape hatch.

The Comment stated that nothing in the rule on confidentiality prevents a lawyer who withdraws from representation from disaffirming or withdrawing his opinions or other documents issued during the representation.[95] According to the Comment's draftsman, Geoffrey Hazard, the Comment was designed to address the problem of ongoing client fraud in which the lawyer's work had been used. But the Comment did not

---

[92] *See* MODEL RULES OF PROF'L CONDUCT R. 1.6 (2002) (allowing disclosure of client confidences only if client consents, if client is going to commit a crime involving death or substantial injury, or to defend the lawyer against charges of wrongdoing). Under this rule, third party allegations that a lawyer aided the client's fraud would be sufficient to relieve a lawyer from his obligation to keep client confidences. But as to revealing undiscovered client fraud, by definition an ongoing crime, in which the lawyer's services are used, the self-defense exception is of no use. If it is undiscovered, there is no one to level charges of complicity against the lawyer.

[93] Hazard, *supra* note 70, at 306.

[94] In states that allow third parties to sue for negligent misrepresentation—the states that have relaxed the requirement of privity—a lawyer might be liable to one who foreseeably relied on the lawyer's opinion (a purchaser or lender, for example) for issuing an opinion negligently. Elsewhere, a lawyer would be liable for issuing an opinion that was used to perpetrate a fraud when the opinion was issued with reckless disregard for its accuracy. *See* HAZARD ET AL., *supra* note 68, at 79–103.

[95] MODEL RULES OF PROF'L CONDUCT R. 1.6 (2002).

explain that. On its face, it gave every withdrawing lawyer the discretion to do so "noisily."[96]

In sum, the original version of the Model Rules did affirm the conduct of the lawyers in O.P.M., in *In re Carter & Johnson,* and in *NSMC*. The lawyers might have, at most, disavowed their work product, but that was not required; they kept quiet, and that is what Model Rule 1.6 said they should do. Yes, Model Rule 1.16 said a lawyer must withdraw when he "knows" that his client is using his services to commit a crime or fraud, and Model Rule 1.2 said that a lawyer must not "knowingly" assist a client in such conduct. But lawyers never "know."

4. *The Savings and Loan Scandals and Their Aftermath.* Charles Keating, the owner of Lincoln Savings & Loan, made assets go round in circles long before Enron. In the era of deregulation and a supposedly booming real estate market, Lincoln had bought land—lots of it—and had made other risky investments. How to turn that land into cash was the question.[97] The answer was to get a friendly appraiser to assess the land high and get someone to buy it. An arms-length purchaser would know better, so Lincoln would lend Company A enough money to buy the land, Company A would lend that money to Company B, and Company B would buy the land from Lincoln. Company B would then default on its loan to Company A, and Company A would "seize" the land bought from Lincoln (land that had been used by Company B to secure its loan from Company A). Company A would then default on its loan to Lincoln, and the land would return to Lincoln. In the end, Lincoln would be left with a big fat "booked" profit from the "sale" of the land, a bad loan, supposedly unconnected to the land, and the land. Lincoln would then send part of the "profit" from the land "sale" to its parent company, American Continental Corporation, where Keating could spend it. Because the land had been "bought" with Lincoln's "own" money, i.e., the savings deposits guaranteed by the federal government, the taxpayers were left footing the bill for this scam. Keating could not have dipped into the federally-insured money without somehow recharacterizing that money as "profit" from a "sale."

---

[96] The Comment to Model Rule 1.6 was a bow to state law: not its content, but its potential force. The text of Model Rule 1.6 defied the idea, embedded in state law, that to prevent the continued use of one's services to commit a fraud, the lawyer must disclose. Moreover, the Comment did not allow forthright disclosure, but only allowed the lawyer to gesture ("wave the red flag," as lawyers sometimes put it) to indicate the client's fraud. To the client and the fraud victim, *successful* gesturing is tantamount to actual disclosure. But for the lawyer, it is not. To be forced to communicate without words is unnatural. Assuming a lawyer avails herself of the Comment's exception to confidentiality, she is thus reminded, at the very moment she is bowing to state law, that what she is doing is taboo for lawyers.

[97] The following description of this scheme relies on testimony given by accountants in the congressional investigation of Lincoln Savings & Loan. *See Investigation of Lincoln Savings & Loan Association: Hearing Before the House Comm. on Banking, Fin. & Urban Affairs*, 101st Cong. 90–99 (1989) (statement on behalf of Kenneth Leventhal & Co., as presented by Roger A. Johnson, Partner, Kenneth Leventhal & Co., and statement of Terry Gilbert, Partner, Kenneth Leventhal & Co.).

Keating was not the only fraud-committing owner of a savings and loan, and the circle scheme just described was not the only way he or others committed fraud. For example, Keating also sold American Continental bonds (based on rosy financial statements, helped considerably by the make-believe land sales) in Lincoln's offices, which left many investors with the impression that the bonds were federally insured, as Lincoln itself was, when in fact the bonds were not.[98] More to the point, Charles Keating and his fellow fraud-committing savings and loan operators had lawyers helping them break the law.

The lawyers all claimed, of course, that they never "knowingly" assisted in unlawful conduct, but the facts suggest that only those constitutionally incapable of seeing illegality could have failed to recognize what was going on. For example, to avoid having its fraudulent conduct detected by bank regulators, Lincoln would "paper" its files with backdated documents purporting to show that loans to companies (with no ability or intent to pay those loans back, as opposed to returning Lincoln's land to it) were justified and to represent corporate resolutions that had not been passed at the relevant period of time.[99] In refusing to grant a motion for summary judgment brought by one of Keating's law firms, Jones, Day, Reavis & Pogue ("Jones Day"), which was being sued for, *inter alia,* aiding fraud, racketeering, and negligent misrepresentation, the court said:

> The testimony suggests that Jones Day partners knew ACC/Lincoln personnel were preparing loan underwriting summaries contemporaneously with Jones Day's regulatory compliance review, even though the loan transactions had already been closed. Moreover, the evidence reveals that Jones Day attorneys participated in creating corporate resolutions to ratify forged and backdated corporate records.[100]

Jones Day settled after the summary judgment motion, paying out tens of millions of dollars for its role in Lincoln's frauds.[101] And Jones Day was not alone. Other well-known firms that settled civil litigation brought against them for having intentionally,

---

[98] *See, e.g.,* Michael Lev, *California Accuses Lincoln of Misleading Bond Buyers,* N.Y. TIMES, Mar. 3, 1990, § 1, at 35.

[99] *In re* Am. Cont'l Corp./Lincoln Sav. & Loan Sec. Litig., 794 F. Supp. 1424, 1450 (D. Ariz. 1992).

[100] *Id.*

[101] *See* Alison Leigh Cowan, *Big Law and Auditing Firms to Pay Millions in S.&L. Suit,* N.Y. TIMES, Mar. 31, 1992, at A1 (reporting that Jones Day agreed to $24 million settlement with investors); *see also* John H. Cushman, Jr., *Law Firm Settles S.&L. Case,* N.Y. TIMES, Apr. 20, 1993, at D1 (noting that Jones Day entered into $51 million settlement with government).

recklessly, or negligently aided some savings and loan operator to commit fraud include Sidley & Austin[102] and Kaye Scholer,[103] and that's hardly a complete list.

The government, in its role as receiver for many of the failed savings and loans, as well as in its role as regulator, sued lawyers at an unprecedented rate. It wanted its money back. But, while some operators of savings and loans were criminally prosecuted and convicted,[104] no law firm or lawyer faced criminal charges for helping them.[105] Once again, the state's commitment to its law was somewhat ambiguous.

The strongest commitment was demonstrated by the Office of Thrift Supervision (OTS), which charged Kaye Scholer with actively helping Charles Keating to mislead bank regulators. The OTS did not just file a complaint; it froze Kaye Scholer's assets pending resolution of the dispute.[106] In contrast to the enforcement gap so often found in cases involving lawyers, this was enforcement on steroids: enforcement before a finding of liability.

The clamor over the forfeiture order served to obscure the fact that the division between the bar and the state was not limited to, or even primarily about, the OTS's decision to enforce first, try later.[107] Put another way, with or without the forfeiture order, I believe the bar would have been outraged by the OTS's complaint against Kaye Scholer and would have created as great, or nearly as great, a furor over it. The OTS's

---

[102] James S. Granelli, *Chicago Law Firm Agrees to Pay up to $34 Million in Lincoln S&L Case*, L.A. TIMES, May 21, 1991, at D5 (reporting that Sidley & Austin agreed to pay $4 million immediately, with an additional $30 million promised if the bondholder plaintiff failed to win damages in future civil suits against other defendants); *see also* Amy Stevens & Jonathan Moses, *Sidley & Austin, RTC Said to Reach Pact*, WALL ST. J., Oct. 31, 1991, at B2 (noting that Sidley & Austin agreed to pay a $7.5 million settlement with federal regulators over its alleged role in Lincoln Savings & Loan failure).

[103] *See* Cowan, *supra* note 101 (stating that Kaye Scholer settled with plaintiffs for $20 million); *see also* James O. Johnston, Jr. & Daniel Scott Schecter, *Introduction: Kaye, Scholer and the OTS—Did Anyone Go Too Far?*, 66 S. CAL. L. REV. 977, 977–78 (1993) (stating that Kaye Scholer settled $275 million government claim for $41 million).

[104] For example, Charles Keating himself was convicted on both state and federal charges stemming from the Lincoln Savings & Loan collapse. Both convictions were later overturned on procedural grounds, and, in 1998, Keating pled guilty in federal court to four counts of fraud. *See* Christian Berthelsen, *Keating Pleads Guilty to 4 Counts of Fraud*, N.Y. TIMES, Apr. 7, 1999, at C2.

[105] Proving a negative is normally difficult. One might expect me to write "I know of no . . . " but that would be to understate the matter. Given the uproar by the bar over the civil forfeiture action by the Office of Thrift Supervision against Kaye Scholer, *see, e.g.*, Symposium, *In the Matter of Kaye, Scholer, Fierman, Hays & Handler: A Symposium on Government Regulation, Lawyers' Ethics, and the Rule of Law*, 66 S. CAL. L. REV. 977 (1993), there is no possibility that I (or any other lawyer) would have missed the outcry from the bar that would have attended a criminal prosecution of a lawyer for work in connection with a savings and loan failure.

[106] *See* Johnston & Schecter, *supra* note 103, at 977.

[107] *See, e.g.*, Steve France, *Just Deserts: Don't Cry for Kaye, Scholer*, LEGAL TIMES, Apr. 6, 1992, at 28, 28–29 (claiming that the furor that erupted over the government's choice of tactics diverted attention away from Kaye Scholer's conduct).

position was that the law it was applying to Kaye Scholer was "unremarkable and well established."[108] The bar's position was that it was novel, unforeseeable, and dangerous.[109]

With Kaye Scholer's settlement and those of so many other law firms, one might think the state won this round, but it didn't. The ABA, during and after the savings and loan litigation, steadfastly refused to amend Model Rule 1.6 to acknowledge that there were some circumstances in which a lawyer should, at least, have the discretion to disclose client fraud or other financial crimes.[110] The bar, in other words, did not look at the behavior of leading law firms in assisting those who committed the fraud that came to light in the wake of the savings and loan debacle, and say, "It is time to reconsider our vision of 'right' lawyer behavior because it is causing so much harm." But the bar did seem to recognize that state law was operating with more force than in the past. Lawyers were scared. So they rallied to change state law, and they managed to do that with a helpful assist from the Supreme Court.

In 1994, the Supreme Court held, in *Central Bank of Denver v. First Interstate Bank of Denver,* that the securities laws did not provide a private cause of action for aiding and abetting securities fraud, despite decades and decades of court cases to the contrary.[111] Congress could have reversed that decision. Indeed, it had the perfect vehicle before it in which to do so. Shortly after *Central Bank,* Congress took up the Private Securities Litigation Reform Act.[112] But instead of reversing *Central Bank,* that Act left the decision in place, and, although Congress did affirm the SEC's long-standing understanding that it could bring civil actions against aiders and abettors, Congress made

---

[108] Harris Weinstein, Remarks Delivered at Pennsylvania Association of Community Bankers (Mar. 23, 1992), *in* ATTORNEYS' LIABILITY ASSURANCE SOCIETY, INC., THE KAYE, SCHOLER CASE AND OTHER SELECTED PROFESSIONAL LIABILITY AND ETHICS ISSUES 133, 134 (Robert E. O'Malley et al. eds., 1992).

[109] *See, e.g.,* John K. Villa, *The Attorney-Client Relationship After Kaye, Scholer: Emerging Theories of Liability for Lending Counsel,* 779 PLI/CORP. 93, 152–57 (1992).

[110] On a number of occasions, the ABA rejected proposals to include an exception allowing a lawyer to disclose financial crimes involving substantial harm to others and in which the lawyer's services have been used. *See, e.g.,* HAZARD ET AL., *supra* note 68, at 287 (stating that in 1991, ABA House of Delegates rejected a proposal to amend Model Rule 1.6 to allow disclosure of client fraud where lawyer's services had been used to further the fraud); Lisa H. Nicholson, *A Hobson's Choice for Securities Lawyers in the Post-Enron Environment: Striking a Balance Between the Obligation of Client Loyalty and Market Gatekeeper,* 16 GEO. J. LEGAL ETHICS 91, 144 (2002) (reporting that in August 2001, ABA House of Delegates rejected a proposed amendment to Model Rule 1.6 that would have allowed disclosure of confidential information "where a client is using the lawyer's services to commit crimes or frauds reasonably certain to result in substantial injury to the financial interests or property of another"); *see also* Morgan Cloud, *Privileges Lost? Privileges Retained?,* 69 TENN. L. REV. 65, 89 (2001) ("[O]nce again the ABA House of Delegates has thwarted attempts to enact a Model Rule 1.6 allowing lawyers to make disclosures [relating to crimes resulting in substantial financial harms] without violating their ethical duties to their clients.").

[111] 511 U.S. 164, 177 (1994).

[112] Private Securities Litigation Reform Act of 1995, Pub. L. No. 104-67, 109 Stat. 737 (codified as amended in scattered sections of 15 U.S.C.).

SEC aiding and abetting actions more difficult, requiring that the SEC show that lawyers (and others) *knowingly* aided fraud, whereas in the past a showing of reckless assistance had been enough. The SEC, which had not instituted any major action against lawyers since its failed attempt in *Carter & Johnson*,[113] needed no further deterrent to picking a fight with the bar. Nonetheless, it got one. Given how aggressive the OTS had been and how the SEC had, once upon a time, shown a fighting spirit, lawyers wanted all the protection they could get. Securing a rule prohibiting a private cause of action for aiding and abetting securities fraud was a big win.[114] Lawyers and bar associations also lobbied heavily for, and secured, state laws limiting the liability of one partner in a law firm for the acts of another—the so-called LLP statutes.[115]

Unbowed and equipped with new legal protections granted by an all-too-cooperative government, lawyers were ready for the boom of the 1990s. They were prepared to help give us Enron.

III. THE FIGHT OVER THE SEC'S NEW LAWYER RULES

A. Round One

Section 307 of the Sarbanes-Oxley Act caught the bar uncharacteristically off-guard. Enron had gone bust, and then WorldCom, but the accountants seemed to be bearing all the heat. Almost no one was talking about the lawyers. The Senate Judiciary Committee had held one hearing devoted to lawyer responsibility for the Enron fiasco, but that hearing was perhaps the only one on Enron to receive virtually no press coverage; it did not even show up in the wee hours of the morning on C-SPAN. I know because I testified at the hearing—the only witness who said lawyers were critical to the success of Enron's schemes and those of other fraud-committing companies. No one was listening. In fact, it was clear to me as I sat there that the Senators were nearly as bored with what I had to say as the press was. I was testifying about lawyer involvement in fraud, the need for the SEC to get back in the lawyer-regulation business, and the need to restore aiding and abetting liability for, at least, lawyers. The Senators were making speeches about bankruptcy, and about how Kenneth Lay or similar people should not be able to declare bankruptcy and keep lavish homes. That was not the subject of the hearing, but it was on the Senators' minds. I went home quite depressed; the hearing had been a waste of time.

---

[113] *See* HAZARD ET AL., *supra* note 68, at 742–43 (noting that, after *Carter & Johnson*, the SEC "has brought very few cases against lawyers").

[114] *See* Paul Braverman, *Who Enabled the Enablers?*, AM. LAW., Oct. 2002, at 87, 88 (stating that, in part because there is no private cause of action for aiding and abetting, a law firm is "a tough target in a securities case").

[115] *See* Walter W. Steele, Jr., *How Lawyers Protect the Family Jewels . . . The Invention of Limited Liability Partnerships*, 39 S. TEX. L. REV. 621, 623 (1998) ("[T]o some observers, a concept that allows partners to share the economic and professional benefits of a partnership without sharing liability in order to save partners' economic hides is more than a contradiction—it is hypocrisy.").

The newspaper stories analyzing the likelihood of legislative "fixes" to the abuses revealed in the Enron mess were in agreement on one thing: There was virtually no chance that Congress would reinstate aiding and abetting liability for securities fraud.[116] Richard Painter, a professor at the University of Illinois, had written a letter to Chairman Pitt at the SEC, which about forty other academics, including me, had signed, urging the SEC to stand by the rule it had tried to enunciate in *Carter & Johnson*. The SEC responded by saying, in effect, that it had gotten out of the lawyer-regulation business years ago, that the bar did not like the SEC trying to regulate it, that bar regulation was really a matter for the states, and that if Congress wanted that changed, it would have to pass a law. The bar had good cause to be breathing easy.

I myself was quite surprised when someone from Senator Edwards's staff called and said that Senator Edwards was interested in doing something to ensure that the SEC would regulate the behavior of securities lawyers faced with clients that commit fraud. And I was even more surprised when the legislation passed, which it did before the bar had a chance to rally. The ABA tried to get the measure removed by the conferees, but somehow, miraculously, the conferees stood firm. It looked as if Congress was intent on finding some vehicle to enforce long-standing principles of state law that had lain dormant for some time. The legislation, in effect, wrote the *Carter & Johnson* rule into law, but strengthened it, eliminating the "maybe this, maybe that" approach that had characterized the SEC's statement of what lawyers should do when faced with fraud-committing managers. The SEC must insist, per Section 307 of the Sarbanes-Oxley Act, that lawyers go up the corporate ladder and report evidence of fraud.[117] And the SEC should issue other rules, too, according to the legislation.

On schedule, the SEC issued its proposed rules. To everyone's surprise, including mine, the rules did not content themselves with requiring up-the-ladder reports. The rules also required a lawyer to make a "noisy withdrawal" to the SEC in the event that the board of directors ignored the lawyer's report. At least, that is what everyone said the rules said—all the newspapers and all the bar organizations talking to those newspapers. And—surprise, surprise—a storm erupted over this supposed duty, which now everyone was calling a duty to disclose client confidences, blow the whistle on one's clients, tell the SEC, turn a client in to the government. Never mind that, since at least 1984, the ABA's own position had been that noisy withdrawal, its own invention, is *not* disclosure. From its first appearance until today, Model Rule 1.6 has forbidden disclosure, but has allowed a withdrawing lawyer to disaffirm any document produced during the representation.[118] There is simply no other way to read Model Rule 1.6 and its Comment except to say that gesturing to indicate that the lawyer's work might be tainted by fraud is *not* disclosing confidential information, however strained that posi-

---

[116] *See* Stephen Labaton, *Now Who, Exactly, Got Us Into This?*, N.Y. TIMES, Feb. 3, 2002, § 3, at 1.

[117] Sarbanes-Oxley Act of 2002, Pub. L. No. 107-204 § 307 (codified at 15 U.S.C. § 7245 (2002)).

[118] *See* MODEL RULES OF PROF'L CONDUCT R. 1.6 & cmt. (2002).

tion may be. All of a sudden, none of that history mattered. Now lawyers and bar associations, including the ABA itself, were stating that to require noisy withdrawal was to require disclosure.

More interesting, even if we accept the bar's newfound realization that gesturing is, in effect, the same as disclosure, the SEC's proposed "disclosure" requirement was a hair short of mandatory in any situation. Any client could avoid its lawyer ever having to noisily withdraw by adopting what the SEC's proposal called a "qualified legal compliance committee" ("QLCC"). Whenever a corporate client had a QLCC, the lawyer's reporting obligations would end with a report to that committee. It was that simple. But one would know that from reading the many overheated press accounts, all describing the government's new rule as requiring lawyers to blow the whistle on their clients. Worthy of a news story, if the proposal actually required whistleblowing, but given that the proposal allowed every client to choose whether its lawyer ever had to make a noisy withdrawal, the news stories were quite sloppy journalism, as I tried in vain to convince every reporter who called me.

The reporters could not be convinced because bar organizations and an impressive list of securities lawyers were telling the reporters that the government was trying to turn them into whistleblowers, trying to alter fundamentally the relationship between lawyers and their clients. Sarbanes-Oxley did not even give the SEC the authority to require "disclosure" to the SEC. The agency was out of control. All Congress had required was reporting within the corporate client—in some circumstances, all the way to the board—but not outside the client. This was regulation gone mad. The world in which clients could trust their lawyers was coming to an end, to hear lawyers tell the tale, and journalists aplenty were listening.

But while journalists were busy writing story after story about the tough (maybe way too tough) SEC proposal, with its "whistleblower" provision, some fellow academics and I were home worrying that the rule was weak, so weak that there might as well have been no rule at all. Congress had told the SEC to issue regulations to govern the conduct of securities lawyers. It said one of those regulations had to require lawyers to report evidence of corporate crimes up the ladder. How much evidence would trigger that responsibility? That was the critical question under any rule. The ABA's own rules had long required lawyers to resign if they *knew* that a client was using the lawyer to commit a crime or fraud, and the rules had always included a prohibition against *knowingly* counseling a client to commit a crime or fraud, but these rules were dead letters. Lawyers never "know" that their client is committing a crime or fraud, not before a court has ruled that way conclusively, and sometimes even not then. Lawyers see it as their job to believe in their client, and they are trained to see the gray in all law.[119] So if lawyers had to "know" before they had to report, there would be no reporting. As one who helped draft the Edwards amendment that eventually became Section 307, I can assure you that that was the reason the section called for lawyers to

---

[119] *See supra* text accompanying notes 39–40.

report "evidence," and not violations of law—specifically to avoid the "lawyers never know" problem.

I was worried about the weakness of the SEC's rule because I was focused on the triggering standard. Did it avoid the "lawyers never know" problem or not? Under the proposal, a lawyer was to report evidence of corporate wrongdoing to the CEO or chief legal officer (the first level of reporting), or, if no satisfactory response was forthcoming from those officers, to the board of directors or the QLCC, when the lawyer "reasonably . . . believe[d]" that a material violation of law "has occurred, is occurring, or is about to occur."[120] Two big problems.

First, "reasonably believes" is a commonly used legal standard, which means that the actor has to have a subjective belief in the existence of a thing, and that belief has to be reasonable. Second, what the lawyer had to "reasonably believe" was, to paraphrase slightly, that *a violation had occurred, was occurring, or was about to occur.* That brings us right back to "know," or worse. One might argue a lawyer need not just "know," which might plausibly be read to include "must have known," but she must actually "believe" that the action in question violates the securities laws. Modifying "believe" with "reasonably" does not negate the need for a belief to be present. It adds the requirement that the actor's subjective "belief" also be "reasonable." It is a standard used in law to deter conduct, not to encourage it.[121] But the point of Section 307 was to encourage, not to deter, lawyer reporting up the corporate ladder. Moreover, it required "evidence" to be reported, not "violations."

Could this be a mere drafting mistake? The agency was, after all, working overtime to keep up with the many new responsibilities Congress had given it under Sarbanes-Oxley, including the drafting of a host of new regulations in specified and short periods of time. I feared not. The rule was not just weak and seemingly contrary to the legislative language, but, rather, it bore the marks of a struggle—a struggle over the standard. The SEC's official comments issued along with the rule purported to redefine the words "reasonably believes" to mean something other than what they always

---

[120] *Implementation of Standards of Professional Conduct for Attorneys,* 67 Fed. Reg. 71,670, 71,704 (proposed Dec. 2, 2002) (to be codified at 17 C.F.R. pt. 205).

[121] As I wrote in comments submitted to the SEC, co-authored with Professors George M. Cohen and Roger C. Cramton and signed by forty-eight other academics:

> The natural and usual use of the "reasonably believes" standard is when the law is trying to *deter* particular conduct, e.g., the law of self-defense in tort and criminal law. In those situations the law wants to impose a heavy burden on an actor: action should not be taken unless the actor believes the action is necessary and, in addition, that the actor's belief is reasonable. Here Congress intended that attorneys be *required* to communicate evidence of a material violation up the corporate ladder, so that higher authority in the company would learn about the major risks involved and handle them appropriately. Using a standard designed to deter action undermines the purpose of § 307.

Comments of Susan P. Koniak et al. on Proposed Rule: Implementation of Standards of Professional Conduct for Attorneys, 17 CFR 205 (Dec. 17, 2002) (on file with the *Columbia Law Review*), *available at* http://www.sec.gov/rules/proposed/s74502/skoniak1.htm.

mean in law, which I described above. The SEC's comments asserted that "reasonably believes" is an objective standard, i.e., what the reasonable lawyer would believe in the circumstances, not what the lawyer actually (and reasonably) believed at the time (the ordinary definition).[122]

This bore all the marks of some "split the baby" compromise. The agency appears to have been torn between a "knows" standard (or "knows plus" standard, i.e., adding "reasonable" on top of "believe") and an objective standard. It split the difference. Well, sort of. Those arguing for an "objective" standard got the short end of the stick, because a comment that seeks to redefine a longstanding legal phrase used in the black-letter rule has little chance of actually doing so. The struggle can even be seen in the comments addressing what the lawyer must believe. The proposed rule defined "evidence" to mean "violation."[123] Here again, the proposed rule redefined a legal term, "evidence," to mean something it does not generally mean: a violation of law. But here, the redefinition was not in a comment but in the rule itself. So those who would weaken the rule triumphed, too. A comment is not likely to change a longstanding definition, but redefining a term in the "definition" section of a rule is, on the other hand, likely to have an effect.

If I were right, and there had been a struggle that the weak-rule folks had won, comments from a bunch of academics pointing out the "inadvertent" confusion with the standard would be highly unlikely to move anybody to "correct" the problem—a compromise is a compromise. We would soon see. Along with my colleagues, George M. Cohen of the University of Virginia and Roger C. Cramton of Cornell University, I spent hours drafting detailed comments, over fifty single-spaced pages, eventually endorsed by forty-eight other academics. The bar wrote more.[124] The SEC was besieged with comments from the bar denouncing the proposed rule, and not just the noisy withdrawal provision, but almost every aspect of the rule. The ABA argued for a

---

[122] *Implementation of Standards of Professional Conduct for Attorneys,* 67 Fed. Reg. at 71,680.

[123] *Id.* at 71,678 (defining evidence of a material violation as "information that would lead an attorney reasonably to believe that a material violation has occurred, is occurring, or is about to occur"). Those who thought "evidence" should mean "evidence" did, however, manage to get into the comments the notion that evidence was different and less than that which would allow one to conclude (reasonably) that the law was broken, *see id.,* but, again, the comments are much less likely to win the day, in a battle over meaning before a court, than the language of the actual rule.

[124] *See, e.g.,* Comments of American Bar Association on Proposed Rule: Implementation of Standards of Professional Conduct for Attorneys (Dec. 18, 2002) (on file with the *Columbia Law Review*), *available at* http://www.sec.gov/rules/proposed/s74502/apcarlton1.htm; Comments of American Corporate Counsel Association on Proposed Rule (Dec. 18, 2002) (on file with the *Columbia Law Review*), *available at* http://www.sec.gov/rules/proposed/s74502/bnagler1.htm; Comments of Attorneys' Liability Assurance Society, Inc., A Risk Retention Group (ALAS) on the U.S. Security and Exchange Commission's Attorney Conduct Rule (Mar. 23, 2003) (on file with the *Columbia Law Review*), *available at* http://www.sec.gov/rules/proposed/s74502/attorneyslia1.htm; Comments of 77 Law Firms (Dec. 18, 2002) (on file with the *Columbia Law Review*), *available at* http://www.sec.gov/rules/proposed/s74502/77lawfirms1.htm.

"lawyer knows" rule; otherwise, the SEC should, preferably, do nothing other than require each company to adopt its own form of internal reporting. Any notion of reporting, or gesturing about, client fraud to the government should, of course, be excised from the rule.[125] On the triggering standard, I think it is fair to say that most (and maybe all) of the bar comments wanted the SEC to remove all vestiges in the rule and comments of the position taken by those I have pictured as losing the battle within the SEC—the strong-rule folks. To my eyes, the bar had already won. The bar, on the other hand, would not be happy without total and absolute surrender.

B. Round Two

The comments were all in. Now the SEC was supposed to issue a final rule. It did, sort of. It issued a rule to cover reporting within the corporate client, but reserved judgment on the entire noisy withdrawal dispute. On that matter, the SEC said that it was persuaded, by the many comments demanding more time for additional comments (against noisy withdrawal), that more time was indeed needed.[126] The SEC is understating just how "persuaded" it was by the clamor over noisy withdrawal. It not only provided more time for comment, it issued an alternative to noisy withdrawal by the lawyer—lawyer withdrawal with reporting (or maybe only noise) *by the company, instead of by the lawyer,* to the SEC.

Now, as I've none too subtly suggested, I believe the entire noisy withdrawal debate has been little more than a distracting sideshow. Not because I think it's a bad idea; I think it's a good one.[127] Having said that, a strong internal reporting requirement would be nearly as good. If a lawyer were required to inform the board of management's refusal to address appropriately evidence of corporate fraud, it would be rare that directors would ignore the lawyer's report or fail to take adequate steps to address the evidence. History suggests that some boards might fire the lawyer and continue business as before, but the real fear of director liability, if not the integrity of most

---

[125] The ABA argued not just for a lawyer "knows" standard and against "noisy withdrawal," but also for the SEC to abandon any specificity about what a lawyer should do when he "knows," leaving it to each company to develop its own standards on lawyer reporting. *See* Comments of American Bar Association, *supra* note 124.

[126] From my reading of the comments, only those commentators who opposed the noisy withdrawal provision—virtually every bar group and lawyer commenting, with the exception of some professors—made this "more time" argument.

[127] Indeed, I would applaud abandoning the charade of gesturing and replacing it with a requirement that a lawyer openly disclose ongoing corporate fraud in which his services had been used whenever the highest authority in the organization-client—in a corporation, that would be the board of directors—refuses to rectify the fraud on its own. Actually, I think the law already requires that of lawyers (as it does of non-lawyers) when, for example, investors are relying on the lawyer's work product to make investment decisions and the lawyer has learned, subsequent to having completed the work, that the work product is materially misleading.

businesspeople, leads me to believe that those boards would be the exception and not the rule.

Given that the internal reporting rule is thus really the heart of the matter, and the SEC's noisy withdrawal "requirement" was never much of a requirement to begin with, as it included the QLCC "out," I have little patience for the entire noisy withdrawal opera. The far more important question is what the SEC did about the trigger for lawyer reporting up the corporate ladder. This is to be found in the part of the rule the SEC did not delay, the part it adopted. The answer is that it made matters worse. If the SEC's first draft revealed the signs of a struggle over the standard, the second draft is so scarred from that internal battle that it is difficult to recognize it as a legal standard, and harder still to imagine it functioning as a rule of law.

Under the adopted portion of the rule, a lawyer must report, first to the CEO or chief legal officer "credible evidence, based upon which it would be unreasonable, under the circumstances, for a prudent and competent attorney not to conclude that it is reasonably likely that a material violation has occurred, is ongoing, or is about to occur."[128]

I wish that were a joke, but it isn't. The SEC said it had taken the professors' comments seriously and eliminated any doubt that it intended the standard to be objective, as the original comment (but not the proposed rule) had said.[129] Unlike the SEC's first try, the standard I just quoted bears the markings of an objective standard, rather than a subjective one, although, as I will explain, I think its "objectivity" is a pose. But objective or subjective, it is incomprehensible. Law is supposed to guide conduct in the world. That requires that the mind be capable of translating the norm into behavior. Need I really say more? Just try translating this rule.

Law is also supposed to be capable of enforcement. Imagine trying to show that it was unreasonable, under the circumstances, for a prudent lawyer *not* to have concluded that a material violation of law had occurred, was occurring, or was about to occur. The double negative, of course, makes this difficult to do, as the rule slips away from you as soon as you try to think about it. But underneath all its contortions, what it seems to require for enforcement is proof that a prudent lawyer would have had to conclude that the law was reasonably likely to have been violated.

As a practical matter, that is equivalent to requiring the agency to show that the lawyer actually concluded (knew) the law was being violated, as in: No reasonable lawyer could have thought anything else. To understand why that is the equivalent of

---

[128] *Implementation of Standards of Professional Conduct for Attorneys,* 68 Fed. Reg. 6296, 6321 (Feb. 6, 2003) (to be codified at 17 C.F.R. pt. 205.2(e)).

[129] In our comments on the proposed rule, we suggested that the SEC adopt a much simpler objective standard. Under our formulation, an attorney would be required to report up the ladder when "confronted with information that a prudent and competent attorney, acting reasonably under the same circumstances, would conclude was credible evidence of a material violation by the issuer." Comments of Susan P. Koniak et al., *supra* note 121.

an actual knowledge (or actual conclusion) standard, remember that knowledge is not proven by x-raying a defendant's brain. It is proven either by an admission by the defendant that he knew (here, concluded) something or, more often, by drawing reasonable inferences about what the defendant knew (or concluded), given the information available to him. In the latter case, the question for the factfinder is what any reasonable lawyer would have had to know in this situation, but that is precisely the standard that seems to be buried under the SEC's convoluted language. True, the ridiculous standard ends by saying that it does not require a conclusion that the law was actually being violated, but rather only a conclusion that it was "reasonably likely" that the law was being violated. But the damage is so serious before that point that it is impossible to praise the agency for this fragment of a good idea, lost in a thicket of gobbledy-gook.

Ugly as the triggering standard is, it is not the only scar on the SEC's adopted rule. Assuming that a lawyer ever imagines that the standard just given has been met and that he has to report evidence of fraud to the CEO or chief legal officer (or that he has already reported the evidence to the company's board), he need not resign (and need not himself report to the board, if he has not already done so), if he is informed that the board or QLCC has hired another lawyer and that lawyer has concluded that he "may, consistent with his or her professional obligations, assert a colorable defense on behalf of the issuer (or the issuer's officer, director, employee, or agent, as the case may be) in any investigation or judicial or administrative proceeding relating to the reported evidence of a material violation."[130]

The comments explain that this language was included to ensure that lawyers acting as advocates in Commission proceedings or in other fora in which the securities laws are in issue are not hamstrung in their duty to represent zealously their clients' interests. Indeed, the Commission notes that some professors, along with many lawyers, had critiqued the SEC's proposal for not adequately distinguishing between lawyers advocating a client's cause in an adversarial setting and lawyers blessing transactions as legal or illegal without the clash of adversarial presentations. Indeed, the SEC was correct in this regard: There is good reason to distinguish between lawyers in an adversarial setting and lawyers acting as advisors. The reason for this distinction inheres in the difference between these two roles.[131] In the adversarial setting, a lawyer is justified in presenting all nonfrivolous arguments, because the opposing party's attorneys, the judge, and the jury all operate as potential checks against abuse. But these checks are all absent when a lawyer is counseling a client on the legality of the clients' contemplated actions.[132]

The problem is that the SEC's solution misses the mark by a mile. If the fraud or other violation of law is past and not ongoing, and an investigation is underway (or,

[130] *Implementation of Standards of Professional Conduct for Attorneys,* 68 Fed. Reg. at 6320 (to be codified at 17 C.F.R. pt. 205.2(b)(3)(ii)).

[131] *See* Comments of Susan P. Koniak et al., *supra* note 121.

[132] *Id.*

maybe, is imminent) or litigation has been commenced (or, maybe, is imminent), then it makes sense to say that a company that gets a report of evidence related to that proceeding need do nothing more than see to it that it is reported to its litigation counsel. But that's true whether or not that counsel can come up with a colorable defense. On the other hand, it makes no sense to say that an appropriate response for a company that has been given a report of evidence of corporate wrongdoing (which is contemplated or ongoing) is to have the board find another lawyer who has a colorable defense to the violation that he "may" assert. If shareholders are buying shares today or tomorrow, based on bogus financial statements, the fact that a lawyer can imagine a colorable defense that might be made if the fraud is ever discovered is no excuse for the company leaving that information outstanding. Moreover, that is true whether or not litigation or an investigation is ongoing. A colorable defense is simply not an acceptable standard for ongoing advice. The SEC's rule states that the existence of a second lawyer, hired by the board, will relieve the reporting lawyer of the obligation to resign (or to go to the board personally and report the evidence), if the second lawyer *either* investigates the matter, recommends rectification, and sees that the company substantially implements those recommendations, or can come up with a colorable defense that "may" be asserted in a subsequent proceeding.[133] These are not alternatives. If rectification is required to stop a fraud, the existence of a colorable defense is simply not a substitute for stopping ongoing illegal conduct.

Thus far, in private conversations, two members of the SEC staff have told me that the "colorable defense" business was intended to address only the vigorous advocate concern raised by many lawyers and by the professors, too. But when the first SEC proposal came out, the staff told me that "reasonably believes" was not an attempt to fudge the standard, but rather was a simple drafting problem. That proved to be wishful thinking, and given the convoluted triggering standard in the adopted rule, I am quite skeptical that the "colorable" problem is some colossal drafting mistake and nothing more. It is just too close to what the bar actually believes, to how lawyers actually behave, to be a result of poor draftsmanship.[134]

---

[133] *Implementation of Standards of Professional Conduct for Attorneys,* 68 Fed. Reg. at 6320 (to be codified at 17 C.F.R. pt. 205.2(b)(3)).

[134] That assessment is, unfortunately, bolstered by a comment in the SEC's new proposal for an alternative to noisy withdrawal—requiring companies to report lawyer withdrawal. The comment asks people to comment on whether it might not be a good idea to relieve companies of the duty to report lawyer withdrawal if the company can find another lawyer to say that the withdrawing lawyer acted unreasonably in thinking that he had to withdraw because the company had made no appropriate response to his report of wrongdoing. *Implementation of Standards of Professional Conduct for Attorneys,* 68 Fed. Reg. 6324, 6329–30 (proposed Feb. 6, 2003) (to be codified at 17 C.F.R. pts. 205, 240, 249). "Acted unreasonably," mind you, in deciding that no reasonable lawyer could fail to conclude that the violation of law was reasonably likely. Given how narrow (to put it kindly) the standard for reporting is already, the suggestion that another layer should be added to further weaken this already-shaky structure is pitiful. But more to the point, that suggestion echoes the "second lawyer says it's okay solution" found in the "colorable defense" provision. That strengthens my suspicion that the "colorable defense" provision was intended to be as broad as it appears.

Congress passed a law demanding that the SEC hold lawyers to account. The SEC proposed something that looked tough, but wasn't. Even that proposal was too much for the bar. It battled back. The SEC says that the fight is not over yet. But the first two rounds surely didn't go its way. We have been here before.

CONCLUSION

The bar's law should be rejected, not because it is contrary to the law of the state, but because the state's law is better. How does one say what "better" is, if, as I do, one abandons the notion that state law is by definition "better" because it is supposedly affirmed by the people, at least in a democracy?[135] Law, the insistent and real demand that norms guide behavior, is designed to affect the world, to change the world to one in which the conduct denounced by a norm is minimized. To judge between two competing laws, one must ask what worlds they create. The bar's law creates a world in which lawyers are and will remain available to help crooked people cheat others. By insisting that lawyers cannot judge their clients except, perhaps, in those rarest of cases when the client virtually announces out loud that he is breaking the law, and then to require only that a lawyer silently resign, the bar helps constitute a world in which wrongdoers will always have lawyers to help them succeed with their plans. If one resigns, another will take over until, perhaps, he has to resign in silence, and then another lawyer, and then another . . . .

Lawyers condemn the state's law on the ground that it would constitute an even worse world. How? In two ways, which the bar often conflates, but which are actually distinct. First, the state would deprive people of champions to fight off state charges of wrongdoing, the first step towards tyrannical rule. That would be true if the state's law on client fraud required lawyers who come in after the fact of wrongdoing or alleged wrongdoing to resign or turn their clients in. It doesn't. To the extent that any state rule did that, I would agree with the bar. Indeed, the comments that I drafted and sent to the SEC, generally supportive of the SEC's approach to corporate lawyers, urged the SEC to make clear that advocates should be free to argue zealously on behalf of their clients.

Second, the bar claims that the state's law would prevent lawyers who facilitate client transactions before the fact and during a transaction's life (before any accusation of wrongdoing) from performing a function is good for the world—in helping people to comply with the law. How? The state's law would discourage clients from telling their lawyers what they were doing. I agree that encouraging compliance with the law

---

[135] I reject this statist view of "better" because I experience it as demonstrably untrue on two levels. First, state law, even in a democracy, is sometimes unquestionably bad. Second, it is fiction, plain and simple, to assert that the people, in any meaningful sense, approve every precept of state law, or even many of the precepts. Most people do not have the slightest idea what the content of state law is, nor do they have any meaningful way to influence it. For a fuller elaboration of why the bar's law on client fraud is inferior to the law of the state, see Susan P. Koniak, *When Courts Refuse to Frame the Law and Others Frame It to Their Will*, 66 S. CAL. L. REV. 1075, 1109–13 (1993).

is good, but there is simply no empirical evidence to suggest that a strong report-up-the-ladder rule, or even a rule requiring outright disclosure of fraud to the SEC, if the board of a company refused to correct its ways, would result in corporate clients telling their lawyers less. Right now, the attorney-client privilege does not protect client confidences aimed at perpetrating a crime or fraud.[136] Right now, most states give lawyers the discretion to disclose confidences when the lawyer believes that criminal fraud is afoot.[137] Right now, every new CEO, a trustee in bankruptcy, or a determined board of directors could order that the corporation waive its entire attorney-client privilege whenever it wanted to make public the conversations between lawyers and management.[138] And corporate managers talk to lawyers. A strong rule on reporting client fraud would not make corporate confidences any more insecure than they already are, nor would it make corporate managers suddenly afraid to talk to lawyers.

But even a strong up-the-ladder rule is not enough. The enforcement gap in the law governing lawyers needs to be closed. Aiding and abetting liability for lawyers must be restored, and the level of *scienter* necessary for liability should be returned to "recklessness" for private suits and for actions brought by the SEC. Helping others cheat people is a serious wrong: That has always been an intentional tort, and there is no excuse to single out securities fraud as the one form of fraud with which one can assist with relative impunity. Criminal prosecutions against one or two law firms involved with fraud should be instituted. There is no reason to accord ministers of the law with *de facto* immunity from criminal prosecution. Lawyers who help others commit crimes are more dangerous than others who aid felons, not less so, if only because lawyers are more likely to prove effective helpers.

The SEC should require that every required filing by a company be signed by a lawyer.[139] Any lawyer should be subject to discipline by the SEC (or a separate lawyer board, if necessary) for negligently certifying that a paper was not materially misleading. The cost to companies? Surely not more than the money now being expended for lawyers helping companies file misleading documents.

Finally, there is an air of unreality about the entire debate on the regulation of securities lawyers. Part of that comes from the bar's protestations that the federal government should leave the regulation of the securities bar to the states. I have been in this field more years than I care to count, and neither I nor any of my colleagues in this area of law know of one single case in which a lawyer from a major law firm has been disciplined by state authorities for aiding a client's securities fraud. Despite all the

---

[136] *See* HAZARD ET AL., *supra* note 68, at 282–83.

[137] *See* THOMAS D. MORGAN & RONALD D. ROTUNDA, 2003 SELECTED STANDARDS ON PROFESSIONAL RESPONSIBILITY 134–44 (2002) (detailing state versions of Model Rule 1.6).

[138] *See* Commodity Futures Trading Comm'n v. Weintraub, 471 U.S. 343, 348, 354 (1985) (observing that power to waive attorney-client privilege is normally exercised by corporation's officers and directors, or by trustee in bankruptcy).

[139] This elegantly simple idea was first suggested to me by Professor John Coates.

settlements after the savings and loan crisis, all the press coverage, and a number of court opinions describing egregious lawyer conduct, there has been not one case of state discipline. The state disciplinary systems lack the expertise in securities law, the staff, and the monetary resources to take on a major law firm. They can't do it, and they don't. Thus, when the bar says "leave securities lawyers to the states," it means "leave them unregulated."

But the unreality has a deeper source than that. The entire debate is so polite, framed as if the question were whether lawyers are in a position to figure out what the client is up to. The facts paint a very different portrait. All too often lawyers don't need to discover what the client is up to; they know, because they are drafting the scripts, structuring the transactions. They are, if you will, in on the ground floor. The problem is not so much knowing what the client is doing; it is respecting that the law has limits that apply to one's client. The problem is that the bar's law has constructed a world in which lawyers believe that it is their job to imagine the client's every objective as being within the law. The bar's law has constructed a world in which lawyers believe it is their duty to contort all law to meet the client's ends. And here is the crux of the matter. In such a world, law is no longer possible. Law, in such a world, does not affect behavior at all; it just recharacterizes it. If lawyers tear down all our laws, where shall we stand? What will protect us then?

The Academics Have It Wrong: Hysteria Is No Substitute for Sound Public Policy Analysis

Lawrence J. Fox*

The recent declassification of the Senator Joseph McCarthy Unamerican Activities Committee tapes of interviews with those accused of being Communists and Communist sympathizers[1] brought to mind the excesses that so often have accompanied hysterical eras in our nation's history. It also raised the question whether we are not engaging in the same trampling of rights and guilt by association as America deals with the pain and the blame for September 11, 2001. How easy, far too easy, it is for us to identify scapegoats, convict without trials, target groups based on no more than religion or national origin, and otherwise deal unfairly to satisfy our need to place responsibility somewhere other than upon ourselves.

The wholesale rounding-up of those who practice the Islamic faith, the suspension of constitutional rights for American citizens, the caging of so-called enemy combatants at Guantanamo, the expansion of surveillance and snooping by the FBI and proposals to expand those powers domestically to the armed forces and the CIA, the denial of the right to counsel, and the effective suspension of the writ of habeas corpus all have numerous precedents in some of the sorriest and most shameful chapters in our nation's history.[2]

---

* © Lawrence J. Fox 2003. All rights reserved. I have been the beneficiary of the largesse of the University of Houston Law Center in inviting me to speak to the faculty on these issues and then of the enthusiastic goading of the Center's indefatigable Dean, Nancy Rapoport, in drafting this article.

[1] Sheryl Gay Stolberg, *Transcripts Detail Secret Questioning in 50's by McCarthy*, N.Y. TIMES, May 6, 2003, at A1.

[2] For example: President Lincoln suspended the privilege of habeas corpus at the start of the Civil War in 1861. This act wasn't declared unconstitutional until 1866, in *Ex Parte Milligan*, 71 U.S. 2 (1866) (mem.). The Espionage Act of 1917 and the Sedition Act of 1918 were enacted to curtail all criticism of the government and the war effort during WWI. The Supreme Court upheld numerous convictions under these acts. *See* Schenck v. United States, 249 U.S. 47 (1919); Frohwerk v. United States, 249 U.S. 204 (1919); Debs v. United States, 249 U.S. 211 (1919); Abrams v. United States, 250 U.S. 616 (1919). During WWII, the Supreme Court found constitutional an order that directed the exclusion of persons of

Several academics now ask us to take a breather from these compelling current events to focus instead upon the crisis in confidence caused by the massive fraud and outsized financial losses that resulted from the various train wrecks that have made the corporate names "Enron," "WorldCom," "Adelphia," and "Tyco" synonymous with the very worst that capitalism has to offer.[3] What the academics criticizing the lawyers don't see is that their entire approach to these matters is the same kind of demonizing of entire categories of people and the same kind of destroying of vital institutions that was the clarion call of Joseph McCarthy in attacking the Communist menace and is the hallmark of John Ashcroft in attacking the terrorist threat. And the same self-righteous indignation that McCarthy and Ashcroft have managed to muster infects the discussion of Enron at every turn.

WHO NEEDS TRIALS TO ASSESS BLAME?

Take a look at what some of these academics say regarding the conduct of the lawyers who represented Enron. Professor Susan Koniak of Boston University is vociferous in her scorn for the lawyers, and she starts by convicting the various players in the Enron debacle, announcing to the entire world:

> But facts are stubborn things. So with or without trials, the legal judgment
> I have made about those facts will abide, as long, that is, as my confidence
> in those facts remains. I repeat, people and institutions broke the laws: lots
> of people, lots of institutions, lots of laws.[4]

Professor Koniak starts with the convictions. She reaches her verdicts based entirely on allegations in complaints and her viewing on television a portion of the hearings conducted in Congress.[5] Nowhere does she acknowledge that allegations are just that—allegations—to say nothing of the fact that the allegations could prove baseless. Nowhere

---

Japanese ancestry from a West coast military area. Korematsu v. United States, 323 U.S. 214 (1944). The Smith Act was used after the end of the war to prosecute individuals charged with Communist Party affiliation. *See* Dennis v. United States, 341 U.S. 494 (1951).

[3] *See, e.g.,* Roger C. Cramton, *Enron and the Corporate Lawyer: A Primer on Legal and Ethical Issues,* 58 BUS. LAW. 143 (2002) [hereinafter Cramton], *reprinted in this book at* 571–623; Robert W. Gordon, *A New Role for Lawyers? The Corporate Counselor After Enron,* 35 CONN. L. REV. 1185 (2003) [hereinafter Gordon], *reprinted in this book at* 763–92; Susan P. Koniak, *When the Hurlyburly's Done: The Bar's Struggle With the SEC,* 103 COL. L. REV. 1236 (2003) [hereinafter Koniak], *reprinted in this book at* 807–49.

[4] Koniak, *supra* note 3, at 1237.

[5] Koniak observes that she watched the testimony of Vinson & Elkins and other assorted law firms. She also watched "every single minute of the testimony given by Citigroup's and J.P. Morgan's managers." Koniak, *supra* note 3, at 1242.

does she admit that the same pandering politicians who lined up to excoriate witness after witness might have been motivated ever so slightly by the fact that most of them had been the willing (yes, even delighted), beneficiaries of Enron largesse and just might have had every reason to play these hearings to the public in a way that would divert attention from that embarrassment.

No. Those facts do not stop her from "convicting" all the lawyers who were anywhere near the scene of these train wrecks. Nor does she hide her idea of a standard of proof. She reads; she observes; she finds bringing charges to the attention of the accused an unnecessary formality; and she certainly sees no need to await hearing from the defenders of these miscreants:

> And they [the lawyers] did it with help. Sure, sure, the accountants pitched in. And some corporate executives, some analysts, some traders, showed entrepreneurial spirit and struck out to break laws on their own or with just a few of their fellows. But others, a good many others, had lawyers showing them the way. Lawyers structuring bogus deals, vouching for nonexistent "sales," writing whitewash reports to keep the sheriff fooled and away. Lawyers going all out for, they would say, their "clients," but as a technical matter, not for their "clients"—rather, for the reckless and dishonest cowboys in control of their clients. The clients of these lawyers were, after all, not corporate executives, but the corporations (some now bankrupt for all their lawyers' tender care)—entities owned by all those duped shareholders.[6]

I'm not the only person who has been frustrated with this rush to judgment, unfettered by any actual findings of facts. In a recent *Wall Street Journal* article, reporter Michael Orey described another such situation.

> Ms. Koniak called Mr. Carroll [a lawyer for Arthur Andersen] . . . to discuss a law-review article she is writing that is based on her Senate testimony. "During our conversation, Ms. Koniak admitted that she didn't have the facts and that she doesn't think that other law firms would have acted any differently," says Mr. Carroll, who adds that the conversation ended cordially. Ms. Koniak says she has enough facts about Davis Polk [and its advice to Andersen] "to draw the conclusions I have drawn and which I stand by."[7]

But Professor Koniak isn't the only academic willing to convict before a trial. Professor Robert Gordon of Yale Law School has observed that

---

[6] *Id.* at 1237.

[7] Michael Orey, *Launching Broadsides at the Bar,* WALL ST. J., May 8, 2002, at B1.

It is clear that the advice both in-house lawyers and outside law firms gave to the managers of Enron and other companies like it was instrumental in enabling those managers to cream off huge profits for themselves while bringing economic ruin to investors, employees, and the taxpaying public. Although the lawyers were not principally responsible for these acts of waste and fraud, their advice was a contributing (and often necessary) cause of those acts. Such fraud could not have been carried out without the lawyers' active approval, passive acquiescence, or failure to inquire and investigate.[8]

But how does Professor Gordon make such clear assertions? Certainly, it is not on the basis of any evidence that has been adduced so far,[9] let alone any finding made by a court of law.

The flaws with this rush to judgment can already be easily demonstrated. Professor Koniak wrote her article before the Enron Examiner's Third Interim Report had come out. In that report, the Examiner concluded that Enron and six banks conspired to keep certain information from Enron's accountant, Arthur Andersen, so that Andersen would sign off on the deals.[10] If Enron and the banks kept information from Andersen, could they not also have kept information from Enron's own lawyers?[11] Alternatively, isn't it possible that Enron deliberately used numerous law firms so that no single law firm could connect the dots with all of Enron's crooked deals? As Professor Gordon grudgingly points out, "[s]ome of their claims of limited knowledge are plausible, however, because Enron never trusted any one set of lawyers with extensive information about its operations—it spread legal work out to over 100 law firms."[12] The truth is that Enron is a complicated matter, and it will take years to get all of the facts. Thus,

---

[8] Gordon, *supra* note 3, at 1190, *reprinted in this book at* 763–92.

[9] Indeed, no privileged communications have been discussed. Until Enron's bankruptcy, Enron itself held the privilege. Upon Enron's bankruptcy, Enron's new manager, Steve Cooper, succeeded to the privilege. *See* Nancy B. Rapoport, *Enron, Titanic, and The Perfect Storm*, 71 FORDHAM L. REV. 1373, 1382 n.54 (2003), *reprinted in this book at* 927–49. To my knowledge, Cooper has not waived the privilege or published Enron's legal advice in any way. The Enron Examiner, Neal Batson, is still working on the issue of whether any of Enron's lawyers would be liable to Enron's estate for misconduct. Batson has indicated (in his Third Interim Report) that he will provide his conclusions about the Enron lawyers in his Fourth Interim Report. *See* Neal Batson, Third Interim Report of Neal Batson, Court-Appointed Examiner, *In re Enron Corp.*, No. 01-16034 (Bankr. S.D.N.Y. June 30, 2003) [hereinafter Third Interim Report].

[10] *See* Third Interim Report, *supra* note 9, at Appendix C, at 38–44.

[11] Based on the Examiner's Third Interim Report, I find it as easy to imagine that the banks' lawyers weren't given all of the information on Enron's side deals (which rendered the deals illegitimate) as Professor Koniak imagines that the banks' lawyers knew all along that the deals were illegitimate. *See* Koniak, *supra* note 3, at 1243.

[12] Gordon, *supra* note 3, at 1193.

it should come as no surprise that I get exasperated when I read of law professors willing to equate "allegations against lawyers in the Enron case"[13] with actual findings of fact.[14]

Given the plea-bargains of two Enron executives, Michael Kopper[15] and Ben Glisan,[16] as well as the Enron Board's own Powers Report,[17] I am willing to say that some of the officers and high-level employees at Enron did some very bad things, and I am even willing to say that more convictions—and some judgments in civil suits—are likely. But I am not willing to condemn Enron's lawyers before the facts are in. And I am certainly not willing to testify before Congress and say, without benefit of any information, beyond the allegations in plaintiffs' complaints, that Enron's lawyers must have been responsible for Enron's actions.[18]

---

[13] Koniak, *supra* note 3, at 1239.

[14] Professor Koniak is not alone in making the cognitive leap from allegations in complaints to findings of facts. Take this passage in Professor Cramton's article:

> The conduct of the inside and outside lawyers who represented Enron, Arthur Andersen, and the many financial institutions involved in the Enron scandal tell the same story that has been told to us by a long string of major financial frauds for fifty years: the professional ideal of "independent professional judgment" does not inform the behavior of some lawyers who represent large corporations in major transactions and high-stakes litigation. These lawyers take the position that they must do everything for the client that the client's managers want them to do, providing the conduct is permitted by law.

Cramton, *supra* note 3, at 173. As far as I can tell from reading the papers, Andersen's conviction was based on the jury's finding that *one* inside (Andersen) lawyer, Nancy Temple, was a wrongdoer. *See* Jonathan Weil, *Andersen: Called to Account; Jury Cuts Off an Andersen Appeals Route—Linking an Employee to Criminal Act Makes Moot the Judge's Risky Procedural Ruling,* WALL ST. J., June 17, 2002, at C13. How, then, do we get from one "corrupt persuader" to all of the "inside and outside lawyers" involved in Enron?

[15] Michael Kopper pleaded guilty to money laundering and conspiracy to commit wire fraud on August 21, 2002. *See* Jonathan Weil, Alexei Barrionuevo, Anita Raghavan & Kathryn Kranhold, *Guilty Plea by Enron's Kopper Increases Scrutiny of Ex-CFO,* WALL ST. J., August 22, 2002, at A1.

[16] Ben Glisan pleaded guilty to criminal charges on September 10, 2003. *See* John R. Emshwiller, *Ex-Treasurer Is First Enron Officer to Go to Prison—Ben Glisan's Guilty Plea Without Cooperation Deal Closes an Avenue in Inquiry,* WALL ST. J., September 11, 2003, at A3.

[17] William C. Powers, Jr., et al., REPORT OF INVESTIGATION BY THE SPECIAL INVESTIGATIVE COMMITTEE OF THE BOARD OF DIRECTORS OF ENRON CORP., 2002 WL 198018 (CORPSCAN 1980818 (ENRON)) [hereinafter Powers Report]. The Powers Report is also available at http://i.cnn.net/cnn/2002/LAW/02/02/enron.report/powers.report.pdf.

[18] The Senate Judiciary Committee had held one hearing devoted to lawyer responsibility for the Enron fiasco, but that hearing was perhaps the only one on Enron to receive virtually no press coverage; it did not even show up in the wee hours of the morning on C-SPAN. I know because I testified at the hearing—the only witness who said lawyers were critical to the success of Enron's schemes and those of other fraud-committing companies.

Koniak, *supra* note 3, at 1269.

Professor Koniak, joined by Professor Roger Cramton, wrote for an *Illinois Law Review* symposium an article that they later withdrew;[19] the unpublished article,[20] nonetheless, reflects the substance of the charges that she made from the podium in Champagne-Urbana (and elsewhere).[21] Professors Koniak and Cramton did not spare Vinson & Elkins in that draft article, any more than either of them does now. Indeed, Vinson & Elkins was attacked on three counts, the first of which was the fact that part of what Vinson & Elkins was investigating related to the firm's prior work for Enron. Koniak and Cramton called this a conflict that they say could not be waived, at least by the individuals at Enron who were requesting the investigation.

The second attack on Vinson & Elkins referred to the "scope" limitations that were placed on the investigation, to wit: this was a "preliminary investigation" to determine whether the Watkins memo "raised new factual information;" there was to be no detailed analysis of each transaction; and the investigation would not involve "the second guessing of the accounting advice and treatment provided"[22] by Arthur Andersen.

Finally, Koniak and Cramton took Vinson & Elkins to task for providing incompetent advice. They argued that, since Vinson & Elkins's underlying role had the effect of compromising any investigation that the firm was undertaking, the firm was remiss for taking any money from Enron to conduct the investigation. They also excoriated the firm for failing to follow leads, all of which, with the benefit of hindsight, look like they might have been promising.

But the at best ambiguous nature of Vinson & Elkins's conduct—as yet undetermined and unadjudicated—did not stop Koniak and Cramton from convicting the entire profession. Not content with defaming Vinson & Elkins, they concluded:

> This is not a [Vinson & Elkins] problem, anymore than our earlier discussion was indicative of a problem at Davis Polk.[23] The problem is sys-

---

[19] *Editors' note:* according to Professors Koniak and Cramton, they withdrew that article for two reasons: one was the law review's delay in publishing their draft, and one was Professor Cramton's health, which prevented him from attending the conference and presenting that paper.

[20] Susan P. Koniak & Roger C. Cramton, *Where Were the Lawyers? Behind the Curtain Wearing Their Magic Caps* (Mar. 30, 2002) (unpublished manuscript, on file with the *University of Illinois Law Review*) [hereinafter *Where Were the Lawyers*].

[21] Professor Koniak delivered a scathing indictment of Vinson & Elkins and Davis Polk and Wardwell at the American Association of Law School convention in D.C. in January 2003; I spoke on the same panel with her at that conference.

[22] *Where Were the Lawyers, supra* note 20, at 25 (citation omitted).

[23] In *Where Were the Lawyers,* Professors Koniak and Cramton also discussed the outside counsel for Arthur Andersen (Davis, Polk & Wardwell). Carefully lining up the dates, they observed that Davis Polk was retained by Andersen on October 9, 2001, and began the firm's work on October 16, seven days "before the major shredding at Andersen began." *Where Were the Lawyers, supra* note 20, at 15.

After questioning why Davis Polk didn't immediately advise Andersen to clarify the in-house counsel's now famous October 12 memo regarding Andersen's document retention policy, they asked: "Why didn't

temic. Law firms that all would count as pillars of the bar and lawyers across the country believe deeply in their magic caps—deeply enough to imagine that they can assess a legal landscape that they were part of, as if they were not there at all, deeply enough to conduct whitewash investigations that keep wrongdoing under wraps and allow fraudulent conduct to continue, deeply enough to imagine obstruction of justice is not a crime that applies to them or to clients armed with some lawyer-drafted policy that invites them to do what the law says they may not. But lawyers have no magic caps and they cannot knit such caps for their clients by running around blessing as legal everything their clients do.[24]

In the view of some academics, the legal landscape is littered with wrongdoers, the problems are everywhere, and lawyers, instead of helping their clients conform their conduct to the law, are blessing whatever the clients choose to do. And it is on the basis of such broadsides (and not the rigorous analysis one should expect in objective scholarship from the academy) that Professor Koniak builds the very weak foundation upon which she erects her attacks on the fundamentals of the practice of law. For what is

---

the law firm, on its own initiative, take steps to see to it that Andersen's notes, drafts, work papers and e-mails on the Enron engagement were preserved and protected from destruction by misguided or criminal actors within Andersen?" *Id.* at 15 n. 51.

What a remarkable observation. Davis Polk, as its first order of business, should have prevented the document destruction, "whether or not anyone asked," them about this topic. *Id.* Ultimately, Koniak and Cramton focused on timing: "that during Davis Polk's engagement massive shredding took place at Andersen." *Id.* at 12. Because Koniak and Cramton "do know the shredding occurred on Davis Polk's *watch,*" *id.* at 16 (emphasis added), they created a new concept of lawyering that should send shivers down the spine of the practicing bar, as well as send its malpractice premiums soaring.

In the view of Professors Koniak and Cramton, Davis Polk was not an aberration; there is a pandemic of such behavior. Read these words carefully:

> More troubling, we believe that virtually every other major law firm in this country would have acted just as Davis Polk did. We believe, to put it bluntly, that lawyers all across this country sit by passively while corporate clients break the law. The problem, in our eyes, is systemic. That is bad news for our economy, our country, and for every American.

Id. at 16.

[24] *Id.* at 38. Professor Koniak reiterated this position in an editorial that she wrote for FORBES:

> Because lawyers are necessary to commit almost any fraud of more than a moment's duration, their firms' survival should be on the line. What's needed is to restore aiding-and-abetting liability, joint-and-several liability, and the recklessness standard, at least for lawyers. . . .
>
> The lawyer problem is systemic: no "few bad apples" here. Neither moral outrage nor proposals for reform have come from the President, our financial wise men like Warren Buffett and Alan Greenspan, or the press. Even companies that suffered greatly from outsize management fraud, all of which should be suing their lawyers for malpractice, aren't and won't—too many skeletons. This is a disgrace.

Susan P. Koniak, *Who Gave Lawyers a Pass?; We haven't blamed the real culprits in corporate scandals,* FORBES, Aug. 12, 2002, at 58.

really distressing is not the broadscale "convictions," but the changes in public policy that these academics assert should follow.

THE "MALEVOLENCE" OF THE BAR'S LAW

Assuming, for the sake of argument, that Enron's lawyers did everything that Enron had asked them to do, with full knowledge that what they were doing was wrong, what new structures do these academics urge upon us to change the way that these evil lawyers practice law? According to Professor Cramton, education about the current rules prohibiting lawyer assistance in client fraud is not sufficient.

> Preaching to lawyers and bar groups about their moral and public responsibilities has proven to be ineffective. Professional discipline, for a variety of reasons, provides virtually no control over the failure of law firms to monitor the partners who are bringing in juicy fees from corporate clients. The spread of limited liability partnerships accentuates the willingness of partners to ignore the risks that other partners are taking. Today's emphasis on "the bottom line," both in corporations and law firms, gives rise to a culture valuing the false sense of prestige and status that flows from being among the leaders in the annual listings of profits per partner. From the vantage point of respect for law and the public responsibilities of lawyers, the current scene runs the risk of being "a race to the bottom." As stated above, there is a systemic problem that requires systemic solutions.[25]

What is that "systemic problem"? Professor Koniak, in one of her earlier articles,[26] suggests that, rather than follow the law of the state, the lawyers follow the law of professional ethics, an approach that is apparently a bad thing. It is not clear to me whether, when Professor Koniak comes up with this construct, she is talking about professional ethics being used on behalf of lawyers or professional ethics being used on behalf of clients. Most of her examples suggest that professional ethics is used in a self-protective way; but in the end, the distinction may not make any difference, because, at least in my view, what she complains about as professional ethics is being employed by lawyers not to benefit themselves but to leave themselves free to independently represent clients.[27] Professor Koniak calls this view of professional ethics the "bar's law."[28] In my view, the beneficiaries of the bar's law are not lawyers, but our clients, though I would gladly concede that, in order to be free to represent our clients effectively, lawyers regularly do have to push back attempts by the state to circumscribe the ambit of permissible lawyer conduct; that is, the more the state can interfere with the

---

[25] Cramton, *supra* note 3, at 175 (footnotes omitted).

[26] *See* Susan P. Koniak, *The Law Between the Bar and the State,* 17 N.C. L. REV.1389, 1396 (1992) [hereinafter *Law Between*].

[27] *See Law Between, supra* note 26, at 1398–1401, 1405–1424.

[28] *Id.*

zealous representation by lawyers of their clients, the more clients will be forced to conform to this concept called "state's law."[29]

I am not alone here. Others have also observed how dangerous it is for lawyers to play both sides of the fence: the client's side and the state's side. Evan Davis, for example, points out the obvious conflict.

> [I]t is very important for the bar to be independent of the political branches of government. It has not been a problem that in the United States the bar has come to be regulated by the judiciary because of the judiciary's own neutrality; it would be a huge problem if the bar were regulated by the Department of Justice or by the various elected or appointed state attorneys general. It would be much harder to resist either gentle or firm governmental pressure if the government's lawyers decided how the bar in general or you, as an attorney, in particular, should behave.[30]

First, let me address what I understand to be Professor Koniak's concept of the state's law. From her examples, it appears she is talking about legislation enacted by Congress, the various state legislatures, or regulations issued by administrative agencies, as well as those agencies' interpretations of both legislation and regulations. Certainly from the examples of conflict between state law and the bar's law that she invokes, that appears to be the case. For example, she takes us through the SEC's *National*

---

[29] However, independence as such is not a legitimate aspiration of the bar. In this world so full of legal complexities and pitfalls, individuals and organizations need legal advisors who owe them a duty of loyalty and in whom they can confide with confidence. Therefore, in a general sense, the bar is right to question proposals that would increase their independence by giving them discretion to reveal client confidences. The question then becomes when an exception should be made. As discussed, an exception for disclosure necessary to prevent the client from committing a crime likely to result in death or serious bodily harm is traditional, and I believe it should be made mandatory. The requirement that a lawyer disclose client perjury to a court is also sound.

What is not sound is seriously damaging the independence of the bar in order to address even important social problems. Other jurisdictions have experimented with compromising the lawyer-client relationship in the pursuit of various policy objectives. In Europe, for example, the European Community has issued a Directive requiring lawyers to report their clients' suspicious activity related to money laundering. Such a measure would no doubt help the government's fight against drug trafficking and organized crime, but it comes at too high a price. There is, however, an exception to preserve legal confidentiality when legal professionals receive information from their clients in connection with legal proceedings. The SEC proposal is more modest since its goal is to require disclosure only of evidence of clear securities law violations, but it does not contain a similar exception. In any event, while different in degree, it is not different in kind. In this area, the independence of the bar should not be compromised even for such an important purpose as to help restore public confidence is corporate accounting and reporting.

Evan A. Davis, *The Meaning of Professional Independence,* 103 COLUM. L. REV.1281, 1291–92 (2003) (footnotes omitted) [hereinafter Davis].

[30] Davis, *supra* note 29, at 1291.

Student Marketing case,[31] the SEC's enforcement proceedings against Carter and Johnson,[32] and the most recent regulatory initiatives following the enactment of Sarbanes-Oxley.[33] In each of those matters, the SEC, as I understand her argument, was carrying the banner of state's law; it was the lawyers who were seeking in each instance to blunt that state's law.

Why is this version of state's law something particularly worthy of respect, veneration, and unquestioning acceptance? Why the SEC's law, and not others? Law in America is a lot more than simply what the legislature says it is or how the regulatory agencies interpret it. First, there are the overlays on this law from laws that conflict and laws that have superior force and effect. All law must be interpreted in context. So if the legislature passes amendments to the Securities Exchange Act of 1934, those amendments must be interpreted in light of related provisions enacted earlier, both in that act and in the other legislation governing the public company world. In addition, that law, as all law, must conform to constitutional principles and, therefore, it is subject to challenge and interpretation in light of those principles. Moreover, to the extent that the federal government has not occupied the field in this area of legislation, the federal enactments must be reconciled with regulation on the state level, where substantive law regarding the conduct of corporations has traditionally resided. When it comes to SEC interpretation of these statutes and its promulgation of regulations, the power of state's law, as that term is defined by Professor Koniak,[34] becomes even more problematic as one challenges whether regulations issued by the SEC are valid exercises of duly delegated authority to that agency and whether the agency interpretations are warranted by the language of the statute.

All of the foregoing does not even address questions relating to the interpretation of language. The meaning of a statute or a regulation is the kind of issue that lawyers, on behalf of clients, should be seeking to address every day. Professor Koniak defines two different ways in which laws might be difficult to interpret: "enforcement gaps"[35] and "example gaps."[36]

> In short, the less committed the state is to its law and the more committed
> a private group is to a competing legal vision, the more likely we are to see

---

[31] SEC v. Nat'l Student Mktg. Corp., 457 F. Supp. 682 (D.D.C. 1978); Koniak, *supra* note 3, at 1248.

[32] *In re* Carter & Johnson, [1981 Transfer Binder] Fed. Sec. L. Rep. (CCH) ¶ 82,847 (Mar. 25, 1981); Koniak, *supra* note 3, at 1256.

[33] 17 C.F.R. pt. 205 (2003); Koniak, *supra* note 3, at 1269.

[34] *See, e.g., Law Between, supra* note 26, at 1463–64.

[35] An "enforcement gap" occurs when "state law whose meaning is clouded by the fact that the state demonstrates continued uncertainty about whether to hold anyone to the meaning it has articulated as 'law.'" Koniak, *supra* note 3, at 1246.

[36] An "example gap" involves "the sparsity (or perceived sparsity) of examples (stamped official by the state, as in court opinions) of what a legal rule means in action." *Id.*

both example and enforcement gaps—in other words, the more likely we are to see unclear state law. In the battle between the bar and the state, the bar is very committed, but the state is weakly committed. Example and enforcement gaps abound, which means it is easy for lawyers to continue to understand their law as "the law," without having to imagine themselves as lawbreakers.

From the perspective of the state, the ethics rules acknowledge the centrality and superiority of state law by insisting that lawyers not aid clients in unlawful activity. But from the bar's perspective, ethical precepts that require lawyers to obey the law and to refrain from helping clients to break it are contingent obligations, not constitutional norms. Example and enforcement gaps are important here, too. What does it mean to obey the law when the meaning of law is never certain? The ethics rules prohibit "knowing" assistance of illegality. Can lawyers ever "know" that X behavior will violate the law?[37]

It is not clear to me, from reading her essay, whether she is blaming the legal profession for the existence of these gaps. It sounds like she is but, on the other hand, one would be hard-pressed to understand how the existence of those gaps was the responsibility of lawyers, rather than legislatures.

On the other hand, Professor Koniak clearly attacks lawyers for taking advantage of these gaps, for raising questions of interpretation, for claiming that—because no case has ever been brought that is quite like the case the lawyer is defending—somehow the complaint should be dismissed, or for capitalizing on the fact that, since no example of the particular conduct in question has been definitively interpreted as violating the law, the lawyer's client charged with this conduct should escape enforcement or criminal action.[38]

As I read Professor Koniak's essay, she has placed—via her "enforcement gap" and "example gap" terminology—a negative connotation upon what, up until now, we all thought were legitimate exercises of exemplary lawyer skills. Indeed, what she is talking about is the very heart of our legal system, both in its common law roots and in its mixed statutory/common law current embodiment. It is precisely these enforcement and example gaps that reflect the fact that our law must grapple with an extraordinary range of human conduct that, in all of its complexity and breadth, could not possibly be codified. Even civil-law nations understand that the entire range of human behavior can never be codified. It is this understanding of human complexity that provides the vitality and dynamic growth that makes our system of justice so healthy.

For sure, the SEC, the Department of Justice, or a private litigant can all announce that in this particular case, it is that party's view that the state's law means that the

---

[37] *Id.* at 1247.

[38] *See id.*

client should go to jail, be suspended from a public company, or pay huge sums in damages; but it is just as vital and just as critical that a champion of that client—even when that client is a lawyer—declare with equal fervor that the state's law goes too far, that it violates the Constitution, that its clear language does not apply, that the language is ambiguous and should be interpreted a particular way, that this case is far closer to the facts of the case in which the defendant was exonerated than it is to the facts of a case in which the defendant was convicted, found liable, or sanctioned.

Every law has enforcement gaps and example gaps, and every system of justice permits the Department of Justice or the SEC (or the Commonwealth of Pennsylvania Department of Environmental Resources, etc.) to announce that the law has been violated. Just as important, every system of justice provides an *equal* opportunity for a lawyer (an ethical lawyer, an effective lawyer), to be available to argue, on behalf of the client whose conduct is challenged, that this announcement of state's law is wrong: in Professor Koniak's words, "to push back the state's law." And then we let the real law (not the state's law and not the bar's law) be determined by our courts, which, in the process of hearing from the parties respectively why the state's law is correct and why the state's law is wrong, fills one more example gap on the road to doing justice.

I am familiar with the adversarial process that would have one side argue in favor of a particular interpretation of state's law and one side argue against it. What I fear that some academics are endorsing, though, is that there is a particular stripe of state law— in connection with the regulation of the governance and conduct of corporate America— that is worthy of special respect. But how would one decide which stripe of law deserves that respect? How do lawyers get up in the morning and decide, either with or on behalf of their clients, those aspects of state law that are particularly worthy? Is there some neutral principle here, or is it simply that the lawyer confronted with one of these matters should pick up the telephone or e-mail Professor Koniak to learn whether, in her view, in this particular matter the lawyer is free to "push back?"

Equally troubling, how should we conduct ourselves when confronted with state law to which this special obeisance is due? Do the lawyer and her client simply throw in the towel and accept whatever result the SEC dictates? Or may the lawyer advocate, just a little bit? You see, the real problem for these unfortunate clients and lawyers who confront this respect-worthy state law is to titrate exactly the quantum of lawyering that is permissible under the "Ivory Tower Justice System": maybe tinkering around the edges while not challenging, heaven forefend, the fundamental principles of the state's law. It might be okay, for example, to argue over the meaning of words, but not to argue that a regulation is unconstitutional! Whatever that level of advocacy should be, our academic friends will make the profession wait until the standards are established, perhaps in some future law review articles.

LAW PROFESSORS, NOISY WITHDRAWAL, AND RULE 307

Lest you think that I am picking on a very few law professors whose views are extreme, or whose views are (forgive the pun) merely academic, consider this: Professor Koniak is one of a large group of law professors who (quite justifiably) claim responsibility for the passage of the now famous § 307 of the notorious Sarbanes-Oxley Act,[39] legislation that, upon careful study, demonstrates the truth of the adage that the American public better beware whenever the Senate passes any bill (other than a declaration of National Halitosis Prevention Month) unanimously.[40]

I am afraid that neither the leader of this group of professors, Professor Richard Painter of the University of Illinois, nor Professor Koniak should get all the credit here. Part of the blame rests with the Ethics 2000 Commission of the American Bar Association: the Commission established by the ABA in 1997 to evaluate and recommend changes to the Model Rules, of which I was a member. That Commission reviewed the Model Rules from stem to stern and invited comments from all interested persons, holding numerous hearings across the country to elicit suggestions for change. Professor Painter was one of those who testified before the Commission. He made the argument—in his characteristically articulate manner—that Model Rule 1.13,[41] the rule governing the ethics of dealing with the organizational client, should be amended to require that the lawyer, when confronted with one of the situations that Rule 1.13 addresses,[42] should go up the corporate ladder, ultimately to the highest authority that can act for the organization (typically, its board of directors).

Ethics 2000 considered seriously the proposal to revise Rule 1.13. To the extent that any one person can speak on behalf of Ethics 2000, it is my recollection that the proposal was unanimously rejected because the present rule—which requires that lawyer "to pro-

---

[39] Pub. L. No. 107-204, 116 Stat. 745 (2002) (codified in scattered sections of 11, 15, 18, 28 and 29 U.S.C.).

[40] The Senate passed Sarbanes-Oxley 97-01 148 Cong. Rec. S6734, S6778–79 (daily ed. July 15, 2002).

[41] Rule 1.13(b) provides:

If a lawyer for an organization knows that an officer, employee or other person associated with the organization is engaged in action, intends to act or refuses to act in a matter related to the representation that is a violation of a legal obligation to the organization, or a violation of law which reasonably might be imputed to the organization, and is likely to result in substantial injury to the organization, the lawyer shall proceed as is reasonably necessary in the best interest of the organization. In determining how to proceed, the lawyer shall give due consideration to the seriousness of the violation and its consequences, the scope and nature of the lawyer's representation, the responsibility in the organization and the apparent motivation of the person involved, the policies of the organization concerning such matters and any other relevant considerations. Any measures taken shall be designed to minimize disruption of the organization and the risk of revealing information relating to the representation to persons outside the organization. . . .

MODEL RULES OF PROF'L CONDUCT R. 1.13(b) (2002).

[42] Rule 1.13 prescribes what the conscientious lawyer should do when a constituent of the organization is acting (or failing to act) in a manner that is either a violation of a legal obligation to the organization, or a violation of law that is likely to be imputed to the organization (and that is likely to result in substantial injury to the organization). *Id.*

ceed as reasonably necessary"—was a far better approach. Instead of mandating the course of action that the lawyer should follow, it was quite enough for the Rules simply to mandate action, with the proper course left to the good judgment of the lawyer.

So Ethics 2000 sent Richard Painter packing, rejecting his alternative formulation with no clue how disastrous would be the results of failing to adopt his change. For when the Congress of the United States decided it must do something about Enron and its progeny, and legislation was crafted allegedly addressing the problems raised by these great frauds, someone suddenly realized that no provision in the legislation addressed the legal profession. This is when Senator Edwards, himself a lawyer, a Presidential candidate, and a man who had never represented a corporation (having made his considerable fortune by suing corporations) latched upon a letter from Professor Painter and 40 of his colleagues, proposing that Congress enact as federal legislation the proposal that the Ethics 2000 Commission had rejected less than a year earlier, despite the fact that there was not a scintilla of evidence (then or now) that Rule 1.13 issues played any role in any of these corporate scandals. Grabbing the Painter proposal as if it were a passing lifeboat, Edwards inserted it into the Sarbanes-Oxley legislation, not as a substantive provision, but as a mandate to the Securities and Exchange Commission to promulgate minimum rules of conduct for those who practice before the SEC, rules that should include an "up the ladder requirement" and such other rules as the Commission might deem appropriate. The world needs no further evidence that Ethics 2000 made a monumental blunder when its members sent away a disappointed Richard Painter, his proposed change to Model Rule 1.13 rejected! Who would have thought a Painter scorned would become the author of such far-sweeping federal legislation?

Not only did the SEC propose and ultimately adopt a regulation that requires lawyers for public companies to go up the corporate ladder, as Professor Painter proposed, but also the SEC adopted a far broader change in its rules, pursuant to the authority granted to the SEC in § 307 of Sarbanes-Oxley. Most important, as I write this essay, the SEC has proposed new rules that would literally destroy the confidentiality between lawyer and corporate client, as well as pre-empt state substantive law addressing fundamental principles of corporate governance.

While I will undoubtedly be accused of being an underminer of state's law and an advocate for the bar's law in challenging the handiwork of the SEC, I firmly believe that, in fact, from the enactment of § 307 through whatever final regulations the SEC issues, we have been presented with one of the great failures of public policy, caused by the hysteria generated by the combination of the outsized losses that innocent investors in fact needlessly suffered, the antipathy of the academy (as reflected in the "findings" of Professors Koniak, Cramton, and Gordon), the self-protective instinct of so many pandering politicians who gleefully accepted Enron contributions and then found themselves embarrassed by that revelation, the need to "do something" (as former Senator John Danforth so eloquently observed),[43] and the failure of the legal profes-

---

[43] John C. Danforth, *When Enforcement Becomes Harassment*, N.Y. TIMES, May 6, 2003, at A31.

sion to rise with one voice to protect our core values, succumbing to public pressure to demonstrate that the lawyers were miscreants, too.

THE PUBLIC POLICY DISASTER

First, no one has sat down, figured out what went wrong, determined that lawyers were involved, and established that existing law did not and does not provide more than adequate remedies for the wrongs, if any, that lawyers perpetrated here. One searches in vain for any connection between the Enron events and the need to amend Rule 1.13. Did one of the lawyers for Enron (or Tyco, or WorldCom, or HealthSouth, or any of the other corporate scandals gracing the papers in 2001, 2002, and 2003) possess the knowledge that would have triggered Rule 1.13? If so, did that lawyer fail to act? If so, then was there a Rule 1.13 violation that the present rule clearly addresses? If not, did the lawyer take any action other than going up the corporate ladder? If so, was that lawyer misled by the present rule's grant of discretion? Finally, if that lawyer had gone up the corporate ladder, would that action have been able to prevent the harm that arose from the debacle that we call Enron (or any of the other current corporate scandals)? It's hard to answer these questions without access to the actual advice that the lawyers gave their clients, and without knowing on what information the lawyers were relying when they gave their advice.[44]

While these might not be precisely the right questions, and professors far more brilliant than I might be able to construct a legal analytical decision tree that is more disciplined and rigorous than mine, the point is that when one reviews the torrent of words that has followed upon the collapse of the "crooked E," there is no one who is approaching the question of whether to change lawyer regulation in this way. The best that we get is the wholesale adoption of mere self-serving allegations in complaints filed against lawyers. Or the wholesale generalization that behind every great fraudster is a lawyer whispering in a client's ear. Or the observations that most of the pieces of paper that documented these transactions were drafted by lawyers. But none of that is helpful to deciding whether the regulation of lawyers should be changed, let alone changed in the fundamental ways that the delegation of authority by the Congress to the SEC has already prompted (and may further prompt) as the SEC goes to the next round of § 307-driven rule-making.

SARBANES-OXLEY § 307

Second, § 307 of the Sarbanes-Oxley legislation itself is deeply flawed. Under a heading eerily captioned "Rules of Professional Responsibility for Lawyers," § 307 mandated that the SEC issue rules "setting forth minimum standards of professional conduct for attorneys appearing and practicing before the Commission in any way in

---

[44] *Cf. supra* note 10 (Enron and banks conspired to keep necessary information from Andersen).

the representation of issuers," including a rule that would require those lawyers to report "evidence of a material violation of the securities laws or breach of fiduciary duty or similar violation by a company or agent thereof" to the chief legal officer or chief executive officer of the company and—if those individuals do not "appropriately respond"—report the evidence to the audit committee of the board of directors.

The very idea of the Senate of the United States enacting or directing others to enact rules of professional responsibility for lawyers should be enough to cause collective professional indigestion and indignation. A foundation of our independent profession is that our rules of professional conduct are promulgated by the states. Time and again, we have quite correctly resisted efforts to have the federal government usurp—even for lawyers employed by the federal government—the traditional role of regulating lawyers through the respective state Supreme Courts. Just a little while ago, the Conference of Chief Justices, as *amicus curiae,* successfully defended this precept yet again when the Eighth Circuit struck down attempts by Janet Reno's Justice Department seeking to apply federal ethical standards to lawyers employed by the federal government.[45] And this was followed by Congress's swift passage of the so-called McDade Amendment, 28 U.S.C. § 530 B, making it clear that federally employed lawyers were required to conform to state rules of professional conduct.

The pre-eminence of state regulation of lawyers is enlightened public policy for a number of reasons. First, lawyers are admitted to practice by the states; states administer bar examinations, and they establish and are the final arbiters of our disciplinary systems. Responsibility for the standards for admission and continuing practice, therefore, should reside within those jurisdictions.

Second, there is no greater threat to lawyer independence than having anyone other than courts establish the lawyer rules for practice. As the so-called "Reno regulations" demonstrated so eloquently,[46] it is impossible for an agency that participates in adversary proceedings to fairly develop the rules that govern that agency's lawyer-adversaries. While some might think of the SEC as an adjucative body, the truth is today that the SEC's law enforcement function makes it just another interested zealous litigant that could not possibly bring the requisite objectivity to promulgating rules for lawyers who practice before (and against) it, particularly when the agency has so much to gain in "efficiency" if these lawyers are rendered eunuchs, simply turning in their clients to the agency for appropriate punishment.

Third, is anything more fundamental to maintaining our professional core values than the content of our rules governing confidentiality, loyalty, and independence? Courts recognize that the lawyer rules fulfill this critical role, but neither the executive nor legislative branches of government are nearly as respectful of the rules, particularly when such core values enhance the effectiveness of our representation of our clients.

---

[45] United States *ex rel.* O'Keefe v. McDonnell Douglas Corp., 132 F.3d 1252 (8th Cir. 1998).

[46] For an interesting discussion of the "Reno rules," see Nancy B. Rapoport, *Our House, Our Rules: The Need for a Uniform Code of Bankruptcy Ethics,* 6 AM. BANKR. INST. L. REV. 45, 57–60 (1998).

In addition, as already noted, there had been no demonstration that any provision like this was even needed. From the highly publicized financial debacles that were the catalyst for this legislative response, there has not been a single suggestion in all the words that have been written that any lawyer *who knew something* failed to report it within the enterprise and, therefore, that disaster inexorably followed. Even now—in late 2003—it appears that our present rules of professional conduct, in all respects, were quite adequate to the task of providing lawyers with the framework for dealing with the multiple issues generated by Enron, WorldCom, and the others. The fact that there have been allegations that lawyers violated our rules—even if those allegations turn out to be true—is no reason to change them right now, before any adjudication.

Finally, § 307, masquerading as a regulation of professional responsibility, in fact had nothing to do with ethics. Rather, it was designed to change those corporate lawyers who appear before the SEC into surveillance operatives and junior regulators. If we had "truth in naming" legislation, § 307 would be captioned "The Lawyer Unlimited Liability Act of 2002."

While § 307 purports only to require reporting within the client organization, its effect is quite different. When, with the benefit of hindsight, it turns out that there were securities law violations or breaches of fiduciary duties by the client, the SEC lawyers for the company will be held responsible for failing to report to the individuals or board committees to whom the legislation requires the lawyer to report. Then creditors, shareholders, and regulators will come along to extract damages or disciplinary relief for the breach by the lawyers of this new obligation.

Given this potential exposure, those retained to represent the company before the SEC will not only undertake the tasks for which they were retained but, as a matter of self-preservation, assume a new regulatory role, erring on the side of reporting far too much and otherwise disrupting the client-organization as a matter of liability avoidance and lawyer protection, rather than as sound practice.

As so many others have done in the context of Enron, the drafters and supporters of § 307 completely confused the responsibilities of lawyers with the responsibilities of their clients. Moreover, § 307 changes the role of the lawyers into one that far more resembles the roles that the accountants and the government regulators should play.

THE SEC REGULATIONS

Third, the regulations issued by the SEC, acting on the authority of § 307, make § 307 look like benign legislation. While the thrust of this essay is to document the public policy failure triggered by Enron, and thus this is no place to catalogue all the horrors generated by the SEC's delight in being invited by Congress to rewrite many of its losses in the courts over the years, these highlights should be more than enough to show that the absence of a demonstrable need for § 307 did not stop the SEC from engaging in not only the worst kind of officious intermeddling into the lawyer-client relationship, but also in exalting the role of the lawyer in the governance of America's public companies into a super-director, with all the authority and incentive to substitute the lawyer's judgment for that of the duly-elected executive officers and directors of these companies.

The breadth of the SEC's regulations is truly stunning. The obligations that the SEC has mandated do not just apply to the lawyers for a public company who provide what we have traditionally considered SEC advice. Rather, they apply to any lawyer who provides advice, the use of which may be incorporated into a filing with the SEC. Thus, even those lawyers who are handling litigation for a public company and are required to respond substantively to an auditor's letter, i.e., by opining other than with the phrase "the probability of success is neither likely nor remote," may find themselves deemed to be practicing before the SEC and, therefore, doomed to be subject to reporting up (and even "reporting out") requirements, if the SEC comes through with its threatened new whistleblower regulations. The latter is a particularly frightening thought in the context of providing a public company with an effective and confidential defense to whatever claims are brought against the company.

The regulations also raise micro-management of the lawyer-client relationship to an art form. The lawyer is required to report evidence of a "material violation of law, breach of fiduciary duty, or similar violation by the issuer or its agent" to the Chief Legal Officer ("CLO") or to the CLO and the CEO. The obligation is not limited to the scope of the lawyer's representation: the lawyer is required to act, in the absence of actual knowledge, if a reasonable lawyer would have acted. And both the concepts of "violation of fiduciary duty" and "other similar violations" literally capture the broadest expanse of misconduct. The failure to reasonably cabin the term "evidence," moreover, means it will be too easy to argue that the reasonable lawyer "should have known" of "evidence" of any of these violations, particularly with the benefit of 20-20 hindsight, something with which the benevolent SEC will always be armed.

Moreover, the SEC's regulations raise serious questions about imputation within a law firm. Is each lawyer in a law firm working on behalf of a public company deemed to know what every other lawyer knows and, therefore, are law firm lawyers subject to "up the ladder" reporting requirements based on this imputed knowledge?

But drafting evils aside—drafting evils that could well become a trap for even the most conscientious lawyer—the real failure of these regulations is formed in what the lawyer who does report to the CLO or CEO must do after these individuals respond. If, in the judgment of the lawyer reporting the alleged misconduct, the lawyer does not receive an "appropriate response," the lawyer is required to go up the corporate ladder to the board or to an appropriate committee thereof. Why should lawyers be making these judgments for the company? Do lawyers even have the expertise to determine what an appropriate response might be? Should the outside lawyer have the authority to trump the risk judgment of in-house counsel? Of the duly elected CEO? On what basis? Did not the board elect the CEO to make judgments like this?

It would be one thing if the lawyer were required to take further action if the trigger were the standard found in Rule 1.13, i.e., that the lawyer "knew" that a constituent of the organization was taking action that is likely to result in substantial injury to the client. But here: (a) the lawyer merely has evidence—and lawyers know how ambiguous "evidence" is; (b) the evidence is merely of a violation, not reasonably limited by the violation's likely effect on the corporation; and (c) there is no opportunity under this rule for the corporation or the decision-trumping lawyer to balance the supposed harm the violations might cause versus any benefit to the corporation of pursuing the chosen course of conduct. It also is sobering to consider the kinds of "judgments" that might be delegated to lawyers under this regime. One entrepreneurial CEO's totally legitimate decision to embark on a new venture, engage in off-balance-sheet financing, or market a new product can, several years later, turn into a claim for breach of fiduciary duty, yet one would think the last person who was qualified to make the risk analysis of pursuing any given course of action would be a lawyer.

Lawyers under this new regime are no longer trusted advisors, acting when violation and damage are certain; they are swashbuckling usurpers, determining the appropriateness of the CEO's response in light of their own fears that—if the lawyers themselves do not make the right decisions about the appropriateness of the CEO's response—the lawyer and the lawyer's law firm colleagues might lose their right to practice before the Commission. Such a cause of action against the lawyers and the lawyers' law firm would allege, in a proceeding brought by this powerful regulatory agency, that the lawyer had evidence and failed to act or acted but then permitted the CEO to make the final decision after the lawyer (wrongly) concluded that the CEO's response was appropriate.

WHISTLEBLOWING, TOO

It would be bad enough if the SEC, under Sarbanes-Oxley, had stopped with regulations governing when the lawyer was required to go to the board. While a rule requiring too many up-the-ladder reports to the board certainly is ill-advised and totally unnecessary, at least when the lawyer (acting out of self-protection) reports too much to the audit committee or the entire board, the only real downside is inefficiency, with reports to the board of directors simply placing decision-making perhaps in the wrong place, but with no compromise of client confidentiality. But the SEC went much further than that (and may go further still). While the Sarbanes-Oxley legislation is totally silent on the question of breaking client confidentiality, the SEC seized this opportunity to provide permission to those lawyers who do not believe that they have received an appropriate response from the board to "report out," presumably to the Commission itself, to the extent that the lawyer reasonably believes necessary to prevent a material violation of law likely to cause substantial injury to the issuer or investors or to prevent the issuer from committing an illegal act—a totally undefined term, with no requirement that the illegal act must cause substantial injury, or to rectify any material violation or illegal act in which the lawyer's services were used.

The effect of this opportunity for permissive disclosure of confidential information is profound. While there is a great debate in the profession whether lawyers ever should be free to disclose confidential client information relating to a fraud—with most jurisdictions permitting some disclosure under certain circumstances, particularly when the lawyer's services have been employed—this provision, which is explicitly designed to supersede state rules of professional conduct for lawyers practicing before the SEC, goes way beyond the disclosure of client confidential information permitted by any jurisdiction's Supreme Court.

While this provision, as the reader will observe, is not yet mandatory (though the Commission is threatening to make it mandatory), it takes no imagination to see how this permission to disclose, which supposedly only governs practice before the Commission and is not supposed to provide a civil remedy against the lawyer, may quickly evolve (with the addition of some easily accessible expert testimony) into a new standard of care for lawyers. The rule in effect provides the lawyers not only with the power to trump the Board's final decision about what is in the best interests of the shareholders (even though it is the directors who should have the responsibility for answering to the shareholders, if the directors are wrong), but also requires the lawyers to do so because failing to act in light of Board action on a close question could easily result in the lawyer being named an additional defendant. Again, the lawyer is forced to change her role from trusted advisor and persuasive remonstrator to a decision-maker whose counsel corporate officers and directors will be reluctant to seek if that advice comes with all of this excess baggage.

The most important concern, however, is the injection into the lawyer-client relationship of this "opportunity" for whistleblowing, an opportunity that may be exercised too often because of the concerns counsel may have if counsel guesses wrong. The lawyer-client relationship is fragile enough; this additional impediment to trust should never have been added to the mix. Its effect on full disclosure by client to lawyer—the essential purpose of having a rule governing confidentiality in the first place—is incalculable. For certain, under the SEC whistleblowing provision, lawyers will have far fewer opportunities to remonstrate with their clients to do the right thing than they enjoy today.

Some academics may rail against the lawyers "pushing back" against the SEC regulations adopted pursuant to the Sarbanes-Oxley legislation. They may believe that the state's law—as reflected in these SEC regulations—is entitled to some special respect, if not observance, and that it is unpatriotic for the lawyers to respond to these proposals with outrage and dismay. But if my essay does not demonstrate the flawed substance of these proposals, it does demonstrate that there are good faith objections to these regulations, regulations that clearly change the lawyer-client relationship as well as our traditional notions of corporate governance, and that, therefore, these objections deserve to be raised in every available forum, if only on behalf of our clients.

CONCLUSION

Enron was a fundamental disaster for creditors, shareholders, employees, officers, and directors. It may turn out to have been a massive fraud. It may turn out that officers, directors, auditors and, yes, even lawyers are liable. It may turn out that some of the lawyers involved violated our rules of professional conduct. It even might turn out that, as a result of Enron, new laws should be enacted and the rules of professional conduct amended. But we will not know of any of those things by jumping to conclusions, convicting without trials, or casting aspersions on participants, let alone all lawyers.

Professor Koniak observes that, unlike chemistry, it is very hard to define law.[47] Professor Koniak then suggests that this definitional problem is similar to that presented by defining what we mean by science. But the difference between science and law could not be more striking, at least as reflected in the way that the two disciplines approach crises.

When the Space Shuttle Columbia tragically broke up on re-entry, dramatically extinguishing the lives of seven talented astronauts, science professors did not hurl epithets at those who designed and maintained the shuttle program. They did not accuse everyone involved of being criminals. They did not trash the scientific method. Rather, they set up a disciplined board of inquiry staffed with talented engineers and scientists. They embarked on an elaborate, painstaking investigation. They developed a list of every possible cause of this great tragedy. They launched hypothesis after hypothesis and then applied the scientific method to determine, through calculations and laboratory experiments, whether those hypotheses held up. They published their tentative results so that others could either replicate or challenge their initial results.

They looked for causes and then searched for solutions. They did not jump to conclusions, and they did not systematically humiliate and defame everyone who had anything to do with the shuttle program. And when they are done—a process not complete as of this writing and which they will undoubtedly permit to take as long as is necessary—I am sure that they will come up with a final report that will identify what went wrong, why it went wrong, and the changes that should be made to avoid these wrongs in the future.

Compare that with what has happened at Enron. Congress holds "show hearings" designed to earn absolution for the acceptance of Enron campaign contributions and to feign sympathy for the shattered shareholders and employees. Legislation is cobbled together overnight. Regulations are promulgated in a matter of months. And scathing broad-brush accusations are flung around. We are presented with overreaction and faux remediation with no clue about what really went wrong and nothing but a hope and a prayer that the knee-jerk solutions will solve the problem.

Isn't that sad? Isn't that a complete failure of public policy? Isn't that the shame of our profession and our professors? Don't the scientists have so much to teach us about civility and, of all things, due process? All of which leads to the biggest question of all: Do we have the will and talent to learn that lesson?

---

[47] Koniak, *supra* note 3, at 1245.

NOTES AND QUESTIONS

1. Go back through the essays in this chapter. You've had an opportunity to read a variety of different views on what happened from the professionals' side. Who do you think has made the best arguments? Why?

2. At what point should the legislature (or other policy-makers) make policy after a crisis? (Should policy-makers try to make policy in the absence of a crisis?) How much evidence should a policy-maker hear before voting on proposed legislation or regulations? What types of evidence should "count"? Would you weigh the testimony of a professor as more important than that of, say, a CEO? A lobbyist? A consumer? How would you decide if the person testifying had ulterior motives? Does it matter if there are ulterior motives?

3. In Enron Bankruptcy Examiner Neal Batson's Final Report,[48] Batson sets out several conclusions, including these:

   • There is sufficient evidence from which a fact-finder could conclude that certain Enron in-house attorneys committed legal malpractice by: (i) failing to advise Enron adequately regarding its disclosure of the SPE transactions, including the related party transactions; (ii) failing to advise adequately Enron's [Board] and certain of its committees with respect to legal and corporate governance issues raised by certain related party transactions; (iii) failing to advise the Enron Board of material facts surrounding Enron's use of SPEs. . . . [The Examiner also suggested that some of Enron's in-house attorneys breached their fiduciary duties by assisting certain officers in *their* breaches of fiduciary duties.] Because Enron's officers participated in the wrongful conduct, however, these attorneys may assert that the actions by the Enron officers should be imputed to Enron and consequently, that claims by Enron should be barred or reduced under comparative fault rules.[49]

   . . . .

   • There is sufficient evidence from which a fact-finder could conclude that certain of Enron's outside attorneys: (i) committed legal malpractice in connection with their legal services provided to Enron with respect to the SPE transactions; or (ii) aided and abetted certain Enron officers in breaching their fiduciary duties. Because Enron's officers participated in the wrongful conduct, however, these attorneys may assert that the actions by the Enron officers should be imputed to Enron and consequently, that claims by Enron should be barred or reduced under comparative fault rules.[50]

---

[48] Neal Batson, Final Report of Neal Batson, Court-Appointed Examiner, *In re* Enron Corp., No. 01-16034 (Bankr. S.D.N.Y. November 4, 2003) [hereinafter Final Report].

[49] *Id.* at 7–8 (footnote omitted).

[50] *Id.* at 8 (footnote omitted).

In Appendix C to the Final Report, the Examiner points out that the final resolution of the culpability of the attorneys will "present issues of fact [to be determined by] the fact-finder."[51] The Final Report, of course, also discusses the culpability of Andersen, Ken Lay, Jeff Skilling, and Enron's directors.[52]

Does the Final Report add anything to any of the essays in this chapter? Are you more or less persuaded by any of the authors based on the Examiner's conclusions? Does it matter to you that the conclusions haven't been tested yet in front of any jury, or is it sufficient that the Examiner, after a thorough (and costly) review of documents and testimony (some, but not all, of which was done under oath), has reached these conclusions?

4. Have the essays in this chapter affected how you might practice law or run your business?

---

[51] *See, e.g.,* Final Report, *supra* note 1, Appendix C at 180.

[52] *See* Final Report, *supra* note 1, and its various appendices.

Chapter 5

Lessons for Society

The premise of our book is that, by using Enron and other recent corporate scandals as case studies (not in the law school sense of studying judicial opinions, but in the business school sense of studying particular organizations), we can draw more universal lessons, thereby preventing the repetition of scandals of these types. This chapter presents some musings on what, exactly, those lessons should be.

There will be more lessons than the essays in this book will describe. (And we'd be interested in hearing some of your ideas about lessons that people should learn from these scandals.)[1] Some of the essays will trigger experiences that you've had in other contexts. That's good: we want these lessons to be transferable to other parts of your life.

For us, Enron represents both a specific fact situation and an opportunity to ask the larger questions that, in our hectic daily lives, we often don't have the leisure to consider. One of the most important questions concerns the dividing line between a rule and the rationale for the rule. Some have argued that the accountants should have paid more attention to the reasons underlying the various accounting rules, rather than merely trying to comply with the technical requirements of the rule. Others have argued that the lawyers' involvement in structuring deals kept them from asking themselves if the structures had gone too far astray. These are important questions, but they are rather abstract. Let's put them in a more concrete context.

The final essay in this book compares Enron to two other historic disasters: the sinking of the *Titanic* in 1912, and three storm systems that collided in October 1991 (which created what Sebastian Junger later called the "Perfect Storm").[2] As you reflect upon all of the essays in our book, you'll notice a theme. Enron sometimes took actions that were outright illegal, but often it simply took advantage of loopholes in

---

1 You can e-mail us at <nrapoport@uh.edu> and <bala@rice.edu>. Please bear with us if it takes us a while to get back to you. Our inboxes are perennially full to overflowing.

[2] SEBASTIAN JUNGER, THE PERFECT STORM: A TRUE STORY OF MEN AGAINST THE SEA (1997).

rules. When the *Titanic* set sail on its maiden (and only) voyage, it had sixteen lifeboats on board, enough to satisfy the legal requirements for safety at the time, but clearly not enough to save all of the souls on that doomed voyage.

Sooner than you might like to think, you will also be making rules and setting policies. Will you be the person who lets an insistence on strict compliance with technicalities doom the lives of others? Will you be strong enough—and knowledgeable enough—to consider the reasons behind the rules?

Everything I Needed to Know About Enron I Learned in Kindergarten (and Graduate School)

George W. Kuney*

INTRODUCTION

Something went wrong at Enron. Whether phrased in terms of a failure of gatekeepers[1] or an aggressive culture of greed based upon bending the rules,[2] the root causes of the problems at Enron were social in nature. And, if the restatement of financial statements at a variety of other companies[3] and other similar business col-

---

* George W. Kuney is an Associate Professor of Law and the Director of the Clayton Center for Entrepreneurial Law at the University of Tennessee College of Law. He holds a J.D. from the University of California's Hastings College of the Law and an M.B.A. from The University of San Diego. Prior to joining the faculty of the University of Tennessee, he was a partner in a large West Coast law firm where his practice focused on business, restructuring, and insolvency. He thanks Matthew Stearns for his factual research regarding Enron, Gena Lewis for her legal research and development of the notes and problems that conclude this piece, and German translation, and Donna C. Looper for insightful analysis and editorial assistance in the preparation of this article. All statements in this article are statements of opinion based upon the facts and opinions as reported or stated in the works of others, as cited.

[1] *See, e.g.,* John C. Coffee, Jr., *Understanding Enron: "It's About the Gatekeepers, Stupid,"* 57 BUS. LAW. 1405, 1405 (2002) ("Properly understood, Enron is a demonstration of gatekeeper failure, and the question it most sharply poses is how this failure should be rectified."); *reprinted in this book at* 125–143.

[2] *See, e.g.,* Anita Raghavan, Kathryn Kranhold & Alexei Barrionuevo, *Full Speed Ahead: How Enron Bosses Created a Culture of Pushing Limits,* WALL ST. J., Aug. 26, 2002, at A1 ("When Enron Corp. was riding high, Chief Financial Officer Andrew Fastow had a Lucite cube on his desk supposedly laying out the company's values. One of these was communication, and the cube's inscription explained what that meant: When Enron says it's going to 'rip your face off,' it said, it will 'rip your face off.' It was a characteristic gesture inside Enron, where the prevailing corporate culture was to push everything to the limits: business practices, laws and personal behavior.").

[3] *See* Huron Consulting Group, *An Analysis of Restatement Matters: Rules, Errors, Ethics, For the Five Years Ended December 31, 2002* (2002), *available at* http://www.huronconsultinggroup.com/uploadedFiles/Huron_RestatementStudy2002.pdf (last visited June 2, 2003).

lapses and restructurings that followed[4] are indicators, these problems probably were not and are not isolated in the remains of the fallen energy-trading giant.

In response to Enron's collapse, there has been an outpouring of sentiment—from the press, the public, and Congress—in support of change. The passage and implementation of the Sarbanes-Oxley Act[5] and other developments will continue to provide an opportunity for a major cultural change in corporate governance.

This essay briefly reviews the facts underlying the Enron debacle.[6] It then describes some of the lessons that can be learned from this chain of events. Reasonable minds can differ on these lessons, but all of the lessons should be borne in mind by the players in corporate America and those who advise them. Drastic revisions of accounting and legal rules and standards are probably not necessary in order to prevent "another Enron"—strictly hewing to existing standards is sufficient. The rules did not fail at Enron; those who were supposed to follow and enforce them failed.

A BRIEF REVIEW OF THE FACTS

Enron was a public company whose shares traded on the New York Stock Exchange ("NYSE"). At its peak stock price of just over $90 a share, Enron was the seventh largest United States corporation in terms of market capitalization.[7] Since Enron's stock was publicly traded, the company was regulated by the Securities and Exchange Commis-

---

[4] For example, *see* Neil H. Aronson, *Symposium: Enron: Lessons and Implications: Preventing Future Enrons: Implementing the Sarbanes-Oxley Act of 2002,* 8 STAN. J. L. BUS. & FIN. 127 (2002).

[5] *See* Sarbanes-Oxley Act of 2002, PL 107-204, 116 Stat. 745 (HR 3763, July 30, 2002) [hereinafter Sarbanes-Oxley].

[6] All factual statements in this article are based upon reports of others and allegations contained in government indictments. *See, e.g.,* PERMANENT SUBCOMMITTEE ON INVESTIGATIONS, COMMITTEE ON GOVERNMENTAL AFFAIRS, THE ROLE OF THE BOARD OF DIRECTORS IN ENRON'S COLLAPSE, S. REP. NO. 107-70 (2002) [hereinafter Report on Board of Directors], *available at* http://news.findlaw.com/hdocs/docs/enron/senpsi70802rpt.pdf (last visited June 2, 2003); NEAL BATSON, THE SECOND INTERIM REPORT OF NEAL BATSON (2003) [hereinafter Batson Report], *available at* 2003 extra lexis 4; WILLIAM C. POWERS, RAYMOND S. TROUBH, HERBERT S. WINOKUR, REPORT OF INVESTIGATION BY THE SPECIAL INVESTIGATIVE COMMITTEE OF THE BOARD OF DIRECTORS OF ENRON CORP. (2002) [hereinafter Powers Report], *available at* http://www.chron.com/content/news/photos/02/02/03/enron-powers report.pdf (last visited June 2, 2003). To the extent that these facts are proven or construed to be otherwise, the author does not dispute those conclusions or contentions. The lessons and opinions stated in this essay are based upon the alleged facts as stated, and if those alleged facts are incorrect, the lessons and conclusions drawn from those alleged facts may need to be adjusted accordingly.

[7] *See* Report on Board of Directors, *supra* note 6 ("At the time of Enron's collapse in December 2001, Enron Corporation was listed as the seventh largest company in the United States, with over 100 billion in gross revenues and more than 20,000 employees worldwide."); *see also* Batson Report, *supra* note 6 ("Until the fall of 2001, Enron was one of the largest companies in the world.").

sion ("SEC").[8] Enron's officers and directors had a fiduciary duty to the company's investors and potential investors to, among other things, record and disclose accurate financial numbers to the investing public in accordance with SEC regulations.[9]

A host of parties in interest, from government prosecutors[10] to Enron's Bankruptcy Examiner, Neal Batson,[11] have alleged that Andrew Fastow, other officers, Arthur Andersen ("Andersen") accountants, and various lawyers devised schemes to defraud the investing public with the ultimate goals of: (1) making Enron appear more financially successful than it actually was, (2) artificially inflating Enron's stock price, (3) avoiding government regulations both to gain undeserved benefits and to avoid legally proper costs, and (4) obtaining personal enrichment. Further, the government claims that Enron's officers attempted to achieve these goals by: (1) engaging in fraudulent transactions involving special purpose entities ("SPEs"), (2) filing false and misleading financial statements with the SEC, (3) making false statements concerning the health of Enron's underlying business model, and (4) exercising control over both the main company and the "independent" SPEs for personal benefit.[12]

---

[8] *See* Batson Report, *supra* note 6, at 54 ("A public company like Enron, in addition to complying with the literal GAAP rules and publishing financial statements that fairly present its financial position, results of operations and cash flows in accordance with GAAP, must also comply with the federal securities laws mandating disclosure."); *see also* Report on Board of Directors, *supra* note 6, at 11 ("Steady revelations since October 2001 have raised questions about numerous aspects of the company's operations from its extensive undisclosed off-the-books dealings . . . to an April 2002 SEC filing announcing that the company's financial statements were unreliable and the book value of its assets would have to be written down as much as 24 billion . . . .").

[9] *See* Report on Board of Directors, *supra* note 6, at 5 ("Among the most important of Board duties is the responsibility the Board shares with the company's management and auditors to ensure that the financial statements provided by the company to its shareholders and the investing public fairly present the financial condition of the company. This responsibility requires more than ensuring the company's technical compliance with generally accepted accounting principles.").

[10] Government prosecutors most recently have handed down indictments against eight former Enron executives, including Andrew Fastow's wife. These indictments also include new charges against Fastow himself. *See* Mary Flood et al., *The Fall of Enron: Fastow's Wife, 6 Others Surrender to Federal Authorities: Charges grow for ex-Enron execs,* HOUS. CHRON., May 2, 2003, at A1 ("Enron prosecutors took a big step forward Thursday by winning indictments against eight more former executives on scores of criminal counts, adding more counts against former Chief Financial Officer Andrew Fastow. One of the eight charged was Fastow's wife, Lea.").

[11] For example, *see* Batson Report, *supra* note 6, at 56 ("The Examiner has found that Enron used SPEs to engineer its financial statements so that they diverged materially from Enron's actual economic condition and performance.")

[12] *See* Report on Board of Directors, *supra* note 6, at 3 (alleging the following failures on the part of Enron's Board of Directors: fiduciary failure, high-risk accounting, inappropriate conflicts of interest, extensive undisclosed off-the-books activity, excessive compensation, and lack of independence).

In essence, much of the alleged fraud revolves around the creation and management of "off balance sheet" partnerships (Chewco, LMJ1, LMJ2, et al.).[13] Enron allegedly used these SPE partnerships to (1) inflate revenues via sham "left-hand to right-hand" transactions and (2) conceal debt.[14] This combination allowed the firm to state fictitiously high earnings.[15] In theory, the liabilities of these SPEs can be left off of the company's consolidated balance sheet if outside investors own 3% or more of the SPE's equity and have the power to control the disposition of the asset in the SPE.[16] Enron allegedly achieved this necessary equity investment both by (1) creating sham entities to provide the capital, and (2) issuing "equity," to outside investors, that closely resembled the intrinsic characteristics of a debt instrument.[17] Additionally, the officers

---

[13] *See* Eric Berger, Mary Flood & Tom Fowler, *The Fall of Enron: Report Details Enron's Deception: Examiner Cites Auditors, Lawyers, and Banks as Part of Scheme,* HOUS. CHRON., March 6, 2003, at B1 ("It is against federal criminal law for executives to knowingly make false material representations about the company's financial condition to the public. The examiner [Neal Batson] several times specifically states Enron broke Securities and Exchange Commission rules, and in the case of special purpose vehicle and prepay transactions, materially misrepresented its financial condition. 'I think the fact he used the word 'materially' is important. It expresses his belief that there is a substantive violation of the criminal law,' said Jacob Frenkel, a former federal prosecutor and SEC lawyer in Washington D.C.").

[14] *See* Batson Report, *supra* note 6, at 15 ("Two factors drove Enron's management of its financial statements: (i) its need for cash and (ii) its need to maintain an investment grade credit rating. Enron was reluctant to issue equity to address these needs for fear of an adverse effect on its stock price and was reluctant to incur debt because of possible adverse effects on its credit ratings.").

[15] For example, Neal Batson, the examiner appointed by the Bankruptcy Court to investigate Enron's prepetition activities, describes how Enron, through the use of SPEs and aggressive accounting practices, so engineered its reported financial position and results of operations that its financial statements bore little resemblance to its actual financial condition or performance. *See* Batson Report, *supra* note 6, at 15.

[16] *See* William W. Bratton, *Enron and the Dark Side of Shareholder Value,* 76 TUL. L. REV. 1275, 1306-07 (2002) ("There is also a critical SEC rule—three percent of the SPE's total capital must come from an outside equity investor who must in addition have the power to control the disposition of the asset in the SPE. This means that the outside equity holder must hold at least a majority of the SPE's equity. In addition, the outside equity holder's capital must be *at risk*—the originator can't guarantee the investment's results. Finally, a legal determination as to the bankruptcy remote status of the SPE from the transferor also must be made."); *see also* Powers Report, *supra* note 6, at 39 ("The SEC staff has taken the position that 3% of total capital is the *minimum* acceptable investment for the substantive residual capital, but that the appropriate level for any particular SPE depends on various facts and circumstances.").

[17] *See* Bratton, *supra* note 16, at 1307 ("Enron used Fastow's limited partnerships as a means to stay in compliance with the SPE rules. Fastow's entities served as the outside equity investor—the source of the qualifying three percent—for SPEs, which served no economic purpose other than to pump up Enron's accounting earnings.").

are accused of making false and misleading statements concerning the SPEs and Andersen's accounting procedures to the board, the SEC, and securities analysts.[18]

For example, in 1993, Enron and the California Public Employee Retirements System ("CalPERS") formed a $500M joint venture, JEDI, to make energy investments. CalPERS owned 50% of the JEDI equity, thus allowing Enron to treat JEDI as a *bona fide* SPE.[19] However, in 1997, as part of its investment into JEDI II, CalPERS decided to liquidate its JEDI investment, and Fastow apparently proposed the creation of a new SPE, Chewco, to buy CalPERS's stake for $383M.[20] However, Chewco was basically an Enron-controlled entity, which would violate the "spirit" of the rule requiring a 3% *outside* equity investment and outside control over deposition of the assets involved.[21]

---

[18] *See* Batson Report, *supra* note 6, at 15 ("The Examiner has concluded that, through pervasive use of structured financing techniques involving SPEs and aggressive accounting practices, Enron so engineered its reported financial position and results of operations that its financial statements bore little resemblance to its actual financial condition or performance. This financial engineering in many cases violated GAAP and applicable disclosure laws, and resulted in financial statements that did not fairly present Enron's financial condition, results of operations or cash flows."); *see also* Report on Board of Directors, *supra* note 8, at 3 ("The Enron Board failed to safeguard Enron shareholders and contributed to the collapse of the seventh largest public company in the United States, by allowing Enron to engage in high-risk accounting, inappropriate conflict of interest transactions, excessive undisclosed off-the-books activities, and excessive executive compensation. The Board witnessed numerous indications of questionable practices by Enron management over several years, but chose to ignore them to the detriment of Enron shareholders, employees and business associates. . . . The Enron Board of Directors knowingly allowed Enron to conduct billions of dollars in off-the-books activity to make its financial condition appear better than it was and failed to ensure adequate public disclosure of material off-the-books liabilities that contributed to Enron's collapse."); *see also* Powers Report, *supra* note 17, at 41 ("The participation of an Enron employee as a principal of Chewco appears to have been accomplished without any presentation to, or approval by, Enron's Board of Directors").

[19] Batson Report, *supra* note 6, at 15.

[20] *See* Powers Report, *supra* note 6, at 43–44 ("In 1997 Enron considered forming a $1 billion dollar partnership with CalPERS called 'JEDI II'. Enron believed that CalPERS would not invest simultaneously in both JEDI and JEDI II, so Enron suggested it buy out CalPERS's interest in JEDI. Enron and CalPERS attempted to value CalPERS's interest (CalPERS retained an investment bank) and discussed an appropriate buy-out price. In order to maintain JEDI as an unconsolidated entity, Enron needed to identify a new limited partner. Fastow initially proposed that he act as the manager of, and an investor in, a new entity called 'Chewco Investments'—named after the Star Wars character 'Chewbacca.' . . . Enron ultimately reached an agreement with CalPERS to redeem its JEDI limited partnership interest for $383 million. In order to close that transaction promptly, Chewco was formed as a Delaware limited liability company on very short notice in early November 1997.").

[21] *See* Powers Report, *supra* note 6, at 41–42 ("Enron Management and Chewco's general partner could not locate third parties willing to invest in the entity. Instead, they created a financing structure for Chewco that—on its face—fell at least $6.6 million (or more than 50%) short of the required third party equity. Despite this shortfall, Enron accounted for Chewco as if it were an unconsolidated SPE from 1997 through March 2001.").

Enron's primary accounting and auditing firm, Andersen, aided in the creation and management of these SPEs.[22] Further, Andersen's Houston office was accused of shredding potentially damning documents relating to the developing Enron scandal in fall 2001.[23] Obstruction of justice charges followed, and Andersen weathered the trial in poor shape. After its conviction, Andersen notified the SEC that it would cease to audit public companies,[24] and consequently shut down its audit practice.[25] Now run by Brian Marsal of the Chicago-based financial restructuring firm Alvarez & Marsal, Andersen is a shell of its former self and exists primarily as a "bundle of accounts receivable, leases and hundreds of Enron-related and other lawsuits."[26] By October 2002, Andersen had "sold off most of its units and shuttered most of its offices."[27] Its principal remaining asset is a 105-acre training facility in St. Charles.[28]

Several of Andersen's accountants and consultants resigned from the firm to work directly for Enron.[29] This had the effect of "blurring the line" between where Enron stopped and its supposedly independent auditing firm started.[30]

---

[22] For example, *see* Batson Report, *supra* note 6, at 39 ("Enron carefully designed its FAS 140 technique with advice from Andersen and Enron's lawyers, with the goal that the asset transfer would qualify for sale treatment under GAAP despite the fact that sale treatment did not reflect the economic substance of the transaction. In fact, Andersen discussed the basic template for the FAS 140 technique with SEC staff accountants in 1999, who indicated that non-consolidation of the SPE and sale treatment were consistent with existing GAAP. The Examiner concluded in the September Report, however, that Enron's failure to disclose the nature of its obligations to repay principal and interest under the debt associated with the transactions was not in compliance with GAAP.").

[23] *See* C. William Thomas, *The Rise and Fall of Enron*, 4/1/02 J. ACCT. 41 (2002), *available at* http://www.aicpa.org/pubs/jofa/apr2002/thomas.htm (last visited June 3, 2003) ("To make matters worse for it, and to the astonishment of many, Andersen admitted it destroyed perhaps thousands of documents and electronic files related to the engagement, in accordance with 'firm policy,' supposedly before the SEC issued a subpoena for them. . . . The firm fired David B. Duncan, partner in charge of the Enron engagement, placed four other partners on leave and replaced the entire management team of the Houston office.").

[24] *See Texas Board Revokes Andersen's License,* N.Y. TIMES, Aug. 17, 2002, at C14 ("Andersen told the Securities and Exchange Commission after the June verdict that it would stop auditing public companies by Aug. 31.").

[25] *See* Jonathan D. Glater, *Last Task at Andersen: Turning Out the Lights,* N.Y. TIMES, Aug. 30, 2002, at C3.

[26] Mike Comerford, *The Lone Gem in Andersen's Fading Empire St. Charles Campus Rethinks Mission,* CHI. DAILY HERALD, April 29, 2003, at B1 [hereinafter Comerford].

[27] *Andersen Holds Almost-Out-of-Business-Sale,* CHI. TRIB. 4 (Oct. 2, 2002).

[28] *See* Comerford ("Its main asset is the 150-acre training facility in St. Charles, a former women's college complete with dormitories, food service and recreational facilities.").

[29] *See* Flynn McRoberts, *Ties to Enron Blinded Andersen: Firm Couldn't Say "No" to Prized Client,* Chi. Trib., Sept. 3, 2002, *available at* 2002 WL 26770980 ("Inside the gleaming Houston headquarters of Enron Corp., it could be hard to distinguish between the energy traders and the Andersen people checking their books. . . . The potential conflicts were only worsened . . . by the close relationships Andersen employees had with the many alumni of the firm who had taken jobs at Enron.").

[30] Of course, the line between Enron and its accountants was not the only line that may have been blurred, *see* Batson Report, *supra* note 6, at 51 ("Enron and its accounting firm Andersen were also aggressive participants in the GAAP standard-setting process").

Enron's primary legal counsel, the independent law firm of Vinson & Elkins, has thus far escaped the wrath of the government prosecutors.[31] The firm's precise role in the Enron scandal is unclear, but it is logical to assume that (1) the firm knew of the existence of these SPEs, and (2) the firm advised Enron on the acceptability or unacceptability of these entities.[32] However, the nature and quality of that counsel is not entirely clear, so it is uncertain if the firm "checked off" or "rubber-stamped" decisions, reports, and opinions regarding the SPEs or if the Enron officers continued to use the entities in spite of warnings by the law firm counseling Enron against using those entities.[33] It appears, however, that the lawyers played a significant role in the creation and management of the SPEs.[34] It is unclear if and when the firm will be forced to produce its relevant documents and testimony. As a practical matter, it is unlikely that the firm or its partners will face legal liability before the completion of the legal actions against the former Enron officers.[35]

---

[31] Civil litigation may be another matter, however. Several class action lawsuits have been filed against Enron on behalf of shareholders and employees. On December 19, 2002, the judge hearing one of these suits denied Vinson and Elkins's motion to dismiss itself from the suit. See Batson Report, *supra* note 6, at 11–12 (fn. 36); *see also Federal Court Rules to Keep Most Defendants in Enron Shareholder's Lawsuit*, Yahoo! Finance (2002), *available at* http://216.239.37.100/search?q=cache:WqznSD1aAVYJ:biz.yahoo.com/prnews/021220/dcf050_1.html (last visited June 3, 2003) ("The federal judge handling the Enron Corp. securities lawsuit ruled today [Dec. 20, 2002] against several major financial institutions, law firms and the Arthur Andersen accounting firm, substantially denying most defendants' motions to be dismissed from the case. . . . Judge Harmon denied in their entirety the motions of . . . Enron's corporate legal counsel, Vincent [sic] and Elkins . . . 'This decision confirms the validity of our legal claims against the major defendants and leaves in the case defendants with resources to pay substantial compensation to the class,' said William Lerach, senior partner at Milberg, Weiss, Bershad, Hynes, & Lerach.").

[32] *See* Powers Report, *supra* note 6, at 173 ("Derrick says that he and Lay both recognized there was a downside to retaining V&E [Vinson & Elkins to investigate Sherron Watkins's letter] because it had been involved in the Raptor and other LJM transactions.").

[33] The Powers Report maintains that Vinson & Elkins shared responsibility for Enron's failure to adequately disclose related party transactions. *See* Powers Report, *supra* note 6, at 178 ("We found significant issues concerning Enron's public disclosures of related-party transactions. Overall, Enron failed to disclose facts that were important for an understanding of the substance of the transactions . . . . We believe that the responsibility for these inadequate disclosures is shared by Enron Management, the Audit and Compliance Committee of the Board, Enron's in-house counsel, Vinson & Elkins, and Andersen.").

[34] For instance, *see* Batson Report, *supra* note 6, at 39 ("Enron carefully designed its FAS 140 technique with advice from Andersen and Enron's lawyers, with the goal that the asset transfer would qualify for sale treatment under GAAP despite the fact that sale treatment did not reflect the economic substance of the transaction. . . . Enron frequently obtained the legal opinions Andersen required. These opinions, however, were limited in scope and analyzed only certain steps and specific entities, rather than the transaction in its entirety. In many of the FAS 140 Transactions, the Examiner believes that legal isolation was not achieved.").

[35] *But see* Batson Report, *supra* note 6, at 129, 131 ("The 'avoidance actions' that are covered by this report are potential claims of the Debtors to avoid, as constructively fraudulent transfers or preferential transfers, payments of money or transfers of property, and to recover the amount avoided. The transfers analyzed by the Examiner as potentially avoidable . . . or (iv) were paid to certain professionals providing legal services to the Debtors or to the Creditors' Committee. . . . [T]he Examiner is in the process of analyzing whether Enron's law firms, accounting firms, banks, investment advisors and others may be considered insiders for the purposes of the application of the avoidance provisions of the Bankruptcy Code.").

Enron conducted investment-banking transactions with many, if not most, of Wall Street's leading firms. The various firms helped create the SPEs, and some of the firms even invested their own capital in the entities.[36] These investments helped Enron meet the necessary level of outside equity investment levels necessary for these SPEs to pass initial legal muster.[37] The investment-banking firms' potential legal liability is largely related to the prolonged "buy" ratings that the firms issued for Enron stock while it was declining in price.[38] This exposure is related to a conflict of interest problem that was (and some would say is) apparently widespread throughout the industry. The same firms that were competing for Enron's lucrative investment-banking fees were also the firms that provided equity investment ratings for Enron's stock.[39] Theoretically, an ethical wall separated the investment-banking operations from the securities

[36] PERMANENT SUBCOMMITTEE ON INVESTIGATIONS, COMMITTEE ON GOVERNMENTAL AFFAIRS, REPORT ON FISHTAIL, BACCHUS, SUNDANCE, AND SLAPSHOP: FOUR ENRON TRANSACTIONS FUNDED AND FACILITATED BY U.S. FINANCIAL INSTITUTIONS, S. Prt. 107-82, at 2 (2003), *available at* http:// levin.senate.gov/enronreport0102.pdf (last visited June 3, 2003) ("The cumulative evidence from the three Subcommittee hearings demonstrates that some U.S. financial institutions have been designing, participating in, and profiting from complex financial transactions explicitly intended to help U.S. public companies engage in deceptive accounting or tax strategies. This evidence also shows that some U.S. financial institutions and public companies have been misusing structured finance vehicles, originally designed to lower financing costs and spread investment risk, to carry out sham transactions that have no legitimate business purpose and mislead investors, analysts, and regulators about the companies' activities, tax obligations, and true financial condition.").

[37] For an example of how banks helped structure transactions and the effect of these transactions on Enron's financial statements, debt ratio, and cash flow, *see* Batson Report, *supra* note 6, at 99 ("Citibank had formed Caymus Trust and funded it with $6 million of 'equity' and $194 million of debt. Enron guaranteed Caymus Trust's obligation to repay the debt to Citibank by entering into a Total Return Swap with Caymus Trust. Enron treated the transfer of the Fishtail Class C equity as a sale to Sonoma and recorded income equal to the $112 million of gain it believed existed in the trading business. The Examiner believes that this transaction did not constitute a 'true sale,' and therefore should have been recorded as a loan. Because of the consolidation of Fishtail and the failure of the transfer of its equity to Sonoma to qualify as a sale, Enron overstated its income in its financial statements by $112 million and understated its debt by $200 million. It also received $208 million of year-end cash flow, $200 million of which it recorded as cash flow from operating activities rather than financing activities.").

[38] *See* William S. Lerach, *Plundering America: How American Investors Got Taken for Trillions by Corporate Insiders, the Rise of the New Corporate Kleptocracy*, 8 STAN. J.L. BUS. & FIN. 69, 115 (2002) ("These banks were not just peddling Enron's worthless securities. Following repeal of Glass-Steagall, these banks were Enron's commercial lenders, its commercial joint venture partners, its investment bankers selling its securities to the public, and its derivative trading counter-parties—all the while, constantly issuing cheerleading analysts' reports about Enron, stressing the skill and integrity of its management, the quality of its balance sheet and reported earnings and its future prospects for strong profit growth.").

[39] *See* Lerach, *supra* note 38, at 115 ("Instead of playing their traditional role as underwriters—gatekeepers to protect the public—prestigious banking firms, including J.P. Morgan Chase, CitiGroup, CS First Boston, Merrill Lynch, CIBC, Deutsche Bank, and Barclays Bank became business partners with Enron, intertwining themselves in every aspect of Enron's business.").

analysis practice, but this separation appears not to have been strictly maintained.[40] Obviously, a firm has a large incentive to issue generous equities ratings, which generate demand for a stock, drive up its price, and please the company's officers, many of whom own the stock or stock options, and who in turn direct the flow of investment-banking business to the firms that issue the "buy" ratings in the first place.

LESSON ONE: THE FRAUD WAS NOT COMPLEX

Anyone who has investigated securities frauds upon the public will report that these frauds and attempts at fraud are, at root, not that complex. They play upon two fundamental tendencies that lie at the core of many people's behavior: greed and laziness.[41] Dangling the promise of vast returns on a passive investment, based upon a supposed new development[42] or inside information, appears to be a lure that vast numbers of otherwise intelligent people cannot resist.

Neither greed nor laziness is that dangerous in isolation. But together, when indulged in by large numbers of people, they lead to stock market, and other market, bubbles.[43] Enron is not the only example, of course. Consider the New Era bankruptcy in Philadelphia. There, the debtor had convinced over 180 charities and institutions of higher education and 150 individual donors that, if they deposited funds in the debtor's accounts, those funds would be matched—i.e. provided with a 100% return—by anonymous donors.[44] Eventually, as with all such things, the scheme collapsed.[45]

---

[40] For example, *see id.* ("Top officials of several Wall Street banks . . . secretly invested with Enron's corrupt (now indicted) CEO in the secret partnerships Fastow ran, which did billions of dollars of deals with Enron, enabling these partnerships to loot Enron. These bank executives secretly took equity positions in those partnerships which self-dealt in Enron's assets. These partnerships produced fantastic returns for these investors. . . .The lowest return on a deal was 150%. The highest was 2,500%.").

[41] Some label these traits "Temptation." Douglas G. Baird & Robert K. Rasmussen, *Four (or Five) Easy Lessons from Enron*, 55 VAND. L.REV. 1787 (2002) [hereinafter Easy Lessons]; *reprinted in this book at* 371–92. (In other contexts, I have also termed them laziness and self-interest, which could also be called utility maximization, the desire for as much good from as little effort as possible.).

[42] *See, e.g.*, ROBERT ZUCCARO, DOW 30,000 BY 2008: WHY IT'S DIFFERENT THIS TIME (Palisade Literary Press 2001) (This book's title is indicative of the "new development" scenario.).

[43] *See* Larry E. Ribstein, *Market vs. Regulatory Responses to Corporate Fraud: A Critique of the Sarbanes-Oxley Act of 2002*, 28. J. CORP. L. 1, 19 (2002) ("Indeed, almost 300 years ago the South Sea Bubble, the high tech of its day, lured investors with, among other things, the hope of riches from the new world, only to collapse amid recriminations against directors and 'stock-jobbers.'"); *see also* Frederick Lewis Allen, *Only Yesterday: an Informal History of the 1920s in America* (1931), *available at* http://xroads.virginia.edu/~Hyper/Allen/ch11.html (last visited June 3, 2003) (describing the Florida Real Estate Bubble of the 1920s).

[44] *See* Evelyn Brody, *The Limits of Charity Fiduciary Law*, 57 MD. L. REV. 1400, 1491 (1998) ("Created by John Bennett in 1989, the Foundation for New Era Philanthropy had been inviting selected charities to contribute funds—but only for a short period. At the end of six months, New Era would return the 'contributed' amount, plus a matching amount of money from anonymous donors.").

[45] *Id.* at 1492–94.

The old saying holds: If it sounds too good to be true, it probably is. So when it sounds too good, it is time for officers, directors, attorneys, accountants, analysts, and investors to start asking tough questions and start demanding answers that make sense.

As Douglas Baird has pointed out, "Enron was not a Ponzi scheme."[46] Like Charles Ponzi, however, Enron offered investors an irresistible combination: huge returns on investments, coupled with the allure of a seemingly heretofore undiscovered business opportunity.[47] Ponzi promised investors returns of more than 50% in 90 days, returns enabled by Ponzi's discovery of "a lucrative arbitrage opportunity in postal coupons."[48] Due to the fluctuating value of currencies after WWI, the value of postal coupons varied from country to country, because the exchange rates for such coupons had been set in 1906.[49] A coupon bought in a country with a depressed currency could be redeemed for greater value in a country whose currency was worth more.[50] In truth, Ponzi wasn't investing in postal coupons at all but was rather paying off earlier investors with subsequent investors' money.[51]

Although Enron did not literally use subsequent investors' money to pay off earlier investors, Enron and Charles Ponzi share some striking similarities, not the least of which is that Enron's business plan also presented a "lucrative arbitrage opportunity." Conservatives "point to insufficient market competition as the cause of the failure" of Enron,[52] but such a claim must bear a degree of irony, since Enron itself was a market, or at least a "market-maker."[53] Indeed, Enron claimed to be a firm that "excelled at creating new markets"[54] and sought to become "a pure financial intermediary"[55] consisting of a "proprietary market place in which Enron matched up energy producers, carriers, and users," and which "Enron was expanding . . . to cover anything which could be traded—pulp, paper, metals, even broadband services."[56]

---

[46] *See* Easy Lessons, *supra* note 41, at 1809.

[47] *Id.* at 1787–92.

[48] *Id.* at 1787.

[49] *Id.*

[50] *Id.*

[51] *Id.*

[52] Lawrence A. Cunnigham, *Sharing Accounting's Burden: Business Lawyers in Enron's Dark Shadows*, 57 BUS. LAW. 1421 (2003) [hereinafter Cunningham].

[53] *See* Easy Lessons, *supra* note 41, at 1790.

[54] *Id.* at 1789.

[55] Bratton, *supra* note 16, at 1287.

[56] *Id.*; *see* Report on Board of Directors, *supra* note 6, at 6 ("It [Enron] had received widespread recognition for its transition from an old-line energy company with pipelines and power plants to a high-tech global enterprise that traded energy contracts like commodities, launched into new industries like broadband communications, and oversaw a multibillion dollar international investment portfolio. One of Enron's key corporate achievements during the 1990s was creation of an online energy trading business that bought and sold contracts to deliver energy products like natural gas, oil or electricity. Enron treated

Market-makers like Enron enable "buyers and sellers to find each other at low cost, eliminating wasted resources through a reduction in transaction costs. The entrepreneur who creates such a market can capture as profit a fair portion of the benefit the initial buyers and sellers enjoy by finding each other."[57] Unlike Ponzi, who never invested in the postal coupons he was supposedly trading, Enron actually did make markets.[58] The problem with being in the business of making markets, however, is that such a business is adverse to competition. Markets cannot be kept secret and can be replicated by competitors at little cost.[59] Thus, "profits are [quickly] competed away."[60]

Making a small profit on each trade was fundamentally not in keeping with Enron's corporate culture, in which "the principals saw themselves in a tournament" where "their job was not just to make money, but to make the most money—to be the superstar firm."[61] Winning the tournament meant "destroying the next firm and much of industrial organization with it, and always delivering good numbers."[62] To deliver these good numbers, Enron embarked upon a course that would lead to its becoming best known "as a company that cooked its books."[63] As Lawrence A. Cunningham notes,

> At the core of the Enron debacle are accounting chicanery related to off-balance sheet financing and related party transactions plus colossal failures of board oversight. In its penumbra are auditing conflicts of interest that may be pervasive, incentivized board members posing as independent directors who could be more widespread than is known, law firms apparently

---

these contracts as marketable commodities comparable to securities or commodities futures, but was able to develop and run the business outside existing controls on investment companies and commodity brokers."); *see also* Batson Report, *supra* note 6, at 16 ("Starting out as a company that had a concentration in natural gas pipelines, it [Enron] became over time a company that depended less on pipelines and transportation and more on *energy trading and investing in new technologies and businesses.*") (emphasis added).

[57] *See* Easy Lessons, *supra* note 41, at 1790.

[58] *Id.*

[59] *Id.*

[60] *Id.*

[61] Bratton, *supra* note 16, at 1286.

[62] *Id.* at 1286–7.

[63] *See* Easy Lessons, *supra* note 41, at 1791; *see also* Powers Report, *supra* note 6, at 4 ("This personal enrichment of Enron employees, however, was merely one aspect of a deeper and more serious problem. . . . Many of the most significant transactions apparently were designed to accomplish favorable financial statement results, not to achieve *bona fide* economic objectives or to transfer risk. . . . Other transactions were implemented—improperly we are informed by our accounting advisors—to offset losses. They allowed Enron to conceal from the market very large losses resulting from Enron's merchant investments by creating an appearance that those investments were hedged—that is, that a third party was obligated to pay Enron the amount of those losses—when in fact that third party was simply an entity in which only Enron had a substantial financial stake.").

asleep at the deal, and political donations and influence peddling that is almost certainly more common than polite politicians prefer to pretend.[64]

Enron has provoked "controversial questions about the values and structures constituting and legitimating American corporate governance, market capitalism, and the globalization of markets and trade."[65] William Lerach, the high-profile plaintiffs' lawyer, observed that, a "few years ago, few could have foreseen the carnage that has recently roiled our securities markets."[66] However, it is not so much that few could have foreseen Enron's collapse and the burst of the stock market bubble, but rather that few wanted to foresee such problems. Like a stock market bubble or a Ponzi scheme, Enron offered investors the opportunity to get rich quick with little effort. Offer people an opportunity for easy money, and you offer them a powerful incentive to believe: Greed. Coupled with laziness (here, in the guise of a fundamental disinclination to raise questions), this combination led investors' belief in the implausible.[67] Fraud is easy when people want to believe. It is time to reaffirm the duty of skepticism of all the watchdogs and gatekeepers that failed to watch and bark,[68] including the investors themselves.

LESSON TWO: AVOID A CULT OF PERSONALITY

Leaders of legendary reputations who have actively participated in the creation of their image rarely produce long-term benefits to a company or other organization.[69]

---

[64] Cunnigham, *supra* note 52, at 1426; *see also* Batson Report, *supra* note 6, at 11 ("In the months immediately following Enron's disclosures, allegations surfaced of securities fraud, accounting irregularities, energy market price manipulation, money laundering, breach of fiduciary duties, misleading financial information, ERISA violations, insider trading, excessive compensation and wrong doing by certain of Enron's bankers.").

[65] Faith Stevelman Kahn, *Bombing Markets, Subverting the Rule of Law: Enron, Financial Fraud, and September 11, 2001*, 76 Tul. L. Rev. 1579, 1634 (2002). There are, perhaps, good reasons for these questions. *See* Report on Board of Directors, *supra* note 6, at 11 ("Steady revelations since October 2001 have raised questions about numerous aspects of the company's operations, from its extensive undisclosed off-the-books dealings, often with companies run by Enron personnel, to an April 2002 SEC filing announcing that the company's financial statements were unreliable and the book value of its assets would have to be written-down as much as $24 billion, to its apparent intention to manipulate the California energy market, to tax strategies which apparently included Enron's ordering its tax department to produce billions of dollars in company earnings through the use of complex tax shelters.").

[66] Lerach, *supra* note 38, at 70.

[67] *See* Report on Board of Directors, *supra* note 6, at 12 ("During their Subcommittee interviews, the Enron Directors seemed to indicate that they were as surprised as anyone by the company's collapse. But a chart produced at the Subcommittee hearing marks more than a dozen incidents over three years that should have raised Board concerns about the activities of the company.").

[68] Harold S. Peckron, *Watchdogs that Failed to Bark: Standards of Tax Review After Enron*, 5 Fla. Tax Rev. 853 (2002).

[69] For a post-modern view, see Jeanne L. Schroeder, *The Four Discourses of Law: A Lacanian Analysis of Legal Practice and Scholarship* 79 Tex. L. Rev. 15, 29 (2000) ("The master signifier is the one signifier that gives meaning to the shifting chain of signifiers. . . . In order to serve this function, the master

One is tempted to look at Mao, Stalin, Marcus Brutus, Kim Jong Il, and other governmental figures whose organizations became too wrapped up in the leader and his self-reflected glory to focus on long-term success and benefit to the stakeholder.[70] But one need not go beyond recent business headlines.[71] Think of Jack Welch, Bill Gates, Martha Stewart.

GE finally ousted Welch in 2001 after disclosures relating to aggressive and questionable earnings management.[72] That ouster possibly freed the company from Welch's focus on GE Capital's growth at the expense of other units.

Microsoft's antitrust case could probably have been resolved faster, with smaller overall legal bills, and with better image management had Bill Gates not been as personally involved in the case and had he been more prepared to be a sympathetic or appealing witness.[73]

And Martha Stewart, a former stockbroker, was brought down as a tippee in an insider trading scam that threatens the goodwill she built up in her company, in spite of her widely reported tendency to have a personal style 180 degrees opposed to the happy, industrious homemaker to whom she was supposed to appeal.[74] These leaders'

---

signifier itself must be totally devoid of meaning. . . . The master signifier itself is the signifier without any signified that can serve as the starting point of the chain. . . . Consequently, within the context of the chain, it has no separate meaning of its own, but is defined by the entire chain of signifiers to which it relates. . . . The classic example of master signifiers [is] political masters who rule through a cult of personality. . . .").

[70] For example, *see* Andrew Roberts, *Lenin's Legacy of Shame*, Daily Mail 8 (1994) ("Political heroes have been deified before, but Lenin was accorded a reputation for infallibility that had not existed since the Roman Empire. It led directly to the cult of personalities which later surrounded Stalin, Hitler, Mao Tse-tung and still exists with Kim Il-Sung in North Korea today [now deceased and replaced by his son Kim Jong Il]. Camps designed especially for the liquidation of political enemies were pioneered by Lenin long before Stalin came to power. They were later to destroy millions of Russian lives in degradation, slavery, torture, and were copied by Hitler and Mao.").

[71] *See* Gary Strauss, *Tyco Events Put Spotlight on Director's Role,* USA TODAY Sept. 16, 2002, at B3, *available at* http://www.usatoday.com/money/industries/manufacturing/2002-09-15-tyco-direct_x.htm (last visited June 3, 2003).

[72] *See* Ameet Sachdev, *Scandal and Upheaval: Corporate America's Image Suffers from Probes, Charges, and Andersen's Convictions,* CHI. TRIB., Dec. 31, 2002, at B1, *available at* 2002 WL 104502193 ("Who would have guessed that a business icon such as Jack Welch, the former CEO of General Electric Co., would come under scrutiny for his retirement perks? A dalliance with the then-editor of the *Harvard Business Review* caused his wife to file for divorce, which led to the revelations of GE picking up the expenses at his Manhattan apartment, including food, wine, cook, and waitstaff. In addition, GE allowed Welch to use the company's Boeing 737 jets and provided tickets to sporting and entertainment events. After the publicity, Welch agreed to pay GE nearly $2.5 million each year for the perks.").

[73] For example, *see* Michael J. Martinez, *Trial and Error? Did 'Attitude' or 'Faith' Cause Microsoft's Downfall?* Associated Press, *at* http://abcnews.go.com/sections/tech/DailyNews/microsoft000612.html (last visited June 3, 2003).

[74] *See* Ameet Sachdev, *Scandal and Upheaval: Corporate America's Image Suffers from Probes, Charges, and Andersen's Convictions,* CHI. TRIB., Dec. 31, 2002, at B1 ("Even the doyenne of domesticity, Martha Stewart, wound up gracing magazine covers—not for her cooking but because of insider trading allegations.").

behaviors were not focused on their company's long-term success, but rather on their own images, agendas, and short-term gains. As one columnist has said, avoid the iconic CEO—or at least the iconic CEO/Chairman of the Board who dominates the officers and directors: "Seek the anonymous plodder."[75]

Charisma and leadership are important in upper management, but these qualities must be balanced with strong self- and company-assessment skills. Senior management needs to make sure that it does not unquestioningly believe its own press. Hubris is not a character flaw reserved only for Greek tragedies or Shakespearean histories. The danger of a cult of personality is not isolated in the cult of an individual leader.

The cult of personality can be a cult of corporate personality, creating a damaged corporate culture. Enron was the Elvis of energy corporations and was to become "far and away the most vigorous agent of change in its industry."[76] The company was formed in 1985 from the merger of a natural gas and a pipeline company. However, the merger that had created Enron saddled the corporation with debt, and deregulation had taken away Enron's exclusive rights to its pipelines.[77] Kenneth Lay, Enron's CEO, needed a "new and innovative business strategy to generate profits and cash flow."[78] The strategy was engineered by Jeffrey Skilling, whose "revolutionary solution to Enron's credit, cash and profit woes" was to reconceive the company as a virtual corporation, or a "gas bank" (in which Enron would buy gas from a network of suppliers and sell it to a network of consumers, contractually guaranteeing both the supply and the price, charging fees for the transactions, and assuming the associated risks).[79] Through Skilling's innovation, Enron "created both a new product and a new paradigm in the industry—the energy derivative."[80]

---

[75] Marianne Jennings, *Remembering the "Business" in Business Ethics*, WASH. POST, Aug. 25, 2002, at B07, *available at* 2002 WL 25998598.

[76] Scott Sherman, *Enron Uncovering the Uncovered Story*, COLUM. JOURNALISM REV. 2228 March/April 2002.

[77] William C. Thomas, *The Rise and Fall of Enron,* J. ACCT. April 2002, at 41 (2002), *available at* http://www.aicpa.org/pubs/jofa/apr2002/thomas.htm (last visited June 3, 2003).

[78] *Id.*

[79] Thomas, *supra* note 77; *see* Batson Report, *supra* note 6, at 16 ("By the mid-1990s, Enron's business and business model changed dramatically. . . . In its 2000 Annual Report, Enron described its four business segments: Wholesale Services, Energy Services, Broadband Services, and Transportation Services. . . . Wholesale Services created trading markets in gas, oil, electricity and other energy products and provided price risk management and other related services."); *see also* Report on Board of Directors, *supra* note 6, at 6 ("It [Enron] had received widespread recognition for its transition from an old-line energy company with pipelines and power plants, to a high-tech global enterprise that traded energy contracts like commodities, launched into new industries like broadband communications, and oversaw a multibillion dollar international investment portfolio.").

[80] Thomas, *supra* note 77, at 2.

Skilling transformed not only Enron's business plan, but also its employees, through the active recruitment of the "best and brightest traders," and through the awarding of "merit based bonuses that had no cap, permitting traders to 'eat what they killed.'"[81] Skilling also instituted the creatively named "rank and yank" employee evaluation system, which "became known as the harshest employee ranking system in the country," where employees who failed to produce large profits were fired.[82] Under "rank and yank," "fierce internal competition prevailed and immediate gratification was prized beyond long-term potential."[83] Just as Skilling transformed Enron's internal culture, so did one of Skilling's earliest hires transform Enron's finances. Andrew Fastow, Enron's CFO, oversaw the corporation's "financing by ever more complicated means."[84]

Lay, Skilling, and Fastow were not anonymous plodders; rather, they took actions and made innovations that transformed a staid energy company into a "new economy" rock star. For this transformation, they and the corporation were lionized. Insiders in the industry voted Enron *Fortune*'s "Most Innovative Company" for six years running.[85] *Business Week* named Lay one of the "25 Top Managers" of 2000, while *Worth*'s survey of the "50 Best CEOs" included Lay and Skilling, with Skilling ranked second.[86] As Scott Sherman states, "The print media coverage of Enron's top executives was pure hagiography."[87]

Enron and its executives do illustrate the perils of conspicuous innovation and hype. "Skilling's relentless push for creativity and competitiveness . . . fostered a growth-at-

---

[81] *Id.*; *see* Report on Board of Directors, *supra* note 6, at 52 ("One Board member said during his interview that Enron's philosophy was to provide 'extraordinary rewards for extraordinary achievement'; others claimed that the company was forced to provide lavish compensation to attract the best and brightest employees.").

[82] Thomas, *supra* note 77, at 42.

[83] *Id.*

[84] Thomas, *supra* note 77. And enriching himself in the process. *See* Powers Report, *supra* note 6, at 166–67 ("Fastow, as CFO, knew what assets Enron's business units wanted to sell, how badly, and how soon they wanted to sell them, and whether they had alternative buyers. He was in a position to exert great pressure and influence, directly or indirectly, on Enron personnel who were negotiating with LJM. We have been told of instances in which he used that pressure to try to obtain better terms for LJM, and where people reporting to him instructed business units that LJM would be the buyer of the assets they wished to sell. . . . This situation led one Fastow subordinate, then-Treasurer Jeff McMahon, to complain to Skilling in March 2000. . . . Skilling has said he recalls the conversation focusing only on McMahon's compensation. Even if that is true, it still may have suggested that Fastow's conflict was placing pressure on an Enron employee.").

[85] Sherman, *supra* note 76, at 24.

[86] *Id.* at 25.

[87] *Id.*; WEBSTER'S THIRD NEW INT'L DICTIONARY 1019 (1986) (defines "hagiography" as "1 a: biography of saints: saint's lives"). A bit ironic, since the Powers Report concluded that, when it came to Enron's management, "no one was minding the store." *See* Powers Report, *supra* note 6, at 166.

any-cost culture, drowning out voices of caution and overriding all checks and balances."[88] Although not as glamorous, the tortoise can win over the hare, and corporations should seek, if not anonymous plodders, then rigorous, methodical individuals to balance charismatic, hard-charging leadership, and should maintain an internal culture that is consistent with notions of responsible stewardship, appropriate disclosure, and maximization of long-term shareholder value.[89] Of all the fabled corporate leaders of the last decade, perhaps the closest to this model is Berkshire Hathaway's Warren Buffett. Berkshire Hathaway, a holding company, is thinly staffed. Buffett focuses on value investing, using quantitative analysis, seeking to acquire companies that are worth more than their market capitalization and that are leaders in currently out-of-favor market segments. Instead of ousting prior management after an acquisition, Buffett largely leaves that management in place, not insisting that they run the business differently from the way they did before the acquisition.[90] Although widely heralded and recognized, Buffett is a picture of solid Midwestern business values and quantitative methods, and the successes that those values and methods can bring—not a charismatic, grandstanding leader that seeks the limelight.

LESSON THREE: ARTIFICIAL ENTITIES ARE ABOUT STEWARDSHIP

CEOs, CFOs, officers, and those attorneys and accountants who advise the company, remember: It is *not* your money! The modern corporation—or limited liability company, partnership, business trust, or other juristic entity formed to conduct business—is an incredible tool for collecting and deploying the capital of a diverse group

---

[88] Tom Fowler, *The Pride and the Fall of Enron*, HOUS. CHRON. Oct. 20, 2002, at A1, *available at* http://www.chron.com/cs/CDA/printstory.hts/special/enron/1624822 (last visited June 3, 2003); *see* Powers Report, *supra* note 6, at 27–28 ("The tragic consequences of the related party transactions and accounting errors were the results at many levels and by many people: a flawed idea, self-enrichment by employees, inadequately defined controls, poor implementation, inattentive oversight, simple (and not-so-simple) accounting mistakes, and overreaching in a culture that appears to have encouraged pushing the limits.").

[89] *See* Batson Report, *supra* note 6, at 13 ("This Report concludes that: . . . certain transfers made to Lay, certain other Enron employees and certain professionals can be avoided as constructively fraudulent transfers and preferential transfers."); *see also* Report on Board of Directors, *supra* note 6, at 49–50 ("Enron provided its executives with lavish compensation. On more than one occasion, it paid tens of millions of dollars to a single executive as a bonus for work on a single deal. Stock options were distributed in large numbers to executives. . . . Mr. Lay alone accumulated more than 6.5 million options on Enron stock. In 2000, Mr. Lay's compensation exceeded $140 million, including $123 million from exercising a portion of his Enron stock options . . . One example of the Compensation Committee's lavish compensation philosophy, combined with its failure to conduct adequate compensation oversight, involves its May 1999 decision to permit Mr. Lay to repay company loans with company stock. . . . In the one-year period from October 2000 to October 2001, Mr. Lay used the credit line to obtain over $77 million in cash from the company and repaid the loans exclusively with Enron stock.").

[90] *See generally* Roger Lowenstein, BUFFETT, THE MAKING OF AN AMERICAN CAPITALIST (1995).

of owners,[91] many of whom are not, and have no interest in being, involved in the day-to-day operations of a business.[92] The corporation is run by its directors, who select officers, for the benefit of the shareholders (or, when the corporation is operating in the zone of insolvency, for the benefit of creditors and shareholders).[93] The role of the officers and directors is to protect and grow the business,[94] not to personally profit at

---

[91] *See* William W. Bratton & Joseph A. McCahery, *Protecting Investors in a Global Economy: Incomplete Contracts Theories of the Firm and Comparative Corporate Governance*, 2 THEORETICAL INQUIRIES L. 745, 750 (2001) ("Market corporate governance systems are characterized by dispersed equity holding, a portfolio orientation among equity holders, and a broad delegation to management of discretion to operate the business. . . . Their shareholders can cheaply reduce their risks through diversification. Relative to shareholders in blockholder systems, they receive high rates of return. Market systems deep trading markets facilitate greater shareholder liquidity); *see also* Ann E. Conaway, *Reexamining the Fiduciary Paradigm at Corporate Insolvency and Dissolution: Defining Directors Duties to Creditors*, 20 DEL. J CORP. L. 1, 113 (1995) ("Generally, stockholders own and indirectly manage the corporation through equity securities of common stock."); *see, e.g.*, Margaret M. Blair and Lynn A. Stout, *A Team Production Theory of Corporate Law* 85 VA. L. REV. 247, 248 (1999) ("Contemporary discussions of corporate governance have come to be dominated by the view that public corporations are little more than bundles of assets collectively owned by shareholders."); *see also* Phillip I. Blumberg, *The Corporate Entity in an Era of Multinational Corporations*, 15 DEL. J. CORP. L. 283, 326 (1990) ("The traditional concept of the corporation as a separate juridical unit clashes violently with reality when applied, not merely to simple corporations with shares owned by individual investors, but to corporations that are members of a corporate group. In such cases, the 'corporation' and the enterprise are no longer identical. The enterprise is no longer being conducted solely by a single corporation but collectively by the coordinated activities of numerous interrelated corporations under common control.").

[92] *See* Stephen M. Bainbridge, *The Board of Directors as Nexus of Contracts*, 88 IOWA L. REV. 1, 3 (2002) ("Shareholders, who are said to 'own' the firm, have virtually no power to control either its day-to-day operations or its long-term policies. Instead, the firm is controlled by its board of directors and subordinate managers, whose equity stake is often small [in comparison to the company's total market capital]"); *see also* Susan Jacqueline Butler, *Models of Modern Corporations: A Comparative Analysis of German and U.S. Corporate Structures*, 17 ARIZ. J. INT'L & COMPARATIVE L. 555, 589 (2000) ("The power to manage the corporation is generally vested in the directors who delegate the day-to-day business to the officers."); *see also* Derek Murphy, *Corporate Governance: The Conflict Between Money and Morality*, 32 HKLJ 233, 234 (2002) ("The financial contributors—the shareholders—rely upon the skill, integrity and resourcefulness of those to whom they have delegated the task of running the business: the company's management and its Board of Directors.").

[93] *See* Ira M. Millstein and Paul W. MacAvoy, *The Active Board of Directors and Performance of the Large Publicly Traded Corporation*, 98 COLUM. L. REV. 1283 (1998); *see also* BLACK'S LAW DICTIONARY 166 (7th ed. 1999) ("board of directors: 1. The Governing body of a corporation, elected by the shareholders to establish corporate policy, appoint executive officers, and make major business and financial decisions."); Rev. Model Bus. Corp. Act § 8.01; *see also* Margaret M. Blair and Lynn A. Stout, *A Team Production Theory of Corporate Law*, 85 VA. L. REV. 247, 262 (1999) ("The owner is understood to delegate residual control rights to her agents (in the corporate context, the board of directors) who in turn are charged with managing the assets in the principal's interest, perhaps through several more layers of delegation.").

[94] *See* Gregory Scott Crespi, *Rethinking Corporate Fiduciary Duties: The Inefficiency of the Shareholder Primacy Norm*, 55 SMU L. Rev. 141 (2002) (summarizing "the conventional understanding among modern courts and commentators" as: fiduciary duties of corporate officers and directors "run exclusively to

the expense of the stakeholders.[95] Like Caesar's wife, they should strive to be beyond reproach.[96]

The use of stock option incentive programs and the mid-1980s to 1990s' shift away from paying dividends and to retaining earnings at the corporate level appear to have increased the temptation to lose sight of this principle of stewardship.[97] With more resources on hand and an immediate, personal reward for creating short-term market gains in the stock's secondary market, positive reinforcement for behavior that falls short of the fiduciary standards applicable to officers and directors may have clouded

---

the corporations' common shareholders, and that other financial claimants of the corporation, such as its bondholders and preferred shareholders, are generally entitled only to enforcement of their express contractual rights. When corporate directors and officers . . . make decisions within the remaining zone of discretion . . . they are regarded as subject to a fiduciary duty to maximize shareholder wealth."); *see also* Francis v. United Jersey Bank, 432 A.2d 814, 824 (1981) ("In general, the relationship of a corporate director to the corporation and its stockholders is that of a fiduciary. Shareholders have a right to expect that directors will exercise reasonable supervision and control over the policies and practices of a corporation."); Rest. 2d. Agency § 387 ("Unless otherwise agreed, an agent is subject to a duty to his principle to act solely for the benefit of the principal in all matters connected with his agency.").

[95] *See infra* notes 105–135 and accompanying text for a detailed discussion of the fiduciary duties of directors and officers; *see also* Butler, *supra* note 92, at 590 ("[T]he duty of loyalty generally requires managers to maximize investors' wealth rather than their own and creates a duty of fair dealing in self-interested transactions. When a conflict arises, it is the management's obligation not to enrich themselves at the corporation's expense."); Murphy, *supra* note 92, at 233 ("It is trite law that directors stand in a fiduciary relationship with their company. They have duties to act in good faith in the interests of the company; they must exercise powers for a proper purpose; and they must avoid conflicts of interest. They must not improperly use information obtained through their position to gain an advantage for themselves or someone else or cause detriment to the corporation."); *see* William Meade Fletcher, 3 FLETCHER CYCLOPEDIA OF PRIVATE CORP. § 837.50 (2002) ("This fiduciary duty runs to shareholders and the corporation, and not to fellow officers or directors except to the extent they are shareholders.").

[96] Or, alternatively, they should behave like Platonic Guardians, *see* Stephen M. Bainbridge, *The Board of Directors as Nexus of Contracts*, 88 IOWA L. REV. 1, 33 (2002).

[97] For an argument from the 1990s arguing for the increased use of stock options, *see* Charles M. Elson, *The Duty of Care, Compensation, and Stock Ownership*, 63 U. Cin. L. Rev. 649, 691 (1995) ("The outside directors must not remain mere observers of the corporate pecuniary interests, but must become active equity participants. If a director's personal capital is potentially affected by inept or corrupt management, that director is much less likely to acquiesce passively to such a group."). For the opposite view, *see* Jeffrey N. Gordon, *What Enron Means for the Management and Control of the Modern Business: Some Initial Reflections*, 69 U. CHI. L. REV. 1233, 1235 (2002) (arguing that Enron "undermines the corporate governance mechanism, the monitoring board, that has been offered as a substitute for unfettered shareholder access to the market for corporate control. In particular, the board's capacity to protect the integrity of financial disclosure has not kept pace with the increasing reliance on stock price performance in measuring and rewarding managerial performance."); *see also* Lerach, *supra* note 38, at 80 ("This explosion of new 'high growth' public companies, plus an executive-compensation system based on meeting predetermined earnings and stock-price appreciation targets, with stock options to be exercised and sold quarterly, created very powerful incentives to falsify results.").

the view of the stewardship model.[98] Stewardship remains the law, however, as well as the fundamental bedrock principle that makes modern corporate capitalism possible.[99] If the public loses its faith that the corporate stewards are acting primarily in the company's and shareholders' best interests, investment falters, the stock market plunges, and it becomes difficult to restart the country's stalled economic engine that, in good times, is fueled by healthy demand from both businesses and consumers.[100]

Enron demonstrates the consequences of lost faith. Trust was essential to the success of Enron's business, and once "there was doubt about the company's ability to perform as a counterpart" to transactions involving "trading in sophisticated energy and other derivatives," both Enron "and the cash flow and profits it generated, rapidly evaporated."[101] Enron relied on "dubious, and at times outrightly fraudulent, accounting

---

[98] *See* Gordon, *supra* note 97, at 1242 ("Recruitment of directors who are qualified to be board members of a large public company may require substantial compensation, especially for directors on time-consuming high-profile committees such as the audit committee. Yet high levels of compensation may compromise director independence, since a director's sharp questioning of senior management may lead to subtle pressures against his/her renomination. Moreover, stock-based director compensation may enhance the board's vigor as a shareholder agent but also increase its ambivalence about uncovering embarrassing facts that will reduce the share price."); *see also Who Dropped the Ball,* FRONTLINE: BIGGER THAN ENRON, *available at* http://www.pbs.org/wgbh/pages/frontline/shows/regulation /watchdogs/ (last visited June 3, 2003) ("In recent years, executives' compensation packages have included large grants of stock options . . . making them even more sensitive to the short-term performance of the company's stock. . . . Although the company's board of directors is supposed to represent the interests of the shareholders, some charge that in recent years they either have been asleep at the wheel or have been seduced by company management. Critics charge that sitting on a corporate board has turned into a lucrative venture with directors receiving consulting fees, sales contracts, donations to their favorite charities, and other assorted side deals that have the potential to compromise their objectivity and make them beholden to management, rather than the other way around.").

[99] *See* T. Jackson Lyons, 3 MS PRAC. ENCYCLOPEDIA MS LAW § 22:168 (2003) ("The fiduciary duties of officers and directors have affirmative obligations. Silence, or concealment, when one ought to speak because of the duty of utmost loyalty and good faith is actionable and the fiduciary may be held liable for any personal benefit or harm to the corporation.").

[100] *See* Kahn, *supra* note 65, at 1585–87 ("By the spring and summer of 2002, concern about the implications of Enron's sudden collapse had escalated into profound, nearly pervasive anxiety about the veracity of corporate reporting and the integrity of corporate governance systems supporting it. . . . Commentators coined the terms 'Enronitis,' and 'the Cockroach theory' to make light of the very serious fact that confidence in the accounting, auditing, disclosure, investment banking, credit ratio, and managerial oversight systems supporting the integrity of the capital markets had been grossly undermined by Enron's failure and the conduct of many of its principals and outside counselors. In the following months, both the capital markets and the general economy teetered at the edge of crisis. . . .").

[101] *Id.* at 1589; *see* Powers Report, *supra* note 6, at 3 ("The LJM1-Chewco-related restatement, like the earlier charge against earnings and reduction of shareholders' equity, was very large. It reduced Enron's reported net income by $28 million in 1997 (of $105 million total), by $133 million in 1998 (of $703 million total), by $248 million in 1999 (of $893 million total), and by $99 million in 2000 (of $979 million total). The restatement reduced reported shareholders' equity by $258 million in 1997, by $391 million in 1998, by $710 million in 1999, and by $754 million in 2000. It increased reported debt by

and disclosure practices, including the immediate recognition of profits on long-term sales contracts of speculative, future value."[102] These faulty systems of "accounting, auditing, and disclosure breached its [Enron's] investors' and employees' rightful expectations of financial transparency."[103]

Enron was seriously destabilized by disclosures of self-dealing transactions involving a raft of side deals connected to "two limited partnerships of which Enron's CFO, Andrew Fastow, was the manager of the general partner."[104] Not only did these deals put $30 million dollars into Fastow's pocket, they also resulted in "an overstatement of Enron's earnings over four years of at least $591 million."[105] The company "used its own high-flying common stock to surmount the sticking point" whenever "economics had gotten in the way of a result it wanted."[106] While employees and investors bore the

---

$71 million in 1997, by $561 million in 1998, by 685 million in 1999, and by $628 million in 2000. Enron also revealed, for the first time, that it had learned that Fastow received more than $30 million from LJM1 and LJM2. These announcements destroyed market confidence and investor trust in Enron. Less than one month later, Enron filed for bankruptcy.").

[102] Kahn, *supra* note 65, at 1589; *see* Batson Report, *supra* note 6, at 15 ("The Examiner has concluded that, through pervasive use of structured finance techniques involving SPEs and aggressive accounting practices, Enron so engineered its reported financial position and results of operations that its financial statements bore little resemblance to its actual financial condition or performance.").

[103] Kahn, *supra* note 65, at 1591; *see* Batson Report, *supra* note 6, at 53, 54, 55 ("As discussed in detail . . . despite Enron's extraordinary efforts to comply with the GAAP rules, in many cases the Examiner has been unable to find a sufficient basis under even the rules-based GAAP standards to support Enron's reported financial accounting . . . the Examiner has concluded that Enron's reporting of many of the SPE transactions did not comply with applicable GAAP rules in the first instance. This failure resulted in Enron's financial statements during the periods it engaged in these transactions not fairly presenting in all material respects its financial position, results of operations and cash flows in accordance with GAAP. . . . The Examiner concludes that, quite apart from questions of whether its accounting for particular SPE transactions was proper, Enron failed in several key respects to provide adequate disclosure to the marketplace for facts and circumstances that were critical to an understanding of its financial condition, operating results and cash flows.").

[104] Bratton, *supra* note 16, at 1305; *see* Powers Report, *supra* note 6, at 8–9 ("In 1999, with Board approval, Enron entered into business relationships with two partnerships in which Fastow was the manager and an investor. The transactions between Enron and the LJM partnerships resulted in Enron increasing its reported financial results by more than a billion dollars, and enriching Fastow and his co-investors by tens of millions of dollars at Enron's expense.").

[105] Bratton, *supra* note 16, at 1305.

[106] Bratton, *supra* note 16, at 1320; *see* Batson Report, *supra* note 6, at 21–22 ("An Enron manager who actively participated in the design and implementation of many of Enron's structured finance transactions confirmed how well he appreciated the importance of financial engineering in a self evaluation memorandum prepared sometime after the close of the 2000 fiscal year. He began the memorandum by pointing out his own contribution to Enron's funds flow and its balance sheet from 1995 through 2000: '. . . While the funds flow metric allows Enron to maintain its current debt rating assuming a certain balance sheet capital structure, of equal importance is the maintenance of that capital structure and maintaining debt ratios which have been generally in the 40% range overt the past five years. To maintain our credit rating, if Enron were to finance itself primarily or solely through simpler, on-balance-sheet reported

brunt of the collapse of Enron stock in 2001, many of Enron's "senior-level insiders had already banked huge financial windfalls."[107] Enron's Chairman and CEO, Kenneth Lay, sold off millions of dollars of Enron stock in 2001 without disclosing the sales.[108] Had he done so, the sales might have "aroused greater scrutiny and concern about what was occurring at Enron. . . . Greater transparency might also have led to management, operational and reporting reforms that might have resolved the problems at Enron before they proved terminal."[109] Instead, as Lay was liquidating his own stock, throughout the late summer and early fall of 2001, he "reassured Enron employees about the positive financial prospects of the firm and even suggested that they would benefit from purchasing more Enron stock."[110]

Such actions undermine confidence in both corporations and markets, since strong markets "depend on healthy investor psychology."[111] When the "fraudsters and charlatans gain prominence, excesses rage and burned investors shy away from markets."[112] Enron was itself a market, and what holds true for Enron holds true for the stock market as well: "no one can believe anything asserted by a firm that covers up losses by entering into sham derivative contracts with itself."[113] Investors won't invest in a market that looks "like the Bulgarian stock market,"[114] and corporate officers like Kenneth

---

structures, 40% of each transaction would be funded by the issuance of new debt and 60% through retained earnings or new equity. . . . For 2000, I was responsible for the Global Finance team that generated approximately $5.5 billion of overall off-balance sheet financing. . . . The value of avoiding $6.1 billion of equity dilution is difficult for me to quantify although, as a shareholder, I know it's reflected in the valuation given the avoided dilution of earnings per share.").

[107] Kahn, *supra* note 65, at 1594; *see* Powers Report, *supra* note 6, at 3 ("Enron employees involved in the partnerships were enriched, in the aggregate, by tens of millions of dollars they should never have received.").

[108] Kahn, *supra* note 65, at 1594.

[109] *Id.* at 1595.

[110] *Id.* at 1594; for instance, *see* Batson Report, *supra* note 6, at 6 ("In an earnings release on October 16, 2001, Kenneth Lay . . . while expressing confidence in Enron's 'strong earnings outlook,' announced, among other things, that Enron was taking 'after-tax-non-recurring charges' of $1.01 billion in the third quarter."). Lay may be paying back some of his ill-gotten gains, however. *See* Batson Report, *supra* note 6, at 131 ("The Examiner's preliminary conclusions are as follows: Enron has a cause of action under Section 548(a)(1)(B) of the Bankruptcy Code (i.e., constructively fraudulent conveyance) against Lay to recover transfers in excess of $74 million made in the year prior to the Petition Date arising out of certain loans made by Enron to Lay and which Lay repaid Enron with Enron stock at a time when Enron was presumed to be insolvent. . . . Enron has a cause of action under Section 547 of the Bankruptcy Code (i.e., preference) against certain employees of the Debtors arising out of Enron's accelerated payments, totaling $53 million, under two deferred compensation plans, made in a 30-day period (commencing on October 30, 2001), at a time when Enron was presumably insolvent.").

[111] Lerach, *supra* note 38, at 120.

[112] *Id.* at 122.

[113] Bratton, *supra* note 16, at 1320.

[114] *See* Lerach, *supra* note 38, at 122.

Lay and Andrew Fastow not only defraud investors, but fundamentally undermine confidence in the market itself.

LESSON FOUR: OFFICERS AND DIRECTORS MUST KNOW AND FULFILL THEIR DUTIES OR FACE LIABILITY

It is black-letter law that the directors and officers of a corporation have fiduciary duties owed to the corporation's stockholders.[115] This statement means that they appoint management, determine management's compensation, and review and approve major investment and operational decisions made by management. In doing so, they must exercise due care and maintain loyalty to the corporation and its stockholders. If they fail in these obligations, they risk liability to the corporation, its shareholders, and its creditors.[116]

An officer may owe a similar set of fiduciary duties to the corporation and its stockholders within the scope of his or her employment, as delegated by the board of directors.[117] Persons simultaneously serving as directors and officers will be held to the standards applicable to directors, and the scope of their responsibilities as officers does not limit the scope or breadth of their duties as directors.

A. The Duty of Care

The duty of care has two component parts: a decision-making duty and an oversight duty. The decision-making duty of care itself has two elements within its scope:

---

[115] When the corporation approaches the zone of insolvency, these fiduciary duties are enhanced and the class of beneficiaries expands beyond stockholders to include creditors. *See* Credit Lyonnais Bank Nederland, N.V. v. Pathe Communications Corp., 1991 WL 277613, 17 Del. J. Corp. L. 1099, 1991 Del. Ch. LEXIS 215 (Del. 1991). Upon bankruptcy they may even expand further to encompass all "parties in interest," a nebulous description indeed.

[116] This liability may be non-dischargeable in a subsequent bankruptcy by the director or officer. *See* Nahman v. Jacks (In re Jacks), 266 B.R. 728 (B.A.P. 9th Cir. 2001) (applying California trust fund doctrine); Flegel v. Burt & Assocs., P.C. (In re Kallmeyer), 242 B.R. 492 (B.A.P. 9th Cir. 1999). By characterizing the trust fund doctrine as one that imposes an express trust, corporate creditors that succeed on a breach of fiduciary duty claim against a director may bring an adversary proceeding in the director's bankruptcy case and have the debt declared non-dischargeable, *i.e.,* determined to be a debt that will *survive* the bankruptcy case and continue to be enforceable against the debtor-director. The non-dischargability of a breach of fiduciary duty claim must be timely and affirmatively sought by the creditor through the bankruptcy adversary proceeding process or the claim will be time barred. *See* 11 U.S.C. § 523(c); *see also* FED. R. BANKR. P. 4004 & 4007 (statute of limitations and procedure for dischargability actions); Katherine S. Kruis, Esq., *The Time Limitation for Objecting to Discharge of Debts: A Trap for the Unwary,* 26 CAL. BANKR. J. 55 (2001).

[117] DEL. CODE ANN. tit. 8, § 141(a) ("The business and affairs of every corporation . . . shall be managed by or under the direction of a board of directors."); *cf.* In re Ben Franklin, 225 B.R. 646, 652 n.10 (Bankr. N.D. Ill. 1998) ("No fiduciary duty governing management of a corporation's affairs can be imposed on persons who have no authority to manage those affairs.").

(1) the duty to be informed of all material information that is reasonably available before making a decision, and (2) the duty to use reasonable care in making the decision itself.[118] The oversight duty requires that directors exercise reasonable care in overseeing and monitoring the performance of corporate officers and the corporation's business.

B. The Duty of Loyalty

The duty of loyalty is even easier to understand than the duty of care. Directors are to act in good faith in the best interest of the corporation and are not to engage in self-dealing or usurp corporate opportunities. If a director desires to engage in a self-dealing transaction or to take advantage of a business opportunity that the corporation would otherwise have the chance to pursue, the director may do so if, after full disclosure of all material facts: (1) the transaction is approved by a majority of the disinterested members of the board of directors, or (2) the transaction is ratified by a wholly disinterested stockholder vote.[119] Absent one of those two conditions being satisfied, the director will bear the burden, in a subsequent lawsuit, of demonstrating that the transaction is objectively and intrinsically fair.[120]

C. The Business Judgment Rule

The business judgment rule is a doctrine creating a rebuttable presumption that a board's decision is one made on an informed basis, with a good-faith belief that the action was taken in the best interests of the corporation.[121] Absent evidence contradicting some portion of this presumption, or a showing that one or more directors with a conflicting interest participated in the decision-making, a reviewing court will not substitute its own judgment for that of the board.[122]

The principal area in which the business judgment rule's protections may be lost involves non-disinterested directors. If a board is dominated or controlled by one or more directors with an undisclosed conflicting interest, the protection of the rule may

---

[118] Smith v. Van Gorkom, 488 A.2d 858, 872–74 (Del. 1985).

[119] DEL. CODE ANN. tit. 8, § 144; CAL. CORP CODE § 310 (1990).

[120] Mills Acquisition Co. v. MacMillan, Inc., 559 A.2d 1261, 1280 (Del. 1989). Delaware's authorization of an exculpatory provision to limit monetary damages for a breach of the duty of care does not apply to breaches of the duty of loyalty or improper self-dealing. DEL. CODE ANN. tit. 8, § 102(b)(7)(i), (iv). By contrast, California's enabling statute contains no such express limitation. See CAL. CORP. CODE § 204(a)(10)(1990).

[121] See CAL. CORP. CODE § 309(a) (1990); Briano v. Rubio, 46 Cal. App. 4th 1167, 54 Cal. Rptr. 2d 408 (1996); Polk v. Good, 507 A.2d 531, 536 (Del. Super. Ct. 1986); Brant v. Hicks, Muse & Co. (In re Healthco International, Inc.), 208 BR 288, 302–07 (Bankr. D. Mass 1997).

[122] Id.

not apply.[123] Additionally, if the board is predominantly composed of members with a financial interest in the transaction, the business judgment rule may not apply.[124]

The business judgment rule is a shield for directors facing claims of breach of the decision-making duty of care. It does not apply to the duty of loyalty if a director pursues a self-interested transaction without either disinterested director approval or stockholder ratification, in each case after full disclosure of all material facts. The business judgment rule does not apply at all to a claim for usurpation of corporate opportunity. If the business judgment rule does not apply to an alleged breach of the duty of loyalty, then the intrinsic or fundamental fairness standard applies, and the non-disinterested director bears the burden of proof that the transaction was both substantively and procedurally fair.[125]

Here's the point: The business judgment rule is a rule for the courtroom; directors should not rely upon it in the boardroom. Although it may apply and protect them if their decisions are later challenged, prudent directors should assume that the rule will not apply and should therefore conduct themselves accordingly, *i.e.,* they should, at all times, exercise the duty of care of a reasonable person in:

(a)   gathering information,
(b)   assessing alternatives and potential outcomes, and
(c)   making decisions,
(d)   all in good faith, and
(e)   *either:*
     (i)   in a disinterested fashion, or
     (ii)   with full disclosure of all conflicts of interest, subject to approval by a majority of disinterested directors or stockholder ratification.

If a lawsuit later arises, the protections of the business judgment rule should supplement an otherwise strong decision-making record.

Finally, a director or officer should not take refuge by resigning from the board or company upon learning of a difficult circumstance or wrongful action. One might especially wish to avoid the example of Jeffery Skilling, who purportedly told Kenneth

---

[123] *See* Cede & Co. v. Technicolor, Inc., 634 A.2d 345, 363, *modified,* 636 A.2d 956 (Del. 1994).

[124] *See* AC Acquisition Co. v. Anderson, Clayton & Co. 519 A.2d 103, 111 (Del. Ch. 1986).

[125] Cinerama, Inc. v. Technicolor, Inc., 1991 WL 111134, at *8–12, (Del. Ch. 1991), *aff'd in part, rev'd in part sub nom* Cede & Co. v. Technicolor, Inc., 634 A.2d 345 (Del. 1993), *modified,* 636 A.2d 956 (Del. 1994) (explaining business judgment rule as a rule that imposes the burden of proof on the plaintiff and, as an alternative, the entire fairness standard of review as imposing the burden of proof on the defendant director). The inquiry into *substantive* fairness focuses on the terms of the transaction and asks, were these terms fair to the corporation? The *procedural* fairness inquiry focuses on whether there was full disclosure and appropriate approval by disinterested directors. To achieve *both* substantive and procedural fairness, boards often employ a committee of disinterested directors to negotiate the transaction with the interested director (or the entity representing his or her interest) and then approve the transaction by a majority of the disinterested members of the entire board.

Lay that he [Skilling] was resigning from Enron for personal reasons, which included his desire to spend more time with his children, and his being kept up at night by Enron's falling stock price.[126] As a director, although one is not irrevocably committed for the ultimate long haul, one has taken on a duty of stewardship to supervise and manage a corporation. Suddenly resigning when the going gets rough is not an action consistent with this notion of stewardship.[127] Further, the protections of the business judgment rule have been held to apply only to director action, not to director inaction, at least under Delaware law.[128] Doing nothing or resigning upon discovery of problems or wrongdoing will rarely be appropriate and should not relieve a director from liability when the plane crashes after he or she bails out.

The behavior of Enron's executives will no doubt become enshrined in that most telling of legends: the cautionary tale. Like Icarus, who flew too close to the sun and perished as a result, Enron's executives will continue to be held up to the business and legal community as examples of what *not* to do. The completion of the cautionary Enron legend will have to await the conclusion of lengthy, civil, criminal, regulatory, and bankruptcy proceedings. The Powers Report "rightly faults Enron's board for defective ongoing monitoring of the LJM transactions,"[129] and Powers himself concluded that "Enron's board of directors breached the fiduciary duty of care it owed to the company's shareholders."[130] By having a "material financial interest in the transactions between Enron and the investment partnerships he created and managed," Andrew Fastow more than likely breached the duty of loyalty.[131] Even managers who did not

---

[126] *See* David Barboza, *Enron's Many Strands: the Former Chief*, N.Y. TIMES, Aug. 22, 2002 at C1 ("In a summary of an interview with lawyers last January, Mr. Lay said that Mr. Skilling told him that he wanted to spend more time with his three children. When he was pressed, the summary stated: 'Skilling said he was under a lot of pressure and felt that Enron's stock price was dropping and he could not do anything about it. Skilling was taking Enron's stock price personally and could not sleep at night.'")

[127] *See* Xerox v Genmoora Corp., 888 F.2d 345 (5th Cir. 1989) (analogizing resignation on the eve of corporate transaction to a pilot bailing out of a commercial airplane after pointing it at a mountain; it is an insufficient defense that one is not at the controls at the moment of impact).

[128] Rabkin v. Philip A. Hunt Chem. Corp., 1987 WL 28436, at *3, LEXIS 522, *3 (Del. Ch. 1987) (The business judgment rule "has no role where directors have either abdicated their functions, or, absent a conscious decision, failed to act.").

[129] Bratton, *supra* note 16, at 1332; *see* Powers Report, *supra* note 6, at 24 ("In sum, the Board did not effectively meet its obligation with respect to the LJM transactions.").

[130] Cheryl L. Wade, *Corporate Governance and the Managerial Duty of Care*, 76 ST. JOHN'S L. REV. 767, 780 (2002); *see* Powers Report, *supra* note 6, at 22 ("With respect to the issues that are the subject of this investigation, the Board of Directors failed, in our judgment, in its oversight duties. This had serious consequences for Enron, its employees, and its shareholders.").

[131] Wade, *supra* note 130, at 781; *see* Powers Report, *supra* note 6, at 18 ("Fastow was Enron's Chief Financial Officer and was involved on both sides of the related-party transactions. What he presented as an arrangement intended to benefit Enron became, over time, a means of both enriching himself personally and facilitating manipulation of Enron's financial statements. Both of these objectives were inconsistent with Fastow's fiduciary duties to Enron and anything the Board authorized.").

benefit monetarily from Enron's transactions with suspect partnerships may have breached the duty of care. Jeffrey Skilling supposedly surrounded himself with "yes men," and it "would be reasonable to argue that the 'yes men,' if they were corporate officers, breached the duty of care by invariably saying yes instead of adequately investigating, monitoring and ensuring compliance with the law."[132] Enron's former CEO, Kenneth Lay, may have breached the duty of care by being out of touch and unfamiliar with many aspects of his own company.[133] The highly competitive, win-at-all-costs culture that Enron fostered "risked the kinds of managerial breaches and possibly criminal conduct that occurred."[134] Enron's leaders "averted their eyes from the manifest implications of their own actions" and as they "stepped across the line to fraud, their belief system trumped reality."[135]

D. The More Organizational Layers, the More Opportunity for Rot

Max Weber's theory of bureaucracy involved the primacy of a social structure that allocated resources according to a set of rules and qualifications, rather than according to rank or status. Bureaucracy was to provide a fair and uniform set of gatekeepers. The theoretical, ideal form of bureaucracy, however, has never materialized. Flawed versions of the model have prevailed. These include the internal governance structure of a corporation and the regulation of that corporation and the information that it discloses to the public by the interaction of officers, directors, lawyers, accountants, and the Securities and Exchange Commission, among others.

In organizational structures like this, there is much to gain by maintaining as "flat" a system as possible. Each layer of bureaucrats and gatekeepers inhibits clear and accu-

---

[132] Wade, *supra* note 130, at 781; *see* Powers Report, *supra* note 6, at 19 ("Individually and collectively, Enron's management failed to carry out its substantive responsibility for ensuring that the transactions were fair to Enron—which in many cases they were not—and its responsibility for implementing a system of oversight and controls over the transactions with the LJM partnerships.").

[133] Wade, *supra* note 130, 781–82; *see* Powers Report, *supra* note 6, at 19 ("For much of the period in question, Lay was the Chief Executive Officer of Enron and, in effect, the captain of the ship. As CEO, he had ultimate responsibility for taking reasonable steps to ensure that the officers reporting to him performed their oversight duties properly. He does not appear to have directed their attention, or his own, to the oversight of the LJM partnerships. Ultimately, a large measure of the responsibility rests with the CEO.").

[134] Wade, *supra* note 130, at 782.

[135] Bratton, *supra* note 16, at 1332. For example, *see* Report on Board of Directors, *supra* note 6, at 13 ("While the evidence indicates that, in some instances, Enron Board members were misinformed or misled, the Subcommittee investigation found that overall the Board received substantial information about Enron's plans and activities and explicitly authorized or allowed many of the questionable Enron strategies, policies and transactions now subject to criticism. Enron's high-risk accounting practices, for example, were not hidden from the Board. The Board knew of them and took no action to prevent Enron from misusing them. . . . Enron's extensive off-the-books activity was not only well known to the Board, but was made possible by Board resolutions authorizing new unconsolidated entities, Enron preferred shares, and Enron stock collateral that was featured in many of the off-the-books deals.").

rate communication and the institutional transparency necessary to root out wrong-doing. A series of Byzantine layers also provides the gatekeepers at each level with more opportunity to indulge in self-dealing. An organization chart that must be printed in "landscape" mode is desirable when one seeks to increase transparency and decrease opportunities for wrongdoing and self-dealing.

The remedy for incompetent or self-dealing management is supposed to be the oversight of a competent and adequately informed board of directors, the major features of which are "independent directors, specialized committees (especially an audit committee) consisting exclusively of independent directors to perform crucial monitoring functions, and clear charter of board authority."[136] On the face of it, Enron's board of directors was a model board, consisting of fourteen members, only two of whom were insiders. The prestigious and qualified directors included the former Chairperson of the Commodity Futures Trading Commission and a former United Kingdom Secretary of State.[137] Enron's Audit Committee had a state-of-the-art charter, giving the committee the power to do everything, from oversee the company's reporting procedures and internal controls, to the power to hire and "retain other accountants, lawyers, or consultants."[138] Both the Board and the Audit Committee, however, were "undermined by side payments of one kind or another."[139] Furthermore, the use of "political contributions to friends and allies of the directors, larger contributions to institutions the directors were associated with, and a lavish equity package for the directors either chloroformed or corrupted Enron's Board."[140] The Board maintained

---

[136] Gordon, *supra* note 97, at 1241; *see* Report on Board of Directors, *supra* note 6, at 5 ("In the United States, the Board of Directors sits at the apex of a company's governing structure. A typical Board's duties include reviewing the company's overall business strategy; selecting and compensating the company's senior executives; evaluating the company's outside auditor; overseeing the company's financial statements; and monitoring overall company performance. According to the Business Roundtable, the Board's 'paramount duty' is to safeguard the interests of the company's shareholders.").

[137] Lerach, *supra* note 38, at 106; *see* Report on Board of Directors, *supra* note 6, at 8 ("The Subcommittee interviews found the Directors to have a wealth of sophisticated business and investment experience and considerable expertise in accounting, derivatives, and structured finance.").

[138] Gordon, *supra* note 97, at 1241.

[139] *Id.* at 1242.

[140] Lerach, *supra* note 38, at 106; *see* Report on Board of Directors, *supra* note 6, 51–52 ("At the May 7 hearing, the expert witnesses testified that the independence and objectivity of the Enron Board had been weakened by financial ties between Enron and certain Directors. . . . A number of corporate governance experts contacted by the Subcommittee staff identified these financial ties as contributing to the Enron Board's lack of independence and reluctance to challenge Enron management. . . . Robert H. Campbell . . . testified that 'consulting arrangements with directors are absolutely incorrect, absolutely wrong' because directors are already paid a substantial fee to be available to management and provide their perspective on company issues. The three experts at the May 7 hearing also criticized the compensation paid to the Board members, noting that $350,000 per year was significantly above the norm and that much of the compensation was in the form of stock options, which enabled the Board members to benefit from stock gains, without risking investment loss.").

that things were going well; so well, in fact, that the proposal to "suspend the corporate ethics code to permit conflicted transactions by a senior executive, an extraordinary request—did not stir the antennae."[141]

If a corporate bureaucracy is meant to function as a system of gatekeepers and checks ensuring honesty and preventing fraud, then the malfunction of that system is illustrated not only by the failure of Enron's board, but also by the failure of Enron's professional gatekeepers: the accountants, lawyers, and bankers who serviced the energy tracking giant.[142] Enron's accounting firm, Author Andersen, was a disaster; for awash "in 27 million in consulting fees on top of 25 million in audit fees at Enron, Andersen, as 'business consultant,' helped structure the very transactions that [it was] to later audit."[143] Enron's lawyers "held themselves out as having special expertise to help put together the kinds of complex structured financial transactions that created million [sic] and millions of dollars of false profits for Enron."[144] Worst of all, however, were the banks. Some of the nation's most prestigious financial institutions "made at least six billion dollars in concealed loans to Enron,"[145] enabling the corporation to

---

[141] Gordon, *supra* note 97, at 1242; *see* Report on Board of Directors, *supra* note 6, at 24 ("The Enron Board's decision to waive the company's code of conduct and allow its Chief Financial Officer (CFO) Andrew Fastow to establish and operate off-the-books entities designed to transact business with Enron was also highly unusual and disturbing."); *see also* Powers Report, *supra* note 17, at 156. ("At bottom, however, the need for such an extensive set of controls said something fundamental about the wisdom of permitting the CFO to take on this conflict of interest. The two members of the Special Committee participating in this review of the Board's actions believe that a conflict of this significance that could be managed only through so many controls and procedures should not have been approved in the first place.").

[142] Lerach, *supra* note 38, 108–117; *see* Powers Report, *supra* note 6, at 148 ("Oversight of the related-party transactions by Enron's Board of Directors and Management failed for many reasons. . . . Enron's outside auditors supposedly examined Enron's internal controls, but did not identify or bring to the Audit Committee's attention the inadequacy in their implementation."); *see also* Report on Board of Directors, *supra* note 8, at 3 ("The Board also failed to ensure the independence of the company's auditor, allowing Andersen to provide internal audit and consulting services while serving as Enron's outside auditor.").

[143] Lerach, *supra* note 38, at 108. For example, *see* Batson Report, *supra* note 6, at 39 ("Enron carefully designed its FAS 140 technique with advice from Andersen and Enron's lawyers, with the goal that the asset transfer would qualify for sale treatment under GAAP despite the fact that sale treatment did not reflect the economic substance of the transaction.").

[144] Lerach, *supra* note 38, at 113. For example, *see* Powers Report, *supra* note 6, at 190 ("Enron had an obligation to disclose the 'amount of [Fastow's] *interest* in the transaction(s)' (emphasis added), not just his income. The lawyers apparently searched for and embraced a technical rationale to avoid that disclosure.").

[145] Lerach, *supra* note 38, at 114. For example, *see* Batson Report, *supra* note 6, at 65–66 ("The financial institutions—specifically, Citibank and JPMorgan—played significant roles in facilitating the Prepay Transactions. They helped Enron structure the transactions, providing the funding either directly or indirectly, and assisted in forming the conduit entities Andersen and Enron deemed necessary to the transactions. Both Citibank and JPMorgan knew that Enron accounted for its obligations under the Prepay Transactions as liabilities from price risk management activities rather than debt. They also believed that Enron reported the cash as cash flow from operating activities rather than financing activities. Nevertheless, both lenders recognized that the Prepay Transactions were essentially loans.").

hide its debt and maintain its investment grade credit rating. With the help of its bankers, Enron raised billions of dollars in fresh capital from investors in the four years before it went bankrupt.[146]

Enron is thus paradigmatic of the systemic problem of failed bureaucracy. A "flatter" corporate structure, and a consequently higher level of transparency, might have prevented, or at least revealed, the problems in the corporation. Smaller committees, like smaller classes in graduate schools, allow for more questioning, more searching inquiries; they allow participants a level of intimacy and comfort that allows them to display their ignorance, to question current practices, and to engage in higher quality learning and decision-making.[147]

The problem with Kafkaesque systems of gatekeepers and gates is not only that they shield the system from outside penetration,[148] but also that the gatekeepers tend to

---

[146] Lerach, *supra* note 38, at 114. Actually, Enron informed its banks of the extent of its debt on November 19, 2001. *See* Batson Report, *supra* note 6, at 9–10 ("On November 19, 2001, the same day Enron filed its third quarter financial statements, senior Enron executives met with certain of Enron's bankers at the Waldorf Astoria hotel in New York City. Enron's objectives for the meeting were to restore creditor confidence, relive its liquidity crisis and discuss its proposed merger with Dynegy, Inc. During this meeting, Enron informed its bankers that, while the debt reflected on its third quarter 2001 balance sheet under GAAP was $12.978 billion, Enron's 'debt' . . . was 38.094 billion. Thus, as Enron noted, $25.116 million of debt was 'off-balance-sheet,' or in some cases reflected on the balance sheet, but classified as something other than debt.").

[147] Professor Warren C. Neal, Director of the Center for Corporate Governance at the University of Tennessee College of Business Administration, Remarks at the Clayton Center for Entrepreneurial Law, the University of Tennessee College of Law, Knoxville, Tennessee (March 24, 2003) (emphasizing the use of small committees and sub-committees to improve the quality of the processes of board deliberation and inquiries of management as a means of improving the quality of corporate governance in U.S. corporations).

[148] The author refers to the following passage from Kafka's *Trial:*

"Don't deceive yourself," said the priest. "What am deceiving myself in?" said K.
"You're deceiving yourself in the court," said the priest, "the introductory writings on the law speak to this deception: A gatekeeper stands before the law. A man from the country comes to the gatekeeper and asks entry into the law. But the gatekeeper says, he cannot guarantee him entry. The man considers and then asks, whether he might enter later. "It's possible," says the gatekeeper, "but not now." Since the door to the law stands open as always and the gatekeeper walks off to the side, the man bends down in order to see through the gate, and into the interior. When the gatekeeper sees that, he laughs and says: "If it tempts you so, try it then, to go in despite my forbidding it. See here though: I am powerful. And I am only the least of the gatekeepers. From chamber to chamber, however, stand gatekeepers, one more powerful than the other. Already the sight of the third is more than even I can bear." The man from the country had not expected such difficulties, the law should be open to each and always he thinks, but as he now looks more closely at the gatekeeper in his fur coat, his big pointed nose, the long, thin, black tartan beard, he decides, he'd better wait until he gets permission to enter. The gatekeeper gives him a stool and lets him sit down beside the door. There he sits for days and years. He makes many attempts to be let in, and tires the gatekeeper out with his requests. The gatekeeper more often holds small interrogations with him, asks him all about his home and about much else besides, they are however disinterested questions, like great lords ask, and at the end he tells him again as always, that he cannot let him in. The man, who had

become friendly with each other and to realize that mutually profitable relationships may spring up within guarded walls. Gatekeepers may not let outsiders in, but, as Enron illustrates, gatekeepers are also not to be trusted to refrain from pillaging that which they are supposed to guard, let alone to continue to watch the other watchers of the gates.

E. Leverage: Great High, Heavy Hangover

All the technical accounting and legal explanations aside, what was the purpose of Enron's SPEs?[149] As Neil Batson points out, the problem was not so much Enron's use of SPEs as Enron's *misuse* of them.[150] ("There is nothing improper about the use of structured finance and SPEs to achieve and report business results. Enron, however, used structured finance to report results it had not achieved.")[151] Enron hid debt. It

---

provisioned himself more than adequately for his trip, expends everything, regardless of its value, in order to bribe the gatekeeper. That one accepts everything, but adds, "I'm only accepting it, so that you won't think that you've wasted something." Over the course of many years, the man observes the gatekeeper almost without interruption. He forgets the other gatekeepers, and this first one seems to him to be the only impediment to entry into the law. He curses the unlucky coincidence out loud in the early years, in the later, when he's old, he grumbles only to himself. He becomes childish, and since during the course of his years-long study of the gatekeeper, he has come to recognize even the fleas in his fur coat, he asks the fleas as well to help him and persuade the gatekeeper. Finally the light in his eyes becomes dim, and he knows not, whether it is really becoming darker around him, or if his eyes deceive him. But in the darkness he now recognizes well a light that inextinguishably breaks forth from the door of the law. He will not live much longer. Before his death the experiences of the whole time all coalesce in his mind into a single question, that until now he had not asked the gatekeeper. He beckons to him, for he can no longer raise his stiffening body. The gatekeeper must bend down deeply to him, for the difference in height has changed very much in the man's favor. "What do you want to know now," asks the gatekeeper. "You are insatiable." "All strive toward the law," says the man, "how come no one except me has requested entry in so many years." The gatekeeper recognizes that the man is already at his end, and in order to reach his fading hearing, he bellows at him, "No one else could gain entry here, for this entrance was meant only for you. I'll go now and close it."

Franz Kafka, *Der Prozess*, *in* FRANZ KAFKA: DIE ROMANE 259, 432–34 (1963) (original translated to English from German).

[149] For a thorough discussion of SPEs, tax review standards, and Enron's accounting practices, *see* Harold S. Peckron, *Watchdogs that Failed to Bark: Standards of Tax Review After Enron*, 5 FLA. TAX REV. 853, 903, 910, 913 (2002) ("Using off-the-books partnerships and maddeningly opaque accounting . . . Enron shielded about 500 million in debt. That helped keep Enron's credit rating high . . . assuming arguendo that some of the Enron special purpose entities that shifted debt off the balance sheet met the realistic possibility standard, still their ethical impact on third parties (e.g. shareholders, creditors, etc.) should have been considered. . . . For instance is it ethically necessary now to consider the impact of the debt-shifting special purpose entity shelter on the publicly traded company's stock price. The creation of special purpose entities . . . acted as tax shelters and off-balance sheet financing vehicles . . . .").

[150] *See* Batson Report, *supra* note 6, at 49–50.

[151] *Id.*

hid leverage. Leverage is not bad in and of itself. Leverage is a tool that can be used to boost returns on equity and reward debt holders with an appropriate rate of interest for the use of their funds.[152] Enron's actual debt-to-equity ratio was on the order of 90%,[153] but for a period, Enron did not report this true figure. Had Enron reported the true figure, the risk associated with such a high degree of leverage would have been factored into the stock price, which would have declined to reflect a more accurate risk premium.[154]

A company's degree of leverage must be accurately assessed and reported at all times, and officers, directors, accountants, and attorneys must be attuned to the possibility that hidden debt and other liabilities are boosting a company's or a unit's reported returns.[155] For those who benefit from high returns, such as managers of strategic business units and others compensated or promoted based upon their unit's performance, the temptation is always there to over-report revenue and under-report expenses and debt. As Ronald Regan once said, in another context, "Trust, but verify." The comment is apt in the corporate governance arena as well.[156]

---

[152] For a thorough discussion of leverage and its benefits, see Robert E. Scott, *The Truth About Secured Financing*, 82 CORNELL L. REV. 1436, 1448–1456 (1997).

[153] *See Testimony of Robert Roach, Chief Investigator: Permanent Subcommittee on Investigations: the Role of Financial Institutions in Enron's Collapse*, at 2, *available at* http://govt-aff.senate.gov/072302roach.pdf (last visited June 5, 2003) ("With the inclusion of the prepays as debt, Enron's debt to equity ratio would have risen from about 69% to about 96%. Its debt to total capital ratio would have risen from 40% to 49%."); *see also* Paul Sperry, *Did Enron insiders smell trouble in '98?: Heavy stock selling began 4 years ago, as company's overseas debt piled up*, WorldNetDaily.com, *available at* http://www.worldnetdaily.com/news/article.asp?ARTICLE_ID=26085 (last visited June 5, 2003) ("Over the same period, Enron's debt-to-equity ratio continued to climb, from 78 percent to 91 percent.").

[154] This was precisely what Enron wanted to avoid, however. *See* Batson Report, *supra* note 6, at 15, 18–19 ("Two key factors drove Enron's management of its financial statements: (i) its need for cash and (ii) its need to maintain an investment grade credit rating. Enron was reluctant to issue equity to address these needs for fear of an adverse effect on its stock price and was reluctant to incur debt because of a possible adverse effect on its stock ratings. Moreover, Enron's use of market-to-market . . . accounting created a large gap between net income and funds flow from operations. . . . By 1999, Enron's Wholesale Services was by far the most significant of Enron's business segments. . . . In order to continue the growth of this business, Enron needed to trade with other market participants without being required to post collateral. Thus, the continued success of Enron's entire business was dependent upon the continued success of its Wholesale Services business segment, which in turn was dependent upon Enron's credit ratings for its senior unsecured long-term debt.").

[155] *See* Batson Report, *supra* note 6, at 54 ("A public company like Enron, in addition to complying with the literal GAAP rules and publishing financial statements that fairly present its financial position, results of operations and cash flows in accordance with GAAP, must also comply with the federal securities laws mandating additional financial disclosure.").

[156] Leverage also has an effect on the legal duties owed by officers and directors. As a company approaches bankruptcy or operates in the zone of insolvency, the fiduciary duties normally owed to shareholders alone shift to include both shareholders and creditors as beneficiaries. This creates a conflict of interest so great that it may be impossible to serve both sets of interests. With few exceptions, when a corporation's balance sheet is leveraged, the creditors and stockholders have fundamentally different stakes

CONCLUSION

The Enron debacle: A concentration of phenomena that, taken together, led to a huge financial collapse. The lessons that can be learned from Enron are many, but they are all simple, fundamental points learned by (or at least taught to) every accounting, business, and law student. Fraud is not complex. If it sounds too good to be true, it probably is. Retain a healthy sense of skepticism and engage in critical analysis of any report or conclusion. Recognize the role of a corporate steward, gatekeeper, or watchdog, and discharge the duties of that role faithfully. Do not establish incentive systems that create conflicts of interest. Prefer flat, transparent organizational structures. Avoid cults of individual or corporate personality. Watch your leverage. Design corporate boards that are, in fact, capable of discharging their fiduciary duties, after reasonable investigation in a disinterested fashion. All you ever needed to know about avoiding another Enron-style situation, you learned in kindergarten—or at least in graduate school.

NOTES AND QUESTIONS

1. The author and others have argued that the problems at Enron were "social in nature." How? What is "culture"? Can a corporation really have a culture, even one based on greed? Or is a corporation just an amalgamation of individuals? Can culture really account for individual wrongdoing, and if so, who is to blame for such wrongdoing—the individual people or the culture? Should we have corporate culture reform? How might such reform be accomplished?

2. The author argues that drastic revisions of accounting and legal rules and standards are probably not necessary. Others have argued that deregulation, and legislation and judicial decisions (making it more difficult for shareholders to sue corporations) are to blame. *See* William S. Lerach, *Plundering America: How American Investors Got Taken for Trillions by Corporate Insiders, the Rise of the New Corporate Kleptocracy*, 8 Stan. J.L. Bus. & Fin. 69 (2002). Are the two views incompatible? Was it that the watchdogs slipped the leash, or that they failed to bark? If the rules did not fail at Enron, how can we make sure in the future that those charged with the enforcement of the rules actually will enforce them?

3. Neal Batson argues that "[m]anaging a corporation's business affairs in order to achieve, and then report, steady earnings growth, healthy cash flow and a strong balance sheet is what good managers are expected to do. These efforts, of course,

and motivations: Stockholders over-value risk (that is the point of leverage) while creditors undervalue it. *See* John D. Ayer & Michael L. Bernstein, *Bankruptcy In Practice* 137 (ABI 2002) (presenting explanation of this conflict of interest and illustrating it with risk-adjusted balance sheet presentation). Stockholders of insolvent corporations—who face the highest risks—always stand to gain from delayed liquidation; it gives them more time for their risk to pay off. *Id.* If a business has debt, this conflict of interest is guaranteed to exist.

must be consistent with GAAP and applicable disclosure standards under the securities laws. There are many tools that business managers have at their disposal to achieve and report earnings and other financial results. Among those tools are structured finance transactions using SPEs. There is nothing improper about the use of structured finance and SPEs to achieve and report business results. Enron, however, used structured finance to report results it had not achieved." Batson Report, *supra* note 6, at 50. Do you agree? Is the distinction between illegitimate and legitimate uses of SPEs a distinction without a difference? If you've earned $10 million, why would you use an SPE to achieve and report those earnings? What makes Enron's use of SPEs illegitimate, and what might a legitimate use of SPEs look like?

4. *What is an SPE, anyway?* There are no hard and fast rules as to what constitutes an SPE. SPEs may take any legally recognized form, including corporations, partnerships, and trusts, and it may be difficult to determine whether or not an entity is a SPE. The Financial Accounting Standards Board, however, tends to conceptualize SPEs as entities whose powers are significantly limited by contractual agreements or their charters. Thus, the length of time an entity is to be in existence and the restrictions placed upon it are prominent factors in the accounting literature on determining whether an entity is an SPE. *See* Powers Report, *supra* note 6, at 37–38. Based on this essay, what other characteristics of SPEs can you infer?

5. The author argues that fraud is not that complex, and that the old adage pertains: if it sounds too good to be true, it probably is. Do you agree? If the author is correct, do investors also bear responsibility for debacles such as Enron? How much? How might people be trained (compelled?) to pay attention to possible fraudulent conduct and to take action to protect themselves from it?

6. *What is a Ponzi scheme?* After World War I and the collapse of the Gold Standard, the relative values of many European currencies and the currencies of those nations pegged to the European currencies were fluctuating. The exchange rates for postal coupons, however, had been set before the war. Thus, a coupon bought in a country with a depressed currency could be redeemed for greater value in a country whose currency was worth more. Charles Ponzi claimed to have discovered a lucrative arbitrage opportunity in these postal coupons, an opportunity that would yield investors a return of more than 50% in 90 days. Ponzi, however, was not investing in postal coupons at all. Instead, he was using present investors' money to pay past investors their 50% returns. This is what is meant by a "pyramid scheme." Incoming funds are used to pay off past investors. *See* Douglas G. Baird & Robert K. Rasmussen, *Four (or Five) Easy Lessons from Enron*, 55 VAND. L. REV. 1787-88 (2002).

   Given that description, is Enron a pyramid or Ponzi scheme? Does the existence of the stock market as an intermediary between investors and the company make any difference in your analysis?

7. Do you agree with the author that the use of stock option incentive programs increased the temptation to lose sight of the principle of stewardship? Why wouldn't

having his personal capital at stake *increase* a director's vigilance in regard to the oversight of management? *See* Charles M. Elson, *The Duty of Care, Compensation, and Stock Ownership,* 63 U. Cin. L. Rev. 649, 690–92 (1995). Based upon what happened at Enron, what reasons might we have for not wanting directors to become active equity participants in the corporate pecuniary interest?

8. You represent Elmer Bloedsinn, the CEO of True Interest Fidelity Corporation ("TIF"). Elmer is not only CEO of TIF, but also sits on TIF's highly regarded board of directors. The Board wants to approve an innovative proposal by TIF's CFO, Laurie Lackluster. Laurie has proposed setting up a Special Purpose Entity (Star Wars Limited Partnership), which will conduct millions of dollars of business with TIF and will enable TIF to transfer some of its debt off-balance-sheet and maintain its credit rating. Laurie proposes that, since she is intimately familiar with TIF and its needs, she is the ideal person to run Star Wars, LLP. The Board recognizes the good sense of this proposal and wishes to allow Laurie to run Star Wars, LLP while remaining CFO of TIF. Elmer thinks this is a wonderful idea (he and Laurie are good friends), but wants to make sure that he will not be doing anything to get himself in trouble. What do you advise him? What duties does Elmer have in this situation, and what liabilities might he face? Who should represent Laurie in any negotiations? Can TIF's general counsel represent Laurie?

9. The author argues for a "flatter" bureaucratic structure. What might such a structure look like? Do you agree that such a structure would help prevent organizational failures such as Enron, or do you think the problem is with bureaucracy itself? If the problem is with bureaucracy itself, what alternative forms of organization might you propose? Are there any reforms in the manner in which boards of directors are formed or operate that could assist them in meeting their fiduciary duties? Does the size of a board matter? What about the size of its committees? What about the ratio of insiders to outsiders on the board as a whole? On committees?

10. You are an attorney in the firm of Drudge, Umber, Mather, and Brown, which represents Lambert International Energy Corporation ("LIE"). LIE wishes to engage in structured finance operations involving "high risk" accounting and SPEs. Having examined these operations, you have determined that LIE's proposals are in technical compliance with GAAP. You also believe, however, that the operations would create an image of the company that did not actually reflect its true financial status. What should you advise LIE in regard to these transactions? What duties and liabilities might you have in regard to the advice you give? What should you do if LIE's CEO rejects your advice?

Lessons for Teaching Energy Law

Jacqueline Lang Weaver*

> Enron was synonymous with Houston, and now it is synonymous with shame.
>
> *—Houston Chronicle* editorial, on the
> anniversary of Enron's bankruptcy[1]

For an energy law professor and former energy economist who has lived in Houston for more than thirty years, writing the two essays in this book has been a painful experience. Two Houstonians have committed suicide—high-ranking executives at Enron and El Paso, respectively, seemingly in despair over what investigations of their companies' activities were disclosing. Their families grieve in ways we cannot fathom. Many Houstonians, especially former employees of Enron, are out of work; the life savings of many others have evaporated in the collapse of this company that everyone once trusted. The office vacancy rate climbs as trading activity moves elsewhere. The city itself discovered that Enron cheated its own hometown to escape a million dollars in local property taxes, claiming that a warehouse on North Shepherd contained items worth only $500 rather then the $20 million worth of computers and telecom equipment stored there, like a Potemkin village, for a falsely painted future.[2]

---

* A.A. White Professor of Law, University of Houston Law Center. This chapter is excerpted, in slightly revised form, from the last section of a longer article, titled *Can Energy Markets Be Trusted?*, with the copyright permission of the *Houston Business and Tax Law Journal*, an electronic journal at the University of Houston Law Center. The full article will appear on this journal's website at www.hbtlj.org in early fall 2003 and printed in hard copy in 4 HOUS. BUS. & TAX L. J. ___ (2004). A longer section of the article appears in this book *supra* at 237–299, and the author's grateful acknowledgments appear in the first footnote of that chapter.

[1] *AFTERMATH/ Enron's Affairs Remain Tangled, but Houston Recovering*, HOUS. CHRON., Dec. 4, 2002, at 42A.

[2] Tom Fowler, *The Fall of Enron/Enron Division to Take Tax Rap/Harris County Due $1 Million*, HOUS. CHRON., Dec. 17, 2002, at 1A. While Enron claimed the warehouse contained virtually nothing for tax purposes, Enron recruiters would visit the warehouse with job candidates to impress them with its plans for broadband expansion by showing them the enormous amount of equipment stored there. *Id.*

Enron Field, the city's spectacular new baseball stadium, is now Minute Maid Park—named for the orange juice company that most didn't even know was headquartered in a Houston suburb. In every lobby of every major art or music institution in the city, the Ken Lay name appears as a chief donor to the city's vibrant arts scene. The museums and opera and symphony scramble for funds that once flowed from Enron's sleek, silvery tower. The society column advises Houston's movers and shakers how to behave when meeting the Lays inadvertently in a restaurant. Some of my students still work at Enron, modeling assets for sale or working on documents for the bankruptcy case. Others are putting in fifteen-hour days of document preparation for lawsuits and regulatory appearances, representing the tangle of energy companies, banks, individuals, and law firms caught in the Enron web. This young city, whose very name connotes the energy capital of the world, is subdued and anxious.

And I wonder: What lessons in lawyering, ethics, money, and greed might be learned from this long, sad and shameful look at the actions of many, many participants, both in the newly restructured energy markets and in the broader financial and securities markets that other essayists have discussed in this book? As we have seen, the new electric markets are intricately intertwined with the financial markets for derivatives and futures and with the capital markets, so essential for an industry requiring massive capital investments to fund long-term infrastructure in transmission and generation.[3] Are there parallel lessons to be drawn from Wall Street and Houston about the regulation of markets?

The financial derivatives and electricity markets are alike in two main respects: they are very complicated, and they allow traders to make "a lifetime of wealth" in just a few transactions. Many sophisticated observers consider this a dangerous combination that threatens the stability of our national economic well-being, not merely the fortunes of some of the companies involved in the deals. Some have called anew for ethical conduct by market participants to guard against this danger. Others have called for a return to principle-based rules for our accounting and tax laws, which will better honor the spirit and intent of the public interest meant to be served by these laws. As a recent Senate committee found, the dense thicket of tax and accounting rules allowed Enron's pool of lawyers, bankers, and accountants to exercise a remarkable ability "to parse the law to produce a result that was contrary to its spirit."[4] Similarly, the dense thicket of market protocols in electricity invites the "best and brightest" of energy market participants to find loopholes to exploit on their way to million-dollar bonuses.

---

[3] *See* Jacqueline Lang Weaver, *Can Energy Markets Be Trusted? The Effect of the Rise and Fall of Enron on Energy Markets, this book* at 237–299, especially Part III, titled *Enron and the California Energy Crisis*.

[4] Staff of Joint Comm. on Taxation, 1 REPORT OF INVESTIGATION OF ENRON CORP. AND RELATED ENTITIES REGARDING FEDERAL TAX AND COMPENSATION ISSUES, AND POLICY RECOMMENDATIONS 22 (Feb. 2003).

To other observers, the key to preventing Enron-type scandals is disclosure.[5] But, what if the transactions are too complex for directors or investors to understand, and too "cancerously intricate"[6] for regulators to monitor? What good is disclosure of something that almost no one can understand? So complex have structured financing transactions become that one expert argues disclosure to investors is necessarily imperfect. The disclosure must either oversimplify the transaction or provide detail beyond the level of even sophisticated investors to understand. In Steven Schwarcz's view, "complexity forces a rethinking of the long-held disclosure paradigm of securities law."[7] Instead, securities law must be revised to eliminate the conflict of interests that can affect management's business judgment in entering into these transactions.

Enron certainly thought complexity would shield it from liability for manipulating California's energy markets. Here are an Enron executive's notes from a meeting in Portland, Oregon with lawyers in late 2000 to discuss Enron's role in the California energy crisis: "No one can prove, given the complexity of our portfolio."[8] In energy markets, industry participants resist broad but vague rules that ban "anticompetitive conduct" or "abuse of market power," and then exploit the legal loopholes in the thicket of protocols that they reverse-engineer and master.

Why do so many actors in the tax, securities, financial, and energy markets find it so easy, ethically and morally, to violate the spirit of laws enacted to protect the public interest? The answer seems simple: Because that's where the really big money is.

---

[5] *See, e.g.,* Diana B. Henriques, *The Brick Stood Up Before, But Now?,* N.Y. TIMES, Mar. 10, 2002, at 1 (quoting Ronald Gilson, a Stanford law professor).

[6] The quoted phrase is by Professor Lawrence Friedman, as noted in Adam Liptak, *Is That Legal?,* N.Y. TIMES, Oct. 6, 2002, Sec. 7, at 20 (reviewing LAWRENCE M. FRIEDMAN, HISTORY OF AMERICAN LAW 1985).

[7] STEVEN L. SCHWARCZ, RETHINKING THE DISCLOSURE PARADIGM IN A WORLD OF COMPLEXITY 1 (Duke Univ. School of Law, Working Paper No. 34, 2002) *available at* www.law.duke.edu/fac/workingpapers.html.

[8] Richard A. Oppel, Jr., *Despite Doubters, Enron Waited to Stop Its Trades, Senate is Told,* N.Y. TIMES, May 16, 2002, at A1. Another example is noteworthy: J.P Morgan Chase, the large bank that facilitated some of Enron's deals, appears to have disguised loans to Enron by burying the loans in its trading books for commodities or equities derivatives where neither the bank nor the eleven insurance companies that guaranteed the bank's repayment by Enron could find them or easily understand them, something that the Vice Chairman of the bank felt "queasy about," but appears nonetheless to have approved. Kurt Eichenwald, *Judge Allows Use of E-Mail as Evidence in Bank Trial,* N.Y. TIMES, Dec. 24, 2002, at 4; Lingling Wei & Colleen Debaise, *Enron Trades Were Circular, J.P. Morgan Official Testifies,* WALL ST. J., Dec. 3, 2002 (online). In January 2003, J.P. Morgan announced it would take a $1.3 billion charge for the fourth quarter, largely to settle litigation over its involvement with Enron, including $400 million that it paid to settle the lawsuit with the insurers, one day before the suit went to a jury. Christopher Oster & Randall Smith, *Enron Deals Cost J.P. Morgan; Bank Plans $1.3 Billion Charge,* WALL ST. J., Jan. 3, 2003, at A1 (online). This bank and others still face class action lawsuits brought by investors alleging the banks participated in Enron's fraud on investors.

Professor Lawrence Friedman, a preeminent scholar of the role of lawyers in America's system of justice, has written: "It is the business of the lawyer to tolerate and master artifice," for lawyers grow rich from their knowledge of these cancerously intricate fields of law.[9] Political scientists have posited that American society is so litigious because our political institutions reflect a Constitutional mistrust of strong centralized power at the federal level.[10] Without powerful regulatory agencies to protect them or to provide social safety nets, Americans turn to the courts to vindicate their rights to be protected from harm and injustice, from discrimination and pollution, from scalding coffee, unsafe cars, unscrupulous sellers, and negligent doctors. "Adversarial legalism" is the "American way of law," premised on the failure of government regulators to protect its citizens.[11] Business launched a successful counter-offensive in the 1990s, pressing for tort reform and other changes to diminish the "litigation explosion" that threatened business' well-being. Congress reacted by making it harder for corporate shareholders to sue accountants. The result: accounting firms became more aggressive in pursuing dubious practices that pleased corporate clients but misled shareholders. Congress removed the right to sue without providing an alternative means of enforcing the law, such as by strengthening the effectiveness of the Securities and Exchange Commission. Class action litigation is now filling the void.

In December 2002, Judge Melinda Harmon of the Federal District Court in Houston refused to dismiss class action lawsuits brought on behalf of investors against defendant banks, investment houses, and law firms that had assisted Enron in structuring its many deals, tax shelters, and Special Purpose Entities.[12] In light of Enron's bank-

---

[9] LAWRENCE M. FRIEDMAN, HISTORY OF AMERICAN LAW 24 (1985); *see also* Gillian K. Hadfield, *The Price of Law: How the Market for Lawyers Distorts the Justice System*, 98 MICH. L. REV. 951 (2000) (analyzing how the complexity of law and legal reasoning creates a "natural" barrier to entry by limiting the number of entrants with the cognitive aptitude to engage in sophisticated, commercial transactions. This effect of legal complexity, coupled with lawyers' state-granted monopoly on coercive dispute resolution, creates powerful incentives to charge legal fees above those that would emerge from a competitive market. The legal profession is "propelled by market forces to devote itself disproportionately to the management of the economic relationships of commerce and not the management of just relations among individuals and the state." *Id.* at 957).

[10] Daphne Eviator, *Is Litigation a Blight, or Built In?*, N.Y. TIMES, Nov. 23, 2002, at A21.

[11] *Id.* (citing the work of Robert A. Kagan, a political science professor and the author of ADVERSARIAL LEGALISM: THE AMERICAN WAY OF LIFE (2001), and THOMAS F. BURKE, LAWYERS, LAWSUITS AND LEGAL RIGHTS: THE BATTLE OVER LITIGATION IN AMERICAN SOCIETY (2002)).

Even sophisticated businessmen and wealthy investors do not appear to understand the caveats and disclaimers that appear after the "comforting assurances" in the opinion letters that law firms write for tax shelters that are being promoted by accounting firms. A new round of litigation brought by wealthy Americans against accounting firms and lawyers seems to prove the American way. David Cay Johnston, *Costly Questions Arise on Legal Opinions for Tax Shelters*, N.Y. TIMES, Feb. 9, 2003, at 25.

[12] *In re* Enron Corp. Securities, Derivatives, and ERISA Litigation, 235 F. Supp. 2d 549 (S.D. Texas 2002).

ruptcy, these entities are the major sources of funds from which injured plaintiffs may be able to recover, should they ultimately prevail. Judge Harmon ruled that the banks and law firms that served as corporate advisors to Enron could be deemed to be substantial participants in a fraud if they constructed transactions with the knowledge that the deals would mislead investors about a company's finances.[13] Some law professors and practicing lawyers have noted that this one decision may accomplish what no amount of regulatory reform has yet achieved: prevent another Enron from happening again.[14] Adversarial legalism aimed at lawyers themselves may be the American way to clean up our securities markets.

There is no analogue, however, for suing those experts, consultants, lobbyists, and advisors who oversold Californians on the dazzling benefits that power markets would bring to its citizens. In electricity markets, it is well to heed the advice of *The Economist*. This respected voice of market-based capitalism surveyed the Enron-related reforms and aftermath and concluded:

> Enronitis showed that there is no substitute for constant scrutiny and questioning [by the individual investor]. . . . [T]he price of the marketplace has to be eternal vigilance.[15]

The same message was delivered in a *Time* magazine cover in a tone more familiar to the American Generation X'ers who sit in our classrooms:

> So many choices, and no one to trust. In today's world . . . YOU'RE ON YOUR OWN, BABY.[16]

---

[13] *Id.* at 704–705:

Vinson & Elkins was necessarily privy to its client's [Enron's] confidences and intimately involved in and familiar with the creation and structure of its numerous businesses, and thus, as a law firm highly sophisticated in commercial matters, had to know of the alleged ongoing illicit and fraudulent conduct. . . . Vinson & Elkins chose to engage in illegal activity for and with its client in return for lucrative fees. Contrary to the Rules of Professional Conduct, it did not resign and thereby violated its professional principles and ethics. Nevertheless, had Vinson & Elkins remained silent publicly, the attorney/client relationship and the traditional rule of privity for suit against lawyers might protect Vinson & Elkins from liability to nonclients. . . . but the complaint goes into great detail to demonstrate that Vinson & Elkins did not remain silent, but chose not once, but frequently, to make statements to the public about Enron's business and financial situation. . . . Vinson & Elkins was not merely a drafter, but essentially a co-author of the documents it created for public consumption. . . .

Id.

[14] Kurt Eichenwald, *A Higher Standard for Corporate Advice*, N.Y. TIMES, Dec. 23, 2002, at A1.

[15] *Investor Self-Protection—Enron a Year On*, THE ECONOMIST, Nov. 30, 2002, at 12.

[16] Cover, TIME, Jan. 2002.

Now that I have the "Power to Choose"[17] my retail electric provider, I sure hope that some regulators are being eternally vigilant on my behalf. It's awfully hard going it alone.

---

[17] This is the name of the website that allows Texas consumers to choose a retail electricity provider. *See* www.powertochoose.org.

Business Education and Corporate Accounting Scandals: Lessons on Accounting Information and Investor Trust

Bala G. Dharan*

1. INTRODUCTION

The Enron failure and other spectacular corporate accounting and governance scandals of recent years have several important lessons for what we need to teach in the classroom and how we should integrate the material across different subjects, such as finance, accounting, law, and ethics. No one is holding the business schools responsible for the dramatic failings of their students who starred in these corporate scandals—not yet, anyway. For every scandal-tainted MBA, one could point to hundreds of other business leaders who are contributing positively to society as good citizens and achievers. But this does not mean that educators should escape without any blame either.

The early reaction of business school professors to the scandals has been to use the scandals enthusiastically as classroom material to supplement whatever is normally taught in the class, or to even offer specific new courses to cover all aspects of the scandals—courses that are marketed as "all Enron, all the time." The scandals have become popular "case studies" for class use in courses such as accounting, auditing, corporate finance, investment banking, business strategy, ethics, and so on. However, as we assimilate the scandals into our case lore, academics need to also ask whether the scandals point to any fundamental problems or weaknesses in the structure of our curriculum and in the way we approach the teaching of fundamental concepts in business. If so, merely including case studies and reading about the scandals in existing classes will not serve as an adequate response to the scandals. Assuming that structural reforms in business curriculum are needed, we will need to address them aggressively and soon, so that future business leaders do not get drawn into the same kinds of business situations and decisions that characterize the current scandals.

* J. Howard Creekmore Professor of Accounting, Jesse H. Jones Graduate School of Management, Rice University, Houston.

917

By curriculum structure, I mean both what is taught in a given course or class and how the different courses are integrated together over the course of the degree program or study plan to achieve the desired goals of education. Curriculum design issues are almost always complex and hard to tackle in a university because they bring up questions about how professors will work together to deliver the desired learning objectives of the school. Surprisingly, pedagogical concepts such as "integrating across courses" are hard to adopt, for most professors. Professors are more used to specializing in one subject and teaching it well in a classroom, and they usually do not want to be bothered with what is taught in other courses. Compounding this notion of specialization, business school faculty members are generally organized in a strict departmental structure. Professors are generally assigned to a department that is their home base for everything—from recruiting to promotion, course allocations, budgets, etc. As a result, curriculum design exercises often turn out to be political land mines. Faculty members may try to defend a particular curriculum issue, with the knowledge that changes may mean some departments winning (and others losing) faculty positions (the ability to hire more faculty members) and budgets. Nevertheless, curriculum changes do take place, albeit infrequently.

The magnitude of investor losses and the complexity of management fraud seen in recent scandals suggest that it may indeed be time to get prepared for one of these infrequent curriculum battles. The scandals and the resulting stock market losses show that there was a huge failure of understanding the important informational role of financial accounting disclosures among corporate managers, their accounting counterparts, the internal control people, the corporate counsel and legal support, and the top management and the board. Such a large-scale abuse of accounting systems, and the corresponding failure of so many business disciplines to understand the role of accounting in our capital markets, clearly suggests the possibility of fundamental flaws in how each of these disciplines approaches its role relative to the corporation and each of the other disciplines. If so, solutions to the crisis must involve not only regulatory reforms and changes in governance procedures, but also reforms and revisions to the system of training and education of managers that might have led so many managers and accountants to abuse the principles of accounting. This in turn suggests the need for us to reexamine business curriculum issues to prevent repeats of the scandals.

2. INVESTOR TRUST AND THE INFORMATIONAL ROLE OF ACCOUNTING

While the typical corporate structure of separation of powers among competing units obviously provides for several built-in conflicts among the units, the potential conflicts between accounting and non-accounting functional areas are especially important for our purpose, since it is accounting's historical role as neutral and objective recorders and transmitters of information that was most likely compromised in Enron and all of the other recent scandal-ridden companies. At the core of these conflicts is a failure by managers to grasp the critical role of accounting disclosures in building and maintaining investor trust, and the equally critical role of investor trust in a company's ability to raise capital and survive as a corporation.

Public companies and public capital markets exist only because investors believe that financial disclosures produced by a company's management are trustworthy. Since investors cannot personally monitor a corporate board or management's decisions, they rely entirely on the financial statements and other financial disclosures from the company to verify that their investments are safeguarded and, more important, to monitor and interpret the future economic prospects of the company. Despite advances in communications, including the advent of the Internet, the fact remains that there is simply no substitute for formal financial reports when it comes to providing reliable and trustworthy information to investors. Company managers are not expected to just use public forums, such as media appearance, webcasts, or press releases, to communicate financial data to investors. These alternative sources of information can and do coexist with accounting disclosures, but investors and regulators have come to regard financial accounting reports produced by company management as the primary source of verifiable and reliable information about a company. Thus, in modern capital markets, investor trust is entirely determined by the ability of corporate financial statements being perceived as neutral and objective while providing useful and timely information. Once accounting information is suspected of not having these fundamental characteristics, public capital market participants have no choice but flee to the exit doors.

It is important to distinguish between what accounting can do and cannot do for a company. Good accounting is not a substitute for a poor business model. Customers of a company do not necessarily read financial reports before buying the products and services. A company must still need to have a well-defined business purpose, a clearly articulated business strategy, products and services that are desired by customers and which can be made and delivered profitably, and effective management to develop and execute strategy. Having reliable financial reporting will not prevent a company from failing if its basic business model and execution are weak. However, as a conveyer of trustworthy and useful information to investors, accounting can and does affect a public company's very existence. While a failure of a business strategy can hurt a company, companies do routinely fix business problems and go on to achieve success. However, failure of accounting to fulfill its role as producer and conveyer of trustworthy and useful information can doom a public company to bankruptcy by shutting down all routes of access to capital markets for the company's financial needs.

Modern industrial societies understand this critical do-or-die role of accounting information for the existence of well-functioning capital markets and public companies. Since trust in financial information is so critical, the United States and most other major countries have developed over the years several layers of corporate governance and regulations to reinforce the system of trust. These layers include requiring audits of financial reports by external auditors, having regulatory systems to monitor and regulate the external auditors, requiring adherence to formal accounting and disclosure standards developed by independent external organizations, such as the Financial Accounting Standards Board ("FASB"), and enforcing the accounting standards and disclosure rules through governmental agencies such as the Securities and Exchange

Commission ("SEC"). Other corporate governance requirements, such as board audit committees consisting of independent directors, and regulatory provisions, such as oversight by stock exchanges, are intended to further strengthen the disclosure system's trustworthiness. But at the core of the entire system of disclosures is the trust placed by investors that corporate management will provide them with reliable and useful information about the company's operations.

3. PRESSURE FOR EARNINGS MANAGEMENT

Corporate managers who fail to grasp the critical role of accounting information in keeping investor trust (or fail to understand the importance of this trust in accessing capital markets) are likely to end up treating the accounting function as just another unit of the corporation to be deployed and managed for shareholder value maximization. This, in turn, will very likely lead to business situations where managers have the temptation to compromise the fundamental informational role of accounting and destroy the desired qualities of accounting information, namely its reliability and investor-relevance, in favor of other corporate objectives of the moment. Managers trying to meet any number of legitimate corporate goals, such as sales targets, cost targets, analysts' earnings expectations, and bonus plan targets, or who are trying to make critical investment and financing decisions to achieve these targets, can suddenly find accounting rules and systems standing in their way. If corporate managers do not understand that even "temporary" compromises of the accounting rules and systems can lead to a deadly loss of investor trust, then there is nothing to stop the pressure on a cost center—such as accounting—to acquiesce and move out of the way.

There is some evidence that, over the past two decades, companies have shifted away from treating accounting as a desirable independent function, and have instead restructured the accounting operations in ways that put internal accounting processes squarely in the way of other competing corporate goals. For example, several studies of Enron's internal control failures have discussed the inherent conflicts that arose every day between the risk assessment and control ("RAC") division of Enron, charged with measuring and monitoring corporate-wide risk and given the power to reject risky projects, and the managers, who were trying to get their projects approved. On the one hand, given the deal-making culture prevalent in the company, operating managers were provided incentives to be dealmakers and were rewarded with large bonuses only when their projects were approved. On the other hand, not only were there no incentives or bonuses for the RAC managers when projects were rejected, the RAC managers were also reporting to senior management, who also benefited with large bonuses when projects were approved by the RAC.

Faced with pressures to cut costs and outsource non-essential functions, corporate managers have resorted to cutting down or even gutting groups such as accounting, which are often viewed by senior managers as non-revenue producing "cost-centers." Accounting managers (controllers, chief accounting officers, etc.) have increasingly been relegated to less visible roles within companies, and their functions are viewed mainly as a non-essential data-processing field that can be outsourced if necessary, rather than as a critical link in the communication chain between the company and investors. Not surprisingly, this has led to more frequent pressures on the accounting system to manage earnings and other disclosures for the purpose of other desired corporate purposes.

4. LESSONS FOR EDUCATING MANAGERS

This discussion of the changing role of corporate accounting suggests that an environment for earnings management is now pervasive in modern corporations. As earnings management escalates, there is an increased risk that the critical informational qualities of accounting reports, including neutrality, objectivity, and informational relevance, will be compromised. Our current regulatory responses to the recent corporate scandals, such as the passage of the Sarbanes-Oxley Act and the creation of the Public Company Accounting Oversight Board ("PCAOB"), have focused mainly on strengthening the systems of checks and balances, especially the corporate board and the external audit functions. However, these measures, while necessary and important, do not address the fundamental structural issues within corporations discussed here— issues that pit accounting against other business functions and create pressures from line managers on accountants to massage the accounting numbers. In addition to the new regulatory changes in auditing and improvements in corporate governance system, we need to also examine how managers are currently educated in business schools about the role of accounting information and consider whether the current business curriculum perhaps reinforces and supports the confrontational environment between managers and accounting that exist in many companies.

We will start with possible problems and needed changes in the way that accounting and finance are taught in business schools. It makes sense to focus on these two subjects first because almost all of the controversial areas of earnings management and accounting abuse in the past three decades have taken place in areas where line management crosses paths with financial accounting and reporting. These intersections include leases, derivatives, consolidation, mergers and acquisitions, pensions, securitization of assets, vendor financing, barter transactions, and convertible debt.

Consider leases as an example. Managers have several incentives to push leases off balance sheet, and this has led to several decades of battles between the accounting profession and corporate management. After more than a decade of debates and inaction in the 1960s, the accounting profession finally passed a rule (FASB Statement No. 13) in 1977 to force the capitalization of certain leases and to put them on balance sheets as assets and liabilities. However, management intent on keeping leases off balance sheet soon responded with dozens of loophole-exploiting implementation tricks. The last twenty-five years have seen a continuing battle between the FASB and the corporate finance world on this issue. Despite the active pursuit of loopholes by the FASB, the net result of the lease accounting battles is that most companies that do not wish to report leases on balance sheets manage to achieve that objective today. For example, according to the 2002 annual report of Delta Airlines, it has only $127 million of leases reported as capital leases, on the balance sheet, representing the present value of about $172 million of payments over the next several years. But the footnotes reveal that an additional $12,744 million of future lease payments are classified as operating leases and are not listed on the balance sheets. In other words, the liabilities representing about 98.7 percent of all future lease payments are kept off balance sheet by the company.

The lease accounting battles were just a precursor to the much larger accounting battles that have followed during the 1980s and 1990s in the areas of acquisition accounting, consolidation of off-balance-sheet entities, derivatives accounting, and accounting for stock options. All of these areas involve corporate management goals that potentially conflict directly with accounting's need to report neutral, objective, and useful information to investors. In acquisition accounting, companies invented the pooling method of accounting instead of using the traditional purchase account-ing to keep goodwill and other intangible assets off balance sheet, thereby understating the actual future reported costs of acquisitions (represented by goodwill amortization and other depreciation charges). Attempts by the FASB to restrict the use of the pool-ing method did not prevent the method from becoming the preferred way to structure merger transactions during the stock market boom of the late 1990s. In a related area, companies trying to keep whole groups of assets off balance sheet have run straight into traditional accounting concepts of entity and consolidation, and have resorted to creative techniques to skirt the consolidation rules. In the case of Enron, this led to the creation of thousands of so-called special purpose entities ("SPEs"). In the stock op-tions area, corporate management wanted to benefit from the incentivizing effect of granting stock options to their employees (and to themselves) but did not want to show the effective cost of the options in their income statements. Finally, in the grow-ing field of risk management and derivatives, corporate managements that are trying to adopt innovative financial products (ones that try to bridge the gap between liabili-ties and equities) have generally come to perceive the traditional accounting rules that make a fundamental distinction between contingent liabilities, liabilities, and equity as major impediments.

An examination of the financial reporting problems in these so-called financial en-gineering areas shows that, in many cases, the auditors and accountants struggling to come up with appropriate accounting rules for a given financial situation are not really aware of the history of the controversy in that area, or of the powerful motivations of managers to skirt existing accounting rules. From an educator's point of view, the problem can be traced back to the compartmentalized way that business courses, such as accounting, finance, and strategy, are taught in most business schools. As a result, students, who are really future business managers, are rarely exposed in the classroom to the potential conflicts between the objectives of corporate management (such as financial engineering) and the objectives of corporate accounting.

To illustrate the types of changes that would need to be made in business school teaching, look at the way that accounting is currently taught in many business schools.

(Of course, a similar detailed analysis of curricula should be done for other areas, such as finance, strategy, and ethics.) Consistent with the traditional focus of accounting on collecting and recording data and producing financial reports, accounting courses in business schools have emphasized a rules-based and transaction-oriented approach to teaching business applications of accounting. For example, in the case of lease accounting, students might learn how to record business transactions related to leases from a lessee's and lessor's point of view, what the rules are for classifying leases as capital leases or operating leases, how lease assets and obligations are estimated in the case of capitalized leases, how the lease payment can be separated into principal and interest, how gains or losses are recognized in a sale-leaseback situation, and how synthetic leases can be reported. What is most clearly missing in this list of learning objectives is getting an appreciation for the business contexts in which lease accounting conflicts between managers and accountants arise.

Other courses, such as finance, do, of course, take up the specific business contexts in which leasing decisions may occur. However, the learning objectives in these courses are usually not designed to use or even complement what has already been taught in accounting. For example, in finance classes, the focus of class discussion is primarily the valuation role of cash flows. The essence of modern corporate finance courses is that only cash flows matter for valuation. To the extent that accounting is perceived as relevant in this approach, the focus is on the deconstruction of accounting data for the construction of cash flows. For example, depreciation, an accounting concept, is introduced in finance classes solely to calculate its "tax-shield" benefit (arising from the tax deductibility of depreciation) and the resulting incremental cash flows, and not for any other informational role that depreciation expense may play in measuring income or investment returns. Similarly, students rarely are given an opportunity to think about the informational role of lease accounting information, such as the effect of reporting lease liabilities on the balance sheet and the corresponding effect on the stock market's perception of the company's risk and the reliability of its information.

In fact, it is not uncommon to find, in popular finance textbooks, statements that categorically dismiss accounting rules and accounting-based financial statements (particularly the income statement) as irrelevant for corporate finance and valuation except for the help they provide in the computation of cash flows. Consider, for example, how a popular finance textbook,[1] widely used in many MBA programs, introduces and explains the purpose of accounting and accounting reports and their uses in finance.

- **Finance is on top, and accounting reports to it**: "In large firms, finance activity is usually associated with a top officer of the firm, such as the vice president and chief financial officer, and some lesser officers. . . . Reporting to the chief financial officer are the treasurer and the controller. . . . The

---

[1] STEPHEN A. ROSS, RANDOLPH W. WESTERFIELD, & JEFFREY JAFFE, CORPORATE FINANCE (6th ed. 2002).

controller handles the accounting function, which includes taxes, cost and financial accounting, and information systems."[2] (Note the subservience of the accounting function to corporate finance, and the lack of mention of the accounting function's role in producing information for investors.)

- **Conflict between accounting rules and corporate goals:** "By generally accepted accounting principles (GAAP), the sale [on credit] is recorded even though the customer has yet to pay. . . . From an accounting perspective [the company] seems to be profitable. However, the perspective of corporate finance is different. It focuses on cash flows. . . . Value creation depends on cash flows."[3] (Note how the old accounting concept of revenue recognition is dismissed.)

- **Questionable use of financial statements for finance:** "Chapter 2 describes the basic accounting statements used for reporting corporate activity. . . . It will become obvious to you in the next several chapters that knowing how to determine cash flow [from the financial statements] helps the financial manager make better decisions."[4]

- **The value-irrelevance of the balance sheet:** "Many users of financial statements, including managers and investors, want to know the value of the firm, not its cost. This is not found on the balance sheet. In fact, many of the true resources of the firm do not appear on the balance sheet. . . ."[5] (Interestingly, even as finance books dismiss the balance sheet as value-irrelevant, finance researchers increasingly are elevating the book value information from the balance sheet to a central role in risk measurement and asset pricing models.)

One could go on. There are dozens more of similar quotes questioning the validity, purpose, and usefulness of financial reports and accounting information. The income statement gets a special trashing.

The purpose here is not to criticize this one book. A cursory examination of any top-selling finance textbook will show a similar sprinkling of statements that often reflect a basic lack of understanding of the critical role of accounting in measuring corporate performance and conveying it to investors in a neutral, believable way. Without meaning to do so, the finance courses start off by, effectively, questioning the very purpose of preparing financial reports using accounting concepts that have been developed over centuries. Rather than trying to help the student understand and integrate the objectives of accounting and finance, the net effect is to paint a corporate picture that dismisses the role of accounting managers as trivial, secondary, and even disruptive to value-creation, even as finance managers nobly try to maximize corpo-

---

[2] *Id.* at 5.

[3] *Id.* at 7.

[4] *Id.* at 22.

[5] *Id.* at 24.

rate value. The student, who may have just come off four months of an accounting course, is left wondering if it was all just a waste of time and tuition dollars.

To summarize, compartmentalized teaching of accounting and finance does not achieve the goal of helping the student learn the business contexts in which financial decisions are made as well as helping the student to understand the importance of measuring and conveying the financial information to market participants. The current failure of accounting education to help students understand the finance and business contexts in which accounting transactions take place has led to the training of primarily rule-oriented accountants. Not surprisingly, these transaction-oriented accountants are quickly sidelined in the corporate world, as the decision-makers try to "get the deals done." The lack of a principles-based learning approach and the lack of mastery of the modern business decision contexts have also led to a generation of auditors who focus more on the strict application of rules rather than on the relevance of the resulting data to decision-makers, such as investors and creditors.

5. CONCLUSION—THE GOOD NEWS

One way to measure the flexible response of a profession to structural changes is to examine the number and variety of new courses offered by the area's faculty over time. On this, the news on the accounting front does not appear encouraging. The bulk of financial accounting courses offered in most business school still consists of introductory accounting, intermediate accounting, advanced accounting, and financial statement analysis, along with a smattering of other traditional courses, such as accounting theory and international accounting. A visitor from the 1950s would find the order of the accounting courses in the curriculum, and often the content, familiar and unchanged. However, despite this appearance of no change, many positive changes are indeed occurring under the surface in many business schools. The good news is that many accounting and business programs nationwide are starting to recognize the shortcomings in business education that arise from the compartmentalized teaching of critical business concepts. For example, a monograph published by the American Accounting Association[6] helped to bring to the attention of academic accountants the need to improve accounting education and to integrate the teaching of critical business concepts in accounting courses. In particular, it effectively addressed the issue of developing a principles-based learning program. This study does not, however, discuss the inherent conflict environment that exists in the corporate world between accounting and other functions or the way in which the compartmentalized teaching of accounting and finance, among others, helps to reinforce these conflicts. As all business areas start to focus on the critical role of accounting reports in an information society and on the need for reliable information to run businesses, it is hoped that further efforts for improvements in business education across several fronts will follow.

---

[6] W. Steve Albrecht and Robert J. Sack, *Accounting Education: Charting the Course through a Perilous Future,* 16 ACCOUNTING EDUCATION SERIES (American Accounting Association 2000).

Enron, Titanic, *and* The Perfect Storm*

*Nancy B. Rapoport***

[Former Enron CEO Jeffrey] Skilling offered a hypothesis for what brought Enron down, calling it a "perfect storm" of events.

He speculated that questions raised about the quality of Enron's accounting and about self-dealing caused a loss of confidence in the financial community. That led to Enron's debt being downgraded.

That downgrade, he said he was told by an Enron executive after he left, meant Enron couldn't access several billion dollars of back-up credit lines. A liquidity crunch followed, he said, even though Enron was solvent and highly profitable.

—Laura Goldberg, *Houston Chronicle*[1]

* Originally published at 71 FORDHAM L. REV. 1373 (2003). Reprinted with permission.

** Dean and Professor of Law at the University of Houston Law Center. All views expressed in this essay are mine alone, and not those of the University of Houston or its faculty, staff, or administration. I want to thank Emily Chan-Nguyen, Kelli Cline, Luddie Collins, Bala Dharan, Patrick Flanagan, Jimmy Halvatzis, Susan Hartman, Michele Hedges, Morris & Shirley Rapoport, Harriet Richman, Jeff Van Niel, and Michelle Wu. I also want to thank the students in my 2002 Seminar on *Special Issues in Ethics:* Sara Alonso Oliver, Justin Berg, Alison Chien, Doug Du Bois, Trevor Fish, Patrick Flanagan (who gets thanked twice, because he was also one of the cite-checkers for this article), Kim Havel, Cathy Helenhouse, Colin Moore, Sandy Oballe, Kevin Powers, Barry Rienstra, Ron Smeberg, and Tiffany Toups.

[1] Laura Goldberg, *Did No Wrong, Skilling Says: Defends His Role in Enron Fall,* HOUS. CHRON., Jan. 17, 2002, *available at* http:// www.chron.com/cs/CDA/story.hts/special/enron/dec01/1183520; *see also Good Morning America* (ABC television broadcast, Feb. 7, 2002) ("All eyes will be on former CEO Jeff Skilling. Skilling blames Enron's collapse on an unfortunate collision of events—the perfect storm. Congressional investigators point out he was at Enron's helm at the time."). Of course, now everyone—and I mean everyone—has latched onto this "perfect storm" metaphor. *See, e.g.,* Federal Document Clearing House, Worldcom CEO John Sidgmore Testifies Before the U.S. Senate Committee on Commerce, Science and Transportation, July 30, 2002, *available at* 2002 WL 1753183, at *3 (statement of John Sidgmore, CEO, WorldCom) ("Several factors . . . converged to create, I'll use Mr. Legere's words, a kind

Of course, we now know the extraordinary combination of circumstances that existed at that time which you would not meet again in 100 years; that they should all have existed just on that particular night shows, of course, that everything was against us.

—Second Officer Charles Lightoller, *RMS Titanic*[2]

I had some misgivings about calling [my book] *The Perfect Storm,* but in the end I decided that the intent was sufficiently clear. I use perfect in the meteorological sense: a storm that could not possibly have been worse.

—Sebastian Junger[3]

Much has been written about the Enron fiasco, from scholarly articles[4] to popular books,[5] and I'm sure that much more will be written about the deals that brought the

---

of perfect storm—and I guarantee you we did not rehearse this—that ripped through the telecommunications industry."); Federal Document Clearing House, *Harming Patient Access to Care: The Impact of Excessive Litigation,* July 17, 2002, *available at* 2002 WL 1584492, at *3 (statement of Richard Anderson, CEO, The Doctor's Company) ("The combination of these factors created . . . the perfect storm . . . for medical liability insurers."); Federal Document Clearing House, *House Committee on Education and the Workforce Holds a Hearing on Enron's Benefits Plan and its Compliance With Laws on Employer-Sponsored Pension Plans,* Feb. 7, 2002, *available at* 2002 WL 203240, at *12 (statement of Teresa Ghilarducci, Associate Professor of Economics, University of Notre Dame) ("The 1990s was the perfect storm for pensions to increase."); Federal Document Clearing House, *U.S. Senate Judiciary Committee Holds Hearing on Accountability Issues: Lessons Learned From Enron's Fall,* Feb. 6, 2002, *available at* 2002 WL 188865, at *11–12 (statement of Christine Gregoire, Attorney General, Washington State) ("In Washington [State,] we feel like Enron has been the gathering of the perfect storm. First, they gouged our consumers and rate payers with highly questionable power prices last year. And now, sadly, they have defrauded our investors and others across the nation.").

One of the coolest things that can happen to a law professor happened to me after I first published this article in the *Fordham Law Review.* I sent a copy to Sebastian Junger, author of THE PERFECT STORM. He read it and said that I was correct in my understanding of the "perfect storm" concept. Thank you, Mr. Junger!

[2] WALTER LORD, THE NIGHT LIVES ON 47 (1987) [hereinafter THE NIGHT LIVES ON].

[3] SEBASTIAN JUNGER, THE PERFECT STORM: A TRUE STORY OF MEN AGAINST THE SEA xiv (1997).

[4] *See, e.g.,* Michelle Chan-Fishel, *After Enron: How Accounting and SEC Reform Can Promote Corporate Accountability While Restoring Public Confidence,* 32 ENVTL. L. REP. 10965 (2002); Timothy P. Duane, *Regulation's Rationale: Learning from the California Energy Crisis,* 19 YALE J. ON REG. 471 (2002); Marisa Rogoway, *Recent Developments, Proposed Reforms to the Regulation of 401(k) Plans in the Wake of the Enron Disaster,* 6 J. SMALL & EMERGING BUS. L. 423 (2002); Marissa P. Viccaro, *Can Regulation Fair Disclosure Survive the Aftermath of Enron?,* 40 DUQ. L. REV. 695 (2002).

[5] *See, e.g.,* DIRK J. BARREVELD, THE ENRON COLLAPSE: CREATIVE ACCOUNTING, WRONG ECONOMICS OR CRIMINAL ACTS? A LOOK INTO THE ROOT CAUSES OF THE LARGEST BANKRUPTCY IN U.S. HISTORY (2002); ROBERT BRYCE, PIPE DREAMS: GREED, EGO, AND THE DEATH OF ENRON (2002); LOREN FOX, ENRON: THE RISE AND FALL (2002); PETER C. FUSARO & ROSS M. MILLER, WHAT WENT WRONG AT ENRON: EVERYONE'S GUIDE TO THE LARGEST BANKRUPTCY IN U.S. HISTORY (2002).

company down, the arrogance of some of the main players, and the ethical and moral issues that seemed to come to light only after the story broke in the media.[6] Enron's collapse, along with the failures of such other mega-businesses as WorldCom and Global Crossing,[7] triggered new legislation[8] and introduced such heretofore arcane acronyms as "SPEs" into the general lexicon.[9] The metaphor most used to describe Enron's quick descent into chapter 11 has been the "perfect storm."

That "perfect storm" metaphor irks me no end. I maintain, and this essay is designed to illustrate, that what brought Enron down—at least as far as we know—wasn't a once-in-a-lifetime alignment of elements beyond its control. Rather, Enron's

---

[6] One of the reasons that I'm sure more will be written is that I'm working on such a project: ENRON: CORPORATE FIASCOS & THEIR IMPLICATIONS (with Bala G. Dharan).

[7] Take a look at the largest bankruptcies, in terms of approximate stated liabilities, in the past twelve months [2001–02]: WorldCom (7/02 bankruptcy filing) ($43 billion, including $2 billion more in liabilities discovered after the bankruptcy filing); Enron (12/01) ($32 billion); NTL, Inc. (5/02) ($23.4 billion); Adelphia (6/02) ($18.6 billion); Global Crossing (1/02) ($12.4 billion); KMart (1/02) ($10.2 billion). *See* American Bankruptcy Institute, *A Look Inside the Mega-Case*, 10th Annual Southwest Bankruptcy Conference, Sept. 12–15, 2002; Bill Atkinson, *Kmart Files Chapter 11 Bankruptcy; No. 3 Discounter Cites Weak Economy, Tough Competition; 'Couldn't Pay the Bills'; Swift Move Surprises; $2 Billion Loan to Aid Firm's Reorganization*, BALT. SUN, Jan. 23, 2002, at 1A ("The Troy, Mich.-based firm listed $17 billion in assets and $11.3 billion in liabilities. . . . [A]lthough Kmart's bankruptcy is large, it pales in comparison to the largest bankruptcy in history, filed last month by Enron Corp . . . [which] listed $49 billion in assets and $31.2 billion in debts."); Julie Creswell, *Going For Broke; Crash! There Goes Another Company into Bankruptcy. How Did We Get Here? (Long Story.) Are We on the Mend? (Don't Bet on It.)*, FORTUNE, Feb. 18, 2002, *available at* 2002 WL 2190302; Lorrie Grant, *Discounter Hopes for Fast Reorganization*, USA TODAY, Jan. 23, 2002, at B02 ("Kmart listed $16.28 billion in assets and $10.34 billion in debts."); Andrew Leckey, *Bankruptcies Leave Investors in the Lurch*, CHI. TRIB., Aug. 27, 2002, *available at* 2002 WL 2689322; Alexandra R. Moses, Chern Yeh Kwok, & Thomas Lee et al., *Retailer Kmart Files for Bankruptcy; Officials Plan to Close Some Stores, Reorganize*, ST. LOUIS POST-DISPATCH, Jan. 23, 2002, at A1 ("[Kmart] has $10.25 billion in debt."); Chris Reidy, *Kmart Tumbles Discount Retail Chain in Record Chap. 11 Filing*, BOSTON GLOBE, Jan. 23, 2002, at C1 ("In its bankruptcy filing, Kmart and its US subsidiaries listed $17 billion in total assets at book value and total liabilities of $11.3 billion as of the quarter ended Oct. 31."); Gary Young, *Major Bankruptcies Filed in New York City*, 228 N.Y. L.J. 5 (Aug. 1, 2002).

[8] *See, e.g.*, Sarbanes-Oxley Act of 2002, Pub. L. No. 107-204, 116 Stat. 745, Corporate and Criminal Fraud Accountability Act of 2002, Pub. L. No. 107-204, 116 Stat. 800 (codified at 18 U.S.C. § 1348, 1514A, 1519–20) [hereinafter Sarbanes-Oxley]; *Framework for Enhancing the Quality of Financial Information Through Improvement of Oversight of the Auditing Process*, 67 Fed. Reg. 44964-01 (proposed July 5, 2002) (to be codified at 17 C.F.R. pt. 210, 229).

[9] If you don't believe me, just do a search in WESTLAW or LEXIS on "SPEs" and see how many documents you get, especially documents dated after October 2001, when the Enron disaster began to break. A search of major newspaper articles (Westlaw database NPMJ) for the terms "special purpose entity" or "special purpose entities" during the year 1999 yielded zero results. The first article in this database appeared in October 2001 and a search of 2002 now yields over 328 results (as of the second week in October 2002, with more being added daily).

demise was a synergistic combination of human errors and hubris: a *"Titanic"*[10] mis-calculation, rather than a "perfect storm."[11]

I. WHY *TITANIC* IS A BETTER METAPHOR FOR ENRON'S EVENTUAL DOWNFALL THAN IS *THE PERFECT STORM*

The story of the *Titanic* is well-known. The ship was, at the time of its maiden (and only) transatlantic voyage, the largest in the world, carrying a microcosm of society.[12] The glitterati of the United States and Europe were on board, as were hundreds of immigrants trying to make their way to a new land. The ship was built with watertight compartments that extended from the keel up several decks (some to D Deck and some to E deck); she also had a double bottom for extra protection.[13] She was designed to float with any two consecutive compartments flooded and even with three of the first five compartments (out of sixteen) flooded,[14] thanks to electronic doors that could be closed by a single command.[15] And she was touted as "unsinkable," at least in some press reports.[16]

But sink she did, based upon a series of miscalculations, no single one of which might have proved fatal, but all of which, taken together, doomed the ship. In a chapter of his follow-up book to *A Night to Remember,* called *The Night Lives On,*[17] Walter Lord enumerates the many individual mistakes made that night:

---

[10] And, no, it wasn't the Leonardo DiCaprio movie (TITANIC (20th Century Fox 1997)) that first piqued my interest in the ship's history. I've been fascinated by it for probably thirty or so years. Among other things, I'm a member of the Titanic Historical Society, and I probably own virtually every book and movie about the ship. If you're wondering if I'm a bit obsessed with the ship and its tale, you're right. But everyone needs a hobby.

[11] I've used the *Titanic* comparison once before. *See, e.g.,* Mike Tolson, *The Fall of Enron/'Convenient whipping boy'/Enron Scandal Offers Fodder for Wide Range of Groups Seeking a Symbol for Their Cause,* HOUS. CHRON., Mar. 3, 2002, at 26, *available at* 2002 WL 3245488. Others have also made the comparison between Enron and the *Titanic. See* Edward J. Cleary, *Lessons For Lawyers From The Enron Debacle,* BENCH & B. MINN., Apr. 2002, at 16 (footnotes omitted) (quoting George F. Will, *Indignation Over Enron is Just the Beginning,* WASH. POST, Jan. 16, 2002) ("Given that Enron employee pensions were decimated with, as one commentator noted, the employees "locked in steerage like the lower orders on the *Titanic,* and given that many state pension funds were among the casualties, both state and national public officials will be forced to act."); Martha Neil, *Partners at Risk,* 88 A.B.A. J. 44 (Aug. 2002) ("The collapse of Enron might give partners at law firms reason to ponder another epic disaster: the sinking of the *Titanic.*").

[12] WALTER LORD, A NIGHT TO REMEMBER 1 (1997) [hereinafter A NIGHT TO REMEMBER].

[13] *Id.* at 174–75. She did not, however, have a double hull. *Id.*

[14] *Id.* at 26.

[15] *Id.* at 8.

[16] *Id.* at 175.

[17] THE NIGHT LIVES ON, *supra* note 2.

- the calm sea, which meant that the lookouts couldn't see any waves breaking against the bergs;[18]
- the numerous, apparently ignored ice warnings from ships already crossing the Atlantic Ocean that were using the same route as the *Titanic;*[19]
- the lack of any systematic procedure to deliver ice and weather warnings from the Marconi telegraph room to the bridge;[20]
- the fact that the lookouts' binoculars had been lost earlier in the trip;[21]
- the failure of the *Titanic's* officers to urge Captain Smith (or each other) to take a more cautious approach to travel, based on the calm sea and rapidly dropping temperature;[22]
- not enough lifeboats for the number of souls aboard;[23]
- Captain Smith's failure to hold lifeboat drills[24] or to do more than a perfunctory test of the ship's braking speed and maneuverability;[25]
- First Wireless Operator Phillips's famous response to an ice warning from the *Californian* (the ship that, according to some accounts, was closest to the *Titanic* when it sunk), "Shut up, shut up . . . I am working Cape Race";[26]
- the fact that lookout Frederic Fleet spotted the berg too late to stop the ship or otherwise to avoid the berg;[27]
- First Officer Murdoch's decision to port around the berg rather than ramming it head-on, a counterintuitive action that might have saved the ship;[28] and
- the *Californian's* decision not to come to the aid of a vessel in enough obvious distress to fire white distress rockets (apparently visible to the *Californian's* crew) at several intervals.[29]

The list of miscalculations goes on and on.[30] But Walter Lord tells it best:

> Given the competitive pressures of the North Atlantic run, the chances taken, the lack of experience with ships of such immense size, the haphaz-

---

[18] *Id.* at 47.

[19] *Id.* at 48–53.

[20] *Id.* at 53.

[21] *Id.* at 60.

[22] *Id.* at 53–54.

[23] *Id.* at 72–80.

[24] A NIGHT TO REMEMBER, *supra* note 12, at 42.

[25] THE NIGHT LIVES ON, *supra* note 2, at 56.

[26] *Id.* at 58.

[27] *Id.* at 59–60.

[28] *Id.* at 59.

[29] *Id.* at 134–59.

[30] And so have I, at some social gatherings, as my very indulgent husband can attest.

ard procedures of the wireless room, the casualness of the bridge, and the misassessment of what speed was safe, it's remarkable that the *Titanic* steamed for two hours and ten minutes through ice-infested waters without coming to grief any sooner.

"Everything was against us?" The wonder is that she lasted as long as she did.[31]

The Perfect Storm, on the other hand, describes a combination of meteorological bad luck and human miscalculation, born less of arrogance than of desperation. Granted, Billy Tyne, captain of the *Andrea Gail,* made a fatal mistake by sailing into the storm,[32] but he did "what ninety percent of us would've done—he battened down the hatches and hung on."[33] Although the signs were clear that bad weather was coming, the sheer magnitude of the storm was far beyond the experience (or imagination) of any of the ship captains in the large area covered by the storm, and each of them had to make a quick decision:

> [The weather bulletin describing Hurricane Grace] reads like an inventory of things fishermen don't want to hear. . . . Every boat in the swordfish fleet receives this information. Albert Johnston, south of the Tail, decides to head northwest into the cold water of the Labrador Current. . . . The rest of the sword fleet stays far to the east, waiting to see what the storm does. They couldn't make it into port in time anyway. The *Contship Holland,* a hundred miles south of Billy, heads straight into the teeth of the thing. Two hundred miles east, . . . the Liberian-registered *Zarah,* also heads for New York. Ray Leonard on the sloop *Sartori* has decided not to head for port; he holds to a southerly course for Bermuda. The *Laurie Dawn 8* keeps plowing out to the fishing grounds and the *Eishin Maru 78,* 150 miles due south of Sable Island, makes for Halifax harbor to the northeast. Billy can either waste several days trying to get out of the way, or he can stay on-course for home. The fact that he has a hold full of fish, and not enough ice, must figure into his decision.[34]

Billy Tyne's decision proved wrong, and the *Andrea Gail* lost all six hands aboard.[35] *Titanic* lost over 1,500 souls, with only 705 saved.[36] Both events were tragic. But only

---

[31] THE NIGHT LIVES ON, *supra* note 2, at 61.

[32] Special thanks to Boyd Henderson for reminding me, at a luncheon, that some human error contributed to the fate of the *Andrea Gail.*

[33] JUNGER, *supra* note 3, at 124 (quoting Captain Tommie Barrie, of the ship *Allison*).

[34] *Id.*

[35] *Id.* at 186.

[36] A NIGHT TO REMEMBER, *supra* note 12, at 176.

the *Titanic* can trace the loss of life directly to human arrogance.[37] When I compare the two tragedies in light of Jeffrey Skilling's claim that the fall of Enron was based on factors outside of the company's control—an economic "perfect storm"—I find that Skilling's claim falls flat.

II. HOW A FAILURE OF CHARACTER CAN TURN "PERFECT STORMS" INTO *TITANIC* MISTAKES

I'm not going to rehash the mechanics of the various Enron deals here. Others have done a good job of describing the problems with the deals,[38] with the Board's lack of oversight of the deals,[39] and with the general culture of Enron that encouraged aggressive risk-taking and short-term profits.[40] We obviously don't know enough about the deals or the people yet to reach any final conclusions, so my comments are going to concentrate on one theme—character. If we are to believe that there is a single root cause of the Enron mess (an arguable point at best in such a complicated situation), failure of character gets my nomination.

---

[37] The Golden Age's love of, and faith in, science contributed to the tragedy as well, as some of the miscalculations that Captain Smith made were based on the scientific advances in ship design.

[38] *See, e.g.*, WILLIAM C. POWERS, JR., ET AL., REPORT OF INVESTIGATION BY THE SPECIAL INVESTIGATIVE COMMITTEE OF THE BOARD OF DIRECTORS OF ENRON CORP., 2002 WL 198018 (CORPSCAN 1980818 (ENRON)) [hereinafter Powers Report]. The Powers Report is also available at http://i.cnn.net/cnn/2002/LAW/02/02/enron.report/powers.report.pdf. There is also a lot of good Congressional testimony on the subject. *See, e.g.*, Federal Document Clearing House, *Strengthening Accounting Oversight: Hearing Before the Subcomm. on Commerce, Trade and Consumer Protection of the House Comm. on Energy and Commerce,* June 26, 2002, *available at* 2002 WL 1381127 (statement of Bala G. Dharan, J. Howard Creekmore Professor of Management, Rice University); Federal Document Clearing House, *U.S. Senate Governmental Affairs Committee Holds a Hearing on the Collapse of Houston-based Enron Corporation,* Jan. 24, 2002, *available at* 2002 WL 93421 (statement of John Langbein, Professor of Law, Yale Law School); Federal Document Clearing House, *Deregulating Capital Markets, Outline of the Testimony of Professor John C. Coffee, Jr., before the Subcommittee on Telecommunications and Finance of the House Commerce Committee,* Nov. 14, 2002, *available at* 2002 WL 1381127 (statement of John C. Coffee, Jr., Columbia University).

[39] *See* SENATE PERMANENT SUBCOMMITTEE ON INVESTIGATIONS OF THE COMMITTEE ON GOVERNMENTAL AFFAIRS, 107TH CONG., THE ROLE OF THE BOARD OF DIRECTORS IN ENRON'S COLLAPSE, July 8, 2002, *available at* http://www.access.gpo.gov/congress/senate/senate12lp107.html [hereinafter Senate Print].

[40] *See, e.g.*, Tom Fowler, *The Pride and the Fall of Enron,* HOUS. CHRON., Oct. 20, 2002, at A25 [hereinafter *The Pride and the Fall*] ("[One manager, told that a deal would take a year, said,] 'I haven't got a year. If I can't do it in three months I won't do it because my bonus depends on it'" since "bonuses were based on the total value of the deal, not the cash it brought in."); Greg Hassell, *The Fall of Enron/The Culture/Pressure Cooker Finally Exploded,* HOUS. CHRON., Dec. 9, 2001, at 1.

Character and leadership are inextricably linked.[41] When the leaders are engaging in self-dealing and side deals,[42] and the supervisors of those leaders are also engaging in side deals,[43] and the gatekeepers are approving those side deals,[44] what should the rank and file be thinking? Given the magnitude of the potentially illegal profits made by CFO Andrew Fastow and CEO Jeffrey Skilling,[45] and the sense of entitlement that Enron encouraged,[46] it must have taken significant strength of character to resist getting on that gravy train. And yet, several people did resist. Who resisted, and why?

By now, those following the Enron case know that Sherron Watkins tried to alert CEO Kenneth Lay to serious concerns that she had about Enron's deals:

> Shortly after Enron announced Skilling's unexpected resignation on August 14, 2001, Watkins sent a one-page anonymous letter to Lay. The letter stated that "Enron has been very aggressive in its accounting—most notably the Raptor transactions." The letter raised serious questions concerning the accounting treatment and economic substance of the Raptor transactions (and transactions between Enron and Condor Trust, a subsidiary of Whitewing Associates), identifying several of the matters discussed in this Report. It concluded that "I am incredibly nervous that we will implode in

---

[41] Mary C. Daly, *Panel Discussion on Enron: What Went Wrong?*, 8 FORDHAM J. CORP. & FIN. L. 1, S28 (2002) ("What the literature teaches is that the ethical behavior is taught from the top down . . . . It is management's commitment to ethical standards that sets the tone.").

[42] The self-dealing by former Enron CFO Andrew Fastow was, apparently, approved by Enron's Board of Directors when the Board waived its ethics rules (more than once) to allow Fastow to head two partnerships that would be negotiating with Enron. *See, e.g.*, Letter from Max Hendrick, III, Vinson & Elkins, to James V. Derrick, Jr., Enron [Re: Preliminary Investigation of Allegations of an Anonymous Employee] (Oct. 15, 2001), *available at* 2001 WL 1764266 (CORPSCAN); *see also* Senate Print, *supra* note 39, at 23–24; Powers Report, *supra* note 38, at *68–71.

[43] The Enron Board apparently had several directors who also had consulting agreements with Enron, enabling a form of double-dipping. *See* Senate Print, *supra* note 39, at 51–55.

[44] *See* Powers Report, *supra* note 38, at *10 ("There was an absence of forceful and effective oversight by Senior Enron Management and in-house counsel, and objective and critical professional advice by outside counsel at Vinson & Elkins, or auditors at Andersen.").

[45] *Fastow Charged With Fraud, Conspiracy in Enron Case*, WASH. POST, Oct. 3, 2002, at A01; April Witt & Peter Behr, *Dream Job Turns Into a Nightmare; Skilling's Success Came at High Price*, WASH. POST, July 29, 2002, at A01; *see also* Senate Print, *supra* note 39, at 24, 34–36; Powers Report, *supra* note 38, at *3, 10.

[46] Enron employees who mastered the art of trading and deal-making could earn fantastic sums. Annual bonuses were as high as $1 million. Shortly after each bonus time, a new crop of silver Porsches—the most favored status symbol at Enron—would appear in the company garage. "I remember one trader going crazy because his bonus was only $500,000. He was cursing and screaming and throwing things at his desk," one former Enron employee recalls. "He thought because he was so brilliant, they should be paying him a lot more."
Hassell, *supra* note 40, at 1.

a wave of accounting scandals." Lay told us that he viewed the letter as thoughtfully written and alarming.[47]

Watkins later told Lay that she had written the letter and met with him regarding her concerns.[48] Lay referred the matter to Enron's General Counsel, James Derrick, a former Vinson & Elkins partner.[49] Derrick in turn asked Vinson & Elkins, one of Enron's key outside law firms, to conduct a preliminary review of the situation—but not to review the underlying transactions that Watkins had discussed in her letter.[50] Within the confines of Derrick's request, Vinson & Elkins conducted an investigation (interviewing Watkins, among others).

V&E concluded that "none of the individuals interviewed could identify any transaction between Enron and LJM that was not reasonable from Enron's standpoint or that was contrary to Enron's best interests." On the accounting issues, V&E said that both Enron and Andersen acknowledge[d] "that the accounting treatment on the Condor/Whitewing and Raptor transactions is creative and aggressive, but no one has

---

[47] Powers Report, *supra* note 38, at 79. Note the new standards of behavior imposed on company attorneys by Sarbanes-Oxley:

> Not later than 180 days after the date of enactment of this Act, the Commission shall issue rules, in the public interest and for the protection of investors, setting forth minimum standards of professional conduct for attorneys appearing and practicing before the Commission in any way in the representation of issuers, including a rule—
>
> (1) requiring an attorney to report evidence of a material violation of securities law or breach of fiduciary duty or similar violation by the company or any agent thereof, to the chief legal counsel or the chief executive officer of the company (or the equivalent thereof); and
>
> (2) if the counsel or officer does not appropriately respond to the evidence (adopting, as necessary, appropriate remedial measures or sanctions with respect to the violation), requiring the attorney to report the evidence to the audit committee of the board of directors of the issuer or to another committee of the board of directors comprised solely of directors not employed directly or indirectly by the issuer, or to the board of directors.

Sarbanes-Oxley Act of 2002 § 307, 15 USC § 7245 (West Supp. 2002). After a whole slew of parties filed objections to the SEC's Proposed Rule regarding attorney conduct (with many of the objections focused on the "noisy withdrawal" provisions of the Proposed Rule, *see* http://www.sec.gov/rules/proposed/s74502.shtml), the SEC apparently abandoned the "noisy withdrawal" provision in its final rule, *see* http://www.sec.gov/news/press/2003-13.htm. As of this writing, I have only seen the press release regarding the final rule, not the actual text of the rule.

The days of taking an issue only partially up the chain of command are over, at least for publicly traded companies. But haven't lawyers always had the responsibility of taking matters all the way up the chain of command? *See* MODEL RULES OF PROF'L CONDUCT R. 1.13 (2002). I wonder whether Ms. Watkins, as an accountant, had a similar duty under her profession's ethics rules. If she did have such a duty, and she didn't go all the way to the Board of Directors (and beyond) with her concerns, was she really a whistleblower? (Mind you, what she did took some guts, even though she was not a whistleblower in the true sense.)

[48] Powers Report, *supra* note 38, at 79.

[49] *See* Ellen Joan Pollock, *Anderson: Called to Account: Enron Lawyers Face Congress Over Their Role,* WALL ST. J., Mar. 15, 2002, at C13 (noting that Derrick used to be a partner at Vinson & Elkins).

[50] Powers Report, *supra* note 38, at 79.

reason to believe that it is inappropriate from a technical standpoint." V&E concluded that the facts revealed in its preliminary investigation did not warrant a "further wide-spread investigation by independent counsel or auditors," although the firm did note that the "bad cosmetics" of the Raptor related-party transactions, coupled with the poor performance of the assets placed in the Raptor vehicles, created "a serious risk of adverse publicity and litigation."[51]

One observation: Vinson & Elkins's undertaking of the investigation had certain restrictions, including Enron's request not to review the bona fides of the underlying transactions.[52] We don't know what sort of give and take occurred between Enron and Vinson & Elkins about the usefulness of such a request.[53] At some point, thanks to the ability of Enron's chapter 11 management to waive the attorney-client privilege,[54] we

---

[51] *Id.* at *80.

[52] *Id.* at *79. "The result of the V&E review was largely predetermined by the scope and nature of the investigation and the process employed . . . . The scope and process of the investigation appear to have been structured with less skepticism than was needed to see through these particularly complex transactions." *Id.* at *81 (footnote omitted).

[53] Jordan Mintz, Enron Global Finance's General Counsel, has stated that Vinson & Elkins "fulfilled its professional duties" in terms of the advice it gave to Enron. Laura Goldberg, *Enron's Words as Relevant as Deeds/Reports May Have Told Partial Truths*, HOUS. CHRON., Feb. 11, 2002, at 1. Because of Vinson & Elkins's ties to Enron's General Counsel James Derrick, though, Mintz hired a separate firm, Fried, Frank, Harris, Shriver & Jacobson, to review the deals of which Watkins had complained. Rone Tempest, *Enron Counsel Warned About Partnerships Probe: Company's Legal Executive Asked Opinion of Law Firm in April. Congressional Investigators Say It Was to 'Halt This Practice,'* L.A. TIMES, Jan. 31, 2002, at C1. I'm not yet ready to get on the bandwagon that denounces all of Enron's lawyers.

[54] The principal case involving privilege in the bankruptcy context is, of course, Commodity Futures Trading Commission v. Weintraub, 471 U.S. 343, 358 (1985) ("[W]e hold that the trustee of a corporation in [a chapter 7] bankruptcy has the power to waive the corporation's attorney-client privilege with respect to pre-bankruptcy communications."). Weintraub answered the question of how much control a chapter 7 trustee had over the corporation's attorney-client privilege. *Id.* Subsequent cases have answered the question about how far the Weintraub holding could go in a chapter 11 context. *See, e.g.,* Am. Metrocomm Corp. v. Duane Morris & Heckscher LLP, 274 B.R. 641, 654–56 (Bankr. D. Dela. 2002) (stating that debtor-in-possession controls attorney-client privilege, and debtor-in-possession can request documents from attorneys even if attorneys raise work product privilege as a defense); *In re* Bame, 251 B.R. 367, 370, 374 (Bankr. D. Minn. 2000) (converting chapter 11 case to chapter 7 case; holding that chapter 7 trustee can access the post-petition, pre-conversion communications between the debtor-in-possession and its lawyers because the privilege is held by the estate, and not by the debtor-in-possession); Whyte v. Williams (In re Williams), 152 B.R. 123, 129 (Bankr. N.D. Tex. 1992) ("The liquidating trustee [under a confirmed chapter 11 plan] controls the power to waive or invoke the evidentiary privileges that arise in connection with the causes of action transferred to the liquidating trust under Article 25.5 of the confirmed plan."); *see also* S. Air Transp., Inc. v. SAT Group, Inc., 255 B.R. 706, 711 (Bankr. S.D. Ohio 2000) (citations omitted).

The Court agrees that a corporate fiduciary is precluded from asserting privileges to protect his own interests that are adverse to those of the corporation. Corporate officers must "exercise the privilege in a manner consistent with their fiduciary capacity to act in the best interests of the corporation and not of themselves individually."

Id. The interesting part about the privilege issue in the Enron bankruptcy context is whether Steve Cooper (the restructuring expert currently running Enron) is going to waive the privilege in order to get

may learn more. But I have to admit, right off the bat, that I have a hard time believing that Vinson & Elkins, or any of Enron's other law firms, knowingly advised Enron to do anything that was clearly illegal. The real issue is how Enron handled the grey areas of the law, based on the advice of all of its lawyers (both its in-house and outside counsel).

Watkins wasn't the lone voice questioning Enron's deals; others, including Enron Global Finance's General Counsel Jordan Mintz, were concerned about the structure and disclosure of the various deals.[55] Apparently, Fastow and Skilling didn't brook disagreement willingly. Those who objected often found themselves the subject of pressure, downright abuse, and exile.[56]

I'd like to put forward one striking similarity between the *Titanic* and Enron: a failure of meaningful communication stemming from a belief that someone else had "taken care of it." Here's how a recent newspaper article described the problem:

> [S]ince most only saw their part of the business, they assumed the problems were isolated. . . . "You understood your piece of the business and maybe what the guy next to you did, but very few understood the big picture. . . .

---

information from the various law firms that represented Enron and then, if the information gives rise to a cause of action against any of Enron's lawyers, use that very information to pursue them in bankruptcy court. Mr. Cooper can also pursue Enron's officers and directors using that privileged information, as the privilege belongs to the client (Enron) and not to any of the client's employees. I've been following the work of the Severed Enron Employees Coalition in the pursuit of the prepetition bonuses paid to certain Enron executives on the theory that the bonuses were fraudulent conveyances. Severed Enron Employees Coalition v. N. Trust Co., No. 02-0267 (S.D. Tex. complaint, filed Jan. 24, 2002). Any privileged advice, on the order of "Should we pay this person a retention bonus? What will we get in terms of a benefit for the retention bonus?," could be helpful in this regard.

[55] *See, e.g.*, Senate Print, *supra* note 39, at 28 n.81 (quoting an internal memorandum from Mintz):

> [T]he Company needs to improve both the process it follows in executing such transactions and implement improved procedures regarding written substantiation supporting and memorializing the Enron/LJM transactions . . . . [F]irst is the need for the Company to implement a more active and systematic effort in pursuing non-LJM sales alternatives before approaching LJM . . . ; the second is to . . . impose a more rigorous testing of the fairness and benefits realized by Enron in transacting with LJM.

Id.; *see also* Dan Feldstein, *Skilling Says He Did No Wrong / Lawyer Told Not to Stick Neck Out*, HOUS. CHRON., Feb. 8, 2002, at 1 (describing how Fastow tried to bully Mintz into blessing irregularities in certain Enron deals).

[56] *See, e.g.*, The Pride and the Fall, *supra* note 40, at 27A (listing three people—Andersen partner Carl Bass, former Enron CFO (after Fastow) Jeff McMahon, and former Merrill Lynch analyst John Olson— who were demoted (Olson was fired) after criticizing the aggressive Enron deals and accounting methods); *see also* Editorial Desk, *Not Quite a Whistle-Blower*, N.Y. TIMES, Feb. 15, 2002, at A20; Andy Geller, *"I Believe Mr. Skilling and Mr. Fastow Duped Mr. Lay"—Enron VP Rips Duo Before Congress*, N.Y. POST, Feb. 15, 2002, at 9; Susan Schmidt, *CEO Was 'Misserved' At Enron, Hill Told; Former Executive Blames Other Top Managers*, WASH. POST, Feb. 15, 2002, at A01; Peter Spiegel, *The Architect of Enron's Downfall: Internal Probe Reveals Andy Fastow as a CFO who Bullied Staff and Even Wall Street Banks, Enriching Himself by More than Dollars 45m in the Process*, FIN. TIMES, May 21, 2002, at A20.

That segmentation allowed us to get work done very quickly, but it isolated that institutional knowledge into the hands of very few people."[57]

Certainly, the Powers Report describes the failure of follow-through regarding several of the Enron deals—the failure to ascertain if the checks and balances, supposedly part of each deal's structure, were in place and working.[58] As John Coffee explains,

> Enron . . . furnish[es] ample evidence of a systematic governance failure. Although other spectacular securities frauds have been discovered from time to time over recent decades, they have not generally disturbed the overall market. In contrast, Enron has clearly roiled the market and created a new investor demand for transparency. Behind this disruption lies the market's discovery that it cannot rely upon the professional gatekeepers—auditors, analysts, and others—whom the market has long trusted to filter, verify and assess complicated financial information. Properly understood, Enron is a demonstration of gatekeeper failure, and the question it most sharply poses is how this failure should be rectified.[59]

Failures of gatekeeper professionals aren't new. The savings and loan crisis, which also represented a significant gatekeeper failure, occurred a mere twenty years ago;[60] the Salomon Brothers Treasury bonds trading scandal occurred just ten years ago.[61]

---

[57] *See, e.g., The Pride and the Fall, supra* note 40, at 27A. Remember that those "very few people" included members of the Board of Directors, which waived Enron's ethics rules more than once to allow self-dealing by some of Enron's executives. *See supra* note 42.

[58] *See* Powers Report, *supra* note 38, at *18–28.

[59] John C. Coffee, Jr., *Understanding Enron: It's About the Gatekeepers, Stupid,* 57 BUS. LAW. 1403 (2002) (footnote omitted), *reprinted in this book at* 125–143.

[60] Now that I wear bifocals, twenty years just doesn't seem that long ago.

[61] Daly, *supra* note 41, at S25–S28; Federal Document Clearing House, *U.S. Senate Committee on Commerce, Science and Transportation Holds a Hearing on Enron Bankruptcy,* Dec. 18, 2001, *available at* 2001 WL 1623334 (statement of John Coffee, Columbia University) ("Well, when a debacle like Enron occurs, the critical question for Congress and for regulators is to ask, as you've been beginning to ask, where were the gatekeepers; where were the watchdogs? . . . Here, all failed, and all failed fairly abysmally.").

> The fallout from [the savings and loan] scandal included a Justice Department action against the prestigious New York firm of Kaye, Scholer, Fierman, Hays & Handler. Kaye, Scholer and partner Peter Fishbein were said to have gone beyond mere aggressive lawyering, and more than one observer viewed their representation as akin to aiding and abetting, while others attributed any errors to simple inattentiveness. Ultimately, the case was settled, with the firm and its malpractice carrier paying $41 million in settlement, and the Keating lawyers paid for their alleged sins, notwithstanding their ability to spread the loss to other lawyers via malpractice insurance coverage.

Jeffrey W. Stempel, *Embracing Descent: The Bankruptcy of a Business Paradigm for Conceptualizing and Regulating the Legal Profession,* 27 FLA. ST. U. L. REV. 25, 111–12 (1999) (footnotes omitted). For a

It's certainly possible that many of the legal and accounting professionals (the in-house and the outside professionals) who advised Enron assumed that Enron's own businesspeople were doing the follow-through; moreover, many of those same professionals may well have thought that it was not the lawyers' or accountants' "place" to bill Enron for continued checks of the system. (I know nothing about the training of accountants, so I'm going to limit the rest of this discussion to the training of lawyers.) If the lawyers saw themselves as morally independent from Enron, rather than morally interdependent, then they might well have believed that it was Enron's job, not theirs, to ensure follow-through. A more complex explanation is that cognitive dissonance— well-documented in social science literature and applied to lawyers by, among others, David Luban—prevented the lawyers from seeing some of these deals more clearly. My hunch is that both concepts (a mistaken belief in moral independence, rather than interdependence, and the effects of cognitive dissonance) played a part in any failures by the gatekeepers.

A. "Moral Independence" Versus "Moral Interdependence" as an Explanation

For the longest time, lawyers have done everything they could to distinguish the client's ends from the means that the lawyers used to achieve those ends. This "moral independence" theory has been used to justify everything from lawyers who take on unpopular causes to lawyers who facilitate shady deals, even though the original theory was never intended to justify shady deals.[62]

---

wonderful discussion of the Kaye, Scholer firm and the savings and loan crisis, see David B. Wilkins, *Making Context Count: Regulating Lawyers After Kaye, Scholer*, 66 S. CAL. L. REV. 1147 (1993). As Clarence Darrow apparently said, "History repeats itself, and that's one of the things that's wrong with history." The Quotations Home Page, *available at* http://www.geocities.com/~spanoudi/topic-h3.html#history.

[62] According to a study by Erwin Smigel, lawyers'

independence derived from two sources. First, "they . . . 'represent' the law and must therefore separate themselves from the client." Second, the commodity they sold was "[i]ndependent legal opinion." Smigel observed that "client[s] desire that a firm maintain its autonomy" so that they can obtain the best advice. Moreover, as the large firms grew older, they increased their number of clients and moved away from fundamentally relying on one or a few clients. This shift "strengthened . . . a firm's ability to retain its independence" because "no one client provid[es] enough income to materially or consciously influence the law office's legal opinion."

Russell G. Pearce, *Lawyers as America's Governing Class: The Formation and Dissolution of the Original Understanding of the American Lawyer's Role*, 8 U. CHI. L. SCH. ROUNDTABLE 381, 406 (2001) (footnotes omitted) [hereinafter Governing Class] (quoting ERWIN O. SMIGEL, THE WALL STREET LAWYER: PROFESSIONAL ORGANIZATION MAN? (1964)).

The fun part about the history of the bar's independence theory is its link with the robber barons of yesteryear. *See, e.g.*, Thomas L. Shaffer, *The Profession as a Moral Teacher*, 18 ST. MARY'S L.J. 195, 222–23 (1986) [hereinafter *Moral Teacher*]; Thomas L. Shaffer, *The Unique, Novel, and Unsound Adversary Ethic*, 41 VAND. L. REV. 697, 703–04 (1988). As Russell Pearce points out,

Several scholars have recognized, though, that the complexity of modern legal practice forces lawyers to take a more active role in shaping not just the clients' advice but the clients' deals and litigation as well.[63] Richard Painter's "moral interdependence" theory of the lawyer-client interaction is a more realistic view of the lawyer's modern role, especially when it comes to complex transactions or complex litigation.[64]

When you overlay the lawyer's moral interdependence on top of a cutthroat culture, you get Enron (and WorldCom, and Tyco, etc.). We still don't know a lot of the facts behind Enron's various deals, including what the various lawyers said, Enron's response to that advice, or how much the accountants' advice contradicted (or supported) the lawyers' advice. But we do know that the structure of Enron itself encouraged a constant pushing of the outside of the envelope.[65] Enron encouraged a "me, first" structure, not a cooperative one.

> "Enron sought to redefine the rules of the industry," said Robert Bruner, a professor at the University of Virginia who has made a case study of Enron's culture. "It was a culture of challenge and confrontation."
>
> . . . .
>
> [Former CEO Jeffrey] Skilling also is responsible, many insiders say, for creating a mercenary, cutthroat culture to stoke the fires beneath the enterprise. One of the hallmarks of the Skilling regime was a performance review process that employees called "rank and yank." The evaluations compared the performance of employees against one another, with the bottom 15 percent getting axed every year.

> In becoming hired guns, elite lawyers abandoned the traditional governing class ideology. They were no longer acting as a disinterested political leadership capable of discerning and pursuing the common good. Instead, they were advocates of private interests. They had violated professionalism's taboo on acting as a servant of big business and could no longer claim the special tie to the public good which distinguished them from those in business.

Pearce, *Governing Class*, *supra*, at 400–10.

[63] Richard W. Painter, *The Moral Interdependence of Corporate Lawyers and Their Clients*, 67 S. Cal. L. Rev. 507, 511, 544–45 (1994); *see also id.* at 526 ("Joint decisionmaking by lawyer and client has become both efficient and prudent.") (footnote omitted).

[64] For example, the Powers Report points out that, with respect to preparing the various disclosure forms that Enron filed, "[w]hile accountants took the lead in preparing the financial statement footnote disclosures, lawyers played a more central role in preparing the proxy statements, including the disclosures of the related-party transactions." Powers Report, *supra* note 38, at 84. This interdependence is by no means limited to the lawyers who worked on Enron's deals. *See Governing Class*, *supra* note 62, at 408–09 (citing Robert A. Kagan and Robert Eli Rosen, *On the Social Significance of Large Law Firm Practice*, 37 Stan. L. Rev. 399 (1985) and Robert L. Nelson, *Ideology, Practice, and Professional Autonomy: Social Values and Client Relationships in the Large Law Firm*, 37 Stan. L. Rev. 503 (1985)). Both the Kagan & Rosen study and the Nelson study are well worth reading.

[65] I first saw this phrase in Tom Wolfe, The Right Stuff 12 (1979).

The evaluations were done by asking employees to judge others' performance. They did so knowing their own promotions and survival hung in the balance.

"Because of that, you never helped one another," said one former Enron employee. "Everyone was in it for themselves. People stabbed you in the back."

Teamwork, once a source of strength, started to disappear.

"It was every man for himself," a former Enron executive said.

What sense of teamwork survived "rank and yank" was undermined by Enron's reward system, which seemed to place no value on group goals but lavishly rewarded individual accomplishment. An employee who could close big deals got big bonuses and promotions. Those who couldn't were shown the door.[66]

Let's take this moral interdependence theory one step further. Add to the theory (1) Enron's culture, and (2) the personality traits of a large number of lawyers (whether or not they ever had Enron as a client), and you have a disaster just waiting to happen. Susan Daicoff has summarized the literature on lawyers' personality traits quite nicely in a series of articles.[67] Lawyers tend to have certain personality characteristics that contribute to their need to "win." They "appear to be more competitive, aggressive, and achievement-oriented, and overwhelmingly Thinkers (instead of Feelers). . . . Lawyers are more often motivated by a need for achievement than are others, which includes a need to compete against an internal or external standard of intelligence."[68] No matter which way you slice it, these gatekeepers were too closely involved with their client[69] to be able to stand up and say, "You shouldn't do that." At some point, we need lawyers to say, "The law lets you do it, but don't. . . . It's a rotten thing to do."[70]

---

[66] Hassell, *supra* note 40. For a masterful compendium of the theories surrounding community norms in monitoring and shaping the roles of lawyers, see W. Bradley Wendel, *Nonlegal Regulation of the Legal Profession: Social Norms in Professional Communities,* 54 VAND. L. REV. 1955 (2001) [hereinafter *Social Norms*].

[67] *See, e.g.,* Susan Daicoff, *Lawyer, Know Thyself: A Review of Empirical Research on Attorney Attributes Bearing on Professionalism,* 46 AM. U. L. REV. 1337 (1997) [hereinafter *Know Thyself*]; Susan Daicoff, *(Oxymoron?) Ethical Decisionmaking by Attorneys: An Empirical Study,* 48 FLA. L. REV. 197, 217–18 (1996).

[68] *Know Thyself, supra* note 67, at 1408–09 (footnotes omitted). According to Daicoff, law students come into law school hard-wired with these traits. *Id.* at 1349–50. Imagine my relief at knowing that law school didn't "ruin" them.

[69] *See, e.g., supra* notes 49–50 and accompanying text.

[70] Sol M. Linowitz, *Moment of Truth for the Legal Profession,* Address at the University of Wisconsin Law School (Oct. 24, 1997), *in* 1997 WIS. L. REV. 1211, 1214–15 ("I believe Elihu Root once again had it exactly right when he told a client: "The law let[s] you do it, but don't . . . . It's a rotten thing to do.").

B. Cognitive Dissonance as an Explanation

Even if the gatekeepers weren't so closely involved with the client, there's yet another reason for their failure to protest the deals that were on (or over) the edge: cognitive dissonance. My sociologist friends[71] tell me that moral development alone—which is an individual trait—can't explain how an individual will react to a particular situation.[72] The situation itself will interact with the traits of the individual, and both the person's individual traits and his situation will affect an outcome.[73]

Peer pressure is one such particular influence. There are some well-regarded studies showing that even relatively obvious physical conclusions, such as the distance from one point to another or the length of a line, can become subject to "groupthink," placing peer pressure on the unbelieving minority to conform to the wrong-headed thinking of the majority.[74] And if hard-wired concepts, such as size and location, are manipulable by the particulars of the situation, what about the fuzzier concept of behavior?

Stanley Milgram's studies on the willingness of experimental subjects to inflict pain (electrical shocks) on complete strangers can give us a glimpse into how powerful the effect of a particular situation can be. In Milgram's best-known study, the actual subject was asked to give a series of progressively more severe shocks to someone who was posing as a fellow experimental subject. Although the actual subject usually agonized about administering the shocks, he went ahead and administered them nonetheless.[75]

In analyzing Milgram's experiment, Lee Ross and Richard Nisbett concluded that the powerful structure of the situation—the authority figure setup; the calm tones of

---

[71] Special thanks go to Julia McQuillan, who guided me through the literature and theories in her field.

[72] *Cf.* Julia McQuillan & Julie Pfeiffer, *Why Anne Makes us Dizzy: Reading Anne of Green Gables from a Gender Perspective*, 16 MOSAIC 34/2, June 2001, at 19 ("In an attempt to explain variation within sex categories, sociologists have argued that external social structures (our actual experiences in the world) organize our behavior more than socialization (how we've been told to behave).").

[73] The thought that moral development alone can predict a person's behavior without regard to the particular situation is called the "fundamental attribution error." *See* DAVID J. LUBAN, THE ETHICS OF WRONGFUL OBEDIENCE, *in* ETHICS IN PRACTICE: LAWYERS' ROLES, RESPONSIBILITIES, AND REGULATION 94, 101 (Deborah L. Rhode ed., 2000) [hereinafter WRONGFUL OBEDIENCE]; *see also* Lee M. Johnson, et al., *General Versus Specific Victim Blaming*, 142 J. OF SOC. PSYCHOL. 249 (Apr. 2002) ("The fundamental attribution error occurs when individuals overemphasize personal attributes and discount environmental attributes in their judgments of others"); LEE ROSS, THE INTUITIVE PSYCHOLOGIST AND HIS SHORTCOMINGS: DISTORTIONS IN THE ATTRIBUTION PROCESS, IN 10 ADVANCES IN EXPERIMENTAL SOCIAL PSYCH. 173 (Leonard Berkowitz ed., 1977); *see generally* DAVID C. FUNDER, PERSONALITY JUDGMENT: A REALISTIC APPROACH TO PERSONAL PERCEPTION (1999).

[74] LEE ROSS & RICHARD E. NISBETT, THE PERSON AND THE SITUATIONS: PERSPECTIVES OF SOCIAL PSYCHOLOGY 30 (1991) ("Our most basic perceptions and judgments about the world are socially conditioned and dictated.") (citing Sherif's "autokinetic effect" studies and Asch's "comparison lines" studies).

[75] *Id.* at 56–57.

the experimenter standing next to the subject who was administrating the shocks; the experimenter's repetition of the phrases, "The experiment requires that you continue; you have no choice"—served to overcome the subjects' expressed desire to stop the experiment before reaching the "severe shock" stage.[76] Most of the subjects were stymied by uncertainty and couldn't overcome the social pressure of the situation. It's not that the subjects were sadists. But the structure of the situation prevented them from acting on their own reluctance to continue the shocks.

David Luban has also described the Milgram experiment and has pointed out that almost two-thirds of the subjects in Milgram's experiments actually did go all the way to 450 volts.[77] He posits that a "corruption of judgment" stemming from cognitive dissonance caused two-thirds of the subjects of Milgram's experiments to "kill" the learner:

> [T]he key to understanding Milgram compliance lies in features of the experimental situation. . . . The teacher moves up the scale of shocks by 15-volt increments, and reaches the 450-volt level only at the thirtieth shock. Among other things, this means that the subjects never confront the question "Should I administer a 330-volt shock to the learner?" The question is "Should I administer a 330-volt shock to the learner given that I've just administered a 315-volt shock?" It seems clear that the latter question is much harder to answer. . . .
>
> Cognitive dissonance theory teaches that when our actions conflict with our self-concept, our beliefs and attitudes change until the conflict is removed. . . . Cognitive dissonance theory suggests that when I have given the learner a series of electrical shocks, I simply won't view giving the next shock as a wrongful act, because I won't admit to myself that the previous shocks were wrong.[78]

Luban's most important point is that lawyers aren't immune to the effects of cognitive dissonance. He does a masterful job of linking the *Berkey Photo-Inc. v. Eastman Kodak Co.*[79] case and Stanley Milgram's experiments on obedience to explain how very well-intentioned lawyers can find themselves slipping into serious breaches of ethics. For those who aren't familiar with this case, Brad Wendel describes it nicely:

---

[76] One of Milgram's later variations on the study involved changing the setting from Yale to an inner-city, run-down, suspicious-looking lab in another town. He recorded approximately the same results, no matter the setting. *See id.* at 55.

[77] WRONGFUL OBEDIENCE, *supra* note 73, at 97 ("In reality, 63 percent of subjects complied all the way to 450 volts. Moreover, this is a robust result: it holds in groups of women as well as men, and experimenters obtained comparable results in Holland, Spain, Italy, Australia, South Africa, Germany, and Jordan. . . .") (footnote omitted).

[78] *Id.* at 102 (footnotes omitted).

[79] 74 F.R.D. 613 (S.D.N.Y. 1977).

The lawyers representing Kodak had retained an economist as an expert witness, expecting that he would testify that Kodak's domination of the market was due to its superior technological innovations, not to anticompetitive behavior. The plaintiff's counsel requested any documents pertinent to the expert's testimony, Kodak's lawyer's resisted, and ultimately a magistrate ordered production of numerous documents including interim reports prepared by the economist. At the economist's deposition, one of Kodak's lawyers stated that he had destroyed the interim reports, which were somewhat unfavorable to Kodak's defense. The lawyer even filed an affidavit in a subsequent discovery dispute in the case, stating under oath that the documents had been destroyed. In fact, the lawyer had not destroyed the documents, but had hidden them in his office and withheld them from production. The affidavit was perjurous. The fallout was a calamity for the firm. Kodak fired it and hired one of its arch-rivals to defend the antitrust case. The firm paid its client over $600,000 to settle Kodak's claims related to its conduct of the litigation. It lost Kodak's business, which had accounted for approximately one-fourth of the firm's billings and had employed thirty lawyers full-time. The partner who had coordinated the firm's preparation of the economist's testimony was released from the firm and spent twenty-seven days in jail for contempt of court.[80]

In his discussion of the *Berkey-Kodak* case, Luban relates the following episode:

> Joseph Fortenberry, the associate working for [Mahlon Perkins, the partner representing Kodak], knew that Perkins was perjuring himself and whispered a warning to him; but when Perkins ignored the warning, Fortenberry did nothing further to correct his misstatements. "What happened" recalls another associate, "was that he saw Perkins lie and really couldn't believe it. And he just had no idea what to do. I mean, he . . . kept thinking there must be a reason. Besides, what do you do? The guy was his boss and a great guy!"[81]

Fortenberry's comments highlight how fledgling lawyers will take many social cues from those more experienced lawyers whom they respect.[82] Of course, the pressure

---

[80] W. Bradley Wendel, *Morality, Motivation, and the Professionalism Movement*, 52 S.C. L. REV. 557, 606–07 (2001) (footnotes omitted); *see also* Walter Kiechell III, *The Strange Case of Kodak's Lawyers*, FORTUNE, May 8, 1978, at 188. If I were a superstitious sort, I'd worry about the fact that one of the two "smoking guns" in the case was Exhibit 666. *Id.* I am *not* making this up.

[81] WRONGFUL OBEDIENCE, *supra* note 73, at 95 (footnotes omitted).

[82] Cognitive dissonance isn't limited to outside counsel. In a study of inside counsel, Hugh and Sally Gunz found that the lawyers' advice was not always independent from the direction that the company itself intended to go:

that the senior lawyers have to keep their clients, maintain their billings, and compete with other elite lawyers at other firms (who are all too happy to steal clients away), is relentless pressure indeed. But if the more senior lawyers can't withstand the pressure, then who will teach the fledgling lawyers to resist?

III. WHERE DO WE GO FROM HERE?

If we want lawyers to spend more time understanding themselves and their relationship to their clients, then we're going to have to lead from the top, with judges, partners, bar associations, and other senior lawyers all singing the same tune. It won't be sufficient for law professors to warn students against the temptations and pressures of law practice. As a matter of fact, it's depressing how little influence law professors have on their students' understanding of legal ethics.

Larry Hellman's study on cognitive dissonance in a legal ethics class is proof of the need to have top lawyers do the preaching, not law professors.[83] Hellman asked the students in his ethics course to keep diaries of possible ethics violations that they observed while working for lawyers during the semester, and those students recounted bad lawyering in an astonishing variety of forms—neglect, incompetence, conflicts of interest, and the like.[84] If we want to train newly minted lawyers to be ethical, it's just not enough for law professors to talk the talk. We must join forces with the lawyers and judges in the "real world," those who can walk the walk.

Lawyers need to behave as true counselors to their clients, rather than as hired guns who are just following orders. Society needs us to take on the role of the social con-

---

From a practitioner standpoint, the model highlights issues surrounding the nature of the advice that organizations can expect to obtain from their in-house counsel when placed in positions of ethical conflict. In our original study of OPC [organizational professional conflict], we suggested that an important implication of our findings was that in-house counsel might not necessarily always provide disinterested professional advice. In their different ways, the Technician and Organization Person might produce superficially helpful advice, which could, under certain circumstances, be dangerously misleading. The Technician, for example, may deliver clever but myopic solutions, and the Observer could well misjudge a situation and remain silent inappropriately. But the Advisor, by avoiding the "cop" aspect of the Lawyer role (in the sense that there is no implication that he or she intends to report the situation to the next level higher within the organization, or to a regulator outside the organization), stays closer to the Lawyer's advice. So the model, as revised, suggests an even greater variety of potential responses than in its initial L[awyer], T[echnician], and O[bserver] form, underlining yet more firmly the need to avoid making simplistic assumptions about the nature of the advice in-house counsel provide their employer[s].

Hugh P. Gunz & Sally P. Gunz, *The Lawyer's Response to Organizational Professional Conflict: An Empirical Study of the Ethical Decision Making of In-House Counsel*, 39 AM. BUS. L.J. 241, 279–80 (2002) (footnotes omitted).

[83] Lawrence K. Hellman, *The Effects of Law Office Work on the Formation of Law Students' Professional Values: Observation, Explanation, Optimization*, 4 GEO. J. LEGAL ETHICS 537 (1991).

[84] *Id.* at 601–05.

science (or, if that sounds too darn highfallutin', the role of the grease that helps society run). As David Luban has pointed out,

> If lawyers have special responsibilities to legal justice, that is not because they are divinely elected, or better and holier that [sic] the rest of us. It is because of how their role fits into an entire division of social labor. Lawyers represent private parties before public institutions, or advise private parties about the requirements of public norms, or reduce private transactions to a publicly-prescribed form, or ratify that transactions are in compliance with public norms. To say that they have special duties of fidelity to those norms is no more ecstatic and supernatural than saying that food-preparers have heightened duties to ensure their hands are clean. It is their social role, not the brush of angels' wings on their foreheads, that requires [food service workers] to wash their hands every time they go to the bathroom.[85]

We used to be better at setting good examples, or so I've heard. In the "golden days" that Tom Shaffer recounts, some of the lawyers that he observed set wonderful examples for their newly minted lawyer colleagues. In my favorite article of his, *The Profession as a Moral Teacher*, he tells story after story of lawyers who did the right thing.[86] The constant choice of ethical over unethical behavior helped mold the lawyer that Shaffer eventually became:

> [Those two partners in my former law firm] were philosophically and temperamentally different and . . . practiced law in different ways. That they were so much alike in these moral matters said something about their personal character, of course, but, in view of their personal differences, it also said something about the way the firm practiced law—about the way the firm functioned as the profession (for me) and, as the profession, functioned (for me) as a moral teacher. It was not, that is, an apprenticeship, in which I was learning my craft, and the morals of my craft, from a master— or at least it didn't seem, then, that it was. It was the profession (the law firm) that was the moral teacher. . . . It was even more like the moral formation a person gets from family, town, and church. Which is to say that, here, code depended on character.[87]

---

[85] David Luban, *Asking the Right Questions*, 72 TEMP. L. REV. 839, 849–50 (1999).

[86] *Moral Teacher, supra* note 62, at 214–17.

[87] *Id.* at 216–17.

From his experience as a young lawyer, Shaffer took the moral lesson that a lawyer should also be a gentleman.[88] Tom Shaffer's view of the "gentlemanly" lawyer, of course, has its critics,[89] including Shaffer himself.[90] And yet, we do understand the concept that he's trying to express:[91] that of a lawyer who understands her role in society as more than just a mere scrivener or functionary, and who tries always to take the moral high ground.[92]

---

[88] Thomas L. Shaffer, *On Being a Professional Elder*, 62 NOTRE DAME L. REV. 624, 630–31 (1987) [hereinafter *Professional Elder*] ("When character is in place, fortified by 'a few rules' that have to do with professional craft, the professional person becomes dependable. Professional character is the connection between virtue and craft. The convention has been to describe that connection with the word gentleman.") (footnotes omitted). If you haven't read Tom Shaffer's work on this topic, you should. For a quick shortcut—not to be confused with reading Shaffer's work—Leslie Gerber has created a good primer. *See* Leslie E. Gerber, *Can Lawyers Be Saved? The Theological Legal Ethics of Thomas Shaffer*, 10 J.L. & RELIGION 347 (1994).

[89] *See, e.g.*, Ann Bartow, *Still Not Behaving Like Gentlemen*, 49 U. KAN. L. REV. 809, 810–11 (2001); Susan Daicoff, *Asking Leopards to Change Their Spots: Should Lawyers Change? A Critique Of Solutions to Problems with Professionalism by Reference to Empirically-Derived Attorney Personality Attributes*, 11 GEO. J. LEGAL ETHICS 547, 582–83 (1998); William J. Wernz, *Does Professionalism Literature Idealize the Past and Over-Rate Civility? Is Zeal a Vice or a Cardinal Virtue?*, 13 PROF. LAW. 1 (2001) (disputing the claim that "back then"—whenever "then" was—lawyers were more professional and more civil).

[90] Thomas L. Shaffer, *The Gentleman in Professional Ethics*, 10 QUEEN'S L.J. 1, 11 (1984).

The 19th century gentleman in North America gave us slavery, Manifest Destiny, the theft of half of Mexico, the subjugation of women, the exploitation of immigrant children, Pinkerton detectives, yellow-dog contracts, and the implacable genocide of American Indians. You could make a case . . . that the gentleman's ethic is not worth taking seriously. If the gentleman has left the professions, the best thing for us would be to bar the door lest he get back in.

Id.; *see also* Thomas L. Shaffer, *Inaugural Howard Lichtenstein Lecture in Legal Ethics: Lawyer Professionalism as a Moral Argument*, 26 GONZ. L. REV. 393, 400 (1991); *Professional Elder, supra* note 88, at 633–34.

[91] Edward McGlynn Gaffney, Jr., *In Praise of a Gentle Soul*, Remarks at the Annual Banquet of the *Journal of Law and Religion* (Oct. 14, 1993), *in* 10 J.L. & RELIGION 279, 284 (1993/1994).

The acid test of [Tom Shaffer's] reliance on the ethics of gentlemen is whether it, too, is not flawed at its core. Is it not by definition limited to males, and does it have any space for minorities? Only one like Shaffer, who by decades of living like a gentleman himself and reflecting carefully on that ethic, could have come to the conclusion that the ethic of the gentleman-lawyer has greater possibilities for the subversion of patriarchy than the ABA's model of professionalism.

Id. (footnotes omitted).

[92] Bill Hodes points out that "[t]he acid test of ethical lawyering is rarely what to do in the face of crisis—a client shows you the buried bodies or drops a bloody knife on your desk or commits perjury or destroys or hides material property asked for in discovery." W. William Hodes, *Accepting and Rejecting Clients—The Moral Autonomy of the Second-to-the-Last Lawyer in Town*, 48 U. KAN. L. REV. 977, 978 (2000) (citing the classic cases of People v. Belge, 372 N.Y.S. 2d 798 (N.Y. Crim. Ct. 1975) (buried bodies), State v. Olwell, 394 P.2d 681 (Wash. 1964) (bloody knife), Nix v. Whiteside, 475 U.S. 157 (1986) (perjury), and Berkey Photo, Inc. v. Eastman Kodak Co., 74 F.R.D. 613 (S.D.N.Y. 1977) (work product)). For a wonderful discussion of how social norms affect lawyering, see *Social Norms, supra* note 66.

What happens when we don't set the right example? We can call doing the right thing "behaving like gentlemen," or we can use some other, less "loaded" phrase. If we don't exert some leadership and emphasize the role of character in the practice of law, some very smart lawyers will continue to do stupid things, and some clients will continue to do stupid (or venal) things. Some of these people will even trot out the hoary (and discredited) old saw that they were "just following orders."[93]

So how do we encourage lawyers to withstand peer pressure and client pressure, especially in those grey areas in which the lawyer gives advice akin to "it's an aggressive interpretation of the law" and the client chooses to use that aggressive interpretation, even at the risk of later litigation? Remember, we're not talking about lawyers who deliberately counsel clients to flout the law. Rather, we're talking about lawyers who say that a particular interpretation could go either in favor of the client or against it.

Personally, I like Russ Pearce's idea that we create a new Model Rule 1.0. His Model Rule 1.0 would provide that "lawyers are morally accountable for their conduct as lawyers."[94] That rule hits the question of moral interdependence head on, and it provides a powerful reminder that "just following orders" is the weakest of excuses.[95]

We can blame part of Enron's downfall on the economy. We can blame part of it on corporate misbehavior, on board malfeasance, and on pure greed. We can blame part of it on a structure that allowed gatekeepers and reputational intermediaries—the board, the accountants, and the lawyers—to rely on the other two categories to understand the overall picture of what Enron was doing. We can even blame the Enron employees who chose to place too much Enron stock in their own 401(k) plans, thereby betting twice with the same money.[96] But one thing we can't blame is fate. Enron's collapse

---

[93] *See, e.g.*, Tom Fowler, *Ex-Andersen auditor defended / Aide: Boss was told to shred files*, HOUS. CHRON., Mar. 7, 2002, at 1 ("An assistant to the Arthur Andersen lead partner who handled the Enron account said she believes her boss was just following orders when he told workers to destroy Enron-related documents last fall."); Marcy Gordon, *SEC, Informal Wall Street System Failed to Detect Enron Failure, Report Finds*, ASSOCIATED PRESS NEWSWIRES, Oct. 7, 2002, Westlaw, Allnewsplus Library (Fastow's lawyer contends that his client was just following orders).

[94] Russell G. Pearce, *Model Rule 1.0: Lawyers are Morally Accountable*, 70 FORDHAM L. REV. 1805, 1807–08 (2002). Pearce points out that Model Rule 1.0 would not take sides in current disputes regarding the lawyer's role. What it would do is move the debates regarding the lawyer's moral duties, like that between Freedman, who favors zealous representation, and Luban, Rhode, and Simon, who favor some significant limits on that representation, to the center of the bar's legal ethics conversations. While the bar currently pays some slight attention to these issues, Model Rule 1.0 would move them to a more prominent place in the bar's official deliberations and continuing legal education courses, as well as in the efforts of the conscientious lawyer to explore her own moral accountability.

[95] I'm not sure how one might enforce a Model Rule 1.0, but at least Pearce is heading in the right direction.

[96] *See, e.g.*, Mark Davis, *The Fallout of a Fallen Enron; Too Much Company Stock in 401(k); Plans Poses Risk*, KAN. CITY STAR, Jan. 20, 2002, at A1; Kaja Whitehouse, *401(k) Woes? Might Be Your Own Fault*, DOW JONES NEWS SERV., Jan. 18, 2002, Westlaw, Allnewsplus Library. Of course, the freeze on selling stock as the value of the stock spiraled downward also had something to do with the losses in the employees' 401(k) plans. *See, e.g.*, Davis, *supra*; Editorial, *Enron and Frontier Justice Fear of Angry Workers Sends Energy Trading Firm to New York to File for Bankruptcy*, PORTLAND OREGONIAN, Dec. 4, 2001, at D06.

wasn't due to a "perfect storm" of mere coincidence—the collapse was caused by humans and their hubris. We need to ensure that hubris doesn't blind us to the first rule of leadership: It's all about character.